# POLITICAL ELITES
## A Select Computerized Bibliography

**M.I.T. STUDIES IN COMPARATIVE POLITICS**

Under the general editorship of Harold D. Lasswell, Daniel Lerner, and Ithiel de Sola Pool.

*The Emerging Elite: A Study of Political Leadership in Ceylon,* Marshall Singer, 1964.

*The Turkish Political Elite,* Frederick W. Frey, 1965.

*World Revolutionary Elites: Studies in Coercive Ideological Movements, Harold D. Lasswell and Daniel Lerner,* editors, 1965.

*Language of Politics: Studies in Quantitative Semantics,* Harold D. Lasswell, Nathan Leites, and Associates, 1965 (reissue).

*The General Inquirer: A Computer Approach to Content Analysis,* Philip J. Stone, Dexter C. Dunphy, Marshall S. Smith, Daniel M. Ogilvie, 1967.

*Political Elites: A Select Computerized Bibliography,* Carl Beck and J. Thomas McKechnie, 1968.

# POLITICAL ELITES
## A Select Computerized Bibliography

Carl Beck and J. Thomas McKechnie

**THE M.I.T. PRESS**
*Massachusetts Institute of Technology*
*Cambridge, Massachusetts and London, England*

# INTRODUCTION

This computerized bibliography stems from a previous survey that examined paradigms used in the categorization and explanation of political elites. Included in that initial survey were a sample inventory of general statements on elite theories and definitions of elites and propositions about the behavior and structure of particular elite groups in various types of political systems.*

The initial survey demonstrated that the accumulation of extensive knowledge about elite behavior required, as a preliminary step, the construction of a more systematic bibliography on political elites. We have constructed such a bibliography. In doing so, we recognized that a bibliographical survey of such a theoretically important and empirically expanding concept as political elite must avoid the imposition of any one definition. We have, therefore, included in the bibliography nonformal as well as formal elite studies. We feel that the bibliography reflects the ideological diversity and theoretical punch carried by the concept of political elite.

We have attempted to include in the bibliography a fair representation of the various conceptual and theoretical areas touched by the study of political elites. Our aim is to give an extensive, representative, but not exhaustive account of the literature. We constructed the bibliography by systematically searching lists of books in print, other bibliographies, and approximately 100 social science journals published in English from 1945 to mid-1967.

The bibliography is divided into three parts. The first part is the KWOC (Key Word Out of Context) title listing. The listing is permuted; the article or book will appear as many times as it contains key words. Next to each title is a reference code consisting of the first four letters of the author's last name, his initials, the year of publication, and the first letters of the first three words in the title. The full citation is available in the second section of the bibliography. The citation can be found by using the reference code in section one as an index to the complete citation listing. The third section of the bibliography is the list of authors.

All titles appear in the bibliography as they appeared in the journals or books. Different methods of spelling and hyphenation are therefore reflected in this bibliography. The scan capabilities of the KWOC program did not allow for precise alphabetical order, hence adjective derivatives sometimes appear before the noun forms.

Two elements of information were added to each citation. When a title was ambiguous concerning the locale under study, either country or area information was added. Each study was further classified according to its relevance to one or more of seven general topics of elite analysis. Acronyms for each of these topics were appended to the citation in the second section of this bibliography as an additional item of information. The seven topics and the acronyms used are as follows:

1. GNELTH    (General Elite Theory)
            This acronym attached to a citation indicates that the item

*For reports of this survey see Carl Beck, James M. Malloy, and William R. Campbell, *A Survey of Elite Studies* (Special Operations Research Office, American University, 1965); and Carl Beck and James M. Malloy, *Political Elites: A Mode of Analysis,* occasional paper published by the Archive on Political Elites in Eastern Europe (Pittsburgh, 1966).

emphasizes the theory of political elites in its widest setting.

2. DEFEL (Definition of Elites)
This acronym attached to a citation indicates that the item contains definitions of the concept of political elite, a particular elite group, or elite-related concept.

3. COMEL (Composition of Elites)
This acronym attached to a citation indicates that the item includes either empirical or hypothesized statements on the social and political composition of elites.

4. ELEL (Elite Elite Relationships)
This acronym attached to a citation indicates that the item refers to structural and behavioral relationships between political elites.

5. ELNOEL (Elite Non-Elite Relationships)
This acronym attached to a citation indicates that the item refers to structural and behavioral relationships between political elites and non-elites.

6. ELPRNOR (Elite Perceptions and Norms)
This acronym attached to a citation indicates that the item refers to elite perceptions, norms, or attitudes.

7. METEL (Methodology of Elites)
This acronym attached to a citation indicates that the item includes methodological suggestions relevant to elite analysis.

In compiling this bibliography, we have had the assistance of several graduate students at the University of Pittsburgh. In particular, we would like to acknowledge the sustained assistance of Richard Allison, Laurie Cummings, Ronald Haver, and Bert Rockman as well as the contributions of William Cunningham, Carl Lieberman, Joanne Miller, John Petersen, David Powers, Michael Quinn, Pamela Quinn, and Myron Rubinoff. We would also like to acknowledge the highly competent assistance of the staff of the International Studies Program at the University of Pittsburgh: Mrs. Suzanne Sega, Miss Patricia McGeary, and Miss Linda R. Fey.

It would only be masochistic to iterate the steps necessary to transform the mounds of cards into the KWOC bibliography. Every system has its idiosyncrasies. In overcoming idiosyncratic behavior we are grateful to George Dunn, Institute of Survey Research, University of Michigan, for generating preliminary runs; Dave Mitchell, Health Law Center, University of Pittsburgh, for adapting the Michigan system to our needs; and Philip Ryave, Computer Center, University of Pittsburgh, for processing the final runs. Without the patience and forbearance of our wives and colleagues this bibliography could not have been compiled.

Carl Beck
J. Thomas McKechnie

*Pittsburgh, Pennsylvania*
*January 1968*

# TABLE OF CONTENTS

ACTIVISTS          (CONTINUATION)
MANHATTAN (UNITED STATES).=
                              FIRSRS-62-PPA

THE POLITICAL IDEAS OF ENGLISH
PARTY ACTIVISTS.=     ROSER -62-PIE

ACTIVITES
PARLIAMENTARY CONTROL OF
ADMINISTRATIVE ACTIVITES IN THE
POLISH PEOPLE'S REPUBLIC.=
                     ROZMS -59-PCA

ACTIVITIES
THE ACTIVITIES OF A SOVIET LEADER.=
                     AKHMH -66-ASL

ACTIVITIES AND ROLE DEFINITIONS OF
GRASSROOTS PARTY OFFICIALS
(UNITED STATES).=    BOWML -66-ARD

LABOR AND POLITICS IN JAPAN -- A
STUDY OF INTEREST GROUP ATTITUDES
AND ACTIVITIES.=     SOUKJR-60-LPJ

ACTIVITY
SELF - DESIGNATED INFLUENTIALITY
AND ACTIVITY.=       ABELHI-58-SDI

THE TRANSFERRED SUDETEN -- GERMANS
AND THEIR POLITICAL ACTIVITY
(GERMANY).=          CELOB -57-TSG

MEASURING THE IMPACT OF LOCAL PARTY
ACTIVITY ON THE GENERAL ELECTION
VOTE (UNITED STATES).=
                     CUTRP -63-MIL

LIMITS OF GOVERNMENT ACTIVITY IN
UNDERDEVELOPED COUNTRIES.=
                     DEYRFJ-57-LGA

THE IMPACT OF LOCAL PARTY ACTIVITY
UPON THE ELECTORATE
(UNITED STATES).=    KATZD -61-ILP

THE STUDY OF EXECUTIVE BEHAVIOR BY
ACTIVITY SAMPLING
(UNITED STATES).=    KELLJ -64-SEB

THE POLITICAL PARTY ACTIVITY OF
WASHINGTON LOBBYISTS
(UNITED STATES).=    MILBLW-58-PPA

A CASE ANALYSIS OF CONGRESSIONAL
ACTIVITY -- CIVIL AVIATION,
1957-1958.=          REDFES-60-CAC

LITIGATION AS A FORM OF PRESSURE
GROUP ACTIVITY.=     VOSECE-58-LFP

ADAPTATION
TRANSITION IN AFRICA -- STUDIES IN
POLITICAL ADAPTATION.=
                     CARTGW-58-TAS

ADAPTION
THE LAWMAKERS -- RECRUITMENT AND
ADAPTION TO LEGISLATIVE LIFE
(UNITED STATES).=    BARBJD-65-LRA

ADAPTIVENESS
SOVIET RUSSIA -- ORTHODOXY AND
ADAPTIVENESS.=       BARGFC-66-SRO

ADENAUER
EQUILIBRIUM, STRUCTURE OF INTERESTS
AND LEADERSHIP -- ADENAUER'S
SURVIVAL AS CHANCELLOR (GERMANY).=
                     MERKPH-62-ESI

ADEQUACY
A TEST OF THE ADEQUACY OF THE POWER

ADEQUACY          (CONTINUATION)
INDEX.=              RIKEWH-59-TAP

ADMINISTERED
THE ADMINISTERED SOCIETY --
TOTALITARIANISM WITHOUT TERROR
(SOVIET UNION).=     KASSA -64-AST

ADMINISTRATION
BOLSHEVIK ADMINISTRATION IN THE
UKRAINE -- 1918.=    ADAMAE-58-BAU

THE LEGAL ASPECTS OF THE CHANGES IN
SOVIET INDUSTRIAL ADMINISTRATION.=
                     ANON -57-LAC

METROPOLITAN ADMINISTRATION IN
TOKYO.=              ANON -62-MAT

THE ORGANIZATION AND ADMINISTRATION
OF THE SOVIET ARMAMENT INDUSTRY.=
                     BARIJJ-57-CAS

INDIGENOUS POLITICS AND COLONIAL
ADMINISTRATION WITH SPECIAL
REFERENCE TO AUSTRALIA.=
                     BARNJA-60-IPC

LEADERSHIP STYLE AS A VARIABLE IN
RESEARCH ADMINISTRATION.=
                     BAUMH -57-LSV

A PROBLEM IN SOVIET BUSINESS
ADMINISTRATION.=     BERLJS-57-PSB

COMMITTEE CHARACTERISTICS AND
LEGISLATIVE OVERSIGHT OF
ADMINISTRATION (UNITED STATES).=
                     BIBBJF-66-CCL

NOTES ON LEADERSHIP PROBLEMS AND
PUBLIC ADMINISTRATION TRAINING IN
INDONESIA.=          BRADJR-63-NLP

ADMINISTRATION AND ECONOMIC
DEVELOPMENT IN INDIA.=
                     BRAIR -63-AED

PROBLEMS OF FIELD ADMINISTRATION IN
THE DEPARTMENT OF LABOR
(PHILIPPINES).=      CALALM-62-PFA

POLITICS AND ADMINISTRATION.=
                     CHAPB -58-PA

THE MO LIAO SYSTEM IN CH'ING
ADMINISTRATION (CHINA).=
                     CHUATS-63-MLS

MEN WHO MANAGE -- FUSIONS OF
FEELING AND THEORY IN
ADMINISTRATION.=     DALTM -59-MWM

TOWARD A PHILOSOPHY OF PUBLIC
ADMINISTRATION IN VIETNAM.=
                     DANGNG-63-TPP

THE REORGANIZATION OF
ADMINISTRATION IN TURKESTAN
(SOVIET UNION).=     DAVLT -63-RAT

PATTERNS IN DECISION-MAKING -- CASE
STUDIES IN PHILIPPINE PUBLIC
ADMINISTRATION.=     DE-GRP-63-PDM

THE DEVELOPMENT AND DECLINE OF
PATRIMONIAL AND BUREAUCRATIC
ADMINISTRATION.=     DELAW -63-DDP

A CASE STUDY OF ADMINISTRATIVE
AUTONOMY -- CONTROLS AND TENSIONS
IN FRENCH ADMINISTRATION.=

ADMINISTRATIVE        (CONTINUATION)
ADMINISTRATIVE ORGANS OF THE
PEOPLE'S COMMITTEES (YUGOSLAVIA).=
                             ANON  -61-TOA

SOURCES OF ADMINISTRATIVE BEHAVIOR
-- SOME SOVIET AND WESTERN
EUROPEAN COMPARISONS.=
                             ARMSJA-65-SAB

RELATIONSHIP BETWEEN PROFESSIONAL
AND ADMINISTRATIVE OFFICERS IN A
GOVERNMENT DEPARTMENT DURING A
PERIOD OF ADMINISTRATIVE CHANGE
(GUYANA).=              BACCMK-67-RBP

RELATIONSHIP BETWEEN PROFESSIONAL
AND ADMINISTRATIVE OFFICERS IN A
GOVERNMENT DEPARTMENT DURING A
PERIOD OF ADMINISTRATIVE CHANGE
(GUYANA).=              BACCMK-67-RBP

LEADERSHIP THEORY AND
ADMINISTRATIVE BEHAVIOR -- THE
PROBLEM OF AUTHORITY.=
                             BENNWG-60-LTA

THE ADMINISTRATIVE ELITE
(GREAT BRITAIN, FRANCE).=
                             BOTTTB-64-AEG

MAINTENANCE OF MEMBERSHIP -- A
STUDY IN ADMINISTRATIVE
STATESMANSHIP (UNITED STATES).=
                             BURNJM-48-MMS

PUBLIC CORPORATIONS AND THE
CLASSIFICATION OF ADMINISTRATIVE
BODIES (GREAT BRITAIN).=
                             CHESON-53-PCC

A CASE STUDY OF ADMINISTRATIVE
AUTONOMY -- CONTROLS AND TENSIONS
IN FRENCH ADMINISTRATION.=
                             DIAMA -58-CSA

THE EXECUTIVE OVERSEAS --
ADMINISTRATIVE ATTITUDES AND
RELATIONSHIPS IN A FOREIGN CULTURE
(MEXICO).=              FAYEJ -59-EOA

THE ITALIAN PREFECTS -- A STUDY IN
ADMINISTRATIVE POLITICS.=
                             FRIERC-63-IPS

THE FRAMEWORK OF ADMINISTRATIVE
RESPONSIBILITY.=        GILBCE-59-FAR

AN ADMINISTRATIVE CENTENARY,
1853-1953 (GREAT BRITAIN).=
                             GLADEN-53-ACG

ADMINISTRATIVE CHANGE IN NEPAL.=
                             GOODMR-66-ACN

ADMINISTRATIVE MANAGEMENT OF PUBLIC
ENTERPRISES IN YUGOSLAVIA.=
                             GROZS -66-AMP

POLITICAL AND ADMINISTRATIVE
LEADERSHIP (UNITED STATES).=
                             GULIL -63-PAL

FOREIGN POLICY-MAKING AND
ADMINISTRATIVE POLITICS
(UNITED STATES).=       HAMMPY-65-FPM

A COMPARATIVE ANALYSIS OF THE
ADMINISTRATIVE SYSTEMS OF CANADA
AND CEYLON.=            HARRRL-64-CAA

THE PHILIPPINE ADMINISTRATIVE

ADMINISTRATIVE        (CONTINUATION)
SYSTEM -- A FUSION OF EAST AND
WEST.=                  HEADF -57-PAS

ADMINISTRATIVE REORGANIZATION AND
THE BUILDING OF COMMUNISM
(SOVIET UNION).=        JURCA -60-ARB

THE SOVIET ADMINISTRATIVE ELITE --
SELECTION AND DEPLOYMENT
PROCEDURES.=            LEBEA -65-SAE

THE CITY MANAGER, ADMINISTRATIVE
THEORY AND POLITICAL POWER
(UNITED STATES).=       LOCKD -62-CMA

RECRUITMENT OF THE ADMINISTRATIVE
CLASS OF THE BRITISH CIVIL
SERVICE.=               MCKIMM-49-RAC

ADMINISTRATIVE ORGANIZATION -- A
COMPARATIVE STUDY OF THE
ORGANIZATION OF PUBLIC
ADMINISTRATION (GREAT BRITAIN,
UNITED STATES).=        MEYEP -57-AOC

SOVIET ADMINISTRATIVE LEGALITY --
THE ROLE OF THE ATTORNEY GENERAL'S
OFFICE.=                MORGGG-62-SAL

THE ADMINISTRATIVE STATE (FRANCE,
GREAT BRITAIN, SWITZERLAND,
UNITED STATES).=        MORSF -57-ASF

ADMINISTRATIVE PROCEDURE IN
NORWAY.=                CS, A -59-APN

ADMINISTRATIVE LEADERSHIP
(UNITED STATES).=       PRICDT-61-ALU

EFFECTS OF LEGISLATIVE AND
ADMINISTRATIVE ACCESSIBILITY ON
INTEREST GROUP POLITICS.=
                             PYE,LW-58-ELA

ADMINISTRATIVE SECRECY --
CONGRESSIONAL DILEMMA
(UNITED STATES).=       ROURFE-60-ASC

PARLIAMENTARY CONTROL OF
ADMINISTRATIVE ACTIVITES IN THE
POLISH PEOPLE'S REPUBLIC.=
                             ROZMS -59-PCA

ADMINISTRATIVE TRUSTIFICATION
(UNITED STATES).=       SALIE -58-ATU

'THE PUBLIC INTEREST' IN
ADMINISTRATIVE DECISION-MAKING
(UNITED STATES).=       SCHUGA-57-PIA

THE CULTURAL FACTORS IN ECONOMIC
AND TECHNOLOGICAL DEVELOPMENT --
AN INDIAN ADMINISTRATIVE
VIEW-POINT.=            SETHSC-65-CFE

ADMINISTRATIVE RESPONSIBILITY --
CONGRESSIONAL PRESCRIPTION OF
INTERAGENCY RELATIONSHIPS
(UNITED STATES).=       SMITJM-57-ARC

METHODS IN THE STUDY OF
ADMINISTRATIVE LEADERSHIP.=
                             STOGRM-55-MSA

DECENTRALIZATION IN RECENT SOVIET
ADMINISTRATIVE PRACTICE.=
                             SWEAHR-62-DRS

SUPREME COURT ATTITUDES TOWARD
FEDERAL ADMINISTRATIVE AGENCIES
(UNITED STATES).=       TANEJ -60-SCA

AFFLICTIONS
AFFLICTIONS OF THE YOUTH LEAGUE
(SOVIET UNION).=          KASSA -58-AYL

AFFLUENCE
AFFLUENCE AND THE BRITISH CLASS
STRUCTURE.=              GOLDJH-63-ABC

AFGHANISTAN
A NEW TRY FOR AFGHANISTAN.=
                         GOCHTS-65-NTA

AFRAID
SURVEY AND JUDICIARIES, OR WHO'S
AFRAID OF THE PURPLE CURTAIN
(UNITED STATES).=        BECKTL-66-SJC

AFRICA
TRIBAL UNIONS IN PARTY POLITICS
(WEST AFRICA).=          ALOBA -54-TUP

THE PROCESSES OF FRAGMENTATION AND
CONSOLIDATION IN SUB-SAHARAN
AFRICA.=                 ANON  -59-PFC

PRESS AND POLITICS OF SOUTH
AFRICA.=                 BROUM -61-PPS

PATTERNS OF AUTHORITY IN WEST
AFRICA.=                 BROWP -51-PAW

AFRICA'S QUEST FOR ORDER.=
                         BURKFG-64-ASO

TRANSITION IN AFRICA -- STUDIES IN
POLITICAL ADAPTATION.=
                         CARTGW-58-TAS

THE POLITICS OF SUB-SAHARA AFRICA.=
                         COLEJS-60-PSS

POLITICAL PARTIES AND NATIONAL
INTEGRATION IN TROPICAL AFRICA.=
                         COLEJS-64-PPN

THE INFLUENCE OF NEWSPAPER AND
TELEVISION IN AFRICA.=
                         COLTJ -63-INT

EDUCATION AND NATION-BUILDING IN
AFRICA.=                 COWALG-65-ENB

HEADMAN AND THE RITUAL OF LAUPULA
VILLAGES (AFRICA).=      CUNNI -56-HRL

HIGHER EDUCATION AND POLITICAL
CHANGE IN EAST AFRICA.=
                         DE BBU-61-HEP

UNIVERSITIES AND NATION BUILDING IN
AFRICA.=                 DILLES-63-UNB

THE SEARCH FOR MODERNITY IN ASIA
AND AFRICA -- A REVIEW ARTICLE.=
                         DORERP-64-SMA

THE GOVERNMENTAL ROLES OF
ASSOCIATIONS AMONG THE YAKO (WEST
AFRICA).=                FORDD -61-GRA

CHANGING POLITICAL LEADERSHIP IN
WEST AFRICA.=            GARIP -54-CPL

OLD SOCIETIES AND NEW STATES -- THE
QUEST FOR MODERNITY IN ASIA AND
AFRICA.=                 GEERC -63-OSN

ASIANS IN EAST AFRICA -- PROBLEMS
AND PROSPECTS.=          GHAID -65-AEA

PORTRAIT OF A MINORITY -- ASIANS IN
EAST AFRICA.=            GHAIDP-65-PMA

AFRICA          (CONTINUATION)
RITUALS OF REBELLION IN SOUTH EAST
AFRICA.=                 GLICM -54-RRS

THE VILLAGE HEADMAN IN BRITISH
CENTRAL AFRICA.=         GLUCM -49-VHB

POLITICAL SYSTEMS AND THE
DISTRIBUTION OF POWER (INDIA,
AFRICA, JAPAN).=         GLUCM -65-PSD

AN AFRICAN ELITE -- A SAMPLE SURVEY
OF 52 FORMER STUDENTS OF MAKERERE
COLLEGE IN EAST AFRICA.=
                         GOLDJE-55-AES

FEUDALISM IN AFRICA.=    GOODJ -63-FA

POLITY, BUREAUCRACY AND INTEREST
GROUPS IN THE NEAR EAST AND NORTH
AFRICA.=                 GRASG -64-PBI

THE 'CLASS STRUGGLE' IN AFRICA --
AN EXAMINATION OF CONFLICTING
THEORIES (WEST AFRICA).=
                         GRUNKW-64-CSA

THE 'CLASS STRUGGLE' IN AFRICA --
AN EXAMINATION OF CONFLICTING
THEORIES (WEST AFRICA).=
                         GRUNKW-64-CSA

NORTH AFRICA -- A NEW PRAGMATISM.=
                         HAHNL -64-NAN

CHIEFTAINSHIP IN TRANSKEIAN
POLITICAL DEVELOPMENT (AFRICA).=
                         HAMMD -64-CTP

SEGMENTATION AND FISSION IN
CAPE NGUNI POLITICAL UNITS
(AFRICA).=               HAMMWD-65-SFC

KGENA CHIEFTAINSHIP IN BASUTOLAND
(AFRICA).=               HAMNI -65-KCB

NATIONALISM IN COLONIAL AFRICA.=
                         HODGT -56-NCA

CHIEFTAINSHIP (AFRICA).=
                         HOWMR -66-CA

THE NEW SOCIETIES OF TROPICAL
AFRICA.=                 HUNTG -63-NST

EDUCATIONAL POLICY AND POLITICAL
DEVELOPMENT IN AFRICA.=
                         HUSSER-46-EPP

THE NEW LEADERS OF AFRICA.=
                         ITALR -61-NLA

THE MILITARY IN THE POLITICAL
DEVELOPMENT OF NEW NATIONS -- AN
ESSAY IN COMPARATIVE ANALYSIS
(ASIA, AFRICA, MIDDLE EAST).=
                         JANOM -64-MPD

THE NEW ELITE IN ASIA AND AFRICA --
A COMPARATIVE STUDY OF INDONESIA
AND AFRICA (GHANA).=     KERST -66-NEA

THE NEW ELITE IN ASIA AND AFRICA --
A COMPARATIVE STUDY OF INDONESIA
AND AFRICA (GHANA).=     KERST -66-NEA

NATIONALISM AND SOCIAL CLASSES IN
BRITISH WEST AFRICA.=    KILSML-58-NSC

DEMOGRAPHIC ASPECTS OF WHITE
SUPREMACY IN SOUTH AFRICA.=
                         KUPEL -50-DAW

AN AFRICAN BOURGEOISIE -- RACE,

6

AFRICA                (CONTINUATION)
  CLASS, AND POLITICS IN SOUTH
  AFRICA.=              KUPEL -65-ABR

  POLITICAL LEADERSHIP IN AFRICA.=
                       LEVIVT-67-PLA

  POLITICS IN WEST AFRICA.=
                       LEWIWA-65-PWA

  THE POLITICAL CLIMATE FOR ECONOMIC
  DEVELOPMENT (AFRICA).=
                       LEYSC -66-PCE

  SACRED KINGSHIP AND GOVERNMENT
  AMONG THE YORUBA (AFRICA).=
                       LLOYPC-60-SKG

  INTRODUCTION -- THE STUDY OF THE
  ELITE (TROPICAL AFRICA).=
                       LLOYPC-66-ISE

  THE NEW ELITES OF TROPICAL AFRICA
  -- STUDIES PRESENTED AND DISCUSSED
  AT THE SIXTH INTERNATIONAL AFRICAN
  SEMINAR AT THE UNIVERSITY OF
  IBADAN.=              LLOYPC-66-NET

  CHIEFS AND POLITICS (AFRICA).=
                       LOVEAJ-59-CPA

  THE TRIBAL ELITE AND THE TRANSKEIAN
  ELECTIONS OF 1963 (SOUTH AFRICA).=
                       MAYEP -66-TET

  THE SOLDIER AND THE STATE IN EAST
  AFRICA -- SOME THEORETICAL
  CONCLUSIONS ON THE ARMY MUTINIES
  OF 1964.=             MAZRAA-7 -SSE

  POLITICAL PARTIES IN
  FRENCH-SPEAKING WEST AFRICA.=
                       MORGRS-64-PPF

  AFRICAN ELITE IN SOUTH AFRICA.=
                       NGCOSB-56-AES

  POLITICS, NATIONALISM AND
  UNIVERSITIES IN AFRICA.=
                       NICOD -63-PNU

  TRADE UNIONS AND POLITICS IN FRENCH
  WEST AFRICA DURING THE FOURTH
  REPUBLIC.=            PFEFG -67-TUP

  KWAME NKRUMAH AND THE FUTURE OF
  AFRICA.=              PHILJ -61-KNF

  THE NATURE OF MODERNIZATION -- THE
  MIDDLE EAST AND AND NORTH AFRICA.=
                       POLKWR-65-NMM

  THE EMERGENCE OF AN ELITE -- A CASE
  STUDY OF A WEST COAST FAMILY (WEST
  AFRICA).=             PRIEM -66-EEC

  NATIONALISM AND THE TRADE UNION IN
  FRENCH NORTH AFRICA.= RF    -52-NTU

  CONSTITUTIONAL REFORM IN FRENCH
  TROPICAL AFRICA.=     ROBIK -58-CRF

  THE ORIGINS OF NATIONALIST
  DISCONTENT IN EAST AND CENTRAL
  AFRICA.=              ROTBRI-63-CND

  THE POLITICS OF THE NEAR EAST --
  SOUTHWEST ASIA AND NORTHERN
  AFRICA.=              RUSTDA-60-PNE

  A WORLD OF NATIONS -- PROBLEMS OF
  POLITICAL MODERNIZATION (ASIA,

AFRICA                (CONTINUATION)
  AFRICA, LATIN AMERICA).=
                       RUSTDA-67-WNP

  SINGLE PARTY SYSTEMS IN WEST
  AFRICA.=              SCHAR -61-SPS

  OPPOSITION IN THE NEW STATES OF
  ASIA AND AFRICA.=     SHILE -66-ONS

  AFRICA'S NEW POLITICAL LEADERS.=
                       SMYTHH-59-ASN

  BLACK AFRICA'S NEW POWER ELITE.=
                       SMYTHH-60-BAS

  THE NON - AFRICAN MINORITY IN
  MODERN AFRICA -- SOCIAL STATUS.=
                       SMYTHH-61-NAM

  SOCIAL CHANGE IN MODERN AFRICA.=
                       SOUTA -61-SCM

  POLITICS IN AFRICA.=  SPIRHJ-62-PA

  AFRICA -- THE PRIMACY OF POLITICS
  (CONGO, NIGERIA).=    SPIRHJ-66-APP

  THE NOTION OF THE ELITE AND THE
  URBAN SOCIAL SURVEY IN AFRICA.=
                       TARDC -56-NEU

  APARTHEID AND POLITICS IN SOUTH
  AFRICA.=              TIRYEQ-60-APS

  POLITICAL INSTITUTIONS AND
  AFRIKANER SOCIAL STRUCTURES IN THE
  REPUBLIC OF SOUTH AFRICA.=
                       TRAPS -63-PIA

  THE ARMED FORCES OF SOUTH AFRICA.=
                       TYLDG -54-AFS

  ELITES IN FRENCH - SPEAKING WEST
  AFRICA -- THE SOCIAL BASIS OF
  IDEAS.=               WALLI -65-EFS

  SHIFTING AUTHORITY IN WEST AFRICA.=
                       WELCCE-66-SAW

  ASPECTS OF BUREAUCRATIZATION IN
  ASHANTI IN THE NINETEENTH CENTURY
  (AFRICA).=            WILKI -66-ABA

  TRADE UNIONS IN AFRICA.=
                       WILLRW-55-TUA

  THE ANALYSIS OF SOCIAL CHANGE --
  BASED ON OBSERVATIONS IN CENTRAL
  AFRICA.=              WILSG -45-ASC

  THE PUBLIC SERVICE IN THE NEW
  STATES -- AFRICA.=    YOUNK -60-PSN

  CREATING POLITICAL ORDER -- THE
  PARTY - STATES OF WEST AFRICA
  (MALI, GHANA, SENEGAL, GUINEA,
  IVORY COAST).=        ZOLBAR-66-CPO

AFRICAN
  THE ISLAMIC FACTOR IN AFRICAN
  POLITICS.=            ABU-I -64-IFA

  DEMOCRACY AND SOCIALISM --
  IDEOLOGIES OF AFRICAN LEADERS.=
                       ANDRCF-64-DSI

  THE INTRODUCTION OF BUREAUCRACY
  INTO AFRICAN POLITICS.=
                       APTHR -60-IBI

  THE ELUSIVENESS OF POWER -- THE

AFRICAN                (CONTINUATION)
AFRICAN SINGLE PARTY STATE.=
                        ASHFDE-65-EPA

BUNYORO -- AN AFRICAN FEUDALITY.=
                        BEATJH-64-BAF

THE AFRICAN PATRICTS -- LEADERSHIP
OF AFRICAN NATIONAL CONGRESS.=
                        BENSM -64-APL

THE AFRICAN PATRICTS -- LEADERSHIP
OF AFRICAN NATIONAL CONGRESS.=
                        BENSM -64-APL

AFRICAN ATTITUDES -- A STUDY OF THE
SOCIAL, RACIAL, AND POLITICAL
ATTITUDES OF SOME MIDDLE CLASS
AFRICANS.=              BRETEA-63-AAS

THE AFRICAN MILITARY BALANCE.=
                        BROWN -64-AMB

NATIONAL UNITY AND REGIONALISM IN
EIGHT AFRICAN STATES (NIGERIA,
NIGER, THE CONGO, GABON, CENTRAL
AFRICAN REPUBLIC, CHAD, UGANDA,
ETHIOPIA).=             CARTGM-66-NUR

NATIONAL UNITY AND REGIONALISM IN
EIGHT AFRICAN STATES (NIGERIA,
NIGER, THE CONGO, GABON, CENTRAL
AFRICAN REPUBLIC, CHAD, UGANDA,
ETHIOPIA).=             CARTGM-66-NUR

AFRICAN ONE PARTY STATES.=
                        CARTGW-62-AOP

THE ROLE OF BUREAUCRATIC NORMS IN
AFRICAN POLITICAL STRUCTURES.=
                        COLSE -58-RBN

THE WEST AFRICAN INTELLECTUAL
COMMUNITY.=             COWVM -62-WAI

FROM EMPIRE TO NATION -- THE RISE
TO SELF-ASSERTION OF ASIAN AND
AFRICAN PEOPLES.=       EMERR -60-ENR

POLITICS IN AN URBAN AFRICAN
COMMUNITY.=             EPSTAL-58-PUA

AFRICAN POLITICAL SYSTEMS.=
                        EVANEE-40-APS

THE PREDICAMENT OF THE MODERN
AFRICAN CHIEF -- AN INSTANCE FROM
UGANDA.=                FALLL -55-PMA

DESPOTISM, STATUS CULTURE AND
SOCIAL MOBILITY IN AN AFRICAN
KINGDOM (UGANDA).=      FALLLA-59-DSC

AUTHORITY, EFFICIENCY, AND ROLE
STRESS -- PROBLEMS IN THE
DEVELOPMENT OF EAST AFRICAN
BUREAUCRACIES (UGANDA, KENYA,
TANGANYIKA).=           FLEMWG-66-AER

THE WEST AFRICAN STUDENT'S UNION --
A STUDY IN CULTURE CONTACT.=
                        GARIP -53-WAS

AN AFRICAN ELITE -- A SAMPLE SURVEY
OF 52 FORMER STUDENTS OF MAKERERE
COLLEGE IN EAST AFRICA.=
                        GOLDJE-55-AES

SOCIAL CONTROL IN AN AFRICAN
SOCIETY (ARUSHA OF TANGANYIKA).=
                        GULLPH-63-SCA

THE DEBATE ON CENTRAL AFRICAN

AFRICAN                (CONTINUATION)
FEDERATION IN RETROSPECT.=
                        GUTTWF-57-DCA

THE POLITICAL ROLE OF AFRICAN ARMED
FORCES -- THE IMPACT OF FOREIGN
MILITARY ASSISTANCE.=   GUTTWF-67-PRA

THE AFRICAN UNIVERSITY AND HUMAN
RESOURCES DEVELOPMENT.=
                        HARKF -65-AUH

TRADE UNIONS IN TRAVAIL -- THE
STORY OF THE BROEDERBOND -
NATIONALIST PLAN TO CONTROL SOUTH
AFRICAN TRADE UNIONS.=
                        HEPPA -54-TUT

AFRICAN POLITICAL PARTIES.=
                        HODGT -61-APP

AFRICAN LEADERSHIP IN TRANSITION --
AN OUTLINE.=            HOWMR -56-ALT

THE SOCIAL BACKGROUND OF A WEST
AFRICAN STUDENT POPULATION -- 1 --
2.=                     JAHOG -54-SBW

THE PRINCIPLES OF AFRICAN TRIBAL
ADMINISTRATION.=        KHAMT -51-PAT

AFRICAN POLITICAL CHANGE AND
MODERNISATION PROCESS.=
                        KILSM -63-APC

POLITICAL CHANGE IN A WEST AFRICAN
STATE -- A STUDY OF THE
MODERNIZATION PROCESS IN
SIERRA LEONE.=          KILSM -66-PCW

AUTHORITARIAN AND SINGLE - PARTY
TENDENCIES IN AFRICAN POLITICS.=
                        KILSML-63-ASP

THE EDUCATED AFRICAN.=
                        KITCH -62-EA

THE WEST AFRICAN SCENE.=
                        KOLAW -61-WAS

AFRICAN ELITES IN INDUSTRIAL
BUREAUCRACY (UGANDA).=
                        KUMAC -66-AEI

THE AFRICAN ARISTOCRACY -- RANK
AMONG THE SWAZI.=       KUPEH -47-AAR

AN AFRICAN BOURGEOISIE -- RACE,
CLASS, AND POLITICS IN SOUTH
AFRICA.=                KUPEL -65-ABR

BEYOND AFRICAN DICTATORSHIP.=
                        LEGUO -65-BAD

BEYOND AFRICAN DICTATORSHIP -- THE
CRISIS OF THE ONE - PARTY STATE.=
                        LEWIWA-65-BAD

THE SIGNIFICANCE OF THE WEST
AFRICAN CREOLE.=        LITTKL-50-SWA

TWO WEST AFRICAN ELITES.=
                        LITTKL-56-TWA

THE ROLE OF VOLUNTARY ASSOCIATIONS
IN WEST AFRICAN URBANISATION.=
                        LITTKL-57-RVA

WEST AFRICAN URBANIZATION -- A
STUDY OF VOLUNTARY ASSOCIATIONS IN
SOCIAL CHANGE.=         LITTKL-65-WAU

THE NEW ELITES OF TROPICAL AFRICA

AFRICAN (CONTINUATION)
-- STUDIES PRESENTED AND DISCUSSED
AT THE SIXTH INTERNATIONAL AFRICAN
SEMINAR AT THE UNIVERSITY OF
IBADAN.= LLOYPC-66-NET

AFRICAN CHIEFS TODAY.=
MAIRLP-58-ACT

PROFILES OF AFRICAN LEADERS.=
MELATP-61-PAL

AFRICAN ELITE IN SOUTH AFRICA.=
NGCOSB-56-AES

SOCIAL DISTANCE ATTITUDES OF SOUTH
AFRICAN STUDENTS.= PETTTF-60-SDA

EAST AFRICAN AGE - CLASS SYSTEMS --
AN INQUIRY INTO THE SOCIAL ORDER
OF GALLA, KIPSIGIS, AND KIKUYU.=
PRINAH-53-EAA

EAST AFRICAN CHIEFS -- A STUDY OF
POLITICAL DEVELOPMENT IN SOME
UGANDA AND TANGANYIKA TRIBES.=
RICHAI-59-EAC

POLITICAL CHANGE IN A TRADITIONAL
AFRICAN CLAN -- A STRUCTURAL
FUNCTIONAL ANALYSIS OF THE NSITS
OF NIGERIA.= SCARJR-65-PCT

THE ADOPTION OF POLITICAL STYLES BY
AFRICAN POLITICIANS IN THE
RHODESIAS.= SCARJR-66-APS

THE POLITICS OF AFRICAN
NATIONALISM.= SHEPGW-62-PAN

NIGERIAN POLITICAL PARTIES -- POWER
IN AN EMERGENT AFRICAN NATION.=
SKLARL-63-NPP

THE NEW AFRICAN LEADERS.=
SMYTHH-61-NAL

THE NCN - AFRICAN MINORITY IN
MODERN AFRICA -- SOCIAL STATUS.=
SMYTHH-61-NAM

SCHISM AND CONTINUITY IN AN AFRICAN
SOCIETY.= TURNVW-57-SCA

AFRICAN ELITES.= UNES -56-AE

CANEVILLE -- THE SOCIAL STRUCTURE
OF A SOUTH AFRICAN TOWN.=
VAN-PL-64-CSS

THE DIVINE KINGDOM OF THE JUKUN --
A RE-EVALUATION OF SOME THEORIES
(EAST AFRICAN).= YOUNMW-66-DKJ

AFRICANS
SOME PSYCHOLOGICAL CONCEPTS OF
URBAN AFRICANS.= BLOOL -64-PCU

AFRICAN ATTITUDES -- A STUDY OF THE
SOCIAL, RACIAL, AND POLITICAL
ATTITUDES OF SOME MIDDLE CLASS
AFRICANS.= BRETEA-63-AAS

KENYA'S FIRST DIRECT ELECTIONS FOR
AFRICANS, MARCH 1957.=
ENGHGF-57-KSF

EDUCATED AFRICANS -- SOME
CONCEPTUAL AND TERMINOLOGICAL
PROBLEMS.= GOLDJE-61-EAC

EDUCATED AFRICANS.= HARGJD-59-EA

AFRIKANER
POLITICAL INSTITUTIONS AND
AFRIKANER SOCIAL STRUCTURES IN THE
REPUBLIC OF SOUTH AFRICA.=
TRAPS -63-PIA

AFRO-ASIAN
THE CHANGING SOVIET PERCEPTION OF
THE DEVELOPMENT PROCESS IN THE
AFRO-ASIAN WORLD.= CARLDS-64-CSP

AGAIN
ON THE LEFT AGAIN (GREAT BRITAIN).=
CROSCA-60-LAG

SOCIAL MOBILITY AGAIN -- AND ELITES
(UNITED STATES, WESTERN EUROPE).=
LUETH -55-SMA

AGAINST
THE STRUGGLE OF SOVIET JURISTS
AGAINST A RETURN TO STALINIST
TERROR.= BERMHJ-63-SSJ

RUSSIANS AGAINST STALIN.=
CHAMWH-52-RAS

WHY THE ODDS ARE AGAINST A
GOVERNOR'S BECOMING PRESIDENT
(UNITED STATES).= HARRL -59-WOA

AGE
BRITISH POLITICS IN THE
COLLECTIVIST AGE.= BEERSH-65-BPC

THE AGE OF CHANGE -- POLITICAL AND
INTELLECTUAL LEADERSHIP IN NORTH
CAROLINA (UNITED STATES).=
BLACR -61-AOP

ARAB ISLAM IN THE MODERN AGE.=
DAWNCE-65-AIM

FROM GENERATION TO GENERATION --
AGE GROUPS AND SOCIAL STRUCTURE.=
EISESN-56-GGA

AGE AS A FACTOR IN THE RECRUITMENT
OF COMMUNIST LEADERSHIP
(SOVIET UNION).= HOLTRT-54-AFR

MAN AND SOCIETY IN AN AGE OF
RECONSTRUCTION.= MANNK -40-MSA

PERMANENT REVOLUTION --
TOTALITARIANISM IN THE AGE OF
WORLD AT WAR (GERMANY).=
NEUMS -65-PRT

FROM YOUTHFUL ZEAL TO MIDDLE AGE
(SOVIET UNION, KOMSOMOL).=
PLOSSI-58-YZM

EAST AFRICAN AGE - CLASS SYSTEMS --
AN INQUIRY INTO THE SOCIAL ORDER
OF GALLA, KIPSIGIS, AND KIKUYU.=
PRINAH-53-EAA

CONSTITUTIONAL DICTATORSHIP IN THE
ATOMIC AGE (UNITED STATES).=
ROSSCL-49-CDA

SCIENTISTS IN THE BUREAUCRATIC
AGE.= SPEYE -57-SBA

THE AGE FACTOR IN THE 1958
CONGRESSIONAL ELECTIONS
(UNITED STATES).= WALKDB-60-AFC

AGENCIES
THE DYNAMICS OF BUREAUCRACY -- A
STUDY OF INTERPERSONAL RELATIONS

9

AGENCIES                    (CONTINUATION)
IN TWC GOVERNMENT AGENCIES
(UNITED STATES).=      BLAUPM-55-CBS

RECRUITMENT ANC SELECTION PRACTICES
IN FOUR GOVERNMENT AGENCIES
(PHILIPPINES).=        FRANGA-57-RSP

BEHIND THE PRESIDENT -- A STUDY OF
THE EXECUTIVE CFFICE AGENCIES
(UNITED STATES).=      HOBBEH-54-BPS

AN APPRCPRIATICNS SUBCOMMITTEE ANC
ITS CLIENT AGENCIES -- A
CCMPARATIVE STUCY CF SUPERVISION
AND CCNTRCL (UNITED STATES).=
                       SHARI -65-ASI

SUPREME COURT ATTITUDES TOWARD
FEDERAL ADMINISTRATIVE AGENCIES
(UNITED STATES).=      TANEJ -60-SCA

CCURTS AS PCLITICAL ANC
GCVERNMENTAL AGENCIES
(UNITED STATES).=      VINEKN-65-CPG

AGENCY
PATTERNS OF INTERACTICN AMONG A
GRCUP CF CFFICIALS IN A GOVERNMENT
AGENCY (UNITED STATES).=
                       BLAUPM-54-PIA

CCNGRESSICNAL CCMMITTEE MEMBERS AS
INDEPENDENT AGENCY CVERSEERS -- A
CASE STUDY (UNITED STATES).=
                       SCHES -60-CCM

REGULATCRY AGENCY CCNTRCL THROUGH
APPOINTMENT -- THE CASE OF THE
EISENHCWER ADMINISTRATICN AND THE
NLRB (UNITED STATES).=
                       SCHES -61-RAC

AGENDA
AGENDA FOR THE STUCY CF POLITICAL
ELITES.=               LASSHD-61-ASP

AGENTS
PROFESSICNAL PCLITICIANS -- A STUCY
CF BRITISH PARTY AGENTS.=
                       COMFGO-58-PPS

AGITATORS
BUREAUCRATS AND AGITATCRS.=
                       GOULAW-65-BA

ADMINISTRATCRS, AGITATCRS, AND
BRCKERS.=              PYE,LW-58-AAB

AGRARIANISM
AGRARIANISM IN ISRAEL'S PARTY
SYSTEM.=               ETZIA -57-AIS

AGREEMENTS
AGREEMENTS BETWEEN LCCAL POLITICAL
PARTIES IN LOCAL GCVERNMENT
MATTERS (GREAT BRITAIN).=
                       THORW -57-ABL

AGRICULTURAL
CONFLICT AND DECISICN-MAKING IN
SCVIET RUSSIA -- A CASE STUDY OF
AGRICULTURAL PCLICY, 1953-1963.
                       PLOSSI-65-CDM

SELECTING LEACERS FCR AGRICULTURAL
PRCGRAMS (UNITED STATES).=
                       WAKERE-47-SLA

AGRICULTURE
REPRESENTATICN IN CCNGRESS -- THE
CASE CF THE HCUSE AGRICULTURE

AGRICULTURE                 (CCNTINUATICN)
CCMMITTEE (UNITED STATES).=
                       JCNECO-61-RCC

THE RECRGANIZATICN CF PARTY
LEADERSHIP IN AGRICULTURE
(SCVIET UNICN).=       KABYS -63-RPL

THE PCLITICS CF SCVIET
AGRICULTURE.=          LAIRRD-64-PSA

AGROVILLE
RURAL RESETTLEMENT IN SCUTH
VIET NAM -- THE AGROVILLE
PRCGRAM.=              ZASLJJ-62-RRS

AGUASCALIENTES
THE MEXICAN REVCLUTICN, 1914-1915
-- THE CONVENTICN CF
AGUASCALIENTES.=       CUIRRE-60-MRC

AIDIT
INDCNESIAN CCMMUNISM UNCER AIDIT.=
                       VAN-JM-58-ICU

AITUTAKI
SOCIAL CHANGE IN THE SCUTH PACIFIC
-- RARCTONGA ANC AITUTAKI.=
                       BEAGE -57-SCS

AL-AZHAR
AL-AZHAR IN THE REVCLUTION
(EGYPT).=              CRECD -66-AAR

ALABAMA
THE ALABAMA SENATCRIAL ELECTICN CF
1962 -- RETURN CF INTER-PARTY
CCMPETITICN (UNITED STATES).=
                       BURNWD-64-ASE

ALBANIAN
FRCM MCNARCHY TC CCMMUNISM -- THE
SCCIAL TRANSFCRMATICN CF THE
ALBANIAN ELITE.=       MOSKCC-65-MCS

ALGERIA
ELITE VALUES ANC ATTITUDINAL CHANGE
IN THE MAGHREB (MCRCCCC, ALGERIA,
TUNISIA).=             ASHFDE-67-EVA

ALGERIA -- REBELLICN AND
REVCLUTION.=           GILLJ -61-ARR

THE DECLINE CF ALGERIA'S FLN
(NATICNAL LIBERATICN FRCNT).=
                       LEWIWH-66-DAS

ALIENATICN
SCME TRENDS IN SCURCES CF
ALIENATICN FRCM THE SCVIET
SYSTEM.=               BAUER -55-TSA

IDECLCGICAL CCRRELATES CF RIGHT
WING PCLITICAL ALIENATICN IN
MEXICC.=               JCHNKF-65-ICR

ITALY -- FRAGMENTATICN, ISCLATION
AND ALIENATICN.=       LAPAJ -66-IFI

THE FUNCTICNS CF ALIENATION IN
LEADERSHIP (UNITED STATES).=
                       LCWRRP-62-FAL

ALIENATION AND FARTICIPATICN -- A
CCMPARISCN CF GROUP LEACERS ANC
THE MASS (UNITED STATES).=
                       RCSEAM-62-APC

ALIENATION ANC REVCLUTICN (CUBA).=
                       ZEITM -66-ARC

ALIGNMENT
NIGERIA -- PCLITICAL NCN-ALIGNMENT

AMERICAN            (CONTINUATION)
  POLICY.=          ALMOGA-60-APF

SOCIAL VALUES OF SOVIET AND
AMERICAN ELITES -- CONTENT
ANALYSIS OF ELITE MEDIA.=
                   ANGERC-64-SVS

POLITICAL LEADERSHIP IN AMERICAN
GOVERNMENT.=       BARBJD-64-PLA

AMERICAN BUSINESS AND PUBLIC POLICY
-- THE POLITICS OF FOREIGN TRADE.=
                   BAUER -63-ABP

THE NEW AMERICAN RIGHT.=
                   BELLD -55-NAR

HIGHER CIVIL SERVANTS IN AMERICAN
SOCIETY.=          BENDR -49-HCS

SOCIAL MOBILITY AND THE AMERICAN
BUSINESS ELITE --1 --2.=
                   BENDR -57-SMA

CIVIL LIBERTIES AND THE AMERICAN
SUPREME COURT.=    BETHLP-58-CLA

THE AMERICAN LAWYER -- A SUMMARY OF
THE SURVEY OF THE LEGAL
PROFESSION.=       BLAUAP-54-ALS

AMERICAN CONSERVATIVES.=
                   BROWBE-51-AC

AMERICAN VOTING BEHAVIOR.=
                   BURDE -59-AVB

THE AMERICAN VOTER.=  CAMPA -60-AV

THE ARABS' VIEW OF POSTWAR AMERICAN
FOREIGN POLICY (EGYPT, IRAN,
JORDAN, LEBANON, SYRIA).=
                   CASTHP-59-AVP

COMMUNITY POWER PERSPECTIVES AND
ROLE DEFINITIONS OF NORTH AMERICAN
EXECUTIVES IN AN ARGENTINE
COMMUNITY.=        CHAME -66-CPP

AMERICAN OPINION AND FOREIGN
POLICY.=           CHANG -55-AOF

AMERICAN CIVILIZATION AND ITS
LEADERSHIP NEEDS, 1960-1990.=
                   CHARJC-59-ACI

CAPITALISM AND AMERICAN
LEADERSHIP.=       COX,CC-62-CAL

LOCALS AND COSMOPOLITANS IN
AMERICAN GRADUATE SCHOOLS.=
                   DAVIJA-62-LCA

MODERN AMERICAN SOCIETY -- READINGS
IN THE PROBLEMS OF ORDER AND
CHANGE.=           DAVIK -49-MAS

INTER - PARTY COMPETITION, ECONOMIC
VARIABLES, AND WELFARE POLICIES IN
THE AMERICAN STATES.=  DAWSRE-63-IPC

PRESSURE GROUPS AND AMERICAN
POLICY.=           DCW  -50-PGA

THE LAWYER AS DECISION-MAKER IN THE
AMERICAN STATE LEGISLATURE.=
                   DERGOR-59-LDM

SOCIAL VALUES OF SOVIET AND
AMERICAN ELITES -- INSIGHTS FROM
SOVIET LITERATURE.=  DUNHVS-64-SVS

AMERICAN            (CONTINUATION)
AMERICAN IMPACT UPON MIDDLE EAST
LEADERSHIP.=       EFIMNM-54-AIU

THE PUBLIC STUDIES DIVISION OF THE
DEPARTMENT OF THE STATE -- PUBLIC
OPINION ANALYSIS IN THE
FORMULATION AND CONDUCT OF
AMERICAN FOREIGN POLICY.=
                   ELDERE-57-PSD

THE POLICY MACHINE -- THE
DEPARTMENT OF STATE AND AMERICAN
FOREIGN POLICY.=   ELDERE-60-PMD

AMERICAN INTEREST GROUPS -- A
SURVEY OF RESEARCH AND SOME
IMPLICATIONS FOR THEORY AND
METHOD.=           ELDESJ-58-AIG

BRITISH MASS PARTIES IN COMPARISON
WITH AMERICAN PARTIES.=
                   EPSTLD-56-BMP

THE POLITICAL SOCIALIZATION OF
AMERICAN STATE LEGISLATORS.=
                   EULAH -59-PSA

CAREER PERSPECTIVES OF AMERICAN
STATE LEGISLATORS.=  EULAH -61-CPA

CIVILIANS, SOLDIERS, AND AMERICAN
MILITARY POLICY.=  FOX,WT-55-CSA

AMERICAN SCIENTISTS AND NUCLEAR
WEAPONS POLICY.=   GILPRG-62-ASN

MACHINE POLITICS IN AMERICAN TRADE
UNIONS.=           GITLAL-52-MPA

SOCIAL CLASS IN AMERICAN
SOCIOLOGY.=        GORDMM-58-SCA

AN UNCERTAIN TRADITION -- AMERICAN
SECRETARIES OF STATE IN THE
TWENTIETH CENTURY.=  GRAENA-61-UTA

AMERICAN POLITICAL PARTIES AND
AMERICAN SYSTEM.=  GRODM -60-APP

AMERICAN POLITICAL PARTIES AND
AMERICAN SYSTEM.=  GRODM -60-APP

THE ELECTED AND THE ANNOINTED --
TWO AMERICAN ELITES.=  HACKA -61-EAT

POPULAR LEADERSHIP IN THE ANGLO -
AMERICAN DEMOCRACIES (CANADA,
GREAT BRITAIN, UNITED STATES).=
                   HARGEC-67-PLA

OPINION LEADERS IN AMERICAN
COMMUNITIES.=      HEROAO-59-OLA

PUBLIC OPINION AND AMERICAN FOREIGN
POLICY -- THE QUEMOY CRISIS OF
1958.=             IRISMD-60-POA

PARTY VOTING IN AMERICAN STATE
LEGISLATURES.=     JEWEME-55-PVA

THE REPUBLICAN PARTY IN AMERICAN
POLITICS.=         JONECO-65-RPA

RECRUITMENT PROBLEMS OF THE FRENCH
HIGHER CIVIL SERVICE -- AN
AMERICAN APPRAISAL.=  JUMPR -57-RPF

THE AMERICAN LEGISLATIVE PROCESS --
CONGRESS AND THE STATES.=
                   KEEFWJ-64-ALP

PUBLIC OPINION AND AMERICAN

AMERICAN          (CONTINUATION)
  DEMOCRACY.=      KEY-VO-61-POA

STRATEGIC POLICY AND AMERICAN
GOVERNMENT -- STRUCTURAL
CONSTRAINTS AND VARIABLES.=
                  KOLOEJ-65-SPA

AMERICAN INTELLECTUALS AND FOREIGN
POLICY.=          KRISI -67-AIF

LABOR'S ROLE IN AMERICAN POLITICS.=
                  LAIDHW-59-LSR

THE AMERICAN LIBERALS AND THE
RUSSIAN REVOLUTION.=   LASCC -62-ALR

THE AMERICAN DEMOCRACY -- A
CONTEMPORARY AND AN
INTERPRETATION.=       LASKHJ-48-ADC

AMERICAN SOCIAL CLASSES --
STATISTICAL STRATA OR SOCIAL
GROUPS.=          LENSGE-52-ASC

AMERICAN INTELLECTUALS -- THEIR
POLITICS AND STATUS.=  LIPSSM-59-AIT

AMERICAN BUSINESS, PUBLIC POLICY,
CASE-STUDIES AND POLITICAL
THEORY.=          LOWITJ-64-ABP

AMERICAN INTELLECTUALS AND U.S.
VIETNAM POLICY.=  LOWRCW-65-AIU

AMERICAN UNIVERSITY STUDENTS -- A
PRESUMPTIVE ELITE.=    MARVD -65-AUS

CONSENSUS AND IDEOLOGY IN AMERICAN
POLITICS.=        MCCLH -64-CIA

AMERICAN MILITARY GOVERNMENT IN
KOREA.=           MEADEG-51-AMG

THE AMERICAN BUSINESS ELITE -- A
COLLECTIVE PORTRAIT.=  MILLCW-54-ABE

THE STRUCTURE OF POWER IN AMERICAN
SOCIETY.=         MILLCW-58-SPA

DECISION-MAKING CLIQUES IN
COMMUNITY POWER STRUCTURES -- A
COMPARATIVE STUDY OF AN AMERICAN
AND AN ENGLISH CITY.=  MILLDC-58-DMC

THE RECRUITMENT OF THE AMERICAN
BUSINESS ELITE.=  MILLW -50-RAB

THE AMERICAN COUNCIL OF ECONOMIC
ADVISERS AND JOINT COMMITTEE ON
THE ECONOMIC REPORT.=  MILNRS-55-ACE

OCCUPATIONAL ROLE STRAINS -- THE
AMERICAN ELECTIVE PUBLIC
OFFICIAL.=        MITCWC-58-ORS

THE AMBIVALENT SOCIAL STATUS OF THE
AMERICAN POLITICIAN.=  MITCWC-59-ASS

THE AMERICAN POLITY -- A SOCIAL AND
CULTURAL INTERPRETATION.=
                  MITCWC-62-APS

SOME CHARACTERISTICS OF AMERICAN
NEGRO LEADERS.=   MONATP-56-CAN

THE MAKERS OF PUBLIC POLICY --
AMERICAN POWER GROUPS AND THEIR
IDEOLOGIES.=      MONSRJ-65-MPP

CONGRESS AND THE COURT -- A CASE
STUDY IN THE AMERICAN POLITICAL

AMERICAN          (CONTINUATION)
  PROCESS.=       MURPWF-62-CCC

AN AMERICAN DILEMMA -- THE NEGRO
PROBLEM AND MODERN DEMOCRACY.=
                  MYRDG -44-ADN

THE DISTRIBUTION OF POWER IN
AMERICAN SOCIETY.=     PARST -57-DPA

AMERICAN POLITICS AND THE RADICAL
RIGHT.=           PAYNT -62-APR

THE AMERICAN LABOUR MOVEMENT -- A
BRITISH VIEW.=    PELLH -54-ALM

PRESIDENTIAL ELECTIONS --
STRATEGIES OF AMERICAN ELECTORAL
POLITICS.=        POLSNW-64-PES

THE AMERICAN GOVERNING CLASS.=
                  POTTA -62-AGC

VERBAL SHIFTS IN THE AMERICAN
PRESIDENCY -- A CONTENT ANALYSIS.=
                  PROTJW-56-VSA

DEMOCRACY AND THE AMERICAN PARTY
SYSTEM.=          RANNA -56-DAP

CLASS IN AMERICAN SOCIETY.=
                  REISL -59-CAS

DONSHIP IN A MEXICAN - AMERICAN
COMMUNITY IN TEXAS.=   ROMAOI-60-DMA

THE POWER STRUCTURE -- POLITICAL
PROCESS IN AMERICAN SOCIETY.=
                  ROSEAM-67-PSP

CONSENSUS-BUILDING IN THE AMERICAN
NATIONAL COMMUNITY -- SOME
HYPOTHESES AND SOME SUPPORTING
DATA.=            ROSEJN-62-CBA

THE AMERICAN PRESIDENCY.=
                  ROSSCL-56-AP

THE ROLE OF THE MILITARY IN
AMERICAN FOREIGN POLICY.=
                  SAPIBM-4 -RMA

LAWYERS AND AMERICAN POLITICS -- A
CLARIFIED VIEW.=  SCHLJA-57-LAP

THE STRUCTURE OF COMPETITION FOR
OFFICE IN THE AMERICAN STATES.=
                  SCHLJA-60-SCC

AN AMERICAN LOOKS AT THE PARTY
CONFERENCES (GREAT BRITAIN).=
                  SHAWM -62-ALP

SOVIET AND AMERICAN FOREIGN POLICY
ATTITUDES -- CONTENT ANALYSIS OF
ELITE ARTICULATIONS.=  SINGDJ-64-SAF

POLITICAL PARTIES IN THE AMERICAN
SYSTEM.=          SORAFJ-64-PPA

THE AMERICAN SYSTEM IN CRISIS.=
                  TRUMDB-59-ASC

THE POLITICAL PARTY AFFILIATION OF
AMERICAN POLITICAL SCIENTISTS.=
                  TURNHA-63-PPA

AMERICAN STATE LEGISLATORS' ROLE
ORIENTATIONS TOWARD PRESSURE
GROUPS.=          WAHLJC-60-ASL

THE AMERICAN FEDERAL EXECUTIVE -- A

AMERICAN                    (CONTINUATION)
STUDY OF SOCIAL AND PERSONAL
CHARACTERISTICS OF THE CIVILIAN
AND MILITARY LEADERS OF THE UNITED
STATES FEDERAL GOVERNMENT.=
                           WARNWL-63-AFE

THE USES OF POWER -- 7 CASES IN
AMERICAN POLITICS.=   WESTAF-62-UPC

POLITICAL ADVANCEMENT IN THE SOUTH
PACIFIC -- A COMPARATIVE STUDY OF
COLONIAL PRACTICE IN FIJI, TAHITI,
AND AMERICAN SAMOA.=   WESTFJ-61-PAS

SOME VARIABLES OF MIDDLE AND LOWER
CLASS IN TWO CENTRAL AMERICAN
CITIES.=              WILLRC-62-VML

AMERICAN BUREAUCRACY.=
                       WOLLP -63-AB

INTEREST GROUPS IN AMERICAN
SOCIETY.=              ZIEGH -64-IGA

AMERICANS
CURRENT LEADERSHIP PROBLEMS AMONG
JAPANESE AMERICANS.=   BURMJH-53-CLP

PATRON - PEON PATTERN AMONG THE
SPANISH AMERICANS OF NEW MEXICO.=
                       KNOWCS-62-PPP

AMERICAS
COLONIAL ELITES -- ROME, SPAIN AND
THE AMERICAS.=         SYMER -58-CER

ANALYSIS
THE JUDICIAL PROCESS -- AN
INTRODUCTORY ANALYSIS OF THE
COURTS OF THE UNITED STATES,
ENGLAND AND FRANCE.=   ABRAHJ-62-JPI

SOCIAL VALUES OF SOVIET AND
AMERICAN ELITES -- CONTENT
ANALYSIS OF ELITE MEDIA.=
                       ANGERC-64-SVS

POLITICAL ELITES -- A MODE OF
ANALYSIS.=             BECKC -66-PEM

POLITICAL ELITES IN COLONIAL
SOUTHEAST ASIA -- AN HISTORICAL
ANALYSIS.=             BENDHJ-64-PEC

AN ANALYSIS OF SOCIAL POWER.=
                       BIERR -50-ASP

COMMUNISM IN SOUTHEAST ASIA -- A
POLITICAL ANALYSIS.=   BRIMJH-59-CSA

ECONOMIC DOMINANTS AND COMMUNITY
POWER -- A COMPARATIVE ANALYSIS
(UNITED STATES).=      CLELDA-64-EDC

YOUTH AND COMMUNISM -- AN
HISTORICAL ANALYSIS OF
INTERNATIONAL COMMUNIST YOUTH
MOVEMENTS.=            CORNR -65-YCH

MODERN POLITICAL ANALYSIS.=
                       DAHLRA-63-MPA

POLITICAL IDEOLOGY AS A TOOL OF
FUNCTIONAL ANALYSIS IN
SOCIO-POLITICAL DYNAMICS.=
                       DIONL -59-PIT

THE NEW CLASS -- AN ANALYSIS OF THE
COMMUNIST SYSTEM (YUGOSLAVIA).=
                       DJILM -57-NCA

A SYSTEMS ANALYSIS OF POLITICAL

ANALYSIS                    (CONTINUATION)
LIFE.=                 EASTD -65-SAP

SOCIAL BACKGROUND IN ELITE ANALYSIS
-- A METHODOLOGICAL INQUIRY
(FRANCE, GERMANY).=    EDINLU-67-SBE

PRIMITIVE POLITICAL SYSTEMS -- A
COMPARATIVE ANALYSIS.=
                       EISESN-59-PPS

THE DEVELOPMENT OF SOCIO-POLITICAL
CENTERS AT THE SECOND STAGE OF
MODERNISATION -- A COMPARATIVE
ANALYSIS OF TWO TYPES.=
                       EISESN-66-DSP

THE PUBLIC STUDIES DIVISION OF THE
DEPARTMENT OF THE STATE -- PUBLIC
OPINION ANALYSIS IN THE
FORMULATION AND CONDUCT OF
AMERICAN FOREIGN POLICY.=
                       ELDERE-57-PSD

POLITICAL PARTIES -- A BEHAVIORAL
ANALYSIS (UNITED STATES).=
                       ELDESJ-64-PPB

A COMPARATIVE ANALYSIS OF COMPLEX
ORGANIZATIONS.=        ETZIA -61-CAC

BASES OF AUTHORITY IN LEGISLATIVE
BODIES -- A COMPARATIVE ANALYSIS
(UNITED STATES).=      EULAH -62-BAL

A SCALE ANALYSIS OF IDEOLOGICAL
FACTORS IN CONGRESSIONAL VOTING
(UNITED STATES).=      FARRCD-58-SAI

THE PRESIDENT'S CABINET -- AN
ANALYSIS IN THE PERIOD FROM WILSON
TO EISENHOWER (UNITED STATES).=
                       FENNRF-59-PSC

THE MATHEMATICAL ANALYSIS OF
SUPREME COURT DECISIONS -- THE USE
AND ABUSE OF QUANTITATIVE METHODS
(UNITED STATES).=      FISHFM-58-MAS

LOCAL PARTY SYSTEMS -- THEORETICAL
CONSIDERATIONS AND A CASE ANALYSIS
(UNITED STATES).=      FREEJL-58-LPS

COSMOPOLITANS AND LOCALS -- TOWARDS
AN ANALYSIS OF LATENT SOCIAL ROLES
(UNITED STATES).=      GOULAW-58-CLT

A FACTOR ANALYSIS OF LEGISLATIVE
BEHAVIOR (UNITED STATES).=
                       GRUMJG-63-FAL

AN ANALYSIS OF CONFLICT IN
DECISION-MAKING GROUPS.=
                       GUETH -53-ACD

A COMPARATIVE ANALYSIS OF THE
ADMINISTRATIVE SYSTEMS OF CANADA
AND CEYLON.=           FARRRL-64-CAA

SCARBOROUGH AND BLACKPOOL -- AN
ANALYSIS OF SOME VOTES AT THE
LABOUR PARTY CONFERENCES OF 1960
AND 1962 (GREAT BRITAIN).=
                       HINDK -62-SBA

DECISIONAL CONFLICTS -- A
THEORETICAL ANALYSIS (GERMANY,
GREAT BRITAIN, UNITED STATES).=
                       JANIIL-59-DCT

THE SYSTEMATIC ANALYSIS OF
POLITICAL BIOGRAPHY.=  JANOM -54-SAP

14

ANALYSIS                (CONTINUATION)
  SOCIAL STRATIFICATION AND THE
  COMPARATIVE ANALYSIS OF ELITES.=
                        JANOM -56-SSC

  THE MILITARY IN THE POLITICAL
  DEVELOPMENT OF NEW NATIONS -- AN
  ESSAY IN COMPARATIVE ANALYSIS
  (ASIA, AFRICA, MIDDLE EAST).=
                        JANOM -64-MPD

  INTERNATIONAL BEHAVIOR -- A
  SOCIAL-PSYCHOLOGICAL ANALYSIS.=
                        KELMHC-65-IBS

  WEALTH AND POWER IN AMERICA -- AN
  ANALYSIS OF SOCIAL CLASS AND
  INCOME DISTRIBUTION.= KOLKG -62-WPA

  OVERCENTRALIZATION IN ECONOMIC
  ADMINISTRATION -- A CRITICAL
  ANALYSIS BASED ON EXPERIENCE IN
  HUNGARIAN LIGHT INDUSTRY.=
                        KORNJ -59-OEA

  PREDICTING SUPREME COURT DECISIONS
  MATHEMATICALLY -- A QUANTITIVE
  ANALYSIS OF THE RIGHT TO COUNSEL
  (UNITED STATES).=     KORTF -57-PSC

  REPLY TO FISHER'S MATHEMATICAL
  ANALYSIS OF SUPREME COURT
  DECISIONS (UNITED STATES).=
                        KORTF -58-RFS

  MODELS FOR THE ANALYSIS OF FACT -
  ACCEPTANCE BY APPELLATE COURTS
  (UNITED STATES).=     KORTF -66-MAF

  THE ANALYSIS OF POLITICAL BEHAVIOR
  -- AN EMPIRICAL APPROACH.=
                        LASSHD-48-APB

  THE DECISION PROCESS -- SEVEN
  CATEGORIES OF FUNCTIONAL
  ANALYSIS.=            LASSHD-56-DPS

  A GAME THEORETIC ANALYSIS OF
  CONGRESSIONAL POWER DISTRIBUTIONS
  FOR A STABLE TWO - PARTY SYSTEM.=
                        LUCERD-56-GTA

  INTEREST GROUPS IN COMPARATIVE
  ANALYSIS.=            MACRRC-61-IGC

  AN ANALYSIS OF POLITICAL CONTROL --
  ACTUAL AND POTENTIAL.=
                        OPPEFE-58-APC

  THE LAPPISH HERDING LEADER -- A
  STRUCTURAL ANALYSIS.= PEHRRN-54-LHL

  THREE PROBLEMS IN THE ANALYSIS OF
  COMMUNITY POWER.=     POLSNW-59-TPA

  THE VERTICAL MOSAIC -- AN ANALYSIS
  OF SOCIAL CLASS AND POWER IN
  CANADA.=              PORTJ -65-VMA

  STATISTICAL ANALYSIS AND
  COMPARATIVE ADMINISTRATION -- THE
  TURKISH COUNSEIL D'ETATE.=
                        PRESRV-58-SAC

  VERBAL SHIFTS IN THE AMERICAN
  PRESIDENCY -- A CONTENT ANALYSIS.=
                        PROTJW-56-VSA

  THE FALL OF KHRUSHCHEV -- TENTATIVE
  ANALYSIS (SOVIET UNION).=
                        REDDPB-65-FKT

  A CASE ANALYSIS OF CONGRESSIONAL

ANALYSIS                (CONTINUATION)
  ACTIVITY -- CIVIL AVIATION,
  1957-1958.=           REDFES-60-CAC

  POLITICAL EXTREMISTS IN IRAN -- A
  SECONDARY ANALYSIS OF
  COMMUNICATIONS DATA.= RINGBB-52-PEI

  EGYPT IN SEARCH OF POLITICAL
  COMMUNITY -- AN ANALYSIS OF THE
  INTELLECTUAL AND POLITICAL
  EVOLUTION OF EGYPT -- 1804-1952.=
                        SAFRN -61-ESP

  POLITICAL CHANGE IN A TRADITIONAL
  AFRICAN CLAN -- A STRUCTURAL
  FUNCTIONAL ANALYSIS OF THE NSITS
  OF NIGERIA.=          SCARJR-65-PCT

  THE 1960-1961 TERM OF THE SUPREME
  COURT -- A PSYCHOLOGICAL ANALYSIS
  (UNITED STATES).=     SCHUG -62-TSC

  QUANTITATIVE ANALYSIS OF JUDICIAL
  BEHAVIOR.=            SCHUGA-59-QAJ

  INTELLIGENTSIA AND REVOLUTION -- AN
  HISTORICAL ANALYSIS.= SETOH -59-IRH

  THE INTELLECTUALS AND THE POWERS --
  SOME PERSPECTIVES FOR COMPARATIVE
  ANALYSIS.=            SHILE -58-IPP

  SOVIET AND AMERICAN FOREIGN POLICY
  ATTITUDES -- CONTENT ANALYSIS OF
  ELITE ARTICULATIONS.= SINGDJ-64-SAF

  AN ANALYSIS OF JUDICIAL ATTITUDES
  IN THE LABOR RELATIONS DECISIONS
  OF THE WARREN COURT.= SPAEHJ-63-AJA

  THE ANALYSIS OF A COUNTER -
  REVOLUTION (FRANCE).= TILLC -64-ACR

  THE ANALYSIS OF BEHAVIOR PATTERNS
  ON THE UNITED STATES SUPREME
  COURT.=               ULMESS-60-ABP

  THE ANALYSIS OF POLITICAL SYSTEMS.=
                        VERNDV-59-APS

  ON THE LOGICAL ANALYSIS OF
  POWER-ATTRIBUTION PROCEDURES.=
                        WALTB -64-LAP

  SUBORDINATE LEADERSHIP IN A
  BICULTURAL COMMUNITY -- AN
  ANALYSIS (UNITED STATES).=
                        WATSJB-54-SLB

  THE ANALYSIS OF SOCIAL CHANGE --
  BASED ON OBSERVATIONS IN CENTRAL
  AFRICA.=              WILSG -45-ASC

  WHO SHALL RULE -- A POLITICAL
  ANALYSIS OF SUCCESSION IN A LARGE
  WELFARE ORGANIZATION
  (UNITED STATES).=     ZALDMN-65-WSR

ANALYZING
  A METHOD FOR ANALYZING LEGISLATIVE
  BEHAVIOR (UNITED STATES).=
                        BELKGM-58-MAL

  A FRAMEWORK FOR ANALYZING ECONOMIC
  AND POLITICAL CHANGE.=
                        HAGGEE-62-FAE

ANATOMY
  THE ANATOMY OF REVOLUTION (FRANCE,
  GREAT BRITAIN, UNITED STATES,
  SOVIET UNION).=       BRINC -60-ARF

15

ANATOMY                     (CONTINUATION)
    CUBA -- ANATOMY OF A REVOLUTION.=
                           HUBELP-61-CAR

    AN ANATOMY OF LEADERSHIP --
    PRINCES, HEROES, AND SUPERMEN
    (UNITED STATES).=     JENNEE-60-ALP

    THE ANATOMY OF BRITAIN TODAY.=
                           SAMPA -65-ABT

ANCHORAGE
    CAREER ANCHORAGE -- MANAGERIAL
    MOBILITY MOTIVATIONS.=
                           TAUSC -65-CAM

ANCIENT
    POLITICAL STRUGGLE IN (ANCIENT)
    BUREAUCRATIC SOCIETIES.=
                           EISESN-56-PSA

    INTERNAL CONTRADICTIONS IN
    BUREAUCRATIC POLITIES (ANCIENT
    CHINA, PERSIA).=      EISESN-58-ICB

    THE DIVINE KINGSHIP IN GHANA AND
    ANCIENT EGYPT.=       MEYELR-60-DKG

ANGLO-AMERICAN
    PARTY AND SOCIETY -- THE
    ANGLO-AMERICAN DEMOCRACIES.=
                           ALFORR-63-PSA

ANGRY
    THE POLITICS OF BRITAIN'S ANGRY
    YOUNG MEN.=           KROLM -61-PBS

    POLAND'S ANGRY AND UNANGRY YOUNG
    MEN.=                 SHERG -58-PSA

ANNOINTED
    THE ELECTED AND THE ANNOINTED --
    TWO AMERICAN ELITES.= HACKA -61-EAT

ANONYMOUS
    THE ANONYMOUS EMPIRE (LOBBYING,
    GREAT BRITAIN).=      FINESE-56-AEL

    ANONYMOUS EMPIRE (GREAT BRITAIN).=
                           FINESE-58-AEG

ANTHROPOLOGICAL
    ANTHROPOLOGICAL STUDY OF PRIMITIVE
    RULING GROUPS --1 --2.=
                           DE-GS -57-ASP

ANTHROPOLOGY
    POLITICAL ANTHROPOLOGY.=
                           EASTD -59-PA

ANTI
    SOCIOLOGICAL ASPECTS OF ANTI -
    INTELLECTUALISM (UNITED STATES).=
                           BARBB -55-SAA

    ANTI - INTELLECTUALISM IN
    GOVERNMENT (UNITED STATES).=
                           CLAPGR-55-AIG

    THE CATHOLIC ANTI - COMMUNIST ROLE
    WITHIN AUSTRALIAN LABOR.=
                           LANGFC-56-CAC

    A PSYCHOLOGICAL APPROACH TO ANTI -
    INTELLECTUALISM.=     MAY,R -55-PAA

    OFFICIAL POLICY AND ANTI -
    INTELLECTUALISM (UNITED STATES).=
                           MCWIC -55-CPA

    A KEY TO SOVIET POLITICS -- THE
    CRISIS OF THE ANTI - PARTY GROUP.=

ANTI                        (CONTINUATION)
                           PETHR -62-KSP

    THE EMERGING ANTI - COLONIAL
    CONSENSUS IN THE UNITED NATIONS.=
                           ROWEET-64-EAC

    PATTERNS OF ANTI - DEMOCRATIC
    THOUGHT.=             SPITO -65-PAD

    KHRUSHCHEV AND THE ANTI - PARTY
    GROUP (SOVIET UNION).=
                           TS    -57-KAP

ANTI-FASCIST
    MUSSOLINI'S ENEMIES -- THE ITALIAN
    ANTI-FASCIST RESISTANCE.=
                           DELZCF-61-MSE

ANTI-SEMITISM
    ANTI-SEMITISM IN POLAND.=
                           MILOC -57-ASP

APARTHEID
    APARTHEID AND POLITICS IN SOUTH
    AFRICA.=              TIRYEQ-60-APS

APOLITICAL
    POLITICAL AND APOLITICAL
    PERSONALITY.=         HENNB -58-PAP

APOLITICALS
    POLITICALS AND APOLITICALS -- SOME
    MEASUREMENT OF PERSONALITY TRAITS
    (UNITED STATES).=     HENNB -59-PAM

APPARATCHIK
    CINCINNATUS AND THE APPARATCHIK
    (UNITED STATES, SOVIET UNION).=
                           BRZEZ -63-CA

APPARATUS
    THE PARTY AND THE PARTY APPARATUS
    (SOVIET UNION).=      ACHMH -58-PPA

    THE PRINCIPLE OF PROFITABILITY AND
    THE SOVIET PARTY APPARATUS.=
                           ACHMH -59-PPS

    THE SOVIET BUREAUCRATIC ELITE -- A
    CASE STUDY OF THE UKRAINIAN
    APPARATUS.=           ARMSJA-59-SBE

    THE COMMUNIST PARTY APPARATUS
    (SOVIET UNION).=      AVTOA -66-CPA

    THE KREMLIN'S PROFESSIONAL STAFF --
    THE 'APPARATUS' OF THE CENTRAL
    COMMITTEE, COMMUNIST PARTY OF THE
    SOVIET UNION.=        NEMZL -50-KSP

    THE CENTRAL APPARATUS OF POLAND'S
    COMMUNIST PARTY.=     STAARF-62-CAP

APPEALS
    THE APPEALS OF COMMUNISM.=
                           ALMOGA-54-AC

    VOTING BEHAVIOR ON THE
    UNITED STATES COURTS OF APPEALS,
    1961-1964.=           GOLDS -66-VBU

APPELLATE
    MODELS FOR THE ANALYSIS OF FACT -
    ACCEPTANCE BY APPELLATE COURTS
    (UNITED STATES).=     KORTF -66-MAF

    REVIEW, DISSENT AND THE APPELLATE
    PROCESS -- A POLITICAL
    INTERPRETATION (UNITED STATES).=
                           RICHRJ-67-RDA

APPLICABLE
    THE APRISTA SEARCH FOR A PROGRAM

16

APPLICABLE          (CONTINUATION)
APPLICABLE TO LATIN AMERICA
(PERU).=              KANTH -52-ASP

APPOINTED
APPOINTED EXECUTIVE LOCAL
GOVERNMENT, THE CALIFORNIA
EXPERIENCE (UNITED STATES).=
                     BOLLJC-52-AEL

TRUSTED LEADERS -- PERCEPTIONS OF
APPOINTED FEDERAL OFFICIALS
(UNITED STATES).=    JENNMK-66-TLP

APPOINTMENT
ELECTION AND APPOINTMENT
(UNITED STATES).=    AKZIB -60-EAU

THE ASSISTANT SECRETARIES --
PROBLEMS AND PROCESSES OF
APPOINTMENT (UNITED STATES).=
                     MANNDE-65-ASP

REGULATORY AGENCY CONTROL THROUGH
APPOINTMENT -- THE CASE OF THE
EISENHOWER ADMINISTRATION AND THE
NLRB (UNITED STATES).=
                     SCHES -61-RAC

APPOINTMENTS
THE ADVICE AND CONSENT OF THE
SENATE -- A STUDY OF THE
CONFIRMATION OF APPOINTMENTS BY
THE UNITED STATES SENATE.=
                     HARRJP-53-ACS

APPRAISAL
THE SOVIET UNION AND DISARMAMENT --
AN APPRAISAL OF SOVIET ATTITUDES
AND INTENTIONS.=     CALLA -64-SUD

RECRUITMENT PROBLEMS OF THE FRENCH
HIGHER CIVIL SERVICE -- AN
AMERICAN APPRAISAL.= JUMPR -57-RPF

EXECUTIVE DEVELOPMENT IN THE
PHILIPPINES -- PERSPECTIVES AND
APPRAISAL.=          SAMOAG-60-EDP

APPRENTICESHIP
A STUDY IN POLITICAL APPRENTICESHIP
(GREAT BRITAIN).=    RICHPG-56-SPA

APPROACH
THE REPUTATIONAL APPROACH IN THE
STUDY OF COMMUNITY POWER -- A
CRITICAL EVALUATION.= ABU-B -65-RAS

CENTRAL AMERICAN POLITICAL PARTIES
-- A FUNCTIONAL APPROACH.=
                     ANDECW-62-CAP

THE TECHNOLOGY - ELITE APPROACH TO
THE DEVELOPMENTAL PROCESS --
PERUVIAN CASE STUDY.= COHEA -66-TEA

MASS COMMUNICATIONS AND THE LOSS OF
FREEDOM IN NATIONAL
DECISION-MAKING -- A POSSIBLE
RESEARCH APPROACH TO INTERSTATE
CONFLICTS.=          DEUTKW-57-MCL

THE REPUTATIONAL APPROACH TO THE
STUDY OF COMMUNITY POWER.=
                     EHRLHJ-61-RAS

A TAXONOMIC APPROACH TO STATE
POLITICAL PARTY STRENGTH.=
                     GOLERT-58-TAS

THE ANALYSIS OF POLITICAL BEHAVIOR
-- AN EMPIRICAL APPROACH.=

APPROACH          (CONTINUATION)
                     LASSHD-48-APB

AN APPROACH TO CONSTRUCTIVE
LEADERSHIP.=         LEVIS -49-ACL

A PSYCHOLOGICAL APPROACH TO ANTI -
INTELLECTUALISM.=    MAY,R -55-PAA

SYSTEM AND NETWORK -- AN APPROACH
TO THE STUDY OF POLITICAL
PROCESS.=            MAYEAC-62-SNA

POLITICAL LEADERSHIP RE-EXAMINED --
AN EXPERIMENTAL APPROACH
(UNITED STATES).=    MOOSM -51-PLR

THE PROBLEM OF LEADERSHIP -- AN
INTERDISCIPLINARY APPROACH.=
                     MORRRT-50-PLI

THE SALA MODEL -- AN ECOLOGICAL
APPROACH TO THE STUDY OF
COMPARATIVE ADMINISTRATION.=
                     RIGGFW-62-SME

AN APPROACH TO A THEORY OF
BUREAUCRACY.=        SELZP -43-ATB

A DECISION-MAKING APPROACH TO THE
STUDY OF POLITICAL PHENOMENA.=
                     SNYDRC-58-DMA

FOREIGN POLICY DECISION-MAKING --
AN APPROACH TO THE STUDY OF
INTERNATIONAL POLITICS.=
                     SNYDRC-62-FPD

AN APPROACH TO THE STUDY OF
ATTITUDINAL DIFFERENCES AS AN
ASPECT OF JUDICIAL BEHAVIOR
(UNITED STATES).=    SPAEHJ-61-ASA

AN EVENT-STRUCTURE APPROACH TO
SOCIAL POWER AND TO THE PROBLEM OF
POWER COMPARABILITY.= TANNAS-62-ESA

LEADERSHIP AND ORGANIZATION -- A
BEHAVIORAL SCIENCE APPROACH.=
                     TANNR -61-LOB

THE BURMESE UNIVERSITY STUDENT --
AN APPROACH TO PERSONALITY AND
SUBCULTURE.=         WOHLJ -66-BUS

APPROACHES
LOCATING LEADERS IN LOCAL
COMMUNITIES -- A COMPARISON OF
SOME ALTERNATIVE APPROACHES
(UNITED STATES).=    FREELC-63-LLL

APPROACHES TO STAFFING THE
PRESIDENCY -- NOTES ON FDR AND JFK
(UNITED STATES).=    NEUSRE-63-ASP

LAW AND POLITICS IN THE SUPREME
COURT -- NEW APPROACHES TO
POLITICAL JURISPRUDENCE
(UNITED STATES).=    SCHAM -64-LPS

INTERGROUP RELATIONS AND LEADERSHIP
-- APPROACHES AND RESEARCH IN
INDUSTRIAL, ETHNIC, CULTURAL, AND
POLITICAL AREAS.=    SHERM -62-IRL

APPROACHING
CHARACTERISTICS OF CANDIDATES FOR
ELECTION IN A COUNTRY APPROACHING
INDEPENDENCE -- THE CASE OF
UGANDA.=             BYRDRO-63-CCE

APPROPRIATIONS
THE APPROPRIATIONS COMMITTEE AS A

APPROPRIATIONS          (CONTINUATION)
POLITICAL SYSTEM (UNITED STATES).=
                              FENNRF-62-ACP

THE POWER OF THE PURSE --
APPROPRIATIONS POLITICS IN
CONGRESS (UNITED STATES).=
                              FENNRF-66-PPA

AN APPROPRIATIONS SUBCOMMITTEE AND
ITS CLIENT AGENCIES -- A
COMPARATIVE STUDY OF SUPERVISION
AND CONTROL (UNITED STATES).=
                              SHARI -65-ASI

APPROVAL
PROCESS SATISFACTION AND POLICY
APPROVAL IN STATE DEPARTMENT --
CONGRESSIONAL RELATIONS
(UNITED STATES).=        ROBIJA-61-PSP

APRA
THE OLD AND THE NEW APRA IN PERU --
MYTH AND REALITY.=      PIKEFB-64-ONA

APRISMO
APRISMO -- PERU'S INDIGENOUS
POLITICAL THEORY.=       KANTH -54-APS

APRISTA
THE LATIN AMERICAN APRISTA
PARTIES.=                ALEXRJ-49-LAA

THE APRISTA SEARCH FOR A PROGRAM
APPLICABLE TO LATIN AMERICA
(PERU).=                 KANTH -52-ASP

THE IDEOLOGY AND PROGRAM OF THE
PERUVIAN APRISTA MOVEMENT.=
                         KANTH -53-IPP

ARAB
THE POLITICAL USAGE OF 'ISLAM' AND
'ARAB CULTURE' (MOROCCO).=
                         ASHFDE-61-PUI

THE USE OF THE ARAB FELLAH.=
                         BASHTM-58-UAF

SOCIAL AND POLITICAL CHANGE IN THE
MOSLEM - ARAB WORLD.=    BERGM -58-SPC

ARAB ISLAM IN THE MODERN AGE.=
                         CAWNCE-65-AIM

THE ROLE OF THE ARMY IN THE
TRANSITIONAL ARAB STATE
(MIDDLE EAST).=          GLUBJ -65-RAT

THE LEAGUE OF ARAB STATES -- A
STUDY IN THE DYNAMICS OF REGIONAL
ORGANIZATION (MIDDLE EAST).=
                         MACDRW-65-LAS

EMERGING GOVERNMENT IN THE ARAB
WORLD.=                  SALEE -62-EGA

THE STRUGGLE FOR SYRIA -- A STUDY
OF POST-WAR ARAB POLITICS,
1945-1948.               SEALP -65-SSS

THE TRANSFORMATION OF IDEOLOGY IN
THE ARAB WORLD.=         SHARH -65-TIA

POWER AND LEADERSHIP IN THE ARAB
WORLD.=                  SHARHB-63-PLA

DILEMMA OF THE ELITE IN ARAB
SOCIETY.=                TANNA -55-DEA

DILEMMAS OF POLITICAL LEADERSHIP IN
THE ARAB MIDDLE EAST -- THE CASE

ARAB                     (CONTINUATION)
OF THE UNITED ARAB REPUBLIC.=
                         VATIPJ-61-DPL

ARABISM
FROM OTTOMANISM TO ARABISM -- THE
ORIGINS OF AN IDEOLOGY
(MIDDLE EAST).=          DAWNCE-61-OAO

THE RISE OF ARABISM IN SYRIA.=
                         DAWNCE-62-RAS

ARABS
THE ARABS' VIEW OF POSTWAR AMERICAN
FOREIGN POLICY (EGYPT, IRAN,
JORDAN, LEBANON, SYRIA).=
                         CASTHP-59-AVP

ARBITER
THE SUPREME COURT AS FINAL ARBITER
IN FEDERAL - STATE RELATIONS
(UNITED STATES).=        SCHMJR-58-SCF

ARCADIA
POLITICAL DECISION-MAKING IN
ARCADIA.=                WALTB -62-PDM

AREA
ALLEGIANCE TO POLITICAL PARTIES --
A STUDY OF THREE PARTIES IN ONE
AREA (GREAT BRITAIN).=
                         PLOWDE-55-APP

AREAS
THE POLITICS OF THE DEVELOPING
AREAS.=                  ALMOGA-60-PDA

COMMUNISM AND THE INTELLIGENTSIA IN
BACKWARD AREAS -- RECENT
LITERATURE (SOVIET UNION).=
                         ARNOGL-55-CIB

ELITES AND PUBLIC OPINION IN AREAS
OF HIGH SOCIAL STRATIFICATION
(CHILE).=                BONIF -58-EPO

THE POLITICAL SYSTEMS OF THE
DEVELOPING AREAS.=       COLEJS-60-PSD

VARIATIONS IN POWER STRUCTURES AND
ORGANIZING EFFICIENCY -- A
COMPARATIVE STUDY OF FOUR AREAS
(UNITED STATES).=        DAKIRE-62-VPS

SOCIAL STRATIFICATION OF RURAL
AREAS -- RESEARCH PROBLEMS
(POLAND).=               GALEB -57-SSR

POLITICAL RECRUITMENT AND
PARTICIPATION -- SOME SUGGESTED
AREAS FOR RESEARCH.=     HANNWG-66-PRP

EDUCATION AND SOCIAL CHANGE IN
TROPICAL AREAS.=         READM -55-ESC

INTERGROUP RELATIONS AND LEADERSHIP
-- APPROACHES AND RESEARCH IN
INDUSTRIAL, ETHNIC, CULTURAL, AND
POLITICAL AREAS.=        SHERM -62-IRL

POLITICAL ACTION BY THE MILITARY IN
THE DEVELOPING AREAS.=
                         VON-FR-61-PAM

ARENA
THE ELECTORAL ARENA (UNITED STATES
CONGRESS).=              PRICHD-65-EAU

THE LITERARY ARENA (SOVIET UNION).=
                         RYWKM -64-LAS

ARGENTINA
THE PERON ERA (ARGENTINA).=

ARGENTINA                    (CONTINUATION)
                        ALEXRJ-51-PEA

PERONISM AND ARGENTINA'S QUEST FOR
LEADERSHIP IN LATIN AMERICA.=
                        ALEXRJ-55-PAS

PERON'S ARGENTINA.=     BLANGI-53-PSA

DICHOTOMIES OF MILITARISM IN
ARGENTINA.=             GOLDM -66-DMA

CHURCH AND STATE IN ARGENTINA --
FACTORS IN PERON'S DOWNFALL.=
                        GP    -56-CSA

CONFLICTING FORCES IN ARGENTINA.=
                        HUELD -62-CFA

CATHOLICISM, NATIONALISM AND
DEMOCRACY IN ARGENTINA.=
                        KENNJJ-58-CND

ARGENTINA AND PERONISM.=
                        KUEBJ -63-AP

STUDENT POLITICS (LATIN AMERICA,
INDIA, POLAND, UNITED STATES,
GERMANY, CHILE, ARGENTINA,
COLUMBIA, FRANCE).=    LIPSSM-67-SPL

THE CHANGING ROLE OF THE MILITARY
IN ARGENTINA.=          POTARA-61-CRM

LEFT AND RIGHT EXTREMISM IN
ARGENTINA.=             WHITAP-63-LRE

ARGENTINE
COMMUNITY POWER PERSPECTIVES AND
ROLE DEFINITIONS OF NORTH AMERICAN
EXECUTIVES IN AN ARGENTINE
COMMUNITY.=             CHAME -66-CPP

ENTREPRENEURSHIP IN ARGENTINE
CULTURE -- 'TORCUATO DI TELLA AND
S.I.A.M.'.=             COCHTC-62-EAC

SOCIAL FACTORS IN ECONOMIC
DEVELOPMENT -- THE ARGENTINE
CASE.=                  FILLTR-61-SFE

THE ARGENTINE TROUBLE -- BETWEEN
SWORD AND STATE.=       FINESE-65-ATB

ARGENTINE POLITICAL PARTIES --
1957-1958.=             POTAA -59-APP

ARGENTINE RADICALISM, 1957-1963.=
                        SNOWG -63-AR

ARGENTINE UPHEAVAL -- PERON'S FALL
AND THE NEW REGIME.=    WHITAP-56-AUP

ARISTOCRACY
THE PROTESTANT ESTABLISHMENT --
ARISTOCRACY AND CAST IN AMERICA.=
                        BALTED-65-PEA

ITALY AND ITS ARISTOCRACY.=
                        BARZL -56-IIA

THE AZTEC ARISTOCRACY IN COLONIAL
MEXICO.=                GIBSC -60-AAC

ARISTOCRACY AND THE MIDDLE CLASS IN
THE BRITISH ELITE, 1886-1916.=
                        GUTTWL-54-AMC

THE AFRICAN ARISTOCRACY -- RANK
AMONG THE SWAZI.=       KUPEH -47-AAR

ENGLAND -- THE CROWN AND THE NEW

ARISTOCRACY             (CONTINUATION)
ARISTOCRACY, 1540-1600.=
                        MACCWT-65-ECN

BUREAUCRACY, ARISTOCRACY, AND
AUTOCRACY -- THE PRUSSIAN
EXPERIENCE, 1660-1815.=
                        ROSEH -66-BAA

ARMAMENT
THE ORGANIZATION AND ADMINISTRATION
OF THE SOVIET ARMAMENT INDUSTRY.=
                        BARIJJ-57-OAS

THREAT - PERCEPTION AND THE
ARMAMENT - TENSION DILEMMA.=
                        SINGDJ-58-TPA

ARMED
THE SOVIET ARMED FORCES.=
                        BARIJJ-63-SAF

THE SIGNIFICANCE OF THE
REESTABLISHMENT OF THE SUPREME
COMMAND OF THE SOVIET ARMED
FORCES.=                GALAN -64-SRS

THE NEW GENERATION IN THE SOVIET
ARMED FORCES.=          GALAN -65-NGS

ARMED FORCES IN NEW STATES.=
                        GUTTWF-63-AFN

THE POLITICAL ROLE OF AFRICAN ARMED
FORCES -- THE IMPACT OF FOREIGN
MILITARY ASSISTANCE.=   GUTTWF-67-PRA

INTERSERVICE COMPETITION AND THE
POLITICAL ROLES OF THE ARMED
SERVICES (UNITED STATES).=
                        HUNTSP-61-ICP

ARMED FORCES IN WESTERN EUROPE --
UNITY AND DIVERSITY.=   JANOM -65-AFW

THE ARMED FORCES OF SOUTH AFRICA.=
                        TYLDG -54-AFS

CHANGES AMONG THE LEADERS OF THE
SOVIET ARMED FORCES.=   VERBV -63-CAL

ARMIES
MIDDLE EASTERN ARMIES AND THE NEW
MIDDLE CLASS.=          HALPM -62-MEA

TWO COMMUNIST ARMIES (CHINA,
SOVIET UNION).=         KASHA -61-TCA

ARMIES IN THE PROCESS OF POLITICAL
MODERNIZATION.=         PYE,LW-62-APP

ARMS
ARMS AND POLITICS IN PAKISTAN.=
                        COHESP-64-APP

INTEGRATION AND ARMS CONTROL IN THE
EUROPEAN POLITICAL ENVIRONMENT --
A SUMMARY REPORT (FRANCE,
GERMANY).=              DEUTKW-66-IAC

THE SETTING FOR EUROPEAN ARMS
CONTROLS -- POLITICAL AND
STRATEGIC CHOICES OF EUROPEAN
ELITES (FRANCE, GERMANY
GREAT BRITAIN, SOVIET UNION,
UNITED STATES).=        GORDM -65-SEA

ARMS AND POLITICS IN
LATIN AMERICA.=         LIEUE -61-APL

ARMY
THE FRENCH ARMY IN POLITICS,

THE ARMY AND PCLITICS IN
INDCNESIA.= ANON -53-API

THE ARMY AND THE SUPREME SOVIET.=
ANON -54-ASS

THE BERIA AFFAIR AND THE ARMY
(SOVIET UNICN).= ANON -54-BAA

THE RED ARMY HIGH CCMMAND
(SCVIET UNICN).= ANON -54-RAH

THE FRENCH ARMY AS A POLITICAL AND
SOCIAL FACTCR.= BEHRE -59-FAP

THE ARMY AND PCLITICS IN FRANCE.=
BROWBE-61-APF

POLITICAL CCNTRCLS IN THE SOVIET
ARMY -- A STUDY BASED CN REPORTS
BY FORMER SCVIET CFFICERS.=
BRZEZK-54-PCS

THE FRENCH ARMY -- FRCM OBEDIENCE
TO INSURRECTICN.= CHALRD-67-FAO

THE NCRTH KCREAN PECPLE'S ARMY AND
THE PARTY.= CHUNK -63-NKP

SUBHAS CHANDRA BOSE AND THE INDIAN
NATIONAL ARMY.= COHESP-63-SCB

THE PCLITICS CF THE PRUSSIAN ARMY
1640-1945.= CRAIGA-55-PPA

JAPANESE ARMY FACTICNALISM IN THE
EARLY 1930'S.= CROWJB-62-JAF

THE FRENCH ARMY IN FCLITICS.=
DOMEJM-61-FAP

THE ARMY AS A SCCIAL STRUCTURE
(UNITED STATES).= FREEFD-48-ASS

DE GAULLE AND THE FRENCH ARMY.=
FURNEJ-64-DGF

THE RCLE OF THE SCVIET ARMY IN THE
CRISIS CF THE CCLLECTIVE
LEADERSHIP.= GALAN -57-RSA

POLITICAL CCNTRCL CF THE CHINESE
ARMY.= GITTJ -63-PCC

THE CHINESE ARMY'S RCLE IN THE
CULTURAL REVCLUTICN.= GITTJ -67-CAS

THE RCLE CF THE CHINESE ARMY.=
GITTJ -67-RCA

THE RCLE OF THE ARMY IN THE
TRANSITIONAL ARAB STATE
(MICCLE EAST).= GLUBJ -65-RAT

THE CCNFLICT BETWEEN CLD AND NEW IN
THE CHINESE ARMY.= JOFFE -64-CBO

PARTY AND ARMY -- PROFESSIONALISM
AND PCLITICAL CCNTRCL IN THE
CHINESE OFFICER CCRPS, 1949-1964.=
JOFFE -65-PAP

POLITICAL PARTIES AND THE FRENCH
ARMY SINCE THE LIBERATICN.=
KATZEL-50-PPF

THE FRENCH ARMY RE-ENTERS POLITICS
1940-1955.= KELLGA-61-FAR

LOST SCLDIERS -- THE FRENCH ARMY

SWORDS AND PLOUGHSHARES -- THE
TURKISH ARMY AS A MCDERNIZING
FORCE.= LERND -60-SPT

THE PCLITICAL RCLE CF THE ARMY IN
INDCNESIA.= LEV,DS-64-PRA

THE SCLDIER AND THE STATE IN EAST
AFRICA -- SCME THECRETICAL
CCNCLUSICNS CN THE ARMY MUTINIES
OF 1964.= MAZRAA-7 -SSE

THE NEW ARMY CF A NEW GERMANY.=
MUHLN -57-NAN

ARMY IN BURMESE PCLITICS.=
PYE,LW-62-ABP

THE IMPERIAL RUSSIAN ARMY OFFICER.=
RAY,CA-61-IRA

LIFE CAREERS, PCWER AND THE
PROFESSIONS -- THE RETIRED ARMY
GENERAL (UNITED STATES).=
REISL -56-LCP

THE ARMY AND THE FCUNDING OF THE
TURKISH REPUBLIC.= RUSTDA-59-AFT

ARMY AND SCCIETY IN ENGLAND
1870-1900 -- A REASSESSMENT OF THE
CARDWELL REFORMS.= TUCKAV-63-ASE

THE PLACE CF THE ARMY IN INCONESIAN
PCLITICS.= VANDJM-57-PAI

THE EGYPTIAN ARMY IN PCLITICS --
THE PATTERN FCR NEW NATIONS.=
VATIPJ-61-EAP

THE NEMESIS CF POWER -- THE GERMAN
ARMY IN PCLITICS 1918-1945.=
WHEEJW-54-NPG

ART
LYNDCN B JCHNSCN AND THE ART OF THE
POSSIBLE.= BRANRL-64-LBJ

GENERALISSIMO STALIN AND THE ART OF
GCVERNMENT (SCVIET UNION).=
UTISO -52-GSA

ARTICULATICNS
SCVIET AND AMERICAN FOREIGN POLICY
ATTITUDES -- CCNTENT ANALYSIS CF
ELITE ARTICULATICNS.= SINGDJ-64-SAF

ARTIFACT
SUBSTANCE AND ARTIFACT -- THE
CURRENT STATUS CF RESEARCH CN
COMMUNITY PCWER STRUCTURE.=
WALTJ -66-SAC

ARTISTS
WRITERS AND ARTISTS CCNFER
(CHINA).= CH-EJ -60-WAC

ARUSHA
SOCIAL CONTRCL IN AN AFRICAN
SCCIETY (ARUSHA CF TANGANYIKA).=
GULLPH-63-SCA

ASCENDANCY
SYRIA CN THE MCVE -- ASCENDANCY OF
THE LEFT WING.= WZL -57-SMA

ASCENT
POLITICAL ASCENT IN A CLASS SCCIETY

ASCENT                    (CONTINUATION)
-- FRENCH DEPUTIES 1870-1958.=
                          DOGAM -61-PAC


ASHANTI
   THE POSITION OF THE CHIEF IN THE
   MODERN POLITICAL SYSTEM OF ASHANTI
   (GOLD COAST).=         BUSIKA-51-PCM

   ASPECTS OF BUREAUCRATIZATION IN
   ASHANTI IN THE NINETEENTH CENTURY
   (AFRICA).=             WILKI -66-ABA

ASIA
   POLITICAL ELITES IN COLONIAL
   SOUTHEAST ASIA -- AN HISTORICAL
   ANALYSIS.=             BENDHJ-64-PEC

   PEASANT MOVEMENTS IN COLONIAL
   SOUTHEAST ASIA.=       BENDHJ-65-PMC

   COMMUNISM IN SOUTHEAST ASIA -- A
   POLITICAL ANALYSIS.=   BRIMJH-59-CSA

   THE SEARCH FOR MODERNITY IN ASIA
   AND AFRICA -- A REVIEW ARTICLE.=
                          CORERP-64-SMA

   SOCIAL FORCES IN SOUTHEAST ASIA.=
                          DUBOCA-59-SFS

   PROBLEMS OF REPRESENTATIVE
   GOVERNMENT IN SOUTHEAST ASIA.=
                          EMERR -53-PRG

   UNIVERSITIES AND THE POLITICAL
   PROCESS IN SOUTHEAST ASIA.=
                          FISCJ -63-UPP

   SOME REQUIREMENTS FOR TECHNICAL
   PROGRESS IN ASIA.=     GADGOR-51-RTP

   LABOR AND ECONOMIC DEVELOPMENT
   (MIDDLE EAST, SOUTHEAST ASIA).=
                          GALEW -59-LED

   OLD SOCIETIES AND NEW STATES -- THE
   QUEST FOR MODERNITY IN ASIA AND
   AFRICA.=               GEERC -63-OSN

   THOUGHTS ON THE CHINESE QUESTION IN
   SOUTHEAST ASIA.=       HALLDG-54-TCC

   ENTREPRENEURSHIP AND TRADITIONAL
   ELITES (ASIA).=        HOSEBF-63-ETE

   TECHNICAL COOPERATION IN
   DEVELOPMENT ADMINISTRATION IN
   SOUTH AND SOUTHEAST ASIA.=
                          HSUESS-66-TCD

   THE MILITARY IN THE POLITICAL
   DEVELOPMENT OF NEW NATIONS -- AN
   ESSAY IN COMPARATIVE ANALYSIS
   (ASIA, AFRICA, MIDDLE EAST).=
                          JANOM -64-MPD

   THE NEW ELITE IN ASIA AND AFRICA --
   A COMPARATIVE STUDY OF INDONESIA
   AND AFRICA (GHANA).=   KERST -66-NEA

   NEW FORCES IN ASIA.=   LASKB -50-NFA

   THE POLITICS OF TRADE UNION
   LEADERSHIP IN SOUTHERN ASIA.=
                          LICHGE-54-PTU

   MALAYSIA -- A NEW FEDERATION IN
   SOUTHEAST ASIA.=       MEANGP-63-MNF

   THE POLITICS OF SOUTHEAST ASIA.=
                          PYE,LW-60-PSA

   THE POLITICS OF THE NEAR EAST --

ASIA                      (CONTINUATION)
   SOUTHWEST ASIA AND NORTHERN
   AFRICA.=               RUSTDA-60-PNE

   A WORLD OF NATIONS -- PROBLEMS OF
   POLITICAL MODERNIZATION (ASIA,
   AFRICA, LATIN AMERICA).=
                          RUSTDA-67-WNP

   THE COMMUNIST REVOLUTION IN ASIA.=
                          SCALRA-65-CRA

   OPPOSITION IN THE NEW STATES OF
   ASIA AND AFRICA.=      SHILE -66-ONS

   SOUTHEAST ASIA FOLLOWS THE LEADER.=
                          THOMV -49-SAF

   THE LEFT WING IN SOUTHEAST ASIA.=
                          THOMV -50-LWS

   MARXISM IN SOUTH-EAST ASIA.=
                          TRAGFN-59-MSE

   THE POLITICS OF SOUTH ASIA.=
                          WEINM -60-PSA

   NATIONALISM AND LEADERSHIP IN
   ASIA.=                 WERTWF-62-NLA

ASIAN
   ASIAN BUREAUCRATIC SYSTEMS EMERGENT
   FROM THE BRITISH IMPERIAL
   TRADITION (INDIA, PAKISTAN, BURMA,
   CEYLON, MALAYA, NEPAL).=
                          BRAIR - -ABS

   THE PROSPECT FOR ASIAN TRADE
   UNIONISM.=             CALLFW-51-PAT

   JAPAN'S ROLE IN SOUTHEAST ASIAN
   NATIONALIST MOVEMENTS, 1940-1945.=
                          ELSBWH-53-JSR

   FROM EMPIRE TO NATION -- THE RISE
   TO SELF-ASSERTION OF ASIAN AND
   AFRICAN PEOPLES.=      EMERR -60-ENR

   THE STUDENT POPULATION OF A
   SOUTHEAST ASIAN UNIVERSITY -- AN
   INDONESIAN EXAMPLE.=   FISCJ -61-SPS

   LEADERSHIP COHESION IN COMMUNIST
   CHINA AND UNDERDEVELOPED ASIAN
   COUNTRIES.=            MACFR -63-LCC

   THE SPLIT BETWEEN ASIAN AND WESTERN
   SOCIALIST.=            SAPODJ-54-SBA

   BALLOT BOX AND BAYONET -- PEOPLE
   AND GOVERNMENT IN EMERGENT ASIAN
   COUNTRIES.=            TINKH -64-BBB

ASIANS
   ASIANS IN EAST AFRICA -- PROBLEMS
   AND PROSPECTS.=        GHAID -65-AEA

   PORTRAIT OF A MINORITY -- ASIANS IN
   EAST AFRICA.=          GHAIDP-65-PMA

ASPIRATIONS
   POLITICAL ASPIRATIONS OF LAW
   STUDENTS (UNITED STATES).=
                          AGGERE-58-PAL

   THE PRESENT SITUATION AND
   ASPIRATIONS OF ELITES IN THE
   GOLD COAST.=           BUSIKA-56-PSA

   ATTITUDES AND ASPIRATIONS OF THE
   CONTEMPORARY IRANIAN
   INTELLECTUAL.=         HAMBG -64-AAC

ATOMIC                    (CONTINUATION)
    ATOMIC AGE (UNITED STATES).=
                            ROSSCL-49-CDA

    GERMAN REARMAMENT AND ATOMIC WAR --
    THE VIEWS OF GERMAN MILITARY AND
    POLITICAL LEADERS.=     SPEIH -57-GRA

ATTEMPT
    DEMOCRACY AND THE PARTY MOVEMENT IN
    PREWAR JAPAN -- THE FAILURE OF THE
    FIRST ATTEMPT.=         SCALRA-53-DPM

    TURKISH POLITICS -- THE ATTEMPT TO
    RECONCILE RAPID MODERNIZATION WITH
    DEMOCRACY.=             ULMAAH-65-TPA

ATTENTIVE
    MAN AND ATTENTIVE OPINION ON
    NUCLEAR WEAPON TESTS AND FALLOUT,
    1954-1963 (UNITED STATES).=
                            ROSIEJ-65-MAC

ATTITUDE
    INTRAPARTY ATTITUDE CONFLICT --
    DEMOCRATIC PARTY LEADERSHIP IN
    CALIFORNIA (UNITED STATES).=
                            COSTE -63-IAC

    ATTITUDE CONSENSUS AND CONFLICT IN
    AN INTEREST -- AN ASSESSMENT OF
    COHESION (UNITED STATES).=
                            LUTTNR-66-ACC

    ILLEGITIMACY OF POWER AND
    POSITIVENESS OF ATTITUDE TOWARDS
    THE POWER PERSON (UNITED STATES).=
                            MULDM -66-IPP

ATTITUDES
    THE POLITICAL ATTITUDES OF WEALTH.=
                            ALMOGA-45-PAW

    THE POLITICAL ATTITUDES OF GERMAN
    BUSINESS.=              ALMOGA-56-PAG

    THE ATTITUDES OF M.P.'S AND ACTIVE
    PEERS (GREAT BRITAIN).=
                            ATTLE -59-AMP

    LEADERSHIP, MOTIVATIONS, AND
    ATTITUDES IN RESEARCH
    LABORATORIES.=          BAUMH -56-LMA

    ATTITUDES OF JAMAICAN ELITES
    TOWARDS THE WEST INDIAN
    FEDERATION.=            BELLW -60-AJE

    EQUALITY AND ATTITUDES OF ELITES IN
    JAMAICA.=               BELLW -62-EAE

    JAMAICAN LEADERS -- POLITICAL
    ATTITUDES IN A NEW NATION.=
                            BELLW -64-JLP

    AFRICAN ATTITUDES -- A STUDY OF THE
    SOCIAL, RACIAL, AND POLITICAL
    ATTITUDES OF SOME MIDDLE CLASS
    AFRICANS.=              BRETEA-63-AAS

    AFRICAN ATTITUDES -- A STUDY OF THE
    SOCIAL, RACIAL, AND POLITICAL
    ATTITUDES OF SOME MIDDLE CLASS
    AFRICANS.=              BRETEA-63-AAS

    ELECTORS' ATTITUDES TOWARDS LOCAL
    GOVERNMENT -- A SURVEY OF A
    GLASGOW CONSTITUENCY
    (GREAT BRITAIN).=       BUDGI -65-EAT

    ATTITUDES TOWARD FOREIGN AFFAIRS AS
    A FUNCTION OF PERSONALITY.=

ATTITUDES                 (CONTINUATION)
                            CHRIB -59-ATF

    THE LINKAGE BETWEEN CONSTITUENCY
    ATTITUDES AND CONGRESSIONAL VOTING
    BEHAVIOR--A CAUSAL MODEL
    (UNITED STATES).=       CNUDCF-66-LBC

    THE SOVIET UNION AND DISARMAMENT --
    AN APPRAISAL OF SOVIET ATTITUDES
    AND INTENTIONS.=        CALLA -64-SUD

    FRANCE, GERMANY, AND THE WESTERN
    ALLIANCE -- A STUDY OF ELITE
    ATTITUDES ON EUROPEAN INTEGRATION
    AND WORLD POLITICS.=    DEUTKW-67-FGW

    THE EXECUTIVE OVERSEAS --
    ADMINISTRATIVE ATTITUDES AND
    RELATIONSHIPS IN A FOREIGN CULTURE
    (MEXICO).=              FAYEJ -59-EOA

    HUNGARIAN SOCIO-POLITICAL ATTITUDES
    AND REVOLUTIONARY ACTION.=
                            GLEIH -60-HSP

    SOCIAL STRATIFICATION IN RELATION
    TO ATTITUDES TOWARD SOURCES OF
    POWER IN A COMMUNITY
    (UNITED STATES).=       HAERJL-56-SSR

    ATTITUDES AND ASPIRATIONS OF THE
    CONTEMPORARY IRANIAN
    INTELLECTUAL.=          HAMBG -64-AAC

    GERMAN OFFICIALS REVISITED --
    POLITICAL VIEWS AND ATTITUDES OF
    THE WESTERN GERMAN CIVIL SERVICE.=
                            HERZJH-54-GOR

    THE SOCIALIZATION OF ATTITUDES
    TOWARD POLITICAL AUTHORITY
    (AUSTRALIA, CHILE, JAPAN,
    PUERTO RICO, UNITED STATES).=
                            HESSRD-63-SAT

    POTENTIAL ELITES IN TURKEY --
    EXPLORING THE VALUES AND ATTITUDES
    OF LISE YOUTH.=         KAZAAM-67-PET

    POLITICAL ATTITUDES AND BEHAVIOR IN
    THE PHILIPPINES.=       LANDCH-59-PAB

    GOVERNMENT AND DEVELOPMENT --
    MANAGERIAL ATTITUDES IN
    LATIN AMERICA.=         LAUTA -65-GDM

    ENTERPRISE IN LATIN AMERICA --
    BUSINESS ATTITUDES IN A DEVELOPING
    ECONOMY.=               LAUTA -66-ELA

    PUBLIC ATTITUDES TOWARD THE
    REPRESENTATIONAL ROLE OF
    LEGISLATORS AND JUDGES
    (UNITED STATES).=       MCMUCD-65-PAT

    SOVIET ATTITUDES TOWARD AUTHORITY.=
                            MEADM -51-SAT

    EGALITARIAN ATTITUDES OF WARSAW
    STUDENTS (POLAND).=     NOWAS -60-EAW

    IN YOUR OPINION -- LEADERS' AND
    VOTERS' ATTITUDES ON DEFENSE AND
    DISARMAMENT (CANADA).=
                            PAULJ -63-YOL

    SOCIAL DISTANCE ATTITUDES OF SOUTH
    AFRICAN STUDENTS.=      PETTTF-60-SDA

    THE BRAZILIAN LAW STUDENT --
    BACKGROUND, HABITS, ATTITUDES.=

AUSTRALIAN          (CCNTINUATION)
  ATTITUDES.=           TRUMT -66-IGA

  SOCIAL ROCTS CF AUSTRALIAN
  NATIONALISM.=          WARDR -56-SRA

  PARTY DISCIPLINE UNDER FEDERALISM
  -- IMPLICATIONS OF AUSTRALIAN
  EXPERIENCE.=          WILDA -61-PDU

AUSTRIA
  PCLITICAL CPPCSITION IN THE WESTERN
  DEMOCRACIES (AUSTRIA, BELGIUM,
  FRANCE, GERMANY, GREAT BRITAIN,
  ITALY, NETHERLANDS, NCRWAY,
  SWEDEN, UNITED STATES).=
                       DAHLRA-66-POW

  AUSTRIA'S SCCIALISTS IN THE TREND
  TCWARD A TWC - PARTY SYSTEM -- AN
  INTERPRETATION CF PCSTWAR
  ELECTIONS.=          GULICA-58-ASS

  THE SCCIALIST PARTY CF AUSTRIA --
  RETREAT FRCM MARX.=    FAHNWF-55-SPA

  BUREAUCRACY (AUSTRIA,
  GREAT BRITAIN, UNITED STATES).=
                       MISELV-44-BAG

AUSTRIAN
  THE ERRAND-RUNNING FUNCTICN OF
  AUSTRIAN LEGISLATCRS.=
                       CRANW -62-ERF

  THE GRCUP BASIS OF AUSTRIAN
  PCLITICS.=           CIAMA -58-GBA

  AUSTRIAN LABCR'S BID FCR POWER --
  THE RCLE OF THE TRADE UNION
  FEDERATION.=         GULICA-58-ALS

  THE AUSTRIAN ELECTCRAL SYSTEM.=
                       KITZUW- -AES

AUTHCRITARIAN
  NCTES CN AUTHCRITARIAN AND
  DEMCCRATIC LEADERSHIP.=
                       BELLD -65-NAD

  STUDIES IN THE SCCPE AND METHCD OF
  THE 'AUTHCRITARIAN PERSCNALITY'.=
                       CHRIR -54-SSM

  THE AUTHCRITARIAN PERSCNALITY IN
  PRCFILE (UNITED STATES).=
                       GLAZN -51-APP

  NEW LIGHT CN 'THE AUTHCRITARIAN
  PERSCNALITY' (GERMANY,
  SCVIET UNICN).=      GLAZN -54-NLA

  PERSCNALITY AND PCLITICAL
  SCCIALIZATICN -- THE THEORIES OF
  AUTHCRITARIAN AND DEMCCRATIC
  CHARACTER.=          GREEFI-65-PPS

  AUTHCRITARIAN AND SINGLE - PARTY
  TENDENCIES IN AFRICAN PCLITICS.=
                       KILSML-63-ASP

  AUTHCRITARIAN PERSCNALITY AND
  FCREIGN PCLICY (UNITED STATES).=
                       LEVICJ-57-APF

  AN AUTHCRITARIAN REGIME -- SPAIN.=
                       LINZJJ-64-ARS


  THE DEMCCRATIC AND THE

AUTHCRITARIAN         (CCNTINUATICN)
  AUTHORITARIAN STATE -- ESSAYS IN
  PCLITICAL AND LEGAL THECRY.=
                       NEUMFL-57-CAS

AUTHCRITARIANISM
  THE MEXICAN ELECTICNS CF 1958 --
  AFFIRMATICN OF AUTHCRITARIANISM.=
                       TAYLP -60-MEA

AUTHCRITIES
  AN HISTCRICAL SKETCH CF EGBA
  TRADITICNAL AUTHCRITIES
  (NIGERIA).=          BICBSO-52-HSE

AUTHCRITY
  AUTHCRITY IN THE 20TH CENTURY.=
                       ARENH -56-ATC

  AUTHCRITY, POWER, AND ABILITY TC
  INFLUENCE.=          BENNWG-58-APA

  LEADERSHIP THECRY AND
  ADMINISTRATIVE BEHAVICR -- THE
  PRCBLEM CF AUTHCRITY.=
                       BENNWG-60-LTA

  THE PRCBLEM CF AUTHCRITY.=
                       BIERR -54-PA

  PATTERNS OF AUTHCRITY IN WEST
  AFRICA.=             BRCWP -51-PAW

  PCLITICAL AUTHCRITY -- ITS EXERCISE
  AND PCSSESSICN.=     CASSCW-61-PAI

  GRCUP STRUCTURE AND AUTHCRITY.=
                       CCCTO -63-GSA

  PCLITICAL AUTHCRITY AND THE
  STRUCTURE CF KINSHIP IN ABORIGINAL
  SAMCA.=              EMBEM -62-PAS

  TYPES CF AUTHCRITY IN A BENGUET
  VILLAGE (LUZCN, PHILIPPINES).=
                       ENCAV -57-TAB

  AUTHCRITY STRUCTURE AND
  CRGANIZATICNAL EFFECTIVENESS.=
                       ETZIA -59-ASC

  BASES CF AUTHCRITY IN LEGISLATIVE
  BCDIES -- A CCMPARATIVE ANALYSIS
  (UNITED STATES).=    EULAH -62-BAL

  A LABCRATORY EXPERIMENT CN
  BUREAUCRATIC AUTHCRITY.=
                       EVANWM-61-LEB

  AUTHCRITY, EFFICIENCY, AND ROLE
  STRESS -- PRCBLEMS IN THE
  DEVELCPMENT OF EAST AFRICAN
  BUREAUCRACIES (UGANDA, KENYA,
  TANGANYIKA).=        FLEMWG-66-AER

  SCME CBSERVATICNS CN KINSHIP AND
  PCLITICAL AUTHCRITY IN SAMOA.=
                       FREED -64-CKP

  AUTHCRITY.=          FRIECJ-58-A

  AUTHCRITY AND CRGANIZATION IN
  GERMAN MANAGEMENT.=  FARTH -59-ACG

  THE SCCIALIZATICN CF ATTITUDES
  TCWARD PCLITICAL AUTHCRITY
  (AUSTRALIA, CHILE, JAPAN,
  PUERTC RICC, UNITED STATES).=
                       HESSRD-63-SAT

  GERMAN ADMINISTRATICN SINCE
  BISMARCK -- CENTRAL AUTHCRITY

BACKBENCH          (CONTINUATION)
COMMONS, 1955-1959
(GREAT BRITAIN).=
                    FINESE-61-BOH

BACKBENCHERS
HONORABLE MEMBERS -- A STUDY OF THE
BRITISH BACKBENCHERS
(GREAT BRITAIN).=    RICHPG-59-HMS

BACKGROUND
REPRESENTATION OF INTERESTS IN
BRITISH GOVERNMENT -- HISTORICAL
BACKGROUND.=         BEERSH-57-RIB

THE CIVIL - RELIGIOUS HIERARCHY IN
MESOAMERICAN COMMUNITIES -- PRE -
SPANISH BACKGROUND AND COLONIAL
DEVELOPMENT.=        CARRP -61-CRH

NIGERIA -- BACKGROUND TO
NATIONALISM.=        COLEJS-58-NBN

THE SOCIAL BACKGROUND OF INDIAN
NATIONALISM.=        DESAAR-49-SBI

THE SOCIAL AND EDUCATIONAL
BACKGROUND OF TURKISH OFFICIALS.=
                    DODOCH-64-SEB

CONTINUITY AND CHANGE IN THE
BACKGROUND OF GERMAN
DECISION-MAKING.=    EDINLJ-61-CCB

SOCIAL BACKGROUND IN ELITE ANALYSIS
-- A METHODOLOGICAL INQUIRY
(FRANCE, GERMANY).=  EDINLU-67-SBE

THE BACKGROUND AND DEVELOPMENT OF
'THE PROLETARIAN CULTURAL
REVOLUTION'.=        HSIAGT-67-BDP

THE SOCIAL BACKGROUND OF A WEST
AFRICAN STUDENT POPULATION -- 1 --
2.=                  JAHOG -54-SBW

RECENT POLITICAL DEVELOPMENTS IN
TURKEY AND THEIR SOCIAL
BACKGROUND.=         KARPKH-62-RPD

THE SOCIAL BACKGROUND OF THE HIGHER
CIVIL SERVICE (GREAT BRITAIN).=
                    KELSRK-54-SBH

THE RELIGIOUS BACKGROUND OF
CANADIAN M.P.'S.=    LAPOJD-58-RBC

ZANZIBAR -- BACKGROUND TO
REVOLUTION.=         LOFCMF-65-ZBR

THE SOCIAL BACKGROUND AND
CONNECTIONS OF 'TOP
DECISION-MAKERS' (GREAT BRITAIN).=
                    LUPTT -59-SBC

THE EDUCATIONAL AND GEOGRAPHICAL
BACKGROUND OF SOME LOCAL LEADERS
(GREAT BRITAIN).=    MUSGF -61-EGB

THE BRAZILIAN LAW STUDENT --
BACKGROUND, HABITS, ATTITUDES.=
                    SCHELR-63-BLS

SCALING SUPREME COURT DECISIONS IN
RELATION TO SOCIAL BACKGROUND
(UNITED STATES).=    SCHMJ -58-SSC

STARE DECISIS, DISSENT AND THE
BACKGROUND OF THE JUSTICES OF THE
SUPREME COURT OF THE
UNITED STATES.=      SCHMJ -62-SDD

RELIGIOUS INFLUENCES IN THE

BACKGROUND          (CONTINUATION)
BACKGROUND OF THE BRITISH LABOUR
PARTY.=
                    SMITRW-57-RIB

THE TAIPING REBELLION -- ITS
ECONOMIC BACKGROUND AND SOCIAL
THEORY.=             TAYLGE-33-TRI

PUBLIC OFFICE IN THE SOCIAL
BACKGROUND OF SUPREME COURT
JUSTICES.=           ULMESS-62-POS

THE SOCIAL BACKGROUND AND
CONNECTIONS OF TOP DECISION-MAKERS
(GREAT BRITAIN).=    WILSCS-59-SBC

BACKGROUNDS
THE EDUCATIONAL BACKGROUNDS AND
CAREER ORIENTATIONS OF THE MEMBERS
OF THE CENTRAL COMMITTEE OF THE
CPSU (SOVIET UNION).= OEHLMP-66-EBC

SOCIAL BACKGROUNDS OF THE BOGOTA
ENTREPRENEUR (COLOMBIA).=
                    LIPMA -65-SBB

THE SOCIAL BACKGROUNDS OF POLITICAL
DECISION MAKERS.=    MATTCR-62-SBP

BACKWARD
COMMUNISM AND THE INTELLIGENTSIA IN
BACKWARD AREAS -- RECENT
LITERATURE (SOVIET UNION).=
                    ARNOGL-55-CIB

THE MORAL BASIS OF A BACKWARD
SOCIETY (ITALY).=    BANFEC-58-MBB

BAERIC
CHANNELS OF COMMUNICATION WITH THE
BAERIC PEOPLE (PHILIPPINES).=
                    PAL,AP-57-CCB

LEADERSHIP IN A PHILIPPINE BAERIC.=
                    SILSWE-57-LPB

BALANCE
UNEASY BALANCE OF DEGAULLE'S
REPUBLIC (FRANCE).=  ALANR -60-UBD

THE AFRICAN MILITARY BALANCE.=
                    BROWN -64-AMB

THE SOCIALIST MERGER AND THE
BALANCE OF PARTIES IN JAPAN.=
                    GRINM -55-SMB

INTERNAL DEVELOPMENTS -- A BALANCE
SHEET (SOVIET UNION).=
                    LECNW -63-IDB

PARTY AND GOVERNMENT REFORMS -- A
PROVISIONAL BALANCE SHEET
(SOVIET UNION).=     MEISB -65-PGR

BALKAN
THE BALKANS IN TRANSITION -- ESSAYS
ON THE DEVELOPMENT OF BALKAN LIFE
AND POLITICS SINCE THE EIGHTEENTH
CENTURY.=            JELAC -63-BTE

THE STRUCTURE OF BALKAN SOCIETY.=
                    TOMAD -46-SBS

BALKANS
THE BALKANS IN TRANSITION -- ESSAYS
ON THE DEVELOPMENT OF BALKAN LIFE
AND POLITICS SINCE THE EIGHTEENTH
CENTURY.=            JELAC -63-BTE

BALLOT
THE INSULATION OF LOCAL POLITICS

BALLOT                    (CONTINUATION)
   UNDER THE NON-PARTISAN BALLOT
   (UNITED STATES).=        ADRICR-59-ILP

   BALLOT BOX AND BAYONET -- PEOPLE
   AND GOVERNMENT IN EMERGENT ASIAN
   COUNTRIES.=             TINKH -64-BBB

   COMMUNIST EXPERIMENTS WITH BALLOT
   (POLAND, YUGOSLAVIA).=
                          WILLP -57-CEB

BALLYBEG
   THE SELECTION OF LEADERS IN
   BALLYBEG, NORTHERN IRELAND.=
                          HARRR -61-SLB

BANGHUAD
   BANGHUAD -- A COMMUNITY STUDY IN
   THAILAND.=             KAUFHK-60-BCS

BANK
   BIG BUSINESS LOBBYING IN JAPAN --
   THE CASE OF CENTRAL BANK REFORM.=
                          LANGFC-61-BBL

BANKING
   GOVERNMENT AND BANKING IN WESTERN
   NIGERIA.=              BROWCV-64-GBW

BANTU
   BANTU BUREAUCRACY -- A STUDY OF
   ROLE CONFLICT AND INSTITUTIONAL
   CHANGE IN THE SOGA POLITICAL
   SYSTEM.=               FALLLA-55-BBS

BAO
   TRIAL OF STRENGTH IN INDO-CHINA --
   THE BAO DAI EXPERIMENT.=
                          ASBO  -50-TSI

   THE BAO DAI EXPERIMENT (VIETNAM).=
                          HAMMEJ-50-BDE

BAR
   THE SOVIET BAR -- PAST AND
   PRESENT.=              SHAPI -61-SBP

   BAR OF POLITICS, JUDICIAL SELECTION
   AND THE REPRESENTATION OF SOCIAL
   INTERESTS (UNITED STATES).=
                          WATSRA-67-BPJ

BARGAINING
   HIERARCHY, BARGAINING, AND
   DEMOCRACY IN POLITICS AND
   ECONOMICS (UNITED STATES).=
                          DAHLRA-55-HBD

   MEASUREMENT OF SOCIAL POWER
   OPPORTUNITY COSTS, AND THE THEORY
   OF TWO-PERSON BARGAINING GAMES.=
                          HARSJC-62-MSP

   BARGAINING AND NEGOTIATION IN
   INTERNATIONAL RELATIONS.=
                          SAWYJ -65-BNI

   COLLECTIVE BARGAINING IN THE USSR.=
                          WOLFC -55-CBU

BARIO
   FOCUS ON THE (PHILIPPINE) BARIO.=
                          ABUEJV-59-FPB

BARKING
   TOWN COUNCILLORS -- A STUDY OF
   BARKING (GREAT BRITAIN).=
                          REESAM-64-TCS

BARREL
   THE PORK BARREL SYSTEM


BARREL                    (CONTINUATION)
   (PHILIPPINES).=         ROXAGM-63-PBS

BARRIERS
   A NOTE ON LEADERSHIP THEORY -- THE
   EFFECT OF SOCIAL BARRIERS BETWEEN
   LEADERS AND FOLLOWERS
   (UNITED STATES).=       FIEDFE-57-NLT

BASES
   BASES OF AUTHORITY IN LEGISLATIVE
   BODIES -- A COMPARATIVE ANALYSIS
   (UNITED STATES).=       EULAH -62-BAL

   THE BASES OF SOCIAL POWER.=
                          FRENJR-59-BSP

   POLITICAL MAN -- THE SOCIAL BASES
   OF POLITICS.=           LIPSSM-60-PMS

   THE SOCIAL BASES OF BUREAUCRATIC
   ORGANIZATION (UNITED STATES).=
                          PRESRV-59-SBB

   THE IDEOLOGICAL BASES OF SOVIET
   FOREIGN POLICY.=        ZINNPE-52-IBS

BASIC
   PAKISTAN'S EXPERIMENT IN BASIC
   DEMOCRACIES.=           FRIEHJ-60-PSE

   ADMINISTRATION AT THE GRASS ROOTS
   -- PAKISTAN'S BASIC DEMOCRACIES.=
                          FRIEHJ-63-AGR

BASIS
   THE MORAL BASIS OF A BACKWARD
   SOCIETY (ITALY).=       BANFEC-58-MBB

   FOUR FORMULAE FOR SELECTING LEADERS
   ON THE BASIS OF PERSONALITY.=
                          CATTRB-54-FFS

   THE GROUP BASIS OF AUSTRIAN
   POLITICS.=              CIAMA -58-GBA

   THE SOCIAL BASIS OF THE CHANGING
   POLITICAL STRUCTURES IN
   LATIN AMERICA.          FITZRH-59-SBC

   THE SOCIAL BASIS OF LEADERSHIP IN A
   CANADIAN HOUSE OF COMMONS.=
                          KORNA -65-SBL

   THE GROUP BASIS OF POLITICS --
   NOTES FOR A THEORY.=    LATHE -52-GBP

   THE COMMUNITY BASIS OF CONFLICT IN
   SCHOOL SYSTEM POLITICS
   (UNITED STATES).=       MINADW-66-CBC

   STRUCTURE AND CONSTITUTIONAL BASIS
   OF THE CHINESE PEOPLES REPUBLIC.=
                          THOMSB-51-SCB

   ELITES IN FRENCH - SPEAKING WEST
   AFRICA -- THE SOCIAL BASIS OF
   IDEAS.=                 WALLI -65-EFS

BASUTOLAND
   KOENA CHIEFTAINSHIP IN BASUTOLAND
   (AFRICA).=              HAMNI -65-KCB

BAYONET
   BALLOT BOX AND BAYONET -- PEOPLE
   AND GOVERNMENT IN EMERGENT ASIAN
   COUNTRIES.=             TINKH -64-BBB

BEGINNING
   THE BEGINNING OF THE END
   (SOVIET UNION).=        TATAM -66-BES

BEGINNINGS
   THE BEGINNINGS OF BUREAUCRACY IN

BEGINNINGS            (CONTINUATION)
  CHINA -- THE ORIGIN OF THE HSIEN.=
                        CREEHG-64-BBC

  FRENCH FIELD ADMINISTRATION -- THE
  BEGINNINGS.=          FELSJW-62-FFA

BEHAVIOR
  RANK EQUILIBRATION AND POLITICAL
  BEHAVIOR.=            ANDEB -64-REP

  SOURCES OF ADMINISTRATIVE BEHAVIOR
  -- SOME SOVIET AND WESTERN
  EUROPEAN COMPARISONS.=
                        ARMSJA-65-SAB

  LEADERSHIP, PSYCHOLOGY, AND
  ORGANIZATIONAL BEHAVIOR.=
                        BASSBM-60-LPC

  A METHOD FOR ANALYZING LEGISLATIVE
  BEHAVIOR (UNITED STATES).=
                        BELKGM-58-MAL

  SCALING LEGISLATIVE BEHAVIOR
  (UNITED STATES).=     BELKGM-58-SLB

  LEADERSHIP THEORY AND
  ADMINISTRATIVE BEHAVIOR -- THE
  PROBLEM OF AUTHORITY.=
                        BENNWG-60-LTA

  AMERICAN VOTING BEHAVIOR.=
                        BURDE -59-AVB

  POWER STRUCTURE AND ITS
  COMMUNICATION BEHAVIOR IN
  SAN JOSE, COSTA RICA.=
                        EDWAHT-67-PSI

  IDENTIFICATION WITH CLASS AND
  POLITICAL ROLE BEHAVIOR
  (UNITED STATES).=     EULAH -56-ICP

  INTER - PARTY CONSTITUENCY
  DIFFERENCES AND CONGRESSIONAL
  VOTING BEHAVIOR (UNITED STATES).=
                        FROMLA-63-IPC

  VOTING BEHAVIOR ON THE
  UNITED STATES COURTS OF APPEALS,
  1961-1964.=           GOLDS -66-VBU

  A FACTOR ANALYSIS OF LEGISLATIVE
  BEHAVIOR (UNITED STATES).=
                        GRUMJG-63-FAL

  CAREER MOBILITY AND MANAGERIAL
  POLITICAL BEHAVIOR
  (UNITED STATES).=     GRUSC -65-CMM

  VARIETIES OF POLITICAL BEHAVIOR
  AMONG NADARS OF TAMILNAD (INDIA).=
                        HARDRL-66-VPB

  THE STUDY OF EXECUTIVE BEHAVIOR BY
  ACTIVITY SAMPLING
  (UNITED STATES).=     KELLJ -64-SEB

  INTERNATIONAL BEHAVIOR -- A
  SOCIAL-PSYCHOLOGICAL ANALYSIS.=
                        KELMHC-65-IBS

  POLITICAL ATTITUDES AND BEHAVIOR IN
  THE PHILIPPINES.=     LANDCH-59-PAB

  THE ANALYSIS OF POLITICAL BEHAVIOR
  -- AN EMPIRICAL APPROACH.=
                        LASSHD-48-APB

  POLITICS -- A STUDY OF CONTROL
  BEHAVIOR (UNITED STATES).=

BEHAVIOR              (CONTINUATION)
                        MCDONA-65-PSC

  IDEOLOGY AND POLITICAL BEHAVIOR.=
                        MINADW-61-IPB

  DIMENSIONS OF VOTING BEHAVIOR IN A
  ONE - PARTY STATE LEGISLATURES
  (UNITED STATES).=     PATTSC-62-DVB

  LEADERSHIP AND INTERPERSONAL
  BEHAVIOR.=            PETRL -61-LIB

  INTERNATIONAL COMMUNICATION AND
  LEGISLATIVE BEHAVIOR -- THE SENATE
  AND THE HOUSE OF COMMONS
  (UNITED STATES, GREAT BRITAIN).=
                        RUSSBM-62-ICL

  THE STUDY OF JUDICIAL
  DECISION-MAKING AS AN ASPECT OF
  POLITICAL BEHAVIOR
  (UNITED STATES).=     SCHUGA-58-SJD

  QUANTITATIVE ANALYSIS OF JUDICIAL
  BEHAVIOR.=            SCHUGA-59-QAJ

  AN APPROACH TO THE STUDY OF
  ATTITUDINAL DIFFERENCES AS AN
  ASPECT OF JUDICIAL BEHAVIOR
  (UNITED STATES).=     SPAEHJ-61-ASA

  JUDICIAL POWER AS A VARIABLE
  MOTIVATING SUPREME COURT BEHAVIOR
  (UNITED STATES).=     SPAEHJ-62-JPV

  LEADERSHIP BEHAVIOR -- ITS
  DESCRIPTION AND MEASUREMENT
  (UNITED STATES).=     STOGRM-57-LBI

  THE ANALYSIS OF BEHAVIOR PATTERNS
  ON THE UNITED STATES SUPREME
  COURT.=               ULMESS-60-ABP

  JUDICIAL REVIEW AS POLITICAL
  BEHAVIOR -- A TEMPORARY CHECK ON
  CONGRESS (UNITED STATES).=
                        ULMESS-60-JRP

  SUPREME COURT BEHAVIOR AND CIVIL
  RIGHTS (UNITED STATES).=
                        ULMESS-60-SCB

  SUPREME COURT BEHAVIOR IN RACIAL
  EXCLUSION CASES -- 1935-1960
  (UNITED STATES).=     ULMESS-62-SCB

  LEGISLATIVE BEHAVIOR -- A READER IN
  THEORY AND RESEARCH.= WAHLJC-59-LBR

  THE LEGISLATIVE SYSTEM --
  EXPLORATIONS IN LEGISLATIVE
  BEHAVIOR (UNITED STATES).=
                        WAHLJC-62-LSE

  THE INFLUENCE OF PRECINCT WORK ON
  VOTING BEHAVIOR (UNITED STATES).=
                        WOLFRE-63-IPW

  SOME UNEXPLORED AVENUES IN FRENCH
  POLITICAL BEHAVIOR.=  WRIGG -58-UAF

BEHAVIORAL
  POLITICAL PARTIES -- A BEHAVIORAL
  ANALYSIS (UNITED STATES).=
                        ELDESJ-64-PPB

  ELEVENTH CENTURY CHINESE
  BUREAUCRATS -- SOME HISTORICAL
  CLASSIFICATIONS AND BEHAVIORAL
  TYPES.=               LIU,  -60-ECC

  LEADERSHIP AND ORGANIZATION -- A

BEHAVIORAL                (CONTINUATION)
  BEHAVIORAL SCIENCE APPROACH.=
                           TANNR -61-LOB

BEHAVIORALISM
  POLITICAL BEHAVIORALISM AND MODERN
  JURISPRUDENCE -- A WORKING THEORY
  AND STUDY IN JUDICIAL
  DECISION-MAKING (UNITED STATES).=
                           BECKTL-64-PBM

BEHAVIOUR
  THOUGHT AND BEHAVIOUR IN MODERN
  JAPANESE POLITICS.=    MARHM -63-TBM

BEIRUT
  A SOCIO-ECONOMIC OPINION POLL IN
  BEIRUT, LEBANON.=      ARMSL -59-SEO

BELGIAN
  THE PROBLEMS OF ELITES IN THE
  BELGIAN CONGO.=        BRAUGE-56-PEB

  POLITICAL AWAKENING IN THE BELGIAN
  CONGO -- THE POLITICS OF
  FRAGMENTATION.=        LEMAR -64-PAB

BELGIUM
  POLITICAL OPPOSITION IN THE WESTERN
  DEMOCRACIES (AUSTRIA, BELGIUM,
  FRANCE, GERMANY, GREAT BRITAIN,
  ITALY, NETHERLANDS, NORWAY,
  SWEDEN, UNITED STATES).=
                           DAHLRA-66-POW

  THE EUROPEAN EXECUTIVE (BELGIUM,
  FRANCE, GERMANY, GREAT BRITAIN,
  UNITED STATES).=       GRAND -62-EEB

  BELGIUM -- LANGUAGE AND CLASS
  OPPOSITION.=           PHILA -66-BLC

BELIEF
  THE NATURE OF BELIEF SYSTEMS IN
  MASS PUBLICS.=         CONVPE-64-NBS

  ASPECTS OF IDEOLOGICAL BELIEF IN
  THE SOVIET UNION.=     REDDPB-66-AIB

BELIEFS
  POLITICIANS' BELIEFS ABOUT VOTERS
  (UNITED STATES).=      KINGJW-67-PBA

BEMBA
  FEDERAL ADMINISTRATION, RANK, AND
  CIVIL STRIFE AMONG BEMBA ROYALS
  AND NOBLES (ZAMBIA).=  WERBRP-67-FAR

BENGAL
  VILLAGE FACTIONS AND POLITICAL
  PARTIES IN RURAL WEST BENGAL
  (INDIA).=              NICHRW-63-VFP

  CHANGING PATTERNS OF POLITICAL
  LEADERSHIP IN WEST BENGAL
  (INDIA).=              WEINM -59-CPP

BENGUET
  TYPES OF AUTHORITY IN A BENGUET
  VILLAGE (LUZON, PHILIPPINES).=
                           ENCAV -57-TAB

BERIA
  THE BERIA AFFAIR AND THE ARMY
  (SOVIET UNION).=       ANON  -54-BAA

  BEHIND THE BERIA AFFAIR
  (SOVIET UNION).=       DEWAM -54-BBA

BERLIN
  IDEOLOGICAL - PRAGMATIC
  ORIENTATIONS OF WEST BERLIN LOCAL

BERLIN                     (CONTINUATION)
  PARTY OFFICIALS (WEST GERMANY).=
                           WRIGWE-67-IPO

BEVAN
  THE LEADERSHIP, THE RANK AND FILE,
  AND MR. BEVAN (GREAT BRITAIN).=
                           YOUNM -53-LRF

BIASES
  SECTIONAL BIASES IN CONGRESS ON
  FOREIGN POLICY (UNITED STATES).=
                           GRASGL-51-SBC

BIBLIOGRAPHICAL
  A BIBLIOGRAPHICAL ESSAY ON
  DECISION-MAKING.=      GOREWJ-59-BEC

BIBLIOGRAPHY
  THE COMPARATIVE STUDY OF ELITES --
  AN INTRODUCTION AND BIBLIOGRAPHY.=
                           LASSH -52-CSE

BICULTURAL
  SUBORDINATE LEADERSHIP IN A
  BICULTURAL COMMUNITY -- AN
  ANALYSIS (UNITED STATES).=
                           WATSJB-54-SLB

BIFACTIONAL
  BIFACTIONAL RIVALRY AS AN
  ALTERNATIVE TO TWO - PARTY
  COMPETITION (UNITED STATES).=
                           SINDAP-55-BRA

BIFURCATION
  PARTY BIFURCATION AND ELITE
  INTERESTS (SOVIET UNION).=
                           ARMSJA-66-PBE

BIG-MAN
  POOR MAN, RICH MAN, BIG-MAN, CHIEF
  -- POLITICAL TYPES IN MELANESIA
  AND POLYNESIA.=        SAHLMD-63-PMR

BIHAR
  INTRA - PARTY CONFLICT IN THE BIHAR
  CONGRESS (INDIA).=     ROY,R -66-IPC

BIOGRAPHICAL
  MACHINE RETRIEVAL OF BIOGRAPHICAL
  DATA (EAST EUROPEAN ELITES).=
                           BECKC -67-MRB

  LAWYERS IN POLITICS -- AN EMPIRICAL
  EXPLORATION OF BIOGRAPHICAL DATA
  ON STATE LEGISLATORS.=
                           GOLDD -61-LPE

  THE INTELLECTUALS - POLITICS NEXUS
  -- STUDIES USING A BIOGRAPHICAL
  TECHNIQUE (BULGARIA,
  SOVIET UNION).=        HANHAM-64-IPN

  MEN WHO GOVERN -- A BIOGRAPHICAL
  PROFILE OF FEDERAL POLITICAL
  EXECUTIVES (UNITED STATES).=
                           STAN  -67-MWG

BIOGRAPHY
  POLITICAL SCIENCE AND POLITICAL
  BIOGRAPHY -- REFLECTIONS ON THE
  STUDY OF LEADERSHIP -- PART 1 --
  PART 2.=               EDINLJ-64-PSP

  THE SYSTEMATIC ANALYSIS OF
  POLITICAL BIOGRAPHY.=  JANOM -54-SAP

BIRTHDAY
  KHRUSHCHEV'S SEVENTIETH BIRTHDAY
  AND THE PROBLEM OF CHOOSING HIS
  SUCCESSOR (SOVIET UNION).=

BIRTHDAY (CONTINUATION)
MARIY -65-KSS

BISMARCK
GERMAN ADMINISTRATION SINCE
BISMARCK -- CENTRAL AUTHORITY
VERSUS LOCAL AUTONOMY.=
JACOH -63-GAS

BITTER
BITTER HARVEST -- THE INTELLECTUAL
REVOLT BEHIND THE IRON CURTAIN
(EAST EUROPE).= STILE -59-BHI

BIZEN
GOVERNMENT AND LOCAL POWER IN JAPAN
-- A STUDY ON BIZEN PROVINCE
500-1700.= HALLJW-66-GLP

BLACK
THE COLUMBIAN 'BLACK HAND' -- A
CASE STUDY OF NEOLIBERALISM IN
LATIN AMERICA.= BAILNA-65-CBH

BLACK MUSLIMS, WHITE LIBERALS
(UNITED STATES).= CUNLM -64-BMW

THE BLACK MUSLIMS -- FROM
REVOLUTION TO INSTITUTION
(UNITED STATES).= PAREM -64-BMR

BLACK AFRICA'S NEW POWER ELITE.=
SMYTHH-60-BAS

BLACKPOOL
SCARBOROUGH AND BLACKPOOL -- AN
ANALYSIS OF SOME VOTES AT THE
LABOUR PARTY CONFERENCES OF 1960
AND 1962 (GREAT BRITAIN).=
HINDK -62-SBA

BLOC
WARSAW AND THE COMMUNIST BLOC
(POLAND).' BIRNI -57-WCB

KHRUSHCHEV'S DISLOYAL OPPOSITION --
STRUCTURAL CHANGE AND POWER
STRUGGLE IN THE COMMUNIST BLOC.=
MICHF -63-KSC

BOARD
THE GOVERNING BOARD OF THE PUBLIC
CORPORATION (GREAT BRITAIN).=
ROBSWA-50-GBP

BODIES
PUBLIC CORPORATIONS AND THE
CLASSIFICATION OF ADMINISTRATIVE
BODIES (GREAT BRITAIN).=
CHESDN-53-PCC

BASES OF AUTHORITY IN LEGISLATIVE
BODIES -- A COMPARATIVE ANALYSIS
(UNITED STATES).= EULAH -62-BAL

A METHOD FOR DETERMINING THE
SIGNIFICANCE OF ROLL CALLS IN
VOTING BODIES.= RIKEWH-59-MDS

BODY
INFLUENCE AND INTERACTION IN A
STATE LEGISLATIVE BODY
(UNITED STATES).= FRANWL-62-IIS

BOGOTA
SOCIAL BACKGROUNDS OF THE BOGOTA
ENTREPRENEUR (COLOMBIA).=
LIPMA -65-SBB

BOLIVIA
BOLIVIA'S SOCIAL REVOLUTION.=
ARNAC -59-BSS

LAND REFORM AND SOCIAL REVOLUTION

BOLIVIA (CONTINUATION)
IN BOLIVIA.= HEATD -59-LRS

BOLIVIA -- A LAND DIVIDED.=
CSBOH -64-BLC

THE 'REVOLUCION NACIONAL' AND THE
MNR IN BOLIVIA.= STOKW -59-RNM

BOLIVIAN
THE BOLIVIAN NATIONAL REVOLUTION.=
ALEXRJ-58-BNR

SOCIAL MOBILITY AND ECONOMIC
DEVELOPMENT -- THE VITAL
PARAMETERS OF THE BOLIVIAN
REVOLUTION.= BERGCF-64-SME

BOLIVIAN ORIENTE
LAND TENURE AND SOCIAL ORGANIZATION
-- AN ETHNOHISTORICAL STUDY FROM
THE BOLIVIAN ORIENTE.=
HEATDB-59-LTS

BOLSHEVIK
BOLSHEVIK ADMINISTRATION IN THE
UKRAINE -- 1918.= ADAMAE-58-BAU

BOLSHEVIK MAN, HIS MOTIVATIONS.=
BELLD -55-BMH

NATIONAL AND SOCIAL COMPOSITION OF
THE MEMBERSHIP OF THE COMMUNIST
PARTY (BOLSHEVIK) OF THE UKRAINE,
1918-1928.= DMYTB -57-NSC

THE ORGANIZATIONAL WEAPON -- A
STUDY OF BOLSHEVIK STRATEGY AND
TACTICS (SOVIET UNION).=
SELZP -52-OWS

INTERRELATIONS BETWEEN BOLSHEVIK
IDEOLOGY AND THE STRUCTURE OF
SOVIET SOCIETY.= TOMAD -51-IBB

BOLSHEVIKI
POWER AND THE SOVIET ELITE -- THE
LETTER OF AN OLD BOLSHEVIKI AND
OTHER ESSAYS.= NICOB -65-PSE

BOLSHEVIKS
THE BOLSHEVIKS.= ULAMAB-65-B

BOLSHEVISM
A STUDY OF BOLSHEVISM
(SOVIET UNION).= LEITN -53-SBS

THE RUSSIAN INTELLIGENTSIA AND
BOLSHEVISM.= STEPF -58-RIB

BOLSHEVISM AND THE INDIVIDUAL
LEADER (SOVIET UNION).=
SWEAH -63-BIL

BOLSHEVIZATION
GOTTWALD AND THE BOLSHEVIZATION OF
THE COMMUNIST PARTY OF
CZECHOSLOVAKIA (1929-1939).=
SKILHG-61-GBC

BOMB
THE ROLE OF THE SCIENTIFIC ELITE IN
THE DECISION TO USE THE ATOMIC
BOMB (UNITED STATES).=
MOORJW-58-RSE

THE DECISION TO USE THE ATOMIC BOMB
(UNITED STATES).= MORTL -57-DUA

BONN
PARTIES AND PRESSURE GROUPS IN
WEIMAR AND BONN (GERMANY).=

31

BCNN (CONTINUATION)
FRYECE-65-PPC

BORDER
INFLUENTIALS IN TWO BORDER CITIES
-- A STUDY IN COMMUNITY
DECISION-MAKING (MEXICO,
UNITED STATES).= D'ANWV-65-ITB

INTEGRATION AND CLEAVAGE AMONG
COMMUNITY INFLUENTIALS IN TWO
BORDER CITIES (MEXICO,
UNITED STATES).= FORMWH-59-ICA

POWER STRUCTURE AND DECISION-MAKING
IN A MEXICAN BORDER CITY.=
KLAPDE-60-PSD

BOSE
SUBHAS CHANDRA BOSE AND THE INDIAN
NATIONAL ARMY.= COHESP-63-SCB

BOSS
THE BOSS AND THE VOTE -- CASE STUDY
IN CITY POLITICS (UNITED STATES).=
BRUNJS-46-BVC

BOSSES
BOSSES, MACHINES, AND ETHNIC GROUPS
(UNITED STATES).= CORNEE-64-BME

CITY BOSSES AND POLITICAL MACHINES
(UNITED STATES).= GREELS-64-CBP

FROM BOSSES TO COSMOPOLITANISM --
CHANGES IN THE RELATIONSHIP OF
URBAN LEADERSHIP TO STATE POLITICS
(UNITED STATES).= HAVAWC-64-BCC

THE BOSSES (UNITED STATES).=
MARTRG-64-BUS

CITY BOSSES IN THE UNITED STATES.=
ZINKH -30-CBU

BOTTLENECKS
THE JULY CENTRAL COMMITTEE PLENUM
AND BOTTLENECKS IN SOVIET
INDUSTRY.= MINYV -60-JCC

BOUGAINVILLE
A SOLOMON ISLAND SOCIETY -- KINSHIP
AND LEADERSHIP AMONG THE SIVAI OF
BOUGAINVILLE.= CLIVOL-58-SIS

BOURGEOIS
POST - BOURGEOIS EUROPE.=
LICHG -63-PBE

BOURGEOISIE
TOWARDS A SOVIET BOURGEOISIE.=
EH -55-TSB

AN AFRICAN BOURGEOISIE -- RACE,
CLASS, AND POLITICS IN SOUTH
AFRICA.= KUPEL -65-ABR

THE CHINESE COMMUNISTS AND THE
'BOURGEOISIE'.= WM -52-CCB

BOW
THE BOW GROUP'S ROLE IN BRITISH
POLITICS.= ROSER -61-BGS

BRAINS
THE ROLE OF BRAINS IN THE TOTAL
STATE.= LERND -53-RBT

BRAZIL
SOCIAL CHANGE IN BRAZIL.=
AZEVT -63-SCB

RACE, SOCIAL MOBILITY AND POLITICS

BRAZIL (CONTINUATION)
IN BRAZIL.= HAMMHR-63-RSM

TOWN AND COUNTRY IN BRAZIL.=
HARRM -56-TCB

REVOLUTION IN BRAZIL -- POLITICS
AND SOCIETY IN A DEVELOPING
NATION.= HOROIL-64-RBP

GOVERNMENT IN CONTEMPORARY BRAZIL.=
LIPSL -56-GCB

THE RISE OF MIDDLE CLASS AND MIDDLE
MANAGEMENT IN BRAZIL.=
PERELC-62-RMC

RACE AND CLASS IN RURAL BRAZIL.=
WAGLC -52-RCR

BRAZILIAN
THE MASTERS AND THE SLAVES -- A
STUDY IN THE DEVELOPMENT OF
BRAZILIAN CIVILIZATION.=
FREYG -46-MSS

BRAZILIAN CAREERS AND SOCIAL
STRUCTURE -- AN EVOLUTIONARY MODEL
AND CASE HISTORY.= LEEDA -64-BCS

TERENA (BRAZILIAN INDIANS) SOCIAL
ORGANIZATIONS AND LAW.=
CLIEK -48-TBI

THE BRAZILIAN LAW STUDENT --
BACKGROUND, HABITS, ATTITUDES.=
SCHELR-63-BLS

DOMINANT POWER COMPONENTS IN THE
BRAZILIAN UNIVERSITY STUDENT
MOVEMENT PRIOR TO APRIL 1964.=
THERLD-65-DPC

TERENTISMO IN THE BRAZILIAN
REVOLUTION OF 1930.= WIRTJD-64-TBR

BRAZILIANS
SOME INTERNATIONAL IMPLICATIONS OF
THE POLITICAL PSYCHOLOGY OF
BRAZILIANS.= FREEL -61-IIP

BRITAIN
POLITICAL PARTIES AND THE PARTY
SYSTEM IN BRITAIN.= BAILSD-52-PPP

PRESSURE GROUPS AND PARTIES IN
BRITAIN.= BEERSH-56-PGP

GROUP REPRESENTATION IN BRITAIN AND
THE UNITED STATES.= BEERSH-58-GRB

WHO GOVERNS BRITAIN.= CHESDN-62-WGB

CABINET REFORM IN IN BRITAIN
1914-1963.= DAALH -63-CRB

CANDIDATE SELECTION IN BRITAIN.=
EPSTLD-59-CSB

BRITAIN'S NEW LABOUR LEADERS.=
JANOGE-63-BSN

INTER - PARTY COMPETITION IN
BRITAIN , 1950-1959.= JONECO-63-IPC

HIGHER CIVIL SERVANTS IN BRITAIN.=
KELSRK-55-HCS

THE POLITICS OF BRITAIN'S ANGRY
YOUNG MEN.= KROLM -61-PBS

CENTRAL ADMINISTRATION IN BRITAIN.=

BRITISH                 (CONTINUATION)
                        GUTTWL-54-AMC

CHANGES IN BRITISH LABOUR
LEADERSHIP.=            GUTTWL-61-CBL

THE BRITISH POLITICAL ELITE.=
                        GUTTWL-63-BPE

TRENDS IN THE BRITISH LABOR
MOVEMENT SINCE 1850.=   HOBSEJ-49-TBL

THE BRITISH COMMUNIST PARTY.=
                        HOBSEJ-54-BCP

UNIFYING THE BRITISH CIVIL SERVICE
-- SOME TRENDS AND PROBLEMS.=
                        HODGJE-48-UBC

NATIONALISM AND SOCIAL CLASSES IN
BRITISH WEST AFRICA.= KILSML-58-NSC

BRITISH POLITICS -- PEOPLE,
PARTIES, AND PARLIAMENT.=
                        KINGA -66-BPP

REPRESENTATIVE BUREAUCRACY -- AN
INTERPRETATION OF THE BRITISH
CIVIL SERVICE.=         KINGJO-44-RBI

THE PRESENT CONDITION OF BRITISH
POLITICAL PARTIES.=    LEWIGK-52-PCB

PROBLEMS IN THE DEVELOPMENT OF
MODERN LEADERSHIP AND LOYALTIES IN
THE BRITISH SOMALILAND
PROTECTORATE AND THE UNITED
NATIONS TRUSTEESHIP TERRITORY OF
SOMALIA.=              LEWIIM-60-PDM

THE TWO - PARTY SYSTEM IN BRITISH
POLITICS.=             LIPSL -53-TPS

THE TRANSFORMATION OF BRITISH
LABOUR PARTY POLICY SINCE 1945.=
                        LOEWG -57-TBL

LEGISLATURES OF THE BRITISH PACIFIC
ISLANDS.=              LUKEH -47-LBP

THE BRITISH CABINET.= MACKJP-62-BC

REPRESENTATION IN PLURAL SOCIETIES
(GREAT BRITAIN, BRITISH
COMMONWEALTH).=        MACKWJ-54-RPS

PRESSURE GROUPS AND BRITISH
GOVERNMENT.=           MACKWJ-55-PGB

THE LEADERSHIP OF THE BRITISH UNION
OF FASCISTS.=          MANDWF-66-LBU

POSTWAR STRAINS ON THE BRITISH
COMMONWEALTH.=         MANSN -48-PSB

FORMAL RECOGNITION OF THE LEADER OF
THE OPPOSITION IN PARLIAMENTS OF
THE BRITISH COMMONWEALTH.=
                        MCHECE-54-FRL

POWER IN BRITISH POLITICAL
PARTIES.=              MCKERT-55-PBP

BRITISH POLITICAL PARTIES -- THE
DISTRIBUTION OF POWER WITHIN THE
CONSERVATIVE AND LABOUR PARTIES.=
                        MCKERT-65-BPP

RECRUITMENT OF THE ADMINISTRATIVE
CLASS OF THE BRITISH CIVIL
SERVICE.=              MCKIMM-49-RAC

THE BRITISH LEFT WING AND FOREIGN


BRITISH                 (CONTINUATION)
POLICY -- A STUDY OF THE INFLUENCE
OF IDEOLOGY.=          MEEHEJ-60-BLW

THE FABIAN SOCIETY AND THE BRITISH
LABOUR PARTY.=         MILBJF-58-FSB

ON THE DANGERS OF COPYING FROM THE
BRITISH.=              NEEDM -62-DCB

BRITISH FOREIGN POLICY AND THE
PARTY SYSTEM.=         NORTFS-60-BFP

THE AMERICAN LABOUR MOVEMENT -- A
BRITISH VIEW.=         PELLH -54-ALM

THE BRITISH COMMUNIST PARTY.=
                        PELLH -58-BCP

BRITISH PRESSURE GROUPS.=
                        POTTA -56-BPG

ORGANIZED GROUPS IN BRITISH
NATIONAL POLITICS.=    POTTAM-60-OGB

INTER - CONSTITUENCY MOVEMENT OF
BRITISH PARLIAMENTARY CANDIDATES,
1951-1959.=            RANNA -64-ICM

THE CENTRAL LEGISLATURE IN BRITISH
INDIA 1921-1947.=      RASHM -65-CLB

RETRENCHMENT AND REVIVAL -- A STUDY
OF THE CONTEMPORARY BRITISH
LIBERAL PARTY.=        RASMJS-64-RRS

HONORABLE MEMBERS -- A STUDY OF THE
BRITISH BACKBENCHERS
(GREAT BRITAIN).=      RICHPG-59-HMS

PATRONAGE IN BRITISH GOVERNMENT.=
                        RICHPG-63-PBG

THE LABOUR GOVERNMENT AND BRITISH
INDUSTRY.=             ROGOAA-55-LGB

THE BOW GROUP'S ROLE IN BRITISH
POLITICS.=             ROSER -61-BGS

STUDIES IN BRITISH POLITICS
                -- A READER IN
POLITICAL SOCIOLOGY.= ROSER -66-SBP

STUDIES IN BRITISH POLITICS
                -- A READER IN
POLITICAL SOCIOLOGY.= ROSER -66-SBP

THE BRITISH LABOR PARTY --
PROSPECTS AND PORTENTS.=
                        ROWSAL-45-BLP

RELIGIOUS INFLUENCES IN THE
BACKGROUND OF THE BRITISH LABOUR
PARTY.=                SMITRW-57-RIB

BRITISH INTELLECTUALS IN THE
WELFARE STATE.=        SPENS -51-BIW

BRITISH PRESSURE GROUPS -- THEIR
ROLE IN RELATION TO THE HOUSE OF
COMMONS.=              STEWJD-58-BPG

THE UNIVERSITY CONSTITUENCIES IN
THE RECENT BRITISH ELECTION.=
                        VEX,MB-46-UCR

AMERICA AND THE BRITISH FOREIGN
POLICY-MAKING ELITE, FROM JOSEPH
CHAMBERLAIN TO ANTHONY EDEN,
1895-1956.=            WATTDC-63-ABF

PERSONALITIES AND POLICIES --

BRITISH (CONTINUATION)
STUDIES IN THE FORMULATION OF
BRITISH FOREIGN POLICY IN THE
TWENTIETH CENTURY.= WATTDC-65-PPS

BRITISH UNIONS AND THE GOVERNMENT.=
WIGHE -59-BUG

PROBABLES AND POSSIBLES (BRITISH
CANDIDATES).= WILCRW-63-PPB

GENTLEMANLY POWER -- BRITISH
LEADERSHIP AND THE PUBLIC SCHOOL
TRADITION -- A COMPARATIVE STUDY
IN THE MAKING OF RULERS.=
WILKR -64-GPB

THE ROUTES OF ENTRY OF NEW MEMBERS
OF THE BRITISH CABINET,
1868-1958.= WILLFM-59-REN

THE BRITISH CRISIS -- A PROBLEM IN
ECONOMIC STATESMANSHIP.=
WILLJH-49-BCP

THE BRITISH GENERAL ELECTION OF
1951 -- CANDIDATES AND PARTIES.=
WILLJR-52-BGE

COMMUNISM AND BRITISH
INTELLECTUALS.= WOODN -59-CBI

BROEDERBOND
TRADE UNIONS IN TRAVAIL -- THE
STORY OF THE BROEDERBOND -
NATIONALIST PLAN TO CONTROL SOUTH
AFRICAN TRADE UNIONS.=
HEPPA -54-TUT

BROKER
THE JAVANESE KIJAJI -- THE CHANGING
ROLE OF A CULTURAL BROKER.=
GEERC -60-JKC

BROKERS
ADMINISTRATORS, AGITATORS, AND
BROKERS.= PYE,LW-58-AAB

BROTHERHOOD
THE MUSLIM BROTHERHOOD (EGYPT).=
KAPLZ -54-MBE

BROTHERHOODS
RELIGIOUS BROTHERHOODS IN MOROCCAN
POLITICS.= VIDAFS-50-RBM

BUDDHISM
BUDDHISM AND POLITICS IN SOUTH
VIETNAM.= ROBEA -65-BPS

BUDDHISM AND SOCIALISM IN JAPAN AND
BURMA.= TOTTGO-60-BSJ

BUDDHISTS
THE BUDDHISTS, THE WAR, AND THE
VIETCONG.= ROBEA -66-BWV

BUDGET
THE CONFERENCE COMMITTEE -- PIVOT
IN THE BUDGET PROCESS
(PHILIPPINES).= DECLCS-63-CCP

THE UNITED STATES BUREAU OF THE
BUDGET.= EGGER -49-USB

THE MILITARY BUDGET --
CONGRESSIONAL PHASE
(UNITED STATES).= GORDBK-61-MBC

BUDGETARY
THE POLITICS OF THE BUDGETARY
PROCESS (UNITED STATES).=

BUDGETARY (CONTINUATION)
WILDA -64-PBP

BUGANDA
THE KING'S MEN -- LEADERSHIP AND
STATUS IN BUGANDA ON THE EVE OF
INDEPENDENCE.= FALLLA-64-KSM

THE CHRISTIAN REVOLUTION IN
BUGANDA.= WRIGCC-59-CRB

BUILDERS
BUILDERS OF EMERGING NATIONS.=
DEANVM-61-BEN

BUILDING
UNIVERSITIES AND NATION BUILDING IN
AFRICA.= DILLES-63-UNB

BUREAUCRACY AND NATION BUILDING IN
TRANSITIONAL SOCIETIES.=
DUBESC-64-BNB

ADMINISTRATIVE REORGANIZATION AND
THE BUILDING OF COMMUNISM
(SOVIET UNION).= JURCA -60-ARB

BUILDING A WELFARE STATE IN BURMA,
1948-1956.= TRAGFN-58-BWS

THE MILITARY ROLE IN NATION
BUILDING AND ECONOMIC
DEVELOPMENT.= UNGEJP-63-MRN

BULGARIA
LEADING PERSONALITIES IN EASTERN
EUROPE -- BULGARIA,
CZECHOSLOVAKIA, HUNGARY, POLAND,
ROMANIA.= ANON -57-LPE

THE POLITICAL SCENE (BULGARIA).=
BROWJF-61-PSB

BULGARIA -- THE VALUE OF
SCAPEGOATS.= CHRIB -62-BVS

THE INTELLECTUALS - POLITICS NEXUS
-- STUDIES USING A BIOGRAPHICAL
TECHNIQUE (BULGARIA,
SOVIET UNION).= HANHAM-64-IPN

THE POLITICS OF THE EUROPEAN
COMMUNIST STATES (BULGARIA,
CZECHOSLOVAKIA, HUNGARY, EAST
GERMANY, POLAND, RUMANIA,
SOVIET UNION, YUGOSLAVIA).=
IONEG -67-PEC

THE COMMUNIST PARTY OF BULGARIA.=
ROTHJ -59-CPB

COMMUNIST-DOMINATED EDUCATION IN
BULGARIA -- A STUDY IN SOCIAL
RELATIONS.= SANDIT-56-CDE

SOCIAL SCIENCE AND THE PARTY
(BULGARIA).= SANDIT-61-SSP

BULGARIAN
LOCAL GOVERNMENT AND ADMINISTRATION
IN THE BULGARIAN PEOPLE'S REPUBLIC
-- 1951-1956. GINSG -63-LGA

BUNDESRAT
POLITICS AND BUREAUCRACY IN THE
WEST GERMAN BUNDESRAT.=
NEURK -59-PBW

LATENT AND MANIFEST BUREAUCRACY IN
THE WEST GERMAN PARLIAMENT -- THE
CASE OF THE BUNDESRAT.=
PINNEL-62-LMB

BUNDESTAG
THE COMPOSITION OF THE GERMAN

BUREAUCRACY          (CONTINUATION)
PUBLIC ADMINISTRATION IN IRAN --
SKETCHES OF A NON-WESTERN
TRANSITIONAL BUREAUCRACY.=
                    GABLRW-61-PAI

WITHER RUSSIA -- A BUREAUCRACY
UNDER FIRE (SOVIET UNION).=
                    GALLG -66-WRB

THE CIVIL SERVICE OF PAKISTAN --
BUREAUCRACY IN A NEW NATION.=
                    GOODHF-64-CSP

THE PROBLEM OF SUCCESSION AND
BUREAUCRACY.=       GOULAW-65-PSB

POLITY, BUREAUCRACY AND INTEREST
GROUPS IN THE NEAR EAST AND NORTH
AFRICA.=            GRASG -64-PBI

BUREAUCRACY AND SMALL ORGANIZATIONS
(UNITED STATES).=   HALLRH-63-BSC

'IMPERIALISM' IN BUREAUCRACY
(UNITED STATES).=   HOLDM -66-IBU

BUREAUCRACY IN A DEMOCRACY
(UNITED STATES).=   HYNECS-50-BDU

BUREAUCRACY AND DEVELOPMENT IN
PAKISTAN.=          INAY(E-63-BDP

MANDARIN BUREAUCRACY AND POLITICS
IN SOUTH VIETNAM.=  JUMPR -57-MBP

THE LEGISLATIVE BUREAUCRACY -- ITS
RESPONSE TO POLITICAL CHANGE
(UNITED STATES).=   KAMPMM-54-LBI

BUREAUCRACY AND ENVIRONMENT IN
CEYLON.=            KEARRN-64-BEC

CEYLON -- THE CONTEMPORARY
BUREAUCRACY.=       KEARRN-66-CCB

REPRESENTATIVE BUREAUCRACY -- AN
INTERPRETATION OF THE BRITISH
CIVIL SERVICE.=     KINGJD-44-RBI

THAILAND'S BUREAUCRACY AND THE
THREAT OF COMMUNIST SUBVERSION.=
                    KINGJK-54-TSB

AFRICAN ELITES IN INDUSTRIAL
BUREAUCRACY (UGANDA).=
                    KUMAC -66-AEI

BUREAUCRACY AND POLITICAL
DEVELOPMENT.=       LAPAJ -63-BPD

AN OVERVIEW OF BUREAUCRACY AND
POLITICAL DEVELOPMENT.=
                    LAPAJ -63-CBP

THE ROLE OF THE BUREAUCRACY IN
JAPAN.=             MAKIJM-47-RBJ

READER IN BUREAUCRACY.=
                    MERTVK-52-RB

BUREAUCRACY IN NEW ZEALAND.=
                    MILNRS-58-BNZ

BUREAUCRACY (AUSTRIA,
GREAT BRITAIN,' UNITED STATES).=
                    MISELV-44-BAG

CHIEF JUSTICE TAFT AND THE LOWER
COURT BUREAUCRACY -- A STUDY IN
JUDICIAL ADMINISTRATION.=
                    MURPWF-62-CJT

BUREAUCRACY AND PROGRESSIVISM --

BUREAUCRACY          (CONTINUATION)
THE EXPERIENCE OF CALIFORNIA,
1899-1933 (UNITED STATES).=
                    NASHGD-60-BPE

FEDERALISM -- WEST GERMAN
BUREAUCRACY.=       NEURK -59-FWG

POLITICS AND BUREAUCRACY IN THE
WEST GERMAN BUNDESRAT.=
                    NEURK -59-PBW

BUREAUCRACY'S OTHER FACE
(UNITED STATES).=   PAGECH-46-BSC

THE BUREAUCRACY AND THE NAZI
PARTY.=             PETEEN-66-BNP

LATENT AND MANIFEST BUREAUCRACY IN
THE WEST GERMAN PARLIAMENT -- THE
CASE OF THE BUNDESRAT.=
                    PINNEL-62-LMB

WEBERIAN V. WELFARE BUREAUCRACY IN
TRADITIONAL SOCIETY (TURKEY).=
                    PRESRV-62-WVW

A STUDY OF ROLE CONCEPTIONS IN
BUREAUCRACY (UNITED STATES).=
                    REISL -49-SRC

BUREAUCRACY, ARISTOCRACY, AND
AUTOCRACY -- THE PRUSSIAN
EXPERIENCE, 1660-1815.=
                    ROSEH -66-BAA

THE THAI BUREAUCRACY.=
                    SCHOEL-61-TB

AN APPROACH TO A THEORY OF
BUREAUCRACY.=       SELZP -43-ATB

THE THAI BUREAUCRACY --
INSTITUTIONAL CHANGE AND
DEVELOPMENT.=       SIFFWJ-66-TBI

CRITERIA FOR RECRUITMENT AND
SUCCESS IN THE JAPANESE
BUREAUCRACY, 1866-1900 --
'TRADITIONAL' AND 'MODERN'
CRITERIA IN BUREAUCRATIC
DEVELOPMENT.=       SILBBS-66-CRS

BUREAUCRACY AND ECONOMIC
DEVELOPMENT.=       SPENJJ-63-BEC

THE RULING SERVANTS -- BUREAUCRACY
IN RUSSIA, FRANCE, AND
GREAT BRITAIN.=     STRAE -61-RSB

THE POLITICS OF BUREAUCRACY
(UNITED STATES).=   TULLG -65-PBU

'BUREAUCRACY' AND 'RATIONALITY' IN
WEBER'S ORGANIZATION THEORY -- AN
EMPIRICAL STUDY.=   UDY,SH-59-BRW

THE RULING BUREAUCRACY OF ORIENTAL
DESPOTISM -- A PHENOMENON THAT
PARALYZED MARX.=    WITTKA-53-RBO

AMERICAN BUREAUCRACY.=
                    WOLLP -63-AB

BUREAUCRAT
THE BUREAUCRAT (UNITED STATES).=
                    CRIDJH-44-BUS

THE BUREAUCRAT AND THE PUBLIC -- A

BUREAUCRAT                (CONTINUATION)
STUDY CF INFORMATICNAL
PERSPECTIVES (UNITED STATES).=
                          JANOM -58-BPS

THE EXECUTIVE -- AUTOCRAT,
BUREAUCRAT, DEMOCRAT
(UNITED STATES).=      JENNEE-62-EAB

THE BUREAUCRAT AND THE ENTHUSIAST
-- AN EXPLORATION CF THE
LEADERSHIP CF SCCIAL MOVEMENTS
(UNITED STATES).=      ROCHJP-55-BEE

FROM REVCLUTICNARY TC SEMI -
BUREAUCRAT -- THE 'REGULARISATION'
CF CADRES (CHINA).=    VOGEEF-67-RSB

BUREAUCRATIC
THE PCLITICAL KINGDCM IN UGANDA --
A STUDY OF BUREAUCRATIC
NATICNALISM.=          APTEDE-61-PKU

THE SCVIET BUREAUCRATIC ELITE -- A
CASE STUDY CF THE UKRAINIAN
APPARATUS.=            ARMSJA-59-SBE

PCWER CLIQUES IN BUREAUCRATIC
SCCIETY.=              BENSJ -62-PCB

ASIAN BUREAUCRATIC SYSTEMS EMERGENT
FROM THE BRITISH IMPERIAL
TRADITICN (INDIA, PAKISTAN, BURMA,
CEYLCN, MALAYA, NEPAL).=
                          BRAIR -  -ABS

THE RCLE CF BUREAUCRATIC NORMS IN
AFRICAN PCLITICAL STRUCTURES.=
                          COLSE -58-RBN

THE U.S.S.R. -- FRCM CHARISMATIC
SECT TC BUREAUCRATIC SOCIETY
(SCVIET UNICN).=       CONTH -62-USS

THE BUREAUCRATIC PHENCMENON -- AN
EXAMINATICN CF BUREAUCRACY IN
MCDERN CRGANIZATICN AND ITS
CULTURAL SETTING IN FRANCE.=
                          CROZM -64-BPE

THE DEVELCPMENT AND DECLINE OF
PATRIMCNIAL AND BUREAUCRATIC
ADMINISTRATICN.=       DELAW -63-DDP

A NCTE CN THE APPEARANCE OF WISDCM
IN LARGE BUREAUCRATIC
CRGANIZATICNS.=        DEUTKW-61-NAW

PCLITICAL STRUGGLE IN (ANCIENT)
BUREAUCRATIC SCCIETIES.=
                          EISESN-56-PSA

INTERNAL CCNTRADICTIONS IN
BUREAUCRATIC PCLITIES (ANCIENT
CHINA, PERSIA).=       EISESN-58-ICB

A LABCRATORY EXPERIMENT ON
BUREAUCRATIC AUTHCRITY.=
                          EVANWM-61-LEB

EQUALITARIANISM AND BUREAUCRATIC
RECRUITMENT.=          CUSFJR-58-EBR

BUREAUCRATIC TRANSFCRMATION IN
BURMA.=                GUYOJF-66-BTB

BUREAUCRATIC CADRES IN A
TRADITICNAL MILIEU (NIGERIA).=
                          KIRKAH-65-BCT

BUREAUCRATIC SUCCESSICN.=
                          LEVEB -61-BS

BUREAUCRATIC MASS MEDIA -- A STUDY

BUREAUCRATIC               (CCNTINUATICN)
CF RCLE DEFINITIONS
(UNITED STATES).=      LYSTMH-56-BMM

HONCR IN BUREAUCRATIC LIFE (FRANCE,
GREAT BRITAIN, UNITED STATES).=
                          MAINLC-64-HBL

CAREER PERSPECTIVES IN A
BUREAUCRATIC SETTING
(UNITED STATES).=      MARVD -54-CPB

HIGHER PUBLIC SERVANTS AND THE
BUREAUCRATIC ELITE IN CANADA.=
                          PORTJ -58-HPS

THE BUREAUCRATIC ELITE -- A REPLY
TC PRCFESSCR RCWAT (CANADA,
GREAT BRITAIN).=       PORTJ -59-BER

BUREAUCRATIC CHANGE IN INDIA.=
                          POTTCC-66-BCI

THE SCCIAL BASES CF BUREAUCRATIC
CRGANIZATICN (UNITED STATES).=
                          PRESRV-59-SBB

THAILAND -- THE MCDERNIZATION OF A
BUREAUCRATIC PCLITY.=  RIGGFW-66-TMB

CN JCHN PCRTER'S 'BUREAUCRATIC
ELITE IN CANADA'.=     RCWADC-59-JPS

THE BUREAUCRATIC REVCLUTION -- THE
RISE CF THE STALINIST STATE
(SCVIET UNICN).=       SCHAM -62-BRR

BUREAUCRATIC PARTY CRGANIZATION
THRCUGH PRCFESSICNAL PCLITICAL
STAFFING (UNITED STATES).=
                          SCHUCE-64-BPC

CRITERIA FCR RECRUITMENT AND
SUCCESS IN THE JAPANESE
BUREAUCRACY, 1866-1900 --
'TRADITIONAL' AND 'MCDERN'
CRITERIA IN BUREAUCRATIC
DEVELCPMENT.=          SILBBS-66-CRS

SCIENTISTS IN THE BUREAUCRATIC
AGE.=                  SPEYE -57-SBA

BUREAUCRATIC TRANSITICN IN MALAYA.=
                          TILMRO-64-BTM

BUREAUCRATIC DEVELCPMENT IN
MALAYA.=               TILMRO-66-BDM

BUREAUCRATIZATICN
PARTY CCNTRCL AND BUREAUCRATIZATION
IN CZECHCSLCVAKIA.=    BECKC -61-PCB

BUREAUCRACY AND BUREAUCRATIZATICN.=
                          EISESN-58-BB

BUREAUCRACY, BUREAUCRATIZATION, AND
DEBUREAUCRATIZATICN.=  EISESN-60-BBD

ASPECTS OF BUREAUCRATIZATION IN
ASHANTI IN THE NINETEENTH CENTURY
(AFRICA).=             WILKI -66-ABA

BUREAUCRATS
BUREAUCRATS AND CITIZENS (MCRCCCO,
TUNISIA, PAKISTAN).=   ASHFDE-65-BCM

WHC ARE THE GCVERNMENT BUREAUCRATS
(UNITED STATES).=      BENDR -65-WAG

BUREAUCRATS AND AGITATCRS.=
                          GOULAW-65-BA

BUSINESSMEN AND BUREAUCRATS

BUREAUCRATS          (CONTINUATION)
(UNITED STATES).=     LANERE-53-BBU

ELEVENTH CENTURY CHINESE
BUREAUCRATS -- SOME HISTORICAL
CLASSIFICATIONS AND BEHAVIORAL
TYPES.=               LIU, -60-ECC

POLITICIANS AND BUREAUCRATS
(UNITED STATES).=     NEUSRE-65-PBU

BUREAUCRATS AND POLITICAL
DEVELOPMENT -- A PARADOXICAL
VIEW.=                RIGGFW-63-BPD

THE RECRUITMENT AND TRAINING OF
BUREAUCRATS IN THE UNITED STATES.=
                      SAYRWS-54-RTB

BURKE
OBSERVATIONS ON THE THEORY OF
EDMUND BURKE (UNITED STATES).=
                      EULAH -59-OTE

BURMA
BURMA'S POLITICAL CRISIS.=
                      BADGJH-58-BSP

BURMA'S RADICAL LEFT -- A STUDY IN
FAILURE.=             BADGJH-61-BSR

ASIAN BUREAUCRATIC SYSTEMS EMERGENT
FROM THE BRITISH IMPERIAL
TRADITION (INDIA, PAKISTAN, BURMA,
CEYLON, MALAYA, NEPAL).=
                      BRAIR - -ABS

THE 1960 ELECTION IN BURMA.=
                      BUTWR -60-EB

BURMA'S MILITARY REGIME.=
                      CADYJF-60-BSM

BURMA'S MILITARY DICTATORSHIP.=
                      CADYJF-65-BSM

BUREAUCRATIC TRANSFORMATION IN
BURMA.=               GUYOJF-66-BTB

THE POLITICAL SIGNIFICANCE OF THE
BURMA WORKERS PARTY.= JOSEA -58-PSB

POLITICAL SYSTEMS OF HIGHLAND BURMA
-- A STUDY OF KACHIN SOCIAL
STRUCTURE.=           LEACER-54-PSH

RELIGION AND AUTHORITY IN MODERN
BURMA.=               MENDEM-60-RAM

POLITICS, PERSONALITY, AND
NATION-BUILDING -- BURMA'S SEARCH
FOR IDENTITY.=        PYE,LW-62-PPN

UNIVERSITY STUDENTS AND POLITICS IN
BURMA.=               SILVJ -64-USP

RELIGION AND POLITICS IN BURMA.=
                      SMITDE-65-RPB

BUDDHISM AND SOCIALISM IN JAPAN AND
BURMA.=               TOTTGO-60-BSJ

BUILDING A WELFARE STATE IN BURMA,
1948-1956.=           TRAGFN-58-BWS

THE POLITICAL SPLIT IN BURMA.=
                      TRAGFN-58-PSB

BURMESE
PORTRAIT OF THE BURMESE
PARLIAMENT.=          MAUNM -57-PBP

ARMY IN BURMESE POLITICS.=

BURMESE               (CONTINUATION)
                      PYE,LW-62-ABP

THE BURMESE UNIVERSITY STUDENT --
AN APPROACH TO PERSONALITY AND
SUBCULTURE.=          WOHLJ -66-BUS

BURUNDI
SOCIAL AND POLITICAL CHANGES IN
BURUNDI.=             LEMAR -66-SPC

BUSINESS
THE POLITICAL ATTITUDES OF GERMAN
BUSINESS.=            ALMOGA-56-PAG

AMERICAN BUSINESS AND PUBLIC POLICY
-- THE POLITICS OF FOREIGN TRADE.=
                      BAUER -63-ABP

SOCIAL MOBILITY AND THE AMERICAN
BUSINESS ELITE --1 --2.=
                      BENDR -57-SMA

THE BUSINESS ELITE -- THEN AND NOW
(UNITED STATES).=     BERGM -56-BET

A PROBLEM IN SOVIET BUSINESS
ADMINISTRATION.=      BERLJS-57-PSB

INTERVIEWING BUSINESS LEADERS.=
                      DEXTLA-59-IBL

ORGANIZED BUSINESS IN FRANCE.=
                      EHRMHW-57-OBF

ORIGINS OF THE MODERN INDIAN
BUSINESS CLASS.=      GADGDR-59-CMI

THE EFFECTS OF SUCCESSION -- A
COMPARATIVE STUDY OF MILITARY AND
BUSINESS ORGANIZATION
(UNITED STATES).=     GRUSO -64-ESC

THE ROLE OF PRIVATE BUSINESS
(LATIN AMERICA).=     HANSSG-66-RPB

U.S. BUSINESS INTERESTS IN CUBA AND
THE RISE OF CASTRO.=  JOHNLL-65-USB

INTERVIEWING THE BUSINESS ELITE.=
                      KINCHB-57-IBE

THE INDIAN BUSINESS COMMUNITIES AND
THE EVOLUTION OF AN INDUSTRIALIST
CLASS.=               LAMBHB-55-IBC

BUSINESS ORGANIZATION AND
LEADERSHIP IN INDIA TODAY.=
                      LAMBHB-59-BOL

BIG BUSINESS LOBBYING IN JAPAN --
THE CASE OF CENTRAL BANK REFORM.=
                      LANGFC-61-BBL

ENTERPRISE IN LATIN AMERICA --
BUSINESS ATTITUDES IN A DEVELOPING
ECONOMY.=             LAUTA -66-ELA

AMERICAN BUSINESS, PUBLIC POLICY,
CASE-STUDIES AND POLITICAL
THEORY.=              LOWITJ-64-ABP

THE BUSINESS ELITE AND FOREIGN
POLICY (UNITED STATES).=
                      MCLEDS-60-BEF

THE AMERICAN BUSINESS ELITE -- A
COLLECTIVE PORTRAIT.= MILLCW-54-ABE

THE RECRUITMENT OF THE AMERICAN
BUSINESS ELITE.=      MILLW -50-RAB

CONSENSUS OR ELITE DOMINATION --

39

BUSINESS                  (CONTINUATION)
THE CASE OF BUSINESS.=
                          NETTJP-65-COE

THE BIG BUSINESS EXECUTIVE
(UNITED STATES).=         NEWCM -55-BBE

ENTREPRENEURS OF LEBANON -- THE
ROLE OF THE BUSINESS LEADER IN A
DEVELOPING ECONOMY.=      SAYIYA-62-ELR

BIG BUSINESS LEADERS IN AMERICA.=
                          WARNWL-55-BBL

BUSINESSMAN
THE PUERTO RICAN BUSINESSMAN -- A
STUDY IN CULTURAL CHANGE.=
                          COCHTC-59-PRB

BUSINESSMAN IN THE STATEHOUSE
(UNITED STATES).=         HODGLH-62-BSU

BUSINESSMEN
BUSINESSMEN AND BUREAUCRATS
(UNITED STATES).=         LANERE-53-BBU

SMALL BUSINESSMEN, POLITICAL
TOLERANCE, AND SUPPORT FOR
MCCARTHY.=                TROWM -58-SBP

BYLAWS
BYLAWS OF THE ELITE -- THE PARTY
STATUTE (SOVIET UNION).=
                          BRUNG -65-BEP

CABINET
CABINET INSTABILITY IN FRANCE.=
                          ADAMW -58-CIF

A SHORT-LIVED CABINET (JAPAN).=
                          ANON  -57-SLC

PRIVY COUNCIL, CABINET AND MINISTRY
IN GREAT BRITAIN AND CANADA.=
                          BANKMA- -PCC

THE SUZUKI CABINET (JAPAN).=
                          BISSTA-45-SCJ

THE CABINET (GREAT BRITAIN).=
                          CLEMRV-65-CGB

MEXICO'S 'NEW CIENTIFICOS' -- THE
DIAZ ORDAZ CABINET.=      COCHJC-67-MSN

CABINET REFORM IN IN BRITAIN
1914-1963.=               DAALH -63-CRB

CABINET GOVERNMENT IN AUSTRALIA.=
                          ENCES -62-CGA

THE WILOPO CABINET -- A TURNING
POINT IN POST REVOLUTIONARY
INDONESIA.=               FEITH -58-WCT

PRESIDENT - CABINET RELATIONS -- A
PATTERN AND A CASE STUDY
(UNITED STATES).=         FENNRF-58-PCR

THE PRESIDENT'S CABINET -- AN
ANALYSIS IN THE PERIOD FROM WILSON
TO EISENHOWER (UNITED STATES).=
                          FENNRF-59-PSC

THE CABINET AND CONGRESS
(UNITED STATES).=         FORNS -60-CCU

CABINET GOVERNMENT
(GREAT BRITAIN).=         JENNWI-59-CGG

THE BRITISH CABINET.=     MACKJP-62-BC

INTRAPARTY DIVISIONS AND CABINET

CABINET                   (CONTINUATION)
COALITIONS IN THE FOURTH FRENCH
REPUBLIC.=                MACRD -63-IDC

CABINET INSTABILITY IN THE FOURTH
REPUBLIC (1946-1951).=
                          MACRRC-52-CIF

CABINET GOVERNMENT IN CANADA.=
                          MALLJM-54-CGC

CABINET REFORM IN BRITAIN,
1914-1963.=               PAALH -63-CRB

CABINET GOVERNMENT IN INDIA.=
                          SHARR -51-CGI

THE ROUTES OF ENTRY OF NEW MEMBERS
OF THE BRITISH CABINET,
1868-1958.=               WILLFM-59-REN

SYRIAN DEPUTIES AND CABINET
MINISTERS, 1919-1959 -- PART 1 --
PART 2.=                  WINDRB-62-SDC

CABINETS
THE FOUR LABOUR CABINETS
(GREAT BRITAIN).=         BONNJ -58-FLC

MINISTERIAL CABINETS OF THE FOURTH
REPUBLIC (FRANCE).=       KINGJB-60-MCF

THE SAIGON POLITICAL ELITE -- FOCUS
ON FOUR CABINETS (SOUTH VIETNAM).=
                          WURFD -67-SPE

CADRE
THE CHINESE COMMUNIST CADRE -- KEY
TO POLITICAL CONTROL.=
                          GOURWE-52-CCC

CADRES
CADRES, BUREAUCRACY AND POLITICAL
POWER IN CHINA.=          BARNAD-67-CBP

BUREAUCRATIC CADRES IN A
TRADITIONAL MILIEU (NIGERIA).=
                          KIRKAH-65-BCT

PARTY CADRES IN COMMUNIST CHINA.=
                          LEWIJW-65-PCC

DEMAGOGUES AND CADRES IN THE
POLITICAL DEVELOPMENT OF THE NEW
STATES.=                  SHILE -63-DCP

FROM REVOLUTIONARY TO SEMI -
BUREAUCRAT -- THE 'REGULARISATION'
OF CADRES (CHINA).=       VOGEEF-67-RSB

CAESARS
THE COMING CAESARS.=      RIENA -57-CC

CALCULATED
THE TWENTIETH CPSU CONGRESS -- A
STUDY IN CALCULATED MODERATION
(SOVIET UNION).=          KENNCD-56-TCC

CALIFORNIA
APPOINTED EXECUTIVE LOCAL
GOVERNMENT, THE CALIFORNIA
EXPERIENCE (UNITED STATES).=
                          BOLLJC-52-AEL

LEGISLATIVE PARTISANSHIP -- THE
DEVIANT CASE OF CALIFORNIA
(UNITED STATES).=         BUCHW -63-LPD

INTRAPARTY ATTITUDE CONFLICT --
DEMOCRATIC PARTY LEADERSHIP IN
CALIFORNIA (UNITED STATES).=
                          COSTE -63-IAC

BUREAUCRACY AND PROGRESSIVISM --

CANADA (CONTINUATION)
PAULJ -63-YOL

ELITE GROUPS -- A SCHEME FOR THE
STUDY CF POWER IN CANADA.=
PORTJ -55-EGS

CONCENTRATION CF ECCNCMIC POWER AND
THE ECCNCMIC ELITE IN CANADA.=
PORTJ -56-CEP

THE ECCNCMIC ELITE AND THE SOCIAL
STRUCTURE IN CANADA.= PORTJ -57-EES

HIGHER PUBLIC SERVANTS AND THE
BUREAUCRATIC ELITE IN CANADA.=
PORTJ -58-HPS

THE BUREAUCRATIC ELITE -- A REPLY
TC PRCFESSCR RCWAT (CANADA,
GREAT BRITAIN).= PORTJ -59-BER

THE VERTICAL MCSAIC -- AN ANALYSIS
CF SCCIAL CLASS AND PCWER IN
CANADA.= PORTJ -65-VMA

CN JCHN PCRTER'S 'BLREAUCRATIC
ELITE IN CANADA'.= ROWADC-59-JPS

PCLITICAL CAREERS AND PARTY
LEACERSHIP (AUSTRALIA, CANADA,
FRANCE, GREAT BRITAIN,
UNITED STATES).= SCHLJA-67-PCP

PARLIAMENTARY REPRESENTATION IN
CANADA.= WARDN -47-PRC

REPRESENTATICN IN THE HCUSE OF
COMMONS CF THE TWENTY-FIRST
PARLIAMENT -- PARTY AND PROVINCE
(CANADA).= WILLJR-52-RHC

CANADIAN
GROUP INTERESTS IN CANADIAN
POLITICS.= CLARSD-63-GIC

THE CANADIAN BUREAUCRACY -- A STUDY
CF CANADIAN CIVIL SERVICE AND
CTHER PUBLIC EMPLCYEES 1939-1947.=
COLET -49-CBS

THE CANADIAN BUREAUCRACY -- A STUDY
CF CANADIAN CIVIL SERVICE AND
CTHER PUBLIC EMPLCYEES 1939-1947.=
COLET -49-CBS

PCLITICAL PARTIES AND THE CANADIAN
SCCIAL STRUCTURE.= ENGLFC-67-PPC

A CCMPARATIVE STUCY CF CANADIAN
PARTIES.= EPSTLD-64-CSC

SCCIAL STRUCTURE AND CANADIAN
PCLITICAL PARTIES -- THE QUEBEC
CASE.= FILLWO-56-SSC

THE SCCIAL BASIS CF LEADERSHIP IN A
CANADIAN HCUSE CF CCMMCNS.=
KORNA -65-SBL

CAUCUS AND CCHESICN IN CANADIAN
PARLIAMENTARY PARTIES.=
KORNA -66-CCC

THE RELIGICUS BACKGRCUND CF
CANADIAN M.P.'S.= LAPCJD-58-RBC

THE FCRMULATICN CF LIBERAL AND
CCNSERVATIVE PRCGRAMMES IN THE
1957 CANADIAN GENERAL ELECTION.=
MEISJ -60-FLC

THE CANADIAN GENERAL ELECTICN CF

CANADIAN (CCNTINUATICN)
1957.= MEISJ -62-CGE

THE STALLEC CMNIBUS -- CANADIAN
PARTIES IN THE 1960'S.=
MEISJ -63-SOC

THE RCLE CF THE LIBERAL PARTY IN
RECENT CANADIAN PCLITICS.=
GUINHF-53-RLP

CCNSENSUS, CCNFLICT, AND THE
CANADIAN PARTY SYSTEM.=
SMILDV-61-CCC

CANDICATE
CANDIDATE SELECTICN IN BRITAIN.=
EPSTLD-59-CSB

DCES A CIVISIVE - PRIMARY HARM A
CANDIDATE'S CHANCES
(UNITED STATES).= HACKA -65-CDP

PATHWAYS TC PARLIAMENT -- CANDICATE
SELECTICN IN BRITAIN.=
RANNA -65-PPC

THE MILITARY HERC AS PRESIDENTIAL
CANDICATE (UNITED STATES).=
SOMIA -48-MHP

CANDICATES
INDEPENDENT CANDIDATES IN 1945,
1950, AND 1951 (GREAT BRITAIN).=
ADLEMK-53-ICA

CHARACTERISTICS OF CANDICATES FOR
ELECTICN IN A CCUNTRY APPROACHING
INDEPENCENCE -- THE CASE OF
UGANDA.= PYRCRO-63-CCE

CANCIDATES MUST MAKE THE ISSUES AND
GIVE THEM MEANING
(UNITED STATES).= DEXTLA-55-CMM

THE CRIENTATICNS CF CCMMUNITY
LEADERS TC PARLIAMENTARY
CANDICATES (GREAT BRITAIN).=
KAVAC -67-CCL

INTER - CCNSTITUENCY MCVEMENT CF
BRITISH PARLIAMENTARY CANDIDATES,
1951-1959.= RANNA -64-ICM

PRCBABLES AND PCSSIBLES (BRITISH
CANDIDATES).= WILCRW-63-PPB

THE BRITISH GENERAL ELECTION CF
1951 -- CANDIDATES AND PARTIES.=
WILLJR-52-BGE

CANEVILLE
CANEVILLE -- THE SCCIAL STRUCTURE
CF A SCUTH AFRICAN TCWN.=
VAN-PL-64-CSS

CAPE NGUNI
SEGMENTATICN AND FISSION IN
CAPE NGUNI PCLITICAL UNITS
(AFRICA).= HAMMWD-65-SFC

CAPITAL
THE RULING CLASS -- A STUDY OF
BRITISH FINANCE CAPITAL.=
AAROS -61-RCS

PCWER IN WASHINGTCN -- A CRITICAL
LCCK AT TCCAY'S STRUGGLE TO GCVERN
IN THE NATICN'S CAPITAL.=
CATED -64-PWC

CAPITAL PUNISHMENT AND BRITISH

CENTRAL                    (CONTINUATION)
                           RANSHH-58-CIN

THE CENTRAL LEGISLATURE IN BRITISH
INDIA 1921-1947.=       RASHM -65-CLB

THE ORIGINS OF NATIONALIST
DISCONTENT IN EAST AND CENTRAL
AFRICA.=                ROTBRI-63-ONC

YOUTH LEAGUES IN CENTRAL EUROPE.=
                        RPH   -55-YLC

THE DEMOCRATIC STATE CENTRAL
COMMITTEE IN MICHIGAN 1949-1959 --
THE RISE OF THE NEW POLITICS AND
THE NEW POLITICAL LEADERSHIP
(UNITED STATES).=       SAWYRL-60-DSC

THE CENTRAL COMMITTEE OF THE UNITED
POLISH WORKERS' PARTY.=
                        STAARF-57-CCU

THE CENTRAL APPARATUS OF POLAND'S
COMMUNIST PARTY.=       STAARF-62-CAP

SOME VARIABLES OF MIDDLE AND LOWER
CLASS IN TWO CENTRAL AMERICAN
CITIES.=                WILLRC-62-VML

THE ANALYSIS OF SOCIAL CHANGE --
BASED ON OBSERVATIONS IN CENTRAL
AFRICA.=                WILSG -45-ASC

CENTRAL AMERICAN
CENTRAL AMERICAN POLITICAL PARTIES
-- A FUNCTIONAL APPROACH.=
                        ANDECW-62-CAP

INTEREST GROUPS IN PANAMA AND THE
CENTRAL AMERICAN COMMON MARKET.=
                        DENTCF-67-IGP

CENTRALIZATION
THE CENTRALIZATION -
DECENTRALIZATION DILEMMA
(SOVIET UNION).=        ANON  -57-CDD

CENTRALIZATION AND THE OPEN SOCIETY
(UNITED STATES).=       CARLWG- -COS

CENTRALIZATION VERSUS
DECENTRALIZATION IN MAINLAND CHINA
AND THE SOVIET UNION.=
                        PERKCH-63-CVD

CENTRALIZED
RELIGIOUS ORGANIZATIONS AND
POLITICAL PROCESS IN CENTRALIZED
EMPIRES (MIDDLE EAST, FAR EAST).=
                        EISESN-62-ROP

CENTURY
AUTHORITY IN THE 20TH CENTURY.=
                        ARENH -56-ATC

THE CHINESE GENTRY, STUDIES ON
THEIR ROLE IN THE NINETEENTH
CENTURY CHINESE SOCIETY.=
                        CHANCL-55-CGS

AN UNCERTAIN TRADITION -- AMERICAN
SECRETARIES OF STATE  IN THE
TWENTIETH CENTURY.=     GRAENA-61-UTA

THE SEIZURE OF POLITICAL POWER IN A
CENTURY OF REVOLUTIONS
(SOVIET UNION).=        GROSF -58-SPP

CONGRESSIONAL RESPONSES TO THE
TWENTIETH CENTURY
(UNITED STATES).=       HUNTSP-65-CRT

CENTURY                    (CONTINUATION)
THE BALKANS IN TRANSITION -- ESSAYS
ON THE DEVELOPMENT OF BALKAN LIFE
AND POLITICS SINCE THE EIGHTEENTH
CENTURY.=               JELAC -63-BTE

ELEVENTH CENTURY CHINESE
BUREAUCRATS -- SOME HISTORICAL
CLASSIFICATIONS AND BEHAVIORAL
TYPES.=                 LIU,  -60-ECC

SUCCESSION IN THE TWENTIETH
CENTURY.=               RUSTDA-64-STC

TWENTIETH CENTURY REVOLUTIONS.=
                        SETOH -51-TCR

PERSONALITIES AND POLICIES --
STUDIES IN THE FORMULATION OF
BRITISH FOREIGN POLICY IN THE
TWENTIETH CENTURY.=     WATTDC-65-PPS

ASPECTS OF BUREAUCRATIZATION IN
ASHANTI IN THE NINETEENTH CENTURY
(AFRICA).=              WILKI -66-ABA

CEYLON
IDEOLOGICAL CHANGE AND SOCIAL
CHANGE IN CEYLON.=      AMESMM-63-ICS

ASIAN BUREAUCRATIC SYSTEMS EMERGENT
FROM THE BRITISH IMPERIAL
TRADITION (INDIA, PAKISTAN, BURMA,
CEYLON, MALAYA, NEPAL).=
                        BRAIR -  -ABS

THE UNORTHODOX LEFT AND THE CEYLON
ELECTIONS.=             GRINM -56-ULC

A BRIEF COMPARISON OF THE PUBLIC
SERVICES OF CANADA AND CEYLON.=
                        HARRRL-63-BCP

A COMPARATIVE ANALYSIS OF THE
ADMINISTRATIVE SYSTEMS OF CANADA
AND CEYLON.=            HARRRL-64-CAA

THE YOUNGER GENERATION IN THE THREE
DOMINICAS (INDIA, PAKISTAN,
CEYLON).=               JACKC -49-YGT

POLITICS IN CEYLON SINCE 1952.=
                        JENNWI-54-PCS

BUREAUCRACY AND ENVIRONMENT IN
CEYLON.=                KEARRN-64-BEC

SINHALESE NATIONALISM AND SOCIAL
CONFLICT IN CEYLON.=    KEARRN-64-SNS

CEYLON -- THE CONTEMPORARY
BUREAUCRACY.=           KEARRN-66-CCB

MILITANT PUBLIC SERVICE TRADE
UNIONISM IN A NEW STATE (CEYLON).=
                        KEARRN-66-MPS

THE LEGISLATURES OF CEYLON,
1928-1948.=             NAMAS -50-LC

STATUS, ACHIEVEMENT, AND EDUCATION
IN CEYLON.=             RYANB -61-SAE

THE EMERGING ELITE -- A STUDY OF
POLITICAL LEADERSHIP IN CEYLON.=
                        SINGMR-64-EES

GROUP PERCEPTION AND SOCIAL CHANGE
IN CEYLON.=             SINGMR-66-GPS

CEYLON GENERAL ELECTIONS, 1956.=
                        WEERID-60-CGE

THE TAMIL FEDERAL PARTY IN CEYLON

CEYLCN          (CCNTINUATICN)
  PCLITICS.=              WILSAJ-66-TFP

CEYLCNESE
  ASPECTS CF CEYLCNESE PARLIAMENTARY
  GCVERNMENT.=            NAMAS -53-ACP

CHAD
  NATICNAL UNITY AND REGICNALISM IN
  EIGHT AFRICAN STATES (NIGERIA,
  NIGER, THE CCNGC, GABCN, CENTRAL
  AFRICAN REPUBLIC, CHAD, UGANDA,
  ETHICPIA).=            CARTGM-66-NUR

CHAIR
  THE HCUSE CF CCMMCNS FRCM THE CHAIR
  (GREAT BRITAIN).=       MILNJ -47-HCC

CHAIRMAN
  THE SCVNARKHCZ CHAIRMAN
  (SCVIET UNICN).=       ANON  -58-SCS

  THE CHAIRMAN'S PANEL
  (GREAT BRITAIN).=       HIGGGM-55-CSP

CHALLENGE
  THE CHALLENGE CF MILITARY
  PRCFESSICNALISM (UNITED STATES).=
                          GINSVN-64-CMP

  THE SCUTHERN GCVERNCR -- CHALLENGE
  TC THE STRCNG EXECUTIVE THEME
  (UNITED STATES).=       HIGHRB-59-SGC

  CHALLENGE TC NEGRC LEADERSHIP
  (UNITED STATES).=       MAYFJ -61-CNL

  CHALLENGE TC THE 'NEW ERA' IN
  PHILIPPINE PCLITICS.=   MEADM -64-CNE

  CHALLENGE FCR INDIAN LEADERSHIP.=
                          PYLEMV-64-CIL

  PCLITICAL PARTIES IN LEBANON -- THE
  CHALLENGE CF A FRAGMENTED
  PCLITICAL CULTURE.=     SULEM -67-PPL

CHALLENGES
  CHALLENGES TC FACTICNALISM IN
  JAPAN'S LIBERAL DEMCCRATIC PARTY.=
                          FARNLW-66-CFJ

CHAMBER
  THE SECCND CHAMBER IN FRANCE.=
                          COBBA -48-SCF

  THE 'SECCND CHAMBER' CUESTICN IN
  THE GCLD CCAST (GHANA).=
                          WRAIRE-54-SCQ

CHAMBERLAIN
  AMERICA AND THE BRITISH FOREIGN
  PCLICY-MAKING ELITE, FRCM JOSEPH
  CHAMBERLAIN TC ANTHCNY EDEN,
  1895-1956.=             WATTDC-63-ABF

CHAMBERS
  CCUNCIL CHAMBERS CF THE GREAT
  PARLIAMENTS.=           PESCK -61-CCG

CHANCELLCR
  THE OFFICE CF LCRD CHANCELLCR
  (GREAT BRITAIN).=       KILMV -56-OLC

  EQUILIBRIUM, STRUCTURE CF INTERESTS
  AND LEADERSHIP -- ADENAUER'S
  SURVIVAL AS CHANCELLCR (GERMANY).=
                          MERKPH-62-ESI

CHANDRA
  SUBHAS CHANDRA BOSE AND THE INDIAN
  NATICNAL ARMY.=         COHESP-63-SCB

CHANGE
  SCCIAL CHANGE IN LATIN AMERICA
  TCDAY -- ITS IMPLICATICNS.= FCR
  U.S. (UNITED STATES) PCLICY.=
                          ADAMRN-  -SCL

  IDECLCGICAL CHANGE AND SOCIAL
  CHANGE IN CEYLCN.=      AMESMM-63-ICS

  IDECLCGICAL CHANGE AND SOCIAL
  CHANGE IN CEYLCN.=      AMESMM-63-ICS

  PCLITICAL CHANGE IN MCRCCCO.=
                          ASHFCE-61-PCM

  ELITE VALUES AND ATTITUDINAL CHANGE
  IN THE MAGHREB (MCRCCCO, ALGERIA,
  TUNISIA).=              ASHFCE-67-EVA

  SCCIAL CHANGE IN BRAZIL.=
                          AZEVT -63-SCB

  RELATICNSHIP BETWEEN PRCFESSIONAL
  AND ADMINISTRATIVE CFFICERS IN A
  GCVERNMENT DEPARTMENT DURING A
  PERICD CF ADMINISTRATIVE CHANGE
  (GUYANA).=              BACCMK-67-RBP

  PCLITICS AND SCCIAL CHANGE, ORISSA
  (INDIA) IN 1959.=       BAILFG-63-PSC

  CCMMUNITY INFLUENCE SYSTEMS --
  STRUCTURE AND CHANGE
  (UNITED STATES).=       BARTEA-61-CIS

  SCCIAL CHANGE IN THE SCUTH PACIFIC
  -- RARCTCNGA AND AITUTAKI.=
                          BEAGE -57-SCS

  SCCIAL CHANGE AND ELITES IN AN
  EMERGENT NATICN (JAMAICA).=
                          BELLW -65-SCE

  SCCIAL AND PCLITICAL CHANGE IN THE
  MCSLEM - ARAB WCRLD.=   BERGM -58-SPC

  MILITARY ELITE AND SOCIAL CHANGE --
  EGYPT SINCE NAPCLECN.=
                          BERGM -60-MES

  SCCIAL STATUS AND SCCIAL CHANGE.=
                          BESHJM-63-SSS

  THE TRANSFCRMATICN CF RUSSIAN
  SCCIETY -- ASPECTS CF SCCIAL
  CHANGE SINCE 1861.=     BLACCE-60-TRS

  PCWER STRUCTURE AND CCMMUNITY
  CHANGE (UNITED STATES).=
                          BOOTDA-62-PSC

  SUCCESSICN IN INDIA 1967 -- THE
  RCUTINIZATICN CF PCLITICAL
  CHANGE.=                BRECM -67-SIR

  THE PUERTC RICAN BUSINESSMAN -- A
  STUDY IN CULTURAL CHANGE.=
                          COCHTC-59-PRB

  THE ENTREPRENEUR IN ECCNOMIC
  CHANGE.=                COCHTC-64-EEC

  SHE WHC RIDES A PEACOCK -- SOCIAL
  CHANGE AND INDIAN STUDENTS.=
                          CORMML-61-SWR

  CHANGE IN LATIN AMERICA -- THE
  MEXICAN AND CUBAN REVCLUTIONS.=
                          COSIO -61-CLA

  RELIGICN, REVCLUTICN AND REFORM --
  NEW FCRCES FCR CHANGE IN

CHARACTERISTICS (CONTINUATION)
UGANDA.=                    BYRDRO-63-CCE

SOME CHARACTERISTICS OF THE YOUNGER
GENERATION IN WESTERN GERMANY.=
                       EBW    -54-CYG

CRITICAL LETTERS TO THE EDITORS OF
THE SOVIET PRESS -- SOCIAL
CHARACTERISTICS AND INTERRELATIONS
OF CRITICS AND THE CRITICIZED.=
                       INKEA -53-CLE

SOME CHARACTERISTICS OF THE SOVIET
LEADERSHIP SYSTEM -- A MATURING
TOTALITARIAN SYSTEM.= LAIRRO-66-CSL

THE SOCIAL CHARACTERISTICS OF AN
EMERGENT ELITE IN HARARE (SOUTHERN
RHODESIA).=            LUKHMB-66-SCE

SOME CHARACTERISTICS OF AMERICAN
NEGRO LEADERS.=        MONATP-56-CAN

TESTING RELATIONS BETWEEN JURIDICAL
CHARACTERISTICS AND JUDICIAL
DECISION MAKING (UNITED STATES).=
                       NAGESS-62-TRB

CHARACTERISTICS OF PARTY LEADERSHIP
(UNITED STATES).=      PATTSC-63-CPL

THE PSYCHOLOGICAL CHARACTERISTICS
OF LEADERSHIP.=        SCHOBN-48-PCL

THE AMERICAN FEDERAL EXECUTIVE -- A
STUDY OF SOCIAL AND PERSONAL
CHARACTERISTICS OF THE CIVILIAN
AND MILITARY LEADERS OF THE UNITED
STATES FEDERAL GOVERNMENT.=
                       WARNWL-63-AFE

CHARISMA
CHARISMA AND RELIGIOUS INNOVATION
-- THE SOCIAL LOCATION OF
ISREALITE PROPHECY.=   BERGPL-63-CRI

FOR A SOCIOLOGICAL CONCEPT OF
CHARISMA.=             FRIEWH-64-SCC

PARTY CHARISMA.=       FOROIL-65-PC

CHARISMA AND FACTIONALISM IN THE
NAZI PARTY (GERMANY.=  NYOMJ -67-CFN

CHARISMA AND POLITICAL LEADERSHIP
(GERMANY).=            RATNKJ-64-CPL

THE CONCENTRATION AND DISPERSION OF
CHARISMA -- THEIR BEARING ON
ECONOMIC POLICY IN UNDERDEVELOPED
COUNTRIES.=            SHILE -58-CDC

CHARISMA, ORDER, AND STATUS.=
                       SHILE -65-COS

CHARISMATIC
CHARISMATIC LEGITIMATION AND
POLITICAL INTEGRATION (GHANA).=
                       AKE,C -66-CLP

THE PSEUDO - CHARISMATIC LEADER IN
SOVIET SOCIETY.=       BAUERA-53-PCL

REFLECTIONS ON CHARISMATIC
LEADERSHIP.=           BENOR -67-RCL

THE U.S.S.R. -- FROM CHARISMATIC
SECT TO BUREAUCRATIC SOCIETY
(SOVIET UNION).=       CONTH -62-USS

CHARISMATIC LEADERSHIP AND CRISIS.=

CHARISMATIC (CONTINUATION)
                       DEVEG -55-CLC

POLITICAL LEADERSHIP AND THE
PROBLEM OF CHARISMATIC POWER
(GERMANY, GREAT BRITAIN, ITALY,
UNITED STATES).=       FRIECJ-61-PLP

CHARISMATIC LEGITIMACY AND ONE -
PARTY RULE IN GHANA.=  RUNCWG-63-CLO

THE RISE AND ROLE OF CHARISMATIC
LEADERS.=              WILLAR-65-RRC

CHEF
THE HAITIAN 'CHEF DE SECTION'.=
                       COMHJL-55-HCD

CHICAGO
FROM COMMERCIAL ELITE TO POLITICAL
ADMINISTRATOR -- THE RECRUITMENT
OF THE MAYORS OF CHICAGO
(UNITED STATES).=      BRADDS-65-CEP

CHIEF
THE PLACE OF THE CHIEF IN THE
GOLD COAST.=           BUSIKA-49-PCC

THE POSITION OF THE CHIEF IN THE
MODERN POLITICAL SYSTEM OF ASHANTI
(GOLD COAST).=         BUSIKA-51-PCM

THE PREDICAMENT OF THE MODERN
AFRICAN CHIEF -- AN INSTANCE FROM
UGANDA.=               FALLL -55-PMA

THE CHIEF EXECUTIVE IN TEXAS -- THE
ORIGINS OF GUBERNATORIAL
LEADERSHIP.=           GANTF -64-CET

THE GOVERNOR AS CHIEF ADMINISTRATOR
IN KENTUCKY (UNITED STATES).=
                       KAMMGM-54-GCA

CHIEF JUSTICE TAFT AND THE LOWER
COURT BUREAUCRACY -- A STUDY IN
JUDICIAL ADMINISTRATION.=
                       MURPWF-62-CJT

POOR MAN, RICH MAN, BIG-MAN, CHIEF
-- POLITICAL TYPES IN MELANESIA
AND POLYNESIA.=        SAHLMD-63-PMR

CHIEFS
CHIEFS AND STRANGERS (SOUTHERN
SUDAN).=               BUXTJC-63-CSS

CHIEFS AND POLITICS (AFRICA).=
                       LOVEAJ-59-CPA

AFRICAN CHIEFS TODAY.=
                       MAIRLP-58-ACT

THE ROLE OF THE CHIEFS AND THE HEAD
MAN AMONG THE LUGBARA OF THE WEST
NILE DISTRICT OF UGANDA.=
                       MIDDJ -56-RCH

EAST AFRICAN CHIEFS -- A STUDY OF
POLITICAL DEVELOPMENT IN SOME
UGANDA AND TANGANYIKA TRIBES.=
                       RICHAI-59-EAC

CHIEFSHIP
CHIEFSHIP AND POLITICS IN THE
MLANJE DISTRICT OF SOUTHERN
NYASALAND.=            WISHRL-61-CPM

CHIEFTAINSHIP
CHIEFTAINSHIP IN TRANSKEIAN
POLITICAL DEVELOPMENT (AFRICA).=
                       HAMMC -64-CTP

KOENA CHIEFTAINSHIP IN BASUTOLAND

CHINA                    (CONTINUATION)
CONQUERORS AND RULERS -- SOCIAL
FORCES IN MEDIEVAL CHINA.=
                          EBERW -52-CRS

INTERNAL CONTRADICTIONS IN
BUREAUCRATIC POLITICS (ANCIENT
CHINA, PERSIA).=          EISESN-58-ICB

THE STUDY OF ORIENTAL DESPOTISMS AS
SYSTEMS OF TOTAL POWER (CHINA).=
                         EISESN-58-SOD

CHINA'S GENTRY -- ESSAYS IN RURAL -
URBAN RELATIONS.=        FEI-  -53-CSG

MAO AND THE PERMANENT PURGE
(CHINA).=                GELMH -66-MPP

WRITERS' CRITICISM OF THE PARTY IN
1942 (CHINA).=           GOLDM -64-WCP

LITERARY DISSENT IN COMMUNIST
CHINA.=                  GOLDM -67-LDC

THE RECTIFICATION CAMPAIGN AT
PEKING UNIVERSITY (CHINA).=
                         GOLDR -62-RCP

THE 'DEMOCRATIC PARTIES' -- END OF
AN EXPERIMENT (CHINA).=
                         HINTHC-58-DPE

INTRA - PARTY POLITICS AND ECONOMIC
POLICY IN COMMUNIST CHINA.=
                         HINTHC-60-IPP

CHINA.=                  HINTHC-63-C

THE CULTURAL REVOLUTION AND
LEADERSHIP CRISIS IN COMMUNIST
CHINA.=                  HSUEC -67-CRL

MINOR PARTIES IN COMMUNIST CHINA.=
                         JAN,GP-62-MPC

PEASANT NATIONALISM AND COMMUNIST
POWER -- THE EMERGENCE OF
REVOLUTIONARY CHINA, 1937-1945.=
                         JOHNCA-62-PNC

TWO COMMUNIST ARMIES (CHINA,
SOVIET UNION).=          KASHA -61-TCA

PEKING'S LEADERS -- A STUDY IN
ISOLATION (CHINA).=      KLEIDW-61-PSL

SUCCESSION AND THE ELITE AND PEKING
(CHINA).=                KLEIDW-64-SEP

WORLD REVOLUTIONARY ELITES --
STUDIES IN COERCIVE IDEOLOGICAL
MOVEMENTS (CHINA, GERMANY, ITALY,
SOVIET UNION).=          LASSHD-66-WRE

INTELLIGENTSIA OF CHINA.=
                         LEE,SC-47-IC

CONFUCIAN CHINA AND ITS MODERN FATE
-- THE PROBLEM OF INTELLECTUAL
CONTINUITY.=             LEVEJR-58-CCI

LEADERSHIP IN COMMUNIST CHINA.=
                         LEWIJW-65-LCC

PARTY CADRES IN COMMUNIST CHINA.=
                         LEWIJW-65-PCC

POLITICAL ASPECTS OF MOBILITY IN
CHINA'S URBAN DEVELOPMENT.=
                         LEWIJW-66-PAM

CHINA, RUSSIA AND THE EXPERTS.=


CHINA                    (CONTINUATION)
                         LICHG -65-CRE

THOUGHT REFORM AND THE PSYCHOLOGY
OF TOTALISM (CHINA).= LIFTRJ-61-TRP

COMMUNIST CHINA'S INTRA - PARTY
DISPUTE.=                MACFR -58-CCS

THE LEADERSHIP IN CHINA.=
                         MACFR -59-LC

LEADERSHIP COHESION IN COMMUNIST
CHINA AND UNDERDEVELOPED ASIAN
COUNTRIES.=              MACFR -63-LCC

THE MANDARINS -- THE CIRCULATION OF
ELITES IN CHINA, 1600-1900.=
                         MARSRM-61-MCE

VALUES, DEMAND, AND SOCIAL MOBILITY
(INDUSTRIAL ELITES, CHINA,
UNITED STATES).=         MARSRM-63-VDS

THE TSUNGLI YAMEN -- ITS
ORGANIZATION AND FUNCTIONS
(CHINA).=                MENGSM-59-TYI

MAO IN STALIN'S FOOTSTEPS (CHINA).=
                         MERTVS-56-MSS

THE STRUGGLE FOR POWER (CHINA).=
                         MICHF -67-SPC

SOCIAL ORIGINS OF DICTATORSHIP AND
DEMOCRACY -- LORD AND PEASANT IN
THE MAKING OF THE MODERN WORLD
(FRANCE, GREAT BRITAIN,
UNITED STATES, CHINA, JAPAN,
INDIA, GERMANY).=        MOORB -66-SOD

THE NEP AND THE NEW DEMOCRACY
(CHINA, USSR).=          NORTRC-51-NND

CHINA -- FORCING THE REVOLUTION TO
A NEW STAGE.=            OKSEM -67-CFR

CENTRALIZATION VERSUS
DECENTRALIZATION IN MAINLAND CHINA
AND THE SOVIET UNION.=
                         PERKDH-63-CVD

THE MILITARY AFFAIRS COMMITTEE AND
PARTY CONTROL OF THE MILITARY IN
CHINA.=                  POWERL-63-MAC

ORGANIZATION AND RESPONSE IN
COMMUNIST CHINA.=        SCHUHF-59-ORC

PEKING'S RECOGNITION OF CRISIS
(CHINA).=                SCHUHF-61-PSR

IDEOLOGY AND ORGANIZATION IN
COMMUNIST CHINA.=        SCHUHF-65-IOC

THE INTELLIGENTSIA IN COMMUNIST
CHINA -- A TENTATIVE COMPARISON.=
                         SCHWBI-60-ICC

THE GREAT PROLETARIAN REVOLUTION
(CHINA).=                SCHWHG-66-GPR

FERMENT AMONG INTELLECTUALS
(CHINA).=                SIMOJ -64-FAI

RED STAR OVER CHINA.=    SNOWE -38-RSO

IDEOLOGY AND POLITICS IN COMMUNIST
CHINA.=                  STEIHA-59-IPC

COMMUNIST CHINA TODAY -- DOMESTIC
AND FOREIGN POLICIES.=

CHINA (CONTINUATION)
TANGPS-57-CCT

THE PURGE CF PROVINCIAL LEADERS
1957-1958 (CHINA).= TEIWFC-66-PPL

CHINA'S RESPONSE TO THE WEST.=
TENGS -54-CSR

RECENT EDUCATIONAL POLICY IN
CHINA.= THOMSB-50-REP

GCVERNMENT AND ADMINISTRATION IN
COMMUNIST CHINA.= THOMSB-53-GAC

THE MAY FOURTH MOVEMENT --
INTELLECTUAL REVOLUTION IN MODERN
CHINA.= TSE-C -60-MFM

THE INTELLECTUAL IN THE NEW CHINA.=
TT -53-INC

FROM REVOLUTICNARY TO SEMI -
BUREAUCRAT -- THE 'REGULARISATION'
OF CADRES (CHINA).= VOGEEF-67-RSB

THE 'WORKING CLASS' IN COMMUNIST
CHINA.= WALKRL-53-WCC

THE INTELLIGENTSIA IN CHANGING
CHINA.= WANGYC-58-ICC

WESTERN IMPACT AND SOCIAL MOBILITY
IN CHINA.= WANGYC-60-WIS

INTELLECTUALS AND SOCIETY IN CHINA
1860-1949.= WANGYC-61-ISC

FROM REVOLUTION TO RESTORATION --
THE TRANSFORMATION OF KUOMINGTANG
IDEOLOGY (CHINA).= WRIGMC-55-RRT

MODERN CHINA IN TRANSITION.=
WRIGMC-59-MCT

CHINESE
THE CHINESE COMMUNISTS AND THE
PEASANTS.= ANON -52-CCP

SOCIAL STRATIFICATION AND ASPECTS
OF PERSCNNEL MANAGEMENT IN THE
CHINESE COMMUNIST BUREAUCRACY.=
BARNAD-66-SSA

CHINESE CLASS STRUCTURE AND ITS
IDEOLOGY.= CH'U -57-CCS

THE CHINESE GENTRY, STUDIES ON
THEIR ROLE IN THE NINETEENTH
CENTURY CHINESE SOCIETY.=
CHANCL-55-CGS

THE CHINESE GENTRY, STUDIES ON
THEIR ROLE IN THE NINETEENTH
CENTURY CHINESE SOCIETY.=
CHANCL-55-CGS

LEADERSHIP IN THE CHINESE COMMUNIST
PARTY.= CHAO -59-LCC

IDEOLOGY OF THE CHINESE
COMMUNISTS.= CHENEK-49-ICC

PROBLEMS CF CHINESE COMMUNIST
LEADERSHIP AS SEEN IN THE SECRET
MILITARY PAPERS.= CHENJC-64-PCC

THE MARXIST REMOLDING CF CHINESE
SOCIETY.= CHENTH-53-MRC

THOUGHT REFORM OF THE CHINESE
INTELLECTUALS.= CHENTH-60-TRC

CHINESE (CONTINUATION)
THE CHINESE GENTRY -- STUDIES ON
THEIR ROLE IN NINETEENTH-CENTURY
CHINESE SOCIETY.= CHUNC -55-CGS

THE CHINESE GENTRY -- STUDIES ON
THEIR ROLE IN NINETEENTH-CENTURY
CHINESE SOCIETY.= CHUNC -55-CGS

CHINESE THOUGHT AND INSTITUTIONS.=
FAIRJK-57-CTI

A FRESH LOOK AT THE CHINESE
REVOLUTION.= FITZCP-63-FLC

MILITARY STATUS IN CHINESE
SOCIETY.= FRIEMH-51-MSC

POLITICAL CONTROL OF THE CHINESE
ARMY.= GITTJ -63-PCC

THE CHINESE ARMY'S ROLE IN THE
CULTURAL REVOLUTION.= GITTJ -67-CAS

THE ROLE OF THE CHINESE ARMY.=
GITTJ -67-RCA

THE CHINESE COMMUNIST CADRE -- KEY
TO POLITICAL CONTROL.=
GOURWE-52-CCC

THOUGHTS ON THE CHINESE QUESTION IN
SOUTHEAST ASIA.= HALLOG-54-TCQ

CHINESE COMMUNIST CONTROL OF THE
PRESS.= HONNFW-58-CCC

THE EIGHTH CENTRAL COMMITTEE OF THE
CHINESE COMMUNIST PARTY -- A STUDY
OF AN ELITE.= HOUNFW-57-ECC

HUANG HSING AND THE CHINESE
REVOLUTION.= HSUEC--61-HHC

THE TRADITIONAL CHINESE CENSORATE
AND THE NEW PEKING REGIME.=
HUCKCO-51-TCC

THE TRAGEDY OF THE CHINESE
REVOLUTION.= ISAAHR-51-TCR

THE CONFLICT BETWEEN OLD AND NEW IN
THE CHINESE ARMY.= JOFFE -64-CBC

PARTY AND ARMY -- PROFESSIONALISM
AND POLITICAL CONTROL IN THE
CHINESE OFFICER CORPS, 1949-1964.=
JOFFE -65-PAP

THE 'NEXT GENERATION' OF CHINESE
COMMUNIST LEADERS.= KLEIOW-62-NGC

THE CHANGING ROLE OF THE CHINESE
INTELLECTUALS -- AN INTRODUCTORY
NOTE.= KRACEA-58-CRC

LEADERSHIP IN THE CHINESE COMMUNIST
PARTY.= KUO-C -59-LCC

THE LEADERSHIP DOCTRINE OF THE
CHINESE COMMUNIST PARTY.=
LEWIJW-63-LDC

THOUGHT REFORM OF CHINESE
INTELLECTUALS -- A PSYCHIATRIC
EVALUATION.= LIFTRJ-56-TRC

ELEVENTH CENTURY CHINESE
BUREAUCRATS -- SOME HISTORICAL
CLASSIFICATIONS AND BEHAVIORAL
TYPES.= LIU, -60-ECC

THE TRADITIONAL CHINESE CLAN

CIVIL                    (CONTINUATION)
  CIVIL LIBERTIES AND THE VINSON
  COURT (UNITED STATES).=
                       PRITCH-54-CLV

  A CASE ANALYSIS OF CONGRESSIONAL
  ACTIVITY -- CIVIL AVIATION,
  1957-1958.=          REDFES-60-CAC

  THE CIVIL SERVICE IN BRITAIN AND
  FRANCE.=             ROBSWA-56-CSB

  THE CIVIL SERVICE OF INDIA.=
                       ROY,NC-58-CSI

  THE POLITICAL ROLE OF PAKISTAN'S
  CIVIL SERVICE.=      SAYEKB-58-PRP

  CIVIL SERVANTS IN WASHINGTON -- 1,
  THE CHARACTER OF THE FEDERAL
  SERVICE --2, THE HIGHER CIVIL
  SERVICE AND ITS FUTURE
  (UNITED STATES).=    SPANRN-53-CSW

  CIVIL SERVANTS IN WASHINGTON -- 1,
  THE CHARACTER OF THE FEDERAL
  SERVICE --2, THE HIGHER CIVIL
  SERVICE AND ITS FUTURE
  (UNITED STATES).=    SPANRN-53-CSW

  COMMUNISM, CONFORMITY, AND CIVIL
  LIBERTIES (UNITED STATES).=
                       STOUSA-55-CCC

  THE EVOLUTION OF MINISTER - CIVIL
  SERVANT RELATIONS IN INDIA.=
                       SUBRV -62-EMC

  SUPREME COURT BEHAVIOR AND CIVIL
  RIGHTS (UNITED STATES).=
                       ULMESS-60-SCB

  FEDERAL ADMINISTRATION, RANK, AND
  CIVIL STRIFE AMONG BEMBA ROYALS
  AND NOBLES (ZAMBIA).= WERBRP-67-FAR

  THE POLITICS OF CIVIL - MILITARY
  RELATIONS IN THE
  DOMINICAN REPUBLIC.=  WIARHJ-65-PCM

CIVIL SERVICE
  GERMAN OFFICIALS REVISITED --
  POLITICAL VIEWS AND ATTITUDES OF
  THE WESTERN GERMAN CIVIL SERVICE.=
                       HERZJH-54-GOR

CIVILIAN
  AN EXPERIMENT WITH CIVILIAN
  DICTATORSHIP IN IRAN -- THE CASE
  OF M. MOSSADAGH.=    EFIMNM-55-ECD

  CIVILIAN CONTROL AND THE
  CONSTITUTION (UNITED STATES,
  MILITARY - CIVIL RELATIONSHIPS).=
                       HUNTSP-56-CCC

  THE AMERICAN FEDERAL EXECUTIVE -- A
  STUDY OF SOCIAL AND PERSONAL
  CHARACTERISTICS OF THE CIVILIAN
  AND MILITARY LEADERS OF THE UNITED
  STATES FEDERAL GOVERNMENT.=
                       WARNWL-63-AFE

CIVILIANS
  CIVILIANS, SOLDIERS, AND AMERICAN
  MILITARY POLICY.=    FOX,WT-55-CSA

CIVILIZATION
  AMERICAN CIVILIZATION AND ITS
  LEADERSHIP NEEDS, 1960-1990.=
                       CHARJC-59-ACI

  THE MASTERS AND THE SLAVES -- A


CIVILIZATION            (CONTINUATION)
  STUDY IN THE DEVELOPMENT OF
  BRAZILIAN CIVILIZATION.=
                       FREYG -46-MSS

CLAN
  THE TRADITIONAL CHINESE CLAN
  RULES.=              LIU,HW-59-TCC

  POLITICAL CHANGE IN A TRADITIONAL
  AFRICAN CLAN -- A STRUCTURAL
  FUNCTIONAL ANALYSIS OF THE NSITS
  OF NIGERIA.=         SCARJR-65-PCT

  CLAN, CHIEFTAINSHIP, AND SLAVERY IN
  LUVALE POLITICAL ORGANIZATION
  (NORTH RHODESIA).=   WHITCM-57-CCS

CLASS
  THE RULING CLASS -- A STUDY OF
  BRITISH FINANCE CAPITAL.=
                       AAROS -61-RCS

  CLASS AND POLITICS
  (GREAT BRITAIN).=    ABRAM -61-CPG

  SOCIAL CLASS AND BRITISH POLITICS.=
                       ABRAM -61-SCB

  THE CLASS STRUCTURE OF THE
  SOVIET UNION.=       ANON  -57-CSS

  SOCIAL STRUCTURE AND RULING CLASS
  -- 1 -- 2.=          ARONR -50-SSR

  THE SOVIET RULING CLASS.=
                       AVTOA -58-SRC

  SOCIAL CLASSES AND CLASS
  CONSCIOUSNESS IN THE USSR.=
                       BEALCP-58-SCC

  IDLE CLASS GOVERNMENT IN CHILE.=
                       BEATCW-62-ICG

  CLASS, STATUS, POWER.=
                       BENDR -53-CSP

  SOCIAL CLASS AND POLITICS IN
  GREENWICH (GREAT BRITAIN).=
                       BENNM -50-SCP

  MASS, CLASS AND BUREAUCRACY -- THE
  EVOLUTION OF CONTEMPORARY
  SOCIETY.=            BENSG -63-MCB

  CASTE, CLASS AND POWER -- CHANGING
  PATTERNS OF STRATIFICATION IN A
  TANJORE VILLAGE (INDIA).=
                       BETEA -  -CCP

  CLASS, STATUS, AND POWER
  REPUTATION.=         BONJCM-64-CSP

  THE BRITISH GOVERNING CLASS AND
  DEMOCRACY.=          BRADA -54-BGC

  AFRICAN ATTITUDES -- A STUDY OF THE
  SOCIAL, RACIAL, AND POLITICAL
  ATTITUDES OF SOME MIDDLE CLASS
  AFRICANS.=           BRETEA-63-AAS

  CHINESE CLASS STRUCTURE AND ITS
  IDEOLOGY.=           CH'U  -57-CCS

  THE SOCIAL DEMOCRATIC PARTY OF
  GERMANY -- FROM WORKING CLASS
  MOVEMENT TO MODERN POLITICAL
  PARTY.=              CHALDA-64-SDP

  CONCEPTION OF THE MIDDLE CLASS
  (GREAT BRITAIN).=    COLEGD-50-CMC

CLASS                    (CONTINUATION)
STUDIES IN CLASS STRUCTURE
(GREAT BRITAIN).=        COLEGC-55-SCS

RECENT CHANGES IN THE CLASS
STRUCTURE CF EUROPEAN SOCIETIES.=
                         DAHRR -64-RCC

CLASS AND CLASS CONFLICT IN
INDUSTRIAL SOCIETY.=    DAHRR -65-CCC

CLASS AND CLASS CONFLICT IN
INDUSTRIAL SOCIETY.=    DAHRR -65-CCC

THE NEW CLASS IN RUSSIA.=
                         DALLDJ-61-NCR

IDECLCGY AND CLASS CONSCIOUSNESS IN
THE MIDDLE CLASS (UNITED STATES).=
                         DEGRG -50-ICC

IDECLCGY AND CLASS CONSCIOUSNESS IN
THE MIDDLE CLASS (UNITED STATES).=
                         DEGRG -50-ICC

CLASS PARAMETERS IN HAITIAN
SOCIETY.=                DEYOM -59-CPH

THE NEW CLASS -- AN ANALYSIS OF THE
COMMUNIST SYSTEM (YUGOSLAVIA).=
                         DJILM -57-NCA

POLITICAL ASCENT IN A CLASS SOCIETY
-- FRENCH DEPUTIES 1870-1958.=
                         DOGAM -61-PAC

THE NEGRO PROFESSIONAL CLASS
(UNITED STATES).=        EDWAFG-59-NPC

BRITISH CLASS CONSCIOUSNESS AND THE
LABOUR PARTY.=           EPSTLD-62-BCC

IDENTIFICATION WITH CLASS AND
POLITICAL ROLE BEHAVIOR
(UNITED STATES).=        EULAH -56-ICP

CLASS AND PARTY IN THE EISENHOWER
YEARS, CLASS ROLES AND PERSPECTIVE
IN THE 1952 AND 1956 ELECTION
(UNITED STATES).=        EULAH -62-CPE

CLASS AND PARTY IN THE EISENHOWER
YEARS, CLASS ROLES AND PERSPECTIVE
IN THE 1952 AND 1956 ELECTION
(UNITED STATES).=        EULAH -62-CPE

THE MIDDLE CLASS FROM A
SOCIOLOGICAL VIEWPOINT
(UNITED STATES).=        FARIRE-60-MCS

ORIGINS OF THE MODERN INDIAN
BUSINESS CLASS.=         GADGDR-59-OMI

MIDDLE CLASS IMPEDIMENTS TO IRANIAN
MODERNIZATION.=          GASTRO-58-MCI

AFFLUENCE AND THE BRITISH CLASS
STRUCTURE.=              GOLDJH-63-ABC

SOCIAL CLASS IN AMERICAN
SOCIOLOGY.=              GORDMM-58-SCA

CLASS AND CONSERVATISM IN THE
ADOPTION OF INNOVATIONS
(UNITED STATES).=        GRAHS -56-CCA

THE CRISIS OF THE MIDDLE CLASS.=
                         GRAYH -55-CMC

THE 'CLASS STRUGGLE' IN AFRICA --
AN EXAMINATION OF CONFLICTING
THEORIES (WEST AFRICA).=

CLASS                    (CONTINUATION)
                         GRUNKW-64-CSA

ARISTOCRACY AND THE MIDDLE CLASS IN
THE BRITISH ELITE, 1886-1916.=
                         GUTTWL-54-AMC

THE METAMORPHOSE OF THE NEW CLASS
(SOVIET UNION, EASTERN EUROPE).=
                         HALPE -59-MNC

MIDDLE EASTERN ARMIES AND THE NEW
MIDDLE CLASS.=           HALPM -62-MEA

CASTE, CLASS, AND MINORITY.=
                         HARRM -59-CCM

RECOVERY OF CLASS THEORY.=
                         HEBER -59-RCT

THE NEW CLASS IN NORTH VIET NAM.=
                         HOAN  -58-NCN

CLASS, STRATUM AND INTELLIGENTSIA.=
                         HODGDC-63-CSI

SOCIAL STRATIFICATION -- CLASS IN
AMERICA.=                HODGHM-64-SSC

THE ENTREPRENEUR CLASS
(MIDDLE EAST).=          ISSAC -55-ECM

BEYOND THE RULING CLASS --
STRATEGIC ELITES IN MODERN
SOCIETY.=                KELLS -63-BRC

ITALIAN COMMUNISM, THE WORKING
CLASS AND ORGANIZED CATHOLICISM.=
                         KOGAN -66-ICW

THE ELITE AND THE RULING CLASS --
PARETO AND MOSCA RE-EXAMINED.=
                         KOLEF -67-ERC

WEALTH AND POWER IN AMERICA -- AN
ANALYSIS OF SOCIAL CLASS AND
INCOME DISTRIBUTION.=    KOLKG -62-WPA

CLASS STRATIFICATION IN THE
SOVIET UNION.=           KULSW -53-CSS

AN AFRICAN BOURGEOISIE -- RACE,
CLASS, AND POLITICS IN SOUTH
AFRICA.=                 KUPEL -65-ABR

THE INDIAN BUSINESS COMMUNITIES AND
THE EVOLUTION OF AN INDUSTRIALIST
CLASS.=                  LAMBHB-55-IBC

CLASS CONSCIOUSNESS AND CLASS
SOLIDARITY IN THE NEW ETHIOPIAN
ELITE.=                  LEVIDN-66-CCC

CLASS CONSCIOUSNESS AND CLASS
SOLIDARITY IN THE NEW ETHIOPIAN
ELITE.=                  LEVIDN-66-CCC

CLASS AND HIERARCHY -- A CRITIQUE
OF MARX.=                LICHG -64-CHC

SOCIAL CHANGE AND SOCIAL CLASS IN
THE SIERRA LEONE PROTECTORATE.=
                         LITTKL-48-SCS

EDUCATION AND FAMILY LIFE IN THE
DEVELOPMENT OF CLASS
IDENTIFICATION AMONG THE YORUBA
(WESTERN NIGERIA).=      LLOYBB-66-EFL

CLASS CONSCIOUSNESS AMONG THE
YORUBA (WESTERN NIGERIA).=
                         LLOYPC-66-CCA

CLASS, CITIZENSHIP AND SOCIAL

CLASS                     (CONTINUATION)
DEVELOPMENT.=            MARSTH-64-CCS

UNITED STATES SENATORS AND THE
CLASS STRUCTURE.=       MATTCR-54-USS

CONSERVATIVE PARTY AND THE CHANGING
CLASS STRUCTURE (GREAT BRITAIN).=
                        MAUDA -53-CPC

RECRUITMENT OF THE ADMINISTRATIVE
CLASS OF THE BRITISH CIVIL
SERVICE.=               MCKIMM-49-RAC

THE MYTH OF THE RULING CLASS --
GAETANO MOSCA AND THE 'ELITE'.=
                        MEISJH-58-MRC

THE INDIAN MIDDLE CLASS -- THEIR
GROWTH IN MODERN TIMES.=
                        MISRBB-61-IMC

SOME ASPECTS OF CLASS, STATUS AND
POWER RELATIONS IN ENGLAND.=
                        MONTGB-51-ACS

THE RULING CLASS.=      MOSCG -39-RC

THE DECLINE AND FALL OF SOCIAL
CLASS.=                 NISBRA-59-DFS

CLASS STRUCTURE IN THE SOCIAL
CONSCIOUSNESS.=         OSSOS -63-CSS

THE NEW CLASS DIVIDED -- RUSSIAN
SCIENCE AND TECHNOLOGY VERSUS
COMMUNISM.=             PARRA -66-NCD

THE RISE OF MIDDLE CLASS AND MIDDLE
MANAGEMENT IN BRAZIL.=
                        PERELC-62-RMC

BELGIUM -- LANGUAGE AND CLASS
OPPOSITION.=            PHILA -66-BLC

ASPECTS OF CLASS RELATIONS IN
CHILE, 1850-1950.=      PIKEFB-63-ACR

THE VERTICAL MOSAIC -- AN ANALYSIS
OF SOCIAL CLASS AND POWER IN
CANADA.=                PORTJ -65-VMA

THE AMERICAN GOVERNING CLASS.=
                        POTTA -62-AGC

EAST AFRICAN AGE - CLASS SYSTEMS --
AN INQUIRY INTO THE SOCIAL ORDER
OF GALLA, KIPSIGIS, AND KIKUYU.=
                        PRINAH-53-EAA

A NEW CLASS IN MALAYA.=
                        PYE,LW-60-NCM

CLASS IN AMERICAN SOCIETY.=
                        REISL -59-CAS

THE SOCIAL DEMOCRATS IN IMPERIAL
GERMANY -- A STUDY IN WORKING
CLASS ISOLATION AND NATIONAL
INTEGRATION.=           ROTHG -63-SDI

THE SPIRIT OF THE NEW SOVIET MIDDLE
CLASS.=                 SANDV -54-SNS

THE SOVIET RULING CLASS.=
                        SETOH -56-SRC

MALAYAN POLITICS -- RACE AND
CLASS.=                 SWIFM -62-MPR

THE NEGRO LEADERSHIP CLASS
(UNITED STATES).=       THOMDC-63-NLC

CLASS                     (CONTINUATION)
SOCIAL CLASS AND SOCIAL CHANGE IN
PUERTO RICO.=           TUMIM -61-SCS

THE CHANGING CLASS STRUCTURE OF
INDONESIA.=             VAN-JM-56-CCS

CLASS STRUCTURE AND COMMUNIST
THEORY.=                VAN-JM-61-CSC

SMALL TOWN IN MASS SOCIETY --
CLASS, POWER AND RELIGION IN A
RURAL COMMUNITY (UNITED STATES).=
                        VIDIAJ-58-STM

JAPAN'S NEW MIDDLE CLASS.=
                        VOGEEF-63-JSN

RACE AND CLASS IN RURAL BRAZIL.=
                        WAGLC -52-RCR

THE DILEMMA OF THE LATIN AMERICAN
MIDDLE CLASS.=          WAGLC -64-DLA

THE 'WORKING CLASS' IN COMMUNIST
CHINA.=                 WALKRL-53-WCC

RULING CLASS AND POWER ELITE.=
                        WESOW -65-RCP

SOME VARIABLES OF MIDDLE AND LOWER
CLASS IN TWO CENTRAL AMERICAN
CITIES.=                WILLRC-62-VML

CLASS STRUCTURE AND CLASS CONFLICT
IN HAITIAN SOCIETY.=    WINGR -65-CSC

CLASS STRUCTURE AND CLASS CONFLICT
IN HAITIAN SOCIETY.=    WINGR -65-CSC

SOCIAL TRANSFORMATIONS IN POLAND --
THE NEW RULING CLASS.=
                        ZAREZ -52-STP

POLITICAL GENERATIONS IN THE CUBAN
WORKING CLASS.=         ZEITM -66-PGC

CLASSES
SOCIAL CLASSES AND CLASS
CONSCIOUSNESS IN THE USSR.=
                        BEALCP-58-SCC

INTELLECTUAL CLASSES AND RULING
CLASSES IN FRANCE.=     BELOM -54-ICR

INTELLECTUAL CLASSES AND RULING
CLASSES IN FRANCE.=     BELOM -54-ICR

NATIONS, COLONIES AND SOCIAL
CLASSES -- THE POSITION OF MARX
AND ENGELS.=            DAVIHB-65-NCS

LEADERSHIP AMONG SOCIAL CLASSES.=
                        GOULAW-65-LAS

THE ROLE OF CLASSES IN HISTORICAL
MATERIALISM.=           HODGDC-59-RCH

LEADERS AND CLASSES IN THE INDIAN
NATIONAL CONGRESS, 1918-1939.=
                        KEMPT -64-LCI

NATIONALISM AND SOCIAL CLASSES IN
BRITISH WEST AFRICA.=   KILSML-58-NSC

SOVIET THEORY OF CLASSES.=
                        KUBAD -61-STC

CLASSES IN THE 'CLASSLESS' STATE
(SOVIET UNION).=        KULSWW-55-CCS

AMERICAN SOCIAL CLASSES --

CLASSES                    (CONTINUATION)
STATISTICAL STRATA CR SOCIAL
GROUPS.=              LENSGE-52-ASC

THE INTEGRATICN OF THE NEW ECCNOMIC
CLASSES WITH LCCAL GCVERNMENT IN
WEST NIGERIA.=        LLOYPC-53-INE

THE NEW URBAN CROUPS -- THE MICCLE
CLASSES (LATIN AMERICA).=
                      RATIL -67-NUC

PCLITICAL PARTIES ANC SCCIAL
CLASSES IN ISRAEL.=   ROSHM -56-PPS

INTELLECTUAL CLASSES ANC RULING
CLASSES IN FRANCE -- A SECOND
LCCK.=                SAX,JW-54-ICR

INTELLECTUAL CLASSES ANC RULINC
CLASSES IN FRANCE -- A SECOND
LCCK.=                SAX,JW-54-ICR

IMPERIALISM ANC SCCIAL CLASSES.=
                      SCHUJ -55-ISC

TWC CITIES CF LATIN AMERICA -- A
CCMPARATIVE CESCRIPTICN OF SOCIAL
CLASSES.=             WHITAH-64-TCL

THE THECRY CF SCCIAL CLASSES.=
                      ZWEIF -58-TSC

CLASSIFICATICN
PUBLIC CORPORATICNS ANC THE
CLASSIFICATION CF ACMINISTRATIVE
BCCIES (GREAT ERITAIN).=
                      CHESCN-53-PCC

CLASSIFICATICNS
ELEVENTH CENTURY CHINESE
BUREAUCRATS -- SCME HISTORICAL
CLASSIFICATICNS ANC BEHAVICRAL
TYPES.=               LIU, -60-ECC

CLASSLESS
CLASSES IN THE 'CLASSLESS' STATE
(SCVIET UNICN).=      KULSWW-55-CCS

CLEARANCE
URBAN RENEWAL PCLITICS -- SLUM
CLEARANCE IN NEWARK
(UNITED STATES).=     KAPLH -63-URP

PRESICENCY ANC LECISLATICN -- THE
GRCWTH CF CENTRAL CLEARANCE
(UNITEC STATES).=     NEUSRE-54-PLG

CLEAVAGE
CCNSENSUS ANC CLEAVAGE IN BRITISH
POLITICAL ICECLCGY.=  CHRIJB-65-CCB

CCMMUNITY LEACERSHIP IN AN ECONCMIC
CRISIS -- TESTING GRCUNC FOR
ICECLCGICAL CLEAVAGE
(UNITEC STATES).=     C'ANWV-66-CLE

INTEGRATICN ANC CLEAVACE AMONG
COMMUNITY INFLUENTIALS IN TWO
BCRCER CITIES (MEXICO,
UNITEC STATES).=      FCRMWH-59-ICA

CCNSENSLS AND CLEAVACE -- PARTY
ALIGNMENT IN GREECE, 1945-1965.=
                      TROMTP-66-CCP

CLIENT
AN APPRCPRIATICNS SUBCOMMITTEE ANC
ITS CLIENT AGENCIES -- A
CCMPARATIVE STUCY CF SUPERVISICN
ANC CCNTRCL (UNITEC STATES).=
                      SHARI -65-ASI

CLIQUES
PCWER CLICUES IN BUREAUCRATIC

CLIQUES                    (CCNTINUATICN)
SCCIETY.=             PENSJ -62-PCB

DECISICN-MAKINC CLICUES IN
COMMUNITY PCWER STRUCTURES -- A
CCMPARATIVE STUCY CF AN AMERICAN
AND AN ENGLISH CITY.= MILLCC-58-CMC

CLUB
THE AMATEUR CEMCCRAT -- CLUB
PCLITICS IN THREE CITIES
(UNITED STATES).=     WILSJQ-62-ADC

CC-CPERATICN
CC-CPERATICN ANC CCNFLICT IN
CCLUMBIAN PARTY PCLITICS.=
                      ANGEA -66-COC

CC-CPERATIVE
MEMBERSHIP PARTICIPATICN IN
PCLICY-MAKING IN THE C.C.F.
(CC-CPERATIVE CCMMCNWEALTH
FEDERATICN, CANADA).= ENGEFC-56-MPP

CC-CPERATIVE PCLITICS IN A
LANCASHIRE CCNSTITUENCY
(GREAT ERITAIN).=     MACKWJ-54-CCP

CC-CRCINATICN
THE CC-CRCINATICN ANC CCNTRCL CF
GOVERNMENT CCRPCRATICNS IN THE
PHILIPPINES.=         MILNRS-61-COC

CCAL
THE EURCPEAN CCAL ANC STEEL
COMMUNITY -- CPERATICNS OF THE
HIGH AUTHORITY.=      MERRHJ-55-ECS

CCALITICNS
INTRAPARTY CIVISICNS ANC CABINET
CCALITICNS IN THE FCURTH FRENCH
REPUBLIC.=            MACRC -63-ICC

THE STABILITY CF CCALITICNS CN ROLL
CALLS IN THE HCUSE CF
REPRESENTATIVES (UNITED STATES).=
                      RIKEWH-62-SCR

THE THECRY CF PCLITICAL
CCALITICNS.=          RIKEWH-62-TPC

CCCE
THE OPERATICNAL CCCE CF THE
PCLITEURC (SCVIET UNICN).=
                      LEITN -51-OCP

CCERCICN
IS COERCICN WITHERING AWAY
(SCVIET UNICN).=      AZRAJR-62-ICW

TCTALITARIANISM WITHCUT COERCICN
(SCVIET UNICN).=      RITVH -60-TWC

CCERCIVE
WCRLD REVCLUTICNARY ELITES --
STUCIES IN COERCIVE ICECLCGICAL
MCVEMENTS (CHINA, GERMANY, ITALY,
SCVIET UNICN).=       LASSHD-66-WRE

CCEXISTENCE
THE CCMMUNIST SLBVERSICN OF
CZECHCSLCVAKIA, 1938-1948 -- THE
FAILURE CF CCEXISTENCE.=
                      KORBJ -59-CSC

CCGNITIVE
THE RCLE CCNCEPT IN LEGISLATURES --
A PROBABILITY MCCEL ANC A NOTE CN
CCGNITIVE STRUCTURE
(UNITED STATES).=     FRANWL-65-RCL

CCHESICN
LEACERSHIP STRATECIES FCR

COHESION                 (CONTINUATION)
LEGISLATIVE PARTY COHESION
(UNITED STATES).=         BARBJD-66-LSL

COHESION OF BRITISH PARLIAMENTARY
PARTIES.=                 EPSTLD-56-CBP

COHESION AND COMMITMENT IN
EMPLOYERS' ORGANIZATIONS (FRANCE,
GERMANY).=               HARTH -59-CCE

CAUCUS AND COHESION IN CANADIAN
PARLIAMENTARY PARTIES.=
                         KORNA -66-CCC

ATTITUDE CONSENSUS AND CONFLICT IN
AN INTEREST -- AN ASSESSMENT OF
COHESION (UNITED STATES).=
                         LUTTNR-66-ACC

LEADERSHIP COHESION IN COMMUNIST
CHINA AND UNDERDEVELOPED ASIAN
COUNTRIES.=              MACFR -63-LCC

COLD
THE COLD WAR ON THE LITERARY FRONT
(SOVIET UNION) -- PART 1, THE
WRITER'S UNDERGROUND -- PART 2,
GROUPS, TRENDS, GENRES, -- PART 3,
THE PARTY AND THE WRITERS.=
                         BURG  -62-CWL

COLLABORATOR
WILLIAM I THOMAS AS A
COLLABORATOR.=           ZNANF -48-WIT

COLLECTION
PARTICIPANT OBSERVATION AND THE
COLLECTION AND INTERPRETATION OF
DATA.=                   VIDIAJ-55-POC

COLLECTIVE
THE POLITICAL LINE OF COLLECTIVE
LEADERSHIP (SOVIET UNION).=
                         ACHMH -54-PLC

WHAT HAPPENED TO COLLECTIVE
LEADERSHIP (SOVIET UNION).=
                         FAINM -59-WHC

LEADERSHIP AND DEMOCRACY IN THE
COLLECTIVE SETTLEMENTS OF ISRAEL.=
                         FEUELS-65-LDC

THE ROLE OF THE SOVIET ARMY IN THE
CRISIS OF THE COLLECTIVE
LEADERSHIP.=             GALAN -57-RSA

NEW FACTORS OF STABILITY IN SOVIET
COLLECTIVE LEADERSHIP.=
                         GILIJM-67-NFS

COLLECTIVE LEADERSHIP
(SOVIET UNION).=         MARIY -54-CLS

UNITED STATES SENATOR -- A
COLLECTIVE PORTRAIT.=    MATTER-61-USS

THE AMERICAN BUSINESS ELITE -- A
COLLECTIVE PORTRAIT.=    MILLCW-54-ABE

THE LOGIC OF COLLECTIVE ACTION --
PUBLIC GOODS AND THE THEORY OF
GROUPS.=                 OLSEM -65-LCA

COLLECTIVE NEGOTIATIONS BETWEEN THE
STATE AND ITS OFFICIALS -- A
COMPARATIVE ESSAY.=      SCHMF -62-CNB

THE JUSTICES OF THE SUPREME COURT
-- A COLLECTIVE PORTRAIT
(UNITED STATES).=        SCHMJR-59-JSC

COLLECTIVE                (CONTINUATION)
CULTS, COUPS, AND COLLECTIVE
LEADERSHIP (SOVIET UNION).=
                         SWEAHR-65-CCC

COLLECTIVE BARGAINING IN THE USSR.=
                         WOLFC -55-CBU

COLLECTIVIST
BRITISH POLITICS IN THE
COLLECTIVIST AGE.=       BEERSH-65-BPC

COLLEGE
AN AFRICAN ELITE -- A SAMPLE SURVEY
OF 52 FORMER STUDENTS OF MAKERERE
COLLEGE IN EAST AFRICA.=
                         GOLDJE-55-AES

THE VALUES OF TURKISH COLLEGE
YOUTH.=                  HYMAH -58-VTC

COLOMBIA
DANCE OF THE MILLIONS -- MILITARY
RULE AND THE SOCIAL REVOLUTION IN
COLOMBIA, 1930-1956.=    FLUHVL-57-DMM

SOCIAL BACKGROUNDS OF THE BOGOTA
ENTREPRENEUR (COLOMBIA).=
                         LIPMA -65-SBB

COLONIAL
INDIGENOUS POLITICS AND COLONIAL
ADMINISTRATION WITH SPECIAL
REFERENCE TO AUSTRALIA.=
                         BARNJA-60-IPC

POLITICAL ELITES IN COLONIAL
SOUTHEAST ASIA -- AN HISTORICAL
ANALYSIS.=               BENCHJ-64-PEC

PEASANT MOVEMENTS IN COLONIAL
SOUTHEAST ASIA.=         BENCHJ-65-PMC

THE CIVIL - RELIGIOUS HIERARCHY IN
MESOAMERICAN COMMUNITIES -- PRE -
SPANISH BACKGROUND AND COLONIAL
DEVELOPMENT.=            CARRP -61-CRH

THE AZTEC ARISTOCRACY IN COLONIAL
MEXICO.=                 GIBSC -60-AAC

NATIONALISM IN COLONIAL AFRICA.=
                         HODGT -56-NCA

THE EMERGING ANTI - COLONIAL
CONSENSUS IN THE UNITED NATIONS.=
                         ROWEET-64-EAC

COLONIAL ELITES -- ROME, SPAIN AND
THE AMERICAS.=           SYMER -58-CER

ASPECTS OF ISLAM IN POST - COLONIAL
INDONESIA -- FIVE ESSAYS.=
                         VAN-CA-58-AIP

POLITICAL ADVANCEMENT IN THE SOUTH
PACIFIC -- A COMPARATIVE STUDY OF
COLONIAL PRACTICE IN FIJI, TAHITI,
AND AMERICAN SAMOA.=     WESTFJ-61-PAS

COLONIES
NATIONS, COLONIES AND SOCIAL
CLASSES -- THE POSITION OF MARX
AND ENGELS.=             DAVIHB-65-NCS

COLUMBIA
THE CHANGING ROLE OF THE MILITARY
IN COLUMBIA.=            HELGJL-61-CRM

STUDENT POLITICS (LATIN AMERICA,
INDIA, POLAND, UNITED STATES,
GERMANY, CHILE, ARGENTINA,

61

COMMITTEE          (CONTINUATION)
                   JONECO-61-RCC

PARTY AND POLICY-MAKING -- THE
HOUSE REPUBLICAN POLICY COMMITTEE
(UNITED STATES).=     JONECO-64-PPM

THE PRESIDING OFFICER AND RULES
COMMITTEE IN LEGISLATURES OF THE
U.S. (UNITED STATES).=
                   LEE,EC-52-POR

THE PARLIAMENTARY AND SCIENTIFIC
COMMITTEE (GREAT BRITAIN).=
                   LINSH -56-PSC

THE HOUSE COMMITTEE ON WAYS AND
MEANS -- CONFLICT MANAGEMENT IN A
CONGRESSIONAL COMMITTEE
(UNITED STATES).=     MANLJF-65-HCW

THE HOUSE COMMITTEE ON WAYS AND
MEANS -- CONFLICT MANAGEMENT IN A
CONGRESSIONAL COMMITTEE
(UNITED STATES).=     MANLJF-65-HCW

COMMITTEE ASSIGNMENTS IN THE HOUSE
OF REPRESENTATIVES
(UNITED STATES).=     MASTNA-61-CAH

THE AMERICAN COUNCIL OF ECONOMIC
ADVISERS AND JOINT COMMITTEE ON
THE ECONOMIC REPORT.= MILNRS-55-ACE

THE JULY CENTRAL COMMITTEE PLENUM
AND BOTTLENECKS IN SOVIET
INDUSTRY.=            MINYV -60-JCC

THE KREMLIN'S PROFESSIONAL STAFF --
THE 'APPARATUS' OF THE CENTRAL
COMMITTEE, COMMUNIST PARTY OF THE
SOVIET UNION.=        NEMZL -50-KSP

THE SOVIET PARTY CENTRAL
COMMITTEE.=           PENNJ -58-SPC

THE MILITARY AFFAIRS COMMITTEE AND
PARTY CONTROL OF THE MILITARY IN
CHINA.=               POWERL-63-MAC

DECISION MAKING IN THE HOUSE RULES
COMMITTEE (UNITED STATES).=
                   ROBIJA-59-DMH

THE ROLE OF THE RULES COMMITTEE IN
ARRANGING THE PROGRAM OF THE U.S.
HOUSE OF REPRESENTATIVES
(UNITED STATES).=     ROBIJA-59-RRC

THE HOUSE RULES COMMITTEE
(UNITED STATES).=     ROBIJA-63-HRC

THE DEMOCRATIC STATE CENTRAL
COMMITTEE IN MICHIGAN 1949-1959 --
THE RISE OF THE NEW POLITICS AND
THE NEW POLITICAL LEADERSHIP
(UNITED STATES).=     SAWYRL-60-DSC

CONGRESSIONAL COMMITTEE MEMBERS AS
INDEPENDENT AGENCY OVERSEERS -- A
CASE STUDY (UNITED STATES).=
                   SCHES -60-CCM

POLITICAL MONEY -- A STUDY OF
CONTRIBUTORS TO THE NATIONAL
COMMITTEE FOR AN EFFECTIVE
CONGRESS (UNITED STATES).=
                   SCOBHM-63-PMS

A METHOD FOR EVALUATING THE
DISTRIBUTION OF POWER IN A
COMMITTEE SYSTEM (UNITED STATES).=

COMMITTEE          (CONTINUATION)
                   SHAPLS-54-MEC

THE ROLE OF THE SELECT COMMITTEE ON
NATIONALIZED INDUSTRY IN
PARLIAMENT (GREAT BRITAIN).=
                   SIMMRH-61-RSC

THE CENTRAL COMMITTEE OF THE UNITED
POLISH WORKERS' PARTY.=
                   STAARF-57-CCU

COMMITTEES
THE TRAINING OF OFFICIALS OF THE
ADMINISTRATIVE ORGANS OF THE
PEOPLE'S COMMITTEES (YUGOSLAVIA).=
                   ANON  -61-TOA

POWER IN COMMITTEES -- AN
EXPERIMENT IN THE GOVERNMENTAL
PROCESS (UNITED STATES).=
                   BARBJD-66-PCE

THE CAPITOL HILL COMMITTEES
(UNITED STATES).=     BONEHA-56-CHC

PARTY COMMITTEES AND NATIONAL
POLITICS (UNITED STATES).=
                   BONEHA-58-PCN

SOME NOTES ON THE STANDING
COMMITTEES OF THE FRENCH NATIONAL
ASSEMBLY.=            BROMPA-57-NSC

LEGISLATIVE COMMITTEES IN POLISH
LAWMAKING.=           CHRYVC-66-LCP

POLITICS WITHOUT POWER -- THE
NATIONAL PARTY COMMITTEES
(UNITED STATES).=     COTTCP-64-PWP

CHANGING MEMBERSHIP PATTERNS IN
HOUSE COMMITTEES (UNITED STATES).=
                   GAWTLC-66-CMP

CONGRESSIONAL AND SENATORIAL
CAMPAIGN COMMITTEES IN THE
MID-TERM ELECTION YEAR 1954
(UNITED STATES).=     HATHGB-56-CSC

ADVISORY COMMITTEES IN THE
LEGISLATIVE PROCESS
(UNITED STATES).=     KAMMGM-53-ACL

COMMITTEES OF THE HOUSE OF COMMONS
(GREAT BRITAIN).=     RYLEM -65-CHC

STANDING COMMITTEES IN THE HOUSE OF
COMMONS, 1945-1950
(GREAT BRITAIN).=     SHEAJG-50-SCH

COMMON
INTEREST GROUPS IN PANAMA AND THE
CENTRAL AMERICAN COMMON MARKET.=
                   CENTCF-67-IGP

COMMONS
THE BRITISH HOUSE OF COMMONS.=
                   BERRHB-61-BHC

FIRST-TIME WINNERS IN THE BRITISH
HOUSE OF COMMONS SINCE 1918.=
                   BUCKPW- -FTW

PARTY DISCILPLINE IN THE HOUSE OF
COMMONS (GREAT BRITAIN).=
                   DOWSR -63-PDH

BACKBENCH OPINION IN THE HOUSE OF
COMMONS, 1955-1959
(GREAT BRITAIN).=     FINESE-61-BOH

THE LABOUR GOVERNMENT AND THE HOUSE

COMMONS                    (CONTINUATION)
OF COMMONS (GREAT BRITAIN).=
                           FITCDG-52-LGH

THE SOCIAL BASIS OF LEADERSHIP IN A
CANADIAN HOUSE OF COMMONS.=
                           KORNA -65-SBL

THE SPEAKER OF THE HOUSE OF COMMONS
(GREAT BRITAIN).=     LAUNP -61-SHC

THE ROLE OF AN INTEREST GROUP
LEADER IN THE HOUSE OF
COMMONS (GREAT BRITAIN).=

                    MILLJH-56-RIG

THE ROLE OF AN INTEREST GROUP
LEADER IN THE HOUSEHE ROLE OF THE
INTEREST GROUP LEADER IN THE HOUSE
OF COMMONS (GREAT BRITAIN).=
COMMONS (GREAT BRITAIN).=
                           MILLJH-56-RIG

NOTES ON FUNCTIONAL REPRESENTATION
IN THE HOUSE OF COMMONS
(GREAT BRITAIN).=     MILLJH-59-NFR

THE HOUSE OF COMMONS FROM THE CHAIR
(GREAT BRITAIN).=     MILNJ -47-HCC

INTERNATIONAL COMMUNICATION AND
LEGISLATIVE BEHAVIOR -- THE SENATE
AND THE HOUSE OF COMMONS
(UNITED STATES, GREAT BRITAIN).=
                           RUSSBM-62-ICL

COMMITTEES OF THE HOUSE OF COMMONS
(GREAT BRITAIN).=     RYLEM -65-CHC

STANDING COMMITTEES IN THE HOUSE OF
COMMONS, 1945-1950
(GREAT BRITAIN).=     SHEAJG-50-SCH

BRITISH PRESSURE GROUPS -- THEIR
ROLE IN RELATION TO THE HOUSE OF
COMMONS.=             STEWJD-58-BPG

REPRESENTATION IN THE HOUSE OF
COMMONS OF THE TWENTY-FIRST
PARLIAMENT -- PARTY AND PROVINCE
(CANADA).=            WILLJR-52-RHC

COMMONWEALTH
MEMBERSHIP PARTICIPATION IN
POLICY-MAKING IN THE C.C.F.
(CO-OPERATIVE COMMONWEALTH
FEDERATION, CANADA).= ENGEFC-56-MPP

INDIRECT RULE AND REPRESENTATIVE
GOVERNMENT (BRITISH COMMONWEALTH
COUNTRIES).=          GUTTWF-59-IRR

REPRESENTATION IN PLURAL SOCIETIES
(GREAT BRITAIN, BRITISH
COMMONWEALTH).=       MACKWJ-54-RPS

POSTWAR STRAINS ON THE BRITISH
COMMONWEALTH.=        MANSN -48-PSB

FORMAL RECOGNITION OF THE LEADER OF
THE OPPOSITION IN PARLIAMENTS OF
THE BRITISH COMMONWEALTH.=
                           MCHEDE-54-FRL

THE HIGHER PUBLIC SERVICE OF THE
COMMONWEALTH OF AUSTRALIA.=
                           SCARHA-57-HPS

BRITAIN AND THE COMMONWEALTH --
ATTITUDES IN PARLIAMENT AND PRESS

COMMONWEALTH          (CONTINUATION)
IN THE UNITED KINGDOM SINCE 1951.=
                           TIERJF-58-BCA

COMMUNAL
COMMUNAL REPRESENTATION IN THE
FIJIAN LEGISLATIVE COUNCIL.=
                           HUGHCA-60-CRF

HINDU COMMUNAL GROUPS IN INDIAN
POLITICS.=            LAMBRO-59-HCG

COMMUNALISM
COMMUNALISM AND COMMUNISM IN
MALAYA.=              CARNFG-53-CCM

COMMUNICATION
PATTERNS OF COMMUNICATION OF
EGYPTIAN CIVIL SERVANTS WITH THE
PUBLIC.=              BERGM -56-PCE

LEADERSHIP AND COMMUNICATION IN THE
CROFTING COMMUNITIES OF THE OUTER
HEBRIDES.=            CAIRJB-61-LCC

CONTINUITY OF LEADERSHIP IN
COMMUNICATION NETWORKS.=
                           COHEAM-61-CLC

POLITICAL COMMUNICATION OF THE
JAPANESE PEACE SETTLEMENT
(UNITED STATES).=     COHEBC-56-PCJ

NATIONALISM AND SOCIAL
COMMUNICATION -- AN INQUIRY INTO
THE FOUNDATIONS OF NATIONALISM.=
                           DEUTKW-53-NSC

THE NERVES OF GOVERNMENT -- MODELS
OF POLITICAL COMMUNICATION AND
CONTROL.=             DEUTKW-63-NGM

POWER STRUCTURE AND ITS
COMMUNICATION BEHAVIOR IN
SAN JOSE, COSTA RICA.=
                           EDWAHT-67-PSI

THE COMMUNICATION OF CONSERVATIVE
POLICY 1957-1959 (GREAT BRITAIN).=
                           HENND -61-CCP

COMMUNICATION AND POLITICAL
AWARENESS IN THE VILLAGES OF
EGYPT.=               HIRAGK-58-CPA

ELITE COMMUNICATION IN SAMOA -- A
STUDY OF LEADERSHIP.= KEESFM-56-ECS

ELITE COMMUNICATION AND THE
GOVERNMENTAL PROCESS
(UNITED STATES, CANADA).=
                           LANERE-58-ECG

SOME REACTIONS OF JAPANESE
UNIVERSITY STUDENTS TO PERSUASIVE
COMMUNICATION.=       MCGIE -65-RJU

LOBBYING AS A COMMUNICATION
PROGRESS (UNITED STATES).=
                           MILBLW-60-LCP

CHANNELS OF COMMUNICATION WITH THE
BAERIO PEOPLE (PHILIPPINES).=
                           PAL,AP-57-CCB

ESOTERIC COMMUNICATION IN SOVIET
POLITICS.=            RUSHM -59-ECS

INTERNATIONAL COMMUNICATION AND
LEGISLATIVE BEHAVIOR -- THE SENATE
AND THE HOUSE OF COMMONS
(UNITED STATES, GREAT BRITAIN).=

COMMUNIST            (CONTINUATION)
ITS FORMATION ABROAD.=
                              AHMAM -60-CPI

THE SOVIET COMMUNIST PARTY'S POLICY
TOWARD SOVIET YOUTH.= ANON -56-SCP

THE COMMUNIST PARTY AND THE
PEASANTRY (SOVIET UNION).=
                              ANON -57-CPP

LEADING POSITIONS AND PERSONALITIES
IN THE COMMUNIST PARTY OF THE
SOVIET UNION AND THE SOVIET
GOVERNMENT.=            ANON -57-LPP

THE COMMUNIST LEAGUE OF YUGOSLAVIA
IN FIGURES.=            AVAKI -59-CLY

STALIN AND THE SOVIET COMMUNIST
PARTY.=                 AVTOA -59-SSC

THE COMMUNIST PARTY APPARATUS
(SOVIET UNION).=        AVTOA -66-CPA

MASS POLITICAL ORGANIZATIONS IN
COMMUNIST CHINA.=       BARNAD-51-MPO

POLITICAL POWER IN COMMUNIST
CHINA.=                 BARNAD-57-PPC

COMMUNIST CHINA IN PERSPECTIVE.=
                        BARNAD-62-CCP

SOCIAL CONTROLS IN COMMUNIST
CHINA.=                 BARNAD-66-SCC

SOCIAL STRATIFICATION AND ASPECTS
OF PERSONNEL MANAGEMENT IN THE
CHINESE COMMUNIST BUREAUCRACY.=
                        BARNAD-66-SSA

EAST EUROPEAN COMMUNIST ELITES --
THEIR CHARACTER AND HISTORY.=
                        BASSR -66-EEC

CHANGING PATTERNS OF POLICY
FORMATION AND IMPLEMENTATION IN
COMMUNIST CHINA.=       BENSO -59-CPP

WARSAW AND THE COMMUNIST BLOC
(POLAND).'             BIRNI -57-WCB

CHILE -- A COMMUNIST BATTLEGROUND.=
                        BLASSC-50-CCB

COMMUNIST IDEOLOGY AND
INTERNATIONAL AFFAIRS
(SOVIET UNION, EAST EUROPE).=
                        BRZEZ -60-CII

CONFLICTS WITHIN THE INDIAN
COMMUNIST PARTY         CARRR -55-CWI

LITERATURE IN COMMUNIST CHINA.=
                        CHANSW-58-LCC

LEADERSHIP IN THE CHINESE COMMUNIST
PARTY.=                 CHAO -59-LCC

PROBLEMS OF CHINESE COMMUNIST
LEADERSHIP AS SEEN IN THE SECRET
MILITARY PAPERS.=       CHENJC-64-PCC

EDUCATION AND PROPAGANDA IN
COMMUNIST CHINA.=       CHENTH-51-EPC

THE 'THREE-ANTI' AND 'FIVE-ANTI'
MOVEMENTS IN COMMUNIST CHINA.=
                        CHENTH-52-TAF

THE THOUGHT REFORM OF INTELLECTUALS

COMMUNIST            (CONTINUATION)
(COMMUNIST CHINA).=    CHENTH-59-TRI

LEADERSHIP IN COMMUNIST CHINA.=
                        CHU,O -57-LCC

THE FRENCH CP (COMMUNIST PARTY) --
SIGNS OF CRISIS.=       COLLM -59-FCC

YOUTH AND COMMUNISM -- AN
HISTORICAL ANALYSIS OF
INTERNATIONAL COMMUNIST YOUTH
MOVEMENTS.=             CORNR -65-YCH

THE TECHNIQUES OF THE COMMUNIST
PARTY IN FRANCE.=      COWALG-49-TCP

GUATEMALA -- LABOR AND THE
COMMUNIST.=            CUMBCC-53-GLC

PARTY RULE IN COMMUNIST CHINA.=
                        DAI,S -62-PRC

THE SECRETARIAT AND THE LOCAL
ORGANIZATIONS IN THE RUSSIAN
COMMUNIST PARTY, 1921-1923.=
                        DANIRV-56-SLO

A STUDY OF 163 OUTSTANDING
COMMUNIST LEADERS (SOVIET UNION).=
                        DAVIJ -29-SOC

INDUSTRIAL ADMINISTRATION IN
COMMUNIST EAST EUROPE.=
                        DITZGW-60-IAC

THE NEW CLASS -- AN ANALYSIS OF THE
COMMUNIST SYSTEM (YUGOSLAVIA).=
                        DJILM -57-NCA

NATIONAL AND SOCIAL COMPOSITION OF
THE MEMBERSHIP OF THE COMMUNIST
PARTY (BOLSHEVIK) OF THE UKRAINE,
1918-1928.=             DMYTB -57-NSC

COMMUNIST CHINA -- THE POLITICS OF
STUDENT OPPOSITION.=   DOOLCJ-64-CCP

LEADERSHIP AND SUCCESSION IN
COMMUNIST CHINA.=      DORRWF-65-LSC

THE FOUNDATION OF THE COMMUNIST
PARTY POLAND.=         DZIEMK-52-FCP

THE COMMUNIST PARTY OF POLAND -- AN
OUTLINE OF HISTORY.=   DZIEMK-59-CPP

POSTWAR ROLE OF THE COMMUNIST PARTY
(SOVIET UNION).=       FAINM -49-PRC

THE COMMUNIST PARTY SINCE STALIN.=
                        FAINM -56-CPS

THE ITALIAN CP (COMMUNIST PARTY) --
CONSERVATISM IN DISGUISE.=
                        GALLG -59-ICC

KADAR AND THE RESURRECTION OF THE
HUNGARIAN COMMUNIST PARTY -- A
STUDY IN POLITICAL TECHNIQUES.=
                        GINSG -64-KRH

THE FATE OF THE FRENCH NON -
COMMUNIST LEFT.=       GODFO -55-FFN

LITERARY DISSENT IN COMMUNIST
CHINA.=                GOLDM -67-LDC

THE CHINESE COMMUNIST CADRE -- KEY
TO POLITICAL CONTROL.=
                        GOURWE-52-CCC

THE CRISIS IN THE BRITISH CP

COMMUNIST          (CONTINUATION)
   (COMMUNIST PARTY).=    GRAIGW-57-CBC

OLIGARCHY IN THE BRITISH COMMUNIST
PARTY.=                  GRAIGW-58-OBC

SOME OBSERVATIONS ON MEMBERSHIP
FIGURES OF THE COMMUNIST PARTY OF
THE SOVIET UNION.=       HANCWS-58-OMF

THE COMMUNIST PARTY OF INDONESIA,
1951-1963.=              HINDD -64-CPI

THE INDONESIAN COMMUNIST PARTY AND
CONFLICT IN THE INTERNATIONAL
COMMUNIST MOVEMENT.=     HINDD -64-ICP

THE INDONESIAN COMMUNIST PARTY AND
CONFLICT IN THE INTERNATIONAL
COMMUNIST MOVEMENT.=     HINDD -64-ICP

INTRA - PARTY POLITICS AND ECONOMIC
POLICY IN COMMUNIST CHINA.=
                         HINTHC-60-IPP

THE BRITISH COMMUNIST PARTY.=
                         HOBSEJ-54-BCP

AGE AS A FACTOR IN THE RECRUITMENT
OF COMMUNIST LEADERSHIP
(SOVIET UNION).=         HOLTRT-54-AFR

CHINESE COMMUNIST CONTROL OF THE
PRESS.=                  HONNFW-58-CCC

THE EIGHTH CENTRAL COMMITTEE OF THE
CHINESE COMMUNIST PARTY -- A STUDY
OF AN ELITE.=            HOUNFW-57-ECC

THE CULTURAL REVOLUTION AND
LEADERSHIP CRISIS IN COMMUNIST
CHINA.=                  HSUEC -67-CRL

THE POLITICS OF THE EUROPEAN
COMMUNIST STATES (BULGARIA,
CZECHOSLOVAKIA, HUNGARY, EAST
GERMANY, POLAND, RUMANIA,
SOVIET UNION, YUGOSLAVIA).=
                         IONEG -67-PEC

MINOR PARTIES IN COMMUNIST CHINA.=
                         JAN,GP-62-MPC

PEASANT NATIONALISM AND COMMUNIST
POWER -- THE EMERGENCE OF
REVOLUTIONARY CHINA, 1937-1945.=
                         JOHNCA-62-PNC

THE COMMUNIST ARMIES (CHINA,
SOVIET UNION).=          KASHA -61-TCA

THE DEFEAT OF THE PRO - SOVIET
FACTION OF THE JAPANESE COMMUNIST
PARTY.=                  KASHA -64-DPS

INDIA'S COMMUNIST PARTY SPLIT.=
                         KATRS -61-ISC

THE SPLIT IN THE CPI (COMMUNIST
PARTY INDIA).=           KAULJM-64-SCC

INDIAN COMMUNIST PARTY STRATEGY
SINCE 1947.=             KAUTJH-55-ICP

MOSCOW AND THE COMMUNIST PARTY OF
INDIA.=                  KAUTJH-56-MCP

THAILAND'S BUREAUCRACY AND THE
THREAT OF COMMUNIST SUBVERSION.=
                         KINGJK-54-TSB

THE JAPAN COMMUNIST PARTY -- ITS


COMMUNIST          (CONTINUATION)
DEVELOPMENT SINCE THE WAR.=
                         KIYOE -58-JCP

THE 'NEXT GENERATION' OF CHINESE
COMMUNIST LEADERS.=      KLEIDW-62-NGC

THE SOVIET MILITARY AND THE
COMMUNIST PARTY.=        KOLKR -67-SMC

THE COMMUNIST SUBVERSION OF
CZECHOSLOVAKIA, 1938-1948 -- THE
FAILURE OF COEXISTENCE.=
                         KORBJ -59-CSC

YOUTH AND THE YOUNG COMMUNIST
LEAGUE.=                 KRUZP -65-YYC

COMMUNIST USE OF THE CZECHOSLOVAK
PARLIAMENT SINCE WORLD WAR II.=
                         KUBAD -61-CUC

PATTERNS OF LEADERSHIP IN A
COMMUNIST STATE -- CZECHOSLOVAKIA
1946-1958.=              KUBAD -61-PLC

LEADERSHIP IN THE CHINESE COMMUNIST
PARTY.=                  KUO-C -59-LCC

THE CATHOLIC ANTI - COMMUNIST ROLE
WITHIN AUSTRALIAN LABOR.=
                         LANGFC-56-CAC

INDEPENDENCE OR SUBORDINATION --
THE JAPANESE COMMUNIST PARTY
BETWEEN MOSCOW AND PEKING.=
                         LANGPF-63-IOS

LEFT WING TRADE UNIONISM -- THE
MATRIX OF COMMUNIST POWER IN
ITALY.=                  LAPAJ -54-LWT

AS IRAQ GOES COMMUNIST.=
                         LAQUWZ-59-IGC

THE COMMUNIST MOVEMENT IN IRAN.=
                         LENCG -47-CMI

THE LEADERSHIP DOCTRINE OF THE
CHINESE COMMUNIST PARTY.=
                         LEWIJW-63-LDC

LEADERSHIP IN COMMUNIST CHINA.=
                         LEWIJW-65-LCC

PARTY CADRES IN COMMUNIST CHINA.=
                         LEWIJW-65-PCC

THE INDONESIAN COMMUNIST MOVEMENT
TODAY.=                  LUBIM -54-ICM

COMMUNIST CHINA'S INTRA - PARTY
DISPUTE.=                MACFR -58-CCS

LEADERSHIP COHESION IN COMMUNIST
CHINA AND UNDERDEVELOPED ASIAN
COUNTRIES.=              MACFR -63-LCC

THE COMMUNIST PARTY IN INDIA -- A
SHORT HISTORY.=          MASAMR-54-CPI

AUTHORITY IN COMMUNIST POLITICAL
SYSTEMS (EASTERN EUROPE,
SOVIET UNION).=          MEYEAG-67-ACP

ORGANIZATION AND LEADERSHIP OF THE
FRENCH COMMUNIST PARTY.=
                         MICACA-52-OLF

KHRUSHCHEV'S DISLOYAL OPPOSITION --
STRUCTURAL CHANGE AND POWER
STRUGGLE IN THE COMMUNIST BLOC.=

COMMUNIST-DOMINATED (CONTINUATION)
RELATIONS.=            SANDIT-56-CDE

COMMUNISTS
THE JACOBIN LEFT AND THE FUTURE OF
THE COMMUNISTS IN LATIN AMERICA.=
ALEXRJ-63-JLF

THE CHINESE COMMUNISTS AND THE
PEASANTS.=            ANON  -52-CCP

IDEOLOGY OF THE CHINESE
COMMUNISTS.=          CHENEK-49-ICC

PIASECKI AND THE POLISH
COMMUNISTS.=          KORAA -57-PPC

NASSER AND THE IRAQI COMMUNISTS.=
LAQUWZ-59-NIC

MOSCOW AND CHINESE COMMUNISTS.=
NORTRC-53-MCC

COMMUNISTS, SOCIALISTS, AND
CHRISTIAN DEMOCRATS
(LATIN AMERICA).=     SZULT -65-CSC

THE COMMUNISTS AND INDIAN LABOR.=
TOOFBM-59-CIL

THE CHINESE COMMUNISTS AND THE
'BOURGEOISIE'.=       WM    -52-CCB

COMMUNITIES
OPINION INFLUENTIALS AND POLITICAL
OPINION FORMATION IN FOUR SWEDISH
COMMUNITIES.=         ANDEB -62-OIP

LEADERSHIP AND COMMUNICATION IN THE
CROFTING COMMUNITIES OF THE OUTER
HEBRIDES.=            CAIRJB-61-LCC

THE CIVIL - RELIGIOUS HIERARCHY IN
MESOAMERICAN COMMUNITIES -- PRE -
SPANISH BACKGROUND AND COLONIAL
DEVELOPMENT.=         CARRP -61-CRH

POPULAR IMAGES OF DECISION-MAKING
IN SUBURBAN COMMUNITIES
(UNITED STATES).=     DYE,TR-62-PID

BRITISH COMMUNITIES.=  FRANR -66-BC

LOCATING LEADERS IN LOCAL
COMMUNITIES -- A COMPARISON OF
SOME ALTERNATIVE APPROACHES
(UNITED STATES).=     FREELC-63-LLL

OPINION LEADERS IN AMERICAN
COMMUNITIES.=         HEROAO-59-OLA

LEADERSHIP FOR ACTION IN RURAL
COMMUNITIES (UNITED STATES).=
KREIBW-60-LAR

THE INDIAN BUSINESS COMMUNITIES AND
THE EVOLUTION OF AN INDUSTRIALIST
CLASS.=               LAMBHB-55-IBC

POWER STRUCTURE AND SOCIOCULTURAL
CHANGE IN LATIN AMERICAN
COMMUNITIES.=         WHITNE-65-PSS

COMMUNITY
THE REPUTATIONAL APPROACH IN THE
STUDY OF COMMUNITY POWER -- A
CRITICAL EVALUATION.= ABU-B -65-RAS

THE INTERRELATIONS BETWEEN LOCAL
GOVERNMENTS AND COMMUNITY
DEVELOPMENT (PHILIPPINES).=
ABUEJV-61-IBL

POWER ATTRIBUTIONS IN THE LOCAL

COMMUNITY            (CONTINUATION)
COMMUNITY -- THEORETICAL AND
RESEARCH CONSIDERATIONS
(UNITED STATES).=     AGGERE-56-PAL

THE POLITICAL STRUCTURE OF A SMALL
COMMUNITY (UNITED STATES).=
AGGERE-56-PSS

COMMUNITY POWER STRUCTURE AND
PARTISANSHIP (UNITED STATES).=
AGGERE-58-CPS

FAMILY STATUS, LOCAL - COMMUNITY
STATUS, AND SOCIAL STRATIFICATION
-- THREE TYPES OF SOCIAL RANKING.=
BARBB -61-FSL

COMMUNITY POWER AND A TYPOLOGY OF
SOCIAL ISSUES.=       BARTEA-59-CPT

POWER STRUCTURE AND THE NEGRO SUB -
COMMUNITY (UNITED STATES).=
BARTEA-59-PSN

COMMUNITY INFLUENCE SYSTEMS --
STRUCTURE AND CHANGE
(UNITED STATES).=     BARTEA-61-CIS

SOCIAL STRATIFICATION AND THE
POLITICAL COMMUNITY.=  BENOR -60-SSP

THE CULTIVATION OF COMMUNITY
LEADERS -- UP FROM THE GRASS ROOTS
(UNITED STATES).=     BIDDWW-53-CCL

ORGANIZATIONAL SUPPORT AND
COMMUNITY POWER STRUCTURE -- THE
HOSPITAL (UNITED STATES).=
BLANLV-62-OSC

COMMUNITY LEADERSHIP -- A CASE
STUDY AND CONCEPTUAL REFINEMENT
(UNITED STATES).=     BONJCM-63-CLC

COMMUNITY LEADERSHIP -- DECISIONS
OF RESEARCH.=         BONJCM-65-CLC

LEGITIMACY AND VISIBILITY --
LEADERSHIP STRUCTURES RELATED TO
FOUR COMMUNITY SYSTEMS
(UNITED STATES).=     BONJCM-65-LVL

POWER STRUCTURE AND COMMUNITY
CHANGE (UNITED STATES).=
BOOTDA-62-PSC

RACIAL DISCRIMINATION AND NEGRO
LEADERSHIP PROBLEMS -- THE CASE OF
A NORTHERN COMMUNITY
(UNITED STATES).=     BOWML -65-RDN

THE POLITICS OF EDUCATION IN THE
LOCAL COMMUNITY (UNITED STATES).=
CAHIRS-64-PEL

COMMUNITY POWER PERSPECTIVES AND
ROLE DEFINITIONS OF NORTH AMERICAN
EXECUTIVES IN AN ARGENTINE
COMMUNITY.=           CHAME -66-CPP

COMMUNITY POWER PERSPECTIVES AND
ROLE DEFINITIONS OF NORTH AMERICAN
EXECUTIVES IN AN ARGENTINE
COMMUNITY.=           CHAME -66-CPP

ECONOMIC DOMINANTS AND COMMUNITY
POWER -- A COMPARATIVE ANALYSIS
(UNITED STATES).=     CLELDA-64-EDC

MEXICAN COMMUNITY STUDIES.=
CLINH -52-MCS

THE INTELLECTUAL AND THE JEWISH

COMMUNITY          (CONTINUATION)
  COMMUNITY (UNITED STATES))=
                      COHEEE-49-IJC

COMMUNITY CONFLICT
(UNITED STATES).=     COLEJS-57-CCU

SCHOOL DESEGREGATION AND NEW
INDUSTRY -- THE SOUTHERN COMMUNITY
LEADER'S VIEWPOINT
(UNITED STATES).=     CRAMMR-63-SDN

DIFFERENTIAL ASSOCIATION AND THE
STRATIFICATION OF THE URBAN
COMMUNITY (UNITED STATES).=
                      CURTRF-63-DAS

THE REPUTATIONAL TECHNIQUE AS A
MEASURE OF COMMUNITY POWER -- AN
EVALUATION BASED ON COMPARATIVE
AND LONGITUDINAL STUDIES.=
                      D'ANWV-62-RTM

INFLUENTIALS IN TWO BORDER CITIES
-- A STUDY IN COMMUNITY
DECISION-MAKING (MEXICO,
UNITED STATES).=      D'ANWV-65-ITB

COMMUNITY LEADERSHIP IN AN ECONOMIC
CRISIS -- TESTING GROUND FOR
IDEOLOGICAL CLEAVAGE
(UNITED STATES).=     D'ANWV-66-CLE

COMMUNITY POWER STRUCTURE --
PROBLEMS AND CONTINUITIES.=
                      DANZMH-64-CPS

A METHOD FOR RANKING COMMUNITY
INFLUENTIALS.=        DICKHR-60-MRC

THE WEST AFRICAN INTELLECTUAL
COMMUNITY.=           DOWVM -62-WAI

INDIA'S CHANGING VILLAGES -- HUMAN
FACTORS IN COMMUNITY DEVELOPMENT.=
                      DUBESC-58-ISC

THE WEEKLY NEWSPAPER'S LEADERSHIP
ROLE AS SEEN BY COMMUNITY LEADER'S
(UNITED STATES).=     EDELAS-63-WNS

THE REPUTATIONAL APPROACH TO THE
STUDY OF COMMUNITY POWER.=
                      EHRLHJ-61-RAS

NEWSPAPER CITATION AND REPUTATION
FOR COMMUNITY LEADERSHIP
(UNITED STATES).=     EHRLHJ-65-NCR

POLITICS IN AN URBAN AFRICAN
COMMUNITY.=           EPSTAL-58-PUA

POLITICAL UNIFICATION -- A
COMPARATIVE STUDY OF LEADERS AND
FOLLOWERS (UNITED ARAB REPUBLIC,
FEDERATION OF THE WEST INDIES,
SCANDINAVIA, EUROPEAN ECONOMIC
COMMUNITY).=          ETZIA -65-PUC

A TYPOLOGY OF COMMUNITY LEADERSHIP
BASED ON INFLUENCE AND INTERACTION
WITHIN THE LEADER SUBSYSTEM
(UNITED STATES).=     FANEAA-56-TCL

NATIONAL ECONOMIC INTEREST AND
POLICY FORMATION IN THE EEC
(EUROPEAN ECONOMIC COMMUNITY).=
                      FELDW -66-NEI

COMMUNITY - POWER STUDIES -- A
CRITIQUE.=            FISHSN-62-CPS

INTEGRATION AND CLEAVAGE AMONG

COMMUNITY          (CONTINUATION)
  COMMUNITY INFLUENTIALS IN TWO
  BORDER CITIES (MEXICO,
  UNITED STATES).=    FORMWH-59-ICA

INDUSTRY, LABOR AND COMMUNITY
(UNITED STATES).=     FORMWH-60-ILC

ORGANIZED LABOR'S IMAGE OF
COMMUNITY POWER STRUCTURE
(UNITED STATES).=     FORMWH-60-OLS

COMMUNITY INFLUENTIALS IN A
MIDDLE-SIZED CITY
(UNITED STATES).=     FORMWH-61-CIM

COMMUNITY AND LABOR INFLUENTIALS --
A COMPARATIVE STUDY OF
PARTICIPATION AND IMAGERY
(UNITED STATES).=     FORMWH-63-CLI

BRITISH COMMUNITY STUDIES --
PROBLEMS OF SYNTHESIS.=
                      FRANR -66-BCS

LOCAL COMMUNITY LEADERSHIP
(UNITED STATES).=     FREELC-60-LCL

REPUTATION AND RESOURCES IN
COMMUNITY POLITICS
(UNITED STATES).=     GAINWA-66-RRC

REPUTATION AND RESOURCES IN
COMMUNITY POLITICS.=  GAMSWA-66-RRC

THE COMMUNITY OF SCHOLARS
(UNITED STATES).=     GOODP -62-CSU

POLITICAL COMMUNITY AND GROUP
INTEREST IN MODERN INDIA.=
                      GUSFJR-65-PCG

SOCIAL STRATIFICATION IN RELATION
TO ATTITUDES TOWARD SOURCES OF
POWER IN A COMMUNITY
(UNITED STATES).=     HAERJL-56-SSR

PREDICTING A COMMUNITY DECISION --
A TEST OF THE MILLER-FORM THEORY
(UNITED STATES).=     HANSRC-59-PCD

COMMUNITY POWER AND URBAN RENEWAL
SUCCESS (UNITED STATES).=
                      HAWLAH-63-CPU

COMMUNITY LEADERSHIP -- THE
REGIONAL PLAN ASSOCIATION OF
NEW YORK.=            HAYSFB-65-CLR

IN THE FOOTSTEPS OF COMMUNITY
POWER.=               HERSLJ-61-FCP

COMMUNITY POWER STRUCTURE -- A
STUDY OF DECISION MAKERS
(UNITED STATES).=     HUNTF -53-CPS

PUBLIC ADMINISTRATION AND THE
PUBLIC -- PERSPECTIVES TOWARD
GOVERNMENT IN A METROPOLITAN
COMMUNITY (UNITED STATES).=
                      JANOM -58-PAP

COMMUNITY POLITICAL SYSTEMS
(UNITED STATES).=     JANOM -61-CPS

COMMUNITY AND 'POLICY SCIENCE'
RESEARCH (UNITED STATES).=
                      JANOM -62-CPS

COMMUNITY INFLUENTIALS -- THE
ELITES OF ATLANTA
(UNITED STATES).=     JENNMK-64-CIE

COMPARATIVE                (CONTINUATION)
                          PRESRV-58-SAC

THE SALA MODEL -- AN ECOLOGICAL
APPROACH TO THE STUDY OF
COMPARATIVE ADMINISTRATION.=
                          RIGGFW-62-SME

COLLECTIVE NEGOTIATIONS BETWEEN THE
STATE AND ITS OFFICIALS -- A
COMPARATIVE ESSAY.=   SCHMF -62-CNB

AN APPROPRIATIONS SUBCOMMITTEE AND
ITS CLIENT AGENCIES -- A
COMPARATIVE STUDY OF SUPERVISION
AND CONTROL (UNITED STATES).=
                      SHARI -65-ASI

THE INTELLECTUALS AND THE POWERS --
SOME PERSPECTIVES FOR COMPARATIVE
ANALYSIS.=            SHILE -58-IPP

CURRENT TRENDS IN COMPARATIVE
COMMUNITY STUDIES.=   SWANBE-62-CTC

COMPARATIVE ADMINISTRATIVE SYSTEMS
-- A SURVEY AND EVALUATION OF
COMPARATIVE RESEARCH.=
                      TICKFJ-58-CAS

COMPARATIVE ADMINISTRATIVE SYSTEMS
-- A SURVEY AND EVALUATION OF
COMPARATIVE RESEARCH.=
                      TICKFJ-58-CAS

TOWARD A COMPARATIVE POLITICS OF
MOVEMENT REGIMES.=    TUCKRC-61-TCP

COMPARATIVE POLITICAL CULTURE.=
                      VERBS -66-CPC

POLITICAL ADVANCEMENT IN THE SOUTH
PACIFIC -- A COMPARATIVE STUDY OF
COLONIAL PRACTICE IN FIJI, TAHITI,
AND AMERICAN SAMOA.=  WESTFJ-61-PAS

THE PERSONALITY OF LAWYERS -- A
COMPARATIVE STUDY OF SUBJECTIVE
FACTORS IN LAW, BASED ON
INTERVIEWS WITH GERMAN LAWYERS.=
                      WEYRWO-64-PLC

TWO CITIES OF LATIN AMERICA -- A
COMPARATIVE DESCRIPTION OF SOCIAL
CLASSES.=             WHITAH-64-TCL

GENTLEMANLY POWER -- BRITISH
LEADERSHIP AND THE PUBLIC SCHOOL
TRADITION -- A COMPARATIVE STUDY
IN THE MAKING OF RULERS.=
                      WILKR -64-GPB

FOUR CITIES -- A STUDY IN
COMPARATIVE POLICY-MAKING
(UNITED STATES).=     WILLOP-63-FCS

ORIENTAL DESPOTISM -- A COMPARATIVE
STUDY OF TOTAL POWER.=
                      WITTK -57-ODC

PARTY FACTIONS AND COMPARATIVE
POLITICS -- SOME PRELIMINARY
OBSERVATIONS.=        ZARIR -60-PFC

COMPARISON
POTENTIAL ELITES IN GHANA AND THE
IVORY COAST -- A PRELIMINARY
COMPARISON.=          CLIGRP-64-PEG

BRITISH MASS PARTIES IN COMPARISON
WITH AMERICAN PARTIES.=
                      EPSTLD-56-BMP

LOCATING LEADERS IN LOCAL

COMPARISON                (CONTINUATION)
COMMUNITIES -- A COMPARISON OF
SOME ALTERNATIVE APPROACHES
(UNITED STATES).=     FREELC-63-LLL

A BRIEF COMPARISON OF THE PUBLIC
SERVICES OF CANADA AND CEYLON.=
                      HARRRL-63-BCP

ALIENATION AND PARTICIPATION -- A
COMPARISON OF GROUP LEADERS AND
THE MASS (UNITED STATES).=
                      ROSEAM-62-APC

THE INTELLIGENTSIA IN COMMUNIST
CHINA -- A TENTATIVE COMPARISON.=
                      SCHWBI-60-ICC

COMPARISONS
SOURCES OF ADMINISTRATIVE BEHAVIOR
-- SOME SOVIET AND WESTERN
EUROPEAN COMPARISONS.=
                      ARMSJA-65-SAB

COMPETENCE
LEADERSHIP STYLE AND POLITICAL
COMPETENCE (ITALY).=  BARNSH-67-LSP

COMPETING
THE LATIN AMERICAN MILITARY AS A
POLITICALLY COMPETING GROUP IN
TRANSITIONAL SOCIETY.=
                      JOHNJJ-62-LAM

COMPETITION
THE ALABAMA SENATORIAL ELECTION OF
1962 -- RETURN OF INTER-PARTY
COMPETITION (UNITED STATES).=
                      BURNWD-64-ASE

INTER - PARTY COMPETITION, ECONOMIC
VARIABLES, AND WELFARE POLICIES IN
THE AMERICAN STATES.= DAWSRE-63-IPC

ELECTORAL COMPETITION AND ELECTORAL
SYSTEMS IN LARGE CITIES
(UNITED STATES).=     GILBCE-62-ECE

INTERSERVICE COMPETITION AND THE
POLITICAL ROLES OF THE ARMED
SERVICES (UNITED STATES).=
                      HUNTSP-61-ICP

INTER - PARTY COMPETITION IN
BRITAIN , 1950-1959.= JONECO-63-IPC

THE STRUCTURE OF COMPETITION FOR
OFFICE IN THE AMERICAN STATES.=
                      SCHLJA-60-SCC

BIFACTIONAL RIVALRY AS AN
ALTERNATIVE TO TWO - PARTY
COMPETITION (UNITED STATES).=
                      SINDAP-55-BRA

INTER - PARTY COMPETITION AND
PRIMARY CONTESTING -- THE CASE OF
INDIANA (UNITED STATES).=
                      STANWH-58-IPC

SPATIAL MODELS OF PARTY
COMPETITION.=         STOKDE-63-SMP

COMPETITIVE
URBANIZATION AND COMPETITIVE PARTY
POLITICS (UNITED STATES).=
                      CUTRP -63-UCP

COMPETITIVE PRESSURE AND DEMOCRATIC
CONSENT -- AN INTERPRETATION OF
THE 1952 PRESIDENTIAL ELECTION
(UNITED STATES).=     JANOM -55-CPD

74

CONFLICT              (CONTINUATION)
                    GULLJT-56-MUC

CONFLICT AND CHANGE IN LITERATURE
(SOVIET UNION).=        HAYWM -63-CCL

THE INDONESIAN COMMUNIST PARTY AND
CONFLICT IN THE INTERNATIONAL
COMMUNIST MOVEMENT.=   HINDD -64-ICP

POLITICAL CONFLICT POTENTIAL,
POLITIZATION, AND THE PEASANTRY IN
THE UNDERDEVELOPED COUNTRIES.=
                    HINDD -65-PCP

DIMENSIONS AND AXES OF SUPREME
COURT DECISIONS -- A STUDY IN THE
SOCIOLOGY OF CONFLICT
(UNITED STATES).=    JESSB -55-DAS

THE CONFLICT BETWEEN OLD AND NEW IN
THE CHINESE ARMY.=   JOFFE -64-CBO

YOUTH VS REGIME -- CONFLICT IN
VALUES (SOVIET UNION).=
                    KASSA -57-YVR

CONSISTENT REACTIVE PARTICIPATION
OF GROUP MEMBERS AND REDUCTION OF
INTERGROUP CONFLICT.= KATZD -59-CRP

SINHALESE NATIONALISM AND SOCIAL
CONFLICT IN CEYLON.=  KEARRN-64-SNS

RACIAL CRISIS IN AMERICA --
LEADERSHIP IN CONFLICT.=
                    KILLL -64-RCA

CONFLICT AND LEADERSHIP -- THE
PROCESS OF DECISION AND THE NATURE
OF AUTHORITY.=     LASSHD-66-CLP

THE ROLE OF SANCTION IN CONFLICT
RESOLUTION.=       LASSHD-67-RSC

LEADERSHIP AND CONFLICT WITHIN THE
FEBRERISTA PARTY OF PARAGUAY.=
                    LEWIPH-67-LCW

THE SOVIET ELITE -- 1 --
GENERATIONS IN CONFLICT.=
                    LEWYB -67-SEG

PARTY CONFLICT IN ZANZIBAR.=
                    LOFCM -63-PCZ

ATTITUDE CONSENSUS AND CONFLICT IN
AN INTEREST -- AN ASSESSMENT OF
COHESION (UNITED STATES).=
                    LUTTNR-66-ACC

THE HOUSE COMMITTEE ON WAYS AND
MEANS -- CONFLICT MANAGEMENT IN A
CONGRESSIONAL COMMITTEE
(UNITED STATES).=   MANLJF-65-HCW

PARTY, REGION AND THE DIMENSION OF
CONFLICT IN THE HOUSE OF
REPRESENTATIVES, 1949-1954
(UNITED STATES).=   MARWG -67-PRD

ISSUE CONFLICT AND CONSENSUS AMONG
PARTY LEADERS AND FOLLOWERS
(UNITED STATES).=   MCCLH -60-ICC

THE COMMUNITY BASIS OF CONFLICT IN
SCHOOL SYSTEM POLITICS
(UNITED STATES).=   MINADW-66-CBC

QUASI - PARTISAN CONFLICT IN A ONE
- PARTY LEGISLATIVE SYSTEM -- THE
FLORIDA SENATE, 1947-1961

CONFLICT            (CONTINUATION)
(UNITED STATES).=   PARSMB-62-QPC

THE CONFLICT BETWEEN CHURCH AND
STATE IN LATIN AMERICA.=
                    PIKEFB-64-CBC

CONFLICT AND DECISION-MAKING IN
SOVIET RUSSIA -- A CASE STUDY OF
AGRICULTURAL POLICY, 1953-1963.
                    PLOSSI-65-CDM

INTRA - PARTY CONFLICT IN THE BIHAR
CONGRESS (INDIA).=   ROY,R -66-IPC

ROLE CONFLICT AND AMBIVALENCE IN
LEADERSHIP.=       SEEMM -53-RCA

REACTION AND REVOLUTION IN
LATIN AMERICA -- THE CONFLICT
SOCIETY.=         SILVKH-61-RRL

CONSENSUS, CONFLICT, AND THE
CANADIAN PARTY SYSTEM.=
                    SMILDV-61-CCC

STATESMANSHIP OR CRAFTSMANSHIP --
CURRENT CONFLICT OVER THE SUPREME
COURT (UNITED STATES).=
                    STEARJ-58-SOC

SOCIAL CONFLICT AND MINORITY
ASPIRATIONS IN INDONESIA.=
                    VAN-JM-50-SCM

IMAGES IN THE CONTEXT OF
INTERNATIONAL CONFLICT -- SOVIET
PERCEPTIONS OF THE U.S. AND THE
U.S.S.R.=         WHITRK-65-ICI

CLASS STRUCTURE AND CLASS CONFLICT
IN HAITIAN SOCIETY.=  WINGR -65-CSC

INTRA - PARTY CONFLICT IN A
DOMINANT PARTY -- THE EXPERIENCE
OF ITALIAN CHRISTIAN DEMOCRACY.=
                    ZARIR -65-IPC

CONFLICTING
CONFLICTING ORIENTATION IN SOVIET
LEADERSHIP.=       BIODJ -61-COS

THE 'CLASS STRUGGLE' IN AFRICA --
AN EXAMINATION OF CONFLICTING
THEORIES (WEST AFRICA).=
                    GRUNKW-64-CSA

CONFLICTING FORCES IN ARGENTINA.=
                    HUELD -62-CFA

CONFLICTS
SOCIAL CONFLICTS AT THE TWENTIETH
PARTY CONGRESS (SOVIET UNION).=
                    ACHMH -56-SCT

CONFLICTS OF POWER IN MODERN
CULTURE -- SEVENTH SYMPOSIUM.=
                    BRYSL -47-CPM

CONFLICTS WITHIN THE INDIAN
COMMUNIST PARTY    CARRR -55-CWI

MASS COMMUNICATIONS AND THE LOSS OF
FREEDOM IN NATIONAL
DECISION-MAKING -- A POSSIBLE
RESEARCH APPROACH TO INTERSTATE
CONFLICTS.=       DEUTKW-57-MCL

DECISIONAL CONFLICTS -- A
THEORETICAL ANALYSIS (GERMANY,
GREAT BRITAIN, UNITED STATES).=
                    JANIIL-59-DCT

CONFORMITY
STUDYING THE STUDENTS -- BETWEEN

CONFORMITY          (CONTINUATION)
CONFORMITY AND DISSENT
(SOVIET UNION).=          CALLT -60-SSB

THE FOLKWAYS OF THE UNITED STATES
SENATE -- CONFORMITY TO GROUP
NORMS AND LEGISLATIVE
EFFECTIVENESS.=          MATTDR-59-FUS

COMMUNISM, CONFORMITY, AND CIVIL
LIBERTIES (UNITED STATES).=
                        STOUSA-55-CCC

CONFUCIAN
CONFUCIAN CHINA AND ITS MODERN FATE
-- THE PROBLEM OF INTELLECTUAL
CONTINUITY.=          LEVEJR-58-CCI

CONFUSION
POLITICS, POWER AND CONFUSION
(UNITED STATES, POWER ELITE
REVIEW).=          HERMFA-56-PPC

CONGO
THE PROBLEMS OF ELITES IN THE
BELGIAN CONGO.=          BRAUGE-56-PEB

NATIONAL UNITY AND REGIONALISM IN
EIGHT AFRICAN STATES (NIGERIA,
NIGER, THE CONGO, GABON, CENTRAL
AFRICAN REPUBLIC, CHAD, UGANDA,
ETHIOPIA).=          CARTGM-66-NUR

POLITICAL AWAKENING IN THE BELGIAN
CONGO -- THE POLITICS OF
FRAGMENTATION.=          LEMAR -64-PAB

AFRICA -- THE PRIMACY OF POLITICS
(CONGO, NIGERIA).=          SPIRHJ-66-APP

CONGRESS
SOCIAL CONFLICTS AT THE TWENTIETH
PARTY CONGRESS (SOVIET UNION).=
                        ACHMH -56-SCT

POLITICAL ASPECTS OF THE NATIONAL
PEOPLE'S CONGRESS (CHINA).=
                        ADIEWA-62-PAN

THE SOCIAL COMPOSITION OF THE
TWENTIETH PARTY CONGRESS
(SOVIET UNION).=          ANON  -56-SCT

TOWARD PERSONAL DICTATORSHIP OR
OLIGARCHY -- SOVIET DOMESTIC
POLITICS SINCE THE TWENTIETH
CONGRESS.=          ARMSJA-58-TPD

KHRUSHCHEV AFTER THE TWENTY-FIRST
PARTY CONGRESS (SOVIET UNION).=
                        AVTOA -59-KAT

CONGRESS AT WORK (UNITED STATES).=
                        BAILSK-52-CWU

THE NEW CONGRESS (UNITED STATES).=
                        BAILSK-66-NCU

THE AFRICAN PATRIOTS -- LEADERSHIP
OF AFRICAN NATIONAL CONGRESS.=
                        BENSM -64-APL

THE 21ST CONGRESS AND SOVIET
POLICY.=          BIALS -59-SCS

PRESIDENT AND CONGRESS
(UNITED STATES).=          BINKWE-47-PCU

FACTIONAL POLITICS IN AN INDIAN
STATE -- THE CONGRESS PARTY IN
UTTAR PRADESH.=          BRASPR-65-FP

EXCELLENCE AND LEADERSHIP IN

CONGRESS          (CONTINUATION)
PRESIDENT AND CONGRESS
(UNITED STATES).=          BURNJM-61-ELP

THE SENIORITY RULE IN CONGRESS
(UNITED STATES).=          CELLE -61-SRC

LEADERSHIP OF THE CONGRESS PARTY
(INDIA).=          CRANRI-59-LCP

CONGRESS AND FOREIGN POLICY
(UNITED STATES).=          DAHLRA-50-CFP

THE POWER OF THE PURSE --
APPROPRIATIONS POLITICS IN
CONGRESS (UNITED STATES).=
                        FENNRF-66-PPA

THE ORGANIZATIONAL DEVELOPMENT OF
INDIA'S CONGRESS PARTY.=
                        FRANMF-62-ODI

THE IMPORTANCE OF INDIVIDUALITY IN
VOTING IN CONGRESS.=          FROMLA-63-IIV

THE SENIORITY SYSTEM IN CONGRESS
(UNITED STATES).=          GOODG -59-SSC

SUBCOMMITTEES -- THE MINIATURE
LEGISLATURES OF CONGRESS
(UNITED STATES).=          GOODG -62-SML

THE CONGRESS PARTY -- A CONCEPTUAL
STUDY (INDIA).=          GOYAOP-64-CPC

SECTIONAL BIASES IN CONGRESS ON
FOREIGN POLICY (UNITED STATES).=
                        GRASGL-51-SBC

THE ROLE OF THE SOVIET PARTY
CONGRESS.=          HO    -52-RSP

THE CABINET AND CONGRESS
(UNITED STATES).=          HORNS -60-CCU

REPRESENTATION IN CONGRESS -- THE
CASE OF THE HOUSE AGRICULTURE
COMMITTEE (UNITED STATES).=
                        JONECO-61-RCC

THE AMERICAN LEGISLATIVE PROCESS --
CONGRESS AND THE STATES.=
                        KEEFWJ-64-ALP

LEADERS AND CLASSES IN THE INDIAN
NATIONAL CONGRESS, 1918-1939.=
                        KEMPT -64-LCI

THE TWENTIETH CPSU CONGRESS -- A
STUDY IN CALCULATED MODERATION
(SOVIET UNION).=          KENNCC-56-TCC

PRESIDENTIAL LEADERSHIP IN CONGRESS
ON FOREIGN POLICY -- A REPLICATION
OF A HYPOTHESIS (UNITED STATES).=
                        KESSM -65-PLC

PROFESSIONAL STAFFS OF CONGRESS.=
                        KOFMK -62-PSC

INDIA -- THE CONGRESS SYSTEM ON
TRIAL.=          KOTHR -67-ICS

THE DEVELOPMENT OF THE INDIAN
NATIONAL CONGRESS AS A MASS
ORGANIZATION, 1919-1923.=
                        KRISG -66-DIN

DIMENSIONS OF CONGRESSIONAL VOTING
-- A STATISTICAL STUDY OF THE
HOUSE OF REPRESENTATIVES IN THE
EIGHTY-FIRST CONGRESS

CONGRESSIONAL          (CONTINUATION)
    CONGRESSIONAL DILEMMA
    (UNITED STATES).=          ROURFE-60-ASC

    CONGRESSIONAL COMMITTEE MEMBERS AS
    INDEPENDENT AGENCY OVERSEERS -- A
    CASE STUDY (UNITED STATES).=
                                SCHES -60-CCM

    ADMINISTRATIVE RESPONSIBILITY --
    CONGRESSIONAL PRESCRIPTION OF
    INTERAGENCY RELATIONSHIPS
    (UNITED STATES).=          SMITJM-57-ARC

    CONGRESSIONAL RECRUITMENT AND
    REPRESENTATION (UNITED STATES).=
                                SNOWLM-66-CRR

    THE CONGRESSIONAL PARTY -- A CASE
    STUDY (UNITED STATES).=
                                TRUMDB-59-CPC

    THE AGE FACTOR IN THE 1958
    CONGRESSIONAL ELECTIONS
    (UNITED STATES).=          WALKDB-60-AFC

CONGRESSMAN
    THE CONGRESSMAN -- HIS WORK AS HE
    SEES IT (UNITED STATES).=
                                CLAPCL-63-CHW

    THE CONGRESSMAN'S CONCEPTION OF HIS
    ROLE (UNITED STATES).=
                                HAWVCF-63-CSC

CONGRESSMEN
    WHAT DO CONGRESSMEN HEAR -- THE
    MAIL (UNITED STATES).=
                                DEXTLA-56-WDC

    CONGRESSMEN AND THE MAKING OF
    MILITARY POLICY (UNITED STATES).=
                                DEXTLA-63-CMM

    CONGRESSMEN AND THEIR
    CONSTITUENCIES (UNITED STATES).=
                                FROMLA- -CTC

    SOUTHERN CONGRESSMEN AND THE 'NEW
    ISOLATIONISM' (UNITED STATES).=
                                LERCCO-60-SCN

    PARTY LOYALTY AMONG CONGRESSMEN --
    THE DIFFERENCE BETWEEN DEMOCRATS
    AND REPUBLICANS, 1947-1962
    (UNITED STATES).=          MAYHOR-66-PLA

    LIBERALISM OF CONGRESSMEN AND THE
    PRESIDENTIAL VOTE IN THEIR
    DISTRICT (UNITED STATES).=
                                WALDLK- 6-LCP

CONNECTIONS
    THE SOCIAL BACKGROUND AND
    CONNECTIONS OF 'TOP
    DECISION-MAKERS' (GREAT BRITAIN).=
                                LUPTT -59-SBC

    THE SOCIAL BACKGROUND AND
    CONNECTIONS OF TOP DECISION-MAKERS
    (GREAT BRITAIN).=          WILSCS-59-SBC

CONQUERORS
    CONQUERORS AND RULERS -- SOCIAL
    FORCES IN MEDIEVAL CHINA.=
                                EBERW -52-CRS

CONSCIOUSNESS
    SOCIAL CLASSES AND CLASS
    CONSCIOUSNESS IN THE USSR.=
                                BEALCP-58-SCC

    IDEOLOGY AND CLASS CONSCIOUSNESS IN

CONSCIOUSNESS       (CONTINUATION)
    THE MIDDLE CLASS (UNITED STATES).=
                                DEGRG -50-ICC

    BRITISH CLASS CONSCIOUSNESS AND THE
    LABOUR PARTY.=            EPSTLD-62-BCC

    CONSCIOUSNESS AND SOCIETY.=
                                HUGHHS-59-CS

    CLASS CONSCIOUSNESS AND CLASS
    SOLIDARITY IN THE NEW ETHIOPIAN
    ELITE.=                    LEVION-66-CCC

    CLASS CONSCIOUSNESS AMONG THE
    YORUBA (WESTERN NIGERIA).=
                                LLOYPC-66-CCA

    LEADERSHIP INTERACTION, GROUP
    CONSCIOUSNESS, AND SOCIAL CHANGE.=
                                LOWRRP-64-LIG

    CLASS STRUCTURE IN THE SOCIAL
    CONSCIOUSNESS.=            CSSOS -63-CSS

CONSENSUS
    PATTERNS OF CONSENSUS IN DEVELOPING
    COUNTRIES.=                ASHFDE-61-PCC

    ELITE CONSENSUS AND DEMOCRACY
    (UNITED STATES).=          BACHP -62-ECC

    CONSENSUS AND CLEAVAGE IN BRITISH
    POLITICAL IDEOLOGY.=       CHRIJB-65-CCB

    ORGANIZATIONAL CONSEQUENCES OF
    PROFESSIONAL CONSENSUS -- LAWYERS
    AND SELECTION OF JUDGES
    (UNITED-STATES).=          LADIJ -66-OCP

    ATTITUDE CONSENSUS AND CONFLICT IN
    AN INTEREST -- AN ASSESSMENT OF
    COHESION (UNITED STATES).=
                                LUTTNR-66-ACC

    ISSUE CONFLICT AND CONSENSUS AMONG
    PARTY LEADERS AND FOLLOWERS
    (UNITED STATES).=          MCCLH -60-ICC

    CONSENSUS AND IDEOLOGY IN AMERICAN
    POLITICS.=                 MCCLH -64-CIA

    CONSENSUS OR ELITE DOMINATION --
    THE CASE OF BUSINESS.=
                                NETTJP-65-COE

    LEADERSHIP AND CONSENSUS IN A NEW
    GUINEA SOCIETY.=           READKE-60-LCN

    THE EMERGING ANTI - COLONIAL
    CONSENSUS IN THE UNITED NATIONS.=
                                ROWEET-64-EAC

    CONSENSUS, CONFLICT, AND THE
    CANADIAN PARTY SYSTEM.=
                                SMILDV-61-CCC

    CONSENSUS AND CLEAVAGE -- PARTY
    ALIGNMENT IN GREECE, 1945-1965.=
                                TROMTP-66-CCP

    CONSENSUS AND MASS COMMUNICATION.=
                                WIRTL -48-CMC

CONSENSUS-BUILDING
    CONSENSUS-BUILDING IN THE AMERICAN
    NATIONAL COMMUNITY -- SOME
    HYPOTHESES AND SOME SUPPORTING
    DATA.=                     ROSEJN-62-CBA

CONSENT
    THE ENGINEERING OF CONSENT

CONTROVERSIAL          (CONTINUATION)
CONTROVERSIAL PORTRAIT.=
                            DE HFU-60-ICP


CONTROVERSY
THE MORSE COMMITTEE ASSIGNMENT
CONTROVERSY -- A STUDY IN SENATE
NORMS (UNITED STATES).=
                            HUITRK-57-MCA

THE ROLE OF THE FEDERAL DISTRICT
COURTS IN THE SEGREGATION
CONTROVERSY (UNITED STATES).=
                            STEARJ-60-RFC


CONURBATION
SIX TRIAL DEFINITIONS --
CONURBATION, ELITE, MIGRATION
PROGRESS, SLUM, UNEMPLOYMENT.=
                            ANON  -55-STD


CONVENTION
NATIONAL CONVENTION LEADERSHIP --
1952 AND 1956 (UNITED STATES).=
                            MARVD -61-NCL

THE MEXICAN REVOLUTION, 1914-1915
-- THE CONVENTION OF
AGUASCALIENTES.=        QUIRRE-60-MRC


CONVENTIONS
TURNOVER IN IOWA STATE PARTY
CONVENTIONS -- AN EXPLORATORY
STUDY (UNITED STATES).=
                            HAHNH -67-TIS

THE EFFECTS OF NOMINATING
CONVENTIONS, ELECTIONS, AND
REFERENCE GROUP IDENTIFICATION
UPON THE PERCEPTIONS OF POLITICAL
FIGURES (UNITED STATES).=
                            RAVEBH-64-ENC

ON THE SUPERIORITY OF NATIONAL
CONVENTIONS.=          WILDAB-62-SNC


CONVERGENCE
LAWYERS IN POLITICS -- A STUDY IN
PROFESSIONAL CONVERGENCE
(UNITED STATES).=      EULAH -64-LPS

URBAN POLITICS -- THE NEW
CONVERGENCE OF POWER
(UNITED STATES).=      SALIRH-64-UPN


COOK ISLANDS
SOCIAL AND POLITICAL CHANGES IN THE
COOK ISLANDS.=        BEAGE -48-SPC


COOLIDGE
COOLIDGE AND PRESIDENTIAL
LEADERSHIP (UNITED STATES).=
                            CORNEE-57-CPL


COOPERATION
TECHNICAL COOPERATION IN
DEVELOPMENT ADMINISTRATION IN
SOUTH AND SOUTHEAST ASIA.=
                            HSUESS-66-TCD


COOPTATION
CONTROL AND COOPTATION IN MEXICAN
POLITICS.=            ANDEB -66-CCM


COORDINATION
THE NATIONAL SECURITY COUNCIL AS A
DEVICE FOR OUTER-DEPARTMENTAL
COORDINATION (UNITED STATES).=
                            HAMMPY-60-NSC


CORRESPONDENTS
LOBBY CORRESPONDENTS


CORRESPONDENTS          (CONTINUATION)
(GREAT BRITAIN).=      EDENG -48-LCG


CORPORATE
CORPORATE GIANTS AND THE POWER
STRUCTURE (UNITED STATES).=
                            BARAMS-56-CGP

INSIDERS AND CONTROLLERS (CORPORATE
ELITE, GREAT BRITAIN).=
                            CROSCA-62-ICC

POWER TO DO WHAT (CORPORATE ELITE,
UNITED STATES).=      HACKA -64-PDW


CORPORATION
THE GOVERNING BOARD OF THE PUBLIC
CORPORATION (GREAT BRITAIN).=
                            ROBSWA-50-GBP


CORPORATIONS
PUBLIC CORPORATIONS AND THE
CLASSIFICATION OF ADMINISTRATIVE
BODIES (GREAT BRITAIN).=
                            CHESON-53-PCC

THE CO-ORDINATION AND CONTROL OF
GOVERNMENT CORPORATIONS IN THE
PHILIPPINES.=          MILNRS-61-COC

THE ROLE OF GOVERNMENT CORPORATIONS
IN THE PHILIPPINES.=  MILNRS-61-RGC

ABSENTEE - OWNED CORPORATIONS AND
COMMUNITY POWER STRUCTURE
(UNITED STATES).=      PELLRJ-56-AOC


CORPS
PARTY AND ARMY -- PROFESSIONALISM
AND POLITICAL CONTROL IN THE
CHINESE OFFICER CORPS, 1949-1964.=
                            JOFFE -65-PAP

PARADES AND POLITICS AT VICHY --
THE FRENCH OFFICERS CORPS UNDER
MARSHAL PETAIN.=      PAXTRO-66-PPV


CORRELATES
IDEOLOGICAL CORRELATES OF RIGHT
WING POLITICAL ALIENATION IN
MEXICO.=              JOHNKF-65-ICR


CORRELATIVES
CORRELATIVES OF LEGISLATIVE VOTING
-- MICHIGAN HOUSE OF
REPRESENTATIVES, 1954-1961
(UNITED STATES).=      BECKRW-62-CLV


CORRUPTION
POWER, CORRUPTION, AND RECTITUDE.=
                            ROGOAA-63-PCR

HISTORICAL AND CULTURAL CONDITIONS
OF POLITICAL CORRUPTION AMONG THE
HAUSA (NORTHERN NIGERIA).=
                            SMITMG-64-HCC


COSMOPOLITAN
LOCAL - COSMOPOLITAN --
UNIDIMENSIONAL OR
MULTIDIMENSIONAL.=    GOLDLC-65-LCU


COSMOPOLITANISM
FROM BOSSES TO COSMOPOLITANISM --
CHANGES IN THE RELATIONSHIP OF
URBAN LEADERSHIP TO STATE POLITICS
(UNITED STATES).=      HAVAWC-64-BCC


COSMOPOLITANS
LOCALS AND COSMOPOLITANS IN
AMERICAN GRADUATE SCHOOLS.=
                            DAVIJA-62-LCA

COSMOPOLITANS AND LOCALS -- TOWARDS

COSMOPOLITANS        (CONTINUATION)
AN ANALYSIS OF LATENT SOCIAL ROLES
(UNITED STATES).=        GOULAW-58-CLT

COSTA RICA
THE PRESIDENTS OF COSTA RICA.=
BUSEJL-61-PCR

POWER STRUCTURE AND ITS
COMMUNICATION BEHAVIOR IN
SAN JOSE, COSTA RICA.=
EDWAHT-67-PSI

SONS OF THE ESTABLISHMENT -- ELITE
YOUTH IN PANAMA AND COSTA RICA.=
GOLDO -66-SEE

COSTS
MEASUREMENT OF SOCIAL POWER
OPPORTUNITY COSTS, AND THE THEORY
OF TWO-PERSON BARGAINING GAMES.=
HARSJC-62-MSP

COUNCIL
PRIVY COUNCIL, CABINET AND MINISTRY
IN GREAT BRITAIN AND CANADA.=
BANKMA-  -PCC

THE LEGISLATIVE COUNCIL
(NEW ZEALAND).=        BENDHJ-49-LCN

THE FRENCH COUNCIL OF STATE --
COMPARATIVE OBSERVATIONS ON THE
PROBLEM OF CONTROLLING BUREAUCRACY
OF THE MODERN STATE.=  DIAMA -51-FCS

THE NATIONAL SECURITY COUNCIL UNDER
TRUMAN, EISENHOWER, AND KENNEDY
(UNITED STATES).=        FALKSL-64-NSC

THE ECONOMIC AND SOCIAL COUNCIL --
POLITICS OF MEMBERSHIP
(UNITED NATIONS, EUROPE).=
GREGRW-63-ESC

THE NATIONAL SECURITY COUNCIL AS A
DEVICE FOR OUTER-DEPARTMENTAL
COORDINATION (UNITED STATES).=
HAMMPY-60-NSC

THE SAUDI ARABIAN COUNCIL OF
MINISTERS.=        HARRCW-58-SAC

COMMUNAL REPRESENTATION IN THE
FIJIAN LEGISLATIVE COUNCIL.=
HUGHCA-60-CRF

THE AMERICAN COUNCIL OF ECONOMIC
ADVISERS AND JOINT COMMITTEE ON
THE ECONOMIC REPORT.=  MILNRS-55-ACE

THE INDIAN COUNCIL OF MINISTERS.=
NORTRC-59-ICM

COUNCIL CHAMBERS OF THE GREAT
PARLIAMENTS.=        PESCK -61-CCG

CROSS - CULTURAL STUDY OF COUNCIL -
MANAGER GOVERNMENT.=  VILLAB-59-CCS

COUNCILLOR
THE WEST AFRICAN COUNCILLOR.=
CAMEID-54-WAC

COUNCILLORS
CONFLICT, DECISION-MAKING AND THE
PERCEPTIONS OF LOCAL COUNCILLORS
(GREAT BRITAIN).=    BLONJ -67-CDM

THE RECRUITMENT OF LOCAL
COUNCILLORS -- A CASE STUDY
(GREAT BRITAIN).=    BOCHJM-66-RLC

COUNCILLORS        (CONTINUATION)
TOWN COUNCILLORS -- A STUDY OF
BARKING (GREAT BRITAIN).=
REESAM-64-TCS

COUNCILMEN
OCCUPATIONAL AFFILIATIONS OF
COUNCILMEN IN SMALL CITIES
(UNITED STATES).=    SPAUCB-51-OAC

CITY COUNCILMEN AND THE GROUP
STRUGGLE -- A TYPOLOGY OF ROLE
ORIENTATIONS (UNITED STATES).=
ZISKBH-65-CCG

COUNCILS
POLISH WORKER'S COUNCILS.=
GRZYK -57-PWS

THE LEGISLATIVE COUNCILS OF PAPUA,
NEW GUINEA.=        HUGHCA-59-LCP

DEFERENCE AND FRIENDSHIP PATTERNS
IN TWO INDIAN MUNICIPAL COUNCILS.=
ROSEDB-66-DFP

COUNSEIL
STATISTICAL ANALYSIS AND
COMPARATIVE ADMINISTRATION -- THE
TURKISH COUNSEIL D'ETATE.=
PRESRV-58-SAC

COUNSEL
PREDICTING SUPREME COURT DECISIONS
MATHEMATICALLY -- A QUANTITIVE
ANALYSIS OF THE RIGHT TO COUNSEL
(UNITED STATES).=    KORTF -57-PSC

COUNTER
THE ANALYSIS OF A COUNTER -
REVOLUTION (FRANCE).=  TILLC -64-ACR

COUNTER-COUP
COUP AND COUNTER-COUP IN THE YAMAN
1948.=        KHADM -52-CCC

COUNTIES
POLITICAL PARTIES AND DECISION
MAKING IN THREE SOUTHERN COUNTIES
(UNITED STATES).=    RHYNEH-58-PPD

COUNTRIES
PATTERNS OF CONSENSUS IN DEVELOPING
COUNTRIES.=        ASHFDE-61-PCD

MASS MEDIA USE BY SUB - ELITES IN
ELEVEN   LATIN AMERICAN COUNTRIES.=
DEUTPJ-61-MMU

LIMITS OF GOVERNMENT ACTIVITY IN
UNDERDEVELOPED COUNTRIES.=
DEYRFJ-57-LGA

INDIRECT RULE AND REPRESENTATIVE
GOVERNMENT (BRITISH COMMONWEALTH
COUNTRIES).=        GUTTWF-59-IRR

DEVELOPMENTALIST TIME AND
LEADERSHIP IN DEVELOPING
COUNTRIES.=        HAHNL -65-DTL

POLITICAL CONFLICT POTENTIAL,
POLITIZATION, AND THE PEASANTRY IN
THE UNDERDEVELOPED COUNTRIES.=
FINDO -65-PCP

POLITICAL CHANGE IN UNDERDEVELOPED
COUNTRIES -- NATIONALISM AND
COMMUNISM.=        KAUTJH-62-PCU

LABOR'S ROLE IN NEWLY DEVELOPING
COUNTRIES.=        LODGGC-59-LSR

CCURT                    (CCNTINUATICN)
  PCLITICAL JURISFRUCENCE
  (UNITED STATES).=        SCHAM -64-LPS

  SCALING SUPREME CCURT DECISIONS IN
  RELATICN TC SCCIAL EACKGROUND
  (UNITED STATES).=        SCHMJ -58-SSC

  STARE DECISIS, CISSENT AND TFE
  BACKGRCUND CF TFE JUSTICES CF TFE
  SUPREME CCURT CF TFE
  UNITEC STATES.=          SCHMJ -62-SCC

  THE SLPREME CCURT AS FINAL ARBITER
  IN FECERAL - STATE RELATICNS
  (UNITED STATES).=        SCHMJR-58-SCF

  THE JUSTICES CF TFE SUPREME COURT
  -- A CCLLECTIVE PCRTRAIT
  (UNITED STATES).=        SCFMJR-59-JSC

  THE SUPREME CCURT -- ITS POLITICS,
  PERSONALITIES, AND PRCCECURES
  (UNITED STATES).=        SCFMJR-60-SCI

  A PSYCHCMETRIC MCCEL CF THE SUPREME
  CCURT (UNITED STATES).=
                          SCHUG -61-PMS

  A SCLUTICN TC INTERMECIATE
  FACTCRIAL RESCLLTICN CFFURSTONE
  AND CEGAN'S STUCY CF THE SUPREME
  COURT (LNITEC STATES).=
                          SCHUG -62-SIF

  THE 196C-1961 TERM CF TFE SUPREME
  CCURT -- A PSYCFCLCGICAL ANALYSIS
  (UNITEC STATES).=        SCHUG -62-TSC

  THE JUCICIAL MINC -- ATTITUDES AND
  IDECLCGIES CF SUPREME CCURT
  JUSTICES 1946-1963
  (UNITED STATES).=        SCFUGA-65-JMA

  THE SLPREME CCURT AND TFE SCUTF
  (UNITED STATES).=        SNISCB-48-SCS

  THE SLPREME CCLRT AS A SMALL GRCUP
  (UNITEC STATES).=        SNYDEC-57-SCS

  UNCERTAINTY ANC TFE SUPREME CCURT'S
  DECISICNS (UNITED STATES).=
                          SNYDEC-59-USC

  PCLITICAL PCWER AND TFE ABILITY TO
  WIN SLPREME CCURT DECISICNS
  (UNITEC STATES).=        SNYDEC-60-PPA

  JUCICIAL PCWER AS A VARIAELE
  MCTIVATING SUPREME CCURT BEHAVICR
  (UNITED STATES).=        SPAEFJ-62-JPV

  AN ANALYSIS CF JUCICIAL ATTITUCES
  IN THE LABCR RELATICNS CECISIONS
  CF THE WARREN CCURT.=    SPAEFJ-63-AJA

  STATESMANSHIP CR CRAFTSMANSFIP --
  CURRENT CCNFLICT CVER TFE SUPREME
  CCURT (LNITED STATES).=
                          STEARJ-58-SOC

  SUPREME CCURT ATTITUCES TCWARC
  FEDERAL ACMINISTRATIVE AGENCIES
  (UNITED STATES).=        TANEJ -60-SCA

  THE ANALYSIS CF BEHAVICR PATTERNS
  CN THE LNITED STATES SUPREME
  CCURT.=                  ULMESS-60-ABP

  SUPREME CCURT BEHAVICR AND CIVIL
  RIGHTS (UNITED STATES).=
                          ULMESS-6C-SCB

HOMECSTATIC TENCENCIES IN TFE

CCURT                    (CCNTINUATICN)
  UNITEC STATES SLPREME CCURT.=
                          ULMESS-61-FTU

  PUBLIC CFFICE IN THE SOCIAL
  BACKGRCUND CF SLPREME CCURT
  JUSTICES.=               ULMESS-62-POS

  SUPREME CCURT BEHAVICR IN RACIAL
  EXCLUSICN CASES -- 1935-1960
  (UNITED STATES).=        ULMESS-62-SCB

CCURTESY
  THE CCURTESY CF THE SENATE
  (UNITED STATES).=        FARRJP-52-CSU

CCURTS
  THE JUDICIAL PRCCESS -- AN
  INTRCDUCTCRY ANALYSIS CF THE
  CCURTS CF TFE UNITED STATES,
  ENGLANC AND FRANCE.=     ABRAFJ-62-JPI

  VCTING BEHAVICR CN THE
  UNITED STATES CCURTS CF APPEALS,
  1961-1964.=              GOLDS -66-VBU

  MCDELS FOR THE ANALYSIS OF FACT -
  ACCEPTANCE BY AFFELLATE COURTS
  (UNITED STATES).=        KCRTF -66-MAF

  CCURTS, JUCGES ANC FCLITICS
  (UNITED STATES).=        MURPWF-61-CJP

  THE RCLE CF THE FECERAL DISTRICT
  CCURTS IN THE SEGREGATICN
  CCNTRCVERSY (UNITED STATES).=
                          STEARJ-6C-RFC

  SECTARIANS IN SCVIET CCURTS.=
                          TAYLPB-65-SSC

  CCURTS AS PCLITICAL ANC
  GCVERNMENTAL ACENCIES
  (UNITED STATES).=        VINEKN-65-CPC

CPSU
  THE ECUCATICNAL BACKGRCUNDS ANC
  CAREER CRIENTATIONS CF TFE MEMBERS
  OF THE CENTRAL CCMMITTEE CF TFE
  CPSL (SCVIET UNICN).=    GEHLMP-66-EBC

  THE TWENTIETH CFSU CCNGRESS -- A
  STUDY IN CALCULATEC MCDERATION
  (SCVIET UNICN).=         KENNCD-56-TCC

  CHANGING RCLES CF TFE CPSU UNCER
  FIRST SECRETARY KFRLSHCFEV
  (SCVIET UNICN).=         SWEAHR-62-CRC

CRAFTING
  LEACERSFIP ANC CCMMUNICATION IN TFE
  CRAFTING CCMMUNITIES CF THE OUTER
  HEBRICES.=               CAIRJB-61-LCC

CRAFTSMANSHIP
  STATESMANSHIP CR CRAFTSMANSFIP --
  CURRENT CCNFLICT CVER TFE SUPREME
  CCURT (LNITED STATES).=
                          STEARJ-58-SOC

CREATINC
  CREATING PCLITICAL CRCER -- TFE
  PARTY - STATES CF WEST AFRICA
  (MALI, GHANA, SENECAL, CUINEA,
  IVCRY CCAST).=           ZCLBAR-66-CPC

CREATIVE
  THE CREATIVE ELITE IN AMERICA.=
                          WEYLN -66-CEA

CRECLE
  THE SIGNIFICANCE CF TFE WEST

CREOLE                (CONTINUATION)
  AFRICAN CREOLE.=       LITTKL-50-SWA

CREOLEDOM
  CREOLEDOM -- A STUDY OF THE
  DEVELOPMENT OF FREETOWN SOCIETY
  (SIERRA LEONE).=       PORTAT-63-CSD

CRESCENT
  THE CRESCENT AND THE RISING SUN --
  INDONESIAN ISLAM UNDER THE
  JAPANESE OCCUPATION 1942-1945.=
                         BENDHJ-58-CRS

CRISES
  LEADERSHIP AND CRISES.=
                         HAMBRL-58-LC

CRISIS
  BURMA'S POLITICAL CRISIS.=
                         BADGJH-58-BSP

  THE IMPLICATIONS OF THE SUCCESSION
  CRISIS IN THE SOVIET UNION FOR
  EAST-WEST RELATIONS.=  BAUERA-53-ISC

  RACIAL AND MORAL CRISIS -- THE ROLE
  OF LITTLE ROCK MINISTERS
  (UNITED STATES).=      CAMPEQ-59-RMC

  THE FRENCH CP (COMMUNIST PARTY) --
  SIGNS OF CRISIS.=      COLLM -59-FCC

  EGYPT FROM THE FALL OF KING FAROUK
  TO THE FEBRUARY 1954 CRISIS.=
                         COLOM -54-EFK

  COMMUNITY LEADERSHIP IN AN ECONOMIC
  CRISIS -- TESTING GROUND FOR
  IDEOLOGICAL CLEAVAGE
  (UNITED STATES).=      D'ANWV-66-CLE

  CHARISMATIC LEADERSHIP AND CRISIS.=
                         DEVEG -55-CLC

  BRITISH M.P.S AND THEIR LOCAL
  PARTIES -- THE SUEZ CRISIS.=
                         EPSTL -63-BMP

  BRITISH POLITICS IN THE SUEZ
  CRISIS.=               EPSTLD-64-BPS

  THE PRESIDENCY -- CRISIS AND
  REGENERATION (UNITED STATES).=
                         FINEH -60-PCR

  THE ROLE OF THE SOVIET ARMY IN THE
  CRISIS OF THE COLLECTIVE
  LEADERSHIP.=           GALAN -57-RSA

  THE CRISIS IN THE BRITISH CP
  (COMMUNIST PARTY).=    GRAIGW-57-CBC

  THE CRISIS OF THE MIDDLE CLASS.=
                         GRAYH -55-CMC

  ZU-AMA AND PARTIES IN THE LEBANESE
  CRISIS OF 1958.=       HOTTA -61-ZAP

  THE CULTURAL REVOLUTION AND
  LEADERSHIP CRISIS IN COMMUNIST
  CHINA.=                HSUEC -67-CRL

  PUBLIC OPINION AND AMERICAN FOREIGN
  POLICY -- THE QUEMOY CRISIS OF
  1958.=                 IRISMO-60-POA

  LOST SOLDIERS -- THE FRENCH ARMY
  AND EMPIRE IN CRISIS, 1947-1962.=
                         KELLGA-65-LSF

  RACIAL CRISIS IN AMERICA --

CRISIS                (CONTINUATION)
  LEADERSHIP IN CONFLICT.=
                         KILLL -64-RCA

  POLITICAL PARTY SYSTEMS AND CRISIS
  GOVERNMENT -- FRENCH AND ITALIAN
  CONTRASTS.=            LAPAJ -58-PPS

  ACADEMIC MIND -- SOCIAL SCIENTISTS
  IN A TIME OF CRISIS
  (UNITED STATES).=      LAZAPF-58-AMS

  A LEADERSHIP CRISIS
  (UNITED STATES).=      LEACRH-65-LCU

  BEYOND AFRICAN DICTATORSHIP -- THE
  CRISIS OF THE ONE - PARTY STATE.=
                         LEWIWA-65-BAD

  CRISIS IN MOSCOW (SOVIET UNION).=
                         LOWER -55-CMS

  THE CRISIS IN NEGRO LEADERSHIP
  (UNITED STATES).=      MABEC -64-CNL

  THE COMING CRISIS IN IRAN.=
                         MAHDH -65-CCI

  THE MONARCH AND THE SELECTION OF A
  PRIME MINISTER -- A RE-EXAMINATION
  OF THE CRISIS OF 1931
  (GREAT BRITAIN).=      MODDGC-57-MSP

  LEADERSHIP AND SOCIAL CRISIS.=
                         NISBRA-65-LSC

  A KEY TO SOVIET POLITICS -- THE
  CRISIS OF THE ANTI - PARTY GROUP.=
                         PETHR -62-KSP

  PEKING'S RECOGNITION OF CRISIS
  (CHINA).=              SCHUHF-61-PSR

  POLITICAL ELITES AND POLITICAL
  MODERNIZATION -- THE CRISIS OF
  TRANSITION (LATIN AMERICA).=
                         SCOTRE-67-PEP

  POWERS OF THE PRESIDENT DURING
  CRISIS (UNITED STATES).=
                         SMITJM-60-PPD

  THE AMERICAN SYSTEM IN CRISIS.=
                         TRUMCB-59-ASC

  THE CRISIS IN THE POLISH COMMUNIST
  PARTY.=                ULAMAB-50-CPC

  THE BRITISH CRISIS -- A PROBLEM IN
  ECONOMIC STATESMANSHIP.=
                         WILLJH-49-BCP

  CRISIS AND COMPROMISE -- POLITICS
  IN THE FOURTH REPUBLIC.=
                         WILLPM-64-CCP

  SOME PSYCHOLOGICAL ASPECTS OF
  CRISIS LEADERSHIP.=    WOLFEV-67-PAC

  IRAN IN CONTINUING CRISIS.=
                         YOUNTC-62-ICC

CRITERIA
  CRITERIA FOR RECRUITMENT AND
  SUCCESS IN THE JAPANESE
  BUREAUCRACY, 1866-1900 --
  'TRADITIONAL' AND 'MODERN'
  CRITERIA IN BUREAUCRATIC
  DEVELOPMENT.=          SILBBS-66-CRS

  CRITERIA FOR RECRUITMENT AND
  SUCCESS IN THE JAPANESE

CURTAIN (CONTINUATION)
THE CURTAIN THAT SHIELDS THE
'DIPLOMAT' (LATIN AMERICA,
UNITED STATES).= HANSSG-51-CTS

INTELLECTUAL UNREST BEHIND THE IRON
CURTAIN (POLAND, HUNGARY).=
KECSP -57-IUB

BITTER HARVEST -- THE INTELLECTUAL
REVOLT BEHIND THE IRON CURTAIN
(EAST EUROPE).= STILE -59-BHI

CZECHOSLOVAK
COMMUNIST USE OF THE CZECHOSLOVAK
PARLIAMENT SINCE WORLD WAR II.=
KUBAC -61-CUC

THE COMINTERN AND CZECHOSLOVAK
COMMUNISM -- 1921-1929.=
SKILHG-60-CCC

CZECHOSLOVAKIA
LEADING PERSONALITIES IN EASTERN
EUROPE -- BULGARIA,
CZECHOSLOVAKIA, HUNGARY, POLAND,
ROMANIA.= ANON -57-LPE

PARTY CONTROL AND BUREAUCRATIZATION
IN CZECHOSLOVAKIA.= BECKC -61-PCB

CZECHOSLOVAKIA -- THE PAST
REBURIED.= CUCHI -62-CPR

THE POLITICAL CONTROL OF
CZECHOSLOVAKIA -- A STUDY IN
SOCIAL CONTROL OF A SOVIET STATE.=
GADOI -53-PCC

RECENT TRENDS IN CZECHOSLOVAKIA --
THE WRITERS' CAMPAIGN OF
CRITICISM.= HANAH -66-RTC

THE POLITICS OF THE EUROPEAN
COMMUNIST STATES (BULGARIA,
CZECHOSLOVAKIA, HUNGARY, EAST
GERMANY, POLAND, RUMANIA,
SOVIET UNION, YUGOSLAVIA).=
IONEG -67-PEC

THE COMMUNIST SUBVERSION OF
CZECHOSLOVAKIA, 1938-1948 -- THE
FAILURE OF COEXISTENCE.=
KORBJ -59-CSC

PATTERNS OF LEADERSHIP IN A
COMMUNIST STATE -- CZECHOSLOVAKIA
1946-1958.= KUBAC -61-PLC

TOTALITARIAN YOUTH MOVEMENT AS A
CAREER MECHANISM -- THE CASE IN
CZECHOSLOVAKIA.= KUBAC -65-TYM

CZECHOSLOVAKIA -- STABLE
SATELLITE.= PICKO -58-CSS

NOTES ON COMMUNIST PERSONALITY
TYPES IN CZECHOSLOVAKIA.=
RODNO -50-NCP

REVOLUTIONS IN PRAGUE
(CZECHOSLOVAKIA).= SKILHG-49-RPC

THE FORMATION OF A COMMUNIST PARTY
IN CZECHOSLOVAKIA.= SKILHG-55-FCP

GOTTWALD AND THE BOLSHEVIZATION OF
THE COMMUNIST PARTY OF
CZECHOSLOVAKIA (1929-1939).=
SKILHG-61-GBC

REVOLUTION AND CONTINUITY IN

CZECHOSLOVAKIA (CONTINUATION)
CZECHOSLOVAKIA 1945-1946.=
SKILHG-61-RCC

CZECHOSLOVAKIA -- OUT OF
STALINISM.= TABOE -64-COS

SOCIOLOGY IN EASTERN EUROPE --
CZECHOSLOVAKIA.= TABOE -65-SEE

DADE
DADE COUNTY -- UNBOSSED,
ERRATICALLY LED (UNITED STATES).=
WOODTJ-64-CCU

DAI
TRIAL OF STRENGTH IN INDO-CHINA --
THE BAO DAI EXPERIMENT.=
ASBO -50-TSI

THE BAO DAI EXPERIMENT (VIETNAM).=
HAMMEJ-50-BDE

DAILY
THE SOVIET CITIZEN -- DAILY LIFE IN
A TOTALITARIAN SOCIETY.=
INKEA -59-SCC

DALLAS
THE DECISION-MAKERS -- THE POWER
STRUCTURE OF DALLAS
(UNITED STATES).= THOMCE-63-DMP

DANCE
DANCE OF THE MILLIONS -- MILITARY
RULE AND THE SOCIAL REVOLUTION IN
COLOMBIA, 1930-1956.= FLUHVL-57-DMM

DANGER
DANGER ON THE RIGHT IN GERMANY.=
COVEHM-50-DRG

DANGERS
ON THE DANGERS OF COPYING FROM THE
BRITISH.= NEEDM -62-DCB

DANISH
AN HISTORICAL STUDY OF THE ORIGINS
AND STRUCTURE OF THE DANISH
INTELLIGENTSIA.= GEIGT -50-HSO

DAR
THE DAR UL-ISLAM MOVEMENT IN
WESTERN JAVA.= VAN- -50-DUI

DARK
DARK GHETTOS -- DILEMMAS OF SOCIAL
POWER (UNITED STATES).=
CLARKB-65-DGD

DATA
MACHINE RETRIEVAL OF BIOGRAPHICAL
DATA (EAST EUROPEAN ELITES).=
BECKC -67-MRB

LAWYERS IN POLITICS -- AN EMPIRICAL
EXPLORATION OF BIOGRAPHICAL DATA
ON STATE LEGISLATORS.=
GOLDD -61-LPE

POLITICAL EXTREMISTS IN IRAN -- A
SECONDARY ANALYSIS OF
COMMUNICATIONS DATA.= RINGBB-52-PEI

CONSENSUS-BUILDING IN THE AMERICAN
NATIONAL COMMUNITY -- SOME
HYPOTHESES AND SOME SUPPORTING
DATA.= ROSEJN-62-CBA

PARTICIPANT OBSERVATION AND THE
COLLECTION AND INTERPRETATION OF
DATA.= VIDIAJ-55-POC

DECISIONS            (CONTINUATION)
ANALYSIS OF SUPREME COURT
DECISIONS (UNITED STATES).=
KORTF -58-RFS

MAJORITY DECISIONS AND MINORITY
RESPONSES IN THE UN GENERAL
ASSEMBLY (UNITED NATIONS).=
MANNCS-66-MDM

DECISIONS IN SYRACUSE
(UNITED STATES).=     MARTRC-61-DSL

POLITICAL PARTY AFFILIATION AND
JUDGE'S DECISIONS
(UNITED STATES).=     NAGESS-61-PPA

POLITICAL DECISIONS IN MODERN
SOCIETY.=             RIEZK -54-PDM

VOTING METHODS AND IRRATIONALITY IN
LEGISLATIVE DECISIONS
(UNITED STATES).=     RIKEWH-58-VMI

SCALING SUPREME COURT DECISIONS IN
RELATION TO SOCIAL BACKGROUND
(UNITED STATES).=     SCHMJ -58-SSC

UNCERTAINTY AND THE SUPREME COURT'S
DECISIONS (UNITED STATES).=
SNYDEC-59-USC

POLITICAL POWER AND THE ABILITY TO
WIN SUPREME COURT DECISIONS
(UNITED STATES).=     SNYDEC-60-PPA

AN ANALYSIS OF JUDICIAL ATTITUDES
IN THE LABOR RELATIONS DECISIONS
OF THE WARREN COURT.= SPAEHJ-63-AJA

THE RELATION OF RESEARCH TO
LEGISLATIVE AND ADMINISTRATIVE
DECISIONS (UNITED STATES).=
TAYLPS-47-RRL

DECISIS
STARE DECISIS, DISSENT AND THE
BACKGROUND OF THE JUSTICES OF THE
SUPREME COURT OF THE
UNITED STATES.=       SCHMJ -62-SDC

DECLINE
THE DEVELOPMENT AND DECLINE OF
PATRIMONIAL AND BUREAUCRATIC
ADMINISTRATION.=      DELAW -63-DDP

THE DECLINE OF CONSTITUTIONAL
DEMOCRACY IN INDONESIA.=
FEITH -62-DCC

THE DECLINE AND FALL OF REVISIONISM
IN EASTERN EUROPE.=   GRIFWE-62-DFR

EVALUATING THE DECLINE OF SOUTHERN
INTERNATIONALISM THROUGH
SENATORIAL ROLL CALL VOTES
(UNITED STATES).=     JEWEME-59-EDS

THE DECLINE OF ALGERIA'S FLN
(NATIONAL LIBERATION FRONT).=
LEWIWH-66-DAS

THE DECLINE AND FALL OF SOCIAL
CLASS.=               NISBRA-59-DFS

DECONTROL
THE PHILIPPINE DECONTROL PROGRAM --
THE GOVERNMENT'S POINT OF VIEW.=
CASTAV-61-PDP

DEFAULT
LEADERSHIP BY DEFAULT

DEFAULT             (CONTINUATION)
(UNITED STATES).=     STONON-64-LDU

DEFEAT
THE DEFEAT OF THE PRO - SOVIET
FACTION OF THE JAPANESE COMMUNIST
PARTY.=               KASHA -64-DPS

DEFEAT AND DEMOCRACY IN JAPAN.=
TAKAY -48-DDJ

DEFENDERS
THE MACHIAVELLIANS -- DEFENDERS OF
FREEDOM.=             BURNJ -63-MDF

DEFENSE
CONGRESSIONAL INNOVATION AND
INTERVENTION IN DEFENSE POLICY --
LEGISLATIVE AUTHORIZATION OF
WEAPONS SYSTEMS (UNITED STATES).=
DAWSRH-62-CII

IN YOUR OPINION -- LEADERS' AND
VOTERS' ATTITUDES ON DEFENSE AND
DISARMAMENT (CANADA).=
PAULJ -63-YOL

DEFENSE AND DIPLOMACY -- THE
SOLDIER AND THE CONDUCT OF FOREIGN
RELATIONS.=           VAGTA -56-DDS

DEFERENCE
DEFERENCE AND FRIENDSHIP PATTERNS
IN TWO INDIAN MUNICIPAL COUNCILS.=
ROSEDB-66-DFP

DEFIANT
HUNGARY'S DEFIANT INTELLECTUALS.=
LANDP -58-HSC

DEFINITION
TOWARD A DEFINITION OF THE EXTREME
RIGHT.=               RUSHGB-63-TDE

DEFINITIONS
SIX TRIAL DEFINITIONS --
CONURBATION, ELITE, MIGRATION
PROGRESS, SLUM, UNEMPLOYMENT.=
ANON  -55-STD

ACTIVITIES AND ROLE DEFINITIONS OF
GRASSROOTS PARTY OFFICIALS
(UNITED STATES).=     BOWML -66-ARD

COMMUNITY POWER PERSPECTIVES AND
ROLE DEFINITIONS OF NORTH AMERICAN
EXECUTIVES IN AN ARGENTINE
COMMUNITY.=           CHAME -66-CPP

BUREAUCRATIC MASS MEDIA -- A STUDY
OF ROLE DEFINITIONS
(UNITED STATES).=     LYSTMH-56-BMM

DEGAN
A SOLUTION TO INTERMEDIATE
FACTORIAL RESOLUTION OFFURSTONE
AND DEGAN'S STUDY OF THE SUPREME
COURT (UNITED STATES).=
SCHUG -62-SIF

DEGAULLE
CAN DEGAULLE CHECK THE GAULLISTS
(FRANCE).=            ALANR -59-CDC

UNEASY BALANCE OF DEGAULLE'S
REPUBLIC (FRANCE).=   ALANR -60-UBC

THE POLITICAL METHODS OF GENERAL
DEGAULLE (FRANCE).=   AROLR -61-PMG

DEGENERATION
THE SOVIET POLITICAL SYSTEM --

DEMOCRACY                (CONTINUATION)
    DEMOCRACY.=              TALMJL-52-RTC

    DEMOCRACY IN FRANCE SINCE 1870.=
                            THOMO -64-DFS

    STABILITY AND VITALITY IN SWEDISH
    DEMOCRACY.=             TINGH -55-SVS

    TURKISH POLITICS -- THE ATTEMPT TO
    RECONCILE RAPID MODERNIZATION WITH
    DEMOCRACY.=             ULMAAH-65-TPA

    A CRITIQUE OF THE ELITIST THEORY OF
    DEMOCRACY.=             WALKJL-66-CET

    INTRA - PARTY CONFLICT IN A
    DOMINANT PARTY -- THE EXPERIENCE
    OF ITALIAN CHRISTIAN DEMOCRACY.=
                            ZARIR -65-IPC

DEMOCRAT
    THE EXECUTIVE -- AUTOCRAT,
    BUREAUCRAT, DEMOCRAT
    (UNITED STATES).=       JENNEE-62-EAB

    THE AMATEUR DEMOCRAT -- CLUB
    POLITICS IN THREE CITIES
    (UNITED STATES).=      WILSJQ-62-ADC

DEMOCRATIC
    DEMOCRATIC LEADERSHIP AND MASS
    MANIPULATION.=          ADORTW-65-DLM

    WHITHER SOCIAL DEMOCRATIC PARTY
    (JAPAN).=              AKIST -59-WSD

    THE VENEZUELAN DEMOCRATIC
    REVOLUTION.=           ALEXRJ-64-VDR

    THE THEORY OF DEMOCRATIC ELITISM.=
                            BACHP -67-TDE

    NOTES ON AUTHORITARIAN AND
    DEMOCRATIC LEADERSHIP.=
                            BELLD -65-NAD

    THE FREE DEMOCRATIC PARTY IN WEST
    GERMAN POLITICS.=      BRAUG -60-FDP

    THE GERMAN SOCIAL DEMOCRATIC PARTY
    AND THE INTERNATIONAL SITUATION
    (GERMANY).=            BRETHL-53-GSC

    THE CHRISTIAN DEMOCRATIC PARTY IN
    ITALIAN POLICY.=       CAPPE -61-CDP

    PUBLIC OPINION POLLS AND DEMOCRATIC
    LEADERSHIP (UNITED STATES).=
                            CARTD -46-POP

    THE SOCIAL DEMOCRATIC PARTY OF
    GERMANY -- FROM WORKING CLASS
    MOVEMENT TO MODERN POLITICAL
    PARTY.=                CHALDA-64-SDP

    INTRAPARTY ATTITUDE CONFLICT --
    DEMOCRATIC PARTY LEADERSHIP IN
    CALIFORNIA (UNITED STATES).=
                            COSTE -63-IAC

    A PREFACE TO DEMOCRATIC THEORY
    (UNITED STATES).=      DAHLRA-56-PDT

    GERMAN EXILE POLITICS -- THE SOCIAL
    DEMOCRATIC EXECUTIVE COMMITTEE IN
    THE NAZI ERA.=         EDINLJ-56-GEP

    CHALLENGES TO FACTIONALISM IN
    JAPAN'S LIBERAL DEMOCRATIC PARTY.=
                            FARNLW-66-CFJ

    PERSONALITY AND POLITICAL

DEMOCRATIC                (CONTINUATION)
    SOCIALIZATION -- THE THEORIES OF
    AUTHORITARIAN AND DEMOCRATIC
    CHARACTER.=             GREEFI-65-PPS

    GROUP LEADERSHIP AND DEMOCRATIC
    ACTION.=               HAIMFS-51-GLD

    THE 'DEMOCRATIC PARTIES' -- END OF
    AN EXPERIMENT (CHINA).=
                            HINTHC-58-DPE

    PARTY RESPONSIBILITY AND LOYALTY --
    NEW RULES IN THE DEMOCRATIC PARTY
    (UNITED STATES).=      HOLTA -60-PRL

    DEMOCRATIC PARTY LEADERSHIP IN THE
    SENATE (UNITED STATES).=
                            HUITRK-61-DPL

    PARTY RULE IN A DEMOCRATIC STATE
    (ITALY).=              IVELV -49-PRD

    COMPETITIVE PRESSURE AND DEMOCRATIC
    CONSENT -- AN INTERPRETATION OF
    THE 1952 PRESIDENTIAL ELECTION
    (UNITED STATES).=      JANOM -55-CPD

    ELEMENTS AND PROBLEMS OF DEMOCRATIC
    LEADERSHIP.=           KUTNB -65-EPD

    WOODROW WILSON AND THE DEMOCRATIC
    PARTY.=                LINKAS-56-WWD

    FREEDOM, POWER, AND DEMOCRATIC
    PLANNING.=             MANNK -50-FPD

    AUSTRALIAN DEMOCRATIC LABOR PARTY
    SUPPORT.=              MCOOCA-65-ADL


    THE DEMOCRATIC AND THE
    AUTHORITARIAN STATE -- ESSAYS IN
    POLITICAL AND LEGAL THEORY.=
                            NEUMFL-57-DAS

    THE POLLSTERS -- PUBLIC OPINION,
    POLITICS, AND DEMOCRATIC
    LEADERSHIP (UNITED STATES).=
                            ROGEL -49-PPO

    THE DEMOCRATIC STATE CENTRAL
    COMMITTEE IN MICHIGAN 1949-1959 --
    THE RISE OF THE NEW POLITICS AND
    THE NEW POLITICAL LEADERSHIP
    (UNITED STATES).=      SAWYRL-60-DSC

    THE GERMAN SOCIAL DEMOCRATIC PARTY
    AFTER WORLD WAR 2 -- THE
    CONSERVATISM OF POWER.=
                            SCHEHK-66-GSD

    DILEMMAS OF LEADERSHIP AND DOCTRINE
    IN DEMOCRATIC PLANNING
    (UNITED STATES).=      SELZP -65-DLC

    PATTERNS OF ANTI - DEMOCRATIC
    THOUGHT.=              SPITD -65-PAD

DEMOCRATICA
    THE DEVELOPMENT OF ACCION
    DEMOCRATICA DE VENEZUELA.=
                            KANTH -59-DAD

    ACCION DEMOCRATICA -- REVOLUTION OF
    A MODERN POLITICAL PARTY IN
    VENEZUELA.=            MARTJD-66-ADR

DEMOCRATIZATION
    THE GROWTH AND DEMOCRATIZATION OF

DEVELCPMENT          (CCNTINUATICN)
    DEVELCPMENT.=          CJCRJ -58-YSR

    THE BUREAUCRACY ANC PCLITICAL
    DEVELCPMENT IN VIETNAM.=
                          CCRSJT-63-BPC

    INDIA'S CHANGING VILLAGES -- FUMAN
    FACTORS IN CCMMLNITY CEVELOPMENT.=
                          CUBESC-58-ISC

    BUREAUCRACY ANC PCLITICAL
    DEVELCPMENT.=          EISESN-63-BPC

    THE DEVELCPMENT CF SCCIC-POLITICAL
    CENTERS AT THE SECCNC STAGE CF
    MCDERNISATICN -- A CCMPARATIVE
    ANALYSIS CF TWC TYPES.=
                          EISESN-66-CSP

    NATICNALISM ANC PCLITICAL
    DEVELCPMENT.=          EMERR -60-NPC

    THE DEVELCPMENT ACMINISTRATCR'S
    RCLE -- SCME CCMMENTS
    (PHILIPPINES).=       ENCAV -62-CAS

    ECCNCMIC CEVELCPMENT ANC SOCIAL
    CHANGE IN SCUTH INCIA.=
                          EPSTTS-62-ECS

    SCCIAL FACTCRS IN ECCNCMIC
    CEVELCPMENT -- THE ARGENTINE
    CASE.=                FILLTR-61-SFE

    AUTHCRITY, EFFICIENCY, ANC ROLE
    STRESS -- PRCBLEMS IN THE
    CEVELCPMENT CF EAST AFRICAN
    BUREAUCRACIES (LGANCA, KENYA,
    TANGANYIKA).=         FLEMWG-66-AER

    CAREER CEVELCPMENT CF FILIPINC
    HIGHER CIVIL SERVANTS.=
                          FRANGA-60-CCF

    THE CRGANIZATICNAL CEVELCPMENT CF
    INCIA'S CCNGRESS PARTY.=
                          FRANMF-62-CCI

    PCLITICAL CEVELCPMENT, PCWER, ANC
    COMMUNICATICNS IN TLRKEY.=
                          FREYFW-63-PDP

    THE MASTERS ANC THE SLAVES -- A
    STUCY IN THE CEVELCPMENT OF
    BRAZILIAN CIVILIZATICN.=
                          FREYG -46-MSS

    LABCR AND ECCNCMIC CEVELOPMENT
    (MICCLE EAST, SCUTHEAST ASIA).=
                          GALEW -59-LEC

    EDUCATICN AND CEVELCPMENT --
    CPINICNS CF SECCNCARY SCHOOL
    TEACHERS (LATIN AMERICA).=
                          GCUVAJ-67-EDC

    CHIEFTAINSHIP IN TRANSKEIAN
    PCLITICAL CEVELCPMENT (AFRICA).=
                          HAMMC -64-CTP

    THE AFRICAN UNIVERSITY AND HUMAN
    RESCURCES DEVELCPMENT.=
                          HARKF -65-AUH

    ENTREPRENEURSHIP ANC LABOR SKILLS
    IN INCCNESIAN ECCNCMIC CEVELOPMENT
    -- A SYMPCSIUM.=      HIGGB -61-ELS

    THE BACKGRCUNC ANC CEVELOPMENT OF
    'THE PRCLETARIAN CULTURAL
    REVCLUTICN'.=         HSIAGT-67-BDP

DEVELCPMENT          (CCNTINUATICN)
    TECHNICAL CCCPERATICN IN
    DEVELCPMENT ACMINISTRATICN IN
    SCUTH AND SCUTHEAST ASIA.=
                          HSUESS-66-TCC

    THE ELECTCRAL PRCCESS ANC PCLITICAL
    DEVELCPMENT IN LEBANCN.=
                          HUCSMC-66-EPP

    EDUCATICNAL PCLICY ANC POLITICAL
    CEVELCPMENT IN AFRICA.=
                          HUSSER-46-EPP

    THE DEVELCPMENT CF CAPITALISM IN
    JAPAN.=               IKE,N -49-CCJ

    BUREAUCRACY ANC DEVELCPMENT IN
    PAKISTAN.=            INAY(E-63-BDP

    THE MILITARY IN THE PCLITICAL
    DEVELCPMENT CF NEW NATICNS -- AN
    ESSAY IN CCMPARATIVE ANALYSIS
    (ASIA, AFRICA, MICCLE EAST).=
                          JANCM -64-MPC

    THE BALKANS IN TRANSITICN -- ESSAYS
    CN THE CEVELCPMENT CF BALKAN LIFE
    ANC PCLITICS SINCE THE EIGHTEENTH
    CENTURY.=             JELAC -63-BTE

    THE DEVELCPMENT CF ACCICN
    CEMCCRATICA CE VENEZUELA.=
                          KANTH -59-CAC

    INDIAN ECCNCMISTS ANC ECCNOMIC
    DEVELCPMENT.=         KITTER-55-IEE

    THE JAPAN CCMMUNIST PARTY -- ITS
    DEVELCPMENT SINCE THE WAR.=
                          KIYOE -58-JCP

    THE DEVELCPMENT CF THE INCIAN
    NATICNAL CCNGRESS AS A MASS
    CRGANIZATICN, 1919-1923.=
                          KRISG -66-CIN

    PCLITICAL ELITES ANC THE PRCCESS OF
    ECCNCMIC CEVELCPMENT
    (UNITEC STATES, WESTERN EUROPE,
    SCVIET LNICN).=       LAMBRK-52-PEP

    BUREAUCRACY ANC PCLITICAL
    DEVELCPMENT.=         LAPAJ -63-BPC

    AN CVERVIEW CF BUREAUCRACY ANC
    PCLITICAL CEVELCPMENT.=
                          LAPAJ -63-CBP

    PCLITICAL PARTIES ANC PCLITICAL
    DEVELCPMENT.=         LAPAJG-65-PPP

    GCVERNMENT AND CEVELCPMENT --
    MANAGERIAL ATTITUCES IN
    LATIN AMERICA.=       LAUTA -65-GCM

    PRCBLEMS IN THE CEVELCPMENT OF
    MCDERN LEADERSHIP ANC LCYALTIES IN
    THE BRITISH SCMALILANC
    PROTECTCRATE ANC THE UNITEC
    NATICNS TRUSTEESHIP TERRITORY CF
    SOMALIA.=             LEWIIM-60-PDM

    PCLITICAL ASPECTS CF MCBILITY IN
    CHINA'S URBAN CEVELCPMENT.=
                          LEWIJW-66-PAM

    THE PCLITICAL CLIMATE FCR ECCNOMIC
    DEVELCPMENT (AFRICA).=
                          LEYSC -66-PCE

    EDUCATICN AND FAMILY LIFE IN THE

100

DEVELOPMENT          (CONTINUATION)
DEVELOPMENT OF CLASS
IDENTIFICATION AMONG THE YORUBA
(WESTERN NIGERIA).=     LLOYBB-66-EFL

THE DEVELOPMENT OF POLITICAL
PARTIES IN WESTERN NIGERIA.=
                         LLOYPC-55-DPP

MEXICAN ECONOMIC AND SOCIAL
DEVELOPMENT.=            MARGHB-65-MES

CLASS, CITIZENSHIP AND SOCIAL
DEVELOPMENT.=            MARSTH-64-CCS

ENTREPRENEURSHIP AND ECONOMIC
DEVELOPMENT IN THE MIDDLE EAST.=
                         MEYEAJ-58-EED

RECENT POLITICAL DEVELOPMENT IN
INDIA -- 2.=            MORRWH-59-RPD

THE HIGHER CIVIL SERVICE AS AN
ACTION GROUP IN WESTERN POLITICAL
DEVELOPMENT.=           MORSF -63-HCS

BLOSSOMS IN THE DUST -- THE HUMAN
FACTOR IN INDIAN DEVELOPMENT.=
                         NAIRK -61-BDH

TRADITIONAL AND MODERN TYPES OF
LEADERSHIP AND ECONOMIC
DEVELOPMENT AMONG THE FIJIANS.=
                         NAYARR-64-TMT

THE POLITICAL DEVELOPMENT OF
MEXICO.=                NEEDMC-61-PDM

POLITICAL DEVELOPMENT AND MILITARY
INTERVENTION IN LATIN AMERICA.=
                         NEEDMC-66-PDM

THE NIGERIAN CONSTITUTION --
HISTORY AND DEVELOPMENT.=
                         ODUMOI-63-NCH

THE STAGES OF POLITICAL
DEVELOPMENT.=           ORGAAF-65-SPD

CRECLEDOM -- A STUDY OF THE
DEVELOPMENT OF FREETOWN SOCIETY
(SIERRA LEONE).=        PORTAT-63-CSD

COMMUNICATIONS AND POLITICAL
DEVELOPMENT.=           PYE,LW-63-CPD

POLITICAL CULTURE AND POLITICAL
DEVELOPMENT.=           PYE,LW-66-PCP

UNIVERSITIES AND SOCIAL DEVELOPMENT
(LATIN AMERICA).=       RIBED -67-USD

EAST AFRICAN CHIEFS -- A STUDY OF
POLITICAL DEVELOPMENT IN SOME
UGANDA AND TANGANYIKA TRIBES.=
                         RICHAI-59-EAC

BUREAUCRATS AND POLITICAL
DEVELOPMENT -- A PARADOXICAL
VIEW.=                  RIGGFW-63-BPD

EXECUTIVE DEVELOPMENT IN THE
PHILIPPINES -- PERSPECTIVES AND
APPRAISAL.=             SAMDAG-60-EDP

ELITE RECRUITMENT AND POLITICAL
DEVELOPMENT.=           SELILG-64-ERP

LEADERSHIP IN A NEW NATION --
POLITICAL DEVELOPMENT IN ISRAEL.=
                         SELILG-64-LNN

THE CULTURAL FACTORS IN ECONOMIC

DEVELOPMENT          (CONTINUATION)
AND TECHNOLOGICAL DEVELOPMENT --
AN INDIAN ADMINISTRATIVE
VIEW-POINT.=            SETHSC-65-CFE

INTERNATIONAL BUREAUCRACIES AND
POLITICAL DEVELOPMENT.=
                         SHARWR-63-IBP

INTELLECTUALS, PUBLIC OPINION AND
ECONOMIC DEVELOPMENT.=
                         SHILE -55-IPO

THE INTELLECTUAL IN THE POLITICAL
DEVELOPMENT OF THE NEW STATES.=
                         SHILE -60-IPD

POLITICAL DEVELOPMENT IN THE NEW
STATES -- 1 -- 2.=      SHILE -60-PDN

INFLUENCE AND WITHDRAWAL -- THE
INTELLECTUALS IN INDIAN POLITICAL
DEVELOPMENT.=           SHILE -61-IWI

THE MILITARY IN THE POLITICAL
DEVELOPMENT OF THE NEW STATES.=
                         SHILE -62-MPC

DEMAGOGUES AND CADRES IN THE
POLITICAL DEVELOPMENT OF THE NEW
STATES.=                SHILE -63-DCP

THE THAI BUREAUCRACY --
INSTITUTIONAL CHANGE AND
DEVELOPMENT.=           SIFFWJ-66-TBI

CRITERIA FOR RECRUITMENT AND
SUCCESS IN THE JAPANESE
BUREAUCRACY, 1866-1900 --
'TRADITIONAL' AND 'MODERN'
CRITERIA IN BUREAUCRATIC
DEVELOPMENT.=           SILBBS-66-CRS

NATIONAL VALUES, DEVELOPMENT,
LEADERS AND FOLLOWERS
(LATIN AMERICA).=       SILVKH-63-NVD

THE INTELLECTUALS IN THE MODERN
DEVELOPMENT OF THE ISLAMIC WORLD.=
                         SMITWC-55-IMD

SECONDARY EDUCATION AND THE
DEVELOPMENT OF ELITES
(LATIN AMERICA).=       SOLAA -67-SED

BUREAUCRACY AND ECONOMIC
DEVELOPMENT.=           SPENJJ-63-BED

THE FUTURE OF UNDER-DEVELOPED
COUNTRIES -- POLITICAL
IMPLICATIONS OF ECONOMIC
DEVELOPMENT.=           STANE -54-FUD

PHILIPPINE INTEREST GROUPS -- AN
INDEX OF POLITICAL DEVELOPMENT.=
                         STAURB-65-PIG

SWAZILAND POLITICAL DEVELOPMENT.=
                         STEVRP-63-SPD

BUREAUCRATIC DEVELOPMENT IN
MALAYA.=                TILMRO-66-BDM

THE MILITARY ROLE IN NATION
BUILDING AND ECONOMIC
DEVELOPMENT.=           UNGEJP-63-MRN

THE COMMUNITY DEVELOPMENT PROGRAM
OF THE PHILIPPINE GOVERNMENT.=
                         VILLBU-57-CDP

PARTY POLITICS IN INDIA -- THE

DEVELOPMENT          (CONTINUATION)
DEVELOPMENT OF A MULTIPARTY
SYSTEM.=                 WEINM -57-PPI

TRADITIONAL ROLE PERFORMANCE AND
THE DEVELOPMENT OF MODERN
POLITICAL PARTIES -- THE INDIAN
CASE.=                   WEINM -64-TRP

THE DEVELOPMENT OF THE LABOR
MOVEMENT IN THE
DOMINICAN REPUBLIC.=     WIARHJ-66-DLM

DEVELOPMENTAL
THE TECHNOLOGY - ELITE APPROACH TO
THE DEVELOPMENTAL PROCESS --
PERUVIAN CASE STUDY.=    COHEA -66-TEA

DEVELOPMENTALIST
DEVELOPMENTALIST TIME AND
LEADERSHIP IN DEVELOPING
COUNTRIES.=              FAHNL -65-DTL

DEVELOPMENTS
POLITICAL DEVELOPMENTS IN IRAN,
1951-1954.=              ATYEH -54-PDI

THE PRESS IN LATIN AMERICA, SPAIN
AND PORTUGAL -- A SUMMARY OF
RECENT DEVELOPMENTS.=    CHILRH-65-PLA

CONSTITUTIONAL DEVELOPMENTS IN
NIGERIA.=                EZERK -64-CDN

RECENT POLITICAL DEVELOPMENTS IN
TURKEY AND THEIR SOCIAL
BACKGROUND.=             KARPKH-62-RPD

INTERNAL DEVELOPMENTS -- A BALANCE
SHEET (SOVIET UNION).=
                         LEONW -63-IDB

DEVELOPMENTS IN THE PRESIDENCY AND
THE CONCEPTION OF POLITICAL
LEADERSHIP (UNITED STATES).=
                         SELILG-55-DPC

RELIGIOUS ELITES --
DIFFERENTIATIONS AND DEVELOPMENTS
IN ROMAN CATHOLICISM
(LATIN AMERICA).=        YALLI -67-RED

DEVIANCY
CDU DEVIANCY IN THE GERMAN
BUNDESTAG.=              RUECGL-62-CDG

DEVIANT
LEGISLATIVE PARTISANSHIP -- THE
DEVIANT CASE OF CALIFORNIA
(UNITED STATES).=        BUCHW -63-LPD

DEVICE
THE NATIONAL SECURITY COUNCIL AS A
DEVICE FOR OUTER-DEPARTMENTAL
COORDINATION (UNITED STATES).=
                         HAMMPY-60-NSC

DIAGNOSIS
WITHER RUSSIA -- NOTES ON AN
AGONIZING DIAGNOSIS
(SOVIET UNION).=         LEONW -66-WRN

DIAZ
MEXICO'S 'NEW CIENTIFICOS' -- THE
DIAZ ORDAZ CABINET.=     COCHJD-67-MSN

DICHOTOMIES
DICHOTOMIES OF MILITARISM IN
ARGENTINA.=              GOLDM -66-DMA

DICTATOR
THE DICTATOR -- 1, THE PRE-MODERN

DICTATOR             (CONTINUATION)
TYRANT -- 2, A MODERN VERSION.=
                         CRAMFH-51-DPM

THE DICTATOR AND TOTALITARIANISM.=
                         TUCKRC-65-DT

DICTATORS
WHY DICTATORS -- THE CAUSES AND
FORMS OF TYRANNICAL RULE SINCE 600
BC.=                     FALLGW-54-WDC

DICTATORSHIP
THE RETURN TO ONE-MAN DICTATORSHIP
IN THE USSR.=            ACHMH -65-ROM

TOWARD PERSONAL DICTATORSHIP OR
OLIGARCHY -- SOVIET DOMESTIC
POLITICS SINCE THE TWENTIETH
CONGRESS.=               ARMSJA-58-TPD

DEMOCRACY AND DICTATORSHIP -- THEIR
PSYCHOLOGY AND PATTERNS OF LIFE.=
                         BARBZ -56-DDT

POLAND'S PECULIAR DICTATORSHIP.=
                         BLITL -59-PSP

DICTATORSHIP AND POLITICAL POLICE
(FRANCE,GERMANY,ITALY).=
                         BRAMEK-45-DPP

BURMA'S MILITARY DICTATORSHIP.=
                         CADYJF-65-BSM

AN EXPERIMENT WITH CIVILIAN
DICTATORSHIP IN IRAN -- THE CASE
OF M. MOSSADAGH.=        EFIMNM-55-ECD

DICTATORSHIP AND DEMOCRACY IN
LATIN AMERICA.=          FITZRH-60-DDL

TOTALITARIAN DICTATORSHIP AND
AUTOCRACY.=              FRIECJ-56-TDA

THE CHANGEABILITY OF A DICTATORSHIP
(SOVIET UNION).=         GERSA -62-CDS

THE PSYCHOLOGY OF DICTATORSHIP --
BASED ON AN EXAMINATION OF THE
LEADERS OF NAZI GERMANY.=
                         GILBGM-50-PCB

DICTATORSHIP IN HAITI.=
                         HERRH -64-CH

FOREIGN FACTORS IN DICTATORSHIP IN
LATIN AMERICA.=          JOHNJJ-51-FFD

THE SICK DICTATORSHIP
(SOVIET UNION).=         KARAA -61-SDS

BEYOND AFRICAN DICTATORSHIP.=
                         LEGUC -65-BAD

BEYOND AFRICAN DICTATORSHIP -- THE
CRISIS OF THE ONE - PARTY STATE.=
                         LEWIWA-65-BAD

TERROR AND PROGRESS, USSR -- SOME
SOURCES OF CHANGE AND STABILITY IN
THE SOVIET DICTATORSHIP.=
                         MOORB -54-TPU

SOCIAL ORIGINS OF DICTATORSHIP AND
DEMOCRACY -- LORD AND PEASANT IN
THE MAKING OF THE MODERN WORLD
(FRANCE, GREAT BRITAIN,
UNITED STATES, CHINA, JAPAN,
INDIA, GERMANY).=        MOORB -66-SOD

CONSTITUTIONAL DICTATORSHIP IN THE

DISSENT                (CONTINUATION)
DOMINANCE AND DISSENT -- THEIR
INTER-RELATIONS IN THE INDIAN
PARTY SYSTEM.=          MORRWH-66-DDT

REVIEW, DISSENT AND THE APPELLATE
PROCESS -- A POLITICAL
INTERPRETATION (UNITED STATES).=
                       RICHRJ-67-RDA

STARE DECISIS, DISSENT AND THE
BACKGROUND OF THE JUSTICES OF THE
SUPREME COURT OF THE
UNITED STATES.=        SCHMJ -62-SDD

THE TROUBLE MAKERS -- DISSENT OVER
FOREIGN POLICY (GREAT BRITAIN).=
                       TAYLAJ-58-TMD

DISSENTERS
THE ESTABLISHED DISSENTERS
(GREAT BRITAIN, UNITED STATES).=
                       PRICCK-65-EDC

DISSOLUTION
THE MONARCH, THE PRIME MINISTER,
AND THE DISSOLUTION OF PARLIAMENT
(GREAT BRITAIN).=      HEASDJ-61-MPM

DISTANCE
SOCIAL DISTANCE ATTITUDES OF SOUTH
AFRICAN STUDENTS.=     PETTTF-60-SDA

DISTRIBUTION
POLITICAL SYSTEM AND THE
DISTRIBUTION OF POWER.=
                       BANTM -65-PSD

THE INTERNAL DISTRIBUTION OF
INFLUENCE -- THE HOUSE
(UNITED STATES).=      FENNRF-65-IDI

POLITICAL SYSTEMS AND THE
DISTRIBUTION OF POWER (INDIA,
AFRICA, JAPAN).=       CLUCM -65-PSD

THE INTERNAL DISTRIBUTION OF
INFLUENCE -- THE SENATE
(UNITED STATES).=      HUITRK-65-IDI

WEALTH AND POWER IN AMERICA -- AN
ANALYSIS OF SOCIAL CLASS AND
INCOME DISTRIBUTION.=  KOLKG -62-WPA

BRITISH POLITICAL PARTIES -- THE
DISTRIBUTION OF POWER WITHIN THE
CONSERVATIVE AND LABOUR PARTIES.=
                       MCKERT-65-BPP

THE DISTRIBUTION OF POWER IN
AMERICAN SOCIETY.=     PARST -57-DPA

SOCIAL ORIENTATION OF RECRUITMENT
AND DISTRIBUTION OF MEMBERSHIP IN
THE COMMUNIST PARTY OF THE
SOVIET UNION.=         RIGBTH-56-SOR

A METHOD FOR EVALUATING THE
DISTRIBUTION OF POWER IN A
COMMITTEE SYSTEM (UNITED STATES).=
                       SHAPLS-54-MED

DISTRIBUTION OF POWER IN
NATIONALIZED INDUSTRIES
(GREAT BRITAIN).=      SMITIH-51-DPN

DISTRIBUTIONS
A GAME THEORETIC ANALYSIS OF
CONGRESSIONAL POWER DISTRIBUTIONS
FOR A STABLE TWO - PARTY SYSTEM.=
                       LUCERD-56-GTA

DISTRICT
CONGRESSIONAL DISTRICT PARTY

DISTRICT                (CONTINUATION)
STRENGTHS AND THE 1962 ELECTIONS
(UNITED STATES).=      COX,EF-62-CDP

THE REPRESENTATIVE AND HIS DISTRICT
(UNITED STATES).=      DEXTLA-57-RHD

ELITE GROUPS IN A SOUTH INDIAN
DISTRICT, 1788-1858.=  FRYKRE-65-EGS

DISTRICT ADMINISTRATION IN INDIA.=
                       KHERSS-64-DAI

OLIGARCHIC PROBLEMS IN A GERMAN
PARTY DISTRICT.=       MAYNR -61-OPG

THE ROLE OF THE CHIEFS AND THE HEAD
MAN AMONG THE LUGBARA OF THE WEST
NILE DISTRICT OF UGANDA.=
                       MIDDJ -56-RCH

THE ROLE OF THE FEDERAL DISTRICT
COURTS IN THE SEGREGATION
CONTROVERSY (UNITED STATES).=
                       STEARJ-60-RFD

LIBERALISM OF CONGRESSMEN AND THE
PRESIDENTIAL VOTE IN THEIR
DISTRICT (UNITED STATES).=
                       WALDLK- 6-LCP

CHIEFSHIP AND POLITICS IN THE
MLANJE DISTRICT OF SOUTHERN
NYASALAND.=            WISHRL-61-CPM

DISTRUST
POLITICS OF DISTRUST IN IRAN.=
                       WESTAF-65-PDI

DISUNITY
THE FUNCTIONS OF DISUNITY -- THE
NEGRO LEADERSHIP IN A SOUTHERN
CITY (UNITED STATES).=
                       WALKJL-63-FDN

DIVERGENT
COPING WITH CUBA -- DIVERGENT
POLICY PREFERENCES OF STATE
POLITICAL LEADERS
(UNITED STATES).=      EKMAP -66-CCD

DIVERSITY
ARMED FORCES IN WESTERN EUROPE --
UNITY AND DIVERSITY.=  JANOM -65-AFW

DIVIDED
FRENCH LABOR DIVIDED.=
                       KERRW -48-FLD

BOLIVIA -- A LAND DIVIDED.=
                       OSBOH -64-BLD

THE NEW CLASS DIVIDED -- RUSSIAN
SCIENCE AND TECHNOLOGY VERSUS
COMMUNISM.=            PARRA -66-NCD

DIVINE
THE DIVINE KINGSHIP IN GHANA AND
ANCIENT EGYPT.=        MEYELR-60-DKG

THE DIVINE KINGDOM OF THE JUKUN --
A RE-EVALUATION OF SOME THEORIES
(EAST AFRICAN).=       YOUNMW-66-DKJ

DIVISION
THE PUBLIC STUDIES DIVISION OF THE
DEPARTMENT OF THE STATE -- PUBLIC
OPINION ANALYSIS IN THE
FORMULATION AND CONDUCT OF
AMERICAN FOREIGN POLICY.=
                       ELDERE-57-PSD

DIVISIONS
INTRAPARTY DIVISIONS AND CABINET

DIVISIONS                    (CONTINUATION)
COALITIONS IN THE FOURTH FRENCH
REPUBLIC.=               MACRC -63-IDC

DIVISIVE
DOES A DIVISIVE - PRIMARY HARM A
CANDIDATE'S CHANCES
(UNITED STATES).=        HACKA -65-DDP

DOCTORS
DOCTORS AND POLITICS
(UNITED STATES).=        GLASWA-60-DPU

DOCTRINE
THE IMPORTANCE OF DOCTRINE
(SOVIET UNION).=         HUNTRN-58-IDS

THE LEADERSHIP DOCTRINE OF THE
CHINESE COMMUNIST PARTY.=
                        LEWIJW-63-LDC

DILEMMAS OF LEADERSHIP AND DOCTRINE
IN DEMOCRATIC PLANNING
(UNITED STATES).=        SELZP -65-DLC

POWER, PRINCIPLE, AND THE DOCTRINE
OF THE MOUVEMENT REPUBLICAIN
POPULAIRE (FRANCE).=     YATEWR-58-PPD

DOMESTIC
TOWARD PERSONAL DICTATORSHIP OR
OLIGARCHY -- SOVIET DOMESTIC
POLITICS SINCE THE TWENTIETH
CONGRESS.=               ARMSJA-58-TPC

THE MOSCOW PATRIARCH IN SOVIET
FOREIGN AND DOMESTIC POLICY.=
                        MARIY -61-MPS

COMMUNIST CHINA TODAY -- DOMESTIC
AND FOREIGN POLICIES.=
                        TANGPS-57-CCT

DOMINANCE
DOMINANCE AND DISSENT -- THEIR
INTER-RELATIONS IN THE INDIAN
PARTY SYSTEM.=           MORRWH-66-DDT

DOMINANT
DOMINANT POWER COMPONENTS IN THE
BRAZILIAN UNIVERSITY STUDENT
MOVEMENT PRIOR TO APRIL 1964.=
                        THERLD-65-DPC

INTRA - PARTY CONFLICT IN A
DOMINANT PARTY -- THE EXPERIENCE
OF ITALIAN CHRISTIAN DEMOCRACY.=
                        ZARIR -65-IPC

DOMINANTS
ECONOMIC DOMINANTS AND COMMUNITY
POWER -- A COMPARATIVE ANALYSIS
(UNITED STATES).=        CLELDA-64-EDC

THE ROLE OF ECONOMIC DOMINANTS IN
COMMUNITY POWER STRUCTURE
(UNITED STATES).=        SCHURO-58-REC

DOMINATION
CONSENSUS OR ELITE DOMINATION --
THE CASE OF BUSINESS.=
                        NETTJP-65-COE

LEADERSHIP OR DOMINATION.=
                        PIGOP -35-LCD

DOMINICAN REPUBLIC
THE POLITICS OF CIVIL - MILITARY
RELATIONS IN THE
DOMINICAN REPUBLIC.=     WIARHJ-65-PCM

THE DEVELOPMENT OF THE LABOR

DOMINICAN REPUBLIC   (CONTINUATION)
MOVEMENT IN THE
DOMINICAN REPUBLIC.=     WIARHJ-66-DLM

DOMINION
AUTOCHTHONOUS ELEMENTS IN THE
EVOLUTION OF DOMINION STATUS --
THE CASE OF NEW ZEALAND.=
                        FIELDK-62-AEE

DOMINIONS
THE YOUNGER GENERATION IN THE THREE
DOMINIONS (INDIA, PAKISTAN,
CEYLON).=                JACKC -49-YGT

DONSHIP
DONSHIP IN A MEXICAN - AMERICAN
COMMUNITY IN TEXAS.=     ROMADI-60-DMA

DOUBLE
THE DOUBLE PATRIOTS -- A STUDY OF
JAPANESE NATIONALISM.=
                        STORR -57-DPS

DRAFTSMANSHIP
LEGISLATIVE DRAFTSMANSHIP
(GREAT BRITAIN).=        ROBSWA-46-LDG

DRAMAS
SYMBOLIC LEADERS -- PUBLIC DRAMAS
AND PUBLIC MEN.=         KLAPOE-64-SLP

DUAL
DUAL LEADERSHIP IN COMPLEX
ORGANIZATIONS.=          ETZIA -65-DLC

REPRESENTATIVES AND EFFICIENCY --
DUAL PROBLEM OF CIVIL - MILITARY
RELATIONS (UNITED STATES).=
                        FOX,WT-61-REC

DUTCH
THE DYNAMICS OF DUTCH POLITICS.=
                        BONERC-62-DDP

THE JAVANESE NOBILITY UNDER THE
DUTCH.=                  PALMLH-60-JNU

DUTIES
DUTIES OF A MEMBER OF PARLIAMENT
(GREAT BRITAIN).=        BALLWM-56-DMP

DUVERGER
A METHODOLOGICAL CRITIQUE OF
DUVERGER'S POLITICAL PARTIES.=
                        WILDAB-59-MCD

DYARCHIC
THE DYARCHIC PATTERN OF GOVERNMENT
AND PAKISTAN'S PROBLEMS.=
                        NEWMKJ-60-DPG

DYNAMICS
THE DYNAMICS OF BUREAUCRACY -- A
STUDY OF INTERPERSONAL RELATIONS
IN TWO GOVERNMENT AGENCIES
(UNITED STATES).=        BLAUPM-55-DBS

THE DYNAMICS OF DUTCH POLITICS.=
                        BONERC-62-DDP

THE DYNAMICS OF COMMUNISM IN
EASTERN EUROPE.=         BURKRV-61-DCE

THE RELATION OF CERTAIN PERSONALITY
DYNAMICS TO LEVELS OF POLITICAL
INTEREST AND ACTION.=    DE-GA -57-RCP

POLITICAL IDEOLOGY AS A TOOL OF
FUNCTIONAL ANALYSIS IN
SOCIO-POLITICAL DYNAMICS.=
                        DIONL -59-PIT

THE LEAGUE OF ARAB STATES -- A

DYNAMICS                    (CONTINUATION)
    STUDY IN THE DYNAMICS OF REGIONAL
    ORGANIZATION (MIDDLE EAST).=
                            MACORW-65-LAS

    THE DYNAMICS OF CHANGE IN
    LATIN AMERICAN POLITICS.=
                            MARTJ -65-DCL

    TUNISIA SINCE INDEPENDENCE -- THE
    DYNAMICS OF ONE - PARTY
    GOVERNMENT.=            MOORCH-65-TSI

    THE DYNAMICS OF DESTALINIZATION
    (SOVIET UNION).=       RITVH -63-DDS

    DYNAMICS OF SOCIALIST LEADERSHIP IN
    INDIA.=                RUSCTA-59-DSL

DYNAMOS
    THE FAULTS IN THE DYNAMOS
    (GREAT BRITAIN).=      MACRN -65-FDG

DYSFUNCTION
    INTERESTS AND INSTITUTIONAL
    DYSFUNCTION IN URUGUAY.=
                            TAYLPB-63-IID

EARLY
    JAPANESE ARMY FACTIONALISM IN THE
    EARLY 1930'S.=         CROWJB-62-JAF

EAST
    EAST EUROPEAN COMMUNIST ELITES --
    THEIR CHARACTER AND HISTORY.=
                            BASSR -66-EEC

    THE NEW ECONOMIC SYSTEM AND THE
    ROLE OF TECHNOCRATS IN THE DDR
    (EAST GERMANY).=       BAYHTA-66-NES

    MACHINE RETRIEVAL OF BIOGRAPHICAL
    DATA (EAST EUROPEAN ELITES).=
                            BECKC -67-MRB

    BUREAUCRACY EAST AND WEST (EGYPT).=
                            BERGM -  -BEW

    EAST EUROPE -- THE SOVIET GRIP
    LOOSENS.=              BROWJF-65-EES

    COMMUNIST IDEOLOGY AND
    INTERNATIONAL AFFAIRS
    (SOVIET UNION, EAST EUROPE).=
                            BRZEZ -60-CII

    THE TOTALITARIAN PARTY
    (SOVIET UNION, EAST EUROPE).=
                            CASSCW-. -TPS

    THE EAST GERMAN ELITE -- RED
    JESUITS AND OTHERS.=   CHILD -66-EGE

    THE SOCIALIST UNITY PARTY OF EAST
    GERMANY.=              CHILD -67-SUP

    EAST GERMAN REVISIONISM -- THE
    SPECTRE AND THE REALITY.=
                            COWAM -62-EGR

    INTELLECTUALS UNDER ULBRICHT (EAST
    GERMANY).=             CROAM -60-IUU

    HIGHER EDUCATION AND POLITICAL
    CHANGE IN EAST AFRICA.=
                            DE BBU-61-HEP

    LITERATURE IN ULBRICHT'S GERMANY
    (EAST GERMANY).=       DEMEP -62-LUS

    INDUSTRIAL ADMINISTRATION IN
    COMMUNIST EAST EUROPE.=

EAST                        (CONTINUATION)
                            DITZGW-60-IAC

    AUTHORITY, EFFICIENCY, AND ROLE
    STRESS -- PROBLEMS IN THE
    DEVELOPMENT OF EAST AFRICAN
    BUREAUCRACIES (UGANDA, KENYA,
    TANGANYIKA).=          FLEMWG-66-AER

    ASIANS IN EAST AFRICA -- PROBLEMS
    AND PROSPECTS.=        GHAID -65-AEA

    PORTRAIT OF A MINORITY -- ASIANS IN
    EAST AFRICA.=          GHAIDP-65-PMA

    RITUALS OF REBELLION IN SOUTH EAST
    AFRICA.=               GLICM -54-RRS

    AN AFRICAN ELITE -- A SAMPLE SURVEY
    OF 52 FORMER STUDENTS OF MAKERERE
    COLLEGE IN EAST AFRICA.=
                            GOLDJE-55-AES

    POLITY, BUREAUCRACY AND INTEREST
    GROUPS IN THE NEAR EAST AND NORTH
    AFRICA.=               GRASG -64-PBI

    THE PHILIPPINE ADMINISTRATIVE
    SYSTEM -- A FUSION OF EAST AND
    WEST.=                 HEADF -57-PAS

    EAST GERMANY -- PROGRESS AND
    PROSPECTS.=            HERZJH-60-EGP

    THE POLITICS OF THE EUROPEAN
    COMMUNIST STATES (BULGARIA,
    CZECHOSLOVAKIA, HUNGARY, EAST
    GERMANY, POLAND, RUMANIA,
    SOVIET UNION, YUGOSLAVIA).=
                            IONEG -67-PEC

    EAST GERMANY TODAY.=   JANIM -63-EGT

    INDIRECT RULE IN EAST INDONESIA.=
                            KAHIGM-49-IRE

    ULBRICHT AND THE INTELLECTUALS
    (EAST GERMANY).=       KERSH -58-UIE

    SOCIOLOGY IN EASTERN EUROPE -- EAST
    GERMANY.=              LUDZPC-65-SEE

    THE SOLDIER AND THE STATE IN EAST
    AFRICA -- SOME THEORETICAL
    CONCLUSIONS ON THE ARMY MUTINIES
    OF 1964.=              MAZRAA-7 -SSE

    SOME STUDENT PROBLEMS IN EAST
    GERMAN UNIVERSITIES.=  NM    -57-SPE

    EAST AFRICAN AGE - CLASS SYSTEMS --
    AN INQUIRY INTO THE SOCIAL ORDER
    OF GALLA, KIPSIGIS, AND KIKUYU.=
                            PRINAH-53-EAA

    THE UNIVERSITIES IN EAST GERMANY.=
                            REINR -62-UEG

    THE ORIGINS AND SIGNIFICANCE OF
    EAST EUROPEAN REVISIONISM.=
                            REYMK -62-OSE

    EAST AFRICAN CHIEFS -- A STUDY OF
    POLITICAL DEVELOPMENT IN SOME
    UGANDA AND TANGANYIKA TRIBES.=
                            RICHAI-59-EAC

    THE ORIGINS OF NATIONALIST
    DISCONTENT IN EAST AND CENTRAL
    AFRICA.=               ROTBRI-63-ONC

    THE POLITICS OF THE NEAR EAST --

ECONOMIC                (CONTINUATION)
  (UNITED STATES).=      CLELDA-64-EDC

    THE ENTREPRENEUR IN ECONOMIC
    CHANGE.=               COCHTC-64-EEC

    COMMUNITY LEADERSHIP IN AN ECONOMIC
    CRISIS -- TESTING GROUND FOR
    IDEOLOGICAL CLEAVAGE
    (UNITED STATES).=      D'ANWV-66-CLE

    INTER - PARTY COMPETITION, ECONOMIC
    VARIABLES, AND WELFARE POLICIES IN
    THE AMERICAN STATES.=  DAWSRE-63-IPC

    IMPEDIMENTS TO ECONOMIC PROGRESS IN
    INDONESIA.=            DE-MH -51-IEP

    AN ECONOMIC THEORY OF DEMOCRACY.=
                          DOWNA -57-ETD

    ECONOMIC DEVELOPMENT AND SOCIAL
    CHANGE IN SOUTH INDIA.=
                          EPSTTS-62-EDS

    POLITICAL UNIFICATION -- A
    COMPARATIVE STUDY OF LEADERS AND
    FOLLOWERS (UNITED ARAB REPUBLIC,
    FEDERATION OF THE WEST INDIES,
    SCANDINAVIA, EUROPEAN ECONOMIC
    COMMUNITY).=           ETZIA -65-PUC

    NATIONAL ECONOMIC INTEREST AND
    POLICY FORMATION IN THE EEC
    (EUROPEAN ECONOMIC COMMUNITY).=
                          FELDW -66-NEI

    NATIONAL ECONOMIC INTEREST AND
    POLICY FORMATION IN THE EEC
    (EUROPEAN ECONOMIC COMMUNITY).=
                          FELDW -66-NEI

    SOCIAL FACTORS IN ECONOMIC
    DEVELOPMENT -- THE ARGENTINE
    CASE.=                 FILLTR-61-SFE

    ECONOMIC PLANNERS (MIDDLE EAST).=
                          FRANPG-55-EPM

    LABOR AND ECONOMIC DEVELOPMENT
    (MIDDLE EAST, SOUTHEAST ASIA).=
                          GALEW -59-LED

    PEDDLERS AND PRINCES -- SOCIAL
    CHANGE AND ECONOMIC MODERNIZATION
    IN TWO INDONESIAN TOWNS.=
                          GEERC -63-PPS

    CHANGING KINSHIP USAGES IN THE
    SETTING OF POLITICAL AND ECONOMIC
    CHANGE AMONG THE NAYARS OF
    MALABAR.=             GOUGEK-52-CKU

    THE ECONOMIC AND SOCIAL COUNCIL --
    POLITICS OF MEMBERSHIP
    (UNITED NATIONS, EUROPE).=
                          GREGRW-63-ESC

    A FRAMEWORK FOR ANALYZING ECONOMIC
    AND POLITICAL CHANGE.=
                          HAGGEE-62-FAE

    ENTREPRENEURSHIP AND LABOR SKILLS
    IN INDONESIAN ECONOMIC DEVELOPMENT
    -- A SYMPOSIUM.=       HIGGB -61-ELS

    INTRA - PARTY POLITICS AND ECONOMIC
    POLICY IN COMMUNIST CHINA.=
                          HINTHC-60-IPP

    ECONOMIC ASPECTS OF POLITICAL
    MOVEMENTS IN NIGERIA AND IN THE

ECONOMIC                (CONTINUATION)
  GOLD COAST, 1918-1939.=
                          HOPKAG-66-EAP

    THE PLACE OF YOUTH IN THE ECONOMIC
    AND CULTURAL CONTEXT OF THE
    CAMEROON.=            IKELJ -64-PYE

    INDIAN ECONOMISTS AND ECONOMIC
    DEVELOPMENT.=          KITTER-55-IEE

    OVERCENTRALIZATION IN ECONOMIC
    ADMINISTRATION -- A CRITICAL
    ANALYSIS BASED ON EXPERIENCE IN
    HUNGARIAN LIGHT INDUSTRY.=
                          KORNJ -59-OEA

    POLITICAL ELITES AND THE PROCESS OF
    ECONOMIC DEVELOPMENT
    (UNITED STATES, WESTERN EUROPE,
    SOVIET UNION).=        LAMBRK-52-PEP

    THE POLITICAL CLIMATE FOR ECONOMIC
    DEVELOPMENT (AFRICA).=
                          LEYSC -66-PCE

    THE INTEGRATION OF THE NEW ECONOMIC
    CLASSES WITH LOCAL GOVERNMENT IN
    WEST NIGERIA.=         LLOYPC-53-INE

    MEXICAN ECONOMIC AND SOCIAL
    DEVELOPMENT.=          MARGHB-65-MES

    ENTREPRENEURSHIP AND ECONOMIC
    DEVELOPMENT IN THE MIDDLE EAST.=
                          MEYEAJ-58-EED

    THE POWER ELITE -- MILITARY,
    ECONOMIC, AND POLITICAL
    (UNITED STATES).=      MILLCW-59-PEM

    THE AMERICAN COUNCIL OF ECONOMIC
    ADVISERS AND JOINT COMMITTEE ON
    THE ECONOMIC REPORT.=  MILNRS-55-ACE

    THE AMERICAN COUNCIL OF ECONOMIC
    ADVISERS AND JOINT COMMITTEE ON
    THE ECONOMIC REPORT.=  MILNRS-55-ACE

    TRADITIONAL AND MODERN TYPES OF
    LEADERSHIP AND ECONOMIC
    DEVELOPMENT AMONG THE FIJIANS.=
                          NAYARR-64-TMT

    CONCENTRATION OF ECONOMIC POWER AND
    THE ECONOMIC ELITE IN CANADA.=
                          PORTJ -56-CEP

    CONCENTRATION OF ECONOMIC POWER AND
    THE ECONOMIC ELITE IN CANADA.=
                          PORTJ -56-CEP

    THE ECONOMIC ELITE AND THE SOCIAL
    STRUCTURE IN CANADA.=  PORTJ -57-EES

    ENTREPRENEURSHIP AND ECONOMIC
    PROGRESS IN JAMAICA.=  RATTS -63-EEP

    THE ROLE OF ECONOMIC DOMINANTS IN
    COMMUNITY POWER STRUCTURE
    (UNITED STATES).=      SCHURO-58-RED

    THE CULTURAL FACTORS IN ECONOMIC
    AND TECHNOLOGICAL DEVELOPMENT --
    AN INDIAN ADMINISTRATIVE
    VIEW-POINT.=           SETHSC-65-CFE

    INTELLECTUALS, PUBLIC OPINION AND
    ECONOMIC DEVELOPMENT.=
                          SHILE -55-IPO

    THE CONCENTRATION AND DISPERSION OF

109

EDUCATION        (CONTINUATION)
  SOLDIERS AND SCHOLARS -- MILITARY
  EDUCATION AND NATIONAL POLICY
  (UNITED STATES).=        MASLJW-57-SSM

  HIGHER EDUCATION IN COMMUNIST
  HUNGARY -- 1948-1956.=
                           MURRE -60-HEC

  POLITICAL EDUCATION IN THE POSTWAR
  KOMSOMOL.=               PLOSSI-56-PEP

  EDUCATION AND THE CIVIL SERVICE IN
  EUROPE.=                 PRICJW-59-ECS

  EDUCATION AND SOCIAL CHANGE IN
  TROPICAL AREAS.=         READM -55-ESC

  STATUS, ACHIEVEMENT, AND EDUCATION
  IN CEYLON.=              RYANB -61-SAE

  EDUCATION FOR COMMUNIST LEADERSHIP
  (SOVIET UNION).=         RYWKMS-58-ECL

  COMMUNIST-DOMINATED EDUCATION IN
  BULGARIA -- A STUDY IN SOCIAL
  RELATIONS.=              SANDIT-56-CDE

  NIGERIAN ELITE -- ROLE OF
  EDUCATION.=              SMYTHH-60-NER

  SECONDARY EDUCATION AND THE
  DEVELOPMENT OF ELITES
  (LATIN AMERICA).=        SOLAA -67-SEC

  THE REORGANIZATION OF SOVIET
  EDUCATION.=              URBAP -62-RSE

  ACADEMIC FREEDOM AND PROBLEMS OF
  HIGHER EDUCATION IN TURKEY.=
                           WEIKWF-62-AFP

  EDUCATION AND POLITICS IN NIGERIA.=
                           WEILHN-64-EPN

EDUCATIONAL
  PUBLIC AFFAIRS OPINION LEADERSHIP
  AMONG EDUCATIONAL TELEVISION
  VIEWERS (UNITED STATES).=
                           CARTRE-62-PAO

  EDUCATIONAL STRATEGY FOR DEVELOPING
  SOCIETIES.=              CURLA -63-ESD

  THE SOCIAL AND EDUCATIONAL
  BACKGROUND OF TURKISH OFFICIALS.=
                           CODOCH-64-SEB

  THE EDUCATIONAL BACKGROUNDS AND
  CAREER ORIENTATIONS OF THE MEMBERS
  OF THE CENTRAL COMMITTEE OF THE
  CPSU (SOVIET UNION).=    GEHLMP-66-EBC

  EDUCATIONAL POLICY AND POLITICAL
  DEVELOPMENT IN AFRICA.=
                           HUSSER-46-EPP

  POLITICAL POWER AND EDUCATIONAL
  DECISION-MAKING (UNITED STATES).=
                           KIMBRB-64-PPE

  THE EDUCATIONAL AND GEOGRAPHICAL
  BACKGROUND OF SOME LOCAL LEADERS
  (GREAT BRITAIN).=        MUSGF -61-EGB

  RECENT EDUCATIONAL POLICY IN
  CHINA.=                  THOMSB-50-REP

EEC
  NATIONAL ECONOMIC INTEREST AND
  POLICY FORMATION IN THE EEC
  (EUROPEAN ECONOMIC COMMUNITY).=

EEC              (CONTINUATION)
                 FELDW -66-NEI

EFFECT
  A NOTE ON LEADERSHIP THEORY -- THE
  EFFECT OF SOCIAL BARRIERS BETWEEN
  LEADERS AND FOLLOWERS
  (UNITED STATES).=        FIEDFE-57-NLT

  EFFECT OF PERSONALITY ON POLITICAL
  PARTICIPATION.=          LASSHD-54-EPP

EFFECTIVE
  POLITICAL MONEY -- A STUDY OF
  CONTRIBUTORS TO THE NATIONAL
  COMMITTEE FOR AN EFFECTIVE
  CONGRESS (UNITED STATES).=
                           SCOBHM-63-PMS

EFFECTIVENESS
  AUTHORITY STRUCTURE AND
  ORGANIZATIONAL EFFECTIVENESS.=
                           ETZIA -59-ASC

  THE FOLKWAYS OF THE UNITED STATES
  SENATE -- CONFORMITY TO GROUP
  NORMS AND LEGISLATIVE
  EFFECTIVENESS.=          MATTOR-59-FUS

EFFECTS
  THE EFFECTS OF SUCCESSION -- A
  COMPARATIVE STUDY OF MILITARY AND
  BUSINESS ORGANIZATION
  (UNITED STATES).=        GRUSO -64-ESC

  EFFECTS OF PARTISANSHIP ON
  PERCEPTIONS OF POLITICAL FIGURES.=
                           MCGRJC-62-EPP

  EFFECTS OF LEGISLATIVE AND
  ADMINISTRATIVE ACCESSIBILITY ON
  INTEREST GROUP POLITICS.=
                           PYE,LW-58-ELA

  THE EFFECTS OF NOMINATING
  CONVENTIONS, ELECTIONS, AND
  REFERENCE GROUP IDENTIFICATION
  UPON THE PERCEPTIONS OF POLITICAL
  FIGURES (UNITED STATES).=
                           RAVEBH-64-ENC

  THE EFFECTS OF LEADERSHIP
  (UNITED STATES).=        SELVHC-60-ELU

  THE POLITICAL EFFECTS OF MILITARY
  PROGRAMS -- SOME INDICATIONS FROM
  LATIN AMERICA.=          WOLFC -65-PEM

EFFICACY
  THE POLITICAL EFFICACY OF JUDICIAL
  SYMBOLISM.=              STUMHP-66-PEJ

EFFICIENCY
  LOCAL PARTY EFFICIENCY AS A FACTOR
  IN THE OUTCOME OF BRITISH
  ELECTIONS.=              BROWJC-58-LPE

  VARIATIONS IN POWER STRUCTURES AND
  ORGANIZING EFFICIENCY -- A
  COMPARATIVE STUDY OF FOUR AREAS
  (UNITED STATES).=        DAKIRE-62-VPS

  AUTHORITY, EFFICIENCY, AND ROLE
  STRESS -- PROBLEMS IN THE
  DEVELOPMENT OF EAST AFRICAN
  BUREAUCRACIES (UGANDA, KENYA,
  TANGANYIKA).=            FLEMWG-66-AER

  REPRESENTATIVES AND EFFICIENCY --
  DUAL PROBLEM OF CIVIL - MILITARY
  RELATIONS (UNITED STATES).=
                           FOX,WT-61-REC

EGALITARIAN
  EGALITARIAN ATTITUDES OF WARSAW

                         BENDR -57-SMA

THE BUSINESS ELITE -- THEN AND NOW
(UNITED STATES).=        BERGM -56-BET

MILITARY ELITE AND SOCIAL CHANGE --
EGYPT SINCE NAPOLEON.=
                         BERGM -60-MES

THE ELITE AND THE ELITES
(UNITED STATES, WESTERN EUROPE).=
                         BETHMW-42-EEU

THE ADMINISTRATIVE ELITE
(GREAT BRITAIN, FRANCE).=
                         BOTTTB-64-AEG

FROM COMMERCIAL ELITE TO POLITICAL
ADMINISTRATOR -- THE RECRUITMENT
OF THE MAYORS OF CHICAGO
(UNITED STATES).=        BRADDS-65-CEP

BYLAWS OF THE ELITE -- THE PARTY
STATUTE (SOVIET UNION).=
                         BRUNG -65-BEP

THE INDUSTRIAL ELITE
(LATIN AMERICA).=        CARDFH-67-IEL

THE SOCIAL ROLE OF THE LITERARY
ELITE (UNITED STATES).=
                         CHARB -50-SRL

THE EAST GERMAN ELITE -- RED
JESUITS AND OTHERS.=     CHILD -66-EGE

THE TECHNOLOGY - ELITE APPROACH TO
THE DEVELOPMENTAL PROCESS --
PERUVIAN CASE STUDY.=    COHEA -66-TEA

INSIDERS AND CONTROLLERS (CORPORATE
ELITE, GREAT BRITAIN).=
                         CROSCA-62-ICC

A CRITIQUE OF THE RULING ELITE
MODEL.=                  DAHLRA-58-CRE

FRANCE, GERMANY, AND THE WESTERN
ALLIANCE -- A STUDY OF ELITE
ATTITUDES ON EUROPEAN INTEGRATION
AND WORLD POLITICS.=     DEUTKW-67-FGW

THE SOVIET POWER ELITE.=
                         DEWAM -60-SPE

SOCIAL BACKGROUND IN ELITE ANALYSIS
-- A METHODOLOGICAL INQUIRY
(FRANCE, GERMANY).=      EDINLU-67-SBE

THE POLITICAL ELITE IN AUSTRALIA.=
                         ENCES -61-PEA

THE TURKISH POLITICAL ELITE.=
                         FREYFW-65-TPE

THE POLITICAL ELITE AND
BUREAUCRACY.=            FRIECJ-63-PEB

ELITE GROUPS IN A SOUTH INDIAN
DISTRICT, 1788-1858.=    FRYKRE-65-EGS

SONS OF THE ESTABLISHMENT -- ELITE
YOUTH IN PANAMA AND COSTA RICA.=
                         GOLDC -66-SEE

AN AFRICAN ELITE -- A SAMPLE SURVEY
OF 52 FORMER STUDENTS OF MAKERERE
COLLEGE IN EAST AFRICA.=
                         GOLDJE-55-AES

THE CHANGING STRUCTURE OF THE

BRITISH POLITICAL ELITE,
1886-1935.=              GUTTWL-51-CSB

ARISTOCRACY AND THE MIDDLE CLASS IN
THE BRITISH ELITE, 1886-1916.=
                         GUTTWL-54-AMC

SOCIAL STRATIFICATION AND POLITICAL
ELITE (GREAT BRITAIN).=
                         GUTTWL-60-SSP

THE BRITISH POLITICAL ELITE.=
                         GUTTWL-63-BPE

POWER TO DO WHAT (CORPORATE ELITE,
UNITED STATES).=         HACKA -64-PDW

THE DILEMMA OF AN ELITE GROUP --
THE INDUSTRIALIST IN
LATIN AMERICA.=          HARBJD-65-DEG

SAINT-SIMON AND THE ROLE OF THE
ELITE.=                  HARTCK-64-SSR

POLITICS, POWER AND CONFUSION
(UNITED STATES, POWER ELITE
REVIEW).=                HERMFA-56-PPC

THE RISE OF THE NATAL INDIAN
ELITE.=                  HEY,PD-61-RNI

ELITE MOBILITY IN THE ROMAN
EMPIRE.=                 HOPKK -65-EMR

THE SOVIET ELITE -- 1, GROUPS AND
INDIVIDUALS -- 2, IN WHOSE HANDS
THE FUTURE.=             HOUGJ -67-SEG

THE TECHNICAL ELITE VS. THE PARTY
(SOVIET UNION).=         HOUGJF-59-TEV

THE EIGHTH CENTRAL COMMITTEE OF THE
CHINESE COMMUNIST PARTY -- A STUDY
OF AN ELITE.=            HOUNFW-57-ECC

THE ELITE CONCEPT IN KARL
MANNHEIM'S SOCIOLOGY OF
EDUCATION.=              HOYLE -64-ECK

FUNCTION OF VALUES IN THE POLICY
PROCESS -- ELITE GROUPS
(UNITED STATES).=        JACOPE-62-FVP

ELITE COMMUNICATION IN SAMOA -- A
STUDY OF LEADERSHIP.=    KEESFM-56-ECS

THE NEW ELITE IN ASIA AND AFRICA --
A COMPARATIVE STUDY OF INDONESIA
AND AFRICA (GHANA).=     KERST -66-NEA

INTERVIEWING THE BUSINESS ELITE.=
                         KINCHB-57-IBE

SUCCESSION AND THE ELITE AND PEKING
(CHINA).=                KLEIDW-64-SEP

THE ELITE AND THE RULING CLASS --
PARETO AND MOSCA RE-EXAMINED.=
                         KOLEF -67-ERC

THE LABOR ELITE -- IS IT
REVOLUTIONARY (LATIN AMERICA).=
                         LANDHA-67-LEI

ELITE COMMUNICATION AND THE
GOVERNMENTAL PROCESS
(UNITED STATES, CANADA).=
                         LANERE-58-ECG

THE NEW PRIESTHOOD -- THE
SCIENTIFIC ELITE AND THE USES OF

ELITE                    (CONTINUATION)
  POWER (UNITED STATES).=
                         LAPPRE-65-NPS

THE SOVIET ADMINISTRATIVE ELITE --
SELECTION AND DEPLOYMENT
PROCEDURES.=            LEREA -65-SAE

THE RISE OF A NEW ELITE AMONGST THE
WOMEN OF NIGERIA.=     LEITS -56-RNE

FRENCH ELITE PERSPECTIVES ON THE
UNITED NATIONS.=       LERND -3 -FEP

THE NAZI ELITE.=       LERND -51-NE

CLASS CONSCIOUSNESS AND CLASS
SOLIDARITY IN THE NEW ETHIOPIAN
ELITE.=                LEVICN-66-CCC

THE SOVIET ELITE -- 1 --
GENERATIONS IN CONFLICT.=
                       LEWYB -67-SEC

INTRODUCTION -- THE STUDY OF THE
ELITE (TROPICAL AFRICA).=
                       LLOYPC-66-ISE

THE SOCIAL CHARACTERISTICS OF AN
EMERGENT ELITE IN HARARE (SOUTHERN
RHODESIA).=            LUKHMB-66-SCE

PAKISTAN'S NEW POWER ELITE.=
                       MAROS -59-PSN

AMERICAN UNIVERSITY STUDENTS -- A
PRESUMPTIVE ELITE.=    MARVD -65-AUS

THE TRIBAL ELITE AND THE TRANSKEIAN
ELECTIONS OF 1963 (SOUTH AFRICA).=
                       MAYEP -66-TET

THE BUSINESS ELITE AND FOREIGN
POLICY (UNITED STATES).=
                       MCLEOS-60-BEF

THE MYTH OF THE RULING CLASS --
GAETANO MOSCA AND THE 'ELITE'.=
                       MEISJH-58-MRC

THE ELITE.=            MICHR -49-E

THE AMERICAN BUSINESS ELITE -- A
COLLECTIVE PORTRAIT.=  MILLCW-54-ABE

THE POWER ELITE (UNITED STATES).=
                       MILLCW-56-PEU

THE POWER ELITE -- COMMENT ON
CRITICISM.=            MILLCW-57-PEC

THE POWER ELITE -- MILITARY,
ECONOMIC, AND POLITICAL
(UNITED STATES).=      MILLCW-59-PEM

THE RECRUITMENT OF THE AMERICAN
BUSINESS ELITE.=       MILLW -50-RAB

THE ROLE OF THE SCIENTIFIC ELITE IN
THE DECISION TO USE THE ATOMIC
BOMB (UNITED STATES).=
                       MOORJW-58-RSE

FROM MONARCHY TO COMMUNISM -- THE
SOCIAL TRANSFORMATION OF THE
ALBANIAN ELITE.=       MOSKCC-65-MCS

THE INDONESIAN ELITE.=
                       MYSBJH-57-IE

THE CONCEPT OF SOCIAL ELITE.=
                       NADESF-56-CSE

CONSENSUS OR ELITE DOMINATION --


ELITE                    (CONTINUATION)
  THE CASE OF BUSINESS.=
                         NETTJP-65-COE

AFRICAN ELITE IN SOUTH AFRICA.=
                       NGCOSB-56-AES

POWER AND THE SOVIET ELITE -- THE
LETTER OF AN OLD BOLSHEVIKI AND
OTHER ESSAYS.=         NICOB -65-PSE

THE CHINESE COMMUNIST ELITE.=
                       NORTRC-51-CCE

A NEW PROGRAM OF IDEOLOGICAL
INSTRUCTION FOR THE ELITE
(SOVIET UNION).=       OLGIL -67-NPI

THE ELITE, INDUSTRIALISM AND
NATIONALISM -- JAPAN.=
                       OLSOL -63-EIN

ELITE GROUPS -- A SCHEME FOR THE
STUDY OF POWER IN CANADA.=
                       PORTJ -55-EGS

CONCENTRATION OF ECONOMIC POWER AND
THE ECONOMIC ELITE IN CANADA.=
                       PORTJ -56-CEP

THE ECONOMIC ELITE AND THE SOCIAL
STRUCTURE IN CANADA.=  PORTJ -57-EES

HIGHER PUBLIC SERVANTS AND THE
BUREAUCRATIC ELITE IN CANADA.=
                       PORTJ -58-HPS

THE BUREAUCRATIC ELITE -- A REPLY
TO PROFESSOR ROWAT (CANADA,
GREAT BRITAIN).=       PORTJ -59-BER

THE ELITE CONCEPT.=    POTTA -66-EC

THE EMERGENCE OF AN ELITE -- A CASE
STUDY OF A WEST COAST FAMILY (WEST
AFRICA).=              PRIEM -66-EEC

ON JOHN PORTER'S 'BUREAUCRATIC
ELITE IN CANADA'.=     ROWADC-59-JPS

ELITE RECRUITMENT AND POLITICAL
DEVELOPMENT.=          SELILG-64-ERP

MINISTERS OF MODERNIZATION -- ELITE
MOBILITY IN THE MEIJI RESTORATION,
1868-1873.=            SILBBS-64-MME

SOVIET AND AMERICAN FOREIGN POLICY
ATTITUDES -- CONTENT ANALYSIS OF
ELITE ARTICULATIONS.=  SINGCJ-64-SAF

THE EMERGING ELITE -- A STUDY OF
POLITICAL LEADERSHIP IN CEYLON.=
                       SINGMR-64-EES

INTERVIEWING A LEGAL ELITE -- THE
WALL STREET LAWYER.=   SMIGEO-58-ILE

THE NIGERIAN ELITE -- SOME
OBSERVATIONS.=         SMYTHH-59-NEO

BLACK AFRICA'S NEW POWER ELITE.=
                       SMYTHH-60-BAS

NIGERIAN ELITE -- ROLE OF
EDUCATION.=            SMYTHH-60-NER

THE NEW NIGERIAN ELITE.=
                       SMYTHH-60-NNE

INTERNATIONAL POLITICAL
COMMUNICATION -- ELITE VS. MASS.=

ELITE (CONTINUATION)
SPEIH -52-IPC

GERMAN REARMAMENT AND THE OLD
MILITARY ELITE.= SPEIH -54-GRO

THE JEWISH ORGANIZATIONAL ELITE OF
ATLANTA, GEORGIA (UNITED STATES).=
SUTKS -52-JOE

DILEMMA OF THE ELITE IN ARAB
SOCIETY.= TANNA -55-DEA

THE NOTION OF THE ELITE AND THE
URBAN SOCIAL SURVEY IN AFRICA.=
TARDO -56-NEU

THE ELITE IN THE WELFARE STATE.=
THOEP -66-EWS

THE EMERGENCE OF THE MODERN
INDONESIAN ELITE.= VAN-R -60-EMI

MARGINAL POLITICS AND ELITE
MANIPULATION IN MOROCCO.=
WATEJ -67-MPE

AMERICA AND THE BRITISH FOREIGN
POLICY-MAKING ELITE, FROM JOSEPH
CHAMBERLAIN TO ANTHONY EDEN,
1895-1956.= WATTDC-63-ABF

RULING CLASS AND POWER ELITE.=
WESOW -65-RCP

THE CREATIVE ELITE IN AMERICA.=
WEYLN -66-CEA

MUSLIM LEGISLATORS IN INDIA --
PROFILE OF A MINORITY ELITE.=
WRIGJR-64-MLI

THE SAIGON POLITICAL ELITE -- FOCUS
ON FOUR CABINETS (SOUTH VIETNAM).=
WURFD -67-SPE

A NEW TYPE OF WHO'S WHO FOR A NEW
ELITE.= ZAWOJK-57-NTW

ELITES
ORIGINS OF AMERICAN OCCUPATIONAL
ELITES, 1900-1955.= ADAMS -57-OAO

SOCIAL VALUES OF SOVIET AND
AMERICAN ELITES -- CONTENT
ANALYSIS OF ELITE MEDIA.=
ANGERC-64-SVS

EAST EUROPEAN COMMUNIST ELITES --
THEIR CHARACTER AND HISTORY.=
BASSR -66-EEC

POLITICAL ELITES -- A MODE OF
ANALYSIS.= BECKC -66-PEM

MACHINE RETRIEVAL OF BIOGRAPHICAL
DATA (EAST EUROPEAN ELITES).=
BECKC -67-MRB

ATTITUDES OF JAMAICAN ELITES
TOWARDS THE WEST INDIAN
FEDERATION.= BELLW -60-AJE

EQUALITY AND ATTITUDES OF ELITES IN
JAMAICA.= BELLW -62-EAE

SOCIAL CHANGE AND ELITES IN AN
EMERGENT NATION (JAMAICA).=
BELLW -65-SCE

NON-WESTERN INTELLIGENTSIAS AS
POLITICAL ELITES.= BENDHJ-60-NWI

ELITES (CONTINUATION)
POLITICAL ELITES IN COLONIAL
SOUTHEAST ASIA -- AN HISTORICAL
ANALYSIS.= BENDHJ-64-PEC

THE ELITE AND THE ELITES
(UNITED STATES, WESTERN EUROPE).=
BETHMW-42-EEU

THE DETERMINATION OF LOCAL POWER
ELITES (UNITED STATES).=
BLUMLA-57-DLP

ELITES AND PUBLIC OPINION IN AREAS
OF HIGH SOCIAL STRATIFICATION
(CHILE).= BONIF -58-EPO

CULTURAL ELITES (LATIN AMERICA).=
BONIF -67-CEL

SIMPLIFYING THE DISCOVERY OF
ELITES.= BOOTDA-61-SDE

ELITES AND SOCIETY.= BOTTTB-64-ES

THE PROBLEMS OF ELITES IN THE
BELGIAN CONGO.= BRAUGE-56-PEB

THE PRESENT SITUATION AND
ASPIRATIONS OF ELITES IN THE
GOLD COAST.= BUSIKA-56-PSA

SOME FRENCH CONCEPTS OF ELITES.=
CLIFM -60-FCE

POTENTIAL ELITES IN GHANA AND THE
IVORY COAST -- A PRELIMINARY
COMPARISON.= CLIGRP-64-PEG

INTERVIEWING POLITICAL ELITES IN
CROSS-CULTURAL COMPARATIVE
RESEARCH.= CRANWW-64-IPE

THE EVOLUTION OF ELITES IN GHANA.=
DE GGR-66-EEG

GERMANY REJOINS THE POWERS -- MASS
OPINION, INTEREST GROUPS AND
ELITES IN CONTEMPORARY GERMAN
FOREIGN POLICY.= DEUTKW-59-GRP

MASS MEDIA USE BY SUB - ELITES IN
ELEVEN LATIN AMERICAN COUNTRIES.=
DEUTPJ-61-MMU

SOCIAL VALUES OF SOVIET AND
AMERICAN ELITES -- INSIGHTS FROM
SOVIET LITERATURE.= DUNHVS-64-SVS

POST - TOTALITARIAN LEADERSHIP --
ELITES IN THE GERMAN FEDERAL
REPUBLIC.= EDINLJ-60-PTL

THE PLACE OF ELITES AND PRIMARY
GROUPS IN THE ABSORPTION OF NEW
IMMIGRANTS IN ISRAEL.=
EISESN-51-PEP

THE FUNCTIONAL DIFFERENTIATION OF
ELITES IN THE KIBBUTZ (ISRAEL).=
ETZIA -59-FDE

THE SETTING FOR EUROPEAN ARMS
CONTROLS -- POLITICAL AND
STRATEGIC CHOICES OF EUROPEAN
ELITES (FRANCE, GERMANY
GREAT BRITAIN, SOVIET UNION,
UNITED STATES).= GORDM -65-SEA

THE ELECTED AND THE ANNOINTED --
TWO AMERICAN ELITES.= HACKA -61-EAT

THE MILITARY ELITES

ELITES            (CONTINUATION)
(LATIN AMERICA).=       FORGIL-67-MEL

ENTREPRENEURSHIP AND TRADITIONAL
ELITES (ASIA).=         FOSEBF-63-ETE

SOCIAL STRATIFICATION AND THE
COMPARATIVE ANALYSIS OF ELITES.=
                JANOM -56-SSC

MILITARY ELITES AND THE STUDY OF
WAR (FRANCE, GERMANY, ITALY,
SOVIET UNION, UNITED STATES).=
                JANOM -57-MES

COMMUNITY INFLUENTIALS -- THE
ELITES OF ATLANTA
(UNITED STATES).=       JENNMK-64-CIE

POTENTIAL ELITES IN TURKEY -- THE
SOCIAL ORIGINS OF LISE YOUTH.=
                KAZAAM-66-PET

POTENTIAL ELITES IN TURKEY --
EXPLORING THE VALUES AND ATTITUDES
OF LISE YOUTH.=         KAZAAM-67-PET

BEYOND THE RULING CLASS --
STRATEGIC ELITES IN MODERN
SOCIETY.=               KELLS -63-BRC

THE POLITICAL SOCIALIZATION OF
NATIONAL LEGISLATIVE ELITES IN THE
UNITED STATES AND CANADA.=
                KORNA -65-PSN

REPRESENTATIVE DEMOCRACY AND
POLITICAL ELITES IN CANADA AND THE
UNITED STATES.=         KORNA -66-RDP

AFRICAN ELITES IN INDUSTRIAL
BUREAUCRACY (UGANDA).=
                KUMAC -66-AEI

POLITICAL ELITES AND THE PROCESS OF
ECONOMIC DEVELOPMENT
(UNITED STATES, WESTERN EUROPE,
SOVIET UNION).=         LAMBRK-52-PEP

THE COMPARATIVE STUDY OF ELITES --
AN INTRODUCTION AND BIBLIOGRAPHY.=
                LASSH -52-CSE

THE COMPARATIVE STUDY OF ELITES.=
                LASSHD-52-CSE

AGENDA FOR THE STUDY OF POLITICAL
ELITES.=                LASSHD-61-ASP

WORLD REVOLUTIONARY ELITES --
STUDIES IN COERCIVE IDEOLOGICAL
MOVEMENTS (CHINA, GERMANY, ITALY,
SOVIET UNION).=         LASSHD-66-WRE

SOCIAL MOBILITY AMONG THE DEAD --
OR POSTHUMOUS CIRCULATION OF
ELITES (SOVIET UNION).=
                LC    -62-SMA

ELITES IN LATIN AMERICA.=
                LIPSSM-67-ELA

THE WEST AFRICAN ELITES.=
                LITTKL-56-TWA

THE NEW ELITES OF TROPICAL AFRICA
-- STUDIES PRESENTED AND DISCUSSED
AT THE SIXTH INTERNATIONAL AFRICAN
SEMINAR AT THE UNIVERSITY OF
IBADAN.=                LLOYPC-66-NET

SOCIAL MOBILITY AGAIN -- AND ELITES

ELITES            (CONTINUATION)
(UNITED STATES, WESTERN EUROPE).=
                LUETH -55-SMA

THE MANDARINS -- THE CIRCULATION OF
ELITES IN CHINA, 1600-1900.=
                MARSRM-61-MCE

VALLES, DEMAND, AND SOCIAL NOBILITY
(INDUSTRIAL ELITES, CHINA,
UNITED STATES).=        MARSRM-63-VDS

EVOLUTION OF SENEGALESE ELITES.=
                MERCP -56-ESE

KUOMINGTANG AND CHINESE COMMUNIST
ELITES.=                NORTRC-52-KCC

ELITES AND POLYARCHIES.=
                PARRG -66-EP

SATELLITE GENERALS -- A STUDY OF
MILITARY ELITES IN THE SOVIET
SPHERE.=                POOLID-55-SGS

ORBITS OF TOLERANCE, INTERVIEWERS,
AND ELITES (UNITED STATES).=
                RIESD -56-OTI

ELITES AND THE METHODOLOGY OF
POLITICS.=              ROSSRG-52-EMP

ELITES AND OLIGARCHIES.=
                RUNCWG-63-EO

THE STUDY OF ELITES -- WHO'S WHO,
WHEN, AND HOW.=         RUSTDA-66-SEW

DEMOCRACY, LEADERSHIP AND ELITES.=
                SARTG -62-DLE

THE DETERMINATION OF LOCAL POWER
ELITES (UNITED STATES).=
                SCHURO-57-DLP

POLITICAL ELITES AND POLITICAL
MODERNIZATION -- THE CRISIS OF
TRANSITION (LATIN AMERICA).=
                SCOTRE-67-PEP

POLITICAL CHANGE -- LEGISLATIVE
ELITES AND PARTIES IN OREGON
(UNITED STATES).=       SELILG-64-PCL

SECONDARY EDUCATION AND THE
DEVELOPMENT OF ELITES
(LATIN AMERICA).=       SCLAA -67-SED

THE CONCEPT OF ELITES AND THEIR
FORMATION IN UGANDA.=   SOUTAW-66-CET

COLONIAL ELITES -- ROME, SPAIN AND
THE AMERICAS.=          SYMER -58-CER

AFRICAN ELITES.=        UNES  -56-AE

RELIGIOUS ELITES IN LATIN AMERICA
-- CATHOLICISM, LEADERSHIP AND
SOCIAL CHANGE.=         VALLI -65-REL

ELITES IN FRENCH - SPEAKING WEST
AFRICA -- THE SOCIAL BASIS OF
IDEAS.=                 WALLI -65-EFS

CONGRESS PARTY ELITES (INDIA).=
                WEINM -67-CPE

ELITES, SCHOLARS, AND
SOCIOLOGISTS.=          WILLSM-66-ESS

RELIGIOUS ELITES --
DIFFERENTIATIONS AND DEVELOPMENTS

ELITES                    (CCNTINUATICN)
  IN ROMAN CATHCLICISM
  (LATIN AMERICA).=         YALLI -67-REC

ELITISM
  THE THECRY CF CEMCCRATIC ELITISM.=
                            BACHP -67-TCE

  DEMCCRACY AND ELITISM.=
                            SIRVHK-67-CE

ELITIST
  FURTHER REFLECTICNS CN 'THE ELITIST
  THEORY CF CEMCCRACY'.=
                            CAHLRA-66-FRE

  A CRITICUE CF THE ELITIST THECRY CF
  DEMCCRACY.=              WALKJL-66-CET

ELUSIVENESS
  THE ELUSIVENESS CF PCWER -- THE
  AFRICAN SINGLE PARTY STATE.=
                            ASHFDE-65-EPA

EMANCIPATICN
  THE EMANCIPATICN CF POWER.=
                            PLESH -64-EP

EMERGENCE
  PEASANT NATICNALISM AND COMMUNIST
  POWER -- THE EMERGENCE CF
  REVCLUTICNARY CHINA, 1937-1945.=
                            JOHNCA-62-PNC

  PCLITICAL CHANGE IN LATIN AMERICA
  -- THE EMERGENCE CF THE MIDDLE
  SECTORS.=                JOHNJJ-58-PCL

  THE EMERGENCE CF MODERN TURKEY.=
                            LEWIB -61-EMT

  JAPAN'S EMERGENCE AS A MODERN
  STATE.=                  NORMEH-46-JSE

  THE EMERGENCE CF AN ELITE -- A CASE
  STUCY CF A WEST CCAST FAMILY (WEST
  AFRICA).=                PRIEM -66-EEC

  THE EMERGENCE CF THE MODERN
  INDONESIAN ELITE.=       VAN-R -60-EMI

EMERGENCY
  EMERGENCY RULE IN INDIA.=
                            SCHOBN-63-ERI

EMERGENT
  SCCIAL CHANGE AND ELITES IN AN
  EMERGENT NATICN (JAMAICA).=
                            BELLW -65-SCE

  ASIAN BUREAUCRATIC SYSTEMS EMERGENT
  FRCM THE BRITISH IMPERIAL
  TRACITICN (INDIA, PAKISTAN, BURMA,
  CEYLCN, MALAYA, NEPAL).=
                            BRAIR -  -ABS

  EDUCATICN CF MILITARY LEADERSHIP IN
  EMERGENT STATES.=        GUTTWF-65-EML

  THE SCCIAL CHARACTERISTICS OF AN
  EMERGENT ELITE IN HARARE (SOUTHERN
  RHCDESIA).=              LUKHMB-66-SCE

  NIGERIAN PCLITICAL PARTIES -- POWER
  IN AN EMERGENT AFRICAN NATION.=
                            SKLARL-63-NPP

  BALLCT BOX AND BAYCNET -- PEOPLE
  AND GCVERNMENT IN EMERGENT ASIAN
  CCUNTRIES.=              TINKH -64-BBB

EMERGING
  BUILDERS CF EMERGING NATICNS.=

EMERGING                    (CCNTINUATICN)
                            CEANVM-61-BEN

  THE EMERGING ANTI - CCLCNIAL
  CCNSENSUS IN THE UNITED NATIONS.=
                            ROWEET-64-EAC

  EMERGING GCVERNMENT IN THE ARAB
  WCRLD.=                  SALEE -62-EGA

  THE EMERGING ELITE -- A STUDY OF
  PCLITICAL LEACERSHIP IN CEYLCN.=
                            SINGMR-64-EES

EMPERCR
  THE NEW EMPERCR SYSTEM (JAPAN).=
                            KENZT -62-NES

EMPIRE
  FRCM EMPIRE TC NATICN -- THE RISE
  TC SELF-ASSERTICN OF ASIAN AND
  AFRICAN PECPLES.=        EMERR -60-ENR

  THE ANCNYMCUS EMPIRE (LCBBYING,
  GREAT BRITAIN).=         FINESE-56-AEL

  ANCNYMCUS EMPIRE (GREAT BRITAIN).=
                            FINESE-58-AEG

  ELITE MCBILITY IN THE RCMAN
  EMPIRE.=                 HOPKK -65-EMR

  LOST SCLDIERS -- THE FRENCH ARMY
  AND EMPIRE IN CRISIS, 1947-1962.=
                            KELLGA-65-LSF

EMPIRES
  RELIGICUS CRGANIZATICNS AND
  PCLITICAL PRCCESS IN CENTRALIZED
  EMPIRES (MICDLE EAST, FAR EAST).=
                            EISESN-62-ROP

  THE PCLITICAL SYSTEMS CF EMPIRES.=
                            EISESN-63-PSE

EMPIRICAL
  LAWYERS IN PCLITICS -- AN EMPIRICAL
  EXPLCRATICN OF BICGRAPHICAL DATA
  CN STATE LEGISLATCRS.=
                            GOLDD -61-LPE

  THE SCCIAL STRUCTURE AND POLITICAL
  PRCCESS OF SUBURBIA -- AN
  EMPIRICAL TEST (UNITEC STATES).=
                            GREES -62-SSP

  AUTHCRITY -- SCME CCNCEPTUAL AND
  EMPIRICAL NCTES.=        KIM,YC-66-ACE

  THE ANALYSIS OF PCLITICAL BEHAVICR
  -- AN EMPIRICAL APPRCACH.=
                            LASSHD-48-APB

  'BUREAUCRACY' AND 'RATICNALITY' IN
  WEBER'S CRGANIZATICN THEORY -- AN
  EMPIRICAL STUDY.=        UDY,SH-59-BRW

EMPLCYEES
  THE CANADIAN BUREAUCRACY -- A STUCY
  CF CANADIAN CIVIL SERVICE AND
  CTHER PUBLIC EMPLCYEES 1939-1947.=
                            COLET -49-CBS

EMPLCYERS
  THE FEDERATICN CF GERMAN EMPLCYERS'
  ASSCCIATICNS -- A PCLITICAL
  INTEREST GRCUP.=         BUNNRF-60-FGE

  CCHESICN AND CCMMITMENT IN
  EMPLCYERS' CRGANIZATICNS (FRANCE,
  GERMANY).=               HARTH -59-CCE

ENEMIES
  MUSSOLINI'S ENEMIES -- THE ITALIAN

FEDERAL            (CONTINUATION)
                   STEARJ-60-RFC

SUPREME COURT ATTITUDES TOWARD
FEDERAL ADMINISTRATIVE AGENCIES
(UNITED STATES).=        TANEJ -60-SCA

THE AMERICAN FEDERAL EXECUTIVE -- A
STUDY OF SOCIAL AND PERSONAL
CHARACTERISTICS OF THE CIVILIAN
AND MILITARY LEADERS OF THE UNITED
STATES FEDERAL GOVERNMENT.=
                         WARNWL-63-AFE

THE AMERICAN FEDERAL EXECUTIVE -- A
STUDY OF SOCIAL AND PERSONAL
CHARACTERISTICS OF THE CIVILIAN
AND MILITARY LEADERS OF THE UNITED
STATES FEDERAL GOVERNMENT.=
                         WARNWL-63-AFE

FEDERAL ADMINISTRATION, RANK, AND
CIVIL STRIFE AMONG BEMBA ROYALS
AND NOBLES (ZAMBIA).= WERBRP-67-FAR

THE TAMIL FEDERAL PARTY IN CEYLON
POLITICS.=              WILSAJ-66-TFP

FEDERALISM
SOVIET PUBLIC ADMINISTRATION AND
FEDERALISM.=            HAZAJN-52-SPA

FEDERALISM -- WEST GERMAN
BUREAUCRACY.=           NEURK -59-FWG

FEDERALISM AND THE PARTY SYSTEM
(UNITED STATES).=       TRUMD -55-FPS

PARTY DISCIPLINE UNDER FEDERALISM
-- IMPLICATIONS OF AUSTRALIAN
EXPERIENCE.=            WILDA -61-PDU

FEDERATION
ATTITUDES OF JAMAICAN ELITES
TOWARDS THE WEST INDIAN
FEDERATION.=            BELLW -60-AJE

THE STUDENT FEDERATION OF CHILE --
50 YEARS OF POLITICAL ACTION.=
                       BONIF -60-SFC

THE FEDERATION OF GERMAN INDUSTRY
IN POLITICS.=          BRAUG -65-FGI

THE FEDERATION OF GERMAN EMPLOYERS'
ASSOCIATIONS -- A POLITICAL
INTEREST GROUP.=       BUNNRF-60-FGE

RACE AND POLITICS -- PARTNERSHIP IN
THE FEDERATION OF RHODESIA
NYASALAND.=            CLEGE -60-RPP

MEMBERSHIP PARTICIPATION IN
POLICY-MAKING IN THE C.C.F.
(CO-OPERATIVE COMMONWEALTH
FEDERATION, CANADA).= ENGLFC-56-MPP

POLITICAL UNIFICATION -- A
COMPARATIVE STUDY OF LEADERS AND
FOLLOWERS (UNITED ARAB REPUBLIC,
FEDERATION OF THE WEST INDIES,
SCANDINAVIA, EUROPEAN ECONOMIC
COMMUNITY).=           ETZIA -65-PUC

AUSTRIAN LABOR'S BID FOR POWER --
THE ROLE OF THE TRADE UNION
FEDERATION.=           GULICA-58-ALS

THE DEBATE ON CENTRAL AFRICAN
FEDERATION IN RETROSPECT.=
                       DUTTWF-57-DCA

MALAYSIA -- A NEW FEDERATION IN

FEDERATION          (CONTINUATION)
SOUTHEAST ASIA.=      MEANGP-63-MNF

PUBLIC SERVICE COMMISSIONS IN THE
FEDERATION OF MALAYA.=
                      TILMRO-61-PSC

FEELING
MEN WHO MANAGE -- FUSIONS OF
FEELING AND THEORY IN
ADMINISTRATION.=      DALTM -59-MWM

FELLAH
THE USE OF THE ARAB FELLAH.=
                      BASHTM-58-UAF

FERMENT
THE INTELLECTUAL FERMENT CONTINUES
(SOVIET UNION).=      ANON  -58-IFC

MOSCOW IN FERMENT (SOVIET UNION).=
                      DEGRJ -62-MFS

FERMENT IN FRANCO SPAIN.=
                      RADIB -59-FFS

FERMENT AMONG INTELLECTUALS
(CHINA).=             SIMOJ -64-FAI

FEUDAL
FEUDAL SOCIETY AND MODERN
LEADERSHIP IN SATSUMA-HAN.=
                      SAKARK-57-FSM

MAX WEBER ON THE SOCIOLOGY OF THE
FEUDAL ORDER.=        ZEITM -60-MWS

FEUDALISM
FEUDALISM IN AFRICA.= GOODJ -63-FA

FEUDALITY
BUNYORO -- AN AFRICAN FEUDALITY.=
                      BEATJH-64-BAF

CONFESSIONALISM AND FEUDALITY IN
LEBANESE POLITICS.=   HESSCG-54-CFL

FEW
THE RULING FEW.=      KELLD -52-RF

FICTION
POLITICAL SCIENCE AND SCIENCE
FICTION (UNITED STATES,
JUDICIARY).=          ROCHJP-58-PSS

FIELD
PROBLEMS OF FIELD ADMINISTRATION IN
THE DEPARTMENT OF LABOR
(PHILIPPINES).=       CALALM-62-PFA

FRENCH FIELD ADMINISTRATION -- THE
BEGINNINGS.=          FELSJW-62-FFA

DECISION MAKING IN A FEDERAL FIELD
OFFICE (UNITED STATES).=
                      GOREWJ-56-DMF

THE UTILITY AND LIMITATIONS OF
INTEREST GROUP THEORY IN
NON-AMERICAN FIELD SITUATIONS.=
                      LAPAJ -60-ULI

FIEVRE
LA FIEVRE DE LA RAISON --
NATIONALISM AND THE FRENCH RIGHT.=
                      WEBEE -58-LFD

FIFTH
FRANCE FROM THE FOURTH TO THE FIFTH
REPUBLIC.=            KIRCO -58-FFF

MOROCCO INDEPENDENT UNDER MOHAMMED

FOREIGN              (CONTINUATION)
  POLICY.=              KRISI -67-AIF

THE PRESS IN WORLD POLITICS AND IN
THE CONDUCT OF FOREIGN POLICY
(GREAT BRITAIN, LATIN AMERICA,
SOVIET UNION, UNITED STATES).=
                       KYDIS -65-PWP

AUTHORITARIAN PERSONALITY AND
FOREIGN POLICY (UNITED STATES).=
                       LEVIDJ-57-APF

NOTES ON THE CAREER FOREIGN SERVICE
(PHILIPPINES).=        MANGRS-57-NCF

THE MOSCOW PATRIARCH IN SOVIET
FOREIGN AND DOMESTIC POLICY.=
                       MARIY -61-MPS

THE PEOPLE OF THE STATE DEPARTMENT
AND FOREIGN SERVICE
(UNITED STATES).=      MCCAJL-54-PSD

THE BUSINESS ELITE AND FOREIGN
POLICY (UNITED STATES).=
                       MCLEDS-60-BEF

THE BRITISH LEFT WING AND FOREIGN
POLICY -- A STUDY OF THE INFLUENCE
OF IDEOLOGY.=          MEEHEJ-60-BLW

THE JAPANESE PEOPLE AND FOREIGN
POLICY -- A STUDY OF PUBLIC
OPINION IN POST-TREATY JAPAN.=
                       MENDCH-61-JPF

BRITISH FOREIGN POLICY AND THE
PARTY SYSTEM.=         NORTFS-60-BFP

CONGRESS AND FOREIGN POLICY-MAKING
-- A STUDY IN LEGISLATIVE
INFLUENCE AND INITIATIVE
(UNITED STATES).=      ROBIJA-62-CFP

OPINION-MAKING AND OPINION MAKERS
IN FOREIGN POLICY
(UNITED STATES).=      ROSEJN-60-OMO

PUBLIC OPINION AND FOREIGN POLICY
(UNITED STATES).=      ROSEJN-61-POF

NATIONAL LEADERSHIP AND FOREIGN
POLICY -- A CASE STUDY IN THE
MOBILIZATION OF PUBLIC SUPPORT
(UNITED STATES).=      ROSEJN-63-NLF

THE ROLE OF THE MILITARY IN
AMERICAN FOREIGN POLICY.=
                       SAPIBM-4 -RMA

SCIENTISTS, FOREIGN POLICY AND
POLITICS (UNITED STATES).=
                       SCHIWR-62-SFP

SOVIET AND AMERICAN FOREIGN POLICY
ATTITUDES -- CONTENT ANALYSIS OF
ELITE ARTICULATIONS.=  SINGDJ-64-SAF

FOREIGN POLICY DECISION-MAKING --
AN APPROACH TO THE STUDY OF
INTERNATIONAL POLITICS.=
                       SNYDRC-62-FPD

WEST GERMAN LEADERSHIP AND FOREIGN
POLICY.=               SPEIH -57-WGL

COMMUNIST CHINA TODAY -- DOMESTIC
AND FOREIGN POLICIES.=
                       TANGPS-57-CCT

THE TROUBLE MAKERS -- DISSENT OVER

FOREIGN              (CONTINUATION)
  FOREIGN POLICY (GREAT BRITAIN).=
                       TAYLAJ-58-TMD

DEFENSE AND DIPLOMACY -- THE
SOLDIER AND THE CONDUCT OF FOREIGN
RELATIONS.=            VAGTA -56-DDS

AMERICA AND THE BRITISH FOREIGN
POLICY-MAKING ELITE, FROM JOSEPH
CHAMBERLAIN TO ANTHONY EDEN,
1895-1956.=            WATTDC-63-ABF

PERSONALITIES AND POLICIES --
STUDIES IN THE FORMULATION OF
BRITISH FOREIGN POLICY IN THE
TWENTIETH CENTURY.=    WATTDC-65-PPS

FOREIGN POLICY AND PARTY POLITICS
-- PEARL HARBOR TO KOREA
(UNITED STATES).=      WESTHB-55-FPP

YOUNG MEN AND THE FOREIGN SERVICE
(UNITED STATES).=      WRISHM-54-YMF

PUBLIC OPINION AND FOREIGN POLICY
(GREAT BRITAIN).=      YOUNK -55-POF

THE IDEOLOGICAL BASES OF SOVIET
FOREIGN POLICY.=       ZINNPE-52-IBS

FOREIGN-EDUCATED
THE FOREIGN-EDUCATED IRANIAN -- A
PROFILE.=              BALDG -63-FEI

FORM
LITIGATION AS A FORM OF PRESSURE
GROUP ACTIVITY.=       VOSECE-58-LFP

FORMAL
FUNCTIONS AND PATHOLOGY OF STATUS
SYSTEMS IN FORMAL ORGANIZATIONS.=
                       BARNCI-46-FPS

IRRATIONAL LEADERSHIP IN FORMAL
ORGANIZATIONS (UNITED STATES).=
                       JOSEE -52-ILF

A STUDY OF THE INFLUENCE OF FORMAL
AND INFORMAL LEADERS IN AN
ELECTION CAMPAIGN
(UNITED STATES).=      LOWEFE-56-SIF

FORMAL RECOGNITION OF THE LEADER OF
THE OPPOSITION IN PARLIAMENTS OF
THE BRITISH COMMONWEALTH.=
                       MCHEDE-54-FRL

THE NEW ZEALAND LABOR PARTY -- ITS
FORMAL STRUCTURE.=     PENFJ -54-NZL

TVA AND THE GRASS ROOTS -- A STUDY
IN THE SOCIOLOGY OF FORMAL
ORGANIZATIONS (UNITED STATES).=
                       SELZP -49-TGR

FORMATION
THE COMMUNIST PARTY OF INDIA AND
ITS FORMATION ABROAD.=
                       AHMAM -60-CPI

OPINION INFLUENTIALS AND POLITICAL
OPINION FORMATION IN FOUR SWEDISH
COMMUNITIES.=          ANDEB -62-OIP

ECONOMIC GROWTH, SOCIAL STRUCTURE,
ELITE FORMATION -- THE CASE OF
POLAND.=               BAUMZ -64-EGS

CHANGING PATTERNS OF POLICY
FORMATION AND IMPLEMENTATION IN
COMMUNIST CHINA.=      BENSO -59-CPP

MINISTERIAL CABINETS OF THE FOURTH
REPUBLIC (FRANCE).= KINGJB-60-MCF

FRANCE FROM THE FOURTH TO THE FIFTH
REPUBLIC.= KIRCO -58-FFF

ON THE GAME OF POLITICS IN FRANCE.=
LEITN -59-GPF

PARLIAMENTARY CONTROL OF
NATIONALIZED INDUSTRY IN FRANCE.=
LEWIEG-57-PCN

STUDENT POLITICS (LATIN AMERICA,
INDIA, POLAND, UNITED STATES,
GERMANY, CHILE, ARGENTINA,
COLUMBIA, FRANCE).= LIPSSM-67-SPL

PARLIAMENT, PARTIES AND SOCIETY IN
FRANCE, 1946-1958.= MACRD -67-PPS

HONOR IN BUREAUCRATIC LIFE (FRANCE,
GREAT BRITAIN, UNITED STATES).=
MAINLC-64-HBL

POLITICAL DECISION-MAKERS (INDIA,
FRANCE, GREAT BRITAIN, GERMANY,
UNITED STATES).= MARVO -61-PDM

THE FALL OF THE REPUBLIC --
MILITARY REVOLT IN FRANCE.=
MEISJH-62-FRM

THE EXECUTIVE IN THE MODERN STATE
(CANADA, FRANCE, GREAT BRITAIN,
SOVIET UNION, UNITED STATES,
YUGOSLAVIA).= MEYNJ -58-EMS

THE 'NEW LEFT' IN FRANCE.=
MICACA-57-NLF

SOCIAL ORIGINS OF DICTATORSHIP AND
DEMOCRACY -- LORD AND PEASANT IN
THE MAKING OF THE MODERN WORLD
(FRANCE, GREAT BRITAIN,
UNITED STATES, CHINA, JAPAN,
INDIA, GERMANY).= MOORB -66-SOD

THE ADMINISTRATIVE STATE (FRANCE,
GREAT BRITAIN, SWITZERLAND,
UNITED STATES).= MORSF -57-ASF

HEROIC LEADERSHIP (EGYPT, FRANCE,
GERMANY, GREAT BRITAIN,
UNITED STATES).= PLAMJ -61-HLE

THE CIVIL SERVICE IN BRITAIN AND
FRANCE.= ROBSWA-56-CSB

INTELLECTUAL CLASSES AND RULING
CLASSES IN FRANCE -- A SECOND
LOOK.= SAX,JW-54-ICR

POLITICAL CAREERS AND PARTY
LEADERSHIP (AUSTRALIA, CANADA,
FRANCE, GREAT BRITAIN,
UNITED STATES).= SCHLJA-67-PCP

STABLE INSTABILITY IN FRANCE.=
SIEGA -56-SIF

THE RULING SERVANTS -- BUREAUCRACY
IN RUSSIA, FRANCE, AND
GREAT BRITAIN.= STRAE -61-RSB

ON POLITICAL STABILITY (FRANCE,
SOVIET UNION).= TANNF -60-PSF

DEMOCRACY IN FRANCE SINCE 1870.=

THE ANALYSIS OF A COUNTER -
REVOLUTION (FRANCE).= TILLC -64-ACR

THE NEW LEFT IN FRANCE.=
VELEVA-61-NLF

POWER, PRINCIPLE, AND THE DOCTRINE
OF THE MOUVEMENT REPUBLICAIN
POPULAIRE (FRANCE).= YATEWR-58-PPD

FRANCO
FRANCO'S SPAIN AND THE NEW EUROPE.=
ALANR -62-FSS

FERMENT IN FRANCO SPAIN.=
RADIB -59-FFS

PRELUDE TO FRANCO (SPAIN).=
RATCDF-57-PFS

FREE
THE FREE DEMOCRATIC PARTY IN WEST
GERMAN POLITICS.= BRAUG -60-FDP

LEADERSHIP IN A FREE SOCIETY.=
WHITTN-44-LFS

FREEDOM
FREEDOM AND CONTROL IN MODERN
SOCIETY.= BERGM -54-FCM

FREEDOM AND CATHOLIC POWER IN SPAIN
AND PORTUGAL.= PLANP -62-FCP

THE MACHIAVELLIANS -- DEFENDERS OF
FREEDOM.= BURNJ -63-MDF

MASS COMMUNICATIONS AND THE LOSS OF
FREEDOM IN NATIONAL
DECISION-MAKING -- A POSSIBLE
RESEARCH APPROACH TO INTERSTATE
CONFLICTS.= DEUTKW-57-MCL

DEMOCRACY -- THE THRESHOLD OF
FREEDOM (UNITED STATES,
GREAT BRITAIN, FRANCE, CANADA,
SCANDINAVIA).= GOSNHF-48-DTF

NATIONAL SECURITY AND INDIVIDUAL
FREEDOM.= LASSHD-O -NSI

FREEDOM, POWER, AND DEMOCRATIC
PLANNING.= MANNK -50-FPD

ACADEMIC FREEDOM AND PROBLEMS OF
HIGHER EDUCATION IN TURKEY.=
WEIKWF-62-AFP

FREETOWN
CREOLEDOM -- A STUDY OF THE
DEVELOPMENT OF FREETOWN SOCIETY
(SIERRA LEONE).= PORTAT-63-CSD

FRENCH
THE FRENCH ARMY IN POLITICS,
1945-1962.= AMBLJS-65-FAP

POLITICS AND THE FRENCH
INTELLECTUAL.= ARONR -50-PFI

THE POLITICS OF FRENCH CHRISTIAN
LABOR.= BARNSH-59-PFC

THE FRENCH ARMY AS A POLITICAL AND
SOCIAL FACTOR.= BEHRE -59-FAP

ON THE FRENCH LEFT.= BLOCJ -63-FL

SOME NOTES ON THE STANDING

FRENCH                     (CONTINUATION)
   CONSTITUTICNAL REFORM IN FRENCH
   TROPICAL AFRICA.=         ROBIK -58-CRF

   THE FRENCH RADICAL SOCIALIST PARTY
   AND THE REPUBLICAN FRONT OF 1956.
                             SCHLJA-58-FRS

   ELITES IN FRENCH - SPEAKING WEST
   AFRICA -- THE SOCIAL BASIS OF
   IDEAS.=                   WALLI -65-EFS

   LA FIEVRE CE LA RAISON --
   NATIONALISM ANC THE FRENCH RIGHT.=
                             WEBEE -58-LFC

   ISSUE DIMENSIONS IN A MULTI - PARTY
   SYSTEM -- THE FRENCH NATIONAL
   ASSEMBLY ANC EUROPEAN
   UNIFICATION.=             WOODCM-64-IDM

   SOME UNEXPLORED AVENUES IN FRENCH
   POLITICAL BEHAVIOR.=     WRIGG -58-UAF

FRENCH-SPEAKING
   POLITICAL PARTIES IN
   FRENCH-SPEAKING WEST AFRICA.=
                             MORGRS-64-PPF

FRIENDSHIP
   DEFERENCE AND FRIENDSHIP PATTERNS
   IN TWO INDIAN MUNICIPAL COUNCILS.=
                             ROSEDB-66-CFP

FRONT
   THE FRENCH POPULAR FRONT.=
                             BURBLB-51-FPF

   THE COLD WAR CN THE LITERARY FRONT
   (SOVIET UNION) -- PART 1, THE
   WRITER'S UNDERGROUND -- PART 2,
   GROUPS, TRENDS, GENRES, -- PART 3,
   THE PARTY ANC THE WRITERS.=
                             BURG  -62-CWL

   THE FRONT AND BACK OF
   ORGANIZATIONAL LEADERSHIP -- A
   CASE STUDY (UNITED STATES).=
                             CICOAV-58-FBC

   THE DECLINE CF ALGERIA'S FLN
   (NATIONAL LIBERATION FRONT).=
                             LEWIWH-66-DAS

   THE FRENCH RADICAL SOCIALIST PARTY
   AND THE REPUBLICAN FRONT OF 1956.
                             SCHLJA-58-FRS

FUNCTICN
   ATTITUDES TOWARD FOREIGN AFFAIRS AS
   A FUNCTION CF PERSONALITY.=
                             CHRIB -59-ATF

   THE ERRAND-RUNNING FUNCTION OF
   AUSTRIAN LEGISLATORS.=
                             CRANW -62-ERF

   CHANGES IN FUNCTION AND LEADERSHIP
   RENEWAL (GREAT BRITAIN).=
                             DENNN -61-CFL

   POWER, FUNCTION AND ORGANIZATION.=
                             CUBIR -63-PFC

   FUNCTION CF VALUES IN THE POLICY
   PROCESS -- ELITE GROUPS
   (UNITED STATES).=        JACOPE-62-FVP

   PARTY LEGISLATIVE REPRESENTATION AS
   A FUNCTION CF ELECTION RESULTS --
   RELATIONSHIP BETWEEN VOTES AND
   LEGISLATIVE REPRESENTATION IN

FUNCTION                   (CONTINUATION)
   ENGLAND AND THE UNITED STATES.=
                             MARCJG-58-PLR

   THE FUNCTION CF FACTIONALISM IN
   JAPANESE POLITICS.=      TOTTGO-65-FFJ

FUNCTIONAL
   CENTRAL AMERICAN POLITICAL PARTIES
   -- A FUNCTIONAL APPROACH.=
                             ANDECW-62-CAP

   POLITICAL IDEOLOGY AS A TOOL CF
   FUNCTIONAL ANALYSIS IN
   SOCIO-POLITICAL DYNAMICS.=
                             CIONL -59-PIT

   THE FUNCTIONAL DIFFERENTIATION OF
   ELITES IN THE KIBBUTZ (ISRAEL).=
                             ETZIA -59-FDE

   SITUATIONAL PRESSURES AND
   FUNCTIONAL ROLE OF THE ETHNIC
   LABOR LEADER.=           GREES -53-SPF

   THE DECISION PROCESS -- SEVEN
   CATEGORIES CF FUNCTIONAL
   ANALYSIS.=               LASSHD-56-DPS

   NOTES ON FUNCTIONAL REPRESENTATION
   IN THE HOUSE CF COMMONS
   (GREAT BRITAIN).=        MILLJH-59-NFR

   POLITICAL CHANGE IN A TRADITIONAL
   AFRICAN CLAN -- A STRUCTURAL
   FUNCTIONAL ANALYSIS CF THE NSITS
   CF NIGERIA.=             SCARJR-65-PCT

FUNCTIONING
   PARLIAMENTARISM IN WESTERN GERMANY
   -- THE FUNCTIONING CF THE
   BUNDESTAG.=              LOEWG -61-PWG

FUNCTIONS
   DIRECTORS AND THEIR FUNCTIONS
   (UNITED STATES).=        BAKEJC-45-DTF

   THE FUNCTIONS CF THE EXECUTIVE.=
                             BARNCI-38-FE

   FUNCTIONS AND PATHOLOGY OF STATUS
   SYSTEMS IN FORMAL ORGANIZATIONS.=
                             BARNCI-46-FPS

   THE FUNCTIONS CF THE PUBLICS IN
   PLATO'S CITIES.=         DAVIM -66-FPP

   THE FUNCTIONS CF LOCAL LABOUR
   PARTIES -- EXPERIMENTS IN RESEARCH
   METHODS (GREAT BRITAIN).=
                             DONNDV-54-FLL

   THE FUNCTIONS CF INFORMAL GROUPS IN
   LEGISLATIVE INSTITUTIONS
   (UNITED STATES).=        FIELA -62-FIG

   THE ETHIOPIAN NC - PARTY STATE -- A
   NOTE CN THE FUNCTIONS CF POLITICAL
   PARTIES IN DEVELOPING STATES.=
                             HESSRL-64-ENP

   THE FUNCTIONS CF ALIENATION IN
   LEADERSHIP (UNITED STATES).=
                             LOWRRP-62-FAL

   THE TSUNGLI YAMEN -- ITS
   ORGANIZATION ANC FUNCTIONS
   (CHINA).=                MENGSM-59-TYI

   THE FUNCTIONS CF POLISH TRADE
   UNIONS -- THEIR PROFESSION TOWARD
   THE SOVIET PATTERN.=     ROSECS-55-FPT

FUNCTIONS          (CONTINUATION)
THE FUNCTIONS CF SCVIET LOCAL
ELECTIONS.=          SWEAHR-61-FSL

CHANGES IN THE STRUCTURE AND
FUNCTIONS CF THE INTELLIGENTSIA
(POLAND).=          SZCZJ -47-CSF

THE FUNCTIONS CF DISUNITY -- THE
NEGRO LEADERSHIP IN A SCUTHERN
CITY (UNITEC STATES).=
                    WALKJL-63-FDN

FUSION
THE PHILIPPINE ADMINISTRATIVE
SYSTEM -- A FUSION CF EAST AND
WEST.=              HEADF -57-PAS

FUSIONS
MEN WHO MANAGE -- FLSIONS OF
FEELING AND THECRY IN
ADMINISTRATION.=    CALTM -59-MWM

FUTILITY
COMMUNISM IN HOLLAND -- A STUDY IN
FUTILITY.=          KOOLF -60-CHS

FUTURE
THE JACOBIN LEFT AND THE FUTURE CF
THE COMMUNISTS IN LATIN AMERICA.=
                    ALEXRJ-63-JLF

BUREAUCRACY AND THE FUTURE.=
                    APPLPH-54-BF

THE FUTURE CF THE LIBERAL-LEFT
(UNITEC STATES).=   CARTMB-60-FLL

THE FUTURE CF THE LEFT
(GREAT BRITAIN).=   CROSCA-60-FLG

REACS TC THE FUTURE
(SOVIET UNICN).=    FAINM -67-RFS

THE FUTURE CF THE LEFT
(GREAT BRITAIN).=   FOOTM -60-FLG

THE SCVIET ELITE -- 1, GROUPS AND
INDIVICUALS -- 2, IN WHCSE HANDS
THE FUTURE.=        HOUGJ -67-SEC

KWAME NKRUMAH AND THE FUTURE CF
AFRICA.=            PHILJ -61-KNF

CIVIL SERVANTS IN WASHINGTON -- 1,
THE CHARACTER CF THE FEDERAL
SERVICE --2, THE HIGHER CIVIL
SERVICE AND ITS FUTURE
(UNITEC STATES).=   SPANRN-53-CSW

INTELLECTUALS AND EURCPE'S FUTURE.=
                    SPENS -47-IES

THE FUTURE CF UNDER-DEVELOPED
COUNTRIES -- POLITICAL
IMPLICATICNS CF ECONCMIC
DEVELCPMENT.=       STANE -54-FUC

THE CONGRESS AND AMERICA'S FUTURE.=
                    TRUMDB-65-CAS

THE FUTURE CF THE LEFT
(GREAT BRITAIN).=   WALKPG-60-FLG

PRCFESSCR CARR'S 'WAVE CF THE
FUTURE'.=           WOLFBC-55-PCS

GABON
NATIONAL UNITY AND REGIONALISM IN
EIGHT AFRICAN STATES (NIGERIA,
NIGER, THE CCNCC, GABCN, CENTRAL
AFRICAN REPUBLIC, CHAD, UGANDA,

GABON              (CCNTINUATICN)
ETHIOPIA).=         CARTGM-66-NUR

GAIN
HCW TCTALITARIANS GAIN ABSOLUTE
POWER (NAZI GERMANY,
SCVIET UNICN).=     KECSP -52-HTG

GALLA
EAST AFRICAN ACE - CLASS SYSTEMS --
AN INCUIRY INTC THE SOCIAL ORDER
CF GALLA, KIPSIGIS, AND KIKUYU.=
                    PRINAH-53-EAA

GAME
CN THE GAME CF POLITICS IN FRANCE.=
                    LEITN -59-GPF

A GAME THECRETIC ANALYSIS OF
CCNGRESSICNAL PCWER CISTRIBUTICNS
FCR A STABLE TWC - PARTY SYSTEM.=
                    LUCERO-56-GTA

GAMES
MEASUREMENT CF SCCIAL PCWER
OPPCRTUNITY CCSTS, AND THE THECRY
CF TWC-PERSCN BARGAINING GAMES.=
                    HARSJC-62-MSP

THE LCCAL CCMMUNITY AS AN ECOLCGY
CF GAMES (UNITEC STATES).=
                    LCNGNE-58-LCE

THE GAMES CF CCMMUNITY POLITICS
(UNITED STATES).=   SMITPA-65-GCP

GAO
MANILA'S MAYCR LOCKS HCRNS WITH THE
GAC (PHILIPPINES).= SCRIK -63-MSM

GARRISCN
THE GARRISCN STATE HYPCTHESIS
TCDAY.=             LASSHD-62-GSH

GASSET
ORTEGA Y GASSET AND THE THEORY CF
THE MASSES.=        MALCM -61-CYG

GATEKEEPERS
NEWSPAPER 'GATEKEEPERS' AND THE
SCURCES CF NEWS.=   CARTRE-58-NGS

GAULLIST
THE GAULLIST REPUBLIC.=
                    ARCNR -63-GR

GAULLISTS
CAN DEGAULLE CHECK THE GAULLISTS
(FRANCE).=          ALANR -59-CDC

GENEALOGICAL
GENEALCGICAL TRCUBLES (HUNGARY).=
                    MERAT -62-GTH

GENEALOGY
THE GENEALCGY CF THE POLISH
INTELLIGENTSIA.=    JELEJA-59-GPI

GENERAL
THE GCVERNCR GENERAL'S PART IN
LEGISLATICN (NEW ZEALAND).=
                    ABRAPL-49-GGS

INTERACTICN IN A CCMMITTEE CF THE
UNITEC NATICNS GENERAL ASSEMBLY.=
                    ALGECF-66-ICU

WCRLC PCLITICS IN THE GENERAL
ASSEMBLY (UNITEC NATICNS).=
                    ALKEHR-65-WPG

THE PCLITICAL METHCCS CF GENERAL

GENERAL (CONTINUATION)
DEGAULLE (FRANCE).= AROLR -61-PMG

THE GENERAL IMPLICATIONS
(SOVIET UNION, KHRUSHCHEV'S
FALL).= AVTOA -64-GIS

MEASURING THE IMPACT OF LOCAL PARTY
ACTIVITY ON THE GENERAL ELECTION
VOTE (UNITED STATES).=
CUTRP -63-MIL

THE LAWYER IN THE INDIANA GENERAL
ASSEMBLY (UNITED STATES).=
CERGOR-62-LIG

HISTORY OF THE GERMAN GENERAL
STAFF, 1657-1945.= GOERW -53-HGG

MAJORITY DECISIONS AND MINORITY
RESPONSES IN THE UN GENERAL
ASSEMBLY (UNITED NATIONS).=
MANNCS-66-MDM

THE GERMAN GENERAL STAFF -- MODEL
OF MILITARY ORGANIZATION.=
MARWA -59-GGS

THE FORMULATION OF LIBERAL AND
CONSERVATIVE PROGRAMMES IN THE
1957 CANADIAN GENERAL ELECTION.=
MEISJ -60-FLC

THE CANADIAN GENERAL ELECTION OF
1957.= MEISJ -62-CGE

INTRODUCTION -- GENERAL STUDY OF
PARLIAMENTARIANS.= MEYNJ -61-IGS

SOVIET ADMINISTRATIVE LEGALITY --
THE ROLE OF THE ATTORNEY GENERAL'S
OFFICE.= MORGGG-62-SAL

INDIAN DEMOCRACY AND THE GENERAL
ELECTION.= PARKRL-52-IDG

THE SIGNIFICANCE OF THE CAMPAIGN IN
GENERAL ELECTIONS
(GREAT BRITAIN).= POLLH -53-SCG

LIFE CAREERS, POWER AND THE
PROFESSIONS -- THE RETIRED ARMY
GENERAL (UNITED STATES).=
REISL -56-LCP

THE KENYA GENERAL ELECTION OF
1963.= SANGC -64-KGE

THE GENERAL ELECTION IN TANZANIA.=
TORDW -66-GET

CEYLON GENERAL ELECTIONS, 1956.=
WEERID-60-CGE

THE BRITISH GENERAL ELECTION OF
1951 -- CANDIDATES AND PARTIES.=
WILLJR-52-BGE

GENERALISSIMO
GENERALISSIMO STALIN AND THE ART OF
GOVERNMENT (SOVIET UNION).=
UTISO -52-GSA

GENERALIZED
YES -- THERE ARE GENERALIZED
OPINION LEADERS.= MARCAS-64-YTA

GENERALS
HITLER AND THE GERMAN GENERALS.=
BOENH -54-HGG

GENERALS AS STATESMEN (FRANCE,

GENERALS (CONTINUATION)
FINLAND, GERMANY UNITED STATES).=
CELLJE-59-GSF

POLITICIANS AND GENERALS
(GREAT BRITAIN).= JONEMW-63-PGG

CONSTITUENCY VERSUS
CONSTITUTIONALISM -- THE
DESEGREGATION ISSUE AND TENSION
AND ASPIRATIONS OF SOUTHERN
ATTORNEY GENERALS
(UNITED STATES).= KRISS -59-CVC

GENERALS VS. PRESIDENTS --
NEOMILITARISM IN LATIN AMERICA.=
LIEUE -64-GVP

SATELLITE GENERALS -- A STUDY OF
MILITARY ELITES IN THE SOVIET
SPHERE.= POOLID-55-SGS

GENERALS AND POLITICIANS IN INDIA.=
RUDOLI-64-GPI

SWORD AND SWASTIKA -- GENERALS AND
NAZIS IN THE THIRD REICH.=
TAYLT -52-SSG

GENERATION
THE YOUNG GENERATION OF SOVIET
WRITERS.= ANON -58-YGS

RIGHT-WING RADICALISM IN WEST
GERMANY'S YOUNGER GENERATION.=
BERGV -62-RWR

SOME CHARACTERISTICS OF THE YOUNGER
GENERATION IN WESTERN GERMANY.=
EBW -54-CYG

FROM GENERATION TO GENERATION --
AGE GROUPS AND SOCIAL STRUCTURE.=
EISESN-56-GGA

FROM GENERATION TO GENERATION --
AGE GROUPS AND SOCIAL STRUCTURE.=
EISESN-56-GGA

THE NEW GENERATION IN THE SOVIET
ARMED FORCES.= GALAN -65-NGS

THE YOUNGER GENERATION IN THE THREE
DOMINIONS (INDIA, PAKISTAN,
CEYLON).= JACKC -49-YGT

THE 'NEXT GENERATION' OF CHINESE
COMMUNIST LEADERS.= KLEIDW-62-NGC

GENERATIONS
THE PROBLEM OF GENERATIONS IN AN
ORGANIZATIONAL STRUCTURE.=
GUSFMR-57-PGG

THREE GENERATIONS OF THE SOVIET
INTELLIGENTSIA.= HAIMLH-58-TGS

THREE GENERATIONS OF THE SOVIET
INTELLIGENTSIA.= HAIMLH-59-TGS

THE SOVIET ELITE -- 1 --
GENERATIONS IN CONFLICT.=
LEWYB -67-SEG

THE PROBLEM OF GENERATIONS IN
FINNISH COMMUNISM.= RINTM -58-PGF

THREE GENERATIONS -- THE EXTREME
RIGHT WING IN FINNISH POLITICS.=
RINTM -62-TGE

POLITICAL GENERATIONS IN THE CUBAN

GERMAN                    (CCNTINUATICN)
                          KNIGME-52-GE

PARLIAMENT IN THE GERMAN POLITICAL
SYSTEM.=                   LOEWG -66-PGP

THE GERMAN GENERAL STAFF -- MCCEL
OF MILITARY CRGANIZATICN.=
                           MARWA -59-GGS

CLIGARCHIC PRCBLEMS IN A GERMAN
PARTY DISTRICT.=           MAYNR -61-CPC

THE RECCRD CF THE GERMAN LEFT.=
                           NEMEPF-45-RGL

FEDERALISM -- WEST GERMAN
BUREAUCRACY.=              NEURK -59-FWG

POLITICS AND BLREAUCRACY IN THE
WEST GERMAN BUNDESRAT.=
                           NEURK -59-PBW

SCME STUDENT PRCBLEMS IN EAST
GERMAN UNIVERSITIES.=  NM    -57-SPE

LATENT AND MANIFEST BUREAUCRACY IN
THE WEST GERMAN PARLIAMENT -- THE
CASE CF THE BUNDESRAT.=
                           PINNEL-62-LMB

THE FEDERAL GERMAN PARLIAMENT.=
                           PRITT -55-FGP

HCW FAR DCES THE GERMAN PARLIAMENT
GCVERN.=                   PRITT -56-HFC

THE WEST GERMAN POLITICAL PARTIES
AND REARMAMENT.=      RS    -53-WGP

CDU DEVIANCY IN THE GERMAN
BUNDESTAG.=                RUECGL-62-CDC

THE GERMAN SOCIAL DEMCCRATIC PARTY
AFTER WCRLD WAR 2 -- THE
CCNSERVATISM OF PCWER.=
                           SCHEFK-66-GSC

THE WILHELMSTRASSE -- A STUDY OF
GERMAN CIPLCMATS UNCER THE NAZI
REGIME.=                   SEABP -54-WSC

GERMAN REARMAMENT AND THE OLD
MILITARY ELITE.=           SPEIH -54-GRC

GERMAN REARMAMENT AND ATOMIC WAR --
THE VIEWS CF GERMAN MILITARY AND
POLITICAL LEADERS.=        SPEIH -57-GRA

GERMAN REARMAMENT AND ATOMIC WAR --
THE VIEWS CF GERMAN MILITARY AND
POLITICAL LEADERS.=        SPEIH -57-GRA

WEST GERMAN LEADERSHIP AND FOREIGN
PCLICY.=                   SPEIH -57-WGL

THE GERMAN CIPLCMATS AND THE NAZI
LEADERSHIP, 1933-1939.=
                           WATTDC-55-GDN

THE PERSONALITY CF LAWYERS -- A
CCMPARATIVE STUCY CF SUEJECTIVE
FACTORS IN LAW, BASED CN
INTERVIEWS WITH GERMAN LAWYERS.=
                           WEYRWO-64-PLC

THE NEMESIS OF PCWER -- THE GERMAN
ARMY IN PCLITICS 1918-1945.=
                           WHEEJW-54-NPC

GERMANS
THE TRANSFERRED SUCETEN -- GERMANS

GERMANS                   (CCNTINUATICN)
AND THEIR PCLITICAL ACTIVITY
(GERMANY).=               CELOB -57-TSC

GERMANY
THE YCUTH MCVEMENT IN THE WEIMAR
REPUBLIC (GERMANY).=   APSLAE-45-YMW

GERMANY'S PCST NAZI INTELLECTUAL
CLIMATE.=                 ARNOGL-55-GSP

THE NEW ECCNOMIC SYSTEM AND THE
RCLE CF TECHNCCRATS IN THE CDR
(EAST GERMANY).=          BAYHTA-66-NES

CHANGES IN THE SOCIAL
STRATIFICATICN CF CCNTEMPORARY
GERMANY.=                 BECKH -50-CSS

RIGHT-WING RADICALISM IN WEST
GERMANY'S YCUNGER GENERATION.=
                          BERGV -62-RWR

REPUBLIC IN SUSPENSE -- POLITICS,
PARTIES, ANC PERSCNALITIES IN
POSTWAR GERMANY.=         BOLLK -64-RSP

DICTATCRSHIP AND PCLITICAL POLICE
(FRANCE,GERMANY,ITALY).=
                          BRAMEK-45-CPP

THE GERMAN SCCIAL DEMCCRATIC PARTY
AND THE INTERNATICNAL SITUATICN
(GERMANY).=               BRETHL-53-GSC

HITLER -- A STUCY IN TYRANNY
(GERMANY).=               BULLA -52-HST

THE TRANSFERRED SUCETEN -- GERMANS
AND THEIR PCLITICAL ACTIVITY
(GERMANY).=               CELOB -57-TSC

THE SCCIAL DEMCCRATIC PARTY OF
GERMANY -- FRCM WCRKING CLASS
MCVEMENT TC MCDERN PCLITICAL
PARTY.=                   CHALDA-64-SDP

THE SCCIALIST UNITY PARTY OF EAST
GERMANY.=                 CHILD -67-SUP

NECFASCISM IN WESTERN GERMANY AND
ITALY.=                   COLET -55-NWG

CANGER CN THE RIGHT IN GERMANY.=
                          COVEHM-50-CRG

INTELLECTUALS UNDER ULBRICHT (EAST
GERMANY).=                CROAM -60-IUU

PCLITICAL CPPCSITICN IN THE WESTERN
DEMCCRACIES (ALSTRIA, BELGIUM,
FRANCE, GERMANY, GREAT BRITAIN,
ITALY, NETHERLANDS, NCRWAY,
SWEDEN, UNITED STATES).=
                          DAHLRA-66-PCW

WHC GCVERNS GERMANY.=  DAHRR -66-WGG

SCCIETY ANC DEMCCRACY IN GERMANY.=
                          DAHRR -67-SDG

LITERATURE IN ULBRICHT'S GERMANY
(EAST GERMANY).=          DEMEP -62-LUS

LITERATURE IN ULBRICHT'S GERMANY
(EAST GERMANY).=          DEMEP -62-LUS

GERMANY REJCINS THE PCWERS -- MASS
CPINICN, INTEREST GRCUPS AND
ELITES IN CCNTEMPCRARY GERMAN
FCREIGN PCLICY.=          DEUTKW-59-GRP

INTEGRATICN AND ARMS CCNTROL IN THE

GREAT                    (CONTINUATION)
                         SOMEDC-53-QGP

GREAT BRITAIN
   CLASS AND POLITICS
   (GREAT BRITAIN).=        ABRAM -61-CPG

   INDEPENDENT CANDIDATES IN 1945,
   1950, AND 1951 (GREAT BRITAIN).=
                            ADLEMK-53-ICA

   THE ETHICS OF TRADE UNION LEADERS
   (GREAT BRITAIN).=        ALLEVL-63-ETU

   THE WORK OF THE PRIVATE SECRETARY
   TO THE MEMBER OF PARLIAMENT
   (GREAT BRITAIN).=        AN MMP-48-WPS

   END OF AN ELITE (GREAT BRITAIN).=
                            ANNAN -66-EEG

   CIVIL SERVANTS, MINISTERS,
   PARLIAMENT AND THE PUBLIC
   (GREAT BRITAIN).=        ATTLCR-54-CSM

   THE ATTITUDES OF M.P.'S AND ACTIVE
   PEERS (GREAT BRITAIN).=
                            ATTLE -59-AMP

   DUTIES OF A MEMBER OF PARLIAMENT
   (GREAT BRITAIN).=        BALLWM-56-DMP

   PRIVY COUNCIL, CABINET AND MINISTRY
   IN GREAT BRITAIN AND CANADA.=
                            BANKMA-  -PCC

   LABOUR PARTY IN ITS SOCIAL CONTEXT
   (GREAT BRITAIN).=        BEALHL-53-LPI

   THE CONSERVATIVE PARTY OF
   GREAT BRITAIN.=          BEERSH-52-CPG

   TREASURY CONTROL (GREAT BRITAIN).=
                            BEERSH-57-TCG

   SOCIAL CLASS AND POLITICS IN
   GREENWICH (GREAT BRITAIN).=
                            BENNM -50-SCP

   SMALL - TOWN POLITICS -- A STUDY OF
   POLITICAL LIFE IN GLOSSOP
   (GREAT BRITAIN).=        BIRCAH-59-STP

   THE CONSERVATIVE ASSOCIATION AND
   THE LABOUR PARTY IN READING
   (GREAT BRITAIN).=        BLONJ -58-CAL

   CONFLICT, DECISION-MAKING AND THE
   PERCEPTIONS OF LOCAL COUNCILLORS
   (GREAT BRITAIN).=        BLONJ -67-CDM

   THE RECRUITMENT OF LOCAL
   COUNCILLORS -- A CASE STUDY
   (GREAT BRITAIN).=        BOCHJM-66-RLC

   THE FOUR LABOUR CABINETS
   (GREAT BRITAIN).=        BONNJ -58-FLC

   THE ADMINISTRATIVE ELITE
   (GREAT BRITAIN, FRANCE).=
                            BOTTTB-64-AEG

   MINISTRY CONTROL AND LOCAL AUTONOMY
   IN EDUCATION (GREAT BRITAIN).=
                            BRANJA-65-MCL

   THE ANATOMY OF REVOLUTION (FRANCE,
   GREAT BRITAIN, UNITED STATES,
   SOVIET UNION).=          BRINC -60-ARF

   M.P.S. IN MINISTERIAL OFFICE
   (GREAT BRITAIN).=        BUCKPW-61-MPS

GREAT BRITAIN            (CONTINUATION)
   ELECTORS' ATTITUDES TOWARDS LOCAL
   GOVERNMENT -- A SURVEY OF A
   GLASGOW CONSTITUENCY
   (GREAT BRITAIN).=        BUDGI -65-EAT

   THE CONSERVATIVE PARTY -- REVOLTS
   AND PRESSURES -- 1955-1961
   (GREAT BRITAIN).=        BURIH -61-CPR

   THE CONSERVATIVES IN POWER
   (GREAT BRITAIN).=        BUTLA -59-CPG

   THE HISTORY AND PRACTICE OF LOBBY
   JOURNALISM (GREAT BRITAIN).=
                            BUTLA -60-HPL

   PARLIAMENT -- A SURVEY
   (GREAT BRITAIN).=        CAMPG -52-PSG

   THE OFFICE OF THE PRIME MINISTER
   (GREAT BRITAIN).=        CARTBE-56-OPM

   ORGANIZATION OF THE NATIONALISED
   INDUSTRIES (GREAT BRITAIN).=
                            CHESON-50-ONI

   PUBLIC CORPORATIONS AND THE
   CLASSIFICATION OF ADMINISTRATIVE
   BODIES (GREAT BRITAIN).=
                            CHESON-53-PCC

   THE RECRUITMENT OF THE NATION'S
   LEADERS (GREAT BRITAIN).=
                            CLAREL-36-RNS

   TRADE UNION OFFICERS
   (GREAT BRITAIN).=        CLEGHA-61-TUO

   THE CABINET (GREAT BRITAIN).=
                            CLEMRV-65-CGB

   CONCEPTION OF THE MIDDLE CLASS
   (GREAT BRITAIN).=        COLEGD-50-CMC

   LABOUR AND STAFF PROBLEMS UNDER
   NATIONALISATION (GREAT BRITAIN).=
                            COLEGD-50-LSP

   STUDIES IN CLASS STRUCTURE
   (GREAT BRITAIN).=        COLEGD-55-SCS

   THE REFORM OF PARLIAMENT
   (GREAT BRITAIN).=        CRICB -65-RPG

   THE FUTURE OF THE LEFT
   (GREAT BRITAIN).=        CROSCA-60-FLG

   ON THE LEFT AGAIN (GREAT BRITAIN).=
                            CROSCA-60-LAG

   INSIDERS AND CONTROLLERS (CORPORATE
   ELITE, GREAT BRITAIN).=
                            CROSCA-62-ICC

   SCIENTISTS IN WHITEHALL
   (GREAT BRITAIN).=        CROSR -64-SWG

   POLITICAL OPPOSITION IN THE WESTERN
   DEMOCRACIES (AUSTRIA, BELGIUM,
   FRANCE, GERMANY, GREAT BRITAIN,
   ITALY, NETHERLANDS, NORWAY,
   SWEDEN, UNITED STATES).=
                            DAHLRA-66-POW

   CHANGES IN FUNCTION AND LEADERSHIP
   RENEWAL (GREAT BRITAIN).=
                            DENNN -61-CFL

   GOVERNMENT ON THE INNER CIRCLE
   (GREAT BRITAIN).=        DEVOE -58-GIC

   THE FUNCTIONS OF LOCAL LABOUR

GREAT BRITAIN          (CONTINUATION)
AND MR. BEVAN (GREAT BRITAIN).=
                    YOUNM -53-LRF


THE RISE OF MERITOCRACY, 1870-2033
(GREAT BRITAIN).=    YOUNM -58-RMG


GREECE
MASS SUPPORT AND COMMUNIST
INSURRECTION (GREECE, MALAYA,
INDOCHINA, PHILIPPINES, SOUTH
VIETNAM).=           SANDR -65-MSC


CONSENSUS AND CLEAVAGE -- PARTY
ALIGNMENT IN GREECE, 1945-1965.=
                    TROMTP-66-CCP


GREENWICH
SOCIAL CLASS AND POLITICS IN
GREENWICH (GREAT BRITAIN).=
                    BENNM -50-SCP


GRENADA
STRATIFICATION IN GRENADA (WEST
INDIES).=            SMITMG-65-SGW


GROUP
PATTERNS OF GROUP DEVELOPMENT IN A
NEW NATION -- MOROCCO.=
                    ASHFCE-61-PGD


GROUP REPRESENTATION IN BRITAIN AND
THE UNITED STATES.=  BEERSH-58-GRB


PATTERNS OF INTERACTION AMONG A
GROUP OF OFFICIALS IN A GOVERNMENT
AGENCY (UNITED STATES).=
                    BLAUPM-54-PIA


THE FEDERATION OF GERMAN EMPLOYERS'
ASSOCIATIONS -- A POLITICAL
INTEREST GROUP.=     BUNNRF-60-FGE


GROUP INTERESTS IN CANADIAN
POLITICS.=           CLARSD-63-GIC


THE GROUP BASIS OF AUSTRIAN
POLITICS.=           DIAMA -58-GBA


GROUP STRUCTURE AND AUTHORITY.=
                    DOCTO -63-GSA


PRESSURE GROUP POLITICS -- THE CASE
OF THE BRITISH MEDICAL
ASSOCIATION.=        ECKSHH-60-PGP


A PRESSURE GROUP AND THE PRESSURED
(UNITED STATES).=    GARCO -54-PGP


POLITICAL COMMUNITY AND GROUP
INTEREST IN MODERN INDIA.=
                    GUSFJR-65-PCG


GROUP LEADERSHIP AND DEMOCRATIC
ACTION.=             HAIMFS-51-GLD


THE DILEMMA OF AN ELITE GROUP --
THE INDUSTRIALIST IN
LATIN AMERICA.=      HARBJD-65-DEG


THE LATIN AMERICAN MILITARY AS A
POLITICALLY COMPETING GROUP IN
TRANSITIONAL SOCIETY.=
                    JOHNJJ-62-LAM


CONSISTENT REACTIVE PARTICIPATION
OF GROUP MEMBERS AND REDUCTION OF
INTERGROUP CONFLICT.= KATZD -59-CRP


A MEXICAN INTEREST GROUP IN
ACTION.=             KLINM -61-MIG


THE UTILITY AND LIMITATIONS OF


GROUP                 (CONTINUATION)
INTEREST GROUP THEORY IN
NON-AMERICAN FIELD SITUATIONS.=
                    LAPAJ -60-ULI


THE GROUP BASIS OF POLITICS --
NOTES FOR A THEORY.=  LATHE -52-GBP


LEADERSHIP INTERACTION, GROUP
CONSCIOUSNESS, AND SOCIAL CHANGE.=
                    LOWRRP-64-LIG


GROUP INTERESTS IN PAKISTAN
POLITICS, 1947-1958.= MANIT -66-GIP


THE FOLKWAYS OF THE UNITED STATES
SENATE -- CONFORMITY TO GROUP
NORMS AND LEGISLATIVE
EFFECTIVENESS.=      MATTDR-59-FUS


THE ROLE OF AN INTEREST GROUP
LEADER IN THE HOUSE OF
COMMONS (GREAT BRITAIN).=


                    MILLJH-56-RIG


THE ROLE OF AN INTEREST GROUP
LEADER IN THE HOUSE OF
COMMONS (GREAT BRITAIN).=


                    MILLJH-56-RIG


THE HIGHER CIVIL SERVICE AS AN
ACTION GROUP IN WESTERN POLITICAL
DEVELOPMENT.=        MORSF -63-HCS


PATTERNS OF INTER-PERSONAL
RELATIONS IN A STATE LEGISLATIVE
GROUP -- THE WISCONSIN ASSEMBLY
(UNITED STATES).=    PATTSC-59-PIP


A KEY TO SOVIET POLITICS -- THE
CRISIS OF THE ANTI - PARTY GROUP.=
                    PETHR -62-KSP


EFFECTS OF LEGISLATIVE AND
ADMINISTRATIVE ACCESSIBILITY ON
INTEREST GROUP POLITICS.=
                    PYE,LW-58-ELA


THE EFFECTS OF NOMINATING
CONVENTIONS, ELECTIONS, AND
REFERENCE GROUP IDENTIFICATION
UPON THE PERCEPTIONS OF POLITICAL
FIGURES (UNITED STATES).=
                    RAVEBH-64-ENC


ALIENATION AND PARTICIPATION -- A
COMPARISON OF GROUP LEADERS AND
THE MASS (UNITED STATES).=
                    ROSEAM-62-APC


THE BOW GROUP'S ROLE IN BRITISH
POLITICS.=           ROSER -61-BGS


GROUP PERCEPTION AND SOCIAL CHANGE
IN CEYLON.=          SINGMR-66-GPS


THE SUPREME COURT AS A SMALL GROUP
(UNITED STATES).=    SNYDEC-57-SCS


LABOR AND POLITICS IN JAPAN -- A
STUDY OF INTEREST GROUP ATTITUDES
AND ACTIVITIES.=     SOUKJR-60-LPJ


USE OF A MULTIPLE REGRESSION MODEL
WITH GROUP DECISION-MAKING.=
                    STONLA-63-UMR


KHRUSHCHEV AND THE ANTI - PARTY

HAND (CONTINUATION)
CASE STUDY CF NECLIBERALISM IN
LATIN AMERICA.= BAILNA-65-CBH

HANDBOOK
HANDBOOK OF ORGANIZATIONS.=
MARCJG-65-HO

HANDS
THE SOVIET ELITE -- 1, GROUPS AND
INDIVIDUALS -- 2, IN WHOSE HANDS
THE FUTURE.= HOUGJ-67-SEG

HARARE
THE SOCIAL CHARACTERISTICS OF AN
EMERGENT ELITE IN HARARE (SOUTHERN
RHODESIA).= LUKHMB-66-SCE

HARM
DOES A DIVISIVE - PRIMARY HARM A
CANDIDATE'S CHANCES
(UNITED STATES).= HACKA-65-DDP

HARVEST
BITTER HARVEST -- THE INTELLECTUAL
REVOLT BEHIND THE IRON CURTAIN
(EAST EUROPE).= STILE-59-BHI

HAUSA
HISTORICAL AND CULTURAL CONDITIONS
OF POLITICAL CORRUPTION AMONG THE
HAUSA (NORTHERN NIGERIA).=
SMITMG-64-HCC

HAWAII
MISSIONARIES TO HAWAII -- SHAPER'S
OF THE ISLAND'S GOVERNMENT.=
MELLN-58-MHS

HEAD
THE ROLE OF THE CHIEFS AND THE HEAD
MAN AMONG THE LUGBARA OF THE WEST
NILE DISTRICT OF UGANDA.=
MIDDJ-56-RCH

HEADMAN
HEADMAN AND THE RITUAL OF LAUPULA
VILLAGES (AFRICA).= CUNNI-56-HRL

THE VILLAGE HEADMAN IN BRITISH
CENTRAL AFRICA.= GLUCM-49-VHB

HEAR
WHAT DO CONGRESSMEN HEAR -- THE
MAIL (UNITED STATES).=
DEXTLA-56-WCC

HEBRIDES
LEADERSHIP AND COMMUNICATION IN THE
CROFTING COMMUNITIES OF THE OUTER
HEBRIDES.= CAIRJB-61-LCC

HERDING
THE LAPPISH HERDING LEADER -- A
STRUCTURAL ANALYSIS.= PEHRRN-54-LHL

HERETICS
THE IDEOLOGY OF THE YUGOSLAV
HERETICS.= SVENTP-60-IYH

HERO
THE ENTREPRENEUR AS CULTURAL HERO.=
HAMID-57-ECH

THE MILITARY HERO AS PRESIDENTIAL
CANDIDATE (UNITED STATES).=
SOMIA-48-MHP

HEROES
AN ANATOMY OF LEADERSHIP --
PRINCES, HEROES, AND SUPERMEN
(UNITED STATES).= JENNEE-60-ALP

HEROIC
HEROIC LEADERSHIP -- THE CASE OF
MODERN FRANCE.= HOFFS-67-HLC

HEROIC LEADERSHIP (EGYPT, FRANCE,
GERMANY, GREAT BRITAIN,
UNITED STATES).= PLAMJ-61-HLE

ON HEROIC LEADERSHIP.=
SCHLA-60-HL

HERRIOT
THE FRENCH RADICAL PARTY -- FROM
HERRIOT TO MENDES-FRANCE.=
DE-TF-61-FRP

HIERARCHICAL
SOME ASPECTS OF HIERARCHICAL
STRUCTURE IN HAITI.= METRR-52-AHS

LEADERSHIP WITHIN A HIERARCHICAL
ORGANIZATION (UNITED STATES).=
PELZD-51-LWH

HIERARCHY
URBAN SOCIAL STRUCTURE AS A SINGLE
HIERARCHY.= BESHJM-63-USS

THE CIVIL - RELIGIOUS HIERARCHY IN
MESOAMERICAN COMMUNITIES -- PRE -
SPANISH BACKGROUND AND COLONIAL
DEVELOPMENT.= CARRP-61-CRH

HIERARCHY, BARGAINING, AND
DEMOCRACY IN POLITICS AND
ECONOMICS (UNITED STATES).=
DAHLRA-55-HBD

THE MINISTERIAL HIERARCHY -- PART 1
(GREAT BRITAIN).= HEASDJ-62-MHP

CLASS AND HIERARCHY -- A CRITIQUE
OF MARX.= LICHG-64-CHC

PERSONAL SENTIMENTS IN A
HIERARCHY.= TURKH-61-PSH

THREE PERSPECTIVES ON HIERARCHY --
POLITICAL THOUGHT AND LEADERSHIP
IN NORTHERN NIGERIA.= WHITCS-65-TPH

HINDU
INDIAN NATIONALISM AND HINDU SOCIAL
REFORM.= HEIMCH-64-INH

HINDU COMMUNAL GROUPS IN INDIAN
POLITICS.= LAMBRD-59-HCG

HINDUISM
MILITANT HINDUISM IN INDIAN
POLITICS -- A STUDY OF THE R.S.S.
(RASHTRIYA SWAYAMSEVAK SANGH).=
CURRJA-51-MHI

HISTORIANS
HISTORY AND THE HISTORIANS
(SOVIET UNION).= MARKK-65-HHS

SOVIET HISTORICAL SCIENCE AND THE
POSITION OF SOVIET HISTORIANS.=
URBAP-64-SHS

HISTORICAL
REPRESENTATION OF INTERESTS IN
BRITISH GOVERNMENT -- HISTORICAL
BACKGROUND.= BEERSH-57-RIB

POLITICAL ELITES IN COLONIAL
SOUTHEAST ASIA -- AN HISTORICAL
ANALYSIS.= BENCHJ-64-PEC

AN HISTORICAL SKETCH OF EGBA

HUNGARY                    (CONTINUATION)
  (HUNGARY).=               MESZJ -58-ERH

  HUNGARY -- CAN THE NEW COURSE
  SURVIVE.=                 MUELG -65-HCN

  HIGHER EDUCATION IN COMMUNIST
  HUNGARY -- 1948-1956.=
                            MURRE -60-HEC

  CHANGES IN THE LEADERSHIP
  (HUNGARY).=               SCHRT -62-CLH

  RIFT AND REVOLT IN HUNGARY.=
                            VALIF -61-RRH

HYPOTHESES
  THE CIVIC ROLE OF THE MILITARY --
  SOME CRITICAL HYPOTHESES.=
                            BOBRCB-66-CRM

  HYPOTHESES FOR A THEORY OF
  POLITICAL POWER.=         FIELGL-51-HTP

  CONSENSUS-BUILDING IN THE AMERICAN
  NATIONAL COMMUNITY -- SOME
  HYPOTHESES AND SOME SUPPORTING
  DATA.=                    ROSEJN-62-CBA

  SOME HYPOTHESES ON THE POLITICS OF
  MODERNIZATION IN INDIA.=
                            WEINM -59-HPM

HYPOTHESIS
  POLITICAL INTEGRATION AND POLITICAL
  STABILITY -- A HYPOTHESIS.=
                            AKE,C -67-PIP

  PRESIDENTIAL LEADERSHIP IN CONGRESS
  ON FOREIGN POLICY -- A REPLICATION
  OF A HYPOTHESIS (UNITED STATES).=
                            KESSM -65-PLC

  THE GARRISON STATE HYPOTHESIS
  TODAY.=                   LASSHD-62-GSH

IATA
  THE IATA SYSTEM IN LEBANON -- A
  COMPARATIVE POLITICAL VIEW.=
                            HARIIF-65-ISL

IBADAN
  THE NEW ELITES OF TROPICAL AFRICA
  -- STUDIES PRESENTED AND DISCUSSED
  AT THE SIXTH INTERNATIONAL AFRICAN
  SEMINAR AT THE UNIVERSITY OF
  IBADAN.=                  LLOYPC-66-NET

IDEA
  'MASS SOCIETY' -- THE LATE STAGES
  OF AN IDEA.=              WALTEV-64-MSL

IDEAS
  THE POLITICAL IDEAS OF CHRISTIAN
  DEMOCRACY.=               ALMOGA-48-PIC

  THE END OF IDEOLOGY -- ON THE
  EXHAUSTION OF POLITICAL IDEAS IN
  THE FIFTIES (UNITED STATES).=
                            BELLD -62-EIE

  MEN OF IDEAS -- A SOCIOLOGIST'S
  VIEW (INTELLECTUALS).=
                            COSELA-65-MIS

  REVISIONISM -- ESSAYS ON THE
  HISTORY OF MARXIST IDEAS.=
                            LABEL -62-REH

  THE POLITICAL IDEAS OF ENGLISH
  PARTY ACTIVISTS.=         ROSER -62-PIE

  ELITES IN FRENCH - SPEAKING WEST

IDEAS                      (CONTINUATION)
  AFRICA -- THE SOCIAL BASIS OF
  IDEAS.=                   WALLI -65-EFS

IDENTIFICATION
  IDENTIFICATION WITH CLASS AND
  POLITICAL ROLE BEHAVIOR
  (UNITED STATES).=         EULAH -56-ICP

  EDUCATION AND FAMILY LIFE IN THE
  DEVELOPMENT OF CLASS
  IDENTIFICATION AMONG THE YORUBA
  (WESTERN NIGERIA).=       LLOYBB-66-EFL

  THE EFFECTS OF NOMINATING
  CONVENTIONS, ELECTIONS, AND
  REFERENCE GROUP IDENTIFICATION
  UPON THE PERCEPTIONS OF POLITICAL
  FIGURES (UNITED STATES).=
                            RAVEBH-64-ENC

IDENTIFYING
  A METHOD FOR IDENTIFYING ISSUES AND
  FACTIONS FROM LEGISLATIVE VOTES
  (UNITED STATES).=         MACRD -59-MII

IDENTITY
  ETHIOPIA -- IDENTITY, AUTHORITY AND
  REALISM.=                 LEVION-66-EIA

  PERSONAL IDENTITY AND POLITICAL
  IDEOLOGY.=                PYE,LW-61-PIP

  POLITICS, PERSONALITY, AND
  NATION-BUILDING -- BURMA'S SEARCH
  FOR IDENTITY.=            PYE,LW-62-PPN

  INTELLECTUAL IDENTITY AND POLITICAL
  IDEOLOGY AMONG UNIVERSITY STUDENTS
  (LATIN AMERICA).=         SOARGA-67-IIP

IDEOLOGICAL
  IDEOLOGICAL CHANGE AND SOCIAL
  CHANGE IN CEYLON.=        AMESMM-63-ICS

  THE IDEOLOGICAL REVOLUTION IN THE
  MIDDLE EAST.=             BINDL -64-IRM

  COMMUNITY LEADERSHIP IN AN ECONOMIC
  CRISIS -- TESTING GROUND FOR
  IDEOLOGICAL CLEAVAGE
  (UNITED STATES).=         D'ANWV-66-CLE

  A SCALE ANALYSIS OF IDEOLOGICAL
  FACTORS IN CONGRESSIONAL VOTING
  (UNITED STATES).=         FARRC-58-SAI

  IDEOLOGICAL CORRELATES OF RIGHT
  WING POLITICAL ALIENATION IN
  MEXICO.=                  JOHNKF-65-ICR

  WORLD REVOLUTIONARY ELITES --
  STUDIES IN COERCIVE IDEOLOGICAL
  MOVEMENTS (CHINA, GERMANY, ITALY,
  SOVIET UNION).=           LASSHD-66-WRE

  A NEW PROGRAM OF IDEOLOGICAL
  INSTRUCTION FOR THE ELITE
  (SOVIET UNION).=          CLGIL -67-NPI

  ASPECTS OF IDEOLOGICAL BELIEF IN
  THE SOVIET UNION.=        REDDPB-66-AIB

  IDEOLOGICAL GROUPS IN THE
  AUSTRALIAN LABOR PARTY AND THEIR
  ATTITUDES.=               TRUMT -66-IGA

  IDEOLOGICAL - PRAGMATIC
  ORIENTATIONS OF WEST BERLIN LOCAL
  PARTY OFFICIALS (WEST GERMANY).=
                            WRIGWE-67-IPO

  THE IDEOLOGICAL BASES OF SOVIET

162

INDIA                        (CCNTINUATICN)
                        LAMBFB-59-POL

STUCENT POLITICS (LATIN AMERICA,
INDIA, POLANC, UNITED STATES,
GERMANY, CHILE, ARGENTINA,
COLUMBIA, FRANCE).=     LIPSSM-67-SPL

PROCESS OF INDEPENDENCE (INDIA,
PAKISTAN, INDONESIA, GHANA).=
                        MANSF -62-PII

CASTE RANKING AND COMMUNITY
STRUCTURE IN FIVE REGICNS OF INDIA
AND PAKISTAN.=          MARRM -60-CRC

POLITICAL DECISION-MAKERS (INDIA,
FRANCE, GREAT BRITAIN, GERMANY,
UNITED STATES).=        MARVC -61-PDM

THE COMMUNIST PARTY IN INDIA -- A
SHORT HISTCRY.=         MASAMR-54-CPI

SOCIAL CRIGINS CF CICTATCRSHIP AND
DEMOCRACY -- LORD AND PEASANT IN
THE MAKING CF TFE MCDERN WORLD
(FRANCE, GREAT BRITAIN,
UNITED STATES, CHINA, JAPAN,
INDIA, GERMANY).=       MOORB -66-SOC

PARLIAMENT IN INDIA.=   MORRWH-57-PI

RECENT POLITICAL CEVELCPMENT IN
INDIA -- 2.=            MORRWH-59-RPC

THE GOVERNMENT AND POLITICS OF
INDIA.=                 MORRWH-64-GPI

INDIA -- RECCNCILIATICN OF THE
RIGHT.=                 MZ    -50-IRR

MINORITY POLITICS IN PUNJAB
(INDIA).=               NAYABR-66-MPP

VILLAGE FACTICNS AND POLITICAL
PARTIES IN RURAL WEST BENGAL
(INDIA).=               NICHRW-63-VFP

COMMUNISM IN INDIA.=    CVERGC-59-CI

PARTIES AND POLITICS IN INDIA.=
                        PANIKM-59-PPI

LEADERSHIP AND POLITICAL
INSTITUTIONS IN INDIA.=
                        PARKRL-59-LPI

POLITICS AND SOCIETY IN INDIA.=
                        PHILCH-62-PSI

BUREAUCRATIC CHANGE IN INDIA.=
                        POTTDC-66-BCI

THE POLITICAL ROLE CF INDIA'S CASTE
ASSCCIATICN.=           RANDLI-60-PRI

NEW SOCIAL FORCES IN INDIA.=
                        RAO,BS-45-NSF

THE CENTRAL LECISLATURE IN BRITISH
INDIA 1921-1947.=       RASHM -65-CLB

THE CIVIL SERVICE CF INDIA.=
                        ROY,NC-58-CSI

INTRA - PARTY CONFLICT IN THE BIHAR
CCNGRESS (INDIA).=      ROY,R -66-IPC

GENERALS AND POLITICIANS IN INDIA.=
                        RUDCLI-64-GPI

DYNAMICS CF SCCIALIST LEADERSHIP IN

INDIA                        (CCNTINUATICN)
INDIA.=                 RUSCTA-59-CSL

TRANSITICN IN INDIA AND OTHER
ESSAYS.=                SANTK -64-TIC

EMERGENCY RULE IN INDIA.=
                        SCHOBN-63-ERI

CASTE AND POLITICAL PROCESS
(INDIA).=               SHAHCJ-66-CPP

CABINET GCVERNMENT IN INDIA.=
                        SHARR -51-CGI

SOCIAL CHANGE IN MCDERN INDIA.=
                        SRINMN-66-SCM

THE EVOLUTICN CF MINISTER - CIVIL
SERVANT RELATICNS IN INDIA.=
                        SUBRV -62-EMC

AUTHCRITY AND COMMUNITY IN VILLACE
INDIA.=                 TINKH -59-ACV

PARTY PCLITICS IN INDIA -- THE
DEVELCPMENT CF A MULTIPARTY
SYSTEM.=                WEINM -57-PPI

CHANGING PATTERNS CF POLITICAL
LEADERSHIP IN WEST BENGAL
(INCIA).=               WEINM -59-CPP

SCME HYPCTHESES CN THE POLITICS OF
MCDERNIZATICN IN INCIA.=
                        WEINM -59-HPM

THE POLITICS OF SCARCITY -- PUBLIC
PRESSURE AND PCLITICAL RESPONSE IN
INDIA.=                 WEINM -62-PSP

CCNGRESS PARTY ELITES (INDIA).=
                        WEINM -67-CPE

THE MEN WHC RULED INDIA -- THE
GUARDIANS.=             WOODP -54-MWR

MUSLIM LEGISLATCRS IN INDIA --
PRCFILE CF A MINCRITY ELITE.=
                        WRIGJR-64-MLI

THE MUSLIM LEACUE IN SCUTH INDIA
SINCE INDEPENDENCE -- A STUDY IN
MINCRITY GRCUP FCLITICAL
STRATEGIES.=            WRIGTP-66-MLS

INDIA AND MILITARY CICTATCRSHIP.=
                        ZINKT -59-IMC

CASTE TCDAY (INCIA).=   ZINKT -62-CTI

INDIA-S
NEHRUISM -- INCIA-S REVCLUTION
WITHOUT FEAR.=          ZINKT -55-NIS

INDIAN
THE INDIAN PRESS AND FOREIGN
PCLICY.=                BALAK -56-IPF

ATTITUCES CF JAMAICAN ELITES
TCWARDS THE WEST INDIAN
FEDERATICN.=            BELLW -60-AJE

FACTICNAL PCLITICS IN AN INDIAN
STATE -- THE CCNGRESS PARTY IN
UTTAR PRADESH.=         BRASPR-65-FPI

TRACITICNAL CCNCEPTS CF INDIAN
LEADERSHIP.=            BROWMC-59-TCI

CCNFLICTS WITHIN THE INDIAN
COMMUNIST PARTY         CARRR -55-CWI

INSTITUTICNALIZATION (CONTINUATICN)
(UNITED STATES).=       SELILG-56-PLI

INSTITUTICNS
EXTRA-PROCESSICNAL EVENTS IN TIV
POLITICAL INSTITUTICNS (NIGERIA).=
BOHAP -58-EPE

CHINESE THOUGHT ANC INSTITUTICNS.=
FAIRJK-57-CTI

THE FUNCTICNS CF INFORMAL GROUPS IN
LEGISLATIVE INSTITUTICNS
(UNITED STATES).=       FIELA -62-FIG

MILITARY INSTITUTICNS ANC POWER IN
THE NEW STATES.=        GUTTWF-65-MIP

CAREERS OF LAWYERS, LAW PRACTICE,
AND LEGAL INSTITUTICNS
(UNITED STATES).=       LACIJ -63-CLL

LEADERSHIP ANC PCLITICAL
INSTITUTICNS IN INCIA.=
PARKRL-59-LPI

PCLITICAL INSTITUTICNS ANC
AFRIKANER SCCIAL STRUCTURES IN THE
REPUBLIC CF SCUTH AFRICA.=
TRAPS -63-PIA

THE STRUGGLE FCR REPRESENTATIVE
INSTITUTICNS IN GERMANY -- PART 1
-- PART 2.=             ULLMRK-49-SRI

INSTRUCTICN
A NEW PROGRAM CF ICECLCGICAL
INSTRUCTION FCR THE ELITE
(SCVIET UNICN).=        CLGIL -67-NPI

INSTRUMENT
RESEARCH -- AN INSTRUMENT OF
PCLITICAL PCWER (UNITED STATES).=
COOKEF-61-RIP

RELIGICN AS AN INSTRUMENT OF
CULTURE CHANGE -- THE PROBLEM CF
THE SECTS IN THE SCVIET UNION.=
CUNNSP-64-RIC

INSULATICN
THE INSULATION CF LOCAL POLITICS
UNDER THE NON-PARTISAN BALLOT
(UNITED STATES).=       ACRICR-59-ILP

INSURRECTICN
THE FRENCH ARMY -- FRCM OBEDIENCE
TO INSURRECTICN.=       CHALRD-67-FAO

MASS SUPPCRT ANC COMMUNIST
INSURRECTICN (GREECE, MALAYA,
INDCCHINA, PHILIPPINES, SOUTH
VIETNAM).=              SANCR -65-MSC

INSURRECTICNS
THE REBELS -- A STUCY CF POST-WAR
INSURRECTICNS.=         CROZB -60-RSP

INTEGRATICN
CHARISMATIC LEGITIMATICN AND
PCLITICAL INTEGRATICN (GHANA).=
AKE,C -66-CLP

POLITICAL INTEGRATICN AND POLITICAL
STABILITY -- A HYPCTHESIS.=
AKE,C -67-PIP

PCLITICAL PARTIES ANC NATIONAL
INTEGRATICN IN TRCPICAL AFRICA.=
COLEJS-64-PPN

INTEGRATICN ANC ARMS CCNTROL IN THE

INTEGRATICN           (CONTINUATICN)
EURCPEAN PCLITICAL ENVIRONMENT --
A SUMMARY REPCRT (FRANCE,
GERMANY).=              CEUTKW-66-IAC

FRANCE, GERMANY, ANC THE WESTERN
ALLIANCE -- A STUCY OF ELITE
ATTITUDES CN EURCPEAN INTEGRATION
AND WCRLD PCLITICS.=    CEUTKW-67-FGW

INTEGRATICN ANC CLEAVAGE AMCNG
COMMUNITY INFLUENTIALS IN TWO
BCRDER CITIES (MEXICC,
UNITEC STATES).=        FORMWH-59-ICA

THE INTEGRATICN CF THE NEW ECCNOMIC
CLASSES WITH LCCAL GCVERNMENT IN
WEST NIGERIA.=          LLCYPC-53-INE

THE RCLE OF TECHNCCRATS IN
LATIN AMERICAN INTEGRATICN.=
MITCC -67-RTL

THE SCCIAL CEMCCRATS IN IMPERIAL
GERMANY -- A STUCY IN WCRKING
CLASS ISCLATICN ANC NATIONAL
INTEGRATICN.=           ROTHG -63-SCI

INTEGRATICN AT THE URBAN LEVEL --
PCLITICAL INFLUENCE ANC THE
DECISICN PRCCESS.=      WHEAWL-64-IUL

MASS PARTIES ANC NATICNAL
INTEGRATICN -- THE CASE OF THE
IVCRY CCAST.=           ZCLBAR-63-MPN

INTEGRATIVE
EGYPT -- THE INTEGRATIVE
REVCLUTION.=            BINDL -66-EIR

INTELLECTUAL
THE REVCLT CF THE MIND -- A CASE
HISTORY OF INTELLECTUAL RESISTANCE
BEHINC THE IRCN CURTAIN.=
ACZET -60-RMC

THE INTELLECTUAL CRIGINS OF
EGYPTIAN NATICNALISM.=
AHMEJM-60-IOE

THE INTELLECTUAL FERMENT CONTINUES
(SCVIET UNICN).=        ANCN  -58-IFC

GERMANY'S PCST NAZI INTELLECTUAL
CLIMATE.=               ARNOGL-55-GSP

PCLITICS ANC THE FRENCH
INTELLECTUAL.=          ARONR -50-PFI

INTELLECTUAL CLASSES ANC RULING
CLASSES IN FRANCE.=     BELOM -54-ICR

THE AGE CF CRANGE -- POLITICAL ANC
INTELLECTUAL LEADERSHIP IN NORTH
CARCLINA (UNITEC STATES).=
BLACR -61-AOP

TOWARD A PCRTRAIT CF THE FRENCH
INTELLECTUAL.=          BRCMV -60-TPF

THE MAY FCURTH MCVEMENT --
INTELLECTUAL REVCLUTICN IN MODERN
CHINA.=                 CHOUT -60-MFM

THE INTELLECTUAL ANC THE JEWISH
COMMUNITY (UNITED STATES))=
COHEEE-49-IJC

THE CULTURAL REVCLUTICN -- NOTES CN
THE CHANGES IN THE INTELLECTUAL
CLIMATE CF FRANCE.=     CROZM -64-CRN

THE WEST AFRICAN INTELLECTUAL

INTELLECTUAL          (CONTINUATION)
  COMMUNITY.=          DOWVM -62-WAI

  THE SCIENTIFIC INTELLECTUAL
  (UNITED STATES).=    FEUELS-63-SIU

  ATTITUDES AND ASPIRATIONS OF THE
  CONTEMPORARY IRANIAN
  INTELLECTUAL.=       HAMBG -64-AAC

  THE ROLE OF THE INTELLECTUAL IN
  FOMENTING CHANGE -- THE UNIVERSITY
  (LATIN AMERICA).=    HARRJP-64-RIF

  THE LOST YOUNG INTELLECTUAL
  (UNITED STATES).=    HOWEI -46-LYI

  IS THE INTELLECTUAL OBSOLETE
  (UNITED STATES).=    HUGHES-56-IIC

  INTELLECTUAL UNREST BEHIND THE IRON
  CURTAIN (POLAND, HUNGARY).=
                       KECSP -57-IUB

  INTELLECTUAL TRENDS IN POLAND.=
                       LABEL -57-ITP

  CONFUCIAN CHINA AND ITS MODERN FATE
  -- THE PROBLEM OF INTELLECTUAL
  CONTINUITY.=         LEVEJR-58-CCI

  THE FRENCH INTELLECTUAL
  MERRY-GO-ROUND.=     MANGS -49-FIM

  THE INTELLECTUAL IN A PEOPLE'S
  DEMOCRACY (POLAND).= MILOC -52-IPS

  THE INTELLECTUAL IN CONTEMPORARY
  SOCIETY.=            MORAJF-59-ICS

  WHAT IS AN INTELLECTUAL.=
                       NISBRA-65-WII

  THE NEGRO INTELLECTUAL AND NEGRO
  NATIONALISM (UNITED STATES).=
                       RECOW -54-NIN

  COMMUNITY AND RACIAL FACTORS IN
  INTELLECTUAL ROLES
  (UNITED STATES).=    RECOW -56-CRF

  INTELLECTUAL AND LITERARY REVIVAL
  IN POLAND.=          REY,L -57-ILR

  EGYPT IN SEARCH OF POLITICAL
  COMMUNITY -- AN ANALYSIS OF THE
  INTELLECTUAL AND POLITICAL
  EVOLUTION OF EGYPT -- 1804-1952.=
                       SAFRN -61-ESP

  INTELLECTUAL CLASSES AND RULING
  CLASSES IN FRANCE -- A SECOND
  LOOK.=               SAX,JW-54-ICR

  THE INTELLECTUAL IN THE POLITICAL
  DEVELOPMENT OF THE NEW STATES.=
                       SHILE -60-IPD

  THE INTELLECTUAL BETWEEN TRADITION
  AND MODERNITY -- THE INDIAN
  SITUATION.=          SHILE -61-IBT

  INTELLECTUAL IDENTITY AND POLITICAL
  IDEOLOGY AMONG UNIVERSITY STUDENTS
  (LATIN AMERICA).=    SOARGA-67-IIP

  BITTER HARVEST -- THE INTELLECTUAL
  REVOLT BEHIND THE IRON CURTAIN
  (EAST EUROPE).=      STILE -59-BHI

  THE MAY FOURTH MOVEMENT --
  INTELLECTUAL REVOLUTION IN MODERN

INTELLECTUAL          (CONTINUATION)
  CHINA.=              TSE-C -60-MFM

  THE INTELLECTUAL IN THE NEW CHINA.=
                       TT    -53-INC

  TWO INTELLECTUAL TRADITIONS.=
                       YABELY-63-TIT

INTELLECTUALISM
  SOCIOLOGICAL ASPECTS OF ANTI -
  INTELLECTUALISM (UNITED STATES).=
                       BARBB -55-SAA

  ANTI - INTELLECTUALISM IN
  GOVERNMENT (UNITED STATES).=
                       CLAPGR-55-AIG

  A PSYCHOLOGICAL APPROACH TO ANTI -
  INTELLECTUALISM.=    MAY,R -55-PAA

  OFFICIAL POLICY AND ANTI -
  INTELLECTUALISM (UNITED STATES).=
                       MCWIC -55-OPA

INTELLECTUALS
  THE OPIUM OF THE INTELLECTUALS.=
                       ARONR -57-CI

  INTELLECTUALS AND POLITICS IN
  WESTERN HISTORY (EUROPE).=
                       BENDHJ-61-IPW

  COMMUNISM AND THE FRENCH
  INTELLECTUALS 1914-1960.=
                       CAUTD -64-CFI

  THE THOUGHT REFORM OF INTELLECTUALS
  (COMMUNIST CHINA).=  CHENTH-59-TRI

  THOUGHT REFORM OF THE CHINESE
  INTELLECTUALS.=      CHENTH-60-TRC

  MEN OF IDEAS -- A SOCIOLOGIST'S
  VIEW (INTELLECTUALS).=
                       COSELA-65-MIS

  INTELLECTUALS UNDER ULBRICHT (EAST
  GERMANY).=           CROAM -60-IUU

  INTELLECTUALS AND THE RUSSIAN
  REVOLUTION.=         DANIRV-61-IRR

  THE INTELLECTUALS -- A
  CONTROVERSIAL PORTRAIT.=
                       DE HHU-60-ICP

  JOHNSON AND THE INTELLECTUALS
  (UNITED STATES).=    FAIRH -65-JIU

  INTELLECTUALS AND DEVELOPING
  SOCIETIES.=          FRIEJ -60-IDS

  A NEW WORLD (SOVIET
  INTELLECTUALS).=     HALAF -52-NWS

  THE INTELLECTUALS - POLITICS NEXUS
  -- STUDIES USING A BIOGRAPHICAL
  TECHNIQUE (BULGARIA,
  SOVIET UNION).=      HANHAM-64-IPN

  CUBA AND THE INTELLECTUALS.=
                       HARTA -61-CI

  POWER ROLES OF INTELLECTUALS -- AN
  INTRODUCTORY STATEMENT.=
                       HARTCL-64-PRI

  HUNGARIAN INTELLECTUALS UNDER
  FIRE.=               IGNOP -59-HIU

  THE REGIME AND THE INTELLECTUALS --

INTERESTS (CONTINUATION)
BRITISH GOVERNMENT -- HISTORICAL
BACKGROUND.= BEERSH-57-RIB

GROUP INTERESTS IN CANADIAN
POLITICS.= CLARSD-63-GIC

FRENCH BUREAUCRACY AND ORGANIZED
INTERESTS.= EHRMHW-61-FBO

U.S. BUSINESS INTERESTS IN CUBA AND
THE RISE OF CASTRO.= JOHNLL-65-USB

ORGANIZED INTERESTS IN JAPAN AND
THEIR INFLUENCE ON POLITICAL
PARTIES.= LANGFC-61-OIJ

GROUP INTERESTS IN PAKISTAN
POLITICS, 1947-1958.= MANIT -66-GIP

EQUILIBRIUM, STRUCTURE OF INTERESTS
AND LEADERSHIP -- ADENAUER'S
SURVIVAL AS CHANCELLOR (GERMANY).=
MERKPH-62-ESI

ST. LOUIS POLITICS -- RELATIONSHIP
AMONG INTERESTS, PARTIES, AND
GOVERNMENTAL STRUCTURE
(UNITED STATES))= SALIRH-60-SLP

INTERESTS AND INSTITUTIONAL
DYSFUNCTION IN URUGUAY.=
TAYLPB-63-IID

THE GOVERNMENTAL PROCESS --
POLITICAL INTERESTS AND PUBLIC
OPINION (UNITED STATES).=
TRUMDB-51-GPP

BAR OF POLITICS, JUDICIAL SELECTION
AND THE REPRESENTATION OF SOCIAL
INTERESTS (UNITED STATES).=
WATSRA-67-BPJ

INTERGOVERNMENTAL
PERSONAL CONTACT IN
INTERGOVERNMENTAL ORGANIZATIONS.=
ALGECF-65-PCI

INTERGROUP
CONSISTENT REACTIVE PARTICIPATION
OF GROUP MEMBERS AND REDUCTION OF
INTERGROUP CONFLICT.= KATZD -59-CRP

INTERGROUP RELATIONS AND LEADERSHIP
-- APPROACHES AND RESEARCH IN
INDUSTRIAL, ETHNIC, CULTURAL, AND
POLITICAL AREAS.= SHERM -62-IRL

INTERMEDIATE
A SOLUTION TO INTERMEDIATE
FACTORIAL RESOLUTION OFHURSTONE
AND DEGAN'S STUDY OF THE SUPREME
COURT (UNITED STATES).=
SCHUG -62-SIF

INTERNAL
INTERNAL CONTRADICTIONS IN
BUREAUCRATIC POLITICS (ANCIENT
CHINA, PERSIA).= EISESN-58-ICB

THE INTERNAL DISTRIBUTION OF
INFLUENCE -- THE HOUSE
(UNITED STATES).= FENNRF-65-IDI

THE INTERNAL DISTRIBUTION OF
INFLUENCE -- THE SENATE
(UNITED STATES).= HUITRK-65-IDI

INTERNAL DEVELOPMENTS -- A BALANCE
SHEET (SOVIET UNION).=
LEONW -63-IDB

INTERNATIONAL
THE ROLE OF THE INTERNATIONAL

INTERNATIONAL (CONTINUATION)
COMMISSION OF JURISTS IN THE
PROMOTION OF WORLD PEACE.=
BOSEV -64-RIC

THE GERMAN SOCIAL DEMOCRATIC PARTY
AND THE INTERNATIONAL SITUATION
(GERMANY).= BRETHL-53-GSD

COMMUNIST IDEOLOGY AND
INTERNATIONAL AFFAIRS
(SOVIET UNION, EAST EUROPE).=
BRZEZ -60-CII

YOUTH AND COMMUNISM -- AN
HISTORICAL ANALYSIS OF
INTERNATIONAL COMMUNIST YOUTH
MOVEMENTS.= CORNR -65-YCH

HOW DECISIONS ARE MADE IN FOREIGN
POLITICS -- PSYCHOLOGY IN
INTERNATIONAL RELATIONS.=
DE BBO-58-HDA

SOME INTERNATIONAL IMPLICATIONS OF
THE POLITICAL PSYCHOLOGY OF
BRAZILIANS.= FREEL -61-IIP

THE INDONESIAN COMMUNIST PARTY AND
CONFLICT IN THE INTERNATIONAL
COMMUNIST MOVEMENT.= HINDD -64-ICP

THE GEOGRAPHIC COMPOSITION OF
INTERNATIONAL SECRETARIATS.=
HOWEJM-48-GCI

THE INTERNATIONAL CIVIL SERVANT AND
HIS LOYALTIES.= JESSPC-55-ICS

INTERNATIONAL BEHAVIOR -- A
SOCIAL-PSYCHOLOGICAL ANALYSIS.=
KELMHC-65-IBS

THE CLIMATE OF INTERNATIONAL
ACTION.= LASSHD-65-CIA

UNION DEMOCRACY -- THE INSIDE
POLITICS OF THE INTERNATIONAL
TYPOGRAPHICAL UNION (NORTH
AMERICA).= LIPSSM-56-UDI

THE NEW ELITES OF TROPICAL AFRICA
-- STUDIES PRESENTED AND DISCUSSED
AT THE SIXTH INTERNATIONAL AFRICAN
SEMINAR AT THE UNIVERSITY OF
IBADAN.= LLOYPC-66-NET

DECISION-MAKING IN INTERNATIONAL
POLITICS.= ROBIJA-65-DMI

INTERNATIONAL COMMUNICATION AND
LEGISLATIVE BEHAVIOR -- THE SENATE
AND THE HOUSE OF COMMONS
(UNITED STATES, GREAT BRITAIN).=
RUSSBM-62-ICL

BARGAINING AND NEGOTIATION IN
INTERNATIONAL RELATIONS.=
SAWYJ -65-BNI

INTERNATIONAL BUREAUCRACIES AND
POLITICAL DEVELOPMENT.=
SHARWR-63-IBP

FOREIGN POLICY DECISION-MAKING --
AN APPROACH TO THE STUDY OF
INTERNATIONAL POLITICS.=
SNYDRC-62-FPD

INTERNATIONAL POLITICAL
COMMUNICATION -- ELITE VS. MASS.=
SPEIH -52-IPC

IMAGES IN THE CONTEXT OF

INTERNATIONAL        (CONTINUATION)
    INTERNATIONAL CONFLICT -- SOVIET
    PERCEPTIONS OF THE U.S. AND THE
    U.S.S.R.=            WHITRK-65-ICI

INTERNATIONALISM
    EVALUATING THE DECLINE OF SOUTHERN
    INTERNATIONALISM THROUGH
    SENATORIAL ROLL CALL VOTES
    (UNITED STATES).=    JEWEME-59-EDS

INTERPARLIAMENTARY
    INTERPARLIAMENTARY CONTACTS IN
    SOVIET FOREIGN POLICY.=
                         JULIPH-61-ICS

INTERPERSONAL
    THE DYNAMICS OF BUREAUCRACY -- A
    STUDY OF INTERPERSONAL RELATIONS
    IN TWO GOVERNMENT AGENCIES
    (UNITED STATES).=    BLAUPM-55-DBS

    LEADERSHIP AND INTERPERSONAL
    BEHAVIOR.=           PETRL -61-LIB

    LEADERSHIP AND INTERPERSONAL CHANGE
    (UNITED STATES).=    YARRLJ-58-LIC

INTERPRETATION
    AUSTRIA'S SOCIALISTS IN THE TREND
    TOWARD A TWO - PARTY SYSTEM -- AN
    INTERPRETATION OF POSTWAR
    ELECTIONS.=          GULICA-58-ASS

    COMPETITIVE PRESSURE AND DEMOCRATIC
    CONSENT -- AN INTERPRETATION OF
    THE 1952 PRESIDENTIAL ELECTION
    (UNITED STATES).=    JANOM -55-CPD

    REPRESENTATIVE BUREAUCRACY -- AN
    INTERPRETATION OF THE BRITISH
    CIVIL SERVICE.=      KINGJD-44-RBI

    THE AMERICAN DEMOCRACY -- A
    CONTEMPORARY AND AN
    INTERPRETATION.=     LASKHJ-48-ADC

    THE SOVIET POLITICAL SYSTEM -- AN
    INTERPRETATION.=     MEYEAG-65-SPS

    THE AMERICAN POLITY -- A SOCIAL AND
    CULTURAL INTERPRETATION.=
                         MITCWC-62-APS

    CHANGING PATTERNS OF POLITICAL
    AUTHORITY -- A PSYCHIATRIC
    INTERPRETATION.=     MITSA -67-CPP

    REVIEW, DISSENT AND THE APPELLATE
    PROCESS -- A POLITICAL
    INTERPRETATION (UNITED STATES).=
                         RICHRJ-67-RDA

    LEADERSHIP IN ADMINISTRATION -- A
    SOCIOLOGICAL INTERPRETATION.=
                         SELZP -57-LAS

    PARTICIPANT OBSERVATION AND THE
    COLLECTION AND INTERPRETATION OF
    DATA.=               VIDIAJ-55-POC

    TWO NEGRO POLITICIANS -- AN
    INTERPRETATION (UNITED-STATES).=
                         WILSJQ-60-TNP

    AN INTERPRETATION OF CHINESE
    ECONOMIC HISTORY.=   WU, T -52-ICE

INTERREGNUM
    TIBETS ADMINISTRATION -- IN THE
    TRANSITION PERIOD, 1951-1954 --
    DURING THE INTERREGNUM,

INTERREGNUM            (CONTINUATION)
    1954-1959.=
                         GINSG -59-TAT

INTERRELATIONS
    THE INTERRELATIONS BETWEEN LOCAL
    GOVERNMENTS AND COMMUNITY
    DEVELOPMENT (PHILIPPINES).=
                         ABUEJV-61-IBL

    CRITICAL LETTERS TO THE EDITORS OF
    THE SOVIET PRESS -- SOCIAL
    CHARACTERISTICS AND INTERRELATIONS
    OF CRITICS AND THE CRITICIZED.=
                         INKEA -53-CLE

    INTERRELATIONS BETWEEN BOLSHEVIK
    IDEOLOGY AND THE STRUCTURE OF
    SOVIET SOCIETY.=     TOMAD -51-IBB

INTERRELATIONSHIP
    THE INTERRELATIONSHIP OF POWER,
    RESPECT, AFFECTION AND RECTITUDE
    IN VICOS (PERU).=    DOUGPL-65-IPR

INTERSERVICE
    INTERSERVICE COMPETITION AND THE
    POLITICAL ROLES OF THE ARMED
    SERVICES (UNITED STATES).=
                         HUNTSP-61-ICP

INTERSTATE
    MASS COMMUNICATIONS AND THE LOSS OF
    FREEDOM IN NATIONAL
    DECISION-MAKING -- A POSSIBLE
    RESEARCH APPROACH TO INTERSTATE
    CONFLICTS.=          DEUTKW-57-MCL

INTERVENTION
    CONGRESSIONAL INNOVATION AND
    INTERVENTION IN DEFENSE POLICY --
    LEGISLATIVE AUTHORIZATION OF
    WEAPONS SYSTEMS (UNITED STATES).=
                         DAWSRH-62-CII

    POLITICS, SOCIAL STRUCTURE, AND
    MILITARY INTERVENTION IN
    LATIN AMERICA.=      GERMG -62-PSS

    POLITICAL DEVELOPMENT AND MILITARY
    INTERVENTION IN LATIN AMERICA.=
                         NEEDMC-66-PDM

INTERVIEW
    THE GOOD WILL OF IMPORTANT PEOPLE
    -- MORE ON THE JEOPARDY OF THE
    INTERVIEW.=          DEXTLA-64-GWI

INTERVIEWERS
    ORBITS OF TOLERANCE, INTERVIEWERS,
    AND ELITES (UNITED STATES).=
                         RIESD -56-OTI

INTERVIEWING
    INTERVIEWING POLITICAL ELITES IN
    CROSS-CULTURAL COMPARATIVE
    RESEARCH.=           CRANWW-64-IPE

    INTERVIEWING BUSINESS LEADERS.=
                         DEXTLA-59-IBL

    INTERVIEWING AT THE COURT
    (UNITED STATES).=    GREYDL-67-ICU

    INTERVIEWING THE BUSINESS ELITE.=
                         KINCHB-57-IBE

    SURVEY INTERVIEWING AMONG MEMBERS
    OF CONGRESS (UNITED STATES).=
                         ROBIJA-60-SIA

    INTERVIEWING A LEGAL ELITE -- THE
    WALL STREET LAWYER.=  SMIGEO-58-ILE

ITALY                    (CONTINUATION)
SWEDEN, UNITED STATES).=
                         DAHLRA-66-POW

TRENDS IN ITALY -- AN OPENING TO
THE LEFT.=               DE-ME -62-TIC

WAR PROPAGANDA, WELFARE VALUE, AND
POLITICAL IDEOLOGIES
(SOVIET UNION, UNITED STATES,
GERMANY, ITALY, GREAT BRITAIN).=
                         ECKHW -65-WPW

FOUR NOBILITIES OF THE OLD REGIME
(ITALY, GERMANY).=       FORSR -65-FNC

SIX ALLIES AND A NEUTRAL (FRANCE,
GREAT BRITAIN, INDIA, ITALY,
JAPAN, UNITED STATES, WEST
GERMANY).=               FREELA-59-SAN

POLITICAL LEADERSHIP AND THE
PROBLEM OF CHARISMATIC POWER
(GERMANY, GREAT BRITAIN, ITALY,
UNITED STATES).=         FRIECJ-61-PLP

THE NEW ITALY AND ITS POLITICS.=
                         HUGHHS-64-NII

PARTY RULE IN A DEMOCRATIC STATE
(ITALY).=                IVELV -49-PRD

MILITARY ELITES AND THE STUDY OF
WAR (FRANCE, GERMANY, ITALY,
SOVIET UNION, UNITED STATES).=
                         JANOM -57-MES

LEFT WING TRADE UNIONISM -- THE
MATRIX OF COMMUNIST POWER IN
ITALY.=                  LAPAJ -54-LWT

ITALY -- FRAGMENTATION, ISOLATION
AND ALIENATION.=         LAPAJ -66-IFI

WORLD REVOLUTIONARY ELITES --
STUDIES IN COERCIVE IDEOLOGICAL
MOVEMENTS (CHINA, GERMANY, ITALY,
SOVIET UNION).=          LASSHD-66-WRE

PARLIAMENTARIANS IN ITALY.=
                         SARTG -61-PI

IVORY COAST
POTENTIAL ELITES IN GHANA AND THE
IVORY COAST -- A PRELIMINARY
COMPARISON.=             CLIGRP-64-PEG

MASS PARTIES AND NATIONAL
INTEGRATION -- THE CASE OF THE
IVORY COAST.=            ZOLBAR-63-MPN

ONE - PARTY GOVERNMENT IN THE
IVORY COAST.=            ZOLBAR-64-OPG

CREATING POLITICAL ORDER -- THE
PARTY - STATES OF WEST AFRICA
(MALI, GHANA, SENEGAL, GUINEA,
IVORY COAST).=           ZOLBAR-66-CPO

JACOBIN
THE JACOBIN LEFT AND THE FUTURE OF
THE COMMUNISTS IN LATIN AMERICA.=
                         ALEXRJ-63-JLF

JAMAICA
EQUALITY AND ATTITUDES OF ELITES IN
JAMAICA.=                BELLW -62-EAE

SOCIAL CHANGE AND ELITES IN AN
EMERGENT NATION (JAMAICA).=
                         BELLW -65-SCE

ENTREPRENEURSHIP AND ECONOMIC

JAMAICA                  (CONTINUATION)
PROGRESS IN JAMAICA.= RATTS -63-EEP

JAMAICAN
ATTITUDES OF JAMAICAN ELITES
TOWARDS THE WEST INDIAN
FEDERATION.=             BELLW -60-AJE

IMAGES OF THE UNITED STATES AND THE
SOVIET UNION HELD BY JAMAICAN
ELITE GROUPS.=           BELLW -60-IUS

JAMAICAN LEADERS -- POLITICAL
ATTITUDES IN A NEW NATION.=
                         BELLW -64-JLP

JAPAN
LEADERS OF MODERN JAPAN -- SOCIAL
ORIGINS AND MOBILITY.=
                         ABEGJ -60-LMJ

WHITHER SOCIAL DEMOCRATIC PARTY
(JAPAN).=                AKIST -59-WSD

A SHORT-LIVED CABINET (JAPAN).=
                         ANON  -57-SLC

BUREAUCRACY ON THE MOVE (JAPAN).=
                         ANON  -59-BMJ

THE UPPER HOUSE ELECTIONS (JAPAN).=
                         ANON  -62-UHE

PARLIAMENT AND PARLIAMENTARIANS IN
JAPAN.=                  BAERPH-64-PPJ

THE POSTWAR STUDENT STRUGGLE IN
JAPAN.=                  BATTLH-56-PSS

INCREASE OF ZAIBATSU PREDOMINANCE
IN WARTIME JAPAN.=       BISSTA-45-IZP

THE SUZUKI CABINET (JAPAN).=
                         BISSTA-45-SCJ

THE ZAIBATSU'S WARTIME ROLE
(JAPAN).=                BISSTA-45-ZSW

SOCIAL STRATIFICATION AND MOBILITY
-- SOME POLITICAL IMPLICATIONS
(JAPAN).=                COLEAB-56-SSM

CONSERVATIVE LEADERSHIP IN JAPAN.=
                         COLTKE-55-CLJ

THE ETHICS OF NEW JAPAN.=
                         CORERP-52-ENJ

POLITICAL LEADERSHIP IN
INDUSTRIALIZED SOCIETIES
(UNITED STATES, SOVIET UNION,
FRANCE, CANADA, GREAT BRITAIN,
AUSTRALIA, JAPAN, PHILIPPINES).=
                         EDINLJ-67-PLI

JAPAN'S ROLE IN SOUTHEAST ASIAN
NATIONALIST MOVEMENTS, 1940-1945.=
                         ELSBWH-53-JSR

CHALLENGES TO FACTIONALISM IN
JAPAN'S LIBERAL DEMOCRATIC PARTY.=
                         FARNLW-66-CFJ

OPINIONS OF PARLIAMENTARIANS IN
INDIA AND JAPAN.=        FREELA-58-OPI

SIX ALLIES AND A NEUTRAL (FRANCE,
GREAT BRITAIN, INDIA, ITALY,
JAPAN, UNITED STATES, WEST
GERMANY).=               FREELA-59-SAN

POLITICAL SYSTEMS AND THE

JAPAN                   (CCNTINUATICN)
DISTRIBUTION CF PCWER (INDIA,
AFRICA, JAPAN).=        GLUCM -65-PSC

THE SCCIALIST MERGER AND THE
BALANCE OF PARTIES IN JAPAN.=
GRINM -55-SMB

THE RESURGENCE CF MILITARY ELEMENTS
IN JAPAN.=              GUILR -52-RME

GCVERNMENT AND LOCAL POWER IN JAPAN
-- A STUDY CN BIZEN PROVINCE
500-1700.=             HALLJW-66-GLP

THE SCCIALIZATICN CF ATTITUCES
TCWARC POLITICAL AUTHCRITY
(AUSTRALIA, CHILE, JAPAN,
PUERTO RICC, UNITEC STATES).=
HESSRD-63-SAT

THE ORIGINS OF ENTREPRENEURSHIP IN
MEIJI JAPAN.=          HIRSJ -64-OEM

SCLDIERS AND GCVERNMENT -- NINE
STUDIES IN CIVIL - MILITARY
RELATICNS (WESTERN EUROPE, USSR,
JAPAN, LATIN AMERICA,
UNITED STATES).=       HOWAM -59-SGN

THE DEVELCPMENT CF CAPITALISM IN
JAPAN.=                IKE,N -49-DCJ

EDUCATICN, VALUES AND PCLITICS IN
JAPAN.=                JANSMB-57-EVP

THE NEW EMPERCR SYSTEM (JAPAN).=
KENZT -62-NES

ECHCES CF MILITARISM IN JAPAN.=
KINOH -53-EMJ

UYOKU, THE RIGHT WING CF JAPAN.=
KINOH -63-URW

THE JAPAN CCMMUNIST PARTY -- ITS
DEVELCPMENT SINCE THE WAR.=
KIYOE -58-JCP

JAPAN'S NEW DIET.=     KURIKK-46-JSN

SCCIABILITY AND PCLITICAL
INVCLVEMENT (JAPAN).=  KUROY -65-SPI

BIG BUSINESS LCBBYING IN JAPAN --
THE CASE CF CENTRAL BANK REFORM.=
LANGFC-61-BBL

CRGANIZED INTERESTS IN JAPAN AND
THEIR INFLUENCE CN POLITICAL
PARTIES.=              LANGFC-61-OIJ

THE RCLE OF THE BUREAUCRACY IN
JAPAN.=                MAKIJM-47-RBJ

GCVERNMENT AND PCLITICS IN JAPAN --
THE RCAD TC DEMCCRACY.=
MAKIJM-62-GPJ

THE JAPANESE PECPLE AND FOREIGN
PCLICY -- A STUCY CF PUBLIC
CPINICN IN PCST-TREATY JAPAN.=
MENDOH-61-JPF

SOCIAL CRIGINS CF DICTATORSHIP AND
DEMCCRACY -- LCRD AND PEASANT IN
THE MAKING CF THE MCDERN WORLD
(FRANCE, GREAT BRITAIN,
UNITED STATES, CHINA, JAPAN,
INDIA, GERMANY).=      MOORB -66-SOD

NATIONALISM AND RIGHT WING IN JAPAN

JAPAN                   (CCNTINUATICN)
-- A STUDY CF PCST-WAR TRENDS.=
MORRII-60-NRW

MCDERN POLITICAL PARTIES (WESTERN
EURCPE, JAPAN) SCVIET UNION,
UNITEC STATES, EASTERN EUROPE).=
NEUMS -56-MPP

JAPAN'S EMERGENCE AS A MCDERN
STATE.=                NORMEH-46-JSE

THE ELITE, INCUSTRIALISM AND
NATICNALISM -- JAPAN.=
CLSOL -63-EIN

THE GREAT PURGE IN JAPAN.=
CUIGHS-47-GPJ

THE UNITED STATES AND JAPAN.=
REISEO-65-USJ

DEMCCRACY AND THE PARTY MOVEMENT IN
PREWAR JAPAN -- THE FAILURE OF THE
FIRST ATTEMPT.=        SCALRA-53-CPM

THE LEFT WING IN JAPAN.
SCALRA-62-LWJ

PARTIES AND PCLITICS IN
CCNTEMPCRARY JAPAN.=   SCALRA-62-PPC

JUDGES AND PCLITICAL LEADERSHIP
(AUSTRALIA, JAPAN, PHILIPPINES,
UNITED STATES).=       SCHUG -67-JPL

LABCR AND PCLITICS IN JAPAN -- A
STUDY CF INTEREST GRCUP ATTITUDES
AND ACTIVITIES.=       SOUKJR-60-LPJ

PCSTWAR PCLITICAL PARTIES IN
JAPAN.=                SPINCN-46-PPP

WITHOUT THE CHRYSANTHEMUM AND THE
SWCRD -- A STUCY CF THE ATTITUDES
OF YOUTH IN PCST-WAR JAPAN.=
STOEJ -55-WCS

COMMUNIST STRENGTH IN JAPAN.=
SWEAR -52-CSJ

DEFEAT AND DEMCCRACY IN JAPAN.=
TAKAY -48-CCJ

BUCDHISM AND SCCIALISM IN JAPAN AND
BURMA.=                TOTTGO-60-BSJ

JAPAN'S NEW MICDLE CLASS.=
VOGEEF-63-JSN

POLITICAL MCDERNIZATICN IN JAPAN
AND TURKEY.=           WARDRE-64-PMJ

JAPAN -- THE CCNTINUITY OF
MCDERNIZATICN.=        WARDRE-66-JCM

A STUDY CF GRCUPS AND PERSONALITIES
IN JAPAN INFLUENCING THE EVENTS
LEACING TC THE SINC-JAPANESE WAR.=
YCUNEP-63-SGP

JAPANESE
JAPANESE STUDENTS AND JAPANESE
PCLITICS.=             ALTBP -63-JSJ

JAPANESE STUDENTS AND JAPANESE
PCLITICS.=             ALTBP -63-JSJ

THE PURGE CF JAPANESE LEADERS UNCER
THE OCCUPATICN.=       BAERHH-59-PJL

THE CRESCENT AND THE RISING SUN --

JUDICIAL                    (CONTINUATION)
                            WATSRA-67-BPJ

JUDICIARIES
  SURVEY AND JUDICIARIES, OR WHO'S
  AFRAID OF THE PURPLE CURTAIN
  (UNITED STATES).=         BECKTL-66-SJO

JUDICIARY
  PUBLIC BUREAUCRACY AND JUDICIARY IN
  PAKISTAN.=                BRAIR -61-PBJ

  POLITICAL SCIENCE AND SCIENCE
  FICTION (UNITED STATES,
  JUDICIARY).=              ROCHJP-58-PSS

JUKUN
  THE DIVINE KINGDOM OF THE JUKUN --
  A RE-EVALUATION OF SOME THEORIES
  (EAST AFRICAN).=          YOUNMW-66-DKJ

JUNKERS
  THE JUNKERS AND THE PRUSSIAN
  ADMINISTRATION, 1918-1939
                            MUNELW-47-JPA

JURIDICAL
  TESTING RELATIONS BETWEEN JURIDICAL
  CHARACTERISTICS AND JUDICIAL
  DECISION MAKING (UNITED STATES).=
                            NAGESS-62-TRB

JURIMETRICS
  THE UNTROUBLED WORLD OF
  JURIMETRICS.=             MENDW -64-UWJ

JURISPRUDENCE
  POLITICAL BEHAVIORALISM AND MODERN
  JURISPRUDENCE -- A WORKING THEORY
  AND STUDY IN JUDICIAL
  DECISION-MAKING (UNITED STATES).=
                            BECKTL-64-PBM

  LAW AND POLITICS IN THE SUPREME
  COURT -- NEW APPROACHES TO
  POLITICAL JURISPRUDENCE
  (UNITED STATES).=         SCHAM -64-LPS

JURISTS
  THE STRUGGLE OF SOVIET JURISTS
  AGAINST A RETURN TO STALINIST
  TERROR.=                  BERMHJ-63-SSJ

  THE ROLE OF THE INTERNATIONAL
  COMMISSION OF JURISTS IN THE
  PROMOTION OF WORLD PEACE.=
                            BOSEV -64-RIC

JUSTICE
  CHIEF JUSTICE TAFT AND THE LOWER
  COURT BUREAUCRACY -- A STUDY IN
  JUDICIAL ADMINISTRATION.=
                            MURPWF-62-CJT

JUSTICES
  STARE DECISIS, DISSENT AND THE
  BACKGROUND OF THE JUSTICES OF THE
  SUPREME COURT OF THE
  UNITED STATES.=           SCHMJ -62-SDD

  THE JUSTICES OF THE SUPREME COURT
  -- A COLLECTIVE PORTRAIT
  (UNITED STATES).=         SCHMJR-59-JSC

  THE JUDICIAL MIND -- ATTITUDES AND
  IDEOLOGIES OF SUPREME COURT
  JUSTICES 1946-1963
  (UNITED STATES).=         SCHUGA-65-JMA

  PUBLIC OFFICE IN THE SOCIAL
  BACKGROUND OF SUPREME COURT
  JUSTICES.=                ULMESS-62-POS

KACHIN
  POLITICAL SYSTEMS OF HIGHLAND BURMA
  -- A STUDY OF KACHIN SOCIAL
  STRUCTURE.=               LEACER-54-PSH

KADAR
  KADAR AND THE RESURRECTION OF THE
  HUNGARIAN COMMUNIST PARTY -- A
  STUDY IN POLITICAL TECHNIQUES.=
                            GINSG -64-KRH

KANSAS
  KANSAS GOVERNORS -- A RESUME OF
  POLITICAL LEADERSHIP
  (UNITED STATES).=         TITUJE-64-KGR

KANSAS CITY
  LEADERSHIP IN A LARGE MANAGER CITY
  -- THE CASE OF KANSAS CITY
  (UNITED STATES).=         GABIST-64-LLM

KAO-JAO
  POWER STRUGGLE IN THE CHINESE CP
  (COMMUNIST PARTY) -- THE KAO-JAO
  PURGE.=                   TANGPS-55-PSC

KAZAKHSTAN
  KAZAKHSTAN -- CHANGES IN
  ADMINISTRATIVE STATUS AND THE
  NATIONAL COMPOSITION OF THE
  POPULATION (SOVIET UNION).=
                            TASKGA-64-KCA

KENNEDY
  THE NATIONAL SECURITY COUNCIL UNDER
  TRUMAN, EISENHOWER, AND KENNEDY
  (UNITED STATES).=         FALKSL-64-NSC

KENTUCKY
  THE GOVERNOR AS CHIEF ADMINISTRATOR
  IN KENTUCKY (UNITED STATES).=
                            KAMMGM-54-GCA

KENYA
  THE DEVELOPMENT OF POLITICAL
  ORGANIZATIONS IN KENYA.=
                            BENNG -57-DPO

  KENYA'S FIRST DIRECT ELECTIONS FOR
  AFRICANS, MARCH 1957.=
                            ENGHGF-57-KSF

  AUTHORITY, EFFICIENCY, AND ROLE
  STRESS -- PROBLEMS IN THE
  DEVELOPMENT OF EAST AFRICAN
  BUREAUCRACIES (UGANDA, KENYA,
  TANGANYIKA).=             FLEMWG-66-AER

  THE PROVINCIAL ADMINISTRATION IN
  KENYA.=                   GERTC -66-PAK

  THE WHITE SETTLER'S ROLE IN KENYA.=
                            HILLMF-60-WSS

  THE KENYA GENERAL ELECTION OF
  1963.=                    SANGC -64-KGE

KEY
  OBITUARIES AS A KEY TO THE SOVIET
  ELITE.=                   AKHMH -61-OKS

  MEN NEAR THE TOP -- FILLING KEY
  POSTS IN THE FEDERAL CIVIL SERVICE
  (UNITED STATES).=         CORSJJ-66-MNT

  THE CHINESE COMMUNIST CADRE -- KEY
  TO POLITICAL CONTROL.=
                            COURWE-52-CCC

  A KEY TO SOVIET POLITICS -- THE
  CRISIS OF THE ANTI - PARTY GROUP.=
                            PETHR -62-KSP

KEYS
  TEN KEYS TO LATIN AMERICA.=

STUDENT POLITICS (LATIN AMERICA,
INDIA, POLAND, UNITED STATES,
GERMANY, CHILE, ARGENTINA,
COLUMBIA, FRANCE).=          LIPSSM-67-SPL

VALUES, EDUCATION, ENTREPRENEURSHIP
(LATIN AMERICA).=           LIPSSM-67-VEE

POLITICS OF CHANGE IN
LATIN AMERICA.=              MAIEJ -64-PCL

SOCIAL CHANGE AND STRUCTURE IN
TRANSITIONAL SOCIETIES
(LATIN AMERICA, MIDDLE EAST).=
                            MARCS -60-SCS

NATIONALISM IN LATIN AMERICA.=
                            MASUG -66-NLA

CIVIL - MILITARY RELATIONS IN
LATIN AMERICA.=             MCALLN-61-CMR

THE MILITARY (LATIN AMERICA).=
                           MCALLN-64-MLA

CHANGING CONCEPTS OF THE ROLE OF
THE MILITARY IN LATIN AMERICA.=
                           MCALLN-65-CCR

POLITICAL SYSTEMS OF
LATIN AMERICA.=             NEEDMC-64-PSL

POLITICAL DEVELOPMENT AND MILITARY
INTERVENTION IN LATIN AMERICA.=
                           NEEDMC-66-PDM

CONTEMPORARY PEASANT MOVEMENTS
(LATIN AMERICA).=           ORBEAQ-67-CPM

PERU -- LATIN AMERICA'S SILENT
REVOLUTION.=                PAYNA -66-PLA

SOCIAL STRUCTURE AND THE POLITICAL
PROCESS IN LATIN AMERICA.=
                           PETERL-63-SSP

PATHOLOGY OF DEMOCRACY IN
LATIN AMERICA -- A SYMPOSIUM.=
                           PIERWW-50-PDL

THE CATHOLIC CHURCH IN
LATIN AMERICA.=             PIKEFB-59-CCL

THE CONFLICT BETWEEN CHURCH AND
STATE IN LATIN AMERICA.=
                           PIKEFB-64-CBC

MILITARY ASSISTANCE AND MILITARISM
IN LATIN AMERICA.=          POWEJD-65-MAM

CAUDILLISM AND CONTINUISM IN
LATIN AMERICA.=             RAI,L -63-CCL

THE NEW URBAN GROUPS -- THE MIDDLE
CLASSES (LATIN AMERICA).=
                           RATIL -67-NUG

UNIVERSITIES AND SOCIAL DEVELOPMENT
(LATIN AMERICA).=           RIBED -67-USD

LATIN AMERICA'S POSTWAR
GOLPES DE ESTADO.=          RIPPJF-65-LAS

LABOR AND DEMOCRACY IN
LATIN AMERICA.=             ROMNS -47-LDL

A WORLD OF NATIONS -- PROBLEMS OF
POLITICAL MODERNIZATION (ASIA,
AFRICA, LATIN AMERICA).=

RELATIONS BETWEEN PUBLIC AND
PRIVATE UNIVERSITIES
(LATIN AMERICA).=           SCHEL -67-RBP

POLITICAL ELITES AND POLITICAL
MODERNIZATION -- THE CRISIS OF
TRANSITION (LATIN AMERICA).=
                           SCOTRE-67-PEP

REACTION AND REVOLUTION IN
LATIN AMERICA -- THE CONFLICT
SOCIETY.=                   SILVKH-61-RRL

NATIONAL VALUES, DEVELOPMENT,
LEADERS AND FOLLOWERS
(LATIN AMERICA).=           SILVKH-63-NVD

INTELLECTUAL IDENTITY AND POLITICAL
IDEOLOGY AMONG UNIVERSITY STUDENTS
(LATIN AMERICA).=           SOARGA-67-IIP

SECONDARY EDUCATION AND THE
DEVELOPMENT OF ELITES
(LATIN AMERICA).=           SOLAA -67-SEC

THE INDUSTRIALISTS
(LATIN AMERICA).=           STRAWP-64-ILA

THE WINDS OF REVOLUTION
(LATIN AMERICA).=           SZULT -63-WRL

COMMUNISTS, SOCIALISTS, AND
CHRISTIAN DEMOCRATS
(LATIN AMERICA).=           SZULT -65-CSC

TEN KEYS TO LATIN AMERICA.=
                           TANNF -65-TKL

EXPLOSIVE FORCES IN LATIN AMERICA.=
                           TEPAJJ-64-EFL

RELIGIOUS ELITES IN LATIN AMERICA
-- CATHOLICISM, LEADERSHIP AND
SOCIAL CHANGE.=             VALLI -65-REL

OBSTACLES TO CHANGE IN
LATIN AMERICA.=             VELIC -65-OCL

POLITICAL SOCIALIZATION IN
UNIVERSITIES (LATIN AMERICA).=
                           WALKKN-67-PSU

STUDENT POLITICS IN LATIN AMERICA
-- THE VENEZUELAN EXAMPLE.=
                           WASHSW-59-SPL

TWO CITIES OF LATIN AMERICA -- A
COMPARATIVE DESCRIPTION OF SOCIAL
CLASSES.=                   WHITAH-64-TCL

THE POLITICAL EFFECTS OF MILITARY
PROGRAMS -- SOME INDICATIONS FROM
LATIN AMERICA.=             WOLFC -65-PEM

RELIGIOUS ELITES --
DIFFERENTIATIONS AND DEVELOPMENTS
IN ROMAN CATHOLICISM
(LATIN AMERICA).=           YALLI -67-RED

LATIN AMERICAN
THE LATIN AMERICAN APRISTA
PARTIES.=                   ALEXRJ-49-LAA

THE RISE OF LATIN AMERICAN
CHRISTIAN DEMOCRACY.=       ALEXRJ-64-RLA

LATIN AMERICAN POLITICS AND
GOVERNMENT.=                ALEXRJ-65-LAP

THE DEVELOPMENT OF LATIN AMERICAN

LATIN AMERICAN          (CONTINUATION)
  PRIVATE ENTERPRISE.=    BRANF -64-CLA

  A CASE STUDY IN LATIN AMERICAN
  COMMUNISM.=             COLECP-55-CSL

  LATIN AMERICAN SOCIAL THOUGHT.=
                          DAVIH -61-LAS

  LATIN AMERICAN LEADERS.=
                          DAVIHE-49-LAL

  MASS MEDIA USE BY SUB - ELITES IN
  ELEVEN LATIN AMERICAN COUNTRIES.=
                          DEUTPJ-61-MMU

  LATIN AMERICAN GOVERNMENT AND
  POLITICS.=              EDELAT-65-LAG

  LATIN AMERICAN EXECUTIVES --
  ESSENCE AND VARIATIONS.=
                          GOMERA-61-LAE

  STRATIFICATION IN A LATIN AMERICAN
  CITY.=                  HAWTAE-48-SLA

  WHITHER THE LATIN AMERICAN MIDDLE
  SECTORS.=               JOHNJJ-61-WLA

  THE LATIN AMERICAN MILITARY AS A
  POLITICALLY COMPETING GROUP IN
  TRANSITIONAL SOCIETY.=
                          JOHNJJ-62-LAM

  THE LATIN AMERICAN NATIONALISM.=
                          JOHNJJ-65-LAN

  NEW ROLES FOR LATIN AMERICAN
  MILITARY.=              LIEUE -60-NRL

  DILEMMAS IN THE STUDY OF
  LATIN AMERICAN POLITICAL PARTIES.=
                          MARTC -64-DSL

  THE DYNAMICS OF CHANGE IN
  LATIN AMERICAN POLITICS.=
                          MARTJ -65-DCL

  THE ROLE OF TECHNOCRATS IN
  LATIN AMERICAN INTEGRATION.=
                          MITCC -67-RTL

  PUTTING LATIN AMERICAN POLITICS IN
  PERSPECTIVE.=           NEEDM -62-PLA

  THE RISE OF THE LATIN AMERICAN
  LABOR MOVEMENT.=        POBLM -60-RLA

  VIOLENCE AS A POWER FACTOR IN
  LATIN AMERICAN POLITICS.=
                          STOKW -52-VPF

  THE DILEMMA OF THE LATIN AMERICAN
  MIDDLE CLASS.=          WAGLC -64-DLA

  POWER STRUCTURE AND SOCIOCULTURAL
  CHANGE IN LATIN AMERICAN
  COMMUNITIES.=           WHITNE-65-PSS

  THE ROLE OF THE MILITARY IN
  LATIN AMERICAN POLITICS.=
                          WYCKT -60-RML

LAUPULA
  HEADMAN AND THE RITUAL OF LAUPULA
  VILLAGES (AFRICA).=     CUNNI -56-HRL

LAW
  POLITICAL ASPIRATIONS OF LAW
  STUDENTS (UNITED STATES).=
                          AGGERE-58-PAL

  THE LAW OF OLIGARCHY.=


LAW                       (CONTINUATION)
                          CASSCW-53-LO

  POLITICS, LAW AND RITUAL IN TRIBAL
  SOCIETY.=               GLUCM -65-PLR

  RADICAL NATIONALISM -- THE
  POLITICAL ORIENTATIONS OF
  PANAMANIAN LAW STUDENTS.=
                          GOLDD -62-RNP

  CAREERS OF LAWYERS, LAW PRACTICE,
  AND LEGAL INSTITUTIONS
  (UNITED STATES).=       LADIJ -63-CLL

  THE MAKING OF CONSTITUTIONAL LAW
  (UNITED STATES).=       LANDJW-64-MCL

  TERENA (BRAZILIAN INDIANS) SOCIAL
  ORGANIZATIONS AND LAW.=
                          OLIEK -48-TBI

  SOCIAL CHANGE AND PRIMITIVE LAW --
  CONSEQUENCES OF A PAPUAN LEGAL
  CASE (NETHERLANDS NEW GUINEA).=
                          POSPL -58-SCP

  LAW AND POLITICS IN THE SUPREME
  COURT -- NEW APPROACHES TO
  POLITICAL JURISPRUDENCE
  (UNITED STATES).=       SCHAM -64-LPS

  THE BRAZILIAN LAW STUDENT --
  BACKGROUND, HABITS, ATTITUDES.=
                          SCHELR-63-BLS

  AN INTRODUCTION TO THE SOCIOLOGY OF
  LAW.=                   TIMANS-39-ISL

  LEADERS, THE LED, AND THE LAW -- A
  CASE STUDY IN SOCIAL CHANGE
  (UNITED STATES).=       TUMIMM-57-LLL

  THE PERSONALITY OF LAWYERS -- A
  COMPARATIVE STUDY OF SUBJECTIVE
  FACTORS IN LAW, BASED ON
  INTERVIEWS WITH GERMAN LAWYERS.=
                          WEYRWO-64-PLC

LAWMAKERS
  THE LAWMAKERS -- RECRUITMENT AND
  ADAPTION TO LEGISLATIVE LIFE
  (UNITED STATES).=       BARBJD-65-LRA

  WASHINGTON STATE'S LAWMAKERS --
  SOME PERSONNEL FACTORS IN THE
  WASHINGTON LEGISLATURE
  (UNITED STATES).=       BECKP -57-WSS

LAWMAKING
  LEGISLATIVE COMMITTEES IN POLISH
  LAWMAKING.=             CHRYVC-66-LCP

LAWS
  LAWS AND MEN IN SOVIET SOCIETY.=
                          HAZAJN-58-LMS

LAWYER
  THE LAWYER AND SOVIET SOCIETY.=
                          BILIA -65-LSS

  THE AMERICAN LAWYER -- A SUMMARY OF
  THE SURVEY OF THE LEGAL
  PROFESSION.=            BLAUAP-54-ALS

  THE LAWYER AS DECISION-MAKER IN THE
  AMERICAN STATE LEGISLATURE.=
                          DERGOR-59-LDM

  THE LAWYER IN THE INDIANA GENERAL
  ASSEMBLY (UNITED STATES).=
                          DERGOR-62-LIG

  INTERVIEWING A LEGAL ELITE -- THE

LAWYER              (CONTINUATION)
  WALL STREET LAWYER.=    SMIGEO-58-ILE

  THE LAWYER IN MICHIGAN STATE
  GOVERNMENT (UNITED STATES).=
                          STEUWL-59-LMS

  THE EXTRA - PROFESSIONAL ROLE OF
  THE LAWYER (UNITED STATES).=
                          WARDWI-56-EPR

LAWYERS
  LAWYERS IN POLITICS
  (UNITED STATES).=       AGGERE-56-LPU

  LAWYERS IN POLITICS -- A STUDY IN
  PROFESSIONAL CONVERGENCE
  (UNITED STATES).=       EULAH -64-LPS

  LAWYERS IN POLITICS -- AN EMPIRICAL
  EXPLORATION OF BIOGRAPHICAL DATA
  ON STATE LEGISLATORS.=
                          GOLDD -61-LPE

  LAWYERS AND JUDGES -- THE ABA AND
  THE POLITICS OF JUDICIAL SELECTION
  (UNITED STATES).=       GROSJB-65-LJA

  CAREERS OF LAWYERS, LAW PRACTICE,
  AND LEGAL INSTITUTIONS
  (UNITED STATES).=       LADIJ -63-CLL

  ORGANIZATIONAL CONSEQUENCES OF
  PROFESSIONAL CONSENSUS -- LAWYERS
  AND SELECTION OF JUDGES
  (UNITED-STATES).=       LADIJ -66-CCP

  LAWYERS IN THE NEW YORK STATE
  LEGISLATURE -- THE URBAN FACTOR
  (UNITED STATES).=       RUCHLI-66-LNY

  LAWYERS AND AMERICAN POLITICS -- A
  CLARIFIED VIEW.=        SCHLJA-57-LAP

  THE PERSONALITY OF LAWYERS -- A
  COMPARATIVE STUDY OF SUBJECTIVE
  FACTORS IN LAW, BASED ON
  INTERVIEWS WITH GERMAN LAWYERS.=
                          WEYRWO-64-PLC

  THE PERSONALITY OF LAWYERS -- A
  COMPARATIVE STUDY OF SUBJECTIVE
  FACTORS IN LAW, BASED ON
  INTERVIEWS WITH GERMAN LAWYERS.=
                          WEYRWO-64-PLC

LEADER
  THE ACTIVITIES OF A SOVIET LEADER.=
                          AKHMH -66-ASL

  THE PSEUDO - CHARISMATIC LEADER IN
  SOVIET SOCIETY.=        BAUERA-53-PCL

  SCHOOL DESEGREGATION AND NEW
  INDUSTRY -- THE SOUTHERN COMMUNITY
  LEADER'S VIEWPOINT
  (UNITED STATES).=       CRAMMR-63-SDN

  THE SUPERIMPOSED LEADER.=
                          DEMADF-47-SL

  THE WEEKLY NEWSPAPER'S LEADERSHIP
  ROLE AS SEEN BY COMMUNITY LEADER'S
  (UNITED STATES).=       EDELAS-63-WNS

  THE LEADER VS. TRADITION -- A CASE
  STUDY (MEXICO).=        ERASCJ-52-LVT

  A TYPOLOGY OF COMMUNITY LEADERSHIP
  BASED ON INFLUENCE AND INTERACTION
  WITHIN THE LEADER SUBSYSTEM
  (UNITED STATES).=       FANEAA-56-TCL

LEADER              (CONTINUATION)
  SITUATIONAL PRESSURES AND
  FUNCTIONAL ROLE OF THE ETHNIC
  LABOR LEADER.=          GREES -53-SPF

  FORMAL RECOGNITION OF THE LEADER OF
  THE OPPOSITION IN PARLIAMENTS OF
  THE BRITISH COMMONWEALTH.=
                          MCHECE-54-FRL

  THE ROLE OF AN INTEREST GROUP
  LEADER IN THE HOUSE OF
  COMMONS (GREAT BRITAIN).=


                          MILLJH-56-RIG

  THE ROLE OF AN INTEREST GROUP
  LEADER IN THE HOUSE OF
  COMMONS (GREAT BRITAIN).=


                          MILLJH-56-RIG

  THE RANK - AND - FILE - LEADER
  (UNITED STATES).=       PECKSM-63-RFL

  THE LAPPISH HERDING LEADER -- A
  STRUCTURAL ANALYSIS.=   PEHRRN-54-LHL

  TWO STRATEGIES OF INFLUENCE --
  CHOOSING A MAJORITY LEADER, 1962
  (UNITED STATES).=       POLSNW-63-TSI

  HOW STRONG IS THE LEADER
  (SOVIET UNION).=        RIGBTH-62-HSI

  ENTREPRENEURS OF LEBANON -- THE
  ROLE OF THE BUSINESS LEADER IN A
  DEVELOPING ECONOMY.=    SAYIYA-62-ELR

  THE LEADER - FOLLOWER
  RELATIONSHIP.=          STEPTE-59-LFR

  BOLSHEVISM AND THE INDIVIDUAL
  LEADER (SOVIET UNION).=
                          SWEAH -63-BIL

  SOUTHEAST ASIA FOLLOWS THE LEADER.=
                          THOMV -49-SAF

LEADERS
  LEADERS OF MODERN JAPAN -- SOCIAL
  ORIGINS AND MOBILITY.=
                          ABEGJ -60-LMJ

  THE LEADERS OF SOVIET RUSSIA.=
                          ALBEVL-53-LSR

  THE ETHICS OF TRADE UNION LEADERS
  (GREAT BRITAIN).=       ALLEVL-63-ETU

  DEMOCRACY AND SOCIALISM --
  IDEOLOGIES OF AFRICAN LEADERS.=
                          ANDRCF-64-DSI

  THE PURGE OF JAPANESE LEADERS UNDER
  THE OCCUPATION.=        BAERHH-59-PJL

  SCREENING LEADERS IN A DEMOCRACY.=
                          BELLD -48-SLD

  JAMAICAN LEADERS -- POLITICAL
  ATTITUDES IN A NEW NATION.=
                          BELLW -64-JLP

  THE CULTIVATION OF COMMUNITY
  LEADERS -- UP FROM THE GRASS ROOTS
  (UNITED STATES).=       BIDDWW-53-CCL

  VOTERS, PARTIES, AND LEADERS -- THE
  SOCIAL FABRIC OF BRITISH

LEADERS          (CONTINUATION)
  POLITICS.=            BLONJ -63-VPL

LEADERS AND LEADERSHIP.=
                       BOGAES-34-LL

SOVIET LEADERS AND MASTERY OVER
MAN.=                  CANTH -60-SLM

FOUR FORMULAE FOR SELECTING LEADERS
ON THE BASIS OF PERSONALITY.=
                       CATTRB-54-FFS

THE RECRUITMENT OF THE NATION'S
LEADERS (GREAT BRITAIN).=
                       CLAREL-36-RNS

LATIN AMERICAN LEADERS.=
                       DAVIHE-49-LAL

A STUDY OF 163 OUTSTANDING
COMMUNIST LEADERS (SOVIET UNION).=
                       DAVIJ -29-SOC

POLITICAL LEADERS AND FOLLOWERS.=
                       DAVIJC-63-PLF

INTERVIEWING BUSINESS LEADERS.=
                       DEXTLA-59-IBL

MILITARY LEADERS AND FOREIGN
POLICY-MAKING.=        EDINLJ-63-MLF

COPING WITH CUBA -- DIVERGENT
POLICY PREFERENCES OF STATE
POLITICAL LEADERS
(UNITED STATES).=      EKMAP -66-CCD

POLITICAL UNIFICATION -- A
COMPARATIVE STUDY OF LEADERS AND
FOLLOWERS (UNITED ARAB REPUBLIC,
FEDERATION OF THE WEST INDIES,
SCANDINAVIA, EUROPEAN ECONOMIC
COMMUNITY).=           ETZIA -65-PUC

POLITICAL POLICY AND PERSUASION --
THE ROLE OF COMMUNICATIONS FROM
POLITICAL LEADERS (SOVIET UNION,
GREAT BRITAIN, UNITED STATES).=
                       FELDMO-58-PPP

A NOTE ON LEADERSHIP THEORY -- THE
EFFECT OF SOCIAL BARRIERS BETWEEN
LEADERS AND FOLLOWERS
(UNITED STATES).=      FIEDFE-57-NLT

LOCAL PARTY LEADERS -- GROUPS OF
LIKE MINDED MEN (UNITED STATES).=
                       FLINTA-65-LPL

LOCATING LEADERS IN LOCAL
COMMUNITIES -- A COMPARISON OF
SOME ALTERNATIVE APPROACHES
(UNITED STATES).=      FREELC-63-LLL

THE PSYCHOLOGY OF DICTATORSHIP --
BASED ON AN EXAMINATION OF THE
LEADERS OF NAZI GERMANY.=
                       GILBGM-50-PCB

THE SELECTION OF LEADERS IN
BALLYBEG, NORTHERN IRELAND.=
                       HARRR -61-SLB

OPINION LEADERS IN AMERICAN
COMMUNITIES.=          HEROAO-59-CLA

LEADERS, GROUPS, AND INFLUENCE.=
                       FOLLEP-64-LGI

THE NEW LEADERS OF AFRICA.=
                       ITALR -61-NLA

BRITAIN'S NEW LABOUR LEADERS.=

LEADERS          (CONTINUATION)
                       JANOGE-63-BSN

TRUSTED LEADERS -- PERCEPTIONS OF
APPOINTED FEDERAL OFFICIALS
(UNITED STATES).=      JENNMK-66-TLP

THE ORIENTATIONS OF COMMUNITY
LEADERS TO PARLIAMENTARY
CANDIDATES (GREAT BRITAIN).=
                       KAVAD -67-OCL

LEADERS AND CLASSES IN THE INDIAN
NATIONAL CONGRESS, 1918-1939.=
                       KEMPT -64-LCI

NEGRO PROTEST LEADERS IN A SOUTHERN
COMMUNITY (UNITED-STATES).=
                       KILLLM-60-NPL

SYMBOLIC LEADERS -- PUBLIC DRAMAS
AND PUBLIC MEN.=       KLAPOE-64-SLP

PEKING'S LEADERS -- A STUDY IN
ISOLATION (CHINA).=    KLEIDW-61-PSL

THE 'NEXT GENERATION' OF CHINESE
COMMUNIST LEADERS.=    KLEIDW-62-NGC

LEADERS, FACTIONS AND PARTIES --
THE STRUCTURE OF PHILIPPINE
POLITICS.=             LANDCH-65-LFP

A STUDY OF THE INFLUENCE OF FORMAL
AND INFORMAL LEADERS IN AN
ELECTION CAMPAIGN
(UNITED STATES).=      LOWEFE-56-SIF

YES -- THERE ARE GENERALIZED
OPINION LEADERS.=      MARCAS-64-YTA

ISSUE CONFLICT AND CONSENSUS AMONG
PARTY LEADERS AND FOLLOWERS
(UNITED STATES).=      MCCLH -60-ICC

THE TRACK OF THE WOLF -- ESSAYS ON
NATIONAL SOCIALISM AND ITS
LEADERS, ADOLPH HITLER (GERMANY).=
                       MCRAJH-65-TWE

PROFILES OF AFRICAN LEADERS.=
                       MELATP-61-PAL

THE NEW MEN OF POWER -- AMERICA'S
LABOR LEADERS.=        MILLCW-48-NMP

SOME CHARACTERISTICS OF AMERICAN
NEGRO LEADERS.=        MONATP-56-CAN

THE EDUCATIONAL AND GEOGRAPHICAL
BACKGROUND OF SOME LOCAL LEADERS
(GREAT BRITAIN).=      MUSGF -61-EGB

DEVELOPING RESPONSIBLE PUBLIC
LEADERS.=              NELSCA-63-DRP

IN YOUR OPINION -- LEADERS' AND
VOTERS' ATTITUDES ON DEFENSE AND
DISARMAMENT (CANADA).=
                       PAULJ -63-YOL

THE NEW CHINESE LEADERS -- POWER
AND PERSONALITY.=      RASEJR-65-NCL

ALIENATION AND PARTICIPATION -- A
COMPARISON OF GROUP LEADERS AND
THE MASS (UNITED STATES).=
                       ROSEAM-62-APC

NATIONAL VALUES, DEVELOPMENT,
LEADERS AND FOLLOWERS
(LATIN AMERICA).=      SILVKH-63-NVD

LEADERS (CONTINUATION)
NEGRO MASSES AND LEADERS
(UNITED STATES).= SMYTHH-50-NML

AFRICA'S NEW POLITICAL LEADERS.=
SMYTHH-59-ASN

THE NEW AFRICAN LEADERS.=
SMYTHH-61-NAL

GERMAN REARMAMENT AND ATOMIC WAR --
THE VIEWS OF GERMAN MILITARY AND
POLITICAL LEADERS.= SPEIH -57-GRA

THE POTENTIAL ROLE OF TURKISH
VILLAGE OPINION LEADERS IN A
PROGRAM OF FAMILY PLANNING.=
SYTCJM-65-PRT

THE PURGE OF PROVINCIAL LEADERS
1957-1958 (CHINA).= TEIWFC-66-PPL

THE SOVIET UNION AFTER STALIN --
LEADERS AND POLICIES.=
TOWSJ -54-SUA

LEADERS, THE LED, AND THE LAW -- A
CASE STUDY IN SOCIAL CHANGE
(UNITED STATES).= TUMIMM-57-LLL

CHANGES AMONG THE LEADERS OF THE
SOVIET ARMED FORCES.= VERBV -63-CAL

SELECTING LEADERS FOR AGRICULTURAL
PROGRAMS (UNITED STATES).=
WAKERE-47-SLA

BIG BUSINESS LEADERS IN AMERICA.=
WARNWL-55-BBL

THE AMERICAN FEDERAL EXECUTIVE -- A
STUDY OF SOCIAL AND PERSONAL
CHARACTERISTICS OF THE CIVILIAN
AND MILITARY LEADERS OF THE UNITED
STATES FEDERAL GOVERNMENT.=
WARNWL-63-AFE

THE RISE AND ROLE OF CHARISMATIC
LEADERS.= WILLAR-65-RRC

LEADERSHIP
THE POLITICAL LINE OF COLLECTIVE
LEADERSHIP (SOVIET UNION).=
ACHMH -54-PLC

DEMOCRATIC LEADERSHIP AND MASS
MANIPULATION.= ADORTW-65-DLM

OUR CHANGING CONCEPT OF LEADERSHIP
(UNITED STATES).= ALBEMH-53-OCC

PERONISM AND ARGENTINA'S QUEST FOR
LEADERSHIP IN LATIN AMERICA.=
ALEXRJ-55-PAS

DECENTRALIZATION OF LEADERSHIP
(SOVIET UNION).= ANON -54-DLS

SOME PROBLEMS OF EXECUTIVE
LEADERSHIP IN THE GOVERNMENT
(PHILIPPINES).= ARANLM-57-PEL

NEO-DESTOUR LEADERSHIP AND THE
'CONFISCATED REVOLUTION'
(TUNISIA).= ASHFDE-65-NDL

DEMOCRACY AND LEADERSHIP
(UNITED STATES).= BABBI -53-DLU

AN UNSTABLE LEADERSHIP
(SOVIET UNION).= BAILS -65-ULS

THE ROLE OF POLITICAL LEADERSHIP IN

LEADERSHIP (CONTINUATION)
THE PASSAGE OF OREGON'S MIGRATORY
LABOR LEGISLATION
(UNITED STATES).= BALMDG-62-RPL

POLITICAL LEADERSHIP IN AMERICAN
GOVERNMENT.= BARBJD-64-PLA

LEADERSHIP STRATEGIES FOR
LEGISLATIVE PARTY COHESION
(UNITED STATES).= BARBJD-66-LSL

LEADERSHIP STYLE AND POLITICAL
COMPETENCE (ITALY).= BARNSH-67-LSP

POLITICAL LEADERSHIP AMONG
SWAT PATHANS (PAKISTAN).=
BARTF -59-PLA

LEADERSHIP, PSYCHOLOGY, AND
ORGANIZATIONAL BEHAVIOR.=
BASSBM-60-LPO

LEADERSHIP, MOTIVATIONS, AND
ATTITUDES IN RESEARCH
LABORATORIES.= BAUMH -56-LMA

LEADERSHIP STYLE AS A VARIABLE IN
RESEARCH ADMINISTRATION.=
BAUMH -57-LSV

NOTES ON AUTHORITARIAN AND
DEMOCRATIC LEADERSHIP.=
BELLD -65-NAD

PUBLIC LEADERSHIP (UNITED STATES).=
BELLW -61-PLU

REFLECTIONS ON CHARISMATIC
LEADERSHIP.= BENDR -67-RCL

LEADERSHIP THEORY AND
ADMINISTRATIVE BEHAVIOR -- THE
PROBLEM OF AUTHORITY.=
BENNWG-60-LTA

REVISIONIST THEORY OF LEADERSHIP.=
BENNWG-61-RTL

THE AFRICAN PATRIOTS -- LEADERSHIP
OF AFRICAN NATIONAL CONGRESS.=
BENSM -64-APL

CONFLICTING ORIENTATION IN SOVIET
LEADERSHIP.= BIODJ -61-COS

COMMUNISM'S DISCORDANT LEADERSHIP
-- MAO AND KHRUSHCHEV (CHINA,
SOVIET UNION).= BJELSN-63-CSD

THE AGE OF CHANGE -- POLITICAL AND
INTELLECTUAL LEADERSHIP IN NORTH
CAROLINA (UNITED STATES).=
BLACR -61-AOP

LEADERS AND LEADERSHIP.=
BOGAES-34-LL

COMMUNITY LEADERSHIP -- A CASE
STUDY AND CONCEPTUAL REFINEMENT
(UNITED STATES).= BONJCM-63-CLC

COMMUNITY LEADERSHIP -- DECISIONS
OF RESEARCH.= BONJCM-65-CLD

LEGITIMACY AND VISIBILITY --
LEADERSHIP STRUCTURES RELATED TO
FOUR COMMUNITY SYSTEMS
(UNITED STATES).= BONJCM-65-LVL

SOME FINDINGS RELEVANT TO THE GREAT
MAN THEORY OF LEADERSHIP.=

LEADERSHIP          (CONTINUATION)
HOMOGENEITY IN ISRAEL.=
                                EISESN-56-PLS

DUAL LEADERSHIP IN COMPLEX
ORGANIZATIONS.=          ETZIA -65-DLC

WHAT HAPPENED TO COLLECTIVE
LEADERSHIP (SOVIET UNION).=
                                FAINM -59-WHC

THE KING'S MEN -- LEADERSHIP AND
STATUS IN BUGANDA ON THE EVE OF
INDEPENDENCE.=          FALLLA-64-KSM

A TYPOLOGY OF COMMUNITY LEADERSHIP
BASED ON INFLUENCE AND INTERACTION
WITHIN THE LEADER SUBSYSTEM
(UNITED STATES).=       FANEAA-56-TCL

LEADERSHIP AND DEMOCRACY IN THE
COLLECTIVE SETTLEMENTS OF ISRAEL.=
                                FEUELS-65-LDC

A NOTE ON LEADERSHIP THEORY -- THE
EFFECT OF SOCIAL BARRIERS BETWEEN
LEADERS AND FOLLOWERS
(UNITED STATES).=       FIEDFE-57-NLT

LEADERSHIP AND CULTURE CHANGE IN
PALAU (AUSTRALIA).=     FORCRW-60-LCC

CHANGING PATTERNS OF POLITICAL
LEADERSHIP IN INDIA.=   FORRDB-66-CPP

NEW CHANGES IN THE SOVIET
LEADERSHIP.=            FRANVS-55-NCS

LOCAL COMMUNITY LEADERSHIP
(UNITED STATES).=       FREELC-60-LCL

POLITICAL LEADERSHIP AND THE
PROBLEM OF CHARISMATIC POWER
(GERMANY, GREAT BRITAIN, ITALY,
UNITED STATES).=        FRIECJ-61-PLP

POWER AND LEADERSHIP.=
                                FRIECJ-63-PL

CONDITIONS FOR PARTY LEADERSHIP --
THE CASE OF THE HOUSE DEMOCRATS
(UNITED STATES).=       FROMLA-65-CPL

LEADERSHIP IN A LARGE MANAGER CITY
-- THE CASE OF KANSAS CITY
(UNITED STATES).=       GABIST-64-LLM

THE ROLE OF THE SOVIET ARMY IN THE
CRISIS OF THE COLLECTIVE
LEADERSHIP.=            GALAN -57-RSA

LEADERSHIP IN THE HOUSE OF
REPRESENTATIVES (UNITED STATES).=
                                GALLGB-59-LHR

THE CHIEF EXECUTIVE IN TEXAS -- THE
ORIGINS OF GUBERNATORIAL
LEADERSHIP.=            GANTF -64-CET

CHANGING POLITICAL LEADERSHIP IN
WEST AFRICA.=           GARIP -54-CPL

THE NAZI PARTY -- ITS LEADERSHIP
AND COMPOSITION (GERMANY).=
                                GERTH -40-NPI

SOCIOLOGY OF LEADERSHIP.=
                                GERTH -54-SL

LEADERSHIP.=            GIBBCA-54-L

NEW FACTORS OF STABILITY IN SOVIET

LEADERSHIP          (CONTINUATION)
COLLECTIVE LEADERSHIP.=
                                GILIJM-67-NFS

POLITICAL RECRUITMENT IN SARAWAK --
A CASE STUDY OF LEADERSHIP IN A
NEW STATE.=             GLICHR-66-PRS

THE PRESIDENCY AS MORAL LEADERSHIP
(UNITED STATES).=       GOLDEF-52-PML

SIGNIFICANT RESEARCH ON
LEADERSHIP.=            GOODCE-51-SRL

LEADERSHIP AMONG SOCIAL CLASSES.=
                                GOULAW-65-LAS

STUDIES IN LEADERSHIP.=
                                GOULAW-65-SL

WHAT IS MEANT BY LEADERSHIP.=
                                GRUNND-62-WIM

GROUPS, LEADERSHIP AND MEN.=
                                GUETH -51-GLM

POLITICAL AND ADMINISTRATIVE
LEADERSHIP (UNITED STATES).=
                                GULIL -63-PAL

EDUCATION OF MILITARY LEADERSHIP IN
EMERGENT STATES.=       GUTTWF-65-EML

CHANGES IN BRITISH LABOUR
LEADERSHIP.=            GUTTWL-61-CBL

DEVELOPMENTALIST TIME AND
LEADERSHIP IN DEVELOPING
COUNTRIES.=             HAHNL -65-DTL

GROUP LEADERSHIP AND DEMOCRATIC
ACTION.=                HAIMFS-51-GLD

LEADERSHIP AND CRISES.=
                                HAMBRL-58-LC

POPULAR LEADERSHIP IN THE ANGLO -
AMERICAN DEMOCRACIES (CANADA,
GREAT BRITAIN, UNITED STATES).=
                                HARGEC-67-PLA

THE POST - KHRUSHCHEV SOVIET
LEADERSHIP -- DILEMMAS AND
ALTERNATIVES.=          HARVML-65-PKS

FROM BOSSES TO COSMOPOLITANISM --
CHANGES IN THE RELATIONSHIP OF
URBAN LEADERSHIP TO STATE POLITICS
(UNITED STATES).=       HAVAWC-64-BCC

COMMUNITY LEADERSHIP -- THE
REGIONAL PLAN ASSOCIATION OF
NEW YORK.=              HAYSFB-65-CLR

PRESIDENTIAL LEADERSHIP
(UNITED-STATES).=       HERRP -40-PLU

HEROIC LEADERSHIP -- THE CASE OF
MODERN FRANCE.=         HOFFS -67-HLC

PRESIDENTIAL LEADERSHIP AND THE
PARTY SYSTEM (UNITED STATES).=
                                HOLCAN-54-PLP

AGE AS A FACTOR IN THE RECRUITMENT
OF COMMUNIST LEADERSHIP
(SOVIET UNION).=        HOLTRT-54-AFR

AFRICAN LEADERSHIP IN TRANSITION --
AN OUTLINE.=            HOWMR -56-ALT

THE CULTURAL REVOLUTION AND

LEADERSHIP                (CONTINUATION)
                          MACFR -59-LC

LEADERSHIP COHESION IN COMMUNIST
CHINA AND UNDERDEVELOPED ASIAN
COUNTRIES.=               MACFR -63-LCC

TRADE UNION LEADERSHIP
(GREAT BRITAIN).=         MACKJA-56-TUL

ROLL CALL VOTES AND LEADERSHIP
(UNITED STATES).=         MACRD -56-RCV

THE LEADERSHIP OF THE BRITISH UNION
OF FASCISTS.=             MANDWF-66-LBU

COLLECTIVE LEADERSHIP
(SOVIET UNION).=          MARIY -54-CLS

NATIONAL CONVENTION LEADERSHIP --
1952 AND 1956 (UNITED STATES).=
                          MARVD -61-NCL

CHALLENGE TO NEGRO LEADERSHIP
(UNITED STATES).=         MAYFJ -61-CNL

EQUILIBRIUM, STRUCTURE OF INTERESTS
AND LEADERSHIP -- ADENAUER'S
SURVIVAL AS CHANCELLOR (GERMANY).=
                          MERKPH-62-ESI

POLITICAL LEADERSHIP
(UNITED STATES).=         MERRCE-49-PLU

ORGANIZATION AND LEADERSHIP OF THE
FRENCH COMMUNIST PARTY.=
                          MICACA-52-OLF

THE JEWISH LEADERSHIP OF LAKEPORT
(UNITED STATES).=         MILLN -65-JLL

POLITICAL LEADERSHIP RE-EXAMINED --
AN EXPERIMENTAL APPROACH
(UNITED STATES).=         MOOSM -51-PLR

THE PROBLEM OF LEADERSHIP -- AN
INTERDISCIPLINARY APPROACH.=
                          MORRRT-50-PLI

TRADITIONAL AND MODERN TYPES OF
LEADERSHIP AND ECONOMIC
DEVELOPMENT AMONG THE FIJIANS.=
                          NAYARR-64-TMT

PRESIDENTIAL POWER -- THE POLITICS
OF LEADERSHIP (UNITED STATES).=
                          NEUSRE-60-PPP

LEADERSHIP AND SOCIAL CRISIS.=
                          NISBRA-65-LSC

CONTEMPORARY TRENDS IN RURAL
LEADERSHIP (UNITED STATES).=
                          NUQUJE-47-CTR

A SOLOMON ISLAND SOCIETY -- KINSHIP
AND LEADERSHIP AMONG THE SIVAI OF
BOUGAINVILLE.=            OLIVDL-58-SIS

ORGANIZATIONAL LEADERSHIP AND
SOCIAL STRUCTURE IN A SMALL CITY
(UNITED STATES).=         OLMSDW-54-OLS

SOCIAL STRUCTURE AND THE LEADERSHIP
FACTOR IN A NEGRO COMMUNITY
(UNITED STATES).=         PAREVJ-56-SSL

LEADERSHIP AND POLITICAL
INSTITUTIONS IN INDIA.=
                          PARKRL-59-LPI

CHARACTERISTICS OF PARTY LEADERSHIP

LEADERSHIP                (CONTINUATION)
(UNITED STATES).=         PATTSC-63-CPL

LEGISLATIVE LEADERSHIP AND
POLITICAL IDEOLOGY
(UNITED STATES).=         PATTSC-63-LLP

A STUDY IN LEADERSHIP AND
PERCEPTION OF CHANGE IN A VILLAGE
CONFRONTED WITH URBANISM
(UNITED STATES).=         PAYNR -63-SLP

PARTY LEADERSHIP CHANGE IN THE
UNITED STATES HOUSE OF
REPRESENTATIVES.=         PEABRL-67-PLC

LEADERSHIP WITHIN A HIERARCHICAL
ORGANIZATION (UNITED STATES).=
                          PELZD -51-LWH

DEMOCRACY AND LEADERSHIP.=
                          PENNJR-60-DL

LEADERSHIP AND INTERPERSONAL
BEHAVIOR.=                PETRL -61-LIB

LEADERSHIP OR DOMINATION.=
                          PIGOP -35-LOD

HEROIC LEADERSHIP (EGYPT, FRANCE,
GERMANY, GREAT BRITAIN,
UNITED STATES).=          PLAMJ -61-HLE

POLITICAL SOCIALIZATION AND
LEADERSHIP SELECTION
(UNITED STATES).=         PREWK -65-PSL

ADMINISTRATIVE LEADERSHIP
(UNITED STATES).=         PRICDT-61-ALU

CHALLENGE FOR INDIAN LEADERSHIP.=
                          PYLEMV-64-CIL

POLITICAL LEADERSHIP IN THE
GOVERNOR'S OFFICE
(UNITED STATES).=         RANSCB-64-PLG

CHARISMA AND POLITICAL LEADERSHIP
(GERMANY).=               RATNKJ-64-CPL

LEADERSHIP AND CONSENSUS IN A NEW
GUINEA SOCIETY.=          READKE-60-LCN

THE BUREAUCRAT AND THE ENTHUSIAST
-- AN EXPLORATION OF THE
LEADERSHIP OF SOCIAL MOVEMENTS
(UNITED STATES).=         ROCHJP-55-BEE

THE POLLSTERS -- PUBLIC OPINION,
POLITICS, AND DEMOCRATIC
LEADERSHIP (UNITED STATES).=
                          ROGEL -49-PPD

NATIONAL LEADERSHIP AND FOREIGN
POLICY -- A CASE STUDY IN THE
MOBILIZATION OF PUBLIC SUPPORT
(UNITED STATES).=         ROSEJN-63-NLF

COMPLEXITIES OF PARTY LEADERSHIP
(GREAT BRITAIN).=         ROSER -63-CPL

DYNAMICS OF SOCIALIST LEADERSHIP IN
INDIA.=                   RUSCTA-59-DSL

EDUCATION FOR COMMUNIST LEADERSHIP
(SOVIET UNION).=          RYWKMS-58-ECL

FEUDAL SOCIETY AND MODERN
LEADERSHIP IN SATSUMA-HAN.=
                          SAKARK-57-FSM

DEMOCRACY, LEADERSHIP AND ELITES.=

LEGISLATIVE          (CONTINUATION)
  (UNITED STATES).=       PATTSC-63-LLP

EFFECTS OF LEGISLATIVE AND
ADMINISTRATIVE ACCESSIBILITY ON
INTEREST GROUP POLITICS.=
                        PYE,LW-58-ELA

VOTING METHODS AND IRRATIONALITY IN
LEGISLATIVE DECISIONS
(UNITED STATES).=       RIKEWH-58-VMI

CONGRESS AND FOREIGN POLICY-MAKING
-- A STUDY IN LEGISLATIVE
INFLUENCE AND INITIATIVE
(UNITED STATES).=       ROBIJA-62-CFP

LEGISLATIVE DRAFTSMANSHIP
(GREAT BRITAIN).=       ROBSWA-46-LDG

INTERNATIONAL COMMUNICATION AND
LEGISLATIVE BEHAVIOR -- THE SENATE
AND THE HOUSE OF COMMONS
(UNITED STATES, GREAT BRITAIN).=
                        RUSSBM-62-ICL

CONDITIONS FOR LEGISLATIVE CONTROL
(UNITED STATES).=       SCHES -63-CLC

POLITICAL CHANGE -- LEGISLATIVE
ELITES AND PARTIES IN OREGON
(UNITED STATES).=       SELILG-64-PCL

THE LEGISLATORS' VIEW OF THE
LEGISLATIVE PROCESS
(UNITED STATES).=       SILVC -54-LVL

THE RELATION OF RESEARCH TO
LEGISLATIVE AND ADMINISTRATIVE
DECISIONS (UNITED STATES).=
                        TAYLPS-47-RRL

LEGISLATIVE BEHAVIOR -- A READER IN
THEORY AND RESEARCH.= WAHLJC-59-LBR

THE LEGISLATIVE SYSTEM --
EXPLORATIONS IN LEGISLATIVE
BEHAVIOR (UNITED STATES).=
                        WAHLJC-62-LSE

THE LEGISLATIVE SYSTEM --
EXPLORATIONS IN LEGISLATIVE
BEHAVIOR (UNITED STATES).=
                        WAHLJC-62-LSE

LEGISLATOR
THE LEGISLATOR -- SOURCE OF EXPERT
INFORMATION (UNITED STATES).=
                        HATTLH-54-LSE

THE ROLE OF THE STATE LEGISLATOR IN
MASSACHUSETTS (UNITED STATES).=
                        MACRD -54-RSL

THE LEGISLATOR AND HIS ENVIRONMENT
(UNITED STATES).=       SHILEA-51-LHE

LEGISLATORS
THE ERRAND-RUNNING FUNCTION OF
AUSTRIAN LEGISLATORS.=
                        CRANW -62-ERF

THE POLITICAL SOCIALIZATION OF
AMERICAN STATE LEGISLATORS.=
                        EULAH -59-PSA

CAREER PERSPECTIVES OF AMERICAN
STATE LEGISLATORS.=     EULAH -61-CPA

LAWYERS IN POLITICS -- AN EMPIRICAL
EXPLORATION OF BIOGRAPHICAL DATA
ON STATE LEGISLATORS.=

LEGISLATORS          (CONTINUATION)
                        GOLDO -61-LPE

JUDGEMENTS OF STATE LEGISLATORS
CONCERNING PUBLIC OPINION
(UNITED STATES).=       HARTGW-45-JSL

LOCAL GOVERNMENT EXPERIENCE OF
LEGISLATORS (GREAT BRITAIN).=
                        MACKWJ-54-LGE

SOME PERSONALITY FACTORS OF STATE
LEGISLATORS IN SOUTH CAROLINA
(UNITED STATES).=       MCCOJB-50-PFS

PUBLIC ATTITUDES TOWARD THE
REPRESENTATIONAL ROLE OF
LEGISLATORS AND JUDGES
(UNITED STATES).=       MCMUCD-65-PAT

THE LEGISLATORS' VIEW OF THE
LEGISLATIVE PROCESS
(UNITED STATES).=       SILVC -54-LVL

PHILIPPINE LEGISLATORS AND THEIR
CHANGING UNIVERSE.=     STAURB-66-PLT

PAIRWISE ASSOCIATION OF JUDGES AND
LEGISLATORS (UNITED STATES).=
                        ULMESS-67-PAJ

AMERICAN STATE LEGISLATORS' ROLE
ORIENTATIONS TOWARD PRESSURE
GROUPS.=                WAHLJC-60-ASL

MUSLIM LEGISLATORS IN INDIA --
PROFILE OF A MINORITY ELITE.=
                        WRIGJR-64-MLI

LEGISLATORS'
LEGISLATORS' SOCIAL STATUS AND
THEIR VOTES (UNITED STATES).=
                        MACRD -61-LSS

LEGISLATURE
WASHINGTON STATE'S LAWMAKERS --
SOME PERSONNEL FACTORS IN THE
WASHINGTON LEGISLATURE
(UNITED STATES).=       BECKP -57-WSS

THE LAWYER AS DECISION-MAKER IN THE
AMERICAN STATE LEGISLATURE.=
                        DERGDR-59-LDM

PARTIES, PARTISANSHIP, AND PUBLIC
POLICY IN THE PENNSYLVANIA
LEGISLATURE.=           KEEFWJ-54-PPP

THE CENTRAL LEGISLATURE IN BRITISH
INDIA 1921-1947.=       RASHM -65-CLB

LAWYERS IN THE NEW YORK STATE
LEGISLATURE -- THE URBAN FACTOR
(UNITED STATES).=       RUCHLI-66-LNY

PARTY POLITICS IN THE IOWA
LEGISLATURE (UNITED STATES).=
                        WIGGCW-67-PPI

LEGISLATURES
THE ROLE CONCEPT IN LEGISLATURES --
A PROBABILITY MODEL AND A NOTE ON
COGNITIVE STRUCTURE
(UNITED STATES).=       FRANWL-65-RCL

SUBCOMMITTEES -- THE MINIATURE
LEGISLATURES OF CONGRESS
(UNITED STATES).=       GOODG -62-SML

PARTY VOTING IN AMERICAN STATE
LEGISLATURES.=          JEWEME-55-PVA

STATE LEGISLATURES IN SOUTHERN

LORD (CONTINUATION)
(FRANCE, GREAT BRITAIN,
UNITED STATES, CHINA, JAPAN,
INDIA, GERMANY).= MOORB -66-SOC

LORDS
THE LABOUR GOVERNMENT AND THE HOUSE
OF LORDS (GREAT BRITAIN).=
HTCOG-48-LGH

THE HOUSE OF LORDS AND CONSERVATIVE
GOVERNMENTS 1951-1964
(GREAT BRITAIN).= PUNNRM-65-HLC

THE COMPOSITION OF THE HOUSE OF
LORDS (GREAT BRITAIN).=
ST-GCF-54-CHL

THE HOUSE OF LORDS
(GREAT BRITAIN).= VINCJR-66-HLG

LOS ANGELES
THE DECENTRALIZED POLITICS OF
LOS ANGELES (UNITED STATES).=
CARNFM-64-DPL

LOUIS
ST. LOUIS POLITICS -- RELATIONSHIP
AMONG INTERESTS, PARTIES, AND
GOVERNMENTAL STRUCTURE
(UNITED STATES))= SALIRH-60-SLP

LOYALTIES
THE INTERNATIONAL CIVIL SERVANT AND
HIS LOYALTIES.= JESSPC-55-ICS

PROBLEMS IN THE DEVELOPMENT OF
MODERN LEADERSHIP AND LOYALTIES IN
THE BRITISH SOMALILAND
PROTECTORATE AND THE UNITED
NATIONS TRUSTEESHIP TERRITORY OF
SOMALIA.= LEWIIM-60-PDM

LOYALTY
DISCIPLINE AND LOYALTY IN THE
FRENCH PARLIAMENT DURING THE PINAY
GOVERNMENT.= CAMPP -53-DLF

PARTY RESPONSIBILITY AND LOYALTY --
NEW RULES IN THE DEMOCRATIC PARTY
(UNITED STATES).= HOLTA -60-PRL

PARTY LOYALTY AMONG CONGRESSMEN --
THE DIFFERENCE BETWEEN DEMOCRATS
AND REPUBLICANS, 1947-1962
(UNITED STATES).= MAYHOR-66-PLA

LOYALTY AND COMMITMENT IN A
TOTALITARIAN PARTY (EAST
GERMANY).= WAGNHR-59-LCT

LUGBARA
THE ROLE OF THE CHIEFS AND THE HEAD
MAN AMONG THE LUGBARA OF THE WEST
NILE DISTRICT OF UGANDA.=
MIDDJ -56-RCH

LUTHER
YOUNG MAN LUTHER -- A STUDY IN
PSYCHOANALYSIS AND HISTORY.=
ERIKEH-58-YML

LUVALE
CLAN, CHIEFTAINSHIP, AND SLAVERY IN
LUVALE POLITICAL ORGANIZATION
(NORTH RHODESIA).= WHITCM-57-CCS

LUZON
TYPES OF AUTHORITY IN A BENGUET
VILLAGE (LUZON, PHILIPPINES).=
ENCAV -57-TAB

MACHIAVELLIANS
THE MACHIAVELLIANS -- DEFENDERS OF

MACHIAVELLIANS (CONTINUATION)
FREEDOM.= BURNJ -63-MOF

MACHINE
MACHINE RETRIEVAL OF BIOGRAPHICAL
DATA (EAST EUROPEAN ELITES).=
BECKC -67-MRB

THE POLICY MACHINE -- THE
DEPARTMENT OF STATE AND AMERICAN
FOREIGN POLICY.= ELDERE-60-PMD

MACHINE POLITICS IN AMERICAN TRADE
UNIONS.= GITLAL-52-MPA

MACHINERY
THE MACHINERY OF GOVERNMENT
1939-1947 (GREAT BRITAIN).=
ROBSWA-48-MGG

MACHINES
BOSSES, MACHINES, AND ETHNIC GROUPS
(UNITED STATES).= CORNEE-64-BME

CITY BOSSES AND POLITICAL MACHINES
(UNITED STATES).= GREELS-64-CBP

MAD
THE 'MAD MULLAH' AND NORTHERN
SOMALIA.= HESSRL-64-MMN

MAGHREB
ELITE VALUES AND ATTITUDINAL CHANGE
IN THE MAGHREB (MOROCCO, ALGERIA,
TUNISIA).= ASHFDE-67-EVA

MAIL
WHAT DO CONGRESSMEN HEAR -- THE
MAIL (UNITED STATES).=
DEXTLA-56-WDC

MAIN STREET
MAIN STREET POLITICS --
POLICY-MAKING AT THE LOCAL LEVEL
(UNITED STATES).= PRESC -62-MSP

MAINLAND
CENTRALIZATION VERSUS
DECENTRALIZATION IN MAINLAND CHINA
AND THE SOVIET UNION.=
PERKDH-63-CVD

MAINTAINING
INITIATING AND MAINTAINING RESEARCH
RELATIONS IN A MILITARY
ORGANIZATION.= DEMENJ-52-IMR

MAINTENANCE
MAINTENANCE OF MEMBERSHIP -- A
STUDY IN ADMINISTRATIVE
STATESMANSHIP (UNITED STATES).=
BURNJM-48-MMS

MAJORITIES
THE TWO MAJORITIES
(UNITED STATES).= KENDW -60-TMU

MAJORITIES AND MINORITIES IN
WESTERN EUROPEAN GOVERNMENTS.=
KIRCO -59-MMW

MAJORITY
MAJORITY DECISIONS AND MINORITY
RESPONSES IN THE UN GENERAL
ASSEMBLY (UNITED NATIONS).=
MANNCS-66-MDM

TWO STRATEGIES OF INFLUENCE --
CHOOSING A MAJORITY LEADER, 1962
(UNITED STATES).= POLSNW-63-TSI

MAKERERE
AN AFRICAN ELITE -- A SAMPLE SURVEY

MAKERERE (CONTINUATION)
OF 52 FORMER STUDENTS OF MAKERERE
COLLEGE IN EAST AFRICA.=
GOLDJE-55-AES

MAKERS
COMMUNITY POWER STRUCTURE -- A
STUDY OF DECISION MAKERS
(UNITED STATES).= HUNTF -53-CPS

THE SOCIAL BACKGROUNDS OF POLITICAL
DECISION MAKERS.= MATTOR-62-SBP

THE MAKERS OF PUBLIC POLICY --
AMERICAN POWER GROUPS AND THEIR
IDEOLOGIES.= MONSRJ-65-MPP

OPINION-MAKING AND OPINION MAKERS
IN FOREIGN POLICY
(UNITED STATES).= ROSEJN-60-OMC

THE TROUBLE MAKERS -- DISSENT OVER
FOREIGN POLICY (GREAT BRITAIN).=
TAYLAJ-58-TMD

THE RUSSIAN INTELLIGENTSIA --
MAKERS OF THE REVOLUTIONARY
STATE.= TOMPSR-57-RIM

MAKING
PHILADELPHIA GENTLEMEN -- THE
MAKING OF A NATIONAL ELITE
(UNITED STATES).= BALTED-58-PGM

THE MAKING OF MODERN MEXICO.=
BRANF -64-MMM

THE INFLUENCE OF NON-GOVERNMENTAL
GROUPS ON FOREIGN POLICY MAKING
(UNITED STATES).= COHEBC-59-ING

CONGRESSMEN AND THE MAKING OF
MILITARY POLICY (UNITED STATES).=
DEXTLA-63-CMM

DECISION MAKING IN A FEDERAL FIELD
OFFICE (UNITED STATES).=
GOREWJ-56-DMF

PUBLIC ADMINISTRATORS AND COMMUNITY
DECISION MAKING.= JENNMK-64-PAC

THE MAKING OF CONSTITUTIONAL LAW
(UNITED STATES).= LANDJW-64-MCL

THE PREDICTION OF ISSUE OUTCOME IN
COMMUNITY DECISION MAKING.=
MILLDC-57-PIC

SOCIAL ORIGINS OF DICTATORSHIP AND
DEMOCRACY -- LORD AND PEASANT IN
THE MAKING OF THE MODERN WORLD
(FRANCE, GREAT BRITAIN,
UNITED STATES, CHINA, JAPAN,
INDIA, GERMANY).= MOORB -66-SOD

TESTING RELATIONS BETWEEN JURIDICAL
CHARACTERISTICS AND JUDICIAL
DECISION MAKING (UNITED STATES).=
NAGESS-62-TRB

POLITICAL PARTIES AND DECISION
MAKING IN THREE SOUTHERN COUNTIES
(UNITED STATES).= RHYNEH-58-PPD

DECISION MAKING IN THE HOUSE RULES
COMMITTEE (UNITED STATES).=
ROBIJA-59-DMH

COMMUNITY DECISION MAKING
(UNITED STATES).= ROSSPH-58-CDM

JUDICIAL DECISION MAKING

MAKING (CONTINUATION)
(UNITED STATES, NORWAY).=
SCHUG -63-JDM

GENTLEMANLY POWER -- BRITISH
LEADERSHIP AND THE PUBLIC SCHOOL
TRADITION -- A COMPARATIVE STUDY
IN THE MAKING OF RULERS.=
WILKR -64-GPB

MALABAR
CHANGING KINSHIP USAGES IN THE
SETTING OF POLITICAL AND ECONOMIC
CHANGE AMONG THE NAYARS OF
MALABAR.= GOUGEK-52-CKU

MALAY
THE ORIGINS OF MALAY NATIONALISM.=
ROFFWR-67-OMN

MALAYA
NATIONALISM AND POLITICS IN
MALAYA.= EAUEPT-47-NPM

ASIAN BUREAUCRATIC SYSTEMS EMERGENT
FROM THE BRITISH IMPERIAL
TRADITION (INDIA, PAKISTAN, BURMA,
CEYLON, MALAYA, NEPAL).=
BRAIR - -ABS

COMMUNALISM AND COMMUNISM IN
MALAYA.= CARNFG-53-CCM

CONSTITUTIONAL REFORM AND ELECTIONS
IN MALAYA.= CARNFG-54-CRE

THE GROWTH OF A PLURAL SOCIETY IN
MALAYA.= FREEM -60-GPS

INDIGENOUS POLITICAL SYSTEMS OF
WESTERN MALAYA.= GUNLJM-58-IPS

TRADE UNIONS AND POLITICS IN
MALAYA.= PARMJN-55-TUP

A NEW CLASS IN MALAYA.=
PYE,LW-60-NCM

MASS SUPPORT AND COMMUNIST
INSURRECTION (GREECE, MALAYA,
INDOCHINA, PHILIPPINES, SOUTH
VIETNAM).= SANDR -65-MSC

PUBLIC SERVICE COMMISSIONS IN THE
FEDERATION OF MALAYA.=
TILMRO-61-PSC

BUREAUCRATIC TRANSITION IN MALAYA.=
TILMRO-64-BTM

BUREAUCRATIC DEVELOPMENT IN
MALAYA.= TILMRO-66-BDM

MALAYAN
MALAYAN POLITICS -- RACE AND
CLASS.= SWIFM -62-MPR

MALAYSIA
MALAYSIA -- A NEW FEDERATION IN
SOUTHEAST ASIA.= MEANGP-63-MNF

MALI
ONE - PARTY GOVERNMENT IN MALI --
TRANSITION TOWARD CONTROL.=
SNYDFG-65-OPG

CREATING POLITICAL ORDER -- THE
PARTY - STATES OF WEST AFRICA
(MALI, GHANA, SENEGAL, GUINEA,
IVORY COAST).= ZOLBAR-66-CPO

MALTESE
FACTIONS, PARTIES AND POLITICS IN A

MALTESE          (CONTINUATION)
  MALTESE VILLAGE.=     BOISJ -64-FPP

MAN
  BOLSHEVIK MAN, HIS MOTIVATIONS.=
               PELLC -55-BMH

  SOME FINDINGS RELEVANT TO THE GREAT
  MAN THEORY OF LEADERSHIP.=
               BORGEF-54-FRG

  SOVIET LEADERS AND MASTERY OVER
  MAN.=          CANTH -60-SLM

  YOUNG MAN LUTHER -- A STUDY IN
  PSYCHOANALYSIS AND HISTORY.=
               ERIKEH-58-YML

  THE MAN ON HORSEBACK -- THE ROLE OF
  THE MILITARY IN POLITICS.=
               FINESE-62-MHR

  THE RED EXECUTIVE--A STUDY OF THE
  ORGANIZATION MAN IN RUSSIAN
  INDUSTRY.=     GRAND -60-RES

  THE ORGANIZATION MAN IN THE
  PRESIDENCY (UNITED STATES).=
               IRISMO-58-CMP

  INDUSTRIALISM AND INDUSTRIAL MAN.=
               KERRC -64-IIM

  POLITICAL MAN -- THE SOCIAL BASES
  OF POLITICS.=    LIPSSM-60-PMS

  MAN AND SOCIETY IN AN AGE OF
  RECONSTRUCTION.=   MANNK -40-MSA

  THE ROLE OF THE CHIEFS AND THE HEAD
  MAN AMONG THE LUGBARA OF THE WEST
  NILE DISTRICT OF UGANDA.=
               MIDDJ -56-RCH

  THE 'NEW MAN' (SOVIET UNION).=
               PISMY -64-NMS

  MAN AND ATTENTIVE OPINION ON
  NUCLEAR WEAPON TESTS AND FALLOUT,
  1954-1963 (UNITED STATES).=
               ROSIEJ-65-MAO

  POOR MAN, RICH MAN, BIG-MAN, CHIEF
  -- POLITICAL TYPES IN MELANESIA
  AND POLYNESIA.=   SAHLMD-63-PMR

  POOR MAN, RICH MAN, BIG-MAN, CHIEF
  -- POLITICAL TYPES IN MELANESIA
  AND POLYNESIA.=   SAHLMD-63-PMR

MANAGE
  MEN WHO MANAGE -- FUSIONS OF
  FEELING AND THEORY IN
  ADMINISTRATION.=   DALTM -59-MWM

MANAGEMENT
  POLITICS AND MANAGEMENT
  (SOVIET UNION).=   AZRAJR-63-PMS

  SOCIAL STRATIFICATION AND ASPECTS
  OF PERSONNEL MANAGEMENT IN THE
  CHINESE COMMUNIST BUREAUCRACY.=
               BARNAD-66-SSA

  ORGANIZATION AND MANAGEMENT.=
               BARNCI-48-OM

  THE LOCAL UNION IN SOVIET INDUSTRY
  -- ITS RELATION WITH MEMBERS,
  PARTY, AND MANAGEMENT.=
               BROWEC-60-LUS

  ADMINISTRATIVE MANAGEMENT OF PUBLIC

MANAGEMENT      (CONTINUATION)
  ENTERPRISES IN YUGOSLAVIA.=
               GROZS -66-AMP

  AUTHORITY AND ORGANIZATION IN
  GERMAN MANAGEMENT.=  HARTH -59-AOO

  TECHNOLOGY AND CAREER MANAGEMENT IN
  THE MILITARY ESTABLISHMENT
  (UNITED STATES).=   LANGK -64-TCM

  THE HOUSE COMMITTEE ON WAYS AND
  MEANS -- CONFLICT MANAGEMENT IN A
  CONGRESSIONAL COMMITTEE
  (UNITED STATES).=   MANLJF-65-HCW

  THE RISE OF MIDDLE CLASS AND MIDDLE
  MANAGEMENT IN BRAZIL.=
               PERELC-62-RMC

MANAGER
  FACTORY AND MANAGER IN THE USSR.=
               BERLJS-57-FMU

  CONTINUITY IN CITY - MANAGER
  CAREERS (UNITED STATES).=
               FLORGK-55-CCM

  LEADERSHIP IN A LARGE MANAGER CITY
  -- THE CASE OF KANSAS CITY
  (UNITED STATES).=   GABIST-64-LLM

  CULTURAL PATTERNS IN THE ROLE OF
  THE MANAGER.=    HAIRM -63-CPR

  THE CITY MANAGER, ADMINISTRATIVE
  THEORY AND POLITICAL POWER
  (UNITED STATES).=   LOCKD -62-CMA

  CROSS - CULTURAL STUDY OF COUNCIL -
  MANAGER GOVERNMENT.=  VILLAB-59-CCS

MANAGERIAL
  MANAGERIAL POWER AND SOVIET
  POLITICS.=     AZRAJR-66-MPS

  THE MANAGERIAL REVOLUTION.=
               BURNJ -60-MR

  CAREER MOBILITY AND MANAGERIAL
  POLITICAL BEHAVIOR
  (UNITED STATES).=   GRUSO -65-CMM

  GOVERNMENT AND DEVELOPMENT --
  MANAGERIAL ATTITUDES IN
  LATIN AMERICA.=   LAUTA -65-GDM

  MANAGERIAL REVOLUTION IN WESTERN
  GERMANY.=     PSJC -51-MRW

  CAREER ANCHORAGE -- MANAGERIAL
  MOBILITY MOTIVATIONS.=
               TAUSC -65-CAM

MANAGERS
  THE 'ILLIBERAL' EDUCATION OF SOVIET
  MANAGERS.=     BAUERA-58-IES

  TYPES OF CITY MANAGERS
  (UNITED STATES).=   FLORGK-54-TCM

  THE MANAGERS (GREAT BRITAIN,
  UNITED STATES, WEST GERMANY).=
               LEWIR -61-MGB

MANDARIN
  THE VIETNAMESE MANDARIN.=
               BUTTJ -58-VM

  MANDARIN BUREAUCRACY AND POLITICS
  IN SOUTH VIETNAM.=  JUMPR -57-MBP

MANDARINS
  THE MANDARINS -- THE CIRCULATION OF

211

MASS                    (CONTINUATION)
NATIONAL CONGRESS AS A MASS
ORGANIZATION, 1919-1923.=
                        KRISG  -66-CIN

BUREAUCRATIC MASS MEDIA -- A STUDY
OF ROLE DEFINITIONS
(UNITED STATES).=       LYSTMH-56-BMM

INTELLECTUALS AND THE MASS MEDIA
(UNITED STATES).=       MCCOT -66-IMM

ALIENATION AND PARTICIPATION -- A
COMPARISON OF GROUP LEADERS AND
THE MASS (UNITED STATES).=
                        ROSEAM-62-APC

MASS SUPPORT AND COMMUNIST
INSURRECTION (GREECE, MALAYA,
INDOCHINA, PHILIPPINES, SOUTH
VIETNAM).=              SANDR -65-MSC

INSTITUTIONAL VULNERABILITY IN MASS
SOCIETY.=               SELZP -51-IVM

INTERNATIONAL POLITICAL
COMMUNICATION -- ELITE VS. MASS.=
                        SPEIH -52-IPC

SMALL TOWN IN MASS SOCIETY --
CLASS, POWER AND RELIGION IN A
RURAL COMMUNITY (UNITED STATES).=
                        VIDIAJ-58-STM

'MASS SOCIETY' -- THE LATE STAGES
OF AN IDEA.=            WALTEV-64-MSL

CONSENSUS AND MASS COMMUNICATION.=
                        WIRTL -48-CMC

MASS PARTIES AND NATIONAL
INTEGRATION -- THE CASE OF THE
IVORY COAST.=           ZOLBAR-63-MPN

MASSACHUSETTS
THE ROLE OF THE STATE LEGISLATOR IN
MASSACHUSETTS (UNITED STATES).=
                        MACRD -54-RSL

THE STATUS REVOLUTION AND
MASSACHUSETTS PROGRESSIVE
LEADERSHIP (UNITED STATES).=
                        SHERRB-63-SRM

MASSES
ORTEGA Y GASSET AND THE THEORY OF
THE MASSES.=            MALOM -61-OYG

THE REVOLT OF THE MASSES.=
                        ORTEY -32-RM

NEGRO MASSES AND LEADERS
(UNITED STATES).=       SMYTHH-50-NML

MASTERS
THE MASTERS AND THE SLAVES -- A
STUDY IN THE DEVELOPMENT OF
BRAZILIAN CIVILIZATION.=
                        FREYG -46-MSS

MASTERY
SOVIET LEADERS AND MASTERY OVER
MAN.=                   CANTH -60-SLM

MATERIALISM
THE ROLE OF CLASSES IN HISTORICAL
MATERIALISM.=           HODGOC-59-RCH

MATHEMATICAL
THE MATHEMATICAL ANALYSIS OF
SUPREME COURT DECISIONS -- THE USE
AND ABUSE OF QUANTITATIVE METHODS

MATHEMATICAL           (CONTINUATION)
(UNITED STATES).=       FISHFM-58-MAS

A MATHEMATICAL PRESENTATION OF
ISRAEL'S POLITICAL PARTIES.=
                        GOODTM-57-MPI

REPLY TO FISHER'S MATHEMATICAL
ANALYSIS OF SUPREME COURT
DECISIONS (UNITED STATES).=
                        KORTF -58-RFS

MATHEMATICALLY
PREDICTING SUPREME COURT DECISIONS
MATHEMATICALLY -- A QUANTITIVE
ANALYSIS OF THE RIGHT TO COUNSEL
(UNITED STATES).=       KORTF -57-PSC

MATRIX
LEFT WING TRADE UNIONISM -- THE
MATRIX OF COMMUNIST POWER IN
ITALY.=                 LAPAJ -54-LWT

MATURING
SOME CHARACTERISTICS OF THE SOVIET
LEADERSHIP SYSTEM -- A MATURING
TOTALITARIAN SYSTEM.=   LAIRRD-66-CSL

MAURITANIA
ONE PARTYISM IN MAURITANIA?=
                        MOORCH-65-OPM

THE ISLAMIC REPUBLIC OF
MAURITANIA.=            EAGLW -65-SRM

MAURITIUS
STRATIFICATION IN PLURAL SOCIETIES
(MAURITIUS).=           BENEB -2 -SPS

MAYOR
MANILA'S MAYOR LOCKS HORNS WITH THE
GAO (PHILIPPINES).=     SORIK -63-MSM

MAYORS
FROM COMMERCIAL ELITE TO POLITICAL
ADMINISTRATOR -- THE RECRUITMENT
OF THE MAYORS OF CHICAGO
(UNITED STATES).=       BRADDS-65-CEP

GOVERNORS, MAYORS, AND COMMUNITY
ETHICS (UNITED STATES).=
                        YOUNWH-52-GMC

MCCARTHY
SMALL BUSINESSMEN, POLITICAL
TOLERANCE, AND SUPPORT FOR
MCCARTHY.=              TROWM -58-SBP

MCCARTHYISM
THEORIES OF MCCARTHYISM -- A SURVEY
(UNITED STATES).=       WRONDH-54-TMS

MEANING
CANDIDATES MUST MAKE THE ISSUES AND
GIVE THEM MEANING
(UNITED STATES).=       DEXTLA-55-CMM

THE PUBLIC INTEREST -- ITS MEANING
IN A DEMOCRACY.=        COWNA -62-PII

THE MEANING OF MILITARISM IN
LATIN AMERICA.=         KNAPFA-64-MML

MEANS
THE HOUSE COMMITTEE ON WAYS AND
MEANS -- CONFLICT MANAGEMENT IN A
CONGRESSIONAL COMMITTEE
(UNITED STATES).=       MANLJF-65-HCW

MEASURE
THE REPUTATIONAL TECHNIQUE AS A

NATIONAL AND SOCIAL COMPOSITION OF
THE MEMBERSHIP OF THE COMMUNIST
PARTY (BOLSHEVIK) OF THE UKRAINE,
1918-1928.=             CMYTB -57-NSC

MEMBERSHIP PARTICIPATION IN
POLICY-MAKING IN THE C.C.F.
(CO-OPERATIVE COMMONWEALTH
FEDERATION, CANADA).= ENGEFC-56-MPP

CHANGING MEMBERSHIP PATTERNS IN
HOUSE COMMITTEES (UNITED STATES).=
                        GAWTLC-66-CMP

THE ECONOMIC AND SOCIAL COUNCIL --
POLITICS OF MEMBERSHIP
(UNITED NATIONS, EUROPE).=
                        GREGRW-63-ESC

SOME OBSERVATIONS ON MEMBERSHIP
FIGURES OF THE COMMUNIST PARTY OF
THE SOVIET UNION.=    HANCWS-58-OMF

POWER STRUCTURE AND MEMBERSHIP
DISPERSION IN UNIONS
(UNITED STATES).=     RAPHEE-65-PSM

SOCIAL ORIENTATION OF RECRUITMENT
AND DISTRIBUTION OF MEMBERSHIP IN
THE COMMUNIST PARTY OF THE
SOVIET UNION.=        RIGBTH-56-SOR

MEN
MEN NEAR THE TOP -- FILLING KEY
POSTS IN THE FEDERAL CIVIL SERVICE
(UNITED STATES).=     CORSJJ-66-MNT

MEN OF IDEAS -- A SOCIOLOGIST'S
VIEW (INTELLECTUALS).=
                        COSELA-65-MIS

MEN WHO MANAGE -- FUSIONS OF
FEELING AND THEORY IN
ADMINISTRATION.=      DALTM -59-MWM

MEN AT THE TOP (UNITED STATES).=
                        ELLIO -59-MTU

THE KING'S MEN -- LEADERSHIP AND
STATUS IN BUGANDA ON THE EVE OF
INDEPENDENCE.=        FALLLA-64-KSM

LOCAL PARTY LEADERS -- GROUPS OF
LIKE MINDED MEN (UNITED STATES).=
                        FLINTA-65-LPL

GROUPS, LEADERSHIP AND MEN.=
                        GUETH -51-GLM

LAWS AND MEN IN SOVIET SOCIETY.=
                        HAZAJN-58-LMS

SYMBOLIC LEADERS -- PUBLIC DRAMAS
AND PUBLIC MEN.=      KLAPCE-64-SLP

THE POLITICS OF BRITAIN'S ANGRY
YOUNG MEN.=           KROLM -61-PBS

THE MEN OF THE POLITBURO
(SOVIET UNION).=      LISTJ -49-MPS

THE NEW MEN OF POWER -- AMERICA'S
LABOR LEADERS.=       MILLCW-48-NMP

MEN AT THE TOP -- A STUDY IN
COMMUNITY POWER (UNITED STATES).=
                        PRESRV-64-MTS

PUBLIC MEN IN AND OUT OF OFFICE
(UNITED STATES).=     SALTJT-46-PMO

POLAND'S ANGRY AND UNANGRY YOUNG

MEN                      (CONTINUATION)
  MEN.=                SHERG -58-PSA

MEN WHO GOVERN -- A BIOGRAPHICAL
PROFILE OF FEDERAL POLITICAL
EXECUTIVES (UNITED STATES).=
                        STAN  -67-MWG

MEN AT WORK.=         WHYTWF-61-MW

THE MEN WHO RULED INDIA -- THE
GUARDIANS.=           WOODP -54-MWR

YOUNG MEN AND THE FOREIGN SERVICE
(UNITED STATES).=     WRISHM-54-YMF

MENDES-FRANCE
THE FRENCH RADICAL PARTY -- FROM
HERRIOT TO MENDES-FRANCE.=
                        DE-TF -61-FRP

MERGER
THE SOCIALIST MERGER AND THE
BALANCE OF PARTIES IN JAPAN.=
                        GRINM -55-SMB

MERIT
MERIT AND POWER IN THE THAI SOCIAL
ORDER.=               HANKLM-62-MPT

MERITOCRACY
THE RISE OF MERITOCRACY, 1870-2033
(GREAT BRITAIN).=     YOUNM -58-RMG

MERRY-GO-ROUND
THE FRENCH INTELLECTUAL
MERRY-GO-ROUND.=      MANGS -49-FIM

MESOAMERICAN
THE CIVIL - RELIGIOUS HIERARCHY IN
MESOAMERICAN COMMUNITIES -- PRE -
SPANISH BACKGROUND AND COLONIAL
DEVELOPMENT.=         CARRP -61-CRH

METAMORPHOSE
THE METAMORPHOSE OF THE NEW CLASS
(SOVIET UNION, EASTERN EUROPE).=
                        HALPE -59-MNC

METAPOLITICS
METAPOLITICS, THE ROOTS OF THE NAZI
MIND.=                VIERPR-61-MRN

METHOD
A COMPARATIVE METHOD FOR THE STUDY
OF POLITICS.=         APTEDE-58-CMS

THE COMMUNITY-STUDY METHOD.=
                        ARENCM-54-CSM

A METHOD FOR ANALYZING LEGISLATIVE
BEHAVIOR (UNITED STATES).=
                        BELKGM-58-MAL

STUDIES IN THE SCOPE AND METHOD OF
THE 'AUTHORITARIAN PERSONALITY'.=
                        CHRIR -54-SSM

A METHOD FOR RANKING COMMUNITY
INFLUENTIALS.=        DICKHR-60-MRC

AMERICAN INTEREST GROUPS -- A
SURVEY OF RESEARCH AND SOME
IMPLICATIONS FOR THEORY AND
METHOD.=              ELDESJ-58-AIG

A METHOD FOR IDENTIFYING ISSUES AND
FACTIONS FROM LEGISLATIVE VOTES
(UNITED STATES).=     MACWD -59-MII

A METHOD FOR DETERMINING THE
SIGNIFICANCE OF ROLL CALLS IN

216

MIDDLE EAST          (CONTINUATION)
RELIGIOUS ORGANIZATIONS AND
POLITICAL PROCESS IN CENTRALIZED
EMPIRES (MIDDLE EAST, FAR EAST).=
                     EISESN-62-ROP

SOCIAL FORCES IN THE MIDDLE EAST.=
                     FISHSN-55-SFM

THE MILITARY IN THE MIDDLE EAST --
PROBLEMS IN SOCIETY AND
GOVERNMENT.=         FISHSN-63-MME

ECONOMIC PLANNERS (MIDDLE EAST).=
                     FRANPG-55-EPM

LABOR AND ECONOMIC DEVELOPMENT
(MIDDLE EAST, SOUTHEAST ASIA).=
                     GALEW -59-LED

LABOR IN DEVELOPING ECONOMICS
(LATIN AMERICA, MIDDLE EAST).=
                     GALEW -62-LDE

THE ROLE OF THE ARMY IN THE
TRANSITIONAL ARAB STATE
(MIDDLE EAST).=      GLUBJ -65-RAT

REVOLUTIONS AND MILITARY RULE IN
THE MIDDLE EAST.=    HADDGM-65-RMR

THE ENTREPRENEUR CLASS
(MIDDLE EAST).=      ISSAC -55-ECM

THE MILITARY IN THE POLITICAL
DEVELOPMENT OF NEW NATIONS -- AN
ESSAY IN COMPARATIVE ANALYSIS
(ASIA, AFRICA, MIDDLE EAST).=
                     JANOM -64-MPD

THE ROLE OF THE MILITARY IN
MIDDLE EAST POLITICS.=
                     KHADM -53-RMM

COMMUNISM AND NATIONALISM IN THE
MIDDLE EAST.=        LAQUWZ-57-CNM

THE PASSING OF TRADITIONAL SOCIETY
(MIDDLE EAST).=      LERND -58-PTS

THE LEAGUE OF ARAB STATES -- A
STUDY IN THE DYNAMICS OF REGIONAL
ORGANIZATION (MIDDLE EAST).=
                     MACDRW-65-LAS

SOCIAL CHANGE AND STRUCTURE IN
TRANSITIONAL SOCIETIES
(LATIN AMERICA, MIDDLE EAST).=
                     MARCS -60-SCS

ENTREPRENEURSHIP AND ECONOMIC
DEVELOPMENT IN THE MIDDLE EAST.=
                     MEYEAJ-58-EED

THE NEW MONARCHIES OF THE
MIDDLE EAST.=        NEWMKJ-59-NMM

THE NATURE OF MODERNIZATION -- THE
MIDDLE EAST AND AND NORTH AFRICA.=
                     POLKWR-65-NMM

PARLIAMENTARY GOVERNMENT AND
MILITARY AUTOCRACY IN THE
MIDDLE EAST.=        SHARHB-60-PGM

POLITICAL EVOLUTION IN THE
MIDDLE EAST.=        SPENW -62-PEM

DILEMMAS OF POLITICAL LEADERSHIP IN
THE ARAB MIDDLE EAST -- THE CASE
OF THE UNITED ARAB REPUBLIC.=
                     VATIPJ-61-DPL

MIDDLE EASTERN
MIDDLE EASTERN ARMIES AND THE NEW

MIDDLE EASTERN        (CONTINUATION)
MIDDLE CLASS.=        HALPM -62-MEA

MIDDLE-SIZED
COMMUNITY INFLUENTIALS IN A
MIDDLE-SIZED CITY
(UNITED STATES).=    FORMWH-61-CIM

MIDDLETOWN
POWER IN MIDDLETOWN -- FACT AND
VALUE IN COMMUNITY RESEARCH
(UNITED STATES).=    POLSNW-60-PMF

MIGRATION
SIX TRIAL DEFINITIONS --
CONURBATION, ELITE, MIGRATION
PROGRESS, SLUM, UNEMPLOYMENT.=
                     ANON  -55-STD

MIGRATORY
THE ROLE OF POLITICAL LEADERSHIP IN
THE PASSAGE OF OREGON'S MIGRATORY
LABOR LEGISLATION
(UNITED STATES).=    BALMDG-62-RPL

MILIEU
BUREAUCRATIC CADRES IN A
TRADITIONAL MILIEU (NIGERIA).=
                     KIRKAH-65-BCT

MILITANT
MILITANT HINDUISM IN INDIAN
POLITICS -- A STUDY OF THE R.S.S.
(RASHTRIYA SWAYAMSEVAK SANGH).=
                     CURRJA-51-MHI

MILITANT PUBLIC SERVICE TRADE
UNIONISM IN A NEW STATE (CEYLON).=
                     KEARRN-66-MPS

MILITARISM
THE STAGES OF MILITARISM IN
LATIN AMERICA.=      ALBAV -62-SML

DICHOTOMIES OF MILITARISM IN
ARGENTINA.=          GOLDM -66-DMA

ECHOES OF MILITARISM IN JAPAN.=
                     KINOH -53-EMJ

THE MEANING OF MILITARISM IN
LATIN AMERICA.=      KNAPFA-64-MML

MILITARISM AND POLITICS IN
LATIN AMERICA.=      LIEUE -62-MPL

MILITARISM IN LATIN AMERICA -- A
THREAT TO THE ALLIANCE FOR
PROGRESS.=           LIEUE -63-MLA

MILITARISM, FASCISM, JAPANISM.=
                     MORRI -63-MFJ

MILITARY ASSISTANCE AND MILITARISM
IN LATIN AMERICA.=   POWEJD-65-MAM

MILITARY
MILITARY ORGANIZATION AND SOCIETY.=
                     ANDRS -54-MOS

IRAQ -- A MILITARY GOVERNMENT WITH
A DIFFERENCE.=       ANON  -53-IMG

MILITARY ELITE AND SOCIAL CHANGE --
EGYPT SINCE NAPOLEON.=
                     BERGM -60-MES

SEQUELS TO A MILITARY CAREER -- THE
RETIRED MILITARY PROFESSIONAL
(UNITED STATES).=    BIDEAD-64-SMC

SEQUELS TO A MILITARY CAREER -- THE

MILITARY          (CCNTINUATICN)
RETIREC MILITARY PRCFESSICNAL
(UNITED STATES).=        BIDEAD-64-SMC

THE CIVIC RCLE CF TFE MILITARY --
SCME CRITICAL FYPCTFESES.=
                         BCBRDB-66-CRM

THE AFRICAN MILITARY BALANCE.=
                         BROWN -64-AMB

BURMA'S MILITARY REGIME.=
                         CADYJF-60-BSM

BURMA'S MILITARY CICTATCRSHIP.=
                         CADYJF-65-BSM

THE PCLITICS CF MILITARY
UNIFICATICN.=        CARDD -66-PMU

PRCBLEMS CF CFINESE CCMMUNIST
LEADERSFIP AS SEEN IN TFE SECRET
MILITARY PAPERS.=        CHENJC-64-PCC

THE MILITARY PCLICY PUBLIC
(UNITED STATES).=        CCHEBC-66-MPP

THE GERMAN MILITARY MINC -- A
SURVEY CF GERMAN MILITARY
WRITING.=        CE-MP -52-GMM

THE GERMAN MILITARY MINC -- A
SURVEY CF GERMAN MILITARY
WRITING.=        CE-MP -52-GMM

INITIATING AND MAINTAINING RESEARCH
RELATICNS IN A MILITARY
CRGANIZATICN.=        CEMENJ-52-IMR

CCNGRESSMEN ANC TFE MAKING CF
MILITARY PCLICY (UNITEC STATES).=
                         CEXTLA-63-CMM

MILITARY LEADERS ANC FCREIGN
PCLICY-MAKING.=        EDINLJ-63-MLF

THE SCVIET FIGF CCMMANC -- A
MILITARY - PCLITICAL FISTCRY.=
                         ERICJ -62-SFC

CRGANIZATICN ANC MILITARY PCWER --
THE JAPANESE FIGH CCMMANC IN WCRLC
WAR II.=        FALKSL-61-CMP

MILITARY SELF-IMAGE IN A
TECHNCLCGICAL ENVIRCNMENT
(UNITED STATES).=        FELDMD-64-MSI

THE MAN CN FCRSEBACK -- TFE RCLE CF
TFE MILITARY IN PCLITICS.=
                         FINESE-62-MHR

THE MILITARY IN TFE MICCLE EAST --
PROBLEMS IN SCCIETY ANC
GCVERNMENT.=        FISHSN-63-MME

DANCE CF THE MILLICNS -- MILITARY
RULE ANC TFE SCCIAL REVCLUTICN IN
CCLCMBIA, 1930-1956.=        FLUHVL-57-CMM

CIVILIANS, SCLCIERS, ANC AMERICAN
MILITARY PCLICY.=        FOX,WT-55-CSA

REPRESENTATIVES ANC EFFICIENCY --
CUAL PRCBLEM CF CIVIL - MILITARY
RELATICNS (UNITED STATES).=
                         FOX,WT-61-REC

MILITARY STATUS IN CHINESE
SCCIETY.=        FRIEMH-51-MSC

MILITARY REPRESENTATICN IN TFE


MILITARY          (CCNTINUATICN)
HIGHER PARTY ECHELCNS (SCVIET
UNICN).=        GALAN -56-MRF

MILITARY REPRESENTATICN CN THE 1958
SUPREME SCVIET CF TFE USSR.=
                         GALAN -58-MRS

THE RCLE CF TFE MILITARY IN RECENT
SCVIET PCLITICS.=        GARTRL-57-RMR

PCLITICS, SCCIAL STRUCTURE, ANC
MILITARY INTERVENTICN IN
LATIN AMERICA.=        GERMC -62-PSS

THE CFALLENGE CF MILITARY
PRCFESSICNALISM (UNITED STATES).=
                         GINSVN-64-CMP

THE MILITARY BUCGET --
CCNGRESSICNAL PFASE
(UNITED STATES).=        GCRDBK-61-MBC

THE EFFECTS CF SUCCESSICN -- A
CCMPARATIVE STUCY CF MILITARY ANC
BUSINESS CRGANIZATICN
(UNITEC STATES).=        GRUSC -64-ESC

THE RESURGENCE CF MILITARY ELEMENTS
IN JAPAN.=        GUILR -52-RME

ECUCATICN CF MILITARY LEACERSFIP IN
EMERGENT STATES.=        GUTTWF-65-EML

MILITARY INSTITUTICNS ANC POWER IN
THE NEW STATES.=        GUTTWF-65-MIP

THE PCLITICAL RCLE CF AFRICAN ARMEC
FCRCES -- TFE IMPACT CF FCREIGN
MILITARY ASSISTANCE.=        GUTTWF-67-PRA

REVCLUTICNS ANC MILITARY RULE IN
THE MICCLE EAST.=        FADCGM-65-RMR

THE RCLE CF TFE MILITARY IN
ISRAEL.=        FALPB -62-RMI

THE CFANGING RCLE CF TFE MILITARY
IN CCLUMBIA.=        FELGJL-61-CRM

THE MILITARY ELITES
(LATIN AMERICA).=        FCRCIL-67-MEL

SCLCIERS ANC GCVERNMENT -- NINE
STUCIES IN CIVIL - MILITARY
RELATICNS (WESTERN EURCPE, USSR,
JAPAN, LATIN AMERICA,
UNITEC STATES).=        FCWAM -59-SGN

CIVIL - MILITARY RELATICNS IN
GREAT BRITAIN ANC TFE
UNITEC STATES, 1945-1958.=
                         FCWAM -60-CMR

CIVILIAN CCNTRCL ANC TFE
CCNSTITUTICN (UNITED STATES,
MILITARY - CIVIL RELATICNSHIPS).=
                         FUNTSP-56-CCC

THE SCLCIER ANC TFE STATE -- TFE
THECRY ANC PCLITICS CF CIVIL -
MILITARY RELATICNS
(UNITEC STATES).=        FUNTSP-57-SST

CHANGING PATTERNS CF MILITARY
PCLITICS.=        FUNTSP-62-CPM

PCWER, EXPERTISE ANC THE MILITARY
PRCFESSICN (UNITEC STATES).=
                         FUNTSP-63-PEM

MILITARY ELITES ANC THE STUCY CF

MILITARY            (CONTINUATION)
WAR (FRANCE, GERMANY, ITALY,
SOVIET UNION, UNITED STATES).=
                    JANOM -57-MES

CHANGING PATTERNS OF ORGANIZATIONAL
AUTHORITY -- THE MILITARY
ESTABLISHMENT (UNITED STATES).=
                    JANOM -59-CPO

THE MILITARY IN THE POLITICAL
DEVELOPMENT OF NEW NATIONS -- AN
ESSAY IN COMPARATIVE ANALYSIS
(ASIA, AFRICA, MIDDLE EAST).=
                    JANCM -64-MPD

THE NEW MILITARY -- CHANGING
PATTERNS OF ORGANIZATION
(UNITED STATES).=    JANOM -64-NMC

SOCIOLOGY AND THE MILITARY
ESTABLISHMENT (UNITED STATES).=
                    JANOM -65-SME

THE LATIN AMERICAN MILITARY AS A
POLITICALLY COMPETING GROUP IN
TRANSITIONAL SOCIETY.=
                    JOHNJJ-62-LAM

THE MILITARY AND SOCIETY IN
LATIN AMERICA.=     JOHNJJ-64-MSL

THE ROLE OF THE MILITARY IN
MIDDLE EAST POLITICS.=
                    KHADM -53-RMM

MILITARY GOVERNMENT IN SUDAN -- THE
PAST THREE YEARS.=   KILNP -62-MGS

THE SOVIET MILITARY AND THE
COMMUNIST PARTY.=   KOLKR -67-SMC

TECHNOLOGY AND CAREER MANAGEMENT IN
THE MILITARY ESTABLISHMENT
(UNITED STATES).=    LANGK -64-TCM

NEW ROLES FOR LATIN AMERICAN
MILITARY.=           LIEUE -60-NRL

THE MILITARY -- A REVOLUTIONARY
FORCE (LATIN AMERICA).=
                    LIEUE -61-MRF

THE NEW CIVIL - MILITARY RELATIONS
(UNITED STATES).=   LYONGM-61-NCM

CIVIL - MILITARY RELATIONS IN THE
UNITED STATES.=     MANSHC-60-CMR

THE GERMAN GENERAL STAFF -- MODEL
OF MILITARY ORGANIZATION.=
                    MARWA -59-GGS

SOLDIERS AND SCHOLARS -- MILITARY
EDUCATION AND NATIONAL POLICY
(UNITED STATES).=    MASLJW-57-SSM

CIVIL - MILITARY RELATIONS IN
LATIN AMERICA.=     MCALLN-61-CMR

THE MILITARY (LATIN AMERICA).=
                    MCALLN-64-MLA

CHANGING CONCEPTS OF THE ROLE OF
THE MILITARY IN LATIN AMERICA.=
                    MCALLN-65-CCR

AMERICAN MILITARY GOVERNMENT IN
KOREA.=             MEADEC-51-AMG

THE FALL OF THE REPUBLIC --
MILITARY REVOLT IN FRANCE.=

MILITARY            (CONTINUATION)
                    MEISJH-62-FRM

CHINESE MILITARY TRADITION -- 1 --
2.=                 MICHFH-46-CMT

THE POWER ELITE -- MILITARY,
ECONOMIC, AND POLITICAL
(UNITED STATES).=    MILLCW-59-PEM

POLITICAL DEVELOPMENT AND MILITARY
INTERVENTION IN LATIN AMERICA.=
                    NEEDMC-66-PDM

MILITARY GOVERNMENT AND THE REVIVAL
OF DEMOCRACY IN GERMANY.=
                    NEUMFL-48-MGR

THE ROLE OF THE MILITARY IN
INDONESIA.=         PAUKGJ-62-RMI

POLITICS AND THE MILITARY IN MODERN
SPAIN.=             PAYNSG-67-PMM

SATELLITE GENERALS -- A STUDY OF
MILITARY ELITES IN THE SOVIET
SPHERE.=            POOLID-55-SGS

THE CHANGING ROLE OF THE MILITARY
IN ARGENTINA.=      POTARA-61-CRM

MILITARY ASSISTANCE AND MILITARISM
IN LATIN AMERICA.=   POWEJC-65-MAM

THE MILITARY AFFAIRS COMMITTEE AND
PARTY CONTROL OF THE MILITARY IN
CHINA.=             POWERL-63-MAC

THE MILITARY AFFAIRS COMMITTEE AND
PARTY CONTROL OF THE MILITARY IN
CHINA.=             POWERL-63-MAC

THE MILITARY AND POLITICS IN
GERMANY.=           RITTG -57-MPG

THE ROLE OF THE MILITARY IN
AMERICAN FOREIGN POLICY.=
                    SAPIBM-4 -RMA

PARLIAMENTARY GOVERNMENT AND
MILITARY AUTOCRACY IN THE
MIDDLE EAST.=       SHARHB-60-PGM

THE MILITARY IN THE POLITICAL
DEVELOPMENT OF THE NEW STATES.=
                    SHILE -62-MPD

THE MILITARY HERO AS PRESIDENTIAL
CANDIDATE (UNITED STATES).=
                    SOMIA -48-MHP

GERMAN REARMAMENT AND THE OLD
MILITARY ELITE.=    SPEIH -54-GRO

GERMAN REARMAMENT AND ATOMIC WAR --
THE VIEWS OF GERMAN MILITARY AND
POLITICAL LEADERS.=  SPEIH -57-GRA

SYRIAN POLITICS AND THE MILITARY,
1945-1958.=         TORRGH-64-SPM

THE ROLE OF THE MILITARY IN CHINESE
GOVERNMENT.=        TUANC -48-RMC

THE MILITARY ROLE IN NATION
BUILDING AND ECONOMIC
DEVELOPMENT.=       UNGEJP-63-MRN

POLITICAL ACTION BY THE MILITARY IN
THE DEVELOPING AREAS.=
                    VON-FR-61-PAM

THE AMERICAN FEDERAL EXECUTIVE -- A

MILITARY                (CONTINUATION)
STUDY CF SCCIAL ANC PERSCNAL
CHARACTERISTICS CF THE CIVILIAN
AND MILITARY LEADERS CF THE UNITEC
STATES FECERAL GCVERNMENT.=
                         WARNWL-63-AFE

THE PCLITICS CF CIVIL - MILITARY
RELATICNS IN THE
DCMINICAN REPUBLIC.=    WIARHJ-65-PCM

THE MILITARY IN THAI PCLITICS.=
                         WILSCA-62-MTP

THE PCLITICAL EFFECTS CF MILITARY
PRCGRAMS -- SCME INCICATIONS FRCM
LATIN AMERICA.=         WOLFC -65-PEM

THE RCLE CF THE MILITARY IN
LATIN AMERICAN PCLITICS.=
                         WYCKT -60-RML

INDIA AND MILITARY CICTATORSHIP.=
                         ZINKT -59-IMC

MILLER-FCRM
PREDICTING A CCMMUNITY CECISICN --
A TEST CF THE MILLER-FCRM THECRY
(UNITEC STATES).=       HANSRC-59-PCC

MILLICNS
DANCE CF THE MILLICNS -- MILITARY
RULE ANC THE SCCIAL REVCLUTION IN
CCLCMBIA, 1930-1956.=   FLUHVL-57-CMM

MILLS
THE NEW SCCICLCGY -- ESSAYS IN
SCCIAL SCIENCE ANC SCCIAL THECRY
IN FCNCR CF C. WRIGHT MILLS.=
                         HORCIL-64-NSE

THE SCCIC-PCLITICAL CRIENTATICNS CF
C. WRIGHT MILLS -- AN EVALUATICN.=
                         SPINW -66-SPC

MIND
THE REVCLT CF THE MIND -- A CASE
HISTORY CF INTELLECTUAL RESISTANCE
BEHINC THE IRCN CURTAIN.=
                         ACZET -60-RMC

THE GERMAN MILITARY MIND -- A
SLRVEY CF GERMAN MILITARY
WRITING.=                CE-MP -52-GMM

ACACEMIC MIND -- SCCIAL SCIENTISTS
IN A TIME CF CRISIS
(UNITEC STATES).=       LAZAPF-58-AMS

THE JUDICIAL MIND -- ATTITUDES AND
ICECLCGIES CF SLPREME CCURT
JUSTICES 1946-1963
(UNITEC STATES).=       SCHUGA-65-JMA

THE SCVIET PCLITICAL MIND.=
                         TUCKRC-63-SPM

METAPCLITICS, THE RCCTS OF THE NAZI
MIND.=                   VIERPR-61-MRN

MINCEC
LCCAL PARTY LEACERS -- GRCUPS CF
LIKE MINDEC MEN (UNITEC STATES).=
                         FLINTA-65-LPL

MINIATURE
SLBCCMMITTEES -- THE MINIATURE
LEGISLATURES CF CCNGRESS
(LNITEC STATES).=       GOODG -62-SML

MINISTER
THE CFFICE CF THE PRIME MINISTER

MINISTER                (CCNTINUATION)
(GREAT ERITAIN).=       CARTBE-56-OPM

THE MCNARCH, THE PRIME MINISTER,
AND THE DISSCLUTICN CF PARLIAMENT
(GREAT ERITAIN).=       FEASCJ-61-MPM

THE PRIME MINISTER AS AN ELECTEC
MCNARCH (GREAT ERITAIN).=
                         HINTRW-60-PME

THE MCNARCH ANC THE SELECTICN CF A
PRIME MINISTER -- A RE-EXAMINATICN
CF THE CRISIS CF 1931
(GREAT ERITAIN).=       MCOCGC-57-MSP

THE QUALITIES CF A CREAT PRIME
MINISTER (GREAT ERITAIN).=
                         SCMEDC-53-CGP

THE EVCLUTICN CF MINISTER - CIVIL
SERVANT RELATICNS IN INCIA.=
                         SUBRV -62-EMC

THE CFFICE CF PUBLIC RELATICNS
ADVISCR TC THE PRIME MINISTER
(GREAT ERITAIN).=       WILLF -56-CPR

MINISTERIAL
M.P.S. IN MINISTERIAL CFFICE
(GREAT ERITAIN).=       BUCKPW-61-MPS

THE MINISTERIAL HIERARCHY -- PART 1
(GREAT ERITAIN).=       FEASCJ-62-MFP

MINISTERIAL CABINETS CF THE FCURTH
REPUBLIC (FRANCE).=     KINGJB-60-MCF

MINISTERS
CIVIL SERVANTS, MINISTERS,
PARLIAMENT ANC THE PUBLIC
(GREAT ERITAIN).=       ATTLCR-54-CSM

RACIAL ANC MCRAL CRISIS -- THE RCLE
CF LITTLE RCCK MINISTERS
(LNITED STATES).=       CAMPEQ-59-RMC

NEW ZEALANC MINISTERS, 1935-1957.=
                         CAMPP -58-NZM

THE SALCI ARABIAN CCUNCIL OF
MINISTERS.=              HARRCW-58-SAC

THE INCIAN CCUNCIL CF MINISTERS.=
                         NORTRC-59-ICM

MINISTERS CF MCCERNIZATION -- ELITE
MCBILITY IN THE MEIJI RESTORATICN,
1868-1873.=             SILBBS-64-MME

SYRIAN CEPLTIES ANC CABINET
MINISTERS, 1919-1959 -- PART 1 --
PART 2.=                 WINCRB-62-SCC

THE GCLC CCAST (GHANA) -- MINISTERS
AND CFFICIALS -- 3.=    WISEHV-57-GCG

MINISTRY
PRIVY CCUNCIL, CABINET AND MINISTRY
IN GREAT BRITAIN ANC CANACA.=
                         BANKMA-  -PCC

MINISTRY CCNTRCL ANC LCCAL AUTCNOMY
IN EDLCATICN (CREAT ERITAIN).=
                         BRANJA-65-MCL

PEKING'S EVCLVING MINISTRY CF
FCREICN AFFAIRS.=       KLEICW-60-PSE

MINCRITIES
MAJCRITIES ANC MINCRITIES IN
WESTERN EURCPEAN GCVERNMENTS.=

MODERN                   (CONTINUATION)
  BUSINESS CLASS.=         GADGDR-59-OMI

  POLITICAL COMMUNITY AND GROUP
  INTEREST IN MODERN INDIA.=
                           GUSFJR-65-PCG

  HEROIC LEADERSHIP -- THE CASE OF
  MODERN FRANCE.=          HOFFS -67-HLC

  BEYOND THE RULING CLASS --
  STRATEGIC ELITES IN MODERN
  SOCIETY.=                KELLS -63-BRC

  THE INTELLIGENTSIA AND MODERN
  CAPITALISM.=             KEMPT -62-IMC

  THE MODERN SENATE OF CANADA,
  1925-1963.=              KUNZFA-65-MSC

  CONFUCIAN CHINA AND ITS MODERN FATE
  -- THE PROBLEM OF INTELLECTUAL
  CONTINUITY.=             LEVEJR-58-CCI

  THE EMERGENCE OF MODERN TURKEY.=
                           LEWIB -61-EMT

  MODERN POLITICAL MOVEMENTS IN
  SOMALILAND -- PART 1 -- PART 2.=
                           LEWIIM-58-MPM

  PROBLEMS IN THE DEVELOPMENT OF
  MODERN LEADERSHIP AND LOYALTIES IN
  THE BRITISH SOMALILAND
  PROTECTORATE AND THE UNITED
  NATIONS TRUSTEESHIP TERRITORY OF
  SOMALIA.=                LEWIIM-60-PDM

  THOUGHT AND BEHAVIOUR IN MODERN
  JAPANESE POLITICS.=      MARHM -63-TBM

  ACCION DEMOCRATICA -- REVOLUTION OF
  A MODERN POLITICAL PARTY IN
  VENEZUELA.=              MARTJD-66-ADR

  RELIGION AND AUTHORITY IN MODERN
  BURMA.=                  MENDEM-60-RAM

  THE EXECUTIVE IN THE MODERN STATE
  (CANADA, FRANCE, GREAT BRITAIN,
  SOVIET UNION, UNITED STATES,
  YUGOSLAVIA).=            MEYNJ -58-EMS

  POLITICAL PARTIES -- A SOCIOLOGICAL
  STUDY OF THE OLIGARCHICAL
  TENDENCIES OF MODERN DEMOCRACY
  (GERMANY).=              MICHR -62-PPS

  THE INDIAN MIDDLE CLASS -- THEIR
  GROWTH IN MODERN TIMES.=
                           MISRBB-61-IMC

  SOCIAL ORIGINS OF DICTATORSHIP AND
  DEMOCRACY -- LORD AND PEASANT IN
  THE MAKING OF THE MODERN WORLD
  (FRANCE, GREAT BRITAIN,
  UNITED STATES, CHINA, JAPAN,
  INDIA, GERMANY).=        MOORB -66-SOD

  AN AMERICAN DILEMMA -- THE NEGRO
  PROBLEM AND MODERN DEMOCRACY.=
                           MYRDG -44-ADN

  TRADITIONAL AND MODERN TYPES OF
  LEADERSHIP AND ECONOMIC
  DEVELOPMENT AMONG THE FIJIANS.=
                           NAYARR-64-TMT

  MODERN POLITICAL PARTIES (WESTERN
  EUROPE, JAPAN) SOVIET UNION,
  UNITED STATES, EASTERN EUROPE).=
                           NEUMS -56-MPP

  JAPAN'S EMERGENCE AS A MODERN

MODERN                   (CONTINUATION)
  STATE.=                  NORMEH-46-JSE

  POLITICS AND THE MILITARY IN MODERN
  SPAIN.=                  PAYNSG-67-PMM

  MEXICO -- A SPANISH - INDIAN
  CULTURE IN A MODERN SETTING.=
                           PS    -49-MSI

  POLITICAL DECISIONS IN MODERN
  SOCIETY.=                RIEZK -54-PDM

  ENGLAND -- A TRADITIONALLY MODERN
  POLITICAL CULTURE.=      ROSER -66-ETM

  FEUDAL SOCIETY AND MODERN
  LEADERSHIP IN SATSUMA-HAN.=
                           SAKARK-57-FSM

  CRITERIA FOR RECRUITMENT AND
  SUCCESS IN THE JAPANESE
  BUREAUCRACY, 1866-1900 --
  'TRADITIONAL' AND 'MODERN'
  CRITERIA IN BUREAUCRATIC
  DEVELOPMENT.=            SILBBS-66-CRS

  THE INTELLECTUALS IN THE MODERN
  DEVELOPMENT OF THE ISLAMIC WORLD.=
                           SMITWC-55-IMD

  THE NON - AFRICAN MINORITY IN
  MODERN AFRICA -- SOCIAL STATUS.=
                           SMYTHH-61-NAM

  SOCIAL CHANGE IN MODERN AFRICA.=
                           SOUTA -61-SCM

  SOCIAL CHANGE IN MODERN INDIA.=
                           SRINMN-66-SCM

  THE MAY FOURTH MOVEMENT --
  INTELLECTUAL REVOLUTION IN MODERN
  CHINA.=                  TSE-C -60-MFM

  THE EMERGENCE OF THE MODERN
  INDONESIAN ELITE.=       VAN-R -60-EMI

  TRADITIONAL ROLE PERFORMANCE AND
  THE DEVELOPMENT OF MODERN
  POLITICAL PARTIES -- THE INDIAN
  CASE.=                   WEINM -64-TRP

  MODERN CHINA IN TRANSITION.=
                           WRIGMC-59-MCT

MODERNISATION
  THE DEVELOPMENT OF SOCIO-POLITICAL
  CENTERS AT THE SECOND STAGE OF
  MODERNISATION -- A COMPARATIVE
  ANALYSIS OF TWO TYPES.=
                           EISESN-66-DSP

  AFRICAN POLITICAL CHANGE AND
  MODERNISATION PROCESS.=
                           KILSM -63-APC

MODERNISM
  TOTALITARIANISM -- A DISEASE OF
  MODERNISM.=              LANGR -55-TDM

MODERNITY
  THE SEARCH FOR MODERNITY IN ASIA
  AND AFRICA -- A REVIEW ARTICLE.=
                           CORERP-64-SMA

  OLD SOCIETIES AND NEW STATES -- THE
  QUEST FOR MODERNITY IN ASIA AND
  AFRICA.=                 GEERC -63-OSN

  TURKEY -- THE MODERNITY OF
  TRADITION.=              RUSTA -65-TMT

MODERNITY (CONTINUATION)
THE INTELLECTUAL BETWEEN TRADITION
AND MODERNITY -- THE INDIAN
SITUATION.= SHILE -61-IBT

MODERNIZATION
THE ROLE OF TRADITIONALISM IN THE
POLITICAL MODERNIZATION OF GHANA
AND UGANDA.= APTEDE-60-RTP

INITIAL INSTITUTIONAL PATTERNS OF
POLITICAL MODERNIZATION -- PART 1
-- PART 2.= EISESN-62-IIP

MIDDLE CLASS IMPEDIMENTS TO IRANIAN
MODERNIZATION.= GASTRO-58-MCI

PEDDLERS AND PRINCES -- SOCIAL
CHANGE AND ECONOMIC MODERNIZATION
IN TWO INDONESIAN TOWNS.=
GEERC -63-PPS

GENESIS AND MODERNIZATION OF
POLITICAL PARTIES IN CHILE.=
GIL,F -62-GMP

THE POLITICAL MODERNIZATION OF
TRADITIONAL MONARCHIES.=
HUNTSP-66-PMT

POLITICAL CHANGE IN A WEST AFRICAN
STATE -- A STUDY OF THE
MODERNIZATION PROCESS IN
SIERRA LEONE.= KILSM -66-PCW

TUNISIA -- THE POLITICS OF
MODERNIZATION.= MICACA-64-TPM

THE NATURE OF MODERNIZATION -- THE
MIDDLE EAST AND AND NORTH AFRICA.=
POLKWR-65-NMM

ARMIES IN THE PROCESS OF POLITICAL
MODERNIZATION.= PYE,LW-62-APP

THAILAND -- THE MODERNIZATION OF A
BUREAUCRATIC POLITY.= RIGGFW-66-TMB

A WORLD OF NATIONS -- PROBLEMS OF
POLITICAL MODERNIZATION (ASIA,
AFRICA, LATIN AMERICA).=
RUSTDA-67-WNP

POLITICAL ELITES AND POLITICAL
MODERNIZATION -- THE CRISIS OF
TRANSITION (LATIN AMERICA).=
SCOTRE-67-PEP

MINISTERS OF MODERNIZATION -- ELITE
MOBILITY IN THE MEIJI RESTORATION,
1868-1873.= SILBBS-64-MME

TURKISH POLITICS -- THE ATTEMPT TO
RECONCILE RAPID MODERNIZATION WITH
DEMOCRACY.= ULMAAH-65-TPA

POLITICAL MODERNIZATION IN JAPAN
AND TURKEY.= WARDRE-64-PMJ

JAPAN -- THE CONTINUITY OF
MODERNIZATION.= WARDRE-66-JCM

SOME HYPOTHESES ON THE POLITICS OF
MODERNIZATION IN INDIA.=
WEINM -59-HPM

MODERNIZING
SWORDS AND PLOUGHSHARES -- THE
TURKISH ARMY AS A MODERNIZING
FORCE.= LERND -60-SPT

MOHAMMED
MOROCCO INDEPENDENT UNDER MOHAMMED

MOHAMMED (CONTINUATION)
THE FIFTH.= LANDR -61-MIU

MONARCH
THE MONARCH, THE PRIME MINISTER,
AND THE DISSOLUTION OF PARLIAMENT
(GREAT BRITAIN).= HEASCJ-61-MPM

THE PRIME MINISTER AS AN ELECTED
MONARCH (GREAT BRITAIN).=
HINTRW-60-PME

THE MONARCH AND THE SELECTION OF A
PRIME MINISTER -- A RE-EXAMINATION
OF THE CRISIS OF 1931
(GREAT BRITAIN).= WOODGC-57-MSP

MONARCHIES
THE POLITICAL MODERNIZATION OF
TRADITIONAL MONARCHIES.=
HUNTSP-66-PMT

THE NEW MONARCHIES OF THE
MIDDLE EAST.= NEWMKJ-59-NMM

MONARCHS
MONARCHS AND SOCIOLOGISTS -- A
REPLY TO PROFESSOR SHILS AND MR.
YOUNG.= BIRNN -55-MSR

MONARCHY
SOME IMPLICATIONS OF THE NEW
CONSTITUTIONAL MONARCHY IN
MOROCCO.= BELIWA-64-INC

FROM MONARCHY TO COMMUNISM -- THE
SOCIAL TRANSFORMATION OF THE
ALBANIAN ELITE.= MOSKCC-65-MCS

MONEY
REFLECTIONS ON MONEY AND PARTY
POLITICS IN BRITAIN.= NEWMFC-57-RMP

POLITICAL MONEY -- A STUDY OF
CONTRIBUTORS TO THE NATIONAL
COMMITTEE FOR AN EFFECTIVE
CONGRESS (UNITED STATES).=
SCOBHM-63-PMS

MONGOLIAN
THE MONGOLIAN PEOPLE'S REPUBLIC --
THE SLOW EVOLUTION.= RUPERA-67-MPS

MONOLITH
THE CHINESE MONOLITH -- PAST AND
PRESENT.= WRIGAF-55-CMP

MORAL
THE MORAL BASIS OF A BACKWARD
SOCIETY (ITALY).= BANFEC-58-MBB

RACIAL AND MORAL CRISIS -- THE ROLE
OF LITTLE ROCK MINISTERS
(UNITED STATES).= CAMPEQ-59-RMC

THE PRESIDENCY AS MORAL LEADERSHIP
(UNITED STATES).= GOLDEF-52-PML

MOROCCAN
MOROCCAN PROFILES -- A NATIONALIST
VIEW.= LANDR -53-MPN

RELIGIOUS BROTHERHOODS IN MOROCCAN
POLITICS.= VIDAFS-50-RBM

MOROCCO
LABOR POLITICS IN A NEW NATION
(MOROCCO).= ASHFOE-60-LPN

A CASE STUDY IN THE DIPLOMACY OF
SOCIAL REVOLUTION (MOROCCO).=
ASHFOE-61-CSD

POLITICAL CHANGE IN MOROCCO.=

MOVEMENT                (CONTINUATION)
                        AL-HMM-56-LMI

THE SOVIET TRADE UNION MOVEMENT.=
                        ANON  -58-STU

THE YOUTH MOVEMENT IN THE WEIMAR
REPUBLIC (GERMANY).=    APSLAE-45-YMW

THE MID-WEST STATE MOVEMENT IN
NIGERIAN POLITICS -- A STUDY IN
PARTY FORMATION.=       BRANJA-65-MWS

THE MRP (MOVEMENT REPUBLICAN
POPULAIRE) AND FRENCH FOREIGN
POLICY.=                CAPERB-63-MMR

THE SOCIAL DEMOCRATIC PARTY OF
GERMANY -- FROM WORKING CLASS
MOVEMENT TO MODERN POLITICAL
PARTY.=                 CHALDA-64-SDP

THE NATIONAL MOVEMENT IN MODERN
CHINA.=                 CHATK -59-NMM

THE MAY FOURTH MOVEMENT --
INTELLECTUAL REVOLUTION IN MODERN
CHINA.=                 CHOUT -60-MFM

THE LABOUR MOVEMENT IN THE SUDAN
1946-1955.=             FAWSSE-57-LMS

THE INDONESIAN COMMUNIST PARTY AND
CONFLICT IN THE INTERNATIONAL
COMMUNIST MOVEMENT.=    HINDD -64-ICP

TRENDS IN THE BRITISH LABOR
MOVEMENT SINCE 1850.=   HOBSEJ-49-TBL

THE IDEOLOGY AND PROGRAM OF THE
PERUVIAN APRISTA MOVEMENT.=
                        KANTH -53-IPP

TOTALITARIAN YOUTH MOVEMENT AS A
CAREER MECHANISM -- THE CASE IN
CZECHOSLOVAKIA.=        KUBAD -65-TYM

THE ITALIAN LABOR MOVEMENT --
PROBLEMS AND PROSPECTS.=
                        LAPAJ -57-ILM

THE COMMUNIST MOVEMENT IN IRAN.=
                        LENCG -47-CMI

THE FRENCH LABOR MOVEMENT.=
                        LORWVR-54-FLM

THE INDONESIAN COMMUNIST MOVEMENT
TODAY.=                 LUBIM -54-ICM

THE GROWTH AND DEMOCRATIZATION OF
THE VENEZUELAN LABOR MOVEMENT.=
                        MARTJD-63-GDV

THE AMERICAN LABOUR MOVEMENT -- A
BRITISH VIEW.=          PELLH -54-ALM

THE RISE OF THE LATIN AMERICAN
LABOR MOVEMENT.=        POBLM -60-RLA

INTER - CONSTITUENCY MOVEMENT OF
BRITISH PARLIAMENTARY CANDIDATES,
1951-1959.=             RANNA -64-ICM

AN IMAGE OF EUROPEAN POLITICS --
THE PEOPLE'S PATRIOTIC MOVEMENT
(FINLAND).=             RINTM -62-IEP

THE TUNISIAN NATIONALIST MOVEMENT
-- FOUR DECADES OF EVOLUTION.=
                        RIVLB -52-TNM

DEMOCRACY AND THE PARTY MOVEMENT IN

MOVEMENT                (CONTINUATION)
PREWAR JAPAN -- THE FAILURE OF THE
FIRST ATTEMPT.=         SCALRA-53-DPM

DOMINANT POWER COMPONENTS IN THE
BRAZILIAN UNIVERSITY STUDENT
MOVEMENT PRIOR TO APRIL 1964.=
                        THERLO-65-DPC

THE MAY FOURTH MOVEMENT --
INTELLECTUAL REVOLUTION IN MODERN
CHINA.=                 TSE-C -60-MFM

TOWARD A COMPARATIVE POLITICS OF
MOVEMENT REGIMES.=      TUCKRC-61-TCP

THE DAR UL-ISLAM MOVEMENT IN
WESTERN JAVA.=          VAN-  -50-DUI

THE PARTISAN MOVEMENT IN POSTWAR
LITHUANIA.=             VARDVS-63-PMP

THE DEVELOPMENT OF THE LABOR
MOVEMENT IN THE
DOMINICAN REPUBLIC.=    WIARHJ-66-DLM

MOVEMENTS
LABOUR MOVEMENTS IN LATIN AMERICA.=
                        ALEXRJ-47-LML

PEASANT MOVEMENTS IN COLONIAL
SOUTHEAST ASIA.=        BENDHJ-65-PMC

THE 'THREE-ANTI' AND 'FIVE-ANTI'
MOVEMENTS IN COMMUNIST CHINA.=
                        CHENTH-52-TAF

YOUTH AND COMMUNISM -- AN
HISTORICAL ANALYSIS OF
INTERNATIONAL COMMUNIST YOUTH
MOVEMENTS.=             CORNR -65-YCH

JAPAN'S ROLE IN SOUTHEAST ASIAN
NATIONALIST MOVEMENTS, 1940-1945.=
                        ELSBWH-53-JSR

ECONOMIC ASPECTS OF POLITICAL
MOVEMENTS IN NIGERIA AND IN THE
GOLD COAST, 1918-1939.=
                        HOPKAG-66-EAP

WORLD REVOLUTIONARY ELITES --
STUDIES IN COERCIVE IDEOLOGICAL
MOVEMENTS (CHINA, GERMANY, ITALY,
SOVIET UNION).=         LASSHD-66-WRE

MODERN POLITICAL MOVEMENTS IN
SOMALILAND -- PART 1 -- PART 2.=
                        LEWIIM-58-MPM

LEADERSHIP AND NEW SOCIAL MOVEMENTS
(CANADA).=              LIPSSM-65-LNS

CONTEMPORARY PEASANT MOVEMENTS
(LATIN AMERICA).=       CRBEAQ-67-CPM

THE BUREAUCRAT AND THE ENTHUSIAST
-- AN EXPLORATION OF THE
LEADERSHIP OF SOCIAL MOVEMENTS
(UNITED STATES).=       ROCHJP-55-BEE

REVITALIZATION MOVEMENTS.=
                        WALLAF-58-RM

MRP
THE MRP (MOVEMENT REPUBLICAN
POPULAIRE) AND FRENCH FOREIGN
POLICY.=                CAPERB-63-MMR

MULLAH
THE 'MAD MULLAH' AND NORTHERN
SOMALIA.=               HESSRL-64-MMN

NATIONAL                (CONTINUATION)
NATIONAL CONGRESS AS A MASS
ORGANIZATION, 1919-1923.=
                        KRISG -66-CIN

NATIONAL SECURITY AND INDIVIDUAL
FREEDOM.=               LASSHD-O -NSI

THE DECLINE OF ALGERIA'S FLN
(NATIONAL LIBERATION FRONT).=
                        LEWIWH-66-DAS

NATIONAL CONVENTION LEADERSHIP --
1952 AND 1956 (UNITED STATES).=
                        MARVD -61-NCL

SOLDIERS AND SCHOLARS -- MILITARY
EDUCATION AND NATIONAL POLICY
(UNITED STATES).=       MASLJW-57-SSM

THE TRACK OF THE WOLF -- ESSAYS ON
NATIONAL SOCIALISM AND ITS
LEADERS, ADOLPH HITLER (GERMANY).=
                        MCRAJH-65-TWE

EUROPEAN ASSEMBLY PARTIES AND
NATIONAL DELEGATIONS.=
                        MERKPH-64-EAP

DECISION THEORY IN THE STUDY OF
NATIONAL ACTION -- PROBLEMS AND A
PROPOSAL.=              PATCM -65-DTS

ORGANIZED GROUPS IN BRITISH
NATIONAL POLITICS.=     POTTAM-60-OGB

CENTRAL INTELLIGENCE AND NATIONAL
SECURITY (UNITED STATES).=
                        RANSHH-58-CIN

CONSENSUS-BUILDING IN THE AMERICAN
NATIONAL COMMUNITY -- SOME
HYPOTHESES AND SOME SUPPORTING
DATA.=                  ROSEJN-62-CBA

NATIONAL LEADERSHIP AND FOREIGN
POLICY -- A CASE STUDY IN THE
MOBILIZATION OF PUBLIC SUPPORT
(UNITED STATES).=       ROSEJN-63-NLF

THE SOCIAL DEMOCRATS IN IMPERIAL
GERMANY -- A STUDY IN WORKING
CLASS ISOLATION AND NATIONAL
INTEGRATION.=           ROTHG -63-SDI

URBANISM AND THE NATIONAL PARTY
ORGANIZATION (UNITED STATES).=
                        ROURFE-65-UNP

POLITICAL MONEY -- A STUDY OF
CONTRIBUTORS TO THE NATIONAL
COMMITTEE FOR AN EFFECTIVE
CONGRESS (UNITED STATES).=
                        SCOBHM-63-PMS

NATIONAL VALUES, DEVELOPMENT,
LEADERS AND FOLLOWERS
(LATIN AMERICA).=       SILVKH-63-NVD

THE PROBLEM OF NATIONAL LEADERSHIP
IN NIGERIA.=            SMYTHH-58-PNL

KAZAKHSTAN -- CHANGES IN
ADMINISTRATIVE STATUS AND THE
NATIONAL COMPOSITION OF THE
POPULATION (SOVIET UNION).=
                        TASKGA-64-KCA

REORGANIZATION IN THE PHILIPPINE
NATIONAL GOVERNMENT PRIOR TO
1954.=                  VILALA-61-RPN

ON THE SUPERIORITY OF NATIONAL

NATIONAL                (CONTINUATION)
CONVENTIONS.=           WILDAB-62-SNC

ISSUE DIMENSIONS IN A MULTI - PARTY
SYSTEM -- THE FRENCH NATIONAL
ASSEMBLY AND EUROPEAN
UNIFICATION.=           WOODDM-64-IDM

MASS PARTIES AND NATIONAL
INTEGRATION -- THE CASE OF THE
IVORY COAST.=           ZOLBAR-63-MPN

NATIONALISATION
LABOUR AND STAFF PROBLEMS UNDER
NATIONALISATION (GREAT BRITAIN).=
                        COLEGD-50-LSP

NATIONALISED
ORGANIZATION OF THE NATIONALISED
INDUSTRIES (GREAT BRITAIN).=
                        CHESDN-50-ONI

NATIONALISM
THE INTELLECTUAL ORIGINS OF
EGYPTIAN NATIONALISM.=
                        AHMEJM-60-IOE

NATIONALISM, GOVERNMENT AND
ECONOMIC GROWTH.=       APTEDE-59-NGE

THE POLITICAL KINGDOM IN UGANDA --
A STUDY OF BUREAUCRATIC
NATIONALISM.=           APTEDE-61-PKU

CONTRADICTIONS OF NATIONALISM AND
NATION-BUILDING IN THE MUSLIM
WORLD.=                 ASHFDE-64-CNN

NATIONALISM AND POLITICS IN
MALAYA.=                BAUEPT-47-NPM

NATIONALISM IN MOROCCO.=
                        CLINWB-47-NM

NIGERIA -- BACKGROUND TO
NATIONALISM.=           COLEJS-58-NBN

NATIONALISM IN IRAN.=   COTTR -64-NI

THE SOCIAL BACKGROUND OF INDIAN
NATIONALISM.=           DESAAR-49-SBI

NATIONALISM AND SOCIAL
COMMUNICATION -- AN INQUIRY INTO
THE FOUNDATIONS OF NATIONALISM.=
                        DEUTKW-53-NSC

NATIONALISM AND SOCIAL
COMMUNICATION -- AN INQUIRY INTO
THE FOUNDATIONS OF NATIONALISM.=
                        DEUTKW-53-NSC

NATIONALISM AND POLITICAL
DEVELOPMENT.=           EMERR -60-NPD

RACE AND NATIONALISM -- THE
STRUGGLE FOR POWER IN
RHODESIA-NYASALAND.=    FRANFM-60-RNS

RADICAL NATIONALISM -- THE
POLITICAL ORIENTATIONS OF
PANAMANIAN LAW STUDENTS.=
                        GOLDD -62-RNP

NATIONALISM AND COMMUNISM IN
CHILE.=                 HALPE -65-NCC

INDIAN NATIONALISM AND HINDU SOCIAL
REFORM.=                HEIMCH-64-INH

NATIONALISM IN COLONIAL AFRICA.=
                        HODGT -56-NCA

PEASANT NATIONALISM AND COMMUNIST

NATIONS             (CONTINUATION)
                    RUSTDA-67-WNP

THE IDEOLOGIES OF THE DEVELOPING
NATIONS.=           SIGMPE-63-IDN

THE EGYPTIAN ARMY IN POLITICS --
THE PATTERN FOR NEW NATIONS.=
                    VATIPJ-61-EAP

NATURE
THE NATURE OF THE SOVIET SYSTEM.=
                    BRZEZ -61-NSS

THE NATURE OF BELIEF SYSTEMS IN
MASS PUBLICS.=      CONVPE-64-NBS

NATURE AND PROSPECTS OF POLITICAL
INTEREST GROUPS.=   DE-GA -58-NPP

THE NATURE OF CANADA'S
PARLIAMENTARY REPRESENTATION.=
                    LAINLH-46-NCS

CONFLICT AND LEADERSHIP -- THE
PROCESS OF DECISION AND THE NATURE
OF AUTHORITY.=      LASSHD-66-CLP

THE NATURE OF KHRUSHCHEV'S POWER
(SOVIET UNION).=    LOWER -60-NKS

THE NATURE OF MODERNIZATION -- THE
MIDDLE EAST AND AND NORTH AFRICA.=
                    POLKWR-65-NMM

REPRESENTATION AND NATURE OF
POLITICAL SYSTEMS.= SUTTFX-59-RNP

NAVY
THE SOVIET NAVY.=   BALDHW-55-SN

NAYARS
CHANGING KINSHIP USAGES IN THE
SETTING OF POLITICAL AND ECONOMIC
CHANGE AMONG THE NAYARS OF
MALABAR.=           GOUGEK-52-CKU

NAZI
GERMANY'S POST NAZI INTELLECTUAL
CLIMATE.=           ARNOGL-55-GSP

THE SOCIAL COMPOSITION OF THE NAZI
LEADERSHIP (GERMANY).=
                    DOBLEM-45-SCN

GERMAN EXILE POLITICS -- THE SOCIAL
DEMOCRATIC EXECUTIVE COMMITTEE IN
THE NAZI ERA.=      EDINLJ-56-GEP

THE NAZI PARTY -- ITS LEADERSHIP
AND COMPOSITION (GERMANY).=
                    GERTH -40-NPI

THE PSYCHOLOGY OF DICTATORSHIP --
BASED ON AN EXAMINATION OF THE
LEADERS OF NAZI GERMANY.=
                    GILBGM-50-PDD

HOW TOTALITARIANS GAIN ABSOLUTE
POWER (NAZI GERMANY,
SOVIET UNION).=     KECSP -52-HTG

THE NAZI ELITE.=    LERND -51-NE

CHARISMA AND FACTIONALISM IN THE
NAZI PARTY (GERMANY.= NYOMJ -67-CFN

THE BUREAUCRACY AND THE NAZI
PARTY.=             PETEEN-66-BNP

THE WILHELMSTRASSE -- A STUDY OF
GERMAN DIPLOMATS UNDER THE NAZI

NAZI                (CONTINUATION)
REGIME.=            SEABP -54-WSG

PARTY AND STATE IN SOVIET RUSSIA
AND NAZI GERMANY.=  UNGEAL-65-PSS

METAPOLITICS, THE ROOTS OF THE NAZI
MIND.=              VIERPR-61-MRN

THE GERMAN DIPLOMATS AND THE NAZI
LEADERSHIP, 1933-1939.=
                    WATTDC-55-GDN

NAZIS
NAZISM AND THE NAZIS.=
                    SAQUW -64-NN

SWORD AND SWASTIKA -- GENERALS AND
NAZIS IN THE THIRD REICH.=
                    TAYLT -52-SSG

NAZISM
NAZISM AND THE NAZIS.=
                    SAQUW -64-NN

NEAR
MEN NEAR THE TOP -- FILLING KEY
POSTS IN THE FEDERAL CIVIL SERVICE
(UNITED STATES).=   CORSJJ-66-MNT

POLITY, BUREAUCRACY AND INTEREST
GROUPS IN THE NEAR EAST AND NORTH
AFRICA.=            GRASG -64-PBI

THE POLITICS OF THE NEAR EAST --
SOUTHWEST ASIA AND NORTHERN
AFRICA.=            RUSTDA-60-PNE

YOUTH AND POLITICS IN THE NEAR
EAST.=              ZNZ   -51-YPN

NEEDS
AMERICAN CIVILIZATION AND ITS
LEADERSHIP NEEDS, 1960-1990.=
                    CHARJC-59-ACI

NEGOTIATION
BARGAINING AND NEGOTIATION IN
INTERNATIONAL RELATIONS.=
                    SAWYJ -65-BNI

PROTEST AND NEGOTIATION -- A CASE
STUDY OF NEGRO LEADERSHIP IN
ATLANTA, GEORGIA (UNITED STATES).=
                    WALKJL-63-PNC

NEGOTIATIONS
COLLECTIVE NEGOTIATIONS BETWEEN THE
STATE AND ITS OFFICIALS -- A
COMPARATIVE ESSAY.= SCHMF -62-CNB

NEGRO
POWER STRUCTURE AND THE NEGRO SUB -
COMMUNITY (UNITED STATES).=
                    BARTEA-59-PSN

RACIAL DISCRIMINATION AND NEGRO
LEADERSHIP PROBLEMS -- THE CASE OF
A NORTHERN COMMUNITY
(UNITED STATES).=   BOWML -65-RDN

NEGRO LEADERSHIP IN A SOUTHERN CITY
(UNITED STATES).=   BURGME-62-NLS

THE NEGRO PROFESSIONAL CLASS
(UNITED STATES).=   EDWAFG-59-NPC

NEGRO PROTEST LEADERS IN A SOUTHERN
COMMUNITY (UNITED-STATES).=
                    KILLLM-60-NPL

NEGRO POLITICAL LEADERSHIP IN THE

NEW MEXICO          (CONTINUATION)
SPANISH AMERICANS CF NEW MEXICO.=
                    KNOWCS-62-PPP

NEW YORK
COMMUNITY LEADERSHIP -- THE
REGIONAL PLAN ASSOCIATION OF
NEW YORK.=          HAYSFB-65-CLR

NEW ZEALAND
THE GOVERNOR GENERAL'S PART IN
LEGISLATION (NEW ZEALAND).=
                    ABRAPL-49-GGS

THE LEGISLATIVE COUNCIL
(NEW ZEALAND).=     BENDHJ-49-LCN

POLITICIANS, PUELIC SERVANTS, AND
THE PEOPLE IN NEW ZEALAND -- 1 --
2.=                 CAMPP -55-PPS

NEW ZEALAND MINISTERS, 1935-1957.=
                    CAMPP -58-NZM

AUTOCHTHONOUS ELEMENTS IN THE
EVOLUTION CF DOMINION STATUS --
THE CASE CF NEW ZEALAND.=
                    FIELCK-62-AEE

THE NEW ZEALAND NATIONAL PARTY.=
                    KELSRN-54-NZN

THE PRIVATE MEMBER CF PARLIAMENT
AND THE FORMATION CF PUELIC POLICY
-- A NEW ZEALAND CASE STUCY.=
                    KELSRN-64-PMP

THE POLITICS CF EQUALITY --
NEW ZEALAND'S ADVENTURES IN
DEMOCRACY.=         LIPSL -48-PEN

TRACE UNIONS IN POLITICS IN
AUSTRALIA AND NEW ZEALAND.=
                    MILBJF-66-TUP

BUREAUCRACY IN NEW ZEALAND.=
                    MILNRS-58-BNZ

THE NEW ZEALAND LABCR PARTY.
                    CVERL -55-NZL

THE NEW ZEALAND LABCR PARTY -- ITS
FORMAL STRUCTURE.=  PENFJ -54-NZL

LEADERSHIP IN THE LABCUR PARTY
(NEW ZEALAND).=     WEBBL -53-LLP

NEWARK
URBAN RENEWAL POLITICS -- SLUM
CLEARANCE IN NEWARK
(UNITED STATES).=   KAPLH -63-URP

NEWLY
LABOR'S ROLE IN NEWLY DEVELOPING
COUNTRIES.=         LOCGGC-59-LSR

NEWS
NEWSPAPER 'GATEKEEPERS' AND THE
SOURCES CF NEWS.=   CARTRE-58-NGS

NEWSPAPER
NEWSPAPER 'GATEKEEPERS' AND THE
SOURCES CF NEWS.=   CARTRE-58-NGS

THE INFLUENCE CF NEWSPAPER AND
TELEVISION IN AFRICA.=
                    COLTJ -63-INT

THE WEEKLY NEWSPAPER'S LEADERSHIP
ROLE AS SEEN BY COMMUNITY LEADER'S
(UNITED STATES).=   EDELAS-63-WNS

NEWSPAPER CITATION AND REPUTATION

NEWSPAPER          (CONTINUATION)
FOR COMMUNITY LEADERSHIP
(UNITED STATES).=   EHRLHJ-65-NCR

HOW THE SOVIET NEWSPAPER OPERATES.=
                    CRULL -56-HSN

NEWSPAPERS
NEWSPAPERS, EDITORS, POLITICIANS
AND POLITICAL SCIENTISTS.=
                    CONNTC-50-NEP

NEXUS
THE INTELLECTUALS - POLITICS NEXUS
-- STUDIES USING A BIOGRAPHICAL
TECHNICLE (BULGARIA,
SOVIET UNION).=     HANHAM-64-IPN

NIGER
NATIONAL UNITY AND REGIONALISM IN
EIGHT AFRICAN STATES (NIGERIA,
NIGER, THE CONGO, GABON, CENTRAL
AFRICAN REPUBLIC, CHAD, UGANDA,
ETHIOPIA).=         CARTGM-66-NUR

NIGERIA
NIGERIA -- POLITICAL NON-ALIGNMENT
AND ECONOMIC ALIGNMENT.=
                    ANGLDG-64-NPN

FEDERAL GOVERNMENT IN NIGERIA.=
                    AWA,EO-64-FGN

AN HISTORICAL SKETCH CF EGBA
TRACITIONAL AUTHORITIES
(NIGERIA).=         BIOBSO-52-HSE

EXTRA-PROCESSIONAL EVENTS IN TIV
POLITICAL INSTITUTIONS (NIGERIA).=
                    BOHAP -58-EPE

GOVERNMENT AND BANKING IN WESTERN
NIGERIA.=           BROWCV-64-GBW

NATIONAL UNITY AND REGIONALISM IN
EIGHT AFRICAN STATES (NIGERIA,
NIGER, THE CONGO, GABON, CENTRAL
AFRICAN REPUBLIC, CHAD, UGANDA,
ETHIOPIA).=         CARTGM-66-NUR

NIGERIA -- BACKGROUND TO
NATIONALISM.=       COLEJS-58-NBN

CONSTITUTIONAL DEVELOPMENTS IN
NIGERIA.=           EZERK -64-CDN

ECONOMIC ASPECTS CF POLITICAL
MOVEMENTS IN NIGERIA AND IN THE
GOLD COAST, 1918-1939.=
                    HOPKAG-66-EAP

BUREAUCRATIC CADRES IN A
TRADITIONAL MILIEU (NIGERIA).=
                    KIRKAH-65-BCT

THE RISE CF A NEW ELITE AMONGST THE
WOMEN CF NIGERIA.=  LEITS -56-RNE

EDUCATION AND FAMILY LIFE IN THE
DEVELOPMENT CF CLASS
IDENTIFICATION AMONG THE YORUBA
(WESTERN NIGERIA).= LLOYBB-66-EFL

THE INTEGRATION CF THE NEW ECONOMIC
CLASSES WITH LOCAL GOVERNMENT IN
WEST NIGERIA.=      LLOYPC-53-INE

THE DEVELOPMENT CF POLITICAL
PARTIES IN WESTERN NIGERIA.=
                    LLOYPC-55-DPP

CLASS CONSCIOUSNESS AMONG THE

NIGERIA                    (CONTINUATION)
YORUBA (WESTERN NIGERIA).=
                    LLOYPC-66-CCA

ELECTORAL TRENDS AND THE TENDENCY
TO A ONE PARTY SYSTEM IN NIGERIA.=
                    MACKJP-62-ETT

POLITICAL CHANGE IN A TRADITIONAL
AFRICAN CLAN -- A STRUCTURAL
FUNCTIONAL ANALYSIS OF THE NSITS
OF NIGERIA.=        SCARJR-65-PCT

HISTORICAL AND CULTURAL CONDITIONS
OF POLITICAL CORRUPTION AMONG THE
HAUSA (NORTHERN NIGERIA).=
                    SMITMG-64-HCC

THE PROBLEM OF NATIONAL LEADERSHIP
IN NIGERIA.=        SMYTHH-58-PNL

SOCIAL STRATIFICATION IN NIGERIA.=
                    SMYTHH-58-SSN

AFRICA -- THE PRIMACY OF POLITICS
(CONGO, NIGERIA).=   SPIRHJ-66-APP

THE PUBLIC SERVICE COMMISSION IN
WESTERN NIGERIA.=   WALLC -61-PSC

EDUCATION AND POLITICS IN NIGERIA.=
                    WEILHN-64-EPN

THREE PERSPECTIVES ON HIERARCHY --
POLITICAL THOUGHT AND LEADERSHIP
IN NORTHERN NIGERIA.=  WHITCS-65-TPH

NIGERIAN
THE MID-WEST STATE MOVEMENT IN
NIGERIAN POLITICS -- A STUDY IN
PARTY FORMATION.=    BRANJA-65-MWS

THE NIGERIAN CONSTITUTION --
HISTORY AND DEVELOPMENT.=
                    COUMOI-63-NCH

NIGERIAN POLITICAL PARTIES -- POWER
IN AN EMERGENT AFRICAN NATION.=
                    SKLARL-63-NPP

CONTRADICTIONS IN THE NIGERIAN
POLITICAL SYSTEM.=   SKLARL-65-CNP

THE NIGERIAN ELITE -- SOME
OBSERVATIONS.=      SMYTHH-59-NEC

NIGERIAN ELITE -- ROLE OF
EDUCATION.=         SMYTHH-60-NER

THE NEW NIGERIAN ELITE.=
                    SMYTHH-60-NNE

NILE
THE ROLE OF THE CHIEFS AND THE HEAD
MAN AMONG THE LUGBARA OF THE WEST
NILE DISTRICT OF UGANDA.=
                    MIDDJ -56-RCH

NILOTIC
NILOTIC KINGS AND THEIR MOTHER'S
KIN (SUDAN).=       LIENG -55-NKT

NINETEENTH-CENTURY
THE CHINESE GENTRY -- STUDIES ON
THEIR ROLE IN NINETEENTH-CENTURY
CHINESE SOCIETY.=    CHUNC -55-CGS

NKRUMAH
KWAME NKRUMAH AND THE FUTURE OF
AFRICA.=            PHILJ -61-KNF

NLRB
REGULATORY AGENCY CONTROL THROUGH

NLRB                      (CONTINUATION)
APPOINTMENT -- THE CASE OF THE
EISENHOWER ADMINISTRATION AND THE
NLRB (UNITED STATES).=
                    SCHES -61-RAC

NOBILITIES
FOUR NOBILITIES OF THE OLD REGIME
(ITALY, GERMANY).=   FORSR -65-FNO

NOBILITY
THE EUROPEAN NOBILITY IN THE MIDDLE
AGES.=              DE-BOF-62-ENM

VALUES, DEMAND, AND SOCIAL NOBILITY
(INDUSTRIAL ELITES, CHINA,
UNITED STATES).=    MARSRM-63-VDS

THE JAVANESE NOBILITY UNDER THE
DUTCH.=             PALMLH-60-JNU

NOBLES
FEDERAL ADMINISTRATION, RANK, AND
CIVIL STRIFE AMONG BEMBA ROYALS
AND NOBLES (ZAMBIA).=  WERBRP-67-FAR

NOBLESSE
SOCIAL MOBILITY AMONG THE FRENCH
NOBLESSE IN THE LATER MIDDLE
AGES.=              PERRE -62-SMA

NOMINATED
HOW PRESIDENTS ARE NOMINATED
(UNITED STATES).=    DRAPED-48-HPA

NOMINATING
PRESIDENTIAL NOMINATING POLITICS IN
1952 (UNITED STATES).=
                    DAVIPT-54-PNP

THE EFFECTS OF NOMINATING
CONVENTIONS, ELECTIONS, AND
REFERENCE GROUP IDENTIFICATION
UPON THE PERCEPTIONS OF POLITICAL
FIGURES (UNITED STATES).=
                    RAVEBH-64-ENC

NON-ALIGNMENT
NIGERIA -- POLITICAL NON-ALIGNMENT
AND ECONOMIC ALIGNMENT.=
                    ANGLOG-64-NPN

NON-AMERICAN
THE UTILITY AND LIMITATIONS OF
INTEREST GROUP THEORY IN
NON-AMERICAN FIELD SITUATIONS.=
                    LAPAJ -60-ULI

NON-GOVERNMENTAL
THE INFLUENCE OF NON-GOVERNMENTAL
GROUPS ON FOREIGN POLICY MAKING
(UNITED STATES).=    COHEBC-59-ING

NON-PARTISAN
THE INSULATION OF LOCAL POLITICS
UNDER THE NON-PARTISAN BALLOT
(UNITED STATES).=    ADRICR-59-ILP

NON-RULE
NON-RULE IN AMERICA.=  BAZEDT-63-NRA

NON-WESTERN
NON-WESTERN INTELLIGENTSIAS AS
POLITICAL ELITES.=   PENDHJ-60-NWI

PUBLIC ADMINISTRATION IN IRAN --
SKETCHES OF A NON-WESTERN
TRANSITIONAL BUREAUCRACY.=
                    GABLRW-61-PAI

NONCONFORMITY
PATTERNS OF NONCONFORMITY

OPINION                    (CONTINUATION)
(UNITED STATES).=      HARTGW-45-JSL

OPINION LEADERS IN AMERICAN
COMMUNITIES.=          HEROAO-59-OLA

PUBLIC OPINION IN SOVIET RUSSIA --
A STUDY IN MASS PERSUASION.=
                       INKEA -50-POS

PUBLIC OPINION AND AMERICAN FOREIGN
POLICY -- THE QUEMOY CRISIS OF
1958.=                 IRISMO-60-POA

PUBLIC OPINION AND AMERICAN
DEMOCRACY.=            KEY-VO-61-POA

PUBLIC OPINION AND DECAY OF
DEMOCRACY (UNITED STATES).=
                       KEY-VO-61-POD

YES -- THERE ARE GENERALIZED
OPINION LEADERS.=      MARCAS-64-YTA

PUBLIC OPINION AND CONGRESSIONAL
ELECTIONS (UNITED STATES).=
                       MCPHWN-62-POC

THE JAPANESE PEOPLE AND FOREIGN
POLICY -- A STUDY OF PUBLIC
OPINION IN POST-TREATY JAPAN.=
                       MENDDH-61-JPF

IN YOUR OPINION -- LEADERS' AND
VOTERS' ATTITUDES ON DEFENSE AND
DISARMAMENT (CANADA).=
                       PAULJ -63-YOL

THE POLLSTERS -- PUBLIC OPINION,
POLITICS, AND DEMOCRATIC
LEADERSHIP (UNITED STATES).=
                       ROGEL -49-PPO

OPINION-MAKING AND OPINION MAKERS
IN FOREIGN POLICY
(UNITED STATES).=      ROSEJN-60-OMC

PUBLIC OPINION AND FOREIGN POLICY
(UNITED STATES).=      ROSEJN-61-POF

MAN AND ATTENTIVE OPINION ON
NUCLEAR WEAPON TESTS AND FALLOUT,
1954-1963 (UNITED STATES).=
                       ROSIEJ-65-MAO

INTELLECTUALS, PUBLIC OPINION AND
ECONOMIC DEVELOPMENT.=
                       SHILE -55-IPO

THE POTENTIAL ROLE OF TURKISH
VILLAGE OPINION LEADERS IN A
PROGRAM OF FAMILY PLANNING.=
                       SYTCJM-65-PRT

THE GOVERNMENTAL PROCESS --
POLITICAL INTERESTS AND PUBLIC
OPINION (UNITED STATES).=
                       TRUMDB-51-GPP

WOODROW WILSON AND PUBLIC OPINION
(UNITED STATES).=      TURNHA-57-WWP

A THEORY OF PUBLIC OPINION.=
                       WILSFG-62-TPO

PUBLIC OPINION AND FOREIGN POLICY
(GREAT BRITAIN).=      YOUNK -55-POF

OPINION-MAKING
OPINION-MAKING AND OPINION MAKERS
IN FOREIGN POLICY
(UNITED STATES).=      ROSEJN-60-OMC

OPINION-POLICY
THE OPINION-POLICY IN DEMOCRACY --
A CRITICAL SUMMARY OF SOME RECENT
LITERATURE.=           HENNB -58-OPO

OPINIONS
OPINIONS OF PARLIAMENTARIANS IN
INDIA AND JAPAN.=      FREELA-58-OPI

EDUCATION AND DEVELOPMENT --
OPINIONS OF SECONDARY SCHOOL
TEACHERS (LATIN AMERICA).=
                       GOUVAJ-67-EDO

OPIUM
THE OPIUM OF THE INTELLECTUALS.=
                       ARONR -57-OI

OPPORTUNITY
MEASUREMENT OF SOCIAL POWER
OPPORTUNITY COSTS, AND THE THEORY
OF TWO-PERSON BARGAINING GAMES.=
                       HARSJC-62-MSP

OPPOSITION
STUDENT OPPOSITION IN
LATIN AMERICA.=        ALBOO -66-SOL

SOME REFLECTIONS ON THE ROLE OF A
POLITICAL OPPOSITION IN NEW
NATIONS.=              APTEDE-62-RRP

GOVERNMENT AND OPPOSITION IN THE
NEW STATES.=           DAALH -66-GON

POLITICAL OPPOSITION IN THE WESTERN
DEMOCRACIES (AUSTRIA, BELGIUM,
FRANCE, GERMANY, GREAT BRITAIN,
ITALY, NETHERLANDS, NORWAY,
SWEDEN, UNITED STATES).=
                       DAHLRA-66-POW

COMMUNIST CHINA -- THE POLITICS OF
STUDENT OPPOSITION.=   DOOLCJ-64-CCP

THE PARLIAMENTARY LABOUR PARTY IN
OPPOSITION (GREAT BRITAIN).=
                       DOWSRE-60-PLP

THE LEFT WING OPPOSITION DURING THE
FIRST TWO LABOUR GOVERNMENTS
(GREAT BRITAIN).=      DOWSRE-61-LWO

SOVIET OPPOSITION TO STALIN -- A
CASE STUDY IN WORLD WAR 11.=
                       FISCG -52-SOS

STUDENT OPPOSITION IN SPAIN.=
                       GALVET-66-SOS

THE WANING OPPOSITION IN
PARLIAMENTARY REGIMES (EUROPE).=
                       KIRCO -57-WOP

FORMAL RECOGNITION OF THE LEADER OF
THE OPPOSITION IN PARLIAMENTS OF
THE BRITISH COMMONWEALTH.=
                       MCHECE-54-FRL

KHRUSHCHEV'S DISLOYAL OPPOSITION --
STRUCTURAL CHANGE AND POWER
STRUGGLE IN THE COMMUNIST BLOC.=
                       MICHF -63-KSD

BELGIUM -- LANGUAGE AND CLASS
OPPOSITION.=           PHILA -66-BLC

POLICY DECISION IN OPPOSITION
(GREAT BRITAIN).=      ROSES -56-PDC

THE ORIGIN OF THE COMMUNIST
AUTOCRACY -- POLITICAL OPPOSITION

ORGANIZATIONS          (CONTINUATION)
IN LARGE BUREAUCRATIC
ORGANIZATIONS.=         CEUTKW-61-NAW

RELIGIOUS ORGANIZATIONS AND
POLITICAL PROCESS IN CENTRALIZED
EMPIRES (MIDDLE EAST, FAR EAST).=
EISESN-62-ROP

A COMPARATIVE ANALYSIS OF COMPLEX
ORGANIZATIONS.=         ETZIA -61-CAC

DUAL LEADERSHIP IN COMPLEX
ORGANIZATIONS.=         ETZIA -65-DLC

BUREAUCRACY AND SMALL ORGANIZATIONS
(UNITED STATES).=       HALLRH-63-BSO

COHESION AND COMMITMENT IN
EMPLOYERS' ORGANIZATIONS (FRANCE,
GERMANY).=              HARTH -59-CCE

IRRATIONAL LEADERSHIP IN FORMAL
ORGANIZATIONS (UNITED STATES).=
JOSEE -52-ILF

HANDBOOK OF ORGANIZATIONS.=
MARCJG-65-HO

TERENA (BRAZILIAN INDIANS) SOCIAL
ORGANIZATIONS AND LAW.=
OLIEK -48-TBI

THE ROLE OF POLITICAL ORGANIZATIONS
IN INDONESIA.=          PAUKGJ-58-RPO

THE PARTY WHIP ORGANIZATIONS IN THE
UNITED STATES HOUSE OF
REPRESENTATIVES.=       RIPLRB-64-PWO

TVA AND THE GRASS ROOTS -- A STUDY
IN THE SOCIOLOGY OF FORMAL
ORGANIZATIONS (UNITED STATES).=
SELZP -49-TGR

ORGANIZED
ORGANIZED LABOR IN LATIN AMERICA.=
ALEXRJ-65-OLL

THE POLITICAL ROLE OF ORGANIZED
LABOR (UNITED STATES).=
CHERJ -56-PRO

ORGANIZED BUSINESS IN FRANCE.=
EHRMHW-57-OBF

FRENCH BUREAUCRACY AND ORGANIZED
INTERESTS.=             EHRMHW-61-FBO

ORGANIZED LABOR'S IMAGE OF
COMMUNITY POWER STRUCTURE
(UNITED STATES).=       FORMWH-60-OLS

ITALIAN COMMUNISM, THE WORKING
CLASS AND ORGANIZED CATHOLICISM.=
KOGAN -66-ICW

ORGANIZED INTERESTS IN JAPAN AND
THEIR INFLUENCE ON POLITICAL
PARTIES.=               LANGFC-61-OIJ

ORGANIZED GROUPS IN BRITISH
NATIONAL POLITICS.=     POTTAM-60-OGB

ORGANIZING
VARIATIONS IN POWER STRUCTURES AND
ORGANIZING EFFICIENCY -- A
COMPARATIVE STUDY OF FOUR AREAS
(UNITED STATES).=       DAKIRE-62-VPS

ORGANS
THE TRAINING OF OFFICIALS OF THE

ORGANS                  (CONTINUATION)
ADMINISTRATIVE ORGANS OF THE
PEOPLE'S COMMITTEES (YUGOSLAVIA).=
ANON -61-TOA

YUGOSLAVIA -- STATUS AND ROLE OF
THE EXECUTIVE ORGANS DURING THE
FIRST STAGE OF YUGOSLAVIA'S
POLITICAL AND CONSTITUTIONAL
DEVELOPMENT.=           DJORJ -58-YSR

THE SOVIET CONCEPT OF THE
RELATIONSHIP BETWEEN THE LOWER
PARTY ORGANS AND THE STATE
ADMINISTRATION.=        HOUGJF-65-SCR

THE 'GOVERNING ORGANS' OF THE UNION
OF SOVIET WRITERS.=     MATLJF-56-GOU

ORIENTAL
THE STUDY OF ORIENTAL DESPOTISMS AS
SYSTEMS OF TOTAL POWER (CHINA).=
EISESN-58-SOD

ORIENTAL DESPOTISM -- A COMPARATIVE
STUDY OF TOTAL POWER.=
WITTK -57-ODC

THE RULING BUREAUCRACY OF ORIENTAL
DESPOTISM -- A PHENOMENON THAT
PARALYZED MARX.=        WITTKA-53-RBO

ORIENTATION
CONFLICTING ORIENTATION IN SOVIET
LEADERSHIP.=            BIDDJ -61-COS

SOCIAL ORIENTATION OF RECRUITMENT
AND DISTRIBUTION OF MEMBERSHIP IN
THE COMMUNIST PARTY OF THE
SOVIET UNION.=          RIGBTH-56-SOR

ORIENTATIONS
THE EDUCATIONAL BACKGROUNDS AND
CAREER ORIENTATIONS OF THE MEMBERS
OF THE CENTRAL COMMITTEE OF THE
CPSU (SOVIET UNION).= GEHLMP-66-EBC

DEVELOPING POLITICAL ORIENTATIONS
OF PANAMANIAN STUDENTS.=
GOLDD -61-DPO

RADICAL NATIONALISM -- THE
POLITICAL ORIENTATIONS OF
PANAMANIAN LAW STUDENTS.=
GOLDD -62-RNP

THE ORIENTATIONS OF COMMUNITY
LEADERS TO PARLIAMENTARY
CANDIDATES (GREAT BRITAIN).=
KAVAD -67-CCL

THE SOCIO-POLITICAL ORIENTATIONS OF
C. WRIGHT MILLS -- AN EVALUATION.=
SPINW -66-SPC

AMERICAN STATE LEGISLATORS' ROLE
ORIENTATIONS TOWARD PRESSURE
GROUPS.=                WAHLJC-60-ASL

IDEOLOGICAL - PRAGMATIC
ORIENTATIONS OF WEST BERLIN LOCAL
PARTY OFFICIALS (WEST GERMANY).=
WRIGWE-67-IPO

CITY COUNCILMEN AND THE GROUP
STRUGGLE -- A TYPOLOGY OF ROLE
ORIENTATIONS (UNITED STATES).=
ZISKBH-65-CCG

ORIGIN
THE BEGINNINGS OF BUREAUCRACY IN
CHINA -- THE ORIGIN OF THE HSIEN.=

ORIGIN                    (CONTINUATION)
                          CREEHG-64-BBC

THE ORIGIN CF THE COMMUNIST CONTROL
COMMISSION (SOVIET UNION).=
                          NEUWM -59-OCC

THE ORIGIN CF THE COMMUNIST
AUTOCRACY -- POLITICAL CPPOSITION
IN THE SOVIET STATE, 1917-1922.=
                          SCHALB-55-OCA

ORIGINS
LEADERS CF MODERN JAPAN -- SOCIAL
CRIGINS AND MOBILITY.=
                          ABEGJ -60-LMJ

ORIGINS OF AMERICAN OCCUPATIONAL
ELITES, 1900-1955.=       ADAMS -57-OAC

THE INTELLECTUAL ORIGINS CF
EGYPTIAN NATICNALISM.=
                          AHMEJM-60-ICE

THE ORIGINS CF TOTALITARIANISM.=
                          ARENH -58-OT

FROM OTTOMANISM TC ARABISM -- THE
ORIGINS OF AN IDECLOGY
(MIDDLE EAST).=           CAWNCE-61-OAC

THE ETHNIC ORIGINS CF ZANDE
OFFICE-HOLDERS (EGYPT,SUDAN).=
                          EVANEE-60-EOZ

CRIGINS OF THE MODERN INDIAN
BUSINESS CLASS.=          GADGOR-59-OMI

THE CHIEF EXECUTIVE IN TEXAS -- THE
ORIGINS OF GUBERNATORIAL
LEADERSHIP.=              GANTF -64-CET

AN HISTORICAL STUDY CF THE ORIGINS
AND STRUCTURE CF THE DANISH
INTELLIGENTSIA.=          GEIGT -50-HSC

THE ORIGINS CF ENTREPRENEURSHIP IN
MEIJI JAPAN.=             HIRSJ -64-OEM

POTENTIAL ELITES IN TURKEY -- THE
SOCIAL CRIGINS CF LISE YOUTH.=
                          KAZAAM-66-PET

THE NEW SOVIET INTELLIGENTSIA --
CRIGINS AND RECRUITMENT.=
                          LABEL -59-NSI

SCCIAL CRIGINS CF DICTATORSHIP AND
DEMOCRACY -- LORD AND PEASANT IN
THE MAKING CF THE MODERN WORLD
(FRANCE, GREAT BRITAIN,
UNITED STATES, CHINA, JAPAN,
INDIA, GERMANY).=         MOORB -66-SOC

THE CRIGINS CF THE LABOUR PARTY
(GREAT BRITAIN).=         PELLH -54-CLP

THE ORIGINS AND SIGNIFICANCE CF
EAST EUROPEAN REVISIONISM.=
                          REYMK -62-CSE

THE CRIGINS OF MALAY NATIONALISM.=
                          ROFFWR-67-OMN

THE ORIGINS OF NATIONALIST
DISCONTENT IN EAST AND CENTRAL
AFRICA.=                  ROTBRI-63-CND

ORISSA
TRADITIONAL SOCIETY AND
REPRESENTATION -- A CASE STUDY IN
ORISSA (INDIA).=          BAILFG-60-TSR

ORISSA                    (CONTINUATION)
POLITICS AND SOCIAL CHANGE, ORISSA
(INDIA) IN 1959.=         BAILFG-63-PSC

ORTHODOXY
SOVIET RUSSIA -- ORTHODOXY AND
ADAPTIVENESS.=            BARGFC-66-SRO

OTTOMANISM
FROM OTTOMANISM TC ARABISM -- THE
ORIGINS OF AN IDECLOGY
(MIDDLE EAST).=           CAWNCE-61-OAC

OUR
OUR CHANGING CONCEPT CF LEADERSHIP
(UNITED STATES).=         ALBEMH-53-OCC

SOVIET SOCIAL SCIENCE AND OUR OWN
(SOVIET UNION, UNITED STATES).=
                          BRODA -57-SSS

THE WORLD REVOLUTION CF OUR TIMES.=
                          LASSHD-51-WRO

SECOND CONSUL -- THE VICE
PRESIDENCY -- CUR GREATEST
POLITICAL PROBLEM
(UNITED-STATES).=         WAUGEW-56-SCV

WHO RUNS CUR TOWN (UNITED STATES).=
                          YAGEJW-63-WRO

OUTCOME
LOCAL PARTY EFFICIENCY AS A FACTOR
IN THE OUTCCME CF BRITISH
ELECTIONS.=               BROWJC-58-LPE

THE PREDICTION CF ISSUE OUTCOME IN
COMMUNITY DECISION MAKING.=
                          MILLDC-57-PIC

CUTER-DEPARTMENTAL
THE NATIONAL SECURITY COUNCIL AS A
DEVICE FOR CUTER-DEPARTMENTAL
COORDINATION (UNITED STATES).=
                          HAMMPY-60-NSC

OUTSIDER
THE ESTABLISHED AND THE OUTSIDER
(GREAT BRITAIN).=         ELIAN -65-EOG

AMONG STUDENTS IN MOSCOW -- AN
OUTSIDER'S REPORT (SOVIET UNION).=
                          HAMMDP-64-ASM

THE CUTSIDER IN THE SENATE -- AN
ALTERNATIVE ROLE (UNITED STATES).=
                          HUITRK-61-OSA

CUTSTATE
METROPOLITAN AND CUTSTATE
ALIGNMENTS IN ILLINOIS AND
MISSOURI LEGISLATIVE DELEGATIONS
(UNITED STATES).=         DERGOR-58-MOA

OVERCENTRALIZATICN
OVERCENTRALIZATION IN ECONOMIC
ADMINISTRATION -- A CRITICAL
ANALYSIS BASED CN EXPERIENCE IN
HUNGARIAN LIGHT INDUSTRY.=
                          KORNJ -59-OEA

OVERSEAS
THE EXECUTIVE OVERSEAS --
ADMINISTRATIVE ATTITUDES AND
RELATIONSHIPS IN A FOREIGN CULTURE
(MEXICO).=                FAYEJ -59-EOA

OVERSEERS
CONGRESSIONAL COMMITTEE MEMBERS AS
INDEPENDENT AGENCY CVERSEERS -- A
CASE STUDY (UNITED STATES).=

OVERSEERS (CONTINUATION)
SCHES -60-CCM

OVERSIGHT
COMMITTEE CHARACTERISTICS AND
LEGISLATIVE OVERSIGHT OF
ADMINISTRATION (UNITED STATES).=
BIBBJF-66-CCL

OVERVIEW
AN OVERVIEW OF BUREAUCRACY AND
POLITICAL DEVELOPMENT.=
LAPAJ -63-OBP

OWNED
ABSENTEE - OWNED CORPORATIONS AND
COMMUNITY POWER STRUCTURE
(UNITED STATES).= PELLRJ-56-AOC

PACIFIC
SOCIAL CHANGE IN THE SOUTH PACIFIC
-- RAROTONGA AND AITUTAKI.=
BEAGE -57-SCS

LEGISLATURES OF THE BRITISH PACIFIC
ISLANDS.= LUKEH -47-LBP

POLITICAL ADVANCEMENT IN THE SOUTH
PACIFIC -- A COMPARATIVE STUDY OF
COLONIAL PRACTICE IN FIJI, TAHITI,
AND AMERICAN SAMOA.= WESTFJ-61-PAS

PAIRWISE
PAIRWISE ASSOCIATION OF JUDGES AND
LEGISLATORS (UNITED STATES).=
ULMESS-67-PAJ

PAKISTAN
GOVERNMENT AND POLITICS IN
PAKISTAN.= AHMAM -59-GPP

BUREAUCRATS AND CITIZENS (MOROCCO,
TUNISIA, PAKISTAN).= ASHFDE-65-BCM

POLITICAL LEADERSHIP AMONG
SWAT PATHANS (PAKISTAN).=
BARTF -59-PLA

RELIGION AND POLITICS IN PAKISTAN.=
BINDL -61-RPP

ASIAN BUREAUCRATIC SYSTEMS EMERGENT
FROM THE BRITISH IMPERIAL
TRADITION (INDIA, PAKISTAN, BURMA,
CEYLON, MALAYA, NEPAL).=
BRAIR - -ABS

PUBLIC BUREAUCRACY AND JUDICIARY IN
PAKISTAN.= BRAIR -61-PBJ

THE HIGHER BUREAUCRACY OF
PAKISTAN.= BRAIR -66-HBP

RESEARCH ON BUREAUCRACY OF
PAKISTAN.= BRIAR -66-RBP

THE ORGANIZATION AND COMPOSITION OF
THE CENTRAL CIVIL SERVICES IN
PAKISTAN.= CHAUMA-60-OCC

FAILURE OF PARLIAMENTARY DEMOCRACY
IN PAKISTAN.= CHOUGW-59-FPD

RESHAPING OF DEMOCRACY IN
PAKISTAN.= CHOUGW-60-RDP

ARMS AND POLITICS IN PAKISTAN.=
COHESP-64-APP

INDIA AND PAKISTAN -- THE
DEMOGRAPHY OF PARTITION.=
DAVIK -49-IPD

PAKISTAN'S EXPERIMENT IN BASIC

PAKISTAN (CONTINUATION)
DEMOCRACIES.= FRIEHJ-60-PSE

ADMINISTRATION AT THE GRASS ROOTS
-- PAKISTAN'S BASIC DEMOCRACIES.=
FRIEHJ-63-AGR

THE CIVIL SERVICE OF PAKISTAN --
BUREAUCRACY IN A NEW NATION.=
GOODHF-64-CSP

BUREAUCRACY AND DEVELOPMENT IN
PAKISTAN.= INAY(E-63-BDP

THE POLITICAL OUTLOOK IN PAKISTAN.=
INNEFM-53-POP

THE YOUNGER GENERATION IN THE THREE
DOMINIONS (INDIA, PAKISTAN,
CEYLON).= JACKC -49-YGT

GROUP INTERESTS IN PAKISTAN
POLITICS, 1947-1958.= MANIT -66-GIP

PROCESS OF INDEPENDENCE (INDIA,
PAKISTAN, INDONESIA, GHANA).=
MANSF -62-PII

PAKISTAN'S NEW POWER ELITE.=
MAROS -59-PSN

CASTE RANKING AND COMMUNITY
STRUCTURE IN FIVE REGIONS OF INDIA
AND PAKISTAN.= MARRM -60-CRC

PAKISTAN'S PREVENTIVE AUTOCRACY AND
ITS CAUSES.= NEWMKJ-59-PSP

THE DYARCHIC PATTERN OF GOVERNMENT
AND PAKISTAN'S PROBLEMS.=
NEWMKJ-60-DPG

ELECTION POLITICS IN PAKISTAN
VILLAGES.= RASHM -66-EPP

THE POLITICAL ROLE OF PAKISTAN'S
CIVIL SERVICE.= SAYEKB-58-PRP

PAKISTAN'S CONSTITUTIONAL
AUTOCRACY.= SAYEKB-64-PSC

PALACE
THE PALACE REVOLUTION IN THE
KREMLIN (SOVIET UNION).=
ANON -64-PRK

THE TECHNIQUE OF THE 'PALACE
REVOLUTION' (SOVIET UNION).=
KRUZP -64-TPR

PALAU
LEADERSHIP AND CULTURE CHANGE IN
PALAU (AUSTRALIA).= FORCRW-60-LCC

STRUCTURE OF POWER IN PALAU.=
USEEJ -50-SPP

PANAMA
INTEREST GROUPS IN PANAMA AND THE
CENTRAL AMERICAN COMMON MARKET.=
CENTCF-67-IGP

SONS OF THE ESTABLISHMENT -- ELITE
YOUTH IN PANAMA AND COSTA RICA.=
GOLDD -66-SEE

PANAMANIAN
DEVELOPING POLITICAL ORIENTATIONS
OF PANAMANIAN STUDENTS.=
GOLDD -61-DPO

RADICAL NATIONALISM -- THE

PANAMANIAN          (CCNTINUATICN)
PCLITICAL CRIENTATICNS CF
PANAMANIAN LAW STUCENTS.=
                    COLDC -62-RNP

PANEL
THE CHAIRMAN'S PANEL
(GREAT BRITAIN).=    HIGGCM-55-CSP

PAPUA
THE LEGISLATIVE CCUNCILS CF PAPUA,
NEW GUINEA.=        HUGHCA-59-LCP

PAPUAN
SCCIAL CHANGE AND PRIMITIVE LAW --
CCNSEQUENCES CF A PAPUAN LEGAL
CASE (NETHERLANCS NEW GUINEA).=
                    POSPL -58-SCP

PARACES
PARADES AND PCLITICS AT VICHY --
THE FRENCH CFFICERS CCRPS UNCER
MARSHAL PETAIN.=    PAXTRC-66-PPV

PARADCX
SCIENTISTS ANC THE PARACCX CF POWER
(UNITEC STATES).=   BERNJ -52-SPP

THE PARADCX CF PART.y CIFFERENCE.=
                    BUTLD -60-PPC

PARADCXICAL
BUREAUCRATS ANC PCLITICAL
CEVELCPMENT -- A PARADCXICAL
VIEW.=              RIGGFW-63-BPC

PARAGUAY
LEADERSHIP AND CCNFLICT WITHIN THE
FEBRERISTA PARTY CF PARAGUAY.=
                    LEWIPH-67-LCW

PARALYZED
THE RULING BUREAUCRACY CF ORIENTAL
DESPOTISM -- A PHENCMENCN THAT
PARALYZED MARX.=    WITTKA-53-RBC

PARAMETERS
SCCIAL MOBILITY AND ECONOMIC
CEVELCPMENT -- THE VITAL
PARAMETERS CF THE BCLIVIAN
REVCLUTICN.=        BERGCF-64-SME

CLASS PARAMETERS IN HAITIAN
SOCIETY.=           CEYCM -59-CPH

PARAPCLITICAL
THE MASS SCCIETY ANC THE
PARAPCLITICAL STRUCTURE.=
                    GREES -62-MSP

PARETC
VILFRED PARETC -- SCCICLOGICAL
WRITINGS.=          FINESE-66-VPS

THE ELITE AND THE RULING CLASS --
PARETC AND MCSCA RE-EXAMINED.=
                    KOLEF -67-ERC

PARETC AND MCSCA.=   MEISJH-65-PM

PARIAH
PCLITICAL CHANGE ANC PARIAH
ENTREPRENEURSHIP (PHILIPPINES).=
                    JIANJP-62-PCP

PARLIAMENT
THE WCRK CF THE PRIVATE SECRETARY
TO THE MEMBER CF PARLIAMENT
(GREAT BRITAIN).=   AN MMP-48-WPS

CIVIL SERVANTS, MINISTERS,
PARLIAMENT ANC THE PUBLIC

PARLIAMENT          (CCNTINUATICN)
(GREAT BRITAIN).=   ATTLCR-54-CSM

PARLIAMENT AND PARLIAMENTARIANS IN
JAPAN.=             BAERHH-64-PPJ

CUTIES CF A MEMBER CF PARLIAMENT
(GREAT BRITAIN).=   BALLWM-56-CMP

PARLIAMENT -- A SURVEY
(GREAT BRITAIN).=   CAMPG -52-PSG

CISCIPLINE AND LCYALTY IN THE
FRENCH PARLIAMENT CURING THE PINAY
GCVERNMENT.=        CAMPP -53-CLF

THE REFCRM CF PARLIAMENT
(GREAT BRITAIN).=   CRICB -65-RPC

PARLIAMENT AND FCREIGN PCLICY IN
SWEDEN.=            ELDEN -53-PFP

PARLIAMENT ANC THE CIVIL SERVICE
(GREAT BRITAIN).=   GLADEN-57-PCS

THE INDIAN PARLIAMENT AND STATES
RECRGANIZATICN.=    GUPTSK-57-IPS

PUBLIC AND PARLIAMENT IN WEST
GERMANY.=           HADLG -56-PPW

MEMBERS OF THE FRENCH PARLIAMENT.=
                    HAMOL -61-MFP

THE MCNARCH, THE PRIME MINISTER,
AND THE DISSCLUTICN CF PARLIAMENT
(GREAT BRITAIN).=   HEASCJ-61-MPM

NORWAY'S THREE 'TINGS'
(PARLIAMENT).=      HOFFG -52-NST

PARLIAMENT (GREAT BRITAIN).=
                    JENNWI-57-PGB

THE PRIVATE MEMBER CF PARLIAMENT
AND THE FORMATICN CF PUBLIC PCLICY
-- A NEW ZEALANC CASE STUCY.=
                    KELSRN-64-PMP

BRITISH PCLITICS -- PECPLE,
PARTIES, ANC PARLIAMENT.=
                    KINGA -66-BPP

COMMUNIST USE CF THE CZECHOSLCVAK
PARLIAMENT SINCE WCRLD WAR II.=
                    KUBAC -61-CUC

THE PCSITICN OF PARLIAMENT IN THE
FCURTH FRENCH REPUBLIC.=
                    LIDDDW-47-PPF

PARLIAMENT IN THE GERMAN POLITICAL
SYSTEM.=            LCEWG -66-PGP

PARLIAMENT, PARTIES ANC SCCIETY IN
FRANCE, 1946-1958.= MACRC -67-PPS

PCRTRAIT CF THE BURMESE
PARLIAMENT.=        MAUNM -57-PBP

PARLIAMENT IN INDIA.= MORRWH-57-PI

LATENT ANC MANIFEST BUREAUCRACY IN
THE WEST GERMAN PARLIAMENT -- THE
CASE CF THE BUNCESRAT.=
                    PINNEL-62-LMB

THE FECERAL GERMAN PARLIAMENT.=
                    PRITT -55-FGP

HCW FAR DCES THE GERMAN PARLIAMENT
GCVERN.=            PRITT -56-HFC

PARTY                (CONTINUATION)
  (SOVIET UNION).=        CLEAJW-64-PPS

RECRUITS TO LABOR -- THE BRITISH
LABOUR PARTY, 1914-1931.=
                        CLINCA-63-RLB

THE FRENCH SOCIALIST PARTY AND THE
WEST.=                  COCDGA-60-FSP

THE FRENCH CP (COMMUNIST PARTY) --
SIGNS OF CRISIS.=       COLLM -59-FCC

PROFESSIONAL POLITICIANS -- A STUDY
OF BRITISH PARTY AGENTS.=
                        COMFGO-58-PPS

INTRAPARTY ATTITUDE CONFLICT --
DEMOCRATIC PARTY LEADERSHIP IN
CALIFORNIA (UNITED STATES).=
                        COSTE -63-IAC

POLITICS WITHOUT POWER -- THE
NATIONAL PARTY COMMITTEES
(UNITED STATES).=       COTTCP-64-PWP

THE TECHNIQUES OF THE COMMUNIST
PARTY IN FRANCE.=       .COWALG-49-TCP

CONGRESSIONAL DISTRICT PARTY
STRENGTHS AND THE 1960 ELECTIONS
(UNITED STATES).=       COX,EF-62-CDP

LEADERSHIP OF THE CONGRESS PARTY
(INDIA).=               CRANRI-59-LCP

A CAVEAT ON ROLL-CALL STUDIES OF
PARTY VOTING (UNITED STATES).=
                        CRANW -60-CRC

PARTY ORGANIZATIONS IN PRIMARY
ELECTIONS (UNITED STATES).=
                        CUTRP -58-POP

MEASURING THE IMPACT OF LOCAL PARTY
ACTIVITY ON THE GENERAL ELECTION
VOTE (UNITED STATES).=
                        CUTRP -63-MIL

URBANIZATION AND COMPETITIVE PARTY
POLITICS (UNITED STATES).=
                        CUTRP -63-UCP

PARTY RULE IN COMMUNIST CHINA.=
                        DAI,S -62-PRC

THE SECRETARIAT AND THE LOCAL
ORGANIZATIONS IN THE RUSSIAN
COMMUNIST PARTY, 1921-1923.=
                        DANIRV-56-SLO

THE AUSTRALIAN POLITICAL PARTY
SYSTEM.=                DAVISR-54-APP

INTER - PARTY COMPETITION, ECONOMIC
VARIABLES, AND WELFARE POLICIES IN
THE AMERICAN STATES.= DAWSRE-63-IPC

THE FRENCH RADICAL PARTY -- FROM
HERRIOT TO MENDES-FRANCE.=
                        DE-TF -61-FRP

SUPPORT FOR THE PARTY SYSTEM BY THE
MASS PUBLIC  (UNITED STATES).=
                        DENNJ -66-SPS

NATIONAL AND SOCIAL COMPOSITION OF
THE MEMBERSHIP OF THE COMMUNIST
PARTY (BOLSHEVIK) OF THE UKRAINE,
1918-1928.=             DMYTB -57-NSC

PARTY DISCIPLINE IN THE HOUSE OF

PARTY                (CONTINUATION)
  COMMONS (GREAT BRITAIN).=
                        DOWSR -63-PCH

THE PARLIAMENTARY LABOUR PARTY IN
OPPOSITION (GREAT BRITAIN).=
                        DOWSRE-60-PLP

PARTY AND WRITERS -- 1956-1958
(SOVIET UNION).=       DRESA -59-PWS

THE DISMANTLING OF PARTY AND STATE
CONTROL AS AN INDEPENDENT PILLAR
OF SOVIET POWER.=       DUEVC -66-DPS

THE FOUNDATION OF THE COMMUNIST
PARTY POLAND.=          DZIEMK-52-FCP

THE COMMUNIST PARTY OF POLAND -- AN
OUTLINE OF HISTORY.=    DZIEMK-59-CPP

BRITISH CLASS CONSCIOUSNESS AND THE
LABOUR PARTY.=          EPSTLD-62-BCC

NEW M.P.S AND THE POLITICS OF THE
PLP (PARLIAMENTARY LABOUR PARTY,
GREAT BRITAIN).=       EPSTLD-62-NMP

WHO MAKES PARTY POLICY -- BRITISH
LABOUR 1960-1961.=      EPSTLD-62-WMP

INDIA'S SWATANTRA PARTY.=
                        ERDMHL-64-ISS

AGRARIANISM IN ISRAEL'S PARTY
SYSTEM.=                ETZIA -57-AIS

CLASS AND PARTY IN THE EISENHOWER
YEARS, CLASS ROLES AND PERSPECTIVE
IN THE 1952 AND 1956 ELECTION
(UNITED STATES).=       EULAH -62-CPE

POSTWAR ROLE OF THE COMMUNIST PARTY
(SOVIET UNION).=       FAINM -49-PRC

THE COMMUNIST PARTY SINCE STALIN.=
                        FAINM -56-CPS

THE PARTY IN THE POST - STALIN ERA
(SOVIET UNION).=       FAINM -58-PPS

PARTY STRENGTH AND POLITICAL
PATRONAGE (UNITED STATES).=
                        FAIROR-64-PSP

CHALLENGES TO FACTIONALISM IN
JAPAN'S LIBERAL DEMOCRATIC PARTY.=
                        FARNLW-66-CFJ

THE PARTY POTPOURRI IN
LATIN AMERICA.=         FITZR -57-PPL

PARTY RESPONSIBILITY IN THE STATES
-- SOME CAUSAL FACTORS
(UNITED STATES).=       FLINTA-64-PRS

LOCAL PARTY LEADERS -- GROUPS OF
LIKE MINDED MEN (UNITED STATES).=
                        FLINTA-65-LPL

THE ORGANIZATIONAL DEVELOPMENT OF
INDIA'S CONGRESS PARTY.=
                        FRANMF-62-ODI

LOCAL PARTY SYSTEMS -- THEORETICAL
CONSIDERATIONS AND A CASE ANALYSIS
(UNITED STATES).=       FREEJL-58-LPS

INTER - PARTY CONSTITUENCY
DIFFERENCES AND CONGRESSIONAL
VOTING BEHAVIOR (UNITED STATES).=
                        FROMLA-63-IPC

CONDITIONS FOR PARTY LEADERSHIP --

PARTY                    (CONTINUATION)
PARTY AND ARMY -- PROFESSIONALISM
AND POLITICAL CONTROL IN THE
CHINESE OFFICER CORPS, 1949-1964.=
                      JOFFE -65-PAP

THE REGIME AND THE INTELLECTUALS --
A WINDOW ON PARTY POLITICS
(SOVIET UNION).=      JOHNP -63-RIW

INTER - PARTY COMPETITION IN
BRITAIN , 1950-1959.= JONECO-63-IPC

PARTY AND POLICY-MAKING -- THE
HOUSE REPUBLICAN POLICY COMMITTEE
(UNITED STATES).=     JONECO-64-PPM

THE REPUBLICAN PARTY IN AMERICAN
POLITICS.=            JONECO-65-RPA

THE POLITICAL SIGNIFICANCE OF THE
BURMA WORKERS PARTY.= JOSEA -58-PSB

THE REORGANIZATION OF PARTY
LEADERSHIP IN AGRICULTURE
(SOVIET UNION).=      KABYS -63-RPL

TURKEY'S POLITICS -- THE TRANSITION
TO MULTI - PARTY SYSTEM.=
                      KARPKH-59-TSP

SOCIALISM AND THE LABOR PARTY OF
TURKEY.=              KARPKH-67-SLP

THE DEFEAT OF THE PRO - SOVIET
FACTION OF THE JAPANESE COMMUNIST
PARTY.=               KASHA -64-DPS

INDIA'S COMMUNIST PARTY SPLIT.=
                      KATRS -61-ISC

THE IMPACT OF LOCAL PARTY ACTIVITY
UPON THE ELECTORATE
(UNITED STATES).=     KATZD -61-ILP

PARTY - POLITICAL EDUCATION IN
SOVIET RUSSIA, 1918-1935.=
                      KATZZ -56-PPE

THE SPLIT IN THE CPI (COMMUNIST
PARTY INDIA).=        KAULJM-64-SCC

INDIAN COMMUNIST PARTY STRATEGY
SINCE 1947.=          KAUTJH-55-ICP

MOSCOW AND THE COMMUNIST PARTY OF
INDIA.=               KAUTJH-56-MCP

THE NEW ZEALAND NATIONAL PARTY.=
                      KELSRN-54-NZN

AUTHORITARIAN AND SINGLE - PARTY
TENDENCIES IN AFRICAN POLITICS.=
                      KILSML-63-ASP

THE JAPAN COMMUNIST PARTY -- ITS
DEVELOPMENT SINCE THE WAR.=
                      KIYOE -58-JCP

THE ITALIAN ACTION PARTY AND THE
INSTITUTIONAL QUESTION.=
                      KOGAN -53-IAP

THE SOVIET MILITARY AND THE
COMMUNIST PARTY.=     KOLKR -67-SMC

THE PROBLEM OF PARTY GROWTH AND
RECRUITMENT (SOVIET UNION).=
                      KRUZP -66-PPG

PARTY PROTECTION AND PRIVILEGED
STATUS IN SOVIET SOCIETY.=

PARTY                    (CONTINUATION)
                      KRYLKA-66-PPP

LEADERSHIP IN THE CHINESE COMMUNIST
PARTY.=               KUO-C -59-LCC

INDEPENDENCE OR SUBORDINATION --
THE JAPANESE COMMUNIST PARTY
BETWEEN MOSCOW AND PEKING.=
                      LANGPF-63-IOS

POLITICAL PARTY SYSTEMS AND CRISIS
GOVERNMENT -- FRENCH AND ITALIAN
CONTRASTS.=           LAPAJ -58-PPS

EXTENSION OF THE POWERS OF
REPUBLICAN PARTY SECOND
SECRETARIES (SOVIET UNION).=
                      LEBEA -63-EPR

SINGLE - PARTY DEMOCRACY
(TANZANIA).=          LEGUC -65-SPD

THE LEADERSHIP DOCTRINE OF THE
CHINESE COMMUNIST PARTY.=
                      LEWIJW-63-LDC

PARTY CADRES IN COMMUNIST CHINA.=
                      LEWIJW-65-PCC

LEADERSHIP AND CONFLICT WITHIN THE
FEBRERISTA PARTY OF PARAGUAY.=
                      LEWIPH-67-LCW

BEYOND AFRICAN DICTATORSHIP -- THE
CRISIS OF THE ONE - PARTY STATE.=
                      LEWIWA-65-BAD

KHRUSHCHEV AND THE PARTY BATTLE
(SOVIET UNION).=      LINDC -63-KPB

WOODROW WILSON AND THE DEMOCRATIC
PARTY.=               LINKAS-56-WWD

THE TWO - PARTY SYSTEM IN BRITISH
POLITICS.=            LIPSL -53-TPS

PARTY SYSTEMS AND THE
REPRESENTATION OF SOCIAL GROUPS.=
                      LIPSSM-60-PSR

THE TRANSFORMATION OF BRITISH
LABOUR PARTY POLICY SINCE 1945.=
                      LOEWG -57-TBL

PARTY CONFLICT IN ZANZIBAR.=
                      LOFCM -63-PCZ

THE LOGIC OF ONE - PARTY RULE
(SOVIET UNION).=      LOWER -58-LOP

A GAME THEORETIC ANALYSIS OF
CONGRESSIONAL POWER DISTRIBUTIONS
FOR A STABLE TWO - PARTY SYSTEM.=
                      LUCERD-56-GTA

COMMUNIST CHINA'S INTRA - PARTY
DISPUTE.=             MACFR -58-CCS

THE PARTY ASPECT OF SOVIET - POLISH
RELATIONS.=           MACKJ -58-PAS

ELECTORAL TRENDS AND THE TENDENCY
TO A ONE PARTY SYSTEM IN NIGERIA.=
                      MACKJP-62-ETT

FRENCH PARTY LITERATURE.=
                      MARCJA-59-FPL

PARTY LEGISLATIVE REPRESENTATION AS
A FUNCTION OF ELECTION RESULTS --
RELATIONSHIP BETWEEN VOTES AND

PATRIARCHATE            (CCNTINUATICN)
  PATRIARCHATE.=          TECCN -6C-PRM

  THE PCLITICAL RCLE CF TFE MCSCCW
  PATRIARCHATE.=          TECCN -65-PRM

PATRIMCNIAL
  THE DEVELCPMENT ANC CECLINE OF
  PATRIMCNIAL ANC BUREAUCRATIC
  ACMINISTRATICN.=        CELAW -63-CCP

PATRICTIC
  AN IMAGE CF EURCPEAN PCLITICS --
  THE PECFLE'S PATRICTIC MOVEMENT
  (FINLAND).=             RINTM -62-IEP

PATRICTS
  THE AFRICAN PATRICTS -- LEACERSHIP
  CF AFRICAN NATICNAL CCNGRESS.=
                          BENSM -64-APL

  THE DCUBLE PATRICTS -- A STUDY CF
  JAPANESE NATICNALISM.=
                          STCRR -57-CPS

PATRCN
  PATRCN - PECN FATTERN AMCNG TFE
  SPANISH AMERICANS CF NEW MEXICC.=
                          KNCWCS-62-PPP

PATRCNAGE
  PARTY STRENGTH ANC PCLITICAL
  PATRCNAGE (UNITED STATES).=
                          FAIRCR-64-PSP

  PATRCNAGE IN BRITISH GCVERNMENT.=
                          RICHPG-63-PBG

PATTERN
  THE PATTERN CF PCLITICAL PURGES
  (EASTERN EURCPE).=      BRZEZ -58-PPP

  PRESIDENT - CABINET RELATIONS -- A
  PATTERN ANC A CASE STUCY
  (UNITED STATES).=       FENNRF-58-PCR

  PATRCN - PECN FATTERN AMCNG TFE
  SPANISH AMERICANS CF NEW MEXICC.=
                          KNCWCS-62-PPP

  THE DYARCHIC PATTERN CF GOVERNMENT
  ANC PAKISTAN'S FRCBLEMS.=
                          NEWMKJ-6C-CPG

  THE FUNCTICNS CF PCLISH TRADE
  UNICNS -- THEIR PRCFESSION TOWARC
  THE SCVIET PATTERN.=    RCSECS-55-FPT

  THE EGYPTIAN ARMY IN PCLITICS --
  THE PATTERN FCR NEW NATICNS.=
                          VATIPJ-61-EAP

  THE PATTERN CF IMPERIALISM -- A
  STUCY IN THE THECRIES CF POWER.=
                          WINSEM-48-PIS

PATTERNS
  PATTERNS CF CCNSENSUS IN CEVELCPING
  CCUNTRIES.=             ASHFCE-61-PCD

  PATTERNS CF GRCUP CEVELCPMENT IN A
  NEW NATICN -- MCRCCCC.=
                          ASHFCE-61-PGC

  DEMCCRACY ANC CICTATORSHIP -- THEIR
  PSYCHCLCGY ANC PATTERNS CF LIFE.=
                          BARBZ -56-CCT

  THE CHRYSANTHEMUM ANC THE SWORC --
  PATTERNS CF JAPANESE CULTURE.=
                          BENER -46-CSP

  CHANGING PATTERNS CF PCLICY

PATTERNS            (CCNTINUATICN)
  FORMATICN ANC IMPLEMENTATION IN
  CCMMUNIST CHINA.=       BENSO -59-CPP

  PATTERNS CF CCMMUNICATICN CF
  EGYPTIAN CIVIL SERVANTS WITH THE
  PUBLIC.=                BERGM -56-PCE

  CASTE, CLASS ANC PCWER -- CHANGING
  PATTERNS CF STRATIFICATION IN A
  TANJCRE VILLAGE (INCIA).=
                          BETEA -  -CCP

  PATTERNS CF INTERACTICN AMCNG A
  GRCUP CF CFFICIALS IN A GOVERNMENT
  AGENCY (UNITEC STATES).=
                          BLAUPM-54-PIA

  RECRUITMENT PATTERNS AMCNG LOCAL
  PARTY CFFICIALS -- A MCCEL ANC
  SCME PRELIMINARY FINCINGS IN
  SELECTEC LCCALES (UNITED STATES).=
                          BCWM -66-RPA

  PATTERNS CF AUTHCRITY IN WEST
  AFRICA.=                PRCWP -51-PAW

  PATTERNS IN CECISICN-MAKING -- CASE
  STUCIES IN FHILIPPINE PUBLIC
  ACMINISTRATICN.=        CE-GRP-63-PCM

  PATTERNS CF LEACERSHIP AND SOCIAL
  HCMCGENEITY IN ISRAEL.=
                          EISESN-56-PLS

  INITIAL INSTITUTICNAL PATTERNS CF
  PCLITICAL MCCERNIZATICN -- PART 1
  -- PART 2.=             EISESN-62-IIP

  CHANGING PATTERNS CF PCLITICAL
  LEACERSHIP IN INCIA.=   FORRCB-66-CPP

  CHANGING MEMBERSHIP PATTERNS IN
  HCUSE CCMMITTEES (UNITEC STATES).=
                          GAWTLC-66-CMP

  CULTURAL PATTERNS IN THE RCLE CF
  THE MANAGER.=           HAIRM -63-CPR

  CHANGING PATTERNS CF MILITARY
  PCLITICS.=              HUNTSP-62-CPM

  PATTERNS CF VICLENCE IN WORLC
  PCLITICS.=              HUNTSP-62-PVW

  CHANGING PATTERNS CF CRGANIZATICNAL
  AUTHCRITY -- TFE MILITARY
  ESTABLISHMENT (UNITEC STATES).=
                          JANCM -59-CPC

  THE NEW MILITARY -- CHANGING
  PATTERNS CF CRGANIZATICN
  (UNITED STATES).=       JANCM -64-NMC

  PATTERNS CF LEACERSHIP IN A
  CCMMUNIST STATE -- CZECHOSLOVAKIA
  1946-1958.=             KUBAC -61-PLC

  CHANGING PATTERNS CF PCLITICAL
  AUTHCRITY -- A FSYCHIATRIC
  INTERPRETATICN.=        MITSA -67-CPP

  PATTERNS CF INTER-PERSCNAL
  RELATICNS IN A STATE LEGISLATIVE
  GRCUP -- THE WISCCNSIN ASSEMBLY
  (UNITED STATES).=       PATTSC-59-PIP

  DEFERENCE ANC FRIENCSHIP PATTERNS
  IN TWC INDIAN MUNICIPAL COUNCILS.=
                          ROSECB-66-CFP

  PATTERNS CF INTER-GRCUP TENSICN IN

PERCEPTIONS        (CONTINUATION)
(GREAT BRITAIN).=      BLONJ -67-CCM

PERCEPTIONS OF THE VIETNAMESE
PUBLIC ADMINISTRATION SYSTEM.=
                       FOX,GH-64-PVP

TRUSTED LEADERS -- PERCEPTIONS OF
APPOINTED FEDERAL OFFICIALS
(UNITED STATES).=      JENNMK-66-TLP

EFFECTS OF PARTISANSHIP ON
PERCEPTIONS OF POLITICAL FIGURES.=
                       MCGRJC-62-EPP

THE EFFECTS OF NOMINATING
CONVENTIONS, ELECTIONS, AND
REFERENCE GROUP IDENTIFICATION
UPON THE PERCEPTIONS OF POLITICAL
FIGURES (UNITED STATES).=
                       RAVEBH-64-ENC

IMAGES IN THE CONTEXT OF
INTERNATIONAL CONFLICT -- SOVIET
PERCEPTIONS OF THE U.S. AND THE
U.S.S.R.=              WHITRK-65-ICI

PERDITION
RESURRECTION AND PERDITION
(SOVIET UNION).=       LABEL -63-RPS

PERFORMANCE
TRADITIONAL ROLE PERFORMANCE AND
THE DEVELOPMENT OF MODERN
POLITICAL PARTIES -- THE INDIAN
CASE.=                 WEINM -64-TRP

PERMANENT
THE 'PERMANENT PURGE' IN THE NEW
PARTY PROGRAM (SOVIET UNION).=
                       AKHMH -61-PPN

THE PURGE -- PERMANENT SOVIET
INSTITUTION.=          DINEHS-54-PPS

MAO AND THE PERMANENT PURGE
(CHINA).=              GELMH -66-MPP

PERMANENT REVOLUTION --
TOTALITARIANISM IN THE AGE OF
WORLD AT WAR (GERMANY).=
                       NEUMS -65-PRT

PERON
THE PERON ERA (ARGENTINA).=
                       ALEXRJ-51-PEA

PERON'S ARGENTINA.=    BLANGI-53-PSA

CHURCH AND STATE IN ARGENTINA --
FACTORS IN PERON'S DOWNFALL.=
                       GP     -56-CSA

THE PERON ERA.=        PIPPLL-64-PE

ARGENTINE UPHEAVAL -- PERON'S FALL
AND THE NEW REGIME.=   WHITAP-56-AUP

PERONISM
PERONISM AND ARGENTINA'S QUEST FOR
LEADERSHIP IN LATIN AMERICA.=
                       ALEXRJ-55-PAS

ARGENTINA AND PERONISM.=
                       KUEBJ -63-AP

PERSIA
INTERNAL CONTRADICTIONS IN
BUREAUCRATIC POLITIES (ANCIENT
CHINA, PERSIA).=       EISESN-58-ICB

THE PARLIAMENTS OF TURKEY AND

PERSIA           (CONTINUATION)
PERSIA.=               PRICMP-48-PTP

PERSISTENCE
THE PERSISTENCE OF STATUS
ADVANTAGES IN SOVIET RUSSIA.=
                       FELDRA-53-PSA

PERSONAL
PERSONAL CONTACT IN
INTERGOVERNMENTAL ORGANIZATIONS.=
                       ALGEOF-65-PCI

TOWARD PERSONAL DICTATORSHIP OR
OLIGARCHY -- SOVIET DOMESTIC
POLITICS SINCE THE TWENTIETH
CONGRESS.=             ARMSJA-58-TPD

PERSONAL IDENTITY AND POLITICAL
IDEOLOGY.=             PYE,LW-61-PIP

PERSONAL GOVERNMENT IN MEXICO.=
                       TANNF -48-PGM

PERSONAL SENTIMENTS IN A
HIERARCHY.=            TURKH -61-PSH

THE AMERICAN FEDERAL EXECUTIVE -- A
STUDY OF SOCIAL AND PERSONAL
CHARACTERISTICS OF THE CIVILIAN
AND MILITARY LEADERS OF THE UNITED
STATES FEDERAL GOVERNMENT.=
                       WARNWL-63-AFE

PERSONALITIES
LEADING PERSONALITIES IN EASTERN
EUROPE -- BULGARIA,
CZECHOSLOVAKIA, HUNGARY, POLAND,
ROMANIA.=              ANON  -57-LPE

LEADING POSITIONS AND PERSONALITIES
IN THE COMMUNIST PARTY OF THE
SOVIET UNION AND THE SOVIET
GOVERNMENT.=           ANON  -57-LPP

REPUBLIC IN SUSPENSE -- POLITICS,
PARTIES, AND PERSONALITIES IN
POSTWAR GERMANY.=      POLLK -64-RSP

POLITICAL SYSTEMS, STYLES AND
PERSONALITIES.=        LASSHD-67-PSS

THE SUPREME COURT -- ITS POLITICS,
PERSONALITIES, AND PROCEDURES
(UNITED STATES).=      SCHMJR-60-SCI

PERSONALITIES AND POLICIES --
STUDIES IN THE FORMULATION OF
BRITISH FOREIGN POLICY IN THE
TWENTIETH CENTURY.=    WATTDC-65-PPS

A STUDY OF GROUPS AND PERSONALITIES
IN JAPAN INFLUENCING THE EVENTS
LEADING TO THE SINO-JAPANESE WAR.=
                       YOUNEP-63-SGP

PERSONALITY
POWER MOTIVATION AND THE POLITICAL
PERSONALITY (UNITED STATES).=
                       BROWRP-64-PMP

FOUR FORMULAE FOR SELECTING LEADERS
ON THE BASIS OF PERSONALITY.=
                       CATTRB-54-FFS

ATTITUDES TOWARD FOREIGN AFFAIRS AS
A FUNCTION OF PERSONALITY.=
                       CHRIB -59-ATF

STUDIES IN THE SCOPE AND METHOD OF
THE 'AUTHORITARIAN PERSONALITY'.=
                       CHRIR -54-SSM

THE RELATION OF CERTAIN PERSONALITY

POLICIES            (CONTINUATION)
VARIABLES, AND WELFARE POLICIES IN
THE AMERICAN STATES.= DAWSRE-63-IPC

COMMUNIST CHINA TODAY -- DOMESTIC
AND FOREIGN POLICIES.=
                      TANGPS-57-CCT

THE SOVIET UNION AFTER STALIN --
LEADERS AND POLICIES.=
                      TOWSJ -54-SUA

PERSONALITIES AND POLICIES --
STUDIES IN THE FORMULATION OF
BRITISH FOREIGN POLICY IN THE
TWENTIETH CENTURY.=   WATTDC-65-PPS

POLICY
SOCIAL CHANGE IN LATIN AMERICA
TODAY -- ITS IMPLICATIONS.= FOR
U.S. (UNITED STATES) POLICY.=
                      ADAMRN-  -SCL

PUBLIC OPINION AND NATIONAL
SECURITY POLICY (UNITED STATES).=
                      ALMOGA-56-PON

THE AMERICAN PEOPLE AND FOREIGN
POLICY.=              ALMOGA-60-APF

THE SOVIET COMMUNIST PARTY'S POLICY
TOWARD SOVIET YOUTH.= ANON  -56-SCP

THE INDIAN PRESS AND FOREIGN
POLICY.=              BALAK -56-IPF

CONGRESSIONAL INITIATIVE IN FOREIGN
POLICY (UNITED STATES).=
                      BALDDA-66-CIF

AMERICAN BUSINESS AND PUBLIC POLICY
-- THE POLITICS OF FOREIGN TRADE.=
                      BAUER -63-ABP

CHANGING PATTERNS OF POLICY
FORMATION AND IMPLEMENTATION IN
COMMUNIST CHINA.=     BENSO -59-CPP

THE 21ST CONGRESS AND SOVIET
POLICY.=              BIALS -59-SCS

THE MRP (MOVEMENT REPUBLICAN
POPULAIRE) AND FRENCH FOREIGN
POLICY.=              CAPERB-63-MMR

THE CHRISTIAN DEMOCRATIC PARTY IN
ITALIAN POLICY.=      CAPPE -61-CDP

THE ARABS' VIEW OF POSTWAR AMERICAN
FOREIGN POLICY (EGYPT, IRAN,
JORDAN, LEBANON, SYRIA).=
                      CASTHP-59-AVP

THE DETERMINANTS OF LIBYAN FOREIGN
POLICY.=              CECICO-65-DLF

AMERICAN OPINION AND FOREIGN
POLICY.=              CHANG -55-AOF

THE PRESS AND FOREIGN POLICY IN THE
UNITED STATES.=       COHEBC-55-PFP

THE POLITICAL PROCESS AND FOREIGN
POLICY (UNITED STATES).=
                      COHEBC-57-PPF

THE INFLUENCE OF NON-GOVERNMENTAL
GROUPS ON FOREIGN POLICY MAKING
(UNITED STATES).=     COHEBC-59-ING

THE PRESS AND FOREIGN POLICY
(UNITED STATES).=     COHEBC-63-PFP

POLICY             (CONTINUATION)
THE MILITARY POLICY PUBLIC
(UNITED STATES).=     COHEBC-66-MPP

POWER AND POLICY IN THE USSR.=
                      CONQR -61-PPU

CONGRESS AND FOREIGN POLICY
(UNITED STATES).=     DAHLRA-50-CFP

CONGRESSIONAL INNOVATION AND
INTERVENTION IN DEFENSE POLICY --
LEGISLATIVE AUTHORIZATION OF
WEAPONS SYSTEMS (UNITED STATES).=
                      DAWSRH-62-CII

PRESSURE GROUPS AND AMERICAN
POLICY.=              DCW   -50-PGA

SOVIET TRADE UNIONS -- THEIR PLACE
IN  SOVIET LABOUR POLICY.=
                      DEUTI -50-STU

GERMANY REJOINS THE POWERS -- MASS
OPINION, INTEREST GROUPS AND
ELITES IN CONTEMPORARY GERMAN
FOREIGN POLICY.=      DEUTKW-59-GRP

CONGRESSMEN AND THE MAKING OF
MILITARY POLICY (UNITED STATES).=
                      DEXTLA-63-CMM

CONGRESSIONAL ISOLATIONISTS AND THE
ROOSEVELT FOREIGN POLICY
(UNITED STATES).=     DONOJC-51-CIR

SCIENCE AND THE NATION -- POLICY
AND POLITICS (UNITED STATES).=
                      DUPRJS-62-SNP

PUBLIC OPINION AND FOREIGN POLICY.=
                      DURAH -55-POF

COPING WITH CUBA -- DIVERGENT
POLICY PREFERENCES OF STATE
POLITICAL LEADERS
(UNITED STATES).=     EKMAP -66-CCD

PARLIAMENT AND FOREIGN POLICY IN
SWEDEN.=              ELDEN -53-PFP

THE PUBLIC STUDIES DIVISION OF THE
DEPARTMENT OF THE STATE -- PUBLIC
OPINION ANALYSIS IN THE
FORMULATION AND CONDUCT OF
AMERICAN FOREIGN POLICY.=
                      ELDERE-57-PSD

THE POLICY MACHINE -- THE
DEPARTMENT OF STATE AND AMERICAN
FOREIGN POLICY.=      ELDERE-60-PMD

THE POLICY MACHINE -- THE
DEPARTMENT OF STATE AND AMERICAN
FOREIGN POLICY.=      ELDERE-60-PMD

WHO MAKES PARTY POLICY -- BRITISH
LABOUR 1960-1961.=    EPSTLD-62-WMP

THE FOREIGN POLICY VIEWS OF THE
INDIAN RIGHT.=        ERDMHL-66-FPV

POLITICAL POLICY AND PERSUASION --
THE ROLE OF COMMUNICATIONS FROM
POLITICAL LEADERS (SOVIET UNION,
GREAT BRITAIN, UNITED STATES).=
                      FELDMC-58-PPP

NATIONAL ECONOMIC INTEREST AND
POLICY FORMATION IN THE EEC
(EUROPEAN ECONOMIC COMMUNITY).=
                      FELDW -66-NEI

CIVILIANS, SOLDIERS, AND AMERICAN

POLICY                    (CONTINUATION)
  MILITARY POLICY.=        FOX,WT-55-CSA

  INTEREST GROUPS AS POLICY SHAPERS
  (UNITED STATES).=        GABLRW-58-IGP

  AMERICAN SCIENTISTS AND NUCLEAR
  WEAPONS POLICY.=         GILPRG-62-ASN

  SECTIONAL BIASES IN CONGRESS ON
  FOREIGN POLICY (UNITED STATES).=
                          GRASGL-51-SBC

  THE ROLE OF THE BRITISH CIVIL
  SERVANT IN POLICY FORMATION.=
                          GRIFR -53-RBC

  THE COMMUNICATION OF CONSERVATIVE
  POLICY 1957-1959 (GREAT BRITAIN).=
                          HENND -61-CCP

  INTRA - PARTY POLITICS AND ECONOMIC
  POLICY IN COMMUNIST CHINA.=
                          HINTHC-60-IPP

  THE CIVIL SERVICE AND POLICY
  FORMATION (NORTH AMERICA).=
                          HODGJE-57-CSP

  EDUCATIONAL POLICY AND POLITICAL
  DEVELOPMENT IN AFRICA.=
                          HUSSER-46-EPP

  PUBLIC OPINION AND AMERICAN FOREIGN
  POLICY -- THE QUEMOY CRISIS OF
  1958.=                  IRISMC-60-POA

  FUNCTION OF VALUES IN THE POLICY
  PROCESS -- ELITE GROUPS
  (UNITED STATES).=        JACOPE-62-FVP

  COMMUNITY AND 'POLICY SCIENCE'
  RESEARCH (UNITED STATES).=
                          JANOM -62-CPS

  THE SENATE REPUBLICAN POLICY
  COMMITTEE AND FOREIGN POLICY
  (UNITED STATES).=        JEWEME-59-SRP

  THE SENATE REPUBLICAN POLICY
  COMMITTEE AND FOREIGN POLICY
  (UNITED STATES).=        JEWEME-59-SRP

  SENATORIAL POLITICS AND FOREIGN
  POLICY (UNITED STATES).=
                          JEWEME-62-SPF

  PARTY AND POLICY-MAKING -- THE
  HOUSE REPUBLICAN POLICY COMMITTEE
  (UNITED STATES).=        JONECO-64-PPM

  INTERPARLIAMENTARY CONTACTS IN
  SOVIET FOREIGN POLICY.=
                          JULIPH-61-ICS

  PARTIES, PARTISANSHIP, AND PUBLIC
  POLICY IN THE PENNSYLVANIA
  LEGISLATURE.=            KEEFWJ-54-PPP

  THE PRIVATE MEMBER OF PARLIAMENT
  AND THE FORMATION OF PUBLIC POLICY
  -- A NEW ZEALAND CASE STUDY.=
                          KELSRN-64-PMP

  PRESIDENTIAL LEADERSHIP IN CONGRESS
  ON FOREIGN POLICY -- A REPLICATION
  OF A HYPOTHESIS (UNITED STATES).=
                          KESSM -65-PLC

  STRATEGIC POLICY AND AMERICAN
  GOVERNMENT -- STRUCTURAL
  CONSTRAINTS AND VARIABLES.=

POLICY                    (CONTINUATION)
                          KOLDEJ-65-SPA

  A TURNING POINT IN THE MOSCOW
  (SOVIET UNION) PATRIARCHATE'S
  POLICY.=                KONSD -63-TPM

  AMERICAN INTELLECTUALS AND FOREIGN
  POLICY.=                KRISI -67-AIF

  THE PRESS IN WORLD POLITICS AND IN
  THE CONDUCT OF FOREIGN POLICY
  (GREAT BRITAIN, LATIN AMERICA,
  SOVIET UNION, UNITED STATES).=
                          KYDIS -65-PWP

  SCIENTISTS AND THE POLICY PROCESS
  (UNITED STATES).=        LEISA -65-SPP

  AUTHORITARIAN PERSONALITY AND
  FOREIGN POLICY (UNITED STATES).=
                          LEVICJ-57-APF

  THE TRANSFORMATION OF BRITISH
  LABOUR PARTY POLICY SINCE 1945.=
                          LOEWG -57-TBL

  AMERICAN BUSINESS, PUBLIC POLICY,
  CASE-STUDIES AND POLITICAL
  THEORY.=                LOWITJ-64-ABP

  AMERICAN INTELLECTUALS AND U.S.
  VIETNAM POLICY.=         LOWRCW-65-AIU

  THE MOSCOW PATRIARCH IN SOVIET
  FOREIGN AND DOMESTIC POLICY.=
                          MARIY -61-MPS

  SOLDIERS AND SCHOLARS -- MILITARY
  EDUCATION AND NATIONAL POLICY
  (UNITED STATES).=        MASLJW-57-SSM

  THE BUSINESS ELITE AND FOREIGN
  POLICY (UNITED STATES).=
                          MCLEDS-60-BEF

  OFFICIAL POLICY AND ANTI -
  INTELLECTUALISM (UNITED STATES).=
                          MCWIC -55-OPA

  THE BRITISH LEFT WING AND FOREIGN
  POLICY -- A STUDY OF THE INFLUENCE
  OF IDEOLOGY.=           MEEHEJ-60-BLW

  THE JAPANESE PEOPLE AND FOREIGN
  POLICY -- A STUDY OF PUBLIC
  OPINION IN POST-TREATY JAPAN.=
                          MENDCH-61-JPF

  THE MAKERS OF PUBLIC POLICY --
  AMERICAN POWER GROUPS AND THEIR
  IDEOLOGIES.=            MONSRJ-65-MPP

  THE FORMULATION OF PARTY POLICY
  (GREAT BRITAIN).=        NICHHG-51-FPP

  BRITISH FOREIGN POLICY AND THE
  PARTY SYSTEM.=           NORTFS-60-BFP

  CONFLICT AND DECISION-MAKING IN
  SOVIET RUSSIA -- A CASE STUDY OF
  AGRICULTURAL POLICY, 1953-1963.=
                          PLOSSI-65-CDM

  THE POLICY IMPLICATIONS OF SOCIAL
  CHANGE IN NON - WESTERN
  SOCIETIES.=              PYE,LW-57-PIS

  PRIVATE PEOPLE AND PUBLIC POLICY
  (UNITED STATES).=        RIESD -59-PPP

  PROCESS SATISFACTION AND POLICY

POLISH                    (CONTINUATION)
THE POLISH REVOLUTION 1956.=
                          SYROK -58-SOS

THE POLISH INTELLIGENTSIA -- PAST
AND PRESENT.=             SZCZJ -62-PIP

POLISH LITERATURE AND THE 'THAW'.=
                          THOMLL-59-PLT

THE CRISIS IN THE POLISH COMMUNIST
PARTY.=                   ULAMAB-50-CPC

POLITBURO
THE EVOLUTION OF THE POLITBURO
(SOVIET UNION).=          BRYNC -49-EPS

PEOPLE OF THE POLITBURO
(SOVIET UNION).=          BRYNC -49-PPS

THE OPERATIONAL CODE OF THE
POLITBURO (SOVIET UNION).=
                          LEITN -51-OCP

POLITBURO IMAGES OF STALIN
(SOVIET UNION).=          LEITN -51-PIS

THE POLITBURO THROUGH WESTERN EYES
(SOVIET UNION).=          LEITN -52-PTW

THE MEN OF THE POLITBURO
(SOVIET UNION).=          LISTJ -49-MPS

THE POLITBURO (SOVIET UNION).=
                          SCHUGK-51-PSU

POLITICAL
THE ROLE OF CONTEMPORARY POLITICAL
PARTIES IN CHILE.=        ABBORS-51-RCP

THE POLITICAL LINE OF COLLECTIVE
LEADERSHIP (SOVIET UNION).=
                          ACHMH -54-PLC

THE CURRENT POLITICAL SCENE IN THE
SOVIET UNION.=            ACHMH -65-CPS

POLITICAL ASPECTS OF THE NATIONAL
PEOPLE'S CONGRESS (CHINA).=
                          ADIEWA-62-PAN

THE POLITICAL STRUCTURE OF A SMALL
COMMUNITY (UNITED STATES).=
                          AGGERE-56-PSS

POLITICAL ASPIRATIONS OF LAW
STUDENTS (UNITED STATES).=
                          AGGERE-58-PAL

THE (PHILIPPINE) POLITICAL PROCESS
AND THE NATIONALIZATION OF THE
RETAIL TRADES.=           AGPARE-62-PPP

CHARISMATIC LEGITIMATION AND
POLITICAL INTEGRATION (GHANA).=
                          AKE,C -66-CLP

POLITICAL INTEGRATION AND POLITICAL
STABILITY -- A HYPOTHESIS.=
                          AKE,C -67-PIP

POLITICAL INTEGRATION AND POLITICAL
STABILITY -- A HYPOTHESIS.=
                          AKE,C -67-PIP

THE RESISTANCE AND THE POLITICAL
PARTIES OF WESTERN EUROPE.=
                          ALMOGA- -RPP

THE POLITICAL ATTITUDES OF WEALTH.=
                          ALMOGA-45-PAW

THE POLITICAL IDEAS OF CHRISTIAN

POLITICAL                 (CONTINUATION)
DEMOCRACY.=               ALMOGA-48-PIC

THE POLITICAL ATTITUDES OF GERMAN
BUSINESS.=                ALMOGA-56-PAG

POLITICAL ACTIVISM IN A RURAL
COUNTY (UNITED STATES).=
                          ALTHP -66-PAR

OPINION INFLUENTIALS AND POLITICAL
OPINION FORMATION IN FOUR SWEDISH
COMMUNITIES.=             ANDEB -62-OIP

RANK EQUILIBRATION AND POLITICAL
BEHAVIOR.=                ANDEB -64-REP

CENTRAL AMERICAN POLITICAL PARTIES
-- A FUNCTIONAL APPROACH.=
                          ANDECW-62-CAP

NIGERIA -- POLITICAL NON-ALIGNMENT
AND ECONOMIC ALIGNMENT.=
                          ANGLOG-64-NPN

PARTY POLITICAL TRAINING IN THE
SOVIET UNION.=            ANON  -55-PPT

THE ROLE OF TRADITIONALISM IN THE
POLITICAL MODERNIZATION OF GHANA
AND UGANDA.=              APTEDE-60-RTP

THE POLITICAL KINGDOM IN UGANDA --
A STUDY OF BUREAUCRATIC
NATIONALISM.=             APTEDE-61-PKU

SOME REFLECTIONS ON THE ROLE OF A
POLITICAL OPPOSITION IN NEW
NATIONS.=                 APTEDE-62-RRP

POLITICAL INSTABILITY IN
LATIN AMERICA.=           ARCIG -55-PIL

THE POLITICAL METHODS OF GENERAL
DEGAULLE (FRANCE).=       AROLR -61-PMG

POLITICAL CHANGE IN MOROCCO.=
                          ASHFDE-61-PCM

THE POLITICAL USAGE OF 'ISLAM' AND
'ARAB CULTURE' (MOROCCO).=
                          ASHFDE-61-PUI

POLITICAL DEVELOPMENTS IN IRAN,
1951-1954.=               ATYEH -54-PDI

BURMA'S POLITICAL CRISIS.=
                          BADGJH-58-BSP

POLITICAL PARTIES AND THE PARTY
SYSTEM IN BRITAIN.=       BAILSD-52-PPP

POLITICAL IMPLICATIONS OF RECENT
SOVIET ECONOMIC REORGANIZATIONS.=
                          BALLWB-61-PIR

THE ROLE OF POLITICAL LEADERSHIP IN
THE PASSAGE OF OREGON'S MIGRATORY
LABOR LEGISLATION
(UNITED STATES).=         BALMOG-62-RPL

POLITICAL INFLUENCE
(UNITED STATES).=         BANFEC-61-PIU

POLITICAL SYSTEM AND THE
DISTRIBUTION OF POWER.=
                          BANTM -65-PSD

POLITICAL LEADERSHIP IN AMERICAN
GOVERNMENT.=              BARBJD-64-PLA

MASS POLITICAL ORGANIZATIONS IN

POLITICAL          (CONTINUATION)
  COMMUNIST CHINA.=        BARNAC-51-MPC

  POLITICAL POWER IN COMMUNIST
  CHINA.=                  BARNAC-57-PPC

  CADRES, BUREAUCRACY AND POLITICAL
  POWER IN CHINA.=         BARNAC-67-CBP

  LEADERSHIP STYLE AND POLITICAL
  COMPETENCE (ITALY).=     BARNSH-67-LSP

  POLITICAL LEADERSHIP AMONG
  SWAT PATHANS (PAKISTAN).=
                           BARTF -59-PLA

  APPLES, ORANGES, AND THE
  COMPARATIVE STUDY OF POLITICAL
  PARTIES (GHANA, INDONESIA).=
                           BAUMRD-67-AOC

  SOCIAL AND POLITICAL CHANGES IN THE
  COOK ISLANDS.=           BEAGE -48-SPC

  BUREAUCRACY AND POLITICAL
  DEVELOPMENT IN EASTERN EUROPE.=
                           BECKC -63-BPD

  POLITICAL ELITES -- A MODE OF
  ANALYSIS.=               BECKC -66-PEM

  POLITICAL BEHAVIORALISM AND MODERN
  JURISPRUDENCE -- A WORKING THEORY
  AND STUDY IN JUDICIAL
  DECISION-MAKING (UNITED STATES).=
                           BECKTL-64-PBM

  THE FRENCH ARMY AS A POLITICAL AND
  SOCIAL FACTOR.=          BEHRE -59-FAP

  POLITICAL POWER RELATIONS IN A
  MID-WEST CITY (UNITED STATES).=
                           BELKGM-56-PPR

  THE END OF IDEOLOGY -- ON THE
  EXHAUSTION OF POLITICAL IDEAS IN
  THE FIFTIES (UNITED STATES).=
                           BELLD -62-EIE

  JAMAICAN LEADERS -- POLITICAL
  ATTITUDES IN A NEW NATION.=
                           BELLW -64-JLP

  NON-WESTERN INTELLIGENTSIAS AS
  POLITICAL ELITES.=       BENDHJ-60-NWI

  POLITICAL ELITES IN COLONIAL
  SOUTHEAST ASIA -- AN HISTORICAL
  ANALYSIS.=               BENDHJ-64-PEC

  SOCIAL STRATIFICATION AND POLITICAL
  POWER.=                  BENDR -52-SSP

  POLITICAL SOCIOLOGY.=    BENDR -57-PS

  SOCIAL STRATIFICATION AND THE
  POLITICAL COMMUNITY.=    BENDR -60-SSP

  THE DEVELOPMENT OF POLITICAL
  ORGANIZATIONS IN KENYA.=
                           BENNG -57-DPO

  SOCIAL AND POLITICAL CHANGE IN THE
  MOSLEM - ARAB WORLD.=    BERGM -58-SPC

  COMMITTEE STACKING AND POLITICAL
  POWER IN FLORIDA (UNITED STATES).=
                           BETHLP-61-CSP

  IRAN -- POLITICAL DEVELOPMENT IN A
  CHANGING SOCIETY.=       BINDL -62-IPD

  SMALL - TOWN POLITICS -- A STUDY OF

POLITICAL          (CONTINUATION)
  POLITICAL LIFE IN GLOSSOP
  (GREAT BRITAIN).=        BIRCAH-59-STP

  THE AGE OF CHANGE -- POLITICAL AND
  INTELLECTUAL LEADERSHIP IN NORTH
  CAROLINA (UNITED STATES).=
                           BLACR -61-AOP

  POLITICAL GROUPS IN LATIN AMERICA.=
                           BLANGI-59-PGL

  THE PROBLEM OF SUCCESSION IN THE
  SOVIET POLITICAL SYSTEM -- THE
  CASE OF KHRUSHCHEV.=     BOCIBR-60-PSS

  EXTRA-PROCESSIONAL EVENTS IN TIV
  POLITICAL INSTITUTIONS (NIGERIA).=
                           BOHAP -58-EPE

  THE STUDENT FEDERATION OF CHILE --
  50 YEARS OF POLITICAL ACTION.=
                           BONIF -60-SFC

  FROM COMMERCIAL ELITE TO POLITICAL
  ADMINISTRATOR -- THE RECRUITMENT
  OF THE MAYORS OF CHICAGO
  (UNITED STATES).=        BRADDS-65-CEP

  DICTATORSHIP AND POLITICAL POLICE
  (FRANCE,GERMANY,ITALY).=
                           BRAMEK-45-DPP

  SUCCESSION IN INDIA 1967 -- THE
  ROUTINIZATION OF POLITICAL
  CHANGE.=                 BRECM -67-SIR

  AFRICAN ATTITUDES -- A STUDY OF THE
  SOCIAL, RACIAL, AND POLITICAL
  ATTITUDES OF SOME MIDDLE CLASS
  AFRICANS.=               BRETEA-63-AAS

  COMMUNISM IN SOUTHEAST ASIA -- A
  POLITICAL ANALYSIS.=     BRIMJH-59-CSA

  SOCIAL STRATIFICATION AND THE
  POLITICAL ORDER.=        BROTHM-59-SSP

  THE POLITICAL SCENE (BULGARIA).=
                           BROWJF-61-PSB

  POWER MOTIVATION AND THE POLITICAL
  PERSONALITY (UNITED STATES).=
                           BROWRP-64-PMP

  THE PATTERN OF POLITICAL PURGES
  (EASTERN EUROPE).=       BRZEZ -58-PPP

  POLITICAL POWER -- USA/USSR
  (UNITED STATES, SOVIET UNION).=
                           BRZEZ -64-PPU

  THE SOVIET POLITICAL SYSTEM --
  TRANSFORMATION OR DEGENERATION.=
                           BRZEZ -66-SPS

  POLITICAL CONTROLS IN THE SOVIET
  ARMY -- A STUDY BASED ON REPORTS
  BY FORMER SOVIET OFFICERS.=
                           BRZEZK-54-PCS

  THE FEDERATION OF GERMAN EMPLOYERS'
  ASSOCIATIONS -- A POLITICAL
  INTEREST GROUP.=         BUNNRF-60-FGE

  THE POSITION OF THE CHIEF IN THE
  MODERN POLITICAL SYSTEM OF ASHANTI
  (GOLD COAST).=           BUSIKA-51-PCM

  TRANSITION IN AFRICA -- STUDIES IN
  POLITICAL ADAPTATION.=
                           CARTGW-58-TAS

  POLITICAL AUTHORITY -- ITS EXERCISE

POLITICAL (CONTINUATION)
TOWARD POLITICAL AUTHORITY
(AUSTRALIA, CHILE, JAPAN,
PUERTO RICO, UNITED STATES).=
HESSRO-63-SAT

THE ETHIOPIAN NO - PARTY STATE -- A
NOTE ON THE FUNCTIONS OF POLITICAL
PARTIES IN DEVELOPING STATES.=
HESSRL-64-ENP

POLITICAL CONFLICT POTENTIAL,
POLITIZATION, AND THE PEASANTRY IN
THE UNDERDEVELOPED COUNTRIES.=
HINDO -65-PCP

POLITICAL POWER AND THE OCTOBER
1965 COUP IN INDONESIA.=
HINDO -67-PPC

COMMUNICATION AND POLITICAL
AWARENESS IN THE VILLAGES OF
EGYPT.= HIRAGK-58-CPA

A PROFILE OF POLITICAL ACTIVISTS IN
MANHATTAN (UNITED STATES).=
HIRSRS-62-PPA

AFRICAN POLITICAL PARTIES.=
HODGT -61-APP

ECONOMIC ASPECTS OF POLITICAL
MOVEMENTS IN NIGERIA AND IN THE
GOLD COAST, 1918-1939.=
HOPKAG-66-EAP

THE ELECTORAL PROCESS AND POLITICAL
DEVELOPMENT IN LEBANON.=
HUDSMC-66-EPP

INTERSERVICE COMPETITION AND THE
POLITICAL ROLES OF THE ARMED
SERVICES (UNITED STATES).=
HUNTSP-61-ICP

THE POLITICAL MODERNIZATION OF
TRADITIONAL MONARCHIES.=
HUNTSP-66-PMT

EDUCATIONAL POLICY AND POLITICAL
DEVELOPMENT IN AFRICA.=
HUSSER-46-EPP

THE POLITICAL OUTLOOK IN PAKISTAN.=
INNEFM-53-POP

THE SYSTEMATIC ANALYSIS OF
POLITICAL BIOGRAPHY.= JANOM -54-SAP

THE PROFESSIONAL SOLDIER -- A
SOCIAL AND POLITICAL PORTRAIT
(UNITED STATES).= JANOM -60-PSS

COMMUNITY POLITICAL SYSTEMS
(UNITED STATES).= JANOM -61-CPS

THE MILITARY IN THE POLITICAL
DEVELOPMENT OF NEW NATIONS -- AN
ESSAY IN COMPARATIVE ANALYSIS
(ASIA, AFRICA, MIDDLE EAST).=
JANOM -64-MPD

POLITICAL CHANGE AND PARIAH
ENTREPRENEURSHIP (PHILIPPINES).=
JIANJP-62-PCP

PARTY AND ARMY -- PROFESSIONALISM
AND POLITICAL CONTROL IN THE
CHINESE OFFICER CORPS, 1949-1964.=
JOFFE -65-PAP

POLITICAL CHANGE IN LATIN AMERICA

POLITICAL (CONTINUATION)
-- THE EMERGENCE OF THE MIDDLE
SECTORS.= JOHNJJ-58-PCL

IDEOLOGICAL CORRELATES OF RIGHT
WING POLITICAL ALIENATION IN
MEXICO.= JOHNKF-65-ICR

THE POLITICAL SIGNIFICANCE OF THE
BURMA WORKERS PARTY.= JOSEA -58-PSB

THE LEGISLATIVE BUREAUCRACY -- ITS
RESPONSE TO POLITICAL CHANGE
(UNITED STATES).= KAMPMM-54-LBI

APRISMO -- PERU'S INDIGENOUS
POLITICAL THEORY.= KANTH -54-APS

RECENT POLITICAL DEVELOPMENTS IN
TURKEY AND THEIR SOCIAL
BACKGROUND.= KARPKH-62-RPD

POLITICAL PARTIES AND THE FRENCH
ARMY SINCE THE LIBERATION.=
KATZEL-50-PPF

PARTY - POLITICAL EDUCATION IN
SOVIET RUSSIA, 1918-1935.=
KATZZ -56-PPE

POLITICAL CHANGE IN UNDERDEVELOPED
COUNTRIES -- NATIONALISM AND
COMMUNISM.= KAUTJH-62-PCU

COMPARATIVE STUDY OF THE ROLE OF
POLITICAL PARTIES IN THE STATE
LEGISLATURES (UNITED STATES).=
KEEFWJ-56-CSR

PROFESSIONAL PUBLIC RELATIONS AND
POLITICAL POWER (UNITED STATES).=
KELLS -56-PPR

AFRICAN POLITICAL CHANGE AND
MODERNISATION PROCESS.=
KILSM -63-APC

POLITICAL CHANGE IN A WEST AFRICAN
STATE -- A STUDY OF THE
MODERNIZATION PROCESS IN
SIERRA LEONE.= KILSM -66-PCW

THE CONCEPT OF POLITICAL CULTURE IN
COMPARATIVE POLITICS.=
KIM,YC-64-CPC

POLITICAL POWER AND EDUCATIONAL
DECISION-MAKING (UNITED STATES).=
KIMBRB-64-PPE

TOWARD A THEORY OF POWER AND
POLITICAL INSTABILITY IN
LATIN AMERICA.= KLINM -56-TTP

THE POLITICAL SOCIALIZATION OF
NATIONAL LEGISLATIVE ELITES IN THE
UNITED STATES AND CANADA.=
KORNA -65-PSN

REPRESENTATIVE DEMOCRACY AND
POLITICAL ELITES IN CANADA AND THE
UNITED STATES.= KORNA -66-RDP

SOCIABILITY AND POLITICAL
INVOLVEMENT (JAPAN).= KUROY -65-SPI

NEGRO POLITICAL LEADERSHIP IN THE
SOUTH (UNITED STATES).=
LADDEC-66-NPL

POLITICAL ELITES AND THE PROCESS OF
ECONOMIC DEVELOPMENT

POLITICAL                (CONTINUATION)
(UNITED STATES, WESTERN EUROPE,
SOVIET UNION).=          LAMBRK-52-PEP

POLITICAL ATTITUDES AND BEHAVIOR IN
THE PHILIPPINES.=        LANDCH-59-PAB

ORGANIZED INTERESTS IN JAPAN AND
THEIR INFLUENCE ON POLITICAL
PARTIES.=                LANGFC-61-OIJ

POLITICAL PARTY SYSTEMS AND CRISIS
GOVERNMENT -- FRENCH AND ITALIAN
CONTRASTS.=              LAPAJ -58-PPS

BUREAUCRACY AND POLITICAL
DEVELOPMENT.=            LAPAJ -63-BPD

AN OVERVIEW OF BUREAUCRACY AND
POLITICAL DEVELOPMENT.=
                        LAPAJ -63-OBP

POLITICAL PARTIES AND POLITICAL
DEVELOPMENT.=            LAPAJG-65-PPP

POLITICAL PARTIES AND POLITICAL
DEVELOPMENT.=            LAPAJG-65-PPP

UNDERSTANDING THE PHILIPPINE
POLITICAL PROCESS.=      LAQUAA-63-UPP

THE ANALYSIS OF POLITICAL BEHAVIOR
-- AN EMPIRICAL APPROACH.=
                        LASSHD-48-APB

POWER AND SOCIETY -- A FRAMEWORK
FOR POLITICAL INQUIRY.=
                        LASSHD-50-PSF

EFFECT OF PERSONALITY ON POLITICAL
PARTICIPATION.=          LASSHD-54-EPP

AGENDA FOR THE STUDY OF POLITICAL
ELITES.=                 LASSHD-61-ASP

POLITICAL SYSTEMS, STYLES AND
PERSONALITIES.=          LASSHD-67-PSS

POLITICAL CONSTITUTION AND
CHARACTER.=              LASWHD-59-PCC

POLITICAL SYSTEMS OF HIGHLAND BURMA
-- A STUDY OF KACHIN SOCIAL
STRUCTURE.=              LEACER-54-PSH

POLITICAL INSTABILITY IN SYRIA.=
                        LEIDC -65-PIS

POLITICAL AWAKENING IN THE BELGIAN
CONGO -- THE POLITICS OF
FRAGMENTATION.=          LEMAR -64-PAB

SOCIAL AND POLITICAL CHANGES IN
BURUNDI.=                LEMAR -66-SPC

THE POLITICAL ROLE OF THE ARMY IN
INDONESIA.=              LEV,DS-64-PRA

THE RELEVANCE OF PERSONALITY FOR
POLITICAL PARTICIPATION.=
                        LEVIDJ-58-RPP

POLITICAL LEADERSHIP IN AFRICA.=
                        LEVIVT-67-PLA

THE PRESENT CONDITION OF BRITISH
POLITICAL PARTIES.=      LEWIGK-52-PCB

MODERN POLITICAL MOVEMENTS IN
SOMALILAND -- PART 1 -- PART 2.=
                        LEWIIM-58-MPM

POLITICAL ASPECTS OF MOBILITY IN

POLITICAL                (CONTINUATION)
CHINA'S URBAN DEVELOPMENT.=
                        LEWIJW-66-PAM

MODELS, THEORIES, AND THE THEORY OF
POLITICAL PARTIES.=      LEYSC -59-MTT

THE POLITICAL CLIMATE FOR ECONOMIC
DEVELOPMENT (AFRICA).=
                        LEYSC -66-PCE

THE RURAL COMMUNITY AND POLITICAL
LEADERSHIP IN SASKATCHEWAN
(CANADA).=               LIPSSM-47-RCP

POLITICAL MAN -- THE SOCIAL BASES
OF POLITICS.=            LIPSSM-60-PMS

THE DEVELOPMENT OF POLITICAL
PARTIES IN WESTERN NIGERIA.=
                        LLOYPC-55-DPP

THE CITY MANAGER, ADMINISTRATIVE
THEORY AND POLITICAL POWER
(UNITED STATES).=        LOCKD -62-CMA

PARLIAMENT IN THE GERMAN POLITICAL
SYSTEM.=                 LOEWG -66-PGP

POLITICAL POWER AND THE
GOVERNMENTAL PROCESS.=
                        LOEWK -57-PPG

POLITICAL PARTIES IN UGANDA
1949-1962.=              LOW,DA-62-PPU

AMERICAN BUSINESS, PUBLIC POLICY,
CASE-STUDIES AND POLITICAL
THEORY.=                 LOWITJ-64-ABP

FEDERAL POLITICAL EXECUTIVES
(UNITED STATES).=        MANNDE-64-FPE

THE SELECTION OF FEDERAL POLITICAL
EXECUTIVES (UNITED STATES).=
                        MANNDE-64-SFP

DILEMMAS IN THE STUDY OF
LATIN AMERICAN POLITICAL PARTIES.=
                        MARTD -64-DSL

ACCION DEMOCRATICA -- REVOLUTION OF
A MODERN POLITICAL PARTY IN
VENEZUELA.=              MARTJD-66-ADR

POLITICAL DECISION-MAKERS (INDIA,
FRANCE, GREAT BRITAIN, GERMANY,
UNITED STATES).=         MARVD -61-PDM

THE SOCIAL BACKGROUNDS OF POLITICAL
DECISION MAKERS.=        MATTDR-62-SBP

SYSTEM AND NETWORK -- AN APPROACH
TO THE STUDY OF POLITICAL
PROCESS.=                MAYEAC-62-SNA

EFFECTS OF PARTISANSHIP ON
PERCEPTIONS OF POLITICAL FIGURES.=
                        MCGRJC-62-EPP

POWER IN BRITISH POLITICAL
PARTIES.=                MCKERT-55-PBP

BRITISH POLITICAL PARTIES -- THE
DISTRIBUTION OF POWER WITHIN THE
CONSERVATIVE AND LABOUR PARTIES.=
                        MCKERT-65-BPP

POLITICAL LEADERSHIP
(UNITED STATES).=        MERRCE-49-PLU

THE SOVIET POLITICAL SYSTEM -- AN

POLITICAL          (CONTINUATION)
  INTERPRETATION.=        MEYEAG-65-SPS

AUTHORITY IN COMMUNIST POLITICAL
SYSTEMS (EASTERN EUROPE,
SOVIET UNION).=         MEYEAG-67-ACP

SOME REFLECTIONS ON THE
SOCIOLOGICAL CHARACTER OF
POLITICAL PARTIES.=     MICHR -27-RSC

POLITICAL PARTIES -- A SOCIOLOGICAL
STUDY OF THE OLIGARCHICAL
TENDENCIES OF MODERN DEMOCRACY
(GERMANY).=             MICHR -62-PPS

THE POLITICAL PARTY ACTIVITY OF
WASHINGTON LOBBYISTS
(UNITED STATES).=       MILBLW-58-PPA

THE POLITICAL ROLE OF LABOR IN
DEVELOPING COUNTRIES.=
                        MILLBH-63-PRL

THE POWER ELITE -- MILITARY,
ECONOMIC, AND POLITICAL
(UNITED STATES).=       MILLCW-59-PEM

IDEOLOGY AND POLITICAL BEHAVIOR.=
                        MINADW-61-IPB

THE POLITICIAN AND THE POLITICAL
SCIENTIST.=             MITCWC-58-PPS

CHANGING PATTERNS OF POLITICAL
AUTHORITY -- A PSYCHIATRIC
INTERPRETATION.=        MITSA -67-CPP

POLITICAL POWER AND SOCIAL THEORY.=
                        MOORB -58-PPS

POLITICAL LEADERSHIP RE-EXAMINED --
AN EXPERIMENTAL APPROACH
(UNITED STATES).=       MOOSM -51-PLR

POLITICAL PARTIES IN
FRENCH-SPEAKING WEST AFRICA.=
                        MORGRS-64-PPF

RECENT POLITICAL DEVELOPMENT IN
INDIA -- 2.=            MORRWH-59-RPD

THE HIGHER CIVIL SERVICE AS AN
ACTION GROUP IN WESTERN POLITICAL
DEVELOPMENT.=           MORSF -63-HCS

CONGRESS AND THE COURT -- A CASE
STUDY IN THE AMERICAN POLITICAL
PROCESS.=               MURPWF-62-CCC

POLITICAL PARTY AFFILIATION AND
JUDGE'S DECISIONS
(UNITED STATES).=       NAGESS-61-PPA

THE POLITICAL DEVELOPMENT OF
MEXICO.=                NEEDMC-61-PDM

POLITICAL SYSTEMS OF
LATIN AMERICA.=         NEEDMC-64-PSL

POLITICAL DEVELOPMENT AND MILITARY
INTERVENTION IN LATIN AMERICA.=
                        NEEDMC-66-PDM

THE DEMOCRATIC AND THE
AUTHORITARIAN STATE -- ESSAYS IN
POLITICAL AND LEGAL THEORY.=
                        NEUMFL-57-DAS

MODERN POLITICAL PARTIES (WESTERN
EUROPE, JAPAN) SOVIET UNION,
UNITED STATES, EASTERN EUROPE).=

POLITICAL          (CONTINUATION)
                        NEUMS -56-MPP

VILLAGE FACTIONS AND POLITICAL
PARTIES IN RURAL WEST BENGAL
(INDIA).=               NICHRW-63-VFP

AN ANALYSIS OF POLITICAL CONTROL --
ACTUAL AND POTENTIAL.=
                        CPPEFE-58-APC

THE STAGES OF POLITICAL
DEVELOPMENT.=           ORGAAF-65-SPD

DEMOCRACY AND THE ORGANIZATION OF
POLITICAL PARTIES, -- VOL. 1,
GREAT BRITAIN -- VOL 2,
UNITED STATES.=         OSTRM -64-DOP

THE MEXICAN POLITICAL SYSTEM.=
                        PADGLV-66-MPS

LEADERSHIP AND POLITICAL
INSTITUTIONS IN INDIA.=
                        PARKRL-59-LPI

LEGISLATIVE LEADERSHIP AND
POLITICAL IDEOLOGY
(UNITED STATES).=       PATTSC-63-LLP

THE ROLE OF POLITICAL ORGANIZATIONS
IN INDONESIA.=          PAUKGJ-58-RPO

THE SOCIOLOGICAL PERSPECTIVE AND
POLITICAL PLURALISM.=   PERRC -64-SPP

SOCIAL STRUCTURE AND THE POLITICAL
PROCESS IN LATIN AMERICA.=
                        PETERL-63-SSP

POLITICAL EDUCATION IN THE POSTWAR
KOMSOMOL.=              PLOSSI-56-PEP

ALLEGIANCE TO POLITICAL PARTIES --
A STUDY OF THREE PARTIES IN ONE
AREA (GREAT BRITAIN).=
                        PLOWDE-55-APP

COMMUNITY POWER AND POLITICAL
THEORY (UNITED STATES).=
                        POLSNW-63-CPP

ARGENTINE POLITICAL PARTIES --
1957-1958.=             POTAA -59-APP

POLITICAL SOCIALIZATION AND
LEADERSHIP SELECTION
(UNITED STATES).=       PREWK -65-PSL

POLITICAL SOCIALIZATION AND
POLITICAL ROLES (UNITED STATES).=
                        PREWK -67-PSP

POLITICAL SOCIALIZATION AND
POLITICAL ROLES (UNITED STATES).=
                        PREWK -67-PSP

THE NON - WESTERN POLITICAL
PROCESS.=               PYE,LW-58-NWP

PERSONAL IDENTITY AND POLITICAL
IDEOLOGY.=              PYE,LW-61-PIP

ARMIES IN THE PROCESS OF POLITICAL
MODERNIZATION.=         PYE,LW-62-APP

COMMUNICATIONS AND POLITICAL
DEVELOPMENT.=           PYE,LW-63-CPD

POLITICAL CULTURE AND POLITICAL
DEVELOPMENT.=           PYE,LW-66-PCP

POLITICAL CULTURE AND POLITICAL

POLITICAL            (CONTINUATION)
  DEVELOPMENT.=           PYE,LW-66-PCP

THE POLITICAL ROLE OF INDIA'S CASTE
ASSOCIATION.=           RANDLI-60-PRI

POLITICAL LEADERSHIP IN THE
GOVERNOR'S OFFICE
(UNITED STATES).=       RANSCB-64-PLG

CHARISMA AND POLITICAL LEADERSHIP
(GERMANY).=             RATNKJ-64-CPL

THE EFFECTS OF NOMINATING
CONVENTIONS, ELECTIONS, AND
REFERENCE GROUP IDENTIFICATION
UPON THE PERCEPTIONS OF POLITICAL
FIGURES (UNITED STATES).=
                        RAVEBH-64-ENC

THE POLITICAL STRUCTURE OF THE
FEDERAL RESERVE SYSTEM
(UNITED STATES).=       REAGMD-61-PSF

POLITICAL PARTIES AND DECISION
MAKING IN THREE SOUTHERN COUNTIES
(UNITED STATES).=       RHYNEH-58-PPD

EAST AFRICAN CHIEFS -- A STUDY OF
POLITICAL DEVELOPMENT IN SOME
UGANDA AND TANGANYIKA TRIBES.=
                        RICHAI-59-EAC

A STUDY IN POLITICAL APPRENTICESHIP
(GREAT BRITAIN).=       RICHPG-56-SPA

REVIEW, DISSENT AND THE APPELLATE
PROCESS -- A POLITICAL
INTERPRETATION (UNITED STATES).=
                        RICHRJ-67-RDA

POLITICAL DECISIONS IN MODERN
SOCIETY.=               RIEZK -54-PDM

BUREAUCRATS AND POLITICAL
DEVELOPMENT -- A PARADOXICAL
VIEW.=                  RIGGFW-63-BPD

THE THEORY OF POLITICAL
COALITIONS.=            RIKEWH-62-TPC

POLITICAL EXTREMISTS IN IRAN -- A
SECONDARY ANALYSIS OF
COMMUNICATIONS DATA.=   RINGBB-52-PEI

POLITICAL SCIENCE AND SCIENCE
FICTION (UNITED STATES,
JUDICIARY).=            ROCHJP-58-PSS

THE POWER STRUCTURE -- POLITICAL
PROCESS IN AMERICAN SOCIETY.=
                        ROSEAM-67-PSP

THE POLITICAL IDEAS OF ENGLISH
PARTY ACTIVISTS.=       ROSER -62-PIE

ENGLAND -- A TRADITIONALLY MODERN
POLITICAL CULTURE.=     ROSER -66-ETM

STUDIES IN BRITISH POLITICS
                -- A READER IN
POLITICAL SOCIOLOGY.=   ROSER -66-SBP

POLITICAL PARTIES AND SOCIAL
CLASSES IN ISRAEL.=     ROSHM -56-PPS

THE WEST GERMAN POLITICAL PARTIES
AND REARMAMENT.=        RS    -53-WGP

POLITICAL SUCCESSION IN THE USSR.=
                        RUSHM -65-PSU

A WORLD OF NATIONS -- PROBLEMS OF

POLITICAL            (CONTINUATION)
  POLITICAL MODERNIZATION (ASIA,
  AFRICA, LATIN AMERICA).=
                        RUSTDA-67-WNP

PSYCHOPATHOLOGY, DECISION-MAKING,
AND POLITICAL INVOLVEMENT
(UNITED STATES).=       RUTHBM-66-PDM

EGYPT IN SEARCH OF POLITICAL
COMMUNITY -- AN ANALYSIS OF THE
INTELLECTUAL AND POLITICAL
EVOLUTION OF EGYPT -- 1804-1952.=
                        SAFRN -61-ESP

EGYPT IN SEARCH OF POLITICAL
COMMUNITY -- AN ANALYSIS OF THE
INTELLECTUAL AND POLITICAL
EVOLUTION OF EGYPT -- 1804-1952.=
                        SAFRN -61-ESP

POOR MAN, RICH MAN, BIG-MAN, CHIEF
-- POLITICAL TYPES IN MELANESIA
AND POLYNESIA.=         SAHLMD-63-PMR

THE DEMOCRATIC STATE CENTRAL
COMMITTEE IN MICHIGAN 1949-1959 --
THE RISE OF THE NEW POLITICS AND
THE NEW POLITICAL LEADERSHIP
(UNITED STATES).=       SAWYRL-60-DSC

THE POLITICAL ROLE OF PAKISTAN'S
CIVIL SERVICE.=         SAYEKB-58-PRP

POLITICAL FORCES IN YUGOSLAVIA
TODAY.=                 SC    -46-PFY

POLITICAL CHANGE IN A TRADITIONAL
AFRICAN CLAN -- A STRUCTURAL
FUNCTIONAL ANALYSIS OF THE NSITS
OF NIGERIA.=            SCARJR-65-PCT

THE ADOPTION OF POLITICAL STYLES BY
AFRICAN POLITICIANS IN THE
RHODESIAS.=             SCARJR-66-APS

THE ORIGIN OF THE COMMUNIST
AUTOCRACY -- POLITICAL OPPOSITION
IN THE SOVIET STATE, 1917-1922.=
                        SCHALB-55-OCA

LAW AND POLITICS IN THE SUPREME
COURT -- NEW APPROACHES TO
POLITICAL JURISPRUDENCE
(UNITED STATES).=       SCHAM -64-LPS

POLITICAL PARTY ORGANIZATION.=
                        SCHLJA-65-PPO

AMBITION AND POLITICS -- POLITICAL
CAREERS IN THE UNITED STATES.=
                        SCHLJA-66-APP

POLITICAL CAREERS AND PARTY
LEADERSHIP (AUSTRALIA, CANADA,
FRANCE, GREAT BRITAIN,
UNITED STATES).=        SCHLJA-67-PCP

BUREAUCRATIC PARTY ORGANIZATION
THROUGH PROFESSIONAL POLITICAL
STAFFING (UNITED STATES).=
                        SCHUCE-64-BPC

JUDGES AND POLITICAL LEADERSHIP
(AUSTRALIA, JAPAN, PHILIPPINES,
UNITED STATES).=        SCHUG -67-JPL

THE STUDY OF JUDICIAL
DECISION-MAKING AS AN ASPECT OF
POLITICAL BEHAVIOR
(UNITED STATES).=       SCHUGA-58-SJD

POLITICAL PARTIES IN SOUTH VIETNAM

POLITICAL          (CONTINUATION)
  UNDER THE REPUBLIC.=   SCIGRC-6C-PPS

  POLITICAL MONEY -- A STUDY OF
  CONTRIBUTORS TO THE NATIONAL
  COMMITTEE FOR AN EFFECTIVE
  CONGRESS (UNITED STATES).=
                          SCOBHM-63-PMS

  POLITICAL ELITES AND POLITICAL
  MODERNIZATION -- THE CRISIS OF
  TRANSITION (LATIN AMERICA).=
                          SCOTRE-67-PEP

  POLITICAL ELITES AND POLITICAL
  MODERNIZATION -- THE CRISIS OF
  TRANSITION (LATIN AMERICA).=
                          SCOTRE-67-PEP

  THE STUDY OF POLITICAL LEADERSHIP.=
                          SELILG-50-SPL

  DEVELOPMENTS IN THE PRESIDENCY AND
  THE CONCEPTION OF POLITICAL
  LEADERSHIP (UNITED STATES).=
                          SELILG-55-DPC

  POLITICAL RECRUITMENT AND PARTY
  STRUCTURE -- A CASE STUDY
  (UNITED STATES).=       SELILG-61-PRP

  ELITE RECRUITMENT AND POLITICAL
  DEVELOPMENT.=           SELILG-64-ERP

  LEADERSHIP IN A NEW NATION --
  POLITICAL DEVELOPMENT IN ISRAEL.=
                          SELILG-64-LNN

  POLITICAL CHANGE -- LEGISLATIVE
  ELITES AND PARTIES IN OREGON
  (UNITED STATES).=       SELILG-64-PCL

  POLITICAL PARTIES AND THE
  RECRUITMENT OF POLITICAL
  LEADERSHIP.=            SELILG-67-PPR

  POLITICAL PARTIES AND THE
  RECRUITMENT OF POLITICAL
  LEADERSHIP.=            SELILG-67-PPR

  CASTE AND POLITICAL PROCESS
  (INDIA).=               SHAHCJ-66-CPP

  THE STUDY OF POLITICAL LEADERSHIP.=
                          SHANJB-49-SPL

  INTERNATIONAL BUREAUCRACIES AND
  POLITICAL DEVELOPMENT.=
                          SHARWR-63-IBP

  INTERGROUP RELATIONS AND LEADERSHIP
  -- APPROACHES AND RESEARCH IN
  INDUSTRIAL, ETHNIC, CULTURAL, AND
  POLITICAL AREAS.=       SHERM -62-IRL

  THE INTELLECTUAL IN THE POLITICAL
  DEVELOPMENT OF THE NEW STATES.=
                          SHILE -60-IPC

  POLITICAL DEVELOPMENT IN THE NEW
  STATES -- 1 -- 2.=      SHILE -60-PDN

  INFLUENCE AND WITHDRAWAL -- THE
  INTELLECTUALS IN INDIAN POLITICAL
  DEVELOPMENT.=           SHILE -61-IWI

  THE MILITARY IN THE POLITICAL
  DEVELOPMENT OF THE NEW STATES.=
                          SHILE -62-MPD

  DEMAGOGUES AND CADRES IN THE
  POLITICAL DEVELOPMENT OF THE NEW

POLITICAL          (CONTINUATION)
  STATES.=                SHILE -63-DCP

  NOTES ON THE OBSERVATION AND
  MEASUREMENT OF POLITICAL POWER.=
                          SIMOHA-53-NOM

  POLITICAL PARTIES IN THE
  UNITED STATES.=         SINDAP-66-PPU

  THE EMERGING ELITE -- A STUDY OF
  POLITICAL LEADERSHIP IN CEYLON.=
                          SINGMR-64-EES

  NIGERIAN POLITICAL PARTIES -- POWER
  IN AN EMERGENT AFRICAN NATION.=
                          SKLARL-63-NPP

  CONTRADICTIONS IN THE NIGERIAN
  POLITICAL SYSTEM.=      SKLARL-65-CNP

  POLITICAL LEADERSHIP IN A NEW
  ENGLAND COMMUNITY
  (UNITED STATES).=       SMITL -55-PLN

  HISTORICAL AND CULTURAL CONDITIONS
  OF POLITICAL CORRUPTION AMONG THE
  HAUSA (NORTHERN NIGERIA).=
                          SMITMG-64-HCC

  LEADERSHIP AND PARTICIPATION IN
  URBAN POLITICAL AFFAIRS
  (UNITED STATES).=       SMUCRH-56-LPU

  AFRICA'S NEW POLITICAL LEADERS.=
                          SMYTHH-59-ASN

  POLITICAL POWER AND THE ABILITY TO
  WIN SUPREME COURT DECISIONS
  (UNITED STATES).=       SNYDEC-60-PPA

  SOCIAL POSITIONS AND IMAGES OF THE
  POLITICAL PROCESS.=     SNYDRC-57-SPI

  A DECISION-MAKING APPROACH TO THE
  STUDY OF POLITICAL PHENOMENA.=
                          SNYDRC-58-DMA

  INTELLECTUAL IDENTITY AND POLITICAL
  IDEOLOGY AMONG UNIVERSITY STUDENTS
  (LATIN AMERICA).=       SOARGA-67-IIP

  POLITICAL PARTIES IN THE AMERICAN
  SYSTEM.=                SORAFJ-64-PPA

  INTERNATIONAL POLITICAL
  COMMUNICATION -- ELITE VS. MASS.=
                          SPEIH -52-IPC

  GERMAN REARMAMENT AND ATOMIC WAR --
  THE VIEWS OF GERMAN MILITARY AND
  POLITICAL LEADERS.=     SPEIH -57-GRA

  POLITICAL EVOLUTION IN THE
  MIDDLE EAST.=           SPENW -62-PEM

  POSTWAR POLITICAL PARTIES IN
  JAPAN.=                 SPINCN-46-PPP

  THE POLITICAL BUREAU OF THE UNITED
  POLISH WORKERS PARTY.=
                          STAARF-56-PBU

  MEN WHO GOVERN -- A BIOGRAPHICAL
  PROFILE OF FEDERAL POLITICAL
  EXECUTIVES (UNITED STATES).=
                          STAN  -67-MWG

  THE FUTURE OF UNDER-DEVELOPED
  COUNTRIES -- POLITICAL
  IMPLICATIONS OF ECONOMIC
  DEVELOPMENT.=           STANE -54-FUD

POLITICS (CONTINUATION)
CARNFM-64-CPL

THE GOVERNMENT AND POLITICS OF
CHINA.= CH'IT--50-GPC

POLITICS AND ADMINISTRATION.=
CHAPB -58-PA

CAPITAL PUNISHMENT AND BRITISH
POLITICS.= CHRIJB-62-CPB

GROUP INTERESTS IN CANADIAN
POLITICS.= CLARSD-63-GIC

RACE AND POLITICS -- PARTNERSHIP IN
THE FEDERATION OF RHODESIA
NYASALAND.= CLEGE -60-RPP

ARMS AND POLITICS IN PAKISTAN.=
COHESP-64-APP

THE LEFT WING IN JAPANESE
POLITICS.= COLBES-52-LWJ

JAPANESE SOCIETY AND POLITICS --
THE IMPACT OF SOCIAL
STRATIFICATION AND MOBILITY ON
POLITICS.= COLEAB-56-JSP

JAPANESE SOCIETY AND POLITICS --
THE IMPACT OF SOCIAL
STRATIFICATION AND MOBILITY ON
POLITICS.= COLEAB-56-JSP

THE POLITICS OF SUB-SAHARA AFRICA.=
COLEJS-60-PSS

POLITICS WITHOUT POWER -- THE
NATIONAL PARTY COMMITTEES
(UNITED STATES).= COTTCP-64-PWP

THE POLITICS OF THE PRUSSIAN ARMY
1640-1945.= CRAIGA-55-PPA

MILITANT HINDUISM IN INDIAN
POLITICS -- A STUDY OF THE R.S.S.
(RASHTRIYA SWAYAMSEVAK SANGH).=
CURRJA-51-MHI

URBANIZATION AND COMPETITIVE PARTY
POLITICS (UNITED STATES).=
CUTRP -63-UCP

PARTIES AND POLITICS IN THE
NETHERLANDS.= DAALH -55-PPN

POLITICS, ECONOMICS, AND WELFARE
(UNITED STATES).= DAHLRA-53-PEW

HIERARCHY, BARGAINING, AND
DEMOCRACY IN POLITICS AND
ECONOMICS (UNITED STATES).=
DAHLRA-55-HBD

CONFLICT AND LIBERTY -- SOME
REMARKS ON THE SOCIAL STRUCTURE OF
GERMAN POLITICS.= DAHRR -63-CLR

PRESIDENTIAL NOMINATING POLITICS IN
1952 (UNITED STATES).=
DAVIPT-54-PNP

HOW DECISIONS ARE MADE IN FOREIGN
POLITICS -- PSYCHOLOGY IN
INTERNATIONAL RELATIONS.=
DE BBO-58-HDA

SOME QUANTITATIVE CONSTRAINTS ON
VALUE ALLOCATION IN SOCIETY AND
POLITICS.= DEUTKW-66-QCV

FRANCE, GERMANY, AND THE WESTERN

POLITICS (CONTINUATION)
ALLIANCE -- A STUDY OF ELITE
ATTITUDES ON EUROPEAN INTEGRATION
AND WORLD POLITICS.= DEUTKW-67-FGW

THE GROUP BASIS OF AUSTRIAN
POLITICS.= DIAMA -58-GBA

THE FRENCH ARMY IN POLITICS.=
DOMEJM-61-FAP

COMMUNIST CHINA -- THE POLITICS OF
STUDENT OPPOSITION.= DOOLCJ-64-CCP

SCIENCE AND THE NATION -- POLICY
AND POLITICS (UNITED STATES).=
DUPRJS-62-SNP

STATE LEGISLATIVE POLITICS
(UNITED STATES).= DYE,TR-65-SLP

THE POLITICS OF THE BRITISH MEDICAL
ASSOCIATION.= ECKSHH-55-PBM

PRESSURE GROUP POLITICS -- THE CASE
OF THE BRITISH MEDICAL
ASSOCIATION.= ECKSHH-60-PGP

LATIN AMERICAN GOVERNMENT AND
POLITICS.= EDELAT-65-LAG

THE SYMBOLIC USES OF POLITICS.=
EDELM -64-SUP

GERMAN EXILE POLITICS -- THE SOCIAL
DEMOCRATIC EXECUTIVE COMMITTEE IN
THE NAZI ERA.= EDINLJ-56-GEP

POLITICS IN AN URBAN AFRICAN
COMMUNITY.= EPSTAL-58-PUA

POLITICS IN WISCONSIN
(UNITED STATES).= EPSTLD-58-PWU

NEW M.P.S AND THE POLITICS OF THE
PLP (PARLIAMENTARY LABOUR PARTY,
GREAT BRITAIN).= EPSTLD-62-NMP

BRITISH POLITICS IN THE SUEZ
CRISIS.= EPSTLD-64-BPS

LAWYERS IN POLITICS -- A STUDY IN
PROFESSIONAL CONVERGENCE
(UNITED STATES).= EULAH -64-LPS

THE POWER OF THE PURSE --
APPROPRIATIONS POLITICS IN
CONGRESS (UNITED STATES).=
FENNRF-66-PPA

THE MAN ON HORSEBACK -- THE ROLE OF
THE MILITARY IN POLITICS.=
FINESE-62-MHR

POLITICS AND PARTIES IN CANADA.=
FOX,PW-59-PPC

THE BUREAUCRACY IN PRESSURE
POLITICS (UNITED STATES).=
FREEJL-58-BPP

THE ITALIAN PREFECTS -- A STUDY IN
ADMINISTRATIVE POLITICS.=
FRIERC-63-IPS

STABILITY AND CHANGE IN LOCAL PARTY
POLITICS (UNITED STATES).=
FROSRT-61-SCL

REPUTATION AND RESOURCES IN
COMMUNITY POLITICS
(UNITED STATES).= GAINWA-66-RRC

POLITICS                (CONTINUATION)
  REPUTATION AND RESOURCES IN
  COMMUNITY POLITICS.=    GAMSWA-66-RRC

  THE ROLE OF THE MILITARY IN RECENT
  SOVIET POLITICS.=       GARTRL-57-RMR

  POLITICS, SOCIAL STRUCTURE, AND
  MILITARY INTERVENTION IN
  LATIN AMERICA.=         GERMG -62-PSS

  NATIONAL POLITICAL ALIGNMENTS AND
  THE POLITICS OF LARGE CITIES
  (UNITED STATES).=       GILBCE-64-NPA

  MACHINE POLITICS IN AMERICAN TRADE
  UNIONS.=                GITLAL-52-MPA

  DOCTORS AND POLITICS
  (UNITED STATES).=       GLASWA-60-DPU

  POLITICS, LAW AND RITUAL IN TRIBAL
  SOCIETY.=               GLUCM -65-PLR

  LAWYERS IN POLITICS -- AN EMPIRICAL
  EXPLORATION OF BIOGRAPHICAL DATA
  ON STATE LEGISLATORS.=
                          GOLDD -61-LPE

  GOVERNMENT AND POLITICS OF
  LATIN AMERICA.=         GOMERA-60-GPL

  PROFESSORS AND POLITICS
  (UNITED STATES).=       GOTTA -61-PPU

  THE ECONOMIC AND SOCIAL COUNCIL --
  POLITICS OF MEMBERSHIP
  (UNITED NATIONS, EUROPE).=
                          GREGRW-63-ESC

  LAWYERS AND JUDGES -- THE ABA AND
  THE POLITICS OF JUDICIAL SELECTION
  (UNITED STATES).=       GROSJB-65-LJA

  MOSLEMS IN INDIAN POLITICS,
  1947-1960.=             GUPTSK-62-MIP

  MASS SOCIETY AND EXTREMIST
  POLITICS.=              GUSFJR-62-MSE

  SOME OBSERVATIONS ON POLITICS AND
  PARTIES IN ISRAEL.=     GUTMEE-61-CPP

  GOVERNMENT, POLITICS, AND SOCIAL
  STRUCTURE IN LAOS -- A STUDY OF
  TRADITION AND INNOVATION.=
                          HALPJM-64-GPS

  RACE, SOCIAL MOBILITY AND POLITICS
  IN BRAZIL.=             HAMMHR-63-RSM

  FOREIGN POLICY-MAKING AND
  ADMINISTRATIVE POLITICS
  (UNITED STATES).=       HAMMPY-65-FPM

  THE INTELLECTUALS - POLITICS NEXUS
  -- STUDIES USING A BIOGRAPHICAL
  TECHNIQUE (BULGARIA,
  SOVIET UNION).=         HANHAM-64-IPN

  FROM BOSSES TO COSMOPOLITANISM --
  CHANGES IN THE RELATIONSHIP OF
  URBAN LEADERSHIP TO STATE POLITICS
  (UNITED STATES).=       HAVAWC-64-BCC

  SUCCESSION AND PARTY POLITICS IN
  WEST GERMANY.=          HEINAJ-64-SPP

  POLITICS, POWER AND CONFUSION
  (UNITED STATES, POWER ELITE
  REVIEW).=               HERMFA-56-PPC

  CONFESSIONALISM AND FEUDALITY IN

POLITICS                (CONTINUATION)
  LEBANESE POLITICS.=     HESSCG-54-CFL

  INTRA - PARTY POLITICS AND ECONOMIC
  POLICY IN COMMUNIST CHINA.=
                          HINTHC-60-IPP

  REVOLUTION IN BRAZIL -- POLITICS
  AND SOCIETY IN A DEVELOPING
  NATION.=                HOROIL-64-RBP

  THE NEW ITALY AND ITS POLITICS.=
                          HUGHHS-64-NII

  THE SOLDIER AND THE STATE -- THE
  THEORY AND POLITICS OF CIVIL -
  MILITARY RELATIONS
  (UNITED STATES).=       HUNTSP-57-SST

  CHANGING PATTERNS OF MILITARY
  POLITICS.=              HUNTSP-62-CPM

  PATTERNS OF VIOLENCE IN WORLD
  POLITICS.=              HUNTSP-62-PVW

  THE POLITICS OF THE EUROPEAN
  COMMUNIST STATES (BULGARIA,
  CZECHOSLOVAKIA, HUNGARY, EAST
  GERMANY, POLAND, RUMANIA,
  SOVIET UNION, YUGOSLAVIA).=
                          IONEG -67-PEC

  EDUCATION, VALUES AND POLITICS IN
  JAPAN.=                 JANSMB-57-EVP

  STUDENTS IN WORLD POLITICS.=
                          JCC   -51-SWP

  THE BALKANS IN TRANSITION -- ESSAYS
  ON THE DEVELOPMENT OF BALKAN LIFE
  AND POLITICS SINCE THE EIGHTEENTH
  CENTURY.=               JELAC -63-BTE

  POLITICS IN CEYLON SINCE 1952.=
                          JENNWI-54-PCS

  THE POLITICS OF REAPPORTIONMENT
  (UNITED STATES).=       JEWEME-62-PR

  SENATORIAL POLITICS AND FOREIGN
  POLICY (UNITED STATES).=
                          JEWEME-62-SPF

  STATE LEGISLATURES IN SOUTHERN
  POLITICS (UNITED STATES).=
                          JEWEME-64-SLS

  THE REGIME AND THE INTELLECTUALS --
  A WINDOW ON PARTY POLITICS
  (SOVIET UNION).=        JOHNP -63-RIW

  ELECTION POLITICS AND SOCIAL CHANGE
  IN ISRAEL.=             JOHNSD-62-EPS

  INTELLECTUALS AND GERMAN POLITICS.=
                          JOLLJ -54-IGP

  THE REPUBLICAN PARTY IN AMERICAN
  POLITICS.=              JONECO-65-RPA

  MANDARIN BUREAUCRACY AND POLITICS
  IN SOUTH VIETNAM.=      JUMPR -57-MBP

  URBAN RENEWAL POLITICS -- SLUM
  CLEARANCE IN NEWARK
  (UNITED STATES).=       KAPLH -63-URP

  TURKEY'S POLITICS -- THE TRANSITION
  TO MULTI - PARTY SYSTEM.=
                          KARPKH-59-TSP

  SOCIETY, ECONOMICS, AND POLITICS IN

CONTEMPORARY TURKEY.= KARPKH-64-SEP

THE FRENCH ARMY RE-ENTERS POLITICS
1940-1955.= KELLGA-61-FAR

POLITICS, PARTIES AND PRESSURE
GROUPS (UNITED STATES).=
KEY-VO-64-PPP

THE ROLE OF THE MILITARY IN
MIDDLE EAST POLITICS.=
KHADM -53-RMM

AUTHORITARIAN AND SINGLE - PARTY
TENDENCIES IN AFRICAN POLITICS.=
KILSML-63-ASP

THE CONCEPT OF POLITICAL CULTURE IN
COMPARATIVE POLITICS.=
KIM,YC-64-CPC

BRITISH POLITICS -- PEOPLE,
PARTIES, AND PARLIAMENT.=
KINGA -66-BPP

THE POLITICS OF MASS SOCIETY.=
KORNW -59-PMS

THE POLITICS OF BRITAIN'S ANGRY
YOUNG MEN.= KROLM -61-PBS

AN AFRICAN BOURGEOISIE -- RACE,
CLASS, AND POLITICS IN SOUTH
AFRICA.= KUPEL -65-ABR

THE PRESS IN WORLD POLITICS AND IN
THE CONDUCT OF FOREIGN POLICY
(GREAT BRITAIN, LATIN AMERICA,
SOVIET UNION, UNITED STATES).=
KYOIS -65-PWP

LABOR'S ROLE IN AMERICAN POLITICS.=
LAIDHW-59-LSR

THE POLITICS OF SOVIET
AGRICULTURE.= LAIRRD-64-PSA

HINDU COMMUNAL GROUPS IN INDIAN
POLITICS.= LAMBRD-59-HCG

LEADERS, FACTIONS AND PARTIES --
THE STRUCTURE OF PHILIPPINE
POLITICS.= LANDCH-65-LFP

INTEREST GROUPS IN ITALIAN
POLITICS.= LAPAJ -64-IGI

PSYCHOPATHOLOGY AND POLITICS.=
LASSHD-30-PP

POLITICS -- WHO GETS WHAT, WHEN,
HOW (UNITED STATES).= LASSHD-36-PWG

THE GROUP BASIS OF POLITICS --
NOTES FOR A THEORY.= LATHE -52-GBP

THE PLACE OF PARTIES IN THE STUDY
OF POLITICS.= LEISA -57-PPS

PARTIES AND POLITICS
(UNITED STATES).= LEISA -58-PPU

ON THE GAME OF POLITICS IN FRANCE.=
LEITN -59-GPF

POLITICAL AWAKENING IN THE BELGIAN
CONGO -- THE POLITICS OF
FRAGMENTATION.= LEMAR -64-PAB

POLITICS IN WEST AFRICA.=
LEWIWA-65-PWA

THE POLITICS OF TRADE UNION

LEADERSHIP IN SOUTHERN ASIA.=
LICHGE-54-PTU

ARMS AND POLITICS IN
LATIN AMERICA.= LIEUE -61-APL

MILITARISM AND POLITICS IN
LATIN AMERICA.= LIEUE -62-MPL

LOCAL POLITICS AND LEADERSHIP IN
EUROPEAN DEMOCRACIES.=
LINZJ -57-LPL

THE POLITICS OF EQUALITY --
NEW ZEALAND'S ADVENTURES IN
DEMOCRACY.= LIPSL -48-PEN

THE TWO - PARTY SYSTEM IN BRITISH
POLITICS.= LIPSL -53-TPS

UNION DEMOCRACY -- THE INSIDE
POLITICS OF THE INTERNATIONAL
TYPOGRAPHICAL UNION (NORTH
AMERICA).= LIPSSM-56-UDI

AMERICAN INTELLECTUALS -- THEIR
POLITICS AND STATUS.= LIPSSM-59-AIT

POLITICAL MAN -- THE SOCIAL BASES
OF POLITICS.= LIPSSM-60-PMS

STUDENT POLITICS (LATIN AMERICA,
INDIA, POLAND, UNITED STATES,
GERMANY, CHILE, ARGENTINA,
COLUMBIA, FRANCE).= LIPSSM-67-SPL

CHIEFS AND POLITICS (AFRICA).=
LOVEAJ-59-CPA

LITERARY POLITICS IN THE SOVIET
UKRAINE, 1917-1934.= LUCKGS-56-LPS

CO-OPERATIVE POLITICS IN A
LANCASHIRE CONSTITUENCY
(GREAT BRITAIN).= MACKWJ-54-COP

POLITICS OF CHANGE IN
LATIN AMERICA.= MAIEJ -64-PCL

GOVERNMENT AND POLITICS IN JAPAN --
THE ROAD TO DEMOCRACY.=
MAKIJM-62-GPJ

GROUP INTERESTS IN PAKISTAN
POLITICS, 1947-1958.= MANIT -66-GIP

THOUGHT AND BEHAVIOUR IN MODERN
JAPANESE POLITICS.= MARHM -63-TBM

INTEREST GROUPS AND CONSERVATIVE
POLITICS (UNITED STATES).=
MARTCW-63-IGC

THE DYNAMICS OF CHANGE IN
LATIN AMERICAN POLITICS.=
MARTJ -65-DCL

AUSTRALIAN POLITICS -- A READER.=
MAYEH -66-APR

CONSENSUS AND IDEOLOGY IN AMERICAN
POLITICS.= MCCLH -64-CIA

THE POLITICS OF SOVIET CULTURE,
1964-1967.= MCCLT -67-PSC

POLITICS -- A STUDY OF CONTROL
BEHAVIOR (UNITED STATES).=
MCDONA-65-PSC

CHALLENGE TO THE 'NEW ERA' IN

POLITICS (CONTINUATION)
IN SOCIAL MANIPULATION AMONG THE
LAKESIDE TONGA OF NYASALAND.=
VELSJV-64-PKS

RELIGIOUS BROTHERHOODS IN MOROCCAN
POLITICS.= VIDAFS-50-RBM

JUDICIAL REVIEW AND POLITICS IN
AUSTRALIA.= VILEMJ-57-JRP

PRESSURE POLITICS (GREAT BRITAIN).=
WALLI -62-PPG

FIVE STUDIES IN JAPANESE POLITICS.=
WARDFE-57-FSJ

STUDENT POLITICS IN LATIN AMERICA
-- THE VENEZUELAN EXAMPLE.=
WASHSW-59-SPL

MARGINAL POLITICS AND ELITE
MANIPULATION IN MOROCCO.=
WATEJ -67-MPE

BAR OF POLITICS, JUDICIAL SELECTION
AND THE REPRESENTATION OF SOCIAL
INTERESTS (UNITED STATES).=
WATSRA-67-BPJ

EDUCATION AND POLITICS IN NIGERIA.=
WEILHN-64-EPN

PARTY POLITICS IN INDIA -- THE
DEVELOPMENT OF A MULTIPARTY
SYSTEM.= WEINM -57-PPI

SOME HYPOTHESES ON THE POLITICS OF
MODERNIZATION IN INDIA.=
WEINM -59-HPM

THE POLITICS OF SOUTH ASIA.=
WEINM -60-PSA

THE POLITICS OF SCARCITY -- PUBLIC
PRESSURE AND POLITICAL RESPONSE IN
INDIA.= WEINM -62-PSP

IDEOLOGY AND LEADERSHIP IN
PUERTO RICAN POLITICS.=
WELLH -55-ILP

ELECTIONS AND POLITICS IN IRAN.=
WESTAF-61-EPI

THE USES OF POWER -- 7 CASES IN
AMERICAN POLITICS.= WESTAF-62-UPC

POLITICS OF DISTRUST IN IRAN.=
WESTAF-65-PDI

FOREIGN POLICY AND PARTY POLITICS
-- PEARL HARBOR TO KOREA
(UNITED STATES).= WESTHB-55-FPP

THE NEMESIS OF POWER -- THE GERMAN
ARMY IN POLITICS 1918-1945.=
WHEEJW-54-NPG

THE POLITICS OF CIVIL - MILITARY
RELATIONS IN THE
DOMINICAN REPUBLIC.= WIARFJ-65-PCM

POLITICS AND SOCIAL CHANGE --
POLAND.= WIATJJ-66-PSC

PARTY POLITICS IN THE IOWA
LEGISLATURE (UNITED STATES).=
WIGGCW-67-PPI

THE POLITICS OF THE BUDGETARY
PROCESS (UNITED STATES).=

POLITICS (CONTINUATION)
WILDA -64-PBP

CRISIS AND COMPROMISE -- POLITICS
IN THE FOURTH REPUBLIC.=
WILLPM-64-CCP

THE TAMIL FEDERAL PARTY IN CEYLON
POLITICS.= WILSAJ-66-TFP

THE MILITARY IN THAI POLITICS.=
WILSDA-62-MTP

NEGRO POLITICS -- THE SEARCH FOR
LEADERSHIP.= WILSJQ-60-NPS

THE AMATEUR DEMOCRAT -- CLUB
POLITICS IN THREE CITIES
(UNITED STATES).= WILSJQ-62-ADC

CHIEFSHIP AND POLITICS IN THE
MLANJE DISTRICT OF SOUTHERN
NYASALAND.= WISHRL-61-CPM

AMERICA'S RADICAL RIGHT -- POLITICS
AND IDEOLOGY.= WOLFRE-64-ASR

EX - SERVICEMEN IN POLITICS
(GREAT BRITAIN).= WOOTG -58-ESP

THE ROLE OF THE MILITARY IN
LATIN AMERICAN POLITICS.=
WYCKT -60-RML

JAPANESE PEOPLE AND POLITICS.=
YANAC -56-JPP

PARTY FACTIONS AND COMPARATIVE
POLITICS -- SOME PRELIMINARY
OBSERVATIONS.= ZARIR -60-PFC

YOUTH AND POLITICS IN THE NEAR
EAST.= ZNZ -51-YPN

POLITIES
INTERNAL CONTRADICTIONS IN
BUREAUCRATIC POLITIES (ANCIENT
CHINA, PERSIA).= EISESN-58-ICB

POLITIZATION
POLITICAL CONFLICT POTENTIAL,
POLITIZATION, AND THE PEASANTRY IN
THE UNDERDEVELOPED COUNTRIES.=
HINDD -65-PCP

POLITY
POLITY, BUREAUCRACY AND INTEREST
GROUPS IN THE NEAR EAST AND NORTH
AFRICA.= GRASG -64-PBI

THE AMERICAN POLITY -- A SOCIAL AND
CULTURAL INTERPRETATION.=
MITCWC-62-APS

THAILAND -- THE MODERNIZATION OF A
BUREAUCRATIC POLITY.= RIGGFW-66-TMB

POLL
A SOCIO-ECONOMIC OPINION POLL IN
BEIRUT, LEBANON.= ARMSL -59-SEO

POLLS
PUBLIC OPINION POLLS AND DEMOCRATIC
LEADERSHIP (UNITED STATES).=
CARTD -46-POP

POLLSTERS
THE POLLSTERS -- PUBLIC OPINION,
POLITICS, AND DEMOCRATIC
LEADERSHIP (UNITED STATES).=
ROGEL -49-PPC

POLYARCHIES
ELITES AND POLYARCHIES.=

POLYARCHIES          (CONTINUATION)
                     PARRG -66-EP

POLYNESIA
  STATUS RIVALRY AND CULTURAL
  EVOLUTION IN POLYNESIA.=
                     GOLDI -55-SRC

  REPRESENTATIONAL ROLE TYPES -- A
  RESEARCH NOTE (MICRONESIA,
  POLYNESIA).=        MELLN -67-RRT

  SOCIAL STRATIFICATION IN
  POLYNESIA.=         SAHLMD-58-SSP

  POOR MAN, RICH MAN, BIG-MAN, CHIEF
  -- POLITICAL TYPES IN MELANESIA
  AND POLYNESIA.=     SAHLMD-63-PMR

POPULAIRE
  THE MRP (MOVEMENT REPUBLICAN
  POPULAIRE) AND FRENCH FOREIGN
  POLICY.=            CAPERB-63-MMR

  POWER, PRINCIPLE, AND THE DOCTRINE
  OF THE MOUVEMENT REPUBLICAIN
  POPULAIRE (FRANCE).= YATEWR-58-PPD

POPULAR
  LEBANON'S POPULAR REVOLUTION.=
                     PRITG -53-LSP

  THE FRENCH POPULAR FRONT.=
                     BURBLB-51-FPF

  POPULAR IMAGES OF DECISION-MAKING
  IN SUBURBAN COMMUNITIES
  (UNITED STATES).=   DYE,TR-62-PID

  POPULAR LEADERSHIP IN THE ANGLO -
  AMERICAN DEMOCRACIES (CANADA,
  GREAT BRITAIN, UNITED STATES).=
                     HARGEC-67-PLA

  POPULAR PARTICIPATION -- MYTHS AND
  REALITY (SOVIET UNION).=
                     SWEAHR-60-PPM

POPULATION
  THE STUDENT POPULATION OF A
  SOUTHEAST ASIAN UNIVERSITY -- AN
  INDONESIAN EXAMPLE.= FISCJ -61-SPS

  THE SOCIAL BACKGROUND OF A WEST
  AFRICAN STUDENT POPULATION -- 1 --
  2.=                 JAHOG -54-SBW

  KAZAKHSTAN -- CHANGES IN
  ADMINISTRATIVE STATUS AND THE
  NATIONAL COMPOSITION OF THE
  POPULATION (SOVIET UNION).=
                     TASKGA-64-KCA

PORK
  THE PORK BARREL SYSTEM
  (PHILIPPINES).=     ROXAGM-63-PBS

PORTENTS
  TERROR IN THE SOVIET SYSTEM --
  TRENDS AND PORTENTS.= LEONW -58-TSS

  THE BRITISH LABOR PARTY --
  PROSPECTS AND PORTENTS.=
                     ROWSAL-45-BLP

PORTER
  ON JOHN PORTER'S 'BUREAUCRATIC
  ELITE IN CANADA'.=  ROWADC-59-JPS

PORTRAIT
  TOWARD A PORTRAIT OF THE FRENCH
  INTELLECTUAL.=      BROMV -60-TPF

PORTRAIT          (CONTINUATION)
  THE INTELLECTUALS -- A
  CONTROVERSIAL PORTRAIT.=
                     DE HFU-60-ICP

  URUGUAY -- PORTRAIT OF A
  DEMOCRACY.=         FITZR -54-UPD

  PORTRAIT OF A MINORITY -- ASIANS IN
  EAST AFRICA.=       GHAIDP-65-PMA

  THE PROFESSIONAL SOLDIER -- A
  SOCIAL AND POLITICAL PORTRAIT
  (UNITED STATES).=   JANOM -60-PSS

  UNITED STATES SENATOR -- A
  COLLECTIVE PORTRAIT.= MATTDR-61-USS

  PORTRAIT OF THE BURMESE
  PARLIAMENT.=        MAUNM -57-PBP

  THE AMERICAN BUSINESS ELITE -- A
  COLLECTIVE PORTRAIT.= MILLCW-54-ABE

  THE JUSTICES OF THE SUPREME COURT
  -- A COLLECTIVE PORTRAIT
  (UNITED STATES).=   SCHMJR-59-JSC

PORTUGAL
  FREEDOM AND CATHOLIC POWER IN SPAIN
  AND PORTUGAL.=      BLANP -62-FCP

  THE PRESS IN LATIN AMERICA, SPAIN
  AND PORTUGAL -- A SUMMARY OF
  RECENT DEVELOPMENTS.= CHILRH-65-PLA

POSITION
  POSITION, ROLE AND STATUS -- A
  REFORMULATION OF CONCEPTS.=
                     BATEFL-56-PRS

  THE POSITION OF THE CHIEF IN THE
  MODERN POLITICAL SYSTEM OF ASHANTI
  (GOLD COAST).=      BUSIKA-51-PCM

  NATIONS, COLONIES AND SOCIAL
  CLASSES -- THE POSITION OF MARX
  AND ENGELS.=        DAVIHB-65-NCS

  THE POSITION OF PARLIAMENT IN THE
  FOURTH FRENCH REPUBLIC.=
                     LIDDCW-47-PPF

  SOVIET HISTORICAL SCIENCE AND THE
  POSITION OF SOVIET HISTORIANS.=
                     URBAP -64-SHS

POSITIONS
  LEADING POSITIONS AND PERSONALITIES
  IN THE COMMUNIST PARTY OF THE
  SOVIET UNION AND THE SOVIET
  GOVERNMENT.=        ANON  -57-LPP

  SCALE POSITIONS AND 'POWER' IN THE
  SENATE (UNITED STATES).=
                     MACRD -59-SPP

  SOCIAL POSITIONS AND IMAGES OF THE
  POLITICAL PROCESS.= SNYDRC-57-SPI

POSITIVENESS
  ILLEGITIMACY OF POWER AND
  POSITIVENESS OF ATTITUDE TOWARD
  THE POWER PERSON (UNITED STATES).=
                     MULCM -66-IPP

POSSESSION
  POLITICAL AUTHORITY -- ITS EXERCISE
  AND POSSESSION.=    CASSCW-61-PAI

POSSIBLE
  LYNDON B JOHNSON AND THE ART OF THE

POSSIBLE                (CCNTINUATICN)
  PCSSIBLE.=            BRANRL-64-LBJ

  MASS COMMUNICATICNS ANC TFE LCSS CF
  FREEDCM IN NATICNAL
  DECISICN-MAKINC -- A PCSSIBLE
  RESEARCH APPRCACH TC INTERSTATE
  CCNFLICTS.=          CEUTKW-57-MCL

POSSIBLES
  PRCBABLES AND FCSSIELES (BRITISH
  CANCICATES).=        WILCRW-63-PPB

PCST
  GERMANY'S PCST NAZI INTELLECTUAL
  CLIMATE.=            ARNOGL-55-GSP

  PCST - TOTALITARIAN LEACERSHIP --
  ELITES IN THE GERMAN FECERAL
  REPUBLIC.=           EDINLJ-60-PTL

  PCST - STALIN TRENCS IN RUSSIAN
  LITERATURE.=         ERLIV -64-PST

  THE PARTY IN TFE PCST - STALIN ERA
  (SCVIET UNICN).=     FAINM -58-PPS

  THE WILCPC CABINET -- A TURNING
  PCINT IN PCST REVCLUTICNARY
  INDCNESIA.=          FEITH -58-WCT

  THE PCST - KHRUSHCFEV SCVIET
  LEACERSHIP -- CILEMMAS ANC
  ALTERNATIVES.=       FARVML-65-PKS

  PCST - BOURGECIS EUROPE.=
                       LICHG -63-PBE

  THE PCST - STALIN ERA
  (SCVIET UNICN).=     MARIY -63-PSE

  REHABILITATICN IN TFE PCST - STALIN
  SCVIET UNICN.=       CPPESA-67-RPS

  ASPECTS CF ISLAM IN PCST - CCLCNIAL
  INDCNESIA -- FIVE ESSAYS.=
                       VAN-CA-58-AIP

PCST-TREATY
  THE JAPANESE PECPLE ANC FCREIGN
  PCLICY -- A STUDY CF PUELIC
  CPINICN IN PCST-TREATY JAPAN.=
                       MENCCF-61-JPF

PCST-WAR
  THE REBELS -- A STUCY CF POST-WAR
  INSURRECTICNS.=      CROZB -60-RSP

  NATICNALISM ANC RIGHT WING IN JAPAN
  -- A STUDY CF PCST-WAR TRENDS.=
                       MORRII-60-NRW

  THE STRUGGLE FCR SYRIA -- A STUDY
  CF PCST-WAR ARAE PCLITICS,
  1945-1948.           SEALP -65-SSS

  WITHOUT THE CHRYSANTHEMUM AND THE
  SWORD -- A STUCY CF TFE ATTITUDES
  CF YOUTH IN PCST-WAR JAPAN.=
                       STCEJ -55-WCS

PCSTHUMCUS
  SCCIAL MCBILITY AMCNG THE DEAC --
  CR PCSTHUMCUS CIRCULATICN OF
  ELITES (SCVIET UNICN).=
                       LC    -62-SMA

PCSTWAR
  THE PCSTWAR STUCENT STRUGGLE IN
  JAPAN.=              EATTLH-56-PSS

  REPUBLIC IN SUSFENSE -- POLITICS,

POSTWAR                (CCNTINUATICN)
  PARTIES, ANC PERSCNALITIES IN
  PCSTWAR GERMANY.=    BCLLK -64-RSP

  THE ARABS' VIEW CF POSTWAR AMERICAN
  FOREIGN PCLICY (EGYPT, IRAN,
  JCRDAN, LEBANCN, SYRIA).=
                       CASTHP-59-AVP

  PCSTWAR RCLE CF TFE CCMMUNIST PARTY
  (SCVIET UNICN).=     FAINM -49-PRC

  AUSTRIA'S SCCIALISTS IN TFE TREND
  TCWARD A TWC - FARTY SYSTEM -- AN
  INTERPRETATICN CF PCSTWAR
  ELECTICNS.=          GULICA-58-ASS

  PCSTWAR STRAINS CN THE ERITISH
  COMMONWEALTF.=       MANSN -48-PSE

  PCLITICAL ECUCATICN IN THE POSTWAR
  KCMSCMCL.=           PLOSSI-56-PEP

  LATIN AMERICA'S PCSTWAR
  GCLPES CE ESTACC.=   RIPPJF-65-LAS

  PCSTWAR PCLITICAL PARTIES IN
  JAPAN.=              SPINCN-46-PPP

  THE PARTISAN MCVEMENT IN POSTWAR
  LITHUANIA.=          VARDVS-63-PMP

PCTENTIAL
  PCTENTIAL ELITES IN GHANA AND TFE
  IVCRY CCAST -- A PRELIMINARY
  CCMPARISON.=         CLIGRP-64-PEG

  PCLITICAL CCNFLICT PCTENTIAL,
  PCLITIZATICN, AND TFE PEASANTRY IN
  THE UNCERDEVELCPEC CCUNTRIES.=
                       FINDC -65-PCP

  PCTENTIAL ELITES IN TURKEY -- TFE
  SCCIAL CRIGINS CF LISE YCUTH.=
                       KAZAAM-66-PET

  PCTENTIAL ELITES IN TURKEY --
  EXPLCRING TFE VALUES ANC ATTITUDES
  CF LISE YCUTH.=      KAZAAM-67-PET

  AN ANALYSIS CF PCLITICAL CONTRCL --
  ACTUAL ANC PCTENTIAL.=
                       CPPEFE-58-APC

  THE PCTENTIAL RCLE CF TURKISH
  VILLAGE CPINICN LEACERS IN A
  PRCGRAM CF FAMILY PLANNING.=
                       SYTCJM-65-PRT

PCTPCURRI
  THE PARTY PCTPCURRI IN
  LATIN AMERICA.=      FITZR -57-PPL

PCUVCIRS
  VERIFICATICN CES PCLVCIRS IN TFE
  FRENCH NATICNAL ASSEMELY.=
                       CAMPP -53-VCP

PCWER
  SCCIAL PCWER ANC CCMMITMENT -- A
  THECRETICAL STATEMENT.=
                       ABRAE -58-SPC

  THE REPUTATICNAL APPRCACH IN TFE
  STUCY CF CCMMUNITY PCWER -- A
  CRITICAL EVALUATICN.=  ABU-B -65-RAS

  PCWER ATTRIBUTICNS IN TFE LOCAL
  CCMMUNITY -- TFECRETICAL ANC
  RESEARCH CCNSICERATICNS
  (UNITED STATES).=    AGGERE-56-PAL

  CCMMUNITY PCWER STRUCTURE ANC

POWER                    (CONTINUATION)
(UNITED STATES, POWER ELITE
REVIEW).=            HERMFA-56-PPC

IN THE FOOTSTEPS OF COMMUNITY
POWER.=              HERSLJ-61-FCP

POLITICAL POWER AND THE OCTOBER
1965 COUP IN INDONESIA.=
                     HINDD -67-PPC

THE POWER OF THE CONTEMPORARY
PRESIDENCY (UNITED STATES).=
                     HIRSRS-61-PCP

THE EXECUTIVE POWER IN
SWITZERLAND.=        HUGHC -56-EPS

DE GAULLE IN POWER (FRANCE).=
                     HUGHES-58-DGP

COMMUNITY POWER STRUCTURE -- A
STUDY OF DECISION MAKERS
(UNITED STATES).=    HUNTF -53-CPS

POWER, EXPERTISE AND THE MILITARY
PROFESSION (UNITED STATES).=
                     HUNTSP-63-PEM

TOWARDS THE EXPLICATION OF THE
CONCEPT OF LEADERSHIP IN TERMS OF
THE CONCEPT OF POWER.=
                     JANDKF-60-TEC

NASSER -- THE RISE TO POWER
(EGYPT).=            JOESJ -60-NRP

PEASANT NATIONALISM AND COMMUNIST
POWER -- THE EMERGENCE OF
REVOLUTIONARY CHINA, 1937-1945.=
                     JOHNCA-62-PNC

THE MYSTERY OF POWER.=
                     KAUFH -54-MP

HOW TOTALITARIANS GAIN ABSOLUTE
POWER (NAZI GERMANY,
SOVIET UNION).=      KECSP -52-HTG

PROFESSIONAL PUBLIC RELATIONS AND
POLITICAL POWER (UNITED STATES).=
                     KELLS -56-PPR

POLITICAL POWER AND EDUCATIONAL
DECISION-MAKING (UNITED STATES).=
                     KIMBRB-64-PPE

POWER STRUCTURE AND DECISION-MAKING
IN A MEXICAN BORDER CITY.=
                     KLAPDE-60-PSD

TOWARD A THEORY OF POWER AND
POLITICAL INSTABILITY IN
LATIN AMERICA.=      KLINM -56-TTP

WEALTH AND POWER IN AMERICA -- AN
ANALYSIS OF SOCIAL CLASS AND
INCOME DISTRIBUTION.=  KOLKG -62-WPA

LEFT WING TRADE UNIONISM -- THE
MATRIX OF COMMUNIST POWER IN
ITALY.=              LAPAJ -54-LWT

THE NEW PRIESTHOOD -- THE
SCIENTIFIC ELITE AND THE USES OF
POWER (UNITED STATES).=
                     LAPPRE-65-NPS

POWER AND PERSONALITY.=
                     LASSHD-48-PP

POWER AND SOCIETY -- A FRAMEWORK


POWER                    (CONTINUATION)
FOR POLITICAL INQUIRY.=
                     LASSHD-50-PSF

POWER SEEKERS.=      LEE,AM-65-PS

THE CITY MANAGER, ADMINISTRATIVE
THEORY AND POLITICAL POWER
(UNITED STATES).=    LOCKD -62-CMA

POLITICAL POWER AND THE
GOVERNMENTAL PROCESS.=
                     LOEWK -57-PPG

THE NATURE OF KHRUSHCHEV'S POWER
(SOVIET UNION).=     LOWER -60-NKS

A GAME THEORETIC ANALYSIS OF
CONGRESSIONAL POWER DISTRIBUTIONS
FOR A STABLE TWO - PARTY SYSTEM.=
                     LUCERD-56-GTA

SCALE POSITIONS AND 'POWER' IN THE
SENATE (UNITED STATES).=
                     MACRD -59-SPP

FREEDOM, POWER, AND DEMOCRATIC
PLANNING.=           MANNK -50-FPD

THE POWER OF POWER.=  MARCJG-66-PP

THE POWER OF POWER.=  MARCJG-66-PP

PAKISTAN'S NEW POWER ELITE.=
                     MAROS -59-PSN

POWER IN BRITISH POLITICAL
PARTIES.=            MCKERT-55-PBP

BRITISH POLITICAL PARTIES -- THE
DISTRIBUTION OF POWER WITHIN THE
CONSERVATIVE AND LABOUR PARTIES.=
                     MCKERT-65-BPP

KHRUSHCHEV'S DISLOYAL OPPOSITION --
STRUCTURAL CHANGE AND POWER
STRUGGLE IN THE COMMUNIST BLOC.=
                     MICHF -63-KSD

THE STRUGGLE FOR POWER (CHINA).=
                     MICHF -67-SPC

THE NEW MEN OF POWER -- AMERICA'S
LABOR LEADERS.=      MILLCW-48-NMP

THE POWER ELITE (UNITED STATES).=
                     MILLCW-56-PEU

THE POWER ELITE -- COMMENT ON
CRITICISM.=          MILLCW-57-PEC

THE STRUCTURE OF POWER IN AMERICAN
SOCIETY.=            MILLCW-58-SPA

THE POWER ELITE -- MILITARY,
ECONOMIC, AND POLITICAL
(UNITED STATES).=    MILLCW-59-PEM

POWER, POLITICS, AND PEOPLE
(GERMANY, UNITED STATES).=
                     MILLCW-63-PPP

DECISION-MAKING CLIQUES IN
COMMUNITY POWER STRUCTURES -- A
COMPARATIVE STUDY OF AN AMERICAN
AND AN ENGLISH CITY.=  MILLDC-58-DMC

TOWN AND GOWN -- THE POWER
STRUCTURE OF A UNIVERSITY TOWN
(UNITED STATES).=    MILLDC-63-TGP

THE SEIZURE OF POWER (GERMANY,

PRAGMATIC          (CONTINUATION)
ORIENTATIONS OF WEST BERLIN LOCAL
PARTY OFFICIALS (WEST GERMANY).=
                    WRIGWE-67-IPC

PRAGMATISM
TUNISIA -- PRAGMATISM AND
PROGRESS.=          HAHNL -62-TPP

NORTH AFRICA -- A NEW PRAGMATISM.=
                    HAHNL -64-NAN

REVISIONISM -- PRAGMATISM --
GOMULKAISM (POLAND).=   JELEKA-58-RPG

PRAGUE
REVOLUTIONS IN PRAGUE
(CZECHOSLOVAKIA).=      SKILHG-49-RPC

PRAVDA
PRAVDA ON THE ROLE OF THE PARTY AND
THE INDIVIDUAL (SOVIET UNION).=
                    ANON  -53-PRP

PRECINCT
THE PRECINCT WORKER
(UNITED STATES).=      FORTS -48-PWU

THE INFLUENCE OF PRECINCT WORK ON
VOTING BEHAVIOR (UNITED STATES).=
                    WOLFRE-63-IPW

PREDICAMENT
THE PREDICAMENT OF THE MODERN
AFRICAN CHIEF -- AN INSTANCE FROM
UGANDA.=            FALLL -55-PMA

PREDICTING
PREDICTING A COMMUNITY DECISION --
A TEST OF THE MILLER-FORM THEORY
(UNITED STATES).=      HANSRC-59-PCD

PREDICTING SUPREME COURT DECISIONS
MATHEMATICALLY -- A QUANTITIVE
ANALYSIS OF THE RIGHT TO COUNSEL
(UNITED STATES).=      KORTF -57-PSC

PREDICTION
THE PREDICTION OF ISSUE OUTCOME IN
COMMUNITY DECISION MAKING.=
                    MILLOC-57-PIO

PREDOMINANCE
INCREASE OF ZAIBATSU PREDOMINANCE
IN WARTIME JAPAN.=     BISSTA-45-IZP

PREFACE
A PREFACE TO DEMOCRATIC THEORY
(UNITED STATES).=      DAHLRA-56-PDT

PREFATORY
A PREFATORY STUDY OF LEADERSHIP
SELECTION IN OREGON
(UNITED STATES).=      SELILG-59-PSL

PREFECTS
THE ITALIAN PREFECTS -- A STUDY IN
ADMINISTRATIVE POLITICS.=
                    FRIERC-63-IPS

PREFERENCES
COPING WITH CUBA -- DIVERGENT
POLICY PREFERENCES OF STATE
POLITICAL LEADERS
(UNITED STATES).=      EKMAP -66-CCD

PRELIMINARY
RECRUITMENT PATTERNS AMONG LOCAL
PARTY OFFICIALS -- A MODEL AND
SOME PRELIMINARY FINDINGS IN
SELECTED LOCALES (UNITED STATES).=
                    BOWM  -66-RPA

POTENTIAL ELITES IN GHANA AND THE

PRELIMINARY         (CONTINUATION)
IVORY COAST -- A PRELIMINARY
COMPARISON.=          CLIGRP-64-PEG

PARTY FACTIONS AND COMPARATIVE
POLITICS -- SOME PRELIMINARY
OBSERVATIONS.=        ZARIR -60-PFC

PRELUDE
THE SUDAN -- PRELUDE TO ELECTIONS.=
                    NYQUTE-65-SPE

THE YOUNG TURKS -- PRELUDE TO THE
REVOLUTION OF 1908.=   RAMSEE-57-YTP

PRELUDE TO FRANCO (SPAIN).=
                    RATCDF-57-PFS

PREPARING
PREPARING FOR POLITICS
(UNITED STATES).=      BELOM -53-PPU

PRESCRIPTION
ADMINISTRATIVE RESPONSIBILITY --
CONGRESSIONAL PRESCRIPTION OF
INTERAGENCY RELATIONSHIPS
(UNITED STATES).=      SMITJM-57-ARC

PRESENT
THE PRESENT SITUATION AND
ASPIRATIONS OF ELITES IN THE
GOLD COAST.=          BUSIKA-56-PSA

VOTERS AND ELECTIONS -- PAST AND
PRESENT.=             CAMPA -64-VEP

POLITICAL FORCES IN PRESENT DAY
FRANCE.=              EHRMHW-48-PFP

THE PRESENT CONDITION OF BRITISH
POLITICAL PARTIES.=    LEWIGK-52-PCB

THE SOVIET BAR -- PAST AND
PRESENT.=             SHAPI -61-SBP

THE POLISH INTELLIGENTSIA -- PAST
AND PRESENT.=         SZCZJ -62-PIP

THE CHINESE MONOLITH -- PAST AND
PRESENT.=             WRIGAF-55-CMP

PRESENTATION
A MATHEMATICAL PRESENTATION OF
ISRAEL'S POLITICAL PARTIES.=
                    GOODTM-57-MPI

PRESENTED
THE NEW ELITES OF TROPICAL AFRICA
-- STUDIES PRESENTED AND DISCUSSED
AT THE SIXTH INTERNATIONAL AFRICAN
SEMINAR AT THE UNIVERSITY OF
IBADAN.=              LLOYPC-66-NET

PRESIDENCY
THE PRESIDENCY (UNITED STATES).=
                    BROGDW-64-PUS

THE PRESIDENCY TODAY
(UNITED STATES).=      CORWES-56-PTU

THE PRESIDENCY -- CRISIS AND
REGENERATION (UNITED STATES).=
                    FINEH -60-PCR

THE PRESIDENCY AS MORAL LEADERSHIP
(UNITED STATES).=      GOLDEF-52-PML

THE PRESIDENCY AND THE EXECUTIVE
OFFICE OF THE PRESIDENT
(UNITED STATES).=      GRAHGA-50-PEC

THE POWER OF THE CONTEMPORARY

295

PRESSURES                (CONTINUATION)
                         TURNJ -51-PCP

PRESUMPTIVE
  AMERICAN UNIVERSITY STUDENTS -- A
  PRESUMPTIVE ELITE.=      MARVC -65-AUS

PREVENTIVE
  PAKISTAN'S PREVENTIVE AUTOCRACY AND
  ITS CAUSES.=             NEWMKJ-59-PSP

PREWAR
  DEMOCRACY AND THE PARTY MOVEMENT IN
  PREWAR JAPAN -- THE FAILURE OF THE
  FIRST ATTEMPT.=          SCALRA-53-DPM

PRICE
  THE ENGINEERS AND THE PRICE
  SYSTEM.=                 VEBLT -21-EPS

PRIESTHOOD
  THE NEW PRIESTHOOD -- THE
  SCIENTIFIC ELITE AND THE USES OF
  POWER (UNITED STATES).=
                          LAPPRE-65-NPS

PRIESTS
  RULERS AND PRIESTS -- A STUDY IN
  CULTURAL CONTROL (INDIA).=
                          COHESP-64-RPS

PRIMACY
  AFRICA -- THE PRIMACY OF POLITICS
  (CONGO, NIGERIA).=       SPIRHJ-66-APP

  POLITICAL PRIMACY VS PROFESSIONAL
  ELAN (SOVIET UNION).= WOLFTW-64-PPV

PRIMARY
  PARTY ORGANIZATIONS IN PRIMARY
  ELECTIONS (UNITED STATES).=
                          CUTRP -58-POP

  THE PLACE OF ELITES AND PRIMARY
  GROUPS IN THE ABSORPTION OF NEW
  IMMIGRANTS IN ISRAEL.=
                          EISESN-51-PEP

  DOES A DIVISIVE - PRIMARY HARM A
  CANDIDATE'S CHANCES
  (UNITED STATES).=        HACKA -65-DDP

  INTER - PARTY COMPETITION AND
  PRIMARY CONTESTING -- THE CASE OF
  INDIANA (UNITED STATES).=
                          STANWH-58-IPC

  TYPES OF PRIMARY AND PARTY
  RESPONSIBILITY (UNITED STATES).=
                          TELFIR-65-TPP

PRIME
  THE OFFICE OF THE PRIME MINISTER
  (GREAT BRITAIN).=        CARTBE-56-OPM

  THE MONARCH, THE PRIME MINISTER,
  AND THE DISSOLUTION OF PARLIAMENT
  (GREAT BRITAIN).=        HEASDJ-61-MPM

  THE PRIME MINISTER AS AN ELECTED
  MONARCH (GREAT BRITAIN).=
                          HINTRW-60-PME

  THE MONARCH AND THE SELECTION OF A
  PRIME MINISTER -- A RE-EXAMINATION
  OF THE CRISIS OF 1931
  (GREAT BRITAIN).=        WOODGC-57-MSP

  THE QUALITIES OF A GREAT PRIME
  MINISTER (GREAT BRITAIN).=
                          SOMEDC-53-QGP

  THE OFFICE OF PUBLIC RELATIONS

PRIME                     (CONTINUATION)
  ADVISOR TO THE PRIME MINISTER
  (GREAT BRITAIN).=        WILLF -56-OPR

PRIMITIVE
  ANTHROPOLOGICAL STUDY OF PRIMITIVE
  RULING GROUPS --1 --2.=
                          EE-GS -57-ASP

  PRIMITIVE POLITICAL SYSTEMS -- A
  COMPARATIVE ANALYSIS.=
                          EISESN-59-PPS

  SOCIAL CHANGE AND PRIMITIVE LAW --
  CONSEQUENCES OF A PAPUAN LEGAL
  CASE (NETHERLANDS NEW GUINEA).=
                          POSPL -58-SCP

PRINCES
  PEDDLERS AND PRINCES -- SOCIAL
  CHANGE AND ECONOMIC MODERNIZATION
  IN TWO INDONESIAN TOWNS.=
                          GEERC -63-PPS

  AN ANATOMY OF LEADERSHIP --
  PRINCES, HEROES, AND SUPERMEN
  (UNITED STATES).=        JENNEE-60-ALP

  PEASANTS, PEDDLERS AND PRINCES IN
  INDONESIA -- A REVIEW ARTICLE.=
                          WERTWF-64-PPP

PRINCIPLE
  THE PRINCIPLE OF PROFITABILITY AND
  THE SOVIET PARTY APPARATUS.=
                          ACHMH -59-PPS

  POWER, PRINCIPLE, AND THE DOCTRINE
  OF THE MOVEMENT REPUBLICAIN
  POPULAIRE (FRANCE).=    YATEWR-58-PPD

PRINCIPLES
  THE PRINCIPLES OF AFRICAN TRIBAL
  ADMINISTRATION.=         KHAMT -51-PAT

PRISMATIC
  PRISMATIC SOCIETY AND FINANCIAL
  ADMINISTRATION.=         RIGGFW-61-PSF

PRIVATE
  THE WORK OF THE PRIVATE SECRETARY
  TO THE MEMBER OF PARLIAMENT
  (GREAT BRITAIN).=        AN MMP-48-WPS

  THE DEVELOPMENT OF LATIN AMERICAN
  PRIVATE ENTERPRISE.=  BRANF -64-DLA

  THE ROLE OF PRIVATE BUSINESS
  (LATIN AMERICA).=        HANSSG-66-RPB

  THE PRIVATE MEMBER OF PARLIAMENT
  AND THE FORMATION OF PUBLIC POLICY
  -- A NEW ZEALAND CASE STUDY.=
                          KELSRN-64-PMP

  PRIVATE PEOPLE AND PUBLIC POLICY
  (UNITED STATES).=        RIESD -59-PPP

  RELATIONS BETWEEN PUBLIC AND
  PRIVATE UNIVERSITIES
  (LATIN AMERICA).=        SCHEL -67-RBP

PRIVILEGED
  PARTY PROTECTION AND PRIVILEGED
  STATUS IN SOVIET SOCIETY.=
                          KRYLKA-66-PPP

PRIVY
  PRIVY COUNCIL, CABINET AND MINISTRY
  IN GREAT BRITAIN AND CANADA.=
                          BANKMA- -PCC

PROBABILITY
  THE ROLE CONCEPT IN LEGISLATURES --

PROBABILITY          (CONTINUATION)
    A PROBABILITY MODEL AND A NOTE ON
    COGNITIVE STRUCTURE
    (UNITED STATES).=     FRANWL-65-PCL

PROBABLES
    PROBABLES AND POSSIBLES (BRITISH
    CANDIDATES).=         WILCRW-63-PPB

PROBLEM
    THE PERENNIAL PROBLEM OF
    REVISIONISM (SOVIET UNION).=
                         ACHMH -59-PPR

    BUREAUCRACY AND THE PROBLEM OF
    POWER.=               BENDR -45-BPP

    BUREAUCRACY -- THE PROBLEM AND ITS
    SETTING.=             BENDR -47-BPI

    LEADERSHIP THEORY AND
    ADMINISTRATIVE BEHAVIOR -- THE
    PROBLEM OF AUTHORITY.=
                         BENNWG-60-LTA

    A PROBLEM IN SOVIET BUSINESS
    ADMINISTRATION.=      BERLJS-57-PSB

    THE PROBLEM OF AUTHORITY.=
                         BIERR -54-PA

    THE PROBLEM OF SUCCESSION IN THE
    SOVIET POLITICAL SYSTEM -- THE
    CASE OF KHRUSHCHEV.=  BOCIBR-60-PSS

    THE FRENCH COUNCIL OF STATE --
    COMPARATIVE OBSERVATIONS ON THE
    PROBLEM OF CONTROLLING BUREAUCRACY
    OF THE MODERN STATE.= CIAMA -51-FCS

    RELIGION AS AN INSTRUMENT OF
    CULTURE CHANGE -- THE PROBLEM OF
    THE SECTS IN THE SOVIET UNION.=
                         CUNNSP-64-RIC

    THE INDONESIAN FEDERAL PROBLEM.=
                         FINKLS-51-IFP

    REPRESENTATIVES AND EFFICIENCY --
    DUAL PROBLEM OF CIVIL - MILITARY
    RELATIONS (UNITED STATES).=
                         FOX,WT-61-REC

    POLITICAL LEADERSHIP AND THE
    PROBLEM OF CHARISMATIC POWER
    (GERMANY, GREAT BRITAIN, ITALY,
    UNITED STATES).=      FRIECJ-61-PLP

    THE PROBLEM OF SUCCESSION AND
    BUREAUCRACY.=         GOULAW-65-PSB

    THE PROBLEM OF GENERATIONS IN AN
    ORGANIZATIONAL STRUCTURE.=
                         GUSFMR-57-PGO

    THE GOVERNANCE OF THE METROPOLIS AS
    A PROBLEM IN DIPLOMACY
    (UNITED STATES).=     HOLDM -64-GMP

    THE PROBLEM OF PARTY GROWTH AND
    RECRUITMENT (SOVIET UNION).=
                         KRUZP -66-PPG

    CONFUCIAN CHINA AND ITS MODERN FATE
    -- THE PROBLEM OF INTELLECTUAL
    CONTINUITY.=          LEVEJR-58-CCI

    KHRUSHCHEV'S SEVENTIETH BIRTHDAY
    AND THE PROBLEM OF CHOOSING HIS
    SUCCESSOR (SOVIET UNION).=
                         MARIY -65-KSS

    THE PROBLEM OF LEADERSHIP -- AN

PROBLEM              (CONTINUATION)
    INTERDISCIPLINARY APPROACH.=
                         MORRRT-50-PLI

    AN AMERICAN DILEMMA -- THE NEGRO
    PROBLEM AND MODERN DEMOCRACY.=
                         MYRDG -44-ADN

    THE PROBLEM OF GENERATIONS IN
    FINNISH COMMUNISM.=   RINTM -58-PGF

    THE KHRUSHCHEV SUCCESSION PROBLEM
    (SOVIET UNION).=      RUSHM -62-KSP

    THE PROBLEM OF NATIONAL LEADERSHIP
    IN NIGERIA.=          SMYTHH-58-PNL

    AN EVENT-STRUCTURE APPROACH TO
    SOCIAL POWER AND TO THE PROBLEM OF
    POWER COMPARABILITY.= TANNAS-62-ESA

    PROBLEM OF LEADERSHIP.=
                         WARDN -46-PL

    SECOND CONSUL -- THE VICE
    PRESIDENCY -- OUR GREATEST
    POLITICAL PROBLEM
    (UNITED-STATES).=     WAUGEW-56-SCV

    THE BRITISH CRISIS -- A PROBLEM IN
    ECONOMIC STATESMANSHIP.=
                         WILLJH-49-BCP

PROBLEMS
    SOME PROBLEMS OF EXECUTIVE
    LEADERSHIP IN THE GOVERNMENT
    (PHILIPPINES).=       ARANLM-57-PEL

    RACIAL DISCRIMINATION AND NEGRO
    LEADERSHIP PROBLEMS -- THE CASE OF
    A NORTHERN COMMUNITY
    (UNITED STATES).=     BOWML -65-RDN

    PROBLEMS OF PARLIAMENTARY DEMOCRACY
    IN EUROPE.=           BRACKD-64-PPD

    NOTES ON LEADERSHIP PROBLEMS AND
    PUBLIC ADMINISTRATION TRAINING IN
    INDONESIA.=           BRADJR-63-NLP

    THE PROBLEMS OF ELITES IN THE
    BELGIAN CONGO.=       BRAUGE-56-PEB

    CURRENT LEADERSHIP PROBLEMS AMONG
    JAPANESE AMERICANS.=  BURMJH-53-CLP

    PROBLEMS OF FIELD ADMINISTRATION IN
    THE DEPARTMENT OF LABOR
    (PHILIPPINES).=       CALALM-62-PFA

    PROBLEMS OF CHINESE COMMUNIST
    LEADERSHIP AS SEEN IN THE SECRET
    MILITARY PAPERS.=     CHENJC-64-PCC

    LABOUR AND STAFF PROBLEMS UNDER
    NATIONALISATION (GREAT BRITAIN).=
                         COLEGD-50-LSP

    COMMUNITY POWER STRUCTURE --
    PROBLEMS AND CONTINUITIES.=
                         DANZMH-64-CPS

    MODERN AMERICAN SOCIETY -- READINGS
    IN THE PROBLEMS OF ORDER AND
    CHANGE.=              DAVIK -49-MAS

    PROBLEMS OF REPRESENTATIVE
    GOVERNMENT IN SOUTHEAST ASIA.=
                         EMERR -53-PRG

    THE MILITARY IN THE MIDDLE EAST --
    PROBLEMS IN SOCIETY AND

PROFESSION                (CONTINUATION)
  PROFESSION.=              BLAUAP-54-ALS

  THE PROFESSION CF GOVERNMENT -- THE
  PUBLIC SERVANT IN (WESTERN)
  EUROPE.=                  CHAPB -59-PGP

  LOBBYISTS -- THE WASTED PROFESSION
  (UNITED STATES).=         EULAH -64-LWP

  POWER, EXPERTISE AND THE MILITARY
  PROFESSION (UNITED STATES).=
                            HUNTSP-63-PEM

  THE FUNCTIONS CF POLISH TRADE
  UNIONS -- THEIR PROFESSION TOWARD
  THE SCVIET PATTERN.=      ROSECS-55-FPT

PROFESSIONAL
  RELATIONSHIP BETWEEN PROFESSIONAL
  AND ADMINISTRATIVE OFFICERS IN A
  GOVERNMENT DEPARTMENT DURING A
  PERIOD CF ADMINISTRATIVE CHANGE
  (GUYANA).=                BACCMK-67-RBP

  SEQUELS TC A MILITARY CAREER -- THE
  RETIRED MILITARY PROFESSIONAL
  (UNITED STATES).=         BIDEAD-64-SMC

  PROFESSIONAL POLITICIANS -- A STUDY
  CF BRITISH PARTY AGENTS.=
                            COMFGO-58-PPS

  SCVIET PROFESSIONAL MANPOWER -- ITS
  EDUCATION, TRAINING AND SUPPLY.=
                            DEWIN -55-SPM

  THE NEGRO PROFESSIONAL CLASS
  (UNITED STATES).=         EDWAFG-59-NPC

  LAWYERS IN POLITICS -- A STUDY IN
  PROFESSIONAL CONVERGENCE
  (UNITED STATES).=         EULAH -64-LPS

  THE PROFESSIONAL SOLDIER -- A
  SOCIAL AND POLITICAL PORTRAIT
  (UNITED STATES).=         JANOM -60-PSS

  PROFESSIONAL PUBLIC RELATIONS AND
  POLITICAL POWER (UNITED STATES).=
                            KELLS -56-PPR

  PROFESSIONAL STAFFS CF CONGRESS.=
                            KOFMK -62-PSC

  ORGANIZATIONAL CONSEQUENCES OF
  PROFESSIONAL CONSENSUS -- LAWYERS
  AND SELECTION CF JUDGES
  (UNITED-STATES).=         LADIJ -66-OCP

  THE KREMLIN'S PROFESSIONAL STAFF --
  THE 'APPARATUS' CF THE CENTRAL
  COMMITTEE, COMMUNIST PARTY OF THE
  SOVIET UNION.=            NEMZL -50-KSP

  BUREAUCRATIC PARTY ORGANIZATION
  THROUGH PROFESSIONAL POLITICAL
  STAFFING (UNITED STATES).=
                            SCHUCE-64-BPO

  THE EXTRA - PROFESSIONAL ROLE CF
  THE LAWYER (UNITED STATES).=
                            WARDWI-56-EPR

  POLITICAL PRIMACY VS PROFESSIONAL
  ELAN (SCVIET UNION).=     WOLFTW-64-PPV

PROFESSIONALISM
  THE CHALLENGE CF MILITARY
  PROFESSIONALISM (UNITED STATES).=
                            GINSVN-64-CMP

  PARTY AND ARMY -- PROFESSIONALISM

PROFESSIONALISM           (CONTINUATION)
  AND POLITICAL CONTROL IN THE
  CHINESE OFFICER CORPS, 1949-1964.=
                            JOFFE -65-PAP

PROFESSIONALIZATION
  THE PROFESSIONALIZATION OF THE NEW
  DIPLOMACY (UNITED STATES).=
                            ROSSR -62-PND

  THE PROFESSIONALIZATION CF
  EVERYONE.=                WILEHL-64-PE

PROFESSIONALS
  AMATEURS AND PROFESSIONALS IN
  BRITISH POLITICS, 1918-1959.=
                            BUCKPW-63-APB

  THE AMBIVALENT CHARACTER OF
  NATIONALISM AMONG EGYPTIAN
  PROFESSIONALS.=           KENDPL-56-ACN

PROFESSIONS
  LIFE CAREERS, POWER AND THE
  PROFESSIONS -- THE RETIRED ARMY
  GENERAL (UNITED STATES).=
                            REISL -56-LCP

PROFESSOR
  MONARCHS AND SOCIOLOGISTS -- A
  REPLY TO PROFESSOR SHILS AND MR.
  YOUNG.=                   BIRNN -55-MSR

  THE BUREAUCRATIC ELITE -- A REPLY
  TO PROFESSOR ROWAT (CANADA,
  GREAT BRITAIN).=          PORTJ -59-BER

  PROFESSOR CARR'S 'WAVE CF THE
  FUTURE'.=                 WOLFBD-55-PCS

PROFESSORS
  PROFESSORS AND POLITICS
  (UNITED STATES).=         COTTA -61-PPU

PROFILE
  THE FOREIGN-EDUCATED IRANIAN -- A
  PROFILE.=                 BALOG -63-FEI

  THE AUTHORITARIAN PERSONALITY IN
  PROFILE (UNITED STATES).=
                            GLAZN -51-APP

  A PROFILE CF POLITICAL ACTIVISTS IN
  MANHATTAN (UNITED STATES).=
                            HIRSRS-62-PPA

  THE EUROPEAN RIGHT -- A HISTORICAL
  PROFILE.=                 ROGEH -65-ERH

  MEN WHO GOVERN -- A BIOGRAPHICAL
  PROFILE CF FEDERAL POLITICAL
  EXECUTIVES (UNITED STATES).=
                            STAN  -67-MWG

  MUSLIM LEGISLATORS IN INDIA --
  PROFILE CF A MINORITY ELITE.=
                            WRIGJR-64-MLI

PROFILES
  MOROCCAN PROFILES -- A NATIONALIST
  VIEW.=                    LANOR -53-MPN

  PROFILES CF AFRICAN LEADERS.=
                            MELATP-61-PAL

PROFITABILITY
  THE PRINCIPLE CF PROFITABILITY AND
  THE SCVIET PARTY APPARATUS.=
                            ACHMH -59-PPS

PROFUMO
  THE RELATIONS CF THE PROFUMO REBELS

PSYCHOLOGY          (CONTINUATION)
THE PSYCHOLOGY OF DICTATORSHIP --
BASED ON AN EXAMINATION OF THE
LEADERS OF NAZI GERMANY.=
                        GILBGM-50-PDB

THOUGHT REFORM AND THE PSYCHOLOGY
OF TOTALISM (CHINA).=    LIFTRJ-61-TRP

PSYCHOMETRIC
A PSYCHOMETRIC MODEL OF THE SUPREME
COURT (UNITED STATES).=
                        SCHUG -61-PMS

PSYCHOPATHOLOGY
PSYCHOPATHOLOGY AND POLITICS.=
                        LASSHD-30-PP

PSYCHOPATHOLOGY, DECISION-MAKING,
AND POLITICAL INVOLVEMENT
(UNITED STATES).=       RUTHBM-66-PDM

PUBLICS
THE NATURE OF BELIEF SYSTEMS IN
MASS PUBLICS.=          CONVPE-64-NBS

THE FUNCTIONS OF THE PUBLICS IN
PLATO'S CITIES.=        CAVIM -66-FPP

PUERTO RICAN
THE PUERTO RICAN BUSINESSMAN -- A
STUDY IN CULTURAL CHANGE.=
                        COCHTC-59-PRB

IDEOLOGY AND LEADERSHIP IN
PUERTO RICAN POLITICS.=
                        WELLH -55-ILP

PUERTO RICO
PARTY POLITICS IN PUERTO RICO.=
                        ANDERW-65-PPP

ADMINISTRATION OF A REVOLUTION
(PUERTO RICO).=         GOODCT-64-ARP

THE SOCIALIZATION OF ATTITUDES
TOWARD POLITICAL AUTHORITY
(AUSTRALIA, CHILE, JAPAN,
PUERTO RICO, UNITED STATES).=
                        HESSRD-63-SAT

SOCIAL CLASS AND SOCIAL CHANGE IN
PUERTO RICO.=           TUMIM -61-SCS

PUNISHMENT
CAPITAL PUNISHMENT AND BRITISH
POLITICS.=              CHRIJB-62-CPB

PUNJAB
MINORITY POLITICS IN PUNJAB
(INDIA).=               NAYABR-66-MPP

PURGE
THE 'PERMANENT PURGE' IN THE NEW
PARTY PROGRAM (SOVIET UNION).=
                        AKHMH -61-PPN

THE PURGE OF JAPANESE LEADERS UNDER
THE OCCUPATION.=        BAERHH-59-PJL

THE PURGE OF MARSHAL ZHUKOV
(SOVIET UNION).=        COCKPM-63-PMZ

THE PURGE -- PERMANENT SOVIET
INSTITUTION.=           DINEHS-54-PPS

MAO AND THE PERMANENT PURGE
(CHINA).=               GELMH -66-MPP

THE GREAT PURGE IN JAPAN.=
                        GUIGHS-47-GPJ

POWER STRUGGLE IN THE CHINESE CP
(COMMUNIST PARTY) -- THE KAO-JAO

PURGE               (CONTINUATION)
PURGE.=                 TANGPS-55-PSC

THE PURGE OF PROVINCIAL LEADERS
1957-1958 (CHINA).=     TEIWFC-66-PPL

PURGES
THE PATTERN OF POLITICAL PURGES
(EASTERN EUROPE).=      BRZEZ -58-PPP

KHRUSHCHEV AND THE PURGES
(SOVIET UNION).=        PISTL -62-KPS

PURPLE
SURVEY AND JUDICIARIES, OR WHO'S
AFRAID OF THE PURPLE CURTAIN
(UNITED STATES).=       BECKTL-66-SJO

PURSE
THE POWER OF THE PURSE --
APPROPRIATIONS POLITICS IN
CONGRESS (UNITED STATES).=
                        FENNRF-66-PPA

PYONGYANG
THE POLITICAL EVOLUTION OF THE
PYONGYANG (KOREAN) GOVERNMENT.=
                        DUBIWB-50-PEP

PYRAMIDS
THE LAND OF PAPER PYRAMIDS
(SOVIET UNION).=        GROSG -55-LPP

QUALITIES
THE QUALITIES OF A GREAT PRIME
MINISTER (GREAT BRITAIN).=
                        SOMEDC-53-QGP

QUANTITATIVE
SOME QUANTITATIVE CONSTRAINTS ON
VALUE ALLOCATION IN SOCIETY AND
POLITICS.=              DEUTKW-66-QCV

THE MATHEMATICAL ANALYSIS OF
SUPREME COURT DECISIONS -- THE USE
AND ABUSE OF QUANTITATIVE METHODS
(UNITED STATES).=       FISHFM-58-MAS

QUANTITATIVE ANALYSIS OF JUDICIAL
BEHAVIOR.=              SCHUGA-59-QAJ

QUANTITIVE
PREDICTING SUPREME COURT DECISIONS
MATHEMATICALLY -- A QUANTITIVE
ANALYSIS OF THE RIGHT TO COUNSEL
(UNITED STATES).=       KORTF -57-PSC

QUEBEC
SOCIAL STRUCTURE AND CANADIAN
POLITICAL PARTIES -- THE QUEBEC
CASE.=                  FILLWO-56-SSC

QUEMOY
PUBLIC OPINION AND AMERICAN FOREIGN
POLICY -- THE QUEMOY CRISIS OF
1958.=                  IRISMD-60-POA

QUEST
PERONISM AND ARGENTINA'S QUEST FOR
LEADERSHIP IN LATIN AMERICA.=
                        ALEXRJ-55-PAS

AFRICA'S QUEST FOR ORDER.=
                        BURKFG-64-ASQ

OLD SOCIETIES AND NEW STATES -- THE
QUEST FOR MODERNITY IN ASIA AND

QUEST (CONTINUATION)
AFRICA.= GEERO -63-OSN

QUESTION
COMMUNISM AND THE NATIONAL QUESTION
IN YUGOSLAVIA.= FRANJ -55-CNC

THOUGHTS ON THE CHINESE QUESTION IN
SOUTHEAST ASIA.= HALLDG-54-TCQ

THE ITALIAN ACTION PARTY AND THE
INSTITUTIONAL QUESTION.=
KOGAN -53-IAP

THE 'SECOND CHAMBER' QUESTION IN
THE GOLD COAST (GHANA).=
WRAIRE-54-SCQ

RACE
RACE AND POWER -- STUDIES OF
LEADERSHIP IN FIVE BRITISH
DEPENDENCIES.= BOW GR-56-RPS

RACE AND POLITICS -- PARTNERSHIP IN
THE FEDERATION OF RHODESIA
NYASALAND.= CLEGG -60-RPP

RACE AND NATIONALISM -- THE
STRUGGLE FOR POWER IN
RHODESIA-NYASALAND.= FRANFM-60-RNS

RACE, SOCIAL MOBILITY AND POLITICS
IN BRAZIL.= HAMMFR-63-RSM

AN AFRICAN BOURGEOISIE -- RACE,
CLASS, AND POLITICS IN SOUTH
AFRICA.= KUPEL -65-ABR

MALAYAN POLITICS -- RACE AND
CLASS.= SWIFM -62-MPR

RACE AND CLASS IN RURAL BRAZIL.=
WAGLC -52-RCR

RACIAL
RACIAL DISCRIMINATION AND NEGRO
LEADERSHIP PROBLEMS -- THE CASE OF
A NORTHERN COMMUNITY
(UNITED STATES).= BOWML -65-RDN

AFRICAN ATTITUDES -- A STUDY OF THE
SOCIAL, RACIAL, AND POLITICAL
ATTITUDES OF SOME MIDDLE CLASS
AFRICANS.= BRETEA-63-AAS

RACIAL AND MORAL CRISIS -- THE ROLE
OF LITTLE ROCK MINISTERS
(UNITED STATES).= CAMPEQ-59-RMC

RACIAL CRISIS IN AMERICA --
LEADERSHIP IN CONFLICT.=
KILLL -64-RCA

COMMUNITY AND RACIAL FACTORS IN
INTELLECTUAL ROLES
(UNITED STATES).= RECOW -56-CRF

SUPREME COURT BEHAVIOR IN RACIAL
EXCLUSION CASES -- 1935-1960
(UNITED STATES).= ULMESS-62-SCB

RADICAL
BURMA'S RADICAL LEFT -- A STUDY IN
FAILURE.= BADGJH-61-BSR

THE FRENCH RADICAL PARTY -- FROM
HERRIOT TO MENDES-FRANCE.=
DE-TF -61-FRP

RADICAL NATIONALISM -- THE
POLITICAL ORIENTATIONS OF
PANAMANIAN LAW STUDENTS.=
GOLDD -62-RNP

AMERICAN POLITICS AND THE RADICAL
RIGHT.= PAYNT -62-APR

THE FRENCH RADICAL SOCIALIST PARTY
AND THE REPUBLICAN FRONT OF 1956.
SCHLJA-58-FRS

THE RADICAL TRADITION
(GREAT BRITAIN).= TAWNRH-64-RTG

AMERICA'S RADICAL RIGHT -- POLITICS
AND IDEOLOGY.= WOLFRE-64-ASR

RADICALISM
RIGHT-WING RADICALISM IN WEST
GERMANY'S YOUNGER GENERATION.=
BERGV -62-RWR

ARGENTINE RADICALISM, 1957-1963.=
SNOWG -63-AR

RAISON
LA FIEVRE DE LA RAISON --
NATIONALISM AND THE FRENCH RIGHT.=
WEBEE -58-LFD

RAKOSI
AFTER RAKOSI -- DISGRACE AND
REHABILITATION (HUNGARY).=
MCCAWO-62-ARD

RANK
RANK EQUILIBRATION AND POLITICAL
BEHAVIOR.= ANDEB -64-REP

THE AFRICAN ARISTOCRACY -- RANK
AMONG THE SWAZI.= KUPEH -47-AAR

THE RANK - AND - FILE - LEADER
(UNITED STATES).= PECKSM-63-RFL

FEDERAL ADMINISTRATION, RANK, AND
CIVIL STRIFE AMONG BEMBA ROYALS
AND NOBLES (ZAMBIA).= WERBRP-67-FAR

THE LEADERSHIP, THE RANK AND FILE,
AND MR. BEVAN (GREAT BRITAIN).=
YOUNM -53-LRF

RANKING
FAMILY STATUS, LOCAL - COMMUNITY
STATUS, AND SOCIAL STRATIFICATION
-- THREE TYPES OF SOCIAL RANKING.=
BARBB -61-FSL

A METHOD FOR RANKING COMMUNITY
INFLUENTIALS.= DICKFR-60-MRC

CASTE RANKING AND COMMUNITY
STRUCTURE IN FIVE REGIONS OF INDIA
AND PAKISTAN.= MARRM -60-CRC

RANKS
DISILLUSIONMENT WITHIN THE RANKS
(CHINA).= COHEAA-63-DWR

RAROTONGA
SOCIAL CHANGE IN THE SOUTH PACIFIC
-- RAROTONGA AND AITUTAKI.=
BEAGE -57-SCS

RASHTRIYA SWAYAMSEVAK
MILITANT HINDUISM IN INDIAN
POLITICS -- A STUDY OF THE R.S.S.
(RASHTRIYA SWAYAMSEVAK SANGH).=
CURRJA-51-MHI

RATIFICATION
THE FRENCH TRADE ASSOCIATIONS AND
THE RATIFICATION OF THE SCHUMAN
PLAN.= EHRMFW-54-FTA

RATIONAL
THE RATIONAL MODEL, THE

RATICNAL                    (CCNTINUATICN)
  SCCICLCGICAL MCCEL, ANC
  METRCPCLITAN REFCRM
  (UNITED STATES).=           GREES -63-RMS

RATICNALITY
  THE RESFCNSIBLE ELECTCRATE --
  RATICNALITY IN FRESICENTIAL VCTING
  1936-1960 (UNITEC STATES).=
                              KEY-VC-66-RER

  'BUREAUCRACY' ANC 'RATICNALITY' IN
  WEBER'S CRGANIZATICN THECRY -- AN
  EMPIRICAL STUCY.=           UDY,SH-59-BRW

RE-ENTERS
  THE FRENCH ARMY RE-ENTERS PCLITICS
  1940-1955.=                 KELLGA-61-FAR

RE-EVALLATICN
  MEXICC'S CNE - FARTY SYSTEM -- A
  RE-EVALLATICN.=             PACGLV-57-MSC

  THE DIVINE KINGCCM CF THE JUKUN --
  A RE-EVALUATICN CF SCME THECRIES
  (EAST AFRICAN).=            YOUNMW-66-CKJ

RE-EXAMINATICN
  THE MCNARCH ANC THE SELECTICN CF A
  PRIME MINISTER -- A RE-EXAMINATICN
  CF THE CRISIS CF 1931
  (GREAT BRITAIN).=           MCCCGC-57-MSP

RE-EXAMINED
  THE ELITE ANC THE RULING CLASS --
  PARETC ANC MCSCA RE-EXAMINEC.=
                              KOLEF -67-ERC

  PCLITICAL LEACERSHIF RE-EXAMINEC --
  AN EXPERIMENTAL APPRCACH
  (UNITEC STATES).=           MCCSM -51-PLR

REACTICN
  RETREAT ANC REACTICN IN EASTERN
  EURCPE.=                    LANCP -58-RRE

  REACTICN ANC REVCLUTICN IN
  LATIN AMERICA -- THE CCNFLICT
  SCCIETY.=                   SILVKH-61-RRL

REACTICNS
  SCME REACTICNS CF JAPANESE
  UNIVERSITY STUCENTS TC PERSUASIVE
  CCMMUNICATICN.=             MCGIE -65-RJU

REACTIVE
  CCNSISTENT REACTIVE PARTICIPATICN
  CF GRCUF MEMBERS ANC REDUCTICN CF
  INTERCRCUP CCNFLICT.=       KATZC -59-CRP

READER
  AUSTRALIAN PCLITICS -- A READER.=
                              MAYEH -66-APR

  REACER IN BUREALCRACY.=
                              MERTVK-52-RB

  STUCIES IN BRITISH FCLITICS
                    -- A READER IN
  POLITICAL SCCICLCGY.=       ROSER -66-SBP

  LEGISLATIVE BEHAVICR -- A READER IN
  THECRY ANC RESEARCH.=       WAHLJC-59-LBR

READING
  THE CCNSERVATIVE ASSCCIATION ANC
  THE LABCUR PARTY IN READING
  (GREAT BRITAIN).=           BLCNJ -58-CAL

READINGS
  MCDERN AMERICAN SCCIETY -- READINGS
  IN THE PRCBLEMS CF CRCER ANC

READINGS                    (CCNTINUATICN)
  CHANGE.=                    CAVIK -49-MAS

REALISM
  CCST CF REALISM -- CCNTEMPORARY
  RESTATEMENT CF CEMCCRACY.=
                              CAVIE -64-CRC

  ETHICPIA -- ICENTITY, ALTHCRITY ANC
  REALISM.=                   LEVICN-66-EIA

REALIST
  THE SEMI-SCVEREIGN FECPLE --
  REALIST'S VIEW CF CEMCCRACY IN
  AMERICA.=                   SCHAEE-60-SSP

REALITIES
  CASTRC'S REVCLLTICN -- MYTHS ANC
  REALITIES.=                 CRAPT -62-CSR

REALITY
  ELECTCRAL MYTH ANC REALITY -- THE
  1964 ELECTICN (UNITEC STATES).=
                              CCNVPE-65-EMR

  EAST CERMAN REVISICNISM -- THE
  SPECTRE ANC THE REALITY.=
                              CCWAM -62-EGR

  THE CLD ANC THE NEW APRA IN PERU --
  MYTH ANC REALITY.=          PIKEFB-64-ONA

  PCPULAR PARTICIFATICN -- MYTHS ANC
  REALITY (SCVIET UNICN).=
                              SWEAHR-60-PPM

  REPUTATICN ANC REALITY IN THE STUCY
  CF 'CCMMUNITY FCWER'
  (UNITEC STATES).=           WOLFRE-60-RRS

REAPPCRTICNMENT
  THE PCLITICS CF REAPPCRTIONMENT
  (UNITEC STATES).=           JEWEME-62-PR

REARMAMENT
  SCCIC-ECCNCMIC ASPECTS CF GERMAN
  REARMAMENT.=                BRANG -65-SEA

  THE WEST GERMAN PCLITICAL PARTIES
  ANC REARMAMENT.=            RS    -53-WGP

  GERMAN REARMAMENT ANC THE CLD
  MILITARY ELITE.=            SPEIH -54-GRC

  GERMAN REARMAMENT ANC ATCMIC WAR --
  THE VIEWS CF GERMAN MILITARY ANC
  PCLITICAL LEACERS.=         SPEIH -57-GRA

REASSESSMENT
  THE SCCICLCGY CF CCMMUNITY POWER --
  A REASSESSMENT (UNITEC STATES).=
                              POLSNW-59-SCP

  ARMY ANC SCCIETY IN ENGLAND
  1870-1900 -- A REASSESSMENT OF THE
  CARCWELL REFCRMS.=          TUCKAV-63-ASE

REBELLING
  THE REBELLING YCUNG SCHCLARS
  (GREAT BRITAIN, UNITEC STATES).=
                              HACKA -60-RYS

REBELLICN
  REBELLICN CF THE YCUNG (FRANCE).=
                              COSWR -65-RYF

  THE ENC OF THE INCCNESIAN
  REBELLICN.=                 FEITH -63-EIR

  ALGERIA -- REBELLICN ANC
  REVCLUTICN.=                GILLJ -61-ARR

  RITUALS CF REBELLICN IN SCUTH EAST

RELATIONSHIP          (CCNTINUATICN)
AMCNG INTERESTS, PARTIES, AND
GCVERNMENTAL STRUCTURE
(UNITED STATES))=          SALIRH-6C-SLP

THE LEADER - FCLLCWER
RELATICNSHIP.=          STEPTE-59-LFR

RELATICNSHIPS
THE EXECUTIVE CVERSEAS --
ADMINISTRATIVE ATTITUDES AND
RELATICNSHIPS IN A FOREIGN CULTURE
(MEXICC).=          FAYEJ -59-EOA

CIVILIAN CCNTRCL AND THE
CCNSTITLTICN (LNITED STATES,
MILITARY - CIVIL RELATICNSHIPS).=
          HUNTSP-56-CCC

ADMINISTRATIVE RESPCNSIBILITY --
CCNGRESSICNAL PRESCRIPTION CF
INTERAGENCY RELATICNSHIPS
(UNITED STATES).=          SMITJM-57-ARC

RELEVANCE
THE RELEVANCE CF PERSCNALITY FCR
PCLITICAL PARTICIPATICN.=
          LEVICJ-58-RPP

RELEVANT
SCME FINDINCS RELEVANT TC THE CREAT
MAN THEORY CF LEADERSHIP.=
          BORGEF-54-FRC

RELIGICN
RELIGICN AND PCLITICS IN PAKISTAN.=
          BINDL -61-RPP

RELIGICN, REVCLLTICN AND REFORM --
NEW FCRCES FCR CHANGE IN
LATIN AMERICA.=          D'ANWV-64-RRR

RELIGICN AS AN INSTRUMENT OF
CULTURE CHANGE -- THE PROBLEM CF
THE SECTS IN THE SCVIET UNICN.=
          CUNNSP-64-RIC

RELIGICN AND AUTHCRITY IN MCDERN
BURMA.=          MENDEM-6O-RAM

RELIGICN AND PCLITICS IN BURMA.=
          SMITDE-65-RPB

SMALL TCWN IN MASS SCCIETY --
CLASS, PCWER AND RELIGICN IN A
RURAL CCMMUNITY (UNITED STATES).=
          VIDIAJ-58-STM

RELIGICUS
CHARISMA AND RELIGICUS INNOVATION
-- THE SOCIAL LCCATICN CF
ISREALITE PRCPHECY.=          BERGPL-63-CRI

THE CIVIL - RELIGICUS HIERARCHY IN
MESCAMERICAN CCMMUNITIES -- PRE -
SPANISH BACKGRCUND AND COLONIAL
DEVELCPMENT.=          CARRP -61-CRH

RELIGICUS SECTARIANISM IN THE
LEBANESE PCLITICAL SYSTEM.=
          CROWRE-62-RSL

RELIGICUS CRGANIZATICNS AND
PCLITICAL PRCCESS IN CENTRALIZED
EMPIRES (MIDDLE EAST, FAR EAST).=
          EISESN-62-ROP

THE PCLITICAL - RELIGICUS SECTS OF
VIETNAM.=          FALLBB-55-PRS

THE RELIGICUS BACKGRCUND CF
CANADIAN M.P.'S.=          LAPCJD-58-RBC

RELIGICLS          (CCNTINUATICN)
RELIGICLS AND SCCICECCNCMIC FACTCRS
IN THE FRENCH VCTE, 1946-1956.=
          MACRD -58-RSF

RELIGICLS INFLUENCES IN THE
BACKGRCLND CF THE BRITISH LABCUR
PARTY.=          SMITRW-57-RIB

RELIGICLS ELITES IN LATIN AMERICA
-- CATHCLICISM, LEADERSHIP AND
SCCIAL CHANGE.=          VALLI -65-REL

RELIGICLS BRCTHERHCCCS IN MCRCCCAN
PCLITICS.=          VICAFS-5C-RBM

RELIGICLS ELITES --
CIFFERENTIATICNS AND CEVELOPMENTS
IN ROMAN CATHCLICISM
(LATIN AMERICA).=          YALLI -67-REC

RENAISSANCE
THE RENAISSANCE CF THE RUSSIAN
INTELLICENTSIA.=          PILLJH-57-RRI

RENEWAL
CHANGES IN FUNCTICN AND LEACERSHIP
RENEWAL (GREAT BRITAIN).=
          DENNN -61-CFL

CCMMUNITY PCWER AND URBAN RENEWAL
SUCCESS (UNITED STATES).=
          HAWLAH-63-CPU

URBAN RENEWAL PCLITICS -- SLUM
CLEARANCE IN NEWARK
(UNITED STATES).=          KAPLH -63-URP

RECRGANIZATICN
THE RECRGANIZATICN CF
ADMINISTRATICN IN TURKESTAN
(SCVIET UNICN).=          DAVLT -63-RAT

THE INDIAN PARLIAMENT AND STATES
RECRGANIZATICN.=          GUPTSK-57-IPS

A HAIRBRAINED SCHEME IN RETRCSPECT
(SCVIET UNICN, PARTY
RECRGANIZATICN).=          HOUGJF-65-HSR

ADMINISTRATIVE RECRGANIZATICN AND
THE BUILDING CF CCMMUNISM
(SCVIET UNICN).=          JURCA -60-ARB

THE RECRGANIZATICN CF PARTY
LEADERSHIP IN AGRICULTURE
(SCVIET UNICN).=          KABYS -63-RPL

THE SCVIET INDUSTRIAL
RECRGANIZATICN.=          NCVEA -57-SIR

THE RECRGANIZATICN CF SCVIET
EDUCATICN.=          URBAP -62-RSE

RECRGANIZATICN IN THE PHILIPPINE
NATICNAL GCVERNMENT PRICR TO
1954.=          VILALA-61-RPN

RECRGANIZATICNS
PCLITICAL IMPLICATICNS CF RECENT
SCVIET ECCNCMIC RECRGANIZATICNS.=
          BALLWB-61-PIR

RECRGANIZED
PARTY CCNTRCLS RECRGANIZED
(SCVIET UNICN).=          RITVH -63-PCR

REPLICATICN
PRESIDENTIAL LEADERSHIP IN CONGRESS
CN FOREIGN PCLICY -- A REPLICATICN
CF A HYPCTHESIS (UNITED STATES).=
          KESSM -65-PLC

REPCRTS
PCLITICAL CCNTRCLS IN THE SOVIET

RHODE ISLAND        (CONTINUATION)
                    GOODJS-67-NLR

RHODESIA
  TRIBAL RULE AND MODERN POLITICS IN
  NORTHERN RHODESIA.=    BILLMG-59-TRM

  RACE AND POLITICS -- PARTNERSHIP IN
  THE FEDERATION OF RHODESIA
  NYASALAND.=            CLEGE -60-RPP

  THE SOCIAL CHARACTERISTICS OF AN
  EMERGENT ELITE IN HARARE (SOUTHERN
  RHODESIA).=           LUKHMB-66-SCE

  CLAN, CHIEFTAINSHIP, AND SLAVERY IN
  LUVALE POLITICAL ORGANIZATION
  (NORTH RHODESIA).=    WHITCM-57-CCS

RHODESIA-NYASALAND
  RACE AND NATIONALISM -- THE
  STRUGGLE FOR POWER IN
  RHODESIA-NYASALAND.=  FRANFM-60-RNS

RHODESIAS
  THE ADOPTION OF POLITICAL STYLES BY
  AFRICAN POLITICIANS IN THE
  RHODESIAS.=           SCARJR-66-APS

RICH
  POOR MAN, RICH MAN, BIG-MAN, CHIEF
  -- POLITICAL TYPES IN MELANESIA
  AND POLYNESIA.=       SAHLMD-63-PMR

RIFT
  RIFT AND REVOLT IN HUNGARY.=
                        VALIF -61-RRH

RIGHT
  THE NEW AMERICAN RIGHT.=
                        BELLD -55-NAR

  DANGER ON THE RIGHT IN GERMANY.=
                        COVEHM-50-DRG

  THE FOREIGN POLICY VIEWS OF THE
  INDIAN RIGHT.=        ERDMHL-66-FPV

  IDEOLOGICAL CORRELATES OF RIGHT
  WING POLITICAL ALIENATION IN
  MEXICO.=              JOHNKF-65-ICR

  UYOKU, THE RIGHT WING OF JAPAN.=
                        KINOH -63-URW

  PREDICTING SUPREME COURT DECISIONS
  MATHEMATICALLY -- A QUANTITIVE
  ANALYSIS OF THE RIGHT TO COUNSEL
  (UNITED STATES).=     KORTF -57-PSC

  NATIONALISM AND RIGHT WING IN JAPAN
  -- A STUDY OF POST-WAR TRENDS.=
                        MORRII-60-NRW

  INDIA -- RECONCILIATION OF THE
  RIGHT.=               MZ    -50-IRR

  AMERICAN POLITICS AND THE RADICAL
  RIGHT.=               PAYNT -62-APR

  THREE GENERATIONS -- THE EXTREME
  RIGHT WING IN FINNISH POLITICS.=
                        RINTM -62-TGE

  THE EUROPEAN RIGHT -- A HISTORICAL
  PROFILE.=             ROGEH -65-ERH

  TOWARD A DEFINITION OF THE EXTREME

RIGHT               (CONTINUATION)
  RIGHT.=               RUSHGB-63-TDE

  CELEBRITY STRUCTURE OF THE FAR
  RIGHT (UNITED STATES).=
                        STEWDK-64-CSF

  LA FIEVRE DE LA RAISON --
  NATIONALISM AND THE FRENCH RIGHT.=
                        WEBEE -58-LFD

  LEFT AND RIGHT EXTREMISM IN
  ARGENTINA.=           WHITAP-63-LRE

  AMERICA'S RADICAL RIGHT -- POLITICS
  AND IDEOLOGY.=        WOLFRE-64-ASR

RIGHT-WING
  RIGHT-WING RADICALISM IN WEST
  GERMANY'S YOUNGER GENERATION.=
                        BERGV -62-RWR

  SOCIAL STRATIFICATION AND
  'RIGHT-WING EXTREMISM'.=
                        LIPSS -59-SSR

RIGHTISTS
  DOWN AMONG THE RIGHTISTS
  (UNITED STATES).=     CROZB -62-DAR

RIGHTS
  SUPREME COURT BEHAVIOR AND CIVIL
  RIGHTS (UNITED STATES).=
                        ULMESS-60-SCB

RIKSDAG
  THE SWEDISH RIKSDAG.= ELDEN -57-SR

RITUAL
  HEADMAN AND THE RITUAL OF LAUPULA
  VILLAGES (AFRICA).=   CUNNI -56-HRL

  POLITICS, LAW AND RITUAL IN TRIBAL
  SOCIETY.=             GLUCM -65-PLR

RITUALS
  RITUALS OF REBELLION IN SOUTH EAST
  AFRICA.=              GLICM -54-RRS

RIVALRY
  STATUS RIVALRY AND CULTURAL
  EVOLUTION IN POLYNESIA.=
                        GOLDI -55-SRC

  BIFACTIONAL RIVALRY AS AN
  ALTERNATIVE TO TWO - PARTY
  COMPETITION (UNITED STATES).=
                        SINDAP-55-BRA

ROAD
  GOVERNMENT AND POLITICS IN JAPAN --
  THE ROAD TO DEMOCRACY.=
                        MAKIJM-62-GPJ

ROADS
  ROADS TO THE FUTURE
  (SOVIET UNION).=      FAINM -67-RFS

ROLE
  THE ROLE OF CONTEMPORARY POLITICAL
  PARTIES IN CHILE.=    ABBORS-51-RCP

  THE ROLE OF IDEOLOGY IN THE SOVIET
  SYSTEM.=              AKHMH -64-RIS

  THE HOUSE FOREIGN AFFAIRS
  COMMITTEE'S ROLE (UNITED STATES).=
                        ALISM -9 -HFA

  PRAVDA ON THE ROLE OF THE PARTY AND
  THE INDIVIDUAL (SOVIET UNION).=
                        ANON  -53-PRP

  THE ROLE OF TRADITIONALISM IN THE

RCLE                    (CONTINUATICN)
POLITICAL MCDERNIZATICN OF GHANA
AND UGADA.=            APTECE-60-RTP

SCME REFLECTICNS CN THE RCLE OF A
PCLITICAL CPPCSITICN IN NEW
NATICNS.=              APTECE-62-RRP

THE SCCIAL RCLE CF THE TECHNICIAN -
INTELLICENTSIA IN SCCIETY.=
                       BAHRHP-61-SRT

THE RCLE CF PCLITICAL LEADERSHIP IN
THE PASSAGE CF CREGCN'S MIGRATCRY
LABCR LEGISLATICN
(UNITED STATES).=      BALMCG-62-RPL

PCSITICN, RCLE AND STATUS -- A
REFCRMULATICN CF CCNCEPTS.=
                       BATEFL-56-PRS

THE NEW ECCNCMIC SYSTEM AND THE
RCLE CF TECHNCCRATS IN THE CCR
(EAST GERMANY).=       BAYHTA-66-NES

THE ZAIBATSU'S WARTIME RCLE
(JAPAN).=              BISSTA-45-ZSW

THE CIVIC RCLE CF THE MILITARY --
SCME CRITICAL HYPCTHESES.=
                       BCBRCB-66-CRM

THE RCLE CF THE INTERNATICNAL
CCMMISSICN CF JURISTS IN THE
PRCMCTICN CF WCRLC PEACE.=
                       BCSEV -64-RIC

ACTIVITIES AND RCLE DEFINITIONS CF
GRASSRCCTS PARTY CFFICIALS
(UNITED STATES).=      BCWML -66-ARC

THE RCLE CF THE UNIVERSITY IN THE
DEVELCPING SCCIETY CF THE WEST
INCIES.=               BRAILE-65-RUC

RACIAL AND MCRAL CRISIS -- THE ROLE
CF LITTLE RCCK MINISTERS
(UNITED STATES).=      CAMPEQ-59-RMC

CCMMUNITY PCWER PERSPECTIVES AND
RCLE CEFINITICNS CF NCRTH AMERICAN
EXECUTIVES IN AN ARCENTINE
CCMMUNITY.=            CHAME -66-CPP

THE CHINESE GENTRY, STUCIES CN
THEIR RCLE IN THE NINETEENTH
CENTURY CHINESE SCCIETY.=
                       CHANCL-55-CGS

THE SCCIAL RCLE CF THE LITERARY
ELITE (UNITED STATES).=
                       CHARB -50-SRL

THE PCLITICAL RCLE CF CRGANIZEC
LABCR (UNITED STATES).=
                       CHERJ -56-PRC

GCING ABCUT PERSECUTING CIVIL
SERVANTS -- THE RCLE CF THE IRISH
PARLIAMENTARY REPRESENTATIVES.=
                       CHUBB -63-GAP

THE CHINESE GENTRY -- STUCIES CN
THEIR RCLE IN NINETEENTH-CENTURY
CHINESE SCCIETY.=      CHUNC -55-CGS

THE RCLE CF BUREAUCRATIC NCRMS IN
AFRICAN PCLITICAL STRUCTURES.=
                       CCLSE -58-RBN

YUGCSLAVIA -- STATUS AND RCLE CF
THE EXECUTIVE CRGANS CURING THE

RCLE                    (CONTINUATICN)
FIRST STAGE CF YUGCSLAVIA'S
PCLITICAL AND CCNSTITUTICNAL
DEVELCPMENT.=          CJORJ -58-YSR

THE WEEKLY NEWSFAPER'S LEADERSHIP
RCLE AS SEEN BY CCMMUNITY LEACER'S
(UNITED STATES).=      ECELAS-63-WNS

JAPAN'S RCLE IN SCUTHEAST ASIAN
NATICNALIST MCVEMENTS, 1940-1945.=
                       ELSBWH-53-JSR

THE DEVELCPMENT ACMINISTRATCR'S
RCLE -- SCME CCMMENTS
(PHILIPPINES).=        ENCAV -62-CAS

IDENTIFICATICN WITH CLASS AND
PCLITICAL RCLE BEHAVICR
(UNITED STATES).=      EULAH -56-ICP

THE CHANGING RCLE CF THE FORMER
JAPANESE LANDLCRC.=    EYREJD-55-CRF

PCSTWAR RCLE CF THE CCMMUNIST PARTY
(SCVIET UNICN).=       FAINM -49-PRC

BANTU BUREAUCRACY -- A STUCY CF
RCLE CCNFLICT AND INSTITUTICNAL
CHANGE IN THE SCGA POLITICAL
SYSTEM.=               FALLLA-55-BBS

PCLITICAL PCLICY AND PERSUASICN --
THE RCLE CF CCMMUNICATICNS FRCM
PCLITICAL LEACERS (SCVIET UNION,
GREAT BRITAIN, UNITED STATES).=
                       FELDMC-58-PPP

THE MAN CN HCRSEBACK -- THE RCLE CF
THE MILITARY IN PCLITICS.=
                       FINESE-62-MHR

AUTHCRITY, EFFICIENCY, AND ROLE
STRESS -- PRCBLEMS IN THE
CEVELCPMENT CF EAST AFRICAN
BUREAUCRACIES (LGANCA, KENYA,
TANGANYIKA).=          FLEMWG-66-AER

THE RCLE CF BUREAUCRACY IN
TRANSITION (GERMANY).=
                       FRANE -66-RBT

THE RCLE CCNCEPT IN LEGISLATURES --
A PRCBABILITY MCDEL AND A NCTE CN
CCGNITIVE STRUCTURE
(UNITED STATES).=      FRANWL-65-RCL

THE RCLE CF THE CCNSTITUTICN-MAKER
AS A REPRESENTATIVE
(UNITED STATES).=      FRIERS-65-RCM

THE RCLE CF THE SCVIET ARMY IN THE
CRISIS CF THE CCLLECTIVE
LEACERSHIP.=           GALAN -57-RSA

THE RCLE CF THE MILITARY IN RECENT
SCVIET PCLITICS.=      GARTRL-57-RMR

THE JAVANESE KIJAJI -- THE CHANGING
RCLE CF A CULTURAL ERCKER.=
                       GEERC -60-JKC

THE CHINESE ARMY'S RCLE IN THE
CULTURAL REVCLUTICN.=  GITTJ -67-CAS

THE RCLE CF THE CHINESE ARMY.=
                       GITTJ -67-RCA

THE RCLE CF THE ARMY IN THE
TRANSITICNAL ARAB STATE
(MICCLE EAST).=        CLUBJ -65-RAT

SITUATICNAL PRESSURES ANC

320

ROLE (CONTINUATION)
FUNCTIONAL ROLE OF THE ETHNIC
LABOR LEADER.= GREES -53-SPF

THE ROLE OF THE BRITISH CIVIL
SERVANT IN POLICY FORMATION.=
GRIFR -53-RBC

THE ROLE OF THE PRESS
(SOVIET UNION).= GRULL -63-RPS

AUSTRIAN LABOR'S BID FOR POWER --
THE ROLE OF THE TRADE UNION
FEDERATION.= GULICA-58-ALS

MEASURING (UNION OFFICIALS') ROLE
CONFLICT (UNITED STATES).=
GULLJT-56-MUO

THE POLITICAL ROLE OF AFRICAN ARMED
FORCES -- THE IMPACT OF FOREIGN
MILITARY ASSISTANCE.= GUTTWF-67-PRA

CULTURAL PATTERNS IN THE ROLE OF
THE MANAGER.= HAIRM -63-CPR

THE ROLE OF THE MILITARY IN
ISRAEL.= HALPB -62-RMI

THE ROLE OF PRIVATE BUSINESS
(LATIN AMERICA).= HANSSG-66-RPB

THE ROLE OF THE INTELLECTUAL IN
FOMENTING CHANGE -- THE UNIVERSITY
(LATIN AMERICA).= HARRJP-64-RIF

SAINT-SIMON AND THE ROLE OF THE
ELITE.= HARTDK-64-SSR

THE CONGRESSMAN'S CONCEPTION OF HIS
ROLE (UNITED STATES).=
HAWVCF-63-CSC

THE ROLE OF THE SOVIET PARTY
CONGRESS.= HD -52-RSP

THE CHANGING ROLE OF THE MILITARY
IN COLUMBIA.= HELGJL-61-CRM

THE WHITE SETTLER'S ROLE IN KENYA.=
HILLMF-60-WSS

THE ROLE OF CLASSES IN HISTORICAL
MATERIALISM.= HODGDC-59-RCH

THE OUTSIDER IN THE SENATE -- AN
ALTERNATIVE ROLE (UNITED STATES).=
HUITRK-61-OSA

TANGANYIKA'S VIEW OF LABOUR'S
ROLE.= KAMAM -64-TSV

COMPARATIVE STUDY OF THE ROLE OF
POLITICAL PARTIES IN THE STATE
LEGISLATURES (UNITED STATES).=
KEEFWJ-56-CSR

THE ROLE OF THE MILITARY IN
MIDDLE EAST POLITICS.=
KHADM -53-RMM

THE CHANGING ROLE OF THE CHINESE
INTELLECTUALS -- AN INTRODUCTORY
NOTE.= KRACEA-58-CRC

ENTREPRENEURS IN LATIN AMERICA AND
THE ROLE OF CULTURAL AND
SITUATIONAL PROCESSES.=
KRIEL -63-ELA

LABOR'S ROLE IN AMERICAN POLITICS.=
LAIDHW-59-LSR

THE CATHOLIC ANTI - COMMUNIST ROLE

ROLE (CONTINUATION)
WITHIN AUSTRALIAN LABOR.=
LANGFC-56-CAC

THE ROLE OF SANCTION IN CONFLICT
RESOLUTION.= LASSHD-67-RSC

THE ROLE OF BRAINS IN THE TOTAL
STATE.= LERND -53-RBT

THE POLITICAL ROLE OF THE ARMY IN
INDONESIA.= LEV,DS-64-PRA

THE ROLE OF THE INTELLECTUALS.=
LICHG -60-RI

THE ROLE OF VOLUNTARY ASSOCIATIONS
IN WEST AFRICAN URBANISATION.=
LITTKL-57-RVA

LABOR'S ROLE IN NEWLY DEVELOPING
COUNTRIES.= LODGGC-59-LSR

BUREAUCRATIC MASS MEDIA -- A STUDY
OF ROLE DEFINITIONS
(UNITED STATES).= LYSTMH-56-BMM

THE ROLE OF THE STATE LEGISLATOR IN
MASSACHUSETTS (UNITED STATES).=
MACRD -54-RSL

THE ROLE OF THE BUREAUCRACY IN
JAPAN.= MAKIJM-47-RBJ

SOCIAL DETERMINANTS OF THE ROLE OF
A CIVIL SERVICE (UNITED STATES,
GREAT BRITAIN).= MARKM -56-SDR

CHANGING CONCEPTS OF THE ROLE OF
THE MILITARY IN LATIN AMERICA.=
MCALLN-65-CCR

THE MOTIVATION AND ROLE OF A
PROPAGANDIST (GREAT BRITAIN).=
MCCOTH-52-MRP

PUBLIC ATTITUDES TOWARD THE
REPRESENTATIONAL ROLE OF
LEGISLATORS AND JUDGES
(UNITED STATES).= MCMUCD-65-PAT

REPRESENTATIONAL ROLE TYPES -- A
RESEARCH NOTE (MICRONESIA,
POLYNESIA).= MELLN -67-RRT

THE ROLE OF THE CHIEFS AND THE HEAD
MAN AMONG THE LUGBARA OF THE WEST
NILE DISTRICT OF UGANDA.=
MIDDJ -56-RCH

THE POLITICAL ROLE OF LABOR IN
DEVELOPING COUNTRIES.=
MILLBH-63-PRL

THE ROLE OF AN INTEREST GROUP
LEADER IN THE HOUSE OF
COMMONS (GREAT BRITAIN).=

MILLJH-56-RIG

THE ROLE OF AN INTEREST GROUP
LEADER IN THE HOUSE OF
COMMONS (GREAT BRITAIN).=

MILLJH-56-RIG

THE ROLE OF GOVERNMENT CORPORATIONS
IN THE PHILIPPINES.= MILNRS-61-RGC

THE ROLE OF TECHNOCRATS IN

RCLE                    (CONTINUATION)
LATIN AMERICAN INTEGRATION.=
                        MITCC -67-RTL

OCCUPATIONAL RCLE STRAINS -- THE
AMERICAN ELECTIVE PUBLIC
OFFICIAL.=              MITCWC-58-ORS

THE RCLE CF THE SCIENTIFIC ELITE IN
THE DECISION TC USE THE ATOMIC
BCMB (UNITED STATES).=
                        MOORJW-58-RSE

SOVIET ADMINISTRATIVE LEGALITY --
THE RCLE CF THE ATTCRNEY GENERAL'S
OFFICE.=               MORGGG-62-SAL

THE RCLE CF THE VILLAGE IN
VIETNAMESE POLITICS.=  MUS,P -49-RVV

THE RCLE CF THE LOBEYIST -- THE
CASE CF OKLAHCMA (UNITED STATES).=
                        PATTSC-63-RLC

THE RCLE CF POLITICAL CRGANIZATIONS
IN INDCNESIA.=          PAUKGJ-58-RPC

THE RCLE CF THE MILITARY IN
INDCNESIA.=            PAUKGJ-62-RMI

THE CHANGING RCLE CF THE MILITARY
IN ARGENTINA.=         POTARA-61-CRM

THE RCLE CF THE LIBERAL PARTY IN
RECENT CANADIAN POLITICS.=
                        CUINHF-53-RLP

THE POLITICAL RCLE CF INDIA'S CASTE
ASSOCIATION.=          RANDLI-6C-PRI

A STUDY CF RCLE CCNCEPTICNS IN
BUREAUCRACY (UNITED STATES).=
                        REISL -49-SRC

THE RCLE CF THE RULES CCMMITTEE IN
ARRANGING THE PROGRAM CF THE U.S.
HCUSE CF REPRESENTATIVES
(UNITED STATES).=       ROBIJA-59-RRC

THE BCW GRCUP'S RCLE IN BRITISH
PCLITICS.=             ROSER -61-BGS

THE RCLE CF THE MILITARY IN
AMERICAN FCREIGN PCLICY.=
                        SAPIBM-4 -RMA

THE PCLITICAL RCLE CF PAKISTAN'S
CIVIL SERVICE.=        SAYEKB-58-PRP

ENTREPRENEURS OF LEBANON -- THE
RCLE CF THE BUSINESS LEADER IN A
DEVELCPING ECCNCMY.=   SAYIYA-62-ELR

THE RCLE CF ECCNCMIC DCMINANTS IN
CCMMUNITY PCWER STRUCTURE
(UNITED STATES).=       SCHURO-58-REC

RCLE CCNFLICT AND AMBIVALENCE IN
LEADERSHIP.=           SEEMM -53-RCA

THE RCLE CF THE INTELLIGENTSIA
(SCVIET UNICN).=        SETOH -62-RIS

THE RCLE CF THE SELECT COMMITTEE ON
NATIONALIZED INDUSTRY IN
PARLIAMENT (GREAT BRITAIN).=
                        SIMMRH-61-RSC

NIGERIAN ELITE -- RCLE CF
EDUCATION.=            SMYTHH-60-NER

THE RCLE CF THE FEDERAL DISTRICT

RCLE                    (CONTINUATION)
COURTS IN THE SEGREGATICN
CCNTRCVERSY (UNITED STATES).=
                        STEARJ-60-RFC

THE RCLE CF THE CHINESE COMMUNIST
PARTY.=                STEIHA-51-RCC

BRITISH PRESSURE GRCUPS -- THEIR
RCLE IN RELATION TO THE HOUSE CF
CCMMONS.=              STEWJC-58-BPG

LEADERSHIP AND RCLE EXPECTATION
(UNITED STATES).=       STOGRM-56-LRE

THE PCTENTIAL RCLE CF TURKISH
VILLAGE CPINICN LEADERS IN A
PROGRAM CF FAMILY PLANNING.=
                        SYTCJM-65-PRT

THE PCLITICAL RCLE CF THE MCSCCW
PATRIARCHATE.=          TEOON -60-PRM

THE PCLITICAL RCLE CF THE MCSCCW
PATRIARCHATE.=          TEOON -65-PRM

THE RCLE CF THE MILITARY IN CHINESE
GOVERNMENT.=            TUANC -48-RMC

THE MILITARY RCLE IN NATION
BUILDING AND ECCNCMIC
DEVELCPMENT.=          UNGEJP-63-MRN

THE RCLE CF ISLAM IN INDONESIAN
NATIONALISM.=          VAN-JM-58-RII

THE RCLE CF THE SOCIALIST
REVCLUTICNARIES IN 1917
(SCVIET UNICN).=        VISHMV-64-RSR

AMERICAN STATE LEGISLATORS' RCLE
ORIENTATIONS TCWARD PRESSURE
GRCUPS.=               WAHLJC-60-ASL

THE EXTRA - PRCFESSICNAL ROLE CF
THE LAWYER (UNITED STATES).=
                        WARDWI-56-EPR

TRADITICNAL RCLE PERFCRMANCE AND
THE DEVELCPMENT OF MODERN
PCLITICAL PARTIES -- THE INDIAN
CASE.=                 WEINM -64-TRP

THE WCRLD RCLE CF UNIVERSITIES.=
                        WIEDEW-62-WRU

THE RISE AND RCLE CF CHARISMATIC
LEADERS.=              WILLAR-65-RRC

LEADERSHIP TYPES, RCLE
DIFFERENTIATICN, AND SYSTEM
PRCBLEMS.=             WILLV -65-LTR

THE RCLE CF THE MILITARY IN
LATIN AMERICAN PCLITICS.=
                        WYCKT -60-RML

CITY CCUNCILMEN AND THE GROUP
STRUGGLE -- A TYPCLCGY CF ROLE
CRIENTATICNS (UNITED STATES).=
                        ZISKBH-65-CCG

THE SERVICE SECRETARY -- HAS HE A
USEFUL RCLE.=          ZUCKEM-66-SSH

RCLES
CLASS AND PARTY IN THE EISENHCWER
YEARS, CLASS RCLES AND PERSPECTIVE
IN THE 1952 AND 1956 ELECTION
(UNITED STATES).=       EULAH -62-CPE

THE GCVERNMENTAL RCLES CF

RUMANIA            (CONTINUATION)
  COMMUNIST STATES (BULGARIA,
  CZECHOSLOVAKIA, HUNGARY, EAST
  GERMANY, POLAND, RUMANIA,
  SOVIET UNION, YUGOSLAVIA).=
                    ICNEG -67-PEC

RUMANIAN
  THE RUMANIAN COMMUNIST LEADERSHIP.=
                    TOMADA-61-RCL

RUNNING
  WHO'S RUNNING THIS TOWN --
  COMMUNITY LEADERSHIP AND SOCIAL
  CHANGE (UNITED STATES).=
                    LOWRRP-65-WSR

RUNS
  WHO RUNS OUR TOWN (UNITED STATES).=
                    YAGEJW-63-WRO

RURAL
  POLITICAL ACTIVISM IN A RURAL
  COUNTY (UNITED STATES).=
                    ALTHP -66-PAR

  CHINA'S GENTRY -- ESSAYS IN RURAL -
  URBAN RELATIONS.=   FEI-  -53-CSG

  SOCIAL STRATIFICATION OF RURAL
  AREAS -- RESEARCH PROBLEMS
  (POLAND).=          GALEB -57-SSR

  LEADERSHIP FOR ACTION IN RURAL
  COMMUNITIES (UNITED STATES).=
                    KREIBW-60-LAR

  THE RURAL COMMUNITY AND POLITICAL
  LEADERSHIP IN SASKATCHEWAN
  (CANADA).=         LIPSSM-47-RCP

  RECRUITMENT CONTRASTS IN RURAL
  CAMPAIGN GROUPS (UNITED STATES).=
                    MARVD -61-RCR

  VILLAGE FACTIONS AND POLITICAL
  PARTIES IN RURAL WEST BENGAL
  (INDIA).=          NICHRW-63-VFP

  CONTEMPORARY TRENDS IN RURAL
  LEADERSHIP (UNITED STATES).=
                    NUQUJE-47-CTR

  SMALL TOWN IN MASS SOCIETY --
  CLASS, POWER AND RELIGION IN A
  RURAL COMMUNITY (UNITED STATES).=
                    VIDIAJ-58-STM

  RACE AND CLASS IN RURAL BRAZIL.=
                    WAGLC -52-RCR

  RURAL RESETTLEMENT IN SOUTH
  VIET NAM -- THE AGROVILLE
  PROGRAM.=          ZASLJJ-62-RRS

RUSSIA
  WILL RUSSIA DEBOLSHEVIZE.=
                    ANINDS-57-WRD

  CHANGES IN RUSSIA -- THE NEED FOR
  PERSPECTIVES.=     BARGFC-66-CRN

  HOW RUSSIANS RULE RUSSIA
  (SOVIET UNION).=   BIALS -64-HRR

  THE NEW CLASS IN RUSSIA.=
                    DALLCJ-61-NCR

  HOW RUSSIA IS RULED.=  FAINM -65-HRI

  WITHER RUSSIA -- A BUREAUCRACY
  UNDER FIRE (SOVIET UNION).=

RUSSIA             (CONTINUATION)
                    GALLG -66-WRB

  RUSSIA -- KHRUSHCHEV AND AFTER.=
                    GASSO -63-RKA

  WHO ARE THE RULERS IN RUSSIA.=
                    KAUFA -54-WAR

  RUSSIA AFTER KHRUSHCHEV.=
                    LABEL -56-RAK

  WITHER RUSSIA -- NOTES ON AN
  AGONIZING DIAGNOSIS
  (SOVIET UNION).=   LEONW -66-WRN

  CHINA, RUSSIA AND THE EXPERTS.=
                    LICHG -65-CRE

  CONFLICT AND DECISION-MAKING IN
  SOVIET RUSSIA -- A CASE STUDY OF
  AGRICULTURAL POLICY, 1953-1963.
                    PLOSSI-65-CDM

  THE RULING SERVANTS -- BUREAUCRACY
  IN RUSSIA, FRANCE, AND
  GREAT BRITAIN.=    STRAE -61-RSB

  PARTY AND STATE IN SOVIET RUSSIA
  AND NAZI GERMANY.=  UNGEAL-65-PSS

RUSSIAN
  THE RENAISSANCE OF THE RUSSIAN
  INTELLIGENTSIA.=   BILLJH-57-RRI

  THE TRANSFORMATION OF RUSSIAN
  SOCIETY -- ASPECTS OF SOCIAL
  CHANGE SINCE 1861.=  BLACCE-60-TRS

  THE TRAGEDY OF THE RUSSIAN
  INTELLIGENTSIA.=   CHAMWH-59-TRI

  THE NEW RUSSIAN INTELLIGENTSIA.=
                    DALLCJ-54-NRI

  THE SECRETARIAT AND THE LOCAL
  ORGANIZATIONS IN THE RUSSIAN
  COMMUNIST PARTY, 1921-1923.=
                    DANIRV-56-SLO

  INTELLECTUALS AND THE RUSSIAN
  REVOLUTION.=       DANIRV-61-IRR

  THE RUSSIAN INTELLIGENTSIA ON THE
  EVE OF THE REVOLUTION.=
                    ELKIB -60-RIE

  POST - STALIN TRENDS IN RUSSIAN
  LITERATURE.=       ERLIV -64-PST

  RUSSIAN LIBERALISM -- FROM GENTRY
  TO INTELLIGENTSIA.=  FISCG -58-RLG

  THE RED EXECUTIVE--A STUDY OF THE
  ORGANIZATION MAN IN RUSSIAN
  INDUSTRY.=         GRAND -60-RES

  THE AMERICAN LIBERALS AND THE
  RUSSIAN REVOLUTION.=  LASCO -62-ALR

  THE NEW CLASS DIVIDED -- RUSSIAN
  SCIENCE AND TECHNOLOGY VERSUS
  COMMUNISM.=        PARRA -66-NCD

  THE HISTORICAL EVOLUTION OF THE
  RUSSIAN INTELLIGENTSIA.=
                    PIPER -60-HER

  THE RUSSIAN INTELLIGENTSIA.=
                    PIPER -60-RI

  THE IMPERIAL RUSSIAN ARMY OFFICER.=

RUSSIAN                (CONTINUATION)
                       RAY,OA-61-IRA

THE RUSSIAN INTELLIGENTSIA AND
BOLSHEVISM.=           STEPF -58-RIB

THE RUSSIAN INTELLIGENTSIA --
MAKERS OF THE REVOLUTIONARY
STATE.=                TOMPSR-57-RIM

RUSSIANS
  HOW RUSSIANS RULE RUSSIA
  (SOVIET UNION).=     BIALS -64-HRR

  RUSSIANS AGAINST STALIN.=
                       CHAMWH-52-RAS

  WHAT THE RUSSIANS MEAN.=
                       CANIRV-62-WRM

SACRED
  SACRED KINGSHIP AND GOVERNMENT
  AMONG THE YORUBA (AFRICA).=
                       LLOYPC-60-SKG

SAFE
  SAFE SEATS, SENIORITY, AND POWER IN
  CONGRESS (UNITED STATES).=
                       WOLFRE-65-SSS

SAIGON
  THE SAIGON POLITICAL ELITE -- FOCUS
  ON FOUR CABINETS (SOUTH VIETNAM).=
                       WURFD -67-SPE

SAINT-SIMON
  SAINT-SIMON AND THE ROLE OF THE
  ELITE.=              HARTOK-64-SSR

SALA
  THE SALA MODEL -- AN ECOLOGICAL
  APPROACH TO THE STUDY OF
  COMPARATIVE ADMINISTRATION.=
                       RIGGFW-62-SME

SALIENCY
  PARTY GOVERNMENT AND THE SALIENCY
  OF CONGRESS (UNITED STATES).=
                       STOKDE-62-PGS

SAMOA
  POLITICAL DEVELOPMENT IN WESTERN
  SAMOA.=              DAVIJW-48-PDW

  POLITICAL AUTHORITY AND THE
  STRUCTURE OF KINSHIP IN ABORIGINAL
  SAMOA.=              EMBEM -62-PAS

  SOME OBSERVATIONS ON KINSHIP AND
  POLITICAL AUTHORITY IN SAMOA.=
                       FREED -64-OKP

  ELITE COMMUNICATION IN SAMOA -- A
  STUDY OF LEADERSHIP.= KEESFM-56-ECS

  POLITICAL ADVANCEMENT IN THE SOUTH
  PACIFIC -- A COMPARATIVE STUDY OF
  COLONIAL PRACTICE IN FIJI, TAHITI,
  AND AMERICAN SAMOA.= WESTFJ-61-PAS

SAMPLE
  AN AFRICAN ELITE -- A SAMPLE SURVEY
  OF 52 FORMER STUDENTS OF MAKERERE
  COLLEGE IN EAST AFRICA.=
                       GOLDJE-55-AES

  UNIVERSITY STUDENTS IN A WORLD OF
  CHANGE -- A COLUMBIAN SAMPLE.=
                       WILLRC-64-USW

SAMPLING
  THE STUDY OF EXECUTIVE BEHAVIOR BY

SAMPLING               (CONTINUATION)
  ACTIVITY SAMPLING
  (UNITED STATES).=    KELLJ -64-SEB

SAN JOSE
  POWER STRUCTURE AND ITS
  COMMUNICATION BEHAVIOR IN
  SAN JOSE, COSTA RICA.=
                       EDWAHT-67-PSI

SANCTION
  THE ROLE OF SANCTION IN CONFLICT
  RESOLUTION.=         LASSHD-67-RSC

SARAWAK
  POLITICAL RECRUITMENT IN SARAWAK --
  A CASE STUDY OF LEADERSHIP IN A
  NEW STATE.=          GLICHR-66-PRS

SARIT
  MARSHAL SARIT AND ABSOLUTIST RULE
  IN THAILAND.=        DARLFC-60-MSA

SASKATCHEWAN
  THE RURAL COMMUNITY AND POLITICAL
  LEADERSHIP IN SASKATCHEWAN
  (CANADA).=           LIPSSM-47-RCP

SATELLITE
  THE SATELLITE POLICE SYSTEM
  (EASTERN EUROPE).=   MP    -52-SPS

  CZECHOSLOVAKIA -- STABLE
  SATELLITE.=          PICKO -58-CSS

  SATELLITE GENERALS -- A STUDY OF
  MILITARY ELITES IN THE SOVIET
  SPHERE.=             POOLID-55-SGS

SATISFACTION
  PROCESS SATISFACTION AND POLICY
  APPROVAL IN STATE DEPARTMENT --
  CONGRESSIONAL RELATIONS
  (UNITED STATES).=    ROBIJA-61-PSP

SATSUMA-HAN
  FEUDAL SOCIETY AND MODERN
  LEADERSHIP IN SATSUMA-HAN.=
                       SAKARK-57-FSM

SAUDI ARABIAN
  THE SAUDI ARABIAN COUNCIL OF
  MINISTERS.=          HARROW-58-SAC

SCALE
  A SCALE ANALYSIS OF IDEOLOGICAL
  FACTORS IN CONGRESSIONAL VOTING
  (UNITED STATES).=    FARRCD-58-SAI

  SCALE POSITIONS AND 'POWER' IN THE
  SENATE (UNITED STATES).=
                       MACRD -59-SPP

SCALING
  SCALING LEGISLATIVE BEHAVIOR
  (UNITED STATES).=    BELKGM-58-SLB

  SCALING SUPREME COURT DECISIONS IN
  RELATION TO SOCIAL BACKGROUND
  (UNITED STATES).=    SCHMJ -58-SSC

  SCALING JUDICIAL CASES -- A
  METHODOLOGICAL NOTE
  (UNITED STATES).=    ULMESS-61-SJC

SCANDINAVIA
  PARLIAMENTARY GOVERNMENT IN
  SCANDINAVIA.=        ELDEN -60-PGS

  POLITICAL UNIFICATION -- A
  COMPARATIVE STUDY OF LEADERS AND

SENATE                 (CCNTINUATICN)
THE MCDERN SENATE CF CANADA,
1925-1963.=              KUNZFA-65-MSC

SCALE PCSITICNS AND 'PCWER' IN THE
SENATE (UNITED STATES).=
                        MACRC -59-SPP

THE FCLKWAYS CF THE UNITED STATES
SENATE -- CCNFCRMITY TC GROUP
NCRMS AND LEGISLATIVE
EFFECTIVENESS.=         MATTCR-59-FUS

QUASI - PARTISAN CCNFLICT IN A CNE
- PARTY LEGISLATIVE SYSTEM -- THE
FLCRICA SENATE, 1947-1961
(UNITED STATES).=       PARSMB-62-QPC

INTERNATICNAL CCMMUNICATION ANC
LEGISLATIVE BEHAVICR -- THE SENATE
AND THE HCUSE CF CCMMCNS
(UNITED STATES, GREAT BRITAIN).=
                        RUSSBM-62-ICL

SENATCR
UNITED STATES SENATCR -- A
CCLLECTIVE PCRTRAIT.=   MATTCR-61-USS

SENATCRIAL
THE ALABAMA SENATCRIAL ELECTICN OF
1962 -- RETURN CF INTER-PARTY
CCMPETITICN (UNITED STATES).=
                        BURNWD-64-ASE

CCNGRESSICNAL AND SENATCRIAL
CAMPAIGN CCMMITTEES IN THE
MID-TERM ELECTICN YEAR 1954
(UNITED STATES).=       HATHGB-56-CSC

EVALUATING THE CECLINE CF SCUTHERN
INTERNATICNALISM THRCUGH
SENATCRIAL RCLL CALL VCTES
(UNITED STATES).=       JEWEME-59-ECS

SENATCRIAL PCLITICS ANC FOREICN
PCLICY (UNITED STATES).=
                        JEWEME-62-SPF

SENATCRS
UNITED STATES SENATCRS ANC THE
CLASS STRUCTURE.=       MATTCR-54-USS

U.S. SENATCRS AND THEIR WCRLD
(UNITED STATES).=       MATTCR-60-USS

SENEGAL
CREATING PCLITICAL CRCER -- THE
PARTY - STATES CF WEST AFRICA
(MALI, GHANA, SENECAL, GUINEA,
IVCRY CCAST).=          ZCLBAR-66-CPC

SENEGALESE
EVCLUTICN CF SENEGALESE ELITES.=
                        MERCP -56-ESE

SENICRITY
THE SENICRITY RULE IN CCNGRESS
(UNITED STATES).=       CELLE -61-SRC

THE SENICRITY SYSTEM IN CCNGRESS
(UNITED STATES).=       GCODG -59-SSC

SAFE SEATS, SENICRITY, AND POWER IN
CCNGRESS (UNITED STATES).=
                        WCLFRE-65-SSS

SENTIMENTS
PERSCNAL SENTIMENTS IN A
HIERARCHY.=             TURKH -61-PSH

SEQUELS
SEQUELS TC A MILITARY CAREER -- THE

SEQUELS                 (CCNTINUATICN)
RETIRED MILITARY PRCFESSICNAL
(UNITED STATES).=       BIDEAC-64-SMC

SERVANT
THE PRCFESSICN CF GCVERNMENT -- THE
PUBLIC SERVANT IN (WESTERN)
EURCPE.=                CHAPB -59-PGP

THE RCLE CF THE BRITISH CIVIL
SERVANT IN PCLICY FCRMATION.=
                        GRIFR -53-RBC

THE INTERNATICNAL CIVIL SERVANT ANC
HIS LOYALTIES.=         JESSPC-55-ICS

THE LESS ENTANGLEC CIVIL SERVANT.=
                        LYNCFL-61-LEC

THE EVCLUTICN CF MINISTER - CIVIL
SERVANT RELATICNS IN INCIA.=
                        SUBRV -62-EMC

SERVANTS
CIVIL SERVANTS, MINISTERS,
PARLIAMENT AND THE PUBLIC
(GREAT BRITAIN).=       ATTLCR-54-CSM

HIGHER CIVIL SERVANTS IN AMERICAN
SCCIETY.=               BENCR -49-HCS

PATTERNS CF CCMMUNICATICN CF
EGYPTIAN CIVIL SERVANTS WITH THE
PUBLIC.=                BERGM -56-PCE

PCLITICIANS, PUBLIC SERVANTS, ANC
THE PECPLE IN NEW ZEALANC -- 1 --
2.=                     CAMPP -55-PPS

GCING ABCUT PERSECUTING CIVIL
SERVANTS -- THE RCLE CF THE IRISH
PARLIAMENTARY REPRESENTATIVES.=
                        CHUBB -63-GAP

CAREER CEVELCPMENT CF FILIPINC
HIGHER CIVIL SERVANTS.=
                        FRANGA-60-CDF

HIGHER CIVIL SERVANTS IN BRITAIN.=
                        KELSRK-55-HCS

HIGHER PUBLIC SERVANTS ANC THE
BUREALCRATIC ELITE IN CANADA.=
                        PORTJ -58-HPS

CIVIL SERVANTS IN WASHINGTCN -- 1,
THE CHARACTER CF THE FECERAL
SERVICE --2, THE HIGHER CIVIL
SERVICE ANC ITS FUTURE
(UNITED STATES).=       SPANRN-53-CSW

THE RULING SERVANTS -- BUREAUCRACY
IN RUSSIA, FRANCE, ANC
GREAT BRITAIN.=         STRAE -61-RSB

SERVICE
THE CIVIL SERVICE IN THE NEW
STATES.=                ADU,A -65-CSN

BUREALCRACY ANC SCCIETY IN MCDERN
EGYPT -- A STUCY CF THE HIGHER
CIVIL SERVICE.=         BERGM -57-BSM

THE CIVIL SERVICE IN FRANCE.=
                        CHATP -54-CSF

THE CANADIAN BUREAUCRACY -- A STUCY
CF CANACIAN CIVIL SERVICE AND
CTHER PUBLIC EMPLCYEES 1939-1947.=
                        COLET -49-CBS

MEN NEAR THE TCP -- FILLING KEY

SERVICE                 (CONTINUATION)
   POSTS IN THE FEDERAL CIVIL SERVICE
   (UNITED STATES).=       CORSJJ-66-MNT

   CIVIL SERVICE IN INDIA.=
                           CROUWW-56-CSI

   SOME THOUGHTS ON THE PUBLIC SERVICE
   (CANADA).=              DEUTJJ-57-TPS

   PARLIAMENT AND THE CIVIL SERVICE
   (GREAT BRITAIN).=       GLADEN-57-PCS

   THE CIVIL SERVICE OF PAKISTAN --
   BUREAUCRACY IN A NEW NATION.=
                           GOODHF-64-CSP

   UNIFYING THE BRITISH CIVIL SERVICE
   -- SOME TRENDS AND PROBLEMS.=
                           HODGJE-48-UBC

   THE CIVIL SERVICE AND POLICY
   FORMATION (NORTH AMERICA).=
                           HODGJE-57-CSP

   RECRUITMENT PROBLEMS OF THE FRENCH
   HIGHER CIVIL SERVICE -- AN
   AMERICAN APPRAISAL.=    JUMPR -57-RPF

   MILITANT PUBLIC SERVICE TRADE
   UNIONISM IN A NEW STATE (CEYLON).=
                           KEARRN-66-MPS

   THE SOCIAL BACKGROUND OF THE HIGHER
   CIVIL SERVICE (GREAT BRITAIN).=
                           KELSRK-54-SBH

   ON THE ESTABLISHMENT OF A EUROPEAN
   CIVIL SERVICE.=         KERNE -59-EEC

   THE IMAGE OF THE FEDERAL SERVICE
   (UNITED STATES).=       KILPFP-64-IFS

   REPRESENTATIVE BUREAUCRACY -- AN
   INTERPRETATION OF THE BRITISH
   CIVIL SERVICE.=         KINGJD-44-RBI

   NOTES ON THE CAREER FOREIGN SERVICE
   (PHILIPPINES).=         MANGRS-57-NCF

   SOCIAL DETERMINANTS OF THE ROLE OF
   A CIVIL SERVICE (UNITED STATES,
   GREAT BRITAIN).=        MARKM -56-SDR

   THE PEOPLE OF THE STATE DEPARTMENT
   AND FOREIGN SERVICE
   (UNITED STATES).=       MCCAJL-54-PSD

   RECRUITMENT OF THE ADMINISTRATIVE
   CLASS OF THE BRITISH CIVIL
   SERVICE.=               MCKIMM-49-RAC

   THE CHINESE CIVIL SERVICE -- CAREER
   OPEN TO TALENT.=        MENZJM-63-CCS

   ADMINISTRATORS, EXPERTS AND
   TRAINING IN THE CIVIL SERVICE
   (UNITED STATES).=       MILNRS-62-AET

   THE HIGHER CIVIL SERVICE AS AN
   ACTION GROUP IN WESTERN POLITICAL
   DEVELOPMENT.=           MORSF -63-HCS

   EDUCATION AND THE CIVIL SERVICE IN
   EUROPE.=                PRICJW-59-ECS

   THE CIVIL SERVICE IN BRITAIN AND
   FRANCE.=                ROBSWA-56-CSB

   THE CIVIL SERVICE OF INDIA.=
                           ROY,NC-58-CSI

   THE POLITICAL ROLE OF PAKISTAN'S

SERVICE                 (CONTINUATION)
   CIVIL SERVICE.=         SAYEKB-58-PRP

   THE HIGHER PUBLIC SERVICE OF THE
   COMMONWEALTH OF AUSTRALIA.=
                           SCARHA-57-HPS

   CIVIL SERVANTS IN WASHINGTON -- 1,
   THE CHARACTER OF THE FEDERAL
   SERVICE --2, THE HIGHER CIVIL
   SERVICE AND ITS FUTURE
   (UNITED STATES).=       SPANRN-53-CSW

   CIVIL SERVANTS IN WASHINGTON -- 1,
   THE CHARACTER OF THE FEDERAL
   SERVICE --2, THE HIGHER CIVIL
   SERVICE AND ITS FUTURE
   (UNITED STATES).=       SPANRN-53-CSW

   PUBLIC SERVICE COMMISSIONS IN THE
   FEDERATION OF MALAYA.=
                           TILMRO-61-PSC

   THE PUBLIC SERVICE COMMISSION IN
   WESTERN NIGERIA.=       WALLC -61-PSC

   YOUNG MEN AND THE FOREIGN SERVICE
   (UNITED STATES).=       WRISHM-54-YMF

   THE PUBLIC SERVICE IN THE NEW
   STATES -- AFRICA.=      YOUNK -60-PSN

   THE SERVICE SECRETARY -- HAS HE A
   USEFUL ROLE.=           ZUCKEM-66-SSH

SERVICEMEN
   EX - SERVICEMEN IN POLITICS
   (GREAT BRITAIN).=       WOOTG -58-ESP

SERVICES
   THE ORGANIZATION AND COMPOSITION OF
   THE CENTRAL CIVIL SERVICES IN
   PAKISTAN.=              CHAUMA-60-OCC

   A BRIEF COMPARISON OF THE PUBLIC
   SERVICES OF CANADA AND CEYLON.=
                           HARRRL-63-BCP

   RECRUITMENT TO THE CIVIL SERVICES
   (GREAT BRITAIN).=       HELSLN-54-RCS

   INTERSERVICE COMPETITION AND THE
   POLITICAL ROLES OF THE ARMED
   SERVICES (UNITED STATES).=
                           HUNTSP-61-ICP

SETTING
   BUREAUCRACY -- THE PROBLEM AND ITS
   SETTING.=               BENDR -47-BPI

   THE BUREAUCRATIC PHENOMENON -- AN
   EXAMINATION OF BUREAUCRACY IN
   MODERN ORGANIZATION AND ITS
   CULTURAL SETTING IN FRANCE.=
                           CROZM -64-BPE

   THE SETTING FOR EUROPEAN ARMS
   CONTROLS -- POLITICAL AND
   STRATEGIC CHOICES OF EUROPEAN
   ELITES (FRANCE, GERMANY
   GREAT BRITAIN, SOVIET UNION,
   UNITED STATES).=        GORDM -65-SEA

   CHANGING KINSHIP USAGES IN THE
   SETTING OF POLITICAL AND ECONOMIC
   CHANGE AMONG THE NAYARS OF
   MALABAR.=               GOUGEK-52-CKU

   CAREER PERSPECTIVES IN A
   BUREAUCRATIC SETTING
   (UNITED STATES).=       MARVC -54-CPB

   MEXICO -- A SPANISH - INDIAN

SITUATION          (CONTINUATION)
  IN SPAIN TODAY.=          MARIJ -60-SIS

  THE INTELLECTUAL BETWEEN TRADITION
  AND MODERNITY -- THE INDIAN
  SITUATION.=              SHILE -61-IBT

SITUATIONAL
  SITUATIONAL PRESSURES AND
  FUNCTIONAL ROLE OF THE ETHNIC
  LABOR LEADER.=           GREES -53-SPF

  SITUATIONAL DETERMINANTS OF
  LEADERSHIP STRUCTURE.=
                          KORTDC-62-SDL

  ENTREPRENEURS IN LATIN AMERICA AND
  THE ROLE OF CULTURAL AND
  SITUATIONAL PROCESSES.=
                          KRIEL -63-ELA

SITUATIONS
  THE UTILITY AND LIMITATIONS OF
  INTEREST GROUP THEORY IN
  NON-AMERICAN FIELD SITUATIONS.=
                          LAPAJ -60-ULI

SIVAI
  A SOLOMON ISLAND SOCIETY -- KINSHIP
  AND LEADERSHIP AMONG THE SIVAI OF
  BOUGAINVILLE.=           OLIVDL-58-SIS

SKETCH
  AN HISTORICAL SKETCH OF EGBA
  TRADITIONAL AUTHORITIES
  (NIGERIA).=              BIOBSO-52-HSE

SKETCHES
  PUBLIC ADMINISTRATION IN IRAN --
  SKETCHES OF A NON-WESTERN
  TRANSITIONAL BUREAUCRACY.=
                          GABLRW-61-PAI

SKILL
  THE STRATEGIC IMPORTANCE OF
  ENLIGHTENMENT AND SKILL FOR POWER
  (PERU).=                 DOBYHF-65-SIE

SKILLS
  ENTREPRENEURSHIP AND LABOR SKILLS
  IN INDONESIAN ECONOMIC DEVELOPMENT
  -- A SYMPOSIUM.=         HIGGB -61-ELS

SLAVERY
  CLAN, CHIEFTAINSHIP, AND SLAVERY IN
  LUVALE POLITICAL ORGANIZATION
  (NORTH RHODESIA).=       WHITCM-57-CCS

SLAVES
  THE MASTERS AND THE SLAVES -- A
  STUDY IN THE DEVELOPMENT OF
  BRAZILIAN CIVILIZATION.=
                          FREYG -46-MSS

SLUM
  SIX TRIAL DEFINITIONS --
  CONURBATION, ELITE, MIGRATION
  PROGRESS, SLUM, UNEMPLOYMENT.=
                          ANON  -55-STD

  URBAN RENEWAL POLITICS -- SLUM
  CLEARANCE IN NEWARK
  (UNITED STATES).=        KAPLH -63-URP

SMALL
  THE POLITICAL STRUCTURE OF A SMALL
  COMMUNITY (UNITED STATES).=
                          AGGERE-56-PSS

  SMALL - TOWN POLITICS -- A STUDY OF
  POLITICAL LIFE IN GLOSSOP
  (GREAT BRITAIN).=        BIRCAH-59-STP

SMALL          (CONTINUATION)
  BUREAUCRACY AND SMALL ORGANIZATIONS
  (UNITED STATES).=        HALLRH-63-BSO

  LEADERSHIP STABILITY AND SOCIAL
  CHANGE -- AN EXPERIMENT SMALL
  GROUPS.=                 KATZE -57-LSS

  ORGANIZATIONAL LEADERSHIP AND
  SOCIAL STRUCTURE IN A SMALL CITY
  (UNITED STATES).=        CLMSDW-54-OLS

  THE SUPREME COURT AS A SMALL GROUP
  (UNITED STATES).=        SNYDEC-57-SCS

  OCCUPATIONAL AFFILIATIONS OF
  COUNCILMEN IN SMALL CITIES
  (UNITED STATES).=        SPAUCB-51-OAC

  SMALL BUSINESSMEN, POLITICAL
  TOLERANCE, AND SUPPORT FOR
  MCCARTHY.=               TROWM -58-SBP

  SMALL TOWN IN MASS SOCIETY --
  CLASS, POWER AND RELIGION IN A
  RURAL COMMUNITY (UNITED STATES).=
                          VIDIAJ-58-STM

  LEADERSHIP IN A SMALL TOWN
  (UNITED STATES).=        WILDA -64-LST

SMOLENSK
  SMOLENSK UNDER SOVIET RULE.=
                          FAINM -58-SUS

SOCIABILITY
  SOCIABILITY AND POLITICAL
  INVOLVEMENT (JAPAN).=    KUROY -65-SPI

SOCIAL-PSYCHOLOGICAL
  INTERNATIONAL BEHAVIOR -- A
  SOCIAL-PSYCHOLOGICAL ANALYSIS.=
                          KELMHC-65-IBS

SOCIALISM
  DEMOCRACY AND SOCIALISM --
  IDEOLOGIES OF AFRICAN LEADERS.=
                          ANDRCF-64-DSI

  SOCIALISM AND THE LABOR PARTY OF
  TURKEY.=                 KARPKH-67-SLP

  THE TRACK OF THE WOLF -- ESSAYS ON
  NATIONAL SOCIALISM AND ITS
  LEADERS, ADOLPH HITLER (GERMANY).=
                          MCRAJH-65-TWE

  CAPITALISM, SOCIALISM AND
  DEMOCRACY.=              SCHUJA-62-CSD

  ISRAELI SOCIALISM AND THE MULTI -
  PARTY SYSTEM.=           SHERA -61-ISM

  BUDDHISM AND SOCIALISM IN JAPAN AND
  BURMA.=                  TOTTGO-60-BSJ

SOCIALIST
  SOCIALIST PARTIES IN
  SOUTH AMERICA.=          ALEXRJ-44-SPS

  THE SOCIALIST UNITY PARTY OF EAST
  GERMANY.=                CHILD -67-SUP

  THE FRENCH SOCIALIST PARTY AND THE
  WEST.=                   CODOGA-60-FSP

  THE SOCIALIST PARTIES AND EUROPEAN
  UNITY                    DWH   -50-SPE

  THE SOVIET PROCURACY AND FORTY
  YEARS OF SOCIALIST LEGALITY.=
                          GINSG -59-SPF

  THE SOCIALIST MERGER AND THE

SOCIALIST                (CONTINUATION)
  BALANCE OF PARTIES IN JAPAN.=
                         GRINM -55-SMB

  THE SOCIALIST PARTY OF AUSTRIA --
  RETREAT FROM MARX.=      FAHNWF-55-SPA

  DYNAMICS OF SOCIALIST LEADERSHIP IN
  INDIA.=                  RUSCTA-59-DSL

  THE SPLIT BETWEEN ASIAN AND WESTERN
  SOCIALIST.=              SAPODJ-54-SBA

  THE FRENCH RADICAL SOCIALIST PARTY
  AND THE REPUBLICAN FRONT OF 1956.
                          SCHLJA-58-FRS

  THE JAPANESE SOCIALIST PARTY UNDER
  NEW LEADERSHIP.=         STOCJA-66-JSP

  PROBLEMS OF JAPANESE SOCIALIST
  LEADERSHIP.=             TOTTGO-55-PJS

  THE ROLE OF THE SOCIALIST
  REVOLUTIONARIES IN 1917
  (SOVIET UNION).=         VISHMV-64-RSR

  THE ITALIAN SOCIALIST PARTY.=
                          ZARIR -62-ISP

SOCIALISTS
  AUSTRIA'S SOCIALISTS IN THE TREND
  TOWARD A TWO - PARTY SYSTEM -- AN
  INTERPRETATION OF POSTWAR
  ELECTIONS.=              GULICA-58-ASS

  COMMUNISTS, SOCIALISTS, AND
  CHRISTIAN DEMOCRATS
  (LATIN AMERICA).=        SZULT -65-CSC

SOCIALIZATION
  THE POLITICAL SOCIALIZATION OF
  AMERICAN STATE LEGISLATORS.=
                          EULAH -59-PSA

  PERSONALITY AND POLITICAL
  SOCIALIZATION (UNITED STATES).=
                          FROMLA-61-PPS

  PERSONALITY AND POLITICAL
  SOCIALIZATION -- THE THEORIES OF
  AUTHORITARIAN AND DEMOCRATIC
  CHARACTER.=              GREEFI-65-PPS

  THE SOCIALIZATION OF ATTITUDES
  TOWARD POLITICAL AUTHORITY
  (AUSTRALIA, CHILE, JAPAN,
  PUERTO RICO, UNITED STATES).=
                          HESSRD-63-SAT

  THE POLITICAL SOCIALIZATION OF
  NATIONAL LEGISLATIVE ELITES IN THE
  UNITED STATES AND CANADA.=
                          KORNA -65-PSN

  POLITICAL SOCIALIZATION AND
  LEADERSHIP SELECTION
  (UNITED STATES).=        PREWK -65-PSL

  POLITICAL SOCIALIZATION AND
  POLITICAL ROLES (UNITED STATES).=
                          PREWK -67-PSP

  POLITICAL SOCIALIZATION IN
  UNIVERSITIES (LATIN AMERICA).=
                          WALKKN-67-PSU

SOCIETIES
  STRATIFICATION IN PLURAL SOCIETIES
  (MAURITIUS).=            BENEB -2 -SPS

  EDUCATIONAL STRATEGY FOR DEVELOPING

SOCIETIES                (CONTINUATION)
  SOCIETIES.=              CURLA -63-ESD

  RECENT CHANGES IN THE CLASS
  STRUCTURE OF EUROPEAN SOCIETIES.=
                          DAHRR -64-RCC

  BUREAUCRACY AND NATION BUILDING IN
  TRANSITIONAL SOCIETIES.=
                          DUBESC-64-BNB

  POLITICAL LEADERSHIP IN
  INDUSTRIALIZED SOCIETIES
  (UNITED STATES, SOVIET UNION,
  FRANCE, CANADA, GREAT BRITAIN,
  AUSTRALIA, JAPAN, PHILIPPINES).=
                          EDINLJ-67-PLI

  POLITICAL STRUGGLE IN (ANCIENT)
  BUREAUCRATIC SOCIETIES.=
                          EISESN-56-PSA

  INTELLECTUALS AND DEVELOPING
  SOCIETIES.=              FRIEJ -60-IDS

  OLD SOCIETIES AND NEW STATES -- THE
  QUEST FOR MODERNITY IN ASIA AND
  AFRICA.=                 GEERC -63-CSN

  THE NEW SOCIETIES OF TROPICAL
  AFRICA.=                 HUNTG -63-NST

  REPRESENTATION IN PLURAL SOCIETIES
  (GREAT BRITAIN, BRITISH
  COMMONWEALTH).=          MACKWJ-54-RPS

  SOCIAL CHANGE AND STRUCTURE IN
  TRANSITIONAL SOCIETIES
  (LATIN AMERICA, MIDDLE EAST).=
                          MARCS -60-SCS

  SOCIAL STRATIFICATION IN TWO
  EQUALITARIAN SOCIETIES --
  AUSTRALIA AND THE UNITED STATES.=
                          MAYEKB-64-SST

  THE POLICY IMPLICATIONS OF SOCIAL
  CHANGE IN NON - WESTERN
  SOCIETIES.=              PYE,LW-57-PIS

  TRADITIONAL, MARKET, AND
  ORGANIZATIONAL SOCIETIES AND THE
  USSR.=                   RIGBTH-64-TMO

SOCIETY
  CHANGES IN THE STRUCTURE OF SOVIET
  SOCIETY.=                AKHMH -63-CSS

  PARTY AND SOCIETY -- THE
  ANGLO-AMERICAN DEMOCRACIES.=
                          ALFORR-63-PSA

  UNDER PRESSURE -- THE WRITER IN
  SOCIETY -- EASTERN EUROPE AND THE
  USA.=                    ALVAA -66-UPW

  MILITARY ORGANIZATION AND SOCIETY.=
                          ANDRS -54-MOS

  SOVIET SOCIETY IN TRANSITION.=
                          ARONR -57-SST

  THE PLACE OF THE TECHNICIAN -
  INTELLIGENTSIA IN SOCIETY.=
                          BAHRHP-60-PTI

  THE SOCIAL ROLE OF THE TECHNICIAN -
  INTELLIGENTSIA IN SOCIETY.=
                          BAHRHP-61-SRT

  TRADITIONAL SOCIETY AND
  REPRESENTATION -- A CASE STUDY IN

SOCIETY                (CONTINUATION)
  ORISSA (INDIA).=        BAILFG-60-TSR

  THE MORAL BASIS OF A BACKWARD
  SOCIETY (ITALY).=       BANFEC-58-MBB

  THE PSEUDO - CHARISMATIC LEADER IN
  SOVIET SOCIETY.=        BAUERA-53-PCL

  THEORY OF MASS SOCIETY.=
                          BELLD -56-TMS

  HIGHER CIVIL SERVANTS IN AMERICAN
  SOCIETY.=               BENDR -49-HCS

  MASS, CLASS AND BUREAUCRACY -- THE
  EVOLUTION OF CONTEMPORARY
  SOCIETY.=               BENSG -63-MCB

  POWER CLIQUES IN BUREAUCRATIC
  SOCIETY.=               BENSJ -62-PCB

  FREEDOM AND CONTROL IN MODERN
  SOCIETY.=               BERGM -54-FCM

  BUREAUCRACY AND SOCIETY IN MODERN
  EGYPT -- A STUDY OF THE HIGHER
  CIVIL SERVICE.=         BERGM -57-BSM

  THE LAWYER AND SOVIET SOCIETY.=
                          BILIA -65-LSS

  IRAN -- POLITICAL DEVELOPMENT IN A
  CHANGING SOCIETY.=      BINDL -62-IPD

  THE TRANSFORMATION OF RUSSIAN
  SOCIETY -- ASPECTS OF SOCIAL
  CHANGE SINCE 1861.=     BLACCE-60-TRS

  ELITES AND SOCIETY.=    BOTTTB-64-ES

  THE ROLE OF THE UNIVERSITY IN THE
  DEVELOPING SOCIETY OF THE WEST
  INDIES.=                BRAILE-65-RUD

  CENTRALIZATION AND THE OPEN SOCIETY
  (UNITED STATES).=       CARLWG- -COS

  THE CHINESE GENTRY, STUDIES ON
  THEIR ROLE IN THE NINETEENTH
  CENTURY CHINESE SOCIETY.=
                          CHANCL-55-CGS

  THE MARXIST REMOLDING OF CHINESE
  SOCIETY.=               CHENTH-53-MRC

  THE CHINESE GENTRY -- STUDIES ON
  THEIR ROLE IN NINETEENTH-CENTURY
  CHINESE SOCIETY.=       CHUNC -55-CGS

  JAPANESE SOCIETY AND POLITICS --
  THE IMPACT OF SOCIAL
  STRATIFICATION AND MOBILITY ON
  POLITICS.=              COLEAB-56-JSP

  THE U.S.S.R. -- FROM CHARISMATIC
  SECT TO BUREAUCRATIC SOCIETY
  (SOVIET UNION).=        CONTH -62-USS

  CLASS AND CLASS CONFLICT IN
  INDUSTRIAL SOCIETY.=    DAHRR -65-CCC

  SOCIETY AND DEMOCRACY IN GERMANY.=
                          DAHRR -67-SDG

  MODERN AMERICAN SOCIETY -- READINGS
  IN THE PROBLEMS OF ORDER AND
  CHANGE.=                DAVIK -49-MAS

  SOME QUANTITATIVE CONSTRAINTS ON
  VALUE ALLOCATION IN SOCIETY AND
  POLITICS.=              DEUTKW-66-QCV

SOCIETY                (CONTINUATION)
  CLASS PARAMETERS IN HAITIAN
  SOCIETY.=               DEYOM -59-CPH

  POLITICAL ASCENT IN A CLASS SOCIETY
  -- FRENCH DEPUTIES 1870-1958.=
                          DOGAM -61-PAC

  THE MILITARY IN THE MIDDLE EAST --
  PROBLEMS IN SOCIETY AND
  GOVERNMENT.=            FISHSN-63-MME

  THE GROWTH OF A PLURAL SOCIETY IN
  MALAYA.=                FREEM -60-GPS

  MILITARY STATUS IN CHINESE
  SOCIETY.=               FRIEMH-51-MSC

  POLITICS, LAW AND RITUAL IN TRIBAL
  SOCIETY.=               GLUCM -65-PLR

  THE MASS SOCIETY AND THE
  PARAPOLITICAL STRUCTURE.=
                          GREES -62-MSP

  SOCIAL CONTROL IN AN AFRICAN
  SOCIETY (ARUSHA OF TANGANYIKA).=
                          GULLPH-63-SCA

  MASS SOCIETY AND EXTREMIST
  POLITICS.=              GUSFJR-62-MSE

  LAWS AND MEN IN SOVIET SOCIETY.=
                          HAZAJN-58-LMS

  REVOLUTION IN BRAZIL -- POLITICS
  AND SOCIETY IN A DEVELOPING
  NATION.=                HOROIL-64-RBP

  CONSCIOUSNESS AND SOCIETY.=
                          HUGHHS-59-CS

  THE SOVIET CITIZEN -- DAILY LIFE IN
  A TOTALITARIAN SOCIETY.=
                          INKEA -59-SCD

  THE LATIN AMERICAN MILITARY AS A
  POLITICALLY COMPETING GROUP IN
  TRANSITIONAL SOCIETY.=
                          JOHNJJ-62-LAM

  THE MILITARY AND SOCIETY IN
  LATIN AMERICA.=         JOHNJJ-64-MSL

  SOCIETY, ECONOMICS, AND POLITICS IN
  CONTEMPORARY TURKEY.=   KARPKH-64-SEP

  THE ADMINISTERED SOCIETY --
  TOTALITARIANISM WITHOUT TERROR
  (SOVIET UNION).=        KASSA -64-AST

  BEYOND THE RULING CLASS --
  STRATEGIC ELITES IN MODERN
  SOCIETY.=               KELLS -63-BRC

  THE POLITICS OF MASS SOCIETY.=
                          KORNW -59-PMS

  PARTY PROTECTION AND PRIVILEGED
  STATUS IN SOVIET SOCIETY.=
                          KRYLKA-66-PPP

  POWER AND SOCIETY -- A FRAMEWORK
  FOR POLITICAL INQUIRY.=
                          LASSHD-50-PSF

  THE PASSING OF TRADITIONAL SOCIETY
  (MIDDLE EAST).=         LERND -58-PTS

  PARLIAMENT, PARTIES AND SOCIETY IN
  FRANCE, 1946-1958.=     MACRD -67-PPS

  MAN AND SOCIETY IN AN AGE OF

SOCIETY          (CONTINUATION)
  RECONSTRUCTION.=          MANNK -40-MSA

  THE FABIAN SOCIETY AND THE BRITISH
  LABOUR PARTY.=           MILBJF-58-FSB

  THE STRUCTURE OF POWER IN AMERICAN
  SOCIETY.=                MILLCW-58-SPA

  THE INTELLECTUAL IN CONTEMPORARY
  SOCIETY.=                MORAJF-59-ICS

  A SOLOMON ISLAND SOCIETY -- KINSHIP
  AND LEADERSHIP AMONG THE SIVAI OF
  BOUGAINVILLE.=           OLIVDL-58-SIS

  THE DISTRIBUTION OF POWER IN
  AMERICAN SOCIETY.=       PARST -57-DPA

  WRITER AND JOURNALIST IN THE
  TRANSITIONAL SOCIETY.=
                           PASSH -63-WJT

  POLITICS AND SOCIETY IN INDIA.=
                           PHILCH-62-PSI

  CRECLEDOM -- A STUDY OF THE
  DEVELOPMENT OF FREETOWN SOCIETY
  (SIERRA LEONE).=         PORTAT-63-CSC

  WEBERIAN V. WELFARE BUREAUCRACY IN
  TRADITIONAL SOCIETY (TURKEY).=
                           PRESRV-62-WVW

  LEADERSHIP AND CONSENSUS IN A NEW
  GUINEA SOCIETY.=         READKE-60-LCN

  CLASS IN AMERICAN SOCIETY.=
                           REISL -59-CAS

  POLITICAL DECISIONS IN MODERN
  SOCIETY.=                RIEZK -54-PDM

  PRISMATIC SOCIETY AND FINANCIAL
  ADMINISTRATION.=         RIGGFW-61-PSF

  THE POWER STRUCTURE -- POLITICAL
  PROCESS IN AMERICAN SOCIETY.=
                           ROSEAM-67-PSP

  FEUDAL SOCIETY AND MODERN
  LEADERSHIP IN SATSUMA-HAN.=
                           SAKARK-57-FSM

  SOCIETY AND POWER.=      SCHERA-61-SP

  INSTITUTIONAL VULNERABILITY IN MASS
  SOCIETY.=                SELZP -51-IVM

  REACTION AND REVOLUTION IN
  LATIN AMERICA -- THE CONFLICT
  SOCIETY.=                SILVKH-61-RRL

  DILEMMA OF THE ELITE IN ARAB
  SOCIETY.=                TANNA -55-DEA

  THE STRUCTURE OF BALKAN SOCIETY.=
                           TOMAD -46-SBS

  INTERRELATIONS BETWEEN BOLSHEVIK
  IDEOLOGY AND THE STRUCTURE OF
  SOVIET SOCIETY.=         TOMAD -51-IBB

  ARMY AND SOCIETY IN ENGLAND
  1870-1900 -- A REASSESSMENT OF THE
  CARDWELL REFORMS.=       TUCKAV-63-ASE

  SCHISM AND CONTINUITY IN AN AFRICAN
  SOCIETY.=                TURNVW-57-SCA

  SOCIETY AND CULTURE IN INDONESIAN
  NATIONALISM.=            VAN-JM-52-SCI

SOCIETY          (CONTINUATION)
  SMALL TOWN IN MASS SOCIETY --
  CLASS, POWER AND RELIGION IN A
  RURAL COMMUNITY (UNITED STATES).=
                           VIDIAJ-58-STM

  'MASS SOCIETY' -- THE LATE STAGES
  OF AN IDEA.=             WALTEV-64-MSL

  INTELLECTUALS AND SOCIETY IN CHINA
  1860-1949.=              WANGYC-61-ISC

  INDONESIAN SOCIETY IN TRANSITION --
  A STUDY OF SOCIAL CHANGE.=
                           WERTWF-59-IST

  LEADERSHIP IN A FREE SOCIETY.=
                           WHITTN-44-LFS

  CLASS STRUCTURE AND CLASS CONFLICT
  IN HAITIAN SOCIETY.=     WINGR -65-CSC

  ASPECTS OF GROUP RELATIONS IN A
  COMPLEX SOCIETY -- MEXICO.=
                           WOLFER-65-AGR

  INTEREST GROUPS IN AMERICAN
  SOCIETY.=                ZIEGH -64-IGA

SOCIO-ECONOMIC
  A SOCIO-ECONOMIC OPINION POLL IN
  BEIRUT, LEBANON.=        ARMSL -59-SEC

  SOCIO-ECONOMIC ASPECTS OF GERMAN
  REARMAMENT.=             BRANG -65-SEA

SOCIO-POLITICAL
  POLITICAL IDEOLOGY AS A TOOL OF
  FUNCTIONAL ANALYSIS IN
  SOCIO-POLITICAL DYNAMICS.=
                           DIONL -59-PIT

  THE DEVELOPMENT OF SOCIO-POLITICAL
  CENTERS AT THE SECOND STAGE OF
  MODERNISATION -- A COMPARATIVE
  ANALYSIS OF TWO TYPES.=
                           EISESN-66-DSP

  HUNGARIAN SOCIO-POLITICAL ATTITUDES
  AND REVOLUTIONARY ACTION.=
                           GLEIH -60-HSP

  THE SOCIO-POLITICAL ORIENTATIONS OF
  C. WRIGHT MILLS -- AN EVALUATION.=
                           SPINW -66-SPO

SOCIOCULTURAL
  POWER STRUCTURE AND SOCIOCULTURAL
  CHANGE IN LATIN AMERICAN
  COMMUNITIES.=            WHITNE-65-PSS

SOCIOECONOMIC
  RELIGIOUS AND SOCIOECONOMIC FACTORS
  IN THE FRENCH VOTE, 1946-1956.=
                           MACRO -58-RSF

SOCIOLOGICAL
  SOCIOLOGICAL ASPECTS OF ANTI -
  INTELLECTUALISM (UNITED STATES).=
                           BARBB -55-SAA

  THE MIDDLE CLASS FROM A
  SOCIOLOGICAL VIEWPOINT
  (UNITED STATES).=        FARIRE-60-MCS

  VILFREO PARETO -- SOCIOLOGICAL
  WRITINGS.=               FINESE-66-VPS

  FOR A SOCIOLOGICAL CONCEPT OF
  CHARISMA.=               FRIEWH-64-SCC

  THE RATIONAL MODEL, THE

SOMALIA                (CONTINUATION)
   MODERN LEADERSHIP AND LOYALTIES IN
   THE BRITISH SOMALILAND
   PROTECTORATE AND THE UNITED
   NATIONS TRUSTEESHIP TERRITORY OF
   SOMALIA.=              LEWIIM-60-PDM

SOMALILAND
   MODERN POLITICAL MOVEMENTS IN
   SOMALILAND -- PART 1 -- PART 2.=
                         LEWIIM-58-MPM

   PROBLEMS IN THE DEVELOPMENT OF
   MODERN LEADERSHIP AND LOYALTIES IN
   THE BRITISH SOMALILAND
   PROTECTORATE AND THE UNITED
   NATIONS TRUSTEESHIP TERRITORY OF
   SOMALIA.=              LEWIIM-60-PDM

SOURCE
   THE LEGISLATOR -- SOURCE OF EXPERT
   INFORMATION (UNITED STATES).=
                         HATTLH-54-LSE

SOURCES
   SOURCES OF ADMINISTRATIVE BEHAVIOR
   -- SOME SOVIET AND WESTERN
   EUROPEAN COMPARISONS.=
                         ARMSJA-65-SAB

   SOME TRENDS IN SOURCES OF
   ALIENATION FROM THE SOVIET
   SYSTEM.=               BAUER -55-TSA

   NEWSPAPER 'GATEKEEPERS' AND THE
   SOURCES OF NEWS.=      CARTRE-58-NGS

   SOCIAL STRATIFICATION IN RELATION
   TO ATTITUDES TOWARD SOURCES OF
   POWER IN A COMMUNITY
   (UNITED STATES).=      HAERJL-56-SSR

   TERROR AND PROGRESS, USSR -- SOME
   SOURCES OF CHANGE AND STABILITY IN
   THE SOVIET DICTATORSHIP.=
                         MOORB -54-TPU

SOUTH
   SOCIAL CHANGE IN THE SOUTH PACIFIC
   -- RAROTONGA AND AITUTAKI.=
                         BEAGE -57-SCS

   PRESS AND POLITICS OF SOUTH
   AFRICA.=               BROUM -61-PPS

   PRESIDENTIAL REPUBLICANISM IN THE
   SOUTH - 1960 (UNITED STATES).=
                         COSMB -62-PRS

   SOUTH KOREA'S SEARCH FOR
   LEADERSHIP.=           DOUGWA-64-SKS

   ECONOMIC DEVELOPMENT AND SOCIAL
   CHANGE IN SOUTH INDIA.=
                         EPSTTS-62-EDS

   ELITE GROUPS IN A SOUTH INDIAN
   DISTRICT, 1788-1858.=  FRYKRE-65-EGS

   RITUALS OF REBELLION IN SOUTH EAST
   AFRICA.=               GLICM -54-RRS

   TRADE UNIONS IN TRAVAIL -- THE
   STORY OF THE BROEDERBOND -
   NATIONALIST PLAN TO CONTROL SOUTH
   AFRICAN TRADE UNIONS.=
                         HEPPA -54-TUT

   NORTH VIET NAM'S WORKERS' PARTY AND
   SOUTH VIET NAM'S PEOPLE'S
   REVOLUTIONARY PARTY.=  HONEPJ-63-NVN

   TECHNICAL COOPERATION IN

SOUTH                  (CONTINUATION)
   DEVELOPMENT ADMINISTRATION IN
   SOUTH AND SOUTHEAST ASIA.=
                         HSUESS-66-TCD

   MANDARIN BUREAUCRACY AND POLITICS
   IN SOUTH VIETNAM.=     JUMPR -57-MBP

   PROBLEMS OF PUBLIC ADMINISTRATION
   IN SOUTH VIETNAM.=     JUMPR -57-PPA

   SECTS AND COMMUNISM IN SOUTH
   VIETNAM.=              JUMPR -59-SCS

   DEMOGRAPHIC ASPECTS OF WHITE
   SUPREMACY IN SOUTH AFRICA.=
                         KUPEL -50-DAW

   AN AFRICAN BOURGEOISIE -- RACE,
   CLASS, AND POLITICS IN SOUTH
   AFRICA.=               KUPEL -65-ABR

   NEGRO POLITICAL LEADERSHIP IN THE
   SOUTH (UNITED STATES).=
                         LADDEC-66-NPL

   THE LEGISLATIVE ASSEMBLY OF NEW
   SOUTH WALES, 1856-1900
   (AUSTRALIA).=          MARTAW-56-LAN

   THE TRIBAL ELITE AND THE TRANSKEIAN
   ELECTIONS OF 1963 (SOUTH AFRICA).=
                         MAYEP -66-TET

   SOME PERSONALITY FACTORS OF STATE
   LEGISLATORS IN SOUTH CAROLINA
   (UNITED STATES).=      MCCOJB-50-PFS

   AFRICAN ELITE IN SOUTH AFRICA.=
                         NGCOSB-56-AES

   SOCIAL DISTANCE ATTITUDES OF SOUTH
   AFRICAN STUDENTS.=     PETTTF-60-SDA

   THE OFFICE OF GOVERNOR IN THE SOUTH
   (UNITED STATES).=      RANSCB-51-OGS

   BUDDHISM AND POLITICS IN SOUTH
   VIETNAM.=              ROBEA -65-BPS

   RESTRUCTURING GOVERNMENT IN SOUTH
   VIETNAM.=              SACKIM-67-RGS

   MASS SUPPORT AND COMMUNIST
   INSURRECTION (GREECE, MALAYA,
   INDOCHINA, PHILIPPINES, SOUTH
   VIETNAM).=             SANDR -65-MSC

   POLITICAL PARTIES IN SOUTH VIETNAM
   UNDER THE REPUBLIC.=   SCIGRC-60-PPS

   THE SUPREME COURT AND THE SOUTH
   (UNITED STATES).=      SNISCB-48-SCS

   APARTHEID AND POLITICS IN SOUTH
   AFRICA.=               TIRYEQ-60-APS

   POLITICAL INSTITUTIONS AND
   AFRIKANER SOCIAL STRUCTURES IN THE
   REPUBLIC OF SOUTH AFRICA.=
                         TRAPS -63-PIA

   THE ARMED FORCES OF SOUTH AFRICA.=
                         TYLDG -54-AFS

   CANEVILLE -- THE SOCIAL STRUCTURE
   OF A SOUTH AFRICAN TOWN.=
                         VAN-PL-64-CSS

   THE POLITICS OF SOUTH ASIA.=
                         WEINM -60-PSA

   POLITICAL ADVANCEMENT IN THE SOUTH

SOUTH                    (CONTINUATION)
PACIFIC -- A COMPARATIVE STUDY OF
COLONIAL PRACTICE IN FIJI, TAHITI,
AND AMERICAN SAMOA.=   WESTFJ-61-PAS

THE MUSLIM LEAGUE IN SOUTH INDIA
SINCE INDEPENDENCE -- A STUDY IN
MINORITY GROUP POLITICAL
STRATEGIES.=           WRIGTP-66-MLS

THE SAIGON POLITICAL ELITE -- FOCUS
ON FOUR CABINETS (SOUTH VIETNAM).=
                       WURFD -67-SPE

RURAL RESETTLEMENT IN SOUTH
VIET NAM -- THE AGROVILLE
PROGRAM.=              ZASLJJ-62-RRS

SOUTH AMERICA
SOCIALIST PARTIES IN
SOUTH AMERICA.=        ALEXRJ-44-SPS

CAUDILLISMO IN NORTHWESTERN
SOUTH AMERICA.=        BLANGI-52-CNS

PARLIAMENTARY GOVERNMENT AND
SOUTH AMERICA.=        PENDG -57-PGS

SOUTH-EAST
MARXISM IN SOUTH-EAST ASIA.=
                       TRAGFN-59-MSE

SOUTHEAST
POLITICAL ELITES IN COLONIAL
SOUTHEAST ASIA -- AN HISTORICAL
ANALYSIS.=             BENDHJ-64-PEC

PEASANT MOVEMENTS IN COLONIAL
SOUTHEAST ASIA.=       BENDHJ-65-PMC

COMMUNISM IN SOUTHEAST ASIA -- A
POLITICAL ANALYSIS.=   BRIMJH-59-CSA

SOCIAL FORCES IN SOUTHEAST ASIA.=
                       DUBOCA-59-SFS

JAPAN'S ROLE IN SOUTHEAST ASIAN
NATIONALIST MOVEMENTS, 1940-1945.=
                       ELSBWH-53-JSR

PROBLEMS OF REPRESENTATIVE
GOVERNMENT IN SOUTHEAST ASIA.=
                       EMERR -53-PRG

THE STUDENT POPULATION OF A
SOUTHEAST ASIAN UNIVERSITY -- AN
INDONESIAN EXAMPLE.=   FISCJ -61-SPS

UNIVERSITIES AND THE POLITICAL
PROCESS IN SOUTHEAST ASIA.=
                       FISCJ -63-UPP

LABOR AND ECONOMIC DEVELOPMENT
(MIDDLE EAST, SOUTHEAST ASIA).=
                       GALEW -59-LED

THOUGHTS ON THE CHINESE QUESTION IN
SOUTHEAST ASIA.=       HALLDG-54-TCQ

TECHNICAL COOPERATION IN
DEVELOPMENT ADMINISTRATION IN
SOUTH AND SOUTHEAST ASIA.=
                       HSUESS-66-TCC

MALAYSIA -- A NEW FEDERATION IN
SOUTHEAST ASIA.=       MEANGP-63-MNF

THE POLITICS OF SOUTHEAST ASIA.=
                       PYE,LW-60-PSA

SOUTHEAST ASIA FOLLOWS THE LEADER.=
                       THOMV -49-SAF

THE LEFT WING IN SOUTHEAST ASIA.=

SOUTHEAST               (CONTINUATION)
                       THOMV -50-LWS

SOUTHERN
NEGRO LEADERSHIP IN A SOUTHERN CITY
(UNITED STATES).=      BURGME-62-NLS

CHIEFS AND STRANGERS (SOUTHERN
SUDAN).=               BUXTJC-63-CSS

THE SOUTHERN POLITICIAN -- 1900 AND
1950 (UNITED STATES).=
                       CARLWG-51-SPU

SCHOOL DESEGREGATION AND NEW
INDUSTRY -- THE SOUTHERN COMMUNITY
LEADER'S VIEWPOINT
(UNITED STATES).=      CRAMMR-63-SDN

SOUTHERN GOVERNORS
(UNITED STATES).=      EWINCA-48-SGU

THE SOUTHERN GOVERNOR -- CHALLENGE
TO THE STRONG EXECUTIVE THEME
(UNITED STATES).=      HIGHRB-59-SGC

EVALUATING THE DECLINE OF SOUTHERN
INTERNATIONALISM THROUGH
SENATORIAL ROLL CALL VOTES
(UNITED STATES).=      JEWEME-59-EDS

STATE LEGISLATURES IN SOUTHERN
POLITICS (UNITED STATES).=
                       JEWEME-64-SLS

NEGRO PROTEST LEADERS IN A SOUTHERN
COMMUNITY (UNITED-STATES).=
                       KILLLM-60-NPL

CONSTITUENCY VERSUS
CONSTITUTIONALISM -- THE
DESEGREGATION ISSUE AND TENSION
AND ASPIRATIONS OF SOUTHERN
ATTORNEY GENERALS
(UNITED STATES).=      KRISS -59-CVC

SOUTHERN CONGRESSMEN AND THE 'NEW
ISOLATIONISM' (UNITED STATES).=
                       LERCCO-60-SCN

THE POLITICS OF TRADE UNION
LEADERSHIP IN SOUTHERN ASIA.=
                       LICHGE-54-PTU

THE SOCIAL CHARACTERISTICS OF AN
EMERGENT ELITE IN HARARE (SOUTHERN
RHODESIA).=            LUKHMB-66-SCE

POLITICAL PARTIES AND DECISION
MAKING IN THREE SOUTHERN COUNTIES
(UNITED STATES).=      RHYNEH-58-PPD

THE FUNCTIONS OF DISUNITY -- THE
NEGRO LEADERSHIP IN A SOUTHERN
CITY (UNITED STATES).=
                       WALKJL-63-FDN

CHIEFSHIP AND POLITICS IN THE
MLANJE DISTRICT OF SOUTHERN
NYASALAND.=            WISHRL-61-CPM

SECTARIANISM IN SOUTHERN
NYASALAND.=            WISHRL-65-SSN

SOUTHWEST
THE POLITICS OF THE NEAR EAST --
SOUTHWEST ASIA AND NORTHERN
AFRICA.=               RUSTDA-60-PNE

SOVIET
THE PRINCIPLE OF PROFITABILITY AND
THE SOVIET PARTY APPARATUS.=

SOVIET UNION (CONTINUATION)
SWEAHR-65-CCC

REVOLT OF THE COMMUNIST
INTELLECTUALS (SOVIET UNION, EAST
EUROPE).= TABOE -57-RCI

ON POLITICAL STABILITY (FRANCE,
SOVIET UNION).= TANNF -60-PSF

KAZAKHSTAN -- CHANGES IN
ADMINISTRATIVE STATUS AND THE
NATIONAL COMPOSITION OF THE
POPULATION (SOVIET UNION).=
TASKGA-64-KCA

THE BEGINNING OF THE END
(SOVIET UNION).= TATAM -66-BES

POLITICAL POWER IN THE
SOVIET UNION.= TIMANS-52-PPS

THE SOVIET UNION AFTER STALIN --
LEADERS AND POLICIES.=
TOWSJ -54-SUA

KHRUSHCHEV AND THE ANTI - PARTY
GROUP (SOVIET UNION).=
TS -57-KAP

PATTERNS OF NONCONFORMITY
(SOVIET UNION).= UTECSV-57-PNS

GENERALISSIMO STALIN AND THE ART OF
GOVERNMENT (SOVIET UNION).=
UTISO -52-GSA

THE ROLE OF THE SOCIALIST
REVOLUTIONARIES IN 1917
(SOVIET UNION).= VISHMV-64-RSR

CAN STALIN HAVE A SUCCESSOR
(SOVIET UNION).= WILLP -53-CSH

STALINISM VERSUS STALIN
(SOVIET UNION).= WOLFBD-56-SVS

POLITICAL PRIMACY VS PROFESSIONAL
ELAN (SOVIET UNION).= WOLFTW-64-PPV

THE SPECTRE OF REVISIONISM
(SOVIET UNION, EAST EUROPE).=
ZAGODS-58-SRS

SOVIETIZATION
POLAND 1942-1962 -- THE
SOVIETIZATION OF A CAPTIVE
PEOPLE.= STAARF-62-PSC

THE CULTURAL SOVIETIZATION OF EAST
GERMANY.= WAGNHR-57-CSE

SOVNARKHOZ
THE SOVNARKHOZ CHAIRMAN
(SOVIET UNION).= ANON -58-SCS

SPAIN
FRANCO'S SPAIN AND THE NEW EUROPE.=
ALANR -62-FSS

FREEDOM AND CATHOLIC POWER IN SPAIN
AND PORTUGAL.= BLANP -62-FCP

THE PRESS IN LATIN AMERICA, SPAIN
AND PORTUGAL -- A SUMMARY OF
RECENT DEVELOPMENTS.= CHILRH-65-PLA

STUDENT OPPOSITION IN SPAIN.=
GALVET-66-SOS

AN AUTHORITARIAN REGIME -- SPAIN.=
LINZJJ-64-ARS

THE SITUATION OF THE INTELLIGENTSIA

SPAIN (CONTINUATION)
IN SPAIN TODAY.= MARIJ -60-SIS

SOCIAL STRUCTURE AND SOCIAL CHANGE
IN NEW SPAIN.= MCALLN-63-SSS

POLITICS AND THE MILITARY IN MODERN
SPAIN.= PAYNSG-67-PMM

FERMENT IN FRANCO SPAIN.=
RADIB -59-FFS

PRELUDE TO FRANCO (SPAIN).=
RATCDF-57-PFS

COLONIAL ELITES -- ROME, SPAIN AND
THE AMERICAS.= SYMER -58-CER

SPANISH
THE CIVIL - RELIGIOUS HIERARCHY IN
MESOAMERICAN COMMUNITIES -- PRE -
SPANISH BACKGROUND AND COLONIAL
DEVELOPMENT.= CARRP -61-CRH

PATRON - PEON PATTERN AMONG THE
SPANISH AMERICANS OF NEW MEXICO.=
KNOWCS-62-PPP

FALANGE -- A HISTORY OF SPANISH
FASCISM.= PAYNSG-61-FHS

MEXICO -- A SPANISH - INDIAN
CULTURE IN A MODERN SETTING.=
PS -49-MSI

SPATIAL
SPATIAL MODELS OF PARTY
COMPETITION.= STOKDE-63-SMP

SPEAKER
THE CHOICE OF SPEAKER IN AUSTRALIAN
PARLIAMENTS.= BOLTG -62-CSA

THE SPEAKER OF THE HOUSE OF COMMONS
(GREAT BRITAIN).= LAUNP -61-SHC

SPEAKING
ELITES IN FRENCH - SPEAKING WEST
AFRICA -- THE SOCIAL BASIS OF
IDEAS.= WALLI -65-EFS

SPEARHEADS
SPEARHEADS OF DEMOCRACY -- LABOR IN
THE DEVELOPING COUNTRIES.=
LODGGC-62-SDL

SPECIAL
INDIGENOUS POLITICS AND COLONIAL
ADMINISTRATION WITH SPECIAL
REFERENCE TO AUSTRALIA.=
BARNJA-60-IPC

SPECTRE
EAST GERMAN REVISIONISM -- THE
SPECTRE AND THE REALITY.=
COWAM -62-EGR

THE SPECTRE OF REVISIONISM
(SOVIET UNION, EAST EUROPE).=
ZAGODS-58-SRS

SPHERE
SATELLITE GENERALS -- A STUDY OF
MILITARY ELITES IN THE SOVIET
SPHERE.= POOLID-55-SGS

SPIRIT
THE SPIRIT OF THE NEW SOVIET MIDDLE
CLASS.= SANDV -54-SNS

SPLIT
INDIA'S COMMUNIST PARTY SPLIT.=

STALIN                    (CONTINUATION)
                          SETOH -54-EES

THE SOVIET UNION AFTER STALIN --
LEADERS AND POLICIES.=
                          TOWSJ -54-SUA

GENERALISSIMO STALIN AND THE ART OF
GOVERNMENT (SOVIET UNION).=
                          UTISO -52-GSA

CAN STALIN HAVE A SUCCESSOR
(SOVIET UNION).=          WILLP -53-CSH

STALINISM VERSUS STALIN
(SOVIET UNION).=          WOLFBD-56-SVS

STALINISM
CZECHOSLOVAKIA -- CULT OF
STALINISM.=               TABOE -64-COS

STALINISM VERSUS STALIN
(SOVIET UNION).=          WOLFBD-56-SVS

STALINIST
THE STRUGGLE OF SOVIET JURISTS
AGAINST A RETURN TO STALINIST
TERROR.=                  BERMHJ-63-SSJ

THE BUREAUCRATIC REVOLUTION -- THE
RISE OF THE STALINIST STATE
(SOVIET UNION).=          SCHAM -62-BRR

POLITICAL LEADERSHIP IN
CONTEMPORARY POLAND -- THE NEO -
STALINIST COURSE.=        TOMAD -61-PLC

STALLED
THE STALLED OMNIBUS -- CANADIAN
PARTIES IN THE 1960'S.=
                          MEISJ -63-SOC

STANDING
SOME NOTES ON THE STANDING
COMMITTEES OF THE FRENCH NATIONAL
ASSEMBLY.=                BROMPA-57-NSC

STANDING COMMITTEES IN THE HOUSE OF
COMMONS, 1945-1950
(GREAT BRITAIN).=         SHEAJG-50-SCH

STAR
RED STAR OVER CHINA.=     SNOWE -38-RSC

STARE
STARE DECISIS, DISSENT AND THE
BACKGROUND OF THE JUSTICES OF THE
SUPREME COURT OF THE
UNITED STATES.=           SCHMJ -62-SDD

STATE
THE ELUSIVENESS OF POWER -- THE
AFRICAN SINGLE PARTY STATE.=
                          ASHFDE-65-EPA

WASHINGTON STATE'S LAWMAKERS --
SOME PERSONNEL FACTORS IN THE
WASHINGTON LEGISLATURE
(UNITED STATES).=         BECKP -57-WSS

THE MID-WEST STATE MOVEMENT IN
NIGERIAN POLITICS -- A STUDY IN
PARTY FORMATION.=         BRANJA-65-MWS

FACTIONAL POLITICS IN AN INDIAN
STATE -- THE CONGRESS PARTY IN
UTTAR PRADESH.=           BRASPR-65-FPI

THE LAWYER AS DECISION-MAKER IN THE
AMERICAN STATE LEGISLATURE.=
                          DERGOR-59-LDM

THE FRENCH COUNCIL OF STATE --

STATE                     (CONTINUATION)
COMPARATIVE OBSERVATIONS ON THE
PROBLEM OF CONTROLLING BUREAUCRACY
OF THE MODERN STATE.=     DIAMA -51-FCS

THE FRENCH COUNCIL OF STATE --
COMPARATIVE OBSERVATIONS ON THE
PROBLEM OF CONTROLLING BUREAUCRACY
OF THE MODERN STATE.=     DIAMA -51-FCS

THE DISMANTLING OF PARTY AND STATE
CONTROL AS AN INDEPENDENT PILLAR
OF SOVIET POWER.=         DUEVO -66-DPS

STATE LEGISLATIVE POLITICS
(UNITED STATES).=         DYE,TR-65-SLP

COPING WITH CUBA -- DIVERGENT
POLICY PREFERENCES OF STATE
POLITICAL LEADERS
(UNITED STATES).=         EKMAP -66-CCD

THE PUBLIC STUDIES DIVISION OF THE
DEPARTMENT OF THE STATE -- PUBLIC
OPINION ANALYSIS IN THE
FORMULATION AND CONDUCT OF
AMERICAN FOREIGN POLICY.=
                          ELDERE-57-PSD

THE POLICY MACHINE -- THE
DEPARTMENT OF STATE AND AMERICAN
FOREIGN POLICY.=          ELDERE-60-PMD

THE POLITICAL SOCIALIZATION OF
AMERICAN STATE LEGISLATORS.=
                          EULAH -59-PSA

CAREER PERSPECTIVES OF AMERICAN
STATE LEGISLATORS.=       EULAH -61-CPA

THE ARGENTINE TROUBLE -- BETWEEN
SWORD AND STATE.=         FINESE-65-ATB

INFLUENCE AND INTERACTION IN A
STATE LEGISLATIVE BODY
(UNITED STATES).=         FRANWL-62-IIS

THE POLITICAL CONTROL OF
CZECHOSLOVAKIA -- A STUDY IN
SOCIAL CONTROL OF A SOVIET STATE.=
                          GADOI -53-PCC

POLAND -- POLITICAL PLURALISM IN A
ONE - PARTY STATE.=       GAMAM -67-PPP

POLITICAL RECRUITMENT IN SARAWAK --
A CASE STUDY OF LEADERSHIP IN A
NEW STATE.=               GLICHR-66-PRS

THE ROLE OF THE ARMY IN THE
TRANSITIONAL ARAB STATE
(MIDDLE EAST).=           GLUBJ -65-RAT

LAWYERS IN POLITICS -- AN EMPIRICAL
EXPLORATION OF BIOGRAPHICAL DATA
ON STATE LEGISLATORS.=
                          GOLDD -61-LPE

A TAXONOMIC APPROACH TO STATE
POLITICAL PARTY STRENGTH.=
                          GOLERT-58-TAS

CHURCH AND STATE IN ARGENTINA --
FACTORS IN PERON'S DOWNFALL.=
                          GP    -56-CSA

AN UNCERTAIN TRADITION -- AMERICAN
SECRETARIES OF STATE   IN THE
TWENTIETH CENTURY.=       GRAENA-61-UTA

TURNOVER IN IOWA STATE PARTY
CONVENTIONS -- AN EXPLORATORY

STATE                    (CONTINUATION)
  STUDY (UNITED STATES).=
                         HAHNH -67-TIS

  JUDGEMENTS OF STATE LEGISLATORS
  CONCERNING PUBLIC OPINION
  (UNITED STATES).=      HARTGW-45-JSL

  FROM BOSSES TO COSMOPOLITANISM --
  CHANGES IN THE RELATIONSHIP OF
  URBAN LEADERSHIP TO STATE POLITICS
  (UNITED STATES).=      HAVAWC-64-BCC

  THE ETHIOPIAN NC - PARTY STATE -- A
  NOTE ON THE FUNCTIONS OF POLITICAL
  PARTIES IN DEVELOPING STATES.=
                         HESSRL-64-ENP

  THE SOVIET CONCEPT OF THE
  RELATIONSHIP BETWEEN THE LOWER
  PARTY ORGANS AND THE STATE
  ADMINISTRATION.=       HOUGJF-65-SCR

  THE SOLDIER AND THE STATE -- THE
  THEORY AND POLITICS OF CIVIL -
  MILITARY RELATIONS
  (UNITED STATES).=      HUNTSP-57-SST

  PARTY RULE IN A DEMOCRATIC STATE
  (ITALY).=              IVELV -49-PRD

  PARTY VOTING IN AMERICAN STATE
  LEGISLATURES.=         JEWEME-55-PVA

  STATE LEGISLATURES IN SOUTHERN
  POLITICS (UNITED STATES).=
                         JEWEME-64-SLS

  MILITANT PUBLIC SERVICE TRADE
  UNIONISM IN A NEW STATE (CEYLON).=
                         KEARRN-66-MPS

  COMPARATIVE STUDY OF THE ROLE OF
  POLITICAL PARTIES IN THE STATE
  LEGISLATURES (UNITED STATES).=
                         KEEFWJ-56-CSR

  POLITICAL CHANGE IN A WEST AFRICAN
  STATE -- A STUDY OF THE
  MODERNIZATION PROCESS IN
  SIERRA LEONE.=         KILSM -66-PCW

  PATTERNS OF LEADERSHIP IN A
  COMMUNIST STATE -- CZECHOSLOVAKIA
  1946-1958.=            KUBAD -61-PLC

  CLASSES IN THE 'CLASSLESS' STATE
  (SOVIET UNION).=       KULSWW-55-CCS

  THE GARRISON STATE HYPOTHESIS
  TODAY.=                LASSHD-62-GSH

  THE ROLE OF BRAINS IN THE TOTAL
  STATE.=                LERND -53-RBT

  BEYOND AFRICAN DICTATORSHIP -- THE
  CRISIS OF THE ONE - PARTY STATE.=
                         LEWIWA-65-BAD

  THE ROLE OF THE STATE LEGISLATOR IN
  MASSACHUSETTS (UNITED STATES).=
                         MACRD -54-RSL

  THE SOLDIER AND THE STATE IN EAST
  AFRICA -- SOME THEORETICAL
  CONCLUSIONS ON THE ARMY MUTINIES
  OF 1964.=              MAZRAA-7 -SSE

  THE PEOPLE OF THE STATE DEPARTMENT
  AND FOREIGN SERVICE
  (UNITED STATES).=      MCCAJL-54-PSD

  SOME PERSONALITY FACTORS OF STATE

STATE                    (CONTINUATION)
  LEGISLATORS IN SOUTH CAROLINA
  (UNITED STATES).=      MCCOJB-50-PFS

  THE EXECUTIVE IN THE MODERN STATE
  (CANADA, FRANCE, GREAT BRITAIN,
  SOVIET UNION, UNITED STATES,
  YUGOSLAVIA).=          MEYNJ -58-EMS

  THE OMNIPOTENT STATE -- RISE OF
  TOTAL STATE AND TOTAL WAR
  (GERMANY).=            MISELV-44-OSR

  THE OMNIPOTENT STATE -- RISE OF
  TOTAL STATE AND TOTAL WAR
  (GERMANY).=            MISELV-44-OSR

  THE ADMINISTRATIVE STATE (FRANCE,
  GREAT BRITAIN, SWITZERLAND,
  UNITED STATES).=       MORSF -57-ASF


  THE DEMOCRATIC AND THE
  AUTHORITARIAN STATE -- ESSAYS IN
  POLITICAL AND LEGAL THEORY.=
                         NEUMFL-57-DAS

  JAPAN'S EMERGENCE AS A MODERN
  STATE.=                NORMEH-46-JSE

  PATTERNS OF INTER-PERSONAL
  RELATIONS IN A STATE LEGISLATIVE
  GROUP -- THE WISCONSIN ASSEMBLY
  (UNITED STATES).=      PATTSC-59-PIP

  DIMENSIONS OF VOTING BEHAVIOR IN A
  ONE - PARTY STATE LEGISLATURES
  (UNITED STATES).=      PATTSC-62-DVB

  THE CONFLICT BETWEEN CHURCH AND
  STATE IN LATIN AMERICA.=
                         PIKEFB-64-CBC

  THE SECRETARY OF STATE
  (UNITED STATES).=      PRICDK-60-SSU

  MOSCOW STATE UNIVERSITY
  (SOVIET UNION).=       ROBED -64-MSU

  PROCESS SATISFACTION AND POLICY
  APPROVAL IN STATE DEPARTMENT --
  CONGRESSIONAL RELATIONS
  (UNITED STATES).=      ROBIJA-61-PSP

  LAWYERS IN THE NEW YORK STATE
  LEGISLATURE -- THE URBAN FACTOR
  (UNITED STATES).=      RUCHLI-66-LNY

  THE DEMOCRATIC STATE CENTRAL
  COMMITTEE IN MICHIGAN 1949-1959 --
  THE RISE OF THE NEW POLITICS AND
  THE NEW POLITICAL LEADERSHIP
  (UNITED STATES).=      SAWYRL-60-DSC

  THE ORIGIN OF THE COMMUNIST
  AUTOCRACY -- POLITICAL OPPOSITION
  IN THE SOVIET STATE, 1917-1922.=
                         SCHALB-55-OCA

  THE BUREAUCRATIC REVOLUTION -- THE
  RISE OF THE STALINIST STATE
  (SOVIET UNION).=       SCHAM -62-BRR

  STATE AND LOCAL PUBLIC
  ADMINISTRATION (WEST GERMANY).=
                         SCHIH -59-SLP

  COLLECTIVE NEGOTIATIONS BETWEEN THE
  STATE AND ITS OFFICIALS -- A
  COMPARATIVE ESSAY.=    SCHMF -62-CNB

STATE                    (CONTINUATION)
    THE SUPREME COURT AS FINAL ARBITER
    IN FEDERAL - STATE RELATIONS
    (UNITED STATES).=         SCHMJR-58-SCF

    CHURCH AND STATE IN POLAND.=
                              SCHOGA-66-CSP

    TRADE UNIONS IN THE SOVIET STATE.=
                              SCHWSM-59-TUS

    BRITISH INTELLECTUALS IN THE
    WELFARE STATE.=           SPENS -51-BIW

    THE LAWYER IN MICHIGAN STATE
    GOVERNMENT (UNITED STATES).=
                              STEUWL-59-LMS

    THE ELITE IN THE WELFARE STATE.=
                              THOEP -66-EWS

    THE RUSSIAN INTELLIGENTSIA --
    MAKERS OF THE REVOLUTIONARY
    STATE.=                   TOMPSR-57-RIM

    BUILDING A WELFARE STATE IN BURMA,
    1948-1956.=               TRAGFN-58-BWS

    THE STATE DELEGATIONS AND THE
    STRUCTURE OF PARTY VOTING IN THE
    UNITED STATES HOUSE OF
    REPRESENTATIVES.=         TRUMDB-56-SDS

    PARTY AND STATE IN SOVIET RUSSIA
    AND NAZI GERMANY.=        UNGEAL-65-PSS

    AMERICAN STATE LEGISLATORS' ROLE
    ORIENTATIONS TOWARD PRESSURE
    GROUPS.=                  WAHLJC-60-ASL

    EXECUTIVE LEADERSHIP IN STATE
    ADMINISTRATION (UNITED STATES).=
                              WRIGDS-67-ELS

STATEHOUSE
    BUSINESSMAN IN THE STATEHOUSE
    (UNITED STATES).=         HODGLH-62-BSU

STATEMENT
    SOCIAL POWER AND COMMITMENT -- A
    THEORETICAL STATEMENT.=
                              ABRAE -58-SPC

    POWER ROLES OF INTELLECTUALS -- AN
    INTRODUCTORY STATEMENT.=
                              HARTCL-64-PRI

STATES
    THE CIVIL SERVICE IN THE NEW
    STATES.=                  ADU,A -65-CSN

    BRITISH UNIVERSITIES AND THE
    STATES.=                  BERDRO-59-BUS

    NATIONAL UNITY AND REGIONALISM IN
    EIGHT AFRICAN STATES (NIGERIA,
    NIGER, THE CONGO, GABON, CENTRAL
    AFRICAN REPUBLIC, CHAD, UGANDA,
    ETHIOPIA).=               CARTGM-66-NUR

    AFRICAN ONE PARTY STATES.=
                              CARTGW-62-AOP

    GOVERNMENT AND OPPOSITION IN THE
    NEW STATES.=              DAALH -66-GON

    INTER - PARTY COMPETITION, ECONOMIC
    VARIABLES, AND WELFARE POLICIES IN
    THE AMERICAN STATES.=     DAWSRE-63-IPC

    PARTY RESPONSIBILITY IN THE STATES
    -- SOME CAUSAL FACTORS

STATES                    (CONTINUATION)
    (UNITED STATES).=         FLINTA-64-PRS

    OLD SOCIETIES AND NEW STATES -- THE
    QUEST FOR MODERNITY IN ASIA AND
    AFRICA.=                  GEERC -63-OSN

    THE INDIAN PARLIAMENT AND STATES
    REORGANIZATION.=          GUPTSK-57-IPS

    ARMED FORCES IN NEW STATES.=
                              GUTTWF-63-AFN

    EDUCATION OF MILITARY LEADERSHIP IN
    EMERGENT STATES.=         GUTTWF-65-EML

    MILITARY INSTITUTIONS AND POWER IN
    THE NEW STATES.=          GUTTWF-65-MIP

    THE ETHIOPIAN NO - PARTY STATE -- A
    NOTE ON THE FUNCTIONS OF POLITICAL
    PARTIES IN DEVELOPING STATES.=
                              HESSRL-64-ENP

    THE POLITICS OF THE EUROPEAN
    COMMUNIST STATES (BULGARIA,
    CZECHOSLOVAKIA, HUNGARY, EAST
    GERMANY, POLAND, RUMANIA,
    SOVIET UNION, YUGOSLAVIA).=
                              IONEG -67-PEC

    THE AMERICAN LEGISLATIVE PROCESS --
    CONGRESS AND THE STATES.=
                              KEEFWJ-64-ALP

    THE LEAGUE OF ARAB STATES -- A
    STUDY IN THE DYNAMICS OF REGIONAL
    ORGANIZATION (MIDDLE EAST).=
                              MACDRW-65-LAS

    THE STRUCTURE OF COMPETITION FOR
    OFFICE IN THE AMERICAN STATES.=
                              SCHLJA-60-SCC

    THE INTELLECTUAL IN THE POLITICAL
    DEVELOPMENT OF THE NEW STATES.=
                              SHILE -60-IPD

    POLITICAL DEVELOPMENT IN THE NEW
    STATES -- 1 -- 2.=        SHILE -60-PDN

    THE MILITARY IN THE POLITICAL
    DEVELOPMENT OF THE NEW STATES.=
                              SHILE -62-MPD

    DEMAGOGUES AND CADRES IN THE
    POLITICAL DEVELOPMENT OF THE NEW
    STATES.=                  SHILE -63-DCP

    OPPOSITION IN THE NEW STATES OF
    ASIA AND AFRICA.=         SHILE -66-ONS

    THE AMERICAN FEDERAL EXECUTIVE -- A
    STUDY OF SOCIAL AND PERSONAL
    CHARACTERISTICS OF THE CIVILIAN
    AND MILITARY LEADERS OF THE UNITED
    STATES FEDERAL GOVERNMENT.=
                              WARNWL-63-AFE

    THE PUBLIC SERVICE IN THE NEW
    STATES -- AFRICA.=        YOUNK -60-PSN

    INTEREST GROUPS IN THE STATES
    (UNITED STATES).=         ZIEGH -65-IGS

    CREATING POLITICAL ORDER -- THE
    PARTY - STATES OF WEST AFRICA
    (MALI, GHANA, SENEGAL, GUINEA,
    IVORY COAST).=            ZOLBAR-66-CPO

STATESMANSHIP
    MAINTENANCE OF MEMBERSHIP -- A

STATESMANSHIP          (CONTINUATION)
STUDY IN ADMINISTRATIVE
STATESMANSHIP (UNITED STATES).=
                    BURNJM-48-MMS

STATESMANSHIP OR CRAFTSMANSHIP --
CURRENT CONFLICT OVER THE SUPREME
COURT (UNITED STATES).=
                    STEARJ-58-SOC

THE BRITISH CRISIS -- A PROBLEM IN
ECONOMIC STATESMANSHIP.=
                    WILLJH-49-BCP

STATESMEN
GENERALS AS STATESMEN (FRANCE,
FINLAND, GERMANY UNITED STATES).=
                    GELLJE-59-GSF

STATISTICAL
AMERICAN SOCIAL CLASSES --
STATISTICAL STRATA OR SOCIAL
GROUPS.=            LENSGE-52-ASC

DIMENSIONS OF CONGRESSIONAL VOTING
-- A STATISTICAL STUDY OF THE
HOUSE OF REPRESENTATIVES IN THE
EIGHTY-FIRST CONGRESS
(UNITED STATES).=   MACRD -58-DCV

THE COMMUNIST PARTY OF UZBEKISTAN,
1959 -- A BRIEF STATISTICAL NOTE
(SOVIET UNION).=    NEWTJA-66-CPU

STATISTICAL ANALYSIS AND
COMPARATIVE ADMINISTRATION -- THE
TURKISH COUNSEIL D'ETATE.=
                    PRESRV-58-SAC

STATUS
FAMILY STATUS, LOCAL - COMMUNITY
STATUS, AND SOCIAL STRATIFICATION
-- THREE TYPES OF SOCIAL RANKING.=
                    BARBB -61-FSL

FAMILY STATUS, LOCAL - COMMUNITY
STATUS, AND SOCIAL STRATIFICATION
-- THREE TYPES OF SOCIAL RANKING.=
                    BARBB -61-FSL

FUNCTIONS AND PATHOLOGY OF STATUS
SYSTEMS IN FORMAL ORGANIZATIONS.=
                    BARNCI-46-FPS

POSITION, ROLE AND STATUS -- A
REFORMULATION OF CONCEPTS.=
                    BATEFL-56-PRS

CLASS, STATUS, POWER.=
                    BENDR -53-CSP

SOCIAL STATUS AND SOCIAL CHANGE.=
                    BESHJM-63-SSS

CLASS, STATUS, AND POWER
REPUTATION.=        BONJCM-64-CSP

YUGOSLAVIA -- STATUS AND ROLE OF
THE EXECUTIVE ORGANS DURING THE
FIRST STAGE OF YUGOSLAVIA'S
POLITICAL AND CONSTITUTIONAL
DEVELOPMENT.=       DJORJ -58-YSR

DESPOTISM, STATUS CULTURE AND
SOCIAL MOBILITY IN AN AFRICAN
KINGDOM (UGANDA).=  FALLLA-59-DSC

THE KING'S MEN -- LEADERSHIP AND
STATUS IN BUGANDA ON THE EVE OF
INDEPENDENCE.=      FALLLA-64-KSM

THE PERSISTENCE OF STATUS

STATUS          (CONTINUATION)
ADVANTAGES IN SOVIET RUSSIA.=
                    FELDRA-53-PSA

AUTOCHTHONOUS ELEMENTS IN THE
EVOLUTION OF DOMINION STATUS --
THE CASE OF NEW ZEALAND.=
                    FIELDK-62-AEE

MILITARY STATUS IN CHINESE
SOCIETY.=           FRIEMH-51-MSC

TYPES OF POWER AND STATUS.=
                    GOLDH -39-TPS

STATUS RIVALRY AND CULTURAL
EVOLUTION IN POLYNESIA.=
                    GOLDI -55-SRC

PARTY PROTECTION AND PRIVILEGED
STATUS IN SOVIET SOCIETY.=
                    KRYLKA-66-PPP

SOCIAL STATUS AND SOCIAL STRUCTURE
-- 1 -- 2.=         LIPSSM-51-SSS

AMERICAN INTELLECTUALS -- THEIR
POLITICS AND STATUS.= LIPSSM-59-AIT

LEGISLATORS' SOCIAL STATUS AND
THEIR VOTES (UNITED STATES).=
                    MACRD -61-LSS

THE AMBIVALENT SOCIAL STATUS OF THE
AMERICAN POLITICIAN.= MITCWC-59-ASS

SOME ASPECTS OF CLASS, STATUS AND
POWER RELATIONS IN ENGLAND.=
                    MONTGB-51-ACS

SOCIAL STATUS AND POWER IN JAVA.=
                    PALMLH-60-SSP

STATUS, ACHIEVEMENT, AND EDUCATION
IN CEYLON.=         RYANB -61-SAE

THE STATUS REVOLUTION AND
MASSACHUSETTS PROGRESSIVE
LEADERSHIP (UNITED STATES).=
                    SHERRB-63-SRM

CHARISMA, ORDER, AND STATUS.=
                    SHILE -65-COS

THE NON - AFRICAN MINORITY IN
MODERN AFRICA -- SOCIAL STATUS.=
                    SMYTHH-61-NAM

KAZAKHSTAN -- CHANGES IN
ADMINISTRATIVE STATUS AND THE
NATIONAL COMPOSITION OF THE
POPULATION (SOVIET UNION).=
                    TASKGA-64-KCA

SUBSTANCE AND ARTIFACT -- THE
CURRENT STATUS OF RESEARCH ON
COMMUNITY POWER STRUCTURE.=
                    WALTJ -66-SAC

STATUTE
BYLAWS OF THE ELITE -- THE PARTY
STATUTE (SOVIET UNION).=
                    BRUNG -65-BEP

STEEL
THE EUROPEAN COAL AND STEEL
COMMUNITY -- OPERATIONS OF THE
HIGH AUTHORITY.=    MERRHJ-55-ECS

STRAINS
POSTWAR STRAINS ON THE BRITISH
COMMONWEALTH.=      MANSN -48-PSB

STRUCTURE          (CONTINUATION)
  (GREAT BRITAIN).=          COLEGC-55-SCS

  CONFLICT AND LIBERTY -- SOME
  REMARKS ON THE SOCIAL STRUCTURE OF
  GERMAN POLITICS.=          DAHRR -63-CLR

  RECENT CHANGES IN THE CLASS
  STRUCTURE OF EUROPEAN SOCIETIES.=
                             DAHRR -64-RCC

  COMMUNITY POWER STRUCTURE --
  PROBLEMS AND CONTINUITIES.=
                             DANZMH-64-CPS

  GROUP STRUCTURE AND AUTHORITY.=
                             DOCTO -63-GSA

  POWER STRUCTURE AND ITS
  COMMUNICATION BEHAVIOR IN
  SAN JOSE, COSTA RICA.=
                             EDWAHT-67-PSI

  YOUTH, CULTURE AND SOCIAL STRUCTURE
  IN ISRAEL.=                EISEEN-51-YCS

  FROM GENERATION TO GENERATION --
  AGE GROUPS AND SOCIAL STRUCTURE.=
                             EISESN-56-GGA

  POLITICAL AUTHORITY AND THE
  STRUCTURE OF KINSHIP IN ABORIGINAL
  SAMOA.=                    EMBEM -62-PAS

  POLITICAL PARTIES AND THE CANADIAN
  SOCIAL STRUCTURE.=         ENGLFC-67-PPC

  AUTHORITY STRUCTURE AND
  ORGANIZATIONAL EFFECTIVENESS.=
                             ETZIA -59-ASC

  SOCIAL STRUCTURE AND CANADIAN
  POLITICAL PARTIES -- THE QUEBEC
  CASE.=                     FILLWO-56-SSC

  ORGANIZED LABOR'S IMAGE OF
  COMMUNITY POWER STRUCTURE
  (UNITED STATES).=          FORMWH-60-CLS

  THE ROLE CONCEPT IN LEGISLATURES --
  A PROBABILITY MODEL AND A NOTE ON
  COGNITIVE STRUCTURE
  (UNITED STATES).=          FRANWL-65-RCL

  THE ARMY AS A SOCIAL STRUCTURE
  (UNITED STATES).=          FREEFD-48-ASS

  AN HISTORICAL STUDY OF THE ORIGINS
  AND STRUCTURE OF THE DANISH
  INTELLIGENTSIA.=           GEIGT -59-HSO

  POLITICS, SOCIAL STRUCTURE, AND
  MILITARY INTERVENTION IN
  LATIN AMERICA.=            GERMG -62-PSS

  AFFLUENCE AND THE BRITISH CLASS
  STRUCTURE.=                GOLDJH-63-ABC

  THE MASS SOCIETY AND THE
  PARAPOLITICAL STRUCTURE.=
                             GREES -62-MSP

  THE SOCIAL STRUCTURE AND POLITICAL
  PROCESS OF SUBURBIA -- AN
  EMPIRICAL TEST (UNITED STATES).=
                             GREES -62-SSP

  THE PROBLEM OF GENERATIONS IN AN
  ORGANIZATIONAL STRUCTURE.=
                             GUSFMR-57-PGC

  THE CHANGING STRUCTURE OF THE
  BRITISH POLITICAL ELITE,
  1886-1935.=                GUTTWL-51-CSB

GOVERNMENT, POLITICS, AND SOCIAL
STRUCTURE IN LAOS -- A STUDY OF
TRADITION AND INNOVATION.=
                           HALPJM-64-GPS

COMMUNITY POWER STRUCTURE -- A
STUDY OF DECISION MAKERS
(UNITED STATES).=          HUNTF -53-CPS

POWER STRUCTURE AND DECISION-MAKING
IN A MEXICAN BORDER CITY.=
                           KLAPOE-60-PSD

SITUATIONAL DETERMINANTS OF
LEADERSHIP STRUCTURE.=
                           KORTDC-62-SDL

THE STRUCTURE OF THE SOVIET
INTELLIGENTSIA.=           LABEL -60-SSI

LEADERS, FACTIONS AND PARTIES --
THE STRUCTURE OF PHILIPPINE
POLITICS.=                 LANDCH-65-LFP

POLITICAL SYSTEMS OF HIGHLAND BURMA
-- A STUDY OF KACHIN SOCIAL
STRUCTURE.=                LEADER-54-PSH

BRAZILIAN CAREERS AND SOCIAL
STRUCTURE -- AN EVOLUTIONARY MODEL
AND CASE HISTORY.=         LEEDA -64-BCS

THE SOCIAL STRUCTURE OF ISLAM.=
                           LEVYR -57-SSI

SOCIAL STATUS AND SOCIAL STRUCTURE
-- 1 -- 2.=                LIPSSM-51-SSS

SOCIAL CHANGE AND STRUCTURE IN
TRANSITIONAL SOCIETIES
(LATIN AMERICA, MIDDLE EAST).=
                           MARCS -60-SCS

CASTE RANKING AND COMMUNITY
STRUCTURE IN FIVE REGIONS OF INDIA
AND PAKISTAN.=             MARRM -60-CRC

UNITED STATES SENATORS AND THE
CLASS STRUCTURE.=          MATTDR-54-USS

CONSERVATIVE PARTY AND THE CHANGING
CLASS STRUCTURE (GREAT BRITAIN).=
                           MAUDA -53-CPC

SOCIAL STRUCTURE AND SOCIAL CHANGE
IN NEW SPAIN.=             MCALLN-63-SSS

EQUILIBRIUM, STRUCTURE OF INTERESTS
AND LEADERSHIP -- ADENAUER'S
SURVIVAL AS CHANCELLOR (GERMANY).=
                           MERKPH-62-ESI

SOME ASPECTS OF HIERARCHICAL
STRUCTURE IN HAITI.=       METRR -52-AHS

THE STRUCTURE OF POWER IN AMERICAN
SOCIETY.=                  MILLCW-58-SPA

TOWN AND GOWN -- THE POWER
STRUCTURE OF A UNIVERSITY TOWN
(UNITED STATES).=          MILLDC-63-TGP

THE YAD VILLAGE -- A STUDY IN THE
SOCIAL STRUCTURE OF A NYASALAND
TRIBE.=                    MITCJC-56-YVS

THE NEO-DESTOUR PARTY OF TUNISIA --
A STRUCTURE FOR DEMOCRACY.=
                           MOORCH-62-NDP

THE THEORY OF SOCIAL STRUCTURE.=
                           NADESF-57-TSS

ORGANIZATIONAL LEADERSHIP AND

SOCIAL STRUCTURE IN A SMALL CITY
(UNITED STATES).=        OLMSDW-54-OLS

CLASS STRUCTURE IN THE SOCIAL
CONSCIOUSNESS.=        CSSOS -63-CSS

ASPECTS OF INDONESIA'S SOCIAL
STRUCTURE.=        PALML -55-AIS

SOCIAL STRUCTURE AND THE LEADERSHIP
FACTOR IN A NEGRO COMMUNITY
(UNITED STATES).=        PAREVJ-56-SSL

POLITICS AND SOCIAL STRUCTURE IN A
NORWEGIAN VILLAGE.=        PARKGK-61-PSS

ABSENTEE - OWNED CORPORATIONS AND
COMMUNITY POWER STRUCTURE
(UNITED STATES).=        PELLRJ-56-AOC

THE NEW ZEALAND LABOR PARTY -- ITS
FORMAL STRUCTURE.=        PENFJ -54-NZL

SOCIAL STRUCTURE AND THE POLITICAL
PROCESS IN LATIN AMERICA.=
                        PETERL-63-SSP

THE ECONOMIC ELITE AND THE SOCIAL
STRUCTURE IN CANADA.=        PORTJ -57-EES

POWER STRUCTURE AND MEMBERSHIP
DISPERSION IN UNIONS
(UNITED STATES).=        RAPHEE-65-PSM

THE POLITICAL STRUCTURE OF THE
FEDERAL RESERVE SYSTEM
(UNITED STATES).=        REAGMD-61-PSF

THE POWER STRUCTURE -- POLITICAL
PROCESS IN AMERICAN SOCIETY.=
                        ROSEAM-67-PSP

POWER AND COMMUNITY STRUCTURE
(UNITED STATES).=        ROSSPH-60-PCS

ST. LOUIS POLITICS -- RELATIONSHIP
AMONG INTERESTS, PARTIES, AND
GOVERNMENTAL STRUCTURE
(UNITED STATES))=        SALIRH-60-SLP

THE STRUCTURE OF COMPETITION FOR
OFFICE IN THE AMERICAN STATES.=
                        SCHLJA-60-SCO

THE ROLE OF ECONOMIC DOMINANTS IN
COMMUNITY POWER STRUCTURE
(UNITED STATES).=        SCHURO-58-REC

POLITICAL RECRUITMENT AND PARTY
STRUCTURE -- A CASE STUDY
(UNITED STATES).=        SELILG-61-PRP

CELEBRITY STRUCTURE OF THE FAR
RIGHT (UNITED STATES).=
                        STEWDK-64-CSF

CHANGES IN THE STRUCTURE AND
FUNCTIONS OF THE INTELLIGENTSIA
(POLAND).=        SZCZJ -47-CSF

THE DECISION-MAKERS -- THE POWER
STRUCTURE OF DALLAS
(UNITED STATES).=        THOMCE-63-DMP

STRUCTURE AND CONSTITUTIONAL BASIS
OF THE CHINESE PEOPLES REPUBLIC.=
                        THOMSB-51-SCB

THE STRUCTURE OF BALKAN SOCIETY.=
                        TOMAD -46-SBS

INTERRELATIONS BETWEEN BOLSHEVIK
IDEOLOGY AND THE STRUCTURE OF

SOVIET SOCIETY.=        TOMAD -51-IBB

THE STATE DELEGATIONS AND THE
STRUCTURE OF PARTY VOTING IN THE
UNITED STATES HOUSE OF
REPRESENTATIVES.=        TRUMDB-56-SDS

STRUCTURE OF POWER IN PALAU.=
                        USEEJ -50-SPP

THE CHANGING CLASS STRUCTURE OF
INDONESIA.=        VAN-JM-56-CCS

CLASS STRUCTURE AND COMMUNIST
THEORY.=        VAN-JM-61-CSC

CANEVILLE -- THE SOCIAL STRUCTURE
OF A SOUTH AFRICAN TOWN.=
                        VAN-PL-64-CSS

SUBSTANCE AND ARTIFACT -- THE
CURRENT STATUS OF RESEARCH ON
COMMUNITY POWER STRUCTURE.=
                        WALTJ -66-SAC

POWER STRUCTURE AND SOCIOCULTURAL
CHANGE IN LATIN AMERICAN
COMMUNITIES.=        WHITNE-65-PSS

CLASS STRUCTURE AND CLASS CONFLICT
IN HAITIAN SOCIETY.=        WINGR -65-CSC

STRUCTURES
LEGITIMACY AND VISIBILITY --
LEADERSHIP STRUCTURES RELATED TO
FOUR COMMUNITY SYSTEMS
(UNITED STATES).=        BONJCM-65-LVL

THE ROLE OF BUREAUCRATIC NORMS IN
AFRICAN POLITICAL STRUCTURES.=
                        COLSE -58-RBN

VARIATIONS IN POWER STRUCTURES AND
ORGANIZING EFFICIENCY -- A
COMPARATIVE STUDY OF FOUR AREAS
(UNITED STATES).=        CLARKE-62-VPS

THE SOCIAL BASIS OF THE CHANGING
POLITICAL STRUCTURES IN
LATIN AMERICA.        FITZRH-59-SBC

DECISION-MAKING CLIQUES IN
COMMUNITY POWER STRUCTURES -- A
COMPARATIVE STUDY OF AN AMERICAN
AND AN ENGLISH CITY.=        MILLDC-58-DMC

STRATEGIES, STRUCTURES, AND
PROCESSES OF ORGANIZATIONAL
DECISION.=        THOMJD-59-SSP

POLITICAL INSTITUTIONS AND
AFRIKANER SOCIAL STRUCTURES IN THE
REPUBLIC OF SOUTH AFRICA.=
                        TRAPS -63-PIA

STRUCTURING
THE STRUCTURING OF POWER IN A
SUBURBAN COMMUNITY
(UNITED STATES).=        SMITTC-60-SPS

STRUGGLE
THE POSTWAR STUDENT STRUGGLE IN
JAPAN.=        BATTLH-56-PSS

THE STRUGGLE OF SOVIET JURISTS
AGAINST A RETURN TO STALINIST
TERROR.=        BERMHJ-63-SSJ

POWER IN WASHINGTON -- A CRITICAL
LOOK AT TODAY'S STRUGGLE TO GOVERN
IN THE NATION'S CAPITAL.=
                        CATED -64-PWC

THE POWER STRUGGLE IN RED CHINA.=

STRUGGLE          (CONTINUATION)
                          CHENC--66-PSR

THE STRUGGLE GOES ON
(SOVIET UNION).=      CONQR -60-SGS

POLITICAL STRUGGLE IN (ANCIENT)
BUREAUCRATIC SOCIETIES.=
                          EISESN-56-PSA

RACE AND NATIONALISM -- THE
STRUGGLE FOR POWER IN
RHODESIA-NYASALAND.=   FRANFM-60-RNS

THE LEGISLATIVE STRUGGLE -- A STUDY
IN SOCIAL COMBAT (UNITED STATES).=
                          GROSBM-53-LSS

THE 'CLASS STRUGGLE' IN AFRICA --
AN EXAMINATION OF CONFLICTING
THEORIES (WEST AFRICA).=
                          GRUNKW-64-CSA

KHRUSHCHEV'S DISLOYAL OPPOSITION --
STRUCTURAL CHANGE AND POWER
STRUGGLE IN THE COMMUNIST BLOC.=
                          MICHF -63-KSD

THE STRUGGLE FOR POWER (CHINA).=
                          MICHF -67-SPC

THE STRUGGLE FOR SYRIA -- A STUDY
OF POST-WAR ARAB POLITICS,
1945-1948.          SEALP -65-SSS

THE POWER STRUGGLE IN IRAQ '' 1, ''
2, '' 3.=         SHWAB -60-PSI

POWER STRUGGLE IN THE CHINESE CP
(COMMUNIST PARTY) -- THE KAO-JAO
PURGE.=          TANGPS-55-PSC

THE STRUGGLE FOR REPRESENTATIVE
INSTITUTIONS IN GERMANY -- PART 1
-- PART 2.=      ULLMRK-49-SRI

THE STRUGGLE FOR THE SOVIET
SUCCESSION.=     WOLFBD-53-SSS

THE STRUGGLE FOR A MULTI - PARTY
GOVERNMENT IN TURKEY.=
                          YALMA -47-SMP

CITY COUNCILMEN AND THE GROUP
STRUGGLE -- A TYPOLOGY OF ROLE
ORIENTATIONS (UNITED STATES).=
                          ZISKBH-65-CCG


STUDENT
STUDENT OPPOSITION IN
LATIN AMERICA.=    ALBOO -66-SOL

THE POSTWAR STUDENT STRUGGLE IN
JAPAN.=          BATTLH-56-PSS

THE MEXICAN STUDENT VIEWS THE
UNITED STATES.=    BEALRL-54-MSV

THE STUDENT FEDERATION OF CHILE --
50 YEARS OF POLITICAL ACTION.=
                          BONIF -60-SFC

COMMUNIST CHINA -- THE POLITICS OF
STUDENT OPPOSITION.=   COOLDJ-64-CCP

THE STUDENT POPULATION OF A
SOUTHEAST ASIAN UNIVERSITY -- AN

STUDENT          (CONTINUATION)
INDONESIAN EXAMPLE.=   FISCJ -61-SPS

STUDENT OPPOSITION IN SPAIN.=
                          GALVET-66-SOS

THE WEST AFRICAN STUDENT'S UNION --
A STUDY IN CULTURE CONTACT.=
                          GARIP -53-WAS

THE SOCIAL BACKGROUND OF A WEST
AFRICAN STUDENT POPULATION -- 1 --
2.=               JAHOG -54-SBW

STUDENT POLITICS (LATIN AMERICA,
INDIA, POLAND, UNITED STATES,
GERMANY, CHILE, ARGENTINA,
COLUMBIA, FRANCE).=  LIPSSM-67-SPL

SOME STUDENT PROBLEMS IN EAST
GERMAN UNIVERSITIES.=  NM    -57-SPE

THE BRAZILIAN LAW STUDENT --
BACKGROUND, HABITS, ATTITUDES.=
                          SCHELR-63-BLS

THE UNIVERSITY STUDENT.=
                          SILVKH-64-US

DOMINANT POWER COMPONENTS IN THE
BRAZILIAN UNIVERSITY STUDENT
MOVEMENT PRIOR TO APRIL 1964.=
                          THERLD-65-DPC

STUDENT POLITICS IN LATIN AMERICA
-- THE VENEZUELAN EXAMPLE.=
                         WASHSW-59-SPL

THE BURMESE UNIVERSITY STUDENT --
AN APPROACH TO PERSONALITY AND
SUBCULTURE.=     WOHLJ -66-BUS

STUDENTS
POLITICAL ASPIRATIONS OF LAW
STUDENTS (UNITED STATES).=
                          AGGERE-58-PAL

JAPANESE STUDENTS AND JAPANESE
POLITICS.=        ALTBP -63-JSJ

STUDYING THE STUDENTS -- BETWEEN
CONFORMITY AND DISSENT
(SOVIET UNION).=    CALLT -60-SSB

SHE WHO RIDES A PEACOCK -- SOCIAL
CHANGE AND INDIAN STUDENTS.=
                          CORMML-61-SWR

EGYPTIAN STUDENTS.=   CRAIJM-53-ES

DEVELOPING POLITICAL ORIENTATIONS
OF PANAMANIAN STUDENTS.=
                          GOLDC -61-DPC

RADICAL NATIONALISM -- THE
POLITICAL ORIENTATIONS OF
PANAMANIAN LAW STUDENTS.=
                          GOLDC -62-RNP

AN AFRICAN ELITE -- A SAMPLE SURVEY
OF 52 FORMER STUDENTS OF MAKERERE
COLLEGE IN EAST AFRICA.=
                          GOLDJE-55-AES

AMONG STUDENTS IN MOSCOW -- AN
OUTSIDER'S REPORT (SOVIET UNION).=
                          HAMMCP-64-ASM

STUDENTS IN WORLD POLITICS.=
                    JCC    -51-SWP

AMERICAN UNIVERSITY STUDENTS -- A

STUDENTS          (CONTINUATION)
  PRESUMPTIVE ELITE.=    MARVD -65-AUS

  SOME REACTIONS CF JAPANESE
  UNIVERSITY STUDENTS TO PERSUASIVE
  COMMUNICATION.=    MCGIE -65-RJU

  EGALITARIAN ATTITUDES OF WARSAW
  STUDENTS (PCLAND).=    NOWAS -60-EAW

  SOCIAL DISTANCE ATTITUDES OF SOUTH
  AFRICAN STUDENTS.=    PETTTF-60-SDA

  UNIVERSITY STUDENTS AND POLITICS IN
  BURMA.=    SILVJ -64-USP

  INTELLECTUAL IDENTITY AND POLITICAL
  IDEOLOGY AMONG UNIVERSITY STUDENTS
  (LATIN AMERICA).=    SOARGA-67-IIP

  STUDENTS, INTELLECTUALS, AND THE
  CHINESE REVOLUTION.=    WALKRL-63-SIC

  UNIVERSITY STUDENTS IN A WORLD OF
  CHANGE -- A COLUMBIAN SAMPLE.=
                         WILLRC-64-USW

STUDYING
  STUDYING THE STUDENTS -- BETWEEN
  CONFORMITY AND DISSENT
  (SOVIET UNION).=    CALLT -60-SSB

  STUDYING YOUR COMMUNITY
  (UNITED STATES).=    WARRRL-55-SYC


STYLE
  LEADERSHIP STYLE AND POLITICAL
  COMPETENCE (ITALY).=    BARNSH-67-LSP

  LEADERSHIP STYLE AS A VARIABLE IN
  RESEARCH ADMINISTRATION.=
                         BAUMH -57-LSV

  JAPANESE POLITICAL STYLE.=
                         TSUNWM-66-JPS

STYLES
  POLITICAL SYSTEMS, STYLES AND
  PERSONALITIES.=    LASSHD-67-PSS

  THE ADOPTION OF POLITICAL STYLES BY
  AFRICAN POLITICIANS IN THE
  RHODESIAS.=    SCARJR-66-APS

SUB-SAHARA
  THE POLITICS OF SUB-SAHARA AFRICA.=
                         COLEJS-60-PSS

SUB-SAHARAN
  THE PROCESSES OF FRAGMENTATION AND
  CONSOLIDATION IN SUB-SAHARAN
  AFRICA.=    ANDN  -59-PFC

SUBCOMMITTEE
  AN APPROPRIATIONS SUBCOMMITTEE AND
  ITS CLIENT AGENCIES -- A
  COMPARATIVE STUDY OF SUPERVISION
  AND CONTROL (UNITED STATES).=
                         SHARI -65-ASI

SUBCOMMITTEES
  SUBCOMMITTEES -- THE MINIATURE
  LEGISLATURES OF CONGRESS
  (UNITED STATES).=    GOODG -62-SML

SUBCULTURE
  THE BURMESE UNIVERSITY STUDENT --

SUBCULTURE          (CONTINUATION)
  AN APPROACH TO PERSONALITY AND
  SUBCULTURE.=    WOHLJ -66-BUS

SUBHAS
  SUBHAS CHANDRA BOSE AND THE INDIAN
  NATIONAL ARMY.=    COHESP-63-SCB

SUBJECT
  PHILOSOPHY STUDIES -- SUBJECT,
  OBJECT, AND ORGANIZATION
  (SOVIET UNION).=    BOCHJM-60-PSS

SUBJECTIVE
  THE PERSONALITY OF LAWYERS -- A
  COMPARATIVE STUDY OF SUBJECTIVE
  FACTORS IN LAW, BASED ON
  INTERVIEWS WITH GERMAN LAWYERS.=
                         WEYRWO-64-PLC

SUBORDINATE
  SUBORDINATE LEADERSHIP IN A
  BICULTURAL COMMUNITY -- AN
  ANALYSIS (UNITED STATES).=
                         WATSJB-54-SLB

SUBORDINATION
  INDEPENDENCE OR SUBORDINATION --
  THE JAPANESE COMMUNIST PARTY
  BETWEEN MOSCOW AND PEKING.=
                         LANGPF-63-IOS

SUBSTANCE
  SUBSTANCE AND ARTIFACT -- THE
  CURRENT STATUS OF RESEARCH ON
  COMMUNITY POWER STRUCTURE.=
                         WALTJ -66-SAC

SUBSYSTEM
  A TYPOLOGY OF COMMUNITY LEADERSHIP
  BASED ON INFLUENCE AND INTERACTION
  WITHIN THE LEADER SUBSYSTEM
  (UNITED STATES).=    FANEAA-56-TCL

SUBURBAN
  POPULAR IMAGES OF DECISION-MAKING
  IN SUBURBAN COMMUNITIES
  (UNITED STATES).=    DYE,TR-62-PID

  THE STRUCTURING OF POWER IN A
  SUBURBAN COMMUNITY
  (UNITED STATES).=    SMITTC-60-SPS

SUBURBIA
  THE SOCIAL STRUCTURE AND POLITICAL
  PROCESS OF SUBURBIA -- AN
  EMPIRICAL TEST (UNITED STATES).=
                         GREES -62-SSP

SUBVERSION
  THAILAND'S BUREAUCRACY AND THE
  THREAT OF COMMUNIST SUBVERSION.=
                         KINGJK-54-TSB

  THE COMMUNIST SUBVERSION OF
  CZECHOSLOVAKIA, 1938-1948 -- THE
  FAILURE OF COEXISTENCE.=
                         KORBJ -59-CSC

SUCCESS
  COMMUNITY POWER AND URBAN RENEWAL
  SUCCESS (UNITED STATES).=
                         HAWLAH-63-CPU

  CRITERIA FOR RECRUITMENT AND
  SUCCESS IN THE JAPANESE
  BUREAUCRACY, 1866-1900 --
  'TRADITIONAL' AND 'MODERN'
  CRITERIA IN BUREAUCRATIC
  DEVELOPMENT.=    SILBBS-66-CRS

SUCCESSION
  THE IMPLICATIONS OF THE SUCCESSION

SYSTEM                    (CONTINUATION)
  MASS PUBLIC (UNITED STATES).=
                          DENNJ -66-SPS

  THE NEW CLASS -- AN ANALYSIS OF THE
  COMMUNIST SYSTEM (YUGOSLAVIA).=
                          DJILM -57-NCA

  THE BRITISH POLITICAL SYSTEM.=
                          ECKSHH-62-BPS

  AGRARIANISM IN ISRAEL'S PARTY
  SYSTEM.=               ETZIA -57-AIS

  BANTU BUREAUCRACY -- A STUDY OF
  ROLE CONFLICT AND INSTITUTIONAL
  CHANGE IN THE SOGA POLITICAL
  SYSTEM.=               FALLLA-55-BBS

  THE APPROPRIATIONS COMMITTEE AS A
  POLITICAL SYSTEM (UNITED STATES).=
                          FENNRF-62-ACP

  PERCEPTIONS OF THE VIETNAMESE
  PUBLIC ADMINISTRATION SYSTEM.=
                          FOX,GH-64-PVP

  THE POLITICAL SYSTEM OF CHILE.=
                          GIL,FG-66-PSC

  THE SENIORITY SYSTEM IN CONGRESS
  (UNITED STATES).=      GOODG -59-SSC

  AMERICAN POLITICAL PARTIES AND
  AMERICAN SYSTEM.=      GROOM -60-APP

  AUSTRIA'S SOCIALISTS IN THE TREND
  TOWARD A TWO - PARTY SYSTEM -- AN
  INTERPRETATION OF POSTWAR
  ELECTIONS.=            GULICA-58-ASS

  THE IATA SYSTEM IN LEBANON -- A
  COMPARATIVE POLITICAL VIEW.=
                          HARIIF-65-ISL

  THE PHILIPPINE ADMINISTRATIVE
  SYSTEM -- A FUSION OF EAST AND
  WEST.=                 HEADF -57-PAS

  PRESIDENTIAL LEADERSHIP AND THE
  PARTY SYSTEM (UNITED STATES).=
                          HOLCAN-54-PLP

  TURKEY'S POLITICS -- THE TRANSITION
  TO MULTI - PARTY SYSTEM.=
                          KARPKH-59-TSP

  THE NEW EMPEROR SYSTEM (JAPAN).=
                          KENZT -62-NES

  THE AUSTRIAN ELECTORAL SYSTEM.=
                          KITZUW- -AES

  INDIA -- THE CONGRESS SYSTEM ON
  TRIAL.=                KOTHR -67-ICS

  SOME CHARACTERISTICS OF THE SOVIET
  LEADERSHIP SYSTEM -- A MATURING
  TOTALITARIAN SYSTEM.=  LAIRRD-66-CSL

  SOME CHARACTERISTICS OF THE SOVIET
  LEADERSHIP SYSTEM -- A MATURING
  TOTALITARIAN SYSTEM.=  LAIRRD-66-CSL

  TERROR IN THE SOVIET SYSTEM --
  TRENDS AND PORTENTS.=  LEONW -58-TSS

  THE TWO - PARTY SYSTEM IN BRITISH
  POLITICS.=             LIPSL -53-TPS

  PARLIAMENT IN THE GERMAN POLITICAL
  SYSTEM.=               LOEWG -66-PGP

SYSTEM                    (CONTINUATION)
  A GAME THEORETIC ANALYSIS OF
  CONGRESSIONAL POWER DISTRIBUTIONS
  FOR A STABLE TWO - PARTY SYSTEM.=
                          LUCERD-56-GTA

  ELECTORAL TRENDS AND THE TENDENCY
  TO A ONE PARTY SYSTEM IN NIGERIA.=
                          MACKJP-62-ETT

  SYSTEM AND NETWORK -- AN APPROACH
  TO THE STUDY OF POLITICAL
  PROCESS.=              MAYEAC-62-SNA

  THE SOVIET POLITICAL SYSTEM -- AN
  INTERPRETATION.=       MEYEAG-65-SPS

  THE COMMUNITY BASIS OF CONFLICT IN
  SCHOOL SYSTEM POLITICS
  (UNITED STATES).=      MINACW-66-CBC

  DOMINANCE AND DISSENT -- THEIR
  INTER-RELATIONS IN THE INDIAN
  PARTY. SYSTEM.=        MORRWH-66-DDT

  THE SATELLITE POLICE SYSTEM
  (EASTERN EUROPE).=     MP      -52-SPS

  BRITISH FOREIGN POLICY AND THE
  PARTY SYSTEM.=         NORTFS-60-BFP

  THE AUSTRALIAN PARTY SYSTEM.=
                          OVERL -52-APS

  MEXICO'S ONE - PARTY SYSTEM -- A
  RE-EVALUATION.=        PADGLV-57-MSO

  THE MEXICAN POLITICAL SYSTEM.=
                          PADGLV-66-MPS

  QUASI - PARTISAN CONFLICT IN A ONE
  - PARTY LEGISLATIVE SYSTEM -- THE
  FLORIDA SENATE, 1947-1961
  (UNITED STATES).=      PARSMB-62-QPC

  THE SOCIAL SYSTEM.=    PARST -51-SS

  DEMOCRACY AND THE AMERICAN PARTY
  SYSTEM.=               RANNA -56-DAP

  THE POLITICAL STRUCTURE OF THE
  FEDERAL RESERVE SYSTEM
  (UNITED STATES).=      REAGMD-61-PSF

  THE PORK BARREL SYSTEM
  (PHILIPPINES).=        ROXAGM-63-PBS

  A METHOD FOR EVALUATING THE
  DISTRIBUTION OF POWER IN A
  COMMITTEE SYSTEM (UNITED STATES).=
                          SHAPLS-54-MEC

  ISRAELI SOCIALISM AND THE MULTI -
  PARTY SYSTEM.=         SHERA -61-ISM

  CONTRADICTIONS IN THE NIGERIAN
  POLITICAL SYSTEM.=     SKLARL-65-CNP

  CONSENSUS, CONFLICT, AND THE
  CANADIAN PARTY SYSTEM.=
                          SMILDV-61-CCC

  POLITICAL PARTIES IN THE AMERICAN
  SYSTEM.=               SORAFJ-64-PPA

  FEDERALISM AND THE PARTY SYSTEM
  (UNITED STATES).=      TRUMD -55-FPS

  THE AMERICAN SYSTEM IN CRISIS.=
                          TRUMDB-59-ASC

  THE ENGINEERS AND THE PRICE

TACTICS                    (CONTINUATION)
  INDONESIA.=              VAN-JM-59-CPT

TAFT
  THE SUPREME COURT FROM TAFT TO
  WARREN (UNITED STATES).=
                          MASOAT-58-SCT

  CHIEF JUSTICE TAFT AND THE LOWER
  COURT BUREAUCRACY -- A STUDY IN
  JUDICIAL ADMINISTRATION.=
                          MURPWF-62-CJT

TAHITI
  POLITICAL ADVANCEMENT IN THE SOUTH
  PACIFIC -- A COMPARATIVE STUDY OF
  COLONIAL PRACTICE IN FIJI, TAHITI,
  AND AMERICAN SAMCA.=    WESTFJ-61-PAS

TAIPING
  THE TAIPING REBELLION -- ITS
  ECONOMIC BACKGROUND AND SOCIAL
  THEORY.=                TAYLGE-33-TRI

TAIWAN
  SUCCESSION AND MYTH IN TAIWAN.=
                          MANCM -64-SMT

TAJISKAN
  THE ESTABLISHMENT OF TAJISKAN
  (SOVIET UNION).=        NEWTJA-63-ETS

TALENT
  THE CHINESE CIVIL SERVICE -- CAREER
  OPEN TO TALENT.=        MENZJM-63-CCS

TAMIL
  THE TAMIL FEDERAL PARTY IN CEYLON
  POLITICS.=              WILSAJ-66-TFP

TAMILNAD
  VARIETIES OF POLITICAL BEHAVIOR
  AMONG NADARS OF TAMILNAD (INDIA).=
                          HARCRL-66-VPB

TANGANYIKA
  AUTHORITY, EFFICIENCY, AND ROLE
  STRESS -- PROBLEMS IN THE
  DEVELOPMENT OF EAST AFRICAN
  BUREAUCRACIES (UGANDA, KENYA,
  TANGANYIKA).=           FLEMWG-66-AER

  SOCIAL CONTROL IN AN AFRICAN
  SOCIETY (ARUSHA OF TANGANYIKA).=
                          GULLPH-63-SCA

  TANGANYIKA'S VIEW OF LABOUR'S
  ROLE.=                  KAMAM -64-TSV

  EAST AFRICAN CHIEFS -- A STUDY OF
  POLITICAL DEVELOPMENT IN SOME
  UGANDA AND TANGANYIKA TRIBES.=
                          RICHAI-59-EAC

TANJORE
  CASTE, CLASS AND POWER -- CHANGING
  PATTERNS OF STRATIFICATION IN A
  TANJORE VILLAGE (INDIA).=
                          BETEA -  -CCP

TANZANIA
  SINGLE - PARTY DEMOCRACY
  (TANZANIA).=            LEDUC -65-SPD

  THE GENERAL ELECTION IN TANZANIA.=
                          TORDW -66-GET

TAXONOMIC
  A TAXONOMIC APPROACH TO STATE
  POLITICAL PARTY STRENGTH.=
                          GOLERT-58-TAS

TEACHERS
  EDUCATION AND DEVELOPMENT --

TEACHERS                   (CONTINUATION)
  OPINIONS OF SECONDARY SCHOOL
  TEACHERS (LATIN AMERICA).=
                          GOUVAJ-67-EDC

TECHNICAL
  SOME REQUIREMENTS FOR TECHNICAL
  PROGRESS IN ASIA.=      GADGDR-51-RTP

  THE TECHNICAL ELITE VS. THE PARTY
  (SOVIET UNION).=        HOUGJF-59-TEV

  TECHNICAL COOPERATION IN
  DEVELOPMENT ADMINISTRATION IN
  SOUTH AND SOUTHEAST ASIA.=
                          HSUESS-66-TCC

TECHNICIAN
  THE PLACE OF THE TECHNICIAN -
  INTELLIGENTSIA IN SOCIETY.=
                          BAHRHP-60-PTI

  THE SOCIAL ROLE OF THE TECHNICIAN -
  INTELLIGENTSIA IN SOCIETY.=
                          BAHRHP-61-SRT

TECHNIQUE
  THE REPUTATIONAL TECHNIQUE AS A
  MEASURE OF COMMUNITY POWER -- AN
  EVALUATION BASED ON COMPARATIVE
  AND LONGITUDINAL STUDIES.=
                          D'ANWV-62-RTM

  THE INTELLECTUALS - POLITICS NEXUS
  -- STUDIES USING A BIOGRAPHICAL
  TECHNIQUE (BULGARIA,
  SOVIET UNION).=         HANHAM-64-IPN

  THE TECHNIQUE OF THE 'PALACE
  REVOLUTION' (SOVIET UNION).=
                          KRUZP -64-TPR

TECHNIQUES
  THE TECHNIQUES OF THE COMMUNIST
  PARTY IN FRANCE.=       COWALG-49-TCP

  TECHNIQUES FOR THE STUDY OF
  LEADERSHIP (UNITED STATES).=
                          EHLEEL-49-TSL

  KADAR AND THE RESURRECTION OF THE
  HUNGARIAN COMMUNIST PARTY -- A
  STUDY IN POLITICAL TECHNIQUES.=
                          GINSG -64-KRH

TECHNOCRATS
  THE NEW ECONOMIC SYSTEM AND THE
  ROLE OF TECHNOCRATS IN THE DDR
  (EAST GERMANY).=        BAYHTA-66-NES

  THE ROLE OF TECHNOCRATS IN
  LATIN AMERICAN INTEGRATION.=
                          MITCC -67-RTL

TECHNOLOGICAL
  MILITARY SELF-IMAGE IN A
  TECHNOLOGICAL ENVIRONMENT
  (UNITED STATES).=       FELDMD-64-MSI

  THE CULTURAL FACTORS IN ECONOMIC
  AND TECHNOLOGICAL DEVELOPMENT --
  AN INDIAN ADMINISTRATIVE
  VIEW-POINT.=            SETHSC-65-CFE

TECHNOLOGY
  THE TECHNOLOGY - ELITE APPROACH TO
  THE DEVELOPMENTAL PROCESS --
  PERUVIAN CASE STUDY.=   COHEA -66-TEA

  TECHNOLOGY AND CAREER MANAGEMENT IN
  THE MILITARY ESTABLISHMENT
  (UNITED STATES).=       LANGK -64-TCM

TRANSITION            (CONTINUATION)
TRANSITION PERIOD, 1951-1954 --
DURING THE INTERREGNUM,
1954-1959.=            GINSG -59-TAT

AFRICAN LEADERSHIP IN TRANSITION --
AN OUTLINE.=          HOWMR -56-ALT

THE BALKANS IN TRANSITION -- ESSAYS
ON THE DEVELOPMENT OF BALKAN LIFE
AND POLITICS SINCE THE EIGHTEENTH
CENTURY.=            JELAC -63-BTE

TURKEY'S POLITICS -- THE TRANSITION
TO MULTI - PARTY SYSTEM.=
KARPKH-59-TSP

TRANSITION IN INDIA AND OTHER
ESSAYS.=            SANTK -64-TIO

MEXICAN GOVERNMENT IN TRANSITION.=
SCOTRE-59-MGT

POLITICAL ELITES AND POLITICAL
MODERNIZATION -- THE CRISIS OF
TRANSITION (LATIN AMERICA).=
SCOTRE-67-PEP

ONE - PARTY GOVERNMENT IN MALI --
TRANSITION TOWARD CONTROL.=
SNYDFG-65-OPG

THE PRESIDENCY IN TRANSITION
(UNITED STATES).=    THE JO-  -PTU

BUREAUCRATIC TRANSITION IN MALAYA.=
TILMRO-64-BTM

INDONESIAN SOCIETY IN TRANSITION --
A STUDY OF SOCIAL CHANGE.=
WERTWF-59-IST

MODERN CHINA IN TRANSITION.=
WRIGMC-59-MCT

TRANSITIONAL
BUREAUCRACY AND NATION BUILDING IN
TRANSITIONAL SOCIETIES.=
DUBESC-64-BNB

PUBLIC ADMINISTRATION IN IRAN --
SKETCHES OF A NON-WESTERN
TRANSITIONAL BUREAUCRACY.=
GABLRW-61-PAI

THE ROLE OF THE ARMY IN THE
TRANSITIONAL ARAB STATE
(MIDDLE EAST).=      GLUBJ -65-RAT

THE LATIN AMERICAN MILITARY AS A
POLITICALLY COMPETING GROUP IN
TRANSITIONAL SOCIETY.=
JOHNJJ-62-LAM

SOCIAL CHANGE AND STRUCTURE IN
TRANSITIONAL SOCIETIES
(LATIN AMERICA, MIDDLE EAST).=
MARCS -60-SCS

WRITER AND JOURNALIST IN THE
TRANSITIONAL SOCIETY.=
PASSH -63-WJT

TRANSKEIAN
CHIEFTAINSHIP IN TRANSKEIAN
POLITICAL DEVELOPMENT (AFRICA).=
HAMMD -64-CTP

THE TRIBAL ELITE AND THE TRANSKEIAN
ELECTIONS OF 1963 (SOUTH AFRICA).=
MAYEP -66-TET

TRAVAIL
TRADE UNIONS IN TRAVAIL -- THE

TRAVAIL            (CONTINUATION)
STORY OF THE BROEDERBOND -
NATIONALIST PLAN TO CONTROL SOUTH
AFRICAN TRADE UNIONS.=
HEPPA -54-TUT

TREADMILL
SOVIET IDEOLOGUES ON THE
TREADMILL.=          KEEPJL-58-SIT

TREASURY
TREASURY CONTROL (GREAT BRITAIN).=
BEERSH-57-TCG

TREND
AUSTRIA'S SOCIALISTS IN THE TREND
TOWARD A TWO - PARTY SYSTEM -- AN
INTERPRETATION OF POSTWAR
ELECTIONS.=          GULICA-58-ASS

TRENDS
SOME TRENDS IN SOURCES OF
ALIENATION FROM THE SOVIET
SYSTEM.=            BAUER -55-TSA

THE COLD WAR ON THE LITERARY FRONT
(SOVIET UNION) -- PART 1, THE
WRITER'S UNDERGROUND -- PART 2,
GROUPS, TRENDS, GENRES, -- PART 3,
THE PARTY AND THE WRITERS.=
BURG  -62-CWL

TRENDS IN ITALY -- AN OPENING TO
THE LEFT.=          DE-ME -62-TIC

POST - STALIN TRENDS IN RUSSIAN
LITERATURE.=         ERLIV -64-PST

RECENT TRENDS IN CZECHOSLOVAKIA --
THE WRITERS' CAMPAIGN OF
CRITICISM.=          HANAH -66-RTC

TRENDS IN THE BRITISH LABOR
MOVEMENT SINCE 1850.= HOBSEJ-49-TBL

UNIFYING THE BRITISH CIVIL SERVICE
-- SOME TRENDS AND PROBLEMS.=
HODGJE-48-UBC

INTELLECTUAL TRENDS IN POLAND.=
LABEL -57-ITP

TERROR IN THE SOVIET SYSTEM --
TRENDS AND PORTENTS.= LEONW -58-TSS

ELECTORAL TRENDS AND THE TENDENCY
TO A ONE PARTY SYSTEM IN NIGERIA.=
MACKJP-62-ETT

NATIONALISM AND RIGHT WING IN JAPAN
-- A STUDY OF POST-WAR TRENDS.=
MORRII-60-NRW

CONTEMPORARY TRENDS IN RURAL
LEADERSHIP (UNITED STATES).=
NUQUJE-47-CTR

CURRENT TRENDS IN COMPARATIVE
COMMUNITY STUDIES.=  SWANBE-62-CTC

TRIAL
SIX TRIAL DEFINITIONS --
CONURBATION, ELITE, MIGRATION
PROGRESS, SLUM, UNEMPLOYMENT.=
ANON  -55-STC

TRIAL OF STRENGTH IN INDO-CHINA --
THE BAO DAI EXPERIMENT.=
ASBO  -50-TSI

INDIA -- THE CONGRESS SYSTEM ON
TRIAL.=            KOTHR -67-ICS

UNITED NATIONS (CONTINUATION)
ASSEMBLY (UNITED NATIONS).=
ALKEHR-65-WPG

THE SECRETARIAT OF THE
UNITED NATIONS.= BAILSD-62-SUN

THE ECONOMIC AND SOCIAL COUNCIL --
POLITICS OF MEMBERSHIP
(UNITED NATIONS, EUROPE).=
GREGRW-63-ESC

HOW UNITED NATIONS DECISIONS ARE
MADE.= HADMJG-61-HUN

FRENCH ELITE PERSPECTIVES ON THE
UNITED NATIONS.= LERND -3 -FEP

MAJORITY DECISIONS AND MINORITY
RESPONSES IN THE UN GENERAL
ASSEMBLY (UNITED NATIONS).=
MANNCS-66-MDM

THE EMERGING ANTI - COLONIAL
CONSENSUS IN THE UNITED NATIONS.=
ROWEET-64-EAC

UNITED STATES
THE JUDICIAL PROCESS -- AN
INTRODUCTORY ANALYSIS OF THE
COURTS OF THE UNITED STATES,
ENGLAND AND FRANCE.= ABRAHJ-62-JPI

SOCIAL CHANGE IN LATIN AMERICA
TODAY -- ITS IMPLICATIONS.= FOR
U.S. (UNITED STATES) POLICY.=
ADAMRN- -SCL

INTEREST AND INFLUENCE IN FOREIGN
AFFAIRS (UNITED STATES).=
ADLEKP-56-IIF

THE INSULATION OF LOCAL POLITICS
UNDER THE NON-PARTISAN BALLOT
(UNITED STATES).= ADRICR-59-ILP

THE RULER AND THE RULED
(UNITED STATES).= AGGER -64-RRU

LAWYERS IN POLITICS
(UNITED STATES).= AGGERE-56-LPU

POWER ATTRIBUTIONS IN THE LOCAL
COMMUNITY -- THEORETICAL AND
RESEARCH CONSIDERATIONS
(UNITED STATES).= AGGERE-56-PAL

THE POLITICAL STRUCTURE OF A SMALL
COMMUNITY (UNITED STATES).=
AGGERE-56-PSS

COMMUNITY POWER STRUCTURE AND
PARTISANSHIP (UNITED STATES).=
AGGERE-58-CPS

POLITICAL ASPIRATIONS OF LAW
STUDENTS (UNITED STATES).=
AGGERE-58-PAL

ELECTION AND APPOINTMENT
(UNITED STATES).= AKZIB -60-EAU

OUR CHANGING CONCEPT OF LEADERSHIP
(UNITED STATES).= ALBEMH-53-OCC

THE EXTERNAL BUREAUCRACY IN
UNITED STATES FOREIGN AFFAIRS.=
ALGEFC-63-EBU

THE HOUSE FOREIGN AFFAIRS
COMMITTEE'S ROLE (UNITED STATES).=
ALISM -9 -HFA

PUBLIC OPINION AND NATIONAL

UNITED STATES (CONTINUATION)
SECURITY POLICY (UNITED STATES).=
ALMOGA-56-PON

POLITICAL ACTIVISM IN A RURAL
COUNTY (UNITED STATES).=
ALTHP -66-PAR

DEMOCRACY AND LEADERSHIP
(UNITED STATES).= BABBI -53-DLU

ELITE CONSENSUS AND DEMOCRACY
(UNITED STATES).= BACHP -62-ECD

CONGRESS AT WORK (UNITED STATES).=
BAILSK-52-CWU

THE NEW CONGRESS (UNITED STATES).=
BAILSK-66-NCU

DIRECTORS AND THEIR FUNCTIONS
(UNITED STATES).= BAKEJC-45-DTF

CONGRESSIONAL INITIATIVE IN FOREIGN
POLICY (UNITED STATES).=
BALDDA-66-CIF

THE ROLE OF POLITICAL LEADERSHIP IN
THE PASSAGE OF OREGON'S MIGRATORY
LABOR LEGISLATION
(UNITED STATES).= BALMDG-62-RPL

PHILADELPHIA GENTLEMEN -- THE
MAKING OF A NATIONAL ELITE
(UNITED STATES).= BALTED-58-PGM

POLITICAL INFLUENCE
(UNITED STATES).= BANFEC-61-PIU

CITY POLITICS (UNITED STATES).=
BANFEC-63-CPU

CORPORATE GIANTS AND THE POWER
STRUCTURE (UNITED STATES).=
BARAMS-56-CGP

SOCIOLOGICAL ASPECTS OF ANTI -
INTELLECTUALISM (UNITED STATES).=
BARBB -55-SAA

THE LAWMAKERS -- RECRUITMENT AND
ADAPTION TO LEGISLATIVE LIFE
(UNITED STATES).= BARBJC-65-LRA

LEADERSHIP STRATEGIES FOR
LEGISLATIVE PARTY COHESION
(UNITED STATES).= BARBJC-66-LSL

POWER IN COMMITTEES -- AN
EXPERIMENT IN THE GOVERNMENTAL
PROCESS (UNITED STATES).=
BARBJC-66-PCE

POWER STRUCTURE AND THE NEGRO SUB -
COMMUNITY (UNITED STATES).=
BARTEA-59-PSN

COMMUNITY INFLUENCE SYSTEMS --
STRUCTURE AND CHANGE
(UNITED STATES).= BARTEA-61-CIS

THE MEXICAN STUDENT VIEWS THE
UNITED STATES.= BEALRL-54-MSV

WASHINGTON STATE'S LAWMAKERS --
SOME PERSONNEL FACTORS IN THE
WASHINGTON LEGISLATURE
(UNITED STATES).= BECKP -57-WSS

CORRELATIVES OF LEGISLATIVE VOTING
-- MICHIGAN HOUSE OF
REPRESENTATIVES, 1954-1961

UNITED STATES          (CONTINUATION)
AND LEGAL INSTITUTIONS
(UNITED STATES).=          LADIJ -63-CLL

POLITICAL ELITES AND THE PROCESS OF
ECONOMIC DEVELOPMENT
(UNITED STATES, WESTERN EUROPE,
SOVIET UNION).=          LAMBRK-52-PEP

THE MAKING OF CONSTITUTIONAL LAW
(UNITED STATES).=          LANDJW-64-MCL

BUSINESSMEN AND BUREAUCRATS
(UNITED STATES).=          LANERE-53-BBL

ELITE COMMUNICATION AND THE
GOVERNMENTAL PROCESS
(UNITED STATES, CANADA).=
                         LANERE-58-ECG

TECHNOLOGY AND CAREER MANAGEMENT IN
THE MILITARY ESTABLISHMENT
(UNITED STATES).=          LANGK -64-TCM

THE NEW PRIESTHOOD -- THE
SCIENTIFIC ELITE AND THE USES OF
POWER (UNITED STATES).=
                         LAPPRE-65-NPS

POLITICS -- WHO GETS WHAT, WHEN,
HOW (UNITED STATES).=     LASSHD-36-PWG

THE SUPREME COURT AND THE SUPREME
PEOPLE (UNITED STATES).=
                         LATHE -54-SCS

ACADEMIC MIND -- SOCIAL SCIENTISTS
IN A TIME OF CRISIS
(UNITED STATES).=          LAZAPF-58-AMS

A LEADERSHIP CRISIS
(UNITED STATES).=          LEACRH-65-LCU

THE PRESIDING OFFICER AND RULES
COMMITTEE IN LEGISLATURES OF THE
U.S. (UNITED STATES).=
                         LEE,EC-52-POR

PARTIES AND POLITICS
(UNITED STATES).=          LEISA -58-PPL

SCIENTISTS AND THE POLICY PROCESS
(UNITED STATES).=          LEISA -65-SPP

SOUTHERN CONGRESSMEN AND THE 'NEW
ISOLATIONISM' (UNITED STATES).=
                         LERCCO-60-SCN

AUTHORITARIAN PERSONALITY AND
FOREIGN POLICY (UNITED STATES).=
                         LEVIDJ-57-APF

THE MANAGERS (GREAT BRITAIN,
UNITED STATES, WEST GERMANY).=
                         LEWIR -61-MGB

ELECTORATES, INTEREST GROUPS, AND
LOCAL GOVERNMENT (UNITED STATES).=
                         LIEBCS-61-EIG

STUDENT POLITICS (LATIN AMERICA,
INDIA, POLAND, UNITED STATES,
GERMANY, CHILE, ARGENTINA,
COLUMBIA, FRANCE).=       LIPSSM-67-SPL

THE CITY MANAGER, ADMINISTRATIVE
THEORY AND POLITICAL POWER
(UNITED STATES).=          LOCKC -62-CMA

THE LOCAL COMMUNITY AS AN ECOLOGY
OF GAMES (UNITED STATES).=
                         LONGNE-58-LCE

A STUDY OF THE INFLUENCE OF FORMAL

UNITED STATES          (CONTINUATION)
AND INFORMAL LEADERS IN AN
ELECTION CAMPAIGN
(UNITED STATES).=          LOWEFE-56-SIF

THE FUNCTIONS OF ALIENATION IN
LEADERSHIP (UNITED STATES).=
                         LOWRRP-62-FAL

WHO'S RUNNING THIS TOWN --
COMMUNITY LEADERSHIP AND SOCIAL
CHANGE (UNITED STATES).=
                         LOWRRP-65-WSR

SOCIAL MOBILITY AGAIN -- AND ELITES
(UNITED STATES, WESTERN EUROPE).=
                         LUETH -55-SMA

ATTITUDE CONSENSUS AND CONFLICT IN
AN INTEREST -- AN ASSESSMENT OF
COHESION (UNITED STATES).=
                         LUTTNR-66-ACC

THE NEW CIVIL - MILITARY RELATIONS
(UNITED STATES).=          LYONGM-61-NCM

BUREAUCRATIC MASS MEDIA -- A STUDY
OF ROLE DEFINITIONS
(UNITED STATES).=          LYSTMH-56-BMM

THE CRISIS IN NEGRO LEADERSHIP
(UNITED STATES).=          MABEC -64-CNL

THE RELATION BETWEEN ROLL CALL
VOTES AND CONSTITUENCIES
(UNITED STATES).=          MACRD -52-RBR

THE ROLE OF THE STATE LEGISLATOR IN
MASSACHUSETTS (UNITED STATES).=
                         MACRD -54-RSL

ROLL CALL VOTES AND LEADERSHIP
(UNITED STATES).=          MACRD -56-RCV

DIMENSIONS OF CONGRESSIONAL VOTING
-- A STATISTICAL STUDY OF THE
HOUSE OF REPRESENTATIVES IN THE
EIGHTY-FIRST CONGRESS
(UNITED STATES).=          MACRD -58-DCV

A METHOD FOR IDENTIFYING ISSUES AND
FACTIONS FROM LEGISLATIVE VOTES
(UNITED STATES).=          MACRD -59-MII

SCALE POSITIONS AND 'POWER' IN THE
SENATE (UNITED STATES).=
                         MACRD -59-SPP

LEGISLATORS- SOCIAL STATUS AND
THEIR VOTES (UNITED STATES).=
                         MACRD -61-LSS

HONOR IN BUREAUCRATIC LIFE (FRANCE,
GREAT BRITAIN, UNITED STATES).=
                         MAINLC-64-HBL

THE HOUSE COMMITTEE ON WAYS AND
MEANS -- CONFLICT MANAGEMENT IN A
CONGRESSIONAL COMMITTEE
(UNITED STATES).=          MANLJF-65-HCW

FEDERAL POLITICAL EXECUTIVES
(UNITED STATES).=          MANNDE-64-FPE

THE SELECTION OF FEDERAL POLITICAL
EXECUTIVES (UNITED STATES).=
                         MANNDE-64-SFP

THE ASSISTANT SECRETARIES --
PROBLEMS AND PROCESSES OF
APPOINTMENT (UNITED STATES).=
                         MANNDE-65-ASP

CIVIL - MILITARY RELATIONS IN THE

UNITED STATES          (CCNTINUATICN)
    UNITED STATES.=          MANSHC-60-CMR

PARTY LEGISLATIVE REPRESENTATION AS
A FUNCTION CF ELECTION RESULTS --
RELATICNSHIP BETWEEN VCTES AND
LEGISLATIVE REFRESENTATICN IN
ENGLAND AND THE UNITED STATES.=
                      MARCJG-58-PLR

SCCIAL CETERMINANTS CF THE RCLE CF
A CIVIL SERVICE (UNITED STATES,
GREAT BRITAIN).=          MARKM -56-SDR

VALUES, DEMAND, AND SCCIAL NOBILITY
(INDUSTRIAL ELITES, CHINA,
UNITED STATES).=          MARSRM-63-VDS

INTEREST GRCUPS AND CCNSERVATIVE
PCLITICS (UNITED STATES).=
                      MARTCW-63-IGC

DECISICNS IN SYRACUSE
(UNITED STATES).=          MARTRC-61-DSU

THE BCSSES (UNITED STATES).=
                      MARTRG-64-BUS

CAREER PERSPECTIVES IN A
BUREAUCRATIC SETTING
(UNITED STATES).=          MARVD -54-CPB

NATICNAL CCNVENTICN LEADERSHIP --
1952 AND 1956 (UNITED STATES).=
                      MARVD -61-NCL

PCLITICAL DECISICN-MAKERS (INDIA,
FRANCE, GREAT BRITAIN, GERMANY,
UNITED STATES).=          MARVD -61-PDM

RECRUITMENT CCNTRASTS IN RURAL
CAMPAIGN GRCUPS (UNITED STATES).=
                      MARVD -61-RCR

PARTY, REGICN AND THE DIMENSICN CF
CCNFLICT IN THE HOUSE CF
REPRESENTATIVES, 1949-1954
(UNITED STATES).=          MARWG -67-PRD

SCLDIERS AND SCHCLARS -- MILITARY
EDUCATICN AND NATIONAL PCLICY
(UNITED STATES).=          MASLJW-57-SSM

THE SUPREME CCURT FRCM TAFT TO
WARREN (UNITED STATES).=
                      MASCAT-58-SCT

CCMMITTEE ASSIGNMENTS IN THE HCUSE
CF REPRESENTATIVES
(UNITED STATES).=          MASTNA-61-CAH

UNITED STATES SENATCRS AND THE
CLASS STRUCTURE.=          MATTCR-54-USS

THE FOLKWAYS CF THE UNITED STATES
SENATE -- CCNFCRMITY TC GROUP
NCRMS AND LEGISLATIVE
EFFECTIVENESS.=          MATTCR-59-FUS

U.S. SENATCRS AND THEIR WCRLD
(UNITED STATES).=          MATTCR-60-USS

UNITED STATES SENATCR -- A
CCLLECTIVE PCRTRAIT.=          MATTCR-61-USS

SCCIAL STRATIFICATICN IN TWC
ECUALITARIAN SCCIETIES --
AUSTRALIA AND THE UNITED STATES.=
                      MAYEKB-64-SST

CHALLENGE TC NEGRC LEADERSHIP
(UNITED STATES).=          MAYFJ -61-CNL

UNITED STATES          (CCNTINUATICN)
    PARTY LCYALTY AMCNG CCNGRESSMEN --
    THE DIFFERENCE BETWEEN DEMOCRATS
    AND REPUBLICANS, 1947-1962
    (UNITED STATES).=          MAYHDR-66-PLA

THE PECPLE CF THE STATE DEPARTMENT
AND FCREIGN SERVICE
(UNITED STATES).=          MCCAJL-54-PSD

THE GCVERNCR AND HIS LEGISLATIVE
PARTY (UNITED STATES).=
                      MCCASP-66-GHL

ISSUE CCNFLICT AND CCNSENSUS AMCNG
PARTY LEADERS AND FCLLCWERS
(UNITED STATES).=          MCCLH -60-ICC

SCME PERSCNALITY FACTORS OF STATE
LEGISLATCRS IN SCUTH CARCLINA
(UNITED STATES).=          MCCOJB-50-PFS

INTELLECTUALS AND THE MASS MEDIA
(UNITED STATES).=          MCCOT -66-IMM

PCLITICS -- A STUDY CF CONTROL
BEHAVICR (UNITED STATES).=
                      MCDONA-65-PSC

THE BUSINESS ELITE AND FOREIGN
PCLICY (UNITED STATES).=
                      MCLEDS-60-BEF

PUBLIC ATTITUDES TCWARD THE
REPRESENTATICNAL RCLE CF
LEGISLATCRS AND JUDGES
(UNITED STATES).=          MCMUCD-65-PAT

PUBLIC CPINICN AND CCNGRESSIONAL
ELECTICNS (UNITED STATES).=
                      MCPHWN-62-POC

CFFICIAL PCLICY AND ANTI -
INTELLECTUALISM (UNITED STATES).=
                      MCWIC -55-OPA

PCLITICAL LEADERSHIP
(UNITED STATES).=          MERRCE-49-PLU

PCLITICS, PLANNING, AND THE PUBLIC
INTEREST (UNITED STATES).=
                      MEYEM -55-PPP

ADMINISTRATIVE CRGANIZATICN -- A
CCMPARATIVE STUDY CF THE
CRGANIZATICN CF PUBLIC
ADMINISTRATICN (GREAT BRITAIN,
UNITED STATES).=          MEYEP -57-AOC

THE EXECUTIVE IN THE MCDERN STATE
(CANADA, FRANCE, GREAT BRITAIN,
SCVIET UNICN, UNITED STATES,
YUGCSLAVIA).=          MEYNJ -58-EMS

THE PCLITICAL PARTY ACTIVITY CF
WASHINGTCN LCBBYISTS
(UNITED STATES).=          MILBLW-58-PPA

LCBBYING AS A CCMMUNICATION
PRCCESS (UNITED STATES).=
                      MILBLW-60-LCP

THE WASHINGTCN LCBBYISTS
(UNITED STATES).=          MILBLW-63-WLU

THE PCWER ELITE (UNITED STATES).=
                      MILLCW-56-PEU

THE PCWER ELITE -- MILITARY,
ECCNOMIC, AND PCLITICAL
(UNITED STATES).=          MILLCW-59-PEM

PCWER, PCLITICS, AND PECPLE

UNITED STATES          (CONTINUATION)
PERCEPTION OF CHANGE IN A VILLAGE
CONFRONTED WITH URBANISM
(UNITED STATES).=        PAYNR -63-SLP

NEW PERSPECTIVES ON THE HOUSE OF
REPRESENTATIVES (UNITED STATES).=
                         PEABRL-63-NPH

PARTY LEADERSHIP CHANGE IN THE
UNITED STATES HOUSE OF
REPRESENTATIVES.=        PEABRL-67-PLC

THE RANK - AND - FILE - LEADER
(UNITED STATES).=        PECKSM-63-RFL

ABSENTEE - OWNED CORPORATIONS AND
COMMUNITY POWER STRUCTURE
(UNITED STATES).=        PELLRJ-56-AOC

LEADERSHIP WITHIN A HIERARCHICAL
ORGANIZATION (UNITED STATES).=
                         PELZD -51-LWH

HEROIC LEADERSHIP (EGYPT, FRANCE,
GERMANY, GREAT BRITAIN,
UNITED STATES).=         PLAMJ -61-HLE

JEWISH CULTURE AND THE
INTELLECTUALS (UNITED STATES).=
                         PODHN -55-JCI

JEWISHNESS AND THE YOUNGER
INTELLECTUALS -- A SYMPOSIUM
(UNITED STATES).=        PODHN -61-JYI

THE SOCIOLOGY OF COMMUNITY POWER --
A REASSESSMENT (UNITED STATES).=
                         POLSNW-59-SCP

POWER IN MIDDLETOWN -- FACT AND
VALUE IN COMMUNITY RESEARCH
(UNITED STATES).=        POLSNW-60-PMF

COMMUNITY POWER AND POLITICAL
THEORY (UNITED STATES).=
                         POLSNW-63-CPP

THE STRATEGIES OF INFLUENCE --
CHOOSING A MAJORITY LEADER, 1962
(UNITED STATES).=        POLSNW-63-TSI

MAIN STREET POLITICS --
POLICY-MAKING AT THE LOCAL LEVEL
(UNITED STATES).=        PRESC -62-MSP

THE SOCIAL BASES OF BUREAUCRATIC
ORGANIZATION (UNITED STATES).=
                         PRESRV-59-SBB

MEN AT THE TOP -- A STUDY IN
COMMUNITY POWER (UNITED STATES).=
                         PRESRV-64-MTS

POLITICAL SOCIALIZATION AND
LEADERSHIP SELECTION
(UNITED STATES).=        PREWK -65-PSL

POLITICAL SOCIALIZATION AND
POLITICAL ROLES (UNITED STATES).=
                         PREWK -67-PSP

THE SECRETARY OF STATE
(UNITED STATES).=        PRICCK-60-SSU

THE ESTABLISHED DISSENTERS
(GREAT BRITAIN, UNITED STATES).=
                         PRICCK-65-EDC

THE SCIENTIFIC ESTATE
(UNITED STATES).=        PRICCK-65-SEL

ADMINISTRATIVE LEADERSHIP

UNITED STATES          (CONTINUATION)
(UNITED STATES).=        PRICDT-61-ALU

THE ELECTORAL ARENA (UNITED STATES
CONGRESS).=              PRICHO-65-EAU

POLITICS AND VALUE SYSTEMS -- THE
SUPREME COURT, 1945-1946
(UNITED STATES).=        PRITCH-46-PVS

THE ROOSEVELT COURT -- A STUDY IN
JUDICIAL POLITICS AND VALUES,
1937-1947 (UNITED STATES).=
                         PRITCH-48-RCS

CIVIL LIBERTIES AND THE VINSON
COURT (UNITED STATES).=
                         PRITCH-54-CLV

THE OFFICE OF GOVERNOR IN THE SOUTH
(UNITED STATES).=        RANSCB-51-OGS

POLITICAL LEADERSHIP IN THE
GOVERNOR'S OFFICE
(UNITED STATES).=        RANSCB-64-PLG

CENTRAL INTELLIGENCE AND NATIONAL
SECURITY (UNITED STATES).=
                         RANSHH-58-CIN

POWER STRUCTURE AND MEMBERSHIP
DISPERSION IN UNIONS
(UNITED STATES).=        RAPHEE-65-PSM

THE EFFECTS OF NOMINATING
CONVENTIONS, ELECTIONS, AND
REFERENCE GROUP IDENTIFICATION
UPON THE PERCEPTIONS OF POLITICAL
FIGURES (UNITED STATES).=
                         RAVEBH-64-ENC

POWER AT THE PENTAGON
(UNITED STATES).=        RAYMJ -64-PPL

THE POLITICAL STRUCTURE OF THE
FEDERAL RESERVE SYSTEM
(UNITED STATES).=        REAGMD-61-PSF

THE NEGRO INTELLECTUAL AND NEGRO
NATIONALISM (UNITED STATES).=
                         RECCW -54-NIN

COMMUNITY AND RACIAL FACTORS IN
INTELLECTUAL ROLES
(UNITED STATES).=        RECCW -56-CRF

THE UNITED STATES AND JAPAN.=
                         REISEO-65-USJ

A STUDY OF ROLE CONCEPTIONS IN
BUREAUCRACY (UNITED STATES).=
                         REISL -49-SRC

LIFE CAREERS, POWER AND THE
PROFESSIONS -- THE RETIRED ARMY
GENERAL (UNITED STATES).=
                         REISL -56-LCP

POLITICAL PARTIES AND DECISION
MAKING IN THREE SOUTHERN COUNTIES
(UNITED STATES).=        RHYNEH-58-PPD

REVIEW, DISSENT AND THE APPELLATE
PROCESS -- A POLITICAL
INTERPRETATION (UNITED STATES).=
                         RICHRJ-67-RDA

ORBITS OF TOLERANCE, INTERVIEWERS,
AND ELITES (UNITED STATES).=
                         RIESD -56-OTI

PRIVATE PEOPLE AND PUBLIC POLICY

UNITED STATES        (CONTINUATION)
(UNITED STATES).=      RIESO -59-PPP

VOTING METHODS AND IRRATIONALITY IN
LEGISLATIVE DECISIONS
(UNITED STATES).=      RIKEWH-58-VMI

THE STABILITY CF COALITIONS ON ROLL
CALLS IN THE HOUSE CF
REPRESENTATIVES (UNITED STATES).=
                       RIKEWH-62-SCR

THE PARTY WHIP ORGANIZATIONS IN THE
UNITED STATES HOUSE CF
REPRESENTATIVES.=      RIPLRB-64-PWO

DECISION MAKING IN THE HOUSE RULES
COMMITTEE (UNITED STATES).=
                       ROBIJA-59-CMH

THE ROLE OF THE RULES COMMITTEE IN
ARRANGING THE PROGRAM CF THE U.S.
HOUSE CF REPRESENTATIVES
(UNITED STATES).=      ROBIJA-59-RRC

SURVEY INTERVIEWING AMONG MEMBERS
OF CONGRESS (UNITED STATES).=
                       ROBIJA-60-SIA

PROCESS SATISFACTION AND POLICY
APPROVAL IN STATE DEPARTMENT --
CONGRESSIONAL RELATIONS
(UNITED STATES).=      ROBIJA-61-PSP

CONGRESS AND FOREIGN POLICY-MAKING
-- A STUDY IN LEGISLATIVE
INFLUENCE AND INITIATIVE
(UNITED STATES).=      ROBIJA-62-CFP

THE HOUSE RULES COMMITTEE
(UNITED STATES).=      ROBIJA-63-HRC

THE BUREAUCRAT AND THE ENTHUSIAST
-- AN EXPLORATION OF THE
LEADERSHIP CF SOCIAL MOVEMENTS
(UNITED STATES).=      ROCHJP-55-BEE

POLITICAL SCIENCE AND SCIENCE
FICTION (UNITED STATES,
JUDICIARY).=           ROCHJP-58-PSS

THE POLLSTERS -- PUBLIC OPINION,
POLITICS, AND DEMOCRATIC
LEADERSHIP (UNITED STATES).=
                       ROGEL -49-PPO

ALIENATION AND PARTICIPATION -- A
COMPARISON CF GROUP LEADERS AND
THE MASS (UNITED STATES).=
                       ROSEAM-62-APC

OPINION-MAKING AND OPINION MAKERS
IN FOREIGN POLICY
(UNITED STATES).=      ROSEJN-60-OMC

PUBLIC OPINION AND FOREIGN POLICY
(UNITED STATES).=      ROSEJN-61-POF

NATIONAL LEADERSHIP AND FOREIGN
POLICY -- A CASE STUDY IN THE
MOBILIZATION CF PUBLIC SUPPORT
(UNITED STATES).=      ROSEJN-63-NLF

THE POLITICIAN AND THE CAREER IN
POLITICS (UNITED STATES).=
                       ROSERM-57-PCP

POLITICIAN AND CONSTITUENCY
(UNITED STATES).=      ROSERM-58-PCU

MAN AND ATTENTIVE OPINION ON
NUCLEAR WEAPON TESTS AND FALLOUT,

UNITED STATES        (CONTINUATION)
1954-1963 (UNITED STATES).=
                       ROSIEJ-65-MAC

WAR, DEPRESSION, AND THE
PRESIDENCY, 1933-1950
(UNITED STATES).=      ROSSC -50-WDP

CONSTITUTIONAL DICTATORSHIP IN THE
ATOMIC AGE (UNITED STATES).=
                       ROSSCL-49-CDA

COMMUNITY DECISION-MAKING
(UNITED STATES).=      ROSSPH-57-CDM

COMMUNITY DECISION MAKING
(UNITED STATES).=      ROSSPH-58-CDM

POWER AND COMMUNITY STRUCTURE
(UNITED STATES).=      ROSSPH-60-PCS

THE PROFESSIONALIZATION OF THE NEW
DIPLOMACY (UNITED STATES).=
                       ROSSR -62-PND

ADMINISTRATIVE SECRECY --
CONGRESSIONAL DILEMMA
(UNITED STATES).=      ROURFE-60-ASC

URBANISM AND THE NATIONAL PARTY
ORGANIZATION (UNITED STATES).=
                       ROURFE-65-UNP

LAWYERS IN THE NEW YORK STATE
LEGISLATURE -- THE URBAN FACTOR
(UNITED STATES).=      RUCHLI-66-LNY

INTERNATIONAL COMMUNICATION AND
LEGISLATIVE BEHAVIOR -- THE SENATE
AND THE HOUSE CF COMMONS
(UNITED STATES, GREAT BRITAIN).=
                       RUSSBM-62-ICL

PSYCHOPATHOLOGY, DECISION-MAKING,
AND POLITICAL INVOLVEMENT
(UNITED STATES).=      RUTHBM-66-PDM

ADMINISTRATIVE TRUSTIFICATION
(UNITED STATES).=      SALIE -58-ATU

THE URBAN PARTY ORGANIZATION MEMBER
(UNITED STATES).=      SALIR -65-UPC

ST. LOUIS POLITICS -- RELATIONSHIP
AMONG INTERESTS, PARTIES, AND
GOVERNMENTAL STRUCTURE
(UNITED STATES)).=     SALIRH-60-SLP

URBAN POLITICS -- THE NEW
CONVERGENCE CF POWER
(UNITED STATES).=      SALIRH-64-UPN

PUBLIC MEN IN AND OUT CF OFFICE
(UNITED STATES).=      SALTJT-46-PMO

THE DEMOCRATIC STATE CENTRAL
COMMITTEE IN MICHIGAN 1949-1959 --
THE RISE CF THE NEW POLITICS AND
THE NEW POLITICAL LEADERSHIP
(UNITED STATES).=      SAWYRL-60-DSC

THE RECRUITMENT AND TRAINING CF
BUREAUCRATS IN THE UNITED STATES.=
                       SAYRWS-54-RTB

GOVERNING NEW YORK CITY
(UNITED STATES).=      SAYRWS-60-GNY

LAW AND POLITICS IN THE SUPREME
COURT -- NEW APPROACHES TO
POLITICAL JURISPRUDENCE
(UNITED STATES).=      SCHAM -64-LPS

UNITED STATES (CONTINUATION)
CONGRESSIONAL COMMITTEE MEMBERS AS
INDEPENDENT AGENCY OVERSEERS -- A
CASE STUDY (UNITED STATES).=
SCHES -60-CCM

REGULATORY AGENCY CONTROL THROUGH
APPOINTMENT -- THE CASE OF THE
EISENHOWER ADMINISTRATION AND THE
NLRB (UNITED STATES).=
SCHES -61-RAC

CONDITIONS FOR LEGISLATIVE CONTROL
(UNITED STATES).= SCHES -63-CLC

SCIENTISTS, FOREIGN POLICY AND
POLITICS (UNITED STATES).=
SCHIWR-62-SFP

HOW THEY BECAME GOVERNOR
(UNITED STATES).= SCHLJA-57-HTB

THE POLITICS OF THE EXECUTIVE
(UNITED STATES).= SCHLJA-65-PEU

AMBITION AND POLITICS -- POLITICAL
CAREERS IN THE UNITED STATES.=
SCHLJA-66-APP

POLITICAL CAREERS AND PARTY
LEADERSHIP (AUSTRALIA, CANADA,
FRANCE, GREAT BRITAIN,
UNITED STATES).= SCHLJA-67-PCP

SCALING SUPREME COURT DECISIONS IN
RELATION TO SOCIAL BACKGROUND
(UNITED STATES).= SCHMJ -58-SSC

STARE DECISIS, DISSENT AND THE
BACKGROUND OF THE JUSTICES OF THE
SUPREME COURT OF THE
UNITED STATES.= SCHMJ -62-SDD

THE SUPREME COURT AS FINAL ARBITER
IN FEDERAL - STATE RELATIONS
(UNITED STATES).= SCHMJR-58-SCF

THE JUSTICES OF THE SUPREME COURT
-- A COLLECTIVE PORTRAIT
(UNITED STATES).= SCHMJR-59-JSC

THE SUPREME COURT -- ITS POLITICS,
PERSONALITIES, AND PROCEDURES
(UNITED STATES).= SCHMJR-60-SCI

BUREAUCRATIC PARTY ORGANIZATION
THROUGH PROFESSIONAL POLITICAL
STAFFING (UNITED STATES).=
SCHUCE-64-BPC

A PSYCHOMETRIC MODEL OF THE SUPREME
COURT (UNITED STATES).=
SCHUG -61-PMS

A SOLUTION TO INTERMEDIATE
FACTORIAL RESOLUTION OFHURSTONE
AND DEGAN'S STUDY OF THE SUPREME
COURT (UNITED STATES).=
SCHUG -62-SIF

THE 1960-1961 TERM OF THE SUPREME
COURT -- A PSYCHOLOGICAL ANALYSIS
(UNITED STATES).= SCHUG -62-TSC

JUDICIAL DECISION MAKING
(UNITED STATES, NORWAY).=
SCHUG -63-JDM

IDEOLOGIES AND ATTITUDES, ACADEMIC
AND JUDICIAL (UNITED STATES).=
SCHUG -67-IAA

JUDGES AND POLITICAL LEADERSHIP

UNITED STATES (CONTINUATION)
(AUSTRALIA, JAPAN, PHILIPPINES,
UNITED STATES).= SCHUG -67-JPL

'THE PUBLIC INTEREST' IN
ADMINISTRATIVE DECISION-MAKING
(UNITED STATES).= SCHUGA-57-PIA

THE STUDY OF JUDICIAL
DECISION-MAKING AS AN ASPECT OF
POLITICAL BEHAVIOR
(UNITED STATES).= SCHUGA-58-SJD

THE JUDICIAL MIND -- ATTITUDES AND
IDEOLOGIES OF SUPREME COURT
JUSTICES 1946-1963
(UNITED STATES).= SCHUGA-65-JMA

THE DETERMINATION OF LOCAL POWER
ELITES (UNITED STATES).=
SCHURO-57-DLP

THE ROLE OF ECONOMIC DOMINANTS IN
COMMUNITY POWER STRUCTURE
(UNITED STATES).= SCHURO-58-RED

POLITICAL MONEY -- A STUDY OF
CONTRIBUTORS TO THE NATIONAL
COMMITTEE FOR AN EFFECTIVE
CONGRESS (UNITED STATES).=
SCOBHM-63-PMS

DEVELOPMENTS IN THE PRESIDENCY AND
THE CONCEPTION OF POLITICAL
LEADERSHIP (UNITED STATES).=
SELILG-55-DPC

PRESIDENTIAL LEADERSHIP -- THE
INNER CIRCLE AND
INSTITUTIONALIZATION
(UNITED STATES).= SELILG-56-PLI

RECRUITMENT IN POLITICS
(UNITED STATES).= SELILG-58-RPU

A PREFATORY STUDY OF LEADERSHIP
SELECTION IN OREGON
(UNITED STATES).= SELILG-59-PSL

POLITICAL RECRUITMENT AND PARTY
STRUCTURE -- A CASE STUDY
(UNITED STATES).= SELILG-61-PRP

POLITICAL CHANGE -- LEGISLATIVE
ELITES AND PARTIES IN OREGON
(UNITED STATES).= SELILG-64-PCL

THE EFFECTS OF LEADERSHIP
(UNITED STATES).= SELVHC-60-ELU

TVA AND THE GRASS ROOTS -- A STUDY
IN THE SOCIOLOGY OF FORMAL
ORGANIZATIONS (UNITED STATES).=
SELZP -49-TGR

DILEMMAS OF LEADERSHIP AND DOCTRINE
IN DEMOCRATIC PLANNING
(UNITED STATES).= SELZP -65-DLD

A METHOD FOR EVALUATING THE
DISTRIBUTION OF POWER IN A
COMMITTEE SYSTEM (UNITED STATES).=
SHAPLS-54-MEC

AN APPROPRIATIONS SUBCOMMITTEE AND
ITS CLIENT AGENCIES -- A
COMPARATIVE STUDY OF SUPERVISION
AND CONTROL (UNITED STATES).=
SHARI -65-ASI

LEADERSHIP AND REPRESENTATION IN
LOCAL GOVERNMENT (UNITED STATES).=

UNIVERSITY            (CONTINUATION)
THE STUDENT POPULATION OF A
SOUTHEAST ASIAN UNIVERSITY -- AN
INDONESIAN EXAMPLE.=    FISCJ -61-SPS

THE RECTIFICATION CAMPAIGN AT
PEKING UNIVERSITY (CHINA).=
                        GOLDR -62-RCP

THE AFRICAN UNIVERSITY AND HUMAN
RESOURCES DEVELOPMENT.=
                        HARKF -65-AUH

THE ROLE OF THE INTELLECTUAL IN
FOMENTING CHANGE -- THE UNIVERSITY
(LATIN AMERICA).=       HARRJP-64-RIF

THE NEW ELITES OF TROPICAL AFRICA
-- STUDIES PRESENTED AND DISCUSSED
AT THE SIXTH INTERNATIONAL AFRICAN
SEMINAR AT THE UNIVERSITY OF
IBADAN.=                LLOYPC-66-NET

AMERICAN UNIVERSITY STUDENTS -- A
PRESUMPTIVE ELITE.=     MARVD -65-AUS

SOME REACTIONS OF JAPANESE
UNIVERSITY STUDENTS TO PERSUASIVE
COMMUNICATION.=         MCGIE -65-RJU

TOWN AND GOWN -- THE POWER
STRUCTURE OF A UNIVERSITY TOWN
(UNITED STATES).=       MILLDC-63-TGP

MOSCOW STATE UNIVERSITY
(SOVIET UNION).=        ROBED -64-MSU

UNIVERSITY STUDENTS AND POLITICS IN
BURMA.=                 SILVJ -64-USP

THE UNIVERSITY STUDENT.=
                        SILVKH-64-US

INTELLECTUAL IDENTITY AND POLITICAL
IDEOLOGY AMONG UNIVERSITY STUDENTS
(LATIN AMERICA).=       SCARGA-67-IIP

DOMINANT POWER COMPONENTS IN THE
BRAZILIAN UNIVERSITY STUDENT
MOVEMENT PRIOR TO APRIL 1964.=
                        THERLD-65-DPC

THE UNIVERSITY CONSTITUENCIES IN
THE RECENT BRITISH ELECTION.=
                        VEX,MB-46-UCR

UNIVERSITY STUDENTS IN A WORLD OF
CHANGE -- A COLUMBIAN SAMPLE.=
                        WILLRC-64-USW

THE BURMESE UNIVERSITY STUDENT --
AN APPROACH TO PERSONALITY AND
SUBCULTURE.=            WOHLJ -66-BUS

UNORTHODOX
THE UNORTHODOX LEFT AND THE CEYLON
ELECTIONS.=             GRINM -56-ULC

UNREST
INTELLECTUAL UNREST BEHIND THE IRON
CURTAIN (POLAND, HUNGARY).=
                        KECSP -57-IUB

UNSTABLE
AN UNSTABLE LEADERSHIP
(SOVIET UNION).=        BAILS -65-ULS

UNTROUBLED
THE UNTROUBLED WORLD OF
JURIMETRICS.=           MENCW -64-UWJ

UPHEAVAL
ARGENTINE UPHEAVAL -- PERON'S FALL

UPHEAVAL            (CONTINUATION)
AND THE NEW REGIME.=    WHITAP-56-AUP

UPPER
THE UPPER HOUSE ELECTIONS (JAPAN).=
                        ANON  -62-UHE

UPRISING
THE UNEXPECTED REVOLUTION -- SOCIAL
FORCES IN THE HUNGARIAN UPRISING.=
                        KECSP -61-URS

URBAN
URBAN SOCIAL STRUCTURE
(UNITED STATES).=       BESHJM-62-USS

URBAN SOCIAL STRUCTURE AS A SINGLE
HIERARCHY.=             BESHJM-63-USS

SOME PSYCHOLOGICAL CONCEPTS OF
URBAN AFRICANS.=        BLOOL -64-PCU

URBAN STRATIFICATION IN HAITI.=
                        COMHS -59-USH

DIFFERENTIAL ASSOCIATION AND THE
STRATIFICATION OF THE URBAN
COMMUNITY (UNITED STATES).=
                        CURTRF-63-DAS

POLITICS IN AN URBAN AFRICAN
COMMUNITY.=             EPSTAL-58-PUA

CHINA'S GENTRY -- ESSAYS IN RURAL -
URBAN RELATIONS.=       FEI-  -53-CSG

FROM BOSSES TO COSMOPOLITANISM --
CHANGES IN THE RELATIONSHIP OF
URBAN LEADERSHIP TO STATE POLITICS
(UNITED STATES).=       HAVAWC-64-BCC

COMMUNITY POWER AND URBAN RENEWAL
SUCCESS (UNITED STATES).=
                        HAWLAH-63-CPU

URBAN LEADERSHIP DURING CHANGE
(UNITED STATES).=       KAMMGM-64-ULC

URBAN RENEWAL POLITICS -- SLUM
CLEARANCE IN NEWARK
(UNITED STATES).=       KAPLH -63-URP

POLITICAL ASPECTS OF MOBILITY IN
CHINA'S URBAN DEVELOPMENT.=
                        LEWIJW-66-PAM

THE NEW URBAN GROUPS -- THE MIDDLE
CLASSES (LATIN AMERICA).=
                        RATIL -67-NUG

LAWYERS IN THE NEW YORK STATE
LEGISLATURE -- THE URBAN FACTOR
(UNITED STATES).=       RUCHLI-66-LNY

THE URBAN PARTY ORGANIZATION MEMBER
(UNITED STATES).=       SALIR -65-UPO

URBAN POLITICS -- THE NEW
CONVERGENCE OF POWER
(UNITED STATES).=       SALIRH-64-UPN

LEADERSHIP AND PARTICIPATION IN
URBAN POLITICAL AFFAIRS
(UNITED STATES).=       SMUCRH-56-LPU

THE NOTION OF THE ELITE AND THE
URBAN SOCIAL SURVEY IN AFRICA.=
                        TARDC -56-NEU

INTEGRATION AT THE URBAN LEVEL --
POLITICAL INFLUENCE AND THE
DECISION PROCESS.=      WHEAWL-64-IUL

URBANISATION
THE ROLE OF VOLUNTARY ASSOCIATIONS
IN WEST AFRICAN URBANISATION.=
                    LITTKL-57-RVA

URBANISM
A STUDY IN LEADERSHIP AND
PERCEPTION OF CHANGE IN A VILLAGE
CONFRONTED WITH URBANISM
(UNITED STATES).=      PAYNR -63-SLP

URBANISM AND THE NATIONAL PARTY
ORGANIZATION (UNITED STATES).=
                    ROURFE-65-UNP

URBANIZATION
URBANIZATION AND COMPETITIVE PARTY
POLITICS (UNITED STATES).=
                    CUTRP -63-UCP

WEST AFRICAN URBANIZATION -- A
STUDY OF VOLUNTARY ASSOCIATIONS IN
SOCIAL CHANGE.=      LITTKL-65-WAU

URUGUAY
URUGUAY -- PORTRAIT OF A
DEMOCRACY.=          FITZR -54-UPD

NATIONAL PERSONNEL ADMINISTRATION
IN URUGUAY.=         KITCJD-60-NPA

GOVERNMENT AND POLITICS OF
URUGUAY.=            TAYLPB-62-GPU

INTERESTS AND INSTITUTIONAL
DYSFUNCTION IN URUGUAY.=
                    TAYLPB-63-IID

USA
UNDER PRESSURE -- THE WRITER IN
SOCIETY -- EASTERN EUROPE AND THE
USA.=                ALVAA -66-UPW

POLITICAL POWER -- USA/USSR
(UNITED STATES, SOVIET UNION).=
                    ERZEZ -64-PPU

TOP LEADERSHIP USA
(UNITED STATES).=    HUNTF -59-TLU

INTELLECTUALS AND POLITICS IN USA
(UNITED STATES).=    NICHAG-54-IPU

PLAINVILLE, USA.=    WESTJ -45-PU

USAGE
THE POLITICAL USAGE OF 'ISLAM' AND
'ARAB CULTURE' (MOROCCO).=
                    ASHFDE-61-PUI

USAGES
CHANGING KINSHIP USAGES IN THE
SETTING OF POLITICAL AND ECONOMIC
CHANGE AMONG THE NAYARS OF
MALABAR.=            GOUGEK-52-CKU

USE
THE USE OF THE ARAB FELLAH.=
                    BASHTM-58-UAF

THE USE OF ELECTRONIC COMPUTERS IN
THE STUDY OF SOCIAL
ORGANIZATIONS.=      COLEJS-65-UEC

MASS MEDIA USE BY SUB - ELITES IN
ELEVEN  LATIN AMERICAN COUNTRIES.=
                    DEUTPJ-61-MMU

THE MATHEMATICAL ANALYSIS OF
SUPREME COURT DECISIONS -- THE USE
AND ABUSE OF QUANTITATIVE METHODS
(UNITED STATES).=    FISHFM-58-MAS

USE                 (CONTINUATION)
COMMUNIST USE OF THE CZECHOSLOVAK
PARLIAMENT SINCE WORLD WAR II.=
                    KUBAO -61-CUC

THE ROLE OF THE SCIENTIFIC ELITE IN
THE DECISION TO USE THE ATOMIC
BOMB (UNITED STATES).=
                    MOORJW-58-RSE

THE DECISION TO USE THE ATOMIC BOMB
(UNITED STATES).=    MORTL -57-DUA

USE OF A MULTIPLE REGRESSION MODEL
WITH GROUP DECISION-MAKING.=
                    STONLA-63-UMR

USEFUL
THE SERVICE SECRETARY -- HAS HE A
USEFUL ROLE.=        ZUCKEM-66-SSH

USES
THE SYMBOLIC USES OF POLITICS.=
                    EDELM -64-SUP

THE NEW PRIESTHOOD -- THE
SCIENTIFIC ELITE AND THE USES OF
POWER (UNITED STATES).=
                    LAPPRE-65-NPS

THE USES OF POWER -- 7 CASES IN
AMERICAN POLITICS.=  WESTAF-62-UPC

USING
THE INTELLECTUALS - POLITICS NEXUS
-- STUDIES USING A BIOGRAPHICAL
TECHNIQUE (BULGARIA,
SOVIET UNION).=      HANHAM-64-IPN

USSR
THE RETURN TO ONE-MAN DICTATORSHIP
IN THE USSR.=        ACHMH -65-ROM

SOCIAL CLASSES AND CLASS
CONSCIOUSNESS IN THE USSR.=
                    BEALCP-58-SCC

THE MOSLEM INTELLIGENTSIA IN THE
USSR.=               BENNA -59-MIU

FACTORY AND MANAGER IN THE USSR.=
                    BERLJS-57-FMU

POLITICAL POWER -- USA/USSR
(UNITED STATES, SOVIET UNION).=
                    ERZEZ -64-PPU

THE COMPOSITION OF THE USSR SUPREME
SOVIET  1958-1966.   CLARRA-67-CUS

POWER AND POLICY IN THE USSR.=
                    CONQR -61-PPU

MILITARY REPRESENTATION ON THE 1958
SUPREME SOVIET OF THE USSR.=
                    GALAN -58-MRS

THE SUPREME SOVIET OF THE USSR AND
ITS MEMBERS.=        GUBIK -61-SSU

SOLDIERS AND GOVERNMENT -- NINE
STUDIES IN CIVIL - MILITARY
RELATIONS (WESTERN EUROPE, USSR,
JAPAN, LATIN AMERICA,
UNITED STATES).=     HOWAM -59-SGN

USSR, INCORPORATED (SOVIET UNION).=
                    MEYEAG-61-UIS

TERROR AND PROGRESS, USSR -- SOME
SOURCES OF CHANGE AND STABILITY IN
THE SOVIET DICTATORSHIP.=

VENEZUELA          (CONTINUATION)
  DEMOCRATICA DE VENEZUELA.=
                        KANTH -59-DAD

  ACCION DEMOCRATICA -- REVOLUTION OF
  A MODERN POLITICAL PARTY IN
  VENEZUELA.=          MARTJD-66-ADR

  THE CHRISTIAN DEMOCRATS OF
  VENEZUELA.=          TUGWF -65-CDV

VENEZUELAN
  THE VENEZUELAN DEMOCRATIC
  REVOLUTION.=         ALEXRJ-64-VDR

  THE GROWTH AND DEMOCRATIZATION OF
  THE VENEZUELAN LABOR MOVEMENT.=
                        MARTJD-63-GDV

  STUDENT POLITICS IN LATIN AMERICA
  -- THE VENEZUELAN EXAMPLE.=
                        WASHSW-59-SPL

VERBAL
  VERBAL SHIFTS IN THE AMERICAN
  PRESIDENCY -- A CONTENT ANALYSIS.=
                        PROTJW-56-VSA

VERIFICATION
  VERIFICATION DES POUVOIRS IN THE
  FRENCH NATIONAL ASSEMBLY.=
                        CAMPP -53-VDP

VERSION
  THE DICTATOR -- 1, THE PRE-MODERN
  TYRANT -- 2, A MODERN VERSION.=
                        CRAMFH-51-DPM

VERTICAL
  THE VERTICAL MOSAIC -- AN ANALYSIS
  OF SOCIAL CLASS AND POWER IN
  CANADA.=             PORTJ -65-VMA

VETERAN
  THE VETERAN IN THE ELECTORAL
  PROCESS -- THE HOUSE OF
  REPRESENTATIVES (UNITED STATES).=
                        SOMIA -57-VEP

VICE
  SECOND CONSUL -- THE VICE
  PRESIDENCY -- OUR GREATEST
  POLITICAL PROBLEM
  (UNITED-STATES).=    WAUGEW-56-SCV

  THE RISE OF THE VICE PRESIDENCY
  (UNITED STATES).=    WILLIG-56-RVP

  THE VICE PRESIDENCY
  (UNITED STATES).=    WILML -53-VPU

VICE-PRESIDENCY
  THE VICE-PRESIDENCY
  (UNITED STATES).=    CURHGH-48-VPU

  OBSERVATIONS ON THE PHILIPPINE
  VICE-PRESIDENCY.=    JACOHB-59-OPV

VICHY
  PARADES AND POLITICS AT VICHY --
  THE FRENCH OFFICERS CORPS UNDER
  MARSHAL PETAIN.=     PAXTRO-66-PPV

VICOS
  THE INTERRELATIONSHIP OF POWER,
  RESPECT, AFFECTION AND RECTITUDE
  IN VICOS (PERU).=    DOUGPL-65-IPR

VICTORIAN
  POLITICAL LEADERSHIP AND THE LATE
  VICTORIAN PUBLIC SCHOOL.=
                        WILKR -62-PLL

VIET MINH
  LOCAL ADMINISTRATION UNDER THE

VIET MINH          (CONTINUATION)
  VIET MINH.=          FALLBB-54-LAU

VIET NAM
  NORTH VIET NAM'S CONSTITUTION AND
  GOVERNMENT.=         FALLBB-60-NVN

  POWER AND PRESSURE GROUPS IN NORTH
  VIET NAM.=           FALLBB-62-PPG

  THE NEW CLASS IN NORTH VIET NAM.=
                        HOAN -58-NCN

  NORTH VIET NAM'S WORKERS' PARTY AND
  SOUTH VIET NAM'S PEOPLE'S
  REVOLUTIONARY PARTY.= HONEPJ-63-NVN

  NORTH VIET NAM'S WORKERS' PARTY AND
  SOUTH VIET NAM'S PEOPLE'S
  REVOLUTIONARY PARTY.= HONEPJ-63-NVN

  RURAL RESETTLEMENT IN SOUTH
  VIET NAM -- THE AGROVILLE
  PROGRAM.=            ZASLJJ-62-RRS

VIETCONG
  THE BUDDHISTS, THE WAR, AND THE
  VIETCONG.=           ROBEA -66-BWV

VIETMINH
  COMMUNIST REVOLUTIONARY WARFARE --
  THE VIETMINH IN INDOCHINA.=
                        TANHGK-62-CRW

VIETNAM
  THE NATIONALIST DILEMMA IN
  VIETNAM.=            CLEMJR-50-NDV

  THE PRESIDENT IN THE CONSTITUTION
  OF THE  REPUBLIC OF VIETNAM.=
                        CORLFJ-61-PCR

  TOWARD A PHILOSOPHY OF PUBLIC
  ADMINISTRATION IN VIETNAM.=
                        DANGNG-63-TPP

  THE BUREAUCRACY AND POLITICAL
  DEVELOPMENT IN VIETNAM.=
                        CORSJT-63-BPD

  THE POLITICAL - RELIGIOUS SECTS OF
  VIETNAM.=            FALLBB-55-PRS

  THE BAO DAI EXPERIMENT (VIETNAM).=
                        HAMMEJ-50-BDE

  MANDARIN BUREAUCRACY AND POLITICS
  IN SOUTH VIETNAM.=   JUMPR -57-MBP

  PROBLEMS OF PUBLIC ADMINISTRATION
  IN SOUTH VIETNAM.=   JUMPR -57-PPA

  SECTS AND COMMUNISM IN SOUTH
  VIETNAM.=            JUMPR -59-SCS

  AMERICAN INTELLECTUALS AND U.S.
  VIETNAM POLICY.=     LOWRCW-65-AIU

  REVOLT OF THE INTELLECTUALS IN
  NORTH VIETNAM.=      PJH -57-RIN

  BUDDHISM AND POLITICS IN SOUTH
  VIETNAM.=            ROBEA -65-BPS

  RESTRUCTURING GOVERNMENT IN SOUTH
  VIETNAM.=            SACKIM-67-RGS

  MASS SUPPORT AND COMMUNIST
  INSURRECTION (GREECE, MALAYA,
  INDOCHINA, PHILIPPINES, SOUTH
  VIETNAM).=           SANDR -65-MSC

  POLITICAL PARTIES IN SOUTH VIETNAM

VIETNAM                    (CONTINUATION)
    UNDER THE REPUBLIC.=    SCIGRC-60-PPS

    THE SAIGON POLITICAL ELITE -- FOCUS
    ON FOUR CABINETS (SOUTH VIETNAM).=
                           WURFD -67-SPE

VIETNAMESE
    THE VIETNAMESE MANDARIN.=
                           BUTTJ -58-VM

    PERCEPTIONS OF THE VIETNAMESE
    PUBLIC ADMINISTRATION SYSTEM.=
                           FOX,GH-64-PVP

    CASES IN VIETNAMESE
    ADMINISTRATION.=       MONTJD-59-CVA

    THE ROLE OF THE VILLAGE IN
    VIETNAMESE POLITICS.=  MUS,P -49-RVV

VIETNAMS
    THE TWO VIETNAMS.=     FALLBB-63-TV

VIEW-POINT
    THE CULTURAL FACTORS IN ECONOMIC
    AND TECHNOLOGICAL DEVELOPMENT --
    AN INDIAN ADMINISTRATIVE
    VIEW-POINT.=           SETHSC-65-CFE

VIEWERS
    PUBLIC AFFAIRS OPINION LEADERSHIP
    AMONG EDUCATIONAL TELEVISION
    VIEWERS (UNITED STATES).=
                           CARTRE-62-PAC

VIEWPOINT
    SCHOOL DESEGREGATION AND NEW
    INDUSTRY -- THE SOUTHERN COMMUNITY
    LEADER'S VIEWPOINT
    (UNITED STATES).=      CRAMMR-63-SDN

    THE MIDDLE CLASS FROM A
    SOCIOLOGICAL VIEWPOINT
    (UNITED STATES).=      FARIRE-60-MCS

VIEWS
    THE MEXICAN STUDENT VIEWS THE
    UNITED STATES.=        BEALRL-54-MSV

    THE FOREIGN POLICY VIEWS OF THE
    INDIAN RIGHT.=         ERDMHL-66-FPV

    GERMAN OFFICIALS REVISITED --
    POLITICAL VIEWS AND ATTITUDES OF
    THE WESTERN GERMAN CIVIL SERVICE.=
                           HERZJH-54-GOR

    JAPANESE VIEWS ON NATIONAL
    SECURITY.=             KAWAK -50-JVN

    POLICY-MAKING IN THE U.S.S.R.
    1953-1961 -- TWO VIEWS
    (SOVIET UNION).=       RIGBTH-62-PMU

    GERMAN REARMAMENT AND ATOMIC WAR --
    THE VIEWS OF GERMAN MILITARY AND
    POLITICAL LEADERS.=    SPEIH -57-GRA

VILFRED
    VILFRED PARETO -- SOCIOLOGICAL
    WRITINGS.=             FINESE-66-VPS

VILLAGE
    CASTE, CLASS AND POWER -- CHANGING
    PATTERNS OF STRATIFICATION IN A
    TANJORE VILLAGE (INDIA).=
                           BETEA -  -CCP

    FACTIONS, PARTIES AND POLITICS IN A
    MALTESE VILLAGE.=      BOISJ -64-FPP

    TYPES OF AUTHORITY IN A BENGUET

VILLAGE                    (CONTINUATION)
    VILLAGE (LUZON, PHILIPPINES).=
                           ENCAV -57-TAB

    THE VILLAGE HEADMAN IN BRITISH
    CENTRAL AFRICA.=       GLUCM -49-VHB

    THE YAO VILLAGE -- A STUDY IN THE
    SOCIAL STRUCTURE OF A NYASALAND
    TRIBE.=                MITCJC-56-YVS

    THE ROLE OF THE VILLAGE IN
    VIETNAMESE POLITICS.=  MUS,P -49-RVV

    VILLAGE FACTIONS AND POLITICAL
    PARTIES IN RURAL WEST BENGAL
    (INDIA).=              NICHRW-63-VFP

    POLITICS AND SOCIAL STRUCTURE IN A
    NORWEGIAN VILLAGE.=    PARKGK-61-PSS

    A STUDY IN LEADERSHIP AND
    PERCEPTION OF CHANGE IN A VILLAGE
    CONFRONTED WITH URBANISM
    (UNITED STATES).=      PAYNR -63-SLP

    THE POTENTIAL ROLE OF TURKISH
    VILLAGE OPINION LEADERS IN A
    PROGRAM OF FAMILY PLANNING.=
                           SYTCJM-65-PRT

    AUTHORITY AND COMMUNITY IN VILLAGE
    INDIA.=                TINKH -59-ACV

    THE SOCIOLOGY OF AN ENGLISH
    VILLAGE.=              WILLWM-56-SEV

VILLAGES
    HEADMAN AND THE RITUAL OF LAUPULA
    VILLAGES (AFRICA).=    CUNNI -56-HRL

    INDIA'S CHANGING VILLAGES -- HUMAN
    FACTORS IN COMMUNITY DEVELOPMENT.=
                           DUBESC-58-ISC

    COMMUNICATION AND POLITICAL
    AWARENESS IN THE VILLAGES OF
    EGYPT.=                HIRAGK-58-CPA

    ELECTION POLITICS IN PAKISTAN
    VILLAGES.=             RASHM -66-EPP

VINSON
    CIVIL LIBERTIES AND THE VINSON
    COURT (UNITED STATES).=
                           PRITCH-54-CLV

VIOLENCE
    PATTERNS OF VIOLENCE IN WORLD
    POLITICS.=             HUNTSP-62-PVW

    VIOLENCE AS A POWER FACTOR IN
    LATIN AMERICAN POLITICS.=
                           STOKW -52-VPF

VISIBILITY
    LEGITIMACY AND VISIBILITY --
    LEADERSHIP STRUCTURES RELATED TO
    FOUR COMMUNITY SYSTEMS
    (UNITED STATES).=      BONJCM-65-LVL

VITAL
    SOCIAL MOBILITY AND ECONOMIC
    DEVELOPMENT -- THE VITAL
    PARAMETERS OF THE BOLIVIAN
    REVOLUTION.=           BERGCF-64-SME

VITALITY
    STABILITY AND VITALITY IN SWEDISH
    DEMOCRACY.=            TINGH -55-SVS

VOCATIONAL
    VOCATIONAL REPRESENTATION AND THE

405

VOTING                    (CONTINUATION)
  LEGISLATIVE DECISIONS
  (UNITED STATES).=       RIKEWH-58-VMI

  A METHOD FOR DETERMINING THE
  SIGNIFICANCE OF ROLL CALLS IN
  VOTING BODIES.=         RIKEWH-59-MDS

  THE STATE DELEGATIONS AND THE
  STRUCTURE OF PARTY VOTING IN THE
  UNITED STATES HOUSE OF
  REPRESENTATIVES.=       TRUMDB-56-SDS

  THE INFLUENCE OF PRECINCT WORK ON
  VOTING BEHAVIOR (UNITED STATES).=
                          WOLFRE-63-IPW

VULNERABILITY
  INSTITUTIONAL VULNERABILITY IN MASS
  SOCIETY.=               SELZP -51-IVM

WALES
  THE LEGISLATIVE ASSEMBLY OF NEW
  SOUTH WALES, 1856-1900
  (AUSTRALIA).=           MARTAW-56-LAN

WALL STREET
  INTERVIEWING A LEGAL ELITE -- THE
  WALL STREET LAWYER.=    SMIGEO-58-ILE

WANING
  THE WANING OPPOSITION IN
  PARLIAMENTARY REGIMES (EUROPE).=
                          KIRCO -57-WOP

WAR
  THE COLD WAR ON THE LITERARY FRONT
  (SOVIET UNION) -- PART 1, THE
  WRITER-S UNDERGROUND -- PART 2,
  GROUPS, TRENDS, GENRES, -- PART 3,
  THE PARTY AND THE WRITERS.=
  BURG  -62-CWL

  WAR PROPAGANDA, WELFARE VALUE, AND
  POLITICAL IDEOLOGIES
  (SOVIET UNION, UNITED STATES,
  GERMANY, ITALY, GREAT BRITAIN).=
  ECKHW -65-WPW

  ORGANIZATION AND MILITARY POWER --
  THE JAPANESE HIGH COMMAND IN WORLD
  WAR II.=                FALKSL-61-CMP

  SOVIET OPPOSITION TO STALIN -- A
  CASE STUDY IN WORLD WAR 11.=
                          FISCG -52-SOS

  MILITARY ELITES AND THE STUDY OF
  WAR (FRANCE, GERMANY, ITALY,
  SOVIET UNION, UNITED STATES).=
                          JANOM -57-MES

  THE JAPAN COMMUNIST PARTY -- ITS
  DEVELOPMENT SINCE THE WAR.=
  KIYOE -58-JCP

  COMMUNIST USE OF THE CZECHOSLOVAK
  PARLIAMENT SINCE WORLD WAR II.=
  KUBAD -61-CUC

  THE CAUSES OF WORLD WAR THREE.=
  MILLCW-58-CWW

  THE OMNIPOTENT STATE -- RISE OF
  TOTAL STATE AND TOTAL WAR
  (GERMANY).=             MISELV-44-OSR

  REBELS IN PARADISE -- INDONESIA'S
  CIVIL WAR.=             MOSSJ -61-RPI

  PERMANENT REVOLUTION --
  TOTALITARIANISM IN THE AGE OF

WAR                       (CONTINUATION)
  WORLD AT WAR (GERMANY).=
                          NEUMS -65-PRT

  THE BUDDHISTS, THE WAR, AND THE
  VIETCONG.=              ROBEA -66-BWV

  WAR, DEPRESSION, AND THE
  PRESIDENCY, 1933-1950
  (UNITED STATES).=       ROSSC -50-WDP

  THE GERMAN SOCIAL DEMOCRATIC PARTY
  AFTER WORLD WAR 2 -- THE
  CONSERVATISM OF POWER.=
                          SCHEHK-66-GSD

  GERMAN REARMAMENT AND ATOMIC WAR --
  THE VIEWS OF GERMAN MILITARY AND
  POLITICAL LEADERS.=     SPEIH -57-GRA

  CHINESE COMMUNIST LEADERSHIP IN WAR
  AND PEACE -- A REVIEW ARTICLE.=
                          STEIHA-63-CCL

  A STUDY OF GROUPS AND PERSONALITIES
  IN JAPAN INFLUENCING THE EVENTS
  LEADING TO THE SINO-JAPANESE WAR.=
                          YOUNEP-63-SGP

WARFARE
  COMMUNIST REVOLUTIONARY WARFARE --
  THE VIETMINH IN INDOCHINA.=
                          TANHGK-62-CRW

WARREN
  THE SUPREME COURT FROM TAFT TO
  WARREN (UNITED STATES).=
                          MASOAT-58-SCT

  AN ANALYSIS OF JUDICIAL ATTITUDES
  IN THE LABOR RELATIONS DECISIONS
  OF THE WARREN COURT.=   SPAEHJ-63-AJA

WARSAW
  WARSAW AND THE COMMUNIST BLOC
  (POLAND).'              BIRNI -57-WCB

  EGALITARIAN ATTITUDES OF WARSAW
  STUDENTS (POLAND).=     NOWAS -60-EAW

WARTIME
  INCREASE OF ZAIBATSU PREDOMINANCE
  IN WARTIME JAPAN.=      BISSTA-45-IZP

  THE ZAIBATSU'S WARTIME ROLE
  (JAPAN).=               BISSTA-45-ZSW

  AN EVALUATION OF WARTIME PERSONNEL
  ADMINISTRATION (UNITED STATES).=
                          KAMMGM-48-EWP

WASHINGTON
  WASHINGTON STATE'S LAWMAKERS --
  SOME PERSONNEL FACTORS IN THE
  WASHINGTON LEGISLATURE
  (UNITED STATES).=       BECKP -57-WSS

  WASHINGTON STATE'S LAWMAKERS --
  SOME PERSONNEL FACTORS IN THE
  WASHINGTON LEGISLATURE
  (UNITED STATES).=       BECKP -57-WSS

  POWER IN WASHINGTON -- A CRITICAL
  LOOK AT TODAY'S STRUGGLE TO GOVERN
  IN THE NATION'S CAPITAL.=
                          CATED -64-PWC

  LOOKING FOR INTELLIGENCE IN
  WASHINGTON (UNITED STATES).=
                          DE MMO-60-LIW

  THE WASHINGTON CONGRESSIONAL

WASHINGTON (CONTINUATION)
DELEGATION (UNITED STATES).=
KESSJH-64-WCD

THE POLITICAL PARTY ACTIVITY OF
WASHINGTON LOBBYISTS
(UNITED STATES).= MILBLW-58-PPA

THE WASHINGTON LOBBYISTS
(UNITED STATES).= MILBLW-63-WLU

CIVIL SERVANTS IN WASHINGTON -- 1,
THE CHARACTER OF THE FEDERAL
SERVICE --2, THE HIGHER CIVIL
SERVICE AND ITS FUTURE
(UNITED STATES).= SPANRN-53-CSW

WAYS
THE HOUSE COMMITTEE ON WAYS AND
MEANS -- CONFLICT MANAGEMENT IN A
CONGRESSIONAL COMMITTEE
(UNITED STATES).= MANLJF-65-HCW

WEALTH
THE POLITICAL ATTITUDES OF WEALTH.=
ALMOGA-45-PAW

WEALTH AND POWER IN AMERICA -- AN
ANALYSIS OF SOCIAL CLASS AND
INCOME DISTRIBUTION.= KOLKG -62-WPA

WEAPON
MAN AND ATTENTIVE OPINION ON
NUCLEAR WEAPON TESTS AND FALLOUT,
1954-1963 (UNITED STATES).=
ROSIEJ-65-MAC

THE ORGANIZATIONAL WEAPON -- A
STUDY OF BOLSHEVIK STRATEGY AND
TACTICS (SOVIET UNION).=
SELZP -52-OWS

WEAPONS
CONGRESSIONAL INNOVATION AND
INTERVENTION IN DEFENSE POLICY --
LEGISLATIVE AUTHORIZATION OF
WEAPONS SYSTEMS (UNITED STATES).=
DAWSRH-62-CII

AMERICAN SCIENTISTS AND NUCLEAR
WEAPONS POLICY.= GILPRG-62-ASN

WEBER
MAX WEBER ON SOCIAL STRATIFICATION
-- A CRITIQUE.= COX,OC-50-MWS

'BUREAUCRACY' AND 'RATIONALITY' IN
WEBER'S ORGANIZATION THEORY -- AN
EMPIRICAL STUDY.= UDY,SH-59-BRW

MAX WEBER ON THE SOCIOLOGY OF THE
FEUDAL ORDER.= ZEITM -60-MWS

WEBERIAN
WEBERIAN V. WELFARE BUREAUCRACY IN
TRADITIONAL SOCIETY (TURKEY).=
PRESRV-62-WVW

WEEKLY
THE WEEKLY NEWSPAPER'S LEADERSHIP
ROLE AS SEEN BY COMMUNITY LEADER'S
(UNITED STATES).= EDELAS-63-WNS

WEIMAR
THE YOUTH MOVEMENT IN THE WEIMAR
REPUBLIC (GERMANY).= APSLAE-45-YMW

PARTIES AND PRESSURE GROUPS IN
WEIMAR AND BONN (GERMANY).=
FRYECE-65-PPG

WELFARE
POLITICS, ECONOMICS, AND WELFARE

WELFARE (CONTINUATION)
(UNITED STATES).= CAHLRA-53-PEW

INTER - PARTY COMPETITION, ECONOMIC
VARIABLES, AND WELFARE POLICIES IN
THE AMERICAN STATES.= DAWSRE-63-IPC

WAR PROPAGANDA, WELFARE VALUE, AND
POLITICAL IDEOLOGIES
(SOVIET UNION, UNITED STATES,
GERMANY, ITALY, GREAT BRITAIN).=
ECKHW -65-WPW

WEBERIAN V. WELFARE BUREAUCRACY IN
TRADITIONAL SOCIETY (TURKEY).=
PRESRV-62-WVW

BRITISH INTELLECTUALS IN THE
WELFARE STATE.= SPENS -51-BIW

THE ELITE IN THE WELFARE STATE.=
THOEP -66-EWS

BUILDING A WELFARE STATE IN BURMA,
1948-1956.= TRAGFN-58-BWS

WHO SHALL RULE -- A POLITICAL
ANALYSIS OF SUCCESSION IN A LARGE
WELFARE ORGANIZATION
(UNITED STATES).= ZALDMN-65-WSR

WEST
TRIBAL UNIONS IN PARTY POLITICS
(WEST AFRICA).= ALOBA -54-TUP

ATTITUDES OF JAMAICAN ELITES
TOWARDS THE WEST INDIAN
FEDERATION.= BELLW -60-AJE

BUREAUCRACY EAST AND WEST (EGYPT).=
BERGM - -BEW

RIGHT-WING RADICALISM IN WEST
GERMANY'S YOUNGER GENERATION.=
BERGV -62-RWR

THE ROLE OF THE UNIVERSITY IN THE
DEVELOPING SOCIETY OF THE WEST
INDIES.= BRAILE-65-RUD

THE FREE DEMOCRATIC PARTY IN WEST
GERMAN POLITICS.= BRAUG -60-FDP

PATTERNS OF AUTHORITY IN WEST
AFRICA.= BROWP -51-PAW

THE FRENCH SOCIALIST PARTY AND THE
WEST.= CODOGA-60-FSP

THE WEST AFRICAN INTELLECTUAL
COMMUNITY.= DOWVM -62-WAI

POLITICAL UNIFICATION -- A
COMPARATIVE STUDY OF LEADERS AND
FOLLOWERS (UNITED ARAB REPUBLIC,
FEDERATION OF THE WEST INDIES,
SCANDINAVIA, EUROPEAN ECONOMIC
COMMUNITY).= ETZIA -65-PUC

THE GOVERNMENTAL ROLES OF
ASSOCIATIONS AMONG THE YAKO (WEST
AFRICA).= FORDD -61-GRA

SIX ALLIES AND A NEUTRAL (FRANCE,
GREAT BRITAIN, INDIA, ITALY,
JAPAN, UNITED STATES, WEST
GERMANY).= FREELA-59-SAN

THE WEST AFRICAN STUDENT'S UNION --
A STUDY IN CULTURE CONTACT.=
GARIP -53-WAS

CHANGING POLITICAL LEADERSHIP IN

YUGOSLAVIA (CONTINUATION)
ADMINISTRATIVE ORGANS OF THE
PEOPLE'S COMMITTEES (YUGOSLAVIA).=
ANON -61-TOA

THE COMMUNIST LEAGUE OF YUGOSLAVIA
IN FIGURES.= AVAKI -59-CLY

THE NEW CLASS -- AN ANALYSIS OF THE
COMMUNIST SYSTEM (YUGOSLAVIA).=
DJILM -57-NCA

LOCAL SELF-GOVERNMENT IN
YUGOSLAVIA.= DJORJ -53-LSG

YUGOSLAVIA -- STATUS AND ROLE OF
THE EXECUTIVE ORGANS DURING THE
FIRST STAGE OF YUGOSLAVIA'S
POLITICAL AND CONSTITUTIONAL
DEVELOPMENT.= DJORJ -58-YSR

YUGOSLAVIA -- STATUS AND ROLE OF
THE EXECUTIVE ORGANS DURING THE
FIRST STAGE OF YUGOSLAVIA'S
POLITICAL AND CONSTITUTIONAL
DEVELOPMENT.= DJORJ -58-YSR

COMMUNISM AND THE NATIONAL QUESTION
IN YUGOSLAVIA.= FRANJ -55-CNQ

ADMINISTRATIVE MANAGEMENT OF PUBLIC
ENTERPRISES IN YUGOSLAVIA.=
GROZS -66-AMP

YUGOSLAVIA AND THE NEW COMMUNISM.=
HOFFGW-62-YNC

THE POLITICS OF THE EUROPEAN
COMMUNIST STATES (BULGARIA,
CZECHOSLOVAKIA, HUNGARY, EAST
GERMANY, POLAND, RUMANIA,
SOVIET UNION, YUGOSLAVIA).=
IONEG -67-PEC

THE EXECUTIVE IN THE MODERN STATE
(CANADA, FRANCE, GREAT BRITAIN,
SOVIET UNION, UNITED STATES,
YUGOSLAVIA).= MEYNJ -58-EMS

THE CENTRAL GOVERNMENT OF
YUGOSLAVIA.= PETRMB-47-CGY

POLITICAL FORCES IN YUGOSLAVIA
TODAY.= SC -46-PFY

PRODUCERS' REPRESENTATION IN
YUGOSLAVIA.= SCOTDJ-54-PRY

PROBLEMS OF PARTY REFORM IN
YUGOSLAVIA.= SHOUP -59-PPR

PEASANTS, POLITICS, AND ECONOMIC
CHANGE IN YUGOSLAVIA.=
SOMAJ -65-PPE

COMMUNIST EXPERIMENTS WITH BALLOT
(POLAND, YUGOSLAVIA).=
WILLP -57-CEB

ZAIBATSU
INCREASE OF ZAIBATSU PREDOMINANCE
IN WARTIME JAPAN.= BISSTA-45-IZP

THE ZAIBATSU'S WARTIME ROLE
(JAPAN).= BISSTA-45-ZSW

ZAMBIA
FEDERAL ADMINISTRATION, RANK, AND
CIVIL STRIFE AMONG BEMBA ROYALS
AND NOBLES (ZAMBIA).= WERBRP-67-FAR

ZANDE
THE ETHNIC ORIGINS OF ZANDE

ZANDE
OFFICE-HOLDERS (EGYPT,SUDAN).=
EVANEE-60-EOZ

ZANZIBAR
PARTY CONFLICT IN ZANZIBAR.=
LOFCM -63-PCZ

ZANZIBAR -- BACKGROUND TO
REVOLUTION.= LOFCMF-65-ZBR

ZEAL
FROM YOUTHFUL ZEAL TO MIDDLE AGE
(SOVIET UNION, KOMSOMOL).=
PLOSSI-58-YZM

ZHUKOV
THE PURGE OF MARSHAL ZHUKOV
(SOVIET UNION).= COCKPM-63-PMZ

ZU-AMA
ZU-AMA AND PARTIES IN THE LEBANESE
CRISIS OF 1958.= HOTTA -61-ZAP

# Section II
# FULL CITATION LISTING

A HOHO-52-COC  A HONG KONG CORRESPONDENT
               THE CENTRAL ORGANIZATION OF THE COMMUNIST PARTY OF CHINA.=
               PROBLEMS OF COMMUNISM, 1, (EXPERIMENTAL ISSUE 1952),       52
                 PP. 20-25.
               COMEL
AAROS -61-RCS  AARONOVITCH, S
               THE RULING CLASS -- A STUDY OF BRITISH FINANCE CAPITAL.=
               LONDON, LAWRENCE AND WISHART, 1961.                        61
               COMEL, ELEL, ELPRNOR
ABBORS-51-RCP  ABBOTT, RS
               THE ROLE OF CONTEMPORARY POLITICAL PARTIES IN CHILE.=
               THE AMERICAN POLITICAL SCIENCE REVIEW, 45, (JUNE 1951),    51
                 PP. 450-463.
               ELEL, ELNOEL
ABEGJ -60-LMJ  ABEGGLEN, J        MANNARI, H
               LEADERS OF MODERN JAPAN -- SOCIAL ORIGINS AND
                 MOBILITY.=
               ECONOMIC DEVELOPMENT AND CULTURAL CHANGE, 9, (OCTOBER      60
                 1960, PART 2), PP. 109-134.
               COMEL, ELEL, ELNOEL, METEL
ABELHI-58-SDI  ABELSON, HI        RUGG, WD
               SELF - DESIGNATED INFLUENTIALITY AND ACTIVITY.=
               THE PUBLIC OPINION QUARTERLY, 22, (WINTER 1958),           58
                 PP. 566-567.
               METEL
ABRAE -58-SPC  ABRAMSON, E        ET AL
               SOCIAL POWER AND COMMITMENT -- A THEORETICAL STATEMENT.=
               AMERICAN SOCIOLOGICAL REVIEW, 23, (FEBRUARY 1958),         58
                 PP. 15-22.
               DEFEL
ABRAHJ-62-JPI  ABRAHAM, HJ
               THE JUDICIAL PROCESS -- AN INTRODUCTORY ANALYSIS OF THE
                 COURTS OF THE UNITED STATES, ENGLAND AND FRANCE.=
               NEW YORK, OXFORD UNIVERSITY PRESS, 1962.                   62
               COMEL, ELEL, ELNOEL
ABRAM -61-CPG  ABRAMS, M
               CLASS AND POLITICS (GREAT BRITAIN).=
               ENCOUNTER, 17, (OCTOBER 1961), PP. 39-43.                  61
               COMEL, ELNOEL
ABRAM -61-SCB  ABRAMS, M
               SOCIAL CLASS AND BRITISH POLITICS.=
               THE PUBLIC OPINION QUARTERLY, 25, (FALL 1961),             61
                 PP. 342-350.
               COMEL, ELNOEL
ABRAP -65-YAB  ABRAMS, P          LITTLE, A
               THE YOUNG ACTIVIST IN BRITISH POLITICS.=
               THE BRITISH JOURNAL OF SOCIOLOGY, 16, (DECEMBER 1965),     65
                 PP. 315-333.
               COMEL
ABRAPL-49-GGS  ABRAHAM, PLR
               THE GOVERNOR GENERAL'S PART IN LEGISLATION (NEW ZEALAND).=
               JOURNAL OF POLITICAL SCIENCE, 1, (MARCH 1949), PP. 20-23. 49
               ELEL, ELNOEL
ABU-B -65-RAS  ABU-LABAN, B
               THE REPUTATIONAL APPROACH IN THE STUDY OF COMMUNITY POWER
                 -- A CRITICAL EVALUATION.=
               PACIFIC SOCIOLOGICAL REVIEW, 8, (SPRING 1965), PP. 35-42. 65
               METEL
ABU-I -64-IFA  ABU-LUGHOD, I
               THE ISLAMIC FACTOR IN AFRICAN POLITICS.=
               ORBIS, 8, (SUMMER 1964), PP. 425-444.                      64
               ELEL, ELPRNOR
ABUEJV-59-FPB  ABUEVA, JV
               FOCUS ON THE (PHILIPPINE) BARIO.=
               MANILA, INSTITUTE OF PUBLIC ADMINISTRATION, UNIVERSITY     59
                 OF THE PHILIPPINES, 1959.
               ELEL, ELNOEL
ABUEJV-61-IBL  ABUEVA, JV
               THE INTERRELATIONS BETWEEN LOCAL GOVERNMENTS AND
                 COMMUNITY DEVELOPMENT (PHILIPPINES).=
               PHILIPPINE JOURNAL OF PUBLIC ADMINISTRATION, 5,            61
                 (JANUARY 1961), PP. 52-58.
               ELEL, ELNOEL
ACHMH -54-PLC  ACHMINOW, H

414

THE POLITICAL LINE OF COLLECTIVE LEADERSHIP
(SOVIET UNION).=
BULLETIN OF THE INSTITUTE FOR THE STUDY OF THE HISTORY      54
AND CULTURE OF THE USSR, 1, (AUGUST 1954), PP. 26-32.
ELEL, ELNOEL
ACHMH -56-SCT    ACHMINOV, H
SOCIAL CONFLICTS AT THE TWENTIETH PARTY CONGRESS
(SOVIET UNION).=
BULLETIN INSTITUTE FOR THE STUDY OF THE USSR, 3,           56
(MAY 1956), PP. 20-29.
ELPRNOR
ACHMH -58-PPA    ACHMINOV, H
THE PARTY AND THE PARTY APPARATUS (SOVIET UNION).=
BULLETIN INSTITUTE FOR THE STUDY OF THE USSR, 5,           58
(JUNE 1958), PP. 12-24.
ELEL
ACHMH -58-SIP    ACHMINOV, H
THE SIGNIFICANCE OF 'INNER-PARTY DEMOCRACY'
(SOVIET UNION).=
BULLETIN INSTITUTE FOR THE STUDY OF THE USSR, 5,           58
(JULY 1958), PP. 3-16.
ELEL
ACHMH -59-PPR    ACHMINOV, H
THE PERENNIAL PROBLEM OF REVISIONISM (SOVIET UNION).=
BULLETIN INSTITUTE FOR THE STUDY OF THE USSR,              59
6, (JULY 1959), PP. 3-12.
ELEL, ELPRNOR
ACHMH -59-PPS    ACHMINOV, H
THE PRINCIPLE OF PROFITABILITY AND THE SOVIET PARTY
APPARATUS.=
BULLETIN INSTITUTE FOR THE STUDY OF THE USSR,              59
6, (FEBRUARY 1959), PP. 3-11.
ELEL
ACHMH -63-SCP    ACHMINOW, H
THE SOVIET COMMUNIST PARTY.=
STUDIES ON THE SOVIET UNION, 2, (1963), PP. 29-41.         63
COMEL, ELEL, ELNOEL
ACHMH -65-CPS    ACHMINOW, H
THE CURRENT POLITICAL SCENE IN THE SOVIET UNION.=
STUDIES ON THE SOVIET UNION, 4, (1965), PP. 16-26.         65
COMEL, ELEL
ACHMH -65-OYW    ACHMINOV, H
ONE YEAR WITHOUT KHRUSHCHEV (SOVIET UNION).=
STUDIES ON THE SOVIET UNION, 5, (1965), PP. 65-81.         65
ELEL
ACHMH -65-ROM    ACHMINOV, H
THE RETURN TO ONE-MAN DICTATORSHIP IN THE USSR.=
STUDIES ON THE SOVIET UNION, 4, (1965), PP. 59-61.         65
ELEL
ACZET -60-RMC    ACZEL, T            MERAY, T
THE REVOLT OF THE MIND -- A CASE HISTORY OF INTELLECTUAL
RESISTANCE BEHIND THE IRON CURTAIN.=
NEW YORK, FREDERICK A PRAEGER, 1960.
ELEL, ELNOEL, ELPRNOR                                      60
ADAMAE-58-BAU    ADAMS, AE
BOLSHEVIK ADMINISTRATION IN THE UKRAINE -- 1918.=
REVIEW OF POLITICS, 20, (JULY 1958), PP. 289-306.          58
ELEL
ADAMRN-  -SCL    ADAMS, RN            ET AL
SOCIAL CHANGE IN LATIN AMERICA TODAY -- ITS IMPLICATIONS.=
FOR U.S. (UNITED STATES) POLICY.=
NEW YORK, HARPER AND ROW, 1960
COMEL, ELEL, ELNOEL
ADAMS -57-OAO    ADAMS, S
ORIGINS OF AMERICAN OCCUPATIONAL ELITES, 1900-1955.=
THE AMERICAN JOURNAL OF SOCIOLOGY, 62, (JANUARY 1957),     57
PP. 360-368.
ELEL, METEL
ADAMW -58-CIF    ADAMS, W
CABINET INSTABILITY IN FRANCE.=
PROD (THE AMERICAN BEHAVIORAL SCIENTIST), 1,               58
(MARCH 1958), PP. 18-21.
ELEL
ADIEWA-62-PAN    ADIE, WAC
POLITICAL ASPECTS OF THE NATIONAL PEOPLE'S CONGRESS
(CHINA).=
THE CHINA QUARTERLY, 11, (JULY-SEPTEMBER 1962), PP. 78-88.62
ELEL, ELNOEL
ADLEKP-56-IIF    ADLER, KP            BOBROW, D
INTEREST AND INFLUENCE IN FOREIGN AFFAIRS
(UNITED STATES).=
THE PUBLIC OPINION QUARTERLY, 20, (SPRING 1956),           56
PP. 89-101.
COMEL, ELEL

ADLEMK-53-ICA  ADLER, MK
               INDEPENDENT CANDIDATES IN 1945, 1950, AND 1951
                  (GREAT BRITAIN).=
               POLITICAL STUDIES, 1, (1953), PP. 80-83.                        53
               COMEL, ELNOEL
ADORTW-65-DLM  ADORNO, TW
               DEMOCRATIC LEADERSHIP AND MASS MANIPULATION.=
               AW GOULDNER (ED), STUDIES IN LEADERSHIP, NEW YORK,              65
                  RUSSELL AND RUSSELL, 1965, PP. 418-435.
               DEFEL, ELNOEL
ADRICR-59-ILP  ADRIAN, CR              WILLIAMS, OP
               THE INSULATION OF LOCAL POLITICS UNDER THE
                  NON-PARTISAN BALLOT (UNITED STATES).=
               THE AMERICAN POLITICAL SCIENCE REVIEW, 53, (DECEMBER           59
                  1959), PP. 1052-1063.
               COMEL, ELNOEL
ADU,A -65-CSN  ADU, A
               THE CIVIL SERVICE IN THE NEW STATES.=
               NEW YORK, FREDERICK A PRAEGER, 1965.                           65
               COMEL, ELEL, ELNOEL
AGGER -64-RRU  AGGER, R               GOLDRICH, D             SWANSON, BE
               THE RULER AND THE RULED (UNITED STATES).=
               NEW YORK, JOHN WILEY AND SONS, 1964.                          64
               GNELTH, DEFEL, COMEL, ELEL, ELNOEL, ELPRNOR, METEL
AGGERE-56-LPU  AGGER, RE
               LAWYERS IN POLITICS (UNITED STATES).=
               TEMPLE LAW QUARTERLY, 4, (SUMMER 1956), PP. 434-452.           56
               COMEL
AGGERE-56-PAL  AGGER, RE
               POWER ATTRIBUTIONS IN THE LOCAL COMMUNITY -- THEORETICAL
                  AND RESEARCH CONSIDERATIONS (UNITED STATES).=
               SOCIAL FORCES, 34, (MAY 1956), PP. 322-331.                    56
               COMEL, METEL
AGGERE-56-PSS  AGGER, RE              OSTOOM, V
               THE POLITICAL STRUCTURE OF A SMALL COMMUNITY
                  (UNITED STATES).=
               THE PUBLIC OPINION QUARTERLY, 20, (SPRING 1956),              56
                  PP. 81-89.
               COMEL, ELEL, ELNOEL, METEL
AGGERE-58-CPS  AGGER, RE              GOLDRICH, D
               COMMUNITY POWER STRUCTURE AND PARTISANSHIP
                  (UNITED STATES).=
               AMERICAN SOCIOLOGICAL REVIEW, 23, (AUGUST 1958),              58
                  PP. 383-392.
               COMEL, ELEL, ELNOEL
AGGERE-58-PAL  AGGER, RE
               POLITICAL ASPIRATIONS OF LAW STUDENTS (UNITED STATES).=
               PROD (THE AMERICAN BEHAVIORAL SCIENTIST), 1,                  58
                  (MARCH 1958), PP. 17-18.
               ELPRNOR
AGPARE-62-PPP  AGPALO, RE
               THE (PHILIPPINE) POLITICAL PROCESS AND THE
                  NATIONALIZATION OF THE RETAIL TRADES.=
               QUEZON CITY, OFFICE OF COORDINATOR OF RESEARCH,                62
                  UNIVERSITY OF THE PHILIPPINES, 1962.
               ELEL, ELNOEL, ELPRNOR
AHH   -51-PIS  AHH
               POLITICS AND INDUSTRY IN SWEDEN.=
               THE WORLD TODAY, 7, (DECEMBER 1951), PP. 529-537.             51
               ELEL
AHMAM -59-GPP  AHMAD, M
               GOVERNMENT AND POLITICS IN PAKISTAN.=
               NEW YORK, INSTITUTE OF PACIFIC RELATIONS, 1959.               59
               ELEL, ELNOEL, ELPRNOR
AHMAM -60-CPI  AHMAD, M
               THE COMMUNIST PARTY OF INDIA AND ITS FORMATION ABROAD.=
               CALCUTTA, THE NATIONAL BOOK AGENCY, 1960.                     60
               COMEL
AHMEJM-60-IOE  AHMED, JM
               THE INTELLECTUAL ORIGINS OF EGYPTIAN NATIONALISM.=
               NEW YORK, OXFORD UNIVERSITY PRESS, 1960.                      60
               COMEL, ELEL, ELPRNOR
AKE,C -66-CLP  AKE, C
               CHARISMATIC LEGITIMATION AND POLITICAL INTEGRATION
                  (GHANA).=
               COMPARATIVE STUDIES IN SOCIETY AND HISTORY, 9, (OCTOBER       66
                  1966), PP. 1-13.
               DEFEL, ELNOEL
AKE,C -67-PIP  AKE, C
               POLITICAL INTEGRATION AND POLITICAL STABILITY -- A
                  HYPOTHESIS.=
               WORLD POLITICS, 19, (APRIL 1967), PP. 486-499.                67
               DEFEL
AKHMH -61-OKS  AKHMINOV, H

```
                    OBITUARIES AS A KEY TO THE SOVIET ELITE.=
                    BULLETIN INSTITUTE FOR THE STUDY OF THE USSR, 8,        61
                       (JULY 1961), PP. 37-43.
                    METEL
AKHMH -61-PPN       AKHMINOV, H
                    THE 'PERMANENT PURGE' IN THE NEW PARTY PROGRAM
                       (SOVIET UNION).=
                    BULLETIN INSTITUTE FOR THE STUDY OF THE USSR, 8,        61
                       (OCTOBER 1961), PP. 32-43.
                    ELEL
AKHMH -63-CSS       AKHMINOV, H
                    CHANGES IN THE STRUCTURE OF SOVIET SOCIETY.=
                    BULLETIN INSTITUTE FOR THE STUDY OF THE USSR, 10,       63
                       (OCTOBER 1963), PP. 3-17.
                    ELEL, ELNOEL
AKHMH -64-RIS       AKHMINOV, H
                    THE ROLE OF IDEOLOGY IN THE SOVIET SYSTEM.=
                    BULLETIN INSTITUTE FOR THE STUDY OF THE USSR, 11,       64
                       (FEBRUARY 1964), PP. 3-15.
                    ELPRNOR
AKHMH -66-ASL       AKHMINOV, H
                    THE ACTIVITIES OF A SOVIET LEADER.=
                    BULLETIN INSTITUTE FOR THE STUDY OF THE USSR, 8,        66
                       (JANUARY 1966), PP. 16-28.
                    ELEL, ELNOEL
AKHMH -67-EPD       AKHMINOV, H
                    AN EXAMPLE OF PARTY DEMOCRACY (SOVIET UNION).=
                    BULLETIN INSTITUTE FOR THE STUDY OF THE USSR, 14        67
                       (APRIL 1967), PP. 35-42.
                    ELEL, ELNOEL
AKIST -59-WSD       AKISADA, T
                    WHITHER SOCIAL DEMOCRATIC PARTY (JAPAN).=
                    CONTEMPORARY JAPAN, 26, (DECEMBER 1959), PP. 228-245.   59
                    ELEL, ELNOEL
AKZIB -60-EAU       AKZIN, B
                    ELECTION AND APPOINTMENT (UNITED STATES).=
                    THE AMERICAN POLITICAL SCIENCE REVIEW, 54,
                       (SEPTEMBER 1960), PP. 705-713.                       60
                    ELEL, ELNOEL
AKZIB -61-KI        AKZIN, B
                    THE KNESSET (ISRAEL).=
                    INTERNATIONAL SOCIAL SCIENCE JOURNAL, 13, (1961),       61
                       PP. 567-582.
                    ELEL
AL-HMM-56-LMI       AL-HABIB, MM
                    THE LABOR MOVEMENT IN IRAQ.=
                    MIDDLE EASTERN AFFAIRS, 7, (APRIL 1956), PP. 137-143.   56
                    ELEL, ELNOEL
ALANR -58-IAC       ALAN, R
                    IRAQ AFTER THE COUP.=
                    COMMENTARY, 20, (SEPTEMBER 1958), PP. 194-199.          58
                    ELEL, ELNOEL, ELPRNOR
ALANR -59-CDC       ALAN, R
                    CAN DEGAULLE CHECK THE GAULLISTS (FRANCE).=
                    COMMENTARY, 27, (JANUARY 1959), PP. 9-16.               59
                    ELEL, ELNOEL, ELPRNOR
ALANR -60-UBD       ALAN, R
                    UNEASY BALANCE OF DEGAULLE'S REPUBLIC (FRANCE).=
                    COMMENTARY, 29, (JANUARY 1960), PP. 29-37.              60
                    ELEL, ELNOEL
ALANR -62-FSS       ALAN, R
                    FRANCO'S SPAIN AND THE NEW EUROPE.=
                    COMMENTARY, 34, (SEPTEMBER 1962), PP. 231-237.          62
                    COMEL, ELEL, ELNOEL
ALBAV -62-SML       ALBA, V
                    THE STAGES OF MILITARISM IN LATIN AMERICA.=
                    JJ JOHNSON (ED), THE ROLE OF THE MILITARY IN
                       UNDERDEVELOPED COUNTRIES, PRINCETON, NEW JERSEY,     62
                       PRINCETON UNIVERSITY PRESS, 1962, PP 165-183.
                    ELEL, ELNOEL, ELPRNOR
ALBEMH-53-OCC       ALBERG, MH
                    OUR CHANGING CONCEPT OF LEADERSHIP (UNITED STATES).=
                    CURRENT HISTORY, N.S., 25, (SEPTEMBER 1953),
                       PP. 157-162.                                        53
                    ELNOEL, ELPRNOR
ALBEVL-53-LSR       ALBERG, VL
                    THE LEADERS OF SOVIET RUSSIA.=
                    CURRENT HISTORY, N.S., 25, (AUGUST 1953), PP. 101-106.  53
                    COMEL, ELPRNOR
ALBOO -66-SOL       ALBORNOZ, O
                    STUDENT OPPOSITION IN LATIN AMERICA.=
                    GOVERNMENT AND OPPOSITION, 2, (NOVEMBER 1966),          66
                       PP. 105-118.
                    COMEL, ELEL, ELPRNOR
```

ALEXRJ-44-SPS    ALEXANDER, RJ
                 SOCIALIST PARTIES IN SOUTH AMERICA.=
                 CANADIAN FORUM, 24, (NOVEMBER 1944), PP. 179-182.          44
                 COMEL, ELNOEL
ALEXRJ-47-LML    ALEXANDER, RJ
                 LABOUR MOVEMENTS IN LATIN AMERICA.=
                 LONDON, FABIAN PUBLICATIONS, 1947.                         47
                 COMEL, ELEL, ELNOEL
ALEXRJ-49-LAA    ALEXANDER, RJ
                 THE LATIN AMERICAN APRISTA PARTIES.=
                 THE POLITICAL QUARTERLY, 20, (JULY 1949), PP. 236-247.     49
                 COMEL, ELNOEL
ALEXRJ-51-PEA    ALEXANDER, RJ
                 THE PERON ERA (ARGENTINA).=
                 NEW YORK, COLUMBIA UNIVERSITY PRESS, 1951.                 51
                 ELEL, ELNOEL
ALEXRJ-55-PAS    ALEXANDER, RJ
                 PERONISM AND ARGENTINA'S QUEST FOR LEADERSHIP IN
                     LATIN AMERICA.=
                 JOURNAL OF INTERNATIONAL AFFAIRS, 9, (1955), PP. 47-55.    55
                 ELEL, ELNOEL
ALEXRJ-57-CLA    ALEXANDER, RJ
                 COMMUNISM IN LATIN AMERICA.=
                 NEW BRUNSWICK, NEW JERSEY, RUTGERS UNIVERSITY PRESS,       57
                     1957.
                 COMEL, ELEL, ELNOEL, ELPRNOR
ALEXRJ-58-BNR    ALEXANDER, RJ
                 THE BOLIVIAN NATIONAL REVOLUTION.=
                 NEW BRUNSWICK, NEW JERSEY, RUTGERS UNIVERSITY PRESS,       58
                     1958.
                 COMEL, ELEL, ELNOEL, ELPRNOR
ALEXRJ-62-PRL    ALEXANDER, RJ
                 PROPHETS OF THE REVOLUTION (LATIN AMERICA).=
                 NEW YORK, MACMILLAN, 1962.                                 62
                 COMEL, ELPRNOR
ALEXRJ-63-JLF    ALEXANDER, RJ
                 THE JACOBIN LEFT AND THE FUTURE OF THE COMMUNISTS IN
                     LATIN AMERICA.=
                 W PETERSEN (ED), THE REALITIES OF WORLD COMMUNISM,         63
                     ENGLEWOOD CLIFFS, NEW JERSEY, PRENTICE HALL, 1963,
                     PP. 188-201.
                 COMEL, ELEL, ELPRNOR
ALEXRJ-64-RLA    ALEXANDER, RJ
                 THE RISE OF LATIN AMERICAN CHRISTIAN DEMOCRACY.=
                 NEW POLITICS, 3, (FALL 1964), PP. 76-84.                   64
                 COMEL, ELPRNOR
ALEXRJ-64-VDR    ALEXANDER, RJ
                 THE VENEZUELAN DEMOCRATIC REVOLUTION.=
                 NEW BRUNSWICK, NEW JERSEY, RUTGERS UNIVERSITY PRESS,       64
                     1964.
                 COMEL, ELEL, ELNOEL, ELPRNOR
ALEXRJ-65-LAP    ALEXANDER, RJ
                 LATIN AMERICAN POLITICS AND GOVERNMENT.=
                 NEW YORK, HARPER AND ROW, 1965.                            65
                 ELEL, ELNOEL
ALEXRJ-65-OLL    ALEXANDER, RJ
                 ORGANIZED LABOR IN LATIN AMERICA.=
                 NEW YORK, THE FREE PRESS, 1965.                            65
                 COMEL, ELEL, ELNOEL, ELPRNOR
ALFORR-63-PSA    ALFORD, RR
                 PARTY AND SOCIETY -- THE ANGLO-AMERICAN DEMOCRACIES.=
                 CHICAGO, RAND MCNALLY, 1963.                               63
                 DEFEL, COMEL, ELEL, ELNOEL
ALGECF-65-PCI    ALGER, CF
                 PERSONAL CONTACT IN INTERGOVERNMENTAL ORGANIZATIONS.=
                 HC KELMAN (ED), INTERNATIONAL BEHAVIOR -- A SOCIAL-        65
                     PSYCHOLOGICAL ANALYSIS, NEW YORK, HOLT, RINEHART AND
                     WINSTON, 1965, PP. 523-547.
                 ELEL
ALGECF-66-ICU    ALGER, CF
                 INTERACTION IN A COMMITTEE OF THE UNITED NATIONS GENERAL
                     ASSEMBLY.=
                 MIDWEST JOURNAL OF POLITICAL SCIENCE, 10, (NOVEMBER        66
                     1966), PP. 411-447.
                 ELEL, ELPRNOR
ALGEFC-63-EBU    ALGER, FC
                 THE EXTERNAL BUREAUCRACY IN UNITED STATES FOREIGN
                     AFFAIRS.=
                 ADMINISTRATIVE SCIENCE QUARTERLY, 7, (1962-1963),          63
                     PP. 50-78.
                 ELEL, ELPRNOR
ALISM -9 -HFA    ALISKY, M
                 THE HOUSE FOREIGN AFFAIRS COMMITTEE'S ROLE
                     (UNITED STATES).=

PROD (THE AMERICAN BEHAVIORAL SCIENTIST), 2,                    59
       (MARCH 1959), PP. 13-14.
       ELEL
ALKEHR-65-WPG   ALKER-JR, HR          RUSSETT, BM
       WORLD POLITICS IN THE GENERAL ASSEMBLY (UNITED NATIONS).=
       NEW HAVEN, YALE UNIVERSITY PRESS, 1965.
          PP. 59-73.                                           65
       COMEL, ELEL, ELNOEL, ELPRNOR
ALLEVL-63-ETU   ALLEN, VL
       THE ETHICS OF TRADE UNION LEADERS (GREAT BRITAIN).=
       THE BRITISH JOURNAL OF SOCIOLOGY, 7, (1963),
          PP. 314-336.                                         63
       ELEL, ELPRNOR
ALMOGA-  -RPP   ALMOND, GA
       THE RESISTANCE AND THE POLITICAL PARTIES OF WESTERN
          EUROPE.=
       POLITICAL SCIENCE QUARTERLY, 62, (MARCH 1947),
          PP. 27-61.
       COMEL, ELEL
ALMOGA-45-PAW   ALMOND, GA
       THE POLITICAL ATTITUDES OF WEALTH.=
       THE JOURNAL OF POLITICS, 7, (AUGUST 1945), PP. 213-255.   45
       ELPRNOR
ALMOGA-48-CPW   ALMOND, GA
       THE CHRISTIAN PARTIES OF WESTERN EUROPE.=
       WORLD POLITICS, 1, (OCTOBER 1948), PP. 30-58.            48
       ELEL, ELNOEL
ALMOGA-48-PIC   ALMOND, GA
       THE POLITICAL IDEAS OF CHRISTIAN DEMOCRACY.=
       THE JOURNAL OF POLITICS, 10, (NOVEMBER 1948), PP. 734-763.48
       ELEL, ELNOEL, ELPRNOR
ALMOGA-54-AC    ALMOND, GA          ET AL
       THE APPEALS OF COMMUNISM.=
       PRINCETON, PRINCETON UNIVERSITY PRESS, 1954.            54
       ELEL, ELNOEL, ELPRNOR
ALMOGA-56-PAG   ALMOND, GA
       THE POLITICAL ATTITUDES OF GERMAN BUSINESS.=
       WORLD POLITICS, 8, (JANUARY 1956), PP. 157-186.          56
       ELPRNOR
ALMOGA-56-PON   ALMOND, GA
       PUBLIC OPINION AND NATIONAL SECURITY POLICY
          (UNITED STATES).=
       THE PUBLIC OPINION QUARTERLY, 20, (SUMMER 1956),         56
          PP. 371-378.
       ELEL, ELNOEL
ALMOGA-60-APF   ALMOND, GA
       THE AMERICAN PEOPLE AND FOREIGN POLICY.=
       NEW YORK, FREDERICK A PRAEGER, 1960.                     60
       COMEL, ELEL ELNOEL, ELPRNOR
ALMOGA-60-PDA   ALMOND, GA          COLEMAN, JS
       THE POLITICS OF THE DEVELOPING AREAS.=
       PRINCETON, PRINCETON UNIVERSITY PRESS, 1960.            60
       DEFEL, ELEL, ELNOEL, ELPRNOR
ALOBA -54-TUP   ALOBA, A
       TRIBAL UNIONS IN PARTY POLITICS (WEST AFRICA).=
       WEST AFRICA, 10, (JULY 1954), PP. 637.                  54
       COMEL, ELEL
ALTBP -63-JSJ   ALTBACH, P
       JAPANESE STUDENTS AND JAPANESE POLITICS.=
       COMPARATIVE EDUCATION REVIEW, 7, (OCTOBER 1963),        63
          PP. 181-188.
       ELEL, ELPRNOR
ALTHP -66-PAR   ALTHOF, P          PATTERSON, SC
       POLITICAL ACTIVISM IN A RURAL COUNTY (UNITED STATES).=
       MIDWEST JOURNAL OF POLITICAL SCIENCE, 10,               66
          (FEBRUARY 1966), PP. 39-51.
       COMEL, ELEL, ELPRNOR
ALVAA -66-UPW   ALVAREZ, A
       UNDER PRESSURE -- THE WRITER IN SOCIETY -- EASTERN
          EUROPE AND THE USA.=
       BALTIMORE, PENGUIN, 1966.                               66
       ELEL, ELPRNOR
AMBLJS-65-FAP   AMBLER, JS
       THE FRENCH ARMY IN POLITICS, 1945-1962.=
       COLUMBUS, OHIO STATE UNIVERSITY PRESS, 1965.            65
       COMEL, ELEL, ELNOEL, ELPRNOR
AMESMM-63-ICS   AMES, MM
       IDEOLOGICAL CHANGE AND SOCIAL CHANGE IN CEYLON.=
       HUMAN ORGANIZATION, 22, (SPRING 1963), PP. 45-53.       63
       ELEL, ELNOEL, ELPRNOR
AN MMP-48-WPS   AN MP'S SECRETARY
       THE WORK OF THE PRIVATE SECRETARY TO THE MEMBER OF
          PARLIAMENT (GREAT BRITAIN).=
       PARLIAMENTARY AFFAIRS, 1, (AUTUMN 1948), PP. 73-77.     48

ELEL, ELNOEL
ANDEB  -62-OIP   ANDERSON, B
OPINION INFLUENTIALS AND POLITICAL OPINION FORMATION IN
   FOUR SWEDISH COMMUNITIES.=
INTERNATIONAL SOCIAL SCIENCE JOURNAL, 14, (1962),                62
   PP. 320-336.
ELEL, ELNOEL, ELPRNOR
ANDEB  -64-REP   ANDERSON, B          ZELDITCH, M
RANK EQUILIBRATION AND POLITICAL BEHAVIOR.=
EUROPEAN JOURNAL OF SOCIOLOGY, S, (1964), PP. 112-125.          64
DEFEL, COMEL, METEL
ANDEB  -66-CCM   ANDERSON, B          COCKROFT, JD
CONTROL AND COOPTATION IN MEXICAN POLITICS.=
INTERNATIONAL JOURNAL OF POLITICAL SOCIOLOGY, 7,                66
   (MARCH 1966), PP. 11-27.
ELEL, ELNOEL, ELPRNOR
ANDECW-62-CAP   ANDERSON, CW
CENTRAL AMERICAN POLITICAL PARTIES -- A FUNCTIONAL
   APPROACH.=
THE WESTERN POLITICAL QUARTERLY, 15, (MARCH 1962),              62
   PP. 125-139.
COMEL, ELEL, ELNOEL
ANDEM  -65-MTH   ANDERSON, M
THE MYTH OF THE 'TWO HUNDRED FAMILIES' (FRANCE).=
POLITICAL STUDIES, 13, (JUNE 1965), PP. 163-178.               65
COMEL
ANDERW-65-PPP   ANDERSON, RW
PARTY POLITICS IN PUERTO RICO.=
STANFORD, STANFORD UNIVERSITY PRESS, 1965.                     65
ELEL, ELNOEL, ELPRNOR
ANDRCF-64-DSI   ANDRAIN, CF
DEMOCRACY AND SOCIALISM -- IDEOLOGIES OF AFRICAN LEADERS.=
DE APTER (ED), IDEOLOGY AND DISCONTENT, LONDON,                64
   THE FREE PRESS, 1964, PP. 155-205.
ELPRNOR
ANDRS  -54-MOS   ANDRZEJEWSKI, S
MILITARY ORGANIZATION AND SOCIETY.=
LONDON, ROUTLEDGE AND KEGAN PAUL, LTD, 1954.                   54
DEFEL, ELEL, ELNOEL
ANGEA  -66-COC   ANGELL, A
CO-OPERATION AND CONFLICT IN COLUMBIAN PARTY POLITICS.=
POLITICAL STUDIES, 14, (FEBRUARY 1966), PP. 53-71.            66
ELEL, ELNOEL
ANGEA  -66-PSL   ANGELL, A
PARTY SYSTEMS IN LATIN AMERICA.=
THE POLITICAL QUARTERLY, 37, (JULY-SEPTEMBER 1966),           66
   PP. 309-323.
ELEL, ELNOEL, ELPRNOR
ANGERC-64-SVS   ANGELL, RC
SOCIAL VALUES OF SOVIET AND AMERICAN ELITES -- CONTENT
   ANALYSIS OF ELITE MEDIA.=
THE JOURNAL OF CONFLICT RESOLUTION, 8, (DECEMBER 1964),        64
   PP. 330-385.
COMEL, ELEL, ELNOEL, ELPRNOR, METEL
ANGLDG-64-NPN   ANGLIN, DG
NIGERIA -- POLITICAL NON-ALIGNMENT AND ECONOMIC
   ALIGNMENT.=
THE JOURNAL OF MODERN AFRICAN STUDIES, 2, (JULY 1964),        64
   PP. 247-263.
ELNOEL, ELPRNOR
ANINDS-57-WRD   ANINE, DS
WILL RUSSIA DEBOLSHEVIZE.=
PROBLEMS OF COMMUNISM, 6, (MAY-JUNE 1957), PP. 9-14.          57
ELEL
ANNAN  -66-EEG   ANNAN, N
END OF AN ELITE (GREAT BRITAIN).=
ENCOUNTER, 26, (JUNE 1966), PP. 10-13.                        66
COMEL, ELEL, ELNOEL
ANON   -52-CCP   ANONYMOUS
THE CHINESE COMMUNISTS AND THE PEASANTS.=
PROBLEMS OF COMMUNISM, 1, (JANUARY-FEBRUARY 1952),            52
   PP. 1-8.
ELNOEL
ANON   -53-API   ANONYMOUS
THE ARMY AND POLITICS IN INDONESIA.=
THE WORLD TODAY, 9, (FEBRUARY 1953), PP. 50-52.               53
ELEL
ANON   -53-IMG   ANONYMOUS
IRAQ -- A MILITARY GOVERNMENT WITH A DIFFERENCE.=
THE WORLD TODAY, 9, (JANUARY 1953), PP. 8-11.                 53
COMEL, ELNOEL
ANON   -53-PRP   ANONYMOUS
PRAVDA ON THE ROLE OF THE PARTY AND THE INDIVIDUAL
   (SOVIET UNION).=

                         SOVIET STUDIES, 5, (OCTOBER 1953), PP. 247-268.            53
                         ELNOEL, ELPRNOR
ANON   -54-ASS   ANONYMOUS
                 THE ARMY AND THE SUPREME SOVIET.=
                 BULLETIN OF THE INSTITUTE FOR THE STUDY OF THE HISTORY      54
                    AND CULTURE OF THE USSR, 1, (APRIL 1954), PP. 23-26.
                 COMEL, ELEL
ANON   -54-BAA   ANONYMOUS
                 THE BERIA AFFAIR AND THE ARMY (SOVIET UNION).=
                 BULLETIN OF THE INSTITUTE FOR THE STUDY OF THE HISTORY      54
                    AND CULTURE OF THE USSR, SPECIAL EDITION (MARCH 1954),
                    PP. 35-36.
                 ELEL
ANON   -54-DLS   ANONYMOUS
                 DECENTRALIZATION OF LEADERSHIP (SOVIET UNION).=
                 BULLETIN OF THE INSTITUTE OF THE STUDY OF THE HISTORY       54
                    AND CULTURE OF THE USSR, 1, (MAY 1954), PP. 27-28.
                 ELEL, ELNOEL
ANON   -54-RAH   ANONYMOUS
                 THE RED ARMY HIGH COMMAND (SOVIET UNION).=
                 BULLETIN OF THE INSTITUTE OF THE STUDY OF THE HISTORY       54
                    AND CULTURE OF THE USSR, 1, (MAY 1954), PP. 25-27.
                 COMEL
ANON   -55-KSY   ANONYMOUS
                 THE KOMSOMOL AND SOVIET YOUTH.=
                 BULLETIN OF THE INSTITUTE FOR THE STUDY OF THE HISTORY      55
                    AND CULTURE OF THE USSR, 2, (JULY 1955), PP. 45-50.
                 ELNOEL, ELPRNOR
ANON   -55-PPT   ANONYMOUS
                 PARTY POLITICAL TRAINING IN THE SOVIET UNION.=
                 BULLETIN OF THE INSTITUTE FOR THE STUDY OF THE HISTORY      55
                    OF THE USSR, 2, (AUGUST 1955), PP. 29-32.
                 COMEL, ELEL
ANON   -55-STD   ANONYMOUS
                 SIX TRIAL DEFINITIONS -- CONURBATION, ELITE, MIGRATION
                    PROGRESS, SLUM, UNEMPLOYMENT.=
                 INTERNATIONAL SOCIAL SCIENCE BULLETIN, 7, (1955),          55
                    PP. 472-483.
                 DEFEL
ANON   -56-SCP   ANONYMOUS
                 THE SOVIET COMMUNIST PARTY'S POLICY TOWARD SOVIET YOUTH.=
                 BULLETIN INSTITUTE FOR THE STUDY OF THE USSR, 3,           56
                    (APRIL 1956), PP. 35-39.
                 ELNOEL, ELPRNOR
ANON   -56-SCT   ANONYMOUS
                 THE SOCIAL COMPOSITION OF THE TWENTIETH PARTY CONGRESS
                    (SOVIET UNION).=
                 BULLETIN INSTITUTE FOR THE STUDY OF THE USSR, 3,           56
                    (MAY 1956), PP. 30-33.
                 COMEL
ANON   -57-CDD   ANONYMOUS
                 THE CENTRALIZATION - DECENTRALIZATION DILEMMA
                    (SOVIET UNION).=
                 BULLETIN INSTITUTE FOR THE STUDY OF THE USSR, 4,           57
                    (APRIL 1957), PP. 27-31.
                 ELEL, ELNOEL, ELPRNOR
ANON   -57-CPP   ANONYMOUS
                 THE COMMUNIST PARTY AND THE PEASANTRY (SOVIET UNION).=
                 BULLETIN INSTITUTE FOR THE STUDY OF THE USSR, 4,           57
                    (JULY 1957), PP. 47-54.
                 ELNOEL, ELPRNOR
ANON   -57-CSS   ANONYMOUS
                 THE CLASS STRUCTURE OF THE SOVIET UNION.=
                 BULLETIN INSTITUTE FOR THE STUDY OF THE USSR, 4,           57
                    (JANUARY 1957), PP. 46-53.
                 COMEL
ANON   -57-LAC   ANONYMOUS
                 THE LEGAL ASPECTS OF THE CHANGES IN SOVIET INDUSTRIAL
                    ADMINISTRATION.=
                 BULLETIN INSTITUTE FOR THE STUDY OF THE USSR, 4,           57
                    (JULY 1957), PP. 29-37.
                 ELNOEL, ELPRNOR
ANON   -57-LPE   ANONYMOUS
                 LEADING PERSONALITIES IN EASTERN EUROPE -- BULGARIA,
                    CZECHOSLOVAKIA, HUNGARY, POLAND, ROMANIA.=
                 WEST NEW YORK, NEW JERSEY, INTERCONTINENTAL PRESS          57
                    SERVICE, 1957.
                 COMEL
ANON   -57-LPP   ANONYMOUS
                 LEADING POSITIONS AND PERSONALITIES IN THE COMMUNIST
                    PARTY OF THE SOVIET UNION AND THE SOVIET GOVERNMENT.=
                 BULLETIN OF THE INSTITUTE FOR THE STUDY OF THE USSR,       57
                    SUPPLEMENT, (OCTOBER 1957), PP. 1-15.
                 COMEL

ANON   -57-SLC   ANONYMOUS
                 A SHORT-LIVED CABINET (JAPAN).=
                 JAPAN QUARTERLY, 4, (APRIL-JUNE 1957), PP. 135-141.          57
                 ELEL
ANON   -58-IFC   ANONYMOUS
                 THE INTELLECTUAL FERMENT CONTINUES (SOVIET UNION).=
                 BULLETIN INSTITUTE FOR THE STUDY OF THE USSR, 5,             58
                    (MAY 1958), PP. 39-43.
                 ELEL, ELNOEL, ELPRNOR
ANON   -58-SCS   ANONYMOUS
                 THE SOVNARKHOZ CHAIRMAN (SOVIET UNION).=
                 BULLETIN INSTITUTE FOR THE STUDY OF THE USSR, 5,             58
                    (MAY 1958), PP. 14-18.
                 ELEL
ANON   -58-SSE   ANONYMOUS
                 THE SUPREME SOVIET ELECTIONS.=
                 BULLETIN INSTITUTE FOR THE STUDY OF THE USSR, 5,             58
                    (APRIL 1958), PP. 30-34.
                 ELEL
ANON   -58-STU   ANONYMOUS
                 THE SOVIET TRADE UNION MOVEMENT.=
                 BULLETIN INSTITUTE FOR THE STUDY OF THE USSR, 5,             58
                    (JANUARY 1958), PP. 35-40.
                 ELEL, ELNOEL, ELPRNOR
ANON   -58-YGS   ANONYMOUS
                 THE YOUNG GENERATION OF SOVIET WRITERS.=
                 BULLETIN INSTITUTE FOR THE STUDY OF THE USSR, 5,             58
                    (SEPTEMBER 1958), PP. 38-42.
                 ELPRNOR
ANON   -59-BMJ   ANONYMOUS
                 BUREAUCRACY ON THE MOVE (JAPAN).=
                 JAPAN QUARTERLY, 6, (JANUARY-MARCH 1959), PP. 1-5.           59
                 ELEL
ANON   -59-PFC   ANONYMOUS
                 THE PROCESSES OF FRAGMENTATION AND CONSOLIDATION IN
                    SUB-SAHARAN AFRICA.=
                 AFRICAN STUDIES BULLETIN, 2, (DECEMBER 1959), PP. 27-33.     59
                 ELEL, ELNOEL, ELPRNOR
ANON   -61-TOA   ANONYMOUS
                 THE TRAINING OF OFFICIALS OF THE ADMINISTRATIVE
                    ORGANS OF THE PEOPLE'S COMMITTEES (YUGOSLAVIA).=
                 INTERNATIONAL SOCIAL SCIENCE JOURNAL, 13, (1961),            61
                 COMEL, ELPRNOR
ANON   -62-MAT   ANONYMOUS
                 METROPOLITAN ADMINISTRATION IN TOKYO.=
                 PHILIPPINE JOURNAL OF PUBLIC ADMINISTRATION, 6,              62
                    (JANUARY 1962), PP. 32-43.
                 ELEL, ELNOEL
ANON   -62-UHE   ANONYMOUS
                 THE UPPER HOUSE ELECTIONS (JAPAN).=
                 JAPAN QUARTERLY, 9, (OCTOBER-DECEMBER 1962), PP. 385-388. 62
                 COMEL, ELEL
ANON   -64-PRK   ANONYMOUS
                 THE PALACE REVOLUTION IN THE KREMLIN (SOVIET UNION).=
                 BULLETIN INSTITUTE FOR THE STUDY OF THE USSR, 11,            64
                    (NOVEMBER 1964), PP. 3-4.
                 ELEL, ELPRNOR
ANON   -64-SMP   ANONYMOUS
                 THE STRUCTURE OF THE MOSCOW PATRIARCHATE (SOVIET UNION).=
                 BULLETIN INSTITUTE FOR THE STUDY OF THE USSR, 11,            64
                    (JANUARY 1964), PP. 31-42.
                 COMEL
ANTOTJ-63-PPL    ANTON, TJ
                 POWER, PLURALISM, AND LOCAL POLITICS.=
                 ADMINISTRATIVE SCIENCE QUARTERLY, 7, (1962-1963),            63
                    PP. 425-457.
                 DEFEL, METEL
APPLPH-54-BF     APPLEBY, PH
                 BUREAUCRACY AND THE FUTURE.=
                 THE ANNALS OF THE AMERICAN ACADEMY OF POLITICAL AND          54
                    SOCIAL SCIENCE, 292, (MARCH 1954), PP. 136-151.
                 DEFEL, ELEL, ELNOEL, ELPRNOR
APSLAE-45-YMW    APSLER, AE
                 THE YOUTH MOVEMENT IN THE WEIMAR REPUBLIC (GERMANY).=
                 SOCIAL SCIENCE, 20, (JANUARY 1945), PP. 31-43.               45
                 ELNOEL, ELPRNOR
APTEDE-55-GCT    APTER, DE
                 THE GOLD COAST IN TRANSITION (GHANA).=
                 PRINCETON, PRINCETON UNIVERSITY PRESS, 1955.                 55
                 ELEL, ELNOEL, ELPRNOR
APTEDE-58-CMS    APTER, DE
                 A COMPARATIVE METHOD FOR THE STUDY OF POLITICS.=
                 THE AMERICAN JOURNAL OF SOCIOLOGY, 64, (NOVEMBER 1958),      58
                    PP. 221-237.

```
                    GNELTH, DEFEL, METEL
APTEDE-59-NGE    APTER, DE
                    NATIONALISM, GOVERNMENT AND ECONOMIC GROWTH.=
                    ECONOMIC DEVELOPMENT AND CULTURAL CHANGE, 7,              59
                      (JANUARY 1959), PP. 17-36.
                    ELEL, ELPRNOR
APTEDE-60-RTP    APTER, DE
                    THE ROLE OF TRADITIONALISM IN THE POLITICAL
                      MODERNIZATION OF GHANA AND UGANDA.=
                    WORLD POLITICS, 13, (OCTOBER 1960) PP. 45-68.            60
                    ELNOEL, ELPRNOR
APTEDE-61-PKU    APTER, DE
                    THE POLITICAL KINGDOM IN UGANDA -- A STUDY OF
                      BUREAUCRATIC NATIONALISM.=
                    PRINCETON, PRINCETON UNIVERSITY PRESS, 1961.             61
                    ELEL, ELNOEL, ELPRNOR
APTEDE-62-RRP    APTER, DE
                    SOME REFLECTIONS ON THE ROLE OF A POLITICAL OPPOSITION IN
                      NEW NATIONS.=
                    COMPARATIVE STUDIES IN SOCIETY AND HISTORY, 4,           62
                      (JANUARY 1962), PP. 154-168.
                    ELEL
APTEDE-64-ID     APTER, DE (ED)
                    IDEOLOGY AND DISCONTENT.=
                    LONDON, THE FREE PRESS, 1964.                            64
                    DEFEL, COMEL, ELEL, ELNOEL, ELPRNOR
APTHR -60-IBI    APTHORPE, R
                    THE INTRODUCTION OF BUREAUCRACY INTO AFRICAN POLITICS.=
                    JOURNAL OF AFRICAN ADMINISTRATION, 12, (JULY 1960)       60
                      PP. 125-134.
                    ELEL, ELNOEL, ELPRNOR
ARANLM-57-PEL    ARANETA, LM
                    SOME PROBLEMS OF EXECUTIVE LEADERSHIP IN THE GOVERNMENT
                      (PHILIPPINES).=
                    PHILIPPINE JOURNAL OF PUBLIC ADMINISTRATION, 1,          57
                      (JULY 1957), PP. 236-240.
                    ELEL, ELPRNOR
ARCIG -55-PIL    ARCINIEGAS, G
                    POLITICAL INSTABILITY IN LATIN AMERICA.=
                    JOURNAL OF INTERNATIONAL AFFAIRS, 9, (1955), PP. 33-36.  55
                    COMEL, ELEL
ARENCM-54-CSM    ARENSBERG, CM
                    THE COMMUNITY-STUDY METHOD.=
                    THE AMERICAN JOURNAL OF SOCIOLOGY, 60, (SEPTEMBER 1954), 54
                      PP. 109-124.
                    METEL
ARENH -50-ME     ARENDT, H
                    MOB AND THE ELITE.=
                    PARTISAN REVIEW, 17, (NOVEMBER 1950), PP. 808-819.       50
                    GNELTH, ELNOEL
ARENH -56-ATC    ARENDT, H
                    AUTHORITY IN THE 20TH CENTURY.=
                    REVIEW OF POLITICS, 18, (OCTOBER 1956), PP. 403-417.     56
                    GNELTH, DEFEL
ARENH -58-OT     ARENDT, H
                    THE ORIGINS OF TOTALITARIANISM.=
                    NEW YORK, HARCOURT, BRACE, 1958.                         58
                    DEFEL, ELEL, ELNOEL, ELPRNOR
ARENH -63-R      ARENDT, H
                    ON REVOLUTION.=
                    NEW YORK, THE VIKING PRESS, 1963                         63
                    GNELTH, ELEL, ELNOEL, ELPRNOR
ARIAA -66-VII    ARIAN, A
                    VOTING AND IDEOLOGY IN ISRAEL.=
                    MIDWEST JOURNAL OF POLITICAL SCIENCE, 10, (AUGUST 1966), 66
                      PP. 265-287.
                    ELNOEL, ELPRNOR
ARMSJA-58-TPD    ARMSTRONG, JA
                    TOWARD PERSONAL DICTATORSHIP OR OLIGARCHY -- SOVIET
                      DOMESTIC POLITICS SINCE THE TWENTIETH CONGRESS.=
                    MIDWEST JOURNAL OF POLITICAL SCIENCE, 2,                 58
                      (NOVEMBER 1958), PP. 345-356.
                    ELEL, ELNOEL
ARMSJA-59-SBE    ARMSTRONG, JA
                    THE SOVIET BUREAUCRATIC ELITE -- A CASE STUDY OF THE
                      UKRAINIAN APPARATUS.=
                    LONDON, STEVENS AND SONS, 1959.                          59
                    COMEL, ELEL, ELPRNOR
ARMSJA-65-SAB    ARMSTRONG, JA
                    SOURCES OF ADMINISTRATIVE BEHAVIOR -- SOME SOVIET AND
                      WESTERN EUROPEAN COMPARISONS.=
                    THE AMERICAN POLITICAL SCIENCE REVIEW, 59, (SEPTEMBER    65
                      1965), PP. 643-655.
                    ELEL, ELNOEL, ELPRNOR
```

ARMSJA-66-PBE    ARMSTRONG, JA
                 PARTY BIFURCATION AND ELITE INTERESTS (SOVIET UNION).=
                 SOVIET STUDIES, 17, (APRIL 1966), PP. 417-430.              66
                 COMEL, ELEL
ARMSL -59-SEO    ARMSTRONG, L
                 A SOCIO-ECONOMIC OPINION POLL IN BEIRUT, LEBANON.=
                 THE PUBLIC OPINION QUARTERLY, 23, (SPRING 1959),            59
                   PP. 18-27.
                 COMEL, ELPRNOR
ARNAC -59-BSS    ARNADE, C
                 BOLIVIA'S SOCIAL REVOLUTION.=
                 JOURNAL OF INTER-AMERICAN STUDIES, 1, (JULY 1959),          59
                   PP. 341-352.
                 COMEL, ELEL, ELNOEL
ARNOGL-55-CIB    ARNOLD, GL
                 COMMUNISM AND THE INTELLIGENTSIA IN BACKWARD
                   AREAS -- RECENT LITERATURE (SOVIET UNION).=
                 PROBLEMS OF COMMUNISM, 9, (SEPTEMBER-OCTOBER 1955),         55
                   PP. 13-17.
                 ELPRNOR
ARNOGL-55-GSP    ARNOLD, GL
                 GERMANY'S POST NAZI INTELLECTUAL CLIMATE.=
                 COMMENTARY, 19, (JANUARY 1955), PP. 78-82.                  55
                 ELEL, ELNOEL, ELPRNOR
AROLR -61-PMG    AROLL, R
                 THE POLITICAL METHODS OF GENERAL DEGAULLE (FRANCE).=
                 INTERNATIONAL AFFAIRS, 37, (JANUARY 1961), PP. 19-28.       61
                 ELEL, ELNOEL, ELPRNOR
ARONR -50-PFI    ARON, R
                 POLITICS AND THE FRENCH INTELLECTUAL.=
                 PARTISAN REVIEW, 17, (JULY 1950), PP. 595-606.              50
                 ELEL, ELPRNOR
ARONR -50-SSR    ARON, R
                 SOCIAL STRUCTURE AND RULING CLASS -- 1 -- 2.=
                 THE BRITISH JOURNAL OF SOCIOLOGY, 1, (1950),                50
                   PP. 1-16, PP. 126-143.
                 GNELTH
ARONR -57-OI     ARON, R
                 THE OPIUM OF THE INTELLECTUALS.=
                 GARDEN CITY, DOUBLDAY, 1957.                                57
                 DEFEL, COMEL, ELPRNOR
ARONR -57-SST    ARON, R
                 SOVIET SOCIETY IN TRANSITION.=
                 PROBLEMS OF COMMUNISM, 6, (NOVEMBER-DECEMBER 1957),         57
                   PP. 5-10.
                 ELEL, ELNOEL, ELPRNOR
ARONR -63-GR     ARON, R
                 THE GAULLIST REPUBLIC.=
                 ENCOUNTER, 20, (MARCH 1963), PP. 4-11.                      63
                 ELEL, ELNOEL, ELPRNOR
ARTEVP-54-STS    ARTEMIER, VP
                 SELECTION AND TRAINING OF SOVIET PERSONNEL FOR TRADE
                   MISSIONS ABROAD -- THE SOVIET TRADE MISSION IN IRAN.=
                 EAST EUROPEAN FUND, RESEARCH PROGRAM ON THE USSR,           54
                   NEW YORK, 1954.
                 ELEL, ELPRNOR
ASBO  -50-TSI    ASBO
                 TRIAL OF STRENGTH IN INDO-CHINA -- THE BAO DAI
                   EXPERIMENT.=
                 THE WORLD TODAY, 6, (MARCH 1950), PP. 127-138.              50
                 COMEL, ELEL, ELNOEL
ASHFDE-60-LPN    ASHFORD, DE
                 LABOR POLITICS IN A NEW NATION (MOROCCO).=
                 WESTERN POLITICAL QUARTERLY, 13, (JUNE 1960),               60
                   PP. 312-331.
                 ELEL, ELNOEL
ASHFDE-61-CSD    ASHFORD, DE
                 A CASE STUDY IN THE DIPLOMACY OF SOCIAL REVOLUTION
                   (MOROCCO).=
                 WORLD POLITICS, 13, (APRIL 1961), PP. 423-434.              61
                 COMEL, ELPRNOR
ASHFDE-61-PCD    ASHFORD, DE
                 PATTERNS OF CONSENSUS IN DEVELOPING COUNTRIES.=
                 THE AMERICAN BEHAVIORAL SCIENTIST, 4, (APRIL 1961),         61
                   PP. 7-10.
                 ELEL, COMEL, ELPRNOR
ASHFDE-61-PCM    ASHFORD, DE
                 POLITICAL CHANGE IN MOROCCO.=
                 PRINCETON, PRINCETON UNIVERSITY PRESS, 1961.                61
                 ELEL, ELNOEL, ELPRNOR
ASHFDE-61-PGD    ASHFORD, DE
                 PATTERNS OF GROUP DEVELOPMENT IN A NEW
                   NATION -- MOROCCO.=
                 THE AMERICAN POLITICAL SCIENCE REVIEW, 55, (JUNE 1961),     61

```
                 PP. 321-332.
                 ELEL, ELNOEL, ELPRNOR
ASHFDE-61-PUI    ASHFORD, DE
                 THE POLITICAL USAGE OF 'ISLAM' AND 'ARAB CULTURE'
                    (MOROCCO).=
                 THE PUBLIC OPINION QUARTERLY. 25, (SPRING 1961),              61
                    PP. 106-114.
                 COMEL, ELPRNOR
ASHFDE-64-CNN    ASHFORD, DE
                 CONTRADICTIONS OF NATIONALISM AND NATION-BUILDING IN
                    THE MUSLIM WORLD.=
                 THE MIDDLE EAST JOURNAL, 18, (AUTUMN 1964), PP. 421-430.      64
                 ELNOEL, ELPRNOR
ASHFDE-65-BCM    ASHFORD, DE
                 BUREAUCRATS AND CITIZENS (MOROCCO, TUNISIA, PAKISTAN).=
                 THE ANNALS OF THE AMERICAN ACADEMY OF POLITICAL AND          65
                    SOCIAL SCIENCE, 358, (MARCH 1965), PP. 89-100.
                 ELNOEL, ELPRNOR
ASHFDE-65-EPA    ASHFORD, DE
                 THE ELUSIVENESS OF POWER -- THE AFRICAN SINGLE PARTY
                    STATE.=
                 ITHACA, CORNELL UNIVERSITY PRESS, 1965.                      65
                 COMEL, ELEL, ELNOEL
ASHFDE-65-MTP    ASHFORD, DE
                 MOROCCO - TUNISIA -- POLITICS AND PLANNING.=
                 SYRACUSE, SYRACUSE UNIVERSITY PRESS, 1965.                   65
                 ELEL, ELNOEL
ASHFDE-65-NDL    ASHFORD, DE
                 NEO-DESTOUR LEADERSHIP AND THE 'CONFISCATED REVOLUTION'
                    (TUNISIA).=
                 WORLD POLITICS, 17, (JANUARY 1965), PP. 215-231.             65
                 ELEL, ELPRNOR
ASHFDE-67-EVA    ASHFORD, DE
                 ELITE VALUES AND ATTITUDINAL CHANGE IN THE MAGHREB
                    (MOROCCO, ALGERIA, TUNISIA).=
                 BLOOMINGTON, THE CARNEGIE SEMINAR ON POLITICAL AND           67
                    ADMINISTRATIVE DEVELOPMENT, DEPARTMENT OF GOVERNMENT,
                    INDIANA UNIVERSITY, 1967.
                 ELEL, ELPRNOR, METEL
ATTLCR-54-CSM    ATTLEE, CR
                 CIVIL SERVANTS, MINISTERS, PARLIAMENT AND THE PUBLIC
                    (GREAT BRITAIN).=
                 THE POLITICAL QUARTERLY, 25, (OCTOBER 1954), PP. 308-315. 54
                 ELEL, ELNOEL
ATTLE -59-AMP    ATTLEE, E
                 THE ATTITUDES OF M.P.'S AND ACTIVE PEERS (GREAT BRITAIN).=
                 THE POLITICAL QUARTERLY, 30, (JANUARY 1959), PP. 29-32.      59
                 ELPRNOR
ATYEH -54-PDI    ATYEO, H
                 POLITICAL DEVELOPMENTS IN IRAN, 1951-1954.=
                 MIDDLE EASTERN AFFAIRS, 5, (AUGUST-SEPTEMBER 1954),          54
                    PP. 249-259.
                 ELEL, ELNOEL
AVAKI -59-CLY    AVAKUMOVIC, I
                 THE COMMUNIST LEAGUE OF YUGOSLAVIA IN FIGURES.=
                 JOURNAL OF CENTRAL EUROPEAN AFFAIRS, 19, (JULY 1959),        59
                    PP. 180-182.
                 COMEL
AVTOA -56-SDC    AVTORKHANOV, A
                 SOCIAL DIFFERENTIATION AND CONTRADICTIONS IN THE
                    (SOVIET) PARTY.=
                 BULLETIN INSTITUTE FOR THE STUDY OF THE USSR, 3,             56
                    (FEBRUARY 1956), PP. 3-17.
                 COMEL, ELEL
AVTOA -57-KCI    AVTORKHANOV, A
                 THE KHRUSHCHEV COUP -- ITS PROSPECTS (SOVIET UNION).=
                 BULLETIN INSTITUTE FOR THE STUDY OF THE USSR, 4,             57
                    (JULY 1957), PP. 3-7.
                 ELEL, ELNOEL
AVTOA -57-SD     AVTORKHANOV, A
                 SOVIET DECENTRALIZATION.=
                 BULLETIN INSTITUTE FOR THE STUDY OF THE USSR, 4,             57
                    (MARCH 1957), PP. 3-12.
                 ELEL, ELNOEL
AVTOA -58-KPC    AVTORKHANOV, A
                 KHRUSHCHEV AND THE PARTY CENTRAL COMMITTEE (SOVIET UNION).=
                 BULLETIN INSTITUTE FOR THE STUDY OF THE USSR, 5,             58
                    (FEBRUARY 1958), PP. 12-18.
                 ELEL
AVTOA -58-SRC    AVTORKHANOV, A
                 THE SOVIET RULING CLASS.=
                 BULLETIN INSTITUTE FOR THE STUDY OF THE USSR, 5,             58
                    (SEPTEMBER 1958), PP. 3-16.
                 COMEL, ELEL, ELNOEL, ELPRNOR
```

AVTOA -59-KAT    AVTORKHANOV, A
                 KHRUSHCHEV AFTER THE TWENTY-FIRST PARTY CONGRESS
                    (SOVIET UNION).=
                 BULLETIN INSTITUTE FOR THE STUDY OF THE USSR,                    59
                    6, (APRIL 1959), PP. 3-15.
                 ELEL
AVTOA -59-SSC    AVTORKHANOV, A
                 STALIN AND THE SOVIET COMMUNIST PARTY.=
                 NEW YORK, FREDERICK A PRAEGER, 1959.                             59
                 ELEL
AVTOA -64-GIS    AVTORKHANOV, A
                 THE GENERAL IMPLICATIONS (SOVIET UNION, KHRUSHCHEV'S
                    FALL).=
                 BULLETIN INSTITUTE FOR THE STUDY OF THE USSR, 11,                64
                    (DECEMBER 1964), PP. 14-18.
                 ELEL, ELNOEL
AVTOA -66-CPA    AVTORKHANOV, A
                 THE COMMUNIST PARTY APPARATUS (SOVIET UNION).=
                 CHICAGO, HENRY REGNERY CO., 1966.                                66
                 COMEL, ELEL, ELNOEL, ELPRNOR
AWA,EO-64-FGN    AWA, EO
                 FEDERAL GOVERNMENT IN NIGERIA.=
                 BERKELEY, UNIVERSITY OF CALIFORNIA PRESS, 1964.                  64
                 ELEL
AZEVT -63-SCB    AZEVEDO, T
                 SOCIAL CHANGE IN BRAZIL.=
                 GAINSVILLE, FLORIDA, UNIVERSITY OF FLORIDA PRESS, 1963.          63
                 COMEL, ELPRNOR
AZRAJR-62-ICW    AZRAEL, JR
                 IS COERCION WITHERING AWAY (SOVIET UNION).=
                 PROBLEMS OF COMMUNISM, 11, (NOVEMBER-DECEMBER 1962),             62
                    PP. 9-17.
                 ELEL, ELNOEL, ELPRNOR
AZRAJR-63-PMS    AZRAEL, JR
                 POLITICS AND MANAGEMENT (SOVIET UNION).=
                 SURVEY--A JOURNAL OF SOVIET AND EAST EUROPEAN STUDIES,           63
                    49, (OCTOBER 1963), PP. 90-101.
                 ELEL, ELPRNOR
AZRAJR-66-MPS    AZRAEL, JR
                 MANAGERIAL POWER AND SOVIET POLITICS.=
                 CAMBRIDGE, HARVARD UNIVERSITY PRESS, 1966.                       66
                 COMEL, ELEL, ELPRNOR
BABBI -53-DLU    BABBITT, I
                 DEMOCRACY AND LEADERSHIP (UNITED STATES).=
                 BOSTON, HOUGHTON MIFFLIN COMPANY, 1953.                          53
                 ELEL, ELNOEL
BACCMK-67-RBP    BACCHUS, MK
                 RELATIONSHIP BETWEEN PROFESSIONAL AND ADMINISTRATIVE
                    OFFICERS IN A GOVERNMENT DEPARTMENT DURING A PERIOD
                    OF ADMINISTRATIVE CHANGE (GUYANA).=
                 THE SOCIOLOGICAL REVIEW, 15, (JULY 1967), PP. 155-178.           67
                 ELEL, ELPRNOR
BACHP -62-ECD    BACHRACH, P
                 ELITE CONSENSUS AND DEMOCRACY (UNITED STATES).=
                 THE JOURNAL OF POLITICS, 24, (AUGUST 1962), PP. 439-452.    62
                 GNELTH, ELEL, ELNOEL
BACHP -62-TFP    BACHRACH, P             BARATZ, MS
                 TWO FACES OF POWER.=
                 THE AMERICAN POLITICAL SCIENCE REVIEW, 56,                       62
                    (DECEMBER 1962), PP. 947-952.
                 GNELTH, COMEL
BACHP -67-TDE    BACHRACH, P
                 THE THEORY OF DEMOCRATIC ELITISM.=
                 BOSTON, LITTLE, BROWN AND COMPANY, 1967.                         67
                 GNELTH, DEFEL, ELEL, ELNOEL, ELPRNOR
BADGJH-58-BSP    BADGLEY, JH
                 BURMA'S POLITICAL CRISIS.=
                 PACIFIC AFFAIRS, 31, (DECEMBER 1958), PP. 336-351.               58
                 ELEL, ELNOEL
BADGJH-61-BSR    BADGLEY, JH
                 BURMA'S RADICAL LEFT -- A STUDY IN FAILURE.=
                 PROBLEMS OF COMMUNISM, 10, (MARCH-APRIL 1961), PP. 47-55. 61
                 ELEL
BAERHH-59-PJL    BAERWALD, HH
                 THE PURGE OF JAPANESE LEADERS UNDER THE OCCUPATION.=
                 BERKELEY, UNIVERSITY OF CALIFORNIA PRESS, 1959.                  59
                 ELEL, ELNOEL
BAERHH-64-PPJ    BAERWALD, HH
                 PARLIAMENT AND PARLIAMENTARIANS IN JAPAN.=
                 PACIFIC AFFAIRS, 37, (FALL 1964), PP. 271-282.                   64
                 ELEL, ELPRNOR
BAHRHP-60-PTI    BAHRDT, HP
                 THE PLACE OF THE TECHNICIAN - INTELLIGENTSIA IN
                    SOCIETY.=

426

THE AMERICAN BEHAVIORAL SCIENTIST, 3, (JANUARY 1960),          60
    P. 7.
ELEL, ELNOEL
BAHRHP-61-SRT   BAHRDT, HP
THE SOCIAL ROLE OF THE TECHNICIAN - INTELLIGENTSIA IN
    SOCIETY.=
THE AMERICAN BEHAVIORAL SCIENTIST, 4, (JANUARY 1961),          61
    PP. 34-35.
COMEL, ELEL, ELNOEL
BAILFG-60-TCN   BAILEY, FG
TRIBE, CASTE, AND NATION (INDIA).=
MANCHESTER, ENGLAND, MANCHESTER UNIVERSITY PRESS, 1960.        60
DEFEL, COMEL, ELEL, ELNOEL, ELPRNOR
BAILFG-60-TSR   BAILEY, FG
TRADITIONAL SOCIETY AND REPRESENTATION -- A CASE STUDY IN
    ORISSA (INDIA).=
EUROPEAN JOURNAL OF SOCIOLOGY, 1, (1960), PP. 121-141.         60
ELEL, ELNOEL, ELPRNOR
BAILFG-63-PSC   BAILEY, FG
POLITICS AND SOCIAL CHANGE, ORISSA (INDIA) IN 1959.=
BERKELEY, UNIVERSITY OF CALIFORNIA PRESS, 1963.               63
ELEL, ELNOEL, ELPRNOR
BAILNA-65-CBH   BAILEY, NA
THE COLUMBIAN 'BLACK HAND' -- A CASE STUDY OF
    NEOLIBERALISM IN LATIN AMERICA.=
THE REVIEW OF POLITICS, 27, (OCTOBER 1965), PP. 445-464.  65
COMEL, ELEL, ELPRNOR
BAILS -65-ULS   BAILER, S
AN UNSTABLE LEADERSHIP (SOVIET UNION).=
PROBLEMS OF COMMUNISM, 14, JULY-AUGUST 1965), PP. 72-74.  65
ELEL
BAILSD-52-PPP   BAILEY, SD (ED)
POLITICAL PARTIES AND THE PARTY SYSTEM IN BRITAIN.=
NEW YORK, FREDERICK A PRAEGER, 1952.                         52
COMEL, ELEL, ELNOEL, ELPRNOR
BAILSD-62-SUN   BAILEY, SD
THE SECRETARIAT OF THE UNITED NATIONS.=
NEW YORK, CARNEGIE ENDOWMENT FOR INTERNATIONAL PEACE,     62
    1962.
COMEL, ELEL, ELPRNOR
BAILSK-52-CWU   BAILEY, SK        SAMUEL, HD
CONGRESS AT WORK (UNITED STATES).=
NEW YORK, HENRY HOLT AND COMPANY, INC, 1952.              52
COMEL, ELEL, ELNOEL
BAILSK-66-NCU   BAILEY, SK
THE NEW CONGRESS (UNITED STATES).=
NEW YORK, ST. MARTIN'S PRESS, 1966.                       66
COMEL, ELEL, ELNOEL, ELPRNOR
BAKEJC-45-DTF   BAKER, JC
DIRECTORS AND THEIR FUNCTIONS (UNITED STATES).=
CAMBRIDGE, HARVARD UNIVERSITY PRESS, 1945.                45
COMEL, ELEL, ELNOEL, ELPRNOR
BALAK -56-IPF   BALARAMAN, K
THE INDIAN PRESS AND FOREIGN POLICY.=
JOURNAL OF INTERNATIONAL AFFAIRS, 10, (1956),             56
    PP. 178-184.
ELEL
BALDDA-66-CIF   BALDWIN, DA
CONGRESSIONAL INITIATIVE IN FOREIGN POLICY
    (UNITED STATES).=
THE JOURNAL OF POLITICS, 28, (NOVEMBER 1966),             66
    PP. 754-773.
ELEL, ELPRNOR
BALDG -63-FEI   BALDWIN, G
THE FOREIGN-EDUCATED IRANIAN -- A PROFILE.=
THE MIDDLE EAST JOURNAL, 17, (SUMMER 1963), PP. 238-244.  63
COMEL
BALDHW-55-SN    BALDWIN, HW
THE SOVIET NAVY.=
FOREIGN AFFAIRS, 33, (JULY 1955), PP. 587-604.            55
COMEL, ELEL
BALLWB-61-PIR   BALLIS, WB
POLITICAL IMPLICATIONS OF RECENT SOVIET ECONOMIC
    REORGANIZATIONS.=
THE REVIEW OF POLITICS, 23, (APRIL 1961), PP. 153-171.    61
ELEL
BALLWM-56-DMP   BALL, WM
DUTIES OF A MEMBER OF PARLIAMENT (GREAT BRITAIN).=
PARLIAMENTARY AFFAIRS, 9, (SPRING 1956), PP. 238-244.     56
ELEL, ELNOEL
BALMDG-62-RPL   BALMER, DG
THE ROLE OF POLITICAL LEADERSHIP IN THE PASSAGE OF
    OREGON'S MIGRATORY LABOR LEGISLATION (UNITED STATES).=
THE WESTERN POLITICAL QUARTERLY, 15, (MARCH 1962),        62

```
                         PP. 146-156.
                         COMEL, ELEL
BALTED-58-PGM   BALTZELL, ED
                PHILADELPHIA GENTLEMEN -- THE MAKING OF A
                   NATIONAL ELITE (UNITED STATES).=
                GLENCOE, THE FREE PRESS, 1958.                          58
                DEFEL, COMEL, ELEL, ELNOEL, ELPRNOR
BALTED-65-PEA   BALTZELL, ED
                THE PROTESTANT ESTABLISHMENT -- ARISTOCRACY AND CAST IN
                   AMERICA.=
                NEW YORK, RANDOM HOUSE, 1965.                           65
                COMEL, ELEL, ELNOEL, ELPRNOR
BANFEC-58-MBB   BANFIELD, EC
                THE MORAL BASIS OF A BACKWARD SOCIETY (ITALY).=
                GLENCOE, THE FREE PRESS, 1958.                          58
                ELNOEL, ELPRNOR
BANFEC-61-PIU   BANFIELD, EC
                POLITICAL INFLUENCE (UNITED STATES).=
                NEW YORK, THE FREE PRESS, 1961.                         61
                DEFEL, COMEL, ELEL, ELNOEL, ELPRNOR
BANFEC-63-CPU   BANFIELD, EC          WILSON, JQ
                CITY POLITICS (UNITED STATES).=
                CAMBRIDGE, HARVARD UNIVERSITY PRESS, 1963.              63
                ELEL, ELNOEL, ELPRNOR
BANKMA-  -PCC   BANKS, MA
                PRIVY COUNCIL, CABINET AND MINISTRY IN GREAT BRITAIN AND
                   CANADA.=
                THE CANADIAN JOURNAL OF ECONOMICS AND POLITICAL SCIENCE,
                   31, (1965), PP. 193-205.
                COMEL, ELEL
BANTM -65-PSD   BANTON, M (ED)
                POLITICAL SYSTEM AND THE DISTRIBUTION OF POWER.=
                NEW YORK, FREDERICK A PRAEGER, 1965.                    65
                DEFEL, COMEL, ELEL, ELNOEL, ELPRNOR
BARAMS-56-CGP   BARATZ, MS
                CORPORATE GIANTS AND THE POWER STRUCTURE (UNITED STATES).=
                THE WESTERN POLITICAL QUARTERLY, 9, (JUNE 1956),        56
                   PP. 406-415.
                ELEL
BARBB -55-SAA   BARBER, B
                SOCIOLOGICAL ASPECTS OF ANTI - INTELLECTUALISM
                   (UNITED STATES).=
                JOURNAL OF SOCIAL ISSUES, 11, (SUMMER 1955), PP. 25-30. 55
                METEL
BARBB -61-FSL   BARBER, B
                FAMILY STATUS, LOCAL - COMMUNITY STATUS, AND SOCIAL
                   STRATIFICATION -- THREE TYPES OF SOCIAL RANKING.=
                PACIFIC SOCIOLOGICAL REVIEW, 4, (1961), PP. 3-10.       61
                METEL
BARBJD-64-PLA   BARBER, JD (ED)
                POLITICAL LEADERSHIP IN AMERICAN GOVERNMENT.=
                BOSTON, LITTLE, BROWN AND COMPANY, 1964.                64
                COMEL, ELEL, ELNOEL, ELPRNOR
BARBJD-65-LRA   BARBER, JD
                THE LAWMAKERS -- RECRUITMENT AND ADAPTION TO LEGISLATIVE
                   LIFE (UNITED STATES).=
                NEW HAVEN, YALE UNIVERSITY PRESS, 1965.                 65
                DEFEL, COMEL, ELEL, ELPRNOR
BARBJD-66-LSL   BARBER, JD
                LEADERSHIP STRATEGIES FOR LEGISLATIVE PARTY COHESION
                   (UNITED STATES).=
                JOURNAL OF POLITICS, 28, (MAY 1966), PP. 347-367.       66
                ELEL
BARBJD-66-PCE   BARBER, JD
                POWER IN COMMITTEES -- AN EXPERIMENT IN THE GOVERNMENTAL
                   PROCESS (UNITED STATES).=
                CHICAGO, RAND MCNALLY, 1966.                            66
                ELEL, ELPRNOR, METEL
BARBZ -56-DDT   BARBU, Z
                DEMOCRACY AND DICTATORSHIP -- THEIR PSYCHOLOGY AND
                   PATTERNS OF LIFE.=
                NEW YORK, GROVE PRESS, 1956.                            56
                DEFEL, ELEL, ELNOEL, ELPRNOR
BARGFC-66-CRN   BARGHOORN, FC
                CHANGES IN RUSSIA -- THE NEED FOR PERSPECTIVES.=
                PROBLEMS OF COMMUNISM, 15, (MAY-JUNE 1966), PP. 39-42.  66
                ELEL, ELPRNOR
BARGFC-66-SRO   BARGHOORN, FC
                SOVIET RUSSIA -- ORTHODOXY AND ADAPTIVENESS.=
                LW PYE AND S VERBA (EDS), POLITICAL CULTURE AND         66
                   POLITICAL DEVELOPMENT, PRINCETON, PRINCETON UNIVERSITY
                   PRESS, 1966, PP. 450-511.
                COMEL, ELEL, ELNOEL, ELPRNOR
BARIJJ-57-OAS   BARITZ, JJ
```

THE ORGANIZATION AND ADMINISTRATION OF THE SOVIET
    ARMAMENT INDUSTRY.=
BULLETIN INSTITUTE FOR THE STUDY OF THE USSR,                    57
    4, (NOVEMBER 1957), PP. 12-21.
COMEL, ELEL, ELNOEL

BARIJJ-63-SAF    BARITZ, JJ
THE SOVIET ARMED FORCES.=
STUDIES ON THE SOVIET UNION, 2, (1963), PP. 16-28.              63
COMEL, ELEL

BARKR -55-TEM    BARKLEY, R
THE THEORY OF THE ELITE AND THE METHODOLOGY OF POWER.=
SCIENCE AND SOCIETY, 19, (SPRING 1955), PP. 97-106.            55
GNELTH, DEFEL, METEL

BARNAD-51-MPO    BARNETT, AD
MASS POLITICAL ORGANIZATIONS IN COMMUNIST CHINA.=
THE ANNALS OF THE AMERICAN ACADEMY OF POLITICAL AND           51
    SOCIAL SCIENCE, 277, (SEPTEMBER 1951), PP. 76-88.
ELNOEL

BARNAD-57-PPC    BARNETT, AD
POLITICAL POWER IN COMMUNIST CHINA.=
JOURNAL OF INTERNATIONAL AFFAIRS, 11, (1957),                 57
    PP. 102-110.
COMEL

BARNAD-62-CCP    BARNETT, AD
COMMUNIST CHINA IN PERSPECTIVE.=
NEW YORK, FREDERICK A PRAEGER, 1962.                          62
ELEL, ELNOEL, ELPRNOR

BARNAD-66-MPC    BARNETT, AD
MECHANISMS FOR PARTY CONTROL IN THE GOVERNMENT
    BUREAUCRACY IN CHINA.=
ASIAN SURVEY, 6, (DECEMBER 1966), PP. 659-674.                66
ELEL, ELNOEL

BARNAD-66-SCC    BARNETT, AD
SOCIAL CONTROLS IN COMMUNIST CHINA.=
FAR EASTERN SURVEY, 22, (APRIL 22, 1966), PP. 45-48.          66
ELNOEL

BARNAD-66-SSA    BARNETT, AD
SOCIAL STRATIFICATION AND ASPECTS OF PERSONNEL MANAGEMENT
    IN THE CHINESE COMMUNIST BUREAUCRACY.=
THE CHINA QUARTERLY, 28, (OCTOBER-DECEMBER 1966),            66
    PP. 8-39.
ELEL, ELNOEL

BARNAD-67-CBP    BARNETT, AD
CADRES, BUREAUCRACY AND POLITICAL POWER IN CHINA.=
NEW YORK, COLUMBIA UNIVERSITY PRESS, 1967.                    67
COMEL, ELEL, ELNOEL, ELPRNOR

BARNCI-38-FE     BARNARD, CI
THE FUNCTIONS OF THE EXECUTIVE.=
CAMBRIDGE, HARVARD UNIVERSITY PRESS, 1938.                    38
ELEL, ELNOEL

BARNCI-46-FPS    BARNARD, CI
FUNCTIONS AND PATHOLOGY OF STATUS SYSTEMS IN FORMAL
    ORGANIZATIONS.=
WF WHYTE (ED), INDUSTRY AND SOCIETY,                          46
    NEW YORK, MCGRAW-HILL, 1946, PP. 207-243.
DEFEL, ELEL, ELNOEL

BARNCI-48-OM     BARNARD, CI
ORGANIZATION AND MANAGEMENT.=
CAMBRIDGE, HARVARD UNIVERSITY PRESS, 1948.                    48
DEFEL, ELEL, ELNOEL

BARNJA-60-IPC    BARNES, JA
INDIGENOUS POLITICS AND COLONIAL ADMINISTRATION WITH
    SPECIAL REFERENCE TO AUSTRALIA.=
COMPARATIVE STUDIES IN SOCIETY AND HISTORY, 2,               60
    (JANUARY 1960), PP. 133-149.
ELNOEL, ELPRNOR

BARNSH-59-PFC    BARNES, SH
THE POLITICS OF FRENCH CHRISTIAN LABOR.=
THE JOURNAL OF POLITICS, 21, (FEBRUARY 1959),               59
    PP. 105-122.
ELEL, ELNOEL, ELPRNOR

BARNSH-67-LSP    BARNES, SH
LEADERSHIP STYLE AND POLITICAL COMPETENCE (ITALY).=
LJ EDINGER (ED), POLITICAL LEADERSHIP IN INDUSTRIALIZED     67
    SOCIETIES, NEW YORK, JOHN WILEY AND SONS, 1967,
    PP. 59-83.
ELEL, ELNOEL, ELPRNOR

BARRR -59-PPM    BARRON, R
PARTIES AND POLITICS IN MODERN FRANCE.=
WASHINGTON, PUBLIC AFFAIRS PRESS, 1959.                      59
ELEL, ELNOEL

BARTEA-59-CPT    BARTH, EAT          JOHNSON, SD
COMMUNITY POWER AND A TYPOLOGY OF SOCIAL ISSUES.=
SOCIAL FORCES, 38, (OCTOBER 1959), PP. 29-32.               59

```
                  ELEL, ELPRNOR, METEL
BARTEA-59-PSN  BARTH, EAT          ABU-LABAN, B
               POWER STRUCTURE AND THE NEGRO SUB - COMMUNITY
                  (UNITED STATES).=
               AMERICAN SOCIOLOGICAL REVIEW, 24, (FEBRUARY 1959),        59
                  PP. 69-76.
                  COMEL
BARTEA-61-CIS  BARTH, EAT
               COMMUNITY INFLUENCE SYSTEMS -- STRUCTURE AND CHANGE
                  (UNITED STATES).=
               SOCIAL FORCES, 40, (OCTOBER 1961), PP. 58-63.              61
                  COMEL, ELNOEL, METEL
BARTF -59-PLA  BARTH, F
               POLITICAL LEADERSHIP AMONG SWAT PATHANS (PAKISTAN).=
               LONDON, ATHLONE PRESS, 1959.                               59
                  COMEL, ELEL, ELNOEL
BARZL -56-IIA  BARZINI, L
               ITALY AND ITS ARISTOCRACY.=
               ENCOUNTER, 6, (JANUARY 1956), PP. 15-32.                   56
                  COMEL, ELEL, ELNOEL, ELPRNOR
BASHTM-58-UAF  BASHEER, TM
               THE USE OF THE ARAB FELLAH.=
               DISSENT, 5, (SUMMER 1958), PP. 260-267.                    58
                  ELEL
BASSBM-60-LPO  BASS, BM
               LEADERSHIP, PSYCHOLOGY, AND ORGANIZATIONAL BEHAVIOR.=
               NEW YORK, HARPER AND ROW, 1960.                            60
                  GNELTH, DEFEL
BASSR -66-EEC  BASS, R
               EAST EUROPEAN COMMUNIST ELITES -- THEIR CHARACTER AND
                  HISTORY.=
               JOURNAL OF INTERNATIONAL AFFAIRS, 20, (1966),              66
                  PP. 106-117.
                  ELEL, ELNOEL
BATEFL-56-PRS  BATES, FL
               POSITION, ROLE AND STATUS -- A REFORMULATION OF
                  CONCEPTS.=
               SOCIAL FORCES, 34, (MAY 1956), PP. 313-321.                56
                  DEFEL, METEL
BATTLH-56-PSS  BATTISTINI, LH
               THE POSTWAR STUDENT STRUGGLE IN JAPAN.=
               TOKYO, CHARLES E TUTTLE COMPANY, 1956.                     56
                  COMEL, ELEL, ELNOEL
BAUEPT-47-NPM  BAUER, PT
               NATIONALISM AND POLITICS IN MALAYA.=
               FOREIGN AFFAIRS, 25, (APRIL 1947), PP. 503-517.            47
                  ELNOEL, ELPRNOR
BAUER -55-TSA  BAUER, R
               SOME TRENDS IN SOURCES OF ALIENATION FROM THE
                  SOVIET SYSTEM.=
               THE PUBLIC OPINION QUARTERLY, 19, (FALL 1955),             55
                  PP. 279-291.
                  ELNOEL
BAUER -56-HSS  BAUER, R           INKELES, A           KLUCKHOHN, C
               HOW THE SOVIET SYSTEM WORKS -- CULTURAL, PSYCHOLOGICAL,
                  AND SOCIAL THEMES.=
               CAMBRIDGE, HARVARD UNIVERSITY PRESS, 1956.                 56
                  COMEL, ELEL, ELNOEL, ELPRNOR
BAUER -63-ABP  BAUER, R           POOL, IS           DEXTER, LA
               AMERICAN BUSINESS AND PUBLIC POLICY -- THE POLITICS OF
                  FOREIGN TRADE.=
               NEW YORK, ATHERTON PRESS, 1963.                            63
                  ELEL
BAUERA-53-ISC  BAUER, RA
               THE IMPLICATIONS OF THE SUCCESSION CRISIS IN THE
                  SOVIET UNION FOR EAST-WEST RELATIONS.=
               SOCIAL PROBLEMS, 1, (OCTOBER 1953), PP. 38-43.             53
                  ELEL
BAUERA-53-PCL  BAUER, RA
               THE PSEUDO - CHARISMATIC LEADER IN SOVIET SOCIETY.=
               PROBLEMS OF COMMUNISM, 2, (NUMBERS 3-4, 1953), PP. 11-14. 53
                  ELEL, ELNOEL
BAUERA-56-PSM  BAUER, RA
               THE PSYCHOLOGY OF THE SOVIET MIDDLE ELITE.=
               C KLUCKHOHN AND HA MURRAY (EDS), PERSONALITY IN NATURE,    56
                  SOCIETY, AND CULTURE, NEW YORK, ALFRED A KNOPF, 1956,
                  PP. 633-650.
                  COMEL, ELPRNOR
BAUERA-58-IES  BAUER, RA           TSCHIRWA, B
               THE 'ILLIBERAL' EDUCATION OF SOVIET MANAGERS.=
               PROD (THE AMERICAN BEHAVIORAL SCIENTIST), 1,               58
                  (JULY 1958), PP. 3-6.
                  ELPRNOR
BAUMH -56-LMA  BAUMGARTEL, H
```

LEADERSHIP, MOTIVATIONS, AND ATTITUDES IN RESEARCH
LABORATORIES.=
JOURNAL OF SOCIAL ISSUES, 12, (1956), PP. 24-31.                    56
METEL
BAUMH -57-LSV    BAUMGARTEL, H
LEADERSHIP STYLE AS A VARIABLE IN
RESEARCH ADMINISTRATION.=
ADMINISTRATIVE SCIENCE QUARTERLY, 2, (DECEMBER 1957),              57
PP. 344-360.
ELPRNOR, METEL
BAUMRD-67-AOC    BAUM, RD
APPLES, ORANGES, AND THE COMPARATIVE STUDY OF POLITICAL
PARTIES (GHANA, INDONESIA).=
THE WESTERN POLITICAL QUARTERLY, 20, (MARCH 1967),               67
PP. 132-148.
ELEL, ELNOEL, ELPRNOR
BAUMZ -64-EGS    BAUMAN, Z
ECONOMIC GROWTH, SOCIAL STRUCTURE, ELITE FORMATION -- THE
CASE OF POLAND.=
INTERNATIONAL SOCIAL SCIENCE JOURNAL, 16, (1964),               64
PP. 203-216.
COMEL, ELEL, ELNOEL
BAYHTA-66-NES    BAYHS, TA
THE NEW ECONOMIC SYSTEM AND THE ROLE OF TECHNOCRATS IN
THE DDR (EAST GERMANY).=
SURVEY--A JOURNAL OF SOVIET AND EAST EUROPEAN STUDIES,          66
61, (OCTOBER 1966), PP. 139-152.
COMEL, ELEL
BAZEDT-63-NRA    BAZELON, DT
NON-RULE IN AMERICA.=
COMMENTARY, 36, (DECEMBER 1963), PP. 438-445.                   63
ELNOEL
BEAGE -48-SPC    BEAGLEHOLE, E
SOCIAL AND POLITICAL CHANGES IN THE COOK ISLANDS.=
PACIFIC AFFAIRS, 21, (DECEMBER 1948), PP. 384-398.              48
ELEL, ELNOEL, ELPRNOR
BEAGE -57-SCS    BEAGLEHOLE, E
SOCIAL CHANGE IN THE SOUTH PACIFIC -- RAROTONGA AND
AITUTAKI.=
NEW YORK, MACMILLAN AND CO., 1957.                              57
COMEL, ELEL, ELNOEL
BEALCP-58-SCC    BEALL, CP
SOCIAL CLASSES AND CLASS CONSCIOUSNESS IN THE USSR.=
THE WESTERN POLITICAL QUARTERLY, 11, (JUNE 1958),              58
PP. 383-385.
COMEL, ELEL, ELPRNOR
BEALHL-53-LPI    BEALES, HL
LABOUR PARTY IN ITS SOCIAL CONTEXT (GREAT BRITAIN).=
THE POLITICAL QUARTERLY, 24, (JANUARY 1953), PP. 90-98.         53
ELEL, ELNOEL, ELPRNOR
BEALRL-53-SSL    BEALS, RL
SOCIAL STRATIFICATION IN LATIN AMERICA.=
THE AMERICAN JOURNAL OF SOCIOLOGY, 58, (SEPTEMBER 1953),        53
PP. 327-339.
COMEL, ELEL, ELNOEL
BEALRL-54-MSV    BEALS, RL
THE MEXICAN STUDENT VIEWS THE UNITED STATES.=
ANNALS OF THE AMERICAN ACADEMY OF POLITICAL AND SOCIAL          54
SCIENCES, 295, (SEPTEMBER 1954), PP. 108-115.
ELPRNOR
BEATDW-62-ICG    BEATTY, DW
IDLE CLASS GOVERNMENT IN CHILE.=
CURRENT HISTORY, N.S., 42, (FEBRUARY 1962), PP. 106-113.  62
COMEL
BEATJH-64-BAF    BEATTIE, JHM
BUNYORO -- AN AFRICAN FEUDALITY.=
JOURNAL OF AFRICAN HISTORY, 5, (1964), PP. 25-35.              64
COMEL, ELNOEL
BECKC -61-PCB    BECK, C
PARTY CONTROL AND BUREAUCRATIZATION IN CZECHOSLOVAKIA.=
THE JOURNAL OF POLITICS, 23, (MAY 1961), PP. 279-294.          61
ELEL, ELNOEL
BECKC -63-BPD    BECK, C
BUREAUCRACY AND POLITICAL DEVELOPMENT IN EASTERN EUROPE.=
J LA PALOMBARA (ED), BUREAUCRACY AND POLITICAL                  63
DEVELOPMENT, PRINCETON, PRINCETON UNIVERSITY
PRESS, 1963, PP. 268-300.
COMEL, ELEL
BECKC -66-PEM    BECK, C               MALLOY, JM
POLITICAL ELITES -- A MODE OF ANALYSIS.=
PITTSBURGH, ARCHIVE ON POLITICAL ELITES IN EASTERN EUROPE,66
OCCASIONAL PAPER, UNIVERSITY OF PITTSBURGH, 1966.
GNELTH, DEFEL, ELEL, ELNOEL
BECKC -67-MRB    BECK, C               STEWART, DK

                    MACHINE RETRIEVAL OF BIOGRAPHICAL DATA (EAST EUROPEAN
                       ELITES).=
                    AMERICAN BEHAVIORAL SCIENTIST, 10, (FEBRUARY 1967),          67
                       PP. 30-32.
                    METEL
BECKH -50-CSS       BECKER, H
                    CHANGES IN THE SOCIAL STRATIFICATION OF
                       CONTEMPORARY GERMANY.=
                    AMERICAN SOCIOLOGICAL REVIEW, 15, (JUNE 1950),               50
                       PP. 333-342.
                    COMEL, ELEL, ELNOEL
BECKP -57-WSS       BECKETT, P              SUNDERLAND, C
                    WASHINGTON STATE'S LAWMAKERS -- SOME PERSONNEL FACTORS IN
                       THE WASHINGTON LEGISLATURE (UNITED STATES).=
                    THE WESTERN POLITICAL QUARTERLY, 10, (MARCH 1957),           57
                       PP. 180-201.
                    COMEL
BECKRW-62-CLV       BECKER, RW              ET AL
                    CORRELATIVES OF LEGISLATIVE VOTING -- MICHIGAN HOUSE OF
                       REPRESENTATIVES, 1954-1961 (UNITED STATES).=
                    MIDWEST JOURNAL OF POLITICAL SCIENCE, 6, (NOVEMBER 1962), 62
                       PP. 384-396.
                    COMEL, ELNOEL, ELPRNOR
BECKTL-64-PBM       BECKER, TL
                    POLITICAL BEHAVIORALISM AND MODERN JURISPRUDENCE -- A
                       WORKING THEORY AND STUDY IN JUDICIAL
                       DECISION-MAKING (UNITED STATES).=
                    CHICAGO, RAND MCNALLY, 1964.                                 64
                    DEFEL, COMEL, ELEL, METEL
BECKTL-66-SJO       BECKER, TL
                    SURVEY AND JUDICIARIES, OR WHO'S AFRAID OF THE PURPLE
                       CURTAIN (UNITED STATES).=
                    LAW AND SOCIETY REVIEW, 1, (NOVEMBER 1966), PP. 133-143.  66
                    METEL
BEERSH-52-CPG       BEER, SH
                    THE CONSERVATIVE PARTY OF GREAT BRITAIN.=
                    THE JOURNAL OF POLITICS, 14, (FEBRUARY 1952), PP. 41-71.  52
                    ELEL, ELNOEL
BEERSH-56-PGP       BEER, SH
                    PRESSURE GROUPS AND PARTIES IN BRITAIN.=
                    THE AMERICAN POLITICAL SCIENCE REVIEW, 50,                   56
                       (MARCH 1956), PP. 1-23.
                    ELEL
BEERSH-57-RIB       BEER, SH
                    REPRESENTATION OF INTERESTS IN BRITISH
                       GOVERNMENT -- HISTORICAL BACKGROUND.=
                    THE AMERICAN POLITICAL SCIENCE REVIEW, 51, (SEPTEMBER        57
                       1957), PP. 613-650.
                    ELEL, ELNOEL
BEERSH-57-TCG       BEER, SH
                    TREASURY CONTROL (GREAT BRITAIN).=
                    2ND ED, OXFORD, CLARENDON PRESS, 1957.                       57
                    ELEL, ELPRNOR
BEERSH-58-GRB       BEER, SH
                    GROUP REPRESENTATION IN BRITAIN AND THE UNITED STATES.=
                    ANNALS OF THE AMERICAN ACADEMY OF POLITICAL AND SOCIAL       58
                       SCIENCE, 319, (SEPTEMBER 1958), PP. 130-140.
                    ELEL, ELNOEL
BEERSH-65-BPC       BEER, SH
                    BRITISH POLITICS IN THE COLLECTIVIST AGE.=
                    NEW YORK, ALFRED A KNOPF, 1965.                              65
                    DEFEL, ELEL, ELNOEL, ELPRNOR
BEHRE -59-FAP       BEHR, E
                    THE FRENCH ARMY AS A POLITICAL AND SOCIAL FACTOR.=
                    INTERNATIONAL AFFAIRS, 35, (OCTOBER 1959),                   59
                       PP. 438-446.
                    ELEL, ELNOEL
BELIWA-64-INC       BELING, WA
                    SOME IMPLICATIONS OF THE NEW CONSTITUTIONAL MONARCHY
                       IN MOROCCO.=
                    THE MIDDLE EAST JOURNAL, 18, (SPRING 1964), PP. 163-179.  64
                    ELEL, ELNOEL
BELKGM-56-PPR       BELKNAP, GM             SMUCKLER, R
                    POLITICAL POWER RELATIONS IN A MID-WEST CITY
                       (UNITED STATES).=
                    THE PUBLIC OPINION QUARTERLY, 20, (SPRING 1956),             56
                       PP. 73-81.
                    COMEL, ELEL
BELKGM-58-MAL       BELKNAP, GM
                    A METHOD FOR ANALYZING LEGISLATIVE BEHAVIOR
                       (UNITED STATES).=
                    MIDWEST JOURNAL OF POLITICAL SCIENCE, 2, (NOVEMBER 1958), 58
                       PP. 377-402.
                    ELPRNOR, METEL

BELKGM-58-SLB    BELKNAP, GM
                 SCALING LEGISLATIVE BEHAVIOR (UNITED STATES).=
                 MIDWEST JOURNAL OF POLITICAL SCIENCE, 2, (NOVEMBER 1958), 58
                    PP. 377-402.
                 METEL
BELLD -48-SLD    BELL, D
                 SCREENING LEADERS IN A DEMOCRACY.=
                 COMMENTARY, 5, (APRIL 1948), PP. 368-375.                    48
                 DEFEL, COMEL, ELPRNOR
BELLD -55-BMH    BELL, D
                 BOLSHEVIK MAN, HIS MOTIVATIONS.=
                 COMMENTARY, 19, (FEBRUARY 1955), PP. 179-187.                55
                 ELNOEL, ELPRNOR
BELLD -55-NAR    BELL, D (ED)
                 THE NEW AMERICAN RIGHT.=
                 NEW YORK, CRITERION PRESS, 1955.                             55
                 DEFEL, COMEL, ELEL, ELNOEL, ELPRNOR
BELLD -56-TMS    BELL, D
                 THEORY OF MASS SOCIETY.=
                 COMMENTARY, 22, (JULY 1956), PP. 75-83.                      56
                 GNELTH, COMEL
BELLD -58-PER    BELL, D
                 THE POWER ELITE -- RECONSIDERED (UNITED STATES).=
                 THE AMERICAN JOURNAL OF SOCIOLOGY, 64, (NOVEMBER 1958),      58
                    PP. 238-250.
                 DEFEL, ELEL, METEL
BELLD -62-EIE    BELL, D
                 THE END OF IDEOLOGY -- ON THE EXHAUSTION OF POLITICAL
                    IDEAS IN THE FIFTIES (UNITED STATES).=
                 NEW YORK, COLLIER BOOKS, 1962.                               62
                 GNELTH, DEFEL, ELEL, ELNOEL, ELPRNOR
BELLD -65-NAD    BELL, D
                 NOTES ON AUTHORITARIAN AND DEMOCRATIC LEADERSHIP.=
                 AW GOULDNER (ED), STUDIES IN LEADERSHIP, NEW YORK,           65
                    RUSSELL AND RUSSELL, 1965, PP. 395-408.
                 GNELTH
BELLW -60-AJE    BELL, W
                 ATTITUDES OF JAMAICAN ELITES TOWARDS THE
                    WEST INDIAN FEDERATION.=
                 ANNALS OF THE NEW YORK ACADEMY OF SCIENCE ,83,               60
                    (1960), PP. 862-879.
                 ELPRNOR
BELLW -60-IUS    BELL, W
                 IMAGES OF THE UNITED STATES AND THE SOVIET UNION
                    HELD BY JAMAICAN ELITE GROUPS.=
                 WORLD POLITICS, 12, (JANUARY 1960), PP. 225-248.             60
                 COMEL, ELEL, ELPRNOR
BELLW -61-PLU    BELL, W            HILL, R              WRIGHT, C
                 PUBLIC LEADERSHIP (UNITED STATES).=
                 SAN FRANCISCO, CHANDLER PUBLISHING, 1961.                    61
                 ELEL, ELNOEL, METEL
BELLW -62-EAE    BELL, W
                 EQUALITY AND ATTITUDES OF ELITES IN JAMAICA.=
                 SOCIAL AND ECONOMIC STUDIES, 11, (1962), PP. 409-432.        62
                 ELPRNOR
BELLW -64-JLP    BELL, W
                 JAMAICAN LEADERS -- POLITICAL ATTITUDES IN A NEW NATION.=
                 BERKELEY, UNIVERSITY OF CALIFORNIA PRESS, 1964.              64
                 COMEL, ELEL, ELPRNOR, METEL
BELLW -65-SCE    BELL, W
                 SOCIAL CHANGE AND ELITES IN AN EMERGENT NATION (JAMAICA).=
                 HR BARRINGER ET AL EDS, SOCIAL CHANGE IN DEVELOPING AREAS,65
                    CAMBRIDGE, SCHENKMAN PUBLISHING CO., 1965,
                    PP. 155-204.
                 COMEL, ELEL
BELOM -53-PPU    BELOFF, M
                 PREPARING FOR POLITICS (UNITED STATES).=
                 PARLIAMENTARY AFFAIRS, 6, (SPRING 1953), PP. 207-210.        53
                 COMEL
BELOM -54-ICR    BELOFF, M
                 INTELLECTUAL CLASSES AND RULING CLASSES IN FRANCE.=
                 OCCIDENTE, 10, (JANUARY-FEBRUARY 1954), PP. 54-64.           54
                 COMEL, ELPRNOR
BENDHJ-49-LCN    BENDA, HJ
                 THE LEGISLATIVE COUNCIL (NEW ZEALAND).=
                 JOURNAL OF POLITICAL SCIENCE, 1, (MARCH 1949), PP. 24-35. 49
                 ELEL, ELNOEL
BENDHJ-58-CRS    BENDA, HJ
                 THE CRESCENT AND THE RISING SUN -- INDONESIAN ISLAM
                    UNDER THE JAPANESE OCCUPATION 1942-1945.=
                 THE HAGUE AND BANDUNG, W VAN HOEVE, 1958.                    58
                 ELEL, ELNOEL, ELPRNOR
BENDHJ-60-NWI    BENDA, HJ
                 NON-WESTERN INTELLIGENTSIAS AS POLITICAL ELITES.=

AUSTRALIAN JOURNAL OF POLITICS AND HISTORY, 6,                    60
   (NOVEMBER 1960), PP. 205-218.
COMEL, ELEL, ELNOEL, ELPRNOR
BENDHJ-61-IPW   BENDA, HJ
INTELLECTUALS AND POLITICS IN WESTERN HISTORY (EUROPE).=
BUCKNELL REVIEW, 10, (MAY 1961), PP. 1-15.                        61
COMEL, ELEL, ELNOEL
BENDHJ-64-PEC   BENDA, HJ
POLITICAL ELITES IN COLONIAL SOUTHEAST ASIA -- AN
   HISTORICAL ANALYSIS.=
COMPARATIVE STUDIES IN SOCIETY AND HISTORY, 7,                    64
   (APRIL 1964), PP. 233-2351.
DEFEL, COMEL
BENDHJ-65-PMC   BENDA, HJ
PEASANT MOVEMENTS IN COLONIAL SOUTHEAST ASIA.=
ASIAN STUDIES, 3, (DECEMBER 1965), PP. 420-424.                  65
ELEL, ELNOEL
BENDR -45-BPP   BENDIX, R
BUREAUCRACY AND THE PROBLEM OF POWER.=
PUBLIC ADMINISTRATION REVIEW, 5, (SUMMER 1945),                  45
   PP. 194-209.
GNELTH, ELEL
BENDR -47-BPI   BENDIX, R
BUREAUCRACY -- THE PROBLEM AND ITS SETTING.=
AMERICAN SOCIOLOGICAL REVIEW, 12, (OCTOBER 1947), PP.            47
   493-507.
GNELTH, ELNOEL
BENDR -49-HCS   BENDIX, R
HIGHER CIVIL SERVANTS IN AMERICAN SOCIETY.=
BOULDER, UNIVERSITY OF COLORADO PRESS, 1949.                     49
COMEL, ELPRNOR
BENDR -52-SSP   BENDIX, R
SOCIAL STRATIFICATION AND POLITICAL POWER.=
THE AMERICAN POLITICAL SCIENCE REVIEW, 46, (JUNE 1952),          52
   PP. 357-375.
GNELTH, ELEL, ELNOEL
BENDR -53-CSP   BENDIX, R          LIPSET, SM
CLASS, STATUS, POWER.=
GLENCOE, THE FREE PRESS, 1953.                                    53
GNELTH, DEFEL, COMEL, ELEL, ELNOEL, ELPRNOR
BENDR -57-PS    BENDIX, R          LIPSET, SM
POLITICAL SOCIOLOGY.=
CURRENT SOCIOLOGY, 6, (1957), PP. 79-169.                        57
DEFEL, METEL
BENDR -57-SMA   BENDIX, R          HOWTON, FW
SOCIAL MOBILITY AND THE AMERICAN BUSINESS ELITE
   --1 --2.=
THE BRITISH JOURNAL OF SOCIOLOGY, 8,9, (DECEMBER 1957,           57
   MARCH 1958), PP. 357-369, PP. 1-14.
COMEL
BENDR -60-SSP   BENDIX, R
SOCIAL STRATIFICATION AND THE POLITICAL COMMUNITY.=
EUROPEAN JOURNAL OF SOCIOLOGY, 1, (1960), PP. 181-210.           60
DEFEL, COMEL, ELNOEL, METEL
BENDR -65-WAG   BENDIX, R
WHO ARE THE GOVERNMENT BUREAUCRATS (UNITED STATES).=
AW GOULDNER (ED), STUDIES IN LEADERSHIP, NEW YORK,               65
   RUSSELL AND RUSSELL, 1965, PP. 330-341.
COMEL, ELEL
BENDR -67-RCL   BENDIX, R
REFLECTIONS ON CHARISMATIC LEADERSHIP.=
ASIAN SURVEY, 7, (JUNE 1967), PP. 341-352.                       67
DEFEL
BENEB -2 -SPS   BENEDICT, B
STRATIFICATION IN PLURAL SOCIETIES (MAURITIUS).=
AMERICAN ANTHROPOLOGIST, 64, (DECEMBER 1962),                    62
   PP. 1235-1246.
DEFEL, ELEL, ELNOEL
BENER -46-CSP   BENEDICT, R
THE CHRYSANTHEMUM AND THE SWORD -- PATTERNS OF
   JAPANESE CULTURE.=
BOSTON, HOUGHTON MIFFLIN COMPANY, 1946.                          46
ELEL, ELNOEL, ELPRNOR
BENNA -59-MIU   BENNIGSEN, A
THE MOSLEM INTELLIGENTSIA IN THE USSR.=
SOVIET SURVEY--A QUARTERLY REVIEW OF CULTURAL TRENDS,            59
   28, (APRIL-JUNE 1959), PP. 3-10.
COMEL, ELEL
BENNG -57-DPO   BENNETT, G
THE DEVELOPMENT OF POLITICAL ORGANIZATIONS IN KENYA.=
POLITICAL STUDIES, 5, (JUNE 1957), PP. 113-130.                  57
COMEL, ELEL, ELNOEL
BENNM -50-SCP   BENNY, M            GEISS, P
SOCIAL CLASS AND POLITICS IN GREENWICH (GREAT BRITAIN).=

```
                         BRITISH JOURNAL OF SOCIOLOGY, 1, (DECEMBER 1950),        50
                            PP. 310-326.
                         ELEL, ELNOEL
BENNP  -63-PCL    BENNO, P
                         THE POLITICS OF CURRENT LITERATURE (SOVIET UNION).=
                         STUDIES ON THE SOVIET UNION, 3, (1963), PP. 20-41.        63
                         ELPRNOR
BENNWG-58-APA     BENNIS, WG          BERKOWITZ, MA        MALONE, M
                         AUTHORITY, POWER, AND ABILITY TO INFLUENCE.=
                         HUMAN RELATIONS, 11, (1958), PP. 143-157.                 58
                         DEFEL, METEL
BENNWG-60-LTA     BENNIS, WG
                         LEADERSHIP THEORY AND ADMINISTRATIVE BEHAVIOR -- THE
                            PROBLEM OF AUTHORITY.=
                         ADMINISTRATIVE SCIENCE QUARTERLY, 4, (1959-1960),         60
                            PP. 259-301.
                         DEFEL, METEL
BENNWG-61-RTL     BENNIS, WG
                         REVISIONIST THEORY OF LEADERSHIP.=
                         HARVARD BUSINESS REVIEW, 39, (JANUARY-FEBRUARY 1961),     61
                            PP. 26-84.
                         GNELTH, ELEL, ELNOEL
BENSG  -63-MCB    BENSMAN, G          ROSENBERG, B
                         MASS, CLASS AND BUREAUCRACY -- THE EVOLUTION OF
                            CONTEMPORARY SOCIETY.=
                         ENGLEWOOD CLIFFS, NEW JERSEY, PRENTICE-HALL, 1963.        63
                         GNELTH, ELEL, ELNOEL, METEL
BENSJ  -62-PCB    BENSMAN, J          VIDICH, A
                         POWER CLIQUES IN BUREAUCRATIC SOCIETY.=
                         SOCIAL RESEARCH, 29, (WINTER 1962), PP. 467-474.          62
                         DEFEL
BENSM  -64-APL    BENSON, M
                         THE AFRICAN PATRIOTS -- LEADERSHIP OF AFRICAN
                            NATIONAL CONGRESS.=
                         JOURNAL OF AFRICAN HISTORY, 5, (1964), PP. 329.           64
                         COMEL, ELEL, ELNOEL
BENSO  -59-CPP    BENSON, O
                         CHANGING PATTERNS OF POLICY FORMATION AND
                            IMPLEMENTATION IN COMMUNIST CHINA.=
                         THE SOUTHWESTERN SOCIAL SCIENCE QUARTERLY, 40,            59
                            (SUPPLEMENT 1959), PP. 66-84.
                         COMEL, ELEL, ELNOEL
BERDRO-59-BUS     BERDAHL, RO
                         BRITISH UNIVERSITIES AND THE STATES.=
                         BERKELEY AND LOS ANGELES, UNIVERSITY OF CALIFORNIA        59
                            PRESS, 1959.
                         COMEL, ELEL, ELNOEL
BEREBR-54-VSO     BERELSON, BR        LAZARSFELD, PF       MCPHEE, WN
                         VOTING -- A STUDY OF OPINION FORMATION IN A PRESIDENTIAL
                            CAMPAIGN (UNITED STATES).=
                         CHICAGO, UNIVERSITY OF CHICAGO PRESS, 1954.               54
                         ELEL, ELNOEL, ELPRNOR
BEREGZ-60-PSE     BEREDAY, GZF        PENNAR, J
                         THE POLITICS OF SOVIET EDUCATION.=
                         NEW YORK, FREDERICK A PRAEGER, 1960.                      60
                         COMEL, ELEL
BERGCF-64-SME     BERGSTEN, CF
                         SOCIAL MOBILITY AND ECONOMIC DEVELOPMENT -- THE VITAL
                            PARAMETERS OF THE BOLIVIAN REVOLUTION.=
                         JOURNAL OF INTER-AMERICAN STUDIES, 6, (JULY 1964),        64
                            PP. 367-375.
                         COMEL, ELNOEL
BERGM  -  -BEW    BERGER, M
                         BUREAUCRACY EAST AND WEST (EGYPT).=
                         ADMINISTRATIVE SCIENCE QUARTERLY,1, (1957),PP. 518-529.
                         DEFEL
BERGM  -54-FCM    BERGER, M           ET AL (EDS)
                         FREEDOM AND CONTROL IN MODERN SOCIETY.=
                         NEW YORK, VAN NOSTRAND, 1954.                             54
                         DEFEL, ELEL, ELNOEL
BERGM  -56-BET    BERGER, M
                         THE BUSINESS ELITE -- THEN AND NOW (UNITED STATES).=
                         COMMENTARY, 22, (OCTOBER 1956), PP. 367-374.              56
                         COMEL, ELEL
BERGM  -56-PCE    BERGER, M
                         PATTERNS OF COMMUNICATION OF EGYPTIAN CIVIL SERVANTS
                            WITH THE PUBLIC.=
                         THE PUBLIC OPINION QUARTERLY, 20, (SPRING 1956),          56
                            PP. 292-298.
                         COMEL, ELEL, ELNOEL, ELPRNOR
BERGM  -57-BSM    BERGER, M
                         BUREAUCRACY AND SOCIETY IN MODERN EGYPT -- A STUDY
                            OF THE HIGHER CIVIL SERVICE.=
                         PRINCETON, PRINCETON UNIVERSITY PRESS, 1957.              57
```

```
                        COMEL, ELEL, ELNOEL, ELPRNOR, METEL
BERGM  -58-SPC   BERGER, M
                 SOCIAL AND POLITICAL CHANGE IN THE MOSLEM - ARAB WORLD.=
                 WORLD POLITICS, 10, (JULY 1958), PP. 629-638.              58
                 ELEL
BERGM  -60-MES   BERGER, M
                 MILITARY ELITE AND SOCIAL CHANGE -- EGYPT SINCE NAPOLEON.=
                 RESEARCH MONOGRAPH, PRINCETON UNIVERSITY, CENTER FOR       60
                    INTERNATIONAL STUDIES, 1960.
                 ELEL, ELNOEL
BERGPL-63-CRI    BERGER, PL
                 CHARISMA AND RELIGIOUS INNOVATION -- THE SOCIAL LOCATION
                    OF ISREALITE PROPHECY.=
                 AMERICAN SOCIOLOGICAL REVIEW, 28, (DECEMBER 1963),         63
                    PP. 940-950.
                 DEFEL
BERGV  -62-RWR   BERGHAHN, V
                 RIGHT-WING RADICALISM IN WEST GERMANY'S
                    YOUNGER GENERATION.=
                 JOURNAL OF CENTRAL EUROPEAN AFFAIRS, 22, (OCTOBER 1962),   62
                    PP. 317-336.
                 ELNOEL, ELPRNOR
BERLAA-59-PWP    BERLE-JR, AA
                 POWER WITHOUT PROPERTY (UNITED STATES).=
                 NEW YORK, HARCOURT, BRACE AND CO., 1959.                   59
                 DEFEL, ELEL, ELNOEL, ELPRNOR
BERLJS-57-FMU    BERLINER, JS
                 FACTORY AND MANAGER IN THE USSR.=
                 CAMBRIDGE, HARVARD UNIVERSITY PRESS, 1957.                 57
                 ELEL, ELNOEL, ELPRNOR
BERLJS-57-PSB    BERLINER, JS
                 A PROBLEM IN SOVIET BUSINESS ADMINISTRATION.=
                 ADMINISTRATIVE SCIENCE QUARTERLY, 1, (1956-1957),          57
                    PP. 86-101.
                 ELEL
BERMHJ-63-SSJ    BERMAN, HJ
                 THE STRUGGLE OF SOVIET JURISTS AGAINST A RETURN TO
                    STALINIST TERROR.=
                 SLAVIC REVIEW, 22, (JUNE 1963), PP. 314-320.               63
                 ELEL, ELPRNOR
BERNEL-47-ECU    BERNAYS, EL
                 THE ENGINEERING OF CONSENT (UNITED STATES).=
                 THE ANNALS OF THE AMERICAN ACADEMY OF POLITICAL AND        47
                    SOCIAL SCIENCE, 250, (MARCH 1947), PP. 113-120.
                 ELNOEL
BERNJ  -52-SPP   BERNARD, J
                 SCIENTISTS AND THE PARADOX OF POWER (UNITED STATES).=
                 SOCIAL FORCES, 31, (OCTOBER 1952), PP. 14-20.              52
                 ELEL
BERNMH-58-JFE    BERNSTEIN, MH
                 THE JOB OF THE FEDERAL EXECUTIVE (UNITED STATES).=
                 WASHINGTON, BROOKINGS INSTITUTION, 1958.                   58
                 ELEL, ELPRNOR
BERRHB-61-BHC    BERRINGTON, HB       FINER, SE
                 THE BRITISH HOUSE OF COMMONS.=
                 INTERNATIONAL SOCIAL SCIENCE JOURNAL, 13, (1961),          61
                    PP. 600-619.
                 COMEL, ELEL
BESHJM-62-USS    BESHERS, JM
                 URBAN SOCIAL STRUCTURE (UNITED STATES).=
                 NEW YORK, THE FREE PRESS OF GLENCOE, 1962.                 62
                 ELEL, ELNOEL, ELPRNOR, METEL
BESHJM-63-SSS    BESHERS, JM          REITER, S
                 SOCIAL STATUS AND SOCIAL CHANGE.=
                 BEHAVIORAL SCIENCE, 8, (JANUARY 1963), PP. 1-13.           63
                 ELEL, ELNOEL
BESHJM-63-USS    BESHERS, JM
                 URBAN SOCIAL STRUCTURE AS A SINGLE HIERARCHY.=
                 SOCIAL FORCES, 41, (MARCH 1963), PP. 223-239.              63
                 ELNOEL, METEL
BETEA  -  -CCP   BETEILLE, A
                 CASTE, CLASS AND POWER -- CHANGING PATTERNS OF
                    STRATIFICATION IN A TANJORE VILLAGE (INDIA).=
                 BERKELEY, UNIVERSITY OF CALIFORNIA PRESS, 1965.
                 COMEL, ELEL, ELNOEL, ELPRNOR
BETHLP-58-CLA    BETH, LP
                 CIVIL LIBERTIES AND THE AMERICAN SUPREME COURT.=
                 POLITICAL STUDIES, 6, (1958), PP. 134-146.                 58
                 ELEL, ELNOEL, ELPRNOR
BETHLP-61-CSP    BETH, LP             HAVARD, WC
                 COMMITTEE STACKING AND POLITICAL POWER IN FLORIDA
                    (UNITED STATES).=
                 THE JOURNAL OF POLITICS, 23, (FEBRUARY 1961), PP. 57-83.   61
                 ELEL
```

BETHMW-42-EEU    BETH, MW
                 THE ELITE AND THE ELITES (UNITED STATES, WESTERN EUROPE).=
                 THE AMERICAN JOURNAL OF SOCIOLOGY, 47, (MARCH 1942),        42
                    PP. 746-755.
                 COMEL, ELEL
BIALS -59-SCS    BIALER, S
                 THE 21ST CONGRESS AND SOVIET POLICY.=
                 PROBLEMS OF COMMUNISM, 8, (MARCH-APRIL 1959), PP. 1-9.      59
                 ELEL, ELPRNOR
BIALS -60-BAM    BIALER, S
                 'BUT SOME ARE MORE EQUAL THAN OTHERS' (SOVIET UNION).=
                 PROBLEMS OF COMMUNISM, 9, (MARCH-APRIL 1960), PP. 40-50.    60
                 COMEL, ELEL
BIALS -64-HRR    BIALER, S
                 HOW RUSSIANS RULE RUSSIA (SOVIET UNION).=
                 PROBLEMS OF COMMUNISM, 13, (SEPTEMBER-OCTOBER 1964),        64
                    PP. 45-52.
                 COMEL, ELEL, ELNOEL
BIBBJF-66-CCL    BIBBY, JF
                 COMMITTEE CHARACTERISTICS AND LEGISLATIVE OVERSIGHT OF
                    ADMINISTRATION (UNITED STATES).=
                 MIDWEST JOURNAL OF POLITICAL SCIENCE, 10,                   66
                    (FEBRUARY 1966), PP. 78-98.
                 COMEL, ELEL, ELPRNOR
BIDDJ -61-COS    BIDDEFORD, J
                 CONFLICTING ORIENTATION IN SOVIET LEADERSHIP.=
                 SIAS REVIEW, 6, (WINTER 1961), PP. 11-19.                   61
                 ELPRNOR
BIDDWW-53-CCL    BIDDLE, WW
                 THE CULTIVATION OF COMMUNITY LEADERS -- UP FROM THE
                    GRASS ROOTS (UNITED STATES).=
                 NEW YORK, HARPER AND BROTHERS, 1953.                        53
                 COMEL, ELPRNOR
BIDEAD-64-SMC    BIDERMAN, AD
                 SEQUELS TO A MILITARY CAREER -- THE RETIRED MILITARY
                    PROFESSIONAL (UNITED STATES).=
                 M JANOWITZ (ED), THE NEW MILITARY--CHANGING PATTERNS OF     64
                    ORGANIZATION, NEW YORK, RUSSELL SAGE FOUNDATION, 1964,
                    PP. 287-338.
                 COMEL, ELEL
BIERR -50-ASP    BIERSTEDT, R
                 AN ANALYSIS OF SOCIAL POWER.=
                 AMERICAN SOCIOLOGICAL REVIEW, 15, (DECEMBER 1950),          50
                    PP. 730-738.
                 GNELTH, DEFEL
BIERR -54-PA     BIERSTEDT, R
                 THE PROBLEM OF AUTHORITY.=
                 M BERGER, ET AL, (EDS), FREEDOM AND CONTROL IN MODERN       54
                    SOCIETY, NEW YORK, VAN NOSTRAND, 1954, PP. 67-81.
                 GNELTH, ELEL, ELNOEL
BILIA -65-LSS    BILINSKY, A
                 THE LAWYER AND SOVIET SOCIETY.=
                 PROBLEMS OF COMMUNISM, 14, (MARCH-APRIL 1965), PP. 62-71. 65
                 ELEL
BILIY -67-RRS    BILINSKY, Y
                 THE RULERS AND THE RULED (SOVIET UNION).=
                 PROBLEMS OF COMMUNISM, 16, (SEPTEMBER-OCTOBER 1967),        67
                    PP. 16-26.
                 COMEL, ELNOEL
BILLJ -63-SEF    BILL, J
                 THE SOCIAL AND ECONOMIC FOUNDATIONS OF POWER IN
                    CONTEMPORARY IRAN.=
                 THE MIDDLE EAST JOURNAL, 17, (FALL 1963), PP. 400-413.      63
                 COMEL, ELEL, ELNOEL
BILLJH-57-RRI    BILLINGTON, JH
                 THE RENAISSANCE OF THE RUSSIAN INTELLIGENTSIA.=
                 FOREIGN AFFAIRS, 35, (APRIL 1957), PP. 525-530.             57
                 ELEL, ELPRNOR
BILLMG-59-TRM    BILLING, MG
                 TRIBAL RULE AND MODERN POLITICS IN NORTHERN RHODESIA.=
                 AFRICAN AFFAIRS, 58, (APRIL 1959), PP. 135-140.             59
                 ELNOEL, ELPRNOR
BINDL -60-ITP    BINDER, L
                 ISLAMIC TRADITION AND POLITICS (MIDDLE EAST).=
                 COMPARATIVE STUDIES IN SOCIETY AND HISTORY, 2,              60
                    (JANUARY 1960), PP. 250-256.
                 ELEL, ELPRNOR
BINDL -61-RPP    BINDER, L
                 RELIGION AND POLITICS IN PAKISTAN.=
                 BERKELEY, UNIVERSITY OF CALIFORNIA PRESS, 1961.             61
                 ELEL, ELPRNOR
BINDL -62-IPD    BINDER, L
                 IRAN -- POLITICAL DEVELOPMENT IN A CHANGING SOCIETY.=
                 BERKELEY, UNIVERSITY OF CALIFORNIA PRESS, 1962.             62

```
                      COMEL, ELEL, ELNOEL, ELPRNOR
BINDL -64-IRM    BINDER, L
                 THE IDEOLOGICAL REVOLUTION IN THE MIDDLE EAST.=
                 NEW YORK, WILEY AND SONS, 1964.                          64
                 CCMEL, ELEL, ELNOEL, ELPRNOR
BINDL -66-EIR    BINDER, L
                 EGYPT -- THE INTEGRATIVE REVOLUTION.=
                 LW PYE AND S VERBA (EDS), POLITICAL CULTURE AND         66
                    POLITICAL DEVELOPMENT, PRINCETON, PRINCETON UNIVERSITY
                    PRESS, 1966, PP. 397-449.
                 COMEL, ELEL, ELNOEL, ELPRNOR
BINDL -66-PL     BINDER, L (ED)
                 POLITICS IN LEBANON.=
                 NEW YORK, JOHN WILEY AND SONS, 1966.                    66
                 COMEL, ELEL, ELNOEL, ELPRNOR
BINKWE-47-PCU    BINKLEY, WE
                 PRESIDENT AND CONGRESS (UNITED STATES).=
                 NEW YORK, ALFRED A KNOPF, 1947.                         47
                 ELEL
BIOBSO-52-HSE    BIOBAKU, SO
                 AN HISTORICAL SKETCH OF EGBA TRADITIONAL AUTHORITIES
                    (NIGERIA).=
                 AFRICA, 22, (1952), PP. 35-49.                          52
                 COMEL
BIRCAH-59-STP    BIRCH, AH
                 SMALL - TOWN POLITICS -- A STUDY OF POLITICAL LIFE IN
                    GLOSSOP (GREAT BRITAIN).=
                 LONDON, OXFORD UNIVERSITY PRESS, 1959.                  59
                 COMEL, ELEL, ELNOEL, ELPRNOR
BIRNI -57-WCB    BIRNBAUM, I
                 WARSAW AND THE COMMUNIST BLOC (POLAND).'
                 PROBLEMS OF COMMUNISM, 6, (MAY-JUNE 1957), PP. 30-35.   57
                 ELEL
BIRNN -55-MSR    BIRNBAUM, N
                 MONARCHS AND SOCIOLOGISTS -- A REPLY TO PROFESSOR SHILS
                    AND MR. YOUNG.=
                 THE SOCIOLOGICAL REVIEW, 3, (JULY 1955), PP. 5-23.      55
                 GNELTH
BISSTA-45-IZP    BISSON, TA
                 INCREASE OF ZAIBATSU PREDOMINANCE IN WARTIME JAPAN.=
                 PACIFIC AFFAIRS, 18, (MARCH 1945), PP. 55-61.           45
                 ELEL, ELPRNOR
BISSTA-45-SCJ    BISSON, TA
                 THE SUZUKI CABINET (JAPAN).=
                 FAR EASTERN SURVEY, 14, (MAY 1945), PP. 105-108.        45
                 COMEL
BISSTA-45-ZSW    BISSON, TA
                 THE ZAIBATSU'S WARTIME ROLE (JAPAN).=
                 PACIFIC AFFAIRS, 18, (MARCH 1945), PP. 355-368.         45
                 COMEL, ELEL, ELPRNOR
BJELSN-63-CSD    BJELAJAC, SN
                 COMMUNISM'S DISCORDANT LEADERSHIP -- MAO AND KHRUSHCHEV
                    (CHINA, SOVIET UNION).=
                 ORBIS, 7, (SUMMER 1963), PP. 386-399.                   63
                 ELEL, ELPRNOR
BLACCE-60-TRS    BLACK, CE
                 THE TRANSFORMATION OF RUSSIAN SOCIETY -- ASPECTS OF
                    SOCIAL CHANGE SINCE 1861.=
                 CAMBRIDGE, HARVARD UNIVERSITY PRESS, 1960.              60
                 COMEL, ELEL, ELNOEL
BLACR -61-AOP    BLACKWELDER, R
                 THE AGE OF ORANGE -- POLITICAL AND INTELLECTUAL LEADERSHIP
                    IN NORTH CAROLINA (UNITED STATES).=
                 CHARLOTTE, NORTH CAROLINA, WILLIAM LAFTIN, 1961.        61
                 COMEL, ELEL, ELNOEL
BLANG -53-ECC    BLANKSTEN, G
                 ECUADOR -- CONSTITUTIONS AND CAUDILLOS.=
                 BERKELEY, UNIVERSITY OF CALIFORNIA PRESS, 1953.         53
                 COMEL, ELEL, ELNOEL, ELPRNOR
BLANGI-52-CNS    BLANKSTEN, GI
                 CAUDILLISMO IN NORTHWESTERN SOUTH AMERICA.=
                 SOUTH ATLANTIC QUARTERLY, 51, (OCTOBER 1952),           52
                    PP. 493-503.
                 COMEL, ELEL, ELNOEL
BLANGI-53-PSA    BLANKSTEN, GI
                 PERON'S ARGENTINA.=
                 CHICAGO, UNIVERSITY OF CHICAGO PRESS, 1953.             53
                 COMEL, ELEL, ELNOEL, ELPRNOR
BLANGI-59-PGL    BLANKSTEN, GI
                 POLITICAL GROUPS IN LATIN AMERICA.=
                 THE AMERICAN POLITICAL SCIENCE REVIEW, 53, (MARCH 1959), 59
                    PP. 106-127.
                 COMEL, ELEL, ELNOEL
BLANLV-62-OSC    BLANKENSHIP, LV      ELLING, RH
```

ORGANIZATIONAL SUPPORT AND COMMUNITY POWER
  STRUCTURE -- THE HOSPITAL (UNITED STATES).=
JOURNAL OF HEALTH AND HUMAN BEHAVIOR, 3, (WINTER 1962),     62
  PP. 257-269.
ELEL, ELNOEL, ELPRNOR, METEL
BLANP  -62-FCP   BLANSHARD, P
FREEDOM AND CATHOLIC POWER IN SPAIN AND PORTUGAL.=
BOSTON, BEACON PRESS, 1962.                                 62
ELEL, ELNOEL
BLASSC-50-CCB   BLASIER, SC
CHILE -- A COMMUNIST BATTLEGROUND.=
POLITICAL SCIENCE QUARTERLY, 65, (SEPTEMBER 1950),          50
  PP. 353-375.
COMEL, ELEL
BLAUAP-54-ALS   BLAUSTEIN, AP        PORTER, CO
THE AMERICAN LAWYER -- A SUMMARY OF THE SURVEY
  OF THE LEGAL PROFESSION.=
CHICAGO, UNIVERSITY OF CHICAGO PRESS, 1954.                 54
COMEL, ELEL, ELNOEL
BLAUPM-54-PIA   BLAU, PM
PATTERNS OF INTERACTION AMONG A GROUP OF OFFICIALS
  IN A GOVERNMENT AGENCY (UNITED STATES).=
HUMAN RELATIONS, 7, (AUGUST 1954), PP. 337-348.             54
ELEL
BLAUPM-55-DBS   BLAU, PM
THE DYNAMICS OF BUREAUCRACY -- A STUDY OF INTERPERSONAL
  RELATIONS IN TWO GOVERNMENT AGENCIES (UNITED STATES).=
CHICAGO, UNIVERSITY OF CHICAGO PRESS, 1955.                 55
ELEL, ELNOEL, ELPRNOR
BLAUPM-64-EPS   BLAU, PM
EXCHANGE AND POWER IN SOCIAL LIFE.=
NEW YORK, JOHN WILEY AND SONS, 1964.                        64
DEFEL, ELEL, ELNOEL
BLITL  -59-PSP   BLIT, L
POLAND'S PECULIAR DICTATORSHIP.=
COMMENTARY, 28, (JULY 1959), PP. 36-41.                     59
ELEL, ELNOEL
BLOCJ  -63-FL   BLOCH-MICHEL, J
ON THE FRENCH LEFT.=
ENCOUNTER, 21, (OCTOBER 1963), PP. 53-54.                   63
COMEL, ELNOEL, ELPRNOR
BLONJ  -58-CAL   BLONDEL, J
THE CONSERVATIVE ASSOCIATION AND THE LABOUR PARTY
  IN READING (GREAT BRITAIN).=
POLITICAL STUDIES, 6, (1958), PP. 101-119.                  58
COMEL, ELEL
BLONJ  -63-VPL   BLONDEL, J
VOTERS, PARTIES, AND LEADERS -- THE SOCIAL FABRIC OF
  BRITISH POLITICS.=
BALTIMORE, PENGUIN BOOKS, 1963.                             63
COMEL, ELEL, ELNOEL, ELPRNOR
BLONJ  -67-CDM   BLONDEL, J        HALL, R
CONFLICT, DECISION-MAKING AND THE PERCEPTIONS OF LOCAL
  COUNCILLORS (GREAT BRITAIN).=
POLITICAL STUDIES, 15, (OCTOBER 1967), PP. 322-350.         67
COMEL, ELEL, ELPRNOR
BLOOL  -64-PCU   BLOOM, L
SOME PSYCHOLOGICAL CONCEPTS OF URBAN AFRICANS.=
ETHNOLOGY, 3, (JANUARY 1964), PP. 66-95.                    64
ELPRNOR
BLUMLA-57-DLP   BLUMBERG, LA        SCHULZE, RO
THE DETERMINATION OF LOCAL POWER ELITES (UNITED STATES).=
THE AMERICAN JOURNAL OF SOCIOLOGY, 63, (NOVEMBER 1957),     57
  PP. 290-296.
DEFEL, ELEL, ELNOEL, METEL
BOBRDB-   -SNS   BOBROW, DB
SOLDIERS AND THE NATION-STATE.=
THE ANNALS OF THE AMERICAN ACADEMY OF POLITICAL AND
  SOCIAL SCIENCE, 358, (MARCH 1965), PP.65-76.              65
ELEL, ELNOEL
BOBRDB-66-CRM   BOBROW, DB
THE CIVIC ROLE OF THE MILITARY -- SOME CRITICAL
  HYPOTHESES.=
THE WESTERN POLITICAL QUARTERLY, 19, (MARCH 1966),          66
  PP. 101-111.
ELEL, ELNOEL
BOCHJM-60-PSS   BOCHENSKI, JM
PHILOSOPHY STUDIES -- SUBJECT, OBJECT, AND ORGANIZATION
  (SOVIET UNION).=
SOVIET SURVEY--A QUARTERLY REVIEW OF CULTURAL TRENDS,       60
  31, (JANUARY-MARCH 1960), PP. 64-74.
ELEL, ELPRNOR
BOCHJM-66-RLC   BOCHEL, JM
THE RECRUITMENT OF LOCAL COUNCILLORS -- A CASE STUDY

(GREAT BRITAIN).=
POLITICAL STUDIES, 14, (OCTOBER 1966), PP. 360-364.                66
COMEL, ELNOEL
BOCIBR-60-PSS    BOCIURKIW, BR
THE PROBLEM OF SUCCESSION IN THE SOVIET POLITICAL
    SYSTEM -- THE CASE OF KHRUSHCHEV.=
CANADIAN JOURNAL OF ECONOMICS AND POLITICAL SCIENCE, 26,         60
    (NOVEMBER 1960), PP. 575-591.
ELEL
BOENH -54-HGG    BOENINGER, H
HITLER AND THE GERMAN GENERALS.=
JOURNAL OF CENTRAL EUROPEAN AFFAIRS, 14, (APRIL 1954),          54
    PP. 19-37.
ELEL
BOGAES-34-LL     BOGARDUS, ES
LEADERS AND LEADERSHIP.=
NEW YORK, APPLETON-CENTURY-CRAFTS, INC, 1934.                   34
GNELTH, DEFEL, COMEL, ELEL, ELNOEL, ELPRNOR
BOHAP -58-EPE    BOHANNAN, P
EXTRA-PROCESSIONAL EVENTS IN TIV POLITICAL INSTITUTIONS
    (NIGERIA).=
AMERICAN ANTHROPOLOGIST, 60, (FEBRUARY 1958), PP. 1-12.         58
COMEL
BOISJ -64-FPP    BOISSEVAIN, J
FACTIONS, PARTIES AND POLITICS IN A MALTESE VILLAGE.=
AMERICAN ANTHROPOLOGIST, 66, (DECEMBER 1964),                  64
    PP. 1275-1287.
ELEL, ELNOEL
BOLLJC-52-AEL    BOLLENS, JC
APPOINTED EXECUTIVE LOCAL GOVERNMENT, THE CALIFORNIA
    EXPERIENCE (UNITED STATES).=
LOS ANGELES, HAYNES FOUNDATION, 1952.                          52
ELEL
BOLLK -64-RSP    BOLLING, K
REPUBLIC IN SUSPENSE -- POLITICS, PARTIES, AND
    PERSONALITIES IN POSTWAR GERMANY.=
NEW YORK, FREDERICK A PRAEGER, 1964.                           64
COMEL, ELEL, ELNOEL, ELPRNOR
BOLTG -62-CSA    BOLTON, G
THE CHOICE OF SPEAKER IN AUSTRALIAN PARLIAMENTS.=
PARLIAMENTARY AFFAIRS, 15, (SUMMER 1962), PP. 355-364.         62
ELEL
BONEHA-56-CHC    BONE, HA
THE CAPITOL HILL COMMITTEES (UNITED STATES).=
PARLIAMENTARY AFFAIRS, 9, (AUTUMN 1956), PP. 388-397.          56
ELEL
BONEHA-58-PCN    BONE, HA
PARTY COMMITTEES AND NATIONAL POLITICS (UNITED STATES).=
SEATTLE, UNIVERSITY OF WASHINGTON PRESS, 1958.                 58
ELEL, ELNOEL
BONERC-62-DDP    BONE, RC
THE DYNAMICS OF DUTCH POLITICS.=
THE JOURNAL OF POLITICS, 24, (FEBRUARY 1962), PP. 23-49.       62
ELEL, ELPRNOR
BONIF -56-WIP    BONILLA, F
WHEN IS PETITION 'PRESSURE' (UNITED STATES).=
THE PUBLIC OPINION QUARTERLY, 20, (SPRING 1956),              56
    PP. 39-48.
ELEL, ELNOEL
BONIF -58-EPO    BONILLA, F
ELITES AND PUBLIC OPINION IN AREAS OF HIGH SOCIAL
    STRATIFICATION (CHILE).=
THE PUBLIC OPINION QUARTERLY, 22, (FALL 1958),               58
    PP. 349-356.
COMEL, ELEL, ELNOEL, ELPRNOR
BONIF -60-SFC    BONILLA, F
THE STUDENT FEDERATION OF CHILE -- 50 YEARS OF
    POLITICAL ACTION.=
JOURNAL OF INTER-AMERICAN STUDIES, 2, (JULY 1960),           60
    PP. 311-334.
ELEL, ELNOEL
BONIF -67-CEL    BONILLA, F
CULTURAL ELITES (LATIN AMERICA).=
SM LIPSET AND A SOLARI (EDS), ELITES IN LATIN AMERICA,        67
    NEW YORK, OXFORD UNIVERSITY PRESS, 1967, PP. 233-255.
COMEL, ELEL, ELPRNOR
BONJCM-63-CLC    BONJEAN, CM
COMMUNITY LEADERSHIP -- A CASE STUDY AND CONCEPTUAL
    REFINEMENT (UNITED STATES).=
THE AMERICAN JOURNAL OF SOCIOLOGY, 68, (MAY 1963),           63
    PP. 672-681.
COMEL, ELEL, ELNOEL, METEL
BONJCM-64-CSP    BONJEAN, CM
CLASS, STATUS, AND POWER REPUTATION.=

SOCIAL SCIENCE RESEARCH, 49, (OCTOBER 1964), PP. 69-75.     64
                     DEFEL
BONJCM-65-CLD   BONJEAN, CM        OLSON, DM
                COMMUNITY LEADERSHIP -- DECISIONS OF RESEARCH.=
                ADMINISTRATIVE SCIENCE QUARTERLY, 9, (1964-1965),            65
                     PP. 278-300.
                DEFEL, METEL
BONJCM-65-LVL   BONJEAN, CM        CARTER, LF
                LEGITIMACY AND VISIBILITY -- LEADERSHIP STRUCTURES
                     RELATED TO FOUR COMMUNITY SYSTEMS (UNITED STATES).=
                PACIFIC SOCIOLOGICAL REVIEW, 8, (SPRING 1965), PP. 16-20. 65
                GNELTH, COMEL, METEL
BONNJ -58-FLC   BONNER, J
                THE FOUR LABOUR CABINETS (GREAT BRITAIN).=
                SOCIOLOGICAL REVIEW (NEW SERIES), 6, (JULY 1958),           58
                     PP. 37-48.
                COMEL, ELEL
BONSAT-49-ECD   BONSCAREN, AT
                THE EUROPEAN CHRISTIAN DEMOCRATS.=
                THE WESTERN POLITICAL QUARTERLY, 2, (MARCH 1949),           49
                COMEL, ELPRNOR
BOOTDA-61-SDE   BOOTH, DA          ADRIAN, CR
                SIMPLIFYING THE DISCOVERY OF ELITES.=
                THE AMERICAN BEHAVIORAL SCIENTIST, 5, (OCTOBER 1961),       61
                     PP. 14-16.
                DEFEL, METEL
BOOTDA-62-PSC   BOOTH, DA          ADRIAN, CR
                POWER STRUCTURE AND COMMUNITY CHANGE (UNITED STATES).=
                MIDWEST JOURNAL OF POLITICAL SCIENCE, 6, (AUGUST 1962),     62
                     PP. 277-296.
                COMEL, ELEL, ELNOEL, METEL
BORGEF-54-FRG   BORGATTA, EF       BALES, RF         COUON, AS
                SOME FINDINGS RELEVANT TO THE GREAT MAN THEORY
                     OF LEADERSHIP.=
                AMERICAN SOCIOLOGICAL REVIEW, 19, (DECEMBER 1954),          54
                     PP. 755-759.
                DEFEL
BOSEV -64-RIC   BOSE, V
                THE ROLE OF THE INTERNATIONAL COMMISSION OF JURISTS
                     IN THE PROMOTION OF WORLD PEACE.=
                WORLD AFFAIRS, 127, (1964), PP. 153-157.                    64
                ELEL
BOTTTB-64-AEG   BOTTOMORE, TB
                THE ADMINISTRATIVE ELITE (GREAT BRITAIN, FRANCE).=
                IL HOROWITZ (ED), THE NEW SOCIOLOGY, NEW YORK, OXFORD       64
                     UNIVERSITY PRESS, 1964, PP. 357-369.
                DEFEL, COMEL, METEL
BOTTTB-64-ES    BOTTOMORE, TB
                ELITES AND SOCIETY.=
                LONDON, C A WATTS AND COMPANY, LTD, 1964.                   64
                GNELTH, DEFEL, COMEL, ELEL, ELNOEL




BOW GR-56-RPS   BOW GROUP
                RACE AND POWER -- STUDIES OF LEADERSHIP IN FIVE BRITISH
                     DEPENDENCIES.=
                LONDON, BOW GROUP, 1956.                                    56
                COMEL, ELEL, ELNOEL
BOWM  -66-RPA   BOWMAN,L           BOYNTON,GR
                RECRUITMENT PATTERNS AMONG LOCAL PARTY OFFICIALS -- A
                     MODEL AND SOME PRELIMINARY FINDINGS IN SELECTED LOCALES
                     (UNITED STATES).=
                THE AMERICAN POLITICAL SCIENCE REVIEW, 60, (SEPTEMBER       66
                     1966), PP. 667-676.
                COMEL, ELNOEL, ELPRNOR
BOWML -65-RDN   BOWMAN, L
                RACIAL DISCRIMINATION AND NEGRO LEADERSHIP PROBLEMS
                     -- THE CASE OF A NORTHERN COMMUNITY (UNITED STATES).=
                SOCIAL FORCES, 44, (DECEMBER 1965), PP. 173-186.            65
                ELEL, ELNOEL
BOWML -66-ARD   BOWMAN, L          BOYNTON, GR
                ACTIVITIES AND ROLE DEFINITIONS OF GRASSROOTS
                     PARTY OFFICIALS (UNITED STATES).=
                THE JOURNAL OF POLITICS, 28, (FEBRUARY 1966), PP. 121-143.66
                ELEL, ELNOEL, ELPRNOR
BRACKD-64-PPD   BRACHER, KD
                PROBLEMS OF PARLIAMENTARY DEMOCRACY IN EUROPE.=
                DAEDALUS, 93, (WINTER 1964), PP. 179-198.                   64
                ELEL, ELNOEL, ELPRNOR
BRADA -54-BGC   BRADY, A
                THE BRITISH GOVERNING CLASS AND DEMOCRACY.=

                CANADIAN JOURNAL OF ECONOMICS AND POLITICAL SCIENCE,     54
                   20, (NOVEMBER 1954), PP. 405-420.
                COMEL

BRADDS-65-CEP  BRADLEY, DS        ZALD, MN
                FROM COMMERCIAL ELITE TO POLITICAL ADMINISTRATOR -- THE
                   RECRUITMENT OF THE MAYORS OF CHICAGO (UNITED STATES).=
                THE AMERICAN JOURNAL OF SOCIOLOGY, 71,             65
                   (SEPTEMBER 1965), PP. 153-167.
                COMEL, ELEL, ELNOEL

BRADJR-63-NLP  BRADY, JR
                NOTES ON LEADERSHIP PROBLEMS AND PUBLIC ADMINISTRATION
                   TRAINING IN INDONESIA.=
                PHILIPPINE JOURNAL OF PUBLIC ADMINISTRATION, 7,       63
                   (JANUARY 1963), PP. 27-35.
                ELEL, ELPRNOR

BRAILE-65-RUD  BRAITHWAITE, LE
                THE ROLE OF THE UNIVERSITY IN THE DEVELOPING SOCIETY
                   OF THE WEST INDIES.=
                SOCIAL AND ECONOMIC STUDIES, 14, (MARCH 1965),        65
                   PP. 76-87.
                ELEL, ELNOEL, ELPRNOR

BRAIR - -ABS   BRAIBANTI, R (ED)
                ASIAN BUREAUCRATIC SYSTEMS EMERGENT FROM THE BRITISH
                   IMPERIAL TRADITION (INDIA, PAKISTAN, BURMA, CEYLON,
                   MALAYA, NEPAL).=
                DURHAM, DUKE UNIVERSITY PRESS, 1966.
                DEFEL, COMEL, ELEL, ELNOEL, ELPRNOR

BRAIR -61-PBJ  BRAIBANTI, R
                PUBLIC BUREAUCRACY AND JUDICIARY IN PAKISTAN.=
                J LA PALOMBARA (ED), BUREAUCRACY AND POLITICAL       61
                   DEVELOPMENT, PRINCETON, PRINCETON UNIVERSITY PRESS,
                   1963, PP. 360-440.
                COMEL, ELEL

BRAIR -63-AED  BRAIBANTI, R        SPENGLER, JJ
                ADMINISTRATION AND ECONOMIC DEVELOPMENT IN INDIA.=
                DURHAM, NORTH CAROLINA, DUKE UNIVERSITY PRESS, 1963.   63
                COMEL, ELEL, ELNOEL, ELPRNOR

BRAIR -66-HBP  BRAIBANTI, R
                THE HIGHER BUREAUCRACY OF PAKISTAN.=
                R BRAIBANTI (ED), ASIAN BUREAUCRATIC SYSTEMS EMERGENT    66
                   FROM THE BRITISH IMPERIAL TRADITION, DURHAM, DUKE
                   UNIVERSITY PRESS, 1966, PP. 209-353.
                COMEL, ELEL, ELPRNOR

BRAMEK-45-DPP  BRAMSTEDT, EK
                DICTATORSHIP AND POLITICAL POLICE (FRANCE,GERMANY,ITALY).=
                LONDON, KEGAN PAUL, TRENCH, TRUBNER, AND COMPANY, 1945.  45
                COMEL, ELEL, ELNOEL, ELPRNOR

BRANF -64-DLA  BRANDENBURG, F
                THE DEVELOPMENT OF LATIN AMERICAN PRIVATE ENTERPRISE.=
                WASHINGTON DC, NATIONAL PLANNING ASSOCIATION, 1964.     64
                ELEL, ELNOEL

BRANF -64-MMM  BRANDENBURG, F
                THE MAKING OF MODERN MEXICO.=
                ENGLEWOOD CLIFFS, NEW JERSEY, PRENTICE-HALL, INC., 1964.  64
                COMEL, ELEL, ELNOEL

BRANG -65-SEA  BRANDT, G
                SOCIO-ECONOMIC ASPECTS OF GERMAN REARMAMENT.=
                EUROPEAN JOURNAL OF SOCIOLOGY, 6, (1965), PP. 294-308.   65
                ELEL, ELPRNOR

BRANJA-65-MCL  BRAND, JA
                MINISTRY CONTROL AND LOCAL AUTONOMY IN EDUCATION
                   (GREAT BRITAIN).=
                THE POLITICAL QUARTERLY, 36, (APRIL-JUNE 1965), PP.    65
                   154-165.
                ELEL, ELNOEL, ELPRNOR

BRANJA-65-MWS  BRAND, JA
                THE MID-WEST STATE MOVEMENT IN NIGERIAN POLITICS -- A
                   STUDY IN PARTY FORMATION.=
                POLITICAL STUDIES, 13, (OCTOBER 1965), PP. 346-365.    65
                ELEL, ELNOEL

BRANRL-64-LBJ  BRANYAN, RL       LEE, RA
                LYNDON B JOHNSON AND THE ART OF THE POSSIBLE.=
                SOUTHWESTERN SOCIAL SCIENCE QUARTERLY, 45,         64
                   (DECEMBER 1964), PP. 213-225.
                ELNOEL, ELPRNOR

BRASPR-65-FPI  BRASS, PR
                FACTIONAL POLITICS IN AN INDIAN STATE -- THE CONGRESS
                   PARTY IN UTTAR PRADESH.=
                BERKELEY, UNIVERSITY OF CALIFORNIA PRESS, 1965.       65
                COMEL, ELEL, ELNOEL, ELPRNOR

BRAUG -60-FDP  BRAUNTHAL, G
                THE FREE DEMOCRATIC PARTY IN WEST GERMAN POLITICS.=
                THE WESTERN POLITICAL QUARTERLY, 13, (JUNE 1960),     60
                   PP. 332-348.

ELEL, ELPRNOR
BRAUG -65-FGI    BRAUNTHAL, G
THE FEDERATION OF GERMAN INDUSTRY IN POLITICS.=
ITHACA, NEW YORK, CORNELL UNIVERSITY PRESS, 1965.
                                                           65
COMEL, ELEL, ELPRNOR
BRAUGE-56-PEB    BRAUSCH, GE
THE PROBLEMS OF ELITES IN THE BELGIAN CONGO.=
INTERNATIONAL SOCIAL SCIENCE BULLETIN, 8, (FALL 1956),     56
     PP. 452-458.
COMEL, ELEL, ELNOEL, ELPRNOR
BRECM -66-NSM    BRECHER, M
NEHRU'S MANTLE -- THE POLITICS OF SUCCESSION IN INDIA.=
NEW YORK, FREDERICK A PRAEGER, 1966.
                                                           66
COMEL, ELEL, ELPRNOR
BRECM -67-SIR    BRECHER, M
SUCCESSION IN INDIA 1967 -- THE ROUTINIZATION OF
     POLITICAL CHANGE.=
ASIAN SURVEY, 7, (JULY 1967), PP. 423-443.                 67
COMEL, ELEL, ELPRNOR
BRETEA-63-AAS    BRETT, EA
AFRICAN ATTITUDES -- A STUDY OF THE SOCIAL, RACIAL, AND
     POLITICAL ATTITUDES OF SOME MIDDLE CLASS AFRICANS.=
JOHANNESBURG, SOUTH AFRICA INSTITUTE OF RACIAL             63
     RELATIONS, 1963.
ELPRNOR
BRETHL-53-GSD    BRETTON, HL
THE GERMAN SOCIAL DEMOCRATIC PARTY AND THE
     INTERNATIONAL SITUATION (GERMANY).=
THE AMERICAN POLITICAL SCIENCE REVIEW, 47,                 53
     (DECEMBER 1953), PP. 980-996.
ELPRNOR
BRIAR -66-RBP    BRAIBANTI, R (ED)
RESEARCH ON BUREAUCRACY OF PAKISTAN.=
DURHAM, DUKE UNIVERSITY PRESS, 1966.                       66
DEFEL, COMEL, ELEL, ELPRNOR, METEL
BRIMJH-59-CSA    BRIMMELL, JH
COMMUNISM IN SOUTHEAST ASIA -- A POLITICAL ANALYSIS.=
NEW YORK, OXFORD UNIVERSITY PRESS, 1959.                   59
ELEL, ELPRNOR
BRINC -60-ARF    BRINTON, C
THE ANATOMY OF REVOLUTION (FRANCE, GREAT BRITAIN,
     UNITED STATES, SOVIET UNION).=
NEW YORK, VINTAGE BOOKS, 1960.                             60
DEFEL, COMEL, ELEL, ELNOEL
BRITG -53-LSP    BRITT, G
LEBANON'S POPULAR REVOLUTION.=
THE MIDDLE EAST JOURNAL, 7, (JANUARY 1953), PP. 1-17.      53
COMEL, ELEL, ELNOEL
BRODA -57-SSS    BRODERSEW, A
SOVIET SOCIAL SCIENCE AND OUR OWN (SOVIET UNION,
     UNITED STATES).=
SOCIAL RESEARCH, 24, (AUTUMN 1957), PP. 253-286.           57
ELEL, ELPRNOR
BROGDW-64-PUS    BROGAN, DW
THE PRESIDENCY (UNITED STATES).=
ENCOUNTER, 22, (JANUARY 1964), PP. 3-11.                   64
ELEL, ELNOEL
BROMA -61-FPP    BROMKE, A
FROM FALANGA TO PAX (POLAND).=
SURVEY--A JOURNAL OF SOVIET AND EAST EUROPEAN STUDIES,     61
     39, (DECEMBER 1961), PP. 29-40.
ELNOEL, ELPRNOR
BROMPA-57-NSC    BROMHEAD, PA
SOME NOTES ON THE STANDING COMMITTEES OF THE
     FRENCH NATIONAL ASSEMBLY.=
POLITICAL STUDIES, 5, (JUNE 1957), PP. 140-157.            57
COMEL, ELEL
BROMV -60-TPF    BROMBERT, V
TOWARD A PORTRAIT OF THE FRENCH INTELLECTUAL.=
PARTISAN REVIEW, 27, (SUMMER 1960), PP. 480-502.           60
ELEL, ELPRNOR
BROTHM-59-SSP    BROTZ, HM
SOCIAL STRATIFICATION AND THE POLITICAL ORDER.=
THE AMERICAN JOURNAL OF SOCIOLOGY, 64, (MAY 1959),         59
     PP. 571-578.
GNELTH, COMEL, ELEL, ELNOEL, ELPRNOR
BROUM -61-PPS    BROUGHTON, M
PRESS AND POLITICS OF SOUTH AFRICA.=
CAPETOWN, PRUNELL AND SONS, 1961.                          61
ELEL, ELNOEL
BROWBE-51-AC     BROWN, BE
AMERICAN CONSERVATIVES.=
NEW YORK, COLUMBIA UNIVERSITY PRESS, 1951.                 51
COMEL, ELEL, ELNOEL, ELPRNOR

BROWBE-61-APF    BROWN, BE
                 THE ARMY AND POLITICS IN FRANCE.=
                 THE JOURNAL OF POLITICS, 23, (MAY 1961), PP. 262-278.        61
                 ELNOEL, ELPRNOR
BROWCG-8 -SL     BROWNE, CG          COHN, TS (EDS)
                 THE STUDY OF LEADERSHIP.=
                 DANVILLE, INTERSTATE PRINTERS AND PUBLISHERS, 1958.          58
                 DEFEL, METEL
BROWCV-64-GBW    BROWN, CV
                 GOVERNMENT AND BANKING IN WESTERN NIGERIA.=
                 IBADAN, OXFORD UNIVERSITY PRESS FOR THE                      64
                    NIGERIAN INSTITUTE FOR SOCIAL AND ECONOMIC RESEARCH,
                    1964.
                 ELEL
BROWEC-60-LUS    BROWN, EC
                 THE LOCAL UNION IN SOVIET INDUSTRY -- ITS RELATION WITH
                    MEMBERS, PARTY, AND MANAGEMENT.=
                 INDUSTRIAL AND LABOR RELATIONS REVIEW, 13,                   60
                    (JANUARY 1960), PP. 192-215.
                 ELEL, ELNOEL
BROWJC-58-LPE    BROWN, JC
                 LOCAL PARTY EFFICIENCY AS A FACTOR IN THE OUTCOME
                    OF BRITISH ELECTIONS.=
                 POLITICAL STUDIES, 6, (JUNE 1958), PP. 174-178.              58
                 ELEL, ELNOEL
BROWJF-61-PSB    BROWN, JF
                 THE POLITICAL SCENE (BULGARIA).=
                 SURVEY--A JOURNAL OF SOVIET AND EAST EUROPEAN STUDIES,       61
                    39, (DECEMBER 1961), PP. 80-85.
                 COMEL, ELEL, ELPRNOR
BROWJF-65-EES    BROWN, JF
                 EAST EUROPE -- THE SOVIET GRIP LOOSENS.=
                 SURVEY--A JOURNAL OF SOVIET AND EAST EUROPEAN STUDIES,       65
                    57, (OCTOBER 1965), PP. 14-25.
                 ELEL
BROWMD-59-TCI    BROWN, MD
                 TRADITIONAL CONCEPTS OF INDIAN LEADERSHIP.=
                 RL PARK AND I TINKER (EDS), LEADERSHIP AND POLITICAL         59
                    INSTITUTIONS IN INDIA, PRINCETON, PRINCETON UNIVERSITY
                    PRESS, 1959, PP. 3-18.
                 DEFEL, ELEL, ELPRNOR
BROWN -64-AMB    BROWN, N            GUTTERIDGE, WF
                 THE AFRICAN MILITARY BALANCE.=
                 LONDON, INSTITUTE OF STRATEGIC STUDIES, 1964.                64
                 COMEL, ELEL
BROWP -51-PAW    BROWN, P
                 PATTERNS OF AUTHORITY IN WEST AFRICA.=
                 AFRICA, 21, (OCTOBER 1951), PP. 261-278.                     51
                 COMEL
BROWRP-64-PMP    BROWNING, RP        JACOB, H
                 POWER MOTIVATION AND THE POLITICAL PERSONALITY
                    (UNITED STATES).=
                 THE PUBLIC OPINION QUARTERLY, 28, (SPRING 1964),             64
                    PP. 75-90.
                 ELNOEL, ELPRNOR, METEL
BROZY -54-DEA    BROZEN, Y
                 DETERMINANTS OF ENTREPRENEURIAL ABILITY.=
                 SOCIAL RESEARCH, 21, (AUTUMN 1954), PP. 339-364.             54
                 DEFEL
BRUNG -65-BEP    BRUNNER, G
                 BYLAWS OF THE ELITE -- THE PARTY STATUTE (SOVIET UNION).=
                 PROBLEMS OF COMMUNISM, 14, (MARCH-APRIL 1965), PP. 48-62. 65
                 ELEL
BRUNJS-46-BVC    BRUNER, JS          KORCHIN, SJ
                 THE BOSS AND THE VOTE -- CASE STUDY IN CITY POLITICS
                    (UNITED STATES).=
                 THE PUBLIC OPINION QUARTERLY, 10, (SPRING 1946),             46
                    PP. 1-23.
                 ELNOEL
BRYNC -49-EPS    BRYNER, C
                 THE EVOLUTION OF THE POLITBURO (SOVIET UNION).=
                 CURRENT HISTORY, N.S., 17, (AUGUST 1949), PP. 71-74.         49
                 COMEL, ELEL, ELPRNOR
BRYNC -49-PPS    BRYNER, C
                 PEOPLE OF THE POLITBURO (SOVIET UNION).=
                 CURRENT HISTORY, N.S., 16, (MAY 1949), PP. 257-261.          49
                 COMEL
BRYSL -47-CPM    BRYSON, L           FINKELSTEIN, L      MACIVER, RM (EDS)
                 CONFLICTS OF POWER IN MODERN CULTURE -- SEVENTH
                    SYMPOSIUM.=
                 NEW YORK, HARPER AND BROTHERS, 1947.                         47
                 GNELTH, DEFEL, COMEL, ELEL, ELNOEL, ELPRNOR, METEL
BRZEZ -58-PPP    BRZEZINSKI, Z
                 THE PATTERN OF POLITICAL PURGES (EASTERN EUROPE).=

                    THE ANNALS OF THE AMERICAN ACADEMY OF POLITICAL AND        58
                       SOCIAL SCIENCE, 317, (MAY 1958), PP. 79-87.
                    COMEL, ELEL
BRZEZ -60-CII      BRZEZINSKI, Z
                    COMMUNIST IDEOLOGY AND INTERNATIONAL AFFAIRS
                       (SOVIET UNION, EAST EUROPE).=
                    THE JOURNAL OF CONFLICT RESOLUTION, 4, (SEPTEMBER 1960),   60
                       PP. 266-290.
                    ELPRNOR
BRZEZ -61-NSS      BRZEZINSKI, Z
                    THE NATURE OF THE SOVIET SYSTEM.=
                    SLAVIC REVIEW, 20, (OCTOBER 1961), PP. 351-368.            61
                    COMEL, ELEL, ELPRNOR
BRZEZ -63-CA       BRZEZINSKI, Z        HUNTINGTON, SP
                    CINCINNATUS AND THE APPARATCHIK
                       (UNITED STATES, SOVIET UNION).=
                    WORLD POLITICS, 16, (OCTOBER 1963), PP. 52-78.             63
                    COMEL, ELEL, ELPRNOR
BRZEZ -64-PPU      BRZEZINSKI, Z        HUNTINGTON, P
                    POLITICAL POWER -- USA/USSR (UNITED STATES,
                       SOVIET UNION).=
                    NEW YORK, VIKING PRESS, 1964.                              64
                    COMEL, ELEL, ELNOEL, ELPRNOR
BRZEZ -66-SPS      BRZEZINSKI, Z
                    THE SOVIET POLITICAL SYSTEM -- TRANSFORMATION OR
                       DEGENERATION.=
                    PROBLEMS OF COMMUNISM, 15, (JANUARY-FEBRUARY 1966),        66
                       PP. 1-15.
                    COMEL, ELEL, ELNOEL, ELPRNOR
BRZEZK-54-PCS      BRZEZINSKI, ZK (ED)
                    POLITICAL CONTROLS IN THE SOVIET ARMY -- A STUDY BASED
                       ON REPORTS BY FORMER SOVIET OFFICERS.=
                    NEW YORK, RESEARCH PROGRAM ON THE USSR, 1954.              54
                    COMEL, ELEL,ELNOEL, ELPRNOR
BRZEZK-56-PU       BRZEZINSKI, ZK
                    THE POLITICS OF UNDERDEVELOPMENT.=
                    WORLD POLITICS, 9, (OCTOBER 1956), PP. 55-75.              56
                    COMEL, ELPRNOR
BRZEZK-62-IPS      BRZEZINSKI, ZK
                    IDEOLOGY AND POWER IN SOVIET POLITICS.=
                    NEW YORK, FREDERICK A PRAEGER, 1962.                       62
                    ELEL, ELNOEL, ELPRNOR
BUCHW -63-LPD      BUCHANAN, W
                    LEGISLATIVE PARTISANSHIP -- THE DEVIANT CASE OF
                       CALIFORNIA (UNITED STATES).=
                    BERKELEY, UNIVERSITY OF CALIFORNIA PRESS, 1963.            63
                    ELEL, ELNOEL, ELPRNOR
BUCKPW-  -FTW      BUCK, PW
                    FIRST-TIME WINNERS IN THE BRITISH HOUSE OF COMMONS
                       SINCE 1918.=
                    THE AMERICAN POLITICAL SCIENCE REVIEW, 58, (SEPTEMBER
                       1964), PP. 662-667.
                    COMEL
BUCKPW-61-MPS      BUCK, PW
                    M.P.S. IN MINISTERIAL OFFICE (GREAT BRITAIN).=
                    POLITICAL STUDIES, 9, (OCTOBER 1961), PP. 300-306.         61
                    COMEL, ELEL
BUCKPW-63-APB      BUCK, PW
                    AMATEURS AND PROFESSIONALS IN BRITISH POLITICS,
                       1918-1959.=
                    CHICAGO, UNIVERSITY OF CHICAGO PRESS, 1963.                63
                    COMEL, ELEL, ELNOEL
BUDGI -65-EAT      BUDGE, I
                    ELECTORS' ATTITUDES TOWARDS LOCAL GOVERNMENT -- A SURVEY
                       OF A GLASGOW CONSTITUENCY (GREAT BRITAIN).=
                    POLITICAL STUDIES, 13, (OCTOBER 1965), PP. 365-372.        65
                    ELNOEL
BULLA -52-HST      BULLOCK, A
                    HITLER -- A STUDY IN TYRANNY (GERMANY).=
                    LONDON, ODHAMS PRESS, 1952.                                52
                    ELEL, ELNOEL, ELPRNOR
BUNNRF-60-FGE      BUNN, RF
                    THE FEDERATION OF GERMAN EMPLOYERS' ASSOCIATIONS -- A
                       POLITICAL INTEREST GROUP.=
                    THE WESTERN POLITICAL QUARTERLY, 13, (SEPTEMBER 1960),     60
                       PP. 325-335.
                    COMEL, ELEL
BURBLB-51-FPF      BURBANK, LB
                    THE FRENCH POPULAR FRONT.=
                    CURRENT HISTORY, N.S., 21, (OCTOBER 1951), PP. 197-201.    51
                    ELEL, ELNOEL
BURDE -59-AVB      BURDICK, E        BRODBECK, AJ    (EDS)
                    AMERICAN VOTING BEHAVIOR.=
                    GLENCOE, ILLINOIS, THE FREE PRESS, 1959.                   59

```
                    DEFEL, ELEL, ENOEL, ELPRNOR, METEL
BURG   -62-CWL      BURG,D
                    THE COLD WAR ON THE LITERARY FRONT (SOVIET UNION)  --
                       PART 1, THE WRITER'S UNDERGROUND -- PART 2, GROUPS,
                       TRENDS, GENRES, -- PART 3, THE PARTY AND THE WRITERS.=
                    PROBLEMS OF COMMUNISM, 11,12, ( JULY-AUGUST 1962,         62
                       SEPTEMBER-OCTOBER 1962, JANUARY-FEBRUARY 1963),
                       PP. 1-14, PP. 33-46, PP. 44-58.
                    ELEL, ELPRNOR
BURGME-62-NLS       BURGESS, ME
                    NEGRO LEADERSHIP IN A SOUTHERN CITY (UNITED STATES).=
                    CHAPEL HILL, UNIVERSITY OF NORTH CAROLINA PRESS, 1962.    62
                    ELEL, ELNOEL, METEL
BURIH  -61-CPR      BURINGTON, H
                    THE CONSERVATIVE PARTY -- REVOLTS AND PRESSURES --
                       1955-1961 (GREAT BRITAIN).=
                    THE POLITICAL QUARTERLY, 33, (OCTOBER-DECEMBER 1961),     61
                       PP. 363-373.
                    ELEL, ELNOEL, ELPRNOR
BURKFG-64-ASQ       BURKE, FG
                    AFRICA'S QUEST FOR ORDER.=
                    ENGLEWOOD CLIFFS, NEW JERSEY, PRENTICE-HALL, 1964.        64
                    COMEL, ELEL, ELNOEL, ELPRNOR
BURKRV-61-DCE       BURKS, RV
                    THE DYNAMICS OF COMMUNISM IN EASTERN EUROPE.=
                    PRINCETON, PRINCETON UNIVERSITY PRESS, 1961.              61
                    COMEL, ELEL, ELNOEL
BURMJH-53-CLP       BURMA, JH
                    CURRENT LEADERSHIP PROBLEMS AMONG JAPANESE AMERICANS.=
                    SOCIOLOGY AND SOCIAL RESEARCH, 37, (JANUARY-FEBRUARY      53
                       1953), PP. 157-163.
                    ELEL, ELPRNOR
BURNC  -62-PPA      BURNS, C
                    PARTIES AND PEOPLE (AUSTRALIA).=
                    PARKVILLE, MELBOURNE UNIVERSITY PRESS--LONDON,            62
                       CAMBRIDGE UNIVERSITY PRESS, 1962.
                    COMEL, ELEL, ELNOEL
BURNJ  -60-MR       BURNHAM, J
                    THE MANAGERIAL REVOLUTION.=
                    BLOOMINGTON, INDIANA UNIVERSITY PRESS, 1960.              60
                    GNELTH, COMEL, ELEL, ELNOEL, ELPRNOR
BURNJ  -63-MDF      BURNHAM, J
                    THE MACHIAVELLIANS -- DEFENDERS OF FREEDOM.=
                    CHICAGO, HENRY REGNERY CO., 1963.                         63
                    GNELTH, DEFEL
BURNJM-48-MMS       BURNS, JM
                    MAINTENANCE OF MEMBERSHIP -- A STUDY IN ADMINISTRATIVE
                       STATESMANSHIP (UNITED STATES).=
                    JOURNAL OF POLITICS, 10, (FEBRUARY 1948), PP. 101-116.    48
                    ELNOEL
BURNJM-61-ELP       BURNS, JM
                    EXCELLENCE AND LEADERSHIP IN PRESIDENT AND CONGRESS
                       (UNITED STATES).=
                    DAEDALUS, 90, (FALL 1961), PP. 734-749.                   61
                    ELEL
BURNWD-64-ASE       BURNHAM, WD
                    THE ALABAMA SENATORIAL ELECTION OF 1962 -- RETURN OF
                       INTER-PARTY COMPETITION (UNITED STATES).=
                    THE JOURNAL OF POLITICS, 26, (NOVEMBER 1964),             64
                       PP. 798-829.
                    ELEL, ELNOEL
BURRRN-  -LAS       BURR, RN (ED)
                    LATIN AMERICA'S NATIONALIST REVOLUTIONS.=
                    THE ANNALS OF THE AMERICAN ACADEMY OF POLITICAL AND
                       SOCIAL SCIENCE, 334, (MARCH 1961), PP. 1-147.
                    ELEL, ELNOEL, ELPRNOR
BUSEJL-61-PCR       BUSEY, JL
                    THE PRESIDENTS OF COSTA RICA.=
                    THE AMERICAS, 18, (JULY 1961), PP. 55-70.                 61
                    COMEL, ELNOEL, ELPRNOR
BUSIKA-49-PCG       BUSIA, KA
                    THE PLACE OF THE CHIEF IN THE GOLD COAST.=
                    ACHIMOTA, GOLD COAST, ACHIMOTA PRESS, 1949.               49
                    ELEL, ELNOEL
BUSIKA-51-PCM       BUSIA, KA
                    THE POSITION OF THE CHIEF IN THE MODERN POLITICAL
                       SYSTEM OF ASHANTI (GOLD COAST).=
                    LONDON, OXFORD UNIVERSITY PRESS, 1951.                    51
                    COMEL, ELEL, ELNOEL
BUSIKA-56-PSA       BUSIA, KA
                    THE PRESENT SITUATION AND ASPIRATIONS OF ELITES IN THE
                       GOLD COAST.=
                    INTERNATIONAL SOCIAL SCIENCE BULLETIN, 8, (1956),         56
                       PP. 424-431.
```

```
                    COMEL, ELEL, ELNOEL, ELPRNOR
     BUTLA -59-CPG  BUTLER, A
                    THE CONSERVATIVES IN POWER (GREAT BRITAIN).=
                    THE POLITICAL QUARTERLY, 30, (OCTOBER-DECEMBER 1959),        59
                       PP. 325-335.
                    ELEL
     BUTLA -60-HPL  BUTLER, A
                    THE HISTORY AND PRACTICE OF LOBBY JOURNALISM
                       (GREAT BRITAIN).=
                    PARLIAMENTARY AFFAIRS, 13, (WINTER 1959-1960),               60
                       PP. 54-60.
                    ELEL
     BUTLD -60-PPD  BUTLER, D
                    THE PARADOX OF PARTY DIFFERENCE.=
                    THE AMERICAN BEHAVIORAL SCIENTIST, 4,                        60
                       (NOVEMBER 1960), PP. 3-5.
                    ELEL, ELNOEL
     BUTTJ -58-VM   BUTTINGER, J
                    THE VIETNAMESE MANDARIN.=
                    DISSENT, 5, (SPRING 1958), PP. 138-147.                      58
                    COMEL, ELEL, ELNOEL
     BUTWR -60-EB   BUTWELL, R           VON-DER-MEHDEN, F
                    THE 1960 ELECTION IN BURMA.=
                    PACIFIC AFFAIRS, 33, (JUNE 1960), PP. 144-157.               60
                    ELEL, ELNOEL, ELPRNOR
     BUXTJC-63-CSS  BUXTON, JC
                    CHIEFS AND STRANGERS (SOUTHERN SUDAN).=
                    OXFORD, CLARENDON PRESS, 1963.                               63
                    COMEL, ELEL, ELNOEL
     BYRDRO-63-CCE  BYRD, RO
                    CHARACTERISTICS OF CANDIDATES FOR ELECTION IN A COUNTRY
                       APPROACHING INDEPENDENCE -- THE CASE OF UGANDA.=
                    MIDWEST JOURNAL OF POLITICAL SCIENCE, 7,                     63
                       (FEBRUARY 1963), PP. 1-27.
                    COMEL, ELNOEL
     CADYJF-60-BSM  CADY, JF
                    BURMA'S MILITARY REGIME.=
                    CURRENT HISTORY, N.S., 38, (FEBRUARY 1960), PP. 75-81.       60
                    COMEL, ELEL, ELNOEL
     CADYJF-65-BSM  CADY, JF
                    BURMA'S MILITARY DICTATORSHIP.=
                    ASIAN STUDIES, 3, (DECEMBER 1965), PP. 490-516.              65
                    COMEL, ELEL, ELPRNOR
     CAHIRS-64-PEL  CAHILL, RS          HENCLEY, SP (EDS)
                    THE POLITICS OF EDUCATION IN THE LOCAL COMMUNITY
                       (UNITED STATES).=
                    DANVILLE, ILLINOIS, INTERSTATE PRINTERS AND PUBLISHERS,      64
                       1964.
                    METEL
     CAIRJB-61-LCC  CAIRD, JB           MOISLEY, HA
                    LEADERSHIP AND COMMUNICATION IN THE CRAFTING COMMUNITIES
                       OF THE OUTER HEBRIDES.=
                    THE SOCIOLOGICAL REVIEW, 9, (MARCH 1961), PP. 85-102.        61
                    ELEL, ELNOEL
     CALALM-62-PFA  CALALANG, LM
                    PROBLEMS OF FIELD ADMINISTRATION IN THE DEPARTMENT
                       OF LABOR (PHILIPPINES).=
                    PHILLIPINE JOURNAL OF PUBLIC ADMINISTRATION, 6,              62
                       (JULY 1962), PP. 215-227.
                    ELEL, ELNOEL
     CALLT -60-SSB  CALLAGHAN, T
                    STUDYING THE STUDENTS -- BETWEEN CONFORMITY AND DISSENT
                       (SOVIET UNION).=
                    SOVIET SURVEY--A QUARTERLY REVIEW OF CULTURAL TRENDS,        60
                    33, (JULY-SEPTEMBER 1960), PP. 12-19.
                    COMEL, ELEL, ELPRNOR
     CAMEID-54-WAC  CAMERON, ID          COPPER, BK
                    THE WEST AFRICAN COUNCILLOR.=
                    OXFORD, OXFORD UNIVERSITY PRESS, 1954.                       54
                    COMEL, ELEL, ELNOEL
     CAMPA -60-AV   CAMPBELL, A          ET AL
                    THE AMERICAN VOTER.=
                    NEW YORK, JOHN WILEY, 1960.                                  60
                    DEFEL, ELEL, ELNOEL, ELPRNOR, METEL
     CAMPA -64-VEP  CAMPBELL, A
                    VOTERS AND ELECTIONS -- PAST AND PRESENT.=
                    THE JOURNAL OF POLITICS, 26, (NOVEMBER 1964),                64
                       PP. 745-757.
                    ELNOEL, METEL
     CAMPAJ-65-LSP  CAMPBELL, AJC
                    THE LEGAL SCENE -- PROCEDURALISTS AND PATERNALISTS
                       (SOVIET UNION).=
                    SURVEY--A JOURNAL OF SOVIET AND EAST EUROPEAN STUDIES,       65
                    57, (OCTOBER 1965), PP. 56-66.
```

```
                    ELEL, ELPRNOR
CAMPEQ-59-RMC       CAMPBELL, EQ         PETTIGREW, TF
                    RACIAL AND MORAL CRISIS -- THE ROLE OF LITTLE ROCK
                      MINISTERS (UNITED STATES).=
                    THE AMERICAN JOURNAL OF SOCIOLOGY, 64, (MARCH 1959),          59
                      PP. 509-516.
                    ELEL, ELNOEL
CAMPG -52-PSG       CAMPION, G           ET AL
                    PARLIAMENT -- A SURVEY (GREAT BRITAIN).=
                    NEW YORK, THE MACMILLAN COMPANY, 1952.                        52
                    ELEL, ELNOEL
CAMPP -53-DLF       CAMPBELL, P
                    DISCIPLINE AND LOYALTY IN THE FRENCH PARLIAMENT DURING
                      THE PINAY GOVERNMENT.=
                    POLITICAL STUDIES, 1, (OCTOBER 1953), PP. 247-257.            53
                    ELEL
CAMPP -53-VDP       CAMPBELL, P
                    VERIFICATION DES POUVOIRS IN THE FRENCH
                      NATIONAL ASSEMBLY.=
                    POLITICAL STUDIES, 1, (1953), PP. 65-79.                      53
                    ELEL
CAMPP -55-PPS       CAMPBELL, P
                    POLITICIANS, PUBLIC SERVANTS, AND THE PEOPLE IN
                      NEW ZEALAND -- 1 -- 2.=
                    POLITICAL STUDIES, 3,4, (OCTOBER 1955, FEBRUARY 1956),        55
                      PP. 193-210, PP. 18-29.
                    COMEL, ELEL, ELNOEL, ELPRNOR
CAMPP -57-FPC       CAMPBELL, P
                    FRENCH PARTY CONGRESSES.=
                    PARLIAMENTARY AFFAIRS, 10, (AUTUMN 1957), PP. 412-423.        57
                    ELEL
CAMPP -58-NZM       CAMPBELL, P
                    NEW ZEALAND MINISTERS, 1935-1957.=
                    POLITICAL SCIENCE, 10, (SEPTEMBER 1958), PP. 65-72.           58
                    COMEL
CAMPP -59-APG       CAMPBELL, P
                    SOME ASPECTS OF PARLIAMENTARY GOVERNMENT IN EUROPE.=
                    PARLIAMENTARY AFFAIRS, 12, (SUMMER AND AUTUMN 1959),          59
                      PP. 405-416.
                    ELEL, ELNOEL, ELPRNOR
CANEE -62-CP        CANETTI, E
                    CROWDS AND POWER.=
                    LONDON, GOLLANCZ, 1962.                                       62
                    ELNOEL
CANTH -58-PDF       CANTRIL, H
                    THE POLITICS OF DESPAIR (FRANCE, ITALY).=
                    NEW YORK, BASIC BOOKS, 1958.                                  58
                    ELNOEL, ELPRNOR
CANTH -60-SLM       CANTRIL, H
                    SOVIET LEADERS AND MASTERY OVER MAN.=
                    NEW BRUNSWICK, RUTGERS UNIVERSITY PRESS, 1960.                60
                    ELEL, ELNOEL, ELPRNOR
CAPERB-63-MMR       CAPELLE, RB
                    THE MRP (MOVEMENT REPUBLICAN POPULAIRE) AND FRENCH
                      FOREIGN POLICY.=
                    NEW YORK, FREDERICK A PRAEGER, 1963.                          63
                    ELEL, ELPRNOR
CAPLT -58-AMU       CAPLON, T           MACGEE, RJ
                    THE ACADEMIC MARKETPLACE (UNITED STATES).=
                    NEW YORK, BASIC BOOKS, 1958.                                  58
                    ELEL
CAPPE -61-CDP       CAPPADOCHA, E
                    THE CHRISTIAN DEMOCRATIC PARTY IN ITALIAN POLICY.=
                    INTERNATIONAL JOURNAL, 16, (AUTUMN 1961), PP. 383-398.        61
                    ELEL, ELNOEL, ELPRNOR
CARDD -66-PMU       CARDAY, D
                    THE POLITICS OF MILITARY UNIFICATION.=
                    NEW YORK, COLUMBIA UNIVERSITY PRESS, 1966.                    66
                    ELEL
CARDFH-67-IEL       CARDOSO, FH
                    THE INDUSTRIAL ELITE (LATIN AMERICA).=
                    SM LIPSET AND A SOLARI (EDS), ELITES IN LATIN AMERICA,        67
                      NEW YORK, OXFORD UNIVERSITY PRESS, 1967, PP. 94-114.
                    COMEL, ELEL, ELNOEL
CARLA -50-SCD       CARLETON, A
                    THE SYRIAN COUPS D'ETAT OF 1949.=
                    THE MIDDLE EAST JOURNAL, 4, (JANUARY 1950), PP. 1-11.         50
                    COMEL, ELEL
CARLDS-64-CSP       CARLISLE, DS
                    THE CHANGING SOVIET PERCEPTION OF THE DEVELOPMENT
                      PROCESS IN THE AFRO-ASIAN WORLD.=
                    MIDWEST JOURNAL OF POLITICAL SCIENCE, 8, (NOVEMBER 1964),     64
                      PP. 385-407.
                    ELPRNOR
```

CARLRO-58-TKJ   CARLSON, RO
                TO TALK WITH KINGS (JORDAN).=
                THE PUBLIC OPINION QUARTERLY, 22, (FALL 1958),              58
                    PP. 224-229.
                METEL
CARLWG-  -COS   CARLETON, WG
                CENTRALIZATION AND THE OPEN SOCIETY (UNITED STATES).=
                POLITICAL SCIENCE QUARTERLY, 75, (JUNE 1960),
                    PP. 244-259.
                ELEL, ELNOEL
CARLWG-51-SPU   CARLETON, WG
                THE SOUTHERN POLITICIAN -- 1900 AND 1950 (UNITED STATES).=
                THE JOURNAL OF POLITICS, 13, (MAY 1951), PP. 215-231.       51
                COMEL, ELNOEL
CARNFG-53-CCM   CARNELL, FG
                COMMUNALISM AND COMMUNISM IN MALAYA.=
                PACIFIC AFFAIRS, 25, (JUNE 1953), PP. 99-117.               53
                ELNOEL, ELPRNOR
CARNFG-54-CRE   CARNELL, FG
                CONSTITUTIONAL REFORM AND ELECTIONS IN MALAYA.=
                PACIFIC AFFAIRS, 27, (SEPTEMBER 1954), PP. 216-235.         54
                ELEL, ELNOEL, ELPRNOR
CARNFM-64-DPL   CARNEY, FM
                THE DECENTRALIZED POLITICS OF LOS ANGELES
                    (UNITED STATES).=
                THE ANNALS OF THE AMERICAN ACADEMY OF POLITICAL AND         64
                    SOCIAL SCIENCE, 353, (MAY 1964), PP. 107-121.
                COMEL
CARRHN-58-HRF   CARROLL, HN
                THE HOUSE OF REPRESENTATIVES AND FOREIGN AFFAIRS
                    (UNITED STATES).=
                PITTSBURGH, UNIVERSITY OF PITTSBURGH PRESS, 1958.           58
                ELEL
CARRP -61-CRH   CARRASCO, P
                THE CIVIL - RELIGIOUS HIERARCHY IN MESOAMERICAN
                    COMMUNITIES -- PRE - SPANISH BACKGROUND AND COLONIAL
                    DEVELOPMENT.=
                AMERICAN ANTHROPOLOGIST, 63, (JUNE 1961), PP. 483-497.      61
                COMEL, ELEL
CARRR -55-CWI   CARR, R
                CONFLICTS WITHIN THE INDIAN COMMUNIST PARTY
                PROBLEMS OF COMMUNISM, 4, (SEPTEMBER-OCTOBER 1955),         55
                    PP. 7-13.
                ELEL, ELPRNOR
CARTBE-56-OPM   CARTER, BE
                THE OFFICE OF THE PRIME MINISTER (GREAT BRITAIN).=
                PRINCETON, PRINCETON UNIVERSITY PRESS, 1956.                56
                COMEL, ELEL, ELNOEL, ELPRNOR
CARTD -46-POP   CARTWRIGHT, D
                PUBLIC OPINION POLLS AND DEMOCRATIC LEADERSHIP
                    (UNITED STATES).=
                JOURNAL OF SOCIAL ISSUES, 2, (MAY 1946), PP. 23-32.         46
                ELEL, ELNOEL
CARTD -5 -ILC   CARTWRIGHT, D
                INFLUENCE, LEADERSHIP, CONTROL.=
                JG MARCH (ED), HANDBOOK OF ORGANIZATIONS, CHICAGO, RAND     65
                    MCNALLY, 1965, PP. 1-48.
                DEFEL, METEL
CARTD -59-SSP   CARTWRIGHT, D (ED)
                STUDIES IN SOCIAL POWER.=
                ANN ARBOR, UNIVERSITY OF MICHIGAN, INSTITUTE FOR SOCIAL     59
                    RESEARCH, 1959.
                GNELTH, DEFEL, ELEL, ELNOEL, ELPRNOR, METEL
CARTGM-66-NUR   CARTER, GM
                NATIONAL UNITY AND REGIONALISM IN EIGHT AFRICAN STATES
                    (NIGERIA, NIGER, THE CONGO, GABON, CENTRAL AFRICAN
                    REPUBLIC, CHAD, UGANDA, ETHIOPIA).=
                ITHACA, CORNELL UNIVERSITY PRESS, 1966.                     66
                ELEL, ELPRNOR
CARTGW-58-TAS   CARTER, GW          BROWN, WO (EDS)
                TRANSITION IN AFRICA -- STUDIES IN POLITICAL ADAPTATION.=
                BOSTON, BOSTON UNIVERSITY PRESS, 1958.                      58
                COMEL, ELEL, ELNOEL, ELPRNOR
CARTGW-62-AOP   CARTER, GW (ED.)
                AFRICAN ONE PARTY STATES.=
                ITHACA, CORNELL UNIVERSITY PRESS, 1962.                     62
                COMEL, ELEL, ELNOEL
CARTMB-60-FLL   CARTER, MB
                THE FUTURE OF THE LIBERAL-LEFT (UNITED STATES).=
                ENCOUNTER, 15, (AUGUST 1960), PP. 33-41.                    60
                COMEL, ELEL, ELNOEL
CARTRE-57-RBP   CARTER-JR, RE
                RELATIONS BETWEEN THE PRESS AND LOCAL GOVERNMENT
                    OFFICIALS IN NORTH CAROLINA.=

                              PROD (THE AMERICAN BEHAVIORAL SCIENTIST), 1,            57
                                 (SEPTEMBER 1957), PP. 23-27.
                              ELEL
CARTRE-58-NGS    CARTER, RE
                              NEWSPAPER 'GATEKEEPERS' AND THE SOURCES OF NEWS.=
                              THE PUBLIC OPINION QUARTERLY, 22, (SUMMER 1958),         58
                                 PP. 133-144.
                              ELEL, ELPRNOR
CARTRE-62-PAO    CARTER, RE            CLARKE, P
                              PUBLIC AFFAIRS OPINION LEADERSHIP AMONG EDUCATIONAL
                                 TELEVISION VIEWERS (UNITED STATES).=
                              AMERICAN SOCIOLOGICAL REVIEW, 27, (DECEMBER 1962),       62
                                 PP. 792-799.
                              COMEL, ELNOEL
CASSCW-. -TPS    CASSINELLI, CW
                              THE TOTALITARIAN PARTY (SOVIET UNION, EAST EUROPE).=
                              THE JOURNAL OF POLITICS, 24, (FEBRUARY 1962), PP. 111-141 .
                              COMEL, ELEL, ELNOEL
CASSCW-53-LO     CASSINELLI, CW
                              THE LAW OF OLIGARCHY.=
                              THE AMERICAN POLITICAL SCIENCE REVIEW, 47, (SEPTEMBER    53
                                 1953), PP. 773-784.
                              GNELTH, ELNOEL
CASSCW-61-PAI    CASSINELLI, CW
                              POLITICAL AUTHORITY -- ITS EXERCISE AND POSSESSION.=
                              THE WESTERN POLITICAL QUARTERLY, 14, (SEPTEMBER 1961),   61
                                 PP. 635-646.
                              ELNOEL, ELPRNOR
CASSTW-61-PTB    CASSTEVENS, TW
                              PARTY THEORIES AND BRITISH PARTIES.=
                              MIDWEST JOURNAL OF POLITICAL SCIENCE, 5, (NOVEMBER 1961), 61
                                 PP. 391-398.
                              COMEL, ELEL
CASTAV-61-PDP    CASTILLO, AV
                              THE PHILIPPINE DECONTROL PROGRAM -- THE GOVERNMENT'S
                                 POINT OF VIEW.=
                              PHILIPPINE JOURNAL OF PUBLIC ADMINISTRATION, 5,          61
                                 (OCTOBER 1961), PP. 287-292.
                              ELEL
CASTHP-59-AVP    CASTLEBERRY, HP
                              THE ARABS' VIEW OF POSTWAR AMERICAN FOREIGN POLICY
                                 (EGYPT, IRAN, JORDAN, LEBANON, SYRIA).=
                              THE WESTERN POLITICAL QUARTERLY, 12, (MARCH1959),        59
                                 PP. 9-36.
                              ELPRNOR
CATED -64-PWC    CATER, D
                              POWER IN WASHINGTON -- A CRITICAL LOOK AT TODAY'S
                                 STRUGGLE TO GOVERN IN THE NATION'S CAPITAL.=
                              NEW YORK, RANDOM HOUSE, 1964.                            64
                              ELEL, ELNOEL, ELPRNOR
CATTRB-54-FFS    CATTELL, RB            STICE, GF
                              FOUR FORMULAE FOR SELECTING LEADERS ON THE BASIS OF
                                 PERSONALITY.=
                              HUMAN RELATIONS, 7, (1954), PP. 493-508.                 54
                              COMEL
CAUTD -64-CFI    CAUTE, D
                              COMMUNISM AND THE FRENCH INTELLECTUALS 1914-1960.=
                              NEW YORK, MACMILLAN, 1964.                               64
                              COMEL, ELEL, ELNOEL, ELPRNOR
CECICO-65-DLF    CECIL, CO
                              THE DETERMINANTS OF LIBYAN FOREIGN POLICY.=
                              THE MIDDLE EAST JOURNAL, 19, (WINTER 1965), PP. 20-34.   65
                              ELEL, ELNOEL
CELLE -61-SRC    CELLER, E
                              THE SENIORITY RULE IN CONGRESS (UNITED STATES).=
                              THE WESTERN POLITICAL QUARTERLY, 14, (MARCH 1961),       61
                                 PP. 1602167.
                              COMEL
CELOB -57-TSG    CELOVSKY, B
                              THE TRANSFERRED SUDETEN -- GERMANS AND THEIR
                                 POLITICAL ACTIVITY (GERMANY).=
                              JOURNAL OF CENTRAL EUROPEAN AFFAIRS, 17, (JULY 1957),    57
                                 PP. 127-149.
                              ELEL, ELNOEL, ELPRNOR
CH-EJ -60-WAC    CH-EN, J
                              WRITERS AND ARTISTS CONFER (CHINA).=
                              THE CHINA QUARTERLY, 4, (OCTOBER-DECEMBER 1960),         60
                                 PP. 76-81.
                              COMEL, ELEL
CH-ESH-60-PGL    CH-EN, SH
                              POETRY AND THE GREAT LEAP FORWARD (CHINA).=
                              THE CHINA QUARTERLY, 3, (JULY-SEPTEMBER 1960), PP. 1-15.  60
                              ELNOEL, ELPRNOR
CH'IT--50-GPC    CH'IEN, T-S

                    THE GOVERNMENT AND POLITICS OF CHINA.=
                    CAMBRIDGE, HARVARD UNIVERSITY PRESS, 1950.                    50
                    ELEL
CH'U   -57-CCS    CH'U-T-UNG-TSU
                    CHINESE CLASS STRUCTURE AND ITS IDEOLOGY.=
                    JK FAIRBANK (ED), CHINESE THOUGHT AND INSTITUTIONS,           57
                       CHICAGO, UNIVERSITY OF CHICAGO PRESS, 1957,
                       PP. 235-250.
                    COMEL, ELEL, ELNOEL, ELPRNOR
CHALDA-64-SDP     CHALMERS, DA
                    THE SOCIAL DEMOCRATIC PARTY OF GERMANY -- FROM WORKING
                       CLASS MOVEMENT TO MODERN POLITICAL PARTY.=
                    NEW HAVEN, YALE UNIVERSITY PRESS, 1964.                       64
                    COMEL, ELEL, ELNOEL, ELPRNOR
CHALRD-67-FAO     CHALLENER, RD
                    THE FRENCH ARMY -- FROM OBEDIENCE TO INSURRECTION.=
                    WORLD POLITICS, 19, (JULY 1967), PP. 678-691.                 67
                    COMEL, ELEL, ELNOEL, ELPRNOR
CHAME -66-CPP     CHAMORRO, E          AGULLA, JC
                    COMMUNITY POWER PERSPECTIVES AND ROLE DEFINITIONS OF
                       NORTH AMERICAN EXECUTIVES IN AN ARGENTINE COMMUNITY.=
                    ADMINISTRATIVE SCIENCE QUARTERLY, 10, (1965-1966),            66
                       PP. 364-380.
                    ELEL, ELPRNOR
CHAMWH-52-RAS     CHAMBERLIN, WH
                    RUSSIANS AGAINST STALIN.=
                    THE RUSSIAN REVIEW, 11, (JANUARY 1952), PP. 16-23.            52
                    COMEL, ELEL
CHAMWH-59-TRI     CHAMBERLIN, WH
                    THE TRAGEDY OF THE RUSSIAN INTELLIGENTSIA.=
                    THE RUSSIAN REVIEW, 18, (APRIL 1959), PP. 89-95.              59
                    ELPRNOR
CHANCL-55-CGS     CHANG, CL
                    THE CHINESE GENTRY, STUDIES ON THEIR ROLE IN THE
                       NINETEENTH CENTURY CHINESE SOCIETY.=
                    SEATTLE, UNIVERSITY OF WASHINGTON PRESS, 1955.                55
                    COMEL, ELEL, ELNOEL, ELPRNOR
CHANG -55-AOF     CHANDLER, G
                    AMERICAN OPINION AND FOREIGN POLICY.=
                    INTERNATIONAL AFFAIRS, 31, (OCTOBER 1955), PP. 447-458.       55
                       PP. 447-458.
                    ELNOEL
CHANSW-58-LCC     CHAN, SW
                    LITERATURE IN COMMUNIST CHINA.=
                    PROBLEMS OF COMMUNISM, 7, (JANUARY-FEBRUARY 1958),            58
                       PP. 44-51.
                    ELEL, ELPRNOR
CHAO   -59-LCC    CHAO-KUO-CHUN
                    LEADERSHIP IN THE CHINESE COMMUNIST PARTY.=
                    THE ANNALS OF THE AMERICAN ACADEMY OF POLITICAL AND           59
                       SOCIAL SCIENCE, 321, (JANUARY 1959), PP. 43-20.
                    COMEL, ELEL, ELPRNOR
CHAPB -58-PA      CHAPMAN, B
                    POLITICS AND ADMINISTRATION.=
                    INTERNATIONAL REVIEW OF ADMINISTRATIVE SCIENCES, 24,          58
                       (1958), PP. 17-20.
                    ELEL, ELNOEL
CHAPB -59-PGP     CHAPMAN, B
                    THE PROFESSION OF GOVERNMENT -- THE PUBLIC SERVANT
                       IN (WESTERN) EUROPE.=
                    NEW YORK, THE MACMILLAN COMPANY, 1959.                        59
                    ELEL, ELPRNOR
CHARB -50-SRL     CHARTIER, B
                    THE SOCIAL ROLE OF THE LITERARY ELITE (UNITED STATES).=
                    SOCIAL FORCES, 29, (DECEMBER 1950), PP. 179-186.              50
                    ELEL, ELNOEL, ELPRNOR
CHARJC-59-ACI     CHARLESWORTH, JC
                    AMERICAN CIVILIZATION AND ITS LEADERSHIP NEEDS,
                       1960-1990.=
                    THE ANNALS OF THE AMERICAN ACADEMY OF POLITICAL AND           59
                       SOCIAL SCIENCE, 325, (SEPTEMBER 1959), PP. 1-123.
                    COMEL, ELEL, ELNOEL, ELPRNOR
CHATK -59-NMM     CHATTEIJI, K
                    THE NATIONAL MOVEMENT IN MODERN CHINA.=
                    CALCUTTA, K L MUKHAPADHYAY, 1959.                             59
                    COMEL, ELEL, ELNOEL
CHATP -54-CSF     CHATENET, P
                    THE CIVIL SERVICE IN FRANCE.=
                    THE POLITICAL QUARTERLY, 25, (OCTOBER 1954), PP. 390-397. 54
                    COMEL, ELEL
CHAUMA-60-OCC     CHAUDHURI, MA
                    THE ORGANIZATION AND COMPOSITION OF THE CENTRAL
                       CIVIL SERVICES IN PAKISTAN.=
                    INTERNATIONAL REVIEW OF ADMINISTRATIVE SCIENCES,              60

```
                        26, (1960), PP. 279-292.
                        COMEL, ELEL
CHENC--66-PSR   CHENG, C-Y
                        THE POWER STRUGGLE IN RED CHINA.=
                        ASIAN SURVEY, 6, (SEPTEMBER 1966), PP. 469-483.              66
                        ELEL
CHENEK-49-ICC   CHEN, EKT
                        IDEOLOGY OF THE CHINESE COMMUNISTS.=
                        THE SOUTHWESTERN SOCIAL SCIENCE QUARTERLY, 30,               49
                            (JUNE 1949), PP. 29-34.
                        COMEL, ELPRNOR
CHENJC-64-PCC   CHENG, JC
                        PROBLEMS OF CHINESE COMMUNIST LEADERSHIP AS SEEN IN THE
                            SECRET MILITARY PAPERS.=
                        ASIAN SURVEY, 4, (JUNE 1964), PP. 861-872.                   64
                        ELEL, ELPRNOR
CHENTH-51-EPC   CHEN, THE
                        EDUCATION AND PROPAGANDA IN COMMUNIST CHINA.=
                        THE ANNALS OF THE AMERICAN ACADEMY OF POLITICAL AND          51
                            SOCIAL SCIENCE, 277, (SEPTEMBER 1951), PP. 135-145.
                        ELNOEL
CHENTH-52-TAF   CHEN, THE            CHEN, WHC
                        THE 'THREE-ANTI' AND 'FIVE-ANTI' MOVEMENTS IN COMMUNIST
                            CHINA.=
                        PACIFIC AFFAIRS, 25, (MARCH 1952), PP. 3-23.                 52
                        ELNOEL
CHENTH-53-MRC   CHEN, THE
                        THE MARXIST REMOLDING OF CHINESE SOCIETY.=
                        THE AMERICAN JOURNAL OF SOCIOLOGY, 58, (JANUARY 1953),       53
                            PP. 340-346.
                        ELNOEL, ELPRNOR
CHENTH-59-TRI   CHEN, THE
                        THE THOUGHT REFORM OF INTELLECTUALS (COMMUNIST CHINA).=
                        THE ANNALS OF THE AMERICAN ACADEMY OF POLITICAL AND          59
                            SOCIAL SCIENCE, 321, (JANUARY 1959), PP. 82-89.
                        ELEL, ELNOEL, ELPRNOR
CHENTH-60-TRC   CHEN, THE
                        THOUGHT REFORM OF THE CHINESE INTELLECTUALS.=
                        NEW YORK, OXFORD UNIVERSITY PRESS, 1960.                     60
                        ELEL, ELNOEL, ELPRNOR
CHENTH-66-NAC   CHEN, TH
                        A NATION IN AGONY (CHINA).=
                        PROBLEMS OF COMMUNISM, 15, (NOVEMBER-DECEMBER 1966),         66
                            PP. 14-20.
                        ELEL, ELNOEL, ELPRNOR
CHERJ -56-PRO   CHERNICK, J
                        THE POLITICAL ROLE OF ORGANIZED LABOR (UNITED STATES).=
                        CURRENT HISTORY, N.S., 31, (AUGUST 1956), PP. 77-83.         56
                        ELEL, ELNOEL
CHESDN-50-ONI   CHESTER, DN
                        ORGANIZATION OF THE NATIONALISED INDUSTRIES
                            (GREAT BRITAIN).=
                        THE POLITICAL QUARTERLY, 21, (1950), PP. 122-134.            50
                        COMEL, ELNOEL
CHESDN-53-PCC   CHESTER, DN
                        PUBLIC CORPORATIONS AND THE CLASSIFICATION OF
                            ADMINISTRATIVE BODIES (GREAT BRITAIN).=
                        POLITICAL STUDIES, 1, (1953), PP. 34-52.                     53
                        ELEL, ELNOEL
CHESDN-62-WGB   CHESTER, DN
                        WHO GOVERNS BRITAIN.=
                        PARLIAMENTARY AFFAIRS, 15, (AUTUMN 1962), PP. 519-527.       62
                        ELEL, ELNOEL
CHIAN -57-IM    CHIAROMONTE, N
                        THE INDIVIDUAL AND THE MASS.=
                        DISSENT, 4, (SPRING 1957), PP. 167-177.                      57
                        DEFEL, ELNOEL
CHILD -66-EGE   CHILDS, D
                        THE EAST GERMAN ELITE -- RED JESUITS AND OTHERS.=
                        THE WORLD TODAY, 22, (JANUARY 1966), PP. 32-41.              66
                        COMEL
CHILD -67-SUP   CHILDS, D
                        THE SOCIALIST UNITY PARTY OF EAST GERMANY.=
                        POLITICAL STUDIES, 15, (OCTOBER 1967), PP. 301-321.          67
                        ELEL, ELPRNOR
CHILRH-65-PLA   CHILCOTE, RH
                        THE PRESS IN LATIN AMERICA, SPAIN AND PORTUGAL -- A
                            SUMMARY OF RECENT DEVELOPMENTS.=
                        STANFORD, INSTITUTE OF HISPANIC AMERICAN AND                 65
                            LUSO-BRAZILIAN STUDIES, 1965.
                        ELEL, ELNOEL
CHOUGW-59-FPD   CHOUDHURY, GW
                        FAILURE OF PARLIAMENTARY DEMOCRACY IN PAKISTAN.=
                        PARLIAMENTARY AFFAIRS, 12, (WINTER 1958-1959),               59
```

```
                        PP. 60-70.
                        ELEL, ELNOEL, ELPRNOR
CHOUGW-60-RDP   CHOUDHURY, GW
                        RESHAPING OF DEMOCRACY IN PAKISTAN.=
                        PARLIAMENTARY AFFAIRS, 13, (SPRING 1960), PP. 227-235.     60
                        ELEL, ELNOEL
CHOUT -60-MFM   CHOU, T
                        THE MAY FOURTH MOVEMENT -- INTELLECTUAL REVOLUTION IN
                           MODERN CHINA.=
                        CAMBRIDGE, HARVARD UNIVERSITY PRESS, 1960.                60
                        ELEL, ELPRNOR
CHRIB -59-ATF   CHRISTIANSEN, B
                        ATTITUDES TOWARD FOREIGN AFFAIRS AS A FUNCTION OF
                           PERSONALITY.=
                        OSLO, OSLO UNIVERSITY PRESS, 1959.                        59
                        COMEL, ELEL, ELPRNOR, METEL
CHRIB -62-BVS   CHRISTOFF, B
                        BULGARIA -- THE VALUE OF SCAPEGOATS.=
                        PROBLEMS OF COMMUNISM, 11, (MAY-JUNE 1962), PP. 13-18.     62
                        ELEL
CHRIJB-62-CPB   CHRISTOPH, JB
                        CAPITAL PUNISHMENT AND BRITISH POLITICS.=
                        LONDON, GEORGE ALLEN AND UNWIN, 1962.                     62
                        COMEL, ELEL, ELNOEL, ELPRNOR
CHRIJB-65-CCB   CHRISTOPH, JB
                        CONSENSUS AND CLEAVAGE IN BRITISH POLITICAL IDEOLOGY.=
                        THE AMERICAN POLITICAL SCIENCE REVIEW, 59, (SEPTEMBER     65
                           1965), PP. 629-642.
                        ELPRNOR
CHRIR -54-SSM   CHRISTIE, R          CHRISTIE, J          CHRISTIE, M (EDS)
                        STUDIES IN THE SCOPE AND METHOD OF THE 'AUTHORITARIAN
                           PERSONALITY'.=
                        GLENCOE, ILLINOIS, FREE PRESS, 1954.                      54
                        COMEL, ELEL, METEL
CHRYVC-66-LCP   CHRYPINSKI, VC
                        LEGISLATIVE COMMITTEES IN POLISH LAWMAKING.=
                        SLAVIC REVIEW, 25, (JUNE 1966), PP. 247-258.              66
                        ELEL, ELPRNOR
CHU-Y -58-ICC   CHU-WANG, Y
                        THE INTELLIGENTSIA IN CHANGING CHINA.=
                        FOREIGN AFFAIRS, 36, (JANUARY 1958), PP. 315-329.         58
                        COMEL, ELEL, ELPRNOR
CHU,D -57-LCC   CHU, D
                        LEADERSHIP IN COMMUNIST CHINA.=
                        CURRENT HISTORY, N.S., (JANUARY 1957), PP. 13-18.         57
                        COMEL
CHUATS-63-MLS   CHUAN, TSENG-YU
                        THE MO LIAO SYSTEM IN CH'ING ADMINISTRATION (CHINA).=
                        PHILLIPINE JOURNAL OF PUBLIC ADMINISTRATION, 7,           63
                           (OCTOBER 1963), PP. 258-267.
                        ELEL, ELNOEL, ELPRNOR
CHUBB -54-VRI   CHUBB, B
                        VOCATIONAL REPRESENTATION AND THE IRISH SENATE.=
                        POLITICAL STUDIES, 2, (JUNE 1954), PP. 97-111.            54
                        COMEL, ELEL
CHUBB -57-IMI   CHUBB, B
                        THE INDEPENDENT MEMBER IN IRELAND.=
                        POLITICAL STUDIES, 5, (JUNE 1957), PP. 131-139            57
                        ELEL, ELNOEL
CHUBB -63-GAP   CHUBB, B
                        GOING ABOUT PERSECUTING CIVIL SERVANTS -- THE ROLE OF THE
                           IRISH PARLIAMENTARY REPRESENTATIVES.=
                        POLITICAL STUDIES, 11, (OCTOBER 1963), PP. 272-286.       63
                        ELEL, ELPRNOR
CHUNC -55-CGS   CHUNG-LI, C
                        THE CHINESE GENTRY -- STUDIES ON THEIR ROLE IN
                           NINETEENTH-CENTURY CHINESE SOCIETY.=
                        SEATTLE, UNIVERSITY OF WASHINGTON PRESS, 1955.            55
                        COMEL, ELEL, ELPRNOR
CHUNK -63-NKP   CHUNG, K
                        THE NORTH KOREAN PEOPLE'S ARMY AND THE PARTY.=
                        THE CHINA QUARTERLY, 14, (APRIL-JUNE 1963), PP. 105-124.  63
                        ELEL
CICOAV-58-FBO   CICOUREL, AV
                        THE FRONT AND BACK OF ORGANIZATIONAL LEADERSHIP -- A
                           CASE STUDY (UNITED STATES).=
                        PACIFIC SOCIOLOGICAL REVIEW, 1, (SPRING 1958), PP. 54-58. 58
                        COMEL, FLPRNOR
CLAPCL-63-CHW   CLAPP, CL
                        THE CONGRESSMAN -- HIS WORK AS HE SEES IT
                           (UNITED STATES).=
                        WASHINGTON, THE BROOKINGS INSTITUTE, 1963.                63
                        COMEL, ELEL, ELNOEL, ELPRNOR
CLAPGR-55-AIG   CLAPP, GR
```

ANTI - INTELLECTUALISM IN GOVERNMENT (UNITED STATES).=
JOURNAL OF SOCIAL ISSUES, 9, (1955), PP. 31-35.                55
ELEL, ELNOEL

CLAREL-36-RNS  CLARKE, EL
THE RECRUITMENT OF THE NATION'S LEADERS (GREAT BRITAIN).=
BRITISH SOCIOLOGICAL REVIEW, 28, (JULY AND OCTOBER          36
1936), PP. 246-266, 333-360.
COMEL

CLARKB-65-DGD  CLARK, KB
DARK GHETTOS -- DILEMMAS OF SOCIAL POWER
(UNITED STATES).=
NEW YORK, HARPER AND ROW, 1965.                             65
ELEL, ELNOEL

CLARRA-67-CUS  CLARKE, RA
THE COMPOSITION OF THE USSR SUPREME SOVIET  1958-1966.
SOVIET STUDIES, 19, (JULY 1967), PP. 53-65.                67
COMEL

CLARSD-63-GIC  CLARK, SD
GROUP INTERESTS IN CANADIAN POLITICS.=
JH AITCHISON (ED), THE POLITICAL PROCESS IN CANADA,        63
UNIVERSITY OF TORONTO PRESS, OXFORD UNIVERSITY PRESS,
1963.
COMEL, ELEL, ELNOEL

CLEAJW-64-PPS  CLEARY, JW
THE PARTS OF THE PARTY (SOVIET UNION).=
PROBLEMS OF COMMUNISM, 13, (JULY-AUGUST 1964), PP. 55-60. 64
ELEL

CLEGE -60-RPP  CLEGG, E
RACE AND POLITICS -- PARTNERSHIP IN THE FEDERATION OF
RHODESIA NYASALAND.=
LONDON, OXFORD UNIVERSITY PRESS, 1960.                     60
COMEL, ELEL, ELNOEL, ELPRNOR

CLEGHA-61-TUO  CLEGG, HA          KILLICK, AJ        ADAMS, R
TRADE UNION OFFICERS (GREAT BRITAIN).=
OXFORD, BASIL BLACKWELL, 1961.                             61
COMEL, ELEL, ELNOEL

CLELDA-64-EDC  CLELLAND, DA         FORM, WH
ECONOMIC DOMINANTS AND COMMUNITY POWER -- A
COMPARATIVE ANALYSIS (UNITED STATES).=
THE AMERICAN JOURNAL OF SOCIOLOGY, 69, (MARCH 1964),       64
PP. 511-521.
ELEL, ELPRNOR

CLEMJR-50-NDV  CLEMENTIN, JR
THE NATIONALIST DILEMMA IN VIETNAM.=
PACIFIC AFFAIRS, 23, (SEPTEMBER 1950), PP. 294-310.        50
ELEL, ELPRNOR

CLEMRV-65-CGB  CLEMENTS, RV
THE CABINET (GREAT BRITAIN).=
POLITICAL STUDIES, 13, (JUNE 1965), PP. 231-234.           65
COMEL, ELEL

CLIFM -60-FCE  CLIFFORD-VAUGHAN, M
SOME FRENCH CONCEPTS OF ELITES.=
THE BRITISH JOURNAL OF SOCIOLOGY, 11, (DECEMBER 1960),     60
PP. 319-331.
GNELTH

CLIGRP-64-PEG  CLIGNET, RP          FOSTER, P
POTENTIAL ELITES IN GHANA AND THE IVORY COAST --
A PRELIMINARY COMPARISON.=
THE AMERICAN JOURNAL OF SOCIOLOGY, 70, (NOVEMBER 1964),    64
PP. 349-362.
DEFEL, COMEL, ELEL, ELPRNOR

CLINCA-63-RLB  CLINE, CA
RECRUITS TO LABOR -- THE BRITISH LABOUR PARTY,
1914-1931.=
SYRACUSE, SYRACUSE UNIVERSITY PRESS, 1963.                 63
COMEL, ELEL

CLINH -52-MCS  CLINE, H
MEXICAN COMMUNITY STUDIES.=
HISPANIC-AMERICAN HISTORICAL REVIEW, 32, (MAY 1952),       52
PP. 212-242.
COMEL, ELEL, ELNOEL, ELPRNOR

CLINWB-47-NM   CLINE, WB
NATIONALISM IN MOROCCO.=
THE MIDDLE EAST JOURNAL, 1, (JANUARY 1947), PP. 18-28.     47
COMEL, ELEL, ELNOEL, ELPRNOR

CNUDCF-66-LBC  CNUDDE, CF           MCCRONE, DJ
THE LINKAGE BETWEEN CONSTITUENCY ATTITUDES AND
CONGRESSIONAL VOTING BEHAVIOR--A CAUSAL MODEL
(UNITED STATES).=
THE AMERICAN POLITICAL SCIENCE REVIEW, 60, (MARCH 1966),   66
PP. 66-72.
ELNOEL, ELPRNOR, METEL

COBBA -48-SCF  COBBAN, A
THE SECOND CHAMBER IN FRANCE.=

THE POLITICAL QUARTERLY, 19, (OCTOBER 1948), PP. 323-335. 48
ELEL

COCHJD-67-MSN    COCHRANE, JD
MEXICO'S 'NEW CIENTIFICOS' -- THE DIAZ ORDAZ CABINET.=
INTER-AMERICAN ECONOMIC AFFAIRS, 21, (SUMMER 1967),          67
    PP. 61-72.
COMEL, ELPRNOR

COCHTC-59-PRB    COCHRAN, TC
THE PUERTO RICAN BUSINESSMAN -- A STUDY IN CULTURAL
    CHANGE.=
PHILADELPHIA, UNIVERSITY OF PENNSYLVANIA PRESS, 1959.        59
COMEL, ELPRNOR

COCHTC-62-EAC    COCHRAN, TC          REINA, RE
ENTREPRENEURSHIP IN ARGENTINE CULTURE --
    'TORCUATO DI TELLA AND S.I.A.M.'.=
PHILADELPHIA, UNIVERSITY OF PENNSYLVANIA PRESS, 1962.        62
ELEL, ELNOEL, ELPRNOR

COCHTC-64-EEC    COCHRAN, TC
THE ENTREPRENEUR IN ECONOMIC CHANGE.=
BEHAVIORAL SCIENCE, 9, (APRIL 1964), PP. 111-119.            64
ELEL, ELNOEL, ELPRNOR

COCKPM-63-PMZ    COCKS, PM
THE PURGE OF MARSHAL ZHUKOV (SOVIET UNION).=
SLAVIC REVIEW, 22, (SEPTEMBER 1963), PP. 483-498.            63
ELEL, ELPRNOR

CODDGA-60-FSP    CODDING, GA
THE FRENCH SOCIALIST PARTY AND THE WEST.=
ORBIS, 4, (WINTER 1960), PP. 478-491.                        60
ELEL, ELPRNOR

COFFTE-44-TCT    COFFIN, TE
THREE COMPONENT THEORIES OF LEADERSHIP.=
JOURNAL OF ABNORMAL AND SOCIAL PSYCHOLOGY, 39.              44
    (JANUARY 1944), PP. 63-83.
DEFEL

COHEA -66-TEA    COHEN, A
THE TECHNOLOGY - ELITE APPROACH TO THE DEVELOPMENTAL
    PROCESS -- PERUVIAN CASE STUDY.=
ECONOMIC DEVELOPMENT AND CULTURAL CHANGE, 14,               66
    (APRIL 1966), PP. 323-333.
COMEL, ELEL, ELPRNOR

COHEAA-63-DWR    COHEN, AA          STEFFENS, CF
DISILLUSIONMENT WITHIN THE RANKS (CHINA).=
PROBLEMS OF COMMUNISM, 12, (MAY-JUNE 1963), PP. 10-17.       63
ELEL, ELPRNOR

COHEAM-61-CLC    COHEN, AM          BENNIS, WG
CONTINUITY OF LEADERSHIP IN COMMUNICATION NETWORKS.=
HUMAN RELATIONS, 14, (1961), PP. 351-367.                    61
METEL

COHEBC-55-PFP    COHEN, BC
THE PRESS AND FOREIGN POLICY IN THE UNITED STATES.=
JOURNAL OF INTERNATIONAL AFFAIRS, 9, (1955),                55
    PP. 128-137.
ELEL, ELPRNOR

COHEBC-56-PCJ    COHEN, BC
POLITICAL COMMUNICATION OF THE JAPANESE PEACE
    SETTLEMENT (UNITED STATES).=
THE PUBLIC OPINION QUARTERLY, 20 (SPRING 1956),             56
    PP. 27-38
ELEL, ELNOEL

COHEBC-57-PPF    COHEN, BC
THE POLITICAL PROCESS AND FOREIGN POLICY (UNITED STATES).=
PRINCETON, PRINCETON UNIVERSITY PRESS, 1957.                57
ELEL, ELNOEL

COHEBC-59-ING    COHEN, BC
THE INFLUENCE OF NON-GOVERNMENTAL GROUPS ON
    FOREIGN POLICY MAKING (UNITED STATES).=
BOSTON, WORLD PEACE FOUNDATION, 1959.                       59
ELEL, ELNOEL

COHEBC-63-PFP    COHEN, BC
THE PRESS AND FOREIGN POLICY (UNITED STATES).=
PRINCETON, NEW JERSEY, PRINCETON UNIVERSITY PRESS, 1963.    63
ELEL, ELNOEL, ELPRNOR

COHEBC-66-MPP    COHEN, BC
THE MILITARY POLICY PUBLIC (UNITED STATES).=
THE PUBLIC OPINION QUARTERLY, 30, (SUMMER 1966),            66
    PP. 200-211.
ELEL, ELNOEL

COHEEE-49-IJC    COHEN, EE
THE INTELLECTUAL AND THE JEWISH COMMUNITY
    (UNITED STATES))=
COMMENTARY, 8, (JULY 1949), PP. 20-30.                      49
COMEL, ELNOEL, ELPRNOR

COHESP-63-SCB    COHEN, SP
SUBHAS CHANDRA BOSE AND THE INDIAN NATIONAL ARMY.=

```
                        PACIFIC AFFAIRS, 36, (WINTER 1963), PP. 411-429.            63
                        ELEL, ELNOEL, ELPRNOR
COHESP-64-APP   COHEN, SP
                        ARMS AND POLITICS IN PAKISTAN.=
                        INDIA QUARTERLY, 20, (OCTOBER-DECEMBER 1964), PP. 403-417.64
                        ELEL, ELNOEL
COHESP-64-RPS   COHEN, SP
                        RULERS AND PRIESTS -- A STUDY IN CULTURAL CONTROL
                          (INDIA).=
                        COMPARATIVE STUDIES IN SOCIETY AND HISTORY, 6,              64
                          (1963-1964), PP. 199-216.
                        ELEL
COLBES-52-LWJ   COLBERT, ES
                        THE LEFT WING IN JAPANESE POLITICS.=
                        NEW YORK, NEW YORK INSTITUTE OF PACIFIC RELATIONS, 1952.    52
                        COMEL, ELEL, ELNOEL, ELPRNOR
COLEAB-56-JSP   COLE, AB
                        JAPANESE SOCIETY AND POLITICS -- THE IMPACT OF SOCIAL
                          STRATIFICATION AND MOBILITY ON POLITICS.=
                        BOSTON, BOSTON UNIVERSITY PRESS, 1956.                      56
                        GNELTH, DEFEL, COMEL, ELEL, ELNOEL, ELPRNOR
COLEAB-56-SSM   COLE, AB
                        SOCIAL STRATIFICATION AND MOBILITY -- SOME POLITICAL
                          IMPLICATIONS (JAPAN).=
                        THE ANNALS OF THE AMERICAN ACADEMY OF POLITICAL            56
                          AND SOCIAL SCIENCE, 308, (NOVEMBER 1956), PP. 121-129.
                        DEFEL, COMEL, ELPRNOR
COLECP-55-CSL   COLEMAN, CP
                        A CASE STUDY IN LATIN AMERICAN COMMUNISM.=
                        PROBLEMS OF COMMUNISM, 4, (SEPTEMBER-OCTOBER 1955),        55
                          PP. 17-26.
                        COMEL, ELEL, ELNOEL
COLEGD-50-CMC   COLE, GDH
                        CONCEPTION OF THE MIDDLE CLASS (GREAT BRITAIN).=
                        THE BRITISH JOURNAL OF SOCIOLOGY, 1, (SEPTEMBER 1950),     50
                          PP. 275-290.
                        GNELTH
COLEGD-50-LSP   COLE, GDH
                        LABOUR AND STAFF PROBLEMS UNDER NATIONALISATION
                          (GREAT BRITAIN).=
                        THE POLITICAL QUARTERLY, 21, (APRIL 1950), PP. 160-170.     50
                        ELEL, ELNOEL
COLEGD-55-SCS   COLE, GDH
                        STUDIES IN CLASS STRUCTURE (GREAT BRITAIN).=
                        LONDON, ROUTLEDGE AND KEGAN PAUL, LTD, 1955.                55
                        GNELTH, DEFEL, COMEL, ELEL, ELNOEL
COLEJS-57-CCU   COLEMAN, JS
                        COMMUNITY CONFLICT (UNITED STATES).=
                        GLENCOE, ILLINOIS, FREE PRESS, 1957.                        57
                        GNELTH, ELEL, ELNOEL
COLEJS-58-NBN   COLEMAN, JS
                        NIGERIA -- BACKGROUND TO NATIONALISM.=
                        BERKELEY, UNIVERSITY OF CALIFORNIA PRESS, 1958.             58
                        COMEL, ELEL, ELNOEL
COLEJS-60-PSD   COLEMAN, JS
                        THE POLITICAL SYSTEMS OF THE DEVELOPING AREAS.=
                        G ALMOND AND JS COLEMAN (EDS), THE POLITICS OF             60
                          DEVELOPING AREAS, PRINCETON, PRINCETON UNIVERSITY
                          PRESS, 1960, PP. 532-576.
                        COMEL, ELEL, ELNOEL
COLEJS-60-PSS   COLEMAN, JS
                        THE POLITICS OF SUB-SAHARA AFRICA.=
                        G ALMOND AND JS COLEMAN (EDS), THE POLITICS OF             60
                          DEVELOPING AREAS, PRINCETON, PRINCETON UNIVERSITY
                          PRESS, 1960, PP. 247-368.
                        COMEL, ELEL, ELNOEL
COLEJS-64-PPN   COLEMAN, JS          ROSBERG, C
                        POLITICAL PARTIES AND NATIONAL INTEGRATION IN TROPICAL
                          AFRICA.=
                        BERKELEY, UNIVERSITY OF CALIFORNIA PRESS, 1964.             64
                        ELEL, ELNOEL, ELPRNOR
COLEJS-65-EPD   COLEMAN, JS (ED)
                        EDUCATION AND POLITICAL DEVELOPMENT.=
                        PRINCETON, PRINCETON UNIVERSITY PRESS, 1965.                65
                        COMEL, METEL, ELPRNOR
COLEJS-65-UEC   COLEMAN, JS
                        THE USE OF ELECTRONIC COMPUTERS IN THE STUDY OF
                          SOCIAL ORGANIZATIONS.=
                        EUROPEAN JOURNAL OF SOCIOLOGY, 6, (1965), PP. 88-107.       65
                        ELEL, ELNOEL, METEL
COLET -49-CBS   COLE, T
                        THE CANADIAN BUREAUCRACY -- A STUDY OF CANADIAN CIVIL
                          SERVICE AND OTHER PUBLIC EMPLOYEES 1939-1947.=
                        DURHAM, NORTH CAROLINA, DUKE UNIVERSITY PRESS, 1949.        49
```

```
                      COMEL
COLET -55-NWG  COLE, T
                      NEOFASCISM IN WESTERN GERMANY AND ITALY.=
                      THE AMERICAN POLITICAL SCIENCE REVIEW, 49, (MARCH 1955),   55
                         PP. 131-144.
                      COMEL, ELEL, ELNOEL, ELPRNOR
COLLM -59-FCC  COLLINET, M
                      THE FRENCH CP (COMMUNIST PARTY) -- SIGNS OF CRISIS.=
                      PROBLEMS OF COMMUNISM, 8, (MAY-JUNE 1959), PP. 22-27.       59
                      ELEL, ELNOEL, ELPRNOR
COLOM -54-EFK  COLOMBE, M
                      EGYPT FROM THE FALL OF KING FAROUK TO THE
                         FEBRUARY 1954 CRISIS.=
                      MIDDLE EASTERN AFFAIRS, 5, (JUNE-JULY 1954), PP. 185-192. 54
                      COMEL, ELEL
COLSE -58-RBN  COLSON, E
                      THE ROLE OF BUREAUCRATIC NORMS IN AFRICAN POLITICAL
                         STRUCTURES.=
                      VF RAY (ED), SYSTEMS OF POLITICAL CONTROL AND BUREAUCRACY 58
                         IN HUMAN SOCIETIES, SEATTLE, PROCEEDINGS OF THE 1958
                         ANNUAL SPRING MEETING OF THE AMERICAN ETHNOLOGICAL
                         SOCIETY, 1958, PP. 42-49.
                      DEFEL, ELEL, ELPRNOR
COLTHK-55-WJD  COLTON, HK
                      THE WORKING OF THE JAPANESE DIET.=
                      PACIFIC AFFAIRS, 28, (DECEMBER 1955), PP. 263-372.          55
                      ELEL
COLTJ -63-INT  COLTART, J
                      THE INFLUENCE OF NEWSPAPER AND TELEVISION IN AFRICA.=
                      AFRICAN AFFAIRS, 62, (JULY 1963), PP. 202-210.              63
                      ELEL, ELNOEL
COLTKE-55-CLJ  COLTON, KE
                      CONSERVATIVE LEADERSHIP IN JAPAN.=
                      FAR EASTERN SURVEY, 24, (JUNE 1955), PP. 90-96.             55
                      COMEL
COMFGO-58-PPS  COMFORT, GO
                      PROFESSIONAL POLITICIANS -- A STUDY OF BRITISH PARTY
                         AGENTS.=
                      WASHINGTON, PUBLIC AFFAIRS PRESS, 1958.                     58
                      COMEL, ELPRNOR
COMHJL-55-HCD  COMHAIRE-SYLVAIN, JL
                      THE HAITIAN 'CHEF DE SECTION'.=
                      AMERICAN ANTHROPOLOGIST, 57, (JUNE 1955), PP. 620-624.      55
                      COMEL, ELEL, ELNOEL
COMHS -59-USH  COMHAIRE-SYLVAIN, S COMHAIRE-SYLVAIN, J
                      URBAN STRATIFICATION IN HAITI.=
                      SOCIAL AND ECONOMIC STUDIES (INSTITUTE OF SOCIAL AND        59
                         ECONOMIC RESEARCH, UNIVERSITY COLLEGE OF THE WEST
                         INDIES), (JUNE 1959), PP. 179-189.
                      COMEL
CONQR -60-SGS  CONQUEST, R
                      THE STRUGGLE GOES ON (SOVIET UNION).=
                      PROBLEMS OF COMMUNISM, 9, (JULY-AUGUST 1960), PP. 7-11.     60
                      ELEL
CONQR -61-PPU  CONQUEST, R
                      POWER AND POLICY IN THE USSR.=
                      NEW YORK, ST. MARTIN'S PRESS, 1961.                         61
                      ELEL, ELNOEL
CONQR -63-AKC  CONQUEST, R
                      AFTER KHRUSHCHEV -- A CONSERVATIVE RESTORATION
                         (SOVIET UNION).=
                      PROBLEMS OF COMMUNISM, 12, (SEPTEMBER-OCTOBER 1963),        63
                         PP. 41-46.
                      COMEL, ELEL
CONQR -65-AFL  CONQUEST, R
                      AFTER THE FALL -- SOME LESSONS (SOVIET UNION).=
                      PROBLEMS OF COMMUNISM, 14, (JANUARY-FEBRUARY 1965),         65
                         PP. 17-22.
                      ELEL, ELNOEL
CONQR -66-IDS  CONQUEST, R
                      IMMOBILISM AND DECAY (SOVIET UNION).=
                      PROBLEMS OF COMMUNISM, 15, (SEPTEMBER-OCTOBER 1966),        66
                         PP. 35-37.
                      ELEL, ELPRNOR
CONTH -62-USS  CONTAS, H
                      THE U.S.S.R. -- FROM CHARISMATIC SECT TO BUREAUCRATIC
                         SOCIETY (SOVIET UNION).=
                      ADMINISTRATIVE SCIENCE QUARTERLY, 6, (1961-1962),           62
                         PP. 282-298.
                      DEFEL, ELEL, ELNOEL
CONVPE-64-NBS  CONVERSE, PE
                      THE NATURE OF BELIEF SYSTEMS IN MASS PUBLICS.=
                      DE APTER (ED), IDEOLOGY AND DISCONTENT, LONDON, THE FREE    64
                         PRESS, 1964, PP. 206-261.
```

```
                    ELNOEL, ELPRNOR
CONVPE-65-EMR  CONVERSE, PE        CLAUSEN, AR        MILLER,WE
               ELECTORAL MYTH AND REALITY -- THE 1964 ELECTION
                  (UNITED STATES).=
               THE AMERICAN POLITICAL SCIENCE REVIEW, 59, (JUNE 1965),   65
                  PP. 321-336.
                    ELNOEL, ELPRNOR
COOKEF-61-RIP  COOKE, EF
               RESEARCH -- AN INSTRUMENT OF POLITICAL POWER
                  (UNITED STATES).=
               POLITICAL SCIENCE QUARTERLY, 76, (MARCH 1961), PP. 69-87. 61
                    ELEL
COOKSD-57-HSL  COOK, SD
               HACKER'S LIBERAL DEMOCRACY AND SOCIAL CONTROL --
                  A CRITIQUE (UNITED STATES).=
               THE AMERICAN POLITICAL SCIENCE REVIEW, 51,                57
                  (DECEMBER 1957), PP. 1027-1039.
                    GNELTH, ELPRNOR
COQUJR-55-PPE  COQUIA, JR
               THE PHILIPPINE PRESIDENTIAL ELECTION OF 1953.=
               MANILA, PHILIPPINE EDUCATION FOUNDATION, INC, AND          55
                  JORGE R COQUIA, 1955.
                    ELEL, ELNOEL, ELPRNOR
CORLFJ-61-PCR  CORLEY, FJ
               THE PRESIDENT IN THE CONSTITUTION OF THE  REPUBLIC
                  OF VIETNAM.=
               PACIFIC AFFAIRS, 34, (SUMMER 1961), PP. 165-174.           61
                    ELEL, ELNOEL
CORMML-61-SWR  CORMACK, ML
               SHE WHO RIDES A PEACOCK -- SOCIAL CHANGE AND INDIAN
                  STUDENTS.=
               NEW YORK, FREDERICK A PRAEGER, 1961.                       61
                    ELEL, ELPRNOR
CORNEE-57-CPL  CORNWELL-JR, EE
               COOLIDGE AND PRESIDENTIAL LEADERSHIP (UNITED STATES).=
               THE PUBLIC OPINION QUARTERLY, 21, (SUMMER 1957),           57
                  PP. 265-277.
                    ELEL, ELNOEL, ELPRNOR
CORNEE-64-BME  CORNWELL-JR, EE
               BOSSES, MACHINES, AND ETHNIC GROUPS (UNITED STATES).=
               THE ANNALS OF THE AMERICAN ACADEMY OF POLITICAL AND        64
                  SOCIAL SCIENCE, 353, (MAY 1964), PP. 27-39.
                    COMEL, ELNOEL
CORNEE-65-PLP  CORNWELL-JR, EE
               PRESIDENTIAL LEADERSHIP OF PUBLIC OPINION
                  (UNITED STATES).=
               BLOOMINGTON, INDIANA UNIVERSITY PRESS, 1965.               65
                    ELEL, ELNOEL, ELPRNOR
CORNR -65-YCH  CORNELL, R
               YOUTH AND COMMUNISM -- AN HISTORICAL ANALYSIS OF
                  INTERNATIONAL COMMUNIST YOUTH MOVEMENTS.=
               NEW YORK, WALKER, 1965.                                    65
                    COMEL, ELEL, ELNOEL, ELPRNOR
CORPOD-57-BP   CORPUZ, OD
               THE BUREAUCRACY IN THE PHILIPPINES.=
               MANILA, INSTITUTE OF PUBLIC ADMINISTRATION, UNIVERSITY     57
                  OF THE PHILIPPINES, 1957.
                    COMEL, ELEL, ELNOEL, ELPRNOR
CORSJJ-66-MNT  CORSON, JJ        PAUL, RS
               MEN NEAR THE TOP -- FILLING KEY POSTS IN THE FEDERAL
                  CIVIL SERVICE (UNITED STATES).=
               BALTIMORE, JOHNS HOPKINS PRESS, 1966.                      66
                    COMEL, ELEL, ELPRNOR
CORWES-56-PTU  CORWIN, ES        KOENIG, LW
               THE PRESIDENCY TODAY (UNITED STATES).=
               NEW YORK, NEW YORK UNIVERSITY PRESS, 1956.                 56
                    ELEL, ELNOEL
COSELA-65-MIS  COSER, LA
               MEN OF IDEAS -- A SOCIOLOGIST'S VIEW (INTELLECTUALS).=
               NEW YORK, THE FREE PRESS, 1965                            65
                    DEFEL, ELEL, ELPRNOR
COSID -61-CLA  COSIO-VILLEGAS, D
               CHANGE IN LATIN AMERICA -- THE MEXICAN AND CUBAN
                  REVOLUTIONS.=
               LINCOLN, NEBRASKA, UNIVERSITY OF NEBRASKA PRESS, 1961.     61
                    ELEL, ELNOEL
COSMB -62-PRS  COSMAN, B
               PRESIDENTIAL REPUBLICANISM IN THE SOUTH - 1960
                  (UNITED STATES).=
               THE JOURNAL OF POLITICS, 24, (MAY 1962), PP. 303-322.      62
                    ELNOEL
COSTE -63-IAC  COSTANTINI, E
               INTRAPARTY ATTITUDE CONFLICT -- DEMOCRATIC PARTY
                  LEADERSHIP IN CALIFORNIA (UNITED STATES).=
```

```
                    THE WESTERN POLITICAL QUARTERLY, 16, (DECEMBER 1963),        63
                       PP. 956-972.
                    ELEL, ELPRNOR
COSWR -65-RYF       COSWELL, R
                    REBELLION OF THE YOUNG (FRANCE).=
                    PROBLEMS OF COMMUNISM, 14, (SEPTEMBER-OCTOBER 1965),         65
                       PP. 11-17.
                    ELNOEL
COTTCP-64-PWP       COTTER, CP           HENNESSY, BC
                    POLITICS WITHOUT POWER -- THE NATIONAL PARTY COMMITTEES
                       (UNITED STATES).=
                    NEW YORK, ATHERTON PRESS, 1964.                             64
                    ELEL
COTTR -64-NI        COTTAM, R
                    NATIONALISM IN IRAN.=
                    PITTSBURGH, UNIVERSITY OF PITTSBURGH PRESS, 1964.            64
                    ELEL, ELNOEL, ELPRNOR
COVEHM-50-DRG       COVERLEY, HM
                    DANGER ON THE RIGHT IN GERMANY.=
                    CURRENT HISTORY, N.S., 18, (MARCH 1950), PP. 138-143.        50
                    COMEL, ELEL, ELNOEL
COWALG-49-TCP       COWAN, LG
                    THE TECHNIQUES OF THE COMMUNIST PARTY IN FRANCE.=
                    INTERNATIONAL JOURNAL, 4, (WINTER 1948-1949),               49
                       PP. 33-46.
                    COMEL, ELNOEL
COWALG-65-ENB       COWAN, LG            O'CONNELL, J          SCANLON, DG (EDS)
                    EDUCATION AND NATION-BUILDING IN AFRICA.=
                    NEW YORK, FREDERICK A PRAEGER, 1965.                        65
                    COMEL, ELEL, ELPRNOR
COWAM -62-EGR       COWAN, M
                    EAST GERMAN REVISIONISM -- THE SPECTRE AND THE REALITY.=
                    L LABEDZ (ED), REVISIONISM, ESSAYS ON THE HISTORY           62
                       OF MARXIST IDEAS, NEW YORK, FREDERICK A PRAEGER,
                       1962, PP. 239-256.
                    COMEL, ELEL, ELNOEL, ELPRNOR
COX,EF-62-CDP       COX, EF
                    CONGRESSIONAL DISTRICT PARTY STRENGTHS AND THE
                       1960 ELECTIONS (UNITED STATES).=
                    THE JOURNAL OF POLITICS, 24, (MAY 1962), PP. 277-302.        62
                    ELNOEL, METEL
COX,OC-50-MWS       COX, OC
                    MAX WEBER ON SOCIAL STRATIFICATION -- A CRITIQUE.=
                    AMERICAN SOCIOLOGICAL REVIEW, 15, (APRIL 1950),             50
                       PP. 223-227.
                    DEFEL
COX,OC-62-CAL       COX, OC
                    CAPITALISM AND AMERICAN LEADERSHIP.=
                    NEW YORK, PHILOSOPHICAL LIBRARY, 1962.                      62
                    COMEL, ELEL, ELPRNOR
COX,OC-65-LAN       COX, OC
                    LEADERSHIP AMONG NEGROES IN THE UNITED STATES.=
                    AW GOULDNER (ED), STUDIES IN LEADERSHIP, NEW YORK,          65
                       RUSSELL AND RUSSELL, 1965, PP. 228-271.
                    ELEL, ELPRNOR
CRAIGA-53-D         CRAIG, GA           GILBERT, F (EDS)
                    THE DIPLOMATS, 1919-1939.=
                    PRINCETON, PRINCETON UNIVERSITY PRESS, 1953.                53
                    ELEL
CRAIGA-55-PPA       CRAIG, GA
                    THE POLITICS OF THE PRUSSIAN ARMY 1640-1945.=
                    OXFORD, CLARENDON PRESS, 1955.                              55
                    COMEL, ELEL, ELNOEL, ELPRNOR
CRAIJM-53-ES        CRAIG, JM
                    EGYPTIAN STUDENTS.=
                    THE MIDDLE EAST JOURNAL, 7, (SUMMER 1953), PP. 293-299.      53
                    COMEL, ELPRNOR
CRAMFH-51-DPM       CRAMER, FH
                    THE DICTATOR -- 1, THE PRE-MODERN TYRANT -- 2, A MODERN
                       VERSION.=
                    CURRENT HISTORY, N.S., 21, (AUGUST 1951, SEPTEMBER 1951), 51
                       PP. 85-91, PP. 151-158.
                    DEFEL, COMEL
CRAMMR-63-SDN       CRAMER, MR
                    SCHOOL DESEGREGATION AND NEW INDUSTRY -- THE SOUTHERN
                       COMMUNITY LEADER'S VIEWPOINT (UNITED STATES).=
                    SOCIAL FORCES, 41, (MAY 1963), PP. 384-389.                 63
                    ELPRNOR
CRANRI-59-LCP       CRANE, RI
                    LEADERSHIP OF THE CONGRESS PARTY (INDIA).=
                    RL PARK AND I TINKER (ED), LEADERSHIP AND POLITICAL         59
                       INSTITUTIONS IN INDIA, PRINCETON, PRINCETON UNIVERSITY
                       PRESS, 1959, PP. 169-187.
                    COMEL, ELNOEL, ELPRNOR
```

```
CRANW -60-CRC    CRANE-JR, W
                 A CAVEAT ON ROLL-CALL STUDIES OF PARTY VOTING
                    (UNITED STATES).=
                 MIDWEST JOURNAL OF POLITICAL SCIENCE, 4, (AUGUST 1960),    60
                    PP. 237-249.
                 ELEL, ELPRNOR, METEL
CRANW -62-ERF    CRANE-JR, W
                 THE ERRAND-RUNNING FUNCTION OF AUSTRIAN LEGISLATORS.=
                 PARLIAMENTARY AFFAIRS, 15, (SPRING 1962), PP. 160-169.      62
                 ELEL
CRANWW-60-DRR    CRANE-JR, WW
                 DO REPRESENTATIVES REPRESENT (UNITED STATES).=
                 THE JOURNAL OF POLITICS, 22, (MAY 1960), PP. 295-299.       60
                 ELNOEL
CRANWW-64-IPE    CRANE, WW            HUNT, WH            WAHLKE, JC
                 INTERVIEWING POLITICAL ELITES IN CROSS-CULTURAL
                    COMPARATIVE RESEARCH.=
                 THE AMERICAN JOURNAL OF SOCIOLOGY, 70, (JULY 1964),         64
                    PP. 59-68.
                 METEL
CRECD -66-AAR    CRECELIUS, D
                 AL-AZHAR IN THE REVOLUTION (EGYPT).=
                 THE MIDDLE EAST JOURNAL, 20, (WINTER 1966), PP. 31-49.      66
                 ELEL, ELNOEL
CREEHG-64-BBC    CREEL, HG
                 THE BEGINNINGS OF BUREAUCRACY IN CHINA -- THE ORIGIN OF
                    THE HSIEN.=
                 THE JOURNAL OF ASIAN STUDIES, 23, (FEBRUARY 1964),          64
                    PP. 155-183.
                 COMEL, ELEL, ELNOEL
CRICB -65-RPG    CRICK, B
                 THE REFORM OF PARLIAMENT (GREAT BRITAIN).=
                 NEW YORK, ANCHOR BOOKS, 1965.                               65
                 ELEL, ELPRNOR
CRIDJH-44-BUS    CRIDER, JH
                 THE BUREAUCRAT (UNITED STATES).=
                 NEW YORK, JB LIPPENCOTT COMPANY, 1944.                      44
                 COMEL, ELPRNOR
CROAM -60-IUU    CROAN, M
                 INTELLECTUALS UNDER ULBRICHT (EAST GERMANY).=
                 SOVIET SURVEY--A QUARTERLY REVIEW OF CULTURAL TRENDS,       60
                    34, (OCTOBER-DECEMBER 1960), PP. 35-45.
                 COMEL, ELEL, ELPRNOR
CROSCA-60-FLG    CROSLAND, CAR
                 THE FUTURE OF THE LEFT (GREAT BRITAIN).=
                 ENCOUNTER, 14, (MARCH 1960), PP. 3-12.                      60
                 COMEL, ELPRNOR
CROSCA-60-LAG    CROSLAND, CAR
                 ON THE LEFT AGAIN (GREAT BRITAIN).=
                 ENCOUNTER, 15, (OCTOBER 1960), PP. 3-12.                    60
                 COMEL, ELEL, ELNOEL
CROSCA-62-ICC    CROSLAND, CAR
                 INSIDERS AND CONTROLLERS (CORPORATE ELITE,
                    GREAT BRITAIN).=
                 CAR CROSLAND, THE CONSERVATIVE ENEMY, NEW YORK,             62
                    SCHOCKEN BOOKS, 1962, PP. 68-96.
                 DEFEL, COMEL, ELEL
CROSR -64-SWG    CROSSMAN, R
                 SCIENTISTS IN WHITEHALL (GREAT BRITAIN).=
                 ENCOUNTER, 23, (JULY 1964), PP. 3-10.                       64
                 ELEL
CROUWW-56-CSI    CROUCH, WW
                 CIVIL SERVICE IN INDIA.=
                 PUBLIC PERSONNEL REVIEW, 17, (APRIL 1956),                  56
                    PP. 84-91.
                 COMEL, ELEL, ELPRNOR
CROWJB-62-JAF    CROWLEY, JB
                 JAPANESE ARMY FACTIONALISM IN THE EARLY 1930'S.=
                 THE JOURNAL OF ASIAN STUDIES, 21, (MAY 1962), PP. 309-326. 62
                 ELEL, ELNOEL
CROWRE-62-RSL    CROW, RE
                 RELIGIOUS SECTARIANISM IN THE LEBANESE POLITICAL SYSTEM.=
                 THE JOURNAL OF POLITICS, 24, (AUGUST 1962), PP. 489-520.    62
                 COMEL, ELEL, ELNOEL, ELPRNOR
CROZB -60-RSP    CROZIER, B
                 THE REBELS -- A STUDY OF POST-WAR INSURRECTIONS.=
                 BOSTON, BEACON PRESS, 1960.                                 60
                 ELEL, ELNOEL, ELPRNOR
CROZB -62-DAR    CROZIER, B
                 DOWN AMONG THE RIGHTISTS (UNITED STATES).=
                 ENCOUNTER, 18, (MARCH 1962), PP. 51-57.                     62
                 ELEL, ELPRNOR
CROZM -64-BPE    CROZIER, M
                 THE BUREAUCRATIC PHENOMENON -- AN EXAMINATION OF
```

                        BUREAUCRACY IN MODERN ORGANIZATION AND ITS CULTURAL
                        SETTING IN FRANCE.=
                        CHICAGO, THE UNIVERSITY OF CHICAGO PRESS, 1964.           64
                        COMEL, ELEL, ELNOEL
CROZM  -64-CRN          CROZIER, M
                        THE CULTURAL REVOLUTION -- NOTES ON THE CHANGES IN THE
                        INTELLECTUAL CLIMATE OF FRANCE.=
                        DAEDALUS, 93, (WINTER 1964), PP. 514-542.                 64
                        ELEL, ELNOEL, ELPRNOR
CUBEJF-54-SSU           CUBER, JF            KENKEL, WF
                        SOCIAL STRATIFICATION IN THE UNITED STATES.=
                        NEW YORK, APPLETON-CENTURY-CROFTS, INC, 1954.             54
                        GNELTH, COMEL, ELEL, ELNOEL, ELPRNOR, METEL
CUMBCC-53-GLC           CUMBERLAND, CC
                        GUATEMALA -- LABOR AND THE COMMUNIST.=
                        CURRENT HISTORY, N.S., 24, (MARCH 1953), PP. 143-148.     53
                        ELNOEL
CUNLM  -64-BMW          CUNLIFFE, M
                        BLACK MUSLIMS, WHITE LIBERALS (UNITED STATES).=
                        ENCOUNTER, 23, (JULY 1964), PP. 3-10.                     64
                        ELEL
CUNNI  -56-HRL          CUNNINSON, I
                        HEADMAN AND THE RITUAL OF LAUPULA VILLAGES (AFRICA).=
                        AFRICA, 26, (1956), PP. 2-16.                             56
                        COMEL, ELPRNOR
CURLA  -63-ESD          CURLE, A
                        EDUCATIONAL STRATEGY FOR DEVELOPING SOCIETIES.=
                        LONDON, TAVISTOCK PUBLICATIONS, 1963.                     63
                        COMEL, ELEL, ELNOEL, ELPRNOR
CURRJA-51-MHI           CURRAN, JA
                        MILITANT HINDUISM IN INDIAN POLITICS -- A STUDY OF THE
                        R.S.S. (RASHTRIYA SWAYAMSEVAK SANGH).=
                        NEW YORK, INSTITUTE OF PACIFIC RELATIONS, 1951.           51
                        ELEL, ELNOEL, ELPRNOR
CURTRF-63-DAS           CURTIS, RF
                        DIFFERENTIAL ASSOCIATION AND THE STRATIFICATION
                        OF THE URBAN COMMUNITY (UNITED STATES).=
                        SOCIAL FORCES, 42, (OCTOBER 1963), PP. 68-77.             63
                        COMEL, ELEL, ELNOEL
CUTRP  -58-GRP          CUTRIGHT, P          ROSSI, PH
                        GRASS ROOTS POLITICIANS AND THE VOTE (UNITED STATES).=
                        AMERICAN SOCIOLOGICAL REVIEW, 23, (APRIL 1958),
                        PP. 171-179.                                             58
                        COMEL, ELNOEL, ELPRNOR
CUTRP  -58-POP          CUTRIGHT, P          ROSSI, PH
                        PARTY ORGANIZATIONS IN PRIMARY ELECTIONS
                        (UNITED STATES).=
                        THE AMERICAN JOURNAL OF SOCIOLOGY, 64, (NOVEMBER 1958),   58
                        PP. 262-269.
                        ELEL, ELNOEL
CUTRP  -63-MIL          CUTRIGHT, P
                        MEASURING THE IMPACT OF LOCAL PARTY ACTIVITY ON THE
                        GENERAL ELECTION VOTE (UNITED STATES).=
                        THE PUBLIC OPINION QUARTERLY, 27, (FALL 1963),            63
                        PP. 372-386.
                        ELNOEL, METEL
CUTRP  -63-UCP          CUTRIGHT, P
                        URBANIZATION AND COMPETITIVE PARTY POLITICS
                        (UNITED STATES).=
                        THE JOURNAL OF POLITICS, 25, (AUGUST 1963), PP. 552-564.  63
                        ELNOEL, METEL
D-SOVS-62-SGO           D-SOUZA, VS
                        SOCIAL GRADING OF OCCUPATIONS IN INDIA.=
                        THE SOCIOLOGICAL REVIEW, 10, (JULY 1962), PP. 145-159.    62
                        COMEL
D'ANWV-61-PDA           D'ANTONIO, WV        EHRLICH, HJ (EDS)
                        POWER AND DEMOCRACY IN AMERICA.=
                        NOTRE DAME, INDIANA, UNIVERSITY OF NOTRE DAME PRESS,      61
                        1961.
                        DEFEL, ELEL, ELNOEL, ELPRNOR, METEL
D'ANWV-62-RTM           D'ANTONIO, WV        ERICKSON, EC
                        THE REPUTATIONAL TECHNIQUE AS A MEASURE OF COMMUNITY
                        POWER -- AN EVALUATION BASED ON COMPARATIVE AND
                        LONGITUDINAL STUDIES.=
                        AMERICAN SOCIOLOGICAL REVIEW, 27, (JUNE 1962),            62
                        PP. 362-376.
                        METEL
D'ANWV-64-RRR           D'ANTONIO, WV        PIKE, FB (EDS)
                        RELIGION, REVOLUTION AND REFORM -- NEW FORCES FOR CHANGE
                        IN LATIN AMERICA.=
                        NEW YORK, FREDERICK A PRAEGER, 1964.                      64
                        COMEL, ELEL, ELNOEL, ELPRNOR
D'ANWV-65-ITB           D'ANTONIO, WV        FORM, WH
                        INFLUENTIALS IN TWO BORDER CITIES -- A STUDY IN

                    COMMUNITY DECISION-MAKING (MEXICO, UNITED STATES).=
                    NOTRE DAME, INDIANA, UNIVERSITY OF NOTRE DAME PRESS,          65
                    1965.
                    DEFEL, COMEL, ELEL, ELPRNOR
D'ANWV-66-CLE    D'ANTONIO, WV
                    COMMUNITY LEADERSHIP IN AN ECONOMIC CRISIS -- TESTING
                    GROUND FOR IDEOLOGICAL CLEAVAGE (UNITED STATES).=
                    THE AMERICAN JOURNAL OF SOCIOLOGY, 71, (MAY 1966),            66
                    PP. 688-700.
                    ELEL, ELNOEL, ELPRNOR, METEL
DAALH -55-PPN    DAALDER, H
                    PARTIES AND POLITICS IN THE NETHERLANDS.=
                    POLITICAL STUDIES, 3, (1955), PP. 1-16.                       55
                    COMEL, ELEL, ELNOEL, ELPRNOR
DAALH -63-CRB    DAALDER, H
                    CABINET REFORM IN IN BRITAIN 1914-1963.=
                    STANFORD, STANFORD UNIVERSITY PRESS, 1963.                    63
                    COMEL, ELEL
DAALH -66-GON    DAALDER, H
                    GOVERNMENT AND OPPOSITION IN THE NEW STATES.=
                    GOVERNMENT AND OPPOSITION, 1, (FEBRUARY 1966),                66
                    PP. 205-226.
                    DEFEL, ELEL, ELNOEL, ELPRNOR
DAHLRA-50-CFP    DAHL, RA
                    CONGRESS AND FOREIGN POLICY (UNITED STATES).=
                    NEW YORK, HARCOURT, BRACE AND COMPANY, 1950.                  50
                    COMEL, ELEL, ELNOEL, ELPRNOR
DAHLRA-53-PEW    DAHL, RA              LINDBLOM, CE
                    POLITICS, ECONOMICS, AND WELFARE (UNITED STATES).=
                    NEW YORK, HARPER AND BROTHERS, 1953.                          53
                    GNELTH, DEFEL
DAHLRA-55-HBD    DAHL, RA
                    HIERARCHY, BARGAINING, AND DEMOCRACY
                    IN POLITICS AND ECONOMICS (UNITED STATES).=
                    BROOKINGS INSTITUTION, RESEARCH FRONTIERS IN POLITICS         55
                    AND GOVERNMENT, WASHINGTON, 1955, PP. 45-69.
                    COMEL, ELEL, ELNOEL, ELPRNOR
DAHLRA-56-PDT    DAHL, RA
                    A PREFACE TO DEMOCRATIC THEORY (UNITED STATES).=
                    CHICAGO, THE UNIVERSITY OF CHICAGO PRESS, 1956.               56
                    GNELTH, DEFEL, METEL
DAHLRA-57-CP     DAHL, RA
                    THE CONCEPT OF POWER.=
                    BEHAVIORAL SCIENCE, 2, (JULY 1957), PP. 201-215.              57
                    GNELTH, DEFEL, METEL
DAHLRA-57-DMD    DAHL, RA
                    DECISION-MAKING IN A DEMOCRACY -- THE SUPREME COURT AS A
                    NATIONAL POLICY-MAKER (UNITED STATES).=
                    JOURNAL OF PUBLIC LAW, 6, (FALL 1957), PP. 279-295.           57
                    GNELTH, DEFEL, COMEL, ELEL, ELNOEL, ELPRNOR
DAHLRA-58-CRE    DAHL, RA
                    A CRITIQUE OF THE RULING ELITE MODEL.=
                    AMERICAN POLITICAL SCIENCE REVIEW, 52, (JUNE 1958),           58
                    PP. 463-469.
                    GNELTH, DEFEL, COMEL, ELEL
DAHLRA-61-WGU    DAHL, RA
                    WHO GOVERNS (UNITED STATES).=
                    NEW HAVEN, YALE UNIVERSITY PRESS, 1961.                       61
                    GNELTH, DEFEL, COMEL, ELEL, ELNOEL, ELPRNOR, METEL
DAHLRA-63-MPA    DAHL, RA
                    MODERN POLITICAL ANALYSIS.=
                    ENGLEWOOD CLIFFS, NEW JERSEY, PRENTICE-HALL, INC, 1963.       63
                    GNELTH, DEFEL, ELEL, ELNOEL
DAHLRA-66-FRE    DAHL, RA
                    FURTHER REFLECTIONS ON 'THE ELITIST THEORY OF DEMOCRACY'.=
                    THE AMERICAN POLITICAL SCIENCE REVIEW, 60, (JUNE 1966),       66
                    PP. 296-305.
                    GNELTH, ELNOEL, METEL
DAHLRA-66-POW    DAHL, RA (ED)
                    POLITICAL OPPOSITION IN THE WESTERN DEMOCRACIES (AUSTRIA,
                    BELGIUM, FRANCE, GERMANY, GREAT BRITAIN, ITALY,
                    NETHERLANDS, NORWAY, SWEDEN, UNITED STATES).=
                    NEW HAVEN, YALE UNIVERSITY PRESS, 1966.                       66
                    DEFEL, COMEL, ELEL, ELPRNOR
DAHRR -63-CLR    DAHRENDORF, R
                    CONFLICT AND LIBERTY -- SOME REMARKS ON THE SOCIAL
                    STRUCTURE OF GERMAN POLITICS.=
                    THE BRITISH JOURNAL OF SOCIOLOGY, 14, (1963), PP. 197-211.63
                    GNELTH, ELPRNOR
DAHRR -64-RCC    DAHRENDORF, R
                    RECENT CHANGES IN THE CLASS STRUCTURE OF EUROPEAN
                    SOCIETIES.=
                    DAEDALUS, 93, (WINTER 1964), PP.225-270.                      64
                    GNELTH, DEFEL, COMEL, ELEL, ELNOEL, ELPRNOR

DAHRR -65-CCC   DAHRENDORF, R
                CLASS AND CLASS CONFLICT IN INDUSTRIAL SOCIETY.=
                STANDFORD, CALIFORNIA, STANDFORD UNIVERSITY PRESS, 1965.   65
                GNELTH, DEFEL, COMEL, ELEL, ELNOEL, ELPRNOR, METEL
DAHRR -66-WGG   DAHRENDORF, R
                WHO GOVERNS GERMANY.=
                GOVERNMENT AND OPPOSITION, 2, (NOVEMBER 1966),            66
                  PP. 119-132.
                DEFEL, COMEL, ELEL, ELPRNOR
DAHRR -67-SDG   DAHRENDORF, R
                SOCIETY AND DEMOCRACY IN GERMANY.=
                GARDEN CITY, DOUBLEDAY AND CO., 1967.                     67
                DEFEL, COMEL, ELEL, ELNOEL, ELPRNOR
DAI,S -62-PRC   DAI, S
                PARTY RULE IN COMMUNIST CHINA.=
                CURRENT HISTORY, N.S., 43, (SEPTEMBER 1962),              62
                  PP. 168-173.
                ELNOEL
DAKIRE-62-VPS   DAKIN, RE
                VARIATIONS IN POWER STRUCTURES AND ORGANIZING EFFICIENCY
                  -- A COMPARATIVE STUDY OF FOUR AREAS (UNITED STATES).=
                THE SOCIOLOGICAL QUARTERLY, 3, (JULY 1962), PP. 228-250.  62
                METEL
DALLA -64-SUD   DALLIN, A           ET AL
                THE SOVIET UNION AND DISARMAMENT -- AN APPRAISAL
                  OF SOVIET ATTITUDES AND INTENTIONS.=
                NEW YORK, FREDERICK A PRAEGER, 1964.
                ELPRNOR                                                   64
DALLDJ-54-NRI   DALLIN, DJ
                THE NEW RUSSIAN INTELLIGENTSIA.=
                YALE REVIEW, 42, (WINTER 1954), PP. 188-203.              54
                COMEL, ELEL
DALLDJ-61-NCR   DALLIN, DJ
                THE NEW CLASS IN RUSSIA.=
                MODERN AGE, 5, (WINTER 1961), PP. 5-13.                   61
                COMEL, ELEL
DALLFW-51-PAT   DALLEY, FW
                THE PROSPECT FOR ASIAN TRADE UNIONISM.=
                PACIFIC AFFAIRS, 24, (SEPTEMBER 1951), PP. 296-306.       51
                COMEL, ELEL
DALTM -59-MWM   DALTON, M
                MEN WHO MANAGE -- FUSIONS OF FEELING AND THEORY IN
                  ADMINISTRATION.=
                NEW YORK, JOHN WILEY AND SONS, 1959.                      59
                ELEL, ELNOEL, ELPRNOR
DANEDJ-67-CIR   DANELSKI, DJ
                CONFLICT AND ITS RESOLUTION IN THE SUPREME COURT
                  (UNITED STATES).=
                THE JOURNAL OF CONFLICT RESOLUTION, 11, (MARCH 1967),     67
                  PP. 70-86.
                ELEL, ELPRNOR, METEL
DANGNG-63-TPP   DANG, NGHIEM
                TOWARD A PHILOSOPHY OF PUBLIC ADMINISTRATION IN VIETNAM.=
                PHILIPPINE JOURNAL OF PUBLIC ADMINISTRATION, 7,           63
                  (APRIL 1963), PP. 67-90.
                ELEL, ELNOEL, ELPRNOR
DANIRV-56-SLO   DANIELS, RV
                THE SECRETARIAT AND THE LOCAL ORGANIZATIONS IN THE
                  RUSSIAN COMMUNIST PARTY, 1921-1923.=
                THE AMERICAN SLAVIC AND EAST EUROPEAN REVIEW, 16,         56
                  (FEBRUARY 1956), PP. 32-49.
                ELEL, ELNOEL
DANIRV-61-IRR   DANIELS, RV
                INTELLECTUALS AND THE RUSSIAN REVOLUTION.=
                THE AMERICAN SLAVIC AND EAST EUROPEAN REVIEW, 20,         61
                  (APRIL 1961), PP. 270-278.
                COMEL, ELEL, ELNOEL
DANIRV-62-WRM   DANIELS, RV
                WHAT THE RUSSIANS MEAN.=
                COMMENTARY, 34, (OCTOBER 1962), PP. 314-323.              62
                ELPRNOR
DANZMH-64-CPS   DANZGER, MH
                COMMUNITY POWER STRUCTURE -- PROBLEMS AND CONTINUITIES.=
                AMERICAN SOCIOLOGICAL REVIEW, 29, (OCTOBER 1964),         64
                  PP. 707-717.
                DEFEL, METEL
DARLFC-60-MSA   DARLING, FC
                MARSHAL SARIT AND ABSOLUTIST RULE IN THAILAND.=
                PACIFIC AFFAIRS, 33, (DECEMBER 1960), PP. 347-360.        60
                COMEL, ELEL, ELNOEL
DAVIE -64-CRC   DAVIS, E
                COST OF REALISM -- CONTEMPORARY RESTATEMENT OF
                  DEMOCRACY.=
                THE WESTERN POLITICAL QUARTERLY, 18, (MARCH 1964),        64

```
                         PP. 37-46.
                         DEFEL, ELNOEL
    DAVIH -61-LAS   DAVIS, H
                         LATIN AMERICAN SOCIAL THOUGHT.=
                         WASHINGTON, D.C., UNIVERSITY PRESS OF WASHINGTON, 1961.   61
                         ELPRNOR
    DAVIHB-65-NCS   DAVIS, HB
                         NATIONS, COLONIES AND SOCIAL CLASSES -- THE POSITION
                            OF MARX AND ENGELS.=
                         SCIENCE AND SOCIETY, 29, (WINTER 1965), PP. 25-43.         65
                         ELNOEL
    DAVIHE-49-LAL   DAVIS, HE
                         LATIN AMERICAN LEADERS.=
                         NEW YORK, H W WILSON COMPANY, 1949.                        49
                         COMEL
    DAVIJ -29-SOC   DAVIS, J
                         A STUDY OF 163 OUTSTANDING COMMUNIST LEADERS
                            (SOVIET UNION).=
                         STUDIES IN QUANTITATIVE AND CULTURAL SOCIOLOGY, 24,        29
                            (1929), PP. 42-55.
                         COMEL
    DAVIJA-62-LCA   DAVIS, JA
                         LOCALS AND COSMOPOLITANS IN AMERICAN GRADUATE SCHOOLS.=
                         INTERNATIONAL JOURNAL OF COMPARATIVE SOCIOLOGY, 2,         62
                            (1962), PP. 212-223.
                         METEL
    DAVIJC-63-PLF   DAVIES, JC
                         POLITICAL LEADERS AND FOLLOWERS.=
                         JC DAVIES, HUMAN NATURE IN POLITICS, NEW YORK,             63
                            JOHN WILEY AND SONS, INC., 1963.
                         COMEL ELEL, ELNOEL, ELPRNOR
    DAVIJW-48-PDW   DAVIDSON, JW
                         POLITICAL DEVELOPMENT IN WESTERN SAMOA.=
                         PACIFIC AFFAIRS, 21, (JUNE 1948), PP. 136-149.             48
                         COMEL, ELEL, ELNOEL
    DAVIK -49-IPD   DAVIS, K
                         INDIA AND PAKISTAN -- THE DEMOGRAPHY OF PARTITION.=
                         PACIFIC AFFAIRS, 22, (1949), PP. 254-264.                  49
                         COMEL, ELEL
    DAVIK -49-MAS   DAVIS, K              BREDEMEIER, HC      LEVY, MJ
                         MODERN AMERICAN SOCIETY -- READINGS IN THE PROBLEMS
                            OF ORDER AND CHANGE.=
                         NEW YORK, RINEHART AND COMPANY, 1949.                      49
                         DEFEL, ELEL, ELNOEL
    DAVIM -66-FPP   DAVIS, M
                         THE FUNCTIONS OF THE PUBLICS IN PLATO'S CITIES.=
                         THE AMERICAN BEHAVIORAL SCIENTIST, 9,                      66
                            (DECEMBER 1965-JANUARY 1966), PP. 9-12.
                         ELEL, ELNOEL
    DAVIPT-54-PNP   DAVID, PT             MOOS, M            GOLDMAN, RM (EDS)
                         PRESIDENTIAL NOMINATING POLITICS IN 1952 (UNITED STATES).=
                         BALTIMORE, THE JOHN HOPKINS PRESS, 1954, 5 VOLUMES.        54
                         ELEL, ELNOEL
    DAVISR-54-APP   DAVIS, SR            ET AL
                         THE AUSTRALIAN POLITICAL PARTY SYSTEM.=
                         LONDON, ANGUS AND ROBERTSON, 1954.                         54
                         ELEL, ELNOEL
    DAVLT -63-RAT   DAVLETSHIN, T
                         THE REORGANIZATION OF ADMINISTRATION IN TURKESTAN
                            (SOVIET UNION).=
                         BULLETIN INSTITUTE FOR THE STUDY OF THE USSR, 10,          63
                            (MAY 1963), PP. 19-30.
                         COMEL, ELEL
    DAWNCE-61-OAO   DAWN, CE
                         FROM OTTOMANISM TO ARABISM -- THE ORIGINS OF AN
                            IDEOLOGY (MIDDLE EAST).=
                         THE REVIEW OF POLITICS, 23, (JULY 1961), PP. 378-400.      61
                         COMEL, ELEL, ELPRNOR
    DAWNCE-62-RAS   DAWN, CE
                         THE RISE OF ARABISM IN SYRIA.=
                         THE MIDDLE EAST JOURNAL, 16, (SPRING 1962), PP. 145-167.   62
                         COMEL, ELEL, ELPRNOR
    DAWNCE-65-AIM   DAWN, CE
                         ARAB ISLAM IN THE MODERN AGE.=
                         THE MIDDLE EAST JOURNAL, 19, (AUTUMN 1965), PP. 435-446.   65
                         ELEL, ELPRNOR
    DAWSRE-63-IPC   DAWSON, RE           ROBINSON, JA
                         INTER - PARTY COMPETITION, ECONOMIC VARIABLES, AND
                            WELFARE POLICIES IN THE AMERICAN STATES.=
                         THE JOURNAL OF POLITICS, 25, (MAY 1963), PP. 265-289.      63
                         DEFEL, ELEL, ELNOEL, ELPRNOR
    DAWSRH-62-CII   DAWSON, RH
                         CONGRESSIONAL INNOVATION AND INTERVENTION IN DEFENSE
                            POLICY -- LEGISLATIVE AUTHORIZATION OF WEAPONS SYSTEMS
```

                    (UNITED STATES).=
                    THE AMERICAN POLITICAL SCIENCE REVIEW, 56, (MARCH 1962),    62
                       PP. 42-57.
                    ELEL
DCW     -50-PGA     DCW
                    PRESSURE GROUPS AND AMERICAN POLICY.=
                    THE WORLD TODAY, 6, (JUNE 1950), PP. 248-255.
                    ELEL                                                        50
DE BBO-58-HDA       DE BOURBON-BUSSET, J
                    HOW DECISIONS ARE MADE IN FOREIGN POLITICS --
                       PSYCHOLOGY IN INTERNATIONAL RELATIONS.=
                    THE REVIEW OF POLITICS, 20, (OCTOBER 1958), PP. 591-614.    58
                    ELEL, ELPRNOR
DE BBU-61-HEP       DE BUNSEN, B
                    HIGHER EDUCATION AND POLITICAL CHANGE IN EAST AFRICA.=
                    AFRICAN AFFAIRS, 60, (OCTOBER 1961), PP. 494-500.           61
                    COMEL, ELEL, ELNOEL
DE GGR-66-EEG       DE GRAFT-JOHNSON, KE
                    THE EVOLUTION OF ELITES IN GHANA.=
                    PC LLOYD (ED), THE NEW ELITES OF TROPICAL AFRICA, LONDON,   66
                       OXFORD UNIVERSITY PRESS, 1966, PP. 104-115.
                    ELEL, ELPRNOR
DE HHU-60-ICP       DE HUSZAR, GB (ED)
                    THE INTELLECTUALS -- A CONTROVERSIAL PORTRAIT.=
                    GLENCOE, ILLINOIS, FREE PRESS, 1960.                        60
                    DEFEL, ELEL, ELNOEL, ELPRNOR
DE MMO-60-LIW       DE MOTT, B
                    LOOKING FOR INTELLIGENCE IN WASHINGTON (UNITED STATES).=
                    COMMENTARY, 30, (OCTOBER 1960), PP. 291-300.                60
                    ELPRNOR
DE RRI-56-CCT       DE RIENCOURT, A
                    THE COMING CEASARS -- TOWARD AUTOCRACY IN THE U.S.
                       (UNITED STATES).=
                    NEW YORK, COWARD-MCCANN, 1956.                              56
                    COMEL, ELEL, ELNOEL
DE-BOF-62-ENM       DE-BATTAGLIA, OF
                    THE EUROPEAN NOBILITY IN THE MIDDLE AGES.=
                    COMPARATIVE STUDIES IN SOCIETY AND HISTORY, 5,              62
                       (OCTOBER 1962), PP. 60-75.
                    COMEL, ELPRNOR
DE-GA -56-LEL       DE-GRAZIA, A
                    THE LIMITS OF EXTERNAL LEADERSHIP OVER A MINORITY
                       ELECTORATE (UNITED STATES).=
                    THE PUBLIC OPINION QUARTERLY, 20, (SPRING 1956),            56
                       PP. 113-128.
                    ELEL, ELNOEL
DE-GA -57-RCP       DE-GRAZIA, A
                    THE RELATION OF CERTAIN PERSONALITY DYNAMICS TO LEVELS OF
                       POLITICAL INTEREST AND ACTION.=
                    PROD (THE AMERICAN BEHAVIORAL SCIENTIST), 1,                57
                       (SEPTEMBER 1957), PP. 13-15.
                    ELPRNOR, METEL
DE-GA -58-NPP       DE-GRAZIA, A
                    NATURE AND PROSPECTS OF POLITICAL INTEREST GROUPS.=
                    THE ANNALS OF THE AMERICAN ACADEMY OF POLITICAL AND         58
                       SOCIAL SCIENCE, 319, (SEPTEMBER 1958), PP. 113-122.
                    DEFEL, ELEL
DE-GRP-63-PDM       DE-GUZMAN, RP (ED)
                    PATTERNS IN DECISION-MAKING -- CASE STUDIES IN
                       PHILIPPINE PUBLIC ADMINISTRATION.=
                    HONOLULU, EAST-WEST CENTER PRESS, 1963.                     63
                    COMEL, ELEL, ELNOEL, ELPRNOR
DE-GS -57-ASP       DE-GRAZIA, S
                    ANTHROPOLOGICAL STUDY OF PRIMITIVE RULING GROUPS --1 --2.=
                    PROD (THE AMERICAN BEHAVIORAL SCIENTIST, 1,                 57
                       (NOVEMBER 1957, JANUARY 1958), PP. 3-6, PP. 26-30.
                    DEFEL, ELEL, ELNOEL, METEL
DE-ME -62-TIO       DE-MARCHI, E
                    TRENDS IN ITALY -- AN OPENING TO THE LEFT.=
                    ORBIS, 5, (WINTER 1962), PP. 411-424.                       62
                    ELEL, ELNOEL
DE-MH -51-IEP       DE-MEEL, H
                    IMPEDIMENTS TO ECONOMIC PROGRESS IN INDONESIA.=
                    PACIFIC AFFAIRS, 24, (MARCH 1951), PP. 39-51.               51
                    ELEL, ELNOEL
DE-MP -52-GMM       DE-MENDELSSOHN, P
                    THE GERMAN MILITARY MIND -- A SURVEY OF GERMAN MILITARY
                       WRITING.=
                    THE POLITICAL QUARTERLY, 23, (1952), PP. 182-190.           52
                    ELEL, ELPRNOR
DE-SMA-54-PGU       DE-SILVA, MA
                    PARLIAMENTARY GOVERNMENT IN UNDER-DEVELOPED DEMOCRACIES.=
                    PARLIAMENTARY AFFAIRS, 7, (AUTUMN 1954), PP. 420-425.       54
                    ELNOEL, ELPRNOR

DE-TF -61-FRP   DE-TARR, F
                THE FRENCH RADICAL PARTY -- FROM HERRIOT TO
                    MENDES-FRANCE.=
                NEW YORK, OXFORD UNIVERSITY PRESS, 1961.                        61
                COMEL, ELEL

DEANVM-61-BEN   DEAN, VM
                BUILDERS OF EMERGING NATIONS.=
                NEW YORK, HOLT RINEHART, AND WINSTON, 1961.                     61
                COMEL, ELPRNOR, ELNOEL

DECLCS-63-CCP   DECLARO, CS
                THE CONFERENCE COMMITTEE -- PIVOT IN THE BUDGET PROCESS
                    (PHILIPPINES).=
                PHILIPPINE JOURNAL OF PUBLIC ADMINISTRATION, 7,                 63
                    (APRIL 1963), PP. 113-121.
                ELEL, ELNOEL, ELPRNOR

DEGRG -50-ICC   DEGRE, G
                IDEOLOGY AND CLASS CONSCIOUSNESS IN THE MIDDLE
                    CLASS (UNITED STATES).=
                SOCIAL FORCES, 29, (DECEMBER 1950), PP. 173-179.                50
                ELPRNOR

DEGRJ -62-MFS   DEGRAS, J
                MOSCOW IN FERMENT (SOVIET UNION).=
                PROBLEMS OF COMMUNISM, 11, (MARCH-APRIL 1962), PP. 1-7.         62
                ELEL, ELPRNOR

DELAW -63-DDP   DELANY, W
                THE DEVELOPMENT AND DECLINE OF PATRIMONIAL AND
                    BUREAUCRATIC ADMINISTRATION.=
                ADMINISTRATIVE SCIENCE QUARTERLY, 7, (1962-1963),               63
                    PP. 458-501.
                DEFEL, ELNOEL

DELZCF-61-MSE   DELZELL, CF
                MUSSOLINI'S ENEMIES -- THE ITALIAN ANTI-FASCIST
                    RESISTANCE.=
                PRINCETON, PRINCETON UNIVERSITY PRESS, 1961.                    61
                COMEL, ELEL, ELNOEL, ELPRNOR

DEMADF-47-SL    DEMARCHE, DF
                THE SUPERIMPOSED LEADER.=
                SOCIOLOGY AND SOCIAL RESEARCH, 31, (JULY-AUGUST 1947),          47
                    PP. 454-457.
                DEFEL

DEMENJ-52-IMR   DEMERATH, NJ
                INITIATING AND MAINTAINING RESEARCH RELATIONS IN A
                    MILITARY ORGANIZATION.=
                JOURNAL OF SOCIAL ISSUES, 8, (1952), PP. 11-23.                 52
                METEL

DEMEP -62-LUS   DEMETZ, P
                LITERATURE IN ULBRICHT'S GERMANY (EAST GERMANY).=
                PROBLEMS OF COMMUNISM, 11, (JULY-AUGUST 1962), PP. 15-21. 62
                ELEL

DENNJ -66-SPS   DENNIS, J
                SUPPORT FOR THE PARTY SYSTEM BY THE MASS PUBLIC
                    (UNITED STATES).=
                THE AMERICAN POLITICAL SCIENCE REVIEW, 60, (SEPTEMBER           66
                    1966), PP. 600-615.
                ELNOEL

DENNN -61-CFL   DENNIS, N
                CHANGES IN FUNCTION AND LEADERSHIP RENEWAL
                    (GREAT BRITAIN).=
                SOCIOLOGICAL REVIEW,N.S., 9, (MARCH 1961), PP.55-84.            61
                DEFEL, ELEL, ELNOEL

DENTCF-67-IGP   DENTON, CF
                INTEREST GROUPS IN PANAMA AND THE CENTRAL AMERICAN
                    COMMON MARKET.=
                INTER-AMERICAN ECONOMIC AFFAIRS, 21, (SUMMER 1967),             67
                    PP. 49-60.
                COMEL, ELPRNOR

DERGDR-58-MOA   DERGE, DR
                METROPOLITAN AND OUTSTATE ALIGNMENTS IN ILLINOIS
                    AND MISSOURI LEGISLATIVE DELEGATIONS (UNITED STATES).=
                THE AMERICAN POLITICAL SCIENCE REVIEW, 52, (DECEMBER            58
                    1958), PP. 1051-1065.
                ELEL, ELNOEL

DERGDR-59-LDM   DERGE, DR
                THE LAWYER AS DECISION-MAKER IN THE AMERICAN
                    STATE LEGISLATURE.=
                THE JOURNAL OF POLITICS, 21, (AUGUST 1959), PP. 408-433.        59
                ELEL, ELPRNOR

DERGDR-62-LIG   DERGE, DR
                THE LAWYER IN THE INDIANA GENERAL ASSEMBLY
                    (UNITED STATES).=
                MIDWEST JOURNAL OF POLITICAL SCIENCE, 6,                        62
                    (FEBRUARY 1962), PP. 19-53.
                DEFEL, COMEL, ELEL, ELPRNOR

DESAAR-49-SBI   DESAI, AR

                    THE SOCIAL BACKGROUND OF INDIAN NATIONALISM.=
                    LONDON, OXFORD UNIVERSITY PRESS, 1949.                      49
                    COMEL, ELEL, ELPRNOR
DEUTI -50-STU       DEUTSCHER, I
                    SOVIET TRADE UNIONS -- THEIR PLACE IN
                      SOVIET LABOUR POLICY.=
                    LONDON AND NEW YORK, ROYAL INSTITUTE OF INTERNATIONAL        50
                    AFFAIRS AND OXFORD UNIVERSITY PRESS, 1950.
                    ELEL
DEUTJJ-57-TPS       DEUTSCH, JJ
                    SOME THOUGHTS ON THE PUBLIC SERVICE (CANADA).=
                    CANADIAN JOURNAL OF ECONOMICS AND POLITICAL SCIENCE,        57
                    23, (FEBRUARY 1957), PP. 83-89.
                    COMEL
DEUTKW-53-NSC       DEUTSCH, KW
                    NATIONALISM AND SOCIAL COMMUNICATION -- AN INQUIRY
                      INTO THE FOUNDATIONS OF NATIONALISM.=
                    NEW YORK, JOHN WILEY AND SONS, 1953.                        53
                    DEFEL, ELNOEL, ELPRNOR, METEL
DEUTKW-57-MCL       DEUTSCH, KW
                    MASS COMMUNICATIONS AND THE LOSS OF FREEDOM IN NATIONAL
                      DECISION-MAKING -- A POSSIBLE RESEARCH APPROACH TO
                      INTERSTATE CONFLICTS.=
                    THE JOURNAL OF CONFLICT RESOLUTION, 1, (JUNE 1957),         57
                      PP. 200-211.
                    METEL
DEUTKW-59-GRP       DEUTSCH, KW              EDINGER, LJ
                    GERMANY REJOINS THE POWERS -- MASS OPINION, INTEREST
                      GROUPS AND ELITES IN CONTEMPORARY GERMAN FOREIGN
                      POLICY.=
                    STANFORD, STANFORD UNIVERSITY PRESS, 1959.                  59
                    COMEL, ELEL, ELNOEL, ELPRNOR
DEUTKW-61-NAW       DEUTSCH, KW             MADON, WG
                    A NOTE ON THE APPEARANCE OF WISDOM IN LARGE
                      BUREAUCRATIC ORGANIZATIONS.=
                    BEHAVIORAL SCIENCE, 6, (JANUARY 1961), PP. 72-78.           61
                    ELEL, ELNOEL, METEL
DEUTKW-63-NGM       DEUTSCH, KW
                    THE NERVES OF GOVERNMENT -- MODELS OF POLITICAL
                      COMMUNICATION AND CONTROL.=
                    NEW YORK, THE FREE PRESS, 1963.                             63
                    GNELTH
DEUTKW-66-IAC       DEUTSCH, KW
                    INTEGRATION AND ARMS CONTROL IN THE EUROPEAN POLITICAL
                      ENVIRONMENT -- A SUMMARY REPORT (FRANCE, GERMANY).=
                    THE AMERICAN POLITICAL SCIENCE REVIEW, 60, (JUNE 1966),     66
                      PP. 354-365.
                    ELEL, ELNOEL, ELPRNOR, METEL
DEUTKW-66-QCV       DEUTSCH, KW
                    SOME QUANTITATIVE CONSTRAINTS ON VALUE ALLOCATION IN
                      SOCIETY AND POLITICS.=
                    BEHAVIORAL SCIENCE, 11, (JULY 1966), PP. 245-252.           66
                    DEFEL, ELEL, ELNOEL, METEL
DEUTKW-67-FGW       DEUTSCH, KW             EDINGER, LJ          ET AL
                    FRANCE, GERMANY, AND THE WESTERN ALLIANCE -- A STUDY OF
                      ELITE ATTITUDES ON EUROPEAN INTEGRATION AND WORLD
                      POLITICS.=
                    NEW YORK, CHARLES SCRIBNER'S SONS, 1967.                    67
                    COMEL, ELEL, ELPRNOR
DEUTPJ-61-MMU       DEUTSCHMANN, PJ      MCNELLY, JT          ELLINGSWORTH, H
                    MASS MEDIA USE BY SUB - ELITES IN ELEVEN
                      LATIN AMERICAN COUNTRIES.=
                    JOURNALISM QUARTERLY, 38, (AUTUMN 1961), PP. 460-472.       61
                    ELEL, ELPRNOR
DEVEG -55-CLC       DEVEREUX, G
                    CHARISMATIC LEADERSHIP AND CRISIS.=
                    W MUENSTERBERGER AND J AXELRAD (EDS), PSYCHOANALYSIS AND     55
                      THE SOCIAL SCIENCES, NEW YORK, INTERNATIONAL UNIVERSITY
                      PRESS, 1955, PP. 145-157.
                    DEFEL, COMEL, ELNOEL
DEVOE -58-GIC       DEVONS, E
                    GOVERNMENT ON THE INNER CIRCLE (GREAT BRITAIN).=
                    INTERNATIONAL REVIEW OF ADMINISTRATIVE SCIENCES, 24,        58
                      (1958), PP. 523-526.
                    ELEL
DEWAM -54-BBA       DEWAR, M
                    BEHIND THE BERIA AFFAIR (SOVIET UNION).=
                    PROBLEMS OF COMMUNISM, 3, (MARCH-APRIL 1954), PP. 17-23.    54
                    ELEL
DEWAM -60-SPE       DEWAR, M
                    THE SOVIET POWER ELITE.=
                    PROBLEMS OF COMMUNISM, 9, (MARCH- APRIL 1960),              60
                      PP. 51-53.
                    DEFEL, ELEL

```
DEWIN  -55-SPM   DEWITT, N
                 SOVIET PROFESSIONAL MANPOWER -- ITS EDUCATION,
                    TRAINING AND SUPPLY.=
                 WASHINGTON, NATIONAL SCIENCE FOUNDATION, 1955.              55
                 COMEL, ELEL, ELNOEL, ELPRNOR
DEXTLA-55-CMM    DEXTER, LA
                 CANDIDATES MUST MAKE THE ISSUES AND GIVE THEM
                    MEANING (UNITED STATES).=
                 THE PUBLIC OPINION QUARTERLY, 19, (WINTER 1955),            55
                    PP. 408-414.
                 ELNOEL, ELPRNOR
DEXTLA-56-WDC    DEXTER, LA
                 WHAT DO CONGRESSMEN HEAR -- THE MAIL (UNITED STATES).=
                 THE PUBLIC OPINION QUARTERLY, 20, (SPRING 1956),            56
                    PP. 16-27
                 ELEL, ELNOEL, ELPRNOR
DEXTLA-57-RHD    DEXTER, LA
                 THE REPRESENTATIVE AND HIS DISTRICT (UNITED STATES).=
                 HUMAN ORGANIZATION, 16, (SPRING 1957), PP. 2-13.            57
                 COMEL, ELNOEL
DEXTLA-59-IBL    DEXTER, LA
                 INTERVIEWING BUSINESS LEADERS.=
                 PROD (AMERICAN BEHAVIORAL SCIENTIST), 2,                    59
                    (JANUARY 1959), PP. 25-29.
                 METEL
DEXTLA-63-CMM    DEXTER, LA
                 CONGRESSMEN AND THE MAKING OF MILITARY POLICY
                    (UNITED STATES).=
                 RL PEABODY AND NW POLSBY (EDS), NEW PERSPECTIVES ON THE     63
                    HOUSE OF REPRESENTATIVES, CHICAGO, RAND MCNALLY, 1963,
                    PP. 305-324.
                 ELEL
DEXTLA-64-GWI    DEXTER, LA
                 THE GOOD WILL OF IMPORTANT PEOPLE -- MORE ON THE
                    JEOPARDY OF THE INTERVIEW.=
                 THE PUBLIC OPINION QUARTERLY, 28, (WINTER 1964),            64
                    PP. 556-563.
                 METEL
DEXTLA-65-SCI    DEXTER, LA
                 SOME STRATEGIC CONSIDERATIONS IN INNOVATING LEADERSHIP.=
                 AW GOULDNER (ED), STUDIES IN LEADERSHIP, NEW YORK,          65
                    RUSSELL AND RUSSELL, 1965, PP. 592-604.
                 ELEL, METEL
DEYOM  -59-CPH   DEYOUNG, M
                 CLASS PARAMETERS IN HAITIAN SOCIETY.=
                 JOURNAL OF INTER-AMERICAN STUDIES, 1, (1959),               59
                    PP. 449-458.
                 DEFEL, COMEL, ELNOEL
DEYRFJ-57-LGA    DEYRUP, FJ
                 LIMITS OF GOVERNMENT ACTIVITY IN UNDERDEVELOPED
                    COUNTRIES.=
                 SOCIAL RESEARCH, 24, (SUMMER 1957), PP. 191-201.            57
                 ELEL, ELNOEL
DIAMA  -51-FCS   DIAMANT, A
                 THE FRENCH COUNCIL OF STATE -- COMPARATIVE OBSERVATIONS
                    ON THE PROBLEM OF CONTROLLING BUREAUCRACY OF
                    THE MODERN STATE.=
                 THE JOURNAL OF POLITICS, 13, (NOVEMBER 1951), PP. 562-588.51
                 ELEL, ELPRNOR
DIAMA  -58-CSA   DIAMANT, A
                 A CASE STUDY OF ADMINISTRATIVE AUTONOMY -- CONTROLS AND
                    TENSIONS IN FRENCH ADMINISTRATION.=
                 POLITICAL STUDIES, 6, (JUNE 1958), PP. 147-166.             58
                 ELEL, ELPRNOR
DIAMA  -58-GBA   DIAMANT, A
                 THE GROUP BASIS OF AUSTRIAN POLITICS.=
                 JOURNAL OF CENTRAL EUROPEAN AFFAIRS, 18, (OCTOBER 1958),    58
                    PP. 134-155.
                 COMEL, ELEL, ELNOEL, ELPRNOR
DIBBVK-61-DCS    DIBBLE, VK        HO, P-T
                 DEBATE -- THE COMPARATIVE STUDY OF SOCIAL MOBILITY
                    (CHINA).=
                 COMPARATIVE STUDIES IN SOCIETY AND HISTORY, 3,              61
                    (APRIL 1961), PP. 315-327.
                 COMEL
DICKHR-60-MRC    DICK, HR
                 A METHOD FOR RANKING COMMUNITY INFLUENTIALS.=
                 AMERICAN SOCIOLOGICAL REVIEW, 25, (JUNE 1960),              60
                    PP. 395-399.
                 METEL
DILLES-63-UNB    DILLION, ES
                 UNIVERSITIES AND NATION BUILDING IN AFRICA.=
                 THE JOURNAL OF MODERN AFRICAN STUDIES, 1, (1963),           63
                    PP. 75-90.
```

```
                      COMEL, ELPRNOR
DINEHS-54-PPS    DINERSTEIN, HS
                 THE PURGE -- PERMANENT SOVIET INSTITUTION.=
                 PROBLEMS OF COMMUNISM, 3, (MAY-JUNE 1954), PP. 30-36.        54
                      ELEL, ELPRNOR
DIONL -59-PIT    DION, L
                 POLITICAL IDEOLOGY AS A TOOL OF FUNCTIONAL ANALYSIS
                      IN SOCIO-POLITICAL DYNAMICS.=
                 CANADIAN JOURNAL OF ECONOMICS AND POLITICAL SCIENCE,         59
                      25, (FEBRUARY 1959), PP. 47-59.
                      GNELTH, DEFEL, COMEL, ELPRNOR
DITZGW-60-IAC    DITZ, GW
                 INDUSTRIAL ADMINISTRATION IN COMMUNIST EAST EUROPE.=
                 ADMINISTRATIVE SCIENCE QUARTERLY, 4, (1959-1960),            60
                      PP. 82-96.
                      ELEL, ELNOEL, ELPRNOR
DJILM -57-NCA    DJILAS, M
                 THE NEW CLASS -- AN ANALYSIS OF THE COMMUNIST
                      SYSTEM (YUGOSLAVIA).=
                 NEW YORK, FREDERICK A PRAEGER, 1957.                         57
                      COMEL, ELEL, ELNOEL, ELPRNOR
DJORJ -53-LSG    DJORDJEVIC, J
                 LOCAL SELF-GOVERNMENT IN YUGOSLAVIA.=
                 THE AMERICAN SLAVIC AND EAST EUROPEAN REVIEW, 12,            53
                      (APRIL 1953), PP. 188-200.
                      ELNOEL
DJORJ -58-YSR    DJORDJEVIC, J
                 YUGOSLAVIA -- STATUS AND ROLE OF THE EXECUTIVE ORGANS
                      DURING THE FIRST STAGE OF YUGOSLAVIA'S POLITICAL
                      AND CONSTITUTIONAL DEVELOPMENT.=
                 INTERNATIONAL SOCIAL SCIENCE BULLETIN, 10, (1958),           58
                      PP. 258-269.
                      COMEL, ELEL, ELNOEL
DMP   -46-FPC    DMP
                 FRENCH PARTIES AND THE CONSTITUTION.=
                 THE WORLD TODAY, 2, (OCTOBER 1946), PP. 445-442.             46
                      ELPRNOR
DMYTB -57-NSC    DMYTRYSHYM, B
                 NATIONAL AND SOCIAL COMPOSITION OF THE MEMBERSHIP OF THE
                      COMMUNIST PARTY (BOLSHEVIK) OF THE UKRAINE, 1918-1928.=
                 JOURNAL OF CENTRAL EUROPEAN AFFAIRS, 17, (JULY 1957),        57
                      PP. 243-258.
                      COMEL, ELNOEL
DOBLEM-45-SCN    DOBLIN, EM          POHLY, C
                 THE SOCIAL COMPOSITION OF THE NAZI LEADERSHIP
                      (GERMANY).=
                 THE AMERICAN JOURNAL OF SOCIOLOGY, 51, (JULY 1945),          45
                      PP. 42-49.
                      COMEL
DOBYHF-65-SIE    DOBYNS, HF
                 THE STRATEGIC IMPORTANCE OF ENLIGHTENMENT AND SKILL FOR
                      POWER (PERU).=
                 THE AMERICAN BEHAVIORAL SCIENTIST, 8, (MARCH 1965),          65
                      PP. 23-27.
                      ELEL, ELPRNOR
DOCTO -63-GSA    DOCTOROW, O
                 GROUP STRUCTURE AND AUTHORITY.=
                 AMERICAN ANTHROPOLOGIST, 65, (1963), PP. 312-322.            63
                      DEFEL
DODDCH-64-SEB    DODD, CH
                 THE SOCIAL AND EDUCATIONAL BACKGROUND OF TURKISH
                      OFFICIALS.=
                 MIDDLE EASTERN STUDIES, 1, (APRIL 1965), PP. 268-276.        64
                      COMEL, METEL
DODDSC-46-SRM    DODD, SC
                 SOCIAL RELATIONS IN THE MIDDLE EAST.=
                 3RD ENGLISH EDITION, BEIRUT, LEBANON,                        46
                      AMERICAN PRESS, 1946.
                      COMEL, ELEL, ELNOEL, ELPRNOR
DODDSC-62-CIS    DODD, SC            KLEIN, LB
                 THE CONCORD INDEX FOR SOCIAL INFLUENCE.=
                 PACIFIC SOCIOLOGICAL REVIEW, 5, ,SPRING 1962), PP. 60-64. 62
                      DEFEL, METEL
DOGAM -61-PAC    DOGAN, M
                 POLITICAL ASCENT IN A CLASS SOCIETY -- FRENCH
                      DEPUTIES 1870-1958.=
                 D MARVICK (ED), POLITICAL DECISION MAKERS, GLENCOE,          61
                      ILLINOIS, THE FREE PRESS, 1961, PP. 57-90.
                      COMEL, ELEL, ELPRNOR
DOMEJM-61-FAP    DOMENACH, JM
                 THE FRENCH ARMY IN POLITICS.=
                 FOREIGN AFFAIRS, 39, (JANUARY 1961), PP. 185-195.            61
                      ELEL
DONNDV-54-FLL    DONNISON, DV        PLOWMAN, DEG
```

THE FUNCTIONS OF LOCAL LABOUR PARTIES -- EXPERIMENTS IN
   RESEARCH METHODS (GREAT BRITAIN).=
POLITICAL STUDIES, 2, (1954), PP. 154-167.                           54
COMEL, FLEL, ELNOEL, METEL
DONNTC-50-NEP  DONNELLY, TC             HOLMES, JE
NEWSPAPERS, EDITORS, POLITICIANS AND POLITICAL
   SCIENTISTS.=
THE WESTERN POLITICAL QUARTERLY, 3, (JUNE 1950),                     50
   PP. 225-232.
ELEL
DONOJC-51-CIR  DONOVAN, JC
CONGRESSIONAL ISOLATIONISTS AND THE ROOSEVELT FOREIGN
   POLICY (UNITED STATES).=
WORLD POLITICS, 3, (JANUARY 1951), PP. 299-316.                      51
ELEL, ELNOEL
DOOBLW-65-PVP  DOOB, LW
PROPAGANDISTS VS PROPAGANDEES.=
AW GOULDNER (ED), STUDIES IN LEADERSHIP, NEW YORK,                   65
   RUSSELL AND RUSSELL, 1965, PP. 439-458.
DEFEL, ELNOEL
DOOLD - -RFC  DOOLIN, D
THE REVIVAL OF THE 100 FLOWERS CAMPAIGN --  1961 (CHINA).=
THE CHINA QUARTERLY, 8, (OCTOBER-DECEMBER 1961),
   PP. 34-41.
COMEL, ELEL
DOOLDJ-64-CCP  DOOLIN, DJ
COMMUNIST CHINA -- THE POLITICS OF STUDENT OPPOSITION.=
STANFORD, HOOVER INSTITUTE MONOGRAPH, 1964.                          64
ELEL, ELNOEL, ELPRNOR
DORERP-52-ENJ  DORE, RP
THE ETHICS OF NEW JAPAN.=
PACIFIC AFFAIRS, 25, (1952), PP. 147-159.                            52
ELEL, ELPRNOR
DORERP-64-SMA  DORE, RP
THE SEARCH FOR MODERNITY IN ASIA AND AFRICA -- A
   REVIEW ARTICLE.=
PACIFIC AFFAIRS, 37, (1964), PP. 161-165.                            64
DEFEL
DORRWF-65-LSC  DORRILL, WF
LEADERSHIP AND SUCCESSION IN COMMUNIST CHINA.=
CURRENT HISTORY, N.S., 49, (SEPTEMBER 1965), PP. 129-135. 65
COMEL, ELEL, ELNOEL
DORSJT-63-BPD  DORSEY, JT
THE BUREAUCRACY AND POLITICAL DEVELOPMENT IN VIETNAM.=
J LAPALOMBARA (ED), BUREAUCRACY AND POLITICAL                        63
   DEVELOPEMENT, PRINCETON, PRINCETON UNIVERSITY PRESS,
   1963, PP. 318-359.
DEFEL, ELEL, ELNOEL
DOUGPL-65-IPR  DOUGHTY, PL
THE INTERRELATIONSHIP OF POWER, RESPECT, AFFECTION
   AND RECTITUDE IN VICOS (PERU).=
THE AMERICAN BEHAVIORAL SCIENTIST, 8, (MARCH 1965),                  65
   PP. 13-17.
ELEL, ELNOEL, ELPRNOR
DOUGWA-64-SKS  DOUGLAS, WA
SOUTH KOREA'S SEARCH FOR LEADERSHIP.=
PACIFIC AFFAIRS, 37, (SPRING 1964), PP. 20-36.                       64
ELEL, ELNOEL
DOWNA -57-ETD  DOWNS, A
AN ECONOMIC THEORY OF DEMOCRACY.=
NEW YORK, HARPER AND ROW, 1957.                                      57
GNELTH, DEFEL, ELPRNOR
DOWNA -62-PII  DOWNS, A
THE PUBLIC INTEREST -- ITS MEANING IN A DEMOCRACY.=
SOCIAL RESEARCH, 29, (SPRING 1962), PP. 1-36.                        62
ELNOEL, ELPRNOR
DOWSR -63-PDH  DOWSE, R             SMITH, T
PARTY DISCILPLINE IN THE HOUSE OF COMMONS
   (GREAT BRITAIN).=
PARLIAMENTARY AFFAIRS, 16, (1963., PP. 159-164.                      63
ELEL, ELPRNOR
DOWSRE-60-PLP  DOWSE, RE
THE PARLIAMENTARY LABOUR PARTY IN OPPOSITION
   (GREAT BRITAIN).=
PARLIAMENTARY AFFAIRS, 13, (AUTUMN 1960), PP. 520-529.    60
ELEL
DOWSRE-61-LWO  DOWSE, RE
THE LEFT WING OPPOSITION DURING THE FIRST TWO
   LABOUR GOVERNMENTS (GREAT BRITAIN).=
PARLIAMENTARY AFFAIRS, 14, (SPRING 1961), PP. 229-243.    61
ELEL, ELNOEL, ELPRNOR
DOWSRE-63-MPH  DOWSE, RE
THE M.P. AND HIS SURGERY (GREAT BRITAIN).=
POLITICAL STUDIES, 11, (OCTOBER 1963), PP. 333-341.       63

```
                    ELEL, ELNOEL, ELPRNOR
DOWVM -62-WAI       DOWVONA, M           SAUNDERS, JT (EDS)
                    THE WEST AFRICAN INTELLECTUAL COMMUNITY.=
                    IBADAN, IBADAN UNIVERSITY PRESS, 1962.                    62
                    COMEL, ELEL
DRAPT -62-CSR       DRAPER, T
                    CASTRO'S REVOLUTION -- MYTHS AND REALITIES.=
                    NEW YORK, FREDERICK A PRAEGER, 1962.                      62
                    ELEL, ELNOEL, ELPRNOR
DRAPT -65-CTP       DRAPER, T
                    CASTROISM -- THEORY AND PRACTICE.=
                    NEW YORK, FREDERICK A PRAEGER, 1965.                      65
                    COMEL, ELEL, ELNOEL, ELPRNOR
DRESA -59-PWS       DRESSLER, A
                    PARTY AND WRITERS -- 1956-1958 (SOVIET UNION).=
                    SOVIET STUDIES, 10, (APRIL 1959), PP. 417-432.           59
                    ELEL
DUBESC-58-ISC       DUBE, SC
                    INDIA'S CHANGING VILLAGES -- HUMAN FACTORS IN COMMUNITY
                       DEVELOPMENT.=
                    ITHACA, CORNELL UNIVERSITY PRESS, 1958.                  58
                    ELEL, ELNOEL
DUBESC-64-BNB       DUBE, SC
                    BUREAUCRACY AND NATION BUILDING IN TRANSITIONAL
                       SOCIETIES.=
                    INTERNATIONAL SOCIAL SCIENCE JOURNAL, 16, (1964),        64
                       PP. 229-236.
                    COMEL, ELEL, ELNOEL
DUBIR -63-PFO       DUBIN, R
                    POWER, FUNCTION AND ORGANIZATION.=
                    PACIFIC SOCIOLOGICAL REVIEW, 6, (1963), PP. 16-24.       63
                    DEFEL, METEL
DUBIWB-50-PEP       DUBIN, WB
                    THE POLITICAL EVOLUTION OF THE PYONGYANG (KOREAN)
                       GOVERNMENT.=
                    PACIFIC AFFAIRS, 23, (DECEMBER 1950), PP. 381-392.       50
                    ELEL
DUBOCA-59-SFS       DUBOIS, CA
                    SOCIAL FORCES IN SOUTHEAST ASIA.=
                    2ND ED., CAMBRIDGE, HARVARD UNIVERSITY PRESS, 1959.      59
                    COMEL, ELEL, ELNOEL, ELPRNOR
DUCHI -62-CPR       DUCHACEK, I
                    CZECHOSLOVAKIA -- THE PAST REBURIED.=
                    PROBLEMS OF COMMUNISM, 11, (MAY-JUNE 1962), PP. 22-26.   62
                    ELEL
DUEVC -66-DPS       DUEVEL, C
                    THE DISMANTLING OF PARTY AND STATE CONTROL AS AN
                       INDEPENDENT PILLAR OF SOVIET POWER.=
                    BULLETIN INSTITUTE FOR THE STUDY OF THE USSR, 8,         66
                       (MARCH 1966), PP. 3-18.
                    ELEL, ELNOEL
DUNCG -63-ND        DUNCAN, G            LUKES, S
                    THE NEW DEMOCRACY.=
                    POLITICAL STUDIES, 11, (JUNE 1963), PP. 156-177.         63
                    DEFEL, ELNOEL
DUNHVS-64-SVS       DUNHAM, VS
                    SOCIAL VALUES OF SOVIET AND AMERICAN ELITES -- INSIGHTS
                       FROM SOVIET LITERATURE.=
                    THE JOURNAL OF CONFLICT RESOLUTION, 8, (DECEMBER 1964),  64
                       PP. 386-410.
                    COMEL, ELEL, ELPRNOR
DUNNSP-64-RIC       DUNN, SP             DUNN, E
                    RELIGION AS AN INSTRUMENT OF CULTURE CHANGE --
                       THE PROBLEM OF THE SECTS IN THE SOVIET UNION.=
                    SLAVIC REVIEW, 23, (SEPTEMBER 1964), PP. 459-478.        64
                    ELNOEL
DUPRJS-62-SNP       DUPRE, JS            LAKOFF, SA
                    SCIENCE AND THE NATION -- POLICY AND POLITICS
                       (UNITED STATES).=
                    ENGLEWOOD CLIFFS, PRENTICE HALL, 1962.                   62
                    ELEL, ELPRNOR
DURAH -55-POF       DURANT, H
                    PUBLIC OPINION AND FOREIGN POLICY.=
                    THE BRITISH JOURNAL OF SOCIOLOGY, 6, (1955), PP. 149-158. 55
                    ELEL, ELNOEL
DURHGH-48-VPU       DURHAM, GH
                    THE VICE-PRESIDENCY (UNITED STATES).=
                    THE WESTERN POLITICAL QUARTERLY, 1, (SEPTEMBER 1948),    48
                       PP. 311-3159
                    ELEL
DWH    -50-SPE      DWH
                    THE SOCIALIST PARTIES AND EUROPEAN UNITY
                    THE WORLD TODAY, 6, (OCTOBER 1950), PP. 415-423.         50
                    COMEL, ELEL, ELNOEL
```

DYACY -61-CCP    DYACHKOV, Y
                 THE CENTRAL COMMITTEE PLENUM (SOVIET UNION).=
                 BULLETIN INSTITUTE FOR THE STUDY OF THE USSR, 8,              61
                    (FEBRUARY 1961), PP. 17-25.
                 ELEL, ELNOEL
DYE,TR-62-PID    DYE, TR
                 POPULAR IMAGES OF DECISION-MAKING IN SUBURBAN
                    COMMUNITIES (UNITED STATES).=
                 SOCIOLOGY AND SOCIAL RESEARCH, 47, (OCTOBER 1962),            62
                    PP. 75-83.
                 ELEL, ELNOEL, ELPRNOR
DYE,TR-65-SLP    DYE, TR
                 STATE LEGISLATIVE POLITICS (UNITED STATES).=
                 H JACOB AND KN VINES (EDS), POLITICS IN THE AMERICAN          65
                    STATES--A COMPARATIVE ANALYSIS, BOSTON, LITTLE, BROWN
                    AND COMPANY, 1965, PP. 151-206.
                 COMEL, ELEL, ELNOEL, ELPRNOR
DZIEMK-52-FCP    DZIEWANOWSKI, MK
                 THE FOUNDATION OF THE COMMUNIST PARTY POLAND.=
                 THE AMERICAN SLAVIC AND EAST EUROPEAN REVIEW, 11,             52
                    (APRIL 1952), PP. 106-122.
                 ELEL
DZIEMK-59-CPP    DZIEWANOWSKI, MK
                 THE COMMUNIST PARTY OF POLAND -- AN OUTLINE OF HISTORY.=
                 CAMBRIDGE, HARVARD UNIVERSITY PRESS, 1959.                    59
                 COMEL, ELEL, ELNOEL, ELPRNOR
EAGLW -65-IRM    EAGLETON-JR, W
                 THE ISLAMIC REPUBLIC OF MAURITANIA.=
                 THE MIDDLE EAST JOURNAL, 19, (WINTER 1965), PP. 45-53.        65
                 COMEL, ELEL, ELPRNOR
EARLEM-51-MF     EARLE, EM (ED)
                 MODERN FRANCE.=
                 PRINCETON, PRINCETON UNIVERSITY PRESS, 1951.                  51
                 COMEL, ELEL, ELNOEL, ELPRNOR
EASTD -59-PA     EASTON, D
                 POLITICAL ANTHROPOLOGY.=
                 BJ SIEGEL (ED), BIENNIAL REVIEW OF ANTHROPOLOGY,              59
                    STANFORD, STANFORD UNIVERSITY PRESS, 1959.
                 DEFEL, METEL
EASTD -65-SAP    EASTON, D
                 A SYSTEMS ANALYSIS OF POLITICAL LIFE.=
                 NEW YORK, JOHN WILEY, 1965.                                   65
                 GNELTH, ELNOEL
EATOJW-47-ETL    EATON, JW
                 EXPERIMENTS IN TESTING FOR LEADERSHIP.=
                 THE AMERICAN JOURNAL OF SOCIOLOGY, 52, (MAY 1947),            47
                    PP. 523-535.
                 METEL
EBERW -52-CRS    EBERHARD, W
                 CONQUERORS AND RULERS -- SOCIAL FORCES IN MEDIEVAL CHINA.=
                 LEIDEN, EJ BRILL, 1952.                                       52
                 GNELTH, ELEL, ELNOEL
EBW   -54-CYG    EBW
                 SOME CHARACTERISTICS OF THE YOUNGER GENERATION IN
                    WESTERN GERMANY.=
                 THE WORLD TODAY, 10, (SEPTEMBER 1954), PP. 406-412.           54
                 COMEL, ELPRNOR
ECKHW -65-WPW    ECKHARDT, W
                 WAR PROPAGANDA, WELFARE VALUE, AND POLITICAL
                    IDEOLOGIES (SOVIET UNION, UNITED STATES, GERMANY,
                    ITALY, GREAT BRITAIN).=
                 THE JOURNAL OF CONFLICT RESOLUTION, 9, (SEPTEMBER 1965),      65
                    PP. 345-358.
                 ELPRNOR
ECKSHH-55-PBM    ECKSTEIN, HH
                 THE POLITICS OF THE BRITISH MEDICAL ASSOCIATION.=
                 THE POLITICAL QUARTERLY, 26, (OCTOBER 1955), PP. 345-359. 55
                 ELEL
ECKSHH-60-PGP    ECKSTEIN, HH
                 PRESSURE GROUP POLITICS -- THE CASE OF THE BRITISH
                    MEDICAL ASSOCIATION.=
                 STANFORD, STANFORD UNIVERSITY PRESS, 1960.                    60
                 ELEL, ELNOEL, ELPRNOR
ECKSHH-62-BPS    ECKSTEIN, HH
                 THE BRITISH POLITICAL SYSTEM.=
                 SH BEER AND AB ULAM (EDS), PATTERNS OF GOVERNMENT, 2ND ED,62
                    NEW YORK, RANDOM HOUSE, 1962, PP. 70-269.
                 ELEL, ELNOEL, ELPRNOR
EDELAS-63-WNS    EDELSTEIN, AS          SCHULZ, JB
                 THE WEEKLY NEWSPAPER'S LEADERSHIP ROLE AS SEEN BY
                    COMMUNITY LEADER'S (UNITED STATES).=
                 JOURNALISM QUARTERLY, 40, (AUTUMN 1963), PP. 565-574.         63
                 ELEL, ELNOEL, ELPRNOR
EDELAT-65-LAG    EDELMANN, AT

                    LATIN AMERICAN GOVERNMENT AND POLITICS.=
                    HOMEWOOD, ILLINOIS, THE DORSEY PRESS, 1965.                    65
                    ELEL, ELNOEL
EDELJD-67-OTU       EDELSTEIN, JD
                    AN ORGANIZATIONAL THEORY OF UNION DEMOCRACY
                    AMERICAN SOCIOLOGICAL REVIEW, 32, (FEBRUARY 1967),           67
                    PP. 19-31.
                    ELEL, ELNOEL, METEL
EDELM -64-SUP       EDELMAN, M
                    THE SYMBOLIC USES OF POLITICS.=
                    URBANA, UNIVERSITY OF ILLINOIS PRESS, 1964.                  64
                    ELEL, ELNOEL, ELPRNOR
EDENG -48-LCG       EDEN, G
                    LOBBY CORESPONDENTS (GREAT BRITAIN).=
                    PARLIAMENTARY AFFAIRS, 2, (WINTER 1948), PP. 25-32.          48
                    ELEL, ELNOEL
EDINLJ-56-GEP       EDINGER, LJ
                    GERMAN EXILE POLITICS -- THE SOCIAL DEMOCRATIC
                    EXECUTIVE COMMITTEE IN THE NAZI ERA.=
                    BERKELEY AND LOS ANGELES, UNIVERSITY OF CALIFORNIA           56
                    PRESS, 1956.
                    ELEL
EDINLJ-60-PTL       EDINGER, LJ
                    POST - TOTALITARIAN LEADERSHIP -- ELITES IN THE
                    GERMAN FEDERAL REPUBLIC.=
                    THE AMERICAN POLITICAL SCIENCE REVIEW, 54, (MARCH 1960),     60
                    PP. 58-82.
                    DEFEL, COMEL, ELEL
EDINLJ-61-CCB       EDINGER, LJ
                    CONTINUITY AND CHANGE IN THE BACKGROUND OF GERMAN
                    DECISION-MAKING.=
                    THE WESTERN POLITICAL QUARTERLY, 14, (MARCH 1961),           61
                    PP. 17-36.
                    COMEL
EDINLJ-63-MLF       EDINGER, LJ
                    MILITARY LEADERS AND FOREIGN POLICY-MAKING.=
                    THE AMERICAN POLITICAL SCIENCE REVIEW, 57, (JUNE 1963),      63
                    PP. 392-405.
                    ELEL, ELNOEL
EDINLJ-64-PSP       EDINGER, LJ
                    POLITICAL SCIENCE AND POLITICAL BIOGRAPHY -- REFLECTIONS
                    ON THE STUDY OF LEADERSHIP -- PART 1 -- PART 2.=
                    THE JOURNAL OF POLITICS, 26, (MAY 1964, AUGUST 1964),        64
                    PP. 423-439, PP. 648-696.
                    COMEL, METEL
EDINLJ-65-KSS       EDINGER, LJ
                    KURT SCHUMACHER -- A STUDY IN PERSONALITY AND POLITICAL
                    STANDFORD, STANDFORD UNIVERSITY PRESS, 1965.                 65
                    BEHAVIOR (GERMANY).=
                    ELEL, ELPRNOR, METEL
EDINLJ-67-ESI       EDINGER, LJ
                    EDITOR'S INTRODUCTION.=
                    LJ EDINGER (ED), POLITICAL LEADERSHIP IN INDUSTRIALIZED      67
                    SOCIETIES, NEW YORK, JOHN WILEY AND SONS, 1967,
                    PP. 1-25.
                    DEFEL, METEL
EDINLJ-67-PLI       EDINGER, LJ
                    POLITICAL LEADERSHIP IN INDUSTRIALIZED SOCIETIES
                    (UNITED STATES, SOVIET UNION, FRANCE, CANADA,
                    GREAT BRITAIN, AUSTRALIA, JAPAN, PHILIPPINES).=
                    NEW YORK, JOHN WILEY AND SONS, 1967.                         67
                    GNELTH, DEFEL, COMEL, ELEL, ELNOEL, ELPRNOR, METEL
EDINLU-67-SBE       EDINGER, LU          SEARING, DD
                    SOCIAL BACKGROUND IN ELITE ANALYSIS -- A METHODOLOGICAL
                    INQUIRY (FRANCE, GERMANY).=
                    THE AMERICAN POLITICAL SCIENCE REVIEW, 61, (JUNE 1967),      67
                    PP. 428-445.
                    DEFEL, COMEL, ELPRNOR, METEL
EDWAFG-59-NPC       EDWARDS, FG
                    THE NEGRO PROFESSIONAL CLASS (UNITED STATES).=
                    GLENCOE, ILLINOIS, THE FREE PRESS, 1959.                     59
                    COMEL, ELPRNOR
EDWAHT-67-PSI       EDWARDS, HT
                    POWER STRUCTURE AND ITS COMMUNICATION BEHAVIOR IN
                    SAN JOSE, COSTA RICA.=
                    JOURNAL OF INTER-AMERICAN STUDIES, 9, (APRIL 1967),          67
                    PP. 236-247.
                    COMEL, ELEL, METEL
EFIMNM-54-AIU       EFIMENCO, NM
                    AMERICAN IMPACT UPON MIDDLE EAST LEADERSHIP.=
                    POLITICAL SCIENCE QUARTERLY, 69, (JUNE 1954), PP. 202-218.54
                    COMEL
EFIMNM-55-ECD       EFIMENCO, NM
                    AN EXPERIMENT WITH CIVILIAN DICTATORSHIP IN IRAN --

                         THE CASE OF M. MOSSADAGH.=
                         THE JOURNAL OF POLITICS, 17, (AUGUST 1955), PP. 390-406.   55
                         ELEL, ELNOEL
EGGER -49-USB    EGGER, R
                         THE UNITED STATES BUREAU OF THE BUDGET.=
                         PARLIAMENTARY AFFAIRS, 3, (WINTER 1949), PP. 39-54.        49
                         ELEL
EH      -55-TSB  EH
                         TOWARDS A SOVIET BOURGEOISIE.=
                         THE WORLD TODAY, 11, (JULY 1955), PP. 300-308.             55
                         COMEL
EHLEEL-49-TSL    EHLE, EL
                         TECHNIQUES FOR THE STUDY OF LEADERSHIP (UNITED STATES).=
                         THE PUBLIC OPINION QUARTERLY, 13, (SPRING 1949),           49
                            PP. 235-240.
                         METEL
EHRLHJ-61-RAS    EHRLICH, HJ
                         THE REPUTATIONAL APPROACH TO THE STUDY OF COMMUNITY
                            POWER.=
                         AMERICAN SOCIOLOGICAL REVIEW, 26, (DECEMBER 1961),         61
                            PP. 926-927.
                         METEL
EHRLHJ-65-NCR    EHRLICH, HJ          BAUER, ML
                         NEWSPAPER CITATION AND REPUTATION FOR COMMUNITY LEADERSHIP
                            (UNITED STATES).=
                         AMERICAN SOCIOLOGICAL REVIEW, 30, (JUNE 1965),             65
                            PP. 411-415.
                         METEL
EHRMHW-48-PFP    EHRMANN, HW
                         POLITICAL FORCES IN PRESENT DAY FRANCE.=
                         SOCIAL RESEARCH, 15, (JUNE 1948), PP. 146-169.             48
                         ELEL
EHRMHW-54-FTA    EHRMANN, HW
                         THE FRENCH TRADE ASSOCIATIONS AND THE RATIFICATION
                            OF THE SCHUMAN PLAN.=
                         WORLD POLITICS, 6, (JULY 1954), PP. 45-47.                 54
                         ELEL
EHRMHW-57-OBF    EHRMANN, HW
                         ORGANIZED BUSINESS IN FRANCE.=
                         PRINCETON, PRINCETON UNIVERSITY PRESS, 1957.               57
                         ELEL, ELNOEL
EHRMHW-58-IGF    EHRMANN, HW (ED)
                         INTEREST GROUPS ON FOUR CONTINENTS.=
                         PITTSBURGH, UNIVERSITY OF PITTSBURGH PRESS, 1958.          58
                         DEFEL, ELEL, ELNOEL, METEL
EHRMHW-61-FBO    EHRMANN, HW
                         FRENCH BUREAUCRACY AND ORGANIZED INTERESTS.=
                         ADMINISTRATIVE SCIENCE QUARTERLY, 5, (MARCH 1961),         61
                            PP. 534-555.
                         ELEL
EHRMHW-63-DDF    EHRMANN, HW
                         DIRECT DEMOCRACY IN FRANCE.=
                         THE AMERICAN POLITICAL SCIENCE REVIEW, 57,                 63
                            (DECEMBER 1963), PP. 883-901.
                         ELNOEL
EISEEN-51-YCS    EISENSTADT, EN
                         YOUTH, CULTURE AND SOCIAL STRUCTURE IN ISRAEL.=
                         THE BRITISH JOURNAL OF SOCIOLOGY, 2, (1951), PP. 105-114. 51
                         COMEL
EISESN-51-PEP    EISENSTADT, SN
                         THE PLACE OF ELITES AND PRIMARY GROUPS IN THE ABSORPTION
                            OF NEW IMMIGRANTS IN ISRAEL.=
                         THE AMERICAN JOURNAL OF SOCIOLOGY, 57, (NOVEMBER 1951),    51
                            PP. 222-231.
                         ELEL, ELNOEL, ELPRNOR
EISESN-56-GGA    EISENSTADT, SN
                         FROM GENERATION TO GENERATION -- AGE GROUPS AND SOCIAL
                            STRUCTURE.=
                         GLENCOE, ILLINOIS, FREE PRESS, 1956.                       56
                         DEFEL, ELEL, ELNOEL, ELPRNOR
EISESN-56-IGT    EISENSTADT, SN        BEN-DAVID, J
                         INTER-GENERATION TENSIONS IN ISRAEL.=
                         INTERNATIONAL SOCIAL SCIENCE BULLETIN, 8, (1956),          56
                            PP. 54-75.
                         COMEL, ELEL, ELNOEL
EISESN-56-PLS    EISENSTADT, SN
                         PATTERNS OF LEADERSHIP AND SOCIAL HOMOGENEITY
                            IN ISRAEL.=
                         INTERNATIONAL SOCIAL SCIENCE BULLETIN, 8, (1956),          56
                            PP. 37-54.
                         COMEL, ELEL, ELNOEL, ELPRNOR
EISESN-56-PSA    EISENSTADT, SN
                         POLITICAL STRUGGLE IN (ANCIENT) BUREAUCRATIC SOCIETIES.=
                         WORLD POLITICS, 9, (OCTOBER 1956), PP. 15-36.              56

                           DEFEL, ELEL, ELPRNOR
EISESN-58-BB     EISENSTADT, SN
                 BUREAUCRACY AND BUREAUCRATIZATION.=
                 CURRENT SOCIOLOGY, 7, (1958), PP. 99-124.
                           ELEL, ELNOEL                                      58
EISESN-58-I      EISENSTADT, SN
                 ISRAEL.=
                 A ROSE (ED), THE INSTITUTIONS OF ADVANCED SOCIETIES,        58
                   MINNEAPOLIS, UNIVERSITY OF MINNESOTA PRESS, 1958,
                   PP. 384-443.
                           COMEL, ELEL, ELNOEL, ELPRNOR
EISESN-58-ICB    EISENSTADT, SN
                 INTERNAL CONTRADICTIONS IN BUREAUCRATIC POLITIES
                   (ANCIENT CHINA, PERSIA).=
                 COMPARATIVE STUDIES IN SOCIETY AND HISTORY,
                   1, (OCTOBER 1958), PP. 58-75.                             58
                           DEFEL, ELEL, ELPRNOR
EISESN-58-SOD    EISENSTADT, SN
                 THE STUDY OF ORIENTAL DESPOTISMS AS SYSTEMS
                   OF TOTAL POWER (CHINA).=
                 THE JOURNAL OF ASIAN STUDIES, 17, (MAY 1958), PP. 435-446.58
                           GNELTH, COMEL, ELEL, ELNOEL
EISESN-59-PPS    EISENSTADT, SN
                 PRIMITIVE POLITICAL SYSTEMS -- A COMPARATIVE ANALYSIS.=
                 AMERICAN ANTHROPOLOGIST, 61, (APRIL 1959), PP. 200-220.     59
                           COMEL, ELEL, ELNOEL
EISESN-60-BBD    EISENSTADT, SN
                 BUREAUCRACY, BUREAUCRATIZATION, AND DEBUREAUCRATIZATION.=
                 ADMINISTRATIVE SCIENCE QUARTERLY, 4, (1959-1960),           60
                   PP. 302-320.
                           DEFEL
EISESN-62-IIP    EISENSTADT, SN
                 INITIAL INSTITUTIONAL PATTERNS OF POLITICAL
                   MODERNIZATION -- PART 1 -- PART 2.=
                 CIVILIZATIONS, 12,13, (1962, 1963),
                   PP. 461-472, PP. 54-75.                                   62
                           COMEL, ELEL, ELNOEL, ELPRNOR
EISESN-62-ROP    EISENSTADT, SN
                 RELIGIOUS ORGANIZATIONS AND POLITICAL PROCESS IN
                   CENTRALIZED EMPIRES (MIDDLE EAST, FAR EAST).=
                 THE JOURNAL OF ASIAN STUDIES, 21, (MAY 1962), PP. 271-294.62
                           ELEL
EISESN-63-BPD    EISENSTADT, SN
                 BUREAUCRACY AND POLITICAL DEVELOPMENT.=
                 J LAPALOMBARA (ED), BUREAUCRACY AND POLITICAL              63
                   DEVELOPMENT, PRINCETON, NEW JERSEY, PRINCETON UNIVERSITY
                   PRESS, 1963, PP. 76-119.
                           DEFEL, ELEL, ELNOEL, ELPRNOR
EISESN-63-PSE    EISENSTADT, SN
                 THE POLITICAL SYSTEMS OF EMPIRES.=
                 NEW YORK, THE FREE PRESS, 1963.
                           DEFEL, COMEL, ELEL, ELNOEL, ELPRNOR               63
EISESN-66-DSP    EISENSTADT, SN
                 THE DEVELOPMENT OF SOCIO-POLITICAL CENTERS AT THE SECOND
                   STAGE OF MODERNISATION -- A COMPARATIVE ANALYSIS OF
                   TWO TYPES.=
                 INTERNATIONAL JOURNAL OF COMPARATIVE SOCIOLOGY, 7,          66
                   (MARCH 1966), PP. 119-137.
                           DEFEL, ELEL, ELPRNOR
EKMAP -66-CCD    EKMAN, P             ET AL
                 COPING WITH CUBA -- DIVERGENT POLICY PREFERENCES OF
                   STATE POLITICAL LEADERS (UNITED STATES).=
                 THE JOURNAL OF CONFLICT RESOLUTION, 10, (JUNE 1966),        66
                   PP. 180-197.
                           COMEL, ELPRNOR, METEL
ELDEN -53-PFP    ELDER, N
                 PARLIAMENT AND FOREIGN POLICY IN SWEDEN.=
                 POLITICAL STUDIES, 1, (1953), PP. 193-206.
                           ELEL, ELNOEL                                      53
ELDEN -57-SR     ELDER, N
                 THE SWEDISH RIKSDAG.=
                 PARLIAMENTARY AFFAIRS, 10, (SUMMER 1957), PP. 288-295.      57
                           ELEL
ELDEN -60-PGS    ELDER, N
                 PARLIAMENTARY GOVERNMENT IN SCANDINAVIA.=
                 PARLIAMENTARY AFFAIRS, 13, (SUMMER 1960), PP. 363-373.      60
                           ELEL, ELNOEL
ELDENC-57-SEO    ELDER, NCM
                 THE SWEDISH ELECTION OF 1956.=
                 POLITICAL STUDIES, 5, (1957), PP. 65-78.                    57
                           ELEL, ELNOEL
ELDERE-57-PSD    ELDEN, RE
                 THE PUBLIC STUDIES DIVISION OF THE DEPARTMENT OF THE
                   STATE -- PUBLIC OPINION ANALYSIS IN THE FORMULATION AND

                        CONDUCT OF AMERICAN FOREIGN POLICY.=
                        THE WESTERN POLITICAL QUARTERLY, 10, (DECEMBER 1957),        57
                        PP. 783-792.
                        ELEL, ELPRNOR
ELDERE-60-PMD   ELDER, RE
                        THE POLICY MACHINE -- THE DEPARTMENT OF STATE AND
                        AMERICAN FOREIGN POLICY.=
                        SYRACUSE, NEW YORK, SYRACUSE UNIVERSITY PRESS, 1960.         60
                        ELEL, ELNOEL, ELPRNOR
ELDESJ-58-AIG   ELDERSVELD, SJ
                        AMERICAN INTEREST GROUPS -- A SURVEY OF RESEARCH AND
                        SOME IMPLICATIONS FOR THEORY AND METHOD.=
                        HW EHRMANN (ED), INTEREST GROUPS ON FOUR CONTINENTS,         58
                        PITTSBURGH, UNIVERSITY OF PITTSBURGH PRESS, 1958.
                        METEL
ELDESJ-64-PPB   ELDERSVELD, SJ
                        POLITICAL PARTIES -- A BEHAVIORAL ANALYSIS
                        (UNITED STATES).=
                        CHICAGO, RAND MCNALLY AND COMPANY, 1964.                     64
                        DEFEL, COMEL, ELEL, ELNOEL, ELPRNOR, METEL
ELIAN -65-EOG   ELIAS, N              SCOTSON, JL
                        THE ESTABLISHED AND THE OUTSIDER (GREAT BRITAIN).=
                        LONDON, FRANK CASS, 1965.                                    65
                        ELEL, ELNOEL
ELKIB -60-RIE   ELKIN, B
                        THE RUSSIAN INTELLIGENTSIA ON THE EVE OF THE REVOLUTION.=
                        DAEDALUS, 89, (SUMMER 1960), PP. 472-486.                    60
                        ELEL, ELPRNOR
ELLIFP-  -WLA   ELLISON, FP
                        THE WRITER (LATIN AMERICA).=
                        JJ JOHNSON (ED), CONTINUITY AND CHANGE IN LATIN AMERICA,
                        STANFORD, STANFORD UNIVERSITY PRESS, 1964, PP. 78-100.  64
                        ELEL, ELPRNOR
ELLIO -59-MTU   ELLIOTT, O
                        MEN AT THE TOP (UNITED STATES).=
                        NEW YORK, HARPER AND ROW, 1959.                              59
                        ELEL, ELNOEL, ELPRNOR
ELSBWH-53-JSR   ELSBREE, WH
                        JAPAN'S ROLE IN SOUTHEAST ASIAN NATIONALIST MOVEMENTS,
                        1940-1945.=
                        CAMBRIDGE, HARVARD UNIVERSITY PRESS, 1953.                   53
                        ELEL, ELNOEL, ELPRNOR
ELSBWH-54-PPE   ELSBREE, WH
                        THE 1953 PHILIPPINE PRESIDENTIAL ELECTIONS.=
                        PACIFIC AFFAIRS, 27, (MARCH 1954), PP. 3-15.                 54
                        ELEL, ELNOEL
ELWELP-49-PPI   ELWELL-SUTTON, LP
                        POLITICAL PARTIES IN IRAN, 1941-1948.=
                        THE MIDDLE EAST JOURNAL, 3, (JANUARY 1949), PP. 45-62.       49
                        COMEL, ELEL, ELNOEL
EMBEM -62-PAS   EMBER, M
                        POLITICAL AUTHORITY AND THE STRUCTURE OF KINSHIP
                        IN ABORIGINAL SAMOA.=
                        AMERICAN ANTHROPOLOGIST, 64, (OCTOBER 1962), PP. 964-971. 62
                        COMEL
EMERR -53-PRG   EMERSON, R
                        PROBLEMS OF REPRESENTATIVE GOVERNMENT IN SOUTHEAST ASIA.=
                        PACIFIC AFFAIRS, 26, (DECEMBER 1953), PP. 291-302.           53
                        ELEL, ELNOEL, ELPRNOR
EMERR -60-ENR   EMERSON, R
                        FROM EMPIRE TO NATION -- THE RISE TO SELF-ASSERTION
                        OF ASIAN AND AFRICAN PEOPLES.=
                        CAMBRIDGE, HARVARD UNIVERSITY PRESS, 1960.                   60
                        ELEL, ELNOEL, ELPRNOR
EMERR -60-NPD   EMERSON, R
                        NATIONALISM AND POLITICAL DEVELOPMENT.=
                        THE JOURNAL OF POLITICS, 22, (FEBRUARY 1960), PP. 3-28.      60
                        ELEL, ELNOEL, ELPRNOR
EMERRM-62-PDR   EMERSON, RM
                        POWER - DEPENDENCE RELATIONS.=
                        AMERICAN SOCIOLOGICAL REVIEW, 27, (FEBRUARY 1962),           62
                        PP. 31-41.
                        DEFEL, METEL
ENCAV -57-TAB   ENCARNACION-JR, V
                        TYPES OF AUTHORITY IN A BENGUET VILLAGE
                        (LUZON, PHILIPPINES).=
                        PHILIPPINE JOURNAL OF PUBLIC ADMINISTRATION, 1,              57
                        (OCTOBER 1957), PP. 379-391.
                        COMEL, ELEL, ELNOEL
ENCAV -62-DAS   ENCARNACION-JR, V
                        THE DEVELOPMENT ADMINISTRATOR'S ROLE -- SOME
                        COMMENTS (PHILIPPINES).=
                        PHILIPPINE JOURNAL OF PUBLIC ADMINISTRATION, 6,              62
                        (APRIL 1962), PP. 122-125.

```
                    ELEL
ENCES -61-PEA   ENCEL, S
                THE POLITICAL ELITE IN AUSTRALIA.=
                POLITICAL STUDIES, 9, (FEBRUARY 1961), PP. 16-36.          61
                DEFEL, COMEL, ELEL
ENCES -62-CGA   ENCEL, S
                CABINET GOVERNMENT IN AUSTRALIA.=
                MELBOURNE, MELBOURNE UNIVERSITY PRESS, 1962.               62
                COMEL, ELEL, ELNOEL
ENGEFC-56-MPP   ENGELMANN, FC
                MEMBERSHIP PARTICIPATION IN POLICY-MAKING IN THE C.C.F.
                  (CO-OPERATIVE COMMONWEALTH FEDERATION, CANADA).=
                CANADIAN JOURNAL OF ECONOMICS AND POLITICAL SCIENCE,       56
                  22, (MAY 1956), PP. 161-173.
                ELEL, ELNOEL, ELPRNOR
ENGHGF-57-KSF   ENGHOLM, GF
                KENYA'S FIRST DIRECT ELECTIONS FOR AFRICANS, MARCH 1957.=
                PARLIAMENTARY AFFAIRS, 10, (AUTUMN 1957), PP. 424-433.     57
                ELNOEL
ENGLFC-67-PPC   ENGLEMANN, FC        SCHWARTZ, MA
                POLITICAL PARTIES AND THE CANADIAN SOCIAL STRUCTURE.=
                ENGLEWOOD CLIFFS, PRENTICE-HALL, 1967.                     67
                COMEL, ELEL, ELNOEL, ELPRNOR
EPSTAL-58-PUA   EPSTEIN, AL
                POLITICS IN AN URBAN AFRICAN COMMUNITY.=
                NEW YORK, HUMANITIES PRESS, 1958                           58
                ELEL, ELNOEL, ELPRNOR
EPSTL -63-BMP   EPSTEIN, L
                BRITISH M.P.S AND THEIR LOCAL PARTIES -- THE SUEZ CRISIS.=
                THE AMERICAN POLITICAL SCIENCE REVIEW, 54, (JUNE 1960),    63
                  PP. 374-391.
                ELEL, ELNOEL, ELPRNOR
EPSTLD-56-BMP   EPSTEIN, LD
                BRITISH MASS PARTIES IN COMPARISON WITH AMERICAN
                  PARTIES.=
                POLITICAL SCIENCE QUARTERLY, 71, (MARCH 1956),             56
                  PP. 97-125.
                ELEL, ELNOEL
EPSTLD-56-CBP   EPSTEIN, LD
                COHESION OF BRITISH PARLIAMENTARY PARTIES.=
                THE AMERICAN POLITICAL SCIENCE REVIEW, 50, (JUNE 1956),     56
                  PP. 360-377.
                ELEL, ELNOEL
EPSTLD-58-PWU   EPSTEIN, LD
                POLITICS IN WISCONSIN (UNITED STATES).=
                MADISON, UNIVERSITY OF WISCONSIN PRESS, 1958.              58
                COMEL, ELEL, ELNOEL
EPSTLD-59-CSB   EPSTEIN, LD
                CANDIDATE SELECTION IN BRITAIN.=
                PROD (THE AMERICAN BEHAVIORAL SCIENTIST), 2,               59
                  (MARCH 1959), PP. 16-18.
                COMEL, ELEL
EPSTLD-62-BCC   EPSTEIN, LD
                BRITISH CLASS CONSCIOUSNESS AND THE LABOUR PARTY.=
                JOURNAL OF BRITISH STUDIES, 1, (MAY 1962), PP. 136-150.    62
                COMEL
EPSTLD-62-NMP   EPSTEIN, LD
                NEW M.P.S AND THE POLITICS OF THE PLP (PARLIAMENTARY
                  LABOUR PARTY, GREAT BRITAIN).=
                POLITICAL STUDIES, 10, (1962), PP. 121-124.                62
                ELEL, ELNOEL, ELPRNOR
EPSTLD-62-WMP   EPSTEIN, LD
                WHO MAKES PARTY POLICY -- BRITISH LABOUR 1960-1961.=
                MIDWEST JOURNAL OF POLITICAL SCIENCE, 6, (MAY 1962),       62
                  PP. 165-182.
                COMEL, ELEL, ELNOEL, ELPRNOR
EPSTLD-64-BPS   EPSTEIN, LD
                BRITISH POLITICS IN THE SUEZ CRISIS.=
                URBANA, ILLINOIS, UNIVERSITY OF ILLINOIS PRESS, 1964.      64
                ELEL, ELNOEL
EPSTLD-64-CSC   EPSTEIN, LD
                A COMPARATIVE STUDY OF CANADIAN PARTIES.=
                THE AMERICAN POLITICAL SCIENCE REVIEW, 58, (MARCH 1964),   64
                  PP. 46-59.
                ELEL, ELNOEL
EPSTTS-62-EDS   EPSTEIN, TS
                ECONOMIC DEVELOPMENT AND SOCIAL CHANGE IN SOUTH INDIA.=
                NEW YORK, THE HUMANITIES PRESS, 1962.                      62
                ELEL, ELNOEL
ERASCJ-52-LVT   ERASMUS, CJ
                THE LEADER VS. TRADITION -- A CASE STUDY (MEXICO).=
                AMERICAN ANTHROPOLIGIST, 54, (APRIL-JUNE 1952),            52
                  PP. 168-178.
                COMEL, ELEL, ELNOEL
```

ERDMHL-64-ISS    ERDMAN, HL
                 INDIA'S SWATANTRA PARTY.=
                 PACIFIC AFFAIRS, 36, (WINTER 1964), PP. 394-410.            64
                 COMEL, ELEL, ELNOEL, ELPRNOR
ERDMHL-66-FPV    ERDMAN, HL
                 THE FOREIGN POLICY VIEWS OF THE INDIAN RIGHT.=
                 PACIFIC AFFAIRS, 39, (SPRING-SUMMER 1966), PP.5-18.          66
                 ELEL, ELPRNOR
ERICJ -62-SHC    ERICKSON, J
                 THE SOVIET HIGH COMMAND -- A MILITARY - POLITICAL
                    HISTORY.=
                 NEW YORK, SAINT MARTIN'S PRESS, 1962.                       62
                 COMEL, ELEL, ELNOEL
ERIKEH-58-YML    ERIKSON, EH
                 YOUNG MAN LUTHER -- A STUDY IN PSYCHOANALYSIS AND
                    HISTORY.=
                 NEW YORK, WW NORTON, 1958.                                  58
                 ELPRNOR, METEL
ERLIV -64-PST    ERLICH, V
                 POST - STALIN TRENDS IN RUSSIAN LITERATURE.=
                 SLAVIC REVIEW, 23, (SEPTEMBER 1964), PP. 405-419.           64
                 ELEL, ELPRNOR
ESMAMJ-47-JAC    ESMAN, MJ
                 JAPANESE ADMINISTRATION -- A COMPARATIVE VIEW.=
                 PUBLIC ADMINISTRATION REVIEW, 7, (SPRING 1947),             47
                    PP. 100-112.
                 COMEL, ELEL
ETZIA -57-AIS    ETZIONI, A
                 AGRARIANISM IN ISRAEL'S PARTY SYSTEM.=
                 THE CANADIAN JOURNAL OF ECONOMICS AND POLITICAL SCIENCE,    57
                    23, (AUGUST 1957), PP. 363-375.
                 COMEL, ELEL
ETZIA -59-ASO    ETZIONI, A
                 AUTHORITY STRUCTURE AND ORGANIZATIONAL EFFECTIVENESS.=
                 ADMINISTRATIVE SCIENCE QUARTERLY, 4, (JUNE 1959),           59
                    PP. 49-69.
                 COMEL, ELEL, ELNOEL
ETZIA -59-FDE    ETZIONI, A
                 THE FUNCTIONAL DIFFERENTIATION OF ELITES IN THE KIBBUTZ
                    (ISRAEL).=
                 THE AMERICAN JOURNAL OF SOCIOLOGY, 64, (1959),              59
                    PP. 476-486.
                 GNETLH, ELEL, ELNOEL, ELPRNOR, METEL
ETZIA -61-CAC    ETZIONI, A
                 A COMPARATIVE ANALYSIS OF COMPLEX ORGANIZATIONS.=
                 NEW YORK, FREE PRESS OF GLENCOE, INC, 1961.                 61
                 GNELTH, DEFEL, ELEL, ELNOEL, ELPRNOR
ETZIA -65-DLC    ETZIONI, A
                 DUAL LEADERSHIP IN COMPLEX ORGANIZATIONS.=
                 AMERICAN SOCIOLOGICAL REVIEW, 30, (OCTOBER 1965),           65
                    PP. 688-698.
                 DEFEL, METEL
ETZIA -65-PUC    ETZIONI, A
                 POLITICAL UNIFICATION -- A COMPARATIVE STUDY OF LEADERS
                    AND FOLLOWERS (UNITED ARAB REPUBLIC, FEDERATION OF THE
                    WEST INDIES, SCANDINAVIA, EUROPEAN ECONOMIC
                    COMMUNITY).=
                 NEW YORK, HOLT, RINEHART AND WINSTON, 1965.                 65
                 GNELTH, DEFEL, ELNOEL, ELPRNOR
EULAH -56-ICP    EULAU, H
                 IDENTIFICATION WITH CLASS AND POLITICAL ROLE BEHAVIOR
                    (UNITED STATES).=
                 THE PUBLIC OPINION QUARTERLY, 20, (FALL 1956),              56
                    PP. 515-530.
                 DEFEL, ELPRNOR, METEL
EULAH -59-OTE    EULAU, H              ET. AL.
                 OBSERVATIONS ON THE THEORY OF EDMUND BURKE
                    (UNITED STATES).=
                 THE AMERICAN POLITICAL SCIENCE REVIEW, 53, (SEPTEMBER       59
                    1959), PP. 742-756.
                 ELEL, ELNOEL, ELPRNOR
EULAH -59-PSA    EULAU, H              BUCHANAN, W          FERGUSON, LC
                 THE POLITICAL SOCIALIZATION OF AMERICAN STATE
                    LEGISLATORS.=
                 MIDWEST JOURNAL OF POLITICAL SCIENCE, 3, (MAY 1959),        59
                    PP. 188-206.
                 COMEL, ELPRNOR
EULAH -61-CPA    EULAU, H              ET AL
                 CAREER PERSPECTIVES OF AMERICAN STATE LEGISLATORS.=
                 D MARVICK (ED), POLITICAL DECISION-MAKERS, GLENCOE, THE     61
                    FREE PRESS, 1961, PP. 218-263.
                 ELPRNOR
EULAH -62-BAL    EULAU, H
                 BASES OF AUTHORITY IN LEGISLATIVE BODIES -- A

                        COMPARATIVE ANALYSIS (UNITED STATES).=
                        ADMINISTRATIVE SCIENCE QUARTERLY, 7, (DECEMBER 1962),        62
                           PP. 309-321.
                        ELEL, ELNOEL, ELPRNOR
EULAH -62-CPE   EULAU, H
                        CLASS AND PARTY IN THE EISENHOWER YEARS, CLASS ROLES
                           AND PERSPECTIVE IN THE 1952 AND 1956 ELECTION
                           (UNITED STATES).=
                        NEW YORK, FREE PRESS, 1962.                                 62
                        COMEL, ELNOEL
EULAH -62-OMP   EULAU, H              KOFF, D
                        OCCUPATIONAL MOBILITY AND POLITICAL CAREER
                           (UNITED STATES).=
                        THE WESTERN POLITICAL QUARTERLY, 15, (SEPTEMBER 1962),       62
                           PP. 507-521.
                        COMEL
EULAH -64-LPS   EULAU, H              SPRAGUE, JD
                        LAWYERS IN POLITICS -- A STUDY IN PROFESSIONAL
                           CONVERGENCE (UNITED STATES).=
                        INDIANAPOLIS, THE BOBBS-MERRILL COMPANY, INC, 1964.          64
                        COMEL, ELEL, ELNOEL, ELPRNOR
EULAH -64-LWP   EULAU, H
                        LOBBYISTS -- THE WASTED PROFESSION (UNITED STATES).=
                        THE PUBLIC OPINION QUARTERLY, 28, (SPRING 1964),             64
                           PP. 27-38.
                        ELEL, ELNOEL, ELPRNOR, METEL
EVANEE-40-APS   EVANS-PRITCHARD, EE
                        AFRICAN POLITICAL SYSTEMS.=
                        LONDON, OXFORD UNIVERSITY PRESS, 1940.                       40
                        COMEL, ELEL, ELNOEL
EVANEE-60-EOZ   EVANS-PRITCHARD, EE
                        THE ETHNIC ORIGINS OF ZANDE OFFICE-HOLDERS (EGYPT,SUDAN).=
                        MAN, 60, (1960), PP. 100-102.                                60
                        COMEL
EVANWM-61-LEB   EVAN, WM              ZELDITCH, M
                        A LABORATORY EXPERIMENT ON BUREAUCRATIC AUTHORITY.=
                        AMERICAN SOCIOLOGICAL REVIEW, 26,                            61
                           (DECEMBER 1961), PP. 883-893.
                        DEFEL, METEL
EWINCA-48-SGU   EWING, CAM
                        SOUTHERN GOVERNORS (UNITED STATES).=
                        THE JOURNAL OF POLITICS, 10, (MAY 1948), PP. 385-409.        48
                        COMEL, ELEL, ELNOEL
EYREJD-55-CRF   EYRE, JD
                        THE CHANGING ROLE OF THE FORMER JAPANESE LANDLORD.=
                        LAND ECONOMICS, 31, (FEBRUARY 1955), PP. 35-46.              55
                        ELNOEL, ELPRNOR
EZERK -64-CDN   EZERA, K
                        CONSTITUTIONAL DEVELOPMENTS IN NIGERIA.=
                        REVISED EDITION, CAMBRIDGE, UNIVERSITY PRESS, 1964.          64
                        ELEL
FAINM -49-PRC   FAINSOD, M
                        POSTWAR ROLE OF THE COMMUNIST PARTY (SOVIET UNION).=
                        THE ANNALS OF THE AMERICAN ACADEMY OF POLITICAL AND          49
                           SOCIAL SCIENCE, 263, (MAY 1949), PP. 20-32.
                        COMEL, ELPRNOR
FAINM -54-SUS   FAINSOD, M
                        THE SOVIET UNION SINCE STALIN.=
                        PROBLEMS OF COMMUNISM, 3, (MARCH-APRIL 1954), PP. 1-10.      54
                        ELEL
FAINM -56-CPS   FAINSOD, M
                        THE COMMUNIST PARTY SINCE STALIN.=
                        THE ANNALS OF THE AMERICAN ACADEMY OF POLITICAL AND          56
                           SOCIAL SCIENCE, 303, (JANUARY 1956), PP. 23-36.
                        COMEL, ELEL
FAINM -58-PPS   FAINSOD, M
                        THE PARTY IN THE POST - STALIN ERA (SOVIET UNION).=
                        PROBLEMS OF COMMUNISM, 7, (JANUARY-FEBRUARY 1958),           58
                           PP. 7-13.
                        ELEL, ELNOEL
FAINM -58-SUS   FAINSOD, M
                        SMOLENSK UNDER SOVIET RULE.=
                        CAMBRIDGE, HARVARD UNIVERSITY PRESS, 1958.                   58
                        ELEL, ELNOEL
FAINM -59-WHC   FAINSOD, M
                        WHAT HAPPENED TO COLLECTIVE LEADERSHIP (SOVIET UNION).=
                        PROBLEMS OF COMMUNISM, 8, (JULY-AUGUST 1959), PP. 1-10.      59
                        ELEL, ELPRNOR
FAINM -61-KRS   FAINSOD, M
                        KHRUSHCHEVISM IN RETROSPECT (SOVIET UNION).=
                        PROBLEMS OF COMMUNISM, 14, (JANUARY-FEBRUARY 1961),          61
                           PP. 1-10.
                        ELEL, ELNOEL
FAINM -65-HRI   FAINSOD, M

                        HOW RUSSIA IS RULED.=
                        REV ED, CAMBRIDGE, HARVARD UNIVERSITY PRESS, 1965.          65
                        GNELTH, ELEL, ELNOEL, ELPRNOR
FAINM -67-RFS           FAINSOD, M
                        ROADS TO THE FUTURE (SOVIET UNION).=
                        PROBLEMS OF COMMUNISM, 16, (JULY-AUGUST 1967), PP. 21-23. 67
                        ELEL, ELNOEL
FAIRDR-64-PSP           FAIR, DR
                        PARTY STRENGTH AND POLITICAL PATRONAGE (UNITED STATES).=
                        SOUTHWESTERN SOCIAL SCIENCE QUARTERLY, 45,                  64
                            (DECEMBER 1964), PP. 264-271.
                        ELEL, ELNOEL
FAIRH -65-JIU           FAIRLIE, H
                        JOHNSON AND THE INTELLECTUALS (UNITED STATES).=
                        COMMENTARY, 40, (OCTOBER 1965), PP. 49-55.                  65
                        ELEL
FAIRJK-57-CTI           FAIRBANK, JK (ED)
                        CHINESE THOUGHT AND INSTITUTIONS.=
                        CHICAGO, UNIVERSITY OF CHICAGO PRESS, 1957.                 57
                        ELPRNOR
FALKSL-61-OMP           FALK, SL
                        ORGANIZATION AND MILITARY POWER -- THE JAPANESE HIGH
                            COMMAND IN WORLD WAR II.=
                        POLITICAL SCIENCE QUARTERLY, 76, (DECEMBER 1961),           61
                            PP. 503-518.
                        COMEL, ELEL, ELNOEL, ELPRNOR
FALKSL-64-NSC           FALK, SL
                        THE NATIONAL SECURITY COUNCIL UNDER TRUMAN, EISENHOWER,
                            AND KENNEDY (UNITED STATES).=
                        POLITICAL SCIENCE QUARTERLY, 79, (SEPTEMBER 1964),          64
                            PP. 403-434.
                        ELEL
FALLBB-54-LAU           FALL, BB
                        LOCAL ADMINISTRATION UNDER THE VIET MINH.=
                        PACIFIC AFFAIRS, 27, (MARCH 1954), PP. 50-57.               54
                        ELEL, ELNOEL, ELPRNOR
FALLBB-55-PRS           FALL, BB
                        THE POLITICAL - RELIGIOUS SECTS OF VIETNAM.=
                        PACIFIC AFFAIRS, 28,(SEPTEMBER 1955), PP. 235-253.          55
                        ELEL
FALLBB-60-NVN           FALL, BB
                        NORTH VIET NAM'S CONSTITUTION AND GOVERNMENT.=
                        PACIFIC AFFAIRS, 33, (SEPTEMBER 1960), PP. 282-290.         60
                        ELEL, ELNOEL
FALLBB-62-PPG           FALL, BB
                        POWER AND PRESSURE GROUPS IN NORTH VIET NAM.=
                        JP HONEY (ED), NORTH VIET NAM TODAY, NEW YORK,              62
                            FREDERICK A PRAEGER, 1962, PP. 60-69.
                        ELEL, ELNOEL
FALLBB-63-TV            FALL, BB
                        THE TWO VIETNAMS.=
                        NEW YORK, FREDERICK A PRAEGER, 1963.                        63
                        ELEL
FALLL -55-PMA           FALLERS, L
                        THE PREDICAMENT OF THE MODERN AFRICAN CHIEF --
                            AN INSTANCE FROM UGANDA.=
                        AMERICAN ANTHROPOLOGIST, 57, (APRIL 1955), PP. 290-305.     55
                        ELEL, ELNOEL
FALLLA-55-BBS           FALLERS, LA
                        BANTU BUREAUCRACY -- A STUDY OF ROLE CONFLICT AND
                            INSTITUTIONAL CHANGE IN THE SOGA POLITICAL SYSTEM.=
                        CAMBRIDGE, ENGLAND, W HEFFER, 1955.                         55
                        ELEL, ELNOEL, ELPRNOR
FALLLA-59-DSC           FALLUS, LA
                        DESPOTISM, STATUS CULTURE AND SOCIAL MOBILITY IN AN
                            AFRICAN KINGDOM (UGANDA).=
                        COMPARATIVE STUDIES IN SOCIETY AND HISTORY, 2,              59
                            (OCTOBER 1959), PP. 11-32.
                        ELEL, ELNOEL, ELPRNOR
FALLLA-64-KSM           FALLERS, LA (ED)
                        THE KING'S MEN -- LEADERSHIP AND STATUS IN BUGANDA ON THE
                            EVE OF INDEPENDENCE.=
                        NEW YORK, OXFORD UNIVERSITY PRESS, 1964.                    64
                        ELEL, ELNOEL, ELPRNOR
FANEAA-56-TCL           FANELLI, AA
                        A TYPOLOGY OF COMMUNITY LEADERSHIP BASED ON INFLUENCE
                            AND INTERACTION WITHIN THE LEADER SUBSYSTEM
                            (UNITED STATES).=
                        SOCIAL FORCES, 34, (MAY 1956), PP. 332-338.                 56
                        COMEL, ELEL, METEL
FARIRE-60-MCS           FARIS, REL
                        THE MIDDLE CLASS FROM A SOCIOLOGICAL VIEWPOINT
                            (UNITED STATES).=
                        SOCIAL FORCES, 39, (OCTOBER 1960), PP. 1-5.                 60

```
                COMEL, ELPRNOR
FARNLW-66-CFJ   FARNSWORTH, LW
                CHALLENGES TO FACTIONALISM IN JAPAN'S LIBERAL DEMOCRATIC
                   PARTY.=
                ASIAN SURVEY, 6, (SEPTEMBER 1966), PP. 501-509.              66
                ELEL, ELPRNOR
FARRCD-58-SAI   FARRIS, CD
                A SCALE ANALYSIS OF IDEOLOGICAL FACTORS IN CONGRESSIONAL
                   VOTING (UNITED STATES).=
                THE JOURNAL OF POLITICS, 20, (MAY 1958), PP. 308-338.        58
                ELPRNOR, METEL
FAWSSE-57-LMS   FAWSI, SED
                THE LABOUR MOVEMENT IN THE SUDAN 1946-1955.=
                LONDON, OXFORD UNIVERSITY PRESS, 1957.                       57
                COMEL, ELEL, ELNOEL
FAYEJ -59-EOA   FAYERWEATHER, J
                THE EXECUTIVE OVERSEAS -- ADMINISTRATIVE ATTITUDES AND
                   RELATIONSHIPS IN A FOREIGN CULTURE (MEXICO).=
                SYRACUSE, SYRACUSE UNIVERSITY PRESS, 1959.                   59
                ELPRNOR
FEDEP -64-RFK   FEDENKO, P
                THE RISE AND FALL OF KHRUSHCHEV (SOVIET UNION).=
                STUDIES ON THE SOVIET UNION, 4, (1964), PP. 3-15.            64
                ELEL, ELNOEL
FEI-  -53-CSG   FEI-HSIAO-TUNG
                CHINA'S GENTRY -- ESSAYS IN RURAL - URBAN RELATIONS.=
                CHICAGO, UNIVERSITY OF CHICAGO PRESS, 1953.                  53
                COMEL, ELEL, ELNOEL, ELPRNOR
FEITH -54-TEI   FEITH, H
                TOWARD ELECTIONS IN INDONESIA.=
                PACIFIC AFFAIRS, 27, (SEPTEMBER 1954), PP. 236-254.          54
                COMEL, ELEL, ELNOEL, ELPRNOR
FEITH -58-WCT   FEITH, H
                THE WILOPO CABINET -- A TURNING POINT IN POST
                   REVOLUTIONARY INDONESIA.=
                NEW YORK, INSTITUTE OF PACIFIC RELATIONS, 1958.              58
                COMEL, ELEL
FEITH -62-DCD   FEITH, H
                THE DECLINE OF CONSTITUTIONAL DEMOCRACY IN INDONESIA.=
                ITHACA, CORNELL UNIVERSITY PRESS, 1962.                      62
                COMEL, ELEL, ELNOEL, ELPRNOR
FEITH -63-EIR   FEITH, H              LEV, DS
                THE END OF THE INDONESIAN REBELLION.=
                PACIFIC AFFAIRS, 26, (SPRING 1963), PP. 32-46.               63
                ELEL, ELNOEL
FEITH -63-ISP   FEITH, H
                INDONESIA'S POLITICAL SYMBOLS AND THEIR WIELDERS.=
                WORLD POLITICS, 16, (OCTOBER 1963), PP. 79-97.               63
                ELNOEL, ELPRNOR
FEJTF -60-HI    FEJTO, F
                THE HUNGARIAN INTELLIGENTSIA.=
                SOVIET SURVEY--A QUARTERLY REVIEW OF CULTURAL TRENDS,        60
                   31, (JANUARY-MARCH 1960), PP. 88-94.
                COMEL, ELEL, ELPRNOR
FELDMD-58-PPP   FELD, MD
                POLITICAL POLICY AND PERSUASION -- THE ROLE OF
                   COMMUNICATIONS FROM POLITICAL LEADERS (SOVIET UNION,
                   GREAT BRITAIN, UNITED STATES).=
                THE JOURNAL OF CONFLICT RESOLUTION, 2, (MARCH 1958),         58
                   PP. 78-89.
                ELNOEL
FELDMD-64-MSI   FELD, MD
                MILITARY SELF-IMAGE IN A TECHNOLOGICAL ENVIRONMENT
                   (UNITED STATES).=
                M JANOWITZ (ED), THE NEW MILITARY--CHANGING PATTERNS OF      64
                   ORGANIZATION, NEW YORK, RUSSELL SAGE FOUNDATION,
                   1964, PP. 159-193.
                ELPRNOR
FELDRA-53-PSA   FELDMESSER, RA
                THE PERSISTENCE OF STATUS ADVANTAGES IN SOVIET RUSSIA.=
                THE AMERICAN JOURNAL OF SOCIOLOGY, 59, (JULY 1953),          53
                   PP. 19-27.
                ELEL, ELNOEL
FELDW -66-NEI   FELD, W
                NATIONAL ECONOMIC INTEREST AND POLICY FORMATION
                   IN THE EEC (EUROPEAN ECONOMIC COMMUNITY).=
                POLITICAL SCIENCE QUARTERLY, 81, (SEPTEMBER 1966),           66
                   PP. 392-412.
                ELEL, ELPRNOR
FELSJW-62-FFA   FELSER, JW
                FRENCH FIELD ADMINISTRATION -- THE BEGINNINGS.=
                COMPARATIVE STUDIES IN SOCIETY AND HISTORY, 5,               62
                   (OCTOBER 1962), PP. 76-111.
                COMEL, ELEL
```

FENNRF-58-PCR  FENNO-JR, RF
               PRESIDENT - CABINET RELATIONS -- A PATTERN AND A CASE
                  STUDY (UNITED STATES).=
               THE AMERICAN POLITICAL SCIENCE REVIEW, 52, (JUNE 1958),     58
                  PP. 388-405.
               ELEL
FENNRF-59-PSC  FENNO-JR, RF
               THE PRESIDENT'S CABINET -- AN ANALYSIS IN THE PERIOD
                  FROM WILSON TO EISENHOWER (UNITED STATES).=
               CAMBRIDGE, HARVARD UNIVERSITY PRESS, 1959.                  59
               COMEL, ELEL, ELNOEL, ELPRNOR
FENNRF-62-ACP  FENNO-JR, RF
               THE APPROPRIATIONS COMMITTEE AS A POLITICAL SYSTEM
                  (UNITED STATES).=
               THE AMERICAN POLITICAL SCIENCE REVIEW, 56, (JUNE 1962),     62
                  PP. 310-324.
               ELEL, ELPRNOR
FENNRF-65-IDI  FENNO-JR, RF
               THE INTERNAL DISTRIBUTION OF INFLUENCE -- THE HOUSE
                  (UNITED STATES).=
               DB TRUMAN (ED), THE CONGRESS AND AMERICA'S FUTURE           65
                  ENGLEWOOD CLIFFS, NEW JERSEY, PRENTICE HALL, 1965,
                  PP. 52-76.
               DEFEL, ELEL
FENNRF-66-PPA  FENNO-JR, RF
               THE POWER OF THE PURSE -- APPROPRIATIONS POLITICS IN
                  CONGRESS (UNITED STATES).=
               BOSTON, LITTLE, BROWN AND CO., 1966.                        66
               COMEL, ELEL, ELPRNOR, METEL
FEUELS-63-SIU  FEUER, LS
               THE SCIENTIFIC INTELLECTUAL (UNITED STATES).=
               NEW YORK, BASIC BOOKS, 1963.                                63
               ELEL
FEUELS-64-MPS  FEUER, LS
               MEETING THE PHILOSOPHERS (SOVIET UNION).=
               SURVEY--A JOURNAL OF SOVIET AND EAST EUROPEAN STUDIES,      64
                  51, (APRIL 1964), PP. 10-23.
               ELPRNOR
FEUELS-65-LDC  FEUER, LS
               LEADERSHIP AND DEMOCRACY IN THE COLLECTIVE SETTLEMENTS OF
                  ISRAEL.=
               AW GOULDNER (ED), STUDIES IN LEADERSHIP, NEW YORK,          65
                  RUSSELL AND RUSSELL, 1965, PP. 363-385.
               COMEL, ELNOEL, ELPRNOR
FF     -55-DSW  FF
               THE DILEMMA OF SOVIET WRITERS.=
               THE WORLD TODAY, 11, (APRIL 1955), PP. 151-163             55
               ELEL, ELPRNOR
FIEDFE-57-NLT  FIEDLER, FE
               A NOTE ON LEADERSHIP THEORY -- THE EFFECT OF SOCIAL
                  BARRIERS BETWEEN LEADERS AND FOLLOWERS (UNITED STATES).=
               SOCIOMETRY, 20, (JUNE 1957), PP. 87-94.                     57
               ELNOEL, ELPRNOR
FIELA  -62-FIG  FIELLIN, A
               THE FUNCTIONS OF INFORMAL GROUPS IN
                  LEGISLATIVE INSTITUTIONS (UNITED STATES).=
               THE JOURNAL OF POLITICS, 24, (FEBRUARY 1962),               62
                  PP. 72-91.
               ELEL, ELPRNOR
FIELDK-62-AEE  FIELDHOUSE, DK
               AUTOCHTHONOUS ELEMENTS IN THE EVOLUTION OF DOMINION
                  STATUS -- THE CASE OF NEW ZEALAND.=
               JOURNAL OF COMMONWEALTH STUDIES, 1, (1962), PP. 85-111.    62
               COMEL, ELEL, ELNOEL, ELPRNOR
FIELGL-51-HTP  FIELD, GL
               HYPOTHESES FOR A THEORY OF POLITICAL POWER.=
               THE AMERICAN POLITICAL SCIENCE REVIEW, 45,                  51
                  (SEPTEMBER 1951), PP. 716-723.
               DEFEL, ELEL, ELNOEL, METEL
FILLTR-61-SFE  FILLOL, TR
               SOCIAL FACTORS IN ECONOMIC DEVELOPMENT -- THE ARGENTINE
                  CASE.=
               CAMBRIDGE, THE MIT PRESS, 1961.                             61
               COMEL, ELEL, ELPRNOR
FILLWO-56-SSC  FILLEY, WO
               SOCIAL STRUCTURE AND CANADIAN POLITICAL PARTIES --
                  THE QUEBEC CASE.=
               THE WESTERN POLITICAL QUARTERLY, 9, (DECEMBER 1956),        56
                  PP. 900-914.
               COMEL, ELNOEL
FINEH  -60-PCR  FINER, H
               THE PRESIDENCY -- CRISIS AND REGENERATION
                  (UNITED STATES).=
               CHICAGO, UNIVERSITY OF CHICAGO PRESS, 1960.                 60

FINESE-56-AEL   ELEL
                FINER, SE
                THE ANONYMOUS EMPIRE (LOBBYING, GREAT BRITAIN).=
                POLITICAL STUDIES, 6, (1956), PP. 16-32.
                ELEL                                                     56
FINESE-58-AEG   FINER, SE
                ANONYMOUS EMPIRE (GREAT BRITAIN).=
                LONDON, PALL MALL PRESS, 1958.
                ELEL, ELNOEL, ELPRNOR                                    58
FINESE-61-BOH   FINER, SE        BERRINGTON, HB        BARTHOLOMEW, DJ
                BACKBENCH OPINION IN THE HOUSE OF COMMONS, 1955-1959
                   (GREAT BRITAIN).=
                NEW YORK, PERGAMON PRESS, 1961.
                COMEL, ELEL, ELPRNOR                                     61
FINESE-62-MHR   FINER, SE
                THE MAN ON HORSEBACK -- THE ROLE OF THE MILITARY
                   IN POLITICS.=
                NEW YORK, FREDERICK A PRAEGER, 1962.                     62
                GNELTH, DEFEL, ELEL, ELNOEL, ELPRNOR
FINESE-65-ATB   FINER, SE
                THE ARGENTINE TROUBLE -- BETWEEN SWORD AND STATE.=
                ENCOUNTER, 25, (SEPTEMBER 1965), PP. 59-66.             65
                ELEL, ELNOEL
FINESE-66-VPS   FINER, SE (ED)
                VILFRED PARETO -- SOCIOLOGICAL WRITINGS.=
                NEW YORK, FREDERICK A PRAEGER, 1966.                     66
                GNELTH, DEFEL, COMEL, ELEL, ELNOEL
FINKLS-51-IFP   FINKELSTEIN, LS
                THE INDONESIAN FEDERAL PROBLEM.=
                PACIFIC AFFAIRS, 24, (SEPTEMBER 1951), PP. 284-295.     51
                ELEL
FISCG -52-SOS   FISCHER, G
                SOVIET OPPOSITION TO STALIN -- A CASE STUDY IN
                   WORLD WAR 11.=
                CAMBRIDGE, HARVARD UNIVERSITY PRESS, 1952.              52
                COMEL, ELEL, ELPRNOR
FISCG -58-RLG   FISCHER, G
                RUSSIAN LIBERALISM -- FROM GENTRY TO INTELLIGENTSIA.=
                CAMBRIDGE, HARVARD UNIVERSITY PRESS, 1958.              58
                COMEL, ELEL, ELPRNOR
FISCJ -61-SPS   FISCHER, J
                THE STUDENT POPULATION OF A SOUTHEAST ASIAN UNIVERSITY --
                   AN INDONESIAN EXAMPLE.=
                INTERNATIONAL JOURNAL OF COMPARATIVE SOCIOLOGY,         61
                   2, (SEPTEMBER 1961), PP. 224-233.
                COMEL
FISCJ -63-UPP   FISCHER, J
                UNIVERSITIES AND THE POLITICAL PROCESS IN SOUTHEAST ASIA.=
                PACIFIC AFFAIRS, 36, (SPRING 1963), PP. 3-15.           63
                COMEL, ELEL, ELPRNOR
FISHFM-58-MAS   FISHER, FM
                THE MATHEMATICAL ANALYSIS OF SUPREME COURT DECISIONS --
                   THE USE AND ABUSE OF QUANTITATIVE METHODS
                   (UNITED STATES).=
                THE AMERICAN POLITICAL SCIENCE REVIEW, 52, (JUNE 1958),  58
                   PP. 321-338.
                METEL
FISHSN-55-SFM   FISHER, SN (ED)
                SOCIAL FORCES IN THE MIDDLE EAST.=
                ITHACA, CORNELL UNIVERSITY PRESS, 1955.                 55
                COMEL, ELEL, ELNOEL
FISHSN-62-CPS   FISHER, SN
                COMMUNITY - POWER STUDIES -- A CRITIQUE.=
                SOCIAL RESEARCH, 29, (WINTER 1962), PP. 449-466.        62
                DEFEL, METEL
FISHSN-63-MME   FISHER, SN (ED)
                THE MILITARY IN THE MIDDLE EAST -- PROBLEMS IN SOCIETY
                   AND GOVERNMENT.=
                COLUMBUS, OHIO STATE UNIVERSITY PRESS, 1963.            63
                COMEL, ELEL, ELNOEL, ELPRNOR
FITCRE-53-IIU   FITCH, RE
                THE ILLUSION OF THE INTELLIGENTSIA (UNITED STATES).=
                COMMENTARY, 16, (DECEMBER 1953), PP. 562-567.           53
                COMEL, ELNOEL, ELPRNOR
FITCRE-54-FIU   FITCH, RE
                THE FEARS OF THE INTELLIGENTSIA (UNITED STATES).=
                COMMENTARY, 18, (OCTOBER 1954), PP. 328-335.            54
                ELEL, ELPRNOR
FITZCP-63-FLC   FITZGERALD, CP
                A FRESH LOOK AT THE CHINESE REVOLUTION.=
                PACIFIC AFFAIRS, 36, (SPRING 1963), PP. 47-53.          63
                ELEL, ELNOEL
FITZR -54-UPD   FITZGIBBON, R
                URUGUAY -- PORTRAIT OF A DEMOCRACY.=

```
                          NEW BRUNSWICK, NEW JERSEY, RUTGERS UNIVERSITY PRESS,         54
                          1954.
                          COMEL, ELEL, ELNOEL
FITZR -57-PPL   FITZGIBBON, R
                THE PARTY POTPOURRI IN LATIN AMERICA.=
                THE WESTERN POLITICAL QUARTERLY, 10, (MARCH 1957),                      57
                          PP. 3-22.
                COMEL, ELEL, ELPRNOR
FITZRH-59-SBC   FITZGIBBON, RH
                THE SOCIAL BASIS OF THE CHANGING POLITICAL STRUCTURES IN
                          LATIN AMERICA.
                SOCIAL SCIENCE, 34, (APRIL 1959), PP. 63-71.                           59
                COMEL, ELEL, ELNOEL
FITZRH-60-DDL   FITZGIBBON, RH
                DICTATORSHIP AND DEMOCRACY IN LATIN AMERICA.=
                INTERNATIONAL AFFAIRS, 36, (JANUARY 1960), PP. 48-60.                   60
                ELEL, ELNOEL, ELPRNOR
FLEMWG-66-AER   FLEMING, WG
                AUTHORITY, EFFICIENCY, AND ROLE STRESS -- PROBLEMS IN THE
                          DEVELOPMENT OF EAST AFRICAN BUREAUCRACIES (UGANDA,
                          KENYA, TANGANYIKA).=
                ADMINISTRATIVE SCIENCE QUARTERLY, 2, (DECEMBER 1966),                  66
                          PP. 386-404.
                ELEL, ELPRNOR
FLINTA-64-PRS   FLINN, TA
                PARTY RESPONSIBILITY IN THE STATES -- SOME CAUSAL FACTORS
                          (UNITED STATES).=
                THE AMERICAN POLITICAL SCIENCE REVIEW, 58, (MARCH 1964),   64
                          PP. 60-71.
                COMEL, ELEL, ELNOEL, ELPRNOR
FLINTA-65-LPL   FLINN, TA                    WIRT, FM
                LOCAL PARTY LEADERS -- GROUPS OF LIKE MINDED MEN
                          (UNITED STATES).=
                MIDWEST JOURNAL OF POLITICAL SCIENCE, 9, (FEBRUARY 1965), 65
                          PP. 77-98.
                ELPRNOR
FLORGK-54-TCM   FLORO, GK
                TYPES OF CITY MANAGERS (UNITED STATES).=
                PUBLIC MANAGEMENT, 36, (OCTOBER 1954), PP. 221-225.                     54
                COMEL, ELEL, ELNOEL, ELPRNOR
FLORGK-55-CCM   FLORO, GK
                CONTINUITY IN CITY - MANAGER CAREERS (UNITED STATES).=
                THE AMERICAN JOURNAL OF SOCIOLOGY, 61, (NOVEMBER 1955),     55
                          PP. 240-246.
                ELEL, ELNOEL, ELPRNOR
FLUHVL-57-DMM   FLUHARTY, VL
                DANCE OF THE MILLIONS -- MILITARY RULE AND THE SOCIAL
                          REVOLUTION IN COLOMBIA, 1930-1956.=
                PITTSBURGH, UNIVERSITY OF PITTSBURGH PRESS, 1957.                       57
                COMEL, ELEL, ELNOEL
FOOTM -60-FLG   FOOT, M
                THE FUTURE OF THE LEFT (GREAT BRITAIN).=
                ENCOUNTER, 15, (JULY 1960), PP. 69-70.                                 60
                COMEL, ELPRNOR
FORCRW-60-LCC   FORCE, RW
                LEADERSHIP AND CULTURE CHANGE IN PALAU (AUSTRALIA).=
                CHICAGO, CHICAGO NATURAL HISTORY MUSEUM, 1960.                          60
                ELEL, ELNOEL, ELPRNOR
FORDD -61-GRA   FORDE, D
                THE GOVERNMENTAL ROLES OF ASSOCIATIONS AMONG THE YAKO
                          (WEST AFRICA).=
                AFRICA, 31, (1961), PP. 309-323.                                       61
                COMEL, ELEL
FORMWH-59-ICA   FORM, WH                     D'ANTONIO, W
                INTEGRATION AND CLEAVAGE AMONG COMMUNITY INFLUENTIALS
                          IN TWO BORDER CITIES (MEXICO, UNITED STATES).=
                AMERICAN SOCIOLOGICAL REVIEW, 24, (1959), PP. 804-814.                 59
                COMEL, ELEL, ELPRNOR
FORMWH-60-ILC   FORM, WH                     MILLER, DC
                INDUSTRY, LABOR AND COMMUNITY (UNITED STATES).=
                NEW YORK, HARPER AND BROTHERS, 1960.                                   60
                COMEL, ELEL, ELNOEL
FORMWH-60-OLS   FORM, WH                     SAUER, WL
                ORGANIZED LABOR'S IMAGE OF COMMUNITY POWER STRUCTURE
                          (UNITED STATES).=
                SOCIAL FORCES, 38, (MAY 1960), PP. 332-341.                            60
                COMEL, ELNOEL, ELPRNOR
FORMWH-61-CIM   FORM, WH                     SAUER, WL
                COMMUNITY INFLUENTIALS IN A MIDDLE-SIZED CITY
                          (UNITED STATES).=
                EAST LANSING, THE INSTITUTE FOR COMMUNITY DEVELOPMENT        61
                          AND SERVICES, 1961.
                COMEL, ELEL, ELNOEL, ELPRNOR
FORMWH-63-CLI   FORM, WH                     SAUER, WL
```

                              COMMUNITY AND LABOR INFLUENTIALS -- A COMPARATIVE STUDY
                                 OF PARTICIPATION AND IMAGERY (UNITED STATES).=
                              INDUSTRIAL AND LABOR RELATIONS REVIEW, 17,                    63
                                 (OCTOBER 1963), PP. 3-19.
                              ELEL, ELNOEL, ELPRNOR
FORMWH-65-IRS        FORM, WH              BLUM, AA
                              INDUSTRIAL RELATIONS AND SOCIAL CHANGE IN LATIN AMERICA.=
                              GAINESVILLE, FLORIDA, UNIVERSITY OF FLORIDA PRESS, 1965.  65
                              ELNOEL, ELPRNOR
FORRDB-66-CPP        FORRESTER, DB
                              CHANGING PATTERNS OF POLITICAL LEADERSHIP IN INDIA.=
                              THE REVIEW OF POLITICS, 28, (JULY 1966), PP. 308-318.       66
                              COMEL, ELEL, ELNOEL, ELPRNOR
FORSR -65-FNO        FORSTER, R            LITCHFIELD, RB
                              FOUR NOBILITIES OF THE OLD REGIME (ITALY, GERMANY).=
                              COMPARATIVE STUDIES IN SOCIETY AND HISTORY,                  65
                                 7, (APRIL 1965), PP. 324-332.
                              COMEL
FORTS -48-PWU        FORTHAL, S
                              THE PRECINCT WORKER (UNITED STATES).=
                              THE ANNALS OF THE AMERICAN ACADEMY OF POLITICAL AND          48
                                 SOCIAL SCIENCE, 259, (SEPTEMBER 1948), PP. 30-45.
                              COMEL, ELNOEL, ELPRNOR
FOX,GH-64-PVP        FOX, GH               JOINER, CA
                              PERCEPTIONS OF THE VIETNAMESE PUBLIC ADMINISTRATION
                                 SYSTEM.=
                              ADMINISTRATIVE SCIENCE QUARTERLY, 8, (1963-1964),            64
                                 PP. 443-481.
                              ELPRNOR
FOX,PW-59-PPC        FOX, PW
                              POLITICS AND PARTIES IN CANADA.=
                              INDIA QUARTERLY, 15, (OCTOBER-DECEMBER 1959),                59
                                 PP. 361-366.
                              ELEL, ELNOEL
FOX,WT-55-CSA        FOX, WTR
                              CIVILIANS, SOLDIERS, AND AMERICAN MILITARY POLICY.=
                              WORLD POLITICS, 7, (APRIL 1955), PP. 402-418.                55
                              ELEL, ELPRNOR
FOX,WT-61-RED        FOX, WTR
                              REPRESENTATIVES AND EFFICIENCY -- DUAL PROBLEM OF
                                 CIVIL - MILITARY RELATIONS (UNITED STATES).=
                              POLITICAL SCIENCE QUARTERLY, 76, (SEPTEMBER 1961),           61
                                 PP. 354-366.
                              ELEL, FLNOEL
FRANC -64-BDN        FRANKEL, C
                              BUREAUCRACY AND DEMOCRACY IN THE NEW EUROPE.=
                              DAEDALUS, 93, (WINTER 1964), PP. 471-492.                    64
                              ELEL, ELNOEL
FRANE -66-RBT        FRANK, E
                              THE ROLE OF BUREAUCRACY IN TRANSITION (GERMANY).=
                              THE JOURNAL OF POLITICS, 28, (NOVEMBER 1966),                66
                                 PP. 725-753.
                              ELEL
FRANFM-60-RNS        FRANCK, FM
                              RACE AND NATIONALISM -- THE STRUGGLE FOR POWER IN
                                 RHODESIA-NYASALAND.=
                              NEW YORK, FORDHAM UNIVERSITY PRESS, 1960.                    60
                              ELEL, ELNOEL
FRANGA-57-RSP        FRANCISCO-JR, GA
                              RECRUITMENT AND SELECTION PRACTICES IN FOUR GOVERNMENT
                                 AGENCIES (PHILIPPINES).=
                              PHILIPPINE JOURNAL OF PUBLIC ADMINISTRATION, 1,              57
                                 (OCTOBER 1957), PP. 403-418.
                              COMEL, ELPRNOR
FRANGA-60-CDF        FRANCISCO-JR, GA
                              CAREER DEVELOPMENT OF FILIPINO HIGHER CIVIL SERVANTS.=
                              PHILIPPINE JOURNAL OF PUBLIC ADMINISTRATION,                 60
                                 4, (JANUARY 1960), PP. 1-18.
                              COMEL, ELEL
FRANJ -55-CNQ        FRANKEL, J
                              COMMUNISM AND THE NATIONAL QUESTION IN YUGOSLAVIA.=
                              JOURNAL OF CENTRAL EUROPEAN AFFAIRS, 15, (APRIL 1955),        55
                                 PP. 50-65.
                              COMEL, ELEL, ELNOEL
FRANMF-62-ODI        FRANDA, MF
                              THE ORGANIZATIONAL DEVELOPMENT OF INDIA'S CONGRESS PARTY.=
                              PACIFIC AFFAIRS, 35, (FALL 1962), PP. 248-260.               62
                              COMEL, ELEL, ELNOEL, ELPRNOR
FRANPG-55-EPM        FRANCK, PG
                              ECONOMIC PLANNERS (MIDDLE EAST).=
                              SN FISHER (ED), SOCIAL FORCES IN THE MIDDLE EAST, ITHACA, 55
                                 CORNELL UNIVERSITY PRESS, 1955, PP. 137-191.
                              COMEL, ELEL, ELPRNOR
FRANR -66-BC         FRANKENBERG, R

                        BRITISH COMMUNITIES.=
                        HARMONDSWORTH, PENGUIN BOOKS, 1966.                              66
                        DEFEL, ELEL, ELNOEL, ELPRNOR, METEL
FRANR -66-BCS    FRANKENBERG, R
                        BRITISH COMMUNITY STUDIES -- PROBLEMS OF SYNTHESIS.=
                        M BARTON (ED), THE SOCIAL ANTHROPOLOGY OF COMPLEX               66
                           SOCIETIES, V. 4, ASA MONOGRAPHS, NEW YORK, FREDERICK,
                           A PRAEGER, 1966, PP. 123-154.
                        DEFEL, ELEL, ELNOEL, ELPRNOR, METEL
FRANVS-55-NCS    FRANK, VS
                        NEW CHANGES IN THE SOVIET LEADERSHIP.=
                        BULLETIN, INSTITUTE FOR THE STUDY AND HISTORY                  55
                           OF THE CULTURE OF THE USSR, 2, (MARCH 1955), PP. 3-12.
                        COMEL
FRANWL-62-IIS    FRANCIS, WL
                        INFLUENCE AND INTERACTION IN A STATE LEGISLATIVE
                           BODY (UNITED STATES).=
                        THE AMERICAN POLITICAL SCIENCE REVIEW, 56, (DECEMBER           62
                           1962), PP. 953-960.
                        ELEL
FRANWL-65-RCL    FRANCIS, WL
                        THE ROLE CONCEPT IN LEGISLATURES -- A PROBABILITY MODEL
                           AND A NOTE ON COGNITIVE STRUCTURE (UNITED STATES).=
                        THE JOURNAL OF POLITICS, 27, (AUGUST 1965), PP. 567-585.       65
                        ELEL, ELNOEL, ELPRNOR, METEL
FREED -64-OKP    FREEMAN, D
                        SOME OBSERVATIONS ON KINSHIP AND POLITICAL AUTHORITY
                           IN SAMOA.=
                        AMERICAN ANTHROPOLOGIST, 66, (JUNE 1964), PP. 553-568.         64
                        COMEL
FREEFD-48-ASS    FREEMAN, FD
                        THE ARMY AS A SOCIAL STRUCTURE (UNITED STATES).=
                        SOCIAL FORCES, 27, (OCTOBER 1948), PP. 78-83.                  48
                        COMEL, ELEL, ELNOEL
FREEJL-58-BPP    FREEMAN, JL
                        THE BUREAUCRACY IN PRESSURE POLITICS (UNITED STATES).=
                        THE ANNALS OF THE AMERICAN ACADEMY OF POLITICAL AND            58
                           AND SOCIAL SCIENCE, 319, (SEPTEMBER 1958), PP. 10-19.
                        ELEL
FREEJL-58-LPS    FREEMAN, JL
                        LOCAL PARTY SYSTEMS -- THEORETICAL CONSIDERATIONS AND A
                           CASE ANALYSIS (UNITED STATES).=
                        THE AMERICAN JOURNAL OF SOCIOLOGY, 64, (NOVEMBER 1958),        58
                           PP. 282-289.
                        ELEL, ELNOEL
FREEJL-65-PPE    FREEMAN, JL
                        THE POLITICAL PROCESS -- EXECUTIVE BUREAU - LEGISLATIVE
                           COMMITTEE RELATIONS (UNITED STATES).=
                        REVISED EDITION, NEW YORK, RANDOM HOUSE, 1965.                 65
                        ELEL, ELPRNOR, METEL
FREEL -61-IIP    FREE, L
                        SOME INTERNATIONAL IMPLICATIONS OF THE POLITICAL
                           PSYCHOLOGY OF BRAZILIANS.=
                        PRINCETON, INSTITUTE FOR INTERNATIONAL SOCIAL RESEARCH,        61
                           1961.
                        ELEL, ELPRNOR
FREELA-58-OPI    FREE, LA
                        OPINIONS OF PARLIAMENTARIANS IN INDIA AND JAPAN.=
                        PRINCETON, INSTITUTE FOR INTERNATIONAL SOCIAL RESEARCH,        58
                           PRINCETON UNIVERSITY, 1958.
                        ELPRNOR
FREELA-59-SAN    FREE, LA
                        SIX ALLIES AND A NEUTRAL (FRANCE, GREAT BRITAIN, INDIA,
                           ITALY, JAPAN, UNITED STATES, WEST GERMANY).=
                        NEW YORK, THE FREE PRESS, 1959.                               59
                        COMEL, ELEL, ELPRNOR
FREELC-60-LCL    FREEMAN, LC        ET AL
                        LOCAL COMMUNITY LEADERSHIP (UNITED STATES).=
                        SYRACUSE, SYRACUSE UNIVERSITY PRESS, 1960.                    60
                        COMEL, ELEL, METEL
FREELC-63-LLL    FREEMAN, LC        ET AL
                        LOCATING LEADERS IN LOCAL COMMUNITIES -- A COMPARISON OF
                           SOME ALTERNATIVE APPROACHES (UNITED STATES).=
                        AMERICAN SOCIOLOGICAL REVIEW, 28, (OCTOBER 1963),             63
                           PP. 791-798.
                        DEFEL, METEL
FREEM -60-GPS    FREEDMAN, M
                        THE GROWTH OF A PLURAL SOCIETY IN MALAYA.=
                        PACIFIC AFFAIRS, 33, (JUNE 1960), PP. 158-168.                60
                        ELEL, ELNOEL, ELPRNOR
FRENJR-59-BSP    FRENCH, JRP          RAVEN, B
                        THE BASES OF SOCIAL POWER.=
                        DORWIN CARTWRIGHT (ED), STUDIES IN SOCIAL POWER,              59
                           ANN ARBOR, MICHIGAN, UNIVERSITY OF MICHIGAN, INSTITUTE

                    FOR SOCIAL RESEARCH, 1959, PP. 150-167.
                    DEFEL
FREUPA-49-USC       FREUND, PA
                    ON UNDERSTANDING THE SUPREME COURT (UNITED STATES).=
                    BOSTON, LITTLE, BROWN, AND COMPANY, 1949.
                    COMEL, ELPRNOR                                              49
FREYFW-63-PDP       FREY, FW
                    POLITICAL DEVELOPMENT, POWER, AND COMMUNICATIONS IN
                       TURKEY.=
                    LW PYE (ED), COMMUNICATIONS AND POLITICAL DEVELOPMENT,      63
                       PRINCETON, PRINCETON UNIVERSITY PRESS, 1963,
                       PP. 298-326.
                    DEFEL, ELEL, ELNOEL, ELPRNOR
FREYFW-65-TPE       FREY, FW
                    THE TURKISH POLITICAL ELITE.=
                    CAMBRIDGE, THE MIT PRESS, 1965.
                    COMEL, ELEL, ELNOEL, ELPRNOR, METEL                        65
FREYG -46-MSS       FREYRE, G
                    THE MASTERS AND THE SLAVES -- A STUDY IN THE
                       DEVELOPMENT OF BRAZILIAN CIVILIZATION.=
                    S PUTNAM (TRANS), NEW YORK, ALFRED A KNOPF. 1946.
                    ELEL, ELNOEL, ELPRNOR                                       46
FRIECJ-56-TDA       FRIEDRICH, CJ          BRZEZINSKI, ZK
                    TOTALITARIAN DICTATORSHIP AND AUTOCRACY.=
                    CAMBRIDGE, HARVARD UNIVERSITY PRESS, 1956.
                    GNELTH, DEFEL, COMEL, ELEL, ELNOEL, ELPRNOR                56
FRIECJ-58-A         FRIEDRICH, CJ (ED)
                    AUTHORITY.=
                    CAMBRIDGE, HARVARD UNIVERSITY PRESS, 1958.
                    DEFEL                                                       58
FRIECJ-61-PLP       FRIEDRICH, CJ
                    POLITICAL LEADERSHIP AND THE PROBLEM OF
                       CHARISMATIC POWER (GERMANY, GREAT BRITAIN, ITALY,
                       UNITED STATES).=
                    THE JOURNAL OF POLITICS, 23, (FEBRUARY 1961), PP. 3-25.    61
                    DEFEL, ELNOEL, ELPRNOR
FRIECJ-63-PEB       FRIEDRICH, CJ
                    THE POLITICAL ELITE AND BUREAUCRACY.=
                    CJ FRIEDRICH, MAN AND HIS GOVERNMENT--AN EMPIRICAL          63
                       THEORY OF POLITICS, NEW YORK, MCGRAW-HILL BOOK CO.,
                       INC., 1963, PP. 315-334
                    DEFEL
FRIECJ-63-PL        FRIEDRICH, CJ
                    POWER AND LEADERSHIP.=
                    CJ FRIEDRICH, MAN AND HIS GOVERNMENT--AN EMPIRICAL          63
                       THEORY OF POLITICS, NEW YORK, MCGRAW-HILL BOOK CO.,
                       INC., 1963, PP. 315-334
                    DEFEL
FRIECJ-63-RR        FRIEDRICH, CJ
                    RULE AND RULERSHIP.=
                    CJ FRIEDRICH, MAN AND HIS GOVERNMENT--AN EMPIRICAL          63
                       THEORY OF POLITICS, NEW YORK, MCGRAW-HILL BOOK CO.,
                       INC., 1963, PP. 180-198.
                    ELNOEL
FRIEHJ-60-PSE       FRIEDMAN, HJ
                    PAKISTAN'S EXPERIMENT IN BASIC DEMOCRACIES.=
                    PACIFIC AFFAIRS, 33, (JANUARY 1960), PP. 107-125.          60
                    ELEL, ELNOEL
FRIEHJ-63-AGR       FRIEDMAN, HJ          RAHENAN, ATR
                    ADMINISTRATION AT THE GRASS ROOTS -- PAKISTAN'S BASIC
                       DEMOCRACIES.=
                    PHILIPPINE JOURNAL OF PUBLIC ADMINISTRATION, 7,            63
                       (JANUARY 1963), PP. 102-112.
                    ELNOEL
FRIEJ -60-IDS       FRIEDMAN, J
                    INTELLECTUALS AND DEVELOPING SOCIETIES.=
                    KYKLOS, 13, (1960), PP. 513-544.
                    DEFEL, ELEL, ELPRNOR                                       60
FRIEMH-51-MSC       FRIED, MH
                    MILITARY STATUS IN CHINESE SOCIETY.=
                    THE AMERICAN JOURNAL OF SOCIOLOGY, 57, (JANUARY 1951),     51
                       PP. 347-355.
                    ELEL, ELNOEL
FRIERC-63-IPS       FRIED, RC
                    THE ITALIAN PREFECTS -- A STUDY IN ADMINISTRATIVE
                       POLITICS.=
                    NEW HAVEN, YALE UNIVERSITY PRESS, 1963.
                    ELEL, ELNOEL, ELPRNOR                                      63
FRIERS-65-RCM       FRIEDMAN, RS          STOKES, SL
                    THE ROLE OF THE CONSTITUTION-MAKER AS A REPRESENTATIVE
                       (UNITED STATES).=
                    MIDWEST JOURNAL OF POLITICAL SCIENCE, 9, (MAY 1965),       65
                       PP. 148-166.
                    COMEL, ELEL, ELNOEL, ELPRNOR

FRIEWH-64-SCC    FRIEDLAND, WH
                 FOR A SOCIOLOGICAL CONCEPT OF CHARISMA.=
                 SOCIAL FORCES, 43, (OCTOBER 1964), PP 18-26.                    64
                 DEFEL, METEL
FROMLA-  -CTC    FROMAN, LA
                 CONGRESSMEN AND THEIR CONSTITUENCIES (UNITED STATES).=
                 CHICAGO, RAND MCNALLY AND COMPANY, 1963.
                 COMEL, ELNOEL, ELPRNOR
FROMLA-61-PPS    FROMAN, LA
                 PERSONALITY AND POLITICAL SOCIALIZATION (UNITED STATES).=
                 THE JOURNAL OF POLITICS, 23, (MAY 1961), PP. 341-352.           61
                 ELPRNOR
FROMLA-63-IIV    FROMAN-JR, LA
                 THE IMPORTANCE OF INDIVIDUALITY IN VOTING IN CONGRESS.=
                 THE JOURNAL OF POLITICS, 25, (MAY 1963), PP. 324-332.           63
                 ELEL, ELNOEL, ELPRNOR, METEL
FROMLA-63-IPC    FROMAN-JR, LA
                 INTER - PARTY CONSTITUENCY DIFFERENCES AND CONGRESSIONAL
                     VOTING BEHAVIOR (UNITED STATES).=
                 THE AMERICAN POLITICAL SCIENCE REVIEW, 57, (MARCH 1963),        63
                     PP. 57-61.
                 ELEL, ELNOEL, ELPRNOR
FROMLA-65-CPL    FROMAN-JR, LA        RIPLEY, RB
                 CONDITIONS FOR PARTY LEADERSHIP -- THE CASE OF THE
                     HOUSE DEMOCRATS (UNITED STATES).=
                 THE AMERICAN POLITICAL SCIENCE REVIEW, 59, (MARCH 1965),        65
                     PP. 52-63.
                 ELEL
FROSRT-61-SCL    FROST, RT
                 STABILITY AND CHANGE IN LOCAL PARTY POLITICS
                     (UNITED STATES).=
                 THE PUBLIC OPINION QUARTERLY, 25, (SUMMER 1961),                61
                     PP. 221-235.
                 COMEL, ELEL, ELNOEL
FRYECE-65-PPG    FRYE, CE
                 PARTIES AND PRESSURE GROUPS IN WEIMAR AND BONN (GERMANY).=
                 WORLD POLITICS, 17, (JULY 1965), PP. 635-655.                   65
                 ELEL, ELNOEL
FRYKRE-65-EGS    FRYKENBERG, RE
                 ELITE GROUPS IN A SOUTH INDIAN DISTRICT, 1788-1858.=
                 THE JOURNAL OF ASIAN STUDIES, 24, (FEBRUARY 1965),              65
                     PP. 261-281.
                 COMEL, ELEL, ELNOEL
FURBH -51-UI     FURBER, H
                 THE UNIFICATION OF INDIA, 1947-1951.=
                 PACIFIC AFFAIRS, 24, (DECEMBER 1951), PP. 352-371.              51
                 ELEL, ELNOEL, ELPRNOR
FURNEJ-64-DGF    FURNISS-JR, EJ
                 DE GAULLE AND THE FRENCH ARMY.=
                 NEW YORK, THE TWENTIETH CENTURY FUND, 1964.                     64
                 ELEL, ELPRNOR
GABIST-64-LLM    GABIS, ST
                 LEADERSHIP IN A LARGE MANAGER CITY -- THE CASE OF
                     KANSAS CITY (UNITED STATES).=
                 THE ANNALS OF THE AMERICAN ACADEMY OF POLITICAL AND             64
                     SOCIAL SCIENCE, 353, (MAY 1964), PP. 52-63.
                 COMEL, ELPRNOR
GABLRW-58-IGP    GABLE, RW
                 INTEREST GROUPS AS POLICY SHAPERS (UNITED STATES).=
                 THE ANNALS OF THE AMERICAN ACADEMY OF POLITICAL AND             58
                     SOCIAL SCIENCE, 319, (SEPTEMBER 1958), PP. 84-93.
                 ELEL
GABLRW-61-PAI    GABLE, RW            STORM, WB
                 PUBLIC ADMINISTRATION IN IRAN -- SKETCHES OF A
                     NON-WESTERN TRANSITIONAL BUREAUCRACY.=
                 PHILIPPINE JOURNAL OF PUBLIC ADMINISTRATION, 5,                 61
                     (JULY 1961), PP. 226-234.
                 ELEL, ELNOEL
GADGDR-51-RTP    GADGIL, DR
                 SOME REQUIREMENTS FOR TECHNICAL PROGRESS IN ASIA.=
                 PACIFIC AFFAIRS, 24, (JUNE 1951), PP. 178-184.                  51
                 ELNOEL
GADGDR-59-OMI    GADGIL, DR
                 ORIGINS OF THE MODERN INDIAN BUSINESS CLASS.=
                 NEW YORK, INSTITUTE OF PACIFIC RELATIONS, 1959.                 59
                 COMEL
GADOI -53-PCC    GADOUREK, I
                 THE POLITICAL CONTROL OF CZECHOSLOVAKIA -- A STUDY IN
                     SOCIAL CONTROL OF A SOVIET STATE.=
                 LEIDEN, HOLLAND, STENFERT KROESE, 1953.                         53
                 ELEL, ELNOEL, ELPRNOR
GAINWA-66-RRC    GAINSON, WA
                 REPUTATION AND RESOURCES IN COMMUNITY POLITICS
                     (UNITED STATES).=

THE AMERICAN JOURNAL OF SOCIOLOGY, 72, (SEPTEMBER 1966), 66
PP. 121-131.
DEFEL, ELEL, ELNOEL

GALAN -56-MRH  GALAY, N
MILITARY REPRESENTATION IN THE HIGHER PARTY
ECHELONS (SOVIET UNION).=
BULLETIN INSTITUTE FOR THE STUDY OF THE USSR, 3,          56
(APRIL 1956), PP. 3-11.
COMEL, ELEL

GALAN -57-RSA  GALAY, N
THE ROLE OF THE SOVIET ARMY IN THE CRISIS OF THE
COLLECTIVE LEADERSHIP.=
BULLETIN INSTITUTE FOR THE STUDY OF THE USSR, 4,          57
(AUGUST 1957), PP. 13-20.
ELEL, ELNOEL

GALAN -58-MRS  GALAY, N
MILITARY REPRESENTATION ON THE 1958 SUPREME SOVIET
OF THE USSR.=
BULLETIN INSTITUTE FOR THE STUDY OF THE USSR, 5,          58
(APRIL 1958), PP. 3-9.
COMEL, ELEL

GALAN -64-SRS  GALAY, N
THE SIGNIFICANCE OF THE REESTABLISHMENT OF THE SUPREME
COMMAND OF THE SOVIET ARMED FORCES.=
BULLETIN INSTITUTE FOR THE STUDY OF THE USSR, 11,         64
(JULY 1964), PP. 19-27.
COMEL, ELEL

GALAN -65-NGS  GALAY, N
THE NEW GENERATION IN THE SOVIET ARMED FORCES.=
STUDIES ON THE SOVIET UNION, 5, (1965), PP. 29-46.        65
COMEL

GALEB -57-SSR  GALESKI, B
SOCIAL STRATIFICATION OF RURAL AREAS -- RESEARCH
PROBLEMS (POLAND).=
INTERNATIONAL SOCIAL SCIENCE BULLETIN, 9, (1957),         57
PP. 193-211.
COMEL, ELNOEL

GALEW -59-LED  GALENSON, W (ED)
LABOR AND ECONOMIC DEVELOPMENT (MIDDLE EAST, SOUTHEAST
ASIA).=
NEW YORK, JOHN WILEY AND SONS, INC, 1959.                 59
COMEL, ELEL, ELNOEL

GALEW -62-LDE  GALENSON, W (ED)
LABOR IN DEVELOPING ECONOMICS (LATIN AMERICA,
MIDDLE EAST).=
BERKELEY, UNIVERSITY OF CALIFORNIA PRESS, 1962.           62
COMEL, ELEL, ELNOEL, ELPRNOR

GALLG -59-ICC  GALLI, G
THE ITALIAN CP (COMMUNIST PARTY) -- CONSERVATISM IN
DISGUISE.=
PROBLEMS OF COMMUNISM, 8, (MAY-JUNE 1959), PP. 27-34.     59
ELEL, ELNOEL, ELPRNOR

GALLG -66-WRB  GALLI, G
WITHER RUSSIA -- A BUREAUCRACY UNDER FIRE (SOVIET UNION).=
PROBLEMS OF COMMUNISM, 15, (SEPTEMBER-OCTOBER 1966),      66
PP. 31-35.
ELEL, ELPRNOR

GALLGB-59-LHR  GALLOWAY, GB
LEADERSHIP IN THE HOUSE OF REPRESENTATIVES
(UNITED STATES).=
THE WESTERN POLITICAL QUARTERLY, 12, (JUNE 1959),         59
PP. 417-441.
COMEL, ELEL

GALVET-66-SOS  GALVAN, ET
STUDENT OPPOSITION IN SPAIN.=
GOVERNMENT AND OPPOSITION, 1, (AUGUST 1966), PP. 467-486. 66
COMEL, ELEL, ELNOEL, ELPRNOR

GAMAM -67-PPP  GAMARNIKOW, M
POLAND -- POLITICAL PLURALISM IN A ONE - PARTY STATE.=
PROBLEMS OF COMMUNISM, 16, (JULY-AUGUST 1967), PP. 1-14.  67
COMEL, ELEL, ELNOEL, ELPRNOR

GAMSWA-66-RRC  GAMSON, WA
REPUTATION AND RESOURCES IN COMMUNITY POLITICS.=
THE AMERICAN JOURNAL OF SOCIOLOGY, 72, (SEPTEMBER 1966),  66
PP. 121-131.
DEFEL, METEL

GANTF -64-CET  GANTT-JR, F
THE CHIEF EXECUTIVE IN TEXAS -- THE ORIGINS OF
GUBERNATORIAL LEADERSHIP.=
AUSTIN, UNIVERSITY OF TEXAS PRESS, 1964.                  64
ELEL, ELNOEL

GARCO -54-PGP  GARCEAU, O         SILVERMAN, C
A PRESSURE GROUP AND THE PRESSURED (UNITED STATES).=
THE AMERICAN POLITICAL SCIENCE REVIEW, 48, (SEPTEMBER     54

                                1954), PP. 672-691.
                                ELEL, ELNOEL, ELPRNOR
            GARFH -59-SSE       GARFINKEL, H
                                SOCIAL SCIENCE EVIDENCE AND THE SCHOOL SEGREGATION
                                    CASES (UNITED STATES).=
                                THE JOURNAL OF POLITICS, 21, (FEBRUARY 1959), PP. 37-59.  59
                                ELEL, ELNOEL, ELPRNOR
            GARIP -53-WAS       GARIGUE, P
                                THE WEST AFRICAN STUDENT'S UNION -- A STUDY IN
                                    CULTURE CONTACT.=
                                AFRICA, 23, (JANUARY 1953), PP. 55-69.                   53
                                COMEL, ELEL
            GARIP -54-CPL       GARIGUE, P
                                CHANGING POLITICAL LEADERSHIP IN WEST AFRICA.=
                                AFRICA, 24, (JULY 1954), PP. 220-232.                    54
                                COMEL, ELEL, ELNOEL
            GARTRL-57-RMR       GARTHOFF, RL
                                THE ROLE OF THE MILITARY IN RECENT SOVIET POLITICS.=
                                THE RUSSIAN REVIEW, 16, (APRIL 1957), PP. 15-24.         57
                                COMEL, ELEL, ELPRNOR
            GARVG -66-TPE       GARVEY, G
                                THE THEORY OF PARTY EQUILIBRIUM (UNITED STATES).=
                                THE AMERICAN POLITICAL SCIENCE REVIEW, 60, (MARCH 1966),  66
                                    PP. 29-38.
                                ELNOEL, ELPRNOR
            GASSO -63-RKA       GASS, O
                                RUSSIA -- KHRUSHCHEV AND AFTER.=
                                COMMENTARY, 36, (NOVEMBER 1963), PP. 353-363.            63
                                ELEL, ELNOEL
            GASTRD-58-MCI       GASTIL, RD
                                MIDDLE CLASS IMPEDIMENTS TO IRANIAN MODERNIZATION.=
                                THE PUBLIC OPINION QUARTERLY, 22, (FALL 1958),           58
                                    PP. 325-329.
                                COMEL, ELEL, ELNOEL, ELPRNOR
            GAWTLC-66-CMP       GAWTHROP, LC
                                CHANGING MEMBERSHIP PATTERNS IN HOUSE COMMITTEES
                                    (UNITED STATES).=
                                THE AMERICAN POLITICAL SCIENCE REVIEW, 60 (JUNE 1966),   66
                                    PP. 366-373.
                                ELEL, ELPRNOR
            GEERC -60-JKC       GEERTZ, C
                                THE JAVANESE KIJAJI -- THE CHANGING ROLE OF A
                                    CULTURAL BROKER.=
                                COMPARATIVE STUDIES IN SOCIETY AND HISTORY, 2,           60
                                    (JANUARY 1960), PP. 228-249.
                                ELEL, ELNOEL, ELPRNOR
            GEERC -63-OSN       GEERTZ, C
                                OLD SOCIETIES AND NEW STATES -- THE QUEST FOR MODERNITY IN
                                    ASIA AND AFRICA.=
                                NEW YORK, THE FREE PRESS, 1963.                          63
                                COMEL, ELEL, ELNOEL, ELPRNOR
            GEERC -63-PPS       GEERTZ, C
                                PEDDLERS AND PRINCES -- SOCIAL CHANGE AND ECONOMIC
                                    MODERNIZATION IN TWO INDONESIAN TOWNS.=
                                CHICAGO, UNIVERSITY OF CHICAGO PRESS, 1963.              63
                                ELEL, ELNOEL, ELPRNOR
            GEHLMP-66-EBC       GEHLEN, MP
                                THE EDUCATIONAL BACKGROUNDS AND CAREER ORIENTATIONS
                                    OF THE MEMBERS OF THE CENTRAL COMMITTEE OF THE
                                    CPSU (SOVIET UNION).=
                                THE AMERICAN BEHAVIORAL SCIENTIST, 9, (APRIL 1966),      66
                                    PP. 11-14.
                                COMEL, ELPRNOR
            GEIGT -50-HSO       GEIGER, T
                                AN HISTORICAL STUDY OF THE ORIGINS AND STRUCTURE OF THE
                                    DANISH INTELLIGENTSIA.=
                                THE BRITISH JOURNAL OF SOCIOLOGY, 1, (1950), PP. 209-220. 50
                                ELEL, ELNOEL, ELPRNOR
            GELLJE-59-GSF       GELLERMANN, JE
                                GENERALS AS STATESMEN (FRANCE, FINLAND, GERMANY
                                    UNITED STATES).=
                                NEW YORK, VINTAGE PRESS, 1959.                           59
                                COMEL, ELPRNOR
            GELMH -66-MPP       GELMAN, H
                                MAO AND THE PERMANENT PURGE (CHINA).=
                                PROBLEMS OF COMMUNISM, 15, (NOVEMBER-DECEMBER 1966),     66
                                    PP. 2-14.
                                ELEL, ELNOEL, ELPRNOR
            GERMDL-59-IFP       GERMINO, DL
                                THE ITALIAN FASCIST PARTY IN POWER.=
                                MINNEAPOLIS, UNIVERSITY OF MINNESOTA PRESS, 1959.        59
                                COMEL, ELEL, ELNOEL
            GERMG -62-PSS       GERMANI, G          SILVERT, K
                                POLITICS, SOCIAL STRUCTURE, AND MILITARY INTERVENTION IN

```
                    LATIN AMERICA.=
                    EUROPEAN JOURNAL OF SOCIOLOGY, 2, (1962), PP. 62-81.        62
                    COMEL, ELEL
    GERSA -62-CDS   GERSCHENKRON, A
                    THE CHANGEABILITY OF A DICTATORSHIP (SOVIET UNION).=
                    WORLD POLITICS, 14, (JULY 1962), PP. 576-604.
                    DEFEL, ELEL, ELNOEL                                         62
    GERTC -66-PAK   GERTZEL, C
                    THE PROVINCIAL ADMINISTRATION IN KENYA.=
                    JOURNAL OF COMMONWEALTH POLITICAL STUDIES, 4,
                      (NOVEMBER 1966), PP. 201-215.                            66
                    ELEL, ELPRNOR
    GERTH -40-NPI   GERTH, H
                    THE NAZI PARTY -- ITS LEADERSHIP AND COMPOSITION
                      (GERMANY).=
                    THE AMERICAN JOURNAL OF SOCIOLOGY, 45, (JANUARY 1940),      40
                      PP. 517-541.
                    COMEL, ELPRNOR
    GERTH -54-SL    GERTH, H            MILLS, CW
                    SOCIOLOGY OF LEADERSHIP.=
                    H GERTH AND CW MILLS, CHARACTER AND SOCIAL STRUCTURE,       54
                      LONDON, ROUTLEDGE AND KEGAN PAUL, 1954, PP. 405-426.
                    DEFEL, COMEL, ELEL, ELNOEL
    GHAID -65-AEA   GHAI, D             GHAI, Y
                    ASIANS IN EAST AFRICA -- PROBLEMS AND PROSPECTS.=
                    THE JOURNAL OF MODERN AFRICAN STUDIES, (MAY 1965),
                      PP. 35-52.                                               65
                    ELEL, ELNOEL
    GHAIDP-65-PMA   GHAI, DP (ED)
                    PORTRAIT OF A MINORITY -- ASIANS IN EAST AFRICA.=
                    LONDON, OXFORD UNIVERSITY PRESS, 1965.                      65
                    ELEL, ELNOEL
    GIBBCA-54-L     GIBB, CA
                    LEADERSHIP.=
                    G LINDZEY (ED), HANDBOOK OF SOCIAL PSYCHOLOGY,             54
                      VOLUME 2, CAMBRIDGE, MASSACHUSETTS,
                      ADDISON-WESLEY, 1954, PP. 877-920.
                    GNETLH, DEFEL, COMEL, ELEL, ELNOEL, ELPRNOR, METEL
    GIBSC -60-AAC   GIBSON, C
                    THE AZTEC ARISTOCRACY IN COLONIAL MEXICO.=
                    COMPARATIVE STUDIES IN SOCIETY AND HISTORY, 2,             60
                      (JANUARY 1960), PP. 169-196.
                    COMEL, ELEL, ELNOEL, ELPRNOR
    GIL,F -62-GMP   GIL, F
                    GENESIS AND MODERNIZATION OF POLITICAL PARTIES IN CHILE.=
                    (LATIN AMERICAN MONOGRAPHS NO. 18), GAINESVILLE,           62
                      UNIVERSITY OF FLORIDA PRESS, 1962.
                    ELEL, ELNOEL
    GIL,FG-66-PSC   GIL, FG
                    THE POLITICAL SYSTEM OF CHILE.=
                    BOSTON, HOUGHTON MIFFLIN, 1966.                            66
                    COMEL, ELEL, ELNOEL, ELPRNOR
    GIL,G -53-RPL   GIL, G
                    RESPONSIBLE PARTIES IN LATIN AMERICA.=
                    THE JOURNAL OF POLITICS, 15, (AUGUST 1953), PP. 333-348.   53
                    COMEL, ELEL, ELNOEL
    GILBCE-59-FAR   GILBERT, CE
                    THE FRAMEWORK OF ADMINISTRATIVE RESPONSIBILITY.=
                    THE JOURNAL OF POLITICS, 21, (AUGUST 1959), PP. 373-407.   59
                    ELEL, METEL
    GILBCE-62-ECE   GILBERT, CE         CLAGUE, C
                    ELECTORAL COMPETITION AND ELECTORAL SYSTEMS IN LARGE
                      CITIES (UNITED STATES).=
                    THE JOURNAL OF POLITICS, 24, (MAY 1962), PP. 323-349.      62
                    ELEL, ELNOEL, METEL
    GILBCE-64-NPA   GILBERT, CE
                    NATIONAL POLITICAL ALIGNMENTS AND THE POLITICS OF
                      LARGE CITIES (UNITED STATES).=
                    POLITICAL SCIENCE QUARTERLY, 79, (MARCH 1964),             64
                      PP. 25-51.
                    ELNOEL
    GILBGM-50-PDB   GILBERT, GM
                    THE PSYCHOLOGY OF DICTATORSHIP -- BASED ON AN EXAMINATION
                      OF THE LEADERS OF NAZI GERMANY.=
                    NEW YORK, RONALD PRESS, 1950.                              50
                    GNELTH, DEFEL, COMEL, ELEL, ELNOEL, ELPRNOR
    GILEB -58-PPT   GILEAD, B
                    POLITICAL PARTIES IN TURKEY.=
                    MIDDLE EASTERN AFFAIRS, 9, (MARCH 1958), PP. 101-107.      58
                    COMEL, ELEL, ELNOEL, ELPRNOR
    GILIJM-67-NFS   GILISON, JM
                    NEW FACTORS OF STABILITY IN SOVIET COLLECTIVE LEADERSHIP.=
                    WORLD POLITICS, 19, (JULY 1967), PP. 563-581.              67
                    DEFEL, ELEL, ELPRNOR
```

GILLJ -61-ARR  GILLESPIE, J
               ALGERIA -- REBELLION AND REVOLUTION.=
               NEW YORK, FREDERICK A PRAEGER, 1961.                        61
               COMEL, ELEL, ELNOEL, ELPRNOR
GILPR -64-SNP  GILPIN, R          WRIGHT, C (EDS)
               SCIENTISTS AND NATIONAL POLICY-MAKING (UNITED STATES).=
               NEW YORK, COLUMBIA UNIVERSITY PRESS, 1964.                  64
               ELEL, ELNOEL, ELPRNOR
GILPRG-62-ASN  GILPIN, RG
               AMERICAN SCIENTISTS AND NUCLEAR WEAPONS POLICY.=
               PRINCETON, PRINCETON UNIVERSITY PRESS, 1962.                62
               ELEL, ELNOEL, ELPRNOR
GINSG -59-SPF  GINSBURGS, G
               THE SOVIET PROCURACY AND FORTY YEARS OF SOCIALIST
                  LEGALITY.=
               THE AMERICAN SLAVIC AND EAST EUROPEAN REVIEW, 18,           59
                  (FEBRUARY 1959), PP. 34-62.
               ELEL
GINSG -59-TAT  GINSBURGS, G          MATHOS, M
               TIBETS ADMINISTRATION -- IN THE TRANSITION PERIOD,
                  1951-1954 -- DURING THE INTERREGNUM, 1954-1959.=
               PACIFIC AFFAIRS, 32, (JUNE 1959, SEPTEMBER 1959),           59
                  PP. 162-176, PP. 249-267.
               ELEL, ELNOEL
GINSG -63-LGA  GINSBURGS, G
               LOCAL GOVERNMENT AND ADMINISTRATION IN THE BULGARIAN
                  PEOPLE'S REPUBLIC -- 1951-1956.
               JOURNAL OF CENTRAL EUROPEAN AFFAIRS, 23, (APRIL 1963),      63
                  PP. 23-51.
               ELNOEL
GINSG -64-KRH  GINSBURGS, G
               KADAR AND THE RESURRECTION OF THE HUNGARIAN COMMUNIST
                  PARTY -- A STUDY IN POLITICAL TECHNIQUES.=
               THE AUSTRALIAN JOURNAL OF POLITICS AND HISTORY, 10,         64
                  (APRIL 1964), PP. 16-32.
               ELEL, ELPRNOR
GINSVN-64-CMP  GINSBURGH, VN
               THE CHALLENGE OF MILITARY PROFESSIONALISM
                  (UNITED STATES).=
               FOREIGN AFFAIRS, 42, (JANUARY 1964), PP. 255-268.           64
               ELEL
GITLAL-52-MPA  GITLOW, AL
               MACHINE POLITICS IN AMERICAN TRADE UNIONS.=
               THE JOURNAL OF POLITICS, 14, (AUGUST 1952), PP. 370-385.    52
               ELEL, ELNOEL
GITTJ -63-PCC  GITTINGS, J
               POLITICAL CONTROL OF THE CHINESE ARMY.=
               THE WORLD TODAY, 19, (AUGUST 1963), PP. 327-336.            63
               ELEL
GITTJ -67-CAS  GITTINGS, J
               THE CHINESE ARMY'S ROLE IN THE CULTURAL REVOLUTION.=
               PACIFIC AFFAIRS, 39, (FALL AND WINTER 1966-1967),           67
                  PP. 269-289.
               ELEL, ELNOEL, ELPRNOR
GITTJ -67-RCA  GITTINGS, J
               THE ROLE OF THE CHINESE ARMY.=
               LONDON, OXFORD UNIVERSITY PRESS, 1967.                      67
               ELEL, ELNOEL, ELPRNOR
GITTM -66-TPM  GITTELL, M
               A TYPOLOGY OF POWER FOR MEASURING SOCIAL CHANGE.=
               THE AMERICAN BEHAVIORAL SCIENTIST, 9, (APRIL 1966),         66
                  PP. 23-28.
               GNELTH, DEFEL
GLADEN-53-ACG  GLADDEN, EN
               AN ADMINISTRATIVE CENTENARY, 1853-1953 (GREAT BRITAIN).=
               PARLIAMENTARY AFFAIRS, 6, (AUTUMN 1953), PP. 318-325.       53
               COMEL, ELEL
GLADEN-57-PCS  GLADDEN, EN
               PARLIAMENT AND THE CIVIL SERVICE (GREAT BRITAIN).=
               PARLIAMENTARY AFFAIRS, 10, (WINTER 1956-1957),              57
                  PP. 165-179.
               ELEL
GLASDV-54-SSS  GLASS, DV
               SOCIAL STRATIFICATION AND SOCIAL MOBILITY.=
               INTERNATIONAL SOCIAL SCIENCE BULLETIN, 6, (1954),           54
                  PP. 12-24.
               ELEL, ELNOEL
GLASWA-60-DPU  GLASER, WA
               DOCTORS AND POLITICS (UNITED STATES).=
               THE AMERICAN JOURNAL OF SOCIOLOGY, 66, (NOVEMBER 1960),     60
                  PP. 230-245.
               ELPRNOR
GLAZN -51-APP  GLAZER, N
               THE AUTHORITARIAN PERSONALITY IN PROFILE (UNITED STATES).=

COMMENTARY, 9, (JUNE 1950), PP. 573-583.                          51
                   ELNOEL, ELPRNOR, METEL
GLAZN -54-NLA      GLAZER, N
                   NEW LIGHT ON 'THE AUTHORITARIAN PERSONALITY' (GERMANY,
                      SOVIET UNION).=
                   COMMENTARY, 17, (MARCH 1954), PP. 289-297.                 54
                   COMEL, ELEL, METEL
GLEIH -60-HSP      GLEITMAN, H          GREENBAUM, JJ
                   HUNGARIAN SOCIO-POLITICAL ATTITUDES AND
                      REVOLUTIONARY ACTION.=
                   THE PUBLIC OPINION QUARTERLY, 24, (SPRING 1960),           60
                      PP. 62-76.
                   ELNOEL, ELPRNOR, METEL
GLICHR-66-PRS      GLICK, HR
                   POLITICAL RECRUITMENT IN SARAWAK -- A CASE
                      STUDY OF LEADERSHIP IN A NEW STATE.=
                   THE JOURNAL OF POLITICS, 28, (FEBRUARY 1966), PP. 81-99.  66
                   COMEL
GLICM -54-RRS      GLICKMAN, M
                   RITUALS OF REBELLION IN SOUTH EAST AFRICA.=
                   MANCHESTER, MANCHESTER UNIVERSITY PRESS, 1954.            54
                   ELEL, ELNOEL, ELPRNOR
GLOCWP-63-PEM      GLOCK, WP            ANDERSON, CW
                   THE POLITICAL ECONOMY OF MEXICO.=
                   MADISON, THE UNIVERSITY OF WISCONSIN PRESS, 1963.         63
                   ELEL, ELNOEL
GLUBJ -65-RAT      GLUBB, J
                   THE ROLE OF THE ARMY IN THE TRANSITIONAL ARAB STATE
                      (MIDDLE EAST).=
                   JOURNAL OF INTERNATIONAL AFFAIRS, 19, (1965), PP. 8-15.   65
                   ELEL
GLUCM -49-VHB      GLUCKMAN, M          MITCHELL, JC         BARNES, JA
                   THE VILLAGE HEADMAN IN BRITISH CENTRAL AFRICA.=
                   AFRICA, 19, (APRIL 1949), PP. 89-106.                     49
                   COMEL, ELPRNOR
GLUCM -65-PLR      GLUCKMAN, M
                   POLITICS, LAW AND RITUAL IN TRIBAL SOCIETY.=
                   CHICAGO, ALDINE PUBLISHING COMPANY, 1965.                 65
                   ELEL, ELPRNOR
GLUCM -65-PSD      GLUCKMAN, M          EGGAN, F (EDS)
                   POLITICAL SYSTEMS AND THE DISTRIBUTION OF POWER
                      (INDIA, AFRICA, JAPAN).=
                   LONDON, TAVISTOCK, 1965.                                  65
                   DEFEL, ELEL, ELNOEL, ELPRNOR
GOCHTS-65-NTA      GOCHENOUR, TS
                   A NEW TRY FOR AFGHANISTAN.=
                   THE MIDDLE EAST JOURNAL, 19, (WINTER 1965), PP. 1-19.     65
                   ELEL, ELNOEL, ELPRNOR
GODFD -55-FFN      GODFREY, D
                   THE FATE OF THE FRENCH NON - COMMUNIST LEFT.=
                   GARDEN CITY, DOUBLEDAY AND COMPANY, INC, 1955.            55
                   ELEL, ELNOEL, ELPRNOR
GOERW -53-HGG      GOERLITZ, W
                   HISTORY OF THE GERMAN GENERAL STAFF, 1657-1945.=
                   NEW YORK, FREDERICK A PRAEGER, 1953.                      53
                   COMEL, ELEL, ELPRNOR
GOLDB -65-CRL      GOLDENBERG, B
                   THE CUBAN REVOLUTION AND LATIN AMERICA.=
                   NEW YORK, FREDERICK A PRAEGER, 1965.                      65
                   COMEL, ELEL, ELNOEL
GOLDD -61-DPO      GOLDRICH, D          SCOTT, EW
                   DEVELOPING POLITICAL ORIENTATIONS OF PANAMANIAN STUDENTS.=
                   THE JOURNAL OF POLITICS, 23, (FEBRUARY 1961), PP. 84-107. 61
                   ELNOEL, ELPRNOR
GOLDD -61-LPE      GOLD, D
                   LAWYERS IN POLITICS -- AN EMPIRICAL EXPLORATION
                      OF BIOGRAPHICAL DATA ON STATE LEGISLATORS.=
                   PACIFIC SOCIOLOGICAL REVIEW, 4, (FALL 1961), PP. 84-86.   61
                   COMEL, METEL
GOLDD -62-RNP      GOLDRICH, D
                   RADICAL NATIONALISM -- THE POLITICAL ORIENTATIONS OF
                      PANAMANIAN LAW STUDENTS.=
                   EAST LANSING, MICHIGAN STATE UNIVERSITY PRESS,            62
                      1962.
                   COMEL, ELPRNOR
GOLDD -64-ROR      GOLDRICH, D
                   REFORM OR REVOLUTION IN LATIN AMERICA.=
                   CHALLENGE, 12, (OCTOBER 1963), PP. 13-16.                 64
                   COMEL, ELPRNOR
GOLDD -66-SEE      GOLDRICH, D
                   SONS OF THE ESTABLISHMENT -- ELITE YOUTH IN PANAMA AND
                      COSTA RICA.=
                   CHICAGO, RAND MCNALLY, 1966.                              66
                   DEFEL, COMEL, ELEL, ELPRNOR, METEL

GOLDEF-52-PML  GOLDMAN, EF
               THE PRESIDENCY AS MORAL LEADERSHIP (UNITED STATES).=
               THE ANNALS OF THE AMERICAN ACADEMY OF POLITICAL AND          52
                  SOCIAL SCIENCE, 280, (MARCH 1952), PP. 37-45.
               COMEL, ELPRNOR
GOLDH -39-TPS  GOLDHAMER, H          SHILS, EA
               TYPES OF POWER AND STATUS.=
               THE AMERICAN JOURNAL OF SOCIOLOGY, 45, (SEPTEMBER 1939),     39
                  PP. 171-182.
               GNELTH, DEFEL, COMEL, ELPRNOR
GOLDH -50-POP  GOLDHAMER, H
               PUBLIC OPINION AND PERSONALITY.=
               THE AMERICAN JOURNAL OF SOCIOLOGY, 55, (JANUARY 1950),       50
                  PP. 346-354.
               ELPRNOR
GOLDI -55-SRC  GOLDMAN, I
               STATUS RIVALRY AND CULTURAL EVOLUTION IN POLYNESIA.=
               AMERICAN ANTHROPOLOGIST, 57, (AUGUST 1955), PP. 680-697.     55
               COMEL, ELEL, ELNOEL
GOLDJE-55-AES  GOLDTHORPE, JE
               AN AFRICAN ELITE -- A SAMPLE SURVEY OF 52 FORMER
                  STUDENTS OF MAKERERE COLLEGE IN EAST AFRICA.=
               THE BRITISH JOURNAL OF SOCIOLOGY, 6, (1955), PP. 31-47.      55
               COMEL
GOLDJE-61-EAC  GOLDTHORPE, JE
               EDUCATED AFRICANS -- SOME CONCEPTUAL AND TERMINOLOGICAL
                  PROBLEMS.=
               A SOUTHALL (ED), SOCIAL CHANGE IN MODERN AFRICA, LONDON,     61
                  OXFORD UNIVERSITY PRESS, 1961, PP. 145-158.
               DEFEL, COMEL, ELPRNOR
GOLDJH-63-ABC  GOLDTHRORPE, JH      LOCKWOOD, D
               AFFLUENCE AND THE BRITISH CLASS STRUCTURE.=
               THE SOCIOLOGICAL REVIEW, 11, (JULY 1963), PP. 133-163.       63
               COMEL, ELEL
GOLDLC-65-LCU  GOLDBERG, LC         BAKER, F          RUBENSTEIN, AH
               LOCAL - COSMOPOLITAN -- UNIDIMENSIONAL OR
                  MULTIDIMENSIONAL.=
               THE AMERICAN JOURNAL OF SOCIOLOGY, 70, (MAY 1965),           65
                  PP. 704-710.
               METEL
GOLDM -64-WCP  GOLDMAN, M
               WRITERS' CRITICISM OF THE PARTY IN 1942 (CHINA).=
               THE CHINA QUARTERLY, 17, (JANUARY-MARCH 1964),               64
                  PP. 205-208.
               ELEL, ELPRNOR
GOLDM -66-DMA  GOLDWERT, M
               DICHOTOMIES OF MILITARISM IN ARGENTINA.=
               ORBIS, 10, (FALL 1966), PP. 930-939.                         66
               ELEL, ELPRNOR
GOLDM -67-LDC  GOLDMAN, M
               LITERARY DISSENT IN COMMUNIST CHINA.=
               CAMBRIDGE, HARVARD UNIVERSITY PRESS, 1967.                   67
               ELEL, ELNOEL, ELPRNOR
GOLDR -62-RCP  GOLDMAN, R
               THE RECTIFICATION CAMPAIGN AT PEKING UNIVERSITY (CHINA).=
               THE CHINA QUARTERLY, 12, (OCTOBER-DECEMBER 1962),            62
                  PP. 138-153.
               ELEL
GOLDS -66-VBU  GOLDMAN, S
               VOTING BEHAVIOR ON THE UNITED STATES COURTS OF APPEALS,
                  1961-1964.=
               THE AMERICAN POLITICAL SCIENCE REVIEW, 60, (JUNE 1966),      66
                  PP. 374-383.
               ELPRNOR, METEL
GOLERT-58-TAS  GOLEMBIEWSKI, RT
               A TAXONOMIC APPROACH TO STATE POLITICAL PARTY STRENGTH.=
               THE WESTERN POLITICAL QUARTERLY, 11, (SEPTEMBER 1958),       58
                  PP. 494-513.
               DEFEL, COMEL, ELEL
GOMERA-60-GPL  GOMEZ, RA
               GOVERNMENT AND POLITICS OF LATIN AMERICA.=
               NEW YORK, RANDOM HOUSE, 1960.                                60
               COMEL, ELEL, ELNOEL
GOMERA-61-LAE  GOMEZ, RA
               LATIN AMERICAN EXECUTIVES -- ESSENCE AND VARIATIONS.=
               JOURNAL OF INTER-AMERICAN STUDIES, 3, (JANUARY 1961),        61
                  PP. 81-95.
               COMEL
GOODCE-51-SRL  GOODE, CE
               SIGNIFICANT RESEARCH ON LEADERSHIP.=
               PERSONNEL, 27, (MARCH 1951), PP. 342-350.                    51
               METEL
GOODCT-64-ARP  GOODSELL, CT
               ADMINISTRATION OF A REVOLUTION (PUERTO RICO).=

```
                        CAMBRIDGE, HARVARD UNIVERSITY PRESS, 1964.               64
                        COMEL, ELEL, ELNOEL, ELPRNOR
GOODG -59-SSC   GOODWIN-JR, G
                        THE SENIORITY SYSTEM IN CONGRESS (UNITED STATES).=
                        THE AMERICAN POLITICAL SCIENCE REVIEW, 53, (JUNE 1959),    59
                            PP. 412-436.
                        COMEL, ELEL, ELNOEL
GOODG -62-SML   GOODWIN-JR, G
                        SUBCOMMITTEES -- THE MINIATURE LEGISLATURES OF CONGRESS
                            (UNITED STATES).=
                        THE AMERICAN POLITICAL SCIENCE REVIEW, 56, (SEPTEMBER      62
                            PP. 596-304.
                        ELEL
GOODHF-64-CSP   GOODNOW, HF
                        THE CIVIL SERVICE OF PAKISTAN -- BUREAUCRACY IN A NEW
                            NATION.=
                        NEW HAVEN, YALE UNIVERSITY PRESS, 1964.                    64
                        COMEL, ELEL, ELNOEL, ELPRNOR
GOODJ -63-FA    GOODY, J
                        FEUDALISM IN AFRICA.=
                        JOURNAL OF AFRICAN HISTORY, 4, (1963), PP. 1-18.           63
                        ELNOEL, COMEL
GOODJS-67-NLR   GOODMAN, JS
                        A NOTE ON LEGISLATIVE RESEARCH -- LABOR REPRESENTATION IN
                            RHODE ISLAND (UNITED STATES).=
                        THE AMERICAN POLITICAL SCIENCE REVIEW, 61, (JUNE 1967),    67
                            PP. 468-473.
                        COMEL, ELPRNOR, METEL
GOODMR-66-ACN   GOODALL, MR
                        ADMINISTRATIVE CHANGE IN NEPAL.=
                        R BRAIBANTI (ED), ASIAN BUREAUCRATIC SYSTEMS EMERGENT      66
                            FROM THE BRITISH IMPERIAL TRADITION, DURHAM, DUKE
                            UNIVERSITY PRESS, 1966, PP. 605-642.
                        ELEL, ELPRNOR
GOODP -62-CSU   GOODMAN, P
                        THE COMMUNITY OF SCHOLARS (UNITED STATES).=
                        NEW YORK, RANDOM HOUSE, 1962.                              62
                        ELEL, ELPRNOR
GOODP -62-IIP   GOODMAN, P
                        THE INEFFECTUALITY OF SOME INTELLIGENT PEOPLE
                            (UNITED STATES).=
                        COMMENTARY, 33, (JUNE 1962), PP. 478-486.                  62
                        ELEL, ELPRNOR
GOODTM-57-MPI   GOODLAND, TM
                        A MATHEMATICAL PRESENTATION OF ISRAEL'S
                            POLITICAL PARTIES.=
                        THE BRITISH JOURNAL OF SOCIOLOGY, 8, (1957), PP. 263-266. 57
                        METEL
GORDBK-61-MBC   GORDON, BK
                        THE MILITARY BUDGET -- CONGRESSIONAL PHASE
                            (UNITED STATES).=
                        THE JOURNAL OF POLITICS, 23, (NOVEMBER 1961),              61
                            PP. 689-710.
                        ELEL
GORDM -65-SEA   GORDEN, M            LERNER, D
                        THE SETTING FOR EUROPEAN ARMS CONTROLS -- POLITICAL AND
                            STRATEGIC CHOICES OF EUROPEAN ELITES (FRANCE, GERMANY
                            GREAT BRITAIN, SOVIET UNION, UNITED STATES).=
                        THE JOURNAL OF CONFLICT RESOLUTION, 9, (DECEMBER 1965),    65
                            PP. 419-433.
                        ELPRNOR
GORDMM-58-SCA   GORDON, MM
                        SOCIAL CLASS IN AMERICAN SOCIOLOGY.=
                        DURHAM, NORTH CAROLINA, DUKE UNIVERSITY PRESS, 1958.       58
                        GNELTH, METEL
GOREWJ-56-DMF   GORE, WJ
                        DECISION MAKING IN A FEDERAL FIELD OFFICE
                            (UNITED STATES).=
                        PUBLIC ADMINISTRATION REVIEW, 16, (AUTUMN 1956),           56
                            PP. 281-291.
                        ELEL, ELNOEL, METEL
GOREWJ-59-BED   GORE, WJ            SILANDER, FS
                        A BIBLIOGRAPHICAL ESSAY ON DECISION-MAKING.=
                        ADMINISTRATIVE SCIENCE QUARTERLY, 4, (JUNE 1959),          59
                            PP. 97-121.
                        COMEL, ELPRNOR, METEL
GOSNHF-48-DTF   GOSNELL, HF
                        DEMOCRACY -- THE THRESHOLD OF FREEDOM (UNITED STATES,
                            GREAT BRITAIN, FRANCE, CANADA, SCANDINAVIA).=
                        NEW YORK, RONALD PRESS, 1948.                              48
                        DEFEL, ELEL, ELNOEL, ELPRNOR, METEL
GOSNHF-50-DCM   GOSNELL, HF
                        DOES CAMPAIGNING MAKE A DIFFERENCE (UNITED STATES).=
                        .THE PUBLIC OPINION QUARTERLY, 14, (FALL 1950),            50
```

```
                        PP. 413-418.
                        ELNOEL
GOTTA  -61-PPU          GOTTFRIED, A
                        PROFESSORS AND POLITICS (UNITED STATES).=
                        THE WESTERN POLITICAL QUARTERLY, 14, (1961),                61
                        PP. 43-45.
                        ELPRNOR
GOUGEK-52-CKU          GOUGH, EK
                        CHANGING KINSHIP USAGES IN THE SETTING OF POLITICAL AND
                        ECONOMIC CHANGE AMONG THE NAYARS OF MALABAR.=
                        JOURNAL OF THE ROYAL ANTHROPOLOGICAL INSTITUTE,            52
                        82, (1952), PP. 71-88.
                        COMEL, ELEL, ELNOEL
GOULAW-58-CLT          GOULDNER, AW
                        COSMOPOLITANS AND LOCALS -- TOWARDS AN ANALYSIS OF LATENT
                        SOCIAL ROLES (UNITED STATES).=
                        ADMINISTRATIVE SCIENCE QUARTERLY, 2, (1957-1958),          58
                        PP. 281-306.
                        ELPRNOR, METEL
GOULAW-65-BA           GOULDNER, AW
                        BUREAUCRATS AND AGITATORS.=
                        AW GOULDNER (ED), STUDIES IN LEADERSHIP, NEW YORK,          65
                        RUSSELL AND RUSSELL, 1965, PP. 53-66.
                        DEFEL, ELEL
GOULAW-65-I            GOULDNER, AW
                        INTRODUCTION.=
                        AW GOULDNER (ED), STUDIES IN LEADERSHIP, NEW YORK,          65
                        RUSSELL AND RUSSELL, 1965, PP. 3-49.
                        GNELTH
GOULAW-65-LAS          GOULDNER, AW
                        LEADERSHIP AMONG SOCIAL CLASSES.=
                        AW GOULDNER (ED), STUDIES IN LEADERSHIP, NEW YORK,          65
                        RUSSELL AND RUSSELL, 1965, PP. 131-143.
                        ELEL, ELNOEL
GOULAW-65-PSB          GOULDNER, AW
                        THE PROBLEM OF SUCCESSION AND BUREAUCRACY.=
                        AW GOULDNER (ED), STUDIES IN LEADERSHIP, NEW YORK           65
                        RUSSELL AND RUSSELL, 1965, PP. 644-659.
                        ELEL
GOULAW-65-SL           GOULDNER, AW (ED)
                        STUDIES IN LEADERSHIP.=
                        NEW YORK, RUSSELL AND RUSSELL, 1965.                        65
                        GNELTH, DEFEL, COMEL, ELEL, ELNOEL, ELPRNOR, METEL
GOURWE-52-CCC          GOURLAY, WE
                        THE CHINESE COMMUNIST CADRE -- KEY TO POLITICAL CONTROL.=
                        PROBLEMS OF COMMUNISM, 1, (JANUARY-FEBRUARY 1952),         52
                        PP. 28-37.
                        ELEL, ELNOEL, ELPRNOR
GOUVAJ-67-EDO          GOUVEIA, AJ
                        EDUCATION AND DEVELOPMENT -- OPINIONS OF SECONDARY SCHOOL
                        TEACHERS (LATIN AMERICA).=
                        SM LIPSET AND A SOLARI (EDS), ELITES IN LATIN AMERICA,     67
                        NEW YORK, OXFORD UNIVERSITY PRESS, 1967, PP. 484-513.
                        ELNOEL, ELPRNOR
GOYAOP-64-CPC          GOYAL, OP            WALLACE, P
                        THE CONGRESS PARTY -- A CONCEPTUAL STUDY (INDIA).=
                        INDIA QUARTERLY, 20, (APRIL-JUNE 1964), PP. 180-201.       64
                        DEFEL, ELEL, ELNOEL, METEL
GP     -56-CSA         GP
                        CHURCH AND STATE IN ARGENTINA -- FACTORS IN PERON'S
                        DOWNFALL.=
                        THE WORLD TODAY, 12, (FEBRUARY 1956), PP. 58-66.           56
                        ELEL
GRAENA-61-UTA          GRAEBNER, NA
                        AN UNCERTAIN TRADITION -- AMERICAN SECRETARIES OF STATE
                        IN THE TWENTIETH CENTURY.=
                        NEW YORK, MCGRAW-HILL, 1961.                               61
                        ELEL, ELPRNOR
GRAHGA-50-PEO          GRAHAM, GA
                        THE PRESIDENCY AND THE EXECUTIVE OFFICE OF THE
                        PRESIDENT (UNITED STATES).=
                        THE JOURNAL OF POLITICS, 12, (NOVEMBER 1950),              50
                        PP. 599-621.
                        ELEL, ELNOEL
GRAHS  -56-CCA         GRAHAM, S
                        CLASS AND CONSERVATISM IN THE ADOPTION OF INNOVATIONS
                        (UNITED STATES).=
                        HUMAN RELATIONS, 9, (FEBRUARY 1956), PP. 91-100.           56
                        ELPRNOR
GRAIGW-57-CBC          GRAINGER, GW
                        THE CRISIS IN THE BRITISH CP (COMMUNIST PARTY).=
                        PROBLEMS OF COMMUNISM, 6, (MARCH-APRIL 1957), PP. 8-14.    57
                        ELEL, ELPRNOR
GRAIGW-58-OBC          GRAINGER, GW
```

```
                    OLIGARCHY IN THE BRITISH COMMUNIST PARTY.=
                    THE BRITISH JOURNAL OF SOCIOLOGY, 9, (JUNE 1958),          58
                       PP. 143-158.
                    COMEL, ELEL, ELNOEL
    GRAND -60-RES    GRANICK, D
                    THE RED EXECUTIVE--A STUDY OF THE ORGANIZATION
                       MAN IN RUSSIAN INDUSTRY.=
                    GARDEN CITY, DOUBLEDAY AND COMPANY, INC, 1960.
                    COMEL, ELEL, ELNOEL, ELPRNOR                               60
    GRAND -62-EEB    GRANICK, D
                    THE EUROPEAN EXECUTIVE (BELGIUM, FRANCE, GERMANY,
                       GREAT BRITAIN, UNITED STATES).=
                    GARDEN CITY, DOUBLEDAY AND COMPANY, INC, 1962.             62
                    COMEL, ELEL, ELNOEL, ELPRNOR
    GRANJA-50-JCL    GRANT, JAC
                    JUDICIAL CONTROL OF THE LEGISLATIVE PROCESS -- THE
                       FEDERAL RULE (UNITED STATES).=
                    THE WESTERN POLITICAL QUARTERLY, 3, (SEPTEMBER 1950),      50
                       PP. 364-389.
                    ELEL
    GRAPED-48-HPA    GRAPER, ED
                    HOW PRESIDENTS ARE NOMINATED (UNITED STATES).=
                    THE ANNALS OF THE AMERICAN ACADEMY OF POLITICAL AND        48
                       SOCIAL SCIENCE, 259, (SEPTEMBER 1948), PP. 53-63.
                    COMEL, ELEL
    GRASG -64-PBI    GRASSMUCK, G
                    POLITY, BUREAUCRACY AND INTEREST GROUPS IN THE NEAR EAST
                       AND NORTH AFRICA.=
                    CAG OCCASIONAL PAPERS, INTERNATIONAL DEVELOPMENT           64
                       RESEARCH CENTER, BLOOMINGTON, INDIANA, 1964.
                    COMEL, ELPRNOR
    GRASGL-51-SBC    GRASSMUCK, GL
                    SECTIONAL BIASES IN CONGRESS ON FOREIGN POLICY
                       (UNITED STATES).=
                    BALTIMORE, JOHNS HOPKINS PRESS, 1951.
                    ELEL, ELNOEL, ELPRNOR                                      51
    GRAYGW-65-CDC    GRAYSON, GW
                    CHRISTIAN DEMOCRATS IN CHILE.=
                    SAIS REVIEW, 9, (WINTER 1965), PP. 12-20.                  65
                    COMEL, ELEL
    GRAYH -55-CMC    GRAYSON, H
                    THE CRISIS OF THE MIDDLE CLASS.=
                    NEW YORK, RINEHART AND COMPANY, 1955.                      55
                    ELEL, ELNOEL
    GREEFI-65-PPS    GREENSTEIN, FI
                    PERSONALITY AND POLITICAL SOCIALIZATION -- THE THEORIES
                       OF AUTHORITARIAN AND DEMOCRATIC CHARACTER.=
                    THE ANNALS OF THE AMERICAN ACADEMY OF                      65
                       POLITICAL AND SOCIAL SCIENCE, 361, (SEPTEMBER 1965),
                       PP. 81-95.
                    DEFEL, ELPRNOR, METEL
    GREELS-64-CBP    GREENE, LS
                    CITY BOSSES AND POLITICAL MACHINES (UNITED STATES).=
                    SOCIAL SCIENCE, 353, (MAY 1964), PP. 1-121.
                    ELEL, ELNOEL                                               64
    GREEP -64-SSN    GREEN, P
                    SOCIAL SCIENTISTS AND NUCLEAR DETERRENCE.=
                    DISSENT, 11, (WINTER 1964), PP. 80-91.                     64
                    COMEL, ELEL, ELPRNOR
    GREERV-63-KES    GREENSLADE, RV
                    KHRUSHCHEV AND THE ECONOMISTS (SOVIET UNION).=
                    PROBLEMS OF COMMUNISM, 12, (MAY-JUNE 1963), PP. 27-33.     63
                    ELEL, ELPRNOR
    GREES -53-SPF    GREER, S
                    SITUATIONAL PRESSURES AND FUNCTIONAL ROLE OF THE ETHNIC
                       LABOR LEADER.=
                    SOCIAL FORCES, 32, (OCTOBER 1953), PP. 41-45.             53
                    ELNOEL
    GREES -62-MSP    GREER, S            ORLEANS, P
                    THE MASS SOCIETY AND THE PARAPOLITICAL STRUCTURE.=
                    AMERICAN SOCIOLOGICAL REVIEW, 27, (OCTOBER 1962),          62
                       PP. 634-646.
                    DEFEL, COMEL, ELEL, ELNOEL, ELPRNOR
    GREES -62-SSP    GREER, S
                    THE SOCIAL STRUCTURE AND POLITICAL PROCESS OF SUBURBIA --
                       AN EMPIRICAL TEST (UNITED STATES).=
                    RURAL SOCIOLOGY, 27, (DECEMBER 1962), PP. 438-459.         62
                    COMEL, ELEL, ELNOEL, ELPRNOR
    GREES -63-MSP    GREER, S
                    METROPOLITICS -- A STUDY OF POLITICAL CULTURE
                       (UNITED STATES).=
                    NEW YORK, JOHN WILEY AND SONS, 1963.                       63
                    ELEL, ELNOEL, ELPRNOR, METEL
    GREES -63-RMS    GREER, S
```

THE RATIONAL MODEL, THE SOCIOLOGICAL MODEL, AND
METROPOLITAN REFORM (UNITED STATES).=
THE PUBLIC OPINION QUARTERLY, 27, (SUMMER 1963),          63
PP. 242-249.
ELEL, ELNOEL, ELPRNOR, METEL

GREGRW-63-ESC    GREGG, RW
THE ECONOMIC AND SOCIAL COUNCIL -- POLITICS OF MEMBERSHIP
(UNITED NATIONS, EUROPE).=
THE WESTERN POLITICAL QUARTERLY, 16, (MARCH 1963),        63
PP. 109-132.
COMEL

GREYDL-67-ICU    GREY, DL
INTERVIEWING AT THE COURT (UNITED STATES).=
THE PUBLIC OPINION QUARTERLY, 31, (SUMMER 1967),          67
PP. 285-289.
METEL

GRIFR -53-RBC    GRIFFITHS, R
THE ROLE OF THE BRITISH CIVIL SERVANT IN POLICY
FORMATION.=
PUBLIC ADMINISTRATION, 12, (DECEMBER 1953), PP. 188-200.  53
ELEL, ELNOEL

GRIFWE-62-DFR    GRIFFITH, WE
THE DECLINE AND FALL OF REVISIONISM IN EASTERN EUROPE.=
L LABEDZ (ED), REVISIONISM, ESSAYS ON THE HISTORY         62
OF MARXIST IDEAS, NEW YORK, FREDERICK A PRAEGER, 1962,
PP. 223-238.
ELEL, ELNOEL, ELPRNOR

GRINM -55-SMB    GRINDROD, M
THE SOCIALIST MERGER AND THE BALANCE OF PARTIES
IN JAPAN.=
THE WORLD TODAY, 11, (MARCH 1955), PP. 458-460.           55
ELEL

GRINM -56-ULC    GRINDROD, M
THE UNORTHODOX LEFT AND THE CEYLON ELECTIONS.=
THE WORLD TODAY, 12, (MAY 1956), PP. 171-172.             56
ELEL, ELNOEL

GRODM -60-APP    GRODZIUS, M
AMERICAN POLITICAL PARTIES AND AMERICAN SYSTEM.=
THE WESTERN POLITICAL QUARTERLY, 13, (DECEMBER 1960),     60
PP. 974-998.
ELEL, ELNOEL

GROSA -64-EEP    GROSSER, A
THE EVOLUTION OF EUROPEAN PARLIAMENTS.=
DAEDALUS, 93, (WINTER 1964), PP. 153-158.                 64
ELEL, ELNOEL

GROSBM-53-LSS    GROSS, BM
THE LEGISLATIVE STRUGGLE -- A STUDY IN SOCIAL COMBAT
(UNITED STATES).=
NEW YORK, MCGRAW HILL, 1953.                              53
ELEL, ELNOEL, ELPRNOR

GROSF -58-SPP    GROSS, F
THE SEIZURE OF POLITICAL POWER IN A CENTURY OF
REVOLUTIONS (SOVIET UNION).=
NEW YORK, PHILOSOPHICAL LIBRARY, 1958.                    58
ELEL, ELNOEL

GROSG -55-LPP    GROSSMAN, G
THE LAND OF PAPER PYRAMIDS (SOVIET UNION).=
PROBLEMS OF COMMUNISM, 4, (JULY-AUGUST 1955), PP. 18-26.  55
ELEL, ELPRNOR

GROSJB-64-FJS    GROSSMAN, JB
FEDERAL JUDICIAL SELECTION -- THE WORK OF THE ABA
COMMITTEE (UNITED STATES).=
MIDWEST JOURNAL OF POLITICAL SCIENCE, 8, (AUGUST 1964),   64
PP. 221-254.
COMEL, ELEL

GROSJB-65-LJA    GROSSMAN, JB
LAWYERS AND JUDGES -- THE ABA AND THE POLITICS OF
JUDICIAL SELECTION (UNITED STATES).=
NEW YORK, JOHN WILEY, 1965.                               65
COMEL, ELEL, ELPRNOR

GROWSL-63-DPP    GROW, SL
THE DEVELOPMEMT OF POLITICAL PARTIES IN UTAH
(UNITED STATES).=
THE WESTERN POLITICAL QUARTERLY, 16, (SEPTEMBER 1963),    63
PP. 39-40.
COMEL

GROZS -66-AMP    GROZDANIC, S
ADMINISTRATIVE MANAGEMENT OF PUBLIC ENTERPRISES IN
YUGOSLAVIA.=
INTERNATIONAL REVIEW OF ADMINISTRATIVE SCIENCES, 32,      66
(1966), PP. 43-57.
ELEL, ELNOEL

GRULL -56-HSN    GRULIOW, L
HOW THE SOVIET NEWSPAPER OPERATES.=

PROBLEMS OF COMMUNISM, 5, (MARCH-APRIL 1956), PP. 3-12.    56
ELEL
GRULL -63-RPS   GRULIOW, L
THE ROLE OF THE PRESS (SOVIET UNION).=
PROBLEMS OF COMMUNISM, 12, (JANUARY-FEBRUARY 1963),    63
PP. 34-40.
ELEL, ELNOEL
GRUMJG-63-FAL   GRUMM, JG
A FACTOR ANALYSIS OF LEGISLATIVE BEHAVIOR
(UNITED STATES).=
MIDWEST JOURNAL OF POLITICAL SCIENCE, 7,    63
(NOVEMBER 1963), PP. 336-356.
ELPRNOR, METEL
GRUNKW-64-CSA   GRUNDY, KW
THE 'CLASS STRUGGLE' IN AFRICA -- AN EXAMINATION OF
CONFLICTING THEORIES (WEST AFRICA).=
THE JOURNAL OF MODERN AFRICAN STUDIES, 2, (NOVEMBER 1964),64
PP. 379-393.
DEFEL, ELEL, ELNOEL, ELPRNOR
GRUNND-62-WIM   GRUNDSTEIN, ND
WHAT IS MEANT BY LEADERSHIP.=
PUBLIC MANAGEMENT, 44, (NOVEMBER 1962), PP. 242-246.    62
DEFEL
GRUSO -64-ESC   GRUSKY, O
THE EFFECTS OF SUCCESSION -- A COMPARATIVE STUDY
OF MILITARY AND BUSINESS ORGANIZATION (UNITED STATES).=
M JANOWITZ (ED), THE NEW MILITARY--CHANGING PATTERNS    64
OF ORGANIZATION, NEW YORK, RUSSELL SAGE FOUNDATION,
1964, PP. 83-118.
COMEL, ELPRNOR
GRUSO -65-CMM   GRUSKY, O
CAREER MOBILITY AND MANAGERIAL POLITICAL BEHAVIOR
(UNITED STATES).=
PACIFIC SOCIOLOGICAL REVIEW, 8, (FALL 1965). PP. 82-89.    65
COMEL, ELPRNOR
GRZYK -57-PWS   GRZYBOWSKI, K
POLISH WORKER'S COUNCILS.=
JOURNAL OF CENTRAL EUROPEAN AFFAIRS, 17, (JULY 1957),    57
PP. 272-286.
ELNOEL
GRZYK -58-RGP   GRZYBOWSKI, K
REFORM OF GOVERNMENT IN POLAND.=
THE AMERICAN SLAVIC AND EAST EUROPEAN REVIEW, 17,    58
(DECEMBER 1958), PP. 454-467.
ELNOEL
GUBIK -61-SSU   GUBIN, K
THE SUPREME SOVIET OF THE USSR AND ITS MEMBERS.=
INTERNATIONAL SOCIAL SCIENCE JOURNAL, 13, (1961),    61
PP. 635-640.
COMEL, ELPRNOR
GUETH -51-GLM   GUETZKOW, H (ED)
GROUPS, LEADERSHIP AND MEN.=
PITTSBURGH, CARNEGIE INSTITUTE OF TECHNOLOGY PRESS, 1951. 51
ELPRNOR, METEL
GUETH -53-ACD   GUETZKOW, H        GYR, J
AN ANALYSIS OF CONFLICT IN DECISION-MAKING GROUPS.=
HUMAN RELATIONS, 7, (AUGUST 1953), PP. 367-382.    53
ELEL, ELNOEL
GUILR -52-RME   GUILLAIN, R
THE RESURGENCE OF MILITARY ELEMENTS IN JAPAN.=
PACIFIC AFFAIRS, 25, (SEPTEMBER 1952), PP. 211-225.    52
ELEL, ELPRNOR
GUIRC -53-SPS   GUIREY, C
THE SHADOW OF POWER (SOVIET UNION, UNITED STATES).=
INDIANAPOLIS, BOBBS-MERRILL, 1953.    53
ELEL
GULICA-58-ALS   GULICK, CA
AUSTRIAN LABOR'S BID FOR POWER -- THE ROLE OF
THE TRADE UNION FEDERATION.=
INDUSTRIAL AND LABOR RELATIONS REVIEW, 12,    58
(OCTOBER 1958), PP. 35-55.
COMEL, ELEL, ELNOEL
GULICA-58-ASS   GULICK, CA
AUSTRIA'S SOCIALISTS IN THE TREND TOWARD A TWO - PARTY
SYSTEM -- AN INTERPRETATION OF POSTWAR ELECTIONS.=
THE WESTERN POLITICAL QUARTERLY, 11, (SEPTEMBER 1958),    58
PP. 539-562.
COMEL, ELEL, ELNOEL
GULIL -63-PAL   GULICK, L
POLITICAL AND ADMINISTRATIVE LEADERSHIP (UNITED STATES).=
PUBLIC MANAGEMENT, 45, (NOVEMBER 1963), PP. 243-247.    63
ELPRNOR, METEL
GULLJT-56-MUO   GULLAHORN, JT
MEASURING (UNION OFFICIALS') ROLE CONFLICT

(UNITED STATES).=
THE AMERICAN JOURNAL OF SOCIOLOGY, 61, (JANUARY 1956),      56
   PP. 299-303.
   METEL
GULLPH-63-SCA    GULLIVER, PH
   SOCIAL CONTROL IN AN AFRICAN SOCIETY (ARUSHA OF
      TANGANYIKA).=
   BOSTON, BOSTON UNIVERSITY PRESS, 1963.                   63
   ELEL, ELNOEL, ELPRNOR
GUNLJM-58-IPS    GUNLICK, JM
   INDIGENOUS POLITICAL SYSTEMS OF WESTERN MALAYA.=
   LONDON, UNIVERSITY OF LONDON, THE ATHLONE PRESS, 1958.   58
   COMEL, ELEL, ELNOEL, ELPRNOR
GUPTSK-57-IPS    GUPTA, SK
   THE INDIAN PARLIAMENT AND STATES REORGANIZATION.=
   PARLIAMENTARY AFFAIRS, 10, (WINTER 1956-1957),           57
      PP. 104-115.
   ELEL, ELPRNOR
GUPTSK-62-MIP    GUPTA, SK
   MOSLEMS IN INDIAN POLITICS, 1947-1960.=
   INDIA QUARTERLY, 18, (OCTOBER-DECEMBER 1962), PP. 355-381.62
   ELEL, ELPRNOR
GURAH -50-LLG    GURADZE, H
   THE LAENDERRAT -- LANDMARK OF GERMAN RECONSTRUCTION.=
   THE WESTERN POLITICAL QUARTERLY, 3, (JUNE 1950),         50
      PP. 190-213.
   COMEL, ELEL
GUSFJR-58-EBR    GUSFIELD, JR
   EQUALITARIANISM AND BUREAUCRATIC RECRUITMENT.=
   ADMINISTRATIVE SCIENCE QUARTERLY, 2, (MARCH 1958),       58
      PP. 521-541.
   DEFEL, COMEL, ELEL, ELNOEL, ELPRNOR
GUSFJR-62-MSE    GUSFIELD, JR
   MASS SOCIETY AND EXTREMIST POLITICS.=
   AMERICAN SOCIOLOGICAL REVIEW, 27, (FEBRUARY 1962),       62
      PP. 19-30.
   DEFEL, ELNOEL
GUSFJR-65-PCG    GUSFIELD, JR
   POLITICAL COMMUNITY AND GROUP INTEREST IN MODERN INDIA.=
   PACIFIC AFFAIRS, 38, (SUMMER 1965), PP. 123-141.         65
   ELEL, ELNOEL
GUSFMR-57-PGO    GUSFIELD, MR
   THE PROBLEM OF GENERATIONS IN AN ORGANIZATIONAL
      STRUCTURE.=
   SOCIAL FORCES, 35, (MAY 1957), PP. 323-330.              57
   COMEL
GUTMEE-61-OPP    GUTMANN, EE
   SOME OBSERVATIONS ON POLITICS AND PARTIES IN ISRAEL.=
   INDIA QUARTERLY, 17, (JANUARY-MARCH 1961), PP. 3-29.     61
   ELEL, ELNEOL
GUTTWF-57-DCA    GUTTERIDGE, WF
   THE DEBATE ON CENTRAL AFRICAN FEDERATION IN RETROSPECT.=
   PARLIAMENTARY AFFAIRS, 10, (SPRING 1957), PP. 210-219.   57
   ELEL, ELPRNOR
GUTTWF-59-IRR    GUTTERIDGE, WF
   INDIRECT RULE AND REPRESENTATIVE GOVERNMENT (BRITISH
      COMMONWEALTH COUNTRIES).=
   PARLIAMENTARY AFFIARS, 12, (SUMMER AND AUTUMN 1959),     59
      PP. 461-468.
   ELEL, ELNOEL, ELPRNOR
GUTTWF-63-AFN    GUTTERIDGE, WF
   ARMED FORCES IN NEW STATES.=
   NEW YORK, OXFORD UNIVERSITY PRESS, 1963.                 63
   DEFEL, COMEL, ELEL, ELNOEL
GUTTWF-65-EML    GUTTERIDGE, WF
   EDUCATION OF MILITARY LEADERSHIP IN EMERGENT STATES.=
   JS COLEMAN  (ED), EDUCATION AND POLITICAL DEVELOPMENT    65
      PRINCETON, NEW JERSEY, PRINCETON UNIVERSITY PRESS,
      1965. PP. 437-462.
   COMEL, ELPRNOR
GUTTWF-65-MIP    GUTTERIDGE, WF
   MILITARY INSTITUTIONS AND POWER IN THE NEW STATES.=
   LONDON, PALL MALL PRESS, 1965.                           65
   DEFEL, COMEL, ELEL, ELNOEL
GUTTWF-67-PRA    GUTTERIDGE, WF
   THE POLITICAL ROLE OF AFRICAN ARMED FORCES -- THE IMPACT
      OF FOREIGN MILITARY ASSISTANCE.=
   AFRICAN AFFAIRS, 66, (APRIL 1967), PP. 93-103.           67
   ELEL, ELPRNOR
GUTTWL-51-CSB    GUTTSMAN, WL
   THE CHANGING STRUCTURE OF THE BRITISH POLITICAL ELITE,
      1886-1935.=
   THE BRITISH JOURNAL OF SOCIOLOGY, 2, (1951), PP. 122-134. 51
   GNELTH, COMEL, ELEL, ELNOEL, ELPRNOR

```
GUTTWL-54-AMC   GUTTSMAN, WL
                ARISTOCRACY AND THE MIDDLE CLASS IN THE BRITISH ELITE,
                   1886-1916.=
                THE BRITISH JOURNAL OF SOCIOLOGY, 5, (1954), PP. 12-32.      54
                ELEL, COMEL
GUTTWL-60-SSP   GUTTSMAN, WL
                SOCIAL STRATIFICATION AND POLITICAL ELITE
                   (GREAT BRITAIN).=
                THE BRITISH JOURNAL OF SOCIOLOGY, 11, (1960), PP. 137-150.60
                GNELTH, COMEL, ELEL,ELNOEL
GUTTWL-61-CBL   GUTTSMAN, WL
                CHANGES IN BRITISH LABOUR LEADERSHIP.=
                D MARVICK (ED), POLITICAL DECISION-MAKERS, GLENCOE, THE      61
                   FREE PRESS, 1961, PP. 91-137.
                COMEL, ELEL, ELPRNOR
GUTTWL-63-BPE   GUTTSMAN, WL
                THE BRITISH POLITICAL ELITE.=
                LONDON, MACGIBBON AND KEE, 1963.
                GNELTH, DEFEL, COMEL, ELEL, ELNOEL, ELPRNOR                   63
GUYOJF-66-BTB   GUYOT, JF
                BUREAUCRATIC TRANSFORMATION IN BURMA.=
                R BRAIBANTI (ED), ASIAN BUREAUCRATIC SYSTEMS EMERGENT        66
                   FROM THE BRITISH IMPERIAL TRADITION, DURHAM, DUKE
                   UNIVERSITY PRESS, 1966, PP. 354-444.
                COMEL, ELEL, ELPRNOR
HACKA -57-LDS   HACKER, A
                LIBERAL DEMOCRACY AND SOCIAL CONTROL (UNITED STATES).=
                THE AMERICAN POLITICAL SCIENCE REVIEW, 51, (DECEMBER         57
                   1957), PP. 1009-1026.
                GNELTH, ELEL, ELNOEL
HACKA -60-RYS   HACKER, A
                THE REBELLING YOUNG SCHOLARS (GREAT BRITAIN,
                   UNITED STATES).=
                COMMENTARY, 30, (NOVEMBER 1960), PP. 404-412.                60
                ELPRNOR
HACKA -61-EAT   HACKER, A
                THE ELECTED AND THE ANNOINTED -- TWO AMERICAN ELITES.=
                THE AMERICAN POLITICAL SCIENCE REVIEW, 55, (SEPTEMBER        61
                   1961), PP. 539-549.
                DEFEL, ELEL, ELNOEL
HACKA -64-PDW   HACKER, A
                POWER TO DO WHAT (CORPORATE ELITE, UNITED STATES).=
                IL HOROWITZ (ED), THE NEW SOCIOLOGY, NEW YORK, OXFORD        64
                   UNIVERSITY PRESS, 1964, PP. 134-146.
                DEFEL
HACKA -65-DDP   HACKER, A
                DOES A DIVISIVE - PRIMARY HARM A CANDIDATE'S CHANCES
                   (UNITED STATES).=
                THE AMERICAN POLITICAL SCIENCE REVIEW, 59, (MARCH 1965),     65
                   PP. 105-110.
                ELNOEL
HADDGM-65-RMR   HADDEN, GM
                REVOLUTIONS AND MILITARY RULE IN THE MIDDLE EAST.=
                NEW YORK, ROBERT SPELLER, 1965.                              65
                ELEL, ELPRNOR
HADLG -56-PPW   HADLEY, G
                PUBLIC AND PARLIAMENT IN WEST GERMANY.=
                PARLIAMENTARY AFFAIRS, 9, (SPRING 1956), PP. 224-229.        56
                ELNOEL
HADMJG-61-HUN   HADMEN, JG    KAUFMAN, J
                HOW UNITED NATIONS DECISIONS ARE MADE.=
                LEYDEN, A W SYTHOFF-LEYDEN, 1961.                            61
                ELEL, ELNOEL, ELPRNOR
HAERJL-56-SSR   HAER, JL
                SOCIAL STRATIFICATION IN RELATION TO ATTITUDES TOWARD
                   SOURCES OF POWER IN A COMMUNITY (UNITED STATES).=
                SOCIAL FORCES, 35, (DECEMBER 1956), PP. 137-142.             56
                ELNOEL, ELPRNOR
HAGEEE-62-TSC   HAGEN, EE
                ON THE THEORY OF SOCIAL CHANGE.=
                HOMEWOOD, ILLINOIS, THE DORSEY PRESS, 1962.                  62
                GNELTH, COMEL, ELEL, ELNOEL, ELPRNOR
HAGGEE-62-FAE   HAGGEN, EE
                A FRAMEWORK FOR ANALYZING ECONOMIC AND POLITICAL CHANGE.=
                RE ASHER (ED), DEVELOPMENT OF THE EMERGING COUNTRIES,        62
                   WASHINGTON, BROOKINGS, 1962, PP. 1-38, PP. 1-38.
                ELEL, ELNOEL, ELPRNOR
HAHNH -67-TIS   HAHN, H
                TURNOVER IN IOWA STATE PARTY CONVENTIONS -- AN
                   EXPLORATORY STUDY (UNITED STATES).=
                MIDWEST JOURNAL OF POLITICAL SCIENCE, 11, (FEBRUARY 1967),67
                   PP. 98-105.
                COMEL
HAHNL -62-TPP   HAHN, L
```

TUNISIA -- PRAGMATISM AND PROGRESS.=
THE MIDDLE EAST JOURNAL, 16, (WINTER 1962), PP. 18-28.          62
ELEL, ELNOEL, ELPRNOR

HAHNL -64-NAN    HAHN, L
NORTH AFRICA -- A NEW PRAGMATISM.=
ORBIS, 8, (SPRING 1964), PP. 125-140.                          64
ELEL, ELPRNOR

HAHNL -65-DTL    HAHN-BEEN, L
DEVELOPMENTALIST TIME AND LEADERSHIP IN
DEVELOPING COUNTRIES.=
CAG OCCASIONAL PAPERS, INTERNATIONAL DEVELOPMENT              65
RESEARCH CENTER, BLOOMINGTON, INDIANA, 1965.
DEFEL, ELPRNOR

HAHNWF-55-SPA    HAHN, WF
THE SOCIALIST PARTY OF AUSTRIA -- RETREAT FROM MARX.=
JOURNAL OF CENTRAL EUROPEAN AFFAIRS, 15, (JULY 1955),         55
PP. 115-133.
COMEL, ELNOEL, ELPRNOR

HAIMFS-51-GLD    HAIMAN, FS
GROUP LEADERSHIP AND DEMOCRATIC ACTION.=
LONDON, HOUGHTON MIFFLIN COMPANY, 1951.                       51
ELEL, ELNOEL

HAIMLH-58-TGS    HAIMSON, LH
THREE GENERATIONS OF THE SOVIET INTELLIGENTSIA.=
HW WINGER (ED), IRON CURTAINS AND SCHOLARSHIP, CHICAGO,       58
UNIVERSITY OF CHICAGO PRESS, 1958.
COMEL, ELEL, ELNOEL

HAIMLH-59-TGS    HAIMSON, LH
THREE GENERATIONS OF THE SOVIET INTELLIGENTSIA.=
FOREIGN AFFAIRS, 37, (JANUARY 1959), PP. 235-246.             59
COMEL, ELEL, ELNOEL

HAIRM -63-CPR    HAIRE, M              ET AL
CULTURAL PATTERNS IN THE ROLE OF THE MANAGER.=
INDUSTRIAL RELATIONS, 2, (FEBRUARY 1963), PP. 95-117.         63
COMEL, ELEL, ELNOEL, ELPRNOR

HALAF -52-NWS    HALAS, F
A NEW WORLD (SOVIET INTELLECTUALS).=
PROBLEMS OF COMMUNISM, 1, (JULY-AUGUST 1952), PP. 4-7.        52
ELEL, ELNOEL, ELPRNOR

HALLDG-54-TCQ    HALL, DGE
THOUGHTS ON THE CHINESE QUESTION IN SOUTHEAST ASIA.=
ASIAN REVIEW, N.S. 50, (JANUARY 1954), PP. 138-148.           54
COMEL, ELEL, ELNOEL, ELPRNOR

HALLGW-54-WDC    HALLGARTEN, GWF
WHY DICTATORS -- THE CAUSES AND FORMS OF TYRANNICAL
RULE SINCE 600 BC.=
NEW YORK, MACMILLAN, 1954.                                    54
DEFEL, COMEL, ELEL, ELNOEL

HALLJW-66-GLP    HALL, JW
GOVERNMENT AND LOCAL POWER IN JAPAN -- A STUDY ON BIZEN
PROVINCE 500-1700.=
PRINCETON, PRINCETON UNIVERSITY PRESS, 1966.                  66
COMEL, ELEL, ELNOEL, ELPRNOR

HALLRH-63-BSO    HALL, RH
BUREAUCRACY AND SMALL ORGANIZATIONS (UNITED STATES).=
SOCIOLOGY AND SOCIAL RESEARCH, 48, (OCTOBER 1963),            63
PP. 38-46.
ELNOEL, METEL

HALPB -62-RMI    HALPERN, B
THE ROLE OF THE MILITARY IN ISRAEL.=
JJ JOHNSON (ED), THE ROLE OF THE MILITARY IN                  62
UNDERDEVELOPED COUNTRIES, PRINCETON, PRINCETON
UNIVERSITY PRESS, 1962, PP. 317-357.
ELEL, ELNOEL

HALPE -59-MNC    HALPERIN, E
THE METAMORPHOSE OF THE NEW CLASS (SOVIET UNION, EASTERN
EUROPE).=
PROBLEMS OF COMMUNISM, 8, (JULY-AUGUST 1959), PP. 17-22.      59
COMEL, ELEL, ELPRNOR

HALPE -65-NCC    HALPERIN, E
NATIONALISM AND COMMUNISM IN CHILE.=
CAMBRIDGE, THE MIT PRESS, 1965.                               65
COMEL, ELEL, ELNOEL, ELPRNOR

HALPJM-64-GPS    HALPERN, JM
GOVERNMENT, POLITICS, AND SOCIAL STRUCTURE IN LAOS -- A
STUDY OF TRADITION AND INNOVATION.=
NEW HAVEN, CONNECTICUT, SOUTHEAST ASIA STUDIES,               64
YALE UNIVERSITY, 1964.
COMEL, ELEL, ELNOEL, ELPRNOR

HALPM -62-MEA    HALPERN, M
MIDDLE EASTERN ARMIES AND THE NEW MIDDLE CLASS.=
JJ JOHNSON (ED), THE ROLE OF THE MILITARY IN                  62
UNDERDEVELOPED COUNTRIES, PRINCETON, PRINCETON
UNIVERSITY PRESS, 1962, PP. 277-316.

```
                     COMEL, ELNOEL, ELPRNOR
HAMBG -64-AAC    HAMBLY, G
                 ATTITUDES AND ASPIRATIONS OF THE CONTEMPORARY IRANIAN
                    INTELLECTUAL.=
                 ROYAL CENTRAL ASIAN JOURNAL, 51, (APRIL 1964),              64
                    PP. 127-140.
                 COMEL, ELEL, ELPRNOR
HAMBRL-58-LC     HAMBLIN, RL
                 LEADERSHIP AND CRISES.=
                 SOCIOMETRY, 21, (1958), PP. 322-335.                       58
                 METEL
HAMID -57-ECH    HAMILTON, D
                 THE ENTREPRENEUR AS CULTURAL HERO.=
                 THE SOUTHWESTERN SOCIAL SCIENCE QUARTERLY, 38,             57
                    (DECEMBER 1957), PP. 248-256.
                 DEFEL, ELEL, ELPRNOR
HAMMD -64-CTP    HAMMOND-TOOKE, D
                 CHIEFTAINSHIP IN TRANSKEIAN POLITICAL DEVELOPMENT
                    (AFRICA).=
                 JOURNAL OF MODERN AFRICAN HISTORY, 2, (DECEMBER 1964),     64
                    PP. 513-530.
                 ELEL, ELNOEL
HAMMDP-64-ASM    HAMMER, DP
                 AMONG STUDENTS IN MOSCOW -- AN OUTSIDER'S REPORT
                    (SOVIET UNION).=
                 PROBLEMS OF COMMUNISM, 13, (JULY-AUGUST 1964), PP. 55-60. 64
                 ELEL, ELPRNOR
HAMMEJ-50-BDE    HAMMER, EJ
                 THE BAO DAI EXPERIMENT (VIETNAM).=
                 PACIFIC AFFAIRS, 23, (MARCH 1950), PP. 46-58.              50
                 ELEL, ELPRNOR
HAMMHR-63-RSM    HAMMOND, HR
                 RACE, SOCIAL MOBILITY AND POLITICS IN BRAZIL.=
                 RACE (JOURNAL OF INSTITUTE OF RACE RELATIONS, LONDON),     63
                    6, (MAY 1963), PP. 3-13.
                 ELNOEL
HAMMPY-60-NSC    HAMMOND, PY
                 THE NATIONAL SECURITY COUNCIL AS A DEVICE FOR
                    OUTER-DEPARTMENTAL COORDINATION (UNITED STATES).=
                 THE AMERICAN POLITICAL SCIENCE REVIEW, 54, (DECEMBER       60
                    1960), PP. 899-910.
                 ELEL
HAMMPY-65-FPM    HAMMOND, PY
                 FOREIGN POLICY-MAKING AND ADMINISTRATIVE POLITICS
                    (UNITED STATES).=
                 WORLD POLITICS, 17, (JULY 1965), PP. 656-671.              65
                 ELEL, METEL
HAMMWD-65-SFC    HAMMOND-TOOKE, WD
                 SEGMENTATION AND FISSION IN CAPE NGUNI POLITICAL UNITS
                    (AFRICA).=
                 AFRICA, 35, (APRIL 1965), PP. 143-166.                     65
                 ELEL, ELNOEL
HAMNI -65-KCB    HAMNETT, I
                 KOENA CHIEFTAINSHIP IN BASUTOLAND (AFRICA).=
                 AFRICA, 35, (JULY 1965), PP. 241-251.                      65
                 COMEL
HAMOL -61-MFP    HAMON, L
                 MEMBERS OF THE FRENCH PARLIAMENT.=
                 INTERNATIONAL SOCIAL SCIENCE JOURNAL, 13, (1961),          61
                    PP. 545-566.
                 COMEL, ELPRNOR
HANAH -66-RTC    HANAK, H
                 RECENT TRENDS IN CZECHOSLOVAKIA -- THE WRITERS'
                    CAMPAIGN OF CRITICISM.=
                 THE WORLD TODAY, 22, (1966), PP. 130-134.                  66
                 ELEL, ELPRNOR
HANCWS-58-OMF    HANCHETT, WS
                 SOME OBSERVATIONS ON MEMBERSHIP FIGURES OF THE
                    COMMUNIST PARTY OF THE SOVIET UNION.=
                 THE AMERICAN POLITICAL SCIENCE REVIEW, 52, (DECEMBER       58
                    1958), PP. 1123-1128.
                 COMEL
HANHAM-64-IPN    HANHARDT-JR, AM    WELSH, WA
                 THE INTELLECTUALS - POLITICS NEXUS -- STUDIES USING A
                    BIOGRAPHICAL TECHNIQUE (BULGARIA, SOVIET UNION).=
                 THE AMERICAN BEHAVIORAL SCIENTIST, 7, (MARCH 1964),        64
                    PP. 2-7.
                 METEL
HANKLM-62-MPT    HANKS, LM
                 MERIT AND POWER IN THE THAI SOCIAL ORDER.=
                 AMERICAN ANTHROPOLOGIST, 64, (DECEMBER 1962),              62
                    PP. 1247-1261.
                 COMEL, ELEL, ELNOEL, ELPRNOR
HANNWG-66-PRP    HANNA, WG
```

```
                    POLITICAL RECRUITMENT AND PARTICIPATION -- SOME
                    SUGGESTED AREAS FOR RESEARCH.=
                    THE PSYCHOANALYTIC REVIEW, 52, (WINTER 1965-1966),          66
                    PP. 407-420.
                    COMEL, ELPRNOR, METEL
HANSRC-59-PCD   HANSON, RC
                    PREDICTING A COMMUNITY DECISION -- A TEST OF THE
                    MILLER-FORM THEORY (UNITED STATES).=
                    AMERICAN SOCIOLOGICAL REVIEW, 24,                           59
                    (OCTOBER 1959), PP. 662-671.
                    METEL
HANSSG-51-CTS   HANSON, SG
                    THE CURTAIN THAT SHIELDS THE 'DIPLOMAT' (LATIN AMERICA,
                    UNITED STATES).=
                    INTER-AMERICAN ECONOMIC AFFAIRS, 4, (SPRING 1951),         51
                    PP. 37-47.
                    ELEL, ELPRNOR
HANSSG-66-RPB   HANSON, SG
                    THE ROLE OF PRIVATE BUSINESS (LATIN AMERICA).=
                    INTER-AMERICAN ECONOMIC AFFAIRS, 20, (AUTUMN 1966),        66
                    PP. 71-78.
                    ELEL
HARBJD-65-DEG   HARBRON, JD
                    THE DILEMMA OF AN ELITE GROUP -- THE INDUSTRIALIST IN
                    LATIN AMERICA.=
                    INTER-AMERICAN ECONOMIC AFFAIRS, 19, (AUTUMN 1965),        65
                    PP. 43-63.
                    COMEL, ELEL, ELPRNOR
HARDRL-66-VPB   HARDGRAVE-JR, RL
                    VARIETIES OF POLITICAL BEHAVIOR AMONG NADARS OF
                    TAMILNAD (INDIA).=
                    ASIAN SURVEY, 6, (NOVEMBER 1966), PP. 614-621.             66
                    COMEL, ELEL
HARGEC-67-PLA   HARGROVE, EC
                    POPULAR LEADERSHIP IN THE ANGLO - AMERICAN DEMOCRACIES
                    (CANADA, GREAT BRITAIN, UNITED STATES).=
                    LJ EDINGER (ED), POLITICAL LEADERSHIP IN INDUSTRIALIZED     67
                    SOCIETIES, NEW YORK, JOHN WILEY AND SONS, 1967,
                    PP. 182-219.
                    ELEL, ELNOEL, ELPRNOR
HARGJD-59-EA    HARGREAVES, JD
                    EDUCATED AFRICANS.=
                    CONTEMPORARY REVIEW, (1959), PP. 210-213.                  59
                    COMEL
HARIIF-65-ISL   HARIK, IF
                    THE IATA SYSTEM IN LEBANON -- A COMPARATIVE
                    POLITICAL VIEW.=
                    THE MIDDLE EAST JOURNAL, 19, (AUTUMN 1965), PP. 405-421.    65
                    COMEL, ELEL, ELNOEL
HARKF -65-AUH   HARKISON, F
                    THE AFRICAN UNIVERSITY AND HUMAN RESOURCES DEVELOPMENT.=
                    THE JOURNAL OF MODERN AFRICAN STUDIES, (MAY 1965),         65
                    PP. 53-62.
                    COMEL
HARRCW-58-SAC   HARRINGTON, CW
                    THE SAUDI ARABIAN COUNCIL OF MINISTERS.=
                    THE MIDDLE EAST JOURNAL, 12, (WINTER 1958), PP. 1-19.       58
                    COMEL, ELEL
HARRJP-52-CSU   HARRIS, JP
                    THE COURTESY OF THE SENATE (UNITED STATES).=
                    POLITICAL SCIENCE QUARTERLY, 67, (MARCH 1952), PP. 36-63. 52
                    ELEL, ELPRNOR
HARRJP-53-ACS   HARRIS, JP
                    THE ADVICE AND CONSENT OF THE SENATE -- A STUDY OF THE
                    CONFIRMATION OF APPOINTMENTS BY THE UNITED STATES
                    SENATE.=
                    BERKELEY, UNIVERSITY OF CALIFORNIA PRESS, 1953.            53
                    ELEL, ELPRNOR
HARRJP-64-RIF   HARRISON, JP
                    THE ROLE OF THE INTELLECTUAL IN FOMENTING CHANGE --
                    THE UNIVERSITY (LATIN AMERICA).=
                    JJ TEPASKE AND SN FISHER (EDS), EXPLOSIVE FORCES IN LATIN 64
                    AMERICA, COLUMBUS, OHIO STATE UNIVERSITY PRESS, 1964,
                    PP. 27-42.
                    COMEL, ELEL, ELNOEL, ELPRNOR
HARRL -59-WOA   HARRIS, L
                    WHY THE ODDS ARE AGAINST A GOVERNOR'S BECOMING
                    PRESIDENT (UNITED STATES).=
                    THE PUBLIC OPINION QUARTERLY, 23, (FALL 1959),             59
                    PP. 361-370.
                    ELEL, ELNOEL
HARRM -56-TCB   HARRIS, M
                    TOWN AND COUNTRY IN BRAZIL.=
                    NEW YORK, COLUMBIA UNIVERSITY PRESS, 1956.                 56
```

```
                    COMEL, ELEL, ELNOEL, ELPRNOR
HARRM -59-CCM    HARRIS, M
                    CASTE, CLASS, AND MINORITY.=
                    SOCIAL FORCES, 37, (MARCH 1959), PP. 248-254.                 59
                    DEFEL, COMEL, ELEL, ELNOEL
HARRM -60-TUL    HARRISON, M
                    TRADE UNIONS AND THE LABOUR PARTY SINCE 1945
                      (GREAT BRITAIN).=
                    DETROIT, WAYNE STATE UNIVERSITY PRESS, 1960.                  60
                    ELEL, ELNOEL
HARRR -61-SLB    HARRIS, R
                    THE SELECTION OF LEADERS IN BALLYBEG, NORTHERN
                      IRELAND.=
                    THE SOCIOLOGICAL REVIEW, 9, (JULY 1961), PP. 137-149.         61
                    COMEL, ELEL, ELNOEL
HARRRL-63-BCP    HARRIS, RL           KERANEY, RN
                    A BRIEF COMPARISON OF THE PUBLIC SERVICES OF CANADA
                      AND CEYLON.=
                    PHILIPPINE JOURNAL OF PUBLIC ADMINISTRATION, 7,               63
                      (JANUARY 1963), PP. 3-10.
                    ELEL
HARRRL-64-CAA    HARRIS, RL           KEARNEY, RN
                    A COMPARATIVE ANALYSIS OF THE ADMINISTRATIVE SYSTEMS OF
                      CANADA AND CEYLON.=
                    ADMINISTRATIVE SCIENCE QUARTERLY, 8, (1963-1964),             64
                      PP. 339-360.
                    COMEL, ELEL, ELNOEL
HARSJC-62-MSP    HARSANYI, JC
                    MEASUREMENT OF SOCIAL POWER OPPORTUNITY COSTS,
                      AND THE THEORY OF TWO-PERSON BARGAINING GAMES.=
                    BEHAVIORAL SCIENCE, 7, (1962), PP. 67-80.                     62
                    DEFEL, METEL
HARTA -61-CI     HARTLEY, A
                    CUBA AND THE INTELLECTUALS.=
                    ENCOUNTER, 17, (AUGUST 1961), PP. 59-63.                      61
                    ELEL, ELPRNOR
HARTCL-64-PRI    HARTER, CL
                    POWER ROLES OF INTELLECTUALS -- AN INTRODUCTORY
                      STATEMENT.=
                    SOCIOLOGY AND SOCIAL RESEARCH, 48, (JANUARY 1964),            64
                      PP. 176-186.
                    DEFEL, ELEL, ELNOEL, ELPRNOR
HARTDK-64-SSR    HART, DK
                    SAINT-SIMON AND THE ROLE OF THE ELITE.=
                    THE WESTERN POLITICAL QUARTERLY, 17, (SEPTEMBER 1964),        64
                      PP. 423-431.
                    GNELTH, ELEL
HARTGW-45-JSL    HARTMANN, GW
                    JUDGEMENTS OF STATE LEGISLATORS CONCERNING PUBLIC
                      OPINION (UNITED STATES).=
                    JOURNAL OF SOCIAL PSYCHOLOGY, 21, (FEBRUARY 1945),            45
                      PP. 105-114.
                    ELNOEL, ELPRNOR
HARTH -59-AOG    HARTMANN, H
                    AUTHORITY AND ORGANIZATION IN GERMAN MANAGEMENT.=
                    PRINCETON, PRINCETON UNIVERSITY PRESS, 1959.                  59
                    ELEL, ELPRNOR
HARTH -59-CCE    HARTMANN, H
                    COHESION AND COMMITMENT IN EMPLOYERS' ORGANIZATIONS
                      (FRANCE, GERMANY).=
                    WORLD POLITICS, 11, (APRIL 1959), PP.475-490.                 59
                    ELEL, ELPRNOR
HARVML-65-PKS    HARVEY, ML
                    THE POST - KHRUSHCHEV SOVIET LEADERSHIP -- DILEMMAS AND
                      ALTERNATIVES.=
                    ORBIS, 8, (WINTER 1965), PP. 745-760.                         65
                    ELEL, ELNOEL
HATHGB-56-CSC    HATHORN, GB
                    CONGRESSIONAL AND SENATORIAL CAMPAIGN COMMITTEES IN THE
                      MID-TERM ELECTION YEAR 1954 (UNITED STATES).=
                    THE SOUTHWESTERN SOCIAL SCIENCE QUARTERLY, 37,                56
                      (DECEMBER 1956), PP. 207-221.
                    ELEL, ELNOEL
HATTLH-54-LSE    HATTERY, LH          HOFHEIMER, S
                    THE LEGISLATOR -- SOURCE OF EXPERT INFORMATION
                      (UNITED STATES).=
                    THE PUBLIC OPINION QUARTERLY, 18, (FALL 1954),                54
                      PP. 301-303.
                    ELEL
HAVAWC-64-BCC    HAVARD, WC
                    FROM BOSSES TO COSMOPOLITANISM -- CHANGES IN THE
                      RELATIONSHIP OF URBAN LEADERSHIP TO STATE POLITICS
                      (UNITED STATES).=
                    THE ANNALS OF THE AMERICAN ACADEMY OF POLITICAL AND           64
```

```
                    SOCIAL SCIENCE, 353, (MAY 1964), PP. 84-94.
                    COMEL, ELEL, ELNOEL, ELPRNOR
HAWLAH-63-CPU   HAWLEY, AH
                    COMMUNITY POWER AND URBAN RENEWAL SUCCESS
                      (UNITED STATES).=
                    THE AMERICAN JOURNAL OF SOCIOLOGY, 68, (JANUARY 1963),      63
                      PP. 422-431.
                    ELEL, ELNOEL, METEL
HAWTAE-48-SLA   HAWTHORNE, AE        HAWTHORNE, HB
                    STRATIFICATION IN A LATIN AMERICAN CITY.=
                    SOCIAL FORCES, 27, (OCTOBER 1948), PP. 19-29.               48
                    COMEL, ELEL, ELNOEL
HAWVCF-63-CSC   HAWVER, CF
                    THE CONGRESSMAN'S CONCEPTION OF HIS ROLE (UNITED STATES).=
                    WASHINGTON, HENNAGE LITHOGRAPH COMPANY, 1963.               63
                    ELPRNOR
HAYSFB-65-CLR   HAYS, FB
                    COMMUNITY LEADERSHIP -- THE REGIONAL PLAN ASSOCIATION
                      OF NEW YORK.=
                    NEW YORK, COLUMBIA UNIVERSITY PRESS, 1965.                  65
                    COMEL, ELEL, ELNOEL, ELPRNOR
HAYWM -63-CCL   HAYWARD, M
                    CONFLICT AND CHANGE IN LITERATURE (SOVIET UNION).=
                    SURVEY--A JOURNAL OF SOVIET AND EAST EUROPEAN STUDIES,      63
                      46, (JANUARY 1963), PP. 9-22.
                    ELEL, ELPRNOR
HAZAJN-52-SPA   HAZARD, JN
                    SOVIET PUBLIC ADMINISTRATION AND FEDERALISM.=
                    THE POLITICAL QUARTERLY, 23, (JANUARY 1952), PP. 4-14.      52
                    ELEL, ELNOEL
HAZAJN-58-LMS   HAZARD, JN
                    LAWS AND MEN IN SOVIET SOCIETY.=
                    FOREIGN AFFAIRS, 36, (JANUARY 1958), PP. 267-276.           58
                    ELNOEL, ELPRNOR
HD    -52-RSP   HD
                    THE ROLE OF THE SOVIET PARTY CONGRESS.=
                    THE WORLD TODAY, 8, (OCTOBER 1952), PP. 412-419.            52
                    ELEL, ELNOEL
HEADF -57-PAS   HEADY, F
                    THE PHILIPPINE ADMINISTRATIVE SYSTEM -- A FUSION OF
                      EAST AND WEST.=
                    PHILIPPINE JOURNAL OF PUBLIC ADMINISTRATION, 1,             57
                      (JANUARY 1957), PP. 27-45.
                    ELEL, ELPRNOR
HEASDJ-61-MPM   HEASMAN, DJ
                    THE MONARCH, THE PRIME MINISTER, AND THE
                      DISSOLUTION OF PARLIAMENT (GREAT BRITAIN).=
                    PARLIAMENTARY AFFAIRS, 14, (WINTER 1960-1961),              61
                      PP. 94-107.
                    ELEL, ELNOEL, ELPRNOR
HEASDJ-62-MHP   HEASMAN, DJ
                    THE MINISTERIAL HIERARCHY -- PART 1 (GREAT BRITAIN).=
                    PARLIAMENTARY AFFAIRS, 15, (SUMMER 1962), PP. 307-330.      62
                    COMEL, ELEL
HEATD -59-LRS   HEATH, D
                    LAND REFORM AND SOCIAL REVOLUTION IN BOLIVIA.=
                    MADISON, UNIVERSITY OF WISCONSIN PRESS, 1959.               59
                    COMEL, ELEL, ELNOEL
HEATDB-59-LTS   HEATH, DB
                    LAND TENURE AND SOCIAL ORGANIZATION -- AN ETHNOHISTORICAL
                      STUDY FROM THE BOLIVIAN ORIENTE.=
                    INTER-AMERICAN ECONOMIC AFFAIRS, 13, (AUTUMN 1959),         59
                      PP. 35-46.
                    COMEL
HEBER -55-FTC   HEBERLE, R
                    FERDINAND TONNIES' CONTRIBUTIONS TO THE SOCIOLOGY OF
                      POLITICAL PARTIES.=
                    THE AMERICAN JOURNAL OF SOCIOLOGY, 61, (SEPTEMBER 1955),    55
                      PP. 213-220.
                    DEFEL, ELEL, ELNOEL
HEBER -59-RCT   HEBERLE, R
                    RECOVERY OF CLASS THEORY.=
                    PACIFIC SOCIOLOGICAL REVIEW, 2, (OCTOBER 1959), PP. 18-24.59
                    GNELTH
HEIDAJ-  -CPF   HEIDENHEIMER, AJ
                    COMPARATIVE PARTY FINANCE -- NOTES ON PRACTICES AND
                      TOWARD A THEORY.=
                    THE JOURNAL OF POLITICS, 25, (FEBRUARY 1963), PP.
                      790-811.
                    ELEL, METEL
HEIDAJ-57-GPF   HEIDENHEIMER, AJ
                    GERMAN PARTY FINANCE -- THE CDU.=
                    THE AMERICAN POLITICAL SCIENCE REVIEW, 51, (JUNE 1957),     57
                      PP. 369-385.
```

                    ELEL
HEIDAJ-63-CPF     HEIDENHEIMER, AJ
                  CITIZENSHIP, PARTIES AND FACTIONS IN GIBRALTAR.=
                  JOURNAL OF COMMONWEALTH POLITICAL STUDIES, 1,              63
                     (1963), PP. 249-265.
                  COMEL, ELEL, ELNOEL
HEIMCH-64-INH     HEIMSATH, CH
                  INDIAN NATIONALISM AND HINDU SOCIAL REFORM.=
                  PRINCETON, NEW JERSEY, PRINCETON UNIVERSITY PRESS, 1964.   64
                  ELEL, ELPRNOR
HEINAJ-64-SPP     HEINDENHEIMER, AJ
                  SUCCESSION AND PARTY POLITICS IN WEST GERMANY.=
                  JOURNAL OF INTERNATIONAL AFFAIRS, 18, (1964), PP. 32-42.   64
                  ELEL
HELGJL-61-CRM     HELGUERA, JL
                  THE CHANGING ROLE OF THE MILITARY IN COLUMBIA.=
                  JOURNAL OF INTER-AMERICAN STUDIES, 3, (JULY 1961),         61
                     PP. 351-358.
                  COMEL, ELEL, ELNOEL
HELSLN-54-RCS     HELSBY, LN
                  RECRUITMENT TO THE CIVIL SERVICES (GREAT BRITAIN).=
                  THE POLITICAL QUARTERLY, 25, (1954), PP. 324-335.          54
                  COMEL, ELEL, ELPRNOR
HENNB -58-OPD     HENNESSY, B
                  THE OPINION-POLICY IN DEMOCRACY -- A CRITICAL SUMMARY
                     OF SOME RECENT LITERATURE.=
                  THE SOUTHWESTERN SOCIAL SCIENCE QUARTERLY, 38,             58
                     (MARCH 1958), PP. 332-343.
                  DEFEL, ELEL
HENNB -58-PAP     HENNESSY, B
                  POLITICAL AND APOLITICAL PERSONALITY.=
                  PROD (THE AMERICAN BEHAVIORAL SCIENTIST), 2,               58
                     (NOVEMBER 1958), PP. 24-26.
                  ELPRNOR
HENNB -59-PAM     HENNESSY, B
                  POLITICALS AND APOLITICALS -- SOME MEASUREMENT OF
                     PERSONALITY TRAITS (UNITED STATES).=
                  MIDWEST JOURNAL OF POLITICAL SCIENCE, 3, (NOVEMBER 1959),  59
                     PP. 336-355.
                  DEFEL, COMEL, ELNOEL, ELPRNOR, METEL
HENND -61-CCP     HENNESSY, D
                  THE COMMUNICATION OF CONSERVATIVE POLICY 1957-1959
                     (GREAT BRITAIN).=
                  THE POLITICAL QUARTERLY, 32, (JULY-SEPTEMBER 1961),        61
                     PP. 238-256.
                  ELNOEL, ELPRNOR
HEPPA -54-TUT     HEPPLE, A
                  TRADE UNIONS IN TRAVAIL -- THE STORY OF THE
                     BROEDERBOND - NATIONALIST PLAN TO CONTROL SOUTH
                     AFRICAN TRADE UNIONS.=
                  JOHANNESBURG, UNITY PUBLICATIONS, 1954.                    54
                  ELEL, ELNOEL
HERMFA-56-PPC     HERMANS, FA
                  POLITICS, POWER AND CONFUSION (UNITED STATES, POWER
                     ELITE REVIEW).=
                  THE REVIEW OF POLITICS, 18, (JULY 1956), PP. 365-368.      56
                  GNELTH, DEFEL, COMEL
HEROAO-59-OLA     HERO, AO
                  OPINION LEADERS IN AMERICAN COMMUNITIES.=
                  BOSTON, WORLD PEACE FOUNDATION, 1959.                      59
                  COMEL, ELPRNOR, ELNOEL
HERRH -64-DH      HERRING, H
                  DICTATORSHIP IN HAITI.=
                  CURRENT HISTORY, N.S., 46, (JANUARY 1964), PP. 34-37.      64
                  ELNOEL
HERRP -40-PLU     HERRING, P
                  PRESIDENTIAL LEADERSHIP (UNITED-STATES).=
                  NEW YORK, RINEHART AND COMPANY, INC, 1940.                 40
                  ELEL, ELNOEL
HERSLJ-61-FCP     HERSON, LJR
                  IN THE FOOTSTEPS OF COMMUNITY POWER.=
                  THE AMERICAN POLITICAL SCIENCE REVIEW, 55, (DECEMBER       61
                     1961), PP. 817-830.
                  DEFEL, METEL
HERTA -51-CEE     HERTZ, A
                  THE CASE OF AN EASTERN EUROPEAN INTELLIGENTSIA (POLAND).=
                  JOURNAL OF CENTRAL EUROPEAN AFFAIRS, 11,                   51
                     (JANUARY-APRIL 1951), PP. 10-26.
                  COMEL, ELEL, ELPRNOR
HERZJH-54-GOR     HERZ, JH
                  GERMAN OFFICIALS REVISITED -- POLITICAL VIEWS AND
                     ATTITUDES OF THE WESTERN GERMAN CIVIL SERVICE.=
                  WORLD POLITICS, 7, (OCTOBER 1954), PP. 63-83.              54
                  COMEL, ELPRNOR

HERZJH-60-EGP    HERZ, JH
                 EAST GERMANY -- PROGRESS AND PROSPECTS.=
                 SOCIAL RESEARCH, 27, (SUMMER 1960), PP. 139-156.                   60
                 COMEL, ELEL
HESSCG-54-CFL    HESS, CG              BODMAN, HL
                 CONFESSIONALISM AND FEUDALITY IN LEBANESE POLITICS.=
                 THE MIDDLE EAST JOURNAL, 8, (1954), PP. 10-26.                     54
                 COMEL, ELEL, ELNOEL
HESSRD-60-CSC    HESS, RD              EASTON, D
                 THE CHILD'S CHANGING IMAGE OF THE PRESIDENT
                    (UNITED STATES).=
                 THE PUBLIC OPINION QUARTERLY, 24, (WINTER 1960),                   60
                    PP. 632-644.
                 ELNOEL, METEL
HESSRD-63-SAT    HESS, RD
                 THE SOCIALIZATION OF ATTITUDES TOWARD POLITICAL
                    AUTHORITY (AUSTRALIA, CHILE, JAPAN, PUERTO RICO,
                    UNITED STATES).=
                 INTERNATIONAL SOCIAL SCIENCE JOURNAL, 15, (1963), PP.              63
                    542-559.
                 ELNOEL, ELPRNOR
HESSRL-64-ENP    HESS, RL              LOEWENBERG, G
                 THE ETHIOPIAN NO - PARTY STATE -- A NOTE ON THE
                    FUNCTIONS OF POLITICAL PARTIES IN DEVELOPING STATES.=
                 THE AMERICAN POLITICAL SCIENCE REVIEW, 58, (DECEMBER              64
                    1964), PP. 947-950.
                 DEFEL, ELEL
HESSRL-64-MMN    HESS, RL
                 THE 'MAD MULLAH' AND NORTHERN SOMALIA.=
                 JOURNAL OF AFRICAN HISTORY, 5, (1964), PP. 415-433.                64
                 COMEL, ELEL
HEY,PD-61-RNI    HEY, PD
                 THE RISE OF THE NATAL INDIAN ELITE.=
                 PIETERMARITZBURG, NAT. WITNESS, 1961.                              61
                 COMEL, ELEL, ELNOEL
HEYWJ -58-Y      HEYWORTH-DUNNE, J
                 THE YEMEN.=
                 MIDDLE EASTERN AFFAIRS, 9, (FEBRUARY 1958), PP. 50-58.             58
                 COMEL, ELEL
HIGGB -61-ELS    HIGGINS, B (ED)
                 ENTREPRENEURSHIP AND LABOR SKILLS IN INDONESIAN
                    ECONOMIC DEVELOPMENT -- A SYMPOSIUM.=
                 NEW HAVEN, YALE UNIVERSITY SOUTHEAST ASIA STUDIES,                 61
                    DETROIT, MICHIGAN, CELLAR BOOK SHOP, 1961.
                 ELEL, ELPRNOR
HIGGGM-55-CSP    HIGGINS, GM
                 THE CHAIRMAN'S PANEL (GREAT BRITAIN).=
                 PARLIAMENTARY AFFAIRS, 8, (AUTUMN 1955), PP. 514-525.              55
                 ELEL, ELNOEL
HIGHRB-59-SGC    HIGHSAW, RB
                 THE SOUTHERN GOVERNOR -- CHALLENGE TO THE STRONG
                    EXECUTIVE THEME (UNITED STATES).=
                 PUBLIC ADMINISTRATION REVIEW, 19, (WINTER 1959),                   59
                    PP. 7-11.
                 ELEL, ELPRNOR
HILLMF-60-WSS    HILL, MF
                 THE WHITE SETTLER'S ROLE IN KENYA.=
                 FOREIGN AFFAIRS, 38, (JULY 1960), PP. 638-645.                     60
                 ELEL, ELNOEL
HILSR -56-SIN    HILSMAN, R
                 STRATEGIC INTELLIGENCE AND NATIONAL DECISIONS.=
                 GLENCOE, ILLINOIS, FREE PRESS, 1956.                               56
                 ELEL, ELNOEL, ELPRNOR
HINDD -64-CPI    HINDLEY, D
                 THE COMMUNIST PARTY OF INDONESIA, 1951-1963.=
                 BERKELEY, UNIVERSITY OF CALIFORNIA PRESS, 1964.                    64
                 COMEL, ELEL, ELNOEL
HINDD -64-ICP    HINDLEY, D
                 THE INDONESIAN COMMUNIST PARTY AND CONFLICT IN THE
                    INTERNATIONAL COMMUNIST MOVEMENT.=
                 THE CHINA QUARTERLY, 19, (JULY-SEPTEMBER 1964),                    64
                    PP. 99-119.
                 ELEL, ELPRNOR
HINDD -65-PCP    HINDLEY, D
                 POLITICAL CONFLICT POTENTIAL, POLITIZATION, AND THE
                    PEASANTRY IN THE UNDERDEVELOPED COUNTRIES.=
                 ASIAN STUDIES, 3, (1965), PP. 470-489.                             65
                 ELNOEL, ELPRNOR
HINDD -67-PPO    HINDLEY, D
                 POLITICAL POWER AND THE OCTOBER 1965 COUP IN INDONESIA.=
                 THE JOURNAL OF ASIA STUDIES, 24, (FEBRUARY 1967),                  67
                    PP. 237-249.
                 COMEL, ELEL, ELNOEL
HINDK -62-SBA    HINDELL, K

```
                    SCARBOROUGH AND BLACKPOOL -- AN ANALYSIS OF SOME VOTES
                       AT THE LABOUR PARTY CONFERENCES OF 1960 AND 1962
                       (GREAT BRITAIN).=
                    THE POLITICAL QUARTERLY, 33, (JULY 1962), PP. 306-320.        62
                    ELEL, ELNOEL
HINTHC-58-DPE       HINTON, HC
                    THE 'DEMOCRATIC PARTIES' -- END OF AN EXPERIMENT
                       (CHINA).=
                    PROBLEMS OF COMMUNISM, 7, (MAY-JUNE 1958), PP. 39-46.         58
                    ELEL, ELNOEL
HINTHC-60-IPP       HINTON, HC
                    INTRA - PARTY POLITICS AND ECONOMIC POLICY IN COMMUNIST
                       CHINA.=
                    WORLD POLITICS, 12, (JULY 1960), PP. 509-524.                 60
                    COMEL, ELEL, ELPRNOR
HINTHC-63-C         HINTON, HC
                    CHINA.=
                    HC HINTON ET AL (EDS), MAJOR GOVERNMENTS OF ASIA, ITHACA,     63
                       CORNELL UNIVERSITY PRESS, 1963, PP. 3-139.
                    ELEL, ELPRNOR
HINTRW-60-PME       HINTON, RWK
                    THE PRIME MINISTER AS AN ELECTED MONARCH (GREAT BRITAIN).=
                    PARLIAMENTARY AFFAIRS, 13, (SUMMER 1960), PP. 297-303.        60
                    ELEL, ELNOEL
HIRAGK-58-CPA       HIRABAYASHI, GK       FATHALLA EL KHATIB M
                    COMMUNICATION AND POLITICAL AWARENESS IN THE
                       VILLAGES OF EGYPT.=
                    THE PUBLIC OPINION QUARTERLY, 22, (FALL 1958),                58
                       PP. 357-363.
                    ELNOEL
HIRSJ -64-OEM       HIRSCHMEIER, J
                    THE ORIGINS OF ENTREPRENEURSHIP IN MEIJI JAPAN.=
                    CAMBRIDGE, HARVARD UNIVERSITY PRESS, 1964.                    64
                    COMEL, ELEL
HIRSRS-61-PCP       HIRSCHFIELD, RS
                    THE POWER OF THE CONTEMPORARY PRESIDENCY (UNITED STATES).=
                    PARLIAMENTARY AFFAIRS, 14, (SUMMER 1961), PP. 353-377.        61
                    COMEL, ELEL, ELNOEL
HIRSRS-62-PPA       HIRSCHFIELD, RS       SWANSON, BE       BLANK, BE
                    A PROFILE OF POLITICAL ACTIVISTS IN MANHATTAN
                       (UNITED STATES).=
                    THE WESTERN POLITICAL QUARTERLY, 15, (SEPTEMBER 1962),        62
                       PP. 489-506.
                    COMEL, ELPRNOR
HITCDG-48-LGH       HITCHNER, DG
                    THE LABOUR GOVERNMENT AND THE HOUSE OF LORDS
                       (GREAT BRITAIN).=
                    THE WESTERN POLITICAL QUARTERLY, 1, (DECEMBER 1948),          48
                       PP. 417-443.
                    ELEL
HITCDG-52-LGH       HITCHNER, DG
                    THE LABOUR GOVERNMENT AND THE HOUSE OF COMMONS
                       (GREAT BRITAIN).=
                    THE WESTERN POLITICAL QUARTERLY, 5, (SEPTEMBER 1952),         52
                       PP. 417-443.
                    COMEL, ELEL
HOAN  -58-NCN       HOANG-VAN-CHI
                    THE NEW CLASS IN NORTH VIET NAM.=
                    SAIGON, CONG DAN PUBLISHING COMPANY, 1958.                    58
                    COMEL, ELEL, ELPRNOR
HOBBEH-54-BPS       HOBBS, EH
                    BEHIND THE PRESIDENT -- A STUDY OF THE EXECUTIVE OFFICE
                       AGENCIES (UNITED STATES).=
                    WASHINGTON, PUBLIC AFFAIRS PRESS, 1954.                       54
                    COMEL, ELEL, ELPRNOR
HOBSEJ-49-TBL       HOBSBAWM, EJ
                    TRENDS IN THE BRITISH LABOR MOVEMENT SINCE 1850.=
                    SCIENCE AND SOCIETY, 13, (1948-1949), PP. 289-312.            49
                    COMEL, ELEL, ELNOEL
HOBSEJ-54-BCP       HOBSBAWM, EJ
                    THE BRITISH COMMUNIST PARTY.=
                    THE POLITICAL QUARTERLY, 25, (JANUARY 1954), PP. 30-43.       54
                    COMEL, ELEL, ELNOEL
HODGDC-59-RCH       HODGES, DC
                    THE ROLE OF CLASSES IN HISTORICAL MATERIALISM.=
                    SCIENCE AND SOCIETY, 23, (WINTER 1959), PP. 16-26.            59
                    DEFEL, ELNOEL, METEL
HODGDC-63-CSI       HODGES, DC
                    CLASS, STRATUM AND INTELLIGENTSIA.=
                    SCIENCE AND SOCIETY, 27, (WINTER 1963), PP. 49-61.            63
                    GNELTH, COMEL, ELEL
HODGHM-64-SSC       HODGES, HM
                    SOCIAL STRATIFICATION -- CLASS IN AMERICA.=
                    CAMBRIDGE, MASSACHUSETTS, SCHENKMAN PUBLISHING COMPANY,       64
```

                        1964.
                        GNELTH, ELNOEL, METEL
HODGJE-48-UBC      HODGETTS, JE
                        UNIFYING THE BRITISH CIVIL SERVICE -- SOME TRENDS AND
                           PROBLEMS.=
                        CANADIAN JOURNAL OF ECONOMICS AND POLITICAL SCIENCE,          48
                           14, (FEBRUARY 1948), PP. 1-19.
                        COMEL
HODGJE-57-CSP      HODGETTS, JE
                        THE CIVIL SERVICE AND POLICY FORMATION (NORTH
                           AMERICA).=
                        CANADIAN JOURNAL OF ECONOMICS AND POLITICAL SCIENCE,          57
                           23, (NOVEMBER 1957), PP. 467-479.
                        ELEL, ELNOEL, ELPRNOR, METEL
HODGLH-62-BSU      HODGES, LH
                        BUSINESSMAN IN THE STATEHOUSE (UNITED STATES).=
                        CHAPEL HILL, THE UNIVERSITY OF NORTH CAROLINA PRESS,          62
                           1962.
                        COMEL, ELEL
HODGT -56-NCA      HODGKIN, T
                        NATIONALISM IN COLONIAL AFRICA.=
                        LONDON, FREDERICK MULLER, 1956.                              56
                        COMEL, ELEL, ELNOEL, ELPRNOR
HODGT -61-APP      HODGKIN, T
                        AFRICAN POLITICAL PARTIES.=
                        LONDON, PENGUIN BOOKS, 1961.                                 61
                        COMEL, ELEL, ELNOEL
HODNG -65-OFS      HODNET, G
                        THE OBKOM FIRST SECRETARIES (SOVIET UNION).=
                        SLAVIC REVIEW, 24, (DECEMBER 1965), PP. 636-652.             65
                        COMEL, ELEL
HOFFD -61-IPD      HOFFMAN, D
                        INTRA - PARTY DEMOCRACY -- A CASE STUDY
                           (UNITED FARMERS OF ONTARIO).=
                        CANADIAN JOURNAL OF ECONOMICS AND POLITICAL SCIENCE,          61
                           27, (MAY 1961), PP. 223-235.
                        ELNOEL
HOFFG -52-NST      HOFF, G
                        NORWAY'S THREE 'TINGS' (PARLIAMENT).=
                        PARLIAMENTARY AFFAIRS, 5, (AUTUMN 1952), PP. 445-448.        52
                        COMEL, ELEL
HOFFGW-62-YNC      HOFFMAN, GW            NEAL, FW
                        YUGOSLAVIA AND THE NEW COMMUNISM.=
                        NEW YORK, THE TWENTIETH CENTURY FUND, 1962.                  62
                        COMEL, ELEL, ELNOEL, ELPRNOR
HOFFS -63-SF       HOFFMAN, S             ET AL
                        IN SEARCH OF FRANCE.=
                        NEW YORK, HARPER AND ROW, 1963.                              63
                        ELEL, ELNOEL, ELPRNOR
HOFFS -67-HLC      HOFFMAN, S
                        HEROIC LEADERSHIP -- THE CASE OF MODERN FRANCE.=
                        LJ EDINGER (ED), POLITICAL LEADERSHIP IN INDUSTRIALIZED       67
                           SOCIETIES, NEW YORK, JOHN WILEY AND SONS, 1967,
                           PP. 108-154.
                        DEFEL, ELEL, ELNOEL, ELPRNOR
HOLCAN-54-PLP      HOLCOMBE, AN
                        PRESIDENTIAL LEADERSHIP AND THE PARTY SYSTEM
                           (UNITED STATES).=
                        YALE REVIEW, 43, (MARCH 1954), PP. 321-335.                  54
                        ELEL, ELNOEL
HOLDM -64-GMP      HOLDEN, M
                        THE GOVERNANCE OF THE METROPOLIS AS A PROBLEM
                           IN DIPLOMACY (UNITED STATES).=
                        THE JOURNAL OF POLITICS, 26, (AUGUST 1964), PP. 627-647. 64
                        DEFEL, ELEL, ELNOEL, ELPRNOR, METEL
HOLDM -66-IBU      HOLDEN-JR, M
                        'IMPERIALISM' IN BUREAUCRACY (UNITED STATES).=
                        THE AMERICAN POLITICAL SCIENCE REVIEW, 60, (DECEMBER          66
                           1966), PP. 943-951.
                        DEFEL, ELEL
HOLLEP-64-LGI      HOLLADER, EP
                        LEADERS, GROUPS, AND INFLUENCE.=
                        NEW YORK, OXFORD UNIVERSITY PRESS, 1964.                     64
                        DEFEL, ELEL, ELNOEL
HOLTA -60-PRL      HOLTZMAN, A
                        PARTY RESPONSIBILITY AND LOYALTY -- NEW RULES IN THE
                           DEMOCRATIC PARTY (UNITED STATES).=
                        THE JOURNAL OF POLITICS, 22, (AUGUST 1960), PP. 485-501. 60
                        ELEL, ELNOEL
HOLTRB-51-FMP      HOLTMAN, RB
                        FRANCE -- MULTI - PARTY DIFFICULTIES.=
                        CURRENT HISTORY, N.S. 20, (JANUARY 1951), PP. 11-15.         51
                        ELEL, ELNOEL
HOLTRT-54-AFR      HOLT, RT

AGE AS A FACTOR IN THE RECRUITMENT OF COMMUNIST
LEADERSHIP (SOVIET UNION).=
THE AMERICAN POLITICAL SCIENCE REVIEW, 48, (SEPTEMBER      54
1954), PP. 486-499.
COMEL
HONEPJ-63-NVN    HONEY, PJ
NORTH VIET NAM'S WORKERS' PARTY AND SOUTH VIET NAM'S
PEOPLE'S REVOLUTIONARY PARTY.=
PACIFIC AFFAIRS, 35, (WINTER 1962-1963), PP. 375-383.      63
ELEL, ELNOEL
HONNFW-58-CCC    HONN, FW
CHINESE COMMUNIST CONTROL OF THE PRESS.=
THE PUBLIC OPINION QUARTERLY, 22, (WINTER 1958),           58
PP. 435-448.
ELEL, ELNOEL
HOPKAG-66-EAP    HOPKINS, AG
ECONOMIC ASPECTS OF POLITICAL MOVEMENTS IN NIGERIA AND IN
THE GOLD COAST, 1918-1939.=
JOURNAL OF AFRICAN HISTORY, 7, (1966), PP. 133-152.        66
COMEL, ELEL
HOPKK -65-EMR    HOPKINS, K
ELITE MOBILITY IN THE ROMAN EMPIRE.=
PAST AND PRESENT, 32, (DECEMBER 1965), PP. 12-26.          65
COMEL
HORNS -60-CCU    HORN, S
THE CABINET AND CONGRESS (UNITED STATES).=
NEW YORK, COLUMBIA UNIVERSITY PRESS, 1960.                 60
ELEL
HOROIL-64-NSE    HOROWITZ, IL (ED)
THE NEW SOCIOLOGY -- ESSAYS IN SOCIAL SCIENCE AND SOCIAL
THEORY IN HONOR OF C. WRIGHT MILLS.=
NEW YORK, OXFORD UNIVERSITY PRESS, 1964.                   64
GNELTH, DEFEL, COMEL, ELEL
HOROIL-64-RBP    HOROWITZ, IL
REVOLUTION IN BRAZIL -- POLITICS AND SOCIETY IN A
DEVELOPING NATION.=
NEW YORK, EP DUTTON AND COMPANY, INC., 1964.               64
ELEL, ELNOEL, ELPRNOR
HOROIL-65-PC     HOROWITZ, IL
PARTY CHARISMA.=
STUDIES IN COMPARATIVE INTERNATIONAL DEVELOPMENT, 1,       65
(1965), PP. 83-97.
DEFEL, ELEL, ELNOEL
HOROIL-67-MEL    HOROWITZ, IL
THE MILITARY ELITES (LATIN AMERICA).=
SM LIPSET AND A SOLARI (EDS), ELITES IN LATIN AMERICA,     67
NEW YORK, OXFORD UNIVERSITY PRESS, 1967, PP. 146-189.
COMEL, ELEL, ELNOEL, ELPRNOR
HOSEBF-63-ETE    HOSELITZ, BF
ENTREPRENEURSHIP AND TRADITIONAL ELITES (ASIA).=
EXPLORATIONS IN ENTREPRENURIAL HISTORY, 1, (FALL 1963),    63
PP. 36-49.
COMEL, ELEL, ELPRNOR
HOTTA -61-ZAP    HOTTINGER, A
ZU-AMA AND PARTIES IN THE LEBANESE CRISIS OF 1958.=
THE MIDDLE EAST JOURNAL, 15, (SPRING 1964), PP. 127-140.   61
COMEL, ELEL, ELNOEL
HOUGJ -67-SEG    HOUGH, J
THE SOVIET ELITE -- 1, GROUPS AND INDIVIDUALS -- 2, IN
WHOSE HANDS THE FUTURE.=
PROBLEMS OF COMMUNISM, 16, (JANUARY-FEBRUARY 1967,         67
APRIL-MARCH 1967), PP. 28-35, PP. 18-25.
COMEL, ELEL, ELPRNOR
HOUGJF-59-TEV    HOUGH, JF
THE TECHNICAL ELITE VS. THE PARTY (SOVIET UNION).=
PROBLEMS OF COMMUNISM, 8, (SEPTEMBER-OCTOBER 1959),        59
PP. 56-59.
COMEL, ELEL
HOUGJF-65-HSR    HOUGH, JF
A HAIRBRAINED SCHEME IN RETROSPECT (SOVIET UNION, PARTY
REORGANIZATION).=
PROBLEMS OF COMMUNISM, 14, (JULY-AUGUST 1965), PP. 26-32.  65
ELEL, ELNOEL
HOUGJF-65-SCR    HOUGH, JF
THE SOVIET CONCEPT OF THE RELATIONSHIP BETWEEN THE
LOWER PARTY ORGANS AND THE STATE ADMINISTRATION.=
SLAVIC REVIEW, 24, (JUNE 1965), PP. 215-240.               65
ELEL, ELNOEL
HOUNFW-57-ECC    HOUN, FW
THE EIGHTH CENTRAL COMMITTEE OF THE CHINESE
COMMUNIST PARTY -- A STUDY OF AN ELITE.=
THE AMERICAN POLITICAL SCIENCE REVIEW, 51, (JUNE 1957),    57
PP. 392-404.
COMEL

HOWAM -59-SGN   HOWARD, M (ED)
                SOLDIERS AND GOVERNMENT -- NINE STUDIES IN CIVIL -
                  MILITARY RELATIONS (WESTERN EUROPE, USSR, JAPAN,
                  LATIN AMERICA, UNITED STATES).=
                BLOOMINGTON, INDIANA UNIVERSITY PRESS, 1959.          59
                COMEL, ELEL, ELNOEL, ELPRNOR
HOWAM -60-CMR   HOWARD, M
                CIVIL - MILITARY RELATIONS IN GREAT BRITAIN AND THE
                  UNITED STATES, 1945-1958.=
                POLITICAL SCIENCE QUARTERLY, 75, (MARCH 1960), PP. 35-46. 60
                ELEL
HOWEI -46-LYI   HOWE, I
                THE LOST YOUNG INTELLECTUAL (UNITED STATES).=
                COMMENTARY, 2, (JULY-DECEMBER 1946), PP. 361-367.     46
                COMEL, ELPRNOR
HOWEJM-48-GCI   HOWE, JM
                THE GEOGRAPHIC COMPOSITION OF INTERNATIONAL
                  SECRETARIATS.=
                COLUMBIA JOURNAL OF INTERNATIONAL AFFAIRS, 2,         48
                  (SPRING 1948), PP. 46-56.
                COMEL
HOWMR -56-ALT   HOWMAN, R
                AFRICAN LEADERSHIP IN TRANSITION -- AN OUTLINE.=
                NADA, 33, (1956), PP. 13-25.                          56
                COMEL, ELEL, ELNOEL
HOWMR -66-CA    HOWMAN, R
                CHIEFTAINSHIP (AFRICA).=
                NADA, 9, (1966), PP. 10-14.                           66
                DEFEL, COMEL
HOYLE -64-ECK   HOYLE, E
                THE ELITE CONCEPT IN KARL MANNHEIM'S SOCIOLOGY OF
                  EDUCATION.=
                THE SOCIOLIGICAL REVIEW, N.S., 12, (MARCH 1964),      64
                  PP. 55-71.
                GNELTH, COMEL
HSIAGT-67-BDP   HSIAO, GT
                THE BACKGROUND AND DEVELOPMENT OF 'THE PROLETARIAN
                  CULTURAL REVOLUTION'.=
                ASIAN SURVEY, 7, (JUNE 1967), PP. 389-404.            67
                ELEL, ELNOEL, ELPRNOR
HSUEC -67-CRL   HSUEH, C
                THE CULTURAL REVOLUTION AND LEADERSHIP CRISIS IN COMMUNIST
                  CHINA.=
                POLITICAL SCIENCE QUARTERLY, 82, (JUNE 1967), PP. 169-190.67
                ELEL, ELNOEL, ELPRNOR
HSUEC--61-HHC   HSUEH, C-T
                HUANG HSING AND THE CHINESE REVOLUTION.=
                STANFORD, STANFORD UNIVERSITY PRESS, 1961.            61
                ELEL, ELNOEL
HSUESS-66-TCD   HSUEH, SS
                TECHNICAL COOPERATION IN DEVELOPMENT ADMINISTRATION IN
                  SOUTH AND SOUTHEAST ASIA.=
                CAG OCCASIONAL PAPERS, BLOOMINGTON, DECEMBER 1966.    66
                DEFEL, ELEL, ELPRNOR
HUBELP-61-CAR   HUBERMAN, LPM
                CUBA -- ANATOMY OF A REVOLUTION.=
                NEW YORK, MONTHLY REVIEW PRESS, 2ND ED., 1961.        61
                COMEL, ELEL, ELNOEL
HUCKCO-51-TCC   HUCKER, CO
                THE TRADITIONAL CHINESE CENSORATE AND THE NEW
                  PEKING REGIME.=
                THE AMERICAN POLITICAL SCIENCE REVIEW, 55, (DECEMBER  51
                  1951), PP. 1041-1057.
                ELNOEL, ELPRNOR
HUDSMC-66-EPP   HUDSON, MC
                THE ELECTORAL PROCESS AND POLITICAL DEVELOPMENT IN
                  LEBANON.=
                THE MIDDLE EAST JOURNAL, 20, (SPRING 1966), PP. 173-186.  66
                COMEL, ELEL, ELNOEL
HUELD -62-CFA   HUELIN, D
                CONFLICTING FORCES IN ARGENTINA.=
                THE WORLD TODAY, 18, (APRIL 1962), PP. 142-152.       62
                ELEL, ELNOEL
HUGHC -56-EPS   HUGHES, C
                THE EXECUTIVE POWER IN SWITZERLAND.=
                PARLIAMENTARY AFFAIRS, 9, (AUTUMN 1956), PP. 439-447. 56
                ELEL
HUGHCA-59-LCP   HUGHES, CA
                THE LEGISLATIVE COUNCILS OF PAPUA, NEW GUINEA.=
                PARLIAMENTARY AFFAIRS, 12, (SPRING 1959), PP. 209-229. 59
                COMEL, ELEL
HUGHCA-60-CRF   HUGHES, CA
                COMMUNAL REPRESENTATION IN THE FIJIAN LEGISLATIVE
                  COUNCIL.=

                    PARLIAMENTARY AFFAIRS, 13, (WINTER 1959-1960), PP. 38-53. 60
                    COMEL, ELEL
HUGHHS-56-IIO      HUGHES, HS
                    IS THE INTELLECTUAL OBSOLETE (UNITED STATES).=
                    COMMENTARY, 22, (OCTOBER 1956), PP. 313-319.                56
                    ELEL, ELNOEL, ELPRNOR
HUGHHS-58-DGP      HUGHES, HS
                    DE GAULLE IN POWER (FRANCE).=
                    COMMENTARY, 26, (SEPTEMBER 1958), PP. 185-193.              58
                    ELEL, ELNOEL, ELPRNOR
HUGHHS-59-CS       HUGHES, HS
                    CONSCIOUSNESS AND SOCIETY.=
                    NEW YORK, ALFRED A KNOPF, 1958.                             59
                    DEFEL
HUGHHS-64-NII      HUGHES, HS
                    THE NEW ITALY AND ITS POLITICS.=
                    COMMENTARY, 38, (OCTOBER 1964), PP. 46-51.                  64
                    ELEL, ELNOEL, ELPRNOR
HUITRK-54-CCC      HUITT, RK
                    THE CONGRESSIONAL COMMITTEE -- A CASE STUDY
                       (UNITED STATES).=
                    THE AMERICAN POLITICAL SCIENCE REVIEW, 48, (JUNE 1954),     54
                       PP. 340-365.
                    ELEL, METEL
HUITRK-57-MCA      HUITT, RK
                    THE MORSE COMMITTEE ASSIGNMENT CONTROVERSY -- A STUDY
                       IN SENATE NORMS (UNITED STATES).=
                    THE AMERICAN POLITICAL SCIENCE REVIEW, 51, (JUNE 1957),     57
                       PP. 313-329.
                    ELEL, ELPRNOR
HUITRK-61-DPL      HUITT, RK
                    DEMOCRATIC PARTY LEADERSHIP IN THE SENATE
                       (UNITED STATES).=
                    THE AMERICAN POLITICAL SCIENCE REVIEW, 55, (JUNE 1961),     61
                       PP. 333-344.
                    ELEL
HUITRK-61-OSA      HUITT, RK
                    THE OUTSIDER IN THE SENATE -- AN ALTERNATIVE ROLE
                       (UNITED STATES).=
                    THE AMERICAN POLITICAL SCIENCE REVIEW, 55, (SEPTEMBER       61
                       1961), PP. 566-575.
                    ELEL, ELPRNOR
HUITRK-65-IDI      HUITT, RK
                    THE INTERNAL DISTRIBUTION OF INFLUENCE -- THE SENATE
                       (UNITED STATES).=
                    DB TRUMAN (ED), THE CONGRESS AND AMERICA'S FUTURE,          65
                       ENGLEWOOD CLIFFS, NEW JERSEY, PRENTICE-HALL,
                       1965, PP. 77-101.
                    DEFEL, ELEL
HULIK -62-KSU      HULICKA, K
                    THE KOMSOMOL (SOVIET UNION).=
                    THE SOUTHWESTERN SOCIAL SCIENCE QUARTERLY, 42,              62
                       (MARCH 1962), PP. 363-373.
                    COMEL, ELEL, ELNOEL
HUNTF -53-CPS      HUNTER, F
                    COMMUNITY POWER STRUCTURE -- A STUDY OF DECISION MAKERS
                       (UNITED STATES).=
                    CHAPEL HILL, UNIVERSITY OF NORTH CAROLINA PRESS, 1953.      53
                    GNELTH, COMEL, ELEL, ELNOEL, ELPRNOR, METEL
HUNTF -59-TLU      HUNTER, F
                    TOP LEADERSHIP USA (UNITED STATES).=
                    CHAPEL HILL, UNIVERSITY OF NORTH CAROLINA PRESS, 1959.      59
                    GNELTH, DEFEL, COMEL, METEL
HUNTG -63-NST      HUNTER, G
                    THE NEW SOCIETIES OF TROPICAL AFRICA.=
                    LONDON, OXFORD UNIVERSITY PRESS, 1963.                      63
                    COMEL, ELEL, ELNOEL
HUNTRN-58-IDS      HUNT, RNC
                    THE IMPORTANCE OF DOCTRINE (SOVIET UNION).=
                    PROBLEMS OF COMMUNISM, 7, (MARCH-APRIL 1958), PP. 10-15.    58
                    ELNOEL, ELPRNOR
HUNTSP-56-CCC      HUNTINGTON, SP
                    CIVILIAN CONTROL AND THE CONSTITUTION (UNITED STATES,
                       MILITARY - CIVIL RELATIONSHIPS).=
                    THE AMERICAN POLITICAL SCIENCE REVIEW, 50,                  56
                       (SEPTEMBER 1956), PP. 676-699.
                    ELEL
HUNTSP-57-SST      HUNTINGTON, SP
                    THE SOLDIER AND THE STATE -- THE THEORY AND POLITICS OF
                       CIVIL - MILITARY RELATIONS (UNITED STATES).=
                    CAMBRIDGE, HARVARD UNIVERSITY PRESS, 1957.                  57
                    DEFEL, ELEL, ELNOEL, ELPRNOR
HUNTSP-61-ICP      HUNTINGTON, SP
                    INTERSERVICE COMPETITION AND THE POLITICAL ROLES OF THE

                         ARMED SERVICES (UNITED STATES).=
                         THE AMERICAN POLITICAL SCIENCE REVIEW, 55,                    61
                            (MARCH 1961), PP. 40-52.
                         ELEL, ELPRNOR
HUNTSP-62-CPM    HUNTINGTON, SP (ED)
                         CHANGING PATTERNS OF MILITARY POLITICS.=
                         NEW YORK, THE FREE PRESS OF GLENCOE, 1962.                    62
                         ELEL, ELNOEL, ELPRNOR
HUNTSP-62-PVW    HUNTINGTON, SP
                         PATTERNS OF VIOLENCE IN WORLD POLITICS.=
                         SP HUNTINGTON (ED), CHANGING PATTERNS OF MILITARY             62
                            POLITICS, GLENCOE, THE FREE PRESS, 1962, PP. 17-51.
                         ELEL, ELNOEL, ELPRNOR
HUNTSP-63-PEM    HUNTINGTON, SP
                         POWER, EXPERTISE AND THE MILITARY PROFESSION
                            (UNITED STATES).=
                         DAEDALUS, 92, (FALL 1963), PP. 785-807.                       63
                         ELEL, ELPRNOR
HUNTSP-65-CRT    HUNTINGTON, SP
                         CONGRESSIONAL RESPONSES TO THE TWENTIETH CENTURY
                            (UNITED STATES).=
                         DB TRUMAN (ED), THE CONGRESS AND AMERICA'S FUTURE,            65
                            ENGLEWOOD CLIFFS, NEW JERSEY, PRENTICE-HALL,
                            1965, PP. 5-31.
                         COMEL, ELEL
HUNTSP-66-PMT    HUNTINGTON, SP
                         THE POLITICAL MODERNIZATION OF TRADITIONAL MONARCHIES.=
                         DAEDALUS, 95, (SUMMER 1966), PP. 763-788.                     66
                         ELEL, ELNOEL, ELPRNOR
HUSSER-46-EPP    HUSSEY, ERJ
                         EDUCATIONAL POLICY AND POLITICAL DEVELOPMENT
                            IN AFRICA.=
                         AFRICA AFFAIRS, 45, (APRIL 1946), PP. 72-79.                  46
                         COMEL, ELPRNOR
HYMAH -58-VTC    HYMAN, H          PAYASLIOGLU, A       FREY, F
                         THE VALUES OF TURKISH COLLEGE YOUTH.=
                         THE PUBLIC OPINION QUARTERLY, 22, (FALL 1958),                58
                            PP. 275-291.
                         ELPRNOR
HYNECS-50-BDU    HYNEMAN, CS
                         BUREAUCRACY IN A DEMOCRACY (UNITED STATES).=
                         NEW YORK, HARPER AND BROTHERS, 1950.                          50
                         COMEL, ELEL, ELNOEL, ELPRNOR
IGNOP -59-HIU    IGNOTUS, P
                         HUNGARIAN INTELLECTUALS UNDER FIRE.=
                         PROBLEMS OF COMMUNISM, 8, (MAY-JUNE 1959), PP. 16-21.         59
                         COMEL, ELEL, ELPRNOR
IGNOP -62-LBA    IGNOTUS, P
                         LITERATURE BEFORE AND AFTER (HUNGARY, REVOLUTION).=
                         SURVEY--A JOURNAL OF SOVIET AND EAST EUROPEAN STUDIES,        62
                            40, (JANUARY 1962), PP. 96-105.
                         ELEL, ELPRNOR
IKE,N -49-DCJ    IKE, N
                         THE DEVELOPMENT OF CAPITALISM IN JAPAN.=
                         PACIFIC AFFAIRS, 22, (JUNE 1949), PP. 185-190.                49
                         ELPRNOR
IKELJ -64-PYE    IKELLE-MATIBA, J
                         THE PLACE OF YOUTH IN THE ECONOMIC AND CULTURAL
                            CONTEXT OF THE CAMEROON.=
                         INTERNATIONAL JOURNAL OF ADULT AND YOUTH EDUCATION,           64
                            16, (OCTOBER 1964), PP. 185-191.
                         ELEL, ELNOEL
INAY(E-63-BDP    INAYATULLAH, (ED)
                         BUREAUCRACY AND DEVELOPMENT IN PAKISTAN.=
                         PESHAWAR, PAKISTAN ACADEMY FOR RURAL DEVELOPMENT, 1963.       63
                         COMEL, ELEL, ELNOEL
INKEA -50-POS    INKELES, A
                         PUBLIC OPINION IN SOVIET RUSSIA -- A STUDY IN MASS
                            PERSUASION.=
                         CAMBRIDGE, HARVARD UNIVERSITY PRESS, 1950.                    50
                         ELNOEL
INKEA -50-SSM    INKELES, A
                         SOCIAL STRATIFICATION AND MOBILITY IN THE
                            SOVIET UNION -- 1945-1950.=
                         AMERICAN SOCIOLOGICAL REVIEW, 15, (AUGUST 1950),              50
                            PP. 465-479.
                         COMEL, ELEL, ELNOEL
INKEA -53-CLE    INKELES, A          GEIGER, K
                         CRITICAL LETTERS TO THE EDITORS OF THE SOVIET PRESS --
                            SOCIAL CHARACTERISTICS AND INTERRELATIONS OF CRITICS
                            AND THE CRITICIZED.=
                         AMERICAN SOCIOLOGICAL REVIEW, 18, (FEBRUARY 1953),            53
                            PP. 12-22.
                         ELNOEL

```
INKEA -59-SCD   INKELES, A          BAUER, RA
                THE SOVIET CITIZEN -- DAILY LIFE IN A TOTALITARIAN
                    SOCIETY.=
                CAMBRIDGE, HARVARD UNIVERSITY PRESS, 1959.            59
                ELNOEL
INNEFM-53-POP   INNES, FM
                THE POLITICAL OUTLOOK IN PAKISTAN.=
                PACIFIC AFFAIRS, 26, (DECEMBER 1953), PP. 303-317.    53
                ELEL, ELNOEL, ELPRNOR
IONEG -67-PEC   IONESCU, G
                THE POLITICS OF THE EUROPEAN COMMUNIST STATES (BULGARIA,
                    CZECHOSLOVAKIA, HUNGARY, EAST GERMANY, POLAND,
                    RUMANIA, SOVIET UNION, YUGOSLAVIA).=
                NEW YORK, FREDERICK A PRAEGER, 1967.                  67
                COMEL, ELEL, ELNOEL
IRISMD-58-OMP   IRISH, MD
                THE ORGANIZATION MAN IN THE PRESIDENCY (UNITED STATES).=
                THE JOURNAL OF POLITICS, 20, (MAY 1958), PP. 259-277.  58
                ELEL, ELNOEL, ELPRNOR
IRISMD-60-POA   IRISH, MD
                PUBLIC OPINION AND AMERICAN FOREIGN POLICY --
                    THE QUEMOY CRISIS OF 1958.=
                THE POLITICAL QUARTERLY, 31, (APRIL-JUNE 1960),       60
                    PP. 151-162.
                ELNOEL
ISAAHR-51-TCR   ISAACS, HR
                THE TRAGEDY OF THE CHINESE REVOLUTION.=
                STANFORD, STANFORD UNIVERSITY PRESS, 1951.            51
                COMEL, ELEL, ELNOEL, ELPRNOR
ISSAC -55-ECM   ISSAWI, C
                THE ENTREPRENEUR CLASS (MIDDLE EAST).=
                ITHACA, CORNELL UNIVERSITY PRESS, 1955, PP. 116-136.  55
                ELEL, ELPRNOR
ITALR -61-NLA   ITALIAANDER, R
                THE NEW LEADERS OF AFRICA.=
                ENGLEWOOD CLIFFS, NEW JERSEY, PRENTICE-HALL, 1961.    61
                COMEL, ELPRNOR
IVELV -49-PRD   IVELLA, V
                PARTY RULE IN A DEMOCRATIC STATE (ITALY).=
                FOREIGN AFFAIRS, 28, (OCTOBER 1949), PP. 75-83.       49
                ELEL, ELNOEL
JACKC -49-YGT   JACKSON, C
                THE YOUNGER GENERATION IN THE THREE DOMINIONS (INDIA,
                    PAKISTAN, CEYLON).=
                ASIATIC REVIEW, N.S., 45, (JUNE 1949), PP. 684-688.   49
                ELEL, ELNOEL, ELPRNOR
JACOCE-63-LPL   JACOB, CE
                THE LIMITS OF PRESIDENTIAL LEADERSHIP (UNITED STATES).=
                SOUTH ATLANTIC QUARTERLY, 62, (AUTUMN 1963), PP. 461-473. 63
                ELEL
JACOH -62-IRE   JACOB, H
                INITIAL RECRUITMENT OF ELECTED OFFICIALS IN THE
                    U.S. (UNITED STATES) -- A MODEL.=
                THE JOURNAL OF POLITICS, 24, (NOVEMBER 1962),         62
                    PP. 703-716.
                DEFEL, COMEL, ELPRNOR, METEL
JACOH -63-GAS   JACOB, H
                GERMAN ADMINISTRATION SINCE BISMARCK -- CENTRAL AUTHORITY
                    VERSUS LOCAL AUTONOMY.=
                NEW HAVEN, YALE UNIVERSITY PRESS, 1963.               63
                DEFEL, ELEL, ELNOEL
JACOHB-59-OPV   JACOBINI, HB
                OBSERVATIONS ON THE PHILIPPINE VICE-PRESIDENCY.=
                PHILIPPINE JOURNAL OF PUBLIC ADMINISTRATION, 3,       59
                    (OCTOBER 1959), PP. 413-425.
                COMEL, ELEL
JACOPE-62-FVP   JACOB, PE         FLICK, JJ          SCHUCKMAN, HL
                FUNCTION OF VALUES IN THE POLICY PROCESS -- ELITE GROUPS
                    (UNITED STATES).=
                THE AMERICAN BEHAVIORAL SCIENTIST, 2,                 62
                    (SUPPLEMENT MAY 1962), PP. 33-34.
                GNELTH
JAHOG -54-SBW   JAHODA, G
                THE SOCIAL BACKGROUND OF A WEST AFRICAN STUDENT
                    POPULATION -- 1 -- 2.=
                THE BRITISH JOURNAL OF SOCIOLOGY, 5,6, (DECEMBER 1954, 54
                    MARCH 1955), PP. 355-365, PP. 71-79.
                COMEL, ELEL, ELNOEL, ELPRNOR
JAMERC-58-TUD   JAMES, RC
                TRADE UNION DEMOCRACY -- INDIAN TEXTILES.=
                THE WESTERN POLITICAL QUARTERLY, 11, (SEPTEMBER 1958), 58
                    PP. 563-573.
                ELEL, ELNOEL, ELPRNOR
JAN,GP-62-MPC   JAN, GP
```

```
                   MINOR PARTIES IN COMMUNIST CHINA.=
                   CURRENT HISTORY, N. S., 43, (SEPTEMBER 1962),                62
                      PP. 174-177.
                   COMEL, ELEL
JANDKF-60-TEC      JANDA, KF
                   TOWARDS THE EXPLICATION OF THE CONCEPT OF LEADERSHIP
                      IN TERMS OF THE CONCEPT OF POWER.=
                   HUMAN RELATIONS, 13, (NOVEMBER 1960), PP. 345-364.           60
                   GNELTH, DEFEL, ELNOEL, METEL
JANIIL-59-DCT      JANIS, IL
                   DECISIONAL CONFLICTS -- A THEORETICAL ANALYSIS (GERMANY,
                      GREAT BRITAIN, UNITED STATES).=
                   JOURNAL OF CONFLICT RESOLUTION, 3, (MARCH 1959), PP. 6-27.59
                   DEFEL, ELEL, ELNOEL, ELPRNOR
JANIM -63-EGT      JANICKE, M
                   EAST GERMANY TODAY.=
                   PROBLEMS OF COMMUNISM, 12, (JULY-AUGUST 1963), PP. 1-8.      63
                   ELNOEL, ELPRNOR
JANOGE-63-BSN      JANOSIK, GE
                   BRITAIN'S NEW LABOUR LEADERS.=
                   ORBIS, 7, (FALL 1963), PP. 518-536.                         63
                   COMEL, ELPRNOR
JANOM -54-SAP      JANOWITZ, M
                   THE SYSTEMATIC ANALYSIS OF POLITICAL BIOGRAPHY.=
                   WORLD POLITICS, 6, (APRIL 1954), PP. 407-412.               54
                   METEL
JANOM -55-CPD      JANOWITZ, M              MARVICK, D
                   COMPETITIVE PRESSURE AND DEMOCRATIC CONSENT -- AN
                      INTERPRETATION OF THE 1952 PRESIDENTIAL ELECTION
                      (UNITED STATES).=
                   THE PUBLIC OPINION QUARTERLY, 19, (WINTER 1955),            55
                      PP. 381-400.
                   ELNOEL
JANOM -56-SSC      JANOWITZ, M
                   SOCIAL STRATIFICATION AND THE COMPARATIVE ANALYSIS
                      OF ELITES.=
                   SOCIAL FORCES, 35, (OCTOBER 1956), PP. 81-85.               56
                   GNELTH, ELEL, ELPRNOR
JANOM -57-MES      JANOWITZ, M
                   MILITARY ELITES AND THE STUDY OF WAR (FRANCE, GERMANY,
                      ITALY, SOVIET UNION, UNITED STATES).=
                   THE JOURNAL OF CONFLICT RESOLUTION, 1, (MARCH 1957),        57
                      PP. 9-18.
                   DEFEL, COMEL, ELEL, ELPRNOR
JANOM -58-BPS      JANOWITZ, M              DELANY, W
                   THE BUREAUCRAT AND THE PUBLIC -- A STUDY OF INFORMATIONAL
                      PERSPECTIVES (UNITED STATES).=
                   ADMINISTRATIVE SCIENCE QUARTERLY, 2, (1957-1958),           58
                      PP. 141-162.
                   ELNOEL, ELPRNOR
JANOM -58-PAP      JANOWITZ, M         WRIGHT, D         DELANY, W
                   PUBLIC ADMINISTRATION AND THE PUBLIC -- PERSPECTIVES
                      TOWARD GOVERNMENT IN A METROPOLITAN COMMUNITY
                      (UNITED STATES).=
                   ANN ARBOR, MICHIGAN, THE UNIVERSITY OF MICHIGAN PRESS,      58
                      INSTITUTE OF PUBLIC ADMINISTRATION, 1958.
                   COMEL, ELNOEL, ELPRNOR
JANOM -58-SSM      JANOWITZ, M
                   SOCIAL STRATIFICATION AND MOBILITY IN WESTERN GERMANY.=
                   THE AMERICAN JOURNAL OF SOCIOLOGY, 64, (JULY 1958),         58
                      PP. 6-24.
                   COMEL, ELEL, ELNOEL
JANOM -59-CPO      JANOWITZ, M
                   CHANGING PATTERNS OF ORGANIZATIONAL AUTHORITY --
                      THE MILITARY ESTABLISHMENT (UNITED STATES).=
                   ADMINISTRATIVE SCIENCE QUARTERLY, 3, (MARCH 1959),          59
                      PP. 473-493.
                   ELEL, ELPRNOR
JANOM -60-PSS      JANOWITZ, M
                   THE PROFESSIONAL SOLDIER -- A SOCIAL AND
                      POLITICAL PORTRAIT (UNITED STATES).=
                   GLENCOE, ILLINOIS, THE FREE PRESS, 1960.                    60
                   COMEL, ELEL, ELPRNOR, METEL
JANOM -61-CPS      JANOWITZ, M (ED)
                   COMMUNITY POLITICAL SYSTEMS (UNITED STATES).=
                   GLENCOE, THE FREE PRESS, 1961.                              61
                   DEFEL, ELEL, ELNOEL, ELPRNOR
JANOM -62-CPS      JANOWITZ, M
                   COMMUNITY AND 'POLICY SCIENCE' RESEARCH
                      (UNITED STATES).=
                   THE PUBLIC OPINION QUARTERLY, 26, (FALL 1962),              62
                      PP. 398-410.
                   METEL
JANOM -64-MPD      JANOWITZ, M (ED)
```

THE MILITARY IN THE POLITICAL DEVELOPMENT OF NEW
  NATIONS -- AN ESSAY IN COMPARATIVE ANALYSIS (ASIA,
  AFRICA, MIDDLE EAST).=
CHICAGO, UNIVERSITY OF CHICAGO PRESS, 1964.                64
DEFEL, COMEL, ELEL, ELNOEL, ELPRNOR
JANOM  -64-NMC   JANOWITZ, M (ED)
THE NEW MILITARY -- CHANGING PATTERNS OF
  ORGANIZATION (UNITED STATES).=
NEW YORK, RUSSELL SAGE FOUNDATION, 1964.                  64
COMEL, ELEL, ELPRNOR
JANOM  -65-AFW   JANOWITZ, M
ARMED FORCES IN WESTERN EUROPE -- UNITY AND DIVERSITY.=
EUROPEAN JOURNAL OF SOCIOLOGY, 68 (1965), PP. 225-237.    65
COMEL, ELEL, ELNOEL, ELPRNOR
JANOM  -65-SME   JANOWITZ, M         LITTLE, R
SOCIOLOGY AND THE MILITARY ESTABLISHMENT (UNITED STATES).=
NEW YORK, RUSSELL SAGE FOUNDATION, 1965.                  65
COMEL, METEL
JANSMB-57-EVP   JANSEN, MB
EDUCATION, VALUES AND POLITICS IN JAPAN.=
FOREIGN AFFAIRS, 35, (JULY 1957), PP. 666-678.            57
ELNOEL, ELPRNOR
JCC    -51-SWP   JCC
STUDENTS IN WORLD POLITICS.=
THE WORLD TODAY, 7, (AUGUST 1951), PP. 346-356.           51
ELEL
JELAC  -63-BTE   JELAVICH, C          JELAVICH, B (EDS)
THE BALKANS IN TRANSITION -- ESSAYS ON THE DEVELOPMENT
  OF BALKAN LIFE AND POLITICS SINCE THE EIGHTEENTH
  CENTURY.=
BERKELEY, UNIVERSITY OF CALIFORNIA PRESS, 1963.           63
COMEL, ELEL, ELNOEL, ELPRNOR
JELEJA-59-GPI   JELENSKI, KA
THE GENEALOGY OF THE POLISH INTELLIGENTSIA.=
SOVIET SURVEY--A QUARTERLY REVIEW OF CULTURAL TRENDS,     59
  29, (JULY-SEPTEMBER 1959), PP. 112-120.
COMEL, ELEL, ELPRNOR
JELEKA-58-RPG   JELENSKI, KA
REVISIONISM -- PRAGMATISM -- GOMULKAISM (POLAND).=
PROBLEMS OF COMMUNISM, 7, (MAY-JUNE 1958), PP. 5-13.      58
COMEL, ELEL, ELPRNOR
JENNEE-60-ALP   JENNINGS, EE
AN ANATOMY OF LEADERSHIP -- PRINCES, HEROES, AND
  SUPERMEN (UNITED STATES).=
NEW YORK, HARPER AND ROW, 1960.                           60
ELPRNOR
JENNEE-62-EAB   JENNINGS, EE
THE EXECUTIVE -- AUTOCRAT, BUREAUCRAT, DEMOCRAT
  (UNITED STATES).=
NEW YORK, HARPER AND ROW, 1962.                           62
COMEL, ELEL, ELNOEL, ELPRNOR
JENNMK-64-CIE   JENNINGS, MK
COMMUNITY INFLUENTIALS -- THE ELITES OF ATLANTA
  (UNITED STATES).=
NEW YORK, THE FREE PRESS OF GLENCOE, 1964.                64
DEFEL, COMEL, ELEL, ELNOEL, ELPRNOR, METEL
JENNMK-64-PAC   JENNINGS, MK
PUBLIC ADMINISTRATORS AND COMMUNITY DECISION MAKING.=
ADMINISTRATIVE SCIENCE QUARTERLY, 8, (1963-1964),         64
  PP. 18-43.
DEFEL, METEL
JENNMK-66-TLP   JENNINGS, MK         CUMMINGS-JR, MC       KILPATRICK, FP
TRUSTED LEADERS -- PERCEPTIONS OF APPOINTED FEDERAL
  OFFICIALS (UNITED STATES).=
THE PUBLIC OPINION QUARTERLY, 30, (FALL 1966),            66
  PP. 368-384.
ELEL, ELNOEL, ELPRNOR
JENNWI-54-PCS   JENNINGS, WI
POLITICS IN CEYLON SINCE 1952.=
PACIFIC AFFAIRS, 27, (DECEMBER 1954), PP. 338-352.        54
ELEL, ELNOEL
JENNWI-57-PGB   JENNINGS, WI
PARLIAMENT (GREAT BRITAIN).=
2ND ED, CAMBRIDGE, CAMBRIDGE UNIVERSITY PRESS, 1957.      57
COMEL, ELEL, ELNOEL, ELPRNOR
JENNWI-59-CGG   JENNINGS, WI
CABINET GOVERNMENT (GREAT BRITAIN).=
LONDON, CAMBRIDGE UNIVERSITY PRESS, 1959.                 59
COMEL, ELEL, ELNOEL, ELPRNOR
JESSB  -55-DAS   JESSIE, B
DIMENSIONS AND AXES OF SUPREME COURT DECISIONS -- A STUDY
  IN THE SOCIOLOGY OF CONFLICT (UNITED STATES).=
SOCIAL FORCES, 34, (OCTOBER 1955), PP. 19-27.             55
ELEL, ELPRNOR, METEL

JESSPC-55-ICS    JESSUP, PC
                 THE INTERNATIONAL CIVIL SERVANT AND HIS LOYALTIES.=
                 JOURNAL OF INTERNATIONAL AFFAIRS, 9, (APRIL 1955),          55
                     PP. 55-61.
                 ELPRNOR
JEWEME-55-PVA    JEWELL, ME
                 PARTY VOTING IN AMERICAN STATE LEGISLATURES.=
                 THE AMERICAN POLITICAL SCIENCE REVIEW, 49, (SEPTEMBER       55
                     1959), PP. 773-791.
                 ELEL, ELNOEL
JEWEME-59-EDS    JEWELL, ME
                 EVALUATING THE DECLINE OF SOUTHERN INTERNATIONALISM
                     THROUGH SENATORIAL ROLL CALL VOTES (UNITED STATES).=
                 THE JOURNAL OF POLITICS, 21, (NOVEMBER 1959), PP. 624-646 59
                 ELEL, ELNOEL, ELPRNOR, METEL
JEWEME-59-SRP    JEWELL, ME
                 THE SENATE REPUBLICAN POLICY COMMITTEE AND FOREIGN
                     POLICY (UNITED STATES).=
                 THE WESTERN POLITICAL QUARTERLY, 12, (DECEMBER 1959),        59
                     PP. 966-980.
                 ELEL, ELPRNOR
JEWEME-62-PR     JEWELL, ME (ED)
                 THE POLITICS OF REAPPORTIONMENT
                     (UNITED STATES).=
                 NEW YORK, ATHERTON PRESS, 1962.                             62
                 COMEL, ELEL, ELNOEL, ELPRNOR
JEWEME-62-SPF    JEWELL, ME
                 SENATORIAL POLITICS AND FOREIGN POLICY (UNITED STATES).=
                 LEXINGTON, KENTUCKY, UNIVERSITY OF KENTUCKY PRESS, 1962.    62
                 ELEL, ELPRNOR
JEWEME-64-SLS    JEWELL, ME
                 STATE LEGISLATURES IN SOUTHERN POLITICS (UNITED STATES).=
                 THE JOURNAL OF POLITICS, 26, (FEBRUARY 1964),               64
                     PP. 177-196.
                 ELEL, ELNOEL, ELPRNOR
JIANJP-62-PCP    JIANG, JPL
                 POLITICAL CHANGE AND PARIAH ENTREPRENEURSHIP
                     (PHILIPPINES).=
                 PHILLIPINE JOURNAL OF PUBLIC ADMINISTRATION, 6,             62
                     (OCTOBER 1962), PP. 289-298.
                 ELEL, ELNOEL
JOESJ -60-NRP    JOESTEN, J
                 NASSER -- THE RISE TO POWER (EGYPT).=
                 LONDON, ODHAMS PRESS, 1960.                                 60
                 COMEL, ELEL, ELNOEL, ELPRNOR
JOFFE -64-CBO    JOFFE, E
                 THE CONFLICT BETWEEN OLD AND NEW IN THE CHINESE ARMY.=
                 THE CHINA QUARTERLY, 18, (APRIL-JUNE 1964), PP. 118-140.    64
                 COMEL, ELEL
JOFFE -65-PAP    JOFFE, E
                 PARTY AND ARMY -- PROFESSIONALISM AND POLITICAL CONTROL IN
                     THE CHINESE OFFICER CORPS, 1949-1964.=
                 CAMBRIDGE, MASSACHUSETTS, EAST ASIAN RESEARCH CENTER,       65
                     HARVARD UNIVERSITY, 1965.
                 COMEL, ELEL, ELPRNOR
JOHNC -66-RC     JOHNSON, C
                 REVOLUTIONARY CHANGE.=
                 BOSTON, LITTLE, BROWN AND CO., 1966.                        66
                 DEFEL, ELEL, ELNOEL, ELPRNOR
JOHNCA-62-PNC    JOHNSON, CA
                 PEASANT NATIONALISM AND COMMUNIST POWER -- THE EMERGENCE
                     OF REVOLUTIONARY CHINA, 1937-1945.=
                 STANFORD, STANFORD UNIVERSITY PRESS, 1962.                  62
                 COMEL, ELEL, ELNOEL, ELPRNOR
JOHNJJ-51-FFD    JOHNSON, JJ
                 FOREIGN FACTORS IN DICTATORSHIP IN LATIN AMERICA.=
                 PACIFIC HISTORICAL REVIEW, 20, (MAY 1951), PP. 127-141.     51
                 COMEL, ELEL
JOHNJJ-58-PCL    JOHNSON, JJ
                 POLITICAL CHANGE IN LATIN AMERICA -- THE EMERGENCE
                     OF THE MIDDLE SECTORS.=
                 STANFORD, STANFORD UNIVERSITY PRESS, 1958.                  58
                 COMEL, ELEL, ELNOEL, ELPRNOR
JOHNJJ-61-WLA    JOHNSON, JJ
                 WHITHER THE LATIN AMERICAN MIDDLE SECTORS.=
                 VIRGINIA QUARTERLY REVIEW, 37, (AUTUMN 1961),               61
                     PP. 508-521.
                 COMEL, ELEL, ELPRNOR
JOHNJJ-62-LAM    JOHNSON, JJ
                 THE LATIN AMERICAN MILITARY AS A POLITICALLY
                     COMPETING GROUP IN TRANSITIONAL SOCIETY.=
                 JJ JOHNSON (ED), THE ROLE OF THE MILITARY IN               62
                     UNDERDEVELOPED COUNTRIES, PRINCETON, NEW JERSEY,
                     PRINCETON UNIVERSITY PRESS, 1962, PP. 91-130.

```
                    ELEL, ELNOEL, ELPRNOR
JOHNJJ-64-CCL       JOHNSON, JJ
                    CONTINUITY AND CHANGE IN LATIN AMERICA.=
                    STANFORD, STANFORD UNIVERSITY PRESS, 1964.                    64
                    COMEL, ELEL, ELPRNOR
JOHNJJ-64-MSL       JOHNSON, JJ
                    THE MILITARY AND SOCIETY IN LATIN AMERICA.=
                    STANFORD, STANFORD UNIVERSITY PRESS, 1964.                    64
                    COMEL, ELEL, ELNOEL, ELPRNOR
JOHNJJ-65-LAN       JOHNSON, JJ
                    THE LATIN AMERICAN NATIONALISM.=
                    YALE REVIEW, 54, (WINTER 1965), PP. 187-204.                  65
                    ELEL, ELPRNOR
JOHNKF-65-ICR       JOHNSON, KF
                    IDEOLOGICAL CORRELATES OF RIGHT WING POLITICAL
                       ALIENATION IN MEXICO.=
                    THE AMERICAN POLITICAL SCIENCE REVIEW, 59, (SEPTEMBER         65
                       1965), PP. 656-664.
                    COMEL, ELEL, ELNOEL, ELPRNOR
-JOHNLL-65-USB      JOHNSON, LL
                    U.S. BUSINESS INTERESTS IN CUBA AND THE RISE OF CASTRO.=
                    WORLD POLITICS, 17, (APRIL 1965), PP. 440-459.                65
                    ELEL, ELPRNOR
JOHNP -63-RIW       JOHNSON, P
                    THE REGIME AND THE INTELLECTUALS -- A WINDOW ON PARTY
                       POLITICS (SOVIET UNION).=
                    PROBLEMS OF COMMUNISM, 12, (WINTER 1962-SUMMER 1963),         63
                       PP. 1-27.
                    ELEL, ELPRNOR
JOHNSD-62-EPS       JOHNSTON, SD
                    ELECTION POLITICS AND SOCIAL CHANGE IN ISRAEL.=
                    THE MIDDLE EAST JOURNAL, 16, (SUMMER 1962), PP. 309-326.      62
                    ELEL, ELNOEL
JOLLJ -54-IGP       JOLL, J
                    INTELLECTUALS AND GERMAN POLITICS.=
                    OCCIDENTE, 10, (JANUARY-FEBRUARY 1954), PP. 28-38.            54
                    ELEL, ELPRNOR
JONECO-61-RCC       JONES, CO
                    REPRESENTATION IN CONGRESS -- THE CASE OF THE HOUSE
                       AGRICULTURE COMMITTEE (UNITED STATES).=
                    THE AMERICAN POLITICAL SCIENCE REVIEW, 55,                    61
                       (JUNE 1961), PP. 358-367.
                    COMEL, ELEL, ELNOEL, ELPRNOR
JONECO-63-IPC       JONES, CO
                    INTER - PARTY COMPETITION IN BRITAIN , 1950-1959.=
                    PARLIAMENTARY AFFAIRS, 17, (1963), PP. 50-56.                 63
                    ELEL
JONECO-64-PPM       JONES, CO
                    PARTY AND POLICY-MAKING -- THE HOUSE REPUBLICAN POLICY
                       COMMITTEE (UNITED STATES).=
                    NEW BRUNSWICK, NEW JERSEY, RUTGERS UNIVERSITY PRESS, 1964.64
                    ELEL, ELPRNOR
JONECO-65-RPA       JONES, CO
                    THE REPUBLICAN PARTY IN AMERICAN POLITICS.=
                    NEW YORK, THE MACMILLAN COMPANY, 1965.                        65
                    ELEL, ELNOEL, ELPRNOR
JONEMW-63-PGG       JONES, MWH
                    POLITICIANS AND GENERALS (GREAT BRITAIN).=
                    CAMBRIDGE JOURNAL, 6, (OCTOBER 1963), PP. 3-22.               63
                    ELEL, ELPRNOR
JORAD -60-SSG       JORAVSKY, D
                    SOVIET SCIENTISTS AND THE GREAT BREAK.=
                    DAEDALUS, 89, (SUMMER 1960), PP. 562-580.                     60
                    ELEL, ELPRNOR
JOSEA -58-PSB       JOSEY, A
                    THE POLITICAL SIGNIFICANCE OF THE BURMA WORKERS PARTY.=
                    PACIFIC AFFAIRS, 31, (DECEMBER 1958), PP. 372-379.            58
                    ELEL, ELNOEL
JOSEE -52-ILF       JOSEPH, E
                    IRRATIONAL LEADERSHIP IN FORMAL ORGANIZATIONS
                       (UNITED STATES).=
                    SOCIAL FORCES, 31, (DECEMBER 1952), PP. 109-117.              52
                    DEFEL
JULIPH-61-ICS       JULIVER, PH
                    INTERPARLIAMENTARY CONTACTS IN SOVIET FOREIGN POLICY.=
                    THE AMERICAN SLAVIC AND EAST EUROPEAN REVIEW, 20,             61
                       (FEBRUARY 1961), PP. 25-39.
                    ELEL
JUMPR -57-MBP       JUMPER, R
                    MANDARIN BUREAUCRACY AND POLITICS IN SOUTH VIETNAM.=
                    PACIFIC AFFAIRS, 30, (MARCH 1957), PP. 47-58.                 57
                    ELEL, ELNOEL
JUMPR -57-PPA       JUMPER, R
                    PROBLEMS OF PUBLIC ADMINISTRATION IN SOUTH VIETNAM.=
```

```
                    FAR EASTERN SURVEY, 26, (DECEMBER 1957), PP. 183-190.        57
                    COMEL, ELEL, ELNOEL
JUMPR -57-RPF       JUMPER, R
                    RECRUITMENT PROBLEMS OF THE FRENCH HIGHER CIVIL
                        SERVICE -- AN AMERICAN APPRAISAL.=
                    THE WESTERN POLITICAL QUARTERLY, 10, (MARCH 1957),           57
                        PP. 38-48.
                    COMEL
JUMPR -59-SCS       JUMPER, R
                    SECTS AND COMMUNISM IN SOUTH VIETNAM.=
                    ORBIS, 3, (SPRING 1959), PP. 85-96.                          59
                    ELEL, ELNOEL
JURCA -60-ARB       JURCZENKO, A
                    ADMINISTRATIVE REORGANIZATION AND THE BUILDING OF
                        COMMUNISM (SOVIET UNION).=
                    BULLETIN INSTITUTE FOR THE STUDY OF THE USSR, 7,             60
                        (FEBRUARY 1960), PP. 14-22.
                    ELEL
KABYS -63-RPL       KABYSH, S
                    THE REORGANIZATION OF PARTY LEADERSHIP IN AGRICULTURE
                        (SOVIET UNION).=
                    BULLETIN INSTITUTE FOR THE STUDY OF THE USSR, 10,            63
                        (MAY 1963), PP. 45-51.
                    COMEL, ELEL
KAHIGM-49-IRE       KAHIN, GM
                    INDIRECT RULE IN EAST INDONESIA.=
                    PACIFIC AFFAIRS, 22, (SEPTEMBER 1949), PP. 227-238.          49
                    ELEL, ELNOEL
KAMAM -64-TSV       KAMALIZA, M
                    TANGANYIKA'S VIEW OF LABOUR'S ROLE.=
                    EAST AFRICA JOURNAL, (NOVEMBER 1964), PP. 9-16.              64
                    ELEL, ELPRNOR
KAMMGM-48-EWP       KAMMERER, GM
                    AN EVALUATION OF WARTIME PERSONNEL ADMINISTRATION
                        (UNITED STATES).=
                    THE JOURNAL OF POLITICS, 10, (FEBRUARY 1948), PP. 49-72.  48
                    ELEL
KAMMGM-53-ACL       KAMMERER, GM
                    ADVISORY COMMITTEES IN THE LEGISLATIVE
                        PROCESS (UNITED STATES).=
                    THE JOURNAL OF POLITICS, 15, (MAY 1953), PP. 171-196.        53
                    ELEL, ELNOEL
KAMMGM-54-GCA       KAMMERER, GM
                    THE GOVERNOR AS CHIEF ADMINISTRATOR IN KENTUCKY
                        (UNITED STATES).=
                    THE JOURNAL OF POLITICS, 16, (MAY 1954), PP. 236-256.        54
                    ELEL, ELNOEL
KAMMGM-64-ULD       KAMMERER, GM          DEGROVE, JM
                    URBAN LEADERSHIP DURING CHANGE (UNITED STATES).=
                    THE ANNALS OF THE AMERICAN ACADEMY OF POLITICAL AND          64
                        SOCIAL SCIENCE, 353, (MAY 1964), PP. 95-106.
                    DEFEL, COMEL
KAMPMM-54-LBI       KAMPELMAN, MM
                    THE LEGISLATIVE BUREAUCRACY -- ITS RESPONSE TO POLITICAL
                        CHANGE (UNITED STATES).=
                    THE JOURNAL OF POLITICS, 16, (AUGUST 1954), PP. 539-550.  54
                    ELEL, ELPRNOR
KANTH -52-ASP       KANTOR, H
                    THE APRISTA SEARCH FOR A PROGRAM APPLICABLE TO
                        LATIN AMERICA (PERU).=
                    THE WESTERN POLITICAL QUARTERLY, 5, (DECEMBER 1952),         52
                        PP. 578-584.
                    ELPRNOR
KANTH -53-IPP       KANTOR, H
                    THE IDEOLOGY AND PROGRAM OF THE PERUVIAN
                        APRISTA MOVEMENT.=
                    BERKELEY, UNIVERSITY OF CALIFORNIA PRESS, 1953.              53
                    COMEL, ELEL, ELNOEL, ELPRNOR
KANTH -54-APS       KANTOR, H
                    APRISMO -- PERU'S INDIGENOUS POLITICAL THEORY.=
                    SOUTH ATLANTIC QUARTERLY, 53, (JANUARY 1954), PP. 1-9.       54
                    ELPRNOR
KANTH -59-DAD       KANTOR, H
                    THE DEVELOPMENT OF ACCION DEMOCRATICA DE VENEZUELA.=
                    JOURNAL OF INTER-AMERICAN STUDIES, 1, (APRIL 1959),          59
                        PP. 237-255.
                    COMEL, ELPRNOR
KAPLH -63-URP       KAPLAN, H
                    URBAN RENEWAL POLITICS -- SLUM CLEARANCE IN NEWARK
                        (UNITED STATES).=
                    NEW YORK, COLUMBIA UNIVERSITY PRESS, 1963.                   63
                    ELEL, ELNOEL, ELPRNOR
KAPLZ -54-MBE       KAPLINSKY, Z
                    THE MUSLIM BROTHERHOOD (EGYPT).=
```

```
                        MIDDLE EASTERN AFFAIRS, 5, (DECEMBER 1954), PP. 377-385.    54
                        ELEL, ELNOEL
KARAA -61-SDS   KARAVAEV, A
                        THE SICK DICTATORSHIP (SOVIET UNION).=
                        BULLETIN INSTITUTE FOR THE STUDY OF THE USSR, 8,             61
                          (DECEMBER 1961), PP. 3-11.
                        ELEL, ELNOEL
KARPKH-59-TSP   KARPAT, KH
                        TURKEY'S POLITICS -- THE TRANSITION TO A
                        MULTI - PARTY SYSTEM.=
                        PRINCETON, PRINCETON UNIVERSITY PRESS, 1959.                 59
                        COMEL, ELEL, ELNOEL, ELPRNOR
KARPKH-62-RPD   KARPAT, KH
                        RECENT POLITICAL DEVELOPMENTS IN TURKEY AND THEIR SOCIAL
                          BACKGROUND.=
                        INTERNATIONAL AFFAIRS, 38, (JULY 1962), PP. 304-323.         62
                        COMEL, ELEL, ELNOEL
KARPKH-64-SEP   KARPAT, KH
                        SOCIETY, ECONOMICS, AND POLITICS IN CONTEMPORARY
                          TURKEY.=
                        WORLD POLITICS 17, (OCTOBER 1964), PP. 50-74.                64
                        COMEL, ELEL, ELNOEL, ELPRNOR
KARPKH-67-SLP   KARPAT, KH
                        SOCIALISM AND THE LABOR PARTY OF TURKEY.=
                        THE MIDDLE EAST JOURNAL, 21, (SPRING 1967), PP. 157-172.     67
                        COMEL, ELEL, ELPRNOR
KASHA -61-TCA   KASHIN, A
                        TWO COMMUNIST ARMIES (CHINA, SOVIET UNION).=
                        BULLETIN INSTITUTE FOR THE STUDY OF THE USSR, 8,             61
                          (MARCH 1961), PP. 34-42.
                        COMEL, ELEL, ELPRNOR
KASHA -64-DPS   KASHIN, A
                        THE DEFEAT OF THE PRO - SOVIET FACTION OF THE JAPANESE
                          COMMUNIST PARTY.=
                        BULLETIN INSTITUTE FOR THE STUDY OF THE USSR, 11,            64
                          (NOVEMBER 1964), PP. 31-35.
                        ELEL, ELPRNOR
KASHA -64-ISS   KASHIN, A
                        THE IMPACT OF SINO-SOVIET RELATIONS (SOVIET UNION).=
                        BULLETIN INSTITUTE FOR THE STUDY OF THE USSR, 11,            64
                          (DECEMBER 1964), PP. 22-26.
                        ELEL, ELNOEL, ELPRNOR
KASSA -57-YVR   KASSOF, A
                        YOUTH VS REGIME -- CONFLICT IN VALUES (SOVIET UNION).=
                        PROBLEMS OF COMMUNISM, 6, (MAY-JUNE 1957), PP. 15-23.        57
                        ELNOEL, ELPRNOR
KASSA -58-AYL   KASSOF, A
                        AFFLICTIONS OF THE YOUTH LEAGUE (SOVIET UNION).=
                        PROBLEMS OF COMMUNISM, 7, (JULY-AUGUST 1958), PP. 17-23.     58
                        ELEL, ELNOEL
KASSA -64-AST   KASSOF, A
                        THE ADMINISTERED SOCIETY -- TOTALITARIANISM
                          WITHOUT TERROR (SOVIET UNION).=
                        WORLD POLITICS, 16, (JULY 1964), PP. 558-575.                64
                        DEFEL
KATRS -61-ISC   KATRAK, S
                        INDIA'S COMMUNIST PARTY SPLIT.=
                        THE CHINA QUARTERLY, 7, (JULY-SEPTEMBER 1961),               61
                          PP. 138-147.
                        ELEL, ELPRNOR
KATTGM-52-NRI   KATTIN, GM
                        NATIONALISM AND REVOLUTION IN INDONESIA.=
                        ITHACA, NEW YORK, CORNELL UNIVERSITY PRESS, 1952.            52
                        ELEL, ELNOEL, ELPRNOR
KATZD -59-CRP   KATZ, D
                        CONSISTENT REACTIVE PARTICIPATION OF GROUP MEMBERS AND
                          REDUCTION OF INTERGROUP CONFLICT.=
                        THE JOURNAL OF CONFLICT RESOLUTION, 3, (MARCH 1959),         59
                          PP. 28-40.
                        DEFEL, ELEL, METEL
KATZD -61-ILP   KATZ, D                    ELDERSVELD, SJ
                        THE IMPACT OF LOCAL PARTY ACTIVITY UPON THE
                          ELECTORATE (UNITED STATES).=
                        THE PUBLIC OPINION QUARTERLY, 25, (SPRING 1961),             61
                          PP. 1-24.
                        COMEL, ELEL, ELNOEL, ELPRNOR,
KATZE -57-LSS   KATZ, E                    ET AL
                        LEADERSHIP STABILITY AND SOCIAL CHANGE -- AN EXPERIMENT
                          SMALL GROUPS.=
                        SOCIOMETRY, 20, (MARCH 1957), PP. 36-50.                     57
                        COMEL, METEL
KATZEL-50-PPF   KATZENBACH-JR, EL
                        POLITICAL PARTIES AND THE FRENCH ARMY
                          SINCE THE LIBERATION.=
```

                    WORLD POLITICS, 2, (JULY 1950), PP. 533-548.                50
                    ELEL
KATZZ -56-PPE    KATZ, Z
                 PARTY - POLITICAL EDUCATION IN SOVIET RUSSIA, 1918-1935.=
                 SOVIET STUDIES, 7, (JANUARY 1956), PP. 237-247.              56
                 COMEL
KAUFA -54-WAR    KAUFMAN, A
                 WHO ARE THE RULERS IN RUSSIA.=
                 DISSENT, 1, (SPRING 1954), PP. 144-156.                      54
                 COMEL, ELEL, ELNOEL
KAUFH -54-MP     KAUFMAN, H              JONES, V
                 THE MYSTERY OF POWER.=
                 PUBLIC ADMINISTRATION REVIEW, 14, (SUMMER 1954),             54
                    PP. 205-212.
                 DEFEL, COMEL, ELEL, ELNOEL, METEL
KAUFHK-60-BCS    KAUFMAN, HK
                 BANGHUAD -- A COMMUNITY STUDY IN THAILAND.=
                 LOCUST VALLEY, NEW YORK, JJ AUGUSTIN INC, 1960.              60
                 ELEL, ELNOEL
KAULJM-64-SCC    KAUL, JM
                 THE SPLIT IN THE CPI (COMMUNIST PARTY INDIA).=
                 INDIA QUARTERLY, 20, (OCTOBER-DECEMBER 1964), PP. 372-390.64
                 COMEL, ELEL
KAUTJH-55-ICP    KAUTSKY, JH
                 INDIAN COMMUNIST PARTY STRATEGY SINCE 1947.=
                 PACIFIC AFFAIRS, 28, (JUNE 1955), PP. 145-160.               55
                 ELEL, ELPRNOR
KAUTJH-56-MCP    KAUTSKY, JH
                 MOSCOW AND THE COMMUNIST PARTY OF INDIA.=
                 BOSTON, JOHN WILEY AND THE TECHNOLOGY PRESS OF M.I.T.,        56
                    1956.
                 ELEL, ELPRNOR
KAUTJH-62-PCU    KAUTSKY, JH
                 POLITICAL CHANGE IN UNDERDEVELOPED COUNTRIES --
                    NATIONALISM AND COMMUNISM.=
                 NEW YORK, JOHN WILEY AND SONS, 1962.                         62
                 GNELTH, DEFEL, COMEL, ELEL, ELNOEL, ELPRNOR
KAVAD -67-OCL    KAVANAGH, D
                 THE ORIENTATIONS OF COMMUNITY LEADERS TO PARLIAMENTARY
                    CANDIDATES (GREAT BRITAIN).=
                 POLITICAL STUDIES, 15, (OCTOBER 1967), PP. 351-356.          67
                 ELEL, ELPRNOR
KAWAK -50-JVN    KAWAI, K
                 JAPANESE VIEWS ON NATIONAL SECURITY.=
                 PACIFIC AFFAIRS, 23, (JUNE 1950), PP. 115-127.               50
                 ELPRNOR
KAZAAM-66-PET    KAZAMIAS, AM
                 POTENTIAL ELITES IN TURKEY -- THE SOCIAL ORIGINS OF
                    LISE YOUTH.=
                 COMPARATIVE EDUCATION REVIEW, 10, (OCTOBER 1966),            66
                    PP. 470-481.
                 COMEL
KAZAAM-67-PET    KAZAMIAS, AM
                 POTENTIAL ELITES IN TURKEY -- EXPLORING THE VALUES AND
                    ATTITUDES OF LISE YOUTH.=
                 COMPARATIVE EDUCATION REVIEW, 11, (FEBRUARY 1967),           67
                    PP. 22-37.
                 COMEL, ELPRNOR
KEARRN-64-BEC    KEARNEY, RN              HARRIS, RL
                 BUREAUCRACY AND ENVIRONMENT IN CEYLON.=
                 JOURNAL OF COMMONWEALTH POLITICAL STUDIES, 2, (1964),        64
                    PP. 253-266.
                 COMEL, ELEL, ELNOEL
KEARRN-64-SNS    KEARNEY, RN
                 SINHALESE NATIONALISM AND SOCIAL CONFLICT IN CEYLON.=
                 PACIFIC AFFAIRS, 37, (SUMMER 1964), PP. 125-136.             64
                 ELEL, ELNOEL
KEARRN-66-CCB    KEARNEY, RN
                 CEYLON -- THE CONTEMPORARY BUREAUCRACY.=
                 R BRAIBANTI (ED), ASIAN BUREAUCRATIC SYSTEMS EMERGENT        66
                    FROM THE BRITISH IMPERIAL TRADITION, DURHAM, DUKE
                    UNIVERSITY PRESS, 1966, PP. 485-549.
                 COMEL, ELEL, ELPRNOR
KEARRN-66-MPS    KEARNEY, RN
                 MILITANT PUBLIC SERVICE TRADE UNIONISM IN A NEW STATE
                    (CEYLON).=
                 THE JOURNAL OF ASIAN STUDIES, 25, (SEPTEMBER 1966),          66
                    PP. 397-412.
                 ELEL, ELNOEL
KECSP -52-HTG    KECSKEMETI, P
                 HOW TOTALITARIANS GAIN ABSOLUTE POWER (NAZI GERMANY,
                    SOVIET UNION).=
                 COMMENTARY, 14, (JULY-DECEMBER 1952), PP. 537-546.           52
                 ELNOEL, ELPRNOR

KECSP -57-IUB    KECSKEMETI, P
                 INTELLECTUAL UNREST BEHIND THE IRON CURTAIN (POLAND,
                    HUNGARY).=
                 COMMENTARY, 24, (NOVEMBER 1957), PP. 397-401.                57
                 ELEL, ELNOEL, ELPRNOR
KECSP -61-URS    KECSKEMETI, P
                 THE UNEXPECTED REVOLUTION -- SOCIAL FORCES IN THE
                    HUNGARIAN UPRISING.=
                 STANFORD, STANFORD UNIVERSITY PRESS, 1961.                   61
                 GNELTH, COMEL, ELEL, ELNOEL, ELPRNOR
KEEFWJ-54-PPP    KEEFE, WJ
                 PARTIES, PARTISANSHIP, AND PUBLIC POLICY IN THE
                    PENNSYLVANIA LEGISLATURE.=
                 THE AMERICAN POLITICAL SCIENCE REVIEW, 48, (JUNE 1954),      54
                    PP. 450-464.
                 ELEL
KEEFWJ-56-CSR    KEEFE, WJ
                 COMPARATIVE STUDY OF THE ROLE OF POLITICAL
                    PARTIES IN THE STATE LEGISLATURES (UNITED STATES).=
                 THE WESTERN POLITICAL QUARTERLY, 9, (SEPTEMBER 1956),        56
                    PP. 726-742.
                 ELEL, METEL
KEEFWJ-64-ALP    KEEFE, WJ          OGUL, MS
                 THE AMERICAN LEGISLATIVE PROCESS -- CONGRESS AND THE
                    STATES.=
                 ENGLEWOOD CLIFFS, NEW JERSEY, PRENTICE-HALL, 1964.           64
                 DEFEL, COMEL, ELEL, ELNOEL, ELPRNOR
KEEPJL-58-SIT    KEEP, JLH
                 SOVIET IDEOLOGUES ON THE TREADMILL.=
                 PROBLEMS OF COMMUNISM, 7, (MARCH-APRIL 1958), PP. 30-35.  58
                 ELEL, ELPRNOR
KEESFM-56-ECS    KEESING, FM          KEESING, MM
                 ELITE COMMUNICATION IN SAMOA -- A STUDY OF LEADERSHIP.=
                 STANFORD, STANFORD UNIVERSITY PRESS, 1956.                   56
                 COMEL, ELEL, ELNOEL, ELPRNOR
KEISNF-58-PRF    KEISER, NF
                 PUBLIC RESPONSIBILITY AND FEDERAL ADVISORY GROUPS --
                    A CASE STUDY (UNITED STATES).=
                 THE WESTERN POLITICAL QUARTERLY, 11, (JUNE 1958),            58
                    PP. 251-264.
                 ELEL, ELNOEL
KELLD -52-RF     KELLY, D
                 THE RULING FEW.=
                 LONDON, HOLLIS AND CARTER, 1952.                             52
                 COMEL, ELPRNOR
KELLGA-61-FAR    KELLY, GA
                 THE FRENCH ARMY RE-ENTERS POLITICS 1940-1955.=
                 POLITICAL SCIENCE QUARTERLY, 76, (SEPTEMBER 1961),           61
                    PP. 323-336.
                 ELEL, ELPRNOR
KELLGA-65-FCS    KELLY, GA
                 FRENCH CANADA'S NEW LEFT.=
                 ORBIS, 9, (FALL 1965), PP. 393-410.                          65
                 COMEL, ELEL, ELNOEL, ELPRNOR
KELLGA-65-LSF    KELLY, GA
                 LOST SOLDIERS -- THE FRENCH ARMY AND EMPIRE IN CRISIS,
                    1947-1962.=
                 CAMBRIDGE, THE MIT PRESS, 1965.                             65
                 COMEL, ELEL, ELNOEL, ELPRNOR
KELLJ -60-CGS    KELLER, J
                 THE CURRENT GERMAN SCENE.=
                 CURRENT HISTORY, 38, (JANUARY 1960), PP. 30-37.             60
                 COMEL, ELEL, ELPRNOR
KELLJ -64-SEB    KELLY, J
                 THE STUDY OF EXECUTIVE BEHAVIOR BY ACTIVITY SAMPLING
                    (UNITED STATES).=
                 HUMAN RELATIONS, 17, (AUGUST 1964), PP. 277-288.            64
                 METEL
KELLS -56-PPR    KELLEY-JR, S
                 PROFESSIONAL PUBLIC RELATIONS AND POLITICAL POWER
                    (UNITED STATES).=
                 BALTIMORE, JOHNS HOPKINS PRESS, 1956.                       56
                 ELNOEL
KELLS -63-BRC    KELLER, S
                 BEYOND THE RULING CLASS -- STRATEGIC ELITES
                    IN MODERN SOCIETY.=
                 NEW YORK, RANDOM HOUSE, 1963.                               63
                 GNELTH, DEFEL, COMEL, ELEL, ELNOEL, ELPRNOR
KELMHC-65-IBS    KELMAN, HC (ED)
                 INTERNATIONAL BEHAVIOR -- A SOCIAL-PSYCHOLOGICAL
                    ANALYSIS.=
                 NEW YORK, HOLT, RINEHART AND WINSTON, 1965.                 65
                 ELEL, ELNOEL, ELPRNOR
KELSRK-54-SBH    KELSALL, RK

THE SOCIAL BACKGROUND OF THE HIGHER CIVIL SERVICE
(GREAT BRITAIN).=
THE POLITICAL QUARTERLY, 25, (OCTOBER-DECEMBER 1954),          54
PP. 382-389.
COMEL, ELPRNOR
KELSRK-55-HCS   KELSALL, RK
HIGHER CIVIL SERVANTS IN BRITAIN.=
LONDON, ROUTLEDGE AND KEGAN PAUL LTD, 1955.                    55
COMEL, ELEL, ELPRNOR
KELSRN-54-NZN   KELSON, RN
THE NEW ZEALAND NATIONAL PARTY.=
POLITICAL SCIENCE, 6, (SEPTEMBER 1954), PP. 3-32.             54
COMEL, ELEL
KELSRN-64-PMP   KELSON, RN
THE PRIVATE MEMBER OF PARLIAMENT AND THE FORMATION OF
PUBLIC POLICY -- A NEW ZEALAND CASE STUDY.=
LONDON, OXFORD UNIVERSITY PRESS, TORONTO, TORONTO              64
UNIVERSITY PRESS, 1964.
ELEL, ELNOEL, ELPRNOR
KEMPT -62-IMC   KEMP, T
THE INTELLIGENTSIA AND MODERN CAPITALISM.=
SCIENCE AND SOCIETY, 26, (SUMMER 1962), PP. 308-325.          62
DEFEL, ELEL, ELPRNOR
KEMPT -64-LCI   KEMP, T
LEADERS AND CLASSES IN THE INDIAN NATIONAL CONGRESS,
1918-1939.=
SCIENCE AND SOCIETY, 28, (WINTER 1964), PP. 1-19.             64
COMEL, ELEL
KENDPL-56-ACN   KENDALL, PL
THE AMBIVALENT CHARACTER OF NATIONALISM AMONG
EGYPTIAN PROFESSIONALS.=
THE PUBLIC OPINION QUARTERLY, 20, (SPRING 1956),             56
PP. 277-289.
ELPRNOR
KENDW -60-TMU   KENDALL, W
THE TWO MAJORITIES (UNITED STATES).=
MIDWEST JOURNAL OF POLITICAL SCIENCE, 4,                     60
COMEL, ELEL, ELNOEL, ELPRNOR
KENNCD-56-TCC   KENNEY, CD
THE TWENTIETH CPSU CONGRESS -- A STUDY IN CALCULATED
MODERATION (SOVIET UNION).=
THE AMERICAN POLITICAL SCIENCE REVIEW, 50,                   56
(DECEMBER 1956), PP. 764-786.
ELEL, ELPRNOR
KENNJJ-58-CND   KENNEDY, JJ
CATHOLICISM, NATIONALISM AND DEMOCRACY IN ARGENTINA.=
NOTRE DAME, INDIANA, UNIVERSITY OF NOTRE DAME PRESS,          58
1958.
COMEL, ELEL, ELPRNOR
KENZT -62-NES   KENZO, T
THE NEW EMPEROR SYSTEM (JAPAN).=
JAPAN QUARTERLY, 9, (JULY-SEPTEMBER 1962), PP. 265-274.   62
ELEL
KERNE -59-EEC   KERN, E
ON THE ESTABLISHMENT OF A EUROPEAN CIVIL SERVICE.=
INTERNATIONAL REVIEW OF ADMINISTRATIVE SCIENCES, 25,         59
(1959), PP. 21-27.
ELEL, ELNOEL
KERRC -64-IIM   KERR, C            ET AL
INDUSTRIALISM AND INDUSTRIAL MAN.=
NEW YORK, OXFORD UNIVERSITY PRESS, 1964.                     64
DEFEL, COMEL, ELPRNOR
KERRW -48-FLD   KERR, W
FRENCH LABOR DIVIDED.=
FOREIGN AFFAIRS, 27, (OCTOBER 1948), PP. 96-103.            48
ELEL, ELPRNOR
KERSH -58-UIE   KERSTEN, H
ULBRICHT AND THE INTELLECTUALS (EAST GERMANY).=
SOVIET SURVEY--A QUARTERLY REVIEW OF CULTURAL TRENDS,        58
25, (JULY-SEPTEMBER 1958), PP. 47-52.
ELEL, ELPRNOR
KERST -66-NEA   KERSTIENS, T
THE NEW ELITE IN ASIA AND AFRICA -- A COMPARATIVE STUDY
OF INDONESIA AND AFRICA (GHANA).=
NEW YORK, FREDERICK A PRAEGER, 1966.                         66
DEFEL, COMEL, ELEL, ELNOEL, ELPRNOR, METEL
KESSJH-64-WCD   KESSEL, JH
THE WASHINGTON CONGRESSIONAL DELEGATION (UNITED STATES).=
MIDWEST JOURNAL OF POLITICAL SCIENCE, 8,                     64
(FEBRUARY 1964), PP. 1-21.
ELEL, ELPRNOR
KESSK -61-PLU   KESSELMAN, K
PRESIDENTIAL LEADERSHIP (UNITED STATES).=
MIDWEST JOURNAL OF POLITICAL SCIENCE, 5, (AUGUST 1961),      61

```
                    PP. 285-289.
                    ELEL, ELPRNOR
KESSM -65-PLC    KESSELMAN, M
                 PRESIDENTIAL LEADERSHIP IN CONGRESS ON FOREIGN POLICY --
                    A REPLICATION OF A HYPOTHESIS (UNITED STATES).=
                 MIDWEST JOURNAL OF POLITICAL SCIENCE, 9, (NOVEMBER 1965), 65
                    PP. 401-406.
                    ELEL, ELPRNOR
KEY-VO-61-POA    KEY-JR, VO
                 PUBLIC OPINION AND AMERICAN DEMOCRACY.=
                 NEW YORK, ALFRED A KNOPF, 1961.                            61
                    DEFEL, COMEL, ELNOEL, ELPRNOR
KEY-VO-61-POD    KEY-JR, VO
                 PUBLIC OPINION AND DECAY OF DEMOCRACY
                    (UNITED STATES).=
                 VIRGINIA QUARTERLY REVIEW, 37, (AUTUMN 1961),             61
                    PP. 481-494.
                    ELNOEL
KEY-VO-64-PPP    KEY-JR, VO
                 POLITICS, PARTIES AND PRESSURE GROUPS (UNITED STATES).=
                 NEW YORK, THOMAS Y CROWELL COMPANY, 1964 (5TH ED).        64
                    ELEL, ELNOEL
KEY-VO-66-RER    KEY-JR, VO
                 THE RESPONSIBLE ELECTORATE -- RATIONALITY IN PRESIDENTIAL
                    VOTING 1936-1960 (UNITED STATES).=
                 CAMBRIDGE, BELKNAP, 1966.                                 66
                    ELNOEL
KHADM -52-CCC    KHADDURI, M
                 COUP AND COUNTER-COUP IN THE YAMAN 1948.=
                 INTERNATIONAL AFFAIRS, 28, (JANUARY 1952), PP. 59-68.     52
                    ELEL
KHADM -53-RMM    KHADDURI, M
                 THE ROLE OF THE MILITARY IN MIDDLE EAST POLITICS.=
                 THE AMERICAN POLITICAL SCIENCE REVIEW, 47, (JUNE 1953),   53
                    PP. 511-524.
                    ELEL, ELNOEL
KHAMT -51-PAT    KHAMA, T
                 THE PRINCIPLES OF AFRICAN TRIBAL ADMINISTRATION.=
                 INTERNATIONAL AFFAIRS, 27, (OCTOBER 1951), PP. 451-456.   51
                    ELEL, ELNOEL
KHERSS-60-AI     KHERA, SSS
                 ADMINISTRATION IN INDIA.=
                 NEW DELHI, INDIAN INSTITUTE OF PUBLIC ADMINISTRATION,     60
                    1960.
                    ELEL, ELNOEL
KHERSS-64-DAI    KHERA, SS
                 DISTRICT ADMINISTRATION IN INDIA.=
                 LONDON, ASIA PUBLISHING HOUSE, 1964.                      64
                    ELNOEL
KILLL -64-RCA    KILLIAN, L          GRIGG, C
                 RACIAL CRISIS IN AMERICA -- LEADERSHIP IN CONFLICT.=
                 ENGLEWOOD CLIFFS, NEW JERSEY, PRENTICE-HALL, 1964.        64
                    ELEL, ELNOEL, ELPRNOR
KILLLM-60-NPL    KILLIAN, LM         SMITH, CU
                 NEGRO PROTEST LEADERS IN A SOUTHERN COMMUNITY
                    (UNITED-STATES).=
                 SOCIAL FORCES, 38, (MARCH 1960), PP. 253-257.             60
                    COMEL, ELPRNOR
KILMV -56-OLC    KILMUIR, V
                 THE OFFICE OF LORD CHANCELLOR (GREAT BRITAIN).=
                 PARLIAMENTARY AFFAIRS, 9, (SPRING 1956), PP. 132-139      56
                    ELEL
KILNP -62-MGS    KILNER, P
                 MILITARY GOVERNMENT IN SUDAN -- THE PAST THREE YEARS.=
                 THE WORLD TODAY, 18, (JUNE 1962) PP. 259-268.             62
                    COMEL, ELEL, ELNOEL
KILPFP-64-IFS    KILPATRICK, FP      CUMMINGS-JR, MC
                 THE IMAGE OF THE FEDERAL SERVICE (UNITED STATES).=
                 WASHINGTON, THE BROOKINGS INSTITUTION, 1964.              64
                    COMEL, ELNOEL, ELPRNOR
KILSM -63-APC    KILSON, M
                 AFRICAN POLITICAL CHANGE AND MODERNISATION PROCESS.=
                 THE JOURNAL OF MODERN AFRICAN STUDIES, 1, (DECEMBER 1963),63
                    PP. 425-440.
                    DEFEL, COMEL, ELEL, ELNOEL, ELPRNOR
KILSM -66-PCW    KILSON, M
                 POLITICAL CHANGE IN A WEST AFRICAN STATE -- A STUDY OF
                    THE MODERNIZATION PROCESS IN SIERRA LEONE.=
                 CAMBRIDGE, HARVARD UNIVERSITY PRESS, 1966.                66
                    COMEL, ELEL, ELNOEL, ELPRNOR
KILSML-58-NSC    KILSON, ML
                 NATIONALISM AND SOCIAL CLASSES IN BRITISH WEST AFRICA.=
                 THE JOURNAL OF POLITICS, 20, (MAY 1958), PP. 368-387.     58
                    COMEL, ELNOEL, ELPRNOR
```

KILSML-63-ASP    KILSON, ML
                 AUTHORITARIAN AND SINGLE - PARTY TENDENCIES
                    IN AFRICAN POLITICS.=
                 WORLD POLITICS, 15, (JANUARY 1963), PP. 262-294.              63
                 COMEL, ELEL, ELNOEL, ELPRNOR
KIM,YC-64-CPC    KIM, YC
                 THE CONCEPT OF POLITICAL CULTURE IN COMPARATIVE POLITICS.=
                 THE JOURNAL OF POLITICS, 26, (MAY 1964), PP. 313-336.         64
                 DEFEL, ELNOEL
KIM,YC-66-ACE    KIM, YC
                 AUTHORITY -- SOME CONCEPTUAL AND EMPIRICAL NOTES.=
                 THE WESTERN POLITICAL QUARTERLY, 19, (1966), PP. 223-234. 66
                 DEFEL
KIMBRB-64-PPE    KIMBROUGH, RB
                 POLITICAL POWER AND EDUCATIONAL DECISION-MAKING
                    (UNITED STATES).=
                 NEW YORK, RAND MCNALLY AND CO., 1964.                         64
                 ELEL, ELNOEL
KIMCJ -64-SLI    KIMCHE, J
                 SUCCESSION AND THE LEGACY IN ISRAEL.=
                 JOURNAL OF INTERNATIONAL AFFAIRS, 18, (APRIL 1964),           64
                    PP. 43-53.
                 ELEL
KINCHB-57-IBE    KINCAID, HB              BRIGHT, N
                 INTERVIEWING THE BUSINESS ELITE.=
                 THE AMERICAN JOURNAL OF SOCIOLOGY, 63, (NOVEMBER 1957),       57
                    PP. 304-311.
                 METEL
KINGA -66-BPP    KING, A (ED)
                 BRITISH POLITICS -- PEOPLE, PARTIES, AND PARLIAMENT.=
                 BOSTON, DC HEATH AND CO., 1966.                               66
                 COMEL, ELEL, ELNOEL, ELPRNOR
KINGA -66-GBS    KING, A
                 GREAT BRITAIN -- THE SEARCH FOR LEADERSHIP.=
                 WG ANDREWS (ED), EUROPEAN POLITICS 1--THE RESTLESS            66
                    SEARCH, PRINCETON, D VAN NOSTRAND CO., 1966, PP. 16-76.
                 COMEL, ELEL, ELPRNOR
KINGJB-60-MCF    KING, JB
                 MINISTERIAL CABINETS OF THE FOURTH REPUBLIC (FRANCE).=
                 THE WESTERN POLITICAL QUARTERLY, 13, (JUNE 1960),             60
                    PP. 433-444.
                 COMEL, ELEL, ELNOEL
KINGJD-44-RBI    KINGSLEY, JD
                 REPRESENTATIVE BUREAUCRACY -- AN INTERPRETATION OF THE
                    BRITISH CIVIL SERVICE.=
                 YELLOW SPRINGS, OHIO, THE ANTIOCH PRESS, 1944.                44
                 COMEL, ELEL, ELPRNOR
KINGJK-54-TSB    KING, JK
                 THAILAND'S BUREAUCRACY AND THE THREAT OF COMMUNIST
                    SUBVERSION.=
                 FAR EASTERN SURVEY, 23, (NOVEMBER 1954), PP. 169-173.         54
                 ELPRNOR
KINGJW-67-PBA    KINGDON, JW
                 POLITICIANS' BELIEFS ABOUT VOTERS (UNITED STATES).=
                 THE AMERICAN POLITICAL SCIENCE REVIEW, 61, (MARCH 1967),      67
                    PP. 137-145.
                 ELNOEL, ELPRNOR
KINOH -53-EMJ    KINOSHITA, H
                 ECHOES OF MILITARISM IN JAPAN.=
                 PACIFIC AFFAIRS, 26, (SEPTEMBER 1953), PP. 224-251.           53
                 COMEL, ELEL, ELPRNOR
KINOH -63-URW    KINOSHITA, H
                 UYOKU, THE RIGHT WING OF JAPAN.=
                 CONTEMPORARY JAPAN (TOKYO), 27, (OCTOBER 1963),               63
                    PP. 701-718.
                 ELEL, ELPRNOR
KIRCO -50-CGB    KIRCHHEIMER, O
                 THE COMPOSITION OF THE GERMAN BUNDESTAG, 1950.=
                 THE WESTERN POLITICAL QUARTERLY, 3, (DECEMBER 1950),          50
                    PP. 590-601.
                 COMEL
KIRCO -57-WOP    KIRCHHEIMER, O
                 THE WANING OPPOSITION IN PARLIAMENTARY REGIMES (EUROPE).=
                 SOCIAL RESEARCH, 24, (SUMMER 1957), PP. 127-156.              57
                 ELEL, ELNOEL
KIRCO -58-FFF    KIRCHHEIMER, O
                 FRANCE FROM THE FOURTH TO THE FIFTH REPUBLIC.=
                 SOCIAL RESEARCH, 25, (WINTER 1958), PP. 379-414.              58
                 ELEL, ELNOEL, ELPRNOR
KIRCO -59-MMW    KIRCHHEIMER, O
                 MAJORITIES AND MINORITIES IN WESTERN EUROPEAN
                    GOVERNMENTS.=
                 THE WESTERN POLITICAL QUARTERLY, 12, (JUNE 1959),             59
                    PP. 492-510.

```
                ELEL, ELNOEL
KIRKAH-65-BCT   KIRK-GREENE, AHM
                BUREAUCRATIC CADRES IN A TRADITIONAL MILIEU (NIGERIA).=
                JS COLEMAN, (ED), EDUCATION AND POLITICAL DEVELOPMENT,      65
                   PRINCETON, NEW JERSEY, PRINCETON UNIVERSITY PRESS, 1965.
                ELEL, ELPRNOR
KITCH -62-EA    KITCHEN, H (ED)
                THE EDUCATED AFRICAN.=
                NEW YORK, FREDERICK A PRAEGER, 1962.                        62
                COMEL
KITCJD-60-NPA   KITCHEN, JD
                NATIONAL PERSONNEL ADMINISTRATION IN URUGUAY.=
                INTER-AMERICAN ECONOMIC AFFAIRS, 4, (SUMMER 1960),          60
                   PP. 45-58.
                COMEL, ELEL, ELPRNOR
KITTER-55-IEE   KITTRELL, ER
                INDIAN ECONOMISTS AND ECONOMIC DEVELOPMENT.=
                THE SOUTHWESTERN SOCIAL SCIENCE QUARTERLY, 35,              55
                   (MARCH 1955), PP. 324-339.
                ELEL, ELPRNOR
KITZUW- -AES    KITZINGER, UW
                THE AUSTRIAN ELECTORAL SYSTEM.=
                PARLIAMENTARY AFFAIRS, 12, (SUMMER AND AUTUMN 1959),
                   PP. 392-404.
                ELEL, ELNOEL
KITZUW-60-SED   KITZINGER, UW
                SWISS ELECTORAL DEMOCRACY.=
                PARLIAMENTARY AFFAIRS, 13, (SUMMER 1960), PP. 335-345.      60
                COMEL, ELEL
KIYOE -58-JCP   KIYOSHI, E
                THE JAPAN COMMUNIST PARTY -- ITS DEVELOPMENT SINCE
                   THE WAR.=
                JAPAN QUARTERLY, 5, (OCTOBER-DECEMBER 1958),                58
                   PP. 426-434.
                ELEL
KLAPOE-60-PSD   KLAPP, OE           PADGETT, LV
                POWER STRUCTURE AND DECISION-MAKING IN A MEXICAN
                   BORDER CITY.=
                THE AMERICAN JOURNAL OF SOCIOLOGY, 65, (JANUARY 1960),      60
                   PP. 400-406.
                COMEL, ELEL, ELNOEL, METEL
KLAPOE-64-SLP   KLAPP, OE
                SYMBOLIC LEADERS -- PUBLIC DRAMAS AND PUBLIC MEN.=
                CHICAGO, ALDINE, 1964.                                      64
                ELEL, ELNOEL, ELPRNOR
KLEIDW-60-PSE   KLEIN, DW
                PEKING'S EVOLVING MINISTRY OF FOREIGN AFFAIRS.=
                THE CHINA QUARTERLY, 4, (OCTOBER-DECEMBER,1960),            60
                   PP. 28-39.
                COMEL, ELEL
KLEIDW-61-PSL   KLEIN, DW
                PEKING'S LEADERS -- A STUDY IN ISOLATION (CHINA).=
                THE CHINA QUARTERLY, 7, (JULY-SEPTEMBER,1961), PP.35-43.    61
                COMEL, ELEL, ELNOEL, ELPRNOR
KLEIDW-62-NGC   KLEIN, DW
                THE 'NEXT GENERATION' OF CHINESE COMMUNIST LEADERS.=
                THE CHINA QUARTERLY, 12, (OCTOBER-DECEMBER 1962),           62
                   PP. 57-74.
                COMEL, ELEL, ELNOEL, ELPRNOR
KLEIDW-64-SEP   KLEIN, DW
                SUCCESSION AND THE ELITE AND PEKING (CHINA).=
                JOURNAL OF INTERNATIONAL, 18, (APRIL 1964), PP. 1-11.       64
                COMEL, ELEL
KLINM -56-TTP   KLING, M
                TOWARD A THEORY OF POWER AND POLITICAL
                   INSTABILITY IN LATIN AMERICA.=
                THE WESTERN POLITICAL QUARTERLY, 9, (MARCH 1956),           56
                   PP. 21-35.
                DEFEL, COMEL, ELEL
KLINM -61-MIG   KLING, M
                A MEXICAN INTEREST GROUP IN ACTION.=
                ENGLEWOOD CLIFFS, NEW JERSEY, PRENTICE-HALL, 1961.          61
                COMEL, ELEL, ELNOEL, ELPRNOR
KNAPFA-64-MML   KNAPP-JR, FA
                THE MEANING OF MILITARISM IN LATIN AMERICA.=
                FOREIGN SERVICE JOURNAL, 41, (DECEMBER 1964),               64
                   PP. 20-26.
                ELEL, ELPRNOR
KNICI -48-LCI   KNICKERBOCKER, I
                LEADERSHIP -- A CONCEPTION AND SOME IMPLICATIONS.=
                THE JOURNAL OF SOCIAL ISSUES, 4, (SUMMER 1948),             48
                   PP. 23-40.
                GNELTH, DEFEL, ELEL, METEL
KNIGME-52-GE    KNIGHT, ME
```

                    THE GERMAN EXECUTIVE 1890-1933.=
                    STANFORD, CALIFORNIA, HOOVER INSTITUTION, STANFORD          52
                       UNIVERSITY, 1952.
                    COMEL, ELEL, ELNOEL, ELPRNOR
     KNOWCS-62-PPP  KNOWLTON, CS
                    PATRON - PEON PATTERN AMONG THE SPANISH AMERICANS
                       OF NEW MEXICO.=
                    SOCIAL FORCES, 41, (OCTOBER 1962), PP. 12-17.                62
                    ELNOEL
     KOENLW-60-IPU  KOENIG, LW
                    THE INVISIBLE PRESIDENCY (UNITED STATES).=
                    NEW YORK, HOLT, RHINEHART AND WINTSTON, 1960.                60
                    ELEL, ELPRNOR
     KOFMK -62-PSC  KOFMEHL, K
                    PROFESSIONAL STAFFS OF CONGRESS.=
                    WEST LAFAYETTE, INDIANA, PURDUE UNIVERSITY PRESS, 1962.      62
                    COMEL, ELEL
     KOGAN -53-IAP  KOGAN, N
                    THE ITALIAN ACTION PARTY AND THE INSTITUTIONAL
                       QUESTION.=
                    THE WESTERN POLITICAL QUARTERLY, 6, (SEPTEMBER 1953),        53
                       PP. 275-295.
                    ELEL, ELNOEL
     KOGAN -66-ICW  KOGAN, N
                    ITALIAN COMMUNISM, THE WORKING CLASS AND ORGANIZED
                       CATHOLICISM.=
                    THE JOURNAL OF POLITICS, 28, (AUGUST 1966), PP. 531-555.     66
                    ELEL, ELPRNOR
     KOLAW -61-WAS  KOLARZ, W
                    THE WEST AFRICAN SCENE.=
                    PROBLEMS OF COMMUNISM, 10, (NOVEMBER-DECEMBER 1961),         61
                       PP. 15-23.
                    COMEL, ELEL, ELNOEL
     KOLEF -67-ERC  KOLEGAR, F
                    THE ELITE AND THE RULING CLASS -- PARETO AND MOSCA
                       RE-EXAMINED.=
                    THE REVIEW OF POLITICS, 29, (JULY 1967), PP. 354-369.        67
                    GNELTH, DEFEL
     KOLKG -62-WPA  KOLKO, G
                    WEALTH AND POWER IN AMERICA -- AN ANALYSIS OF SOCIAL CLASS
                       AND INCOME DISTRIBUTION.=
                    NEW YORK, FREDERICK A PRAEGER, 1962.                         62
                    COMEL, ELEL, ELNOEL
     KOLKR -67-SMC  KOLKOWICZ, R
                    THE SOVIET MILITARY AND THE COMMUNIST PARTY.=
                    PRINCETON, PRINCETON UNIVERSITY PRESS, 1967.                 67
                    ELEL, ELNOEL, ELPRNOR
     KOLOEJ-65-SPA  KOLODZIEJ, EJ
                    STRATEGIC POLICY AND AMERICAN GOVERNMENT -- STRUCTURAL
                       CONSTRAINTS AND VARIABLES.=
                    THE REVIEW OF POLITICS, 27, (OCTOBER 1965), PP. 465-490.     65
                    ELEL
     KONSD -63-TPM  KONSTANTINOV, D
                    A TURNING POINT IN THE MOSCOW (SOVIET UNION)
                       PATRIARCHATE'S POLICY.=
                    BULLETIN INSTITUTE FOR THE STUDY OF THE USSR, 10,            63
                       (MARCH 1963), PP. 20-27.
                    ELEL, ELPRNOR
     KOOLF -60-CHS  KOOL, F
                    COMMUNISM IN HOLLAND -- A STUDY IN FUTILITY.=
                    PROBLEMS OF COMMUNISM, 9, (SEPTEMBER-OCTOBER 1960),          60
                       PP. 17-24.
                    ELEL
     KORAA -56-PSI  KORAB, A
                    POLAND -- THE SEARCH FOR INDEPENDENCE.=
                    PROBLEMS OF COMMUNISM, 5, (NOVEMBER-DECEMBER 1956),          56
                       PP. 10-16.
                    COMEL, ELEL, ELNOEL, ELPRNOR
     KORAA -57-PPC  KORAB, A
                    PIASECKI AND THE POLISH COMMUNISTS.=
                    PROBLEMS OF COMMUNISM, 6, (NOVEMBER-DECEMBER 1957),          57
                       PP. 33-38.
                    ELNOEL
     KORBJ -59-CSC  KORBEL, J
                    THE COMMUNIST SUBVERSION OF CZECHOSLOVAKIA, 1938-1948 --
                       THE FAILURE OF COEXISTENCE.=
                    PRINCETON, PRINCETON UNIVERSITY PRESS, 1959.                 59
                    COMEL, ELEL, ELNOEL
     KORMF -56-HSR  KORMENDI, F
                    HUNGARY'S REBELLIOUS MUSE.=
                    PROBLEMS OF COMMUNISM, 5, (MAY-JUNE 1956), PP. 31-36.        56
                    COMEL, ELEL, ELNOEL, ELPRNOR
     KORNA -65-PSN  KORNBERG, A          THOMAS, N
                    THE POLITICAL SOCIALIZATION OF NATIONAL LEGISLATIVE

ELITES IN THE UNITED STATES AND CANADA.=
THE JOURNAL OF POLITICS, 27, (NOVEMBER 1965), PP. 761-775.65
COMEL, ELPRNOR

KORNA -65-SBL    KORNBERG, A
THE SOCIAL BASIS OF LEADERSHIP IN A CANADIAN HOUSE
OF COMMONS.=
THE AUSTRALIAN JOURNAL OF POLITICS AND HISTORY, 11,          65
(DECEMBER 1965), PP. 324-334.
COMEL

KORNA -66-CCC    KORNBERG, A
CAUCUS AND COHESION IN CANADIAN PARLIAMENTARY PARTIES.=
THE AMERICAN POLITICAL SCIENCE REVIEW, 60, (MARCH 1966),     66
PP. 83-92.
ELEL

KORNA -66-RDP    KORNBERG, A          THOMAS, N
REPRESENTATIVE DEMOCRACY AND POLITICAL ELITES IN CANADA
AND THE UNITED STATES.=
PARLIAMENTARY AFFAIRS, 19, (WINTER 1965-1966), PP. 91-102.66
COMEL

KORNJ -59-OEA    KORNAI, J
OVERCENTRALIZATION IN ECONOMIC ADMINISTRATION -- A
CRITICAL ANALYSIS BASED ON EXPERIENCE IN HUNGARIAN
LIGHT INDUSTRY.=
J KNAPP (TRANS), LONDON, OXFORD UNIVERSITY PRESS, 1959.      59
ELEL

KORNW -59-PMS    KORNHAUSER, W
THE POLITICS OF MASS SOCIETY.=
GLENCOE, THE FREE PRESS, 1959.                               59
GNELTH, DEFEL, COMEL, ELEL, ELNOEL, ELPRNOR

KORTDC-62-SDL    KORTON, DC
SITUATIONAL DETERMINANTS OF LEADERSHIP STRUCTURE.=
THE JOURNAL OF CONFLICT RESOLUTION, 6, (SEPTEMBER 1962),     62
PP. 222-235.
DEFEL, ELEL

KORTF -57-PSC    KORT, F
PREDICTING SUPREME COURT DECISIONS MATHEMATICALLY -- A
QUANTITIVE ANALYSIS OF THE RIGHT TO COUNSEL
(UNITED STATES).=
THE AMERICAN POLITICAL SCIENCE REVIEW, 51, (MARCH 1957),     57
PP. 1-12.
ELPRNOR, METEL

KORTF -58-RFS    KORT, F
REPLY TO FISHER'S MATHEMATICAL ANALYSIS OF SUPREME COURT
DECISIONS (UNITED STATES).=
THE AMERICAN POLITICAL SCIENCE REVIEW, 52, (JUNE 1958),      58
PP. 339-348.
METEL

KORTF -66-MAF    KORT, F
MODELS FOR THE ANALYSIS OF FACT - ACCEPTANCE BY
APPELLATE COURTS (UNITED STATES).=
THE AMERICAN BEHAVIORAL SCIENTIST, 9, (APRIL 1966),          66
PP. 8-10.
ELPRNOR, METEL

KOTHR -66-CSI    KOTHARI, R           MARU, R
CASTE AND SECULARISM IN INDIA.=
JOURNAL OF ASIAN STUDIES, 25, (1965-1966), PP. 33-50.        66
COMEL, ELEL, ELNOEL, ELPRNOR

KOTHR -67-ICS    KOTHARI, R
INDIA -- THE CONGRESS SYSTEM ON TRIAL.=
ASIAN SURVEY, 7, (JANUARY 1967), PP. 83-96.                  67
ELEL, ELPRNOR

KRACEA-58-CRC    KRACKE, EA
THE CHANGING ROLE OF THE CHINESE INTELLECTUALS --
AN INTRODUCTORY NOTE.=
COMPARATIVE STUDIES IN SOCIETY AND HISTORY, 1,               58
(OCTOBER 1958), PP. 23-25.
COMEL, ELEL, ELNOEL

KREIBW-60-LAR    KREITLOW, BW          AITON, EW            TORRENCE, AP
LEADERSHIP FOR ACTION IN RURAL COMMUNITIES
(UNITED STATES).=
DANVILLE, ILLINOIS, INTERSTATE PRINTERS AND PUBLISHERS,      60
1960.
COMEL, ELNOEL

KRIEL -63-ELA    KRIESBERG, L
ENTREPRENEURS IN LATIN AMERICA AND THE ROLE OF
CULTURAL AND SITUATIONAL PROCESSES.=
INTERNATIONAL SOCIAL SCIENCE JOURNAL, 15, (OCTOBER 1963), 63
PP. 581-594.
ELEL, ELNOEL, ELPRNOR

KRISG -66-DIN    KRISHNA, G
THE DEVELOPMENT OF THE INDIAN NATIONAL CONGRESS AS A MASS
ORGANIZATION, 1919-1923.=
THE JOURNAL OF ASIAN STUDIES, 25, (SEPTEMBER 1966),          66
PP. 413-430.

```
                    COMEL, ELEL, ELPRNOR
    KRISI  -67-AIF  KRISTOL, I
                    AMERICAN INTELLECTUALS AND FOREIGN POLICY.=
                    FOREIGN AFFAIRS, 45, (JULY 1967), PP. 594-609.              67
                    ELEL, ELPRNOR
    KRISS  -59-CVC  KRISLOV, S
                    CONSTITUENCY VERSUS CONSTITUTIONALISM -- THE
                        DESEGREGATION ISSUE AND TENSION AND ASPIRATIONS OF
                        SOUTHERN ATTORNEY GENERALS (UNITED STATES).=
                    MIDWEST JOURNAL OF POLITICAL SCIENCE, 3, (FEBRUARY 1959), 59
                        PP. 75-92.
                    COMEL, ELEL, ELNOEL, ELPRNOR
    KROLM  -61-PBS  KROLL, M
                    THE POLITICS OF BRITAIN'S ANGRY YOUNG MEN.=
                    SOCIAL SCIENCE, 36, (JUNE 1961), PP. 157-166.                61
                    ELEL, ELNOEL, ELPRNOR
    KRUZP  -64-TPR  KRUZHIN, P
                    THE TECHNIQUE OF THE 'PALACE REVOLUTION' (SOVIET UNION).=
                    BULLETIN INSTITUTE FOR THE STUDY OF THE USSR, 11,           64
                        (DECEMBER 1964), PP. 3-14.
                    ELEL, ELNOEL
    KRUZP  -65-YYC  KRUZHIN, P
                    YOUTH AND THE YOUNG COMMUNIST LEAGUE.=
                    STUDIES ON THE SOVIET UNION, 4, (1965), PP. 87-94.          65
                    ELPRNOR
    KRUZP  -66-PPG  KRUZHIN, P
                    THE PROBLEM OF PARTY GROWTH AND RECRUITMENT
                        (SOVIET UNION).=
                    BULLETIN INSTITUTE FOR THE STUDY OF THE USSR, 8,            66
                        (JANUARY 1966), PP. 33-36.
                    COMEL, ELEL, ELPRNOR
    KRYLKA-66-PPP   KRYLOV, KA
                    PARTY PROTECTION AND PRIVILEGED STATUS IN SOVIET SOCIETY.=
                    BULLETIN INSTITUTE FOR THE STUDY OF THE USSR, 8,            66
                        (MARCH 1966), PP. 39-43.
                    ELEL, ELNOEL
    KUBAD  -61-CUC  KUBAT, D
                    COMMUNIST USE OF THE CZECHOSLOVAK PARLIAMENT SINCE
                        WORLD WAR II.=
                    SLAVIC REVIEW, 20, (DECEMBER 1961), PP. 695-700.            61
                    COMEL, ELEL
    KUBAD  -61-PLC  KUBAT, D
                    PATTERNS OF LEADERSHIP IN A COMMUNIST STATE --
                        CZECHOSLOVAKIA 1946-1958.=
                    JOURNAL OF CENTRAL EUROPEAN AFFAIRS, 21, (OCTOBER 1961),    61
                        PP. 305-318.
                    COMEL, ELEL
    KUBAD  -61-STC  KUBAT, D
                    SOVIET THEORY OF CLASSES.=
                    SOCIAL FORCES, 40, (OCTOBER 1961), PP. 417-421.             61
                    ELPRNOR
    KUBAD  -65-TYM  KUBAT, D
                    TOTALITARIAN YOUTH MOVEMENT AS A CAREER MECHANISM --
                        THE CASE IN CZECHOSLOVAKIA.=
                    SOCIAL FORCES, 43, (MAY 1965), PP. 417-421.                 65
                    COMEL
    KUEBJ  -63-AP   KUEBLER, J
                    ARGENTINA AND PERONISM.=
                    EDITORIAL RESEARCH REPORTS, 1, (MAY 15, 1963),              63
                        PP. 367-383.
                    ELNOEL, ELPRNOR
    KULSW  -53-CSS  KULSKI, W
                    CLASS STRATIFICATION IN THE SOVIET UNION.=
                    FOREIGN AFFAIRS, 32, (OCTOBER 1953), PP. 144-153.           53
                    COMEL, ELEL, ELNOEL
    KULSWW-55-CCS   KULSKI, WW
                    CLASSES IN THE 'CLASSLESS' STATE (SOVIET UNION).=
                    PROBLEMS OF COMMUNISM, 4, (JANUARY-FEBRUARY 1955),          55
                        PP. 20-28.
                    COMEL, ELEL, ELNOEL, ELPRNOR
    KUMAC  -66-AEI  KUMALO, C
                    AFRICAN ELITES IN INDUSTRIAL BUREAUCRACY (UGANDA).=
                    PC LLOYD (ED), THE NEW ELITES OF TROPICAL AFRICA, LONDON, 66
                        OXFORD UNIVERSITY PRESS, 1966, PP. 216-226.
                    COMEL, ELPRNOR
    KUNZFA-65-MSC   KUNZ, FA
                    THE MODERN SENATE OF CANADA, 1925-1963.=
                    TORONTO, UNIVERSITY OF TORONTO PRESS, 1965.                 65
                    COMEL, ELEL, ELPRNOR
    KUO-C  -59-LCC  KUO-CHUN, C
                    LEADERSHIP IN THE CHINESE COMMUNIST PARTY.=
                    THE ANNALS OF THE AMERICAN ACADEMY OF POLITICAL AND         59
                        SOCIAL SCIENCE, 321, (JANUARY 1959), PP. 40-50.
                    COMEL, ELEL, ELNOEL
```

KUPEH -47-AAR    KUPER, H
                 THE AFRICAN ARISTOCRACY -- RANK AMONG THE SWAZI.=
                 LONDON, OXFORD UNIVERSITY PRESS, 1947.                    47
                 COMEL, ELEL, ELNOEL, ELPRNOR
KUPEL -50-DAW    KUPER, L
                 DEMOGRAPHIC ASPECTS OF WHITE SUPREMACY IN SOUTH AFRICA.=
                 THE BRITISH JOURNAL OF SOCIOLOGY, 1, (MARCH 1950),        50
                    PP. 144-153.
                 COMEL
KUPEL -65-ABR    KUPER, L
                 AN AFRICAN BOURGEOISIE -- RACE, CLASS, AND POLITICS IN
                    SOUTH AFRICA.=
                 NEW HAVEN, YALE UNIVERSITY PRESS, 1965.                   65
                 COMEL, ELEL, ELNOEL, ELPRNOR
KURIKK-46-JSN    KURIHARA, KK
                 JAPAN'S NEW DIET.=
                 FAR EASTERN SURVEY, 15, (MAY 22, 1946), PP. 145-148.      46
                 COMEL
KUROY -65-SPI    KURODA, Y
                 SOCIABILITY AND POLITICAL INVOLVEMENT (JAPAN).=
                 MIDWEST JOURNAL OF POLITICAL SCIENCE, 9, (MAY 1965),      65
                    PP. 133-147.
                 COMEL, ELEL, ELNOEL, METEL
KUTNB -65-EPD    KUTNER, B
                 ELEMENTS AND PROBLEMS OF DEMOCRATIC LEADERSHIP.=
                 AW GOULDNER (ED), STUDIES IN LEADERSHIP, NEW YORK,        65
                    RUSSELL AND RUSSELL, 1965, PP. 459-467.
                 DEFEL
KYDIS -65-PWP    KYDIS, S
                 THE PRESS IN WORLD POLITICS AND IN THE CONDUCT
                    OF FOREIGN POLICY (GREAT BRITAIN, LATIN AMERICA,
                    SOVIET UNION, UNITED STATES).=
                 JOURNAL OF INTERNATIONAL AFFAIRS, 10, (SEPTEMBER 1965),   65
                    PP. 201-210.
                 ELEL
L     -57-SI     L
                 THE SOVIET INTELLIGENTSIA.=
                 FOREIGN AFFAIRS, 36, (OCTOBER 1957), PP. 122-130.         57
                 ELPRNOR
LABEL -56-RAK    LABEDZ, L
                 RUSSIA AFTER KHRUSHCHEV.=
                 THE REVIEW OF POLITICS, 18, (OCTOBER 1956), PP. 473-486.  56
                 ELEL, ELPRNOR
LABEL -57-ITP    LABEDZ, L
                 INTELLECTUAL TRENDS IN POLAND.=
                 DISSENT, 4, (SPRING 1957), PP. 113-121.                   57
                 ELEL, ELPRNOR
LABEL -59-NSI    LABEDZ, L
                 THE NEW SOVIET INTELLIGENTSIA -- ORIGINS AND RECRUITMENT.=
                 SOVIET SURVEY--A QUARTERLY REVIEW OF CULTURAL TRENDS,     59
                    29, (JULY-SEPTEMBER 1959), PP. 103-111.
                 COMEL, ELEL
LABEL -60-SSI    LABEDZ, L
                 THE STRUCTURE OF THE SOVIET INTELLIGENTSIA.=
                 DAEDALUS, 89, (SUMMER 1960), PP. 503-519.                 60
                 COMEL, ELPRNOR
LABEL -62-REH    LABEDZ, L (ED.)
                 REVISIONISM -- ESSAYS ON THE HISTORY OF MARXIST IDEAS.=
                 NEW YORK, FREDERICK A PRAEGER, 1962.                      62
                 ELEL, ELPRNOR
LABEL -63-RPS    LABEDZ, L
                 RESURRECTION AND PERDITION (SOVIET UNION).=
                 PROBLEMS OF COMMUNISM, 12, (MARCH-APRIL 1963), PP. 48-59. 63
                 ELEL
LADDEC-66-NPL    LADD-JR, EC
                 NEGRO POLITICAL LEADERSHIP IN THE SOUTH
                    (UNITED STATES).=
                 ITHACA, CORNELL UNIVERSITY PRESS, 1966.                   66
                 COMEL, ELNOEL, ELPRNOR
LADIJ -63-CLL    LADINSKY, J
                 CAREERS OF LAWYERS, LAW PRACTICE, AND LEGAL
                    INSTITUTIONS (UNITED STATES).=
                 AMERICAN SOCIOLOGICAL REVIEW, 28, (FEBRUARY 1963),        63
                    PP. 47-54.
                 COMEL
LADIJ -66-OCP    LADINSKY, J          GROSSMAN, JB
                 ORGANIZATIONAL CONSEQUENCES OF PROFESSIONAL CONSENSUS --
                    LAWYERS AND SELECTION OF JUDGES (UNITED-STATES).=
                 ADMINISTRATIVE SCIENCE QUARTERLY, 11, (JUNE 1966),        66
                    PP. 79-106.
                 COMEL, ELEL, ELPRNOR
LAIDHW-59-LSR    LAIDLER, HW
                 LABOR'S ROLE IN AMERICAN POLITICS.=
                 CURRENT HISTORY, N.S., 36, (JUNE 1959), PP. 321-327.      59

ELEL, ELNOEL
LAINLH-46-NCS   LAING, LH
THE NATURE OF CANADA'S PARLIAMENTARY REPRESENTATION.=
CANADIAN JOURNAL OF ECONOMICS AND POLITICAL SCIENCE,          46
   12, (NOVEMBER 1946), PP. 509-516.
COMEL
LAIRRD-64-PSA   LAIRD, RD
THE POLITICS OF SOVIET AGRICULTURE.=
STUDIES ON THE SOVIET UNION, 3, (1964), PP. 147-158.         64
ELEL, ELPRNOR
LAIRRD-66-CSL   LAIRD, RD
SOME CHARACTERISTICS OF THE SOVIET LEADERSHIP SYSTEM --
   A MATURING TOTALITARIAN SYSTEM.=
MIDWEST JOURNAL OF POLITICAL SCIENCE, 10,                    66
   (FEBRUARY 1966), PP. 29-38.
ELEL, ELNOEL
LAMBHB-55-IBC   LAMB, HB
THE INDIAN BUSINESS COMMUNITIES AND THE EVOLUTION OF
   AN INDUSTRIALIST CLASS.=
PACIFIC AFFAIRS, 28, (JUNE 1955), PP. 101-106.               55
COMEL, ELEL, ELPRNOR
LAMBHB-59-BOL   LAMB, HB
BUSINESS ORGANIZATION AND LEADERSHIP IN INDIA TODAY.=
RL PARK AND I TINKER (EDS), LEADERSHIP AND POLITICAL         59
   INSTITUTIONS IN INDIA, PRINCETON, PRINCETON
   UNIVERSITY PRESS, 1959, PP. 251-267.
COMEL, ELEL, ELNOEL
LAMBRD-59-HCG   LAMBERT, RD
HINDU COMMUNAL GROUPS IN INDIAN POLITICS.=
RL RARK AND I TINKER (EDS), LEADERSHIP AND POLITICAL         59
   INSTITUTIONS IN INDIA, PRINCETON, PRINCETON UNIVERSITY
   PRESS, 1959, PP. 211-225.
ELEL, ELPRNOR
LAMBRK-52-PEP   LAMB, RK
POLITICAL ELITES AND THE PROCESS OF ECONOMIC DEVELOPMENT
   (UNITED STATES, WESTERN EUROPE, SOVIET UNION).=
B HOSELITZ (ED), THE PROGRESS OF UNDERDEVELOPED AREAS,       52
   CHICAGO, UNIVERSITY OF CHICAGO PRESS, 1952, PP. 33-53.
GNELTH, COMEL, ELPRNOR
LANDCH-59-PAB   LANDE, CH
POLITICAL ATTITUDES AND BEHAVIOR IN THE PHILIPPINES.=
PHILIPPINE JOURNAL OF PUBLIC ADMINISTRATION, 3,              59
   (JULY 1959), PP. 341-365.
ELNOEL, ELPRNOR
LANDCH-65-LFP   LANDE, CH
LEADERS, FACTIONS AND PARTIES -- THE STRUCTURE OF
   PHILIPPINE POLITICS.=
NEW HAVEN, YALE UNIVERSITY PRESS, 1965.                      65
COMEL, ELEL, ELNOEL, ELPRNOR
LANDHA-67-LEI   LANDSBERGER, HA
THE LABOR ELITE -- IS IT REVOLUTIONARY (LATIN AMERICA).=
SM LIPSET AND A SOLARI (EDS), ELITES IN LATIN AMERICA,       67
   NEW YORK, OXFORD UNIVERSITY PRESS, 1967, PP. 256-300.
ELEL, ELNOEL, ELPRNOR
LANDJW-64-MCL   LANDYNSKI, JW
THE MAKING OF CONSTITUTIONAL LAW (UNITED STATES).=
SOCIAL RESEARCH, 31, (SPRING 1964), PP. 23-44.               64
COMEL, ELEL, ELPRNOR
LANDP -58-HSD   LANDY, P
HUNGARY'S DEFIANT INTELLECTUALS.=
PROBLEMS OF COMMUNISM, 7, (JANUARY-FEBRUARY 1958),           58
   PP. 52-57.
COMEL, ELEL
LANDP -58-RRE   LANDY, P
RETREAT AND REACTION IN EASTERN EUROPE.=
PROBLEMS OF COMMUNISM, 7, (JULY-AUGUST 1958), PP. 8-15.      58
ELEL, ELPRNOR
LANDP -62-HPA   LANDY, P
HUNGARY -- PRESSURES FROM ABOVE.=
PROBLEMS OF COMMUNISM, 11, (MAY-JUNE 1962), PP. 27-32.       62
ELEL, ELNOEL
LANDR -53-MPN   LANDAU, R
MOROCCAN PROFILES -- A NATIONALIST VIEW.=
THE MIDDLE EAST JOURNAL, 7, (WINTER 1953)) PP. 45-57.        53
COMEL, ELPRNOR
LANDR -61-MIU   LANDAU, R
MOROCCO INDEPENDENT UNDER MOHAMMED THE FIFTH.=
HOLLYWOOD BY THE SEA, FLORIDA, TRANSATLANTIC ARTS, 1961.     61
COMEL
LANERE-49-NTL   LANE, RE
NOTES ON THE THEORY OF THE LOBBY.=
THE WESTERN POLITICAL QUARTERLY, 2, (MARCH 1949),            49
   PP. 154-162.
ELEL, ELNOEL, ELPRNOR

LANERE-53-BBU   LANE, RE
                BUSINESSMEN AND BUREAUCRATS (UNITED STATES).=
                SOCIAL FORCES, 32, (DECEMBER 1953), PP. 145-152.          53
                ELEL
LANERE-58-ECG   LANE, RE
                ELITE COMMUNICATION AND THE GOVERNMENTAL PROCESS
                    (UNITED STATES, CANADA).=
                WORLD POLITICS, 10, (APRIL 1958), PP. 430-437.            58
                COMEL, ELEL
LANGFC-56-CAC   LANGDON, FC
                THE CATHOLIC ANTI - COMMUNIST ROLE WITHIN AUSTRALIAN
                    LABOR.=
                THE WESTERN POLITICAL QUARTERLY, 9, (DECEMBER 1956),      56
                    PP. 884-889.
                ELEL, ELNOEL, ELPRNOR
LANGFC-61-BBL   LANGDON, FC
                BIG BUSINESS LOBBYING IN JAPAN -- THE CASE OF CENTRAL
                    BANK REFORM.=
                THE AMERICAN POLITICAL SCIENCE RECIEW, 55, (JUNE 1961),   61
                    PP. 527-538.
                ELEL
LANGFC-61-OIJ   LANGDON, FC
                ORGANIZED INTERESTS IN JAPAN AND THEIR INFLUENCE ON
                    POLITICAL PARTIES.=
                PACIFIC AFFAIRS, 34, (FALL 1961), PP. 271-278.            61
                ELEL, ELNOEL
LANGK -64-TCM   LANG, K
                TECHNOLOGY AND CAREER MANAGEMENT IN THE MILITARY
                    ESTABLISHMENT (UNITED STATES).=
                M JANOWITZ (ED), THE NEW MILITARY--CHANGING PATTERNS OF   64
                    ORGANIZATION, NEW YORK, RUSSELL SAGE FOUNDATION, 1964,
                    PP. 39-82.
                COMEL
LANGPF-63-IOS   LANGER, PF
                INDEPENDENCE OR SUBORDINATION -- THE JAPANESE
                    COMMUNIST PARTY BETWEEN MOSCOW AND PEKING.=
                AD BARNETT (ED), COMMUNIST STRATEGIES IN ASIA, NEW YORK,  63
                    FREDERICK A PRAEGER, 1963, PP. 63-100.
                COMEL, ELEL, ELPRNOR
LANGR -55-TDM   LANGBAUM, R
                TOTALITARIANISM -- A DISEASE OF MODERNISM.=
                COMMENTARY, 19, (MAY 1955), PP. 487-494.                  55
                ELEL, ELNOEL, ELPRNOR
LANPE -57-SR    LANPERT, E
                STUDIES IN REBELLION.=
                NEW YORK, FREDERICK A PRAEGER, 1957.                      57
                ELNOEL
LAPAJ -54-LWT   LAPALOMBARA, J
                LEFT WING TRADE UNIONISM -- THE MATRIX OF COMMUNIST
                    POWER IN ITALY.=
                THE WESTERN POLITICAL QUARTERLY, 7, (JUNE 1954),          54
                    PP. 202-226.
                COMEL
LAPAJ -57-IFB   LAPALOMBARA, J         DORSEY, JT
                ON THE ITALIAN AND FRENCH BUREAUCRACIES.=
                PROD (THE AMERICAN BEHAVIORAL SCIENTIST), 1,              57
                    (SEPTEMBER 1957), PP. 35-40.
                ELEL
LAPAJ -57-ILM   LAPALOMBARA, J
                THE ITALIAN LABOR MOVEMENT -- PROBLEMS AND PROSPECTS.=
                ITHACA, CORNELL UNIVERSITY PRESS, 1957.                   57
                COMEL, ELEL, ELNOEL
LAPAJ -58-PPS   LAPALOMBARA, J
                POLITICAL PARTY SYSTEMS AND CRISIS GOVERNMENT --
                    FRENCH AND ITALIAN CONTRASTS.=
                MIDWEST JOURNAL OF POLITICAL SCIENCE, 2, (MAY 1958),      58
                    PP. 117-142.
                ELEL, ELNOEL, ELPRNOR
LAPAJ -60-ULI   LAPALOMBARA, J
                THE UTILITY AND LIMITATIONS OF INTEREST GROUP THEORY
                    IN NON-AMERICAN FIELD SITUATIONS.=
                THE JOURNAL OF POLITICS, 22, (FEBRUARY 1960), PP. 29-49.  60
                ELEL, METEL
LAPAJ -63-BPD   LAPALOMBARA, J (ED)
                BUREAUCRACY AND POLITICAL DEVELOPMENT.=
                PRINCETON, PRINCETON UNIVERSITY PRESS, 1963.              63
                GNELTH, DEFEL, COMEL, ELEL, ELNOEL, ELPRNOR
LAPAJ -63-OBP   LAPALOMBARA, J
                AN OVERVIEW OF BUREAUCRACY AND POLITICAL DEVELOPMENT.=
                J LAPALOMBARA (ED), BUREAUCRACY AND POLITICAL            63
                    DEVELOPMENT, PRINCETON, PRINCETON UNIVERSITY PRESS,
                    1963, PP. 3-33.
                DEFEL, ELEL, ELNOEL, ELPRNOR
LAPAJ -64-IGI   LAPALOMBARA, J

                         INTEREST GROUPS IN ITALIAN POLITICS.=
                         PRINCETON, PRINCETON UNIVERSITY PRESS, 1964.              64
                         ELEL, ELNOEL
LAPAJ  -66-IFI   LAPALOMBARA, J
                         ITALY -- FRAGMENTATION, ISOLATION AND ALIENATION.=
                         LW PYE AND S VERBA (EDS), POLITICAL CULTURE AND           66
                           POLITICAL DEVELOPMENT, PRINCETON, PRINCETON UNIVERSITY
                           PRESS, 1966, PP. 282-329.
                         COMEL, ELNOEL, ELPRNOR
LAPAJG-65-PPP    LAPALOMBARA, JG      WEINER, M
                         POLITICAL PARTIES AND POLITICAL DEVELOPMENT.=
                         PRINCETON, NEW JERSEY, PRINCETON UNIVERSITY PRESS, 1965.  65
                         DEFEL, ELEL, ELNOEL
LAPIRT-65-SC     LAPIERE, RT
                         SOCIAL CHANGE.=
                         NEW YORK, MCGRAW-HILL, 1965.                              65
                         DEFEL, ELEL, COMEL, ELNOEL
LAPOJD-58-RBC    LAPONCE, JD
                         THE RELIGIOUS BACKGROUND OF CANADIAN M.P.'S.=
                         POLITICAL STUDIES, 6, (1958), PP. 253-258.                58
                         COMEL, ELPRNOR
LAPPRE-65-NPS    LAPP, RE
                         THE NEW PRIESTHOOD -- THE SCIENTIFIC ELITE AND THE USES
                           OF POWER (UNITED STATES).=
                         NEW YORK, HARPER, 1965.                                   65
                         ELEL, ELNOEL
LAQUAA-63-UPP    LAQUIAN, AA
                         UNDERSTANDING THE PHILIPPINE POLITICAL PROCESS.=
                         PHILIPPINE JOURNAL OF PUBLIC ADMINISTRATION, 7,           63
                           (APRIL 1963), PP. 133-137.
                         ELEL, ELNOEL, ELPRNOR
LAQUWZ-57-CNM    LAQUER, WZ
                         COMMUNISM AND NATIONALISM IN THE MIDDLE EAST.=
                         NEW YORK, FREDERICK A PRAEGER, 1957.                      57
                         COMEL, ELEL, ELNOEL, ELPRNOR
LAQUWZ-59-IGC    LAQUEUR, WZ
                         AS IRAQ GOES COMMUNIST.=
                         COMMENTARY, 27, (MAY 1959), PP. 369-375.                  59
                         ELEL, ELNOEL
LAQUWZ-59-NIC    LAQUEUR, WZ
                         NASSER AND THE IRAQI COMMUNISTS.=
                         COMMENTARY, 27, (FEBRUARY 1959), PP. 101-108.             59
                         ELEL, ELNOEL
LASCC  -62-ALR   LASCH, C
                         THE AMERICAN LIBERALS AND THE RUSSIAN REVOLUTION.=
                         NEW YORK, COLUMBIA UNIVERSITY PRESS, 1962.                62
                         ELPRNOR
LASKB  -50-NFA   LASKER, B
                         NEW FORCES IN ASIA.=
                         NEW YORK, H W WILSON COMPANY, 1950.                       50
                         COMEL, ELEL, ELNOEL, ELPRNOR
LASKHJ-48-ADC    LASKI, HJ
                         THE AMERICAN DEMOCRACY -- A CONTEMPORARY AND AN
                           INTERPRETATION.=
                         NEW YORK, VIKING PRESS, 1948.                             48
                         DEFEL, COMEL, ELEL, ELNOEL, ELPRNOR
LASSH  -52-CSE   LASSWELL, H        LERNER, D         ROTHELL, EC
                         THE COMPARATIVE STUDY OF ELITES -- AN INTRODUCTION AND
                           BIBLIOGRAPHY.=
                         STANFORD, STANFORD UNIVERSITY PRESS, 1952.                52
                         GNELTH, DEFEL, COMEL, ELEL, ELNOEL, ELPRNOR, METEL
LASSHD-0 -NSI    LASSWELL, HD
                         NATIONAL SECURITY AND INDIVIDUAL FREEDOM.=
                         NEW YORK, MCGRAW-HILL, 1950.                              50
                         DEFEL, COMEL, ELEL
LASSHD-30-PP     LASSWELL, HD
                         PSYCHOPATHOLOGY AND POLITICS.=
                         CHICAGO, UNIVERSITY OF CHICAGO PRESS, 1930.               30
                         DEFEL, ELPRNOR, METEL
LASSHD-36-PWG    LASSWELL, HD
                         POLITICS -- WHO GETS WHAT, WHEN, HOW (UNITED STATES).=
                         NEW YORK, MCGRAW-HILL, 1936.                              36
                         GNELTH, COMEL, ELEL, ELNOEL, ELPRNOR
LASSHD-48-APB    LASSWELL, HD
                         THE ANALYSIS OF POLITICAL BEHAVIOR --
                           AN EMPIRICAL APPROACH.=
                         LONDON, KEGAN PAUL, TRENCH, TRUBNER AND COMPANY, 1948.    48
                         DEFEL, COMEL, ELEL, ELNOEL, ELPRNOR, METEL
LASSHD-48-PP     LASSWELL, HD
                         POWER AND PERSONALITY.=
                         NEW YORK, W W NORTON AND COMPANY, INC, 1948.              48
                         COMEL, ELPRNOR
LASSHD-50-PSF    LASSWELL, HD
                         POWER AND SOCIETY -- A FRAMEWORK FOR POLITICAL INQUIRY.=

```
                    NEW HAVEN, YALE UNIVERSITY PRESS, 1950.                    50
                    GNELTH, METEL
LASSHD-51-WRO       LASSWELL, HD
                    THE WORLD REVOLUTION OF OUR TIMES.=
                    STANFORD, STANFORD UNIVERSITY PRESS, 1951.                 51
                    DEFEL, ELNOEL, ELPRNOR
LASSHD-52-CSE       LASSWELL, HD
                    THE COMPARATIVE STUDY OF ELITES.=
                    STANFORD, HOOVER INSTITUTE ELITE STUDIES SERIES,           52
                      STANFORD UNIVERSITY PRESS, 1952.
                    GNELTH, DEFEL, COMEL, ELEL, ELNOEL, ELPRNOR, METEL
LASSHD-52-CSS       LASSWELL, HD
                    THE COMPARATIVE STUDY OF SYMBOLS.=
                    STANFORD, STANFORD UNIVERSITY PRESS, 1952.                 52
                    DEFEL, COMEL, ELEL, ELNOEL, ELPRNOR
LASSHD-54-EPP       LASSWELL, HD
                    EFFECT OF PERSONALITY ON POLITICAL PARTICIPATION.=
                    R CHRISTIE AND M JAHODA (EDS), STUDIES IN THE SCOPE AND    54
                      METHOD OF 'THE AUTHORITARIAN PERSONALITY', GLENCOE,
                      THE FREE PRESS, 1954, PP. 197-225.
                    ELPRNOR, METEL
LASSHD-56-DPS       LASSWELL, HD
                    THE DECISION PROCESS -- SEVEN CATEGORIES
                      OF FUNCTIONAL ANALYSIS.=
                    UNIVERSITY PARK, BUREAU OF GOVERNMENT RESEARCH,            56
                      UNIVERSITY OF MARYLAND, 1956.
                    METEL
LASSHD-61-ASP       LASSWELL, HD
                    AGENDA FOR THE STUDY OF POLITICAL ELITES.=
                    D MARVICK (ED), POLITICAL DECISION MAKERS, GLENCOE,        61
                      THE FREE PRESS, 1961, PP. 264-287.
                    METEL
LASSHD-62-GSH       LASSWELL, HD
                    THE GARRISON STATE HYPOTHESIS TODAY.=
                    SP HUNTINGTON (ED), CHANGING PATTERNS OF MILITARY          62
                      POLITICS, GLENCOE, THE FREE PRESS, 1962, PP. 51-71.
                    COMEL, ELEL, ELNOEL, ELPRNOR
LASSHD-65-CIA       LASSWELL, HD
                    THE CLIMATE OF INTERNATIONAL ACTION.=
                    INTERNATIONAL BEHAVIOR--A SOCIAL-PSYCHOLOGICAL ANALYSIS,   65
                      HERBERT C KELMAN (ED), NEW YORK, HOLT, RINEHART AND
                      WINSTON, 1965, PP. 339-353.
                    ELEL, ELNOEL, METEL
LASSHD-66-CLP       LASSWELL, HD
                    CONFLICT AND LEADERSHIP -- THE PROCESS OF DECISION AND
                      THE NATURE OF AUTHORITY.=
                    AVS DEREUCK AND J KNIGHT (EDS), CIBA FOUNDATION SYMPOSIUM 66
                      ON CONFLICT IN SOCIETY, LONDON, J AND A CHURCHILL,
                      PP. 210-228.
                    GNELTH, DEFEL
LASSHD-66-WRE       LASSWELL, HD          LERNER, D (EDS)
                    WORLD REVOLUTIONARY ELITES -- STUDIES IN COERCIVE
                      IDEOLOGICAL MOVEMENTS (CHINA, GERMANY, ITALY,
                      SOVIET UNION).=
                    CAMBRIDGE, THE MIT PRESS, 1966.                           66
                    GNELTH, DEFEL, COMEL, ELEL, ELPRNOR
LASSHD-67-PSS       LASSWELL, HD
                    POLITICAL SYSTEMS, STYLES AND PERSONALITIES.=
                    LJ EDINGER (ED), POLITICAL LEADERSHIP IN INDUSTRIALIZED    67
                      SOCIETIES, NEW YORK, JOHN WILEY AND SONS, 1967,
                      PP. 315-347.
                    GNELTH, DEFEL
LASSHD-67-RSC       LASSWELL, HD          ARENS, R
                    THE ROLE OF SANCTION IN CONFLICT RESOLUTION.=
                    THE JOURNAL OF CONFLICT RESOLUTION, 11, (MARCH 1967),      67
                      PP. 27-39.
                    DEFEL, METEL
LASWHD-59-PCC       LASWELL, HD
                    POLITICAL CONSTITUTION AND CHARACTER.=
                    PSYCHOANALYSIS AND PSYCHOANALYTIC REVIEW, 46,              59
                      (WINTER 1959), PP. 3-18.
                    DEFEL, ELPRNOR, METEL
LATHE -52-GBP       LATHAM, E
                    THE GROUP BASIS OF POLITICS -- NOTES FOR A THEORY.=
                    THE AMERICAN POLITICAL SCIENCE REVIEW, 46, (JUNE 1952),    52
                      PP. 376-397.
                    DEFEL, ELEL, ELNOEL
LATHE -54-SCS       LATHAM, E
                    THE SUPREME COURT AND THE SUPREME PEOPLE (UNITED STATES).=
                    THE JOURNAL OF POLITICS, 16, (MAY 1954), PP. 207-235.      54
                    ELEL, ELNOEL
LATISA-53-ISC       LATIF, SA
                    ISLAM AND SOCIAL CHANGE.=
                    INTERNATIONAL SOCIAL SCIENCE BULLETIN, 5, (1953),          53
```

                          PP. 691-697.
                          ELNOEL, ELPRNOR
LAUNP -61-SHC    LAUNDY, P
                          THE SPEAKER OF THE HOUSE OF COMMONS (GREAT BRITAIN).=
                          PARLIAMENTARY AFFAIRS, 14, (WINTER 1960-1961),                    61
                          PP. 72-79.
                          ELEL, ELNOEL
LAUTA -65-GDM    LAUTERBACH, A
                          GOVERNMENT AND DEVELOPMENT -- MANAGERIAL ATTITUDES IN
                          LATIN AMERICA.=
                          JOURNAL OF INTER-AMERICAN STUDIES, 7, (APRIL 1965),            65
                          PP. 201-225.
                          COMEL, ELPRNOR
LAUTA -66-ELA    LAUTERBACH, A
                          ENTERPRISE IN LATIN AMERICA -- BUSINESS ATTITUDES IN A
                          DEVELOPING ECONOMY.=
                          ITHACA, CORNELL UNIVERSITY PRESS, 1966.                              66
                          COMEL, ELEL, ELNOEL, ELPRNOR
LAVIH -59-SRC    LAVINE, H
                          SOCIAL REVOLUTION IN CUBA.=
                          COMMENTARY, 28, (OCTOBER 1959), PP. 324-341.                     59
                          ELNOEL, ELPRNOR
LAZAPF-58-AMS    LAZARSFELD, PF        THIELENS, W (EDS)
                          ACADEMIC MIND -- SOCIAL SCIENTISTS IN A TIME OF CRISIS
                          (UNITED STATES).=
                          GLENCOE, ILLINOIS, FREE PRESS, 1958.                                 58
                          COMEL, ELEL, ELPRNOR
LC      -62-SMA    LC
                          SOCIAL MOBILITY AMONG THE DEAD -- OR POSTHUMOUS
                          CIRCULATION OF ELITES (SOVIET UNION).=
                          DISSENT, 9, (WINTER 1962), PP. 82-83.                                62
                          ELNOEL
LEACER-54-PSH    LEACH, ER
                          POLITICAL SYSTEMS OF HIGHLAND BURMA -- A STUDY OF KACHIN
                          SOCIAL STRUCTURE.=
                          CAMBRIDGE, HARVARD UNIVERSITY PRESS, 1954.                       54
                          COMEL, ELEL, ELNOEL, ELPRNOR, METEL
LEACRH-65-LCU    LEACH, RH
                          A LEADERSHIP CRISIS (UNITED STATES).=
                          NATIONAL CIVIC REVIEW, 54, (MAY 1965), PP. 244-252.          65
                          COMEL
LEBEA -63-EPR    LEBED, A
                          EXTENSION OF THE POWERS OF REPUBLICAN PARTY SECOND
                          SECRETARIES (SOVIET UNION).=
                          BULLETIN INSTITUTE FOR THE STUDY OF THE USSR, 10,            63
                          (AUGUST 1963), PP. 34-37.
                          COMEL, ELEL
LEBEA -65-SAE    LEBED, A
                          THE SOVIET ADMINISTRATIVE ELITE -- SELECTION AND
                          DEPLOYMENT PROCEDURES.=
                          STUDIES ON THE SOVIET UNION, 5, (1965), PP. 47-55.         65
                          COMEL, ELEL
LEE,AM-65-PS     LEE, AM
                          POWER SEEKERS.=
                          AW GOULDNER (ED), STUDIES IN LEADERSHIP, NEW YORK           65
                          RUSSELL AND RUSSELL, 1965, PP. 667-678.
                          DEFEL
LEE,EC-52-POR    LEE, EC
                          THE PRESIDING OFFICER AND RULES COMMITTEE IN
                          LEGISLATURES OF THE U.S. (UNITED STATES).=
                          BERKELEY, BUREAU OF PUBLIC ADMINISTRATION, UNIVERSITY OF  52
                          CALIFORNIA PRESS, 1952.
                          ELEL, ELPRNOR
LEE,SC-47-IC     LEE, SC
                          INTELLIGENTSIA OF CHINA.=
                          THE AMERICAN JOURNAL OF SOCIOLOGY, 52,                           47
                          (MAY 1947), PP. 489-497.
                          COMEL, ELEL, ELPRNOR
LEEDA -64-BCS    LEEDS, A
                          BRAZILIAN CAREERS AND SOCIAL STRUCTURE -- AN EVOLUTIONARY
                          MODEL AND CASE HISTORY.=
                          AMERICAN ANTHROPOLOGIST, 66, (OCTOBER 1964),                  64
                          PP. 1321-1347.
                          COMEL, ELEL, ELNOEL
LEGUC -65-BAD    LEGUM, C            LEWIS, A
                          BEYOND AFRICAN DICTATORSHIP.=
                          ENCOUNTER, 25, (DECEMBER 1965), PP. 51-54.                       65
                          ELEL, ELNOEL
LEGUC -65-SPD    LEGUM, C
                          SINGLE - PARTY DEMOCRACY (TANZANIA).=
                          THE WORLD TODAY, 21, (DECEMBER 1965), PP. 526-533.        65
                          COMEL, ELEL, ELNOEL
LEIDC -65-PIS    LEIDEN, C
                          POLITICAL INSTABILITY IN SYRIA.=

                    THE SOUTHWESTERN SOCIAL SCIENCE QUARTERLY, 45, (MARCH        65
                       1965), PP. 353-360.
                    ELEL, ELNOEL
LEIGAH-65-LSS       LEIGHTON, AH
                    LEADERSHIP IN A STRESS SITUATION.=
                    AW GOULDNER (ED), STUDIES IN LEADERSHIP, NEW YORK,           65
                       RUSSELL AND RUSSELL, 1965, PP. 605-614.
                    METEL
LEISA -57-PPS       LEISERSON, A
                    THE PLACE OF PARTIES IN THE STUDY OF POLITICS.=
                    THE AMERICAN POLITICAL SCIENCE REVIEW, 51, (DECEMBER         57
                       1957), PP. 143-954.
                    METEL
LEISA -58-PPU       LEISERSON, A
                    PARTIES AND POLITICS (UNITED STATES).=
                    NEW YORK, ALFRED KNOPF, 1958.                                58
                    COMEL, ELEL, ELNOEL, ELPRNOR
LEISA -65-SPP       LEISERSON, A
                    SCIENTISTS AND THE POLICY PROCESS (UNITED STATES).=
                    THE AMERICAN POLITICAL SCIENCE REVIEW, 59, (JUNE 1965),      65
                       PP. 408-416.
                    COMEL, ELEL, ELPRNOR
LEITN -51-OCP       LEITES, N
                    THE OPERATIONAL CODE OF THE POLITBURO (SOVIET UNION).=
                    NEW YORK, MAGRAW-HILL BOOK COMPANY, 1951.                    51
                    ELEL, ELNOEL, ELPRNOR, METEL
LEITN -51-PIS       LEITES, N                BERNAUT, E            GARTHOFF, RL
                    POLITBURO IMAGES OF STALIN (SOVIET UNION).=
                    WORLD POLITICS, 3, (JANUARY 1951), PP. 317-339.              51
                    ELEL, ELPRNOR
LEITN -52-PTW       LEITES, N
                    THE POLITBURO THROUGH WESTERN EYES (SOVIET UNION).=
                    WORLD POLITICS, 4, (JANUARY 1952), PP. 159-185.              52
                    ELPRNOR
LEITN -53-SBS       LEITES, N
                    A STUDY OF BOLSHEVISM (SOVIET UNION).=
                    GLENCOE, ILLINOIS, FREE PRESS, 1953.                         53
                    ELPRNOR, METEL
LEITN -59-GPF       LEITES, N
                    ON THE GAME OF POLITICS IN FRANCE.=
                    STANFORD, STANFORD UNIVERSITY PRESS, 1959.                   59
                    COMEL, ELEL, ELNOEL, ELPRNOR
LEITS -56-RNE       LEITH-ROSS, S
                    THE RISE OF A NEW ELITE AMONGST THE WOMEN OF NIGERIA.=
                    INTERNATIONAL SOCIAL SCIENCE BULLETIN, 8, (1956),            56
                       PP. 481-488.
                    COMEL, ELEL, ELNOEL
LEMAR -64-PAB       LEMARCHAND, R
                    POLITICAL AWAKENING IN THE BELGIAN CONGO -- THE POLITICS
                       OF FRAGMENTATION.=
                    BERKELEY, UNIVERSITY OF CALIFORNIA PRESS, 1964.              64
                    COMEL, ELEL, ELNOEL, ELPRNOR
LEMAR -66-SPC       LEMARCHAND, R
                    SOCIAL AND POLITICAL CHANGES IN BURUNDI.=
                    THE JOURNAL OF MODERN AFRICAN STUDIES, 4, (DECEMBER 1966),66
                       PP. 401-433.
                    COMEL, ELEL, ELPRNOR
LENCG -47-CMI       LENCZOWSKI, G
                    THE COMMUNIST MOVEMENT IN IRAN.=
                    THE MIDDLE EAST JOURNAL, 1, (JANUARY 1947), PP. 29-45.       47
                    COMEL, ELEL, ELNOEL
LENSGE-52-ASC       LENSKI, GE
                    AMERICAN SOCIAL CLASSES -- STATISTICAL STRATA
                       OR SOCIAL GROUPS.=
                    THE AMERICAN JOURNAL OF SOCIOLOGY, 58, (SEPTEMBER 1952),     52
                       PP. 139-144.
                    METEL
LEONW -58-TSS       LEONHARD, W
                    TERROR IN THE SOVIET SYSTEM -- TRENDS AND PORTENTS.=
                    PROBLEMS OF COMMUNISM, 7, (NOVEMBER-DECEMBER 1958),          58
                       PP. 1-7.
                    ELPRNOR
LEONW -63-IDB       LEONHARD, W
                    INTERNAL DEVELOPMENTS -- A BALANCE SHEET (SOVIET UNION).=
                    PROBLEMS OF COMMUNISM, 12, (MARCH-APRIL 1963), PP. 2-9.      63
                    ELEL, ELPRNOR
LEONW -66-WRN       LEONHARD, W
                    WITHER RUSSIA -- NOTES ON AN AGONIZING DIAGNOSIS
                       (SOVIET UNION).=
                    PROBLEMS OF COMMUNISM, 15, (JULY-AUGUST 1966), PP. 36-42. 66
                    FLEL, ELPRNOR
LERCCO-60-SCN       LERCHE-JR, CO
                    SOUTHERN CONGRESSMEN AND THE 'NEW ISOLATIONISM'
                       (UNITED STATES).=

                    POLITICAL SCIENCE QUARTERLY, 75, (SEPTEMBER 1960),          60
                       PP. 321-337.
                    ELNOEL, ELPRNOR, METEL
LERND -3 -FEP    LERNER, D              KRAMER, MN
                    FRENCH ELITE PERSPECTIVES ON THE UNITED NATIONS.=
                    INTERNATIONAL ORGANIZATION, 17, (WINTER 1963), PP. 54-74.63
                    ELPRNOR
LERND -51-NE     LERNER, D
                    THE NAZI ELITE.=
                    STANFORD, HOOVER INSTITUTE ELITE STUDIES SERIES,            51
                       STANFORD UNIVERSITY PRESS, 1951.
                    COMEL
LERND -53-RBT    LERNER, D
                    THE ROLE OF BRAINS IN THE TOTAL STATE.=
                    COMMENTARY, 16, (AUGUST 1953), PP. 167-173.                 53
                    DEFEL, COMEL, ELEL, ELNOEL
LERND -58-PTS    LERNER, D
                    THE PASSING OF TRADITIONAL SOCIETY (MIDDLE EAST).=
                    GLENCOE, THE FREE PRESS, 1958.                              58
                    GNELTH, DEFEL, COMEL, ELEL, ELNOEL, ELPRNOR
LERND -60-SPT    LERNER, D              ROBINSON, R
                    SWORDS AND PLOUGHSHARES -- THE TURKISH ARMY
                       AS A MODERNIZING FORCE.=
                    WORKD POLITICS, 13, (OCTOBER 1960), PP. 19-44.              60
                    COMEL, ELEL, ELNOEL, ELPRNOR
LEV,DS-64-PRA    LEV, DS
                    THE POLITICAL ROLE OF THE ARMY IN INDONESIA.=
                    PACIFIC AFFAIRS, 36, (WINTER 1963-1964), PP. 349-364.       64
                    ELEL, ELPRNOR
LEVEB -61-BS     LEVENSON, B
                    BUREAUCRATIC SUCCESSION.=
                    A ETZIONI (ED), COMPLEX ORGANIZATIONS, NEW YORK,            61
                       HOLT, RINEHART, AND WINSTON, 1961, PP. 362-375.
                    COMEL, ELEL
LEVEJR-58-CCI    LEVENSON, JR
                    CONFUCIAN CHINA AND ITS MODERN FATE -- THE PROBLEM OF
                       INTELLECTUAL CONTINUITY.=
                    BERKELEY, UNIVERSITY OF CALIFORNIA PRESS, 1958.             58
                    COMEL, ELEL, ELNOEL, ELPRNOR
LEVIDJ-57-APF    LEVINSON, DJ
                    AUTHORITARIAN PERSONALITY AND FOREIGN POLICY
                       (UNITED STATES).=
                    THE JOURNAL OF CONFLICT RESOLUTION, 1, (MARCH 1957),        57
                       PP. 37-47.
                    ELPRNOR, METEL
LEVIDJ-58-RPP    LEVINSON, DJ
                    THE RELEVANCE OF PERSONALITY FOR POLITICAL PARTICIPATION.=
                    THE PUBLIC OPINION QUARTERLY, 22, (SPRING 1958),            58
                       PP. 3-10.
                    METEL
LEVIDN-66-CCC    LEVINE, DN
                    CLASS CONSCIOUSNESS AND CLASS SOLIDARITY IN THE NEW
                       ETHIOPIAN ELITE.=
                    PC LLOYD (ED), THE NEW ELITES OF TROPICAL AFRICA, LONDON, 66
                       OXFORD UNIVERSITY PRESS, PP. 312-325.
                    COMEL, ELEL, ELNOEL
LEVIDN-66-EIA    LEVINE, DN
                    ETHIOPIA -- IDENTITY, AUTHORITY AND REALISM.=
                    LW PYE AND S VERBA (EDS), POLITICAL CULTURE AND             66
                       POLITICAL DEVELOPMENT, PRINCETON, PRINCETON UNIVERSITY
                       PRESS, 1966, PP. 245-281.
                    COMEL, ELEL, ELNOEL, ELPRNOR
LEVIS -49-ACL    LEVINE, S
                    AN APPROACH TO CONSTRUCTIVE LEADERSHIP.=
                    JOURNAL OF SOCIAL ISSUES, 5, (WINTER 1949), PP. 46-53.      49
                    DEFEL, COMEL
LEVIVT-67-PLA    LEVINE, VT
                    POLITICAL LEADERSHIP IN AFRICA.=
                    STANDFORD, STANDFORD UNIVERSITY PRESS, 1967.                67
                    DEFEL, COMEL, ELEL, ELPRNOR
LEVYR -57-SSI    LEVY, R
                    THE SOCIAL STRUCTURE OF ISLAM.=
                    CAMBRIDGE, CAMBRIDGE UNIVERSITY PRESS, 1957.                57
                    COMEL, ELPRNOR
LEWIB -61-EMT    LEWIS, B
                    THE EMERGENCE OF MODERN TURKEY.=
                    NEW YORK, OXFORD UNIVERSITY PRESS, 1961.                    61
                    COMEL, ELEL, ELNOEL, ELPRNOR
LEWIEG-57-PCN    LEWIS, EG
                    PARLIAMENTARY CONTROL OF NATIONALIZED INDUSTRY IN FRANCE.=
                    THE AMERICAN POLITICAL SCIENCE REVIEW, 51, (SEPTEMBER       57
                       1957), PP. 669-683.
                    ELEL
LEWIGK-52-PCB    LEWIS, GK

                        THE PRESENT CONDITION OF BRITISH POLITICAL PARTIES.=
                        THE WESTERN POLITICAL QUARTERLY, 5, (JUNE 1952),          52
                        PP. 231-257.
                        COMEL
LEWIIM-58-MPM           LEWIS, IM
                        MODERN POLITICAL MOVEMENTS IN SOMALILAND
                        -- PART 1 -- PART 2.=
                        AFRICA, 28, (JULY 1958, OCTOBER 1958),                   58
                        PP. 244-261, PP. 344-363.
                        COMEL, ELEL, ELNOEL
LEWIIM-60-PDM           LEWIS, IM
                        PROBLEMS IN THE DEVELOPMENT OF MODERN LEADERSHIP
                        AND LOYALTIES IN THE BRITISH SOMALILAND PROTECTORATE
                        AND THE UNITED NATIONS TRUSTEESHIP TERRITORY
                        OF SOMALIA.=
                        CIVILISATIONS, 10, (1960), PP. 49-60.                    60
                        COMEL, ELEL, ELNOEL, ELPRNOR
LEWIJW-63-LDC           LEWIS, JW
                        THE LEADERSHIP DOCTRINE OF THE CHINESE COMMUNIST PARTY.=
                        ASIAN SURVEY, 3, (OCTOBER 1963), PP. 457-464.            63
                        ELNOEL, ELPRNOR
- LEWIJW-65-LCC         LEWIS, JW
                        LEADERSHIP IN COMMUNIST CHINA.=
                        ITHACA, CORNELL UNIVERSITY PRESS, 1965.                  65
                        COMEL, ELEL, ELNOEL, ELPRNOR
LEWIJW-65-PCC           LEWIS, JW
                        PARTY CADRES IN COMMUNIST CHINA.=
                        JS COLEMAN (ED), EDUCATION AND POLITICAL DEVELIOMENT,    65
                        PRINCETON, PRINCETON UNIVERSITY PRESS, 1965,
                        PP. 408-436.
                        COMEL, ELEL, ELNOEL, ELPRNOR
LEWIJW-66-PAM           LEWIS, JW
                        POLITICAL ASPECTS OF MOBILITY IN CHINA'S URBAN
                        DEVELOPMENT.=
                        THE AMERICAN POLITICAL SCIENCE REVIEW, 60, (DECEMBER     66
                        1966), PP. 899-912.
                        COMEL, ELNOEL, ELPRNOR
LEWIPH-67-LCW           LEWIS, PH
                        LEADERSHIP AND CONFLICT WITHIN THE FEBRERISTA PARTY OF
                        PARAGUAY.=
                        JOURNAL OF INTER-AMERICAN STUDIES, 9, (APRIL 1967),      67
                        PP. 283-295.
                        COMEL, ELEL, ELPRNOR
LEWIR -61-MGB           LEWIS, R                 STEWART, R
                        THE MANAGERS (GREAT BRITAIN, UNITED STATES,
                        WEST GERMANY).=
                        NEW YORK, MENTOR BOOKS, 1961.                            61
                        COMEL, ELEL, ELNOEL
LEWIWA-65-BAD           LEWIS, WA
                        BEYOND AFRICAN DICTATORSHIP -- THE CRISIS OF THE
                        ONE - PARTY STATE.=
                        ENCOUNTER, 25, (AUGUST 1965), PP. 3-18.                  65
                        ELEL, ELNOEL
LEWIWA-65-PWA           LEWIS, WA
                        POLITICS IN WEST AFRICA.=
                        LONDON, ALLEN AND UNWIN, 1965.                           65
                        COMEL, ELEL, ELNOEL, ELPRNOR
LEWIWH-66-DAS           LEWIS, WH
                        THE DECLINE OF ALGERIA'S FLN (NATIONAL LIBERATION FRONT).=
                        THE MIDDLE EAST JOURNAL, 20, (SPRING 1966), PP. 161-172. 66
                        ELEL
LEWYB -67-SEG           LEWYTZKYJ, B
                        THE SOVIET ELITE -- 1 -- GENERATIONS IN CONFLICT.=
                        PROBLEMS OF COMMUNISM, 16, (JANUARY-FEBRUARY 1967),      67
                        PP. 36-40.
                        COMEL, ELEL
LEYSC -57-EN            LEYS, C
                        AN ELECTION IN NYASALAND.=
                        POLITICAL STUDIES, 5, (MARCH 1957), PP. 258-280.         57
                        COMEL, ELEL, ELNOEL
LEYSC -59-MTT           LEYS, C
                        MODELS, THEORIES, AND THE THEORY OF POLITICAL PARTIES.=
                        POLITICAL STUDIES, 7, (1959), PP. 129-146.               59
                        DEFEL, ELEL, ELNOEL, METEL
LEYSC -66-PCE           LEYS, C
                        THE POLITICAL CLIMATE FOR ECONOMIC DEVELOPMENT (AFRICA).=
                        AFRICAN AFFAIRS, 65, (JANUARY 1966), PP. 55-66.          66
                        ELEL, ELNOEL, ELPRNOR
LICHG -60-RI            LICHTHEIM, G
                        THE ROLE OF THE INTELLECTUALS.=
                        COMMENTARY, 29, (APRIL 1960), PP. 295-307.               60
                        ELEL, ELNOEL, ELPRNOR
LICHG -62-WGT           LICHTHEIM, G
                        WEST GERMANY TODAY.=

                        COMMENTARY, 34, (JULY 1962), PP. 28-38.                          62
                        ELEL, ELNOEL, ELPRNOR
LICHG -63-PBE   LICHTHEIM, G
                        POST - BOURGEOIS EUROPE.=
                        COMMENTARY, 35, (JANUARY 1963), PP. 1-9.                         63
                        COMEL
LICHG -63-TSL   LICHTHEIM, G
                        THE TORY SUCCESSION -- A LONDON LETTER (GREAT BRITAIN).=
                        COMMENTARY, 36, (DECEMBER 1963), PP. 468-472.                    63
                        ELEL, ELNOEL, ELPRNOR
LICHG -64-CHC   LICHTHEIM, G
                        CLASS AND HIERARCHY -- A CRITIQUE OF MARX.=
                        EUROPEAN JOURNAL OF SOCIOLOGY, 5, (1964), PP. 101-111.            64
                        DEFEL, COMEL ELNOEL
LICHG -65-CRE   LICHTHEIM, G
                        CHINA, RUSSIA AND THE EXPERTS.=
                        COMMENTARY, 39, (MARCH 1965), PP. 62-66.                          65
                        ELEL, ELNOEL
LICHGE-54-PTU   LICHTBLAU, GE
                        THE POLITICS OF TRADE UNION LEADERSHIP IN SOUTHERN ASIA.=
                        WORLD POLITICS, 7, (OCTOBER 1954), PP. 84-101.                    54
                        COMEL, ELEL, ELNOEL, ELPRNOR
LIDDDW-47-PPF   LIDDERDALE, DWS
                        THE POSITION OF PARLIAMENT IN THE FOURTH FRENCH REPUBLIC.=
                        PARLIAMENTARY AFFAIRS, 1, (WINTER 1947), PP. 24-34.               47
                        ELEL
LIEBCS-61-EIG   LIEBMAN, CS
                        ELECTORATES, INTEREST GROUPS, AND LOCAL GOVERNMENT
                            (UNITED STATES).=
                        THE AMERICAN BEHAVIORAL SCIENTIST, 4, (JANUARY 1961),             61
                            PP. 9-11.
                        ELEL, ELNOEL
LIENG -55-NKT   LIENHARDT, G
                        NILOTIC KINGS AND THEIR MOTHER'S KIN (SUDAN).=
                        AFRICA, 25, (JANUARY 1955), PP. 29-42.                            55
                        COMEL
LIEUE -60-NRL   LIEUWEN, E
                        NEW ROLES FOR LATIN AMERICAN MILITARY.=
                        WORLD AFFAIRS, 123, (FALL 1960),  PP. 78-83.                      60
                        ELEL, ELNOEL
LIEUE -61-APL   LIEUWEN, E
                        ARMS AND POLITICS IN LATIN AMERICA.=
                        NEW YORK, FREDERICK A PRAGGER, 1961                               61
                        COMEL, ELEL, ELPRNOR
LIEUE -61-MRF   LIEUWEN, E
                        THE MILITARY -- A REVOLUTIONARY FORCE (LATIN AMERICA).=
                        THE ANNALS OF THE AMERICAN ACADEMY OF POLITICAL AND               61
                            SOCIAL SCIENCE, 334, (MARCH 1961), PP. 30-40.
                        COMEL, ELEL, ELNOEL, ELPRNOR
LIEUE -62-MPL   LIEUWEN, E
                        MILITARISM AND POLITICS IN LATIN AMERICA.=
                        JJ JOHNSON (ED), THE ROLE OF THE MILITARY IN                      62
                            UNDERDEVELOPED COUNTRIES, PRINCETON, PRINCETON
                            UNIVERSITY PRESS, 1962, PP. 131-164.
                        COMEL, ELEL, ELPRNOR
LIEUE -63-MLA   LIEUWEN, E
                        MILITARISM IN LATIN AMERICA -- A THREAT TO THE ALLIANCE
                            FOR PROGRESS.=
                        THE WORLD TODAY, 19, (MAY 1963), PP. 193-199.                     63
                        ELEL, ELNOEL, ELPRNOR
LIEUE -64-GVP   LIEUWEN, E
                        GENERALS VS. PRESIDENTS -- NEOMILITARISM IN
                            LATIN AMERICA.=
                        NEW YORK, FREDERICK A PRAEGER, 1964.                              64
                        COMEL, ELEL, ELNOEL, ELPRNOR
LIFTRJ-56-TRC   LIFTON, RJ
                        THOUGHT REFORM OF CHINESE INTELLECTUALS -- A
                            PSYCHIATRIC EVALUATION.=
                        THE JOURNAL OF ASIAN STUDIES, 16, (NOVEMBER 1956),                56
                            PP. 75-88.
                        ELPRNOR
LIFTRJ-61-TRP   LIFTON, RJ
                        THOUGHT REFORM AND THE PSYCHOLOGY OF TOTALISM (CHINA).=
                        NEW YORK, W W NORTON AND COMPANY, INC, 1961.                      61
                        ELEL, ELNOEL
LINDC -63-KPB   LINDEN, C
                        KHRUSHCHEV AND THE PARTY BATTLE (SOVIET UNION).=
                        PROBLEMS OF COMMUNISM, 12, (SEPTEMBER-OCTOBER 1963),              63
                            PP. 27-35.
                        ELEL, ELPRNOR
LINDCA-66-KSL   LINDEN, CA
                        KHRUSHCHEV AND THE SOVIET LEADERSHIP 1957-1964.=
                        BALTIMORE, THE JOHN HOPKINS PRESS, 1966.                          66
                        DEFEL, COMEL, ELEL, ELPRNOR

```
LINKAS-56-WWD   LINK, AS
                WOODROW WILSON AND THE DEMOCRATIC PARTY.=
                THE REVIEW OF POLITICS, 18, (APRIL 1956), PP. 146-156.      56
                ELEL
LINSH -56-PSC   LINSTEAD, H
                THE PARLIAMENTARY AND SCIENTIFIC COMMITTEE
                   (GREAT BRITAIN).=
                PARLIAMENTARY AFFAIRS, 9, (AUTUMN 1956), PP. 465-469.       56
                ELEL
LINZJ -57-LPL   LINZ, J
                LOCAL POLITICS AND LEADERSHIP IN EUROPEAN DEMOCRACIES.=
                PROD (THE AMERICAN BEHAVIORAL SCIENTIST), 1,                57
                   (SEPTEMBER 1957), PP. 32-35.
                ELEL, ELNOEL
LINZJJ-64-ARS   LINZ, JJ
                AN AUTHORITARIAN REGIME -- SPAIN.=
                E ALARDT AND Y LITTUNEN (EDS), CLEAVAGES, IDEOLOGIES AND    64
                   PARTY SYSTEMS--CONTRIBUTIONS TO COMPARATIVE POLITICAL
                   SOCIOLOGY, HELSINSKI, WESTERMARCK SOCIETY, 1964.
                DEFEL, COMEL, ELEL, ELNOEL, ELPRNOR
LIPMA -65-SBB   LIPMAN, A
                SOCIAL BACKGROUNDS OF THE BOGOTA ENTREPRENEUR (COLOMBIA).=
                JOURNAL OF INTER-AMERICAN AFFAIRS, 7, (APRIL 1965),         65
                   PP. 227-236.
                COMEL, ELPRNOR
LIPPW -55-EPP   LIPPMANN, W
                ESSAYS IN THE PUBLIC PHILOSOPHY.=
                BOSTON, LITTLE, BROWN AND COMPANY, 1955.                    55
                GNELTH, COMEL, ELEL, ELNOEL, ELPRNOR
LIPSL -48-PEN   LIPSON, L
                THE POLITICS OF EQUALITY -- NEW ZEALAND'S ADVENTURES IN
                   DEMOCRACY.=
                CHICAGO, UNIVERSITY OF CHICAGO PRESS, 1948.                 48
                DEFEL, COMEL, ELEL, ELPRNOR
LIPSL -53-TPS   LIPSON, L
                THE TWO - PARTY SYSTEM IN BRITISH POLITICS.=
                THE AMERICAN POLITICAL SCIENCE REVIEW, 47, (JUNE 1953),     53
                   PP. 337-358.
                ELEL, ELNOEL, ELPRNOR
LIPSL -56-GCB   LIPSON, L
                GOVERNMENT IN CONTEMPORARY BRAZIL.=
                CANADIAN JOURNAL OF ECONOMICS AND POLITICAL SCIENCE,        56
                   22, (MAY 1956), PP. 183-198.
                ELEL, ELNOEL
LIPSS -59-SSR   LIPSET, S
                SOCIAL STRATIFICATION AND 'RIGHT-WING EXTREMISM'.=
                THE BRITISH JOURNAL OF SOCIOLOGY, 10, (1959), PP. 346-382.59
                COMEL
LIPSSM-47-RCP   LIPSET, SM
                THE RURAL COMMUNITY AND POLITICAL LEADERSHIP IN
                   SASKATCHEWAN (CANADA).=
                CANADIAN JOURNAL OF ECONOMICS AND POLITICAL SCIENCE,        47
                   13, (AUGUST 1947), PP. 410-428.
                COMEL
LIPSSM-51-SSS   LIPSET, SM           BENDIX, R
                SOCIAL STATUS AND SOCIAL STRUCTURE -- 1 -- 2.=
                THE BRITISH JOURNAL OF SOCIOLOGY, 2, (1951),                51
                    PP. 150-168, PP. 230-254.
                COMEL
LIPSSM-56-UDI   LIPSET, SM           TROW, M           COLEMAN, J
                UNION DEMOCRACY -- THE INSIDE POLITICS OF THE
                   INTERNATIONAL TYPOGRAPHICAL UNION (NORTH AMERICA).=
                GLENCOE, ILLINOIS, THE FREE PRESS 1956.                     56
                DEFEL, COMEL, ELEL, ELPRNOR
LIPSSM-59-AIT   LIPSET, SM
                AMERICAN INTELLECTUALS -- THEIR POLITICS AND STATUS.=
                DAEDALUS, 88, (SUMMER 1959), PP. 460-486.                   59
                COMEL, ELEL, ELNOEL, ELPRNOR
LIPSSM-60-PMS   LIPSET, SM
                POLITICAL MAN -- THE SOCIAL BASES OF POLITICS.=
                GARDEN CITY, NEW YORK, DOUBLEDAY, 1960.                     60
                DEFEL, COMEL, ELEL, ELNOEL, ELPRNOR
LIPSSM-60-PSR   LIPSET, SM
                PARTY SYSTEMS AND THE REPRESENTATION OF SOCIAL GROUPS.=
                EUROPEAN JOURNAL OF SOCIOLOGY, 1, (1960), PP. 50-86.        60
                ELEL, ELNOEL, ELPRNOR
LIPSSM-62-I     LIPSET, SM
                INTRODUCTION.=
                R MICHELS, POLITICAL PARTIES--A SOCIOLOGICAL STUDY OF       62
                   OLIGARCHICAL TENDENCIES OF MODERN DEMOCRACY,
                   NEW YORK, THE FREE PRESS, 1962, PP. 15-39.
                GNELTH, ELEL, ELNOEL
LIPSSM-65-LNS   LIPSET, SM
                LEADERSHIP AND NEW SOCIAL MOVEMENTS (CANADA).=
```

                         AW GOULDNER (ED), STUDIES IN LEADERSHIP, NEW YORK,         65
                            RUSSELL AND RUSSELL, 1965, PP. 342-362.
                         COMEL, ELNOEL
LIPSSM-67-ELA    LIPSET, SM              SOLARI, A (EDS)
                         ELITES IN LATIN AMERICA.=
                         NEW YORK, OXFORD UNIVERSITY PRESS, 1967.                   67
                         DEFEL, COMEL, ELEL, ELNOEL, ELPRNOR
LIPSSM-67-SPL    LIPSET, SM (ED)
                         STUDENT POLITICS (LATIN AMERICA, INDIA, POLAND,
                            UNITED STATES, GERMANY, CHILE, ARGENTINA, COLUMBIA,
                            FRANCE).=
                         NEW YORK, BASIC BOOKS, 1967.                               67
                         DEFEL, COMEL, ELEL, ELNOEL, ELPRNOR
LIPSSM-67-VEE    LIPSET, SM
                         VALUES, EDUCATION, ENTREPRENEURSHIP (LATIN AMERICA).=
                         SM LIPSET AND A SOLARI (EDS), ELITES IN LATIN AMERICA.=    67
                            NEW YORK, OXFORD UNIVERSITY PRESS, 1967, PP. 3-60.
                         DEFEL, COMEL, ELEL, ELPRNOR
LISSM -64-SLR    LISSAK, M
                         SELECTED LITERATURE OF REVOLUTIONS AND COUPS D'ETAT
                            IN THE DEVELOPING NATIONS.=
                         M JANOWITZ (ED), THE NEW MILITARY--CHANGING PATTERNS OF    64
                            ORGANIZATION, NEW YORK, RUSSELL SAGE FOUNDATION,
                            1964, PP. 339-362.
                         ELEL, ELPRNOR
LISTJ -49-MPS    LISTOWEL, J
                         THE MEN OF THE POLITBURO (SOVIET UNION).=
                         SOUNDING, 24, (MARCH 1949), PP. 22-30.                     49
                         COMEL, ELPRNOR
LITTKL-48-SCS    LITTLE, KL
                         SOCIAL CHANGE AND SOCIAL CLASS IN THE SIERRA LEONE
                            PROTECTORATE.=
                         THE AMERICAN JOURNAL OF SOCIOLOGY, 54, (JULY 1948),        48
                            PP. 10-21.
                         COMEL, ELNOEL, ELPRNOR
LITTKL-50-SWA    LITTLE, KL
                         THE SIGNIFICANCE OF THE WEST AFRICAN CREOLE.=
                         AFRICAN AFFAIRS, 49, (OCTOBER 1950), PP. 308-318.          50
                         COMEL, ELEL, ELNOEL
LITTKL-55-SCS    LITTLE, KL
                         STRUCTURAL CHANGE IN SIERRA LEONE PROTECTORATE.=
                         AFRICA, 25, (JULY 1955), PP. 217-233.                      55
                         COMEL, ELNOEL
LITTKL-56-TWA    LITTLE, KL
                         TWO WEST AFRICAN ELITES.=
                         INTERNATIONAL SOCIAL SCIENCE BULLETIN, 8, (1956),          56
                            PP. 495-498.
                         COMEL
LITTKL-57-RVA    LITTLE, KL
                         THE ROLE OF VOLUNTARY ASSOCIATIONS IN WEST AFRICAN
                            URBANISATION.=
                         AMERICAN ANTHROPOLOGIST, 59, (AUGUST 1957), PP. 579-596.   57
                         ELEL, ELNOEL, ELPRNOR
LITTKL-65-WAU    LITTLE, KL
                         WEST AFRICAN URBANIZATION -- A STUDY OF VOLUNTARY
                            ASSOCIATIONS IN SOCIAL CHANGE.=
                         LONDON, CAMBRIDGE UNIVERSITY PRESS, 1965.                  65
                         COMEL, ELEL, ELNOEL
LIU,  -60-ECC    LIU,JTC
                         ELEVENTH CENTURY CHINESE BUREAUCRATS -- SOME HISTORICAL
                            CLASSIFICATIONS AND BEHAVIORAL TYPES.=
                         ADMINISTRATIVE SCIENCE QUARTERLY, 4, (1959-1960),          60
                            PP. 207-226.
                         DEFEL
LIU,HW-59-TCC    LIU, HW
                         THE TRADITIONAL CHINESE CLAN RULES.=
                         LOCUST VALLEY, NEW YORK, JJ AUGUSTIN, 1959.                59
                         COMEL, ELEL, ELNOEL, ELPRNOR, METEL
LIVIWS-59-MPM    LIVINGSTON, WS
                         MINOR PARTIES AND MINORITY M.P.'S (GREAT BRITAIN).=
                         THE WESTERN POLITICAL QUARTERLY, 12, (DECEMBER 1959),      59
                            PP. 1017-1038.
                         COMEL, ELEL
LLOYBB-66-EFL    LLOYD, BB
                         EDUCATION AND FAMILY LIFE IN THE DEVELOPMENT OF CLASS
                            IDENTIFICATION AMONG THE YORUBA (WESTERN NIGERIA).=
                         PC LLOYD (ED), THE NEW ELITES OF TROPICAL AFRICA, LONDON,  66
                            OXFORD UNIVERSITY PRESS, 1966, PP. 163-181.
                         COMEL, ELPRNOR
LLOYPC-53-INE    LLOYD, PC
                         THE INTEGRATION OF THE NEW ECONOMIC CLASSES WITH
                            LOCAL GOVERNMENT IN WEST NIGERIA.=
                         AFRICAN AFFAIRS, 52, (OCTOBER 1953), PP. 327-333.          53
                         ELEL

LLOYPC-55-DPP   LLOYD, PC
                THE DEVELOPMENT OF POLITICAL PARTIES IN WESTERN
                    NIGERIA.=
                THE AMERICAN POLITICAL SCIENCE REVIEW, 49, (SEPTEMBER        55
                    1955), PP. 693-707.
                COMEL, ELEL, ELNOEL
LLOYPC-60-SKG   LLOYD, PC
                SACRED KINGSHIP AND GOVERNMENT AMONG THE YORUBA (AFRICA).=
                AFRICA, 30, (JULY 1960), PP. 221-237.                        60
                COMEL, ELEL, ELNOEL
LLOYPC-66-CCA   LLOYD, PC
                CLASS CONSCIOUSNESS AMONG THE YORUBA (WESTERN NIGERIA).=
                PC LLOYD (ED), THE NEW ELITES OF TROPICAL AFRICA, LONDON,    66
                    OXFORD UNIVERSITY PRESS, PP. 328-340.
                COMEL, ELEL, ELNOEL, ELPRNOR
LLOYPC-66-ISE   LLOYD, PC
                INTRODUCTION -- THE STUDY OF THE ELITE (TROPICAL AFRICA).=
                PC LLOYD (ED), THE NEW ELITES OF TROPICAL AFRICA, LONDON,    66
                    OXFORD UNIVERSITY PRESS, 1966, PP. 1-65.
                DEFEL, ELEL, ELPRNOR, METEL
LLOYPC-66-NET   LLOYD, PC (ED)
                THE NEW ELITES OF TROPICAL AFRICA -- STUDIES PRESENTED
                    AND DISCUSSED AT THE SIXTH INTERNATIONAL AFRICAN SEMINAR
                    AT THE UNIVERSITY OF IBADAN.=
                LONDON, OXFORD UNIVERSITY PRESS, 1966.                       66
                GNELTH, DEFEL, COMEL, ELEL, ELNOEL, ELPRNOR, METEL
LOCKD -62-CMA   LOCKARD, D
                THE CITY MANAGER, ADMINISTRATIVE THEORY AND
                    POLITICAL POWER (UNITED STATES).=
                POLITICAL SCIENCE QUARTERLY, 77, (JUNE 1962), PP. 224-236.62
                DEFEL, ELEL, ELNOEL
LODGGC-59-LSR   LODGE, GC
                LABOR'S ROLE IN NEWLY DEVELOPING COUNTRIES.=
                FOREIGN AFFAIRS, 37, (JULY 1959), PP. 660-671.               59
                ELEL, ELNOEL
LODGGC-62-SDL   LODGE, GC
                SPEARHEADS OF DEMOCRACY -- LABOR IN THE DEVELOPING
                    COUNTRIES.=
                NEW YORK, HARPER AND ROW, 1962.                             62
                ELEL, ELNOEL, ELPRNOR
LOEWG -57-TBL   LOEWENBERG, G
                THE TRANSFORMATION OF BRITISH LABOUR PARTY POLICY
                    SINCE 1945.=
                THE JOURNAL OF POLITICS, 19, (MAY 1957), PP. 206-226.        57
                ELEL, ELNOEL, ELPRNOR
LOEWG -61-PWG   LOEWENBERG, G
                PARLIAMENTARISM IN WESTERN GERMANY -- THE FUNCTIONING OF
                    THE BUNDESTAG.=
                THE AMERICAN POLITICAL SCIENCE REVIEW, 55, (MARCH 1961),     61
                    PP. 87-102.
                ELEL, ELNOEL
LOEWG -66-PGP   LOEWENBERG, G
                PARLIAMENT IN THE GERMAN POLITICAL SYSTEM.=
                ITHACA, CORNELL UNIVERSITY PRESS, 1966.                      66
                COMEL, ELEL, ELNOEL, ELPRNOR
LOEWK -57-PPG   LOEWENSTEIN, K
                POLITICAL POWER AND THE GOVERNMENTAL PROCESS.=
                CHICAGO, UNIVERSITY OF CHICAGO PRESS, 1957.                  57
                DEFEL, ELEL, ELNOEL, ELPRNOR
LOFCM -63-PCZ   LOFCHIE, M
                PARTY CONFLICT IN ZANZIBAR.=
                THE JOURNAL OF MODERN AFRICAN STUDIES, 1, (JUNE 1963),       63
                    PP. 185-207.
                COMEL, ELEL, ELNOEL, ELPRNOR
LOFCMF-65-ZBR   LOFCHIE, MF
                ZANZIBAR -- BACKGROUND TO REVOLUTION.=
                PRINCETON, PRINCETON UNIVERSITY PRESS, 1965.                 65
                COMEL, ELEL, ELNOEL, ELPRNOR
LONGNE-58-LCE   LONG, NE
                THE LOCAL COMMUNITY AS AN ECOLOGY OF GAMES
                    (UNITED STATES).=
                THE AMERICAN JOURNAL OF SOCIOLOGY, 64, (NOVEMBER 1958),      58
                    PP. 251-261.
                DEFEL, ELEL, ELNOEL, METEL
LORWVR-54-FLM   LORWIN, VR
                THE FRENCH LABOR MOVEMENT.=
                CAMBRIDGE, HARVARD UNIVERSITY PRESS, 1954.                   54
                ELEL, ELNOEL
LOVEAJ-59-CPA   LOVERIDGE, AJ
                CHIEFS AND POLITICS (AFRICA).=
                JOURNAL OF AFRICAN ADMINISTRATION, 11,                       59
                    (OCTOBER 1959), PP. 201-207.
                ELEL, ELNOEL, ELPRNOR
LOW,DA-62-PPU   LOW, DA

                    POLITICAL PARTIES IN UGANDA 1949-1962.=
                    LONDON, THE ATHLONE PRESS, 1962.                          62
                    COMEL, ELEL, ELNOEL
LOWEFE-56-SIF    LOWE, FE           MCCORMICK, TC
                    A STUDY OF THE INFLUENCE OF FORMAL AND INFORMAL LEADERS
                       IN AN ELECTION CAMPAIGN (UNITED STATES).=
                    THE PUBLIC OPINION QUARTERLY, 20, (WINTER 1956),          56
                       PP. 651-662.
                    ELNOEL, ELPRNOR
LOWER -55-CMS    LOWENTHAL, R
                    CRISIS IN MOSCOW (SOVIET UNION).=
                    PROBLEMS OF COMMUNISM, 4, (MAY-JUNE 1955), PP. 1-8.       55
                    COMEL, ELEL
LOWER -56-ROE    LOWENTHAL, R
                    REVOLUTION OVER EASTERN EUROPE.=
                    PROBLEMS OF COMMUNISM, 5, (NOVEMBER-DECEMBER 1956),       56
                       PP. 4-9.
                    ELEL, ELNOEL, ELPRNOR
LOWER -58-KCS    LOWENTHAL, R
                    KHRUSHCHEV IN COMMAND (SOVIET UNION).=
                    COMMENTARY, 25, (JUNE 1958), PP. 504-511.                 58
                    ELEL, ELNOEL
LOWER -58-LOP    LOWENTHAL, R
                    THE LOGIC OF ONE - PARTY RULE (SOVIET UNION).=
                    PROBLEMS OF COMMUNISM, 7, (MARCH-APRIL 1958), PP. 21-30.  58
                    ELEL, ELPRNOR
LOWER -59-KSF    LOWENTHAL, R
                    KHRUSHCHEV'S FLEXIBLE COMMUNISM (SOVIET UNION).=
                    COMMENTARY, 27, (APRIL 1959), PP. 277-284.                59
                    ELEL, ELNOEL, ELPRNOR
LOWER -60-NKS    LOWENTHAL, R
                    THE NATURE OF KHRUSHCHEV'S POWER (SOVIET UNION).=
                    PROBLEMS OF COMMUNISM, 9, (JULY-AUGUST 1960), PP. 1-7.    60
                    ELEL
LOWER -60-TR     LOWENTHAL, R
                    TOTALITARIANISM RECONSIDERED.=
                    COMMENTARY, 29, (JUNE 1960), PP. 504-512.                 60
                    DEFEL, COMEL, ELEL
LOWER -65-RWA    LOWENTHAL, R
                    THE REVOLUTION WITHERS AWAY (SOVIET UNION).=
                    PROBLEMS OF COMMUNISM, 14, (JANUARY-FEBRUARY 1965),       65
                       PP. 10-17.
                    ELEL
LOWITJ-64-ABP    LOWI, TJ
                    AMERICAN BUSINESS, PUBLIC POLICY, CASE-STUDIES
                       AND POLITICAL THEORY.=
                    WORLD POLITICS, 16, (JULY 1964), PP. 677-715.             64
                    DEFEL, COMEL, ELEL
LOWRCW-65-AIU    LOWRY, CW
                    AMERICAN INTELLECTUALS AND U.S. VIETNAM POLICY.=
                    WORLD AFFAIRS, 128, (APRIL-JUNE 1965), PP. 21-27.         65
                    ELEL, ELPRNOR
LOWRRP-62-FAL    LOWRY, RP
                    THE FUNCTIONS OF ALIENATION IN LEADERSHIP
                       (UNITED STATES).=
                    SOCIOLOGY AND SOCIAL RESEARCH, 46, (JULY 1962),           62
                       PP. 426-435.
                    DEFEL, COMEL, ELPRNOR
LOWRRP-64-LIG    LOWRY, RP
                    LEADERSHIP INTERACTION, GROUP CONSCIOUSNESS, AND
                       SOCIAL CHANGE.=
                    PACIFIC SOCIOLOGICAL REVIEW, 7, (SPRING 1964), PP. 22-29  64
                    COMEL, ELEL, ELNOEL
LOWRRP-65-WSR    LOWRY, RP
                    WHO'S RUNNING THIS TOWN -- COMMUNITY LEADERSHIP AND SOCIAL
                       CHANGE (UNITED STATES).=
                    NEW YORK, HARPER AND ROW, 1965.                           65
                    DEFEL, COMEL, ELEL, ELPRNOR, METEL
LUBIM -54-ICM    LUBIS, M
                    THE INDONESIAN COMMUNIST MOVEMENT TODAY.=
                    FAR EASTERN SURVEY, 23, (NOVEMBER 1954), PP. 161-164.     54
                    COMEL, ELEL, ELNOEL
LUCERD-56-GTA    LUCE, RD           ROGOW, AA
                    A GAME THEORETIC ANALYSIS OF CONGRESSIONAL POWER
                       DISTRIBUTIONS FOR A STABLE TWO - PARTY SYSTEM.=
                    BEHAVIORAL SCIENCE, 1, (JANUARY 1956), PP. 83-95.         56
                    DEFEL, ELEL, METEL
LUCKGS-56-LPS    LUCKYJ, GSN
                    LITERARY POLITICS IN THE SOVIET UKRAINE, 1917-1934.=
                    NEW YORK, COLUMBIA UNIVERSITY PRESS, 1956.                56
                    ELEL
LUDZPC-65-SEE    LUDZ, PC
                    SOCIOLOGY IN EASTERN EUROPE -- EAST GERMANY.=
                    PROBLEMS OF COMMUNISM, 14, (JANUARY-FEBRUARY 1965),       65

PP. 66-70.
ELEL, ELPRNOR

LUETH -55-SMA    LUETHY, H
THE SOCIAL MOBILITY AGAIN -- AND ELITES (UNITED STATES,
WESTERN EUROPE).=
COMMENTARY, 20, (SEPTEMBER 1955), PP. 270-273.                55
DEFEL, COMEL, ELNOEL, ELPRNOR

LUKEH -47-LBP    LUKE, H
LEGISLATURES OF THE BRITISH PACIFIC ISLANDS.=
PARLIAMENTARY AFFAIRS, 1, (WINTER 1947), PP. 38-50.          47
ELEL

LUKHMB-66-SCE    LUKHERO, MB
THE SOCIAL CHARACTERISTICS OF AN EMERGENT ELITE IN
HARARE (SOUTHERN RHODESIA).=
PC LLOYD (ED), THE NEW ELITES OF TROPICAL AFRICA, LONDON, 66
OXFORD UNIVERSITY PRESS, 1966, PP. 126-137.
COMEL

LUPTT -59-SBC    LUPTON, T              WILSON, CS
THE SOCIAL BACKGROUND AND CONNECTIONS OF 'TOP
DECISION-MAKERS' (GREAT BRITAIN).=
MANCHESTER SCHOOL OF ECONOMIC AND SOCIAL STUDIES,           59
27, (1959).
COMEL, ELEL

LUTTNR-66-ACC    LUTTBERG, NR           ZEIGLER, H
ATTITUDE CONSENSUS AND CONFLICT IN AN INTEREST GROUP --
AN ASSESSMENT OF COHESION  (UNITED STATES).=
THE AMERICAN POLITICAL SCIENCE REVIEW, 60, (SEPTEMBER       66
1966), PP. 655-666.
ELNOEL, ELPRNOR

LYMARW-57-FLG    LYMAN, RW
THE FIRST LABOUR GOVERNMENT, 1924 (GREAT BRITAIN).=
LONDON, CHAPMAN AND HALL, 1957.                             57
COMEL, ELEL

LYNCFL-61-LEC    LYNCH, FL
THE LESS ENTANGLED CIVIL SERVANT.=
PHILIPPINE JOURNAL OF PUBLIC ADMINISTRATION, 5,             61
(JULY 1961), PP. 201-209.
ELNOEL, ELPRNOR

LYONGM-61-NCM    LYONS, GM
THE NEW CIVIL - MILITARY RELATIONS (UNITED STATES).=
THE AMERICAN POLITICAL SCIENCE REVIEW, 55, (MARCH 1955),    61
PP. 53-63.
COMEL, ELEL, ELPRNOR

LYSTMH-56-BMM    LYSTAD, MH             STONE, RC
BUREAUCRATIC MASS MEDIA -- A STUDY OF ROLE
DEFINITIONS (UNITED STATES).=
SOCIAL FORCES, 34, (MAY 1956), PP. 356-367.                 56
COMEL, ELPRNOR, METEL

MABEC -64-CNL    MABEE, C
THE CRISIS IN NEGRO LEADERSHIP (UNITED STATES).=
ANTIOCH REVIEW, 24, (FALL 1964), PP. 365-378.               64
COMEL, ELEL, ELNOEL

MACCWT-65-ECN    MACCAFFREY, WT
ENGLAND -- THE CROWN AND THE NEW ARISTOCRACY, 1540-1600.=
PAST AND PRESENT, 30, (APRIL 1965), PP. 52-64.              65
DEFEL, COMEL, ELPRNOR

MACDRW-65-LAS    MACDONALD, RW
THE LEAGUE OF ARAB STATES -- A STUDY IN THE DYNAMICS OF
REGIONAL ORGANIZATION (MIDDLE EAST).=
PRINCETON, PRINCETON UNIVERSITY PRESS, 1965.                65
ELEL, ELPRNOR

MACFR -58-CCS    MACFARQUHAR, R
COMMUNIST CHINA'S INTRA - PARTY DISPUTE.=
PACIFIC AFFAIRS, 31, (DECEMBER 1958), PP. 223-335.          58
ELEL, ELPRNOR

MACFR -59-LC     MACFARQUHAR, R
THE LEADERSHIP IN CHINA.=
THE WORLD TODAY, 15, (AUGUST 1959), PP. 310-323.            59
ELEL, ELPRNOR

MACFR -60-HFC    MACFARQUHAR, R
THE HUNDRED FLOWERS CAMPAIGN AND THE CHINESE
INTELLECTUALS.=
NEW YORK, FREDERICK A PRAEGER, 1960.                        60
ELEL, ELPRNOR

MACFR -63-LCC    MACFARQUHAR, R
LEADERSHIP COHESION IN COMMUNIST CHINA AND
UNDERDEVELOPED ASIAN COUNTRIES.=
K LONDON (ED), NEW NATIONS IN A DIVIDED WORLD, NEW YORK,    63
FREDERICK A PRAEGER, 1963, PP. 222-235.
ELEL, ELPRNOR

MACKJ -58-PAS    MACKIEWICZ, J
THE PARTY ASPECT OF SOVIET - POLISH RELATIONS.=
BULLETIN INSTITUTE FOR THE STUDY OF THE USSR, 5,            58
(MARCH 1958), PP. 26-31.

```
                    ELEL
MACKJA-56-TUL       MACK, JA
                    TRADE UNION LEADERSHIP (GREAT BRITAIN).=
                    THE POLITICAL QUARTERLY, 27, (JANUARY-MARCH 1956),        56
                       PP. 71-81.
                    COMEL, ELEL
MACKJP-62-BC        MACKINTOSH, JP
                    THE BRITISH CABINET.=
                    TORONTO, UNIVERSITY OF TORONTO PRESS, 1962.               62
                    COMEL, ELEL, ELPRNOR
MACKJP-62-ETT       MACKINTOSH, JP
                    ELECTORAL TRENDS AND THE TENDENCY TO A ONE PARTY
                       SYSTEM IN NIGERIA.=
                    JOURNAL OF COMMONWEALTH POLITICAL STUDIES, 1, (1962),      62
                       PP. 194-210.
                    COMEL
MACKWJ-54-COP       MACKENZIE, WJM        ARDITTI, C
                    CO-OPERATIVE POLITICS IN A LANCASHIRE CONSTITUENCY
                       (GREAT BRITAIN).=
                    POLITICAL STUDIES, 2, (1954), PP. 112-127.                54
                    ELEL, ELNOEL
MACKWJ-54-LGE       MACKENZIE, WJM
                    LOCAL GOVERNMENT EXPERIENCE OF LEGISLATORS
                       (GREAT BRITAIN).=
                    PUBLIC ADMINISTRATION, 32, (WINTER 1954), PP. 409-423.     54
                    COMEL
MACKWJ-54-RPS       MACKENZIE, WJM
                    REPRESENTATION IN PLURAL SOCIETIES (GREAT BRITAIN,
                       BRITISH COMMONWEALTH).=
                    POLITICAL STUDIES, 2, (1954), PP. 54-69.                   54
                    ELNOEL
MACKWJ-55-PGB       MACKENZIE, WJM
                    PRESSURE GROUPS AND BRITISH GOVERNMENT.=
                    THE BRITISH JOURNAL OF SOCIOLOGY, 6, (1955), PP. 133-148. 55
                    ELEL
MACKWJ-59-CAB       MACKENZIE, WJM        GROVE, JW
                    CENTRAL ADMINISTRATION IN BRITAIN.=
                    LONDON, LONGMANS, 1959.                                    59
                    ELEL, ELNOEL, ELPRNOR
MACRD -52-RBR       MACRAE-JR, D
                    THE RELATION BETWEEN ROLL CALL VOTES AND CONSTITUENCIES
                       (UNITED STATES).=
                    THE AMERICAN POLITICAL SCIENCE REVIEW, 46, (DECEMBER       52
                    1952), PP. 1046-1055.
                    ELNOEL
MACRD -54-RSL       MACRAE-JR, D
                    THE ROLE OF THE STATE LEGISLATOR IN MASSACHUSETTS
                       (UNITED STATES).=
                    AMERICAN SOCIOLOGICAL REVIEW, 19, (APRIL 1954),            54
                       PP. 185-194.
                    COMEL, ELEL, ELNOEL, ELPRNOR
MACRD -56-RCV       MACRAE-JR, D
                    ROLL CALL VOTES AND LEADERSHIP (UNITED STATES).=
                    THE PUBLIC OPINION QUARTERLY, 20, (FALL 1956),             56
                       PP. 543-558.
                    ELEL, ELNOEL, METEL
MACRD -58-DCV       MACRAE-JR, D
                    DIMENSIONS OF CONGRESSIONAL VOTING -- A STATISTICAL
                       STUDY OF THE HOUSE OF REPRESENTATIVES IN THE
                       EIGHTY-FIRST CONGRESS (UNITED STATES).=
                    UNIVERSITY OF CALIFORNIA PUBLICATIONS IN SOCIOLOGY AND     58
                       SOCIAL INSTITUTIONS, VOL 1, NO. 3, PP. 203-390,
                       BERKELEY, UNIVERSITY OF CALIFORNIA PRESS, 1958.
                    ELNOEL, ELPRNOR, METEL
MACRD -58-RSF       MACRAE-JR, D
                    RELIGIOUS AND SOCIOECONOMIC FACTORS IN THE FRENCH VOTE,
                       1946-1956.=
                    THE AMERICAN JOURNAL OF SOCIOLOGY, 64, (NOVEMBER 1958),    58
                       PP. 290-298.
                    ELNOEL, METEL
MACRD -59-MII       MACRAE-JR, D
                    A METHOD FOR IDENTIFYING ISSUES AND FACTIONS FROM
                       LEGISLATIVE VOTES (UNITED STATES).=
                    THE AMERICAN POLITICAL SCIENCE REVIEW, 59, (DECEMBER       59
                    1956), PP. 909-926.
                    ELEL, METEL
MACRD -59-SPP       MACRAE-JR, D          PRICE, HD
                    SCALE POSITIONS AND 'POWER' IN THE SENATE
                       (UNITED STATES).=
                    BEHAVIORAL SCIENCE, 4, (JULY 1959), PP. 212-218.           59
                    DEFEL, ELEL, METEL
MACRD -61-LSS       MACRAE-JR, D          MACRAE, EK
                    LEGISLATORS' SOCIAL STATUS AND THEIR VOTES
                       (UNITED STATES).=
```

```
                    THE AMERICAN JOURNAL OF SOCIOLOGY, 66, (MAY 1961),         61
                       PP. 599-683.
                    ELEL, ELPRNOR
MACRD  -63-IDC   MACRAE-JR, D
                    INTRAPARTY DIVISIONS AND CABINET COALITIONS IN THE
                       FOURTH FRENCH REPUBLIC.=
                    COMPARATIVE STUDIES IN SOCIETY AND HISTORY, 5,             63
                       (JANUARY 1963), PP. 164-211.
                    ELEL
MACRD  -67-PPS   MACRAE-JR, D
                    PARLIAMENT, PARTIES AND SOCIETY IN FRANCE, 1946-1958.=
                    NEW YORK, ST. MARTIN-S PRESS, 1967.                       67
                    COMEL, ELEL, ELNOEL, ELPRNOR
MACRN  -65-FDG   MACRE, N
                    THE FAULTS IN THE DYNAMOS (GREAT BRITAIN).=
                    ENCOUNTER, 25, (JULY 1965), PP. 22-27.                    65
                    ELPRNOR
MACRRC-52-CIF   MACRIDIS, RC
                    CABINET INSTABILITY IN THE FOURTH REPUBLIC (1946-1951).=
                    THE JOURNAL OF POLITICS, 14, (NOVEMBER 1952),             52
                       PP. 643-658.
                    ELEL, ELNOEL
MACRRC-61-IGC   MACRIDIS, RC
                    INTEREST GROUPS IN COMPARATIVE ANALYSIS.=
                    THE JOURNAL OF POLITICS, 23, (FEBRUARY 1961), PP. 25-45.  61
                    DEFEL, ELEL
MAHDH  -65-CCI   MAHDAVY, H
                    THE COMING CRISIS IN IRAN.=
                    FOREIGN AFFAIRS, 44, (OCTOBER 1965), PP. 134-146.         65
                    COMEL, ELEL, ELNOEL
MAIEJ  -64-PCL   MAIER, J              WEATHERHEAD, RW
                    POLITICS OF CHANGE IN LATIN AMERICA.=
                    NEW YORK, FREDERICK A PRAEGER, 1964.                      64
                    ELEL, ELNOEL, ELPRNOR
MAINLC-64-HBL   MAINZER, LC
                    HONOR IN BUREAUCRATIC LIFE (FRANCE,
                       GREAT BRITAIN, UNITED STATES).=
                    THE REVIEW OF POLITICS, 26, (JANUARY 1964), PP. 70-90.    64
                    ELPRNOR
MAIRLP-58-ACT   MAIR, LP
                    AFRICAN CHIEFS TODAY.=
                    AFRICA, 28, (JULY 1958), PP. 195-205.                     58
                    COMEL
MAKIJM-47-RBJ   MAKI, JM
                    THE ROLE OF THE BUREAUCRACY IN JAPAN.=
                    PACIFIC AFFAIRS, 20, (DECEMBER 1947), PP. 391-406.        47
                    COMEL, ELEL, ELNOEL, ELPRNOR
MAKIJM-62-GPJ   MAKI, JM
                    GOVERNMENT AND POLITICS IN JAPAN -- THE ROAD TO
                       DEMOCRACY.=
                    NEW YORK, FREDERICK A PRAEGER, 1962.                      62
                    COMEL, ELEL, ELNOEL, ELPRNOR
MALDM  -61-OYG   MALDONADO-DENIS, M
                    ORTEGA Y GASSET AND THE THEORY OF THE MASSES.=
                    THE WESTERN POLITICAL QUARTERLY, 14, (SEPTEMBER 1961),    61
                       PP. 676-690.
                    GNELTH, COMEL, ELEL, ELNOEL
MALIM  -60-WII   MALIA, M
                    WHAT IS THE INTELLIGENTSIA (SOVIET UNION).=
                    DAEDALUS, 89, (SUMMER 1960) PP. 441-458.                  60
                    DEFEL, COMEL, ELPRNOR
MALLJM-54-CGC   MALLORY, JM
                    CABINET GOVERNMENT IN CANADA.=
                    POLITICAL STUDIES, 2, (1954), PP. 142-153.                54
                    COMEL, ELEL, ELNOEL
MANCM  -64-SMT   MANCALL, M
                    SUCCESSION AND MYTH IN TAIWAN.=
                    JOURNAL OF INTERNATIONAL AFFAIRS, 18, (JANUARY-MARCH      64
                       1964), PP. 12-20.
                    COMEL, ELEL, ELPRNOR
MANDJ  -64-SDT   MANDER, J
                    THE STRANGE DEATH OF TORY ENGLAND.=
                    COMMENTARY, 38, (DECEMBER 1964), PP. 41-45.               64
                    ELNOEL, ELPRNOR
MANDWF-66-LBU   MANDLE, WF
                    THE LEADERSHIP OF THE BRITISH UNION OF FASCISTS.=
                    THE AUSTRALIAN JOURNAL OF POLITICS AND HISTORY, 12,       66
                       (DECEMBER 1966), PP. 360-383.
                    COMEL, ELPRNOR
MANGRS-57-NCF   MANGLAPUS, RS
                    NOTES ON THE CAREER FOREIGN SERVICE (PHILIPPINES).=
                    PHILIPPINE JOURNAL OF PUBLIC ADMINISTRATION, 1,           57
                       (APRIL 1957), PP. 127-130.
                    COMEL, ELEL
```

MANGS -49-FIM    MANGAN, S
                 THE FRENCH INTELLECTUAL MERRY-GO-ROUND.=
                 COMMENTARY, 7, (JUNE 1949), PP. 550-558.                      49
                 COMEL, ELEL, ELPRNOR
MANIT -66-GIP    MANIRUZZMAN, T
                 GROUP INTERESTS IN PAKISTAN POLITICS, 1947-1958.=
                 PACIFIC AFFAIRS, 39, (SPRING-SUMMER 1966), PP. 83-98.         66
                 COMEL, ELEL, ELPRNOR
MANLJF-65-HCW    MANLEY, JF
                 THE HOUSE COMMITTEE ON WAYS AND MEANS -- CONFLICT
                    MANAGEMENT IN A CONGRESSIONAL COMMITTEE
                    (UNITED STATES).=
                 THE AMERICAN POLITICAL SCIENCE REVIEW, 59, (DECEMBER          65
                    1965), PP. 927-939.
                 ELEL, ELPRNOR
MANNCS-66-MDM    MANNO, CS
                 MAJORITY DECISIONS AND MINORITY RESPONSES IN THE
                    UN GENERAL ASSEMBLY (UNITED NATIONS).=
                 THE JOURNAL OF CONFLICT RESOLUTION, 10, (MARCH 1966),         66
                    PP. 1-20.
                 ELEL, ELPRNOR, METEL
MANNDE-64-FPE    MANN, DE
                 FEDERAL POLITICAL EXECUTIVES (UNITED STATES).=
                 WASHINGTON, BROOKINGS INSTITUTION, 1964.                      64
                 COMEL, ELEL, ELPRNOR
MANNDE-64-SFP    MANN, DE
                 THE SELECTION OF FEDERAL POLITICAL EXECUTIVES
                    (UNITED STATES).=
                 THE AMERICAN POLITICAL SCIENCE REVIEW, 58, (MARCH 1964),      64
                    PP. 81-99.
                 COMEL
MANNDE-65-ASP    MANN, DE
                 THE ASSISTANT SECRETARIES -- PROBLEMS AND PROCESSES OF
                    APPOINTMENT (UNITED STATES).=
                 WASHINGTON, BROOKINGS INSTITUTION, 1965.                      65
                 COMEL, ELEL
MANNK -40-MSA    MANNHEIM, K
                 MAN AND SOCIETY IN AN AGE OF RECONSTRUCTION.=
                 NEW YORK, HARCOURT, BRACE AND CO., 1940.                      40
                 GNELTH, DEFEL, COMEL, ELPRNOR
MANNK -50-FPD    MANNHEIM, K
                 FREEDOM, POWER, AND DEMOCRATIC PLANNING.=
                 NEW YORK, OXFORD UNIVERSITY PRESS, 1950.                      50
                 GNELTH, DEFEL, COMEL, ELEL, ELNOEL, ELPRNOR
MANNK -66-IU     MANNHEIM, K
                 IDEOLOGY AND UTOPIA.=
                 NEW YORK, HARCOURT, BRACE AND WORLD, 1966.                    66
                 GNELTH, DEFEL, COMEL, ELEL, ELNOEL, ELPRNOR
MANSF -62-PII    MANSUR, F
                 PROCESS OF INDEPENDENCE (INDIA, PAKISTAN, INDONESIA,
                    GHANA).=
                 NEW YORK, HUMANITIES PRESS, 1962.                            62
                 DEFEL, ELEL, ELNOEL, ELPRNOR
MANSHC-60-CMR    MANSFIELD, HC
                 CIVIL - MILITARY RELATIONS IN THE UNITED STATES.=
                 CURRENT HISTORY, N.S., 38, (APRIL 1960), PP. 228-233.         60
                 ELEL, ELNOEL
MANSN -48-PSB    MANSERGH, N
                 POSTWAR STRAINS ON THE BRITISH COMMONWEALTH.=
                 FOREIGN AFFAIRS, 27, (OCTOBER 1948), PP. 129-142.             48
                 ELEL
MARCAS-64-YTA    MARCUS, AS           BAUER, RA
                 YES -- THERE ARE GENERALIZED OPINION LEADERS.=
                 THE PUBLIC OPINION QUARTERLY, 28, (WINTER 1964),              64
                    PP. 628-632.
                 DEFEL, METEL
MARCJA-59-FPL    MARCUM, JA
                 FRENCH PARTY LITERATURE.=
                 THE WESTERN POLITICAL QUARTERLY, 12, (MARCH 1959),            59
                    PP. 168-177.
                 ELEL, ELNOEL, ELPRNOR
MARCJG-55-ITM    MARCH, JG
                 AN INTRODUCTION TO THE THEORY AND MEASUREMENT OF
                    INFLUENCE.=
                 THE AMERICAN POLITICAL SCIENCE REVIEW, 49, (JUNE 1955),       55
                    PP. 431-451.
                 DEFEL, METEL
MARCJG-57-MCT    MARCH, JG
                 MEASUREMENT CONCEPTS IN THE THEORY OF INFLUENCE.=
                 THE JOURNAL OF POLITICS, 19, (MAY 1957), PP. 202-226.         57
                 DEFEL, METEL
MARCJG-58-PLR    MARCH, JG
                 PARTY LEGISLATIVE REPRESENTATION AS A FUNCTION OF
                    ELECTION RESULTS -- RELATIONSHIP BETWEEN VOTES AND

```
                    LEGISLATIVE REPRESENTATION IN ENGLAND AND THE
                    UNITED STATES.=
                    THE PUBLIC OPINION QUARTERLY, 21, (WINTER 1957-1958),        58
                       PP. 521-542.
                    ELNOEL
MARCJG-65-HO        MARCH, JG (ED)
                    HANDBOOK OF ORGANIZATIONS.=
                    CHICAGO, RAND MCNALLY, 1965                                  65
                    DEFEL, COMEL, ELEL, ELNOEL, ELPRNOR, METEL
MARCJG-66-PP        MARCH, JG
                    THE POWER OF POWER.=
                    D EASTON ED., VARIETIES OF POLITICAL THEORY, ENGLEWOOD       66
                       CLIFFS, PRENTICE-HALL, 1966, PP. 39-70.
                    DEFEL, METEL
MARCS -60-SCS       MARCSON, S
                    SOCIAL CHANGE AND STRUCTURE IN TRANSITIONAL SOCIETIES
                       (LATIN AMERICA, MIDDLE EAST).=
                    INTERNATIONAL JOURNAL OF COMPARATIVE SOCIOLOGY,              60
                       1, (SEPTEMBER 1960), PP. 248-253.
                    COMEL
MARGHB-65-MES       MARGAIN, HB
                    MEXICAN ECONOMIC AND SOCIAL DEVELOPMENT.=
                    THE ANNALS OF THE AMERICAN ACADEMY OF POLITICAL AND          65
                       SOCIAL SCIENCE, 360, (JULY 1965), PP. 68-77.
                    ELEL, ELPRNOR
MARHM -63-TBM       MARHYAMA, M           MORRIS, I (EDS)
                    THOUGHT AND BEHAVIOUR IN MODERN JAPANESE POLITICS.=
                    NEW YORK, OXFORD UNIVERSITY PRESS, 1963.                     63
                    ELEL, ELPRNOR
MARIJ -60-SIS       MARIAS, J
                    THE SITUATION OF THE INTELLIGENTSIA IN SPAIN TODAY.=
                    DAEDALUS, 89, (SUMMER 1960), PP. 622-631.                    60
                    COMEL, ELEL, ELNOEL
MARILC-57-CLA       MARIANO, LC
                    CONGRESS AND LOCAL AUTONOMY (PHILIPPINES).=
                    PHILIPPINE JOURNAL OF PUBLIC ADMINISTRATION, 1,              57
                       (OCTOBER 1957), PP. 363-378.
                    ELEL, ELNOEL
MARILC-58-SCL       MARIANO, LC
                    THE SUPREME COURT AND LOCAL AUTONOMY (PHILIPPINES).=
                    PHILIPPINE JOURNAL OF PUBLIC ADMINISTRATION, 2,              58
                       (JANUARY 1958), PP. 38-53.
                    ELEL, ELNOEL
MARIY -54-CLS       MARIN, Y
                    COLLECTIVE LEADERSHIP (SOVIET UNION).=
                    BULLETIN OF THE INSTITUTE FOR THE STUDY OF THE HISTORY       54
                       AND CULTURE OF THE USSR, 1, (MAY 1954), PP. 3-7.
                    ELEL
MARIY -61-MPS       MARIN, Y
                    THE MOSCOW PATRIARCH IN SOVIET FOREIGN
                       AND DOMESTIC POLICY.=
                    BULLETIN INSTITUTE FOR THE STUDY OF THE USSR, 8,             61
                       (FEBRUARY 1961), PP. 32-38.
                    ELEL, ELPRNOR
MARIY -63-PSE       MARIN, Y
                    THE POST - STALIN ERA (SOVIET UNION).=
                    STUDIES ON THE SOVIET UNION, 2, (1963), PP. 5-15.            63
                    ELEL, ELNOEL
MARIY -65-KSS       MARIN, Y
                    KHRUSHCHEV'S SEVENTIETH BIRTHDAY AND THE PROBLEM OF
                       CHOOSING HIS SUCCESSOR (SOVIET UNION).=
                    STUDIES ON THE SOVIET UNION, 4, (1965), PP. 100-104.         65
                    ELEL
MARKK -65-HHS       MARKO, K
                    HISTORY AND THE HISTORIANS (SOVIET UNION).=
                    SURVEY--A JOURNAL OF SOVIET AND EAST EUROPEAN STUDIES,       65
                       56, (JULY 1965), PP. 71-82.
                    ELEL, ELPRNOR
MARKM -56-SDR       MARK, M
                    SOCIAL DETERMINANTS OF THE ROLE OF A CIVIL SERVICE
                       (UNITED STATES, GREAT BRITAIN).=
                    THE SOUTHWESTERN SOCIAL SCIENCE QUARTERLY, 36,               56
                       (MARCH 1956), PP. 376-384.
                    COMEL, ELEL, ELPRNOR
MAROS -59-PSN       MARON, S
                    PAKISTAN'S NEW POWER ELITE.=
                    FOREIGN POLICY BULLETIN, 38, (JULY 1959), PP. 153-154,160.59
                    COMEL, ELEL, ELPRNOR
MARQD -62-LRG       MARQUAND, D
                    THE LIBERAL REVIVAL (GREAT BRITAIN).=
                    ENCOUNTER, 19, (JULY 1962), PP. 63-68.                       62
                    COMEL, ELEL, ELPRNOR
MARRM -60-CRC       MARRIOTT, M
                    CASTE RANKING AND COMMUNITY STRUCTURE IN FIVE REGIONS OF
```

                        INDIA AND PAKISTAN.=
                        POONA, DECCAN COLLEGE PRESS, 1960.                        60
                        COMEL, ELEL, ELNOEL
MARSRM-61-MCE   MARSH, RM
                        THE MANDARINS -- THE CIRCULATION OF ELITES IN CHINA,
                            1600-1900.=
                        GLENCOE, THE FREE PRESS, 1961.                           61
                        COMEL, ELEL, ELNOEL
MARSRM-63-VDS   MARSH, RM
                        VALUES, DEMAND, AND SOCIAL MOBILITY (INDUSTRIAL ELITES,
                            CHINA, UNITED STATES).=
                        AMERICAN SOCIOLOGICAL REVIEW, 28, (AUGUST 1963),        63
                            PP. 565-575.
                        COMEL, ELEL
MARSTH-64-CCS   MARSHALL, TH
                        CLASS, CITIZENSHIP AND SOCIAL DEVELOPMENT.=
                        NEW YORK, DOUBLEDAY, 1964.                               64
                        DEFEL, ELNOEL, ELPRNOR
MARTAW-56-LAN   MARTIN, AW
                        THE LEGISLATIVE ASSEMBLY OF NEW SOUTH WALES,
                            1856-1900 (AUSTRALIA).=
                        AUSTRALIAN JOURNAL OF POLITICS AND HISTORY, 2,          56
                            (MAY 1956), PP. 46-67
                        COMEL, ELEL, ELNOEL, ELPRNOR
MARTCW-63-IGC   MARTIN, CW
                        INTEREST GROUPS AND CONSERVATIVE POLITICS
                            (UNITED STATES).=
                        THE WESTERN POLITICAL QUARTERLY, 16, (SUPPLEMENT,       63
                            SEPTEMBER 1963), PP. 68-69.
                        ELEL, ELPRNOR
MARTD -64-DSL   MARTZ, D
                        DILEMMAS IN THE STUDY OF LATIN AMERICAN POLITICAL
                            PARTIES.=
                        THE JOURNAL OF POLITICS, 26, (AUGUST 1964),             64
                            PP. 509-531.
                        DEFEL, ELNOEL
MARTJ -65-DCL   MARTZ, J (ED)
                        THE DYNAMICS OF CHANGE IN LATIN AMERICAN POLITICS.=
                        ENGLEWOOD CLIFFS, NEW JERSEY, PRENTICE-HALL, 1965.      65
                        ELEL, ELNOEL, ELPRNOR
MARTJD-63-GDV   MARTZ, JD
                        THE GROWTH AND DEMOCRATIZATION OF THE VENEZUELAN LABOR
                            MOVEMENT.=
                        INTER-AMERICAN ECONOMIC AFFAIRS, 17,                    63
                            (AUTUMN 1963), PP. 3-18.
                        ELEL, ELNOEL
MARTJD-66-ADR   MARTZ, JD
                        ACCION DEMOCRATICA -- REVOLUTION OF A MODERN POLITICAL
                            PARTY IN VENEZUELA.=
                        PRINCETON, PRINCETON UNIVERSITY PRESS, 1966.            66
                        ELEL, ELNOEL, ELPRNOR
MARTK -63-BSC   MARTIN, K
                        BRITAIN IN THE SIXTIES -- THE CROWN AND THE
                            ESTABLISHMENT.=
                        LONDON, PEQUIN BOOKS, 1963.                             63
                        COMEL, ELEL, ELPRNOR
MARTRC-61-DSU   MARTIN, RC          MUNGER, FJ          ET AL
                        DECISIONS IN SYRACUSE (UNITED STATES).=
                        BLOOMINGTON, INDIANA, INDIANA UNIVERSITY PRESS, 1961.   61
                        COMEL, ELEL, ELNOEL, ELPRNOR
MARTRG-64-BUS   MARTIN, RG
                        THE BOSSES (UNITED STATES).=
                        NEW YORK, GP PUTNAM'S SONS, 1964.                       64
                        ELEL, ELPRNOR
MARTRM-63-TUL   MARTIN, RM
                        TRADE UNIONS AND LABOUR GOVERNMENTS IN AUSTRALIA.=
                        JOURNAL OF COMMONWEALTH POLITICAL STUDIES, 2,           63
                            (1963), PP. 59-78.
                        COMEL, ELEL, ELPRNOR
MARVD -54-CPB   MARVICK, D
                        CAREER PERSPECTIVES IN A BUREAUCRATIC SETTING
                            (UNITED STATES).=
                        ANN ARBOR, MICHIGAN, UNIVERSITY OF MICHIGAN PRESS, 1954.  54
                        COMEL, ELEL, ELNOEL, ELPRNOR
MARVD -61-NCL   MARVICK, D          ELDERSVELD, SJ
                        NATIONAL CONVENTION LEADERSHIP -- 1952 AND 1956
                            (UNITED STATES).=
                        THE WESTERN POLITICAL QUARTERLY, 14, (MARCH 1961),      61
                            PP. 176-194.
                        COMEL, ELEL, ELPRNOR
MARVD -61-PDM   MARVICK, D (ED)
                        POLITICAL DECISION-MAKERS (INDIA, FRANCE, GREAT BRITAIN,
                            GERMANY, UNITED STATES).=
                        GLENCOE, THE FREE PRESS, 1961.                          61

```
                    GNELTH, DEFEL, COMEL, ELEL, ELNOEL, ELPRNOR, METEL
MARVD -61-RCR       MARVICK, D          NIXON, C
                    RECRUITMENT CONTRASTS IN RURAL CAMPAIGN GROUPS
                       (UNITED STATES).=
                    D MARVICK (ED), POLITICAL DECISION-MAKERS, GLENCOE, THE    61
                       FREE PRESS, 1961, PP. 193-217.
                    COMEL, ELNOEL, ELPRNOR
MARVD -65-AUS       MARVICK, D
                    AMERICAN UNIVERSITY STUDENTS -- A PRESUMPTIVE ELITE.=
                    JS COLEMAN (ED), EDUCATION AND POLITICAL DEVELOPMENT,      65
                       PRINCETON, PRINCETON UNIVERSITY PRESS, 1965,
                       PP. 463-497.
                    COMEL, ELPRNOR
MARWA -59-GGS       MARWALD, A
                    THE GERMAN GENERAL STAFF -- MODEL OF MILITARY
                       ORGANIZATION.=
                    ORBIS, 3, (SPRING 1959), PP. 38-62.                        59
                    ELEL
MARWG -67-PRD       MARWELL, G
                    PARTY, REGION AND THE DIMENSION OF CONFLICT IN THE HOUSE
                       OF REPRESENTATIVES, 1949-1954 (UNITED STATES).=
                    THE AMERICAN POLITICAL SCIENCE REVIEW, 61, (JUNE 1967),    67
                       PP. 380-399.
                    ELEL, ELPRNOR, METEL
MASAMR-54-CPI       MASANI, MR
                    THE COMMUNIST PARTY IN INDIA -- A SHORT HISTORY.=
                    LONDON, DEREK VERSCHOYIE, 1954.                            54
                    COMEL, ELEL, ELPRNOR
MASLJW-57-SSM       MASLAND, JW         RADWAY, LI
                    SOLDIERS AND SCHOLARS -- MILITARY EDUCATION AND NATIONAL
                       POLICY (UNITED STATES).=
                    PRINCETON, PRINCETON UNIVERSITY PRESS, 1957.               57
                    ELEL, ELPRNOR
MASOAT-58-SCT       MASON, AT
                    THE SUPREME COURT FROM TAFT TO WARREN (UNITED STATES).=
                    BATON ROUGE, LOUISIANA STATE UNIVERSITY PRESS, 1958.       58
                    ELEL
MASTNA-61-CAH       MASTERS, NA
                    COMMITTEE ASSIGNMENTS IN THE HOUSE OF REPRESENTATIVES
                       (UNITED STATES).=
                    THE AMERICAN POLITICAL SCIENCE REVIEW, 55, (JUNE 1961),    61
                       PP. 345-357.
                    ELEL
MASUG -66-NLA       MASUR, G
                    NATIONALISM IN LATIN AMERICA.=
                    NEW YORK, MACMILLAN, 1966.                                 66
                    COMEL, ELEL, ELNOEL, ELPRNOR
MATLJF-56-GOU       MATLOCK-JR, JF
                    THE 'GOVERNING ORGANS' OF THE UNION OF SOVIET WRITERS.=
                    THE AMERICAN SLAVIC AND EAST EUROPEAN REVIEW, 15,          56
                       (OCTOBER 1956), PP. 382-399.
                    ELEL, ELNOEL
MATTDR-54-USS       MATTHEWS, DR
                    UNITED STATES SENATORS AND THE CLASS STRUCTURE.=
                    THE PUBLIC OPINION QUARTERLY, 18, (SPRING 1954),           54
                       PP. 5-22.
                    COMEL, ELNOEL
MATTDR-59-FUS       MATTHEWS, DR
                    THE FOLKWAYS OF THE UNITED STATES SENATE --
                       CONFORMITY TO GROUP NORMS AND LEGISLATIVE
                       EFFECTIVENESS.=
                    THE AMERICAN POLITICAL SCIENCE REVIEW, 53, (DECEMBER       59
                       1959), PP. 1064-1089.
                    ELEL, ELPRNOR
MATTDR-60-USS       MATTHEWS, DR
                    U.S. SENATORS AND THEIR WORLD (UNITED STATES).=
                    NEW YORK, RANDOM HOUSE, INC, 1960.                         60
                    COMEL, ELEL, ELNOEL, ELPRNOR, METEL
MATTDR-61-USS       MATTHEWS, DR
                    UNITED STATES SENATOR -- A COLLECTIVE PORTRAIT.=
                    INTERNATIONAL SOCIAL SCIENCE JOURNAL, 13, (OCTOBER-        61
                       DECEMBER 1961), PP. 620-634.
                    COMEL, ELEL
MATTDR-62-SBP       MATTHEWS, DR
                    THE SOCIAL BACKGROUNDS OF POLITICAL DECISION MAKERS.=
                    NEW YORK, RANDOM HOUSE, 1962.                              62
                    COMEL, ELEL, ELNOEL, METEL
MAUDA -53-CPC       MAUDE, A
                    CONSERVATIVE PARTY AND THE CHANGING CLASS STRUCTURE
                       (GREAT BRITAIN).=
                    THE POLITICAL QUARTERLY, 18, (APRIL 1953), PP. 139-147.    53
                    COMEL, ELEL, ELNOEL, ELPRNOR
MAUNM -57-PBP       MAUNG, M
                    PORTRAIT OF THE BURMESE PARLIAMENT.=
```

                        PARLIAMENTARY AFFAIRS, 10, (SPRING 1957), PP. 204-209.      57
                        ELEL, ELNOEL
MAY,JD-65-DOM    MAY, JD
                        DEMOCRACY, ORGANIZATION, MICHELS.=
                        THE AMERICAN POLITICAL SCIENCE REVIEW, 59, (JUNE 1965),     65
                           PP. 417-429.
                        DEFEL, ELEL, ELNOEL
MAY,R -55-PAA    MAY, R
                        A PSYCHOLOGICAL APPROACH TO ANTI - INTELLECTUALISM.=
                        THE JOURNAL OF SOCIAL ISSUES, 9, (SUMMER 1955), PP. 41-47.55
                        METEL
MAYEAC-62-SNA    MAYER, AC
                        SYSTEM AND NETWORK -- AN APPROACH TO THE STUDY OF
                           POLITICAL PROCESS.=
                        TN MADAN AND G SARENA (EDS), INDIAN ANTHROPOLOGY,           62
                           BOMBAY, ASIA, 1962.
                        GNELTH, ELEL, ELNOEL, METEL
MAYEH -66-APR    MAYER, H
                        AUSTRALIAN POLITICS -- A READER.=
                        MELBOURNE, FW CHESHIRE, 1966.                               66
                        COMEL, ELEL, ELNOEL, ELPRNOR
MAYEKB-64-SST    MAYER, KB
                        SOCIAL STRATIFICATION IN TWO EQUALITARIAN SOCIETIES --
                           AUSTRALIA AND THE UNITED STATES.=
                        SOCIAL RESEARCH, 31, (WINTER 1964), PP. 435-465.            64
                        COMEL
MAYEP -66-TET    MAYER, P
                        THE TRIBAL ELITE AND THE TRANSKEIAN ELECTIONS OF 1963
                           (SOUTH AFRICA).=
                        PC LLOYD (ED), THE NEW ELITES OF TROPICAL AFRICA, LONDON, 66
                           OXFORD UNIVERSITY PRESS, 1966, PP. 286-308.
                        COMEL, ELEL, ELNOEL, ELPRNOR
MAYFJ -61-CNL    MAYFIELD, J
                        CHALLENGE TO NEGRO LEADERSHIP (UNITED STATES).=
                        COMMENTARY, 31, (APRIL 1961), PP. 297-305.                  61
                        ELEL, ELNOEL, ELPRNOR
MAYHDR-66-PLA    MAYHEW, DR
                        PARTY LOYALTY AMONG CONGRESSMEN -- THE DIFFERENCE
                           BETWEEN DEMOCRATS AND REPUBLICANS, 1947-1962
                           (UNITED STATES).=
                        CAMBRIDGE, HARVARD UNIVERSITY PRESS, U9LL.                  66
                        ELEL, ELNOEL, ELPRNOR
MAYNR -61-OPG    MAYNTZ, R
                        OLIGARCHIC PROBLEMS IN A GERMAN PARTY DISTRICT.=
                        D MARVICK (ED), POLITICAL DECISION MAKERS, GLENCOE,         61
                           THE FREE PRESS, 1961, PP. 138-192.
                        COMEL, ELEL, ELNOEL
MAZRAA-7 -SSE    MAZRUI, AA          ROTHCHILD, D
                        THE SOLDIER AND THE STATE IN EAST AFRICA -- SOME
                           THEORETICAL CONCLUSIONS ON THE ARMY MUTINIES OF 1964.=
                        THE WESTERN POLITICAL QUARTERLY, 20, (MARCH 1967),          67
                           PP. 82-96.
                        ELEL, ELPRNOR
MCALLN-61-CMR    MCALISTER, LN
                        CIVIL - MILITARY RELATIONS IN LATIN AMERICA.=
                        JOURNAL OF INTER-AMERICAN STUDIES, 3, (JULY 1961),          61
                           PP. 341-350.
                        ELEL, ELNOEL, ELPRNOR
MCALLN-63-SSS    MCALISTER, LN
                        SOCIAL STRUCTURE AND SOCIAL CHANGE IN NEW SPAIN.=
                        THE HISPANIC AMERICAN HISTORICAL REVIEW, 43, (AUGUST,       63
                           1963), PP. 349-370.
                        DEFEL, ELEL, ELNOEL, ELPRNOR
MCALLN-64-MLA    MCALISTER, LN
                        THE MILITARY (LATIN AMERICA).=
                        JJ JOHNSON (ED), CONTINUITY AND CHANGE IN LATIN AMERICA,    64
                           STANDFORD, STANDFORD UNIVERSITY PRESS, 1964,
                           PP. 136-160.
                        COMEL, ELEL, ELPRNOR
MCALLN-65-CCR    MCALISTER, LN
                        CHANGING CONCEPTS OF THE ROLE OF THE MILITARY IN
                           LATIN AMERICA.=
                        THE ANNALS OF THE AMERICAN ACADEMY OF POLITICAL AND         65
                           SOCIAL SCIENCE, 360, (JULY 1965), PP. 85-98.
                        COMEL, ELEL, ELPRNOR
MCCAJL-54-PSD    MCCAMY, JL          CORRADINI, A
                        THE PEOPLE OF THE STATE DEPARTMENT AND FOREIGN
                           SERVICE (UNITED STATES).=
                        THE AMERICAN POLITICAL SCIENCE REVIEW, 48,                  54
                           (DECEMBER 1954), PP. 1067-1082.
                        COMEL, ELPRNOR
MCCASP-66-GHL    MCCALLY, SP
                        THE GOVERNOR AND HIS LEGISLATIVE PARTY (UNITED STATES).=
                        THE AMERICAN POLITICAL SCIENCE REVIEW, 60, (DECEMBER        66

                                      1966), PP. 923-942.
                                      ELEL, METEL
MCCAWO-62-ARD   MCCAGG, WO
                AFTER RAKOSI -- DISGRACE AND REHABILITATION (HUNGARY).=
                SURVEY--A JOURNAL OF SOVIET AND EAST EUROPEAN STUDIES,        62
                    40, (JANUARY 1962), PP. 124-132.
                COMEL, ELEL
MCCLH -60-ICC   MCCLOSKY, H          HOFFMAN, PJ          O'HARA, R
                ISSUE CONFLICT AND CONSENSUS AMONG PARTY LEADERS AND
                    FOLLOWERS (UNITED STATES).=
                THE AMERICAN POLITICAL SCIENCE REVIEW, 54, (JUNE 1960),       60
                    PP. 406-427.
                ELEL, ELNOEL, ELPRNOR, METEL
MCCLH -64-CIA   MCCLOSKY, H
                CONSENSUS AND IDEOLOGY IN AMERICAN POLITICS.=
                THE AMERICAN POLITICAL SCIENCE REVIEW, 58, (JUNE 1964),       64
                    PP. 361-382.
                ELNOEL, ELPRNOR
MCCLT -67-PSC   MCCLURE, T
                THE POLITICS OF SOVIET CULTURE, 1964-1967.=
                PROBLEMS OF COMMUNISM, 16, (MARCH-APRIL 1967), PP. 26-43. 67
                ELEL, ELPRNOR
MCCOCA-65-ADL   MCCOY, CA
                AUSTRALIAN DEMOCRATIC LABOR PARTY SUPPORT.=
                JOURNAL OF COMMONWEALTH POLITICAL STUDIES, 3, (1965),         65
                    PP. 199-208.
                ELEL, ELNOEL
MCCOJB-50-PFS   MCCONAUGHY, JB
                SOME PERSONALITY FACTORS OF STATE LEGISLATORS IN SOUTH
                    CAROLINA (UNITED STATES).=
                THE AMERICAN POLITICAL SCIENCE REVIEW, 44,                    50
                    (DECEMBER 1950), PP. 897-903.
                COMEL, ELPRNOR
MCCOT -66-IMM   MCCORMACK, T
                INTELLECTUALS AND THE MASS MEDIA (UNITED STATES).=
                THE AMERICAN BEHAVIORAL SCIENTIST, 9, (DECEMBER 1965-         66
                    JANUARY 1966), PP. 31-36.
                COMEL, ELEL, ELPRNOR
MCCOTH-52-MRP   MCCORMACK, TH
                THE MOTIVATION AND ROLE OF A PROPAGANDIST
                    (GREAT BRITAIN).=
                SOCIAL FORCES, 30, (MAY 1952), PP. 388-394.                   52
                ELPRNOR
MCDONA-65-PSC   MCDONALD, NA
                POLITICS -- A STUDY OF CONTROL BEHAVIOR (UNITED STATES).=
                NEW BRUNSWICK, NEW JERSEY, RUTGERS UNIVERSITY PRESS, 1965 65
                DEFEL
MCGIE -65-RJU   MCGINNIES, E
                SOME REACTIONS OF JAPANESE UNIVERSITY STUDENTS TO
                    PERSUASIVE COMMUNICATION.=
                THE JOURNAL OF CONFLICT RESOLUTION, 9, (DECEMBER 1965),       65
                    PP. 482-490.
                ELPRNOR, METEL
MCGRJC-62-EPP   MCGRATH, JC          MCGRATH, MF
                EFFECTS OF PARTISANSHIP ON PERCEPTIONS OF POLITICAL
                    FIGURES.=
                THE PUBLIC OPINION QUARTERLY, 26, (SUMMER 1962),              62
                    PP. 236-248.
                ELNOEL
MCHEDE-54-FRL   MCHENRY, DE
                FORMAL RECOGNITION OF THE LEADER OF THE OPPOSITION IN
                    PARLIAMENTS OF THE BRITISH COMMONWEALTH.=
                POLITICAL SCIENCE QUARTERLY, 69, (SEPTEMBER 1954),            54
                    PP. 438-542.
                ELEL
MCKERT-55-PBP   MCKENZIE, RT
                POWER IN BRITISH POLITICAL PARTIES.=
                THE BRITISH JOURNAL OF SOCIOLOGY, 6, (1955), PP. 123-132. 55
                ELEL
MCKERT-65-BPP   MCKENZIE, RT
                BRITISH POLITICAL PARTIES -- THE DISTRIBUTION OF POWER
                    WITHIN THE CONSERVATIVE AND LABOUR PARTIES.=
                2ND EDITION, NEW YORK, FREDERICK A PRAEGER, 1965.             65
                COMEL, ELEL, ELNOEL, ELPRNOR
MCKIMM-49-RAC   MCKINNEY, MM
                RECRUITMENT OF THE ADMINISTRATIVE CLASS OF THE BRITISH
                    CIVIL SERVICE.=
                THE WESTERN POLITICAL QUARTERLY, 2, (SEPTEMBER 1949),         49
                    PP. 345-357.
                COMEL
MCLEDS-60-BEF   MCLELLAN, DS          WOODHOUSE, CE
                THE BUSINESS ELITE AND FOREIGN POLICY (UNITED STATES).=
                THE WESTERN POLITICAL QUARTERLY, 13, (MARCH 1960),            60
                    PP. 172-190.

```
                    ELEL, ELPRNOR
MCLEH -63-ERH   MCLEAN, H
                ET RESURREXERUNT -- HOW WRITERS RISE FROM THE DEAD
                    (SOVIET UNION).=
                PROBLEMS OF COMMUNISM, 13, (MAY-JUNE 1963), PP. 33-41.     63
                    ELEL, ELPRNOR
MCMUCD-65-PAT   MCMURRAY, CD         PARSONS, MB
                PUBLIC ATTITUDES TOWARD THE REPRESENTATIONAL ROLE OF
                    LEGISLATORS AND JUDGES (UNITED STATES).=
                MIDWEST JOURNAL OF POLITICAL SCIENCE, 9, (MAY 1965),       65
                    PP. 167-185.
                    ELNOEL
MCPHWN-61-NCS   MCPHEE, WN
                NOTE ON A CAMPAIGN SIMULATOR.=
                THE PUBLIC OPINION QUARTERLY, 25, (SUMMER 1961),           61
                    PP. 184-193.
                    METEL
MCPHWN-62-POC   MCPHEE, WN           GLASER, WA (EDS)
                PUBLIC OPINION AND CONGRESSIONAL ELECTIONS
                    (UNITED STATES).=
                NEW YORK, THE FREE PRESS, 1962.                           62
                    ELEL, ELNOEL, ELPRNOR, METEL
MCRAJH-65-TWE   MCRANDLE, JH
                THE TRACK OF THE WOLF -- ESSAYS ON NATIONAL SOCIALISM
                    AND ITS LEADERS, ADOLPH HITLER (GERMANY).=
                EVANSTON, NORTHWESTERN UNIVERSITY PRESS, 1965.            65
                    ELPRNOR, METEL
MCWIC -55-OPA   MCWILLIAMS, C
                OFFICIAL POLICY AND ANTI - INTELLECTUALISM
                    (UNITED STATES).=
                THE JOURNAL OF SOCIAL ISSUES, 9, (SUMMER 1955), PP. 18-21.55
                    ELEL
MD    -51-PDE   MD
                PARTY DISCIPLINE IN EASTERN EUROPE.=
                THE WORLD TODAY, 7, (OCTOBER 1951), PP. 430-439.           51
                    COMEL
MEADEG-51-AMG   MEADE, EG
                AMERICAN MILITARY GOVERNMENT IN KOREA.=
                NEW YORK, KING'S CROWN, 1951.                             51
                    ELEL, ELNOEL
MEADM -51-SAT   MEAD, M
                SOVIET ATTITUDES TOWARD AUTHORITY.=
                NEW YORK, MCGRAW-HILL, 1951.                              51
                    ELNOEL, ELPRNOR
MEADM -64-CNE   MEADOWS, M
                CHALLENGE TO THE 'NEW ERA' IN PHILIPPINE POLITICS.=
                PACIFIC AFFAIRS, 37, (FALL 1964), PP. 296-306.            64
                    ELEL, ELNOEL
MEANGP-63-MNF   MEANS, GP
                MALAYSIA -- A NEW FEDERATION IN SOUTHEAST ASIA.=
                PACIFIC AFFAIRS, 36, (SUMMER 1963), PP. 138-159.          63
                    COMEL, ELEL
MEEHEJ-60-BLW   MEEHAN, EJ
                THE BRITISH LEFT WING AND FOREIGN POLICY -- A STUDY
                    OF THE INFLUENCE OF IDEOLOGY.=
                NEW BRUNSWICK, NEW JERSEY, RUTGERS UNIVERSITY             60
                    PRESS, 1960.
                    ELEL, ELPRNOR
MEISB -65-PGR   MEISSNER, B
                PARTY AND GOVERNMENT REFORMS -- A PROVISIONAL BALANCE
                    SHEET (SOVIET UNION).=
                SURVEY--A JOURNAL OF SOVIET AND EAST EUROPEAN STUDIES,     65
                    56, (JULY 1965), PP. 31-45.
                    ELEL, ELNOEL
MEISB -66-TRS   MEISSNER, B
                TOTALITARIAN RULE AND SOCIAL CHANGE (SOVIET UNION).=
                PROBLEMS OF COMMUNISM, 15, (NOVEMBER-DECEMBER 1966),       66
                    PP. 56-61.
                    COMEL, ELEL, ELNOEL, ELPRNOR
MEISJ -60-FLC   MEISEL, J
                THE FORMULATION OF LIBERAL AND CONSERVATIVE PROGRAMMES
                    IN THE 1957 CANADIAN GENERAL ELECTION.=
                CANADIAN JOURNAL OF ECONOMICS AND POLITICAL SCIENCE,       60
                    26, (NOVEMBER 1960), PP. 565-574.
                    ELEL, ELNOEL, ELPRNOR
MEISJ -62-CGE   MEISEL, J
                THE CANADIAN GENERAL ELECTION OF 1957.=
                TORONTO, UNIVERSITY OF TORONTO PRESS, 1962.               62
                    COMEL, ELEL, ELNOEL
MEISJ -63-SOC   MEISEL, J
                THE STALLED OMNIBUS -- CANADIAN PARTIES IN THE 1960'S.=
                SOCIAL RESEARCH, 30, (AUTUMN 1963), PP. 367-390.          63
                    ELEL, ELNOEL
MEISJH-58-MRC   MEISEL, JH
```

```
                    THE MYTH OF THE RULING CLASS -- GAETANO MOSCA AND
                        THE 'ELITE'.=
                    ANN ARBOR, THE UNIVERSITY OF MICHIGAN, 1958.            58
                    GNELTH, DEFEL
MEISJH-62-FRM       MEISEL, JH
                    THE FALL OF THE REPUBLIC -- MILITARY REVOLT IN FRANCE.=
                    ANN ARBOR, UNIVERSITY OF MICHIGAN PRESS, 1962.         62
                    ELEL, ELNOEL, ELPRNOR
MEISJH-65-PM        MEISEL, JH
                    PARETO AND MOSCA.=
                    EDGEWOOD CLIFFS, NEW JERSEY, PRENTICE-HALL, INC, 1965.  65
                    GNELTH, DEFEL, ELEL, ELNOEL
MELATP-61-PAL       MELADY, TP
                    PROFILES OF AFRICAN LEADERS.=
                    NEW YORK, THE MACMILLAN CO., 1961.                     61
                    ELEL, ELPRNOR
MELLN -58-MHS       MELLER, N
                    MISSIONARIES TO HAWAII -- SHAPER'S OF THE ISLAND'S
                        GOVERNMENT.=
                    THE WESTERN POLITICAL QUARTERLY, 11, (DECEMBER 1958),   58
                        PP. 788-799.
                    ELEL, ELNOEL
MELLN -67-RRT       MELLER, N
                    REPRESENTATIONAL ROLE TYPES -- A RESEARCH NOTE
                        (MICRONESIA, POLYNESIA).=
                    THE AMERICAN POLITICAL SCIENCE REVIEW, 61, (JUNE 1967)  67
                        PP. 474-477.
                    ELPRNOR, METEL
MENDDH-59-BJE       MENDEL, DH
                    BEHIND THE 1959 JAPANESE ELECTIONS.=
                    PACIFIC AFFAIRS, 32, (SEPTEMBER 1959), PP. 298-306.     59
                    ELEL, ELNOEL
MENDDH-61-JPF       MENDEL, DH
                    THE JAPANESE PEOPLE AND FOREIGN POLICY -- A STUDY OF
                        PUBLIC OPINION IN POST-TREATY JAPAN.=
                    BERKELEY AND LOS ANGELES, UNIVERSITY OF CALIFORNIA,     61
                        1961.
                    ELEL, ELNOEL
MENDEM-60-RAM       MENDELSON, EM
                    RELIGION AND AUTHORITY IN MODERN BURMA.=
                    THE WORLD TODAY, 16, (MARCH 1960), PP. 110-118.         60
                    ELEL, ELNOEL, ELPRNOR
MENDW -64-UWJ       MENDELSON, W
                    THE UNTROUBLED WORLD OF JURIMETRICS.=
                    THE JOURNAL OF POLITICS, 26, (NOVEMBER 1964),           64
                        PP. 914-922.
                    METEL
MENGSM-59-TYI       MENG, SM
                    THE TSUNGLI YAMEN -- ITS ORGANIZATION AND FUNCTIONS
                        (CHINA).=
                    CAMBRIDGE, HARVARD UNIVERSITY PRESS, 1959.             59
                    COMEL, ELEL, ELNOEL
MENZJM-63-CCS       MENZEL, JM
                    THE CHINESE CIVIL SERVICE -- CAREER OPEN TO TALENT.=
                    BOSTON, HEATH, 1963.                                   63
                    COMEL
MERAT -62-GTH       MERAY, T
                    GENEALOGICAL TROUBLES (HUNGARY).=
                    SURVEY--A JOURNAL OF SOVIET AND EAST EUROPEAN STUDIES,  62
                        40, (JANUARY 1962), PP. 106-113.
                    COMEL, ELEL, ELPRNOR
MERCP -56-ESE       MERCER, P
                    EVOLUTION OF SENEGALESE ELITES.=
                    INTERNATIONAL SOCIAL SCIENCE BULLETIN, 8, (JULY-SEPTEMBER 56
                        1956), PP. 441-452.
                    COMEL, ELEL, ELNOEL, ELPRNOR, METEL
MERKPH-62-ESI       MERKL, PH
                    EQUILIBRIUM, STRUCTURE OF INTERESTS AND LEADERSHIP --
                        ADENAUER'S SURVIVAL AS CHANCELLOR (GERMANY).=
                    THE AMERICAN POLITICAL SCIENCE REVIEW, 6, (SEPTEMBER    62
                        1962), PP. 634-650.
                    ELEL, ELNOEL, ELPRNOR
MERKPH-64-EAP       MERKL, PH
                    EUROPEAN ASSEMBLY PARTIES AND NATIONAL DELEGATIONS.=
                    THE JOURNAL OF CONFLICT RESOLUTION, 8, (MARCH 1964),    64
                        PP. 50-64.
                    ELEL, ELPRNOR
MERRCE-49-PLU       MERRIAM, CE
                    POLITICAL LEADERSHIP (UNITED STATES).=
                    RC SNYDER AND HH WILSON (EDS), ROOTS OF POLITICAL       49
                        BEHAVIOR, NEW YORK, AMERICAN BOOK CO., 1949,
                        PP. 141-145.
                    ELEL, ELPRNOR
MERRHJ-55-ECS       MERRY, HJ
```

THE EUROPEAN COAL AND STEEL COMMUNITY -- OPERATIONS OF THE
   HIGH AUTHORITY.=
THE WESTERN POLITICAL QUARTERLY, 8, (JUNE 1955),     55
   PP. 166-185.
ELEL

MERTVK-52-RB   MERTON, VK      ET AL (EDS)
READER IN BUREAUCRACY.=
GLENCOE, ILLINOIS, FREE PRESS, 1952.     52
GNELTH, DEFEL, ELEL, ELNOEL, ELPRNOR, METEL

MERTVS-56-MSS   MERTSALOV, VS
MAO IN STALIN'S FOOTSTEPS (CHINA).=
BULLETIN INSTITUTE FOR THE STUDY OF THE USSR, 3,     56
   (FEBRUARY 1956), PP. 18-25.
ELEL

MESZJ -58-ERH   MESZAROS, J
ON THE EVE OF A REVOLUTION (HUNGARY).=
JOURNAL OF CENTRAL EUROPEAN AFFAIRS, 18, (APRIL 1958),     58
   PP. 48-67.
ELEL, ELNOEL, ELPRNOR

METRR -52-AHS   METRAUX, R
SOME ASPECTS OF HIERARCHICAL STRUCTURE IN HAITI.=
S TAX (ED), ACCULTURATION IN THE AMERICAS, PROCEEDINGS AND52
   SELECTED PAPERS OF THE 29TH INTERNATIONAL CONGRESS OF
   AMERICANISTS, VOL. 2, CHICAGO, UNIVERSITY OF CHICAGO
   PRESS, 1952, PP. 185-194.
COMEL, ELNOEL

MEYEAG-61-UIS   MEYER, AG
USSR, INCORPORATED (SOVIET UNION).=
SLAVIC REVIEW, 20, (OCTOBER 1961), PP. 369-376.     61
ELEL, ELNOEL

MEYEAG-65-SPS   MEYER, AG
THE SOVIET POLITICAL SYSTEM -- AN INTERPRETATION.=
NEW YORK, RANDOM HOUSE, 1965.     65
COMEL, ELEL, ELNOEL, ELPRNOR

MEYEAG-67-ACP   MEYER, AG
AUTHORITY IN COMMUNIST POLITICAL SYSTEMS (EASTERN EUROPE,
   SOVIET UNION).=
LJ EDINGER (ED), POLITICAL LEADERSHIP IN INDUSTRIALIZED     67
   SOCIETIES, NEW YORK, JOHN WILEY AND SONS, 1967,
   PP. 84-107.
DEFEL, ELEL, ELNOEL

MEYEAJ-58-EED   MEYER, AJ
ENTREPRENEURSHIP AND ECONOMIC DEVELOPMENT IN THE
   MIDDLE EAST.=
THE PUBLIC OPINION QUARTERLY, 22, (FALL 1958),     58
   PP. 391-396.
ELEL, ELNOEL, ELPRNOR

MEYELR-60-DKG   MEYEROWITZ, LR
THE DIVINE KINGSHIP IN GHANA AND ANCIENT EGYPT.=
LONDON, FABER AND FABER, 1960.     60
COMEL

MEYEM -55-PPP   MEYERSON, M      BANFIELD, EC
POLITICS, PLANNING, AND THE PUBLIC INTEREST
   (UNITED STATES).=
GLENCOE, ILLINOIS, FREE PRESS, 1955.     55
DEFEL, ELEL, ELNOEL, ELPRNOR, METEL

MEYEP -57-AOC   MEYER, P
ADMINISTRATIVE ORGANIZATION -- A COMPARATIVE STUDY OF THE
   ORGANIZATION OF PUBLIC ADMINISTRATION (GREAT BRITAIN,
   UNITED STATES).=
LONDON, STEVENS AND SONS, 1957.     57
ELEL

MEYNJ -58-EMS   MEYNAUD, J
THE EXECUTIVE IN THE MODERN STATE (CANADA, FRANCE,
   GREAT BRITAIN, SOVIET UNION, UNITED STATES,
   YUGOSLAVIA).=
INTERNATIONAL SOCIAL SCIENCE BULLETIN, 10, (APRIL-     58
   JUNE 1958), PP. 171-198.
COMEL, ELEL, ELNOEL

MEYNJ -61-IGS   MEYNAUD, J
INTRODUCTION -- GENERAL STUDY OF PARLIAMENTARIANS.=
INTERNATIONAL SOCIAL SCIENCE JOURNAL, 13, (OCTOBER     61
   DECEMBER 1961), PP. 513-543.
DEFEL, METEL

MICACA-52-OLF   MICAUD, CA
ORGANIZATION AND LEADERSHIP OF THE FRENCH
   COMMUNIST PARTY.=
WORLD POLITICS, 4, (APRIL 1952), PP. 318-355.     52
COMEL, ELEL

MICACA-54-FIC   MICAUD, CA
FRENCH INTELLECTUALS AND COMMUNISM.=
SOCIAL RESEARCH, 21, (AUTUMN 1954), PP. 286-296.     54
ELEL, ELPRNOR

MICACA-57-NLF   MICAUD, CA

```
                    THE 'NEW LEFT' IN FRANCE.=
                    WORLD POLITICS, 10, (DECEMBER 1957), PP. 537-559.          57
                    COMEL, DEFEL, ELEL, ELPRNOR
MICACA-63-CFL       MICAUD, CA
                    COMMUNISM AND THE FRENCH LEFT.=
                    NEW YORK, FREDERICK A PRAEGER, 1963.                       63
                    COMEL, ELEL, ELNOEL, ELPRNOR
MICACA-64-TPM       MICAUD, CA          ET AL
                    TUNISIA -- THE POLITICS OF MODERNIZATION.=
                    NEW YORK, FREDERICK A PRAEGER, 1964.                       64
                    DEFEL, COMEL, ELEL, ELNOEL, ELPRNOR
MICHF -63-KSD       MICHAEL, F
                    KHRUSHCHEV'S DISLOYAL OPPOSITION -- STRUCTURAL CHANGE
                       AND POWER STRUGGLE IN THE COMMUNIST BLOC.=
                    ORBIS, 7, (SPRING 1963), PP. 49-76.                        63
                    ELEL
MICHF -67-SPC       MICHAEL, F
                    THE STRUGGLE FOR POWER (CHINA).=
                    PROBLEMS OF COMMUNISM, 16, (MAY-JUNE 1967), PP. 12-21.      67
                    ELEL, ELPRNOR
MICHFH-46-CMT       MICHAEL, FH
                    CHINESE MILITARY TRADITION -- 1 -- 2.=
                    FAR EASTERN SURVEY, 15, (MARCH 13, 1946, MARCH 27, 1946),  46
                       PP. 65-69, PP. 84-87.
                    COMEL, ELPRNOR
MICHR -27-RSC       MICHELS, R
                    SOME REFLECTIONS ON THE SOCIOLOGICAL CHARACTER OF
                       POLITICAL PARTIES.=
                    THE AMERICAN POLITICAL SCIENCE REVIEW, 21, (NOVEMBER       27
                       1927), PP. 753-772.
                    DEFEL, COMEL, ELEL, ELNOEL
MICHR -49-E         MICHELS, R
                    THE ELITE.=
                    A DE-GRAZIA (TRANS), R MICHELS, FIRST LECTURES             49
                       IN POLITICAL SOCIOLOGY, MINNEAPOLIS, UNIVERSITY OF
                       MINNESOTA PRESS, 1949, PP. 63-87.
                    GNELTH, COMEL, ELEL
MICHR -62-PPS       MICHELS, R
                    POLITICAL PARTIES -- A SOCIOLOGICAL STUDY OF THE
                       OLIGARCHICAL TENDENCIES OF MODERN DEMOCRACY (GERMANY).=
                    NEW YORK, THE FREE PRESS, 1962.                            62
                    GNELTH, DEFEL, COMEL, ELEL, ELNOEL, ELPRNOR
MIDDJ -56-RCH       MIDDLETON, J
                    THE ROLE OF THE CHIEFS AND THE HEAD MAN AMONG THE LUGBARA
                       OF THE WEST NILE DISTRICT OF UGANDA.=
                    JOURNAL OF AFRICAN ADMINISTRATION, 8,                      56
                       (JANUARY 1956), PP. 32-38.
                    ELEL, ELNOEL
MIKUMW-64-PSS       MIKULAK, MW
                    PHILOSOPHY AND SCIENCE (SOVIET UNION).=
                    SURVEY--A JOURNAL OF SOVIET AND EAST EUROPEAN STUDIES,     64
                       52, (JULY 1964), PP. 147-156.
                    ELEL, ELPRNOR
MILBJF-58-FSB       MILBURN, JF
                    THE FABIAN SOCIETY AND THE BRITISH LABOUR PARTY.=
                    THE WESTERN POLITICAL QUARTERLY, 11, (JUNE 1958),          58
                       PP. 319-339.
                    ELEL, ELPRNOR
MILBJF-66-TUP       MILBURN, JF
                    TRADE UNIONS IN POLITICS IN AUSTRALIA AND NEW ZEALAND.=
                    THE WESTERN POLITICAL QUARTERLY, 19, (DECEMBER 1966),      66
                       PP. 672-687.
                    ELEL
MILBLW-58-PPA       MILBRATH, LW
                    THE POLITICAL PARTY ACTIVITY OF WASHINGTON
                       LOBBYISTS (UNITED STATES).=
                    THE JOURNAL OF POLITICS, 20, (MAY 1958), PP. 339-352.      58
                    ELEL
MILBLW-60-LCP       MILBRATH, LW
                    LOBBYING AS A COMMUNICATION PROGRESS (UNITED STATES).=
                    THE PUBLIC OPINION QUARTERLY, 24, (SPRING 1960),           60
                       PP. 32-53.
                    COMEL, ELEL, ELPRNOR
MILBLW-63-WLU       MILBRATH, LW
                    THE WASHINGTON LOBBYISTS (UNITED STATES).=
                    CHICAGO, RAND MCNALLY AND COMPANY, 1963.                   63
                    COMEL, ELEL, ELPRNOR
MILLBH-63-PRL       MILLEN, BH
                    THE POLITICAL ROLE OF LABOR IN DEVELOPING COUNTRIES.=
                    WASHINGTON, THE BROOKINGS INSTITUTION, 1963.               63
                    COMEL, ELEL, ELNOEL, ELPRNOR, METEL
MILLCW-48-NMP       MILLS, CW
                    THE NEW MEN OF POWER -- AMERICA'S LABOR LEADERS.=
                    NEW YORK, HARCOURT, BRACE AND COMPANY, 1948.               48
```

```
                    COMEL, ELEL, ELNOEL, ELPRNOR
MILLCW-54-ABE   MILLS, CW
                THE AMERICAN BUSINESS ELITE -- A COLLECTIVE PORTRAIT.=
                JOURNAL OF ECONOMIC HISTORY, 5, (SUPPL), (1954).            54
                COMEL
MILLCW-56-PEU   MILLS, CW
                THE POWER ELITE (UNITED STATES).=
                NEW YORK, OXFORD UNIVERSITY PRESS, 1956.                    56
                GNELTH, DEFEL, COMEL, ELEL, ELNOEL, ELPRNOR
MILLCW-57-PEC   MILLS, CW
                THE POWER ELITE -- COMMENT ON CRITICISM.=
                DISSENT, 4, (WINTER 1957), PP. 22-34.                      57
                GNELTH, DEFEL, METEL
MILLCW-58-CWW   MILLS, CW
                THE CAUSES OF WORLD WAR THREE.=
                NEW YORK, SIMON AND SCHUSTER, 1958.                        58
                GNELTH, ELEL, ELPRNOR
MILLCW-58-SPA   MILLS, CW
                THE STRUCTURE OF POWER IN AMERICAN SOCIETY.=
                THE BRITISH JOURNAL OF SOCIOLOGY, 9, (1958), PP. 29-41.    58
                DEFEL, COMEL
MILLCW-59-PEM   MILLS, CW
                THE POWER ELITE -- MILITARY, ECONOMIC, AND POLITICAL
                    (UNITED STATES).=
                A KORNHAUSER (ED), PROBLEMS OF POWER IN AMERICAN           59
                    DEMOCRACY, DETROIT, WAYNE STATE UNIVERSITY PRESS,
                    1959, PP. 145-183.
                GNELTH, DEFEL, COMEL, ELEL, ELPRNOR
MILLCW-63-PPP   MILLS, CW
                POWER, POLITICS, AND PEOPLE (GERMANY, UNITED STATES).=
                NEW YORK, OXFORD UNIVERSITY PRESS, 1963.                   63
                DEFEL, COMEL, ELEL, ELNOEL, ELPRNOR
MILLDC-57-PIO   MILLER, DC
                THE PREDICTION OF ISSUE OUTCOME IN COMMUNITY
                    DECISION MAKING.=
                PROCEEDINGS OF THE PACIFIC SOCIOLOGICAL SOCIETY,           57
                    RESEARCH STUDIES OF THE STATE COLLEGE OF WASHINGTON,
                    (JUNE 1957), PP. 137-147.
                METEL
MILLDC-58-DMC   MILLER, DC
                DECISION-MAKING CLIQUES IN COMMUNITY POWER STRUCTURES
                    -- A COMPARATIVE STUDY OF AN AMERICAN AND AN ENGLISH
                    CITY.=
                THE AMERICAN JOURNAL OF SOCIOLOGY, 64, (NOVEMBER 1958),    58
                    PP. 299-310.
                DEFEL, ELEL, ELNOEL, METEL
MILLDC-63-TGP   MILLER, DC
                TOWN AND GOWN -- THE POWER STRUCTURE OF A UNIVERSITY TOWN
                    (UNITED STATES).=
                THE AMERICAN JOURNAL OF SOCIOLOGY, 68, (JANUARY 1963),     63
                    PP. 432-443.
                DEFEL, COMEL, ELEL, METEL
MILLJ -65-TSI   MILLER, J
                TOMORROW'S INDUSTRIALISTS (SOVIET UNION).=
                STUDIES ON THE SOVIET UNION, 5, (1965), PP. 23-28.         65
                COMEL
MILLJH-56-RIG   MILLET, JH
                THE ROLE OF AN INTEREST GROUP LEADER IN THE HOUSE
                    OF COMMONS (GREAT BRITAIN).=

                THE WESTERN POLITICAL QUARTERLY, 9, (DECEMBER 1956),       56
                    PP. 915-916.
                ELEL, ELPRNOR
MILLJH-59-NFR   MILLETT, JH
                NOTES ON FUNCTIONAL REPRESENTATION IN THE
                    HOUSE OF COMMONS (GREAT BRITAIN).=
                THE SOUTHWESTERN SOCIAL SCIENCE QUARTERLY, 40,             59
                    (SEPTEMBER 1959), PP. 113-124.
                COMEL, ELEL, ELNOEL
MILLN -65-JLL   MILLER, N
                THE JEWISH LEADERSHIP OF LAKEPORT (UNITED STATES).=
                AW GOULDNER (ED), STUDIES IN LEADERSHIP, NEW YORK,         65
                    RUSSELL AND RUSSELL, 1965, PP. 195-227.
                COMEL, ELEL, ELNOEL, ELPRNOR
MILLW -50-RAB   MILLER, W
                THE RECRUITMENT OF THE AMERICAN BUSINESS ELITE.=
                QUARTERLY JOURNAL OF ECONOMICS, 64, (MAY 1950),            50
                    PP. 242-253.
                ELEL, ELPRNOR
MILLWB-55-TCA   MILLER, WB
                TWO CONCEPTS OF AUTHORITY.=
                AMERICAN ANTHROPOGIST, 57, (APRIL 1955), PP. 271-289.      55
                DEFEL, ELNOEL
MILLWE-63-CIC   MILLER, WE              STOKES, DE
```

                    CONSTITUENCY INFLUENCE IN CONGRESS (UNITED STATES).=
                    THE AMERICAN POLITICAL SCIENCE REVIEW, 57, (MARCH 1963),   63
                       PP. 45-56.
                    ELEL, ELNOEL, ELPRNOR
MILNJ -47-HCC       MILNER, J
                    THE HOUSE OF COMMONS FROM THE CHAIR (GREAT BRITAIN).=
                    PARLIAMENTARY AFFAIRS, 1, (WINTER 1947), PP. 59-66.        47
                    ELEL, ELPRNOR
MILNRS-55-ACE       MILNE, RS
                    THE AMERICAN COUNCIL OF ECONOMIC ADVISERS AND JOINT
                       COMMITTEE ON THE ECONOMIC REPORT.=
                    POLITICAL STUDIES, 3, (1955), PP. 123-142.                 55
                    ELEL
MILNRS-58-BNZ       MILNE, RS
                    BUREAUCRACY IN NEW ZEALAND.=
                    LONDON, OXFORD UNIVERSITY PRESS, 1958.                     58
                    ELEL, ELNOEL
MILNRS-61-COC       MILNE, RS
                    THE CO-ORDINATION AND CONTROL OF GOVERNMENT
                       CORPORATIONS IN THE PHILIPPINES.=
                    PHILIPPINE JOURNAL OF PUBLIC ADMINISTRATION, 5,            61
                       (OCTOBER 1961), PP. 293-320.
                    ELEL
MILNRS-61-RGC       MILNE, RS
                    THE ROLE OF GOVERNMENT CORPORATIONS IN THE PHILIPPINES.=
                    PACIFIC AFFAIRS, 34, (FALL 1961), PP. 257-270.             61
                    ELEL, ELNOEL
MILNRS-62-AET       MILNE, RS
                    ADMINISTRATORS, EXPERTS AND TRAINING IN THE CIVIL
                       SERVICE (UNITED STATES).=
                    PHILIPPINE JOURNAL OF PUBLIC ADMINISTRATION, 6,            62
                       (OCTOBER 1962), PP. 272-278.
                    COMEL, ELEL
MILOC -52-IPS       MILOSZ, C
                    THE INTELLECTUAL IN A PEOPLE'S DEMOCRACY (POLAND).=
                    PROBLEMS OF COMMUNISM, 1, (NUMBER 4, 1952), PP. 1-3.       52
                    ELEL, ELNOEL
MILOC -55-SPG       MILOSZ, C
                    THE SEIZURE OF POWER (GERMANY, POLAND, SOVIET UNION).=
                    NEW YORK, CRITERION BOOKS, 1955.                           55
                    COMEL, ELEL, ELNOEL
MILOC -56-PVD       MILOSZ, C
                    POLAND -- VOICES OF DISILLUSION.=
                    PROBLEMS OF COMMUNISM, 5, (MAY-JUNE 1956), PP. 24-30.      56
                    ELEL, ELPRNOR
MILOC -57-ASP       MILOSZ, C
                    ANTI-SEMITISM IN POLAND.=
                    PROBLEMS OF COMMUNISM, 6, (MAY-JUNE 1957), PP. 35-40.      57
                    ELEL, ELNOEL, ELPRNOR
MINADW-61-IPB       MINAR, DW
                    IDEOLOGY AND POLITICAL BEHAVIOR.=
                    MIDWEST JOURNAL OF POLITICAL SCIENCE, 5, (NOVEMBER 1961), 61
                       PP. 317-331.
                    ELEL, ELPRNOR
MINADW-66-CBC       MINAR, DW
                    THE COMMUNITY BASIS OF CONFLICT IN SCHOOL SYSTEM
                       POLITICS (UNITED STATES).=
                    AMERICAN SOCIOLOGICAL REVIEW, 60, (DECEMBER 1966),         66
                       PP. 822-835.
                    ELEL, ELNOEL, ELPRNOR
MINDM -58-ISI       MINDLIN, M
                    ISRAEL'S INTELLECTUALS.=
                    COMMENTARY, 25, (MARCH 1958), PP. 217-225.                 58
                    COMEL, ELEL, ELNOEL, ELPRNOR
MINYV -60-JCC       MINYAILO, V
                    THE JULY CENTRAL COMMITTEE PLENUM AND BOTTLENECKS IN
                       SOVIET INDUSTRY.=
                    BULLETIN INSTITUTE FOR THE STUDY OF THE USSR, 7,           60
                       (AUGUST 1960), PP. 18-20.
                    ELNOEL, ELPRNOR
MISELV-44-BAG       MISES, LV
                    BUREAUCRACY (AUSTRIA, GREAT BRITAIN, UNITED STATES).=
                    NEW HAVEN, YALE UNIVERSITY PRESS, 1944.                    44
                    ELEL
MISELV-44-OSR       MISES, LV
                    THE OMNIPOTENT STATE -- RISE OF TOTAL STATE AND TOTAL
                       WAR (GERMANY).=
                    NEW HAVEN, YALE UNIVERSITY PRESS, 1944.                    44
                    DEFEL, ELEL, ELNOEL, ELPRNOR
MISRBB-61-IMC       MISRA, BB
                    THE INDIAN MIDDLE CLASS -- THEIR GROWTH IN MODERN
                       TIMES.=
                    LONDON, OXFORD UNIVERSITY PRESS, 1961.                     61
                    COMEL, ELEL, ELNOEL

MITCC -67-RTL    MITCHELL, C
                 THE ROLE OF TECHNOCRATS IN LATIN AMERICAN INTEGRATION.=
                 INTER-AMERICAN ECONOMIC AFFAIRS, 21, (SUMMER 1967),        67
                    PP. 3-29.
                 COMEL, ELEL, ELPRNOR
MITCJC-56-YVS    MITCHELL, JC
                 THE YAO VILLAGE -- A STUDY IN THE SOCIAL STRUCTURE OF A
                    NYASALAND TRIBE.=
                 MANCHESTER, MANCHESTER UNIVERSITY PRESS, 1956.             56
                 ELEL, ELNOEL
MITCWC-58-ORS    MITCHELL, WC
                 OCCUPATIONAL ROLE STRAINS -- THE AMERICAN ELECTIVE
                    PUBLIC OFFICIAL.=
                 ADMINISTRATIVE SCIENCE QUARTERLY, 3, (SEPTEMBER 1958),     58
                    PP. 210-228.
                 COMEL, ELPRNOR
MITCWC-58-PPS    MITCHELL, WC
                 THE POLITICIAN AND THE POLITICAL SCIENTIST.=
                 PROD (THE AMERICAN BEHAVIORAL SCIENTIST), 1,               58
                    (JULY 1958), PP. 30-33.
                 ELEL
MITCWC-59-ASS    MITCHELL, WC
                 THE AMBIVALENT SOCIAL STATUS OF THE AMERICAN POLITICIAN.=
                 THE WESTERN POLITICAL QUARTERLY, 12, (SEPTEMBER 1959),     59
                    PP. 683-698.
                 COMEL
MITCWC-59-RTL    MITCHELL, WC
                 REDUCTION OF TENSIONS IN LEGISLATURES (UNITED STATES).=
                 PROD (THE AMERICAN BEHAVIORAL SCIENTIST), 2,               59
                    (JANUARY 1959), PP. 3-6.
                 ELEL, ELPRNOR
MITCWC-62-APS    MITCHELL, WC
                 THE AMERICAN POLITY -- A SOCIAL AND CULTURAL
                    INTERPRETATION.=
                 NEW YORK, THE FREE PRESS, 1962.                            62
                 DEFEL, ELEL, ELNOEL
MITSA -67-CPP    MITSCHERLICH, A
                 CHANGING PATTERNS OF POLITICAL AUTHORITY -- A PSYCHIATRIC
                    INTERPRETATION.=
                 LJ EDINGER (ED), POLITICAL LEADERSHIP IN INDUSTRIALIZED    67
                    SOCIETIES, NEW YORK, JOHN WILEY AND SONS, 1967,
                    PP. 26-58.
                 DEFEL, COMEL, ELEL, ELNOEL, ELPRNOR
MONATP-56-CAN    MONAHAN, TP        MONAHAN, EH
                 SOME CHARACTERISTICS OF AMERICAN NEGRO LEADERS.=
                 AMERICAN SOCIOLOGICAL REVIEW, 21, (OCTOBER 1956),          56
                    PP. 588-596.
                 COMEL
MONSRJ-65-MPP    MONSEN-JR, RJ        CANNON, MW
                 THE MAKERS OF PUBLIC POLICY -- AMERICAN POWER GROUPS AND
                    THEIR IDEOLOGIES.=
                 NEW YORK, MCGRAW-HILL, 1965.                               65
                 ELEL, ELPRNOR
MONTGB-51-ACS    MONTAGUE-JR, GB
                 SOME ASPECTS OF CLASS, STATUS AND POWER RELATIONS
                    IN ENGLAND.=
                 SOCIAL FORCES, 30, (DECEMBER 1951), PP. 134-140.           51
                 COMEL, ELEL, ELNOEL
MONTJD-59-CVA    MONTGOMERY, JD (ED)
                 CASES IN VIETNAMESE ADMINISTRATION.=
                 SAIGON, MICHIGAN STATE UNIVERSITY, VIETNAM ADVISORY        59
                    GROUP, 1959.
                 ELEL
MOODGC-57-MSP    MOODIE, GC
                 THE MONARCH AND THE SELECTION OF A PRIME MINISTER -- A
                    RE-EXAMINATION OF THE CRISIS OF 1931 (GREAT BRITAIN).=
                 POLITICAL STUDIES, 5, (1957), PP. 1-20.                    57
                 ELEL
MOORB -50-SPD    MOORE-JR, B
                 SOVIET POLITICS -- THE DILEMMA OF POWER.=
                 CAMBRIDGE, HARVARD UNIVERSITY PRESS, 1950.                 50
                 ELEL, ELNOEL, ELPRNOR
MOORB -54-TPU    MOORE-JR, B
                 TERROR AND PROGRESS, USSR -- SOME SOURCES OF CHANGE AND
                    STABILITY IN THE SOVIET DICTATORSHIP.=
                 CAMBRIDGE, HARVARD UNIVERSITY PRESS, 1954.                 54
                 ELEL, ELNOEL, ELPRNOR
MOORB -55-STC    MOORE-JR, B
                 SOCIOLOGICAL THEORY AND CONTEMPORARY POLITICS.=
                 THE AMERICAN JOURNAL OF SOCIOLOGY, 61, (SEPTEMBER 1955),   55
                    PP. 107-115.
                 METEL
MOORB -58-PPS    MOORE-JR, B
                 POLITICAL POWER AND SOCIAL THEORY.=

```
                    LONDON, OXFORD UNIVERSITY PRESS, 1958.                    58
                    DEFEL
MOORB -66-SOD       MOORE-JR, B
                    SOCIAL ORIGINS OF DICTATORSHIP AND DEMOCRACY -- LORD AND
                        PEASANT IN THE MAKING OF THE MODERN WORLD (FRANCE,
                        GREAT BRITAIN, UNITED STATES, CHINA, JAPAN, INDIA,
                        GERMANY).=
                    BOSTON, BEACON PRESS, 1966.                               66
                    DEFEL, ELEL, ELNOEL
MOORCH-62-NDP       MOORE, CH
                    THE NEO-DESTOUR PARTY OF TUNISIA -- A STRUCTURE
                        FOR DEMOCRACY.=
                    WORLD POLITICS, 14, (APRIL 1962), PP. 461-482.            62
                    ELEL, ELNOEL
MOORCH-65-OPM       MOORE, CH
                    ONE PARTYISM IN MAURITANIA.=
                    THE JOURNAL OF MODERN AFRICAN STUDIES, 3, (OCTOBER 1965), 65
                        PP. 409-420.
                    ELEL, ELNOEL
MOORCH-65-TSI       MOORE, CH
                    TUNISIA SINCE INDEPENDENCE -- THE DYNAMICS OF ONE - PARTY
                        GOVERNMENT.=
                    BERKELEY, UNIVERSITY OF CALIFORNIA, 1965.                 65
                    COMEL, ELEL, ELNOEL, ELPRNOR
MOORJW-58-RSE       MOORE, JW          MOORE, BM
                    THE ROLE OF THE SCIENTIFIC ELITE IN THE DECISION
                        TO USE THE ATOMIC BOMB (UNITED STATES).=
                    SOCIAL PROBLEMS, 6, (SUMMER 1958), PP. 78-85.             58
                    COMEL, ELEL, ELNOEL
MOORSF-58-PPI       MOORE, SF
                    POWER AND PROPERTY IN INCA PERU.=
                    NEW YORK, COLUMBIA UNIVERSITY PRESS, 1958.                58
                    COMEL, ELEL, ELPRNOR
MOOSM -51-PLR       MOOS, M            KOSLIN, B
                    POLITICAL LEADERSHIP RE-EXAMINED -- AN EXPERIMENTAL
                        APPROACH (UNITED STATES).=
                    THE PUBLIC OPINION QUARTERLY, 15, (FALL 1951),            51
                        PP. 563-574.
                    DEFEL, METEL
MORAJF-59-ICS       MORA, JF
                    THE INTELLECTUAL IN CONTEMPORARY SOCIETY.=
                    ETHICS, 69, (JANUARY 1959), PP. 94-101.                   59
                    DEFEL
MORGGG-62-SAL       MORGAN, GG
                    SOVIET ADMINISTRATIVE LEGALITY -- THE ROLE OF THE
                        ATTORNEY GENERAL'S OFFICE.=
                    STANFORD, STANFORD UNIVERSITY PRESS, 1962.                62
                    ELEL
MORGRS-64-PPF       MORGENTHAU, RS
                    POLITICAL PARTIES IN FRENCH-SPEAKING WEST AFRICA.=
                    OXFORD, CLARENDON PRESS, 1964.                            64
                    COMEL, ELEL, ELNOEL, ELPRNOR
MORRI -63-MFJ       MORRIS, I (ED).
                    MILITARISM, FASCISM, JAPANISM.=
                    BOSTON, HEATH, 1963.                                      63
                    COMEL, ELEL, ELNOEL, ELPRNOR
MORRII-60-NRW       MORRIS, II
                    NATIONALISM AND RIGHT WING IN JAPAN -- A STUDY OF
                        POST-WAR TRENDS.=
                    NEW YORK, OXFORD UNIVERSITY PRESS, 1960.                  60
                    COMEL, ELEL, ELNOEL, ELPRNOR
MORRRT-50-PLI       MORRIS, RT         SEEMAN, M
                    THE PROBLEM OF LEADERSHIP -- AN INTERDISCIPLINARY
                        APPROACH.=
                    THE AMERICAN JOURNAL OF SOCIOLOGY, 56, (SEPTEMBER 1950),  50
                        PP. 149-155.
                    METEL
MORRWH-57-PI        MORRIS-JONES, WH
                    PARLIAMENT IN INDIA.=
                    LONDON, LONGMANS, GREEN AND COMPANY, LTD, 1957.           57
                    COMEL, ELEL, ELNOEL, ELPRNOR
MORRWH-59-RPD       MORRIS-JONES, WH
                    RECENT POLITICAL DEVELOPMENT IN INDIA -- 2.=
                    PARLIAMENTARY AFFAIRS, 12, (WINTER 1958-1959), PP.        59
                        71-82.
                    ELEL, ELNOEL, ELPRNOR
MORRWH-64-GPI       MORRIS-JONES, WH
                    THE GOVERNMENT AND POLITICS OF INDIA.=
                    LONDON, HUTCHISON UNIVERSITY LIBRARY, 1964.               64
                    ELEL, ELPRNOR
MORRWH-66-DDT       MORRIS-JONES, WH
                    DOMINANCE AND DISSENT -- THEIR INTER-RELATIONS IN THE
                        INDIAN PARTY SYSTEM.=
                    GOVERNMENT AND OPPOSITION, 1, (AUGUST 1966), PP. 451-466. 66
```

```
                    ELEL, ELNOEL, ELPRNOR
     MORSF -57-ASF  MORSTEIN-MARX, F
                    THE ADMINISTRATIVE STATE (FRANCE, GREAT BRITAIN,
                       SWITZERLAND, UNITED STATES).=
                    CHICAGO, THE UNIVERSITY OF CHICAGO PRESS, 1957.            57
                    ELEL, ELNOEL
     MORSF -63-HCS  MORSTEIN-MARX, F
                    THE HIGHER CIVIL SERVICE AS AN ACTION GROUP
                       IN WESTERN POLITICAL DEVELOPMENT.=
                    J LAPALOMBARA (ED), BUREAUCRACY AND POLITICAL DEVELOPMENT,63
                       PRINCETON, NEW JERSEY, PRINCETON UNIVERSITY PRESS, 1963.
                       PP. 62-95.
                    ELEL, ELNOEL, ELPRNOR
     MORTL -57-DUA  MORTON, L
                    THE DECISION TO USE THE ATOMIC BOMB (UNITED STATES).=
                    FOREIGN AFFAIRS, 35, (JANUARY 1957), PP. 334-353.          57
                    ELEL
     MOSCG -39-RC   MOSCA, G
                    THE RULING CLASS.=
                    A.LIVINGSTON (ED), NEW YORK, MCGRAW-HILL BOOK CO., INC.,    39
                       1939.
                    GNELTH, DEFEL, COMEL, ELEL, ELNOEL, ELPRNOR, METEL
     MOSKCC-65-MCS  MOSKOS-JR, CC
                    FROM MONARCHY TO COMMUNISM -- THE SOCIAL TRANSFORMATION
                       OF THE ALBANIAN ELITE.=
                    HR BARRINGER ET AL EDS, SOCIAL CHANGE IN DEVELOPING AREAS,65
                       CAMBRIDGE, SCHENKMAN PUBLISHING CO., 1965,
                       PP. 205-221.
                    COMEL
     MOSSJ -61-RPI  MOSSMAN, J
                    REBELS IN PARADISE -- INDONESIA'S CIVIL WAR.=
                    LONDON, JONATHAN CAPE, 1961.                               61
                    ELEL, ELPRNOR
     MP    -52-SPS  MP
                    THE SATELLITE POLICE SYSTEM (EASTERN EUROPE).=
                    THE WORLD TODAY, 8, (1952), PP. 504-512.                   52
                    COMEL, ELEL, ELNOEL
     MU-F  -62-WHF  MU-FU-SHENG
                    THE WILTING OF THE HUNDRED FLOWERS -- THE CHINESE
                       INTELLIGENTSIA UNDER MAO.=
                    NEW YORK, FREDERICK A PRAEGER, 1962.                       62
                    ELEL, ELPRNOR
     MUELA -57-HRP  MUELLER-DEHAM, A
                    HUMAN RELATIONS AND POWER.=
                    NEW YORK, PHILOSOPHICAL LIBRARY, 1957.                     57
                    DEFEL, ELEL, ELNOEL
     MUELG -65-HCN  MUELLER, G          SINGER, H
                    HUNGARY -- CAN THE NEW COURSE SURVIVE.=
                    PROBLEMS OF COMMUNISM, 14, (JANUARY-FEBRUARY 1965),        65
                       PP. 32-38.
                    ELEL
     MUHLN -57-NAN  MUHLEN, N
                    THE NEW ARMY OF A NEW GERMANY.=
                    ORBIS, 1, (FALL 1957), PP. 278-290.                        57
                    ELEL, ELNOEL
     MULDM -66-IPP  MULDER, M           ET AL
                    ILLEGITIMACY OF POWER AND POSITIVENESS OF ATTITUDE
                       TOWARDS THE POWER PERSON (UNITED STATES).=
                    HUMAN RELATIONS, 19, (JANUARY-MARCH 1966) PP. 21-38.       66
                    ELEL, ELNOEL, ELPRNOR
     MUNELW-47-JPA  MUNEY, LW
                    THE JUNKERS AND THE PRUSSIAN ADMINISTRATION, 1918-1939
                    THE REVIEW OF POLITICS, 9, (OCTOBER 1947), PP. 485-501.    47
                    ELEL
     MURPWF-61-CJP  MURPHY, WF          PRITCHETT, CH
                    COURTS, JUDGES AND POLITICS (UNITED STATES).=
                    NEW YORK, RANDOM HOUSE, 1961.                              61
                    ELEL, ELPRNOR
     MURPWF-62-CCC  MURPHY, WF
                    CONGRESS AND THE COURT -- A CASE STUDY IN THE
                       AMERICAN POLITICAL PROCESS.=
                    CHICAGO, UNIVERSITY OF CHICAGO PRESS, 1962.                62
                    ELEL, ELNOEL
     MURPWF-62-CJT  MURPHY, WF
                    CHIEF JUSTICE TAFT AND THE LOWER COURT BUREAUCRACY
                       -- A STUDY IN JUDICIAL ADMINISTRATION.=
                    THE JOURNAL OF POLITICS, 24, (AUGUST 1962), PP. 453-476.   62
                    ELEL, ELPRNOR
     MURPWF-64-EJS  MURPHY, WF
                    ELEMENTS OF JUDICIAL STRATEGY (UNITED STATES).=
                    CHICAGO, UNIVERSITY OF CHICAGO PRESS, 1964.                64
                    ELEL, ELPRNOR
     MURRE -60-HEC  MURRAY, E
                    HIGHER EDUCATION IN COMMUNIST HUNGARY -- 1948-1956.=
```

THE AMERICAN SLAVIC AND EAST EUROPEAN REVIEW, 19,
   (OCTOBER 1960), PP. 395-413.                                60
COMEL, ELNOEL, ELPRNOR
MUS,P  -49-RVV  MUS, P
THE ROLE OF THE VILLAGE IN VIETNAMESE POLITICS.=
PACIFIC AFFAIRS, 22, (SEPTEMBER 1949), PP. 265-272.
COMEL, ELNOEL                                                 49
MUSGF -61-EGB  MUSGROVE, F
THE EDUCATIONAL AND GEOGRAPHICAL BACKGROUND OF
   SOME LOCAL LEADERS (GREAT BRITAIN).=
THE BRITISH JOURNAL OF SOCIOLOGY, 12, (1961),
   PP. 363-374.                                               61
DEFEL, COMEL, ELEL, ELNOEL
MYRDG -44-ADN  MYRDAL, G
AN AMERICAN DILEMMA -- THE NEGRO PROBLEM
   AND MODERN DEMOCRACY.=
2 VOLUMES, NEW YORK, HARPER AND SONS, 1944.                   44
DEFEL, ELNOWL, ELPRNOR
MYSBJH-57-IE   MYSBERGH, JH
THE INDONESIAN ELITE.=
FAR EASTERN SURVEY, 26, (MARCH 1957), PP. 38-42.              57
ELPRNOR
MZ     -50-IRR  MZ
INDIA -- RECONCILIATION OF THE RIGHT.=
THE WORLD TODAY, 6, (1950), PP. 340-347.                      50
ELEL, ELPRNOR
NADESF-56-CSE  NADEL, SF
THE CONCEPT OF SOCIAL ELITE.=
INTERNATIONAL SOCIAL SCIENCE BULLETIN, 8, (FALL 1956),        56
   PP. 413-424.
GNELTH, DEFEL, METEL
NADESF-57-TSS  NADEL, SF
THE THEORY OF SOCIAL STRUCTURE.=
GLENCOE, THE FREE PRESS, 1957.                                57
GNELTH, ELEL, METEL
NAGESS-61-PPA  NAGEL, SS
POLITICAL PARTY AFFILIATION AND JUDGE'S DECISIONS
   (UNITED STATES).=
THE AMERICAN POLITICAL SCIENCE REVIEW, 55, (DECEMBER          61
   1961), PP. 843-850.
COMEL, ELPRNOR
NAGESS-62-EAJ  NAGEL, SS
ETHNIC AFFILIATIONS AND JUDICIAL PROPENSITIES
   (UNITED STATES).=
THE JOURNAL OF POLITICS, 24, (FEBRUARY 1962),
   PP. 92-110.                                                62
COMEL, ELPRNOR
NAGESS-62-TRB  NAGEL, SS
TESTING RELATIONS BETWEEN JURIDICAL CHARACTERISTICS AND
   JUDICIAL DECISION MAKING (UNITED STATES).=
THE WESTERN POLITICAL QUARTERLY, 15, (SEPTEMBER 1962),        62
   PP. 425-437.
METEL
NAIRK -61-BDH  NAIR, K
BLOSSOMS IN THE DUST -- THE HUMAN FACTOR IN INDIAN
   DEVELOPMENT.=
NEW YORK, FREDERICK A PRAEGER, 1961.                          61
COMEL, ELEL, ELNOEL, ELPRNOR
NAMAS -50-LC   NAMASIVAYAM, S
THE LEGISLATURES OF CEYLON, 1928-1948.=
LONDON, FABER AND FABER, 1950.                                50
COMEL, ELEL
NAMAS -53-ACP  NAMASIVAYAM, S
ASPECTS OF CEYLONESE PARLIAMENTARY GOVERNMENT.=
PACIFIC AFFAIRS, 26, (1953), PP. 76-83.                       53
ELEL, ELPRNOR
NASHGD-60-BPE  NASH, GD
BUREAUCRACY AND PROGRESSIVISM -- THE EXPERIENCE OF
   CALIFORNIA, 1899-1933 (UNITED STATES).=
THE WESTERN POLITICAL QUARTERLY, 13, (SEPTEMBER 1960),        60
   PP. 678-691.
ELEL, ELPRNOR
NAYABR-66-MPP  NAYAR, BR
MINORITY POLITICS IN PUNJAB (INDIA).=
PRINCETON, PRINCETON UNIVERSITY PRESS, 1966.                  66
ELEL, ELNOEL, ELPRNOR
NAYARR-64-TMT  NAYACAKADOU, RR
TRADITIONAL AND MODERN TYPES OF LEADERSHIP AND ECONOMIC
   DEVELOPMENT AMONG THE FIJIANS.=
INTERNATIONAL SOCIAL SCIENCE JOURNAL, 16, (1964),             64
   PP. 261-272.
COMEL, ELEL, ELNOEL
NEEDM -62-DCB  NEEDLER, M
ON THE DANGERS OF COPYING FROM THE BRITISH.=

                        POLITICAL SCIENCE QUARTERLY, 77, (SEPTEMBER 1962),        62
                           PP. 379-396.
                        ELEL, ELNOEL
NEEDM -62-PLA    NEEDLER, M
                        PUTTING LATIN AMERICAN POLITICS IN PERSPECTIVE.=
                        INTER-AMERICAN ECONOMIC AFFAIRS, 16, (AUTUMN 1962),        62
                           PP. 41-50.
                        COMEL, ELEL, ELNOEL
NEEDMC-61-PDM    NEEDLER, MC
                        THE POLITICAL DEVELOPMENT OF MEXICO.=
                        THE AMERICAN POLITICAL SCIENCE REVIEW, 55, (JUNE 1961),    61
                           PP. 308-312.
                        ELEL, ELNOEL, ELPRNOR
NEEDMC-64-PSL    NEEDLER, MC (ED)
                        POLITICAL SYSTEMS OF LATIN AMERICA.=
                        PRINCETON, NEW JERSEY, D VAN NOSTRAND, 1964.               64
                        COMEL, ELEL, ELNOEL
NEEDMC-66-PDM    NEEDLER, MC
                        POLITICAL DEVELOPMENT AND MILITARY INTERVENTION IN
                           LATIN AMERICA.=
                        THE AMERICAN POLITICAL SCIENCE REVIEW, 60, (SEPTEMBER      66
                           1966), PP. 616-626.
                        ELEL, ELPRNOR
NELSCA-63-DRP    NELSON, CA
                        DEVELOPING RESPONSIBLE PUBLIC LEADERS.=
                        DOBBS FERRY, NEW YORK, OCEANA PUBLICATIONS, 1963.          63
                        METEL
NEMEPF-45-RGL    NEMENYI, PF
                        THE RECORD OF THE GERMAN LEFT.=
                        CURRENT HISTORY, N.S. 9, (NOVEMBER 1945), PP. 439-446.     45
                        COMEL, ELPRNOR
NEMZL -50-KSP    NEMZER, L
                        THE KREMLIN'S PROFESSIONAL STAFF -- THE 'APPARATUS' OF THE
                           CENTRAL COMMITTEE, COMMUNIST PARTY OF THE
                           SOVIET UNION.=
                        THE AMERICAN POLITICAL SCIENCE REVIEW, 44, (MARCH 1950),   50
                           PP. 64-85.
                        COMEL, ELEL, ELNOEL
NETTJP-65-COE    NETTL, JP
                        CONSENSUS OR ELITE DOMINATION -- THE CASE OF BUSINESS.=
                        POLITICAL STUDIES, 13, (FEBRUARY 1965), PP. 22-44.         65
                        COMEL, ELEL, ELNOEL, ELPRNOR




NEUMFL-48-MGR    NEUMANN, FL
                        MILITARY GOVERNMENT AND THE REVIVAL OF DEMOCRACY
                           IN GERMANY.=
                        COLUMBIA JOURNAL OF INTERNATIONAL AFFAIRS, 2,              48
                           (WINTER 1948), PP. 3-20.
                        ELEL, ELNOEL
NEUMFL-57-DAS    NEUMANN, FL
                        THE DEMOCRATIC AND THE AUTHORITARIAN STATE -- ESSAYS IN
                           POLITICAL AND LEGAL THEORY.=
                        GLENCOE, ILLINOIS, FREE PRESS, 1957.                       57
                        DEFEL, ELEL, ELNOEL
NEUMS -56-MPP    NEUMANN, S (ED)
                        MODERN POLITICAL PARTIES (WESTERN EUROPE, JAPAN)
                           SOVIET UNION, UNITED STATES, EASTERN EUROPE).=
                        CHICAGO, UNIVERSITY OF CHICAGO, 1956.                      56
                        COMEL, ELEL, ELNOEL, ELPRNOR
NEUMS -65-PRT    NEUMANN, S
                        PERMANENT REVOLUTION -- TOTALITARIANISM IN THE AGE OF
                           WORLD AT WAR (GERMANY).=
                        2ND ED., NEW YORK, FREDERICK A PRAEGER, 1965               65
                        DEFEL, COMEL, ELEL, ELNOEL, ELPRNOR
NEURK -59-FWG    NEUREITHER, K
                        FEDERALISM -- WEST GERMAN BUREAUCRACY.=
                        POLITICAL STUDIES, 7, (OCTOBER 1959), PP. 233-245.         59
                        ELEL, ELNOEL, ELPRNOR
NEURK -59-PBW    NEUREITHER, K
                        POLITICS AND BUREAUCRACY IN THE WEST GERMAN BUNDESRAT.=
                        THE AMERICAN POLITICAL SCIENCE REVIEW, 53, (SEPTEMBER      59
                           1959), PP. 713-731.
                        ELEL, ELPRNOR
NEUSRE-54-PLG    NEUSTADT, RE
                        PRESIDENCY AND LEGISLATION -- THE GROWTH OF CENTRAL
                           CLEARANCE (UNITED STATES).=
                        THE AMERICAN POLITICAL SCIENCE REVIEW, 48,                 54
                           (SEPTEMBER 1954), PP. 641-671.
                        ELEL
NEUSRE-60-PPP    NEUSTADT, RE
                        PRESIDENTIAL POWER -- THE POLITICS OF LEADERSHIP

(UNITED STATES).=
NEW YORK, JOHN WILEY AND SONS, 1960.                          60
ELEL, ELNOEL, ELPRNOR
NEUSRE-63-ASP  NEUSTADT, RE
APPROACHES TO STAFFING THE PRESIDENCY -- NOTES ON FDR
AND JFK (UNITED STATES).=
THE AMERICAN POLITICAL SCIENCE REVIEW, 57, (DECEMBER         63
1963, PP. 855-862.
ELEL
NEUSRE-65-PBU  NEUSTADT, RE
POLITICIANS AND BUREAUCRATS (UNITED STATES).=
DB TRUMAN (ED), THE CONGRESS AND AMERICA'S FUTURE,           65
ENGLEWOOD CLIFFS, NEW JERSEY, PRENTICE HALL, 1965,
PP. 102-120.
ELEL, ELNOEL
NEUWM -59-OCC  NEUWILD, M
THE ORIGIN OF THE COMMUNIST CONTROL COMMISSION
(SOVIET UNION).=
THE AMERICAN SLAVIC AND EAST EUROPEAN REVIEW, 18,           59
(OCTOBER 1959), PP. 315-333.
COMEL, ELEL, ELNOEL
NEWCM -55-BBE  NEWCOMER, M
THE BIG BUSINESS EXECUTIVE (UNITED STATES).=
NEW YORK, COLUMBIA UNIVERSITY PRESS, 1955.                  55
COMEL, ELPRNOR
NEWMFC-57-RMP  NEWMAN, FC
REFLECTIONS ON MONEY AND PARTY POLITICS IN BRITAIN.=
PARLIAMENTARY AFFAIRS, 10, (SUMMER 1957), PP. 308-332.      57
ELEL, ELPRNOR
NEWMKJ-59-NMM  NEWMAN, KJ
THE NEW MONARCHIES OF THE MIDDLE EAST.=
JOURNAL OF INTERNATIONAL AFFAIRS, 13, (SPRING 1959),        59
PP. 157-168.
ELEL, ELPRNOR
NEWMKJ-59-PSP  NEWMAN, KJ
PAKISTAN'S PREVENTIVE AUTOCRACY AND ITS CAUSES.=
PACIFIC AFFAIRS, 32, (MARCH 1959), PP. 18-33.               59
ELEL, ELNOEL, ELPRNOR
NEWMKJ-60-DPG  NEWMAN, KJ
THE DYARCHIC PATTERN OF GOVERNMENT AND PAKISTAN'S
PROBLEMS.=
POLITICAL SCIENCE QUARTERLY, 75, (MARCH 1960), PP. 94-108.60
ELEL, ELPRNOR
NEWTJA-63-ETS  NEWTH, JA
THE ESTABLISHMENT OF TAJISKAN (SOVIET UNION).=
SOVIET STUDIES, 15, (JULY 1963), PP. 72-81.                 63
COMEL
NEWTJA-66-CPU  NEWTH, JA
THE COMMUNIST PARTY OF UZBEKISTAN, 1959 -- A BRIEF
STATISTICAL NOTE (SOVIET UNION).=
SOVIET STUDIES, 17, (APRIL 1966), PP. 484-489.              66
COMEL
NGCOSB-56-AES  NGCOBO, SB
AFRICAN ELITE IN SOUTH AFRICA.=
INTERNATIONAL SOCIAL SCIENCE BULLETIN, 8, (1956),           56
PP. 431-440.
COMEL
NICHAG-54-IPU  NICHOLAS, AG
INTELLECTUALS AND POLITICS IN USA (UNITED STATES).=
OCCIDENTE (TORINO), (JANUARY-FEBRUARY 1954). (NO PAGES)     54
COMEL, ELPRNOR
NICHHG-51-FPP  NICHOLAS, HG
THE FORMULATION OF PARTY POLICY (GREAT BRITAIN).=
PARLIAMENTARY AFFAIRS, 5, (WINTER 1951), PP. 142-453.       51
ELEL, ELPRNOR
NICHRW-63-VFP  NICHOLAS, RW
VILLAGE FACTIONS AND POLITICAL PARTIES IN RURAL WEST
BENGAL (INDIA).=
JOURNAL OF COMMONWEALTH POLITICAL STUDIES, 2, (1963),       63
PP. 17-32.
COMEL, ELEL, ELNOEL
NICOB -65-PSE  NICOLAEVSKY, B
POWER AND THE SOVIET ELITE -- THE LETTER OF AN OLD
BOLSHEVIKI AND OTHER ESSAYS.=
NEW YORK, FREDERICK A PRAEGER, 1965.                        65
ELEL, ELPRNOR
NICOD -63-PNU  NICOL, D
POLITICS, NATIONALISM AND UNIVERSITIES IN AFRICA.=
AFRICA AFFAIRS, 62, (JANUARY 1963), PP. 20-28.              63
COMEL, ELEL, ELPRNOR
NIEBHL-62-EAC  NIEBERG, HL
THE EISENHOWER AEC AND CONGRESS (UNITED STATES).=
MIDWEST JOURNAL OF POLITICAL SCIENCE, 6, (MAY 1962),        62
PP. 115-148.

```
                        COMEL, ELEL, ELPRNOR
NISBRA-59-DFS   NISBET, RA
                THE DECLINE AND FALL OF SOCIAL CLASS.=
                PACIFIC SOCIOLOGICAL REVIEW, 2, (SPRING 1959), PP. 11-17. 59
                GNELTH
NISBRA-65-LSC   NISBET, RA
                LEADERSHIP AND SOCIAL CRISIS.=
                AW GOULDNER (ED), STUDIES IN LEADERSHIP, NEW YORK       65
                    RUSSELL AND RUSSELL, 1965, PP. 702-720.
                GNELTH
NISBRA-65-WII   NISBET, RA
                WHAT IS AN INTELLECTUAL.=
                COMMENTARY, 40, (DEBEMBER 1965), PP. 93-104.           65
                DEFEL, ELPRNOR
NM     -57-SPE  NM
                SOME STUDENT PROBLEMS IN EAST GERMAN UNIVERSITIES.=
                THE WORLD TODAY, 13, (NOVEMBER 1957), PP. 481-489.      57
                COMEL, ELPRNOR
NORMEH-46-JSE   NORMAN, EH
                JAPAN'S EMERGENCE AS A MODERN STATE.=
                NEW YORK, INSTITUTE OF PACIFIC RELATIONS, 1946.         46
                ELEL, ELNOEL, ELPRNOR
NORTFS-60-BFP   NORTHEDGE, FS
                BRITISH FOREIGN POLICY AND THE PARTY SYSTEM.=
                THE AMERICAN POLITICAL SCIENCE REVIEW, 54, (SEPTEMBER   60
                    1960), PP. 635-646.
                ELEL, ELNOEL
NORTRC-51-CCE   NORTH, RC
                THE CHINESE COMMUNIST ELITE.=
                THE ANNALS OF THE AMERICAN ACADEMY OF POLITICAL AND     51
                    SOCIAL SCIENCE, 277, (SEPTEMBER 1951), PP. 67-75.
                COMEL
NORTRC-51-NND   NORTH, RC
                THE NEP AND THE NEW DEMOCRACY (CHINA, USSR).=
                PACIFIC AFFAIRS, 24, (MARCH 1951), PP. 52-60.           51
                ELEL, ELNOEL
NORTRC-52-KCC   NORTH, RC
                KUOMINGTANG AND CHINESE COMMUNIST ELITES.=
                STANFORD, STANFORD UNIVERSITY PRESS, 1952.              52
                COMEL, ELEL, ELPRNOR
NORTRC-53-MCC   NORTH, RC
                MOSCOW AND CHINESE COMMUNISTS.=
                STANFORD, STANFORD UNIVERSITY PRESS, 1953.              53
                COMEL, ELEL, ELNOEL
NORTRC-59-ICM   NORTH, RC
                THE INDIAN COUNCIL OF MINISTERS.=
                RL PARK AND I TINKER (EDS), LEADERSHIP AND POLITICAL    59
                    INSTITUTIONS IN INDIA, PRINCETON, NEW JERSEY,
                    PRINCETON UNIVERSITY PRESS, 1959, PP. 103-114.
                COMEL, ELEL
NOVEA -57-SIR   NOVE, A
                THE SOVIET INDUSTRIAL REORGANIZATION.=
                PROBLEMS OF COMMUNISM, 6, (NOVEMBER-DECEMBER 1957),     57
                    PP. 19-25.
                ELNOEL
NOWAS -60-EAW   NOWAK, S
                EGALITARIAN ATTITUDES OF WARSAW STUDENTS (POLAND).=
                AMERICAN SOCIOLOGICAL REVIEW, 25,                       60
                    (APRIL 1960), PP. 219-231.
                COMEL, ELPRNOR
NUQUJE-47-CTR   NUQUIST, JE
                CONTEMPORARY TRENDS IN RURAL LEADERSHIP (UNITED STATES).=
                RURAL SOCIOLOGY, 12, (SEPTEMBER 1947), PP. 273-284.     47
                COMEL, ELNOEL
NYOMJ -67-CFN   NYOMARKAY, J
                CHARISMA AND FACTIONALISM IN THE NAZI PARTY (GERMANY.=
                MINNEAPOLIS, UNIVERSITY OF MINNESOTA PRESS, 1967.       67
                DEFEL, ELEL, ELNOEL, ELPRNOR
NYQUTE-65-SPE   NYQUIST, TE
                THE SUDAN -- PRELUDE TO ELECTIONS.=
                THE MIDDLE EAST JOURNAL, 19, (SUMMER 1965), PP. 263-272. 65
                COMEL, ELEL, ELNOEL
ODUMOI-63-NCH   ODUMOSU, OI
                THE NIGERIAN CONSTITUTION -- HISTORY AND DEVELOPMENT.=
                LONDON, SWEET AND MAXWELL, 1963.                        63
                COMEL, ELEL, ELNOEL
OKSEM -67-CFR   OKSENBERG, M
                CHINA -- FORCING THE REVOLUTION TO A NEW STAGE.=
                ASIAN SURVEY, 7, (JANUARY 1967), PP. 1-15.              67
                ELEL, ELNOEL, ELPRNOR
OLGIC -63-SSP   OLGIN, C
                A SURVEY OF SOVIET PHILOSOPHY IN 1962.=
                STUDIES ON THE SOVIET UNION, 3, (1963), PP. 124-136.    63
                ELPRNOR
```

```
OLGIL  -67-NPI   OLGIN, L
                 A NEW PROGRAM OF IDEOLOGICAL INSTRUCTION FOR THE
                   ELITE (SOVIET UNION).=
                 BULLETIN INSTITUTE FOR THE STUDY OF THE USSR, 14,      67
                   (APRIL 1967), PP. 3-18.
                 ELEL, ELPRNOR
OLIEK  -48-TBI   OLIENG, K
                 TERENA (BRAZILIAN INDIANS) SOCIAL ORGANIZATIONS AND LAW.=
                 AMERICAN ANTHROPOLOGIST, 50, (APRIL-JUNE 1948),         48
                   PP. 283-291.
                 COMEL, ELEL, ELNOEL
OLIVDL-58-SIS    OLIVER, DL
                 A SOLOMON ISLAND SOCIETY -- KINSHIP AND LEADERSHIP
                   AMONG THE SIVAI OF BOUGAINVILLE.=
                 CAMBRIDGE, HARVARD UNIVERSITY PRESS, 1958.             58
                 COMEL, ELEL, ELNOEL
OLMSDW-54-OLS    OLMSTED, DW
                 ORGANIZATIONAL LEADERSHIP AND SOCIAL STRUCTURE IN A
                   SMALL CITY (UNITED STATES).=
                 AMERICAN SOCIOLOGICAL REVIEW, 19, (JUNE 1954),         54
                   PP. 273-281.
                 COMEL, ELEL, ELNOEL, METEL
OLSEM  -65-LCA   OLSEN, M
                 THE LOGIC OF COLLECTIVE ACTION -- PUBLIC GOODS AND THE
                   THEORY OF GROUPS.=
                 CAMBRIDGE, HARVARD UNIVERSITY PRESS, 1965.             65
                 DEFEL
OLSOL  -63-EIN   OLSON, L
                 THE ELITE, INDUSTRIALISM AND NATIONALISM -- JAPAN.=
                 KH SILVERT (ED), EXPECTANT PEOPLES--NATIONALISM AND    63
                   DEVELOPMENT, NEW YORK, RANDOM HOUSE, 1963, PP. 398-426.
                 COMEL, ELEL, ELPRNOR
OPPEFE-58-APC    OPPENHEIM, FE
                 AN ANALYSIS OF POLITICAL CONTROL -- ACTUAL AND POTENTIAL.=
                 THE JOURNAL OF POLITICS, 20, (AUGUST 1958), PP. 514-534. 58
                 DEFEL, ELEL, ELNOEL
OPPESA-67-RPS    OPPENHEIM, SA
                 REHABILITATION IN THE POST - STALIN SOVIET UNION.=
                 THE WESTERN POLITICAL QUARTERLY, 20, (MARCH 1967),     67
                   PP. 97-115.
                 COMEL, ELEL
ORBEAQ-67-CPM    ORBEGON, AQ
                 CONTEMPORARY PEASANT MOVEMENTS (LATIN AMERICA).=
                 SM LIPSET AND A SOLARI (EDS), ELITES IN LATIN AMERICA, 67
                   NEW YORK, OXFORD UNIVERSITY PRESS, 1967, PP. 301-304.
                 ELEL, ELNOEL, ELPRNOR
ORGAAF-65-SPD    ORGANSKI, AFK
                 THE STAGES OF POLITICAL DEVELOPMENT.=
                 NEW YORK, ALFRED A KNOPF, 1965.                        65
                 DEFEL, COMEL, ELEL, ELNOEL, ELPRNOR
ORTEY  -32-RM    ORTEGA Y GASSET, J
                 THE REVOLT OF THE MASSES.=
                 NEW YORK, WW NORTON, U9OI.                             32
                 DEFEL, ELEL, ELNOEL, ELPRNOR
OS, A  -59-APN   OS, A
                 ADMINISTRATIVE PROCEDURE IN NORWAY.=
                 INTERNATIONAL REVIEW OF ADMINISTRATIVE SCIENCES, 25,   59
                   (1959), PP. 67-78.
                 ELEL
OSBOH  -64-BLD   OSBORNE, H
                 BOLIVIA -- A LAND DIVIDED.=
                 LONDON, OXFORD UNIVERSITY PRESS, 1964.                 64
                 COMEL, ELEL, ELNOEL
OSSOS  -63-CSS   OSSOWOSKI, S
                 CLASS STRUCTURE IN THE SOCIAL CONSCIOUSNESS.=
                 S PATTERSON (TRANS), NEW YORK, FREE PRESS, 1963.       63
                 GNELTH, DEFEL, COMEL, ELEL, ELNOEL, ELPRNOR
OSTRM  -64-DOP   OSTROGORSKI, M
                 DEMOCRACY AND THE ORGANIZATION OF POLITICAL PARTIES,
                   -- VOL. 1, GREAT BRITAIN -- VOL 2, UNITED STATES.=
                 NEW YORK, ANCHOR BOOKS, 1964.                          64
                 DEFEL, ELEL, ELNOEL
OVERGD-59-CI     OVERSTREET, GD      WINDMILLER, M
                 COMMUNISM IN INDIA.=
                 BERKELEY, UNIVERSITY OF CALIFORNIA PRESS, 1959.        59
                 COMEL, ELEL, ELNOEL, ELPRNOR
OVERL  -52-APS   OVERACKER, L
                 THE AUSTRALIAN PARTY SYSTEM.=
                 NEW HAVEN, YALE UNIVERSITY PRESS, 1952.                52
                 COMEL, ELEL, ELNOEL
OVERL  -55-NZL   OVERACKER, L
                 THE NEW ZEALAND LABOR PARTY.
                 THE AMERICAN POLITICAL SCIENCE REVIEW, 49, (SEPTEMBER  55
                   1955), PP. 708-733.
```

```
                        COMEL, ELEL, ELNOEL
PAALH -63-CRB    PAALDER, H
                 CABINET REFORM IN BRITAIN, 1914-1963.=
                 STANFORD, STANFORD UNIVERSITY PRESS, 1963.                 63
                 ELEL, ELNOEL
PADGLV-57-MSO    PADGETT, LV
                 MEXICO'S ONE - PARTY SYSTEM -- A RE-EVALUATION.=
                 THE AMERICAN POLITICAL SCIENCE REVIEW, 51, (DECEMBER      57
                     1957), PP. 995-1008.
                 COMEL, ELNOEL, ELPRNOR
PADGLV-66-MPS    PADGETT, LV
                 THE MEXICAN POLITICAL SYSTEM.=
                 BOSTON, HOUGHTON MIFFLIN, 1966.                            66
                 ELEL, ELNOEL, ELPRNOR
PADOSK-58-WFF    PADOVER, SK
                 THE WORLD OF THE FOUNDING FATHERS (UNITED STATES).=
                 SOCIAL RESEARCH, 25, (SUMMER 1958), PP. 191-214.           58
                 COMEL, ELPRNOR
PAGECH-46-BSO    PAGE, CH
                 BUREAUCRACY'S OTHER FACE (UNITED STATES).=
                 SOCIAL FORCES, 25, (OCTOBER 1946), PP. 88-94.              46
                 COMEL, ELPRNOR
PAL,AP-57-CCB    PAL, AP
                 CHANNELS OF COMMUNICATION WITH THE BAERIO PEOPLE
                     (PHILIPPINES).=
                 PHILIPPINE JOURNAL OF PUBLIC ADMINISTRATION, 1,            57
                     (APRIL 1957), PP. 160-164.
                 ELNOEL
PALML -55-AIS    PALMIER, L
                 ASPECTS OF INDONESIA'S SOCIAL STRUCTURE.=
                 PACIFIC AFFAIRS, 28, (JUNE 1955), PP. 117-131.             55
                 ELEL, ELNOEL, ELPRNOR
PALMLH-60-JNU    PALMIER, LH
                 THE JAVANESE NOBILITY UNDER THE DUTCH.=
                 COMPARATIVE STUDIES IN SOCIETY AND HISTORY, 2,             60
                     (JANUARY 1960), PP. 197-227.
                 ELEL, ELNOEL, ELPRNOR
PALMLH-60-SSP    PALMIER, LH
                 SOCIAL STATUS AND POWER IN JAVA.=
                 LONDON, UNIVERSITY OF LONDON ATHLONE PRESS, 1960.          60
                 COMEL, ELEL, ELNOEL, ELPRNOR
PALMM -66-UAR    PALMER, M
                 THE UNITED ARAB REPUBLIC -- AN ASSESSMENT OF ITS FAILURE.=
                 THE MIDDLE EAST JOURNAL, 20, (WINTER 1966), PP. 50-67.     66
                 ELEL, ELNOEL
PANIKM-59-PPI    PANIKKAR, KM
                 PARTIES AND POLITICS IN INDIA.=
                 CURRENT HISTORY, N.S., 36, (MARCH 1959), PP. 153-157.      59
                 COMEL, ELNOEL
PAREM -64-BMR    PARENTI, M
                 THE BLACK MUSLIMS -- FROM REVOLUTION TO INSTITUTION
                     (UNITED STATES).=
                 SOCIAL RESEARCH, 32, (SUMMER 1964), PP. 175-194.           64
                 ELEL, ELNOEL, ELPRNOR
PAREVJ-56-SSL    PARENTON, VJ          PELLEGRIN, VJ
                 SOCIAL STRUCTURE AND THE LEADERSHIP FACTOR IN A
                     NEGRO COMMUNITY (UNITED STATES).=
                 PHYLON, 17, (MARCH 1956), PP. 74-78.                       56
                 ELEL, ELNOEL
PARKGK-61-PSS    PARK, GK              SOLTOW, C
                 POLITICS AND SOCIAL STRUCTURE IN A NORWEGIAN VILLAGE.=
                 THE AMERICAN JOURNAL OF SOCIOLOGY, 67, (SEPTEMBER 1961),   61
                     PP. 152-162.
                 COMEL, ELNOEL
PARKRL-52-IDG    PARK, RL
                 INDIAN DEMOCRACY AND THE GENERAL ELECTION.=
                 PACIFIC AFFAIRS, 25, (JUNE 1952), PP. 130-139.             52
                 ELEL, ELNOEL
PARKRL-59-LPI    PARK, RL              TINKER, I (EDS)
                 LEADERSHIP AND POLITICAL INSTITUTIONS IN INDIA.=
                 PRINCETON, PRINCETON UNIVERSITY PRESS, 1959.               59
                 COMEL, ELEL, ELNOEL, ELPRNOR
PARMJN-55-TUP    PARMER, JN
                 TRADE UNIONS AND POLITICS IN MALAYA.=
                 FAR EASTERN SURVEY, 24, (MARCH 1955), PP. 33-39.           55
                 COMEL, ELPRNOR
PARRA -66-NCD    PARRY, A
                 THE NEW CLASS DIVIDED -- RUSSIAN SCIENCE AND TECHNOLOGY
                     VERSUS COMMUNISM.=
                 NEW YORK, MACMILLAN, 1966.                                 66
                 COMEL, ELEL, ELPRNOR
PARRA -66-STV    PARRY, A
                 SCIENCE AND TECHNOLOGY VERSUS COMMUNISM (SOVIET UNION).=
                 THE RUSSIAN REVIEW, 25, (JULY 1966), PP. 227-241.          66
```

```
                    COMEL, ELEL, ELPRNOR
PARRG  -66-EP    PARRY, G
                    ELITES AND POLYARCHIES.=
                    JOURNAL OF COMMONWEALTH POLITICAL STUDIES, 4,            66
                       (NOVEMBER 1966), PP. 163-179.
                    GNELTH, METEL
PARSMB-62-QPC    PARSONS, MB
                    QUASI - PARTISAN CONFLICT IN A ONE - PARTY LEGISLATIVE
                       SYSTEM -- THE FLORIDA SENATE, 1947-1961
                       (UNITED STATES).=
                    THE AMERICAN POLITICAL SCIENCE REVIEW, 56,               62
                       (SEPTEMBER 1962), PP. 605-614.
                    ELEL, ELNOEL
PARST  -51-SS    PARSONS, T
                    THE SOCIAL SYSTEM.=
                    GLENCOE, THE FREE PRESS, 1951.                           51
                    GNELTH, DEFEL, COMEL, ELEL, ELNOEL
PARST  -57-DPA   PARSONS, T
                    THE DISTRIBUTION OF POWER IN AMERICAN SOCIETY.=
                    WORLD POLITICS, 10, (OCTOBER 1957), PP. 123-143.         57
                    GNELTH, DEFEL
PARST  -63-CI    PARSONS, T
                    ON THE CONCEPT OF INFLUENCE.=
                    THE PUBLIC OPINION QUARTERLY, 27, (SPRING 1963),         63
                       PP. 37-62.
                    GNELTH, DEFEL
PARTPH-63-NCP    PARTRIDGE, PH
                    SOME NOTES ON THE CONCEPT OF POWER.=
                    POLITICAL STUDIES, 11, (1963), PP. 107-125.              63
                    DEFEL, METEL
PASSH  -63-WJT   PASSIN, H
                    WRITER AND JOURNALIST IN THE TRANSITIONAL SOCIETY.=
                    LW PYE (ED), COMMUNICATIONS AND POLITICAL DEVELOPMENT,   63
                       PRINCETON, PRINCETON UNIVERSITY PRESS, 1963, PP. 82-123.
                    COMEL, ELEL, ELNOEL, ELPRNOR
PATCM  -65-DTS   PATCHEN, M
                    DECISION THEORY IN THE STUDY OF NATIONAL ACTION --
                       PROBLEMS AND A PROPOSAL.=
                    THE JOURNAL OF CONFLICT RESOLUTION, 9, (JUNE 1965),      65
                       PP. 164-176.
                    DEFEL, METEL
PATTSC-59-PIP    PATTERSON, SC
                    PATTERNS OF INTER-PERSONAL RELATIONS IN A STATE
                       LEGISLATIVE GROUP -- THE WISCONSIN ASSEMBLY
                       (UNITED STATES).=
                    THE PUBLIC OPINION QUARTERLY, 25, (SPRING 1959),         59
                       PP. 101-109.
                    ELEL
PATTSC-62-DVB    PATTERSON, SC
                    DIMENSIONS OF VOTING BEHAVIOR IN A ONE - PARTY STATE
                       LEGISLATURES (UNITED STATES).=
                    THE PUBLIC OPINION QUARTERLY, 26, (SUMMER 1962),         62
                       PP. 185-200.
                    ELEL, FLNOEL, ELPRNOR
PATTSC-63-CPL    PATTERSON, SC
                    CHARACTERISTICS OF PARTY LEADERSHIP (UNITED STATES).=
                    THE WESTERN POLITICAL QUARTERLY, 16, (JUNE 1963)         63
                       PP. 332-352.
                    COMEL, ELPRNOR
PATTSC-63-LLP    PATTERSON, SC
                    LEGISLATIVE LEADERSHIP AND POLITICAL IDEOLOGY
                       (UNITED STATES).=
                    THE PUBLIC OPINION QUARTERLY, 27, (FALL 1963),           63
                       PP. 399-410.
                    ELEL, ELNOEL, ELPRNOR
PATTSC-63-RLC    PATTERSON, SC
                    THE ROLE OF THE LOBBYIST -- THE CASE OF OKLAHOMA
                       (UNITED STATES).=
                    THE JOURNAL OF POLITICS, 25, (FEBRUARY 1963), PP. 72-92. 63
                    COMEL, ELPRNOR
PAUKGJ-58-RPO    PAUKER, GJ
                    THE ROLE OF POLITICAL ORGANIZATIONS IN INDONESIA.=
                    FAR EASTERN SURVEY, 27, (SEPTEMBER 1958), PP. 129-142.   58
                    ELNOEL
PAUKGJ-62-RMI    PAUKER, GJ
                    THE ROLE OF THE MILITARY IN INDONESIA.=
                    JJ JOHNSON (ED), THE ROLE OF THE MILITARY IN             62
                       UNDERDEVELOPED COUNTRIES, PRINCETON, NEW JERSEY,
                       PRINCETON UNIVERSITY PRESS, 1962, PP. 185-230.
                    COMEL, ELEL, ELNOEL, ELPRNOR
PAULJ  -63-YOL   PAUL, J            LAULICHT, J
                    IN YOUR OPINION -- LEADERS' AND VOTERS' ATTITUDES ON
                       DEFENSE AND DISARMAMENT (CANADA).=
                    VOL 1, CLARKSON, ONTARIO, CANADIAN PEACE RESEARCH        63
```

```
                         INSTITUTE, 1963.
                         ELPRNOR, METEL
PAXTRO-66-PPV   PAXTON, RO
                         PARADES AND POLITICS AT VICHY -- THE FRENCH OFFICERS CORPS
                            UNDER MARSHAL PETAIN.=
                         PRINCETON, PRINCETON UNIVERSITY PRESS, 1966.                   66
                         ELEL, ELNOEL, ELPRNOR
PAYNA -66-PLA   PAYNE, A
                         PERU -- LATIN AMERICA'S SILENT REVOLUTION.=
                         INTER-AMERICAN ECONOMIC AFFAIRS, 20, (WINTER 1966),            66
                            PP. 69-78.
                         COMEL, ELEL
PAYNJL-65-LPP   PAYNE, JL
                         LABOR AND POLITICS IN PERU.=
                         NEW HAVEN, YALE UNIVERSITY PRESS  1965.                        65
                         COMEL, ELEL, ELNOEL, ELPRNOR
PAYNR -63-SLP   PAYNE, R
                         A STUDY IN LEADERSHIP AND PERCEPTION OF CHANGE IN
                            A VILLAGE CONFRONTED WITH URBANISM (UNITED STATES).=
                         SOCIAL FORCES, 41, (MARCH 1963), PP. 264-269.                  63
                         COMEL, ELEL, ELNOEL
PAYNSG-61-FHS   PAYNE, SG
                         FALANGE -- A HISTORY OF SPANISH FASCISM.=
                         STANFORD, STANFORD UNIVERSITY PRESS, 1961.                     61
                         ELEL, ELNOEL
PAYNSG-67-PMM   PAYNE, SG
                         POLITICS AND THE MILITARY IN MODERN SPAIN.=
                         STANFORD, STANFORD UNIVERSITY PRESS, 1967.                     67
                         COMEL, ELEL, ELPRNOR
PAYNT -62-APR   PAYNE, T
                         AMERICAN POLITICS AND THE RADICAL RIGHT.=
                         THE WESTERN POLITICAL QUARTERLY, 15, (SEPTEMBER 1962),         62
                            SUPP. PP. 20-21.
                         ELPRNOR
PEABRL-63-NPH   PEABODY, RL          POLSBY, NW (ED)
                         NEW PERSPECTIVES ON THE HOUSE OF REPRESENTATIVES
                            (UNITED STATES).=
                         CHICAGO, RAND MCNALLY, 1963.                                   63
                         ELEL, ELNOEL, ELPRNOR
PEABRL-67-PLC   PEABODY, RL
                         PARTY LEADERSHIP CHANGE IN THE UNITED STATES HOUSE OF
                            REPRESENTATIVES.=
                         THE AMERICAN POLITICAL SCIENCE REVIEW, 61,                     67
                            (SEPTEMBER 1967), PP. 675-693.
                         ELEL, ELPRNOR
PECKSM-63-RFL   PECK, SM
                         THE RANK - AND - FILE - LEADER (UNITED STATES).=
                         NEW HAVEN, CONNECTICUT, COLLEGE AND UNIVERSITY PRESS,          63
                            1963.
                         ELEL, ELNOEL, ELPRNOR, METEL
PEHRRN-54-LHL   PEHRSON, RN
                         THE LAPPISH HERDING LEADER -- A STRUCTURAL ANALYSIS.=
                         AMERICAN ANTHROPLOLGIST, 56, (DECEMBER 1954),                  54
                            PP. 1076-1080.
                         COMEL, ELNOEL
PELCZ -57-PP    PELCZYNSKI, Z
                         PARLIAMENTARIANISM IN POLAND.=
                         PARLIAMENTARY AFFAIRS, 10, (AUTUMN 1957), PP. 495-504.         57
                         ELEL
PELLH -54-ALM   PELLING, H
                         THE AMERICAN LABOUR MOVEMENT -- A BRITISH VIEW.=
                         POLITICAL STUDIES, 2, (1954), PP. 227-241.                     54
                         ELEL, ELNOEL, ELPRNOR
PELLH -54-OLP   PELLING, H
                         THE ORIGINS OF THE LABOUR PARTY (GREAT BRITAIN).=
                         NEW YORK, ST. MARTIN'S PRESS, 1954.                            54
                         COMEL, ELEL, ELNOEL
PELLH -58-BCP   PELLING, H
                         THE BRITISH COMMUNIST PARTY.=
                         LONDON, ADAM AND CHARLES BLACK, 1958.                          58
                         COMEL, ELEL, ELNOEL, ELPRNOR
PELLRJ-56-AOC   PELLEGRIN, RJ          COATES, CH
                         ABSENTEE - OWNED CORPORATIONS AND COMMUNITY POWER
                            STRUCTURE (UNITED STATES).=
                         THE AMERICAN JOURNAL OF SOCIOLOGY, 61, (MARCH 1956),           56
                            PP. 413-419.
                         COMEL, ELEL, ELNOEL, ELPRNOR
PELZD -51-LWH   PELZ, D
                         LEADERSHIP WITHIN A HIERARCHICAL ORGANIZATION
                            (UNITED STATES).=
                         THE JOURNAL OF SOCIAL ISSUES, 12, (JULY-SEPTEMBER 1951),       51
                            PP. 49-55.
                         DEFEL, COMEL
PENDG -57-PGS   PENDLE, G
```

PARLIAMENTARY GOVERNMENT AND SOUTH AMERICA.=
PARLIAMENTARY AFFAIRS, 10, (WINTER 1956-1957),                    57
      PP. 75-80.
      ELNOEL, ELPRNOR
PENFJ  -54-NZL  PENFOLD, J
THE NEW ZEALAND LABOR PARTY -- ITS FORMAL STRUCTURE.=
POLITICAL SCIENCE, 6, (MARCH 1954), PP. 3-16.                     54
      COMEL, ELEL
PENNJ  -58-SPC  PENNAR, J
THE SOVIET PARTY CENTRAL COMMITTEE.=
BULLETIN INSTITUTE FOR THE STUDY OF THE USSR, 5,                  58
      (JUNE 1958), PP. 25-28.
      ELEL
PENNJR-60-DL   PENNOCK, JR
DEMOCRACY AND LEADERSHIP.=
WN CHAMBERS AND RH SALISBURY (EDS), DEMOCRACY IN THE              60
      MID-TWENTIETH CENTURY, SAINT LOUIS, THE WASHINGTON
      UNIVERSITY PRESS, 1960, PP. 95-125.
      DEFEL, ELEL, ELNOEL, ELPRNOR
PERELC-62-RMC  PEREIRA, LCB
THE RISE OF MIDDLE CLASS AND MIDDLE MANAGEMENT IN BRAZIL.=
JOURNAL OF INTER-AMERICAN STUDIES, 4, (JULY 1962),               62
      PP. 313-326.
      COMEL, ELEL, ELPRNOR
PERKDH-63-CVD  PERKINS, DH
CENTRALIZATION VERSUS DECENTRALIZATION IN MAINLAND
      CHINA AND THE SOVIET UNION.=
THE ANNALS OF THE AMERICAN ACADEMY OF POLITICAL AND              63
      SOCIAL SCIENCE, 349, (SEPTEMBER 1963), PP. 70-80.
      ELEL, ELPRNOR
PERRC  -64-SPP  PERROW, C
THE SOCIOLOGICAL PERSPECTIVE AND POLITICAL PLURALISM.=
SOCIAL RESEARCH, 31, (WINTER 1964), PP. 411-422.
      DEFEL                                                      64
PERRE  -62-SMA  PERROY, E
SOCIAL MOBILITY AMONG THE FRENCH NOBLESSE IN THE LATER
      MIDDLE AGES.=
PAST AND PRESENT, 21, (APRIL 1962), PP. 25-38.                   62
      COMEL
PESCK  -61-CCG  PESCHEL, K
COUNCIL CHAMBERS OF THE GREAT PARLIAMENTS.=
PARLIAMENTARY AFFAIRS, 14, (AUTUMN 1961), PP. 518-541.           61
      ELEL, ELNOEL
PETEEN-66-BNP  PETERSON, EN
THE BUREAUCRACY AND THE NAZI PARTY.=
THE REVIEW OF POLITICS, 28, (APRIL 1966), PP. 172-192.           66
      COMEL, ELPRNOR, ELEL
PETERL-63-SSP  PETERSON, RL
SOCIAL STRUCTURE AND THE POLITICAL PROCESS IN
      LATIN AMERICA.=
THE WESTERN POLITICAL QUARTERLY, 16, (DECEMBER 1963),            63
      PP. 885-896.
      GNELTH, COMEL, ELEL, ELNOEL
PETHR  -62-KSP  PETHYBRIDGE, R
A KEY TO SOVIET POLITICS -- THE CRISIS OF THE ANTI - PARTY
      GROUP.=
NEW YORK, FREDERICK A PRAEGER, 1962.                             62
      ELEL, ELPRNOR
PETRL  -61-LIB  PETRULLO, L        BASS, BM (EDS)
LEADERSHIP AND INTERPERSONAL BEHAVIOR.=
NEW YORK, HOLT, RINEHART AND WINSTON, 1961.                      61
      DEFEL, ELEL, ELNOEL
PETRMB-47-CGY  PETROVICH, MB
THE CENTRAL GOVERNMENT OF YUGOSLAVIA.=
POLITICAL SCIENCE QUARTERLY, 62, (DECEMBER 1947),                47
      PP. 504-530.
      COMEL, ELEL
PETRT  -63-CIS  PETRAN, T
THE COUPS IN IRAQ AND SYRIA.=
MONTHLY REVIEW, 15, (MAY 1963), PP. 31-39.                       63
      ELEL
PETTGS-38-PR   PETTEE, GS
THE PROCESS OF REVOLUTION.=
NEW YORK, HARPER BROS., 1938.                                    38
      DEFEL, ELEL, ELNOEL, ELPRNOR
PETTTF-60-SDA  PETTIGREW, TF
SOCIAL DISTANCE ATTITUDES OF SOUTH AFRICAN STUDENTS.=
SOCIAL FORCES, 38, (MARCH 1960), PP. 246-253.                    60
      ELPRNOR
PFEFG  -67-TUP  PFEFFERMANN, G
TRADE UNIONS AND POLITICS IN FRENCH WEST AFRICA DURING
      THE FOURTH REPUBLIC.=
AFRICAN AFFAIRS, 66, (JULY 1967), PP. 213-230.                   67
      ELEL, ELNOEL, ELPRNOR

```
PHILA -66-BLC    PHILIPPART, A
                 BELGIUM -- LANGUAGE AND CLASS OPPOSITION.=
                 GOVERNMENT AND OPPOSITION, 2, (NOVEMBER 1966),                66
                    PP. 63-81.
                 COMEL, ELNOEL, ELPRNOR
PHILCH-62-PSI    PHILIPS, CH (ED)
                 POLITICS AND SOCIETY IN INDIA.=
                 NEW YORK, FREDERICK A PRAEGER, 1962.                          62
                 ELNOEL, ELPRNOR
PHILJ -61-KNF    PHILLIPS, J
                 KWAME NKRUMAH AND THE FUTURE OF AFRICA.=
                 NEW YORK, FREDERICK A PRAEGER, 1961.                          61
                 COMEL, ELNOEL, ELPRNOR
PICHU -63-RAS    PICHT, U
                 REHABILITATIONS AFTER STALIN'S DEATH.=
                 STUDIES ON THE SOVIET UNION, 2, (1963), PP. 23-34.            63
                 ELEL, ELNOEL
PICKD -54-FP     PICKLES, D
                 THE FRENCH PRESIDENCY.=
                 THE POLITICAL QUARTERLY, 25, (APRIL 1954), PP. 105-115.       54
                 ELEL
PICKO -58-CSS    PICK, O
                 CZECHOSLOVAKIA -- STABLE SATELLITE.=
                 PROBLEMS OF COMMUNISM, 7, (JULY-AUGUST 1958), PP. 32-39.      58
                 ELEL, ELNOEL
PIERWW-50-PDL    PIERSON, WW (ED)
                 PATHOLOGY OF DEMOCRACY IN LATIN AMERICA -- A SYMPOSIUM.=
                 THE AMERICAN POLITICAL SCIENCE REVIEW, 44, (MARCH 1950),      50
                    PP. 100-149.
                 COMEL, ELEL, ELNOEL
PIGOP -35-LOD    PIGORS, P
                 LEADERSHIP OR DOMINATION.=
                 BOSTON, HOUGHTON MIFFLIN, 1935.                               35
                 DEFEL, ELEL, ELNOEL
PIKEFB-59-CCL    PIKE, FB
                 THE CATHOLIC CHURCH IN LATIN AMERICA.=
                 THE REVIEW OF POLITICS, 21, (JANUARY 1959), PP. 83-113.       59
                 ELEL
PIKEFB-63-ACR    PIKE, FB
                 ASPECTS OF CLASS RELATIONS IN CHILE, 1850-1950.=
                 HISPANIC-AMERICAN HISTORICAL REVIEW, 43,                      63
                    (FEBRUARY 1963), PP. 14-33.
                 COMEL, ELEL, ELNOEL
PIKEFB-64-CBC    PIKE, FB (ED)
                 THE CONFLICT BETWEEN CHURCH AND STATE IN LATIN AMERICA.=
                 NEW YORK, ALFRED A KNOPF, 1964.                               64
                 COMEL, ELEL, ELPRNOR
PIKEFB-64-ONA    PIKE, FB
                 THE OLD AND THE NEW APRA IN PERU -- MYTH AND REALITY.=
                 INTER-AMERICAN ECONOMIC AFFAIRS, 18, (AUTUMN 1964),           64
                    PP. 3-45.
                 COMEL, ELPRNOR
PINNEL-62-LMB    PINNEY, EL
                 LATENT AND MANIFEST BUREAUCRACY IN THE WEST GERMAN
                    PARLIAMENT -- THE CASE OF THE BUNDESRAT.=
                 MIDWEST JOURNAL OF POLITICAL SCIENCE, 6, (MAY 1962),          62
                    PP. 149-164.
                 COMEL, ELEL, ELPRNOR
PIPER -60-HER    PIPES, R
                 THE HISTORICAL EVOLUTION OF THE RUSSIAN INTELLIGENTSIA.=
                 DAEDALUS, 89, (SUMMER 1960), PP. 487-502.                     60
                 COMEL, ELPRNOR
PIPER -60-RI     PIPES, R (ED)
                 THE RUSSIAN INTELLIGENTSIA.=
                 NEW YORK, COLUMBIA UNIVERSITY PRESS, 1960.                    60
                 COMEL, ELEL, ELPRNOR
PIPPLL-64-PE     PIPPRIN, LLR
                 THE PERON ERA.=
                 STANFORD, CALIFORNIA, INSTITUTE OF HISPANIC AMERICAN          64
                    AND LUSO-BRAZILIAN STUDIES, 1964.
                 COMEL, ELEL, ELNOEL, ELPRNOR
PISMG -64-EAS    PISMENNY, G
                 THE ELECTIONS TO THE ACADEMY OF SCIENCES OF THE USSR.=
                 BULLETIN INSTITUTE FOR THE STUDY OF THE USSR, 11,             64
                    (NOVEMBER 1964), PP. 42-46.
                 COMEL
PISMY -64-NMS    PISMENNY, Y
                 THE 'NEW MAN' (SOVIET UNION).=
                 STUDIES ON THE SOVIET UNION, 4, (1964), PP. 49-58.            64
                 ELPRNOR
PISTL -61-GTK    PISTRAK, L
                 THE GREAT TACTICIAN -- KHRUSHCHEV'S RISE TO POWER
                    (SOVIET UNION).=
                 NEW YORK, FREDERICK A PRAEGER, 1961.                          61
```

```
                ELEL, ELNOEL
PISTL  -62-KPS  PISTRAK, L
                KHRUSHCHEV AND THE PURGES (SOVIET UNION).=
                PROBLEMS OF COMMUNISM, 11, (JANUARY-FEBRUARY 1962),          62
                   PP. 21-27.
                ELEL
PIZZA  -64-IME  PIZZORNO, A
                THE INDIVIDUALISTIC MOBILIZATION OF EUROPE.=
                DAEDALUS, 93, (WINTER 1964), PP. 199-224.
                                                                             64
                COMEL, ELEL, ELNOEL
PJH    -57-RIN  PJH
                REVOLT OF THE INTELLECTUALS IN NORTH VIETNAM.=
                THE WORLD TODAY, 13, (JUNE 1957), PP. 250-260.               57
                ELEL, ELPRNOR
PLAMJ  -61-HLE  PLAMENATZ, J
                HEROIC LEADERSHIP (EGYPT, FRANCE, GERMANY, GREAT BRITAIN,
                   UNITED STATES).=
                ENCOUNTER, 17, (SEPTEMBER 1961), PP. 64-65.                  61
                DEFEL, ELNOEL
PLESH  -64-EP   PLESSNER, H
                THE EMANCIPATION OF POWER.=
                SOCIAL RESEARCH, 32, (SUMMER 1964), PP. 153-174.
                                                                             64
                DEFEL
PLOSSI-56-PEP   PLOSS, SI
                POLITICAL EDUCATION IN THE POSTWAR KOMSOMOL.=
                THE AMERICAN SLAVIC AND EAST EUROPEAN REVIEW, 15,            56
                   (DECEMBER 1956), PP. 489-505.
                ELNOEL
PLOSSI-58-YZM   PLOSS, SI
                FROM YOUTHFUL ZEAL TO MIDDLE AGE (SOVIET UNION,
                   KOMSOMOL).=
                PROBLEMS OF COMMUNISM, 7, (JULY-AUGUST 1958), PP. 8-17.      58
                ELEL, ELNOEL, ELPRNOR
PLOSSI-65-CDM   PLOSS, SI
                CONFLICT AND DECISION-MAKING IN SOVIET RUSSIA -- A CASE
                   STUDY OF AGRICULTURAL POLICY, 1953-1963.
                PRINCETON, PRINCETON UNIVERSITY PRESS, 1965.                 65
                ELEL, ELPRNOR
PLOWDE-55-APP   PLOWMAN, DEG
                ALLEGIANCE TO POLITICAL PARTIES -- A STUDY OF THREE
                   PARTIES IN ONE AREA (GREAT BRITAIN).=
                POLITICAL STUDIES, 3, (OCTOBER 1955), PP. 222-234.           55
                ELEL, ELNOEL
POBLM  -60-RLA  POBLETE-TRONCOSO, M BURNETT, BG
                THE RISE OF THE LATIN AMERICAN LABOR MOVEMENT.=
                NEW YORK, BOOKMAN ASSOCIATES, 1960.
                                                                             60
                COMEL, ELEL, ELNOEL
PODHN  -55-JCI  PODHORETZ, N
                JEWISH CULTURE AND THE INTELLECTUALS (UNITED STATES).=
                COMMENTARY, 19, (MAY 1955), PP. 451-457.                     55
                ELNOEL, ELPRNOR
PODHN  -61-JYI  PODHORETZ, N (ED)
                JEWISHNESS AND THE YOUNGER INTELLECTUALS -- A SYMPOSIUM
                   (UNITED STATES).=
                COMMENTARY, 31, (APRIL 1961), PP. 306-359.                   61
                COMEL, ELEL, ELNOEL, ELPRNOR
POLKWR-65-NMM   POLK, WR
                THE NATURE OF MODERNIZATION -- THE MIDDLE EAST AND
                   AND NORTH AFRICA.=
                FOREIGN AFFAIRS, 44, (OCTOBER 1965), PP. 100-110.            65
                COMEL, ELEL, ELNOEL
POLLH  -53-SCG  POLLINS, H
                THE SIGNIFICANCE OF THE CAMPAIGN IN GENERAL
                   ELECTIONS (GREAT BRITAIN).=
                POLITICAL STUDIES, 1, (1953), PP. 207-215.                   53
                ELEL, ELNOEL, ELPRNOR
POLSNW-59-SCP   POLSBY, NW
                THE SOCIOLOGY OF COMMUNITY POWER -- A REASSESSMENT
                   (UNITED STATES).=
                SOCIAL FORCES, 37, (MARCH 1959), PP. 232-236.                59
                DEFEL, COMEL, ELEL, ELPRNOR
POLSNW-59-TPA   POLSBY, NW
                THREE PROBLEMS IN THE ANALYSIS OF COMMUNITY POWER.=
                AMERICAN SOCIOLOGICAL REVIEW, 24,                            59
                   (DECEMBER 1959), PP. 796-803.
                COMEL, METEL
POLSNW-60-HSC   POLSBY, NW
                HOW TO STUDY COMMUNITY POWER -- THE PLURALISTIC
                   ALTERNATIVE.=
                THE JOURNAL OF POLITICS, 22, (AUGUST 1960), PP. 474-484.     60
                METEL
POLSNW-60-PMF   POLSBY, NW
                POWER IN MIDDLETOWN -- FACT AND VALUE
                   IN COMMUNITY RESEARCH (UNITED STATES).=
```

                CANADIAN JOURNAL OF ECONOMICS AND POLITICAL SCIENCE, 26,  60<br>
                (NOVEMBER 1960), PP. 592-603.<br>
                COMEL, ELEL<br>
POLSNW-63-CPP  POLSBY, NW<br>
                COMMUNITY POWER AND POLITICAL THEORY (UNITED STATES).=<br>
                NEW HAVEN, YALE UNIVERSITY PRESS, 1963.                63<br>
                GNELTH, DEFEL, COMEL, ELEL, ELNOEL, ELPRNOR, METEL<br>
POLSNW-63-TSI  POLSBY, NW<br>
                TWO STRATEGIES OF INFLUENCE -- CHOOSING A MAJORITY LEADER,<br>
                   1962 (UNITED STATES).=<br>
                RL PEABODY AND NW POLSBY (EDS), NEW PERSPECTIVES ON THE     63<br>
                   HOUSE OF REPRESENTATIVES, CHICAGO, RAND MCNALLY, 1963,<br>
                   PP. 237-270.<br>
                DEFEL, ELEL<br>
POLSNW-64-PES  POLSBY, NW            WILDAVSKY, A<br>
                PRESIDENTIAL ELECTIONS -- STRATEGIES OF AMERICAN<br>
                   ELECTORAL POLITICS.=<br>
                NEW YORK, CHARLES SCRIBNER'S SONS, 1964.                64<br>
                ELEL, ELNOEL, ELPRNOR<br>
POOLID-52-SD   POOL, IDS          ET AL<br>
                SYMBOLS OF DEMOCRACY.=<br>
                STANFORD, CALIFORNIA, HOOVER INSTITUTION, STANFORD       52<br>
                   UNIVERSITY, 1952.<br>
                ELNOEL, ELPRNOR<br>
POOLID-55-SGS  POOL, IDS<br>
                SATELLITE GENERALS -- A STUDY OF MILITARY ELITES<br>
                   IN THE SOVIET SPHERE.=<br>
                STANFORD, STANFORD UNIVERSITY PRESS, 1955.             55<br>
                COMEL, ELEL, ELNOEL, ELPRNOR<br>
PORTAT-63-CSD  PORTER, AT<br>
                CREOLEDOM -- A STUDY OF THE DEVELOPMENT OF FREETOWN<br>
                   SOCIETY (SIERRA LEONE).=<br>
                LONDON, OXFORD UNIVERSITY PRESS, 1963.                63<br>
                COMEL, ELEL, ELNOEL<br>
PORTJ -55-EGS  PORTER, J<br>
                ELITE GROUPS -- A SCHEME FOR THE STUDY OF POWER IN<br>
                   CANADA.=<br>
                CANADIAN JOURNAL OF ECONOMICS AND POLITICAL SCIENCE,       55<br>
                   21, (NOVEMBER 1955), PP. 498-512.<br>
                GNELTH, DEFEL, METEL<br>
PORTJ -56-CEP  PORTER, J<br>
                CONCENTRATION OF ECONOMIC POWER AND THE ECONOMIC ELITE<br>
                   IN CANADA.=<br>
                CANADIAN JOURNAL OF ECONOMICS AND POLITICAL SCIENCE,       56<br>
                   22, (MAY 1956), PP. 199-220.<br>
                DEFEL, COMEL<br>
PORTJ -57-EES  PORTER, J<br>
                THE ECONOMIC ELITE AND THE SOCIAL STRUCTURE IN CANADA.=<br>
                CANADIAN JOURNAL OF ECONOMICS AND POLITICAL SCIENCE,       57<br>
                   23, (AUGUST 1957), PP. 376-394.<br>
                DEFEL, COMEL<br>
PORTJ -58-HPS  PORTER, J<br>
                HIGHER PUBLIC SERVANTS AND THE BUREAUCRATIC ELITE IN<br>
                   CANADA.=<br>
                CANADIAN JOURNAL OF ECONOMICS AND POLITICAL SCIENCE,       58<br>
                   24, (NOVEMBER 1958), PP. 483-501.<br>
                COMEL<br>
PORTJ -59-BER  PORTER, J<br>
                THE BUREAUCRATIC ELITE -- A REPLY TO PROFESSOR ROWAT<br>
                   (CANADA, GREAT BRITAIN).=<br>
                CANADIAN JOURNAL OF ECONOMICS AND POLITICAL SCIENCE, 25,  59<br>
                 (MAY 1959), PP. 207-209.<br>
                COMEL<br>
PORTJ -65-VMA  PORTER, J<br>
                THE VERTICAL MOSAIC -- AN ANALYSIS OF SOCIAL CLASS AND<br>
                   POWER IN CANADA.=<br>
                TORONTO, UNIVERSITY OF TORONTO PRESS, 1965.           65<br>
                GNELTH, DEFEL, COMEL, ELEL, ELNOEL<br>
POSPL -58-SCP  POSPISIL, L<br>
                SOCIAL CHANGE AND PRIMITIVE LAW -- CONSEQUENCES OF A<br>
                   PAPUAN LEGAL CASE (NETHERLANDS NEW GUINEA).=<br>
                AMERICAN ANTHROPOLOGIST, 60, (OCTOBER 1958), PP. 832-837. 58<br>
                ELNOEL, ELPRNOR<br>
POTAA -59-APP  POTASH, A<br>
                ARGENTINE POLITICAL PARTIES -- 1957-1958.=<br>
                JOURNAL OF INTER-AMERICAN STUDIES, 1, (OCTOBER 1959),      59<br>
                 PP. 515-524.<br>
                COMEL, ELEL<br>
POTARA-61-CRM  POTASH, RA<br>
                THE CHANGING ROLE OF THE MILITARY IN ARGENTINA.=<br>
                JOURNAL OF INTER-AMERICAN STUDIES, 3, (OCTOBER 1961),      61<br>
                 PP. 571-578.<br>
                ELEL, ELNOEL<br>
POTTA -56-BPG  POTTER, A

BRITISH PRESSURE GROUPS.=
PARLIAMENTARY AFFAIRS, 9, (AUTUMN 1956), PP. 418-426.      56
ELEL, ELNOEL
POTTA -62-AGC    POTTER, A
THE AMERICAN GOVERNING CLASS.=
THE BRITISH JOURNAL OF SOCIOLOGY, 13, (1962), PP. 309-319.62
COMEL
POTTA -66-EC    POTTER, A
THE ELITE CONCEPT.=
POLITICAL STUDIES, 14, (OCTOBER 1966), PP. 373-375.       66
DEFEL
POTTAM-60-OGB    POTTER, AM
ORGANIZED GROUPS IN BRITISH NATIONAL POLITICS.=
LONDON, FABER AND FABER, 1960.
ELNOEL, METEL                                             60
POTTDC-66-BCI    POTTER, DC
BUREAUCRATIC CHANGE IN INDIA.=
R BRAIBANTI (ED), ASIAN BUREAUCRATIC SYSTEMS EMERGENT     66
   FROM THE BRITISH IMPERIAL TRADITION, DURHAM, DUKE
   UNIVERSITY PRESS, 1966, PP. 141-208.
ELEL, ELPRNOR
POWEJD-65-MAM    POWELL, JD
MILITARY ASSISTANCE AND MILITARISM IN LATIN AMERICA.=
THE WESTERN POLITICAL QUARTERLY, 18, (JUNE 1965),
   PP. 382-092.                                           65
COMEL
POWERL-63-MAC    POWELL, RL
THE MILITARY AFFAIRS COMMITTEE AND PARTY CONTROL OF THE
   MILITARY IN CHINA.=
ASIAN SURVEY, 3, (JULY 1963), PP. 347-356.                63
ELEL
PRESC -62-MSP    PRESS, C
MAIN STREET POLITICS -- POLICY-MAKING AT THE LOCAL LEVEL
   (UNITED STATES).=
EAST LANSING, MICHIGAN STATE UNIVERSITY, 1962.            62
ELEL, ELNOEL, METEL
PRESRV-58-SAC    PRESTHUS, RV        EREM, S
STATISTICAL ANALYSIS AND COMPARATIVE ADMINISTRATION --
   THE TURKISH COUNSEIL D'ETATE.=
ITHACA, CORNELL UNIVERSITY PRESS, 1958.                   58
COMEL, METEL
PRESRV-59-SBB    PRESTHUS, RV
THE SOCIAL BASES OF BUREAUCRATIC ORGANIZATION
   (UNITED STATES).=
SOCIAL FORCES, 38, (DECEMBER 1959), PP. 103-109.          59
DEFEL, COMEL, ELEL, ELNOEL, ELPRNOR
PRESRV-62-WVW    PRESTHUS, RV
WEBERIAN V. WELFARE BUREAUCRACY IN TRADITIONAL
   SOCIETY (TURKEY).=
ADMINISTRATIVE SCIENCE QUARTERLY, 6, (1961-1962),         62
   PP. 1-24.
DEFEL
PRESRV-64-MTS    PRESTHUS, RV
MEN AT THE TOP -- A STUDY IN COMMUNITY POWER
   (UNITED STATES).=
NEW YORK, OXFORD UNIVERSITY PRESS, 1964.                  64
GNELTH, DEFEL, COMEL, ELEL, ELNOEL, ELPRNOR, METEL
PREWK -65-PSL    PREWITT, K
POLITICAL SOCIALIZATION AND LEADERSHIP SELECTION
   (UNITED STATES).=
THE ANNALS OF THE AMERICAN ACADEMY OF POLITICAL AND SOCIAL65
   SCIENCE, 361, (SEPTEMBER 1965), PP. 96-111.
DEFEL, COMEL, ELPRNOR, METEL
PREWK -67-PSP    PREWITT, K        EULAU, H        ZISK, BH
POLITICAL SOCIALIZATION AND POLITICAL ROLES
   (UNITED STATES).=
THE PUBLIC OPINION QUARTERLY, 30, (WINTER 1966-1967),     67
   PP. 569-582.
COMEL, ELPRNOR, METEL
PRICDK-60-SSU    PRICE, DK (ED)
THE SECRETARY OF STATE (UNITED STATES).=
NEW YORK, PRENTICE-HALL, 1960.
ELEL, ELNOEL, ELPRNOR                                     60
PRICDK-65-EDG    PRICE, DK
THE ESTABLISHED DISSENTERS (GREAT BRITAIN,
   UNITED STATES).=
DAEDALUS, 94, (WINTER 1965), PP. 84-116.                  65
ELEL, ELPRNOR
PRICDK-65-SEU    PRICE, DK
THE SCIENTIFIC ESTATE (UNITED STATES).=
CAMBRIDGE, BELKNAP PRESS, 1965.                           65
COMEL, ELEL, ELNOEL, ELPRNOR
PRICDT-61-ALU    PRICE, DT
ADMINISTRATIVE LEADERSHIP (UNITED STATES).=

                              DAEDALUS, 90, (FALL 1961), PP. 750-763.                    61
                              ELEL, ELPRNOR
PRICHD-65-EAU    PRICE, HD
                              THE ELECTORAL ARENA (UNITED STATES CONGRESS).=
                              DB TRUMAN, (ED), THE CONGRESS AND AMERICA'S FUTURE,         65
                                  ENGLEWOOD CLIFFS, NEW JERSEY, PRENTICE-HALL, 1965,
                                  PP. 32-51.
                              ELEL, ELNOEL, ELPRNOR
PRICJW-59-ECS    PRICE, JW
                              EDUCATION AND THE CIVIL SERVICE IN EUROPE.=
                              THE WESTERN POLITICAL QUARTERLY, 10, (DECEMBER 1957),       59
                                  PP. 317-832.
                              COMEL
PRICMP-48-PTP    PRICE, MP
                              THE PARLIAMENTS OF TURKEY AND PERSIA.=
                              PARLIAMENTARY AFFAIRS, 1, (SUMMER 1948), PP. 43-50.         48
                              ELEL
PRIEM -66-EEC    PRIESTLY, M
                              THE EMERGENCE OF AN ELITE -- A CASE STUDY OF A WEST COAST
                                  FAMILY (WEST AFRICA).=
                              PC LLOYD (ED), THE NEW ELITES OF TROPICAL AFRICA, LONDON, 66
                                  OXFORD UNIVERSITY PRESS, 1966, PP. 87-100.
                              COMEL, ELEL, ELPRNOR
PRINAH-53-EAA    PRINS, AHJ
                              EAST AFRICAN AGE - CLASS SYSTEMS -- AN INQUIRY INTO
                                  THE SOCIAL ORDER OF GALLA, KIPSIGIS, AND KIKUYU.=
                              DIAKARTIA, JB WOLTERS, 1953.                                53
                              COMEL, ELEL, ELNOEL
PRINKH-62-CCY    PRINGSHELM, KH
                              CHINESE COMMUNIST YOUTH LEAGUES (1920-1949).=
                              THE CHINA QUARTERLY, 12, (OCTOBER-DECEMBER 1962),           62
                                  PP. 75-91.
                              COMEL, ELEL, ELNOEL
PRITCH-46-PVS    PRITCHETT, CH
                              POLITICS AND VALUE SYSTEMS -- THE SUPREME COURT,
                                  1945-1946 (UNITED STATES).=
                              THE JOURNAL OF POLITICS, 8, (NOVEMBER 1946), PP. 499-519. 46
                              ELEL, ELNOEL, ELPRNOR
PRITCH-48-RCS    PRITCHETT, CH
                              THE ROOSEVELT COURT -- A STUDY IN JUDICIAL POLITICS
                                  AND VALUES, 1937-1947 (UNITED STATES).=
                              NEW YORK, THE MACMILLAN COMPANY, 1948.                      48
                              COMEL, ELEL, ELNOEL, ELPRNOR
PRITCH-54-CLV    PRITCHETT, CH
                              CIVIL LIBERTIES AND THE VINSON COURT (UNITED STATES).=
                              CHICAGO, THE UNIVERSITY OF CHICAGO PRESS, 1954.             54
                              ELEL, ELPRNOR
PRITT -55-FGP    PRITTIE, T
                              THE FEDERAL GERMAN PARLIAMENT.=
                              PARLIAMENTARY AFFAIRS, 8, (SPRING 1955), PP. 235-239.       55
                              ELEL
PRITT -56-HFD    PRITTIE, T
                              HOW FAR DOES THE GERMAN PARLIAMENT GOVERN.=
                              PARLIAMENTARY AFFAIRS, 10, (WINTER 1956-1957), PP) 57-64. 56
                              ELEL
PROTJW-56-VSA    PROTHRO, JW
                              VERBAL SHIFTS IN THE AMERICAN PRESIDENCY -- A CONTENT
                                  ANALYSIS.=
                              THE AMERICAN POLITICAL SCIENCE REVIEW, 50, (SEPTEMBER       56
                                  1956), PP. 726-739.
                              ELPRNOR, METEL
PS      -49-MSI  PS
                              MEXICO -- A SPANISH - INDIAN CULTURE IN A MODERN
                                  SETTING.=
                              THE WORLD TODAY, 5, (1949), PP. 108-114.                    49
                              COMEL, ELPRNOR
PSJC    -51-MRW  PSJC
                              MANAGERIAL REVOLUTION IN WESTERN GERMANY.=
                              THE WORLD TODAY, 7, (JUNE 1951), PP. 249-262.               51
                              COMEL
PUNNRM-65-HLC    PUNNETT, RM
                              THE HOUSE OF LORDS AND CONSERVATIVE GOVERNMENTS
                                  1951-1964 (GREAT BRITAIN).=
                              POLITICAL STUDIES, 13, (1965), PP. 85-88.                   65
                              ELEL
PYE,LW-57-PIS    PYE, LW
                              THE POLICY IMPLICATIONS OF SOCIAL CHANGE IN
                                  NON - WESTERN SOCIETIES.=
                              CAMBRIDGE, MIT PRESS, 1957.                                 57
                              DEFEL, ELEL, ELNOEL
PYE,LW-58-AAB    PYE, LW
                              ADMINISTRATORS, AGITATORS, AND BROKERS.=
                              THE PUBLIC OPINION QUARTERLY, 22, (FALL 1958),              58
                                  PP. 342-348.

PYE,LW-58-ELA
                        DEFEL, ELEL, ELPRNOR
                        PYE, LW
                        EFFECTS OF LEGISLATIVE AND ADMINISTRATIVE ACCESSIBILITY
                            ON INTEREST GROUP POLITICS.=
                        PROD (THE AMERICAN BEHAVIORAL SCIENTIST), 1,           58
                            (JANUARY 1958), PP. 11-13.
                        ELEL, ELPRNOR
PYE,LW-58-NWP           PYE, LW
                        THE NON - WESTERN POLITICAL PROCESS.=
                        THE JOURNAL OF POLITICS, 20, (AUGUST 1958), PP. 468-486.  58
                        DEFEL, COMEL, ELEL, ELNOEL, ELPRNOR
PYE,LW-60-NCM           PYE, LW
                        A NEW CLASS IN MALAYA.=
                        NEW LEADER, 43, (MAY 1960), PP. 12-14.                 60
                        COMEL, ELEL, ELNOEL, ELPRNOR
PYE,LW-60-PSA           PYE, LW
                        THE POLITICS OF SOUTHEAST ASIA.=
                        GA ALMOND AND JS COLEMAN (EDS), THE POLITICS OF THE     60
                            DEVELOPING AREAS, PRINCETON, PRINCETON UNIVERSITY
                            PRESS, 1960, PP. 65-152.
                        COMEL, ELEL, ELNOEL, ELPRNOR
PYE,LW-61-PIP           PYE, LW
                        PERSONAL IDENTITY AND POLITICAL IDEOLOGY.=
                        D MARVICK (ED), POLITICAL DECISION-MAKERS, GLENCOE, THE  61
                            FREE PRESS, PP. 290-313.
                        METEL
PYE,LW-62-ABP           PYE, LW
                        ARMY IN BURMESE POLITICS.=
                        JJ JOHNSON, (ED), THE ROLE OF THE MILITARY IN           62
                            UNDERDEVELOPED COUNTRIES, PRINCETON, PRINCETON
                            UNIVERSITY PRESS, 1962, PP. 231-252.
                        ELEL, ELNOEL, ELPRNOR
PYE,LW-62-APP           PYE, LW
                        ARMIES IN THE PROCESS OF POLITICAL MODERNIZATION.=
                        JJ JOHNSON (ED), THE ROLE OF THE MILITARY IN            62
                            UNDERDEVELOPED COUNTRIES, PRINCETON, PRINCETON
                            UNIVERSITY PRESS, 1962, PP. 69-91.
                        ELEL, ELNOEL, ELPRNOR
PYE,LW-62-PPN           PYE, LW
                        POLITICS, PERSONALITY, AND NATION-BUILDING --
                            BURMA'S SEARCH FOR IDENTITY.=
                        NEW HAVEN, YALE UNIVERSITY PRESS, 1962.                62
                        ELEL, ELNOEL, ELPRNOR
PYE,LW-63-CPD           PYE, LW
                        COMMUNICATIONS AND POLITICAL DEVELOPMENT.=
                        PRINCETON, PRINCETON UNIVERSITY PRESS, 1963.           63
                        DEFEL, COMEL, ELEL, ELNOEL, ELPRNOR
PYE,LW-66-PCP           PYE, LW            VERBA,S (EDS)
                        POLITICAL CULTURE AND POLITICAL DEVELOPMENT.=
                        PRINCETON, PRINCETON UNIVERSITY PRESS, 1966.           66
                        DEFEL, COMEL, ELEL, ELNOEL, ELPRNOR
PYLEMV-64-CIL           PYLEE, MV
                        CHALLENGE FOR INDIAN LEADERSHIP.=
                        CURRENT HISTORY, N.S., 46, (FEBRUARY 1964), PP. 78-82.  64
                        ELEL, ELNOEL
QUIGHS-47-GPJ           QUIGLEY, HS
                        THE GREAT PURGE IN JAPAN.=
                        PACIFIC AFFAIRS, 20, (SEPTEMBER 1947), PP. 299-308.     47
                        ELEL
QUINHF-53-RLP           QUINN, HF
                        THE ROLE OF THE LIBERAL PARTY IN RECENT
                            CANADIAN POLITICS.=
                        POLITICAL SCIENCE QUARTERLY, 68, (SEPTEMBER 1953),     53
                            PP. 396-418.
                        ELEL, ELNOEL
QUIRRE-60-MRC           QUIRK, RE
                        THE MEXICAN REVOLUTION, 1914-1915 -- THE CONVENTION
                            OF AGUASCALIENTES.=
                        BLOOMINGTON, UNIVERSITY OF INDIANA PRESS, 1960.        60
                        COMEL, ELEL, ELNOEL
RADIB -59-FFS           RADITSA, B
                        FERMENT IN FRANCO SPAIN.=
                        COMMENTARY, 27, (JUNE 1959), PP. 500-507.              59
                        ELEL, ELNOEL, ELPRNOR
RAI,L -63-CCL           RAI, L
                        CAUDILLISM AND CONTINUISM IN LATIN AMERICA.=
                        FOREIGN AFFAIRS REPORTS (INDIA), 13, (SEPTEMBER 1963),  63
                            PP. 66-77.
                        COMEL, ELNOEL
RAMSEE-57-YTP           RAMSAUR, EE
                        THE YOUNG TURKS -- PRELUDE TO THE REVOLUTION OF 1908.=
                        PRINCETON, PRINCETON UNIVERSITY PRESS, 1957.           57
                        COMEL, ELEL, ELPRNOR
RANDLI-60-PRI           RANDOLPH, LI           RUDOLPH, SH

                        THE POLITICAL ROLE OF INDIA'S CASTE ASSOCIATION.=
                        PACIFIC AFFAIRS, 33, (MARCH 1960), PP. 5-22.                60
                        COMEL, ELEL, ELNOEL
RANNA -56-DAP           RANNEY, A              KENDALL, W
                        DEMOCRACY AND THE AMERICAN PARTY SYSTEM.=
                        NEW YORK, HARCOURT, BRACE AND COMPANY, 1956.               56
                        DEFEL, ELEL, ELNOEL
RANNA -64-ICM           RANNEY, A
                        INTER - CONSTITUENCY MOVEMENT OF BRITISH PARLIAMENTARY
                           CANDIDATES, 1951-1959.=
                        THE AMERICAN POLITICAL SCIENCE REVIEW, 58, (MARCH 1964),   64
                           PP. 36-45.
                        COMEL
RANNA -65-PPC           RANNEY, A
                        PATHWAYS TO PARLIAMENT -- CANDIDATE SELECTION IN BRITAIN.=
                        MADISON AND MILWAUKEE, THE UNIVERSITY OF WISCONSIN         65
                           PRESS, 1965.
                        COMEL, ELEL, ELPRNOR
RANSCB-51-OGS           RANSONE-JR, CB
                        THE OFFICE OF GOVERNOR IN THE SOUTH (UNITED STATES).=
                        UNIVERSITY, ALABAMA, UNIVERSITY OF ALABAMA, 1951.          51
                        COMEL, ELEL, ELNOEL, ELPRNOR
RANSCB-64-PLG           RANSONE-JR, CB
                        POLITICAL LEADERSHIP IN THE GOVERNOR'S OFFICE
                           (UNITED STATES).=
                        THE JOURNAL OF POLITICS, 26, (FEBRUARY 1964),              64
                           PP. 197-220.
                        ELEL, ELNOEL
RANSHH-58-CIN           RANSOM, HH
                        CENTRAL INTELLIGENCE AND NATIONAL SECURITY
                           (UNITED STATES).=
                        CAMBRIDGE, HARVARD UNIVERSITY PRESS, 1958.                 58
                        ELEL, ELNOEL
RAO,BS-45-NSF           RAO, BS
                        NEW SOCIAL FORCES IN INDIA.=
                        FOREIGN AFFAIRS, 23, (JULY 1945), PP. 635-644.             45
                        COMEL, ELEL, ELNOEL
RAPHEE-65-PSM           RAPHAEL, EE
                        POWER STRUCTURE AND MEMBERSHIP DISPERSION IN UNIONS
                           (UNITED STATES).=
                        THE AMERICAN JOURNAL OF SOCIOLOGY, 71, (NOVEMBER 1965),    65
                           PP. 274-283.
                        ELEL, ELNOEL
RASEJR-65-NCL           RASER, JR
                        THE NEW CHINESE LEADERS -- POWER AND PERSONALITY.=
                        THE JOURNAL OF SOCIAL ISSUES, 21, (JULY 1965),             65
                           PP. 118-135.
                        COMEL, ELEL, ELPRNOR, METEL
RASHM -65-CLB           RASHIDUZZAMAN, M
                        THE CENTRAL LEGISLATURE IN BRITISH INDIA 1921-1947.=
                        DACCA, MULLIER BROTHERS, 1965.                             65
                        COMEL, ELEL, ELPRNOR
RASHM -66-EPP           RASHIDUZZAMAN, M
                        ELECTION POLITICS IN PAKISTAN VILLAGES.=
                        JOURNAL OF COMMONWEALTH POLITICAL STUDIES, 4,              66
                           (NOVEMBER 1966), PP. 191-200.
                        COMEL, ELNOEL, ELPRNOR
RASMJS-64-RRS           RASMUSSEN, JS
                        RETRENCHMENT AND REVIVAL -- A STUDY OF THE CONTEMPORARY
                           BRITISH LIBERAL PARTY.=
                        TUCSON, UNIVERSITY OF ARIZONA PRESS, 1964.=                64
                        COMEL, ELEL, ELNOEL, ELPRNOR
RASMJS-66-RPR           RASMUSSEN, JS
                        THE RELATIONS OF THE PROFUMO REBELS WITH THEIR LOCAL
                           PARTIES (GREAT BRITAIN).=
                        TUCSON, UNIVERSITY OF ARIZONA PRESS, 1966.                 66
                        ELEL, ELNOEL, ELPRNOR
RATCDF-57-PFS           RATCLIFF, DF
                        PRELUDE TO FRANCO (SPAIN).=
                        NEW YORK, LAS AMERICAS PUBLISHING COMPANY, 1957.           57
                        ELEL, ELNOEL, ELPRNOR
RATIL -67-NUG           RATINOFF, L
                        THE NEW URBAN GROUPS -- THE MIDDLE CLASSES
                           (LATIN AMERICA).=
                        SM LIPSET AND A SOLARI (EDS), ELITES IN LATIN AMERICA,     67
                           NEW YORK, OXFORD UNIVERSITY PRESS, 1967, PP. 61-93.
                        COMEL, ELEL, ELNOEL, ELPRNOR
RATNKJ-64-CPL           RATNAM, KJ
                        CHARISMA AND POLITICAL LEADERSHIP (GERMANY).=
                        POLITICAL STUDIES, 12, (MARCH 1964), PP. 341-354.          64
                        DEFEL, ELNOEL
RATTS -63-EEP           RATTENBERG, S
                        ENTREPRENEURSHIP AND ECONOMIC PROGRESS IN JAMAICA.=
                        INTER-AMERICAN ECONOMIC AFFAIRS, 7, (AUTUMN 1963),         63

PP. 74-79.
ELNOEL, ELPRNOR
RAVEBH-64-ENC    RAVEN, BH          GALLO, PS
THE EFFECTS OF NOMINATING CONVENTIONS, ELECTIONS, AND
    REFERENCE GROUP IDENTIFICATION UPON THE PERCEPTIONS
    OF POLITICAL FIGURES (UNITED STATES).=
HUMAN RELATIONS, 18, (AUGUST 1965), PP. 217-231.          64
ELNOEL, ELPRNOR
RAY,OA-61-IRA    RAY, OA
THE IMPERIAL RUSSIAN ARMY OFFICER.=
POLITICAL SCIENCE QUARTERLY, 76, (DECEMBER 1961),          61
    PP. 576-592.
COMEL, ELEL, ELPRNOR
RAYMJ  -64-PPU    RAYMOND, J
POWER AT THE PENTAGON (UNITED STATES).=
NEW YORK, HARPER AND ROW, 1964.
ELEL                                                       64
READHA-57-SIT    READ, HA
SECULARISM AND ISLAM IN TURKISH POLITICS.=
CURRENT HISTORY, N.S., 32, (JUNE 1957), PP. 333-338.       57
ELEL, ELNOEL, ELPRNOR
READKE-60-LCN    READ, KE
LEADERSHIP AND CONSENSUS IN A NEW GUINEA SOCIETY.=
AMERICAN ANTHROPOLOGIST, 61, (JUNE 1960), PP. 425-436.     60
COMEL, ELNOEL, ELPRNOR
READM  -55-ESC    READ, M
EDUCATION AND SOCIAL CHANGE IN TROPICAL AREAS.=
LONDON, NELSON, 1955.
COMEL, ELEL, ELNOEL                                        55
REAGMD-61-PSF    REAGAN, MD
THE POLITICAL STRUCTURE OF THE FEDERAL RESERVE SYSTEM
    (UNITED STATES).=
THE AMERICAN POLITICAL SCIENCE REVIEW, 55, (MARCH 1961),   61
    PP. 64-76.
COMEL, ELEL
RECOW  -54-NIN    RECORD, W
THE NEGRO INTELLECTUAL AND NEGRO NATIONALISM
    (UNITED STATES).=
SOCIAL FORCES, 33, (OCTOBER 1954), PP. 10-18.              54
COMEL, ELPRNOR
RECOW  -56-CRF    RECORD, W
COMMUNITY AND RACIAL FACTORS IN INTELLECTUAL ROLES
    (UNITED STATES).=
SOCIOLOGY AND SOCIAL RESEARCH, 41, (SEPTEMBER-OCTOBER      56
    1956), PP. 33-38.
COMEL, ELPRNOR
REDDPB-65-FKT    REDDAWAY, PB
THE FALL OF KHRUSHCHEV -- TENTATIVE ANALYSIS
    (SOVIET UNION).=
SURVEY--A JOURNAL OF SOVIET AND EAST EUROPEAN STUDIES,     65
    56, (JULY 1965), PP. 11-30.
ELEL, ELPRNOR
REDDPB-66-AIB    REDDAWAY, PB
ASPECTS OF IDEOLOGICAL BELIEF IN THE SOVIET UNION.=
SOVIET STUDIES, 17, (APRIL 1966), PP. 473-783.            66
ELPRNOR
REDFES-60-CAC    REDFORD, ES
A CASE ANALYSIS OF CONGRESSIONAL ACTIVITY -- CIVIL
    AVIATION, 1957-1958.=
THE JOURNAL OF POLITICS, 22, (MAY 1960), PP. 228-258.      60
ELEL, ELNOEL
REESAM-64-TCS    REES, AM          SMITH, T
TOWN COUNCILLORS -- A STUDY OF BARKING (GREAT BRITAIN).=
LONDON, THE ACTION SOCIETY TRUST, 1964.                   64
COMEL, ELEL, ELPRNOR
REESG  -63-AGG    REES, G
AMATEURS AND GENTLEMEN (GREAT BRITAIN).=
ENCOUNTER, 21, (JULY 1963), PP. 20-25.                    63
COMEL, ELEL, ELNOEL
REEVWD-52-PAS    REEVE, WD
PUBLIC ADMINISTRATION IN SIAM.=
NEW YORK, THE ROYAL INSTITUTE OF INTERNATIONAL AFFAIRS,   52
    1952.
COMEL
REINR  -62-UEG    REINHARDT, R
THE UNIVERSITIES IN EAST GERMANY.=
SURVEY--A JOURNAL OF SOVIET AND EAST EUROPEAN STUDIES,     62
    40, (JANUARY 1962), PP. 68-76.
COMEL, ELEL
REISEO-65-JC    REISCHAUER, EO
THE JAPANESE CHARACTER.=
EO REISCHAUER (ED), 3RD ED, THE UNITED STATES AND JAPAN,   65
    CAMBRIDGE, HARVARD UNIVERSITY PRESS, 1965, PP.
ELEL, ELNOEL, ELPRNOR

REISEO-65-USJ    REISCHAUER, EO
                 THE UNITED STATES AND JAPAN.=
                 CAMBRIDGE, HARVARD UNIVERSITY PRESS, 1965.                    65
                 ELEL, ELNOEL, ELPRNOR
REISL -49-SRC    REISSMAN, L
                 A STUDY OF ROLE CONCEPTIONS IN BUREAUCRACY
                    (UNITED STATES).=
                 SOCIAL FORCES, 27, (MARCH 1949), PP. 305-310.                 49
                 ELPRNOR
REISL -56-LCP    REISSMAN, L
                 LIFE CAREERS, POWER AND THE PROFESSIONS -- THE RETIRED
                    ARMY GENERAL (UNITED STATES).=
                 AMERICAN SOCIOLOGICAL REVIEW, 21, (APRIL 1956),               56
                    PP. 215-221.
                 COMEL
REISL -59-CAS    REISSMAN, L
                 CLASS IN AMERICAN SOCIETY.=
                 GLENCOE, THE FREE PRESS, 1959.                                59
                 GNELTH, DEFEL, COMEL, ELEL, ELNOEL, ELPRNOR, METEL
REY,L -57-ILR    REY, L
                 INTELLECTUAL AND LITERARY REVIVAL IN POLAND.=
                 PROBLEMS OF COMMUNISM, 6, (NOVEMBER-DECEMBER 1957),           57
                    PP. 26-33.
                 ELEL, ELPRNOR
REYMK -62-OSE    REYMAN, K        SINGER, H
                 THE ORIGINS AND SIGNIFICANCE OF EAST EUROPEAN
                    REVISIONISM.=
                 L LABEDZ (ED), REVISIONISM, ESSAYS ON THE HISTORY            62
                 OF MARXIST IDEAS, NEW YORK, FREDERICK A PRAEGER,
                 1962, PP. 215-222.
                 ELEL, ELNOEL, ELPRNOR
RF       -52-NTU RF
                 NATIONALISM AND THE TRADE UNION IN FRENCH NORTH AFRICA.=
                 THE WORLD TODAY, 9, (JUNE 1952), PP. 249-257.                 52
                 ELPRNOR
RHYNEH-58-PPD    RHYNE, EH
                 POLITICAL PARTIES AND DECISION MAKING IN THREE SOUTHERN
                    COUNTIES (UNITED STATES).=
                 THE AMERICAN POLITICAL SCIENCE REVIEW, 52, (DECEMBER         58
                    1958), PP. 1091-1107.
                 COMEL, ELEL, ELNOEL
RIBED -67-USD    RIBEIRO, D
                 UNIVERSITIES AND SOCIAL DEVELOPMENT (LATIN AMERICA).=
                 SM LIPSET AND A SOLARI (EDS), ELITES IN LATIN AMERICA,       67
                 NEW YORK, OXFORD UNIVERSITY PRESS, 1967, PP. 343-381.
                 ELEL, ELNOEL, ELPRNOR
RICHAI-59-EAC    RICHARDS, AI (ED)
                 EAST AFRICAN CHIEFS -- A STUDY OF POLITICAL DEVELOPMENT
                    IN SOME UGANDA AND TANGANYIKA TRIBES.=
                 NEW YORK, FREDERICK A PRAEGER, 1959.                          59
                 ELEL, ELNOEL, ELPRNOR, METEL
RICHPG-56-SPA    RICHARDS, PG
                 A STUDY IN POLITICAL APPRENTICESHIP (GREAT BRITAIN).=
                 PARLIAMENTARY AFFAIRS, 9, (SUMMER 1956), PP. 353-357.         56
                 COMEL, ELEL, ELNOEL
RICHPG-59-HMS    RICHARDS, PG
                 HONORABLE MEMBERS -- A STUDY OF THE BRITISH BACKBENCHERS
                    (GREAT BRITAIN).=
                 NEW YORK, FREDERICK A PRAEGER, 1959.                          59
                 COMEL, ELEL, ELNOEL, ELPRNOR
RICHPG-63-PBG    RICHARDS, PG
                 PATRONAGE IN BRITISH GOVERNMENT.=
                 TORONTO, UNIVERSITY OF TORONTO PRESS, 1963.                   63
                 COMEL, ELEL, ELNOEL
RICHRJ-67-RDA    RICHARDSON, RJ       VINES, KN
                 REVIEW, DISSENT AND THE APPELLATE PROCESS -- A POLITICAL
                    INTERPRETATION (UNITED STATES).=
                 THE JOURNAL OF POLITICS, 29, (AUGUST 1967), PP. 597-616.  67
                 ELEL, ELNOEL, ELPRNOR
RIENA -57-CC     RIENCOURT, A
                 THE COMING CAESARS.=
                 NEW YORK, COWARD-MCCANN, 1957.                                57
                 GNELTH, DEFEL, COMEL, ELEL, ELNOEL
RIESD -56-OTI    RIESMAN, D
                 ORBITS OF TOLERANCE, INTERVIEWERS, AND ELITES
                    (UNITED STATES).=
                 THE PUBLIC OPINION QUARTERLY, 20, (SPRING 1956),             56
                    PP. 49-73.
                 ELEL, ELNOEL, METEL
RIESD -59-PPP    RIESMAN, D
                 PRIVATE PEOPLE AND PUBLIC POLICY (UNITED STATES).=
                 BULLETIN OF ATOMIC SCIENTISTS, 15, (MAY 1959), PP.          59
                    203-208.
                 ELEL, ELNOEL

RIEZK -54-PDM  RIEZLER, K
               POLITICAL DECISIONS IN MODERN SOCIETY.=
               ETHICS, 64, (JANUARY 1954), PP. 1-55.
                                                                    54
               COMEL, ELEL, ELNOEL, ELPRNOR
RIGBTH-53-CCS  RIGBY, TH
               CHANGING COMPOSITION OF THE SUPREME SOVIET.=
               THE POLITICAL QUARTERLY, 24, (JULY 1953), PP. 307-316.   53
               COMEL, ELPRNOR
RIGBTH-56-SOR  RIGBY, TH
               SOCIAL ORIENTATION OF RECRUITMENT AND DISTRIBUTION OF
                  MEMBERSHIP IN THE COMMUNIST PARTY OF THE SOVIET UNION.=
               THE AMERICAN SLAVIC AND EAST EUROPEAN REVIEW, 16,       56
                  (OCTOBER 1957), PP. 275-290.
               ELNOEL, ELPRNOR
RIGBTH-62-HSI  RIGBY, TH
               HOW STRONG IS THE LEADER (SOVIET UNION).=
               PROBLEMS OF COMMUNISM, 11, (SEPTEMBER-OCTOBER 1962),    62
                  PP. 1-8.
               ELEL
RIGBTH-62-PMU  RIGBY, TH              CHURCHWARD, LG
               POLICY-MAKING IN THE U.S.S.R. 1953-1961 -- TWO VIEWS
                  (SOVIET UNION).=
               MELBOURNE, LANDSDOWNE PRESS, 1962.
                                                                    62
               ELEL, ELNOEL, ELPRNOR
RIGBTH-63-ELA  RIGBY, TH
               THE EXTENT AND LIMITS OF AUTHORITY (SOVIET UNION).=
               PROBLEMS OF COMMUNISM, 12, (SEPTEMBER-OCTOBER 1963),    63
                  PP. 36-40.
               ELEL, ELNOEL, ELPRNOR
RIGBTH-64-TMO  RIGBY, TH
               TRADITIONAL, MARKET, AND ORGANIZATIONAL SOCIETIES AND
                  THE USSR.=
               WORLD POLITICS, 16, (JULY 1964), PP. 539-557.
                                                                    64
               DEFEL
RIGGFW-61-PSF  RIGGS, FW
               PRISMATIC SOCIETY AND FINANCIAL ADMINISTRATION.=
               ADMINISTRATIVE SCIENCE QUARTERLY, 5, (1960-1961),       61
                  PP. 1-46.
               DEFEL
RIGGFW-62-SME  RIGGS, FW
               THE SALA MODEL -- AN ECOLOGICAL APPROACH TO THE STUDY
                  OF COMPARATIVE ADMINISTRATION.=
               PHILIPPINE JOURNAL OF PUBLIC ADMINISTRATION, 6,         62
                  (JANUARY 1962), PP. 3-16.
               METEL
RIGGFW-63-BPD  RIGGS, FW
               BUREAUCRATS AND POLITICAL DEVELOPMENT --
                  A PARADOXICAL VIEW.=
               J LA PALOMBARA  (ED), BUREAUCRACY AND POLITICAL         63
                  DEVELOPMENT, PRINCETON, PRINCETON UNIVERSITY
                  PRESS, 1963, PP. 120-167.
               COMEL, ELEL, ELNOEL, ELPRNOR
RIGGFW-64-ADC  RIGGS, FW
               ADMINISTRATION IN DEVELOPING COUNTRIES.=
               BOSTON, HOUGHTON MIFFLIN COMPANY, 1964.                 64
               DEFEL, COMEL, ELEL, ELNOEL, ELPRNOR
RIGGFW-66-TMB  RIGGS, FW
               THAILAND -- THE MODERNIZATION OF A BUREAUCRATIC POLITY.=
               HONOLULU, EAST-WEST PRESS, 1966.                        66
               DEFEL, COMEL, ELEL, ELNOEL, ELPRNOR
RIKEWH-58-VMI  RIKER, WH
               VOTING METHODS AND IRRATIONALITY IN LEGISLATIVE
                  DECISIONS (UNITED STATES).=
               THE AMERICAN POLITICAL SCIENCE REVIEW, 52, (JUNE 1958), 58
                  PP. 349-366.
               ELEL, METEL
RIKEWH-59-MDS  RIKER, WH
               A METHOD FOR DETERMINING THE SIGNIFICANCE OF ROLL
                  CALLS IN VOTING BODIES.=
               JC WAHLKE AND H EULAU, (EDS), LEGISLATIVE BEHAVIOR--A    59
                  READER IN THEORY AND RESEARCH, GLENCOE, ILLINOIS,
                  THE FREE PRESS, 1959, PP. 377-384.
               METEL
RIKEWH-59-TAP  RIKER, WH
               A TEST OF THE ADEQUACY OF THE POWER INDEX.=
               BEHAVIORAL SCIENCE, 4, (APRIL 1959), PP. 120-131.       59
               METEL
RIKEWH-62-SCR  RIKER, WH              NIEMI, D
               THE STABILITY OF COALITIONS ON ROLL CALLS IN THE
                  HOUSE OF REPRESENTATIVES (UNITED STATES).=
               THE AMERICAN POLITICAL SCIENCE REVIEW, 56, (MARCH 1962), 62
                  PP. 58-65.
               ELPRNOR
RIKEWH-62-TPC  RIKER, WH

```
                    THE THEORY OF POLITICAL COALITIONS.=
                    NEW HAVEN, CONNECTICUT, YALE UNIVERSITY PRESS, 1962.      62
                    DEFEL, ELEL, ELPRNOR
RINGBB-52-PEI   RINGER, BB              SILLS, DL
                    POLITICAL EXTREMISTS IN IRAN -- A SECONDARY
                      ANALYSIS OF COMMUNICATIONS DATA.=
                    THE PUBLIC OPINION QUARTERLY, 16, (WINTER 1952),          52
                      PP. 689-701.
                    COMEL, ELEL, ELNOEL, ELPRNOR
RINTM -58-PGF   RINTALA, M
                    THE PROBLEM OF GENERATIONS IN FINNISH COMMUNISM.=
                    THE AMERICAN SLAVIC AND EAST EUROPEAN REVIEW, 17,         58
                      (APRIL 1958), PP. 190-202.
                    COMEL, ELEL, ELPRNOR
RINTM -62-IEP   RINTALA, M
                    AN IMAGE OF EUROPEAN POLITICS -- THE PEOPLE'S PATRIOTIC
                      MOVEMENT (FINLAND).=
                    JOURNAL OF CENTRAL EUROPEAN AFFAIRS, 22, (OCTOBER 1962),  62
                      PP. 308-316.
                    COMEL, ELNOEL, ELPRNOR
RINTM -62-TGE   RINTALA, M
                    THREE GENERATIONS -- THE EXTREME RIGHT WING IN FINNISH
                      POLITICS.=
                    BLOOMINGTON, INDIANA UNIVERSITY PRESS, 1962.             62
                    COMEL, ELEL, ELPRNOR
RIPLRB-64-PWO   RIPLEY, RB
                    THE PARTY WHIP ORGANIZATIONS IN THE UNITED STATES
                      HOUSE OF REPRESENTATIVES.=
                    THE AMERICAN POLITICAL SCIENCE REVIEW, 58, (SEPTEMBER    64
                      1964), PP. 561-576.
                    ELEL
RIPPJF-65-LAS   RIPPY, JF
                    LATIN AMERICA'S POSTWAR GOLPES DE ESTADO.=
                    INTER-AMERICAN ECONOMIC AFFAIRS, 19, (WINTER 1965),      65
                      PP. 73-80.
                    ELEL
RITTG -57-MPG   RITTER, G
                    THE MILITARY AND POLITICS IN GERMANY.=
                    JOURNAL OF CENTRAL EUROPEAN AFFAIRS, 17, (JULY 1957),    57
                      PP. 259-271.
                    ELEL, ELPRNOR
RITVH -60-TWC   RITVO, H
                    TOTALITARIANISM WITHOUT COERCION (SOVIET UNION).=
                    PROBLEMS OF COMMUNISM, 9, (NOVEMBER-DECEMBER 1960),      60
                      PP. 19-29.
                    ELEL, ELNOEL
RITVH -61-TFP   RITVO, H
                    TWENTY-FIRST PARTY CONGRESS (SOVIET UNION) -- BEFORE AND
                      AFTER -- PART ONE -- PART TWO.=
                    THE AMERICAN SLAVIC AND EAST EUROPEAN REVIEW, 20,        61
                      (APRIL 1961, OCTOBER 1961), PP. 203-219, PP. 436-453.
                    COMEL, ELEL, ELNOEL, ELPRNOR
RITVH -63-DDS   RITVO, H
                    THE DYNAMICS OF DESTALINIZATION (SOVIET UNION).=
                    SURVEY--A JOURNAL OF SOVIET AND EAST EUROPEAN STUDIES,   63
                      47, (APRIL 1963), PP. 13-23.
                    ELEL
RITVH -63-PCR   RITVO, H
                    PARTY CONTROLS REORGANIZED (SOVIET UNION).=
                    SURVEY--A JOURNAL OF SOVIET AND EAST EUROPEAN STUDIES,   63
                      49, (OCTOBER 1963), PP. 78-89.
                    ELEL, ELNOEL
RIVLB -52-TNM   RIVLIN, B
                    THE TUNISIAN NATIONALIST MOVEMENT -- FOUR DECADES
                      OF EVOLUTION.=
                    THE MIDDLE EAST JOURNAL, 6, (1952), PP. 167-193.         52
                    ELEL, ELNOEL, ELPRNOR
ROBEA -65-BPS   ROBERTS, A
                    BUDDHISM AND POLITICS IN SOUTH VIETNAM.=
                    THE WORLD TODAY, 21, (JUNE 1965), PP. 240-250.           65
                    ELEL, ELNOEL, ELPRNOR
ROBEA -66-BWV   ROBERTS, A
                    THE BUDDHISTS, THE WAR, AND THE VIETCONG.=
                    THE WORLD TODAY, 22, (MAY 1966), PP. 214-222.            66
                    ELEL
ROBEBC-56-TUG   ROBERTS, BC
                    TRADE UNIONS, GOVERNMENT AND ADMINISTRATION IN
                      GREAT BRITAIN.=
                    CAMBRIDGE, HARVARD UNIVERSITY PRESS, 1956.               56
                    ELEL
ROBED -64-MSU   ROBERT, D
                    MOSCOW STATE UNIVERSITY (SOVIET UNION).=
                    SURVEY--A JOURNAL OF SOVIET AND EAST EUROPEAN STUDIES,   64
                      51, (APRIL 1964), PP. 24-31.
```

```
                    ELPRNOR
ROBIJA-59-DMH       ROBINSON, JA
                    DECISION MAKING IN THE HOUSE RULES COMMITTEE
                       (UNITED STATES).=
                    ADMINISTRATIVE SCIENCE QUARTERLY, 3, (1958-1959),            59
                       PP. 73-86.
                    ELEL, ELPRNOR
ROBIJA-59-RRC       ROBINSON, JA
                    THE ROLE OF THE RULES COMMITTEE IN ARRANGING THE PROGRAM
                       OF THE U.S. HOUSE OF REPRESENTATIVES (UNITED STATES).=
                    THE WESTERN POLITICAL QUARTERLY, 12, (SEPTEMBER 1959),       59
                       PP. 653-669.
                    ELEL
ROBIJA-60-SIA       ROBINSON, JA
                    SURVEY INTERVIEWING AMONG MEMBERS OF CONGRESS
                       (UNITED STATES).=
                    THE PUBLIC OPINION QUARTERLY, 24, (SPRING 1960),             60
                       PP. 127-138.
                    METEL
ROBIJA-61-PSP       ROBINSON, JA
                    PROCESS SATISFACTION AND POLICY APPROVAL IN STATE
                       DEPARTMENT -- CONGRESSIONAL RELATIONS (UNITED STATES).=
                    THE AMERICAN JOURNAL OF SOCIOLOGY, 67, (NOVEMBER 1961),      61
                       PP. 278-283.
                    ELEL, ELPRNOR
ROBIJA-62-CFP       ROBINSON, JA
                    CONGRESS AND FOREIGN POLICY-MAKING -- A STUDY IN
                       LEGISLATIVE INFLUENCE AND INITIATIVE (UNITED STATES).=
                    HOMEWOOD, ILLINOIS, THE DORSEY PRESS, 1962.
                    COMEL, ELEL, ELPRNOR, METEL                                  62
ROBIJA-63-HRC       ROBINSON, JA
                    THE HOUSE RULES COMMITTEE (UNITED STATES).=
                    INDIANAPOLIS, BOBBS-MERRILL, 1963.
                    ELEL, ELPRNOR                                                63
ROBIJA-65-DMI       ROBINSON, JA           SNYDER, RC
                    DECISION-MAKING IN INTERNATIONAL POLITICS.=
                    HC KELMAN, (ED), INTERNATIONAL BEHAVIOR-- A                  65
                       SOCIAL-PSYCHOLOGICAL ANALYSIS, NEW YORK, HOLT,
                       RINEHART AND WINSTON, 1965, PP. 435-463.
                    COMEL, ELEL, ELNOEL, ELPRNOR
ROBIK -58-CRF       ROBINSON, K
                    CONSTITUTIONAL REFORM IN FRENCH TROPICAL AFRICA.=
                    POLITICAL STUDIES, 6, (FALL 1958), PP. 45-69.                58
                    ELEL, ELPRNOR
ROBSWA-46-LDG       ROBSON, WA
                    LEGISLATIVE DRAFTSMANSHIP (GREAT BRITAIN).=
                    THE POLITICAL QUARTERLY, 17, (OCTOBER 1946), PP. 330-342. 46
                    ELEL
ROBSWA-48-MGG       ROBSON, WA
                    THE MACHINERY OF GOVERNMENT 1939-1947 (GREAT BRITAIN).=
                    THE POLITICAL QUARTERLY, 19, (JANUARY 1948), PP. 1-13.       48
                    COMEL, ELEL, ELNOEL
ROBSWA-50-GBP       ROBSON, WA
                    THE GOVERNING BOARD OF THE PUBLIC CORPORATION
                       (GREAT BRITAIN).=
                    THE POLITICAL QUARTERLY, 21, (APRIL 1950), PP. 135-149.      50
                    COMEL, ELEL, ELNOEL, ELPRNOR
ROBSWA-53-LLG       ROBSON, WA
                    LABOUR AND LOCAL GOVERNMENT (GREAT BRITAIN).=
                    THE POLITICAL QUARTERLY, 24, (JANUARY 1953), PP. 45-69.      53
                    ELEL, ELNOEL
ROBSWA-56-CSB       ROBSON, WA (ED)
                    THE CIVIL SERVICE IN BRITAIN AND FRANCE.=
                    NEW YORK, MACMILLAN AND CO., 1956.
                    COMEL, ELEL                                                  56
ROBSWA-64-GG        ROBSON, WA
                    THE GOVERNORS AND THE GOVERNED.=
                    BATON ROUGE, LOUSIANA STATE UNIVERSITY PRESS, 1964.          64
                    ELEL, ELNOEL, ELPRNOR
ROCHJP-55-BEE       ROCHE, JP
                    THE BUREAUCRAT AND THE ENTHUSIAST -- AN EXPLORATION OF
                       THE LEADERSHIP OF SOCIAL MOVEMENTS (UNITED STATES).=
                    THE WESTERN POLITICAL QUARTERLY, 8, (JUNE 1955),             55
                       PP. 248-261.
                    COMEL, ELPRNOR
ROCHJP-58-PSS       ROCHE, JP
                    POLITICAL SCIENCE AND SCIENCE FICTION
                       (UNITED STATES, JUDICIARY).=
                    THE AMERICAN POLITICAL SCIENCE REVIEW, 52, (DECEMBER         58
                       1958), PP. 1026-1029.
                    METEL
RODND -50-NCP       RODNICK, D             RODNICK, E
                    NOTES ON COMMUNIST PERSONALITY TYPES IN CZECHOSLOVAKIA.=
                    THE PUBLIC OPINION QUARTERLY, 14, (SPRING 1950),             50
```

                              PP. 81-88.
                              COMEL, ELPRNOR
ROFFWR-67-OMN    ROFF, WR
                 THE ORIGINS OF MALAY NATIONALISM.=
                 NEW HAVEN, YALE UNIVERSITY PRESS, 1967.                    67
                 COMEL, ELEL, ELNOEL, ELPRNOR
ROGEH -65-ERH    ROGERS, H            WEBER, E (EDS)
                 THE EUROPEAN RIGHT -- A HISTORICAL PROFILE.=
                 BERKELEY AND LOS ANGELES, UNIVERSITY OF CALIFORNIA         65
                    PRESS, 1965.
                 COMEL, ELPRNOR
ROGEL -49-PPO    ROGERS, L
                 THE POLLSTERS -- PUBLIC OPINION, POLITICS, AND
                    DEMOCRATIC LEADERSHIP (UNITED STATES).=
                 NEW YORK, ALFRED A KNOPF, 1949.                            49
                 ELEL, ELNOEL
ROGOAA-55-LGB    ROGOW, AA
                 THE LABOUR GOVERNMENT AND BRITISH INDUSTRY.=
                 ITHACA, CORNELL UNIVERSITY PRESS, 1955.                    55
                 ELEL
ROGOAA-63-PCR    ROGOW, AA            LASSWELL, HD
                 POWER, CORRUPTION, AND RECTITUDE.=
                 ENGLEWOOD CLIFFS, PRENTICE-HALL, 1963.                     63
                 ELEL, ELNOEL
ROMAOI-60-DMA    ROMANO, OI
                 DONSHIP IN A MEXICAN - AMERICAN COMMUNITY IN TEXAS.=
                 AMERICAN ANTHROPOLOGIST, 62, (DECEMBER 1960), PP. 966-976.60
                 COMEL
ROMNS -47-LDL    ROMNALDI, S
                 LABOR AND DEMOCRACY IN LATIN AMERICA.=
                 FOREIGN AFFAIRS, 25, (APRIL 1947), PP. 477-489.            47
                 COMEL, ELEL, ELNOEL, ELPRNOR
ROSEAM-62-APC    ROSE, AM
                 ALIENATION AND PARTICIPATION -- A COMPARISON OF GROUP
                    LEADERS AND THE MASS (UNITED STATES).=
                 AMERICAN SOCIOLOGICAL REVIEW, 27, (DECEMBER 1962),         62
                    PP. 834-841.
                 COMEL, ELNOEL, ELPRNOR
ROSEAM-67-PSP    ROSE, AM
                 THE POWER STRUCTURE -- POLITICAL PROCESS IN AMERICAN
                    SOCIETY.=
                 NEW YORK, OXFORD UNIVERSITY PRESS, 1967.                   67
                 DEFEL, COMEL, ELEL, ELNOEL, ELPRNOR, METEL
ROSECS-55-FPT    ROSENTHAL, CS
                 THE FUNCTIONS OF POLISH TRADE UNIONS -- THEIR PROFESSION
                    TOWARD THE SOVIET PATTERN.=
                 THE BRITISH JOURNAL OF SOCIOLOGY, 6, (SEPTEMBER 1955),     55
                    PP. 264-276.
                 ELEL
ROSEDB-66-DFP    ROSENTHAL, DB
                 DEFERENCE AND FRIENDSHIP PATTERNS IN TWO INDIAN
                    MUNICIPAL COUNCILS.=
                 SOCIAL FORCES, 45, (DECEMBER 1966), PP) 178-192.           66
                 COMEL, ELEL, ELPRNOR
ROSEDB-66-FAI    ROSENTHAL, DB
                 FACTIONS AND ALLIANCES IN INDIAN CITY POLITICS.=
                 MIDWEST JOURNAL OF POLITICAL SCIENCE, 10, (AUGUST 1966),   66
                    PP. 321-347.
                 COMEL, ELEL
ROSEH -66-BAA    ROSENBURG, H
                 BUREAUCRACY, ARISTOCRACY, AND AUTOCRACY -- THE
                    PRUSSIAN EXPERIENCE, 1660-1815.=
                 BOSTON, BEACON PRESS, 1966.                                66
                 ELEL
ROSEJN-60-OMO    ROSENAU, JN
                 OPINION-MAKING AND OPINION MAKERS IN FOREIGN POLICY
                    (UNITED STATES).=
                 NEW YORK, RANDOM HOUSE, 1960.                              60
                 ELEL, ELNOEL
ROSEJN-61-POF    ROSENAU, JN
                 PUBLIC OPINION AND FOREIGN POLICY (UNITED STATES).=
                 NEW YORK, RANDOM HOUSE, 1961.                              61
                 DEFEL, ELNOEL, ELPRNOR
ROSEJN-62-CBA    ROSENAU, JN
                 CONSENSUS-BUILDING IN THE AMERICAN NATIONAL COMMUNITY
                    -- SOME HYPOTHESES AND SOME SUPPORTING DATA.=
                 THE JOURNAL OF POLITICS, 24, (NOVEMBER 1962),              62
                    PP. 639-661.
                 ELEL, ELNOEL
ROSEJN-63-NLF    ROSENAU, JN
                 NATIONAL LEADERSHIP AND FOREIGN POLICY -- A CASE STUDY
                    IN THE MOBILIZATION OF PUBLIC SUPPORT (UNITED STATES).=
                 PRINCETON, PRINCETON UNIVERSITY PRESS, 1963.               63
                 ELEL, ELNOEL, METEL

ROSELE-63-NSE    ROSE, LE
                 NEPAL'S EXPERIMENT WITH 'TRADITIONAL DEMOCRACY'.=
                 PACIFIC AFFAIRS, (SPRING 1963), PP. 16-31.
                 ELEL, ELNOEL                                               63
ROSER -61-BGS    ROSE, R
                 THE BOW GROUP'S ROLE IN BRITISH POLITICS.=
                 THE WESTERN POLITICAL QUARTERLY, 14, (DECEMBER 1961),      61
                    PP. 868-878.
                 ELEL, ELPRNOR
ROSER -62-PIE    ROSE, R
                 THE POLITICAL IDEAS OF ENGLISH PARTY ACTIVISTS.=
                 THE AMERICAN POLITICAL SCIENCE REVIEW, 56, (JUNE 1962),    62
                    PP. 360-371.
                 ELPRNOR
ROSER -63-CPL    ROSE, R
                 COMPLEXITIES OF PARTY LEADERSHIP (GREAT BRITAIN).=
                 PARLIAMENTARY AFFAIRS, 16, (SUMMER 1963), PP. 257-273.     63
                 COMEL, ELEL, ELNOEL
ROSER -64-PFT    ROSE, R
                 PARTIES, FACTIONS, AND TENDENCIES IN BRITAIN.,
                 POLITICAL STUDIES, 12, (1964), PP. 33-46.                  64
                 DEFEL, ELEL
ROSER -66-ETM    ROSE, R
                 ENGLAND -- A TRADITIONALLY MODERN POLITICAL CULTURE.=
                 LW PYE AND S VERBA (EDS), POLITICAL CULTURE AND            66
                    POLITICAL DEVELOPMENT, PRINCETON, PRINCETON UNIVERSITY
                    PRESS, 1966, PP. 83-129.
                 COMEL, ELEL, ELNOEL, ELPRNOR
ROSER -66-SBP    ROSE, R (ED)

                 STUDIES IN BRITISH POLITICS -- A READER IN POLITICAL
                    SOCIOLOGY.=
                 NEW YORK, ST MARTIN-S PRESS, 1966.
                 COMEL, ELEL, ELNOEL, ELPRNOR                               66
ROSERM-57-PCP    ROSENZWEIG, RM
                 THE POLITICIAN AND THE CAREER IN POLITICS
                    (UNITED STATES).=
                 MIDWEST JOURNAL OF POLITICAL SCIENCE, 1, (AUGUST 1957),    57
                    PP. 163-172.
                 COMEL, ELEL, ELNOEL
ROSERM-58-PCU    ROSENZWEIG, RM
                 POLITICIAN AND CONSTITUENCY (UNITED STATES).=
                 PROD (THE AMERICAN BEHAVIORAL SCIENTIST), 1,               58
                    (MAY 1958), PP. 29-32.
                 ELNOEL
ROSES -56-PDO    ROSE, S
                 POLICY DECISION IN OPPOSITION (GREAT BRITAIN).=
                 POLITICAL STUDIES, 4, (JUNE 1956), PP. 128-138.            56
                 ELEL, ELPRNOR
ROSHM -56-PPS    ROSHWALD, M
                 POLITICAL PARTIES AND SOCIAL CLASSES IN ISRAEL.=
                 SOCIAL RESEARCH, 23, (SUMMER 1956), PP. 199-218.           56
                 ELNOEL
ROSIEJ-65-MAO    ROSI, EJ
                 MAN AND ATTENTIVE OPINION ON NUCLEAR WEAPON TESTS AND
                    FALLOUT, 1954-1963 (UNITED STATES).=
                 THE PUBLIC OPINION QUARTERLY, 29, (SUMMER 1965),           65
                    PP. 280-297.
                 ELEL, ELNOEL
ROSSC -50-WDP    ROSSITER, C
                 WAR, DEPRESSION, AND THE PRESIDENCY,
                    1933-1950 (UNITED STATES).=
                 SOCIAL RESEARCH, 17, (WINTER 1950), PP. 417-440.           50
                 ELEL
ROSSCL-49-CDA    ROSSITER, CL
                 CONSTITUTIONAL DICTATORSHIP IN THE ATOMIC AGE
                    (UNITED STATES).=
                 REVIEW OF POLITICS, 11, (OCTOBER 1949), PP. 395-418.       49
                 ELNOEL
ROSSCL-56-AP     ROSSITER, CL
                 THE AMERICAN PRESIDENCY.=
                 NEW YORK, HARCOURT, BRACE AND COMPANY, 1956.               56
                 ELEL, ELNOEL
ROSSPH-57-CDM    ROSSI, PH
                 COMMUNITY DECISION-MAKING (UNITED STATES).=
                 ADMINISTRATIVE SCIENCE QUARTERLY, 1, (MARCH 1957),         57
                    PP. 415-443.
                 METEL
ROSSPH-58-CDM    ROSSI, PH
                 COMMUNITY DECISION MAKING (UNITED STATES).=
                 R YOUNG (ED), APPROACHES TO THE STUDY OF POLITICS,         58
                    EVANSTON, NORTHWESTERN UNIVERSITY PRESS, 1958.
                 METEL
ROSSPH-60-PCS    ROSSI, PH

                    POWER AND COMMUNITY STRUCTURE (UNITED STATES).=
                    MIDWEST JOURNAL OF POLITICAL SCIENCE, 4, (NOVEMBER 1960), 60
                        PP. 390-401.
                    ELEL, ELNOEL, METEL
ROSSR -62-PND   ROSSOW, R
                    THE PROFESSIONALIZATION OF THE NEW DIPLOMACY
                        (UNITED STATES).=
                    WORLD POLITICS, 14, (JULY 1962), PP. 561-575.              62
                    ELPRNOR
ROSSRG-52-EMP   ROSS, RG
                    ELITES AND THE METHODOLOGY OF POLITICS.=
                    THE PUBLIC OPINION QUARTERLY, 16, (SPRING 1952),          52
                        PP. 27-32.
                    METEL
ROTBRI-63-OND   ROTBERG, RI
                    THE ORIGINS OF NATIONALIST DISCONTENT IN EAST AND
                        CENTRAL AFRICA.=
                    THE JOURNAL OF NEGRO HISTORY, 48, (APRIL 1963), PP.       63
                        130-141.
                    ELNOEL, ELPRNOR
ROTHG -63-SDI   ROTH, G
                    THE SOCIAL DEMOCRATS IN IMPERIAL GERMANY -- A STUDY IN
                        WORKING CLASS ISOLATION AND NATIONAL INTEGRATION.=
                    TOTOWA, NEW JERSEY, BEDMINSTER PRESS, 1963.               63
                    ELEL, ELNOEL
ROTHJ -59-CPB   ROTHSCHILD, J
                    THE COMMUNIST PARTY OF BULGARIA.=
                    NEW YORK, COLUMBIA UNIVERSITY PRESS, 1959.                59
                    COMEL, ELEL, ELNOEL, ELPRNOR
ROURFE-60-ASC   ROURKE, FE
                    ADMINISTRATIVE SECRECY -- CONGRESSIONAL DILEMMA
                        (UNITED STATES).=
                    THE AMERICAN POLITICAL SCIENCE REVIEW, 54, (SEPTEMBER     60
                        1960), PP. 684-694.
                    ELEL
ROURFE-65-UNP   ROURKE, FE
                    URBANISM AND THE NATIONAL PARTY ORGANIZATION
                        (UNITED STATES).=
                    THE WESTERN POLITICAL QUARTERLY, 18, (JUNE 1965),         65
                        PP. 149-163.
                    ELNOEL
ROWADC-59-JPS   ROWAT, DC
                    ON JOHN PORTER'S 'BUREAUCRATIC ELITE IN CANADA'.=
                    CANADIAN JOURNAL OF ECONOMICS AND POLITICAL SCIENCE, 25,  59
                        (MAY 1959), PP. 204-207.
                    COMEL, METEL
ROWEET-64-EAC   ROWE, ET
                    THE EMERGING ANTI - COLONIAL CONSENSUS IN THE
                        UNITED NATIONS.=
                    THE JOURNAL OF CONFLICT RESOLUTION, 8, (JUNE 1964),       64
                        PP. 209-230.
                    ELEL, ELPRNOR
ROWSAL-45-BLP   ROWSE, AL
                    THE BRITISH LABOR PARTY -- PROSPECTS AND PORTENTS.=
                    FOREIGN AFFAIRS, 23, (JULY 1945), PP. 658-667.            45
                    ELEL
ROXAGM-63-PBS   ROXAS, GM
                    THE PORK BARREL SYSTEM (PHILIPPINES).=
                    PHILIPPINE JOURNAL OF PUBLIC ADMINISTRATION, 7,           63
                        (OCTOBER 1963), PP. 254-257.
                    ELEL, ELNOEL, ELPRNOR
ROY,NC-58-CSI   ROY, NC
                    THE CIVIL SERVICE OF INDIA.=
                    CALCUTTA, KL MUKHOPADHYAY, 1958.                          58
                    COMEL, ELEL
ROY,R -66-IPC   ROY, R
                    INTRA - PARTY CONFLICT IN THE BIHAR CONGRESS (INDIA).=
                    ASIAN SURVEY, 6, (DECEMBER 1966), PP. 706-715.            66
                    ELEL, ELPRNOR
ROZMS -59-PCA   ROZMARYN, S
                    PARLIAMENTARY CONTROL OF ADMINISTRATIVE ACTIVITES IN THE
                        POLISH PEOPLE'S REPUBLIC.=
                    POLITICAL STUDIES, 7, (1959), PP. 70-85.                  59
                    ELEL
RPH    -55-YLC  RPH                     PK
                    YOUTH LEAGUES IN CENTRAL EUROPE.=
                    THE WORLD TODAY, 11, (SEPTEMBER 1955), PP. 380-390.       55
                    COMEL, ELEL
RS     -53-WGP  RS
                    THE WEST GERMAN POLITICAL PARTIES AND REARMAMENT.=
                    THE WORLD TODAY, 9, (FEBRUARY 1953), PP. 53-64.           53
                    ELEL, ELPRNOR
RUCHLI-66-LNY   RUCHELMAN, LI
                    LAWYERS IN THE NEW YORK STATE LEGISLATURE -- THE URBAN

```
                     FACTOR (UNITED STATES).=
                     MIDWEST JOURNAL OF POLITICAL SCIENCE, 10, (NOVEMBER        66
                     1966), PP. 484-497.
                     COMEL
RUDOLI-64-GPI   RUDOLPH, LI           RUDOLPH, SH
                     GENERALS AND POLITICIANS IN INDIA.=
                     PACIFIC AFFAIRS, 37, (SPRING 1964), PP. 3-19.               64
                     ELEL, ELNOEL
RUECGL-62-CDG   RUECKER, GL           CRANE W
                     CDU DEVIANCY IN THE GERMAN BUNDESTAG.=
                     THE JOURNAL OF POLITICS, 24, (AUGUST 1962), PP. 477-488.    62
                     ELEL, ELNOEL, ELPRNOR
RUNCWG-63-CLO   RUNCIMAN, WG
                     CHARISMATIC LEGITIMACY AND ONE - PARTY RULE IN GHANA.=
                     EUROPEAN JOURNAL OF SOCIOLOGY, 4, (1963), PP. 148-165.      63
                     DEFEL, ELEL, ELPRNOR
RUNCWG-63-EO    RUNCIMAN, WG
                     ELITES AND OLIGARCHIES.=
                     WG RUNCIMAN, SOCIAL SCIENCE AND POLITICAL THEORY,           63
                        CAMBRIDGE, CAMBRIDGE UNIVERSITY PRESS, 1963, PP. 64-88.
                     GNELTH, ELEL, ELNOEL
RUPERA-67-MPS   RUPEN, RA
                     THE MONGOLIAN PEOPLE'S REPUBLIC -- THE SLOW EVOLUTION.=
                     ASIAN SURVEY, 7, (JANUARY 1967), PP. 16-20.                 67
                     COMEL
RUSCTA-59-DSL   RUSCH, TA
                     DYNAMICS OF SOCIALIST LEADERSHIP IN INDIA.=
                     RL PARK AND I TINKER  (ED), LEADERSHIP AND POLITICAL        59
                        INSTITUTIONS IN INDIA, PRINCETON, PRINCETON UNIVERSITY
                        PRESS, 1959, PP. 188-211.
                     ELEL, ELPRNOR
RUSHGB-63-TDE   RUSH, GB
                     TOWARD A DEFINITION OF THE EXTREME RIGHT.=
                     PACIFIC SOCIOLOGICAL REVIEW, 6, (FALL 1963), PP. 64-73.     63
                     DEFEL, COMEL
RUSHM -58-RKS   RUSH, M
                     THE RISE OF KHRUSHCHEV (SOVIET UNION).=
                     WASHINGTON, PUBLIC AFFAIRS PRESS, 1958.                     58
                     ELEL, ELNOEL
RUSHM -59-ECS   RUSH, M
                     ESOTERIC COMMUNICATION IN SOVIET POLITICS.=
                     WORLD POLITICS, 11, (JULY 1959), PP. 614-620.               59
                     ELEL
RUSHM -62-KSP   RUSH, M
                     THE KHRUSHCHEV SUCCESSION PROBLEM (SOVIET UNION).=
                     WORLD POLITICS, 14, (JANUARY 1962), PP. 259-282.            62
                     ELEL
RUSHM -65-PSU   RUSH, M
                     POLITICAL SUCCESSION IN THE USSR.=
                     NEW YORK, COLUMBIA UNIVERSITY PRESS, 1965.                  65
                     ELEL, ELNOEL
RUSSBM-62-ICL   RUSSETT, BM
                     INTERNATIONAL COMMUNICATION AND LEGISLATIVE BEHAVIOR --
                        THE SENATE AND THE HOUSE OF COMMONS (UNITED STATES,
                        GREAT BRITAIN).=
                     THE JOURNAL OF CONFLICT RESOLUTION, 6, (DECEMBER 1962),     62
                        PP. 291-307.
                     ELPRNOR, METEL
RUSTA -65-TMT   RUSTOW, A
                     TURKEY -- THE MODERNITY OF TRADITION.=
                     L PYE AND S VERBA (EDS), POLITICAL CULTURE AND              65
                        POLITICAL DEVELOPMENT, PRINCETON, PRINCETON UNIVERSITY
                        PRESS, (1965), PP. 171-198.
                     COMEL, ELEL, ELNOEL, ELPRNOR
RUSTD -63-TSS   RUSTOW, D
                     TURKEY'S SECOND TRY AT DEMOCRACY.=
                     YALE REVIEW,52, (JUNE 1963), PP 518-538.                    63
                     ELEL, ELNOEL
RUSTDA-59-AFT   RUSTOW, DA
                     THE ARMY AND THE FOUNDING OF THE TURKISH REPUBLIC.=
                     WORLD POLITICS, 11, (JULY 1959), PP. 513-552.               59
                     COMEL, ELEL, ELNOEL
RUSTDA-60-PNE   RUSTOW, DA
                     THE POLITICS OF THE NEAR EAST -- SOUTHWEST ASIA
                        AND NORTHERN AFRICA.=
                     GA ALMOND AND JS COLEMAN  (EDS), THE POLITICS OF            60
                        THE DEVELOPING AREAS, PRINCETON, PRINCETON
                        UNIVERSITY PRESS, 1960, PP. 369-454.
                     COMEL, ELEL, ELNOEL, ELPRNOR
RUSTDA-64-STC   RUSTOW, DA
                     SUCCESSION IN THE TWENTIETH CENTURY.=
                     JOURNAL OF INTERNATIONAL AFFAIRS, 18, (1964),               64
                        PP. 104-113.
                     COMEL, ELEL
```

RUSTDA-66-SEW    RUSTOW, DA
                 THE STUDY OF ELITES -- WHO'S WHO, WHEN, AND HOW.=
                 WORLD POLITICS, 18, (JULY 1966), PP. 690-717.            66
                 COMEL, METEL
RUSTDA-67-WNP    RUSTOW, DA
                 A WORLD OF NATIONS -- PROBLEMS OF POLITICAL
                    MODERNIZATION (ASIA, AFRICA, LATIN AMERICA).=
                 WASHINGTON, THE BROOKINGS INSTITUTION, 1967.            67
                 COMEL, ELEL, ELNOEL, ELPRNOR
RUTHBM-66-PDM    RUTHERFORD, BM
                 PSYCHOPATHOLOGY, DECISION-MAKING, AND POLITICAL
                    INVOLVEMENT (UNITED STATES).=
                 THE JOURNAL OF CONFLICT RESOLUTION, 10, (DECEMBER 1966),  66
                    PP. 387-407.
                 DEFEL, METEL
RYANB -61-SAE    RYAN, B
                 STATUS, ACHIEVEMENT, AND EDUCATION IN CEYLON.=
                 THE JOURNAL OF ASIAN STUDIES, 20, (AUGUST 1961),         61
                    PP. 463-476.
                 COMEL, ELPRNOR
RYLEM -65-CHC    RYLE, M
                 COMMITTEES OF THE HOUSE OF COMMONS (GREAT BRITAIN).=
                 THE POLITICAL QUARTERLY, 36, (JULY-OCTOBER 1965),        65
                    PP. 295-308.
                 ELEL
RYWKM -64-LAS    RYWKIN, M
                 THE LITERARY ARENA (SOVIET UNION).=
                 PROBLEMS OF COMMUNISM, 13, (JULY-AUGUST 1964), PP. 1-10.  64
                 ELPRNOR
RYWKMS-58-ECL    RYWKIN, MS
                 EDUCATION FOR COMMUNIST LEADERSHIP (SOVIET UNION).=
                 CURRENT HISTORY, N.S., 34, (JULY 1958), PP. 35-39.       58
                 COMEL
SACKIM-67-RGS    SACKS, IM
                 RESTRUCTURING GOVERNMENT IN SOUTH VIETNAM.=
                 ASIAN SURVEY, 7, (AUGUST 1967), PP. 515-526.             67
                 ELEL, ELPRNOR
SAFRN -61-ESP    SAFRAN, N
                 EGYPT IN SEARCH OF POLITICAL COMMUNITY -- AN ANALYSIS
                    OF THE INTELLECTUAL AND POLITICAL EVOLUTION OF
                    EGYPT -- 1804-1952.=
                 CAMBRIDGE, HARVARD UNIVERSITY PRESS, 1961.               61
                 ELEL, ELNOEL, ELPRNOR
SAHLMD-58-SSP    SAHLIN, MD
                 SOCIAL STRATIFICATION IN POLYNESIA.=
                 SEATTLE, UNIVERSITY OF WASHINGTON PRESS, 1958.           58
                 COMEL
SAHLMD-63-PMR    SAHLINS, MD
                 POOR MAN, RICH MAN, BIG-MAN, CHIEF -- POLITICAL TYPES
                    IN MELANESIA AND POLYNESIA.=
                 COMPARATIVE STUDIES IN SOCIETY AND HISTORY,              63
                    5, (APRIL 1963), PP. 285-303.
                 COMEL, ELNOEL
SAKARK-57-FSM    SAKAI, RK
                 FEUDAL SOCIETY AND MODERN LEADERSHIP IN SATSUMA-HAN.=
                 THE JOURNAL OF ASIAN STUDIES, 16, (MAY 1957),            57
                    PP. 365-376.
                 COMEL, ELEL, ELNOEL, ELPRNOR
SALEE -62-EGA    SALEM, E
                 EMERGING GOVERNMENT IN THE ARAB WORLD.=
                 ORBIS, 6, (SPRING 1962), PP. 102-118.                    62
                 ELEL, ELNOEL, ELPRNOR
SALIE -58-ATU    SALITAN, E
                 ADMINISTRATIVE TRUSTIFICATION (UNITED STATES).=
                 THE WESTERN POLITICAL QUARTERLY, 11, (DECEMBER 1958),    58
                    PP. 857-874.
                 COMEL, ELEL
SALIR -65-UPO    SALISBURY, R
                 THE URBAN PARTY ORGANIZATION MEMBER (UNITED STATES).=
                 THE PUBLIC OPINION QUARTERLY, 29, (WINTER 1965),         65
                    PP. 550-564.
                 COMEL, ELEL, ELNOEL
SALIRH-60-SLP    SALISBURY, RH
                 ST. LOUIS POLITICS -- RELATIONSHIP AMONG INTERESTS,
                    PARTIES, AND GOVERNMENTAL STRUCTURE (UNITED STATES))=
                 THE WESTERN POLITICAL QUARTERLY, 13, (JUNE 1960),        60
                    PP. 498-507.
                 ELEL, ELNOEL
SALIRH-64-UPN    SALISBURY, RH
                 URBAN POLITICS -- THE NEW CONVERGENCE OF POWER
                    (UNITED STATES).=
                 THE JOURNAL OF POLITICS, 26, (NOVEMBER 1964),            64
                    PP. 775-797.
                 DEFEL, COMEL, ELEL, ELNOEL, METEL

SALTJT-46-PMO    SALTER, JT (ED)
                 PUBLIC MEN IN AND OUT OF OFFICE (UNITED STATES).=
                 CHAPEL HILL, THE UNIVERSITY OF NORTH CAROLINA PRESS,      46
                    1946.
                 COMEL, ELEL, ELNOEL
SAMOAG-60-EDP    SAMONTE, AG
                 EXECUTIVE DEVELOPMENT IN THE PHILIPPINES --
                    PERSPECTIVES AND APPRAISAL.=
                 PHILIPPINE JOURNAL OF PUBLIC ADMINISTRATION,              60
                    4, (JULY 1960), PP. 203-219.
                 COMEL, ELEL
SAMPA -65-ABT    SAMPSON, A
                 THE ANATOMY OF BRITAIN TODAY.=
                 NEW YORK, HARPER AND ROW, 1965.                          65
                 COMEL, ELEL, ELNOEL, ELPRNOR
SANDIT-56-CDE    SANDERS, IT
                 COMMUNIST-DOMINATED EDUCATION IN BULGARIA -- A STUDY IN
                    SOCIAL RELATIONS.=
                 THE AMERICAN SLAVIC AND EAST EUROPEAN REVIEW, 15,         56
                    (OCTOBER 1956), PP. 364-381.
                 ELNOEL
SANDIT-61-SSP    SANDERS, IT
                 SOCIAL SCIENCE AND THE PARTY (BULGARIA).=
                 SURVEY--A JOURNAL OF SOVIET AND EAST EUROPEAN STUDIES,    61
                    39, (DECEMBER 1961), PP. 96-104.
                 ELEL, ELPRNOR
SANDR -65-MSC    SANDERS, R
                 MASS SUPPORT AND COMMUNIST INSURRECTION (GREECE, MALAYA,
                    INDOCHINA, PHILIPPINES, SOUTH VIETNAM).=
                 ORBIS, 9, (SPRING 1965), PP. 214-231.
                 ELNOEL                                                    65
SANDV -54-SNS    SANDOMIRSKY, V
                 THE SPIRIT OF THE NEW SOVIET MIDDLE CLASS.=
                 THE RUSSIAN REVIEW, 13, (JULY 1954), PP. 193-202.         54
                 ELPRNOR
SANGC -64-KGE    SANGER, C             NOTTINGHAM, J
                 THE KENYA GENERAL ELECTION OF 1963.=
                 THE JOURNAL OF MODERN AFRICAN STUDIES, 2, (MARCH 1964),   64
                    PP. 1-40.
                 COMEL, ELEL, ELNOEL
SANTK -64-TIO    SANTHANAM, K
                 TRANSITION IN INDIA AND OTHER ESSAYS.=
                 NEW YORK, ASIA PUBLISHING HOUSE, 1964.                    64
                 ELEL, ELPRNOR
SAPIBM-4 -RMA    SAPIN, BM                SNYDER, RC
                 THE ROLE OF THE MILITARY IN AMERICAN FOREIGN POLICY.=
                 GARDEN CITY, DOUBLEDAY, 1954.                             54
                 ELEL, ELNOEL, ELPRNOR
SAPODJ-54-SBA    SAPOSS, DJ
                 THE SPLIT BETWEEN ASIAN AND WESTERN SOCIALIST.=
                 FOREIGN AFFAIRS, 32, (JULY 1954), PP. 588-594.            54
                 ELEL, ELPRNOR
SAQUW -64-NN     SAQUEUR, W
                 NAZISM AND THE NAZIS.=
                 ENCOUNTER, 22, (APRIL 1964), PP. 39-49.                   64
                 COMEL, ELPRNOR
SARTG -61-PI     SARTORI, G
                 PARLIAMENTARIANS IN ITALY.=
                 INTERNATIONAL SOCIAL SCIENCE JOURNAL, 13, (1961),         61
                    PP. 583-599.
                 COMEL, ELPRNOR
SARTG -62-DLE    SARTORI, G
                 DEMOCRACY, LEADERSHIP AND ELITES.=
                 G SARTORI, DEMOCRATIC THEORY, DETROIT, WAYNE STATE        62
                    UNIVERSITY PRESS, 1962, PP. 96-134.
                 GNELTH, ELEL, ELNOEL
SAWYJ -65-BNI    SAWYER, J              GUETZKOW, H
                 BARGAINING AND NEGOTIATION IN INTERNATIONAL RELATIONS.=
                 HC KELMAN (ED), INTERNATIONAL BEHAVIOR--A                 65
                    SOCIAL-PSYCHOLOGICAL ANALYSIS, NEW YORK,
                    HOLT, RINEHART AND WINSTON, 1965, PP. 466-520.
                 ELEL
SAWYRL-60-DSC    SAWYER-JR, RL
                 THE DEMOCRATIC STATE CENTRAL COMMITTEE IN MICHIGAN
                    1949-1959 -- THE RISE OF THE NEW POLITICS AND THE NEW
                    POLITICAL LEADERSHIP (UNITED STATES).=
                 ANN ARBOR, UNIVERSITY OF MICHIGAN PRESS, 1960.            60
                 COMEL, METEL
SAX,JW-54-ICR    SAX, JW
                 INTELLECTUAL CLASSES AND RULING CLASSES IN FRANCE --
                    A SECOND LOOK.=
                 OCCIDENTE, 10, (MAY-JUNE 1954), PP. 265-270.              54
                 ELEL
SAYEKB-58-PRP    SAYEED, KB

```
                        THE POLITICAL ROLE OF PAKISTAN'S CIVIL SERVICE.=
                        PACIFIC AFFAIRS (JUNE 1958), PP. 131-446.                      58
                        ELEL, ELNOEL
SAYEKB-64-PSC   SAYEED, KB
                        PAKISTAN'S CONSTITUTIONAL AUTOCRACY.=
                        PACIFIC AFFAIRS (WINTER 1963-1964), PP. 365-377.               64
                        ELEL, ELNOEL
SAYIYA-62-ELR   SAYIGH, YA
                        ENTREPRENEURS OF LEBANON -- THE ROLE OF THE BUSINESS
                           LEADER IN A DEVELOPING ECONOMY.=
                        CAMBRIDGE, HARVARD UNIVERSITY PRESS, 1962.                     62
                        COMEL, ELEL, ELPRNOR
SAYRWS-54-RTB   SAYRE, WS
                        THE RECRUITMENT AND TRAINING OF BUREAUCRATS IN THE
                           UNITED STATES.=
                        THE ANNALS OF THE AMERICAN ACADEMY OF POLITICAL AND            54
                           SOCIAL SCIENCE, 292, (MARCH 1954), PP. 39-44.
                        COMEL
SAYRWS-60-GNY   SAYRE, WS            KAUFMAN, H
                        GOVERNING NEW YORK CITY (UNITED STATES).=
                        NEW YORK, RUSSELL SAGE FOUNDATION, 1960.                       60
                        COMEL, ELEL, ELNOEL
SC    -46-PFY   SC
                        POLITICAL FORCES IN YUGOSLAVIA TODAY.=
                        THE WORLD TODAY, 2, (NOVEMBER 1946), PP. 535-545.              46
                        ELEL, ELNOEL
SCALRA-52-JDT   SCALAPINO, RA
                        THE JAPANESE DIET TODAY.=
                        PARLIAMENTARY AFFAIRS, 5, (SUMMER 1952), PP. 347-355.          52
                        ELEL, ELPRNOR
SCALRA-53-DPM   SCALAPINO, RA
                        DEMOCRACY AND THE PARTY MOVEMENT IN PREWAR JAPAN -- THE
                           FAILURE OF THE FIRST ATTEMPT.=
                        BERKELEY, UNIVERSITY OF CALIFORNIA PRESS, 1953.                53
                        ELEL, ELNOEL
SCALRA-62-LWJ   SCALAPINO, RA
                        THE LEFT WING IN JAPAN.
                        SURVEY, 43, (AUGUST 1962), PP. 102-111.                        62
                        ELPRNOR
SCALRA-62-PPC   SCALAPINO, RA          MASUMI, J
                        PARTIES AND POLITICS IN CONTEMPORARY JAPAN.=
                        BERKELEY, UNIVERSITY OF CALIFORNIA PRESS, 1962.                62
                        COMEL, ELEL, ELNOEL, ELPRNOR
SCALRA-65-CRA   SCALAPINO, RA
                        THE COMMUNIST REVOLUTION IN ASIA.=
                        ENGLEWOOD CLIFFS, PRENTICE HALL, 1965                          65
                        COMEL, ELPRNOR
SCARHA-57-HPS   SCARROW, HA
                        THE HIGHER PUBLIC SERVICE OF THE COMMONWEALTH OF
                           AUSTRALIA.=
                        DURHAM, DUKE UNIVERSITY PRESS, 1957.                           57
                        COMEL, ELEL, ELNOEL, ELPRNOR
SCARJR-65-PCT   SCARRITT, JR
                        POLITICAL CHANGE IN A TRADITIONAL AFRICAN CLAN -- A
                           STRUCTURAL FUNCTIONAL ANALYSIS OF THE NSITS OF
                           NIGERIA.=
                        DENVER, UNIVERSITY OF DENVER PRESS, 1965.                      65
                        ELNOEL, ELPRNOR
SCARJR-66-APS   SCARRITT, JR
                        THE ADOPTION OF POLITICAL STYLES BY AFRICAN
                           POLITICIANS IN THE RHODESIAS.=
                        MIDWEST JOURNAL OF POLITICAL SCIENCE, 10,                      66
                           (FEBRUARY 1966), PP. 1-28.
                        COMEL, ELEL, ELPRNOR, METEL
SCHAEE-60-SSP   SCHATTSCHNEIDER, EE
                        THE SEMI-SOVEREIGN PEOPLE -- REALIST'S VIEW OF
                           DEMOCRACY IN AMERICA.=
                        NEW YORK, HOLT, RINEHART AND WINSTON, 1960.                    60
                        DEFEL, COMEL, ELEL, ELNOEL, ELPRNOR
SCHAL -60-PRI   SCHAPIRO, L
                        THE PRE - REVOLUTIONARY INTELLIGENTSIA AND THE LEGAL
                           ORDER (SOVIET UNION).=
                        DAEDALUS, 89, (SUMMER 1960), PP. 459-471.                      60
                        COMEL, ELPRNOR
SCHALB-55-OCA   SCHAPIRO, LB
                        THE ORIGIN OF THE COMMUNIST AUTOCRACY -- POLITICAL
                           OPPOSITION IN THE SOVIET STATE, 1917-1922.=
                        CAMBRIDGE, HARVARD UNIVERSITY PRESS, 1955.                     55
                        DEFEL, COMEL, ELEL
SCHALB-60-CPS   SCHAPIRO, LB
                        THE COMMUNIST PARTY OF THE SOVIET UNION.=
                        NEW YORK, RANDOM HOUSE, INC, 1960.                             60
                        COMEL, ELEL, ELNOEL, ELPRNOR
SCHALB-65-GPS   SCHAPIRO, LB
```

THE GOVERNMENT AND POLITICS OF THE SOVIET UNION.=
LONDON, HUTCHINSON UNIVERSITY LIBRARY, 1965.                          65
ELEL, ELNOEL
SCHAM -62-BRR  SCHACTMAN, M
THE BUREAUCRATIC REVOLUTION -- THE RISE OF THE STALINIST
    STATE (SOVIET UNION).=
NEW YORK, DONALD PRESS, 1962.                                        62
ELEL, ELNOEL
SCHAM -64-LPS  SCHAPIRO, M
LAW AND POLITICS IN THE SUPREME COURT -- NEW APPROACHES
    TO POLITICAL JURISPRUDENCE (UNITED STATES).=
NEW YORK, THE FREE PRESS, 1964.                                     64
ELEL, ELPRNOR, METEL
SCHAR -61-SPS  SCHACHTER, R
SINGLE PARTY SYSTEMS IN WEST AFRICA.=
THE AMERICAN POLITICAL SCIENCE REVIEW, 55, (JUNE 1961),    61
    PP. 294-308.
COMEL, ELEL, ELNOEL
SCHEHK-66-GSD  SCHELLENGER-JR, HK
THE GERMAN SOCIAL DEMOCRATIC PARTY AFTER WORLD WAR 2 --
    THE CONSERVATISM OF POWER.=
THE WESTERN POLITICAL QUARTERLY, 19, (JUNE 1966),            66
    PP. 251-265.
COMEL, ELPRNOR
SCHEL -67-RBP  SCHERZ-GARCIA, L
RELATIONS BETWEEN PUBLIC AND PRIVATE UNIVERSITIES
    (LATIN AMERICA).=
SM LIPSET AND A SOLARI (EDS), ELITES IN LATIN AMERICA,      67
    NEW YORK, OXFORD UNIVERSITY PRESS, 1967, PP. 382-407.
ELEL, ELNOEL
SCHELR-63-BLS  SCHEMEN, LR
THE BRAZILIAN LAW STUDENT -- BACKGROUND, HABITS,
    ATTITUDES.=
JOURNAL OF INTER-AMERICAN STUDIES, 5, (JULY 1963),          63
    PP. 333-356.
COMEL, ELPRNOR
SCHERA-61-SP  SCHERMERHORN, RA
SOCIETY AND POWER.=
NEW YORK, RANDOM HOUSE, 1961.                                61
DEFEL, ELNOEL, ELPRNOR
SCHES -60-CCM  SCHER, S
CONGRESSIONAL COMMITTEE MEMBERS AS INDEPENDENT AGENCY
    OVERSEERS -- A CASE STUDY (UNITED STATES).=
THE AMERICAN POLITICAL SCIENCE REVIEW, 54, (DECEMBER       60
    1960), PP. 911-920
ELEL
SCHES -61-RAC  SCHER, S
REGULATORY AGENCY CONTROL THROUGH APPOINTMENT -- THE CASE
    OF THE EISENHOWER ADMINISTRATION AND THE NLRB
    (UNITED STATES).=
THE JOURNAL OF POLITICS, 23, (NOVEMBER 1961),               61
    PP. 667-688.
ELEL, ELNOEL
SCHES -63-CLC  SCHER, S
CONDITIONS FOR LEGISLATIVE CONTROL (UNITED STATES).=
THE JOURNAL OF POLITICS, 25, (AUGUST 1963), PP. 526-551.   63
ELEL, ELNOEL, ELPRNOR
SCHIH -59-SLP  SCHIRRMACHER, H
STATE AND LOCAL PUBLIC ADMINISTRATION (WEST GERMANY).=
INTERNATIONAL REVIEW OF ADMINISTRATIVE SCIENCES, 25,       59
    (1959), PP. 142-149.
ELEL, ELNOEL
SCHIWR-62-SFP  SCHILLING, WR
SCIENTISTS, FOREIGN POLICY AND POLITICS (UNITED STATES).=
THE AMERICAN POLITICAL SCIENCE REVIEW, 56, (JUNE 1962),    62
    PP. 287-300.
ELEL
SCHLA -60-HL  SCHLESINGER-JR, A
ON HEROIC LEADERSHIP.=
ENCOUNTER, 15, (DECEMBER 1960), PP. 3-11.                   60
DEFEL, ELNOEL
SCHLJA-57-HTB  SCHLESINGER, JA
HOW THEY BECAME GOVERNOR (UNITED STATES).=
EAST LANSING, MICHIGAN, GOVERNMENTAL RESEARCH BUREAU,      57
    MICHIGAN STATE UNIVERSITY, 1957.
COMEL, ELEL, ELNOEL, ELPRNOR
SCHLJA-57-LAP  SCHLESINGER, JA
LAWYERS AND AMERICAN POLITICS -- A CLARIFIED VIEW.=
MIDWEST JOURNAL OF POLITICAL SCIENCE, 1, (MAY 1957),       57
    PP. 26-39.
COMEL
SCHLJA-58-FRS  SCHLESINGER, JA
THE FRENCH RADICAL SOCIALIST PARTY AND THE REPUBLICAN
    FRONT OF 1956.

THE WESTERN POLITICAL QUARTERLY, 11, (MARCH 1958),              58
   PP. 71-85.
COMEL, ELEL
SCHLJA-60-SCO  SCHLESINGER, JA
THE STRUCTURE OF COMPETITION FOR OFFICE IN THE
   AMERICAN STATES.=
BEHAVIORAL SCIENCE, 5, (JULY 1960), PP. 197-210.              60
DEFEL, ELEL, ELNOEL, METEL
SCHLJA-65-PEU  SCHLESINGER, JA
THE POLITICS OF THE EXECUTIVE (UNITED STATES).=
H JACOB AND KN VINES (EDS), POLITICS IN THE AMERICAN         65
   STATES--A COMPARATIVE ANALYSIS, BOSTON, LITTLE, BROWN
   AND COMPANY, 1965, PP. 207-237.
COMEL, ELEL, ELNOEL, ELPRNOR
SCHLJA-65-PPO  SCHLESINGER, JA
POLITICAL PARTY ORGANIZATION.=
JG MARCH (ED), HANDBOOK OF ORGANIZATIONS, CHICAGO, RAND      65
   MCNALLY, 1965, PP. 764-801.
COMEL, ELEL, ELNOEL, ELPRNOR
SCHLJA-66-APP  SCHLESINGER, JA
AMBITION AND POLITICS -- POLITICAL CAREERS IN THE
   UNITED STATES.=
CHICAGO, RAND MCNALLY AND CO., 1966.                         66
COMEL, ELEL, ELPRNOR
SCHLJA-67-PCP  SCHLESINGER, JA
POLITICAL CAREERS AND PARTY LEADERSHIP (AUSTRALIA, CANADA,
   FRANCE, GREAT BRITAIN, UNITED STATES).=
LJ EDINGER (ED), POLITICAL LEADERSHIP IN INDUSTRIALIZED      67
   SOCIETIES, NEW YORK, JOHN WILEY AND SONS, 1967,
   PP. 266-293.
COMEL, ELEL, ELNOEL, ELPRNOR
SCHMF -62-CNB  SCHMIDT, F
COLLECTIVE NEGOTIATIONS BETWEEN THE STATE AND ITS
   OFFICIALS -- A COMPARATIVE ESSAY.=
INTERNATIONAL REVIEW OF ADMINISTRATIVE SCIENCES, 28,         62
   (1962), PP. 296-305.
ELEL
SCHMJ -58-SSC  SCHMIDHAUSER, J       GOLD, D
SCALING SUPREME COURT DECISIONS IN RELATION TO SOCIAL
   BACKGROUND (UNITED STATES).=
PROD (THE AMERICAN BEHAVIORAL SCIENTIST), 1, (MAY 1958),     58
   PP. 6-7.
METEL
SCHMJ -62-SDD  SCHMIDHAUSER, J
STARE DECISIS, DISSENT AND THE BACKGROUND OF THE JUSTICES
   OF THE SUPREME COURT OF THE UNITED STATES.=
UNIVERSITY OF TORONTO LAW JOURNAL, 14, (1962),               62
   PP. 194-212.
COMEL, ELPRNOR
SCHMJR-58-SCF  SCHMIDHAUSER, JR
THE SUPREME COURT AS FINAL ARBITER IN FEDERAL - STATE
   RELATIONS (UNITED STATES).=
CHAPEL HILL, UNIVERSITY OF NORTH CAROLINA PRESS, 1958.       58
ELEL, ELPRNOR
SCHMJR-59-JSC  SCHMIDHAUSER, JR
THE JUSTICES OF THE SUPREME COURT -- A COLLECTIVE
   PORTRAIT (UNITED STATES).=
MIDWEST JOURNAL OF POLITICAL SCIENCE, 3, (FEBRUARY 1959),    59
   PP. 1-57.
COMEL, ELEL, ELPRNOR
SCHMJR-60-SCI  SCHMIDHAUSER, JR
THE SUPREME COURT -- ITS POLITICS, PERSONALITIES, AND
   PROCEDURES (UNITED STATES).=
NEW YORK, HOLT, RINEHART AND WINSTON, 1960.                  60
COMEL, ELEL, ELPRNOR
SCHNRM-58-CG  SCHNEIDER, RM
COMMUNISM IN GUATEMALA, 1944-1954.=
NEW YORK, FREDERICK A PRAEGER, 1958.                         58
COMEL, ELEL
SCHOBN-48-PCL  SCHOENFELD-JR, BN
THE PSYCHOLOGICAL CHARACTERISTICS OF LEADERSHIP.=
SOCIAL FORCES, 26, (MAY 1948), PP. 391-396.                  48
COMEL, ELPRNOR
SCHOBN-63-ERI  SCHOENFELD, BN
EMERGENCY RULE IN INDIA.=
PACIFIC AFFAIRS, 36, (FALL 1963), PP. 221-237.               63
ELEL, ELNOEL, ELPRNOR
SCHOEL-61-TB  SCHOR, EL
THE THAI BUREAUCRACY.=
ADMINISTRATIVE SCIENCE QUARTERLY, 5, (1960-1961),            61
   PP. 66-86.
ELEL, ELNOEL, ELPRNOR
SCHOGA-66-CSP  SCHOPFLIN, GA
CHURCH AND STATE IN POLAND.=

THE WORLD TODAY, 22, (MAY 1966), PP. 177-180.                66
ELEL

SCHRT -62-CLH   SCHREIBER, T
CHANGES IN THE LEADERSHIP (HUNGARY).=
SURVEY--A JOURNAL OF SOVIET AND EAST EUROPEAN STUDIES,        62
40, (JANUARY 1962), PP. 114-123.
COMEL, ELEL

SCHUCE-64-BPO   SCHULZ, CE
BUREAUCRATIC PARTY ORGANIZATION THROUGH PROFESSIONAL
POLITICAL STAFFING (UNITED STATES).=
MIDWEST JOURNAL OF POLITICAL SCIENCE, 8, (MAY 1964),         64
PP. 127-142.
COMEL, ELEL, ELNOEL

SCHUG -61-PMS   SCHUBERT, G
A PSYCHOMETRIC MODEL OF THE SUPREME COURT
(UNITED STATES).=
AMERICAN BEHAVIORAL SCIENTISTS, 5, (NOVEMBER 1961),          61
PP. 14-18.
METEL

SCHUG -62-SIF   SCHUBERT, G
A SOLUTION TO INTERMEDIATE FACTORIAL RESOLUTION OF
THURSTONE AND DEGAN'S STUDY OF THE SUPREME COURT
(UNITED STATES).=
BEHAVIORAL SCIENCE, 7, (OCTOBER 1962), PP. 448-458.          62
METEL

SCHUG -62-TSC   SCHUBERT, G
THE 1960-1961 TERM OF THE SUPREME COURT --
A PSYCHOLOGICAL ANALYSIS (UNITED STATES).=
THE AMERICAN POLITICAL SCIENCE REVIEW, 56, (MARCH 1962),     62
PP. 90-107.
ELPRNOR, METEL

SCHUG -63-JDM   SCHUBERT, G
JUDICIAL DECISION MAKING (UNITED STATES, NORWAY).=
NEW YORK, THE FREE PRESS, 1963.                              63
ELEL, ELPRNOR, METEL

SCHUG -67-IAA   SCHUBERT, G
IDEOLOGIES AND ATTITUDES, ACADEMIC AND JUDICIAL
(UNITED STATES).=
THE JOURNAL OF POLITICS, 29, (FEBRUARY 1967), PP. 3-40.      67
ELPRNOR, METEL

SCHUG -67-JPL   SCHUBERT, G
JUDGES AND POLITICAL LEADERSHIP (AUSTRALIA, JAPAN,
PHILIPPINES, UNITED STATES).=
LJ EDINGER (ED), POLITICAL LEADERSHIP IN INDUSTRIALIZED      67
SOCIETIES, NEW YORK, JOHN WILEY AND SONS, 1967,
PP. 220-265.
COMEL, ELEL, ELPRNOR

SCHUGA-57-PIA   SCHUBERT, GA
'THE PUBLIC INTEREST' IN ADMINISTRATIVE DECISION-MAKING
(UNITED STATES).=
THE AMERICAN POLITICAL SCIENCE REVIEW, 51, (JUNE 1957),      57
PP. 346-368.
ELEL, ELNOEL, ELPRNOR

SCHUGA-58-SJD   SCHUBERT, GA
THE STUDY OF JUDICIAL DECISION-MAKING AS AN ASPECT
OF POLITICAL BEHAVIOR (UNITED STATES).=
AMERICAN POLITICAL SCIENCE REVIEW, 52, (DECEMBER 1958),      58
PP. 1007-1025.
METEL

SCHUGA-58-TPI   SCHUBERT-JR, GA
THE THEORY OF PUBLIC INTEREST.=
PROD (THE AMERICAN BEHAVIORAL SCIENTIST), 1,                 58
(MAY 1958), PP. 34-36.
DEFEL, METEL

SCHUGA-59-QAJ   SCHUBERT, GA
QUANTITATIVE ANALYSIS OF JUDICIAL BEHAVIOR.=
GLENCOE, THE FREE PRESS, 1959.                               59
ELEL, ELPRNOR, METEL

SCHUGA-65-JMA   SCHUBERT, GA
THE JUDICIAL MIND -- ATTITUDES AND IDEOLOGIES OF
SUPREME COURT JUSTICES 1946-1963 (UNITED STATES).=
EVANSTON, ILLINOIS, NORTHWESTERN UNIVERSITY PRESS, 1965.     65
COMEL, ELEL, ELPRNOR, METEL

SCHUGK-51-PSU   SCHUELLER, GK
THE POLITBURO (SOVIET UNION).=
STANFORD, STANFORD UNIVERSITY PRESS, 1951.                   51
COMEL, ELEL, ELPRNOR

SCHUHF-59-ORC   SCHURMANN, HF
ORGANIZATION AND RESPONSE IN COMMUNIST CHINA.=
THE ANNALS OF THE AMERICAN ACADEMY OF POLITICAL AND          59
SOCIAL SCIENCE, 321, (JANUARY 1959), PP. 51-61.
ELNOEL, ELPRNOR

SCHUHF-61-PSR   SCHURMANN, HF
PEKING'S RECOGNITION OF CRISIS (CHINA).=

```
                    PROBLEMS OF COMMUNISM, 10, (SEPTEMBER-OCTOBER 1961),        61
                       PP. 5-14.
                    ELEL, ELNOEL
SCHUHF-65-IOC       SCHURMANN, HF
                    IDEOLOGY AND ORGANIZATION IN COMMUNIST CHINA.=
                    BERKELEY, UNIVERSITY OF CALIFORNIA, 1965                     65
                    COMEL, ELEL, ELNOEL, ELPRNOR
SCHUJ -55-ISC       SCHUMPTER, J
                    IMPERIALISM AND SOCIAL CLASSES.=
                    NEW YORK, MERIDIAN BOOKS, 1955.                              55
                    DEFEL, COMEL
SCHUJA-62-CSD       SCHUMPETER, JA
                    CAPITALISM, SOCIALISM AND DEMOCRACY.=
                    NEW YORK, HARPER AND ROW, 1962.                              62
                    DEFEL, ELEL, ELNOEL, ELPRNOR
SCHURO-57-DLP       SCHULZE, RO          BLUMBERG, LU
                    THE DETERMINATION OF LOCAL POWER ELITES (UNITED STATES).=
                    THE AMERICAN JOURNAL OF SOCIOLOGY, 63, (NOVEMBER 1957),      57
                       PP. 290-296.
                    METEL
SCHURO-58-RED       SCHULZE, RO
                    THE ROLE OF ECONOMIC DOMINANTS IN COMMUNITY POWER
                       STRUCTURE (UNITED STATES).=
                    AMERICAN SOCIOLOGICAL REVIEW, 23, (FEBRUARY 1958),           58
                       PP. 3-9.
                    COMEL, ELEL, ELNOEL, METEL
SCHWBI-51-CCR       SCHWARTZ, BI
                    CHINESE COMMUNISM AND THE RISE OF MAO.=
                    CAMBRIDGE, HARVARD UNIVERSITY PRESS, 1951.                   51
                    COMEL, ELEL, ELNOEL, ELPRNOR
SCHWBI-60-ICC       SCHWARTZ, BI
                    THE INTELLIGENTSIA IN COMMUNIST CHINA -- A TENTATIVE
                       COMPARISON.=
                    DAEDALUS, 89, (SUMMER 1960), PP. 604-621.                    60
                    DEFEL, COMEL, ELEL
SCHWHG-66-GPR       SCHWARTZ, HG
                    THE GREAT PROLETARIAN REVOLUTION (CHINA).=
                    ORBIS, 10, (FALL 1966), PP. 803-822.                         66
                    ELEL, ELNOEL, ELPRNOR
SCHWSM-53-CPS       SCHWARZ, SM
                    THE COMMUNIST PARTY AND THE SOVIET STATE.=
                    PROBLEMS OF COMMUNISM, 2, (JANUARY 1953), PP. 8-13.          53
                    COMEL, ELEL
SCHWSM-53-NLC       SCHWARZ, SM
                    NEW LIGHT ON THE COMMUNIST PARTY OF THE SOVIET UNION.=
                    PROBLEMS OF COMMUNISM, 2, (NUMBER 2, 1953), PP. 11-13.       53
                    COMEL
SCHWSM-59-TUS       SCHWARZ, SM
                    TRADE UNIONS IN THE SOVIET STATE.=
                    CURRENT HISTORY, 37, (AUGUST 1959), PP. 79-84.               59
                    ELEL
SCIGRC-60-PPS       SCIGLIANO, RC
                    POLITICAL PARTIES IN SOUTH VIETNAM UNDER THE REPUBLIC.=
                    PACIFIC AFFAIRS, 33, (DECEMBER 1960), PP. 327-346.           60
                    COMEL, ELEL, ELNOEL, ELPRNOR
SCOBHM-63-PMS       SCOBLE, HM
                    POLITICAL MONEY -- A STUDY OF CONTRIBUTORS TO THE
                       NATIONAL COMMITTEE FOR AN EFFECTIVE CONGRESS
                       (UNITED STATES).=
                    MIDWEST JOURNAL OF POLITICAL SCIENCE, 7, (AUGUST 1963),      63
                       PP. 229-253.
                    COMEL, ELEL, ELNOEL, ELPRNOR
SCOTDJ-54-PRY       SCOTT, DJR
                    PRODUCERS' REPRESENTATION IN YUGOSLAVIA.=
                    POLITICAL STUDIES, 2, (1954), PP. 210-226.                   54
                    COMEL, ELEL, ELNOEL
SCOTRE-59-MGT       SCOTT, RE
                    MEXICAN GOVERNMENT IN TRANSITION.=
                    URBANA, UNIVERSITY OF ILLINOIS PRESS, 1959.                  59
                    DEFEL, COMEL, ELEL, ELNOEL, ELPRNOR
SCOTRE-66-MER       SCOTT, RE
                    MEXICO -- THE ESTABLISHED REVOLUTION.=
                    LW PYE AND S VERBA (EDS), POLITICAL CULTURE AND              66
                       POLITICAL DEVELOPMENT, PRINCETON, PRINCETON UNIVERSITY
                       PRESS, 1966, PP. 330-395.
                    COMEL, FLEL, ELNOEL, ELPRNOR
SCOTRE-67-PEP       SCOTT, RE
                    POLITICAL ELITES AND POLITICAL MODERNIZATION --
                       THE CRISIS OF TRANSITION (LATIN AMERICA).=
                    SM LIPSET AND A SOLARI (EDS), ELITES IN LATIN AMERICA,       67
                       NEW YORK, OXFORD UNIVERSITY PRESS, 1967, PP. 117-145.
                    DEFEL, COMEL, ELEL, ELNOEL, ELPRNOR
SCRIT -58-LOS       SCRIVEN, T
                    THE 'LITERARY OPPOSITION' (SOVIET UNION).=
```

                         PROBLEMS OF COMMUNISM, 7, (JANUARY-FEBRUARY 1958),        58
                            PP. 28-34.
                         ELEL, ELPRNOR
SEABP  -54-WSG           SEABURY, P
                         THE WILHELMSTRASSE -- A STUDY OF GERMAN DIPLOMATS
                            UNDER THE NAZI REGIME.=
                         BERKELEY, UNIVERSITY OF CALIFORNIA PRESS, 1954.           54
                         COMEL, ELEL, ELNOEL, ELPRNOR
SEALP  -65-SSS           SEALE, P
                         THE STRUGGLE FOR SYRIA -- A STUDY OF POST-WAR ARAB
                            POLITICS, 1945-1948.
                         LONDON, OXFORD UNIVERSITY PRESS, 1965.                    65
                         ELEL, ELPRNOR
SEEMM  -53-RCA           SEEMAN, M
                         ROLE CONFLICT AND AMBIVALENCE IN LEADERSHIP.=
                         AMERICAN SOCIOLOGICAL REVIEW, 18, (AUGUST 1953),          53
                            PP. 373-380.
                         DEFEL, METEL
SELILG-50-SPL            SELIGMAN, LG
                         THE STUDY OF POLITICAL LEADERSHIP.=
                         THE AMERICAN POLITICAL SCIENCE REVIEW, 44,                50
                            (DECEMBER 1950), PP. 904-916.
                         DEFEL, METEL
SELILG-55-DPC            SELIGMAN, LG
                         DEVELOPMENTS IN THE PRESIDENCY AND THE CONCEPTION
                            OF POLITICAL LEADERSHIP (UNITED STATES).=
                         AMERICAN SOCIOLOGICAL REVIEW, 20, (DECEMBER 1955),        55
                            PP. 706-712.
                         ELEL, ELNOEL, METEL
SELILG-56-PLI            SELIGMAN, LG
                         PRESIDENTIAL LEADERSHIP -- THE INNER CIRCLE AND
                            INSTITUTIONALIZATION (UNITED STATES).=
                         THE JOURNAL OF POLITICS, 18, (AUGUST 1956), PP. 410-426.   56
                         ELEL, ELNOEL, ELPRNOR
SELILG-58-RPU            SELIGMAN, LG
                         RECRUITMENT IN POLITICS (UNITED STATES).=
                         PROD, 1, (MARCH 1958), PP. 14-17.                         58
                         DEFEL, ELNOEL
SELILG-59-PSL            SELIGMAN, LG
                         A PREFATORY STUDY OF LEADERSHIP SELECTION IN OREGON
                            (UNITED STATES).=
                         THE WESTERN POLITICAL QUARTERLY, 12, (MARCH 1959),        59
                            PP. 153-167.
                         COMEL
SELILG-61-PRP            SELIGMAN, LG
                         POLITICAL RECRUITMENT AND PARTY STRUCTURE -- A CASE
                            STUDY (UNITED STATES).=
                         THE AMERICAN POLITICAL SCIENCE REVIEW, 55, (MARCH 1961),   61
                            PP. 77-86.
                         COMEL, ELEL
SELILG-64-ERP            SELIGMAN, LG
                         ELITE RECRUITMENT AND POLITICAL DEVELOPMENT.=
                         THE JOURNAL OF POLITICS, 26, (AUGUST 1964), PP. 612-626.   64
                         DEFEL, ELEL, ELNOEL, ELPRNOR
SELILG-64-LNN            SELIGMAN, LG
                         LEADERSHIP IN A NEW NATION -- POLITICAL DEVELOPMENT
                            IN ISRAEL.=
                         NEW YORK, ATHERTON PRESS, 1964.                           64
                         COMEL, ELEL, ELNOEL, ELPRNOR
SELILG-64-PCL            SELIGMAN, LG
                         POLITICAL CHANGE -- LEGISLATIVE ELITES AND PARTIES
                            IN OREGON (UNITED STATES).=
                         THE WESTERN POLITICAL QUARTERLY, 17, (JUME 1964),         64
                            PP. 177-187.
                         COMEL, ELEL, ELNOEL
SELILG-67-PPR            SELIGMAN, LG
                         POLITICAL PARTIES AND THE RECRUITMENT OF POLITICAL
                            LEADERSHIP.=
                         LJ EDINGER (ED), POLITICAL LEADERSHIP IN INDUSTRIALIZED   67
                            SOCIETIES, NEW YORK, JOHN WILEY AND SONS, 1967,
                            PP. 294-315.
                         DEFEL, ELEL, ELNOEL
SELVHC-60-ELU            SELVIN, HC
                         THE EFFECTS OF LEADERSHIP (UNITED STATES).=
                         GLENCOE, ILLINOIS, THE FREE PRESS, 1960.                  60
                         ELEL, ELNOEL, ELPRNOR, METEL
SELZP  -43-ATB           SELZNICK, P
                         AN APPROACH TO A THEORY OF BUREAUCRACY.=
                         AMERICAN SOCIOLOGICAL REVIEW, 8, (FEBRUARY 1943), PP.      43
                            47-54.
                         DEFEL, ELEL, METEL
SELZP  -49-TGR           SELZNICK, P
                         TVA AND THE GRASS ROOTS -- A STUDY IN THE SOCIOLOGY OF
                            FORMAL ORGANIZATIONS (UNITED STATES).=

```
                        BERKELEY, UNIVERSITY OF CALIFORNIA PRESS, 1949.            49
            ELEL, ELPRNOR
SELZP -51-IVM   SELZNICK, P
                INSTITUTIONAL VULNERABILITY IN MASS SOCIETY.=
                THE AMERICAN JOURNAL OF SOCIOLOGY, 56, (JANUARY 1951),        51
                    PP. 320-331.
                DEFEL, ELEL, ELNOEL
SELZP -52-OWS   SELZNICK, P
                THE ORGANIZATIONAL WEAPON -- A STUDY OF
                    BOLSHEVIK STRATEGY AND TACTICS (SOVIET UNION).=
                NEW YORK, MCGRAW-HILL BOOK COMPANY, INC, 1952.               52
                COMEL, ELEL, ELNOEL, ELPRNOR
SELZP -57-LAS   SELZNICK, P
                LEADERSHIP IN ADMINISTRATION -- A SOCIOLOGICAL
                    INTERPRETATION.=
                EVANSTON, ROW, PETERSON, 1957.                              57
                GNELTH, DEFEL, METEL
SELZP -65-DLD   SELZNICK, P
                DILEMMAS OF LEADERSHIP AND DOCTRINE IN DEMOCRATIC
                    PLANNING (UNITED STATES).=
                AW GOULDNER (ED), STUDIES IN LEADERSHIP, NEW YORK,          65
                    RUSSELL AND RUSSELL, 1965, PP. 560-591.
                ELEL, ELNOEL, ELPRNOR
SENIDA-64-OSR   SENIOR, DA
                THE ORGANISATION OF SCIENTIFIC RESEARCH (SOVIET UNION).=
                SURVEY--A JOURNAL OF SOVIET AND EAST EUROPEAN STUDIES,       64
                    52, (JULY 1964), PP. 19-35.
                COMEL, ELEL
SERER -62-R     SERENO, R
                THE RULERS.=
                NEW YORK, FREDERICK A PRAEGER, 1962.                        62
                GNELTH
SETHSC-65-CFE   SETH, SC
                THE CULTURAL FACTORS IN ECONOMIC AND TECHNOLOGICAL
                    DEVELOPMENT -- AN INDIAN ADMINISTRATIVE VIEW-POINT.=
                JOURNAL OF SOCIAL RESEARCH, 8, (MARCH 1965),                65
                    PP. 104-122.
                COMEL, ELPRNOR
SETOH -51-TCR   SETON-WATSON, H
                TWENTIETH CENTURY REVOLUTIONS.=
                THE POLITICAL QUARTERLY, 22, (JULY-SEPTEMBER 1951),         51
                    PP. 251-265.
                COMEL, ELEL, ELNOEL
SETOH -54-EES   SETON-WATSON, H
                EASTERN EUROPE SINCE STALIN.=
                PROBLEMS OF COMMUNISM, 3, (MARCH-APRIL 1954),               54
                    PP. 10-17.
                ELEL, ELNOEL
SETOH -56-SRC   SETON-WATSON, H
                THE SOVIET RULING CLASS.=
                PROBLEMS OF COMMUNISM, 5, (MAY-JUNE 1956), PP. 10-16.        56
                ELEL, ELNOEL, ELPRNOR
SETOH -59-IRH   SETON-WATSON, H
                INTELLIGENTSIA AND REVOLUTION -- AN HISTORICAL ANALYSIS.=
                SOVIET SURVEY, 29, (SEPTEMBER 1959), PP. 90-96.             59
                DEFEL, COMEL, ELEL
SETOH -61-FYA   SETON-WATSON, H
                FIVE YEARS AFTER OCTOBER (EASTERN EUROPE).=
                PROBLEMS OF COMMUNISM, 10, (SEPTEMBER-OCTOBER 1961),        61
                    PP. 15-21.
                ELEL, ELNOEL
SETOH -62-RIS   SETON-WATSON, H
                THE ROLE OF THE INTELLIGENTSIA (SOVIET UNION).=
                SURVEY--A JOURNAL OF SOVIET AND EAST EUROPEAN STUDIES,       62
                    43, (AUGUST 1962), PP. 23-30.
                ELEL, ELPRNOR
SHAHDJ-66-CPP   SHAH, DJ
                CASTE AND POLITICAL PROCESS (INDIA).=
                ASIAN SURVEY, (SEPTEMBER 1966), PP. 516-522.                66
                DEFEL
SHANJB-49-SPL   SHANNON, JB
                THE STUDY OF POLITICAL LEADERSHIP.=
                JB SHANNON ET AL., THE STUDY OF COMPARATIVE GOVERNMENT,      49
                    NEW YORK, APPLETON-CENTURY-CROFTS, 1949, PP. 314-330.
                DEFEL, ELEL, METEL
SHAPI -61-SBP   SHAPIRO, I
                THE SOVIET BAR -- PAST AND PRESENT.=
                THE RUSSIAN REVIEW, 20, (APRIL 1961), PP. 143-150.          61
                COMEL, ELPRNOR
SHAPLS-54-MED   SHAPLEY, LS          SHUBIK, M
                A METHOD FOR EVALUATING THE DISTRIBUTION OF POWER IN A
                    COMMITTEE SYSTEM (UNITED STATES).=
                THE AMERICAN POLITICAL SCIENCE REVIEW, 48,                  54
                    (SEPTEMBER 1954), PP. 787-792.
```

SHARBA-62-IP    DEFEL, METEL
                SHARMA, BAV         VALECHA, NM
                THE INDIAN PRESIDENT.=
                THE POLITICAL QUARTERLY, 33, (1962), PP. 59-73.              62
                ELEL, ELNOEL
SHARH -65-TIA   SHARABI, H
                THE TRANSFORMATION OF IDEOLOGY IN THE ARAB WORLD.=
                THE MIDDLE EAST JOURNAL, 19, (SUMMER 1965), PP. 471-486.    65
                ELEL, ELNOEL, ELPRNOR
SHARHB-60-PGM   SHARABI, HB
                PARLIAMENTARY GOVERNMENT AND MILITARY AUTOCRACY IN
                    THE MIDDLE EAST.=
                ORBIS, 4, (FALL 1960), PP. 338-355.
                ELEL                                                        60
SHARHB-63-PLA   SHARABI, HB
                POWER AND LEADERSHIP IN THE ARAB WORLD.=
                ORBIS, 7, (FALL 1963), PP. 583-595.
                COMEL, ELEL, ELNOEL                                         63
SHARI -65-ASI   SHARKANSKY, I
                AN APPROPRIATIONS SUBCOMMITTEE AND ITS CLIENT AGENCIES --
                    A COMPARATIVE STUDY OF SUPERVISION AND CONTROL
                    (UNITED STATES).=
                THE AMERICAN POLITICAL SCIENCE REVIEW, 59, (SEPTEMBER       65
                    1965), PP. 622-628.
                ELEL
SHARLJ-66-LRL   SHARPE, LJ
                LEADERSHIP AND REPRESENTATION IN LOCAL GOVERNMENT
                    (UNITED STATES).=
                THE POLITICAL QUARTERLY, 37, (APRIL-JUNE 1966),             66
                    PP. 149-158.
                ELEL, ELNOEL, ELPRNOR
SHARR -51-CGI   SHARMA, R
                CABINET GOVERNMENT IN INDIA.=
                PARLIAMENTARY AFFAIRS, 4, (1950-1951), PP. 116-126.         51
                ELEL
SHARWR-63-IBP   SHARP, WR
                INTERNATIONAL BUREAUCRACIES AND POLITICAL DEVELOPMENT.=
                J LAPALOMBARA (ED), BUREAUCRACY AND POLITICAL               63
                    DEVELOPMENT, PRINCETON, PRINCETON UNIVERSITY PRESS,
                    1963, PP. 441-474.
                ELEL, ELPRNOR
SHAWM -62-ALP   SHAW, M
                AN AMERICAN LOOKS AT THE PARTY CONFERENCES
                    (GREAT BRITAIN).=
                PARLIAMENTARY AFFAIRS, 15, (SPRING 1962), PP. 203-212.      62
                ELEL, ELNOEL
SHEAJG-50-SCH   SHEARER, JGS
                STANDING COMMITTEES IN THE HOUSE OF COMMONS, 1945-1950
                    (GREAT BRITAIN).=
                PARLIAMENTARY AFFAIRS, 3, (AUTUMN 1950), PP. 558-568.       50
                ELEL
SHEPGW-62-PAN   SHEPHERD, GW
                THE POLITICS OF AFRICAN NATIONALISM.=
                NEW YORK, FREDERICK A PRAEGER, 1962.                        62
                COMEL, ELEL, ELNOEL, ELPRNOR
SHERA -61-ISM   SHERMAN, A
                ISRAELI SOCIALISM AND THE MULTI - PARTY SYSTEM.=
                THE WORLD TODAY, 17, (MAY 1961), PP. 217-226.               61
                COMEL
SHERFP-66-LT    SHERWOOD, FP
                LEADERSHIP AND TIME.=
                CAG OCCASIONAL PAPERS, INTERNATIONAL DEVELOPMENT            66
                    RESEARCH CENTER, BLOOMINGTON, INDIANA, 1966.
                DEFEL, ELPRNOR
SHERG -58-PSA   SHERMAN, G
                POLAND'S ANGRY AND UNANGRY YOUNG MEN.=
                PROBLEMS OF COMMUNISM, 7, (MAY-JUNE 1958), PP. 30-38.       58
                ELNOEL, ELPRNOR
SHERM -62-IRL   SHERIF, M (ED)
                INTERGROUP RELATIONS AND LEADERSHIP -- APPROACHES AND
                    RESEARCH IN INDUSTRIAL, ETHNIC, CULTURAL, AND
                    POLITICAL AREAS.=
                NEW YORK, JOHN WILEY, 1962.                                 62
                DEFEL, ELEL, METEL
SHERRB-63-SRM   SHERMAN, RB
                THE STATUS REVOLUTION AND MASSACHUSETTS
                    PROGRESSIVE LEADERSHIP (UNITED STATES).=
                POLITICAL SCIENCE QUARTERLY, 78, (MARCH 1963), PP. 59-65. 63
                COMEL, ELPRNOR
SHILE -55-IPO   SHILS, E
                INTELLECTUALS, PUBLIC OPINION AND ECONOMIC DEVELOPMENT.=
                WORLD POLITICS, 10, (JUNE 1955), PP. 232-255.               55
                COMEL, ELEL, ELPRNOR
SHILE -58-CDC   SHILS, E

THE CONCENTRATION AND DISPERSION OF CHARISMA -- THEIR
BEARING ON ECONOMIC POLICY IN UNDERDEVELOPED COUNTRIES.=
WORLD POLITICS, 11, (OCTOBER 1958), PP. 1-19.                58
DEFEL, ELEL, ELNOEL, ELPRNOR

SHILE -58-IPP    SHILS, E
THE INTELLECTUALS AND THE POWERS -- SOME PERSPECTIVES
FOR COMPARATIVE ANALYSIS.=
COMPARATIVE STUDIES IN SOCIETY AND HISTORY, 1, (1958),      58
PP. 5-22.
DEFEL, ELEL, METEL

SHILE -60-IPD    SHILS, E
THE INTELLECTUAL IN THE POLITICAL DEVELOPMENT OF
THE NEW STATES.=
WORLD POLITICS, 12, (APRIL 1960), PP. 329-368.             60
COMEL, ELEL, ELNOEL, ELPRNOR

SHILE -60-PDN    SHILS, E
POLITICAL DEVELOPMENT IN THE NEW STATES -- 1 -- 2.=
COMPARATIVE STUDIES IN SOCIETY AND HISTORY, 2,             60
(APRIL 1960, JULY 1960), PP. 265-292, PP. 379-4119.
ELEL, ELNOEL, ELPRNOR

SHILE -61-IBT    SHILS, E
THE INTELLECTUAL BETWEEN TRADITION AND MODERNITY -- THE
INDIAN SITUATION.=
THE HAGUE, MOUTON AND COMPANY, 1961.                       61
COMEL, ELEL, ELPRNOR

SHILE -61-IWI    SHILS, E
INFLUENCE AND WITHDRAWAL -- THE INTELLECTUALS IN INDIAN
POLITICAL DEVELOPMENT.=
D MARVICK (ED), POLITICAL DECISION MAKERS, GLENCOE,        61
THE FREE PRESS, 1961, PP. 29-55.
COMEL, ELEL, ELNOEL

SHILE -62-MPD    SHILS, E
THE MILITARY IN THE POLITICAL DEVELOPMENT OF THE
NEW STATES.=
JJ JOHNSON (ED), THE ROLE OF THE MILITARY IN              62
UNDERDEVELOPED COUNTRIES, PRINCETON, PRINCETON
UNIVERSITY PRESS, 1962, PP. 7-69.
DEFEL, ELEL, ELNOEL

SHILE -62-PSG    SHILS, E
POLITICIANS AND SCIENTISTS (GREAT BRITAIN).=
ENCOUNTER, 18, (JANUARY 1962), PP. 103-106.               62
ELEL, ELPRNOR

SHILE -63-DCP    SHILS, E
DEMAGOGUES AND CADRES IN THE POLITICAL DEVELOPMENT
OF THE NEW STATES.=
LW PYE (ED), COMMUNICATIONS AND POLITICAL DEVELOPMENT,    63
PRINCETON, PRINCETON UNIVERSITY PRESS, 1963, PP.64-77.
DEFEL, COMEL, ELEL, ELNOEL, ELPRNOR

SHILE -65-COS    SHILS, E
CHARISMA, ORDER, AND STATUS.=
AMERICAN SOCIOLOGICAL REVIEW, 30, (APRIL 1965),           65
PP. 199-213.
GNELTH

SHILE -66-ONS    SHILS, E
OPPOSITION IN THE NEW STATES OF ASIA AND AFRICA.=
GOVERNMENT AND OPPOSITION, 1, (FEBRUARY 1966),            66
PP. 175-204.
COMEL, ELEL, ELNOEL, ELPRNOR

SHILEA-51-LHE    SHILS, EA
THE LEGISLATOR AND HIS ENVIRONMENT (UNITED STATES).=
UNIVERSITY OF CHICAGO LAW REVIEW, 18, (SPRING 1951),      51
PP. 571-584.
ELEL, ELPRNOR

SHILEA-59-PI     SHILS, EA
THE PROSPECTS FOR INTELLECTUALS.=
SOVIET SURVEY--A QUARTERLY REVIEW OF CULTURAL TRENDS,     59
29, (JULY-SEPTEMBER 1959), PP. 81-89.
DEFEL

SHIRJR-65-CKA    SHIRLEY, JR
CONTROL OF THE KUOMINGTANG AFTER SUN YAT-SEN'S DEATH.=
THE JOURNAL OF ASIAN STUDIES, 25, (NOVEMBER 1965),        65
PP. 69-82.
COMEL, ELEL, ELNOEL

SHOUP -59-PPR    SHOUP, P
PROBLEMS OF PARTY REFORM IN YUGOSLAVIA.=
THE AMERICAN SLAVIC AND EAST EUROPEAN REVIEW, 18,         59
(OCTOBER 1959), PP. 334-350.
ELNOEL

SHULMD-56-ISU    SHULMAN, MD

```
                    IS THE SOVIET UNION CHANGING.=
                    PROBLEMS OF COMMUNISM, 5, (MAY-JUNE 1956), PP. 16-23.          56
                    COMEL, ELEL
SHUVJT-56-PIG       SHUVAL, JT
                    PATTERNS OF INTER-GROUP TENSION IN ISRAEL.=
                    INTERNATIONAL SOCIAL SCIENCE BULLETIN, 8, (1956),              56
                       PP. 75-123.
                    ELEL, ELNOEL
SHWAB -57-KJB       SHWADRAN, B
                    THE KINGDOM OF JORDAN -- TO BE OR NOT TO BE.=
                    MIDDLE EASTERN AFFAIRS, 8, (AUGUST-SEPTEMBER 1957),            57
                       PP. 270-288.
                    ELEL, ELNOEL, ELPRNOR
SHWAB -60-PSI       SHWADRAN, B
                    THE POWER STRUGGLE IN IRAQ '' 1, '' 2, '' 3.=
                    MIDDLE EASTERN AFFAIRS, 11, (FEBRUARY, APRIL, MAY 1960),       60
                       PP. 38-63, PP. 106-123, PP. 150-161.
                    ELEL, ELNOEL
SIEGA -56-SIF       SIEGFRIED, A
                    STABLE INSTABILITY IN FRANCE.=
                    FOREIGN AFFAIRS, 34, (APRIL 1956), PP. 394-404.                56
                    ELEL, ELNOEL
SIFFWJ-66-TBI       SIFFIN, WJ
                    THE THAI BUREAUCRACY -- INSTITUTIONAL CHANGE
                       AND DEVELOPMENT.=
                    HONOLULU, EAST-WEST CENTER PRESS, 1966.                        66
                    ELEL
SIGMPE-63-IDN       SIGMUND, PE
                    THE IDEOLOGIES OF THE DEVELOPING NATIONS.=
                    NEW YORK, FREDERICK A PRAEGER, 1963.                           63
                    DEFEL, ELPRNOR
SILBBS-64-MME       SILBERMAN, BS
                    MINISTERS OF MODERNIZATION -- ELITE MOBILITY IN THE
                       MEIJI RESTORATION, 1868-1873.=
                    TUSCON, UNIVERSITY OF ARIZONA PRESS, 1964.                     64
                    COMEL, ELEL, ELNOEL, ELPRNOR, METEL
SILBBS-66-CRS       SILBERMAN, BS
                    CRITERIA FOR RECRUITMENT AND SUCCESS IN THE JAPANESE
                       BUREAUCRACY, 1866-1900 -- 'TRADITIONAL' AND 'MODERN'
                       CRITERIA IN BUREAUCRATIC DEVELOPMENT.=
                    ECONOMIC DEVELOPMENT AND CULTURAL CHANGE, 14,                  66
                       (JANUARY 1966), PP. 158-173.
                    COMEL, ELEL, ELPRNOR
SILBL -59-DS        SILBERMAN, L
                    DEMOCRACY IN THE SUDAN.=
                    PARLIAMENTARY AFFAIRS, 12, (SUMMER-AUTUMN 1959),               59
                       PP. 349-376.
                    ELEL, ELNOEL
SILSWE-57-LPB       SILSLEY, WE
                    LEADERSHIP IN A PHILIPPINE BAERIO.=
                    PHILIPPINE JOURNAL OF PUBLIC ADMINISTRATION, 1,                57
                       (APRIL 1957), PP. 154-159.
                    COMEL, ELNOEL, ELPRNOR
SILVC -54-LVL       SILVERMAN, C
                    THE LEGISLATORS' VIEW OF THE LEGISLATIVE PROCESS
                       (UNITED STATES).=
                    THE PUBLIC OPINION QUARTERLY, 18, (SUMMER 1954),               54
                       PP. 180-190.
                    ELPRNOR
SILVJ -64-USP       SILVERSTEIN, J       WOHL, J
                    UNIVERSITY STUDENTS AND POLITICS IN BURMA.=
                    PACIFIC AFFAIRS, 37, (SPRING 1964), PP. 50-65.                 64
                    ELEL, ELNOEL, ELPRNOR
SILVKH-54-SGG       SILVERT, KH
                    A STUDY IN GOVERNMENT -- GUATEMALA.=
                    NEW ORLEANS, TULANE UNIVERSITY PRESS, 1954.                    54
                    COMEL, ELEL, ELNOEL
SILVKH-61-RRL       SILVERT, KH
                    REACTION AND REVOLUTION IN LATIN AMERICA -- THE
                       CONFLICT SOCIETY.=
                    NEW ORLEANS, HANSER PRESS, 1961.                               61
                    COMEL, ELEL, ELNOEL, ELPRNOR
SILVKH-63-NVD       SILVERT, KH
                    NATIONAL VALUES, DEVELOPMENT, LEADERS AND FOLLOWERS
                       (LATIN AMERICA).=
                    INTERNATIONAL SOCIAL SCIENCE JOURNAL, 15, (1963),              63
                       PP. 560-570.
                    DEFEL, COMEL, ELNOEL, ELPRNOR
SILVKH-64-US        SILVERT, KH
                    THE UNIVERSITY STUDENT.=
                    JJ JOHNSON (ED), CONTINUITY AND CHANGE IN LATIN AMERICA,       64
                       STANFORD, CALIFORNIA, STANFORD UNIVERSITY PRESS, 1964,
                       PP. 206-226.
                    COMEL, ELEL, ELNOEL
```

```
SIMMRH-61-RSC    SIMMONS, RH
                 THE ROLE OF THE SELECT COMMITTEE ON NATIONALIZED
                   INDUSTRY IN PARLIAMENT (GREAT BRITAIN).=
                 THE WESTERN POLITICAL QUARTERLY, 14, (SEPTEMBER 1961),      61
                   PP. 741-747.
                 ELEL
SIMOHA-53-NOM    SIMON, HA
                 NOTES ON THE OBSERVATION AND MEASUREMENT OF POLITICAL
                   POWER.=
                 JOURNAL OF POLITICS, 15, (NOVEMBER 1953), PP. 500-516.      53
                 DEFEL, METEL
SIMOJ -64-FAI    SIMON, J
                 FERMENT AMONG INTELLECTUALS (CHINA).=
                 PROBLEMS OF COMMUNISM, 13, (SEPTEMBER-OCTOBER 1964),        64
                   PP. 29-37.
                 ELEL, ELPRNOR
SINDAP-55-BRA    SINDLER, AP
                 BIFACTIONAL RIVALRY AS AN ALTERNATIVE TO TWO - PARTY
                   COMPETITION (UNITED STATES).=
                 THE AMERICAN POLITICAL SCIENCE REVIEW, 49, (SEPTEMBER       55
                   1955), PP. 641-662.
                 COMEL, ELEL
SINDAP-66-PPU    SINDLER, AP
                 POLITICAL PARTIES IN THE UNITED STATES.=
                 NEW YORK, ST. MARTIN'S PRESS, 1966.                        66
                 COMEL, ELEL, ELNOEL
SINGDJ-58-TPA    SINGER, DJ
                 THREAT - PERCEPTION AND THE ARMAMENT - TENSION DILEMMA.=
                 THE JOURNAL OF CONFLICT RESOLUTION, 2, (MARCH 1958), PP.    58
                   90-105.
                 ELEL, ELPRNOR, METEL
SINGDJ-64-SAF    SINGER, DJ
                 SOVIET AND AMERICAN FOREIGN POLICY ATTITUDES -- CONTENT
                   ANALYSIS OF ELITE ARTICULATIONS.=
                 THE JOURNAL OF CONFLICT RESOLUTION, 8, (DECEMBER 1964),     64
                   PP. 424-485.
                 ELPRNOR, METEL
SINGMR-64-EES    SINGER, MR
                 THE EMERGING ELITE -- A STUDY OF POLITICAL LEADERSHIP
                   IN CEYLON.=
                 CAMBRIDGE, MIT PRESS, 1964.                                64
                 GNELTH, DEFEL, COMEL, ELEL, ELNOEL, ELPRNOR
SINGMR-66-GPS    SINGER, MR
                 GROUP PERCEPTION AND SOCIAL CHANGE IN CEYLON.=
                 INTERNATIONAL JOURNAL OF COMPARATIVE SOCIOLOGY, 7,          66
                   (MARCH 1966), PP. 209-226.
                 COMEL, ELEL, ELPRNOR
SIRVHK-67-DE     SIRVETZ, HK
                 DEMOCRACY AND ELITISM.=
                 NEW YORK, CHARLES SCRIBNER'S SONS, 1967.                   67
                 GNELTH, DEFEL
SK    -59-ICP    SK
                 THE INDIAN COMMUNIST PARTY TODAY.=
                 THE WORLD TODAY, 15, (JULY 1959), PP. 277-286.             59
                 COMEL, ELEL, ELNOEL, ELPRNOR
SKILHG-49-RPC    SKILLING, HG
                 REVOLUTIONS IN PRAGUE (CZECHOSLOVAKIA).=
                 INTERNATIONAL JOURNAL, 4, (SPRING 1949), PP. 119-136.      49
                 ELEL, ELNOEL
SKILHG-55-FCP    SKILLING, HG
                 THE FORMATION OF A COMMUNIST PARTY IN CZECHOSLOVAKIA.=
                 THE AMERICAN SLAVIC AND EAST EUROPEAN REVIEW, 14,           55
                   (OCTOBER 1955), PP. 346-358.
                 ELEL
SKILHG-60-CCC    SKILLING, HG
                 THE COMINTERN AND CZECHOSLOVAK COMMUNISM -- 1921-1929.=
                 THE AMERICAN SLAVIC AND EAST EUROPEAN REVIEW, 19,           60
                   (APRIL 1960), PP. 234-247.
                 ELEL
SKILHG-61-GBC    SKILLING, HG
                 GOTTWALD AND THE BOLSHEVIZATION OF THE COMMUNIST PARTY
                   OF CZECHOSLOVAKIA (1929-1939).=
                 SLAVIC REVIEW, 20, (DECEMBER 1961), PP. 641-655.           61
                 COMEL, ELEL, ELNOEL
SKILHG-61-RCC    SKILLING, HG
                 REVOLUTION AND CONTINUITY IN CZECHOSLOVAKIA 1945-1946.=
                 JOURNAL OF CENTRAL EUROPEAN AFFAIRS, 20, (JANUARY 1961),    61
                   PP. 357-377.
                 COMEL, ELEL
SKILHG-66-IGC    SKILLING, HG
                 INTEREST GROUPS AND COMMUNIST POLITICS.=
                 WORLD POLITICS, 18, (APRIL 1966), PP. 435-451.             66
                 DEFEL, ELEL
SKINGW-58-LPC    SKINNER, GW
```

LEADERSHIP AND POWER IN THE CHINESE COMMUNITY
   OF THAILAND.=
ITHACA, CORNELL UNIVERSITY PRESS FOR THE
   ASSOCIATION OF ASIAN STUDIES, 1958.    58
COMEL, ELEL, ELNOEL, ELPRNOR, METEL

SKLARL-63-NPP  SKLAR, RL
NIGERIAN POLITICAL PARTIES -- POWER IN AN EMERGENT
   AFRICAN NATION.=
PRINCETON, PRINCETON UNIVERSITY PRESS, 1963.    63
COMEL, ELEL, ELNOEL, ELPRNOR

SKLARL-65-CNP  SKLAR, RL
CONTRADICTIONS IN THE NIGERIAN POLITICAL SYSTEM.=
THE JOURNAL OF MODERN AFRICAN STUDIES, 3, (AUGUST 1965),  65
   PP. 201-213.
ELEL, ELNOEL, ELPRNOR

SMIGEO-58-ILE  SMIGEL, EO
INTERVIEWING A LEGAL ELITE -- THE WALL STREET LAWYER.=
THE AMERICAN JOURNAL OF SOCIOLOGY, 64, (SEPTEMBER 1958),  58
   PP. 159-164.
METEL

SMILDV-61-CCC  SMILEY, DV
CONSENSUS, CONFLICT, AND THE CANADIAN PARTY SYSTEM.=
CANADIAN FORUM, 40, (JANUARY 1961), PP. 223-224.    61
ELEL, ELPRNOR

SMITDE-65-RPB  SMITH, DE
RELIGION AND POLITICS IN BURMA.=
PRINCETON, PRINCETON UNIVERSITY PRESS, 1965.    65
ELEL, ELPRNOR

SMITIH-51-DPN  SMITH, IH        CHESTER, IE
DISTRIBUTION OF POWER IN NATIONALIZED INDUSTRIES
   (GREAT BRITAIN).=
THE BRITISH JOURNAL OF SOCIOLOGY, 2, (1951), PP. 275-293.  51
COMEL, ELEL

SMITJM-57-ARC  SMITH, JM        COTTER, CP
ADMINISTRATIVE RESPONSIBILITY -- CONGRESSIONAL
   PRESCRIPTION OF INTERAGENCY RELATIONSHIPS
   (UNITED STATES).=
THE WESTERN POLITICAL QUARTERLY, 10, (DECEMBER 1957)    57
   PP. 765-782.
ELEL

SMITJM-60-PPD  SMITH, JM        COTTER, CP (EDS)
POWERS OF THE PRESIDENT DURING CRISIS (UNITED STATES).=
WASHINGTON, PUBLIC AFFAIRS PRESS, 1960.    60
ELEL, ELNOEL, ELPRNOR

SMITL -55-PLN  SMITH, L
POLITICAL LEADERSHIP IN A NEW ENGLAND COMMUNITY
   (UNITED STATES).=
THE REVIEW OF POLITICS, 17, (JULY 1955), PP. 392-409.    55
COMEL, ELPRNOR

SMITMG-64-HCC  SMITH, MG
HISTORICAL AND CULTURAL CONDITIONS OF POLITICAL
   CORRUPTION AMONG THE HAUSA (NORTHERN NIGERIA).=
COMPARATIVE STUDIES IN SOCIETY AND HISTORY, 6,    64
   (1963-1964), PP. 164-194.
ELEL, ELNOEL, ELPRNOR

SMITMG-65-SGW  SMITH, MG
STRATIFICATION IN GRENADA (WEST INDIES).=
BERKELEY, UNIVERSITY OF CALIFORNIA PRESS, 1965.    65
COMEL, ELEL, ELNOEL, ELPRNOR

SMITPA-65-GCP  SMITH, PA
THE GAMES OF COMMUNITY POLITICS (UNITED STATES).=
MIDWEST JOURNAL OF POLITICAL SCIENCE, 9,    65
   (FEBRUARY 1965), PP. 37-60.
ELNOEL, ELPRNOR, METEL

SMITRW-57-RIB  SMITH, RW
RELIGIOUS INFLUENCES IN THE BACKGROUND OF THE BRITISH
   LABOUR PARTY.=
THE SOUTHWESTERN SOCIAL SCIENCE QUARTERLY, 37,    57
   (MARCH 1957), PP. 355-369.
COMEL, ELPRNOR

SMITTC-60-SPS  SMITH, TC
THE STRUCTURING OF POWER IN A SUBURBAN COMMUNITY
   (UNITED STATES).=
PACIFIC SOCIOLOGICAL REVIEW, 3, (FALL 1960), PP. 83-88.  60
DEFEL, COMEL, ELEL, ELNOEL, ELPRNOR

SMITWC-55-IMD  SMITH, WC
THE INTELLECTUALS IN THE MODERN DEVELOPMENT
   OF THE ISLAMIC WORLD.=
SN FISHER (ED), SOCIAL FORCES IN THE MIDDLE EAST,    55
   ITHACA, CORNELL UNIVERSITY PRESS, 1955, PP. 190-204.
COMEL, ELEL, ELNOEL, ELPRNOR

SMUCRH-56-LPU  SMUCKLER, RH        BELKNAP, GM
LEADERSHIP AND PARTICIPATION IN URBAN POLITICAL AFFAIRS
   (UNITED STATES).=

                EAST LANSING, THE GOVERNMENT RESEARCH BUREAU, 1956.      56
                COMEL, ELEL, ELNOEL
SMYTHH-50-CPN  SMYTHE, HH
                CHANGING PATTERNS IN NEGRO LEADERSHIP
                  (UNITED STATES).=
                SOCIAL FORCES, 29, (DECEMBER 1950), PP. 191-197.       50
                COMEL
SMYTHH-50-NML  SMYTHE, HH
                NEGRO MASSES AND LEADERS (UNITED STATES).=
                SOCIOLOGY AND SOCIAL RESEARCH, 35, (SEPTEMBER-OCTOBER    50
                  1950), PP. 31-37.
                ELNOEL, ELPRNOR
SMYTHH-58-PNL  SMYTHE, HH
                THE PROBLEM OF NATIONAL LEADERSHIP IN NIGERIA.=
                SOCIAL RESEARCH, 25, (SUMMER 1958), PP. 215-227.       58
                COMEL, ELEL
SMYTHH-58-SSN  SMYTHE, HH
                SOCIAL STRATIFICATION IN NIGERIA.=
                SOCIAL FORCES, 37, (DECEMBER 1958), PP. 168-171.       58
                COMEL, ELNOEL
SMYTHH-59-ASN  SMYTHE, HH
                AFRICA'S NEW POLITICAL LEADERS.=
                PROD (THE AMERICAN BEHAVIORAL SCIENTIST), 2,          59
                  (MAY 1959), PP. 17-19.
                COMEL, METEL
SMYTHH-59-NEO  SMYTHE, HH         SMYTHE, MM
                THE NIGERIAN ELITE -- SOME OBSERVATIONS.=
                SOCIOLOGY AND SOCIAL RESEARCH, 44,             59
                  (SEPTEMBER-OCTOBER 1959), PP. 42-45.
                DEFEL, COMEL, ELEL
SMYTHH-60-BAS  SMYTHE, HH         SMYTHE, MM
                BLACK AFRICA'S NEW POWER ELITE.=
                THE SOUTH ATLANTIC QUARTERLY, 59, (SPRING 1960),     60
                  PP. 13-23.
                COMEL, ELPRNOR
SMYTHH-60-NER  SMYTHE, HH
                NIGERIAN ELITE -- ROLE OF EDUCATION.=
                SOCIOLOGY AND SOCIAL RESEARCH, 45, (OCTOBER 1960),   60
                  PP. 71-73.
                COMEL
SMYTHH-60-NNE  SMYTHE, HH         SMYTHE, MM
                THE NEW NIGERIAN ELITE.=
                STANFORD, STANFORD UNIVERSITY PRESS, 1960.         60
                DEFEL, COMEL, ELEL, ELNOEL, ELPRNOR
SMYTHH-61-NAL  SMYTHE, HH         SMYTHE, MM
                THE NEW AFRICAN LEADERS.=
                YALE REVIEW, 51, (DECEMBER 1961), PP. 227-235.      61
                COMEL, ELEL, ELNOEL
SMYTHH-61-NAM  SMYTHE, HH         SMYTHE, MM
                THE NON - AFRICAN MINORITY IN MODERN AFRICA --
                  SOCIAL STATUS.=
                SOCIOLOGY AND SOCIAL RESEARCH, 45, (APRIL 1961),    61
                  PP. 310-315.
                COMEL, ELEL
SNISCB-48-SCS  SNISHER, CB
                THE SUPREME COURT AND THE SOUTH (UNITED STATES).=
                THE JOURNAL OF POLITICS, 10, (MAY 1948), PP. 282-305.    48
                ELNOEL
SNOWCP-61-SGG  SNOW, CP
                SCIENCE AND GOVERNMENT (GREAT BRITAIN).=
                CAMBRIDGE, HARVARD UNIVERSITY PRESS, 1961.         61
                COMEL, ELEL, ELPRNOR
SNOWE -38-RSO  SNOW, E
                RED STAR OVER CHINA.=
                NEW YORK, RANDOM HOUSE, 1938.             38
                ELEL, ELNOEL
SNOWG -63-AR  SNOW, G
                ARGENTINE RADICALISM, 1957-1963.=
                JOURNAL OF INTER-AMERICAN STUDIES, 5, (OCTOBER 1963),   63
                  PP. 507-531.
                COMEL, ELEL, ELPRNOR
SNOWLM-66-CRR  SNOWISS, LM
                CONGRESSIONAL RECRUITMENT AND REPRESENTATION
                  (UNITED STATES).=
                THE AMERICAN POLITICAL SCIENCE REVIEW, 60, (SEPTEMBER   66
                  1966), PP. 627-639.
                COMEL, ELPRNOR
SNYDEC-57-SCS  SNYDER, EC
                THE SUPREME COURT AS A SMALL GROUP (UNITED STATES).=
                SOCIAL FORCES, 36, (DECEMBER 1957), PP. 232-238.       57
                ELEL, METEL
SNYDEC-59-USC  SNYDER, EC
                UNCERTAINTY AND THE SUPREME COURT'S DECISIONS
                  (UNITED STATES).=

THE AMERICAN JOURNAL OF SOCIOLOGY, 65, (NOVEMBER 1959),    59
    PP. 241-245.
    ELEL, ELNOEL, ELPRNOR
SNYDEC-60-PPA   SNYDER, EC
    POLITICAL POWER AND THE ABILITY TO WIN SUPREME COURT
        DECISIONS (UNITED STATES).=
    SOCIAL FORCES, 39, (OCTOBER 1960), PP. 36-40.            60
    ELNOEL
SNYDFG-65-OPG   SNYDER, FG
    ONE - PARTY GOVERNMENT IN MALI -- TRANSITION TOWARD
        CONTROL.=
    NEW HAVEN, YALE UNIVERSITY PRESS, 1965.                  65
    DEFEL, COMEL, ELEL, ELNOEL, ELPRNOR, METEL
SNYDRC-57-SPI   SNYDER, RC
    SOCIAL POSITIONS AND IMAGES OF THE POLITICAL PROCESS.=
    PROD (THE AMERICAN BEHAVIORAL SCIENTIST), 1,             57
        (SEPTEMBER 1957), PP. 9-10)
    ELPRNOR
SNYDRC-58-DMA   SNYDER, RC
    A DECISION-MAKING APPROACH TO THE STUDY
        OF POLITICAL PHENOMENA.=
    R YOUNG (ED), APPROACHES TO THE STUDY OF POLITICS,       58
        EVANSTON, ILLINOIS, NORTHWESTERN UNIVERSITY PRESS,
        1958, PP. 3-38.
    DEFEL, COMEL, ELPRNOR, METEL
SNYDRC-62-FPD   SNYDER, RC            ET. AL.
    FOREIGN POLICY DECISION-MAKING -- AN APPROACH TO THE STUDY
        OF INTERNATIONAL POLITICS.=
    GLENCOE, THE FREE PRESS, 1962.                           62
    COMEL, ELEL, ELNOEL, ELPRNOR
SOARGA-67-IIP   SOARES, GAC
    INTELLECTUAL IDENTITY AND POLITICAL IDEOLOGY AMONG
        UNIVERSITY STUDENTS (LATIN AMERICA).=
    SM LIPSET AND A SOLARI (EDS), ELITES IN LATIN AMERICA,   67
        NEW YORK, OXFORD UNIVERSITY PRESS, 1967, PP. 431-453.
    ELEL, ELPRNOR
SOFEE -61-PML   SOFEN, E
    PROBLEMS OF METROPOLITAN LEADERSHIP -- THE MIAMI
        EXPERIENCE (UNITED STATES).=
    MIDWEST JOURNAL OF POLITICAL SCIENCE, 5,                 61
        (FEBRUARY 1961), PP. 18-38.
    ELEL, ELNOEL
SOLAA -67-SED   SOLARI, A
    SECONDARY EDUCATION AND THE DEVELOPMENT OF ELITES
        (LATIN AMERICA).=
    SM LIPSET AND A SOLARI (EDS), ELITES IN LATIN AMERICA,   67
    NEW YORK, OXFORD UNIVERSITY PRESS, 1967, PP. 457-483.
    COMEL, ELEL, ELPRNOR
SOLOSR-60-GUS   SOLOMON, SR
    GOVERNORS -- 1950-1960 (UNITED STATES).=
    NATIONAL CIVIC REVIEW, 49, (SEPTEMBER 1960),             60
        PP. 410-416.
    COMEL
SOMAJ -65-PPE   SOMASEVICH, J
    PEASANTS, POLITICS, AND ECONOMIC CHANGE IN YUGOSLAVIA.=
    STANFORD, STANFORD UNIVERSITY PRESS, 1965.               65
    ELEL, ELNOEL, ELPRNOR
SOMEDC-53-QGP   SOMERVELL, DC
    THE QUALITIES OF A GREAT PRIME MINISTER (GREAT BRITAIN).=
    PARLIAMENTARY AFFAIRS, 6, (SUMMER 1953), PP. 242-249.    53
    COMEL
SOMIA -48-MHP   SOMIT, A
    THE MILITARY HERO AS PRESIDENTIAL CANDIDATE
        (UNITED STATES).=
    THE PUBLIC OPINION QUARTERLY, 12, (SUMMER 1948),         48
        PP. 192-200.
    COMEL, ELNOEL
SOMIA -57-VEP   SOMIT, A              TANENHAUS, J
    THE VETERAN IN THE ELECTORAL PROCESS -- THE HOUSE OF
        REPRESENTATIVES (UNITED STATES).=
    THE JOURNAL OF POLITICS, 19, (MAY 1957), PP. 184-201.    57
    COMEL, ELEL, ELNOEL
SORAFJ-63-PRU   SORAUF, FJ
    PARTY AND REPRESENTATION (UNITED STATES).=
    NEW YORK, ATHERTON PRESS, 1963.                          63
    COMEL, ELNOEL, ELPRNOR
SORAFJ-64-PPA   SORAUF, FJ
    POLITICAL PARTIES IN THE AMERICAN SYSTEM.=
    BOSTON, LITTLE, BROWN AND COMPANY, 1964.                 64
    DEFEL, COMEL, ELEL, ELNOEL, ELPRNOR
SORIK -63-MSM   SORIANO-JR, K
    MANILA'S MAYOR LOCKS HORNS WITH THE GAO (PHILIPPINES).=
    PHILIPPINE JOURNAL OF PUBLIC ADMINISTRATION, 7,          63
        (APRIL 1963), PP. 122-132.

                         ELEL, ELPRNOR
SOUKJR-60-LPJ    SOUKUP, JR
                 LABOR AND POLITICS IN JAPAN -- A STUDY OF INTEREST GROUP
                    ATTITUDES AND ACTIVITIES.=
                 THE JOURNAL OF POLITICS, 22, (MAY 1960), PP. 314-337.      60
                 ELEL, ELNOEL, ELPRNOR
SOUTA -61-SCM    SOUTHALL, A (ED)
                 SOCIAL CHANGE IN MODERN AFRICA.=
                 LONDON, OXFORD UNIVERSITY PRESS, 1961.                     61
                 DEFEL, COMEL, ELEL, ELNOEL, ELPRNOR
SOUTAW-66-CET    SOUTHALL, AW
                 THE CONCEPT OF ELITES AND THEIR FORMATION IN UGANDA.=
                 PC LLOYD (ED), THE NEW ELITES OF TROPICAL AFRICA, LONDON,  66
                    OXFORD UNIVERSITY PRESS, PP. 342-366.
                 DEFEL, COMEL, ELEL, ELPRNOR
SPAEHJ-61-ASA    SPAETH, HJ
                 AN APPROACH TO THE STUDY OF ATTITUDINAL DIFFERENCES AS AN
                    ASPECT OF JUDICIAL BEHAVIOR (UNITED STATES).=
                 MIDWEST JOURNAL OF POLITICAL SCIENCE, 5, (MAY 1961),       61
                    PP. 165-180.
                 ELEL, ELPRNOR, METEL
SPAEHJ-62-JPV    SPAETH, HJ
                 JUDICIAL POWER AS A VARIABLE MOTIVATING SUPREME
                    COURT BEHAVIOR (UNITED STATES).=
                 MIDWEST JOURNAL OF POLITICAL SCIENCE, 6, (FEBRUARY 1962),  62
                    PP. 54-82.
                 ELEL, ELPRNOR, METEL
SPAEHJ-63-AJA    SPAETH, HJ
                 AN ANALYSIS OF JUDICIAL ATTITUDES IN THE LABOR
                    RELATIONS DECISIONS OF THE WARREN COURT.=
                 THE JOURNAL OF POLITICS, 25, (MAY 1963), PP. 290-311.      63
                 ELEL, ELNOEL, ELPRNOR
SPANRN-53-CSW    SPANN, RN
                 CIVIL SERVANTS IN WASHINGTON -- 1, THE CHARACTER OF THE
                    FEDERAL SERVICE --2, THE HIGHER CIVIL SERVICE AND
                    ITS FUTURE (UNITED STATES).=
                 POLITICAL STUDIES, 1, (1953), PP. 143-161, PP. 238-246.    53
                 COMEL, ELEL, ELPRNOR
SPAUCB-51-OAC    SPAULDING, CB
                 OCCUPATIONAL AFFILIATIONS OF COUNCILMEN IN SMALL CITIES
                    (UNITED STATES).=
                 SOCIOLOGY AND SOCIAL RESEARCH, 35, (JANUARY-FEBRUARY       51
                    1951), PP. 194-200.
                 COMEL
SPEIH -52-IPC    SPEIER, H
                 INTERNATIONAL POLITICAL COMMUNICATION -- ELITE VS. MASS.=
                 WORLD POLITICS, 4, (APRIL 1952), PP. 305-317.              52
                 ELNOEL, ELPRNOR
SPEIH -54-GRO    SPEIER, H
                 GERMAN REARMAMENT AND THE OLD MILITARY ELITE.=
                 WORLD POLITICS, 6, (JANUARY 1954), PP. 147-168.            54
                 COMEL, ELPRNOR
SPEIH -57-GRA    SPEIER, H
                 GERMAN REARMAMENT AND ATOMIC WAR -- THE VIEWS OF GERMAN
                    MILITARY AND POLITICAL LEADERS.=
                 EVANSTON, ILLINOIS, ROW, PETERSON AND COMPANY, 1957.       57
                 COMEL, ELEL, ELPRNOR
SPEIH -57-WGL    SPEIER, H          DAVISON, WP (EDS)
                 WEST GERMAN LEADERSHIP AND FOREIGN POLICY.=
                 EVANSTON, ILLINOIS, ROW, PETERSON AND COMPANY, 1957.       57
                 ELEL, ELNOEL, ELPRNOR
SPENJJ-63-BED    SPENGLER, JJ
                 BUREAUCRACY AND ECONOMIC DEVELOPMENT.=
                 J LA PALOMBARA (ED), BUREAUCRACY AND POLITICAL             63
                    DEVELOPMENT, PRINCETON, PRINCETON UNIVERSITY
                    PRESS, 1963, PP. 199-232.
                 DEFEL, COMEL, ELFL, ELNOEL, ELPRNOR
SPENS -47-IES    SPENDER, S
                 INTELLECTUALS AND EUROPE'S FUTURE.=
                 COMMENTARY, 3, (JANUARY 1947), PP. 7-12.                   47
                 ELEL, ELNOEL, ELPRNOR
SPENS -51-BIW    SPENDER, S
                 BRITISH INTELLECTUALS IN THE WELFARE STATE.=
                 COMMENTARY, 12, (NOVEMBER 1951), PP. 425-430.              51
                 ELEL, ELNOEL, ELPRNOR
SPENW -62-PEM    SPENCER, W
                 POLITICAL EVOLUTION IN THE MIDDLE EAST.=
                 PHILADELPHIA, J B LIPPENCOTT COMPANY, 1962.                62
                 COMEL, ELEL, ELNOEL, ELPRNOR
SPEYE -57-SBA    SPEYER, E
                 SCIENTISTS IN THE BUREAUCRATIC AGE.=
                 DISSENT, 4, (AUTUMN 1957), PP. 402-413.                    57
                 ELEL, ELPRNOR
SPINCN-46-PPP    SPINKS, CN

POSTWAR POLITICAL PARTIES IN JAPAN.=
PACIFIC AFFAIRS, 19, (SEPTEMBER 1946., PP. 250-259.                46
ELEL, ELNOEL

SPINW -66-SPO   SPINRAD, W
THE SOCIO-POLITICAL ORIENTATIONS OF C. WRIGHT MILLS --
   AN EVALUATION.=
THE BRITISH JOURNAL OF SOCIOLOGY, 17, (MARCH 1966),               66
   PP. 46-59
GNELTH

SPIRHJ-62-PA   SPIRO, HJ
POLITICS IN AFRICA.=
ENGLEWOOD CLIFFS, NEW JERSEY, PRENTICE-HALL, 1962.                62
COMEL, ELEL, ELNOEL

SPIRHJ-66-APP   SPIRO, HJ (ED)
AFRICA -- THE PRIMACY OF POLITICS (CONGO, NIGERIA).=
NEW YORK, RANDOM HOUSE, 1966.                                     66
DEFEL, COMEL, ELEL, ELNOEL, ELPRNOR

SPITD -65-PAD   SPITZ, D
PATTERNS OF ANTI - DEMOCRATIC THOUGHT.=
NEW YORK, THE FREE PRESS, 1965.                                   65
DEFEL

SRINMN-66-SCM   SRINIVAS, MN
SOCIAL CHANGE IN MODERN INDIA.=
BERKELEY, UNIVERSITY OF CALIFORNIA PRESS, 1966.                   66
COMEL, ELEL, ELNOEL, ELPRNOR

ST-GCF-54-CHL   ST-GEORGE, CFL
THE COMPOSITION OF THE HOUSE OF LORDS (GREAT BRITAIN).=
PARLIAMENTARY AFFAIRS, 7, (WINTER 1953-1954), PP. 60-68.   54
COMEL

STAARF-55-SUP   STAAR, RF
THE SECRETARIAT OF THE UNITED POLISH WORKER'S PARTY.=
JOURNAL OF CENTRAL EUROPEAN AFFAIRS, 15, (OCTOBER 1955),   55
   PP. 272-285.
COMEL, ELEL

STAARF-56-PBU   STAAR, RF
THE POLITICAL BUREAU OF THE UNITED POLISH WORKERS PARTY.=
THE AMERICAN SLAVIC AND EAST EUROPEAN REVIEW, 15,
   (APRIL 1956), PP. 206-215.                                     56
COMEL, ELEL

STAARF-57-CCU   STAAR, RF
THE CENTRAL COMMITTEE OF THE UNITED POLISH WORKERS' PARTY.=
JOURNAL OF CENTRAL EUROPEAN AFFAIRS, 16, (JANUARY 1957),   57
   PP. 371-383.
COMEL, ELEL

STAARF-60-TCP   STAAR, RF
THIRD CONGRESS OF THE POLISH COMMUNIST PARTY.=
THE AMERICAN SLAVIC AND EAST EUROPEAN REVIEW, 19,
   (FEBRUARY 1960), PP. 63-73.                                    60
COMEL, ELEL

STAARF-62-CAP   STAAR, RF
THE CENTRAL APPARATUS OF POLAND'S COMMUNIST PARTY.=
JOURNAL OF CENTRAL EUROPEAN AFFAIRS, 22, (OCTOBER 1962),   62
   PP. 337-348.
COMEL, ELEL

STAARF-62-PSC   STAAR, RF
POLAND 1942-1962 -- THE SOVIETIZATION OF A CAPTIVE
   PEOPLE.=
NEW ORLEANS, LOUISIANA STATE UNIVERSITY PRESS, 1962.             62
COMEL, ELEL, ELNOEL, ELPRNOR

STAN  -67-MWG   STANLEY,DT          MANN, DE          DOIG, JW
MEN WHO GOVERN -- A BIOGRAPHICAL PROFILE OF FEDERAL
   POLITICAL EXECUTIVES (UNITED STATES).=
WASHINGTON, THE BROOKINGS INSTITUTION, 1967.                     67
COMEL

STANE -54-FUD   STANLEY, E
THE FUTURE OF UNDER-DEVELOPED COUNTRIES -- POLITICAL
   IMPLICATIONS OF ECONOMIC DEVELOPMENT.=
NEW YORK, COUNCIL ON FOREIGN RELATIONS AND HARPER AND            54
   BROTHERS, 1954.
ELEL, ELPRNOR

STANWH-58-IPC   STANDING, WH          ROBINSON, JA
INTER - PARTY COMPETITION AND PRIMARY CONTESTING --
   THE CASE OF INDIANA (UNITED STATES).=
THE AMERICAN POLITICAL SCIENCE REVIEW, 52,
   (DECEMBER 1958), PP. 1066-1077.                                58
ELEL, ELNOEL

STAURB-65-PIG   STAUFFER, RB
PHILIPPINE INTEREST GROUPS -- AN INDEX OF
   POLITICAL DEVELOPMENT.=
ASIAN STUDIES, 3, (1965), PP. 193-220.                           65
ELEL, ELPRNOR

STAURB-66-PLT   STAUFFER, RB
PHILIPPINE LEGISLATORS AND THEIR CHANGING UNIVERSE.=
THE JOURNAL OF POLITICS, 28, (AUGUST 1966), PP. 556-597.   66

COMEL

STEARJ-58-SOC STEAMER, RJ
STATESMANSHIP OR CRAFTSMANSHIP -- CURRENT CONFLICT
OVER THE SUPREME COURT (UNITED STATES).=
THE WESTERN POLITICAL QUARTERLY, 11, (JUNE 1958),            58
PP. 265-277.
ELEL, ELPRNOR

STEARJ-60-RFD STEAMER, RJ
THE ROLE OF THE FEDERAL DISTRICT COURTS IN THE
SEGREGATION CONTROVERSY (UNITED STATES).=
THE JOURNAL OF POLITICS, 22, (AUGUST 1960), PP. 417-438.     60
ELNOEL

STEIE -63-DUD STEIN, E
THE DILEMMA OF UNION DEMOCRACY (UNITED STATES).=
THE ANNALS OF THE AMERICAN ACADEMY OF POLITICAL AND          63
SOCIAL SCIENCE, 350, (NOVEMBER 1963), PP. 46-54.
ELNOEL

STEIHA-51-RCC STEINER, HA
THE ROLE OF THE CHINESE COMMUNIST PARTY.=
THE ANNALS OF THE AMERICAN ACADEMY OF POLITICAL AND          51
SOCIAL SCIENCE, 277, (SEPTEMBER 1951), PP. 56-66.
COMEL, ELEL, ELNOEL

STEIHA-59-IPC STEINER, HA
IDEOLOGY AND POLITICS IN COMMUNIST CHINA.=
THE ANNALS OF THE AMERICAN ACADEMY OF POLITICAL AND          59
SOCIAL SCIENCE, 321, (JANUARY 1959), PP. 29-39.
DEFEL, ELPRNOR

STEIHA-63-CCL STEINER, HA
CHINESE COMMUNIST LEADERSHIP IN WAR AND PEACE --
A REVIEW ARTICLE.=
PACIFIC AFFAIRS, 35, (WINTER 1962-1963), PP. 384-390.        63
ELEL, ELNOEL, ELPRNOR

STEIJW-51-SI STEIN, JW
THE SOVIET INTELLIGENTSIA.=
THE RUSSIAN REVIEW, 10, (OCTOBER 1951), PP. 283-292.         51
COMEL, ELEL

STEPF -58-RIB STEPUN, F
THE RUSSIAN INTELLIGENTSIA AND BOLSHEVISM.=
THE RUSSIAN REVIEW, 17, (OCTOBER 1958), PP. 263-277.         58
ELEL, ELPRNOR

STEPRP-50-PSP STEPHENS, RP
THE PROSPECT FOR SOCIAL PROGRESS IN THE PHILIPPINES.=
PACIFIC AFFAIRS, 23, (JUNE 1950), PP. 139-152.               50
ELEL, ELNOEL, ELPRNOR

STEPTE-59-LFR STEPHENSON, TE
THE LEADER - FOLLOWER RELATIONSHIP.=
THE SOCIOLOGICAL REVIEW, 7, (DECEMBER 1959), PP. 179-195. 59
DEFEL, ELNOEL

STEUWL-59-LMS STEUDE, WL
THE LAWYER IN MICHIGAN STATE GOVERNMENT (UNITED STATES).=
ANN ARBOR, THE INSTITUTE OF PUBLIC ADMINISTRATION,           59
UNIVERSITY OF MICHIGAN PRESS, 1959.
COMEL

STEVRP-63-SPD STEVENS, RP
SWAZILAND POLITICAL DEVELOPMENT.=
THE JOURNAL OF MODERN AFRICAN STUDIES, 1, (SEPTEMBER         63
PP. 327-350.
COMEL, ELEL, ELNOEL, ELPRMOR

STEWDK-64-CSF STEWART, DK          SMITH, TC
CELEBRITY STRUCTURE OF THE FAR RIGHT (UNITED STATES).=
THE WESTERN POLITICAL QUARTERLY, 17, (JUNE 1964),            64
PP. 349-355.
COMEL, ELEL

STEWJD-58-BPG STEWART, JD
BRITISH PRESSURE GROUPS -- THEIR ROLE IN RELATION TO THE
HOUSE OF COMMONS.=
LONDON, OXFORD UNIVERSITY PRESS, 1958.                       58
ELEL, ELNOEL

STILE -59-BHI STILLMAN, E (ED)
BITTER HARVEST -- THE INTELLECTUAL REVOLT BEHIND
THE IRON CURTAIN (EAST EUROPE).=
NEW YORK, FREDERICK A PRAEGER, 1959.                         59
ELEL, ELNOEL, ELPRNOR

STOCJA-66-JSP STOCKWIN, JAA
THE JAPANESE SOCIALIST PARTY UNDER NEW LEADERSHIP.=
ASIAN SURVEY, 6, (APRIL 1966), PP. 187-200.                  66
ELEL, ELPRNOR

STOEJ -55-WCS STOETZEL, J
WITHOUT THE CHRYSANTHEMUM AND THE SWORD -- A STUDY OF THE
ATTITUDES OF YOUTH IN POST-WAR JAPAN.=
NEW YORK, UNESCO (COLUMBIA UNIVERSITY PRESS), 1955.          55
ELEL, ELNOEL, ELPRNOR, METEL

STOGRM-55-MSA STOGDILL, RM          SHARTLE, CL
METHODS IN THE STUDY OF ADMINISTRATIVE LEADERSHIP.=

COLUMBUS, OHIO, BUREAU OF BUSINESS RESEARCH, OHIO STATE    55
   UNIVERSITY, 1955.
   METEL
STOGRM-56-LRE    STOGDILL, RM        SCOTT, EL        JAYNES, W
   LEADERSHIP AND ROLE EXPECTATION (UNITED STATES).=
   COLUMBUS, OHIO STATE UNIVERSITY, RESEARCH MONOGRAPH 86,    56
   1956.
   ELPRNOR
STOGRM-57-LBI    STOGDILL, RM        COONS, AE
   LEADERSHIP BEHAVIOR -- ITS DESCRIPTION AND MEASUREMENT
   (UNITED STATES).=
   COLUMBUS, OHIO, OHIO STATE UNIVERSITY, 1957.    57
   DEFEL, ELPRNOR, METEL
STOKDE-62-PGS    STOKES, DE        MILLER, WE
   PARTY GOVERNMENT AND THE SALIENCY OF CONGRESS
   (UNITED STATES).=
   THE PUBLIC OPINION QUARTERLY, 26, (WINTER 1962),    62
   PP. 531-546.
   ELEL, ELNOEL
STOKDE-63-SMP    STOKES, DE
   SPATIAL MODELS OF PARTY COMPETITION.=
   THE AMERICAN POLITICAL SCIENCE REVIEW, 57, (JUNE 1963),    63
   PP. 368-377.
   METEL
STOKW -52-VPF    STOKES, W
   VIOLENCE AS A POWER FACTOR IN LATIN AMERICAN POLITICS.=
   THE WESTERN POLITICAL QUARTERLY, 5, (SEPTEMBER 1952),    52
   PP. 445-468.
   ELEL, ELPRNOR
STOKW -59-RNM    STOKES, W
   THE 'REVOLUCION NACIONAL' AND THE MNR IN BOLIVIA.=
   INTER-AMERICAN ECONOMIC AFFAIRS, 12, (SPRING 1959),    59
   PP. 28-53.
   COMEL, ELEL, ELNOEL
STONCN-64-LDU    STONE, CN
   LEADERSHIP BY DEFAULT (UNITED STATES).=
   NATIONAL CIVIC REVIEW, 53, (JULY 1964), PP. 360-364.    64
   COMEL
STONLA-63-UMR    STONE, LA
   USE OF A MULTIPLE REGRESSION MODEL WITH GROUP
   DECISION-MAKING.=
   HUMAN RELATIONS, 16, (MAY 1963), PP. 183-188.    63
   METEL
STORR -57-DPS    STORRY, R
   THE DOUBLE PATRIOTS -- A STUDY OF JAPANESE NATIONALISM.=
   BOSTON, HOUGHTON MIFFLIN, 1957.    57
   ELEL, ELPRNOR
STOUSA-55-CCC    STOUFFER, SA
   COMMUNISM, CONFORMITY, AND CIVIL LIBERTIES
   (UNITED STATES).=
   GARDEN CITY, NEW YORK, DOUBLEDAY, 1955.    55
   ELEL, ELNOEL, ELPRNOR
STRAE -61-RSB    STRAUSS, E
   THE RULING SERVANTS -- BUREAUCRACY IN RUSSIA, FRANCE,
   AND GREAT BRITAIN.=
   NEW YORK, FREDERICK A PRAEGER, 1961.    61
   COMEL, ELEL, ELNOEL, ELPRNOR
STRAL -63-T    STRAUSS, L
   ON TYRANNY.=
   GLENCOE, ILLINOIS, THE FREE PRESS, 1963.    63
   DEFEL
STRAR -56-PC    STRAUSZ-HUPE, R
   POWER AND COMMUNITY.=
   NEW YORK, FREDERICK A PRAEGER, 1956.    56
   GNELTH
STRAWP-64-ILA    STRASSMAN, WP
   THE INDUSTRIALISTS (LATIN AMERICA).=
   JJ JOHNSON (ED), CONTINUITY AND CHANGE IN LATIN AMERICA,    64
   STANFORD, STABNFORD UNIVERSITY PRESS, 1964,
   PP. 161-185.
   COMEL, ELEL, ELPRNOR
STUMHP-66-PEJ    STUMPF, HP
   THE POLITICAL EFFICACY OF JUDICIAL SYMBOLISM.=
   THE WESTERN POLITICAL QUARTERL, 19, (JUNE 1966),    66
   PP. 293-303.
   ELEL, ELPRNOR
SUBRV -62-EMC    SUBRAMANIAM, V
   THE EVOLUTION OF MINISTER - CIVIL SERVANT RELATIONS IN
   INDIA.=
   JOURNAL OF COMMONWEALTH POLITICAL STUDIES, 1,    62
   (1962), PP. 223-232.
   COMEL, ELEL, ELNOEL
SUKIW -63-ESR    SUKIENNICKI, W
   THE ESTABLISHMENT OF THE SOVIET REGIME IN EASTERN POLAND

              IN 1939.=
              JOURNAL OF CENTRAL EUROPEAN AFFAIRS, 23, (JULY 1963),    63
                PP. 191-218.
              ELNOEL

SULEM -67-PPL   SULEIMAN, M
              POLITICAL PARTIES IN LEBANON -- THE CHALLENGE OF A
                FRAGMENTED POLITICAL CULTURE.=
              ITHACA, CORNELL UNIVERSITY PRESS, 1967.         67
              COMEL, ELEL, ELNOEL, ELPRNOR

SULEMW-67-ECD   SULEIMAN, MW
              ELECTIONS IN A CONFESSIONAL DEMOCRACY (LEBANON).=
              THE JOURNAL OF POLITICS, 29, (FEBRUARY 1967), PP. 109-128.67
              COMEL, ELNOEL, ELPRNOR

SUTKS -52-JOE   SUTKER, S
              THE JEWISH ORGANIZATIONAL ELITE OF ATLANTA, GEORGIA
                (UNITED STATES).=
              SOCIAL FORCES, 31, (DECEMBER 1952), PP. 136-144.      52
              COMEL, ELPRNOR

SUTTFX-59-RNP   SUTTON, FX
              REPRESENTATION AND NATURE OF POLITICAL SYSTEMS.=
              COMPARATIVE STUDIES IN SOCIETY AND HISTORY, 2,        59
                (OCTOBER 1959), PP. 1-10.
              DEFEL, ELNOEL

SVENTP-60-IYH   SVENNEVIG, TP
              THE IDEOLOGY OF THE YUGOSLAV HERETICS.=
              SOCIAL RESEARCH, 27, (SPRING 1960), PP. 39-48.      60
              ELPRNOR

SWANBE-62-CTC   SWANSON, BE (ED)
              CURRENT TRENDS IN COMPARATIVE COMMUNITY STUDIES.=
              KANSAS CITY, MISSOURI, COMMUNITY STUDIES, INC, 1962.    62
              DEFEL, COMEL, ELEL, ELNOEL, ELPRNOR, METEL

SWAYH -62-PCL   SWAYZE, H
              POLITICAL CONTROL OF LITERATURE IN THE USSR,
                1946-1959.=
              CAMBRIDGE, HARVARD UNIVERSITY PRESS, 1962.       62
              ELEL, ELPRNOR

SWEAH -63-BIL   SWEARER, H
              BOLSHEVISM AND THE INDIVIDUAL LEADER (SOVIET UNION).=
              PROBLEMS OF COMMUNISM, 12, (MARCH-APRIL 1963), PP. 84-99. 63
              ELEL, ELPRNOR

SWEAHR-60-PPM   SWEARER, HR
              POPULAR PARTICIPATION -- MYTHS AND REALITY
                (SOVIET UNION).=
              PROBLEMS OF COMMUNISM, 9, (SEPTEMBER-OCTOBER 1960),   60
                PP. 42-51.
              ELNOEL

SWEAHR-61-FSL   SWEARER, HR
              THE FUNCTIONS OF SOVIET LOCAL ELECTIONS.=
              MIDWEST JOURNAL OF POLITICAL SCIENCE, 5, (MAY 1961),   61
                PP. 129-149.
              COMEL, ELNOEL

SWEAHR-62-CRC   SWEARER, HR
              CHANGING ROLES OF THE CPSU UNDER FIRST SECRETARY
                KHRUSHCHEV (SOVIET UNION).=
              WORLD POLITICS, 15, (OCTOBER 1962), PP. 20-43.      62
              ELEL

SWEAHR-62-DRS   SWEARER, HR
              DECENTRALIZATION IN RECENT SOVIET ADMINISTRATIVE
                PRACTICE.=
              SLAVIC REVIEW, 21, (SEPTEMBER 1962), PP. 456-470.    62
              ELEL, ELNOEL

SWEAHR-64-PSU   SWEARER, HR
              THE POLITICS OF SUCCESSION IN THE U.S.S.R.=
              BOSTON, LITTLE BROWN AND COMPANY, 1964.        64
              COMEL, ELEL, ELNOEL, ELPRNOR

SWEAHR-65-CCC   SWEARER, HR
              CULTS, COUPS, AND COLLECTIVE LEADERSHIP (SOVIET UNION).=
              CURRENT HISTORY, N.S., 49, (OCTOBER 1965), PP. 193-200.  65
              COMEL, ELEL

SWEAR -52-CSJ   SWEARINGEN, R
              COMMUNIST STRENGTH IN JAPAN.=
              CURRENT HISTORY, N.S., 23, (JULY 1952), PP. 1-6.     52
              COMEL, ELEL, ELNOEL, ELPRNOR

SWIFM -62-MPR   SWIFT, M
              MALAYAN POLITICS -- RACE AND CLASS.=
              CIVILISATIONS, 12, (1962), PP. 237-245.         62
              COMEL, ELEL, ELPRNOR

SWISE -58-CIW   SWISHER, E
              CHINESE INTELLECTUALS AND THE WESTERN IMPACT, 1838-1900.=
              COMPARATIVE STUDIES IN SOCIETY AND HISTORY, 1, (1958),   58
                PP. 26-37.
              ELEL, ELPRNOR

SYMER -39-RR   SYME, R
              THE ROMAN REVOLUTION.=

```
                   OXFORD, CLARENDON PRESS, 1939.                            39
                   COMEL, ELEL, ELPRNOR, METEL
SYMER -58-CER   SYME, R
                   COLONIAL ELITES -- ROME, SPAIN AND THE AMERICAS.=
                   LONDON, OXFORD UNIVERSITY PRESS, 1958.                    58
                   DEFEL, COMEL, ELEL, ELNOEL, ELPRNOR, METEL
SYROK -58-SOS   SYROP, K
                   SPRING IN OCTOBER -- THE STORY OF THE POLISH REVOLUTION
                      1956.=
                   NEW YORK, FREDERICK A PRAEGER, 1958.                      58
                   ELEL, ELNOEL, ELPRNOR
SYTCJM-65-PRT   SYTCOS, JM
                   THE POTENTIAL ROLE OF TURKISH VILLAGE OPINION LEADERS
                      IN A PROGRAM OF FAMILY PLANNING.=
                   THE PUBLIC OPINION QUARTERLY, 29, (SPRING 1965),          65
                      PP. 120-130.
                   ELEL, ELNOEL, ELPRNOR
SZCZJ -47-CSF   SZCZEPANSKI, J
                   CHANGES IN THE STRUCTURE AND FUNCTIONS OF THE
                      INTELLIGENTSIA (POLAND).=
                   INTERNATIONAL SOCIAL SCIENCE BULLETIN, 9, (1947),         47
                      PP. 180-192.
                   COMEL, ELEL, ELNOEL
SZCZJ -62-PIP   SZCZEPANSKI, J
                   THE POLISH INTELLIGENTSIA -- PAST AND PRESENT.=
                   WORLD POLITICS, 14, (APRIL 1962), PP. 406-420.            62
                   COMEL
SZULT -63-WRL   SZULC, T
                   THE WINDS OF REVOLUTION (LATIN AMERICA).=
                   NEW YORK, FREDERICK A PRAEGER, 1963.                      63
                   ELEL, ELNOEL, ELPRNOR
SZULT -65-CSC   SZULC, T
                   COMMUNISTS, SOCIALISTS, AND CHRISTIAN DEMOCRATS
                      (LATIN AMERICA).=
                   ANNALS OF THE AMERICAN ACADEMY OF POLITICAL AND SOCIAL    65
                      SCIENCES, 360, (JULY 1965), PP. 99-109.
                   COMEL, ELEL, ELPRNOR
TABOE -57-RCI   TABORSKY, E
                   REVOLT OF THE COMMUNIST INTELLECTUALS (SOVIET UNION,
                      EAST EUROPE).=
                   THE REVIEW OF POLITICS, 19, (JULY 1957), PP. 308-329.     57
                   ELEL, ELPRNOR
TABOE -64-COS   TABORSKY, E
                   CZECHOSLOVAKIA -- OUT OF STALINISM.=
                   PROBLEMS OF COMMUNISM, 13, (MAY-JUNE 1964), PP. 4-14.     64
                   ELEL, ELNOEL
TABOE -65-SEE   TABORSKY, E
                   SOCIOLOGY IN EASTERN EUROPE -- CZECHOSLOVAKIA.=
                   PROBLEMS OF COMMUNISM, 14, (JANUARY-FEBRUARY 1965),       65
                      PP. 62-66.
                   ELEL, ELPRNOR
TAITD -58-TWR   TAIT, D              MIDDLETON, J (EDS)
                   TRIBES WITHOUT RULERS.=
                   LONDON, ROUTLEDGE AND KEGAN PAUL, 1958.                   58
                   COMEL, ELEL, ELNOEL, ELPRNOR
TAKAY -48-DDJ   TAKAGI, Y
                   DEFEAT AND DEMOCRACY IN JAPAN.=
                   FOREIGN AFFAIRS, 26, (JULY 1948), PP. 645-652.            48
                   ELEL, ELPRNOR
TALMJL-52-RTD   TALMON, JL
                   THE RISE OF TOTALITARIAN DEMOCRACY.=
                   BOSTON, BEACON PRESS, 1952.                               52
                   DEFEL, ELPRNOR
TANEJ -60-SCA   TANENHAUS, J
                   SUPREME COURT ATTITUDES TOWARD FEDERAL ADMINISTRATIVE
                      AGENCIES (UNITED STATES).=
                   THE JOURNAL OF POLITICS, 22, (AUGUST 1960), PP. 502-524.  60
                   ELEL, ELPRNOR, METEL
TANGPS-55-PSC   TANG, PSH
                   POWER STRUGGLE IN THE CHINESE CP (COMMUNIST PARTY) --
                      THE KAO-JAO PURGE.=
                   PROBLEMS OF COMMUNISM, 4, (NOVEMBER-DECEMBER 1955),       55
                      PP. 18-25.
                   ELEL
TANGPS-57-CCT   TANG, PSH
                   COMMUNIST CHINA TODAY -- DOMESTIC AND FOREIGN POLICIES.=
                   WASHINGTON, DC, RESEARCH INSTITUTE ON THE SINO-SOVIET     57
                      BLOC, 1957, PP. 71-455.
                   COMEL, ELEL, ELNOEL, ELPRNOR
TANHGK-62-CRW   TANHAM, GK
                   COMMUNIST REVOLUTIONARY WARFARE -- THE VIETMINH IN
                      INDOCHINA.=
                   NEW YORK, FREDERICK A PRAEGER, 1962.                      62
                   ELNOEL
```

TANNA -55-DEA    TANNOUS, A
                 DILEMMA OF THE ELITE IN ARAB SOCIETY.=
                 HUMAN ORGANIZATION, 14, (FALL 1955), PP. 11-15.                55
                 ELEL, ELNOEL
TANNAS-62-ESA    TANNENBAUM, AS
                 AN EVENT-STRUCTURE APPROACH TO SOCIAL POWER AND TO THE
                    PROBLEM OF POWER COMPARABILITY.=
                 BEHAVIORAL SCIENCE, 7, (JULY 1962), PP. 315-331.              62
                 DEFEL, ELEL, ELNOEL, METEL
TANNF -48-PGM    TANNENBAUM, F
                 PERSONAL GOVERNMENT IN MEXICO.=
                 FOREIGN AFFAIRS, 27, (OCTOBER 1948), PP. 44-57.               48
                 COMEL, ELEL, ELNOEL
TANNF -60-PSF    TANNENBAUM, F
                 ON POLITICAL STABILITY (FRANCE, SOVIET UNION).=
                 POLITICAL SCIENCE QUARTERLY, 75, (JUNE 1960),                 60
                    PP. 161-180.
                 ELEL, ELNOEL, ELPRNOR
TANNF -65-TKL    TANNENBAUM, F
                 TEN KEYS TO LATIN AMERICA.=
                 NEW YORK, ALFRED A KNOPF, 1965.                               65
                 COMEL, ELEL, ELNOEL, ELPRNOR
TANNR -57-LFR    TANNENBAUM, R        MASARIK, F
                 LEADERSHIP -- A FRAME OF REFERENCE.=
                 MANAGEMENT SCIENCE, 4, (OCTOBER 1957), PP. 1-19.              57
                 DEFEL, ELPRNOR
TANNR -61-LOB    TANNENBAUM, R        WESCHLER, IR        MASSARIK, F
                 LEADERSHIP AND ORGANIZATION -- A BEHAVIORAL SCIENCE
                    APPROACH.=
                 NEW YORK, MCGRAW HILL, 1961.                                  61
                 GNELTH, COMEL, ELEL, ELNOEL, ELPRNOR
TANNT -62-CSC    TANNENBAUM, T
                 CASTRO AND SOCIAL CHANGE (CUBA).=
                 POLITICAL SCIENCE QUARTERLY, 77, (JUNE 1962),                 62
                    PP. 178-204.
                 ELEL, ELNOEL
TARDC -56-NEU    TARDITS, C
                 THE NOTION OF THE ELITE AND THE URBAN SOCIAL SURVEY
                    IN AFRICA.=
                 INTERNATIONAL SOCIAL SCIENCE BULLETIN, 8, (1956),             56
                    PP. 492-495.
                 DEFEL, COMEL, ELEL, ELNOEL, METEL
TASKGA-64-KCA    TASKIN, GA
                 KAZAKHSTAN -- CHANGES IN ADMINISTRATIVE STATUS AND THE
                    NATIONAL COMPOSITION OF THE POPULATION (SOVIET UNION).=
                 BULLETIN INSTITUTE FOR THE STUDY OF THE USSR, 11,             64
                    (FEBRUARY 1964), PP. 33-41.
                 COMEL
TATAM -66-BES    TATAU, M
                 THE BEGINNING OF THE END (SOVIET UNION).=
                 PROBLEMS OF COMMUNISM, 15, (MARCH-APRIL 1966), PP. 44-47. 66
                 ELEL, ELPRNOR
TATAM -66-SER    TATAU, M
                 SOVIET (ECONOMIC) REFORMS -- THE DEBATE GOES ON.=
                 PROBLEMS OF COMMUNISM, 15, (JANUARY-FEBRUARY 1966),           66
                    PP. 28-34.
                 ELEL, ELPRNOR
TAUSC -65-CAM    TAUSKY, C            DUBIN, R
                 CAREER ANCHORAGE -- MANAGERIAL MOBILITY MOTIVATIONS.=
                 AMERICAN SOCIOLOGICAL REVIEW, 30, (OCTOBER 1965),             65
                    PP. 725-735.
                 COMEL, ELPRNOR, METEL
TAWNRH-64-RTG    TAWNEY, RH
                 THE RADICAL TRADITION (GREAT BRITAIN).=
                 NEW YORK, PANTHEON, 1964.                                     64
                 ELEL, ELNOEL, ELPRNOR
TAYLAJ-58-TMD    TAYLOR, AJP
                 THE TROUBLE MAKERS -- DISSENT OVER FOREIGN POLICY
                    (GREAT BRITAIN).=
                 BLOOMINGTON, INDIANA UNIVERSITY PRESS, 1958.                  58
                 ELEL, ELPRNOR
TAYLGE-33-TRI    TAYLOR, GE
                 THE TAIPING REBELLION -- ITS ECONOMIC BACKGROUND
                    AND SOCIAL THEORY.=
                 CHINESE SOCIAL AND POLITICAL SCIENCE REVIEW, 16,              33
                    (JANUARY 1933), PP. 545-614.
                 DEFEL, COMEL, ELEL, ELNOEL, ELPRNOR
TAYLP -60-MEA    TAYLOR, P
                 THE MEXICAN ELECTIONS OF 1958 -- AFFIRMATION OF
                    AUTHORITARIANISM.=
                 THE WESTERN POLITICAL QUARTERLY, 13, (SEPTEMBER 1960),        60
                    PP. 722-744.
                 COMEL, ELEL, ELNOEL
TAYLPB-62-GPU    TAYLOR-JR, PB

GOVERNMENT AND POLITICS OF URUGUAY.=
NEW ORLEANS, TULANE UNIVERSITY PRESS, 1962.
COMEL, ELEL, ELNOEL                                               62

TAYLPB-63-IID    TAYLOR-JR, PB
INTERESTS AND INSTITUTIONAL DYSFUNCTION IN URUGUAY.=
THE AMERICAN POLITICAL SCIENCE REVIEW, 57, (MARCH 1963),   63
  PP.62-74.
COMEL, ELPRNOR

TAYLPB-65-SSC    TAYLOR, PB
SECTARIANS IN SOVIET COURTS.=
THE RUSSIAN REVIEW, 24, (JULY 1965), PP. 278-288.            65
ELPRNOR

TAYLPS-47-RRL    TAYLOR, PS
THE RELATION OF RESEARCH TO LEGISLATIVE AND
  ADMINISTRATIVE DECISIONS (UNITED STATES).=
JOURNAL OF SOCIAL ISSUES, 3, (FALL 1947), PP. 49-56.        47
ELNOEL

TAYLT -52-SSG    TAYLOR, T
SWORD AND SWASTIKA -- GENERALS AND NAZIS IN THE
  THIRD REICH.=
NEW YORK, SIMON AND SCHUSTER, 1952.
COMEL, ELEL, ELNOEL, ELPRNOR                                 52

TEIWFC-66-PPL    TEIWES, FC
THE PURGE OF PROVINCIAL LEADERS 1957-1958 (CHINA).=
THE CHINA QUARTERLY, 26, (JULY-SEPTEMBER 1966),
  PP. 14-32.                                                 66
ELEL, ELPRNOR

TELFIR-65-TPP    TELFORD, IR
TYPES OF PRIMARY AND PARTY RESPONSIBILITY
  (UNITED STATES).=
THE AMERICAN POLITICAL SCIENCE REVIEW, 59, (MARCH 1965),   65
PP. 117-118.
ELNOEL

TENGS -54-CSR    TENG, S            FAIRBANK, JK
CHINA'S RESPONSE TO THE WEST.=
CAMBRIDGE, HARVARD UNIVERSITY PRESS, 1954.
ELPRNOR                                                      54

TEODN -60-PRM    TEODOROVICH, N
THE POLITICAL ROLE OF THE MOSCOW PATRIARCHATE.=
BULLETIN INSTITUTE FOR THE STUDY OF THE USSR, 7,
  (SEPTEMBER 1960), PP. 44-50.                               60
ELEL, ELPRNOR

TEODN -65-PRM    TEODOROVICH, N
THE POLITICAL ROLE OF THE MOSCOW PATRIARCHATE.=
STUDIES ON THE SOVIET UNION, 4, (1965), PP. 241-247.        65
ELEL, ELPRNOR

TEPAJJ-64-EFL    TEPASKE, JJ         FISHER, SN (EDS)
EXPLOSIVE FORCES IN LATIN AMERICA.=
COLUMBUS, OHIO STATE UNIVERSITY PRESS, 1964.
COMEL, ELEL, ELNOEL, ELPRNOR                                 64

TERRFW-59-TMR    TERRIEN, FW
TOO MUCH ROOM AT THE TOP (UNITED STATES).=
SOCIAL FORCES, 37, (MAY 1959), PP. 298-305.                 59
COMEL

THE JO-  -PTU    THE JOURNAL OF POLITICS--FEBRUARY 1949
THE PRESIDENCY IN TRANSITION (UNITED STATES).=
THE JOURNAL OF POLITICS, 11, (FEBRUARY 1949).
ELEL, ELNOEL, ELPRNOR

THERLD-65-DPC    THERRY, LD
DOMINANT POWER COMPONENTS IN THE BRAZILIAN UNIVERSITY
  STUDENT MOVEMENT PRIOR TO APRIL 1964.=
JOURNAL OF INTER-AMERICAN STUDIES, 7, (JANUARY 1965),      65
  PP. 27-48.
COMEL, ELEL, ELPRNOR

THOEP -66-EWS    THOENES, P
THE ELITE IN THE WELFARE STATE.=
NEW YORK, THE FREE PRESS, 1966.                             66
GNELTH, DEFEL

THOMCE-63-DMP    THOMETZ, CE
THE DECISION-MAKERS -- THE POWER STRUCTURE OF DALLAS
  (UNITED STATES).=
DALLAS, SOUTHERN METHODIST UNIVERSITY PRESS, 1963.         63
COMEL, ELEL, ELNOEL, METEL

THOMD -64-DFS    THOMSON, D
DEMOCRACY IN FRANCE SINCE 1870.=
NEW YORK, OXFORD UNIVERSITY PRESS, 1964.                    64
COMEL, ELEL, ELNOEL, ELPRNOR

THOMDC-63-NLC    THOMPSON, DC
THE NEGRO LEADERSHIP CLASS (UNITED STATES).=
ENGLEWOOD CLIFFS, PRENTICE-HALL, 1963.                      63
COMEL,  ELEL, ELNOEL, ELPRNOR

THOMH -59-EGB    THOMAS, H
THE ESTABLISHMENT (GREAT BRITAIN).=
LONDON, BLOND, 1959.                                        59

COMEL, ELEL, ELPRNOR
THOMJD-59-SSP  THOMPSON, JD        TUDEN, A
STRATEGIES, STRUCTURES, AND PROCESSES OF ORGANIZATIONAL
    DECISION.=
JD THOMPSON, ET AL (EDS), COMPARATIVE STUDIES IN                59
    ADMINISTRATION, PITTSBURGH, UNIVERSITY OF PITTSBURGH
    PRESS, 1959, PP.195-216.
DEFEL, ELEL, ELPRNOR
THOMLL-59-PLT  THOMAS, LL
POLISH LITERATURE AND THE 'THAW'.=
THE AMERICAN SLAVIC AND EAST EUROPEAN REVIEW, 18,              59
    (OCTOBER 1959), PP. 394-416.
ELEL, ELPRNOR
THOMSB-50-REP  THOMAS, SB
RECENT EDUCATIONAL POLICY IN CHINA.=
PACIFIC AFFAIRS, 23, (MARCH 1950), PP. 21-33.                  50
ELPRNOR
THOMSB-51-SCB  THOMAS, SB
STRUCTURE AND CONSTITUTIONAL BASIS OF THE CHINESE
    PEOPLES REPUBLIC.=
THE ANNALS OF THE AMERICAN ACADEMY OF POLITICAL AND            51
    SOCIAL SCIENCE, 277, (SEPTEMBER 1951), PP. 46-55.
COMEL, ELEL, ELNOEL
THOMSB-53-GAC  THOMAS, SB
GOVERNMENT AND ADMINISTRATION IN COMMUNIST CHINA.=
NEW YORK, INTERNATIONAL SECRETARIAT, INSTITUTE OF             53
    PACIFIC RELATIONS, 1953.
COMEL, ELEL, ELNOEL
THOMV -49-SAF  THOMPSON, V        ADLOFF, R
SOUTHEAST ASIA FOLLOWS THE LEADER.=
FAR EASTERN SURVEY, 18, (NOVEMBER 2, 1949),                    49
    PP. 253-257.
COMEL, ELPRNOR
THOMV -50-LWS  THOMPSON, V        ADLOFF, R
THE LEFT WING IN SOUTHEAST ASIA.=
NEW YORK, WILLIAM SLOANE ASSOCIATES, 1950.                    50
COMEL, ELEL, ELNOEL, ELPRNOR
THORW -57-ABL  THORNHILL, W
AGREEMENTS BETWEEN LOCAL POLITICAL PARTIES IN LOCAL
    GOVERNMENT MATTERS (GREAT BRITAIN).=
POLITICAL STUDIES, 5, (1957), PP. 83-88.                      57
ELEL, ELPRNOR
TICKFJ-58-CAS  TICKNER, FJ
COMPARATIVE ADMINISTRATIVE SYSTEMS -- A SURVEY AND
    EVALUATION OF COMPARATIVE RESEARCH.=
PUBLIC ADMINISTRATION REVIEW, 19, (WINTER 1958),              58
    PP. 19-25.
METEL
TIERJF-58-BCA  TIERNEY, JF
BRITAIN AND THE COMMONWEALTH -- ATTITUDES IN
    PARLIAMENT AND PRESS IN THE UNITED KINGDOM SINCE 1951.=
POLITICAL STUDIES, 6, (1958), PP. 220-233.                    58
ELEL, ELPRNOR
TILLC -64-ACR  TILLY, C
THE ANALYSIS OF A COUNTER - REVOLUTION (FRANCE).=
HISTORY AND THEORY, 3, (1963-1964), PP. 30-58.                64
COMEL, ELEL, ELNOEL
TILMRO-61-PSC  TILMAN, RO
PUBLIC SERVICE COMMISSIONS IN THE FEDERATION OF MALAYA.=
THE JOURNAL OF ASIAN STUDIES, 20, (FEBRUARY 1961),            61
    PP. 181-196.
COMEL
TILMRO-64-BTM  TILMAN, RO
BUREAUCRATIC TRANSITION IN MALAYA.=
DURHAM, NORTH CAROLINA, DUKE UNIVERSITY PRESS, 1964.          64
COMEL, ELEL, ELNOEL
TILMRO-66-BDM  TILMAN, RO
BUREAUCRATIC DEVELOPMENT IN MALAYA.=
R BRAIBANTI (ED), ASIAN BUREAUCRATIC SYSTEMS EMERGENT         66
    FROM THE BRITISH IMPERIAL TRADITION, DURHAM, DUKE
    UNIVERSITY PRESS, 1966, PP. 550-604.
COMEL, ELEL, ELPRNOR
TIMANS-39-ISL  TIMASHEFF, NS
AN INTRODUCTION TO THE SOCIOLOGY OF LAW.=
CAMBRIDGE, HARVARD UNIVERSITY PRESS, 1939.                    39
DEFEL, ELEL
TIMANS-52-PPS  TIMASHEFF, NS
POLITICAL POWER IN THE SOVIET UNION.=
THE REVIEW OF POLITICS, 14, (JANUARY 1952), PP. 15-24.        52
COMEL, ELEL, ELNOEL
TINGH -55-SVS  TINGSTEN, H
STABILITY AND VITALITY IN SWEDISH DEMOCRACY.=
THE POLITICAL QUARTERLY, 26, (APRIL-JUNE 1955),               55
    PP. 140-151.

```
                 ELNOEL, ELPRNOR
TINKH -59-ACV    TINKER, H
                 AUTHORITY AND COMMUNITY IN VILLAGE INDIA.=
                 PACIFIC AFFAIRS, 32, (DECEMBER 1959), PP. 354-375.              59
                 ELEL, ELNOEL
TINKH -64-BBB    TINKER, H
                 BALLOT BOX AND BAYONET -- PEOPLE AND GOVERNMENT IN
                    EMERGENT ASIAN COUNTRIES.=
                 LONDON, OXFORD UNIVERSITY PRESS, 1964.                          64
                 DEFEL, ELEL, ELNOEL, ELPRNOR
TIRYEQ-60-APS    TIRYAKIAN, EQ
                 APARTHEID AND POLITICS IN SOUTH AFRICA.=
                 THE JOURNAL OF POLITICS, 22, (NOVEMBER 1960),
                    PP. 682-697.                                                 60
                 ELNOEL, ELPRNOR
TITUJE-64-KGR    TITUS, JE
                 KANSAS GOVERNORS -- A RESUME OF POLITICAL LEADERSHIP
                    (UNITED STATES).=
                 THE WESTERN POLITICAL QUARTERLY, 17, (JUNE 1964),
                    PP. 356-370.                                                 64
                 COMEL, ELPRNOR
TOMAD -46-SBS    TOMASIC, D
                 THE STRUCTURE OF BALKAN SOCIETY.=
                 THE AMERICAN JOURNAL OF SOCIOLOGY, 52, (SEPTEMBER 1946),  46
                    PP. 132-140.
                 ELEL, ELNOEL
TOMAD -51-IBB    TOMASIC, D
                 INTERRELATIONS BETWEEN BOLSHEVIK IDEOLOGY AND THE
                    STRUCTURE OF SOVIET SOCIETY.=
                 AMERICAN SOCIOLOGICAL REVIEW, 16, (APRIL 1951),
                    PP. 137-148.                                                 51
                 ELNOEL, ELPRNOR
TOMAD -61-PLC    TOMASIC, D
                 POLITICAL LEADERSHIP IN CONTEMPORARY POLAND --
                    THE NEO - STALINIST COURSE.=
                 JOURNAL OF HUMAN RELATIONS, 9, (WINTER 1961), PP. 191-205 61
                 COMEL, ELEL, ELNOEL
TOMADA-48-PCE    TOMASIC, DA
                 PERSONALITY AND CULTURE IN EASTERN EUROPEAN POLITICS.=
                 NEW YORK, GW STEWART, INC, 1948.                                48
                 COMEL, ELEL, ELNOEL, ELPRNOR
TOMADA-61-RCL    TOMASIC, DA
                 THE RUMANIAN COMMUNIST LEADERSHIP.=
                 SLAVIC REVIEW, 20, (OCTOBER 1961), PP. 477-494.                 61
                 COMEL, ELEL
TOMPSR-57-RIM    TOMPKINS, SR
                 THE RUSSIAN INTELLIGENTSIA -- MAKERS OF THE
                    REVOLUTIONARY STATE.=
                 NORMAN, UNIVERSITY OF OKLAHOMA PRESS, 1957.                     57
                 COMEL, ELEL, ELNOEL, ELPRNOR
TOOFBM-59-CIL    TOOFAN, BM
                 THE COMMUNISTS AND INDIAN LABOR.=
                 PROBLEMS OF COMMUNISM, 8, (MARCH-APRIL 1959), PP. 35-43.   59
                 ELNOEL
TORDW -66-GET    TORDOFF, W
                 THE GENERAL ELECTION IN TANZANIA.=
                 JOURNAL OF COMMONWEALTH POLITICAL STUDIES, 4,
                    (MARCH 1966), PP. 47-64.                                     66
                 ELEL, ELNOEL, ELPRNOR
TORRGH-64-SPM    TORREY, GH
                 SYRIAN POLITICS AND THE MILITARY, 1945-1958.=
                 COLUMBUS, OHIO STATE UNIVERSITY PRESS, 1964.                    64
                 ELEL, ELPRNOR
TOTTGO-55-PJS    TOTTEN, GO
                 PROBLEMS OF JAPANESE SOCIALIST LEADERSHIP.=
                 PACIFIC AFFAIRS, 28, (JUNE 1955), PP. 160-169.                  55
                 COMEL, ELEL
TOTTGO-60-BSJ    TOTTEN, GO
                 BUDDHISM AND SOCIALISM IN JAPAN AND BURMA.=
                 COMPARATIVE STUDIES IN SOCIETY AND HISTORY, 2,
                    (APRIL 1960), PP. 293-304.                                   60
                 ELEL, ELPRNOR
TOTTGO-65-FFJ    TOTTEN, GO            KUWAHAMI, T
                 THE FUNCTION OF FACTIONALISM IN JAPANESE POLITICS.=
                 PACIFIC AFFAIRS, 38, (SPRING 1965), PP. 109-122.               65
                 ELEL, ELPRNOR
TOWSJ -54-SUA    TOWSTER, J
                 THE SOVIET UNION AFTER STALIN -- LEADERS AND POLICIES.=
                 THE AMERICAN SLAVIC AND EAST EUROPEAN REVIEW, 13,
                    (DECEMBER 1954), PP. 471-499.                                54
                 ELEL, ELPRNOR
TRAGFN-58-BWS    TRAGER, FN
                 BUILDING A WELFARE STATE IN BURMA, 1948-1956.=
                 NEW YORK, INSTITUTE OF PACIFIC RELATIONS, 1958.                 58
```

```
                    COMEL, ELEL, ELNOEL, ELNOEL, ELPRNOR
TRAGFN-58-PSB    TRAGER, FN
                    THE POLITICAL SPLIT IN BURMA.=
                    FAR EASTERN SURVEY, 27, (OCTOBER 1958), PP. 145-155.          58
                    ELEL
TRAGFN-59-MSE    TRAGER, FN (ED)
                    MARXISM IN SOUTH-EAST ASIA.=
                    STANFORD, STANFORD UNIVERSITY PRESS, 1959.                    59
                    ELEL, ELNOEL, ELPRNOR
TRAPS -63-PIA    TRAPIDO, S
                    POLITICAL INSTITUTIONS AND AFRIKANER SOCIAL STRUCTURES
                       IN THE REPUBLIC OF SOUTH AFRICA.=
                    THE AMERICAN POLITICAL SCIENCE REVIEW, 57, (MARCH 1963),      63
                       PP. 75-87.
                    COMEL, ELNOEL
TRL    -55-CLE   TRL
                    CHANGE OF LEADERSHIP IN EGYPT.=
                    THE WORLD TODAY, 11, (FEBRUARY 1955), PP. 51-60.              55
                    ELEL
TROMTP-66-CCP    TROMBETAS, TP
                    CONSENSUS AND CLEAVAGE -- PARTY ALIGNMENT IN GREECE,
                       1945-1965.=
                    PARLIAMENTARY AFFAIRS, 19, (SUMMER 1966), PP. 295-311.        66
                    ELEL, ELPRNOR
TROWM -58-SBP    TROW, M
                    SMALL BUSINESSMEN, POLITICAL TOLERANCE, AND SUPPORT FOR
                       MCCARTHY.=
                    THE AMERICAN JOURNAL OF SOCIOLOGY, 64, (NOVEMBER 1958),       58
                       PP. 270-281.
                    ELNOEL, ELPRNOR
TRUMD -55-FPS    TRUMAN, D
                    FEDERALISM AND THE PARTY SYSTEM (UNITED STATES).=
                    AW MACMAHON (ED), FEDERALISM, MATURE AND EMERGENT,            55
                       GARDEN CITY, NEW YORK, DOUBLEDAY, 1955, PP. 115-136.
                    ELEL, ELNOEL
TRUMDB-51-GPP    TRUMAN, DB
                    THE GOVERNMENTAL PROCESS -- POLITICAL INTERESTS AND
                       PUBLIC OPINION (UNITED STATES).=
                    NEW YORK, ALFRED A KNOPF, 1951.                               51
                    DEFEL, COMEL, ELEL, ELNOEL, ELPRNOR
TRUMDB-56-SDS    TRUMAN, DB
                    THE STATE DELEGATIONS AND THE STRUCTURE OF PARTY VOTING
                       IN THE UNITED STATES HOUSE OF REPRESENTATIVES.=
                    THE AMERICAN POLITICAL SCIENCE REVIEW, 50, (DECEMBER          56
                       1956), PP. 1023-1045.
                    ELEL, ELNOEL
TRUMDB-59-ASC    TRUMAN, DB
                    THE AMERICAN SYSTEM IN CRISIS.=
                    POLITICAL SCIENCE QUARTERLY, 74, (DECEMBER 1959),             59
                       PP. 481-497.
                    GNELTH, ELEL, ELNOEL
TRUMDB-59-CPC    TRUMAN, DB
                    THE CONGRESSIONAL PARTY -- A CASE STUDY (UNITED STATES).=
                    NEW YORK, JOHN WILEY AND SONS, 1959.                          59
                    COMEL, ELEL, ELPRNOR
TRUMDB-65-CAS    TRUMAN, DB (ED)
                    THE CONGRESS AND AMERICA'S FUTURE.=
                    ENGLEWOOD CLIFFS, NEW JERSEY, PRENTICE-HALL, 1965.            65
                    COMEL, ELEL, ELNOEL, ELPRNOR
TRUMT -59-CPA    TRUMAN, T
                    CATHOLICS AND POLITICS IN AUSTRALIA.=
                    THE WESTERN POLITICAL QUARTERLY, 12, (JUNE 1959),             59
                       PP. 527-534.
                    ELEL, ELPRNOR
TRUMT -66-IGA    TRUMAN, T
                    IDEOLOGICAL GROUPS IN THE AUSTRALIAN LABOR PARTY
                       AND THEIR ATTITUDES.=
                    BRISBANE, WATSON FERGUSON AND COMPANY, 1966.                  66
                    ELEL, ELPRNOR
TS     -57-KAP   TS
                    KHRUSHCHEV AND THE ANTI - PARTY GROUP (SOVIET UNION).=
                    THE WORLD TODAY, 13, (SEPTEMBER 1957), PP. 377-388.           57
                    ELEL
TSE-C -60-MFM    TSE-TSUNG, C
                    THE MAY FOURTH MOVEMENT -- INTELLECTUAL REVOLUTION IN
                       MODERN CHINA.=
                    CAMBRIDGE, HARVARD UNIVERSITY PRESS, 1960.                    60
                    COMEL, ELEL, ELPRNOR
TSUNWM-66-JPS    TSUNEISHI, WM
                    JAPANESE POLITICAL STYLE.=
                    NEW YORK, HARPER AND ROW, 1966.                               66
                    ELEL, ELNOEL, ELPRNOR
TT     -53-INC   TT
                    THE INTELLECTUAL IN THE NEW CHINA.=
```

```
                    PROBLEMS OF COMMUNISM, 2, (NUMBER 2, 1953), PP. 1-7.        53
                    ELEL, ELPRNOR
TUANC -48-RMC       TUAN-SHENG, C
                    THE ROLE OF THE MILITARY IN CHINESE GOVERNMENT.=
                    PACIFIC AFFAIRS, 21, (SEPTEMBER 1948), PP. 239-251.         48
                    COMEL, ELEL, ELNOEL, ELPRNOR
TUCKAV-63-ASE       TUCKER, AV
                    ARMY AND SOCIETY IN ENGLAND 1870-1900 -- A REASSESSMENT
                        OF THE CARDWELL REFORMS.=
                    JOURNAL OF BRITISH STUDIES, 2, (MAY 1963), PP. 110-141.      63
                    COMEL
TUCKRC-61-TCP       TUCKER, RC
                    TOWARD A COMPARATIVE POLITICS OF MOVEMENT REGIMES.=
                    THE AMERICAN POLITICAL SCIENCE REVIEW, 60, (JUNE 1961),      61
                        PP. 281-289.
                    DEFEL, COMEL, ELEL, ELPRNOR
TUCKRC-63-SPM       TUCKER, RC
                    THE SOVIET POLITICAL MIND.=
                    NEW YORK, FREDERICK A PRAEGER, 1963.                         63
                    DEFEL, COMEL, ELEL, ELPRNOR
TUCKRC-65-DT        TUCKER, RC
                    THE DICTATOR AND TOTALITARIANISM.=
                    WORLD POLITICS, 17, (JULY 1965), PP. 555-583.                65
                    DEFEL
TUGWF -65-CDV       TUGWELL, F
                    THE CHRISTIAN DEMOCRATS OF VENEZUELA.=
                    JOURNAL OF INTER-AMERICAN STUDIES, 7, (APRIL 1965),          65
                        PP. 245-267.
                    COMEL, ELEL, ELNOEL
TUGWRG-64-HTB       TUGWELL, RG
                    HOW THEY BECAME PRESIDENT (UNITED STATES).=
                    NEW YORK, SIMON AND SCHUSTER, 1964.                          64
                    COMEL, ELEL, ELNOEL, ELPRNOR
TULLG -65-PBU       TULLOCK, G
                    THE POLITICS OF BUREAUCRACY (UNITED STATES).=
                    WASHINGTON, PUBLIC AFFAIRS PRESS, 1965.                      65
                    ELEL, ELNOEL, ELPRNOR
TUMIM -61-SCS       TUMIN, M             FELDMAN, AS
                    SOCIAL CLASS AND SOCIAL CHANGE IN PUERTO RICO.=
                    PRINCETON, PRINCETON UNIVERSITY PRESS, 1961.                 61
                    COMEL, ELEL, ELNOEL
TUMIMM-57-LLL       TUMIN, MM            ROTBERG, R
                    LEADERS, THE LED, AND THE LAW -- A CASE STUDY IN SOCIAL
                        CHANGE (UNITED STATES).=
                    THE PUBLIC OPINION QUARTERLY, 21, (FALL 1957),               57
                        PP. 354-370.
                    ELNOEL, ELPRNOR, METEL
TURKH -61-PSH       TURK, H              TURK, T
                    PERSONAL SENTIMENTS IN A HIERARCHY.=
                    SOCIAL FORCES, 40, (SEPTEMBER 1961), PP. 137-140.            61
                    ELPRNOR
TURKH -62-TTR       TURK, H              LEFCOWITZ, MJ
                    TOWARDS A THEORY OF REPRESENTATION BETWEEN GROUPS.=
                    SOCIAL FORCES, 40, (MAY 1962), PP. 337-341.                  62
                    METEL
TURNHA-57-WWP       TURNER, HA
                    WOODROW WILSON AND PUBLIC OPINION (UNITED STATES).=
                    THE PUBLIC OPINION QUARTERLY, 21, (WINTER 1957),             57
                        PP. 505-520.
                    ELEL, ELNOEL
TURNHA-63-PPA       TURNER, HA           MCCLINTOCK, CG        SPAULDING, CB
                    THE POLITICAL PARTY AFFILIATION OF AMERICAN POLITICAL
                        SCIENTISTS.=
                    THE WESTERN POLITICAL QUARTERLY, 16, (SEPTEMBER 1963),       63
                        PP. 650-665.
                    ELNOEL, ELPRNOR
TURNJ -51-PCP       TURNER, J
                    PARTY AND CONSTITUENCY -- PRESSURES ON CONGRESS
                        (UNITED STATES).=
                    BALTIMORE, JOHNS HOPKINS PRESS, 1951.                        51
                    ELEL, ELNOEL, ELPRNOR
TURNVW-57-SCA       TURNER, VW
                    SCHISM AND CONTINUITY IN AN AFRICAN SOCIETY.=
                    MANCHESTER, MANCHESTER UNIVERSITY PRESS, 1957.               57
                    ELEL, ELNOEL, ELPRNOR
TYLDG -54-AFS       TYLDEN, G
                    THE ARMED FORCES OF SOUTH AFRICA.=
                    JOHANNESBURG, AFRICANA MUSEUM, FRANK CONNOCK                 54
                        PUBLICATIONS, 1954.
                    COMEL, ELEL, ELNOEL
UDY,SH-59-BRW       UDY, SH
                    'BUREAUCRACY' AND 'RATIONALITY' IN WEBER'S ORGANIZATION
                        THEORY -- AN EMPIRICAL STUDY.=
                    AMERICAN SOCIOLOGICAL REVIEW, 24,                            59
```

                              (DECEMBER 1959), PP. 791-795.
                              DEFEL
ULAMAB-50-CPC   ULAM, AB
                THE CRISIS IN THE POLISH COMMUNIST PARTY.=
                REVIEW OF POLITICS, 12, (JANUARY 1950), PP. 83-98.              50
                ELEL
ULAMAB-65-B     ULAM, AB
                THE BOLSHEVIKS.=
                NEW YORK, MACMILLAN, 1965.                                      65
                DEFEL, COMEL, ELPRNOR
ULLMRK-49-SRI   ULLMANN, RK
                THE STRUGGLE FOR REPRESENTATIVE INSTITUTIONS IN GERMANY
                  -- PART 1 -- PART 2.=
                PARLIMENTARY AFFAIRS, 2,3, (AUTUMN 1949, SPRING 1950),          49
                  PP. 361-377, PP. 321-338.
                ELEL, ELNOEL
ULMAAH-65-TPA   ULMAN, AH            TACHAV, F
                TURKISH POLITICS -- THE ATTEMPT TO RECONCILE RAPID
                  MODERNIZATION WITH DEMOCRACY.=
                THE MIDDLE EAST JOURNAL, 19, (SPRING 1965), PP. 153-168.        65
                ELEL, ELNOEL
ULMESS-60-ABP   ULMER, SS
                THE ANALYSIS OF BEHAVIOR PATTERNS ON THE UNITED STATES
                  SUPREME COURT.=
                THE JOURNAL OF POLITICS, 22, (NOVEMBER 1960),                   60
                  PP. 629-653.
                ELEL, METEL
ULMESS-60-JRP   ULMER, SS
                JUDICIAL REVIEW AS POLITICAL BEHAVIOR -- A TEMPORARY CHECK
                  ON CONGRESS (UNITED STATES).=
                ADMINISTRATIVE SCIENCE QUARTERLY, 4, (1959-1960),               60
                  PP. 426-445.
                ELEL, ELPRNOR
ULMESS-60-SCB   ULMER, SS
                SUPREME COURT BEHAVIOR AND CIVIL RIGHTS (UNITED STATES).=
                THE WESTERN POLITICAL QUARTERLY, 13, (JUNE 1960),               60
                  PP. 288-311.
                ELPRNOR, METEL
ULMESS-61-HTU   ULMER, SS
                HOMEOSTATIC TENDENCIES IN THE UNITED STATES SUPREME
                  COURT.=
                SS ULMER (ED), INTRODUCTORY READINGS IN POLITICAL              61
                  BEHAVIOR, CHICAGO, RAND MCNALLY, 1961, PP. 167-188.
                ELPRNOR, METEL
ULMESS-61-SJC   ULMER, SS
                SCALING JUDICIAL CASES -- A METHODOLOGICAL NOTE
                  (UNITED STATES).=
                AMERICAN BEHAVIORAL SCIENTIST, 4, (APRIL 1961), PP. 31-35.61
                METEL
ULMESS-62-POS   ULMER, SS
                PUBLIC OFFICE IN THE SOCIAL BACKGROUND OF SUPREME COURT
                  JUSTICES.=
                AMERICAN JOURNAL OF ECONOMICS AND SOCIOLOGY, 21,                62
                  (JANUARY 1962), PP. 57-68.
                COMEL, ELEL
ULMESS-62-SCB   ULMER, SS
                SUPREME COURT BEHAVIOR IN RACIAL EXCLUSION CASES --
                  1935-1960 (UNITED STATES).=
                THE AMERICAN POLITICAL SCIENCE REVIEW, 56, (JUNE 1966),         62
                  PP. 325-330.
                ELEL, METEL
ULMESS-67-PAJ   ULMER, SS
                PAIRWISE ASSOCIATION OF JUDGES AND LEGISLATORS
                  (UNITED STATES).=
                MIDWEST JOURNAL OF POLITICAL SCIENCE, 11, (FEBRUARY 1967),67
                  PP. 106-115.
                METEL
UNES   -56-AE   UNESCO
                AFRICAN ELITES.=
                INTERNATIONAL SOCIAL SCIENCE BULLETIN, 8, (1956),               56
                  PP. 413-498.
                GNELTH, DEFEL, COMEL, ELEL, ELNOEL, ELPRNOR
UNGEAL-65-PSS   UNGER, AL
                PARTY AND STATE IN SOVIET RUSSIA AND NAZI GERMANY.=
                THE POLITICAL QUARTERLY, 36, (OCTOBER-DECEMBER 1965),           65
                  PP. 441-459.
                COMEL, ELEL, ELNOEL, ELPRNOR
UNGEJP-63-MRN   UNGER, JP
                THE MILITARY ROLE IN NATION BUILDING AND ECONOMIC
                  DEVELOPMENT.=
                CAG OCCASIONAL PAPERS, INTERNATIONAL DEVELOPMENT               63
                  RESEARCH CENTER, BLOOMINGTON, INDIANA, 1963.
                COMEL, ELPRNOR
URBAP  -62-RSE   URBAN, P

                    THE REORGANIZATION OF SOVIET EDUCATION.=
                    STUDIES ON THE SOVIET UNION, 2, (1962), PP. 89-103.          62
                    ELPRNOR
URBAP -64-SHS   URBAN, P
                    SOVIET HISTORICAL SCIENCE AND THE POSITION OF SOVIET
                       HISTORIANS.=
                    BULLETIN INSTITUTE FOR THE STUDY OF THE USSR, 11,            64
                       (SEPTEMBER 1964), PP. 24-32.
                    COMEL, ELEL
USEEJ -50-SPP   USEEM, J
                    STRUCTURE OF POWER IN PALAU.=
                    SOCIAL FORCES, 29, (DECEMBER 1950), PP. 141-148.             50
                    COMEL, ELEL, ELNOEL
UTECSV-57-PNS   UTECHIN, SV           UTECHIN, P
                    PATTERNS OF NONCONFORMITY (SOVIET UNION).=
                    PROBLEMS OF COMMUNISM, 6, (MAY-JUNE 1957), PP. 23-29.        57
                    ELNOEL
UTISO -52-GSA   UTIS, O
                    GENERALISSIMO STALIN AND THE ART OF GOVERNMENT
                       (SOVIET UNION).=
                    FOREIGN AFFAIRS, 30, (JANUARY 1952), PP. 197-214.            52
                    ELEL, ELNOEL, ELPRNOR
VAGTA -56-DDS   VAGTS, A
                    DEFENSE AND DIPLOMACY -- THE SOLDIER AND THE CONDUCT OF
                       FOREIGN RELATIONS.=
                    NEW YORK, KING'S CROWN PRESS, 1956.                          56
                    ELEL, ELNOEL
VALEH -65-PPN   VALEN, H             KATZ, D
                    POLITICAL PARTIES IN NORWAY.=
                    LONDON, TAVISTOCK PUBLICATIONS, 1965.                        65
                    COMEL, ELEL, ELNOEL, ELPRNOR
VALIF -61-RRH   VALI, F
                    RIFT AND REVOLT IN HUNGARY.=
                    CAMBRIDGE, HARVARD UNIVERSITY PRESS, 1961.                   61
                    ELEL, ELNOEL
VALLI -65-REL   VALLIER, I
                    RELIGIOUS ELITES IN LATIN AMERICA -- CATHOLICISM,
                       LEADERSHIP AND SOCIAL CHANGE.=
                    AMERICA LATINA, 8, (OCTOBER-DECEMBER 1965), PP. 93-115.      65
                    ELEL, ELNOEL, ELPRNOR
VAN-  -50-DUI   VAN-NIEUWENHUIJZE, CAO
                    THE DAR UL-ISLAM MOVEMENT IN WESTERN JAVA.=
                    PACIFIC AFFAIRS, 23, (1950), PP. 169-183.                    50
                    ELNOEL, ELPRNOR
VAN-CA-58-AIP   VAN-NIEUWENHUIJZE, CAO
                    ASPECTS OF ISLAM IN POST - COLONIAL INDONESIA -- FIVE
                       ESSAYS.=
                    THE HAGUE AND BANDUNG, W VAN HOEVE, 1958.                    58
                    ELEL, ELNOEL, ELPRNOR
VAN-GV-66-CNW   VAN-DEN-BERGH, GVB
                    CONTEMPORARY NATIONALISM IN THE WESTERN WORLD.=
                    DAEDALUS, 95, (1966), PP. 828-861.                          66
                    ELPRNOR
VAN-JM-50-SCM   VAN-DER-KROEF, JM
                    SOCIAL CONFLICT AND MINORITY ASPIRATIONS IN INDONESIA.=
                    THE AMERICAN JOURNAL OF SOCIOLOGY, 55, (1950),               50
                       PP. 450-463.
                    ELEL, ELNOEL, ELPRNOR
VAN-JM-52-SCI   VAN-DER-KROEF, JM
                    SOCIETY AND CULTURE IN INDONESIAN NATIONALISM.=
                    THE AMERICAN JOURNAL OF SOCIOLOGY, 58, (JULY 1952),          52
                       PP. 11-24.
                    ELNOEL, ELPRNOR
VAN-JM-56-CCS   VAN-DER-KROEF, JM
                    THE CHANGING CLASS STRUCTURE OF INDONESIA.=
                    AMERICAN SOCIOLOGICAL REVIEW, 21, (APRIL 1956),              56
                       PP. 138-148.
                    COMEL, ELEL, ELNOEL
VAN-JM-57-II    VAN-DER-KROEF, JM
                    INSTABILITY IN INDONESIA.=
                    FAR EASTERN SURVEY, 26, (APRIL 1957), PP. 49-62.             57
                    ELEL
VAN-JM-58-ICU   VAN-DER-KROEF, JM
                    INDONESIAN COMMUNISM UNDER AIDIT.=
                    PROBLEMS OF COMMUNISM, 7, (NOVEMBER-DECEMBER 1958),          58
                       PP. 15-23.
                    ELPRNOR
VAN-JM-58-ISE   VAN-DER-KROEF, JM
                    INDONESIAN SOCIAL EVOLUTION -- SOME PSYCHOLOGICAL
                       CONSIDERATIONS.=
                    AMSTERDAM-ANTWERP, WERLD-BIBLIOTHEEK, 1958.                  58
                    ELPRNOR, METEL
VAN-JM-58-RII   VAN-DER-KROEF, JM
                    THE ROLE OF ISLAM IN INDONESIAN NATIONALISM.=

                          THE WESTERN POLITICAL QUARTERLY, 11, (MARCH 1958),        58
                             PP. 33-54.
                          ELEL, ELPRNOR
VAN-JM-59-CPT    VAN-DER-KROEF, JM
                 COMMUNIST POLICY AND TACTICS IN INDONESIA.=
                 THE AUSTRALIAN JOURNAL OF POLITICS AND HISTORY, 5,              59
                    (NOVEMBER 1959), PP. 163-179.
                 ELEL, ELNOEL
VAN-JM-60-ICP    VAN-DER-KROEF, JM
                 INDONESIAN COMMUNIST POLICY AND THE SIXTH PARTY CONGRESS.=
                 PACIFIC AFFAIRS, 33, (SEPTEMBER 1960), PP. 227-249.            60
                 COMEL, ELEL, ELPRNOR
VAN-JM-61-CSC    VAN-DER-KROEF, JM
                 CLASS STRUCTURE AND COMMUNIST THEORY.=
                 THE AMERICAN BEHAVIORAL SCIENTIST, 4, (MAY 1961),              61
                    PP. 19-23.
                 DEFEL
VAN-JM-61-NPW    VAN-DER-KROEF, JM
                 NATIONALISM AND POLITICS IN WEST NEW GUINEA.=
                 PACIFIC AFFAIRS, 34, (SPRING 1961), PP. 38-53.                 61
                 ELEL, ELNOEL
VAN-JM-62-DIC    VAN-DER-KROEF, JM
                 DILEMMAS OF INDONESIAN COMMUNISM.=
                 PACIFIC AFFAIRS, 35, (1962), PP. 141-159.                      62
                 ELEL, ELPRNOR
VAN-JM-65-CPI    VAN-DER-KROEF, JM
                 THE COMMUNIST PARTY OF INDONESIA.=
                 VANCOUVER, UNIVERSITY OF BRITISH COLUMBIA, 1965.               65
                 COMEL, ELEL, ELNOEL, ELPRNOR
VAN-PL-64-CSS    VAN-DEN-BERGHE, PL
                 CANEVILLE -- THE SOCIAL STRUCTURE OF A SOUTH AFRICAN
                    TOWN.=
                 MIDDLETOWN, CONNECTICUT, WESLEYAN UNIVERSITY PRESS, 1964. 64
                 COMEL
VAN-PW-63-PAW    VAN-DER-VEUR, PW
                 POLITICAL AWAKENING IN WEST NEW GUINEA.=
                 PACIFIC AFFAIRS, 36, (SPRING 1963), PP. 54-73.                 63
                 ELEL, ELNOEL, ELPRNOR
VAN-R  -60-EMI   VAN-NEIL, R
                 THE EMERGENCE OF THE MODERN INDONESIAN ELITE.=
                 CHICAGO, QUADRANGLE BOOKS, 1960.                               60
                 COMEL, ELEL, ELNOEL, ELPRNOR
VANDJM-57-PAI    VAN-DER-KROEF, JM
                 THE PLACE OF THE ARMY IN INDONESIAN POLITICS.=
                 EASTERN WORLD, 2, (JANUARY 1957), PP. 13-18.                   57
                 ELEL
VARDVS-63-PMP    VARDYS, VS
                 THE PARTISAN MOVEMENT IN POSTWAR LITHUANIA.=
                 SLAVIC REVIEW, 22, (SEPTEMBER 1963), PP. 499-522.              63
                 ELNOEL
VATIPJ-61-DPL    VATIKIOTIS, PJ
                 DILEMMAS OF POLITICAL LEADERSHIP IN THE ARAB
                    MIDDLE EAST -- THE CASE OF THE UNITED ARAB REPUBLIC.=
                 THE AMERICAN POLITICAL SCIENCE REVIEW, 55, (MARCH 1961),       61
                    PP. 103-111.
                 ELEL, ELNOEL, ELPRNOR
VATIPJ-61-EAP    VATIKIOTIS, PJ
                 THE EGYPTIAN ARMY IN POLITICS -- THE PATTERN FOR NEW
                    NATIONS.=
                 BLOOMINGTON, INDIANA UNIVERSITY PRESS, 1961.                   61
                 COMEL, ELEL, ELNOEL, ELPRNOR
VEBLT  -21-EPS   VEBLEN, T
                 THE ENGINEERS AND THE PRICE SYSTEM.=
                 NEW YORK, BB HUEBACH, 1921.                                    21
                 DEFEL, COMEL, ELEL, ELPRNOR
VELEVA-61-NLF    VELEN, VA
                 THE NEW LEFT IN FRANCE.=
                 FOREIGN AFFAIRS, 40, (OCTOBER 1961), PP. 71-82.                61
                 COMEL, ELEL
VELIC  -65-OCL   VELIZ, C (ED)
                 OBSTACLES TO CHANGE IN LATIN AMERICA.=
                 LONDON, OXFORD UNIVERSITY PRESS, 1965.                         65
                 COMEL, ELEL, ELNOEL, ELPRNOR
VELSJV-64-PKS    VELSEN, JV
                 THE POLITICS OF KINSHIP -- A STUDY IN SOCIAL
                    MANIPULATION AMONG THE LAKESIDE TONGA OF NYASALAND.=
                 MANCHESTER, MANCHESTER UNIVERSITY PRESS, 1964.                 64
                 ELEL, ELNOEL
VERBS  -66-CPC   VERBA, S
                 COMPARATIVE POLITICAL CULTURE.=
                 LW PYE AND S VERBA (EDS), POLITICAL CULTURE AND                66
                    POLITICAL DEVELOPMENT, PRINCETON, PRINCETON UNIVERSITY
                    PRESS, 1966, PP. 512-560.
                 DEFEL, ELPRNOR, METEL

VERBS -66-GRP    VERBA, S
                 GERMANY -- THE REMAKING OF THE POLITICAL CULTURE.=
                 LW PYE AND S VERBA (EDS), POLITICAL CULTURE AND            66
                    POLITICAL DEVELOPMENT, PRINCETON, PRINCETON UNIVERSITY
                    PRESS, 1966, PP. 130-170.
                 ELNOEL, ELPRNOR
VERBV -63-CAL    VERBIN, V
                 CHANGES AMONG THE LEADERS OF THE SOVIET ARMED FORCES.=
                 BULLETIN INSTITUTE FOR THE STUDY OF THE USSR, 10,          63
                    (JUNE 1963), PP. 36-40.
                 COMEL, ELEL
VERNDV-59-APS    VERNEY, DV
                 THE ANALYSIS OF POLITICAL SYSTEMS.=
                 LONDON, ROUTLEDGE AND KEGAN PAUL, LTD., 1959.              59
                 ELEL, ELNOEL, METEL
VEX,MB-46-UCR    VEX, MB
                 THE UNIVERSITY CONSTITUENCIES IN THE RECENT
                    BRITISH ELECTION.=
                 THE JOURNAL OF POLITICS, 8, (FEBRUARY 1946), PP. 201-211. 46
                 ELEL, ELNOEL
VIDAFS-50-RBM    VIDAL, FS
                 RELIGIOUS BROTHERHOODS IN MOROCCAN POLITICS.=
                 MIDDLE EAST JOURNAL, 4, (1950), PP. 427-446.               50
                 COMEL, ELEL
VIDIAJ-55-POC    VIDICH, AJ
                 PARTICIPANT OBSERVATION AND THE COLLECTION AND
                    INTERPRETATION OF DATA.=
                 THE AMERICAN JOURNAL OF SOCIOLOGY, 60, (JANUARY 1955),     55
                    PP. 354-360.
                 METEL
VIDIAJ-58-STM    VIDICH, AJ          BENSMAN, J
                 SMALL TOWN IN MASS SOCIETY -- CLASS, POWER AND RELIGION
                    IN A RURAL COMMUNITY (UNITED STATES).=
                 PRINCETON, NEW JERSEY, PRINCETON UNIVERSITY PRESS, 1958.   58
                 ELEL, ELNOEL
VIDIAJ-64-RCS    VIDICH, AJ          ET AL (EDS)
                 REFLECTIONS ON COMMUNITY STUDIES (UNITED STATES).=
                 NEW YORK, JOHN WILEY AND SONS, 1964.                       64
                 DEFEL, METEL
VIERPR-53-SGI    VIERECK, PR
                 SHAME AND GLORY OF THE INTELLECTUALS -- BABBIT JR VS THE
                    REDISCOVERY OF VALUES.=
                 BOSTON, BEACON PRESS, 1953.                                53
                 ELNOEL, ELPRNOR
VIERPR-61-MRN    VIERECK, PRE
                 METAPOLITICS, THE ROOTS OF THE NAZI MIND.=
                 REVISED EDITION, NEW YORK, CAPRICORN BOOKS, 1961.          61
                 COMEL, ELEL, ELNOEL, ELPRNOR
VILALA-61-RPN    VILARIA, LA
                 REORGANIZATION IN THE PHILIPPINE NATIONAL GOVERNMENT
                    PRIOR TO 1954.=
                 PHILIPPINE JOURNAL OF PUBLIC ADMINISTRATION, 5,            61
                    (JANUARY 1961), PP. 31-51.
                 ELEL
VILEMJ-57-JRP    VILE, MJC
                 JUDICIAL REVIEW AND POLITICS IN AUSTRALIA.=
                 THE AMERICAN POLITICAL SCIENCE REVIEW, 51, (JUNE 1957),    57
                    PP. 386-391.
                 ELEL
VILLAB-59-CCS    VILLANUEVA, AB
                 CROSS - CULTURAL STUDY OF COUNCIL - MANAGER GOVERNMENT.=
                 PROD (THE AMERICAN BEHAVIORAL SCIENTIST), 2, (MAY 1959),   59
                    PP. 9-10.
                 METEL
VILLBU-57-CDP    VILLANUEVA, BU
                 THE COMMUNITY DEVELOPMENT PROGRAM OF THE
                    PHILIPPINE GOVERNMENT.=
                 PHILIPPINE JOURNAL OF PUBLIC ADMINISTRATION, 1,            57
                    (APRIL 1957), PP. 144-153.
                 ELEL, ELNOEL
VINCJR-66-HLG    VINCENT, JR
                 THE HOUSE OF LORDS (GREAT BRITAIN).=
                 PARLIAMENTARY AFFAIRS, 19, (AUTUMN 1966), PP. 475-485.     66
                 COMEL, ELPRNOR
VINEKN-65-CPG    VINES, KN
                 COURTS AS POLITICAL AND GOVERNMENTAL AGENCIES
                    (UNITED STATES).=
                 H JACOB AND KN VINES (EDS), POLITICS IN THE AMERICAN       65
                    STATES--A COMPARATIVE ANALYSIS,
                    BOSTON, LITTLE, BROWN AND COMPANY, 1965, PP. 239-287.
                 COMEL, ELEL, ELNOEL, ELPRNOR
VISHMV-64-RSR    VISHNYAK, MV
                 THE ROLE OF THE SOCIALIST REVOLUTIONARIES IN 1917
                    (SOVIET UNION).=

                    STUDIES ON THE SOVIET UNION, 3, (1964), PP. 172-182.          64
                    ELEL, ELNOEL
VOGEEF-63-JSN    VOGEL, EF
                    JAPAN'S NEW MIDDLE CLASS.=
                    BERKELEY, UNIVERSITY OF CALIFORNIA PRESS, 1963.               63
                    ELNOEL, ELPRNOR
VOGEEF-67-RSB    VOGEL, EF
                    FROM REVOLUTIONARY TO SEMI - BUREAUCRAT -- THE
                    'REGULARISATION' OF CADRES (CHINA).=
                    THE CHINA QUARTERLY, 29, (JANUARY-MARCH 1967), PP. 36-60. 67
                    COMEL, ELEL, ELPRNOR
VON-FR-61-PAM    VON-DER-MEHDEN, FR    ANDERSON, CW
                    POLITICAL ACTION BY THE MILITARY IN THE DEVELOPING AREAS.=
                    SOCIAL RESEARCH, 28, (WINTER 1961), PP. 459-479.              61
                    COMEL, ELEL, ELPRNOR
VOROS -64-SYS    VORONITSYN, S
                    SOVIET YOUTH IN THE SINO-SOVIET DISPUTE.=
                    BULLETIN INSTITUTE FOR THE STUDY OF THE USSR, 11,             64
                    (MAY 1964), PP. 25-28.
                    ELPRNOR
VOROS -66-KPE    VORONITSYN, S
                    KOMSOMOL PROBLEMS ON THE EVE OF THE TWENTY-THIRD
                    PARTY CONGRESS.=
                    BULLETIN INSTITUTE FOR THE STUDY OF THE USSR, 8,              66
                    (MARCH 1966), PP. 44-48.
                    ELEL, ELNOEL, ELPRNOR
VOSECE-58-LFP    VOSE, CE
                    LITIGATION AS A FORM OF PRESSURE GROUP ACTIVITY.=
                    THE ANNALS OF THE AMERICAN ACADEMY OF POLITICAL AND           58
                    SOCIAL SCIENCE, 319, (SEPTEMBER 1958), PP. 20-31.
                    ELEL
VOSECE-66-IGJ    VOSE, CE
                    INTEREST GROUPS, JUDICIAL REVIEW, AND LOCAL GOVERNMENT.=
                    THE WESTERN POLITICAL QUARTERLY, (MARCH 1966),                66
                    PP. 85-100.
                    ELEL
VUCIA -56-SAS    VUCINICH, A
                    THE SOVIET ACADEMY OF SCIENCES.=
                    STANFORD, STANFORD UNIVERSITY PRESS, 1956.                    56
                    COMEL, ELEL, ELNOEL, ELPRNOR
WAGLC -52-RCR    WAGLEY, C (ED)
                    RACE AND CLASS IN RURAL BRAZIL.=
                    NEW YORK, COLUMBIA UNIVERSITY PRESS, 1952.                    52
                    ELEL, ELNOEL, ELPRNOR
WAGLC -64-DLA    WAGLEY, C
                    THE DILEMMA OF THE LATIN AMERICAN MIDDLE CLASS.=
                    PROCEEDINGS OF THE ACADEMY OF POLITICAL SCIENCE, 27,          64
                    (MAY 1964), PP. 2-10.
                    ELEL, ELPRNOR
WAGNHR-57-CSE    WAGNER, HR
                    THE CULTURAL SOVIETIZATION OF EAST GERMANY.=
                    SOCIAL RESEARCH, 24, (WINTER 1957), PP. 395-426.              57
                    ELNOEL
WAGNHR-59-LCT    WAGNER, HR
                    LOYALTY AND COMMITMENT IN A TOTALITARIAN PARTY
                    (EAST GERMANY).=
                    SOCIAL RESEARCH, 26, (AUTUMN 1959), PP. 272-282.              59
                    ELEL, ELNOEL, ELPRNOR
WAHLJC-59-LBR    WAHLKE, JC            EULAU, H
                    LEGISLATIVE BEHAVIOR -- A READER IN THEORY AND RESEARCH.=
                    GLENCOE, ILLINOIS, THE FREE PRESS, 1959.                      59
                    DEFEL, ELEL, ELNOEL, ELPRNOR, METEL
WAHLJC-60-ASL    WAHLKE, JC           BUCHANAN, W            EULAU, H
                    AMERICAN STATE LEGISLATORS' ROLE ORIENTATIONS TOWARD
                    PRESSURE GROUPS.=
                    THE JOURNAL OF POLITICS, 22, (MAY 1960), PP. 203-227.         60
                    ELEL, ELNOEL, ELPRNOR
WAHLJC-62-LSE    WAHLKE, JC           ET AL
                    THE LEGISLATIVE SYSTEM -- EXPLORATIONS IN LEGISLATIVE
                    BEHAVIOR (UNITED STATES).=
                    NEW YORK, JOHN WILEY AND SONS, INC, 1962.                     62
                    COMEL, ELEL, ELNOEL, ELPRNOR, METEL
WAKERE-47-SLA    WAKELEY, RE
                    SELECTING LEADERS FOR AGRICULTURAL PROGRAMS
                    (UNITED STATES).=
                    SOCIOMETRY, 10, (NOVEMBER 1947), PP. 384-395.                 47
                    COMEL, ELNOEL
WALDLK- 6-LCP    WALDMAN, LK
                    LIBERALISM OF CONGRESSMEN AND THE PRESIDENTIAL VOTE IN
                    THEIR DISTRICT (UNITED STATES).=
                    MIDWEST JOURNAL OF POLITICAL SCIENCE, 11, (FEBRUARY 1967), 6
                    PP. 73-85.
                    ELNOEL, ELPRNOR
WALKDB-60-AFC    WALKER, DB

THE AGE FACTOR IN THE 1958 CONGRESSIONAL ELECTIONS
(UNITED STATES).=
MIDWEST JOURNAL OF POLITICAL SCIENCE, 4,                          60
(FEBRUARY 1960), PP. 1-26.
COMEL, ELNOEL

WALKJL-63-FDN  WALKER, JL
THE FUNCTIONS OF DISUNITY -- THE NEGRO LEADERSHIP IN A
SOUTHERN CITY (UNITED STATES).=
JOURNAL OF NEGRO EDUCATION, (SUMMER 1963),                       63
PP. 227-236.
COMEL, ELEL, ELNOEL

WALKJL-63-PNC  WALKER, JL
PROTEST AND NEGOTIATION -- A CASE STUDY OF NEGRO
LEADERSHIP IN ATLANTA, GEORGIA (UNITED STATES).=
MIDWEST JOURNAL OF POLITICAL SCIENCE, 7, (MAY 1963),             63
PP. 99-124.
COMEL, ELNOEL, ELPRNOR

WALKJL-66-CET  WALKER, JL
A CRITIQUE OF THE ELITIST THEORY OF DEMOCRACY.=
THE AMERICAN POLITICAL SCIENCE REVIEW, 60, (JUNE 1966),          66
PP. 285-295.
GNELTH, ELNOEL, METEL

WALKKN-67-PSU  WALKER, KN
POLITICAL SOCIALIZATION IN UNIVERSITIES (LATIN AMERICA).=
SM LIPSET AND A SOLARI (EDS), ELITES IN LATIN AMERICA,           67
NEW YORK, OXFORD UNIVERSITY PRESS, 1967, PP. 408-430.
ELEL, ELNOEL, ELPRNOR

WALKPG-60-FLG  WALKER, PG
THE FUTURE OF THE LEFT (GREAT BRITAIN).=
ENCOUNTER, 15, (JULY 1960), PP. 71-72.                           60
COMEL, ELPRNOR

WALKRL-53-WCC  WALKER, RL
THE 'WORKING CLASS' IN COMMUNIST CHINA.=
PROBLEMS OF COMMUNISM, 2, (NUMBERS 3-4, 1953), PP. 42-50. 53
COMEL, ELNOEL

WALKRL-63-SIC  WALKER, RL
STUDENTS, INTELLECTUALS, AND THE CHINESE REVOLUTION.=
JJ KIRKPATRICK (ED), THE STRATEGY OF DECEPTION--A STUDY          63
IN WORLD-WIDE COMMUNIST TACTICS, NEW YORK, FARRAR,
STRAUS AND COMPANY, 1963, PP. 87-108.
ELEL, ELPRNOR

WALLAF-58-RM  WALLACE, AFC
REVITALIZATION MOVEMENTS.=
AMERICAN ANTHROPOLOGIST, 58, (APRIL 1956), PP. 264-281.          58
COMEL

WALLC -61-PSC  WALLIS, C
THE PUBLIC SERVICE COMMISSION IN WESTERN NIGERIA.=
AFRICAN AFFAIRS, 60, (1961), PP. 532-538.                        61
COMEL, ELEL, ELNOEL

WALLI -62-PPG  WALLER, I
PRESSURE POLITICS (GREAT BRITAIN).=
ENCOUNTER, 19, (AUGUST 1962), PP. 3-15.                          62
ELEL, ELPRNOR

WALLI -65-EFS  WALLERSTEIN, I
ELITES IN FRENCH - SPEAKING WEST AFRICA -- THE SOCIAL
BASIS OF IDEAS.=
THE JOURNAL OF MODERN AFRICAN STUDIES, 3, (MAY 1965),            65
PP. 1-33.
DEFEL, COMEL, ELEL, ELPRNOR

WALTB -62-PDM  WALTER, B
POLITICAL DECISION-MAKING IN ARCADIA.=
FS CHAPIN AND SF WEISS (EDS), URBAN GROWTH DYNAMICS,             62
NEW YORK, JOHN WILEY AND SONS, 1962.
ELEL, ELNOEL, METEL

WALTB -64-LAP  WALTER, B
ON THE LOGICAL ANALYSIS OF POWER-ATTRIBUTION
PROCEDURES.=
THE JOURNAL OF POLITICS, 26, (NOVEMBER 1964),                    64
PP. 850-866.
DEFEL, ELEL, ELNOEL, METEL

WALTEV-64-MSL  WALTER, EV
'MASS SOCIETY' -- THE LATE STAGES OF AN IDEA.=
SOCIAL RESEARCH, 31, (WINTER 1964), PP. 391-410.                 64
DEFEL

WALTJ -66-SAC  WALTON, J
SUBSTANCE AND ARTIFACT -- THE CURRENT STATUS OF RESEARCH
ON COMMUNITY POWER STRUCTURE.=
THE AMERICAN JOURNAL OF SOCIOLOGY, 71, (JANUARY 1966),           66
PP. 430-438.
DEFEL, METEL

WANGTC-66-CIW  WANG, TC
CHINESE INTELLECTUALS AND THE WEST, 1872-1949.
CHAPEL HILL, UNIVERSITY OF NORTH CAROLINA PRESS, 1966.           66
COMEL, ELELE, ELPRNOR

WANGYC-58-ICC  WANG, YC
               THE INTELLIGENTSIA IN CHANGING CHINA.=
               FOREIGN AFFAIRS, 36, (JANUARY 1958), PP. 315-329.            58
               ELEL, ELNOEL, ELPRNOR
WANGYC-60-WIS  WANG, YC
               WESTERN IMPACT AND SOCIAL MOBILITY IN CHINA.=
               AMERICAN SOCIOLOGICAL REVIEW, 25, (DECEMBER 1960),           60
                 PP. 843-855.
               COMEL, ELPRNOR
WANGYC-61-ISC  WANG, YC
               INTELLECTUALS AND SOCIETY IN CHINA 1860-1949.=
               COMPARATIVE STUDIES IN SOCIETY AND HISTORY, 3,               61
                 (JUNE 1961), PP. 395-426.
               COMEL, ELPRNOR
WARDFE-57-FSJ  WARD, FE (ED)
               FIVE STUDIES IN JAPANESE POLITICS.=
               ANN ARBOR, MICHIGAN, CENTER FOR JAPANESE STUDIES,            57
                 UNIVERSITY OF MICHIGAN, 1957.
               ELEL, ELPRNOR
WARDN -46-PL   WARD, N
               PROBLEM OF LEADERSHIP.=
               SOCIOLOGY AND SOCIAL RESEARCH, 30, (MARCH-APRIL 1946),       46
                 PP. 275-281.
               DEFEL, COMEL
WARDN -47-PRC  WARD, N
               PARLIAMENTARY REPRESENTATION IN CANADA.=
               CANADIAN JOURNAL OF ECONOMICS AND POLITICAL SCIENCE, 13,     47
                 (AUGUST 1947), PP. 447-464.
               COMEL
WARDR -56-SRA  WARD, R
               SOCIAL ROOTS OF AUSTRALIAN NATIONALISM.=
               THE AUSTRALIAN JOURNAL OF POLITICS AND HISTORY, 1,           56
                 (MAY 1956), PP. 179-195.
               COMEL, ELPRNOR
WARDRE-64-PMJ  WARD, RE          RUSTOW, DA (EDS)
               POLITICAL MODERNIZATION IN JAPAN AND TURKEY.=
               PRINCETON, PRINCETON UNIVERSITY PRESS, 1964.                 64
               ELEL, ELNOEL, ELPRNOR
WARDRE-66-JCM  WARD, RE
               JAPAN -- THE CONTINUITY OF MODERNIZATION.=
               LW PYE AND S VERBA (EDS), POLITICAL CULTURE AND              66
                 POLITICAL DEVELOPMENT, PRINCETON UNIVERSITY
                 PRESS, 1966, PP. 27-82.
               ELEL, ELNOEL, ELPRNOR
WARDWI-56-EPR  WARDWELL, WI        WOOD, AL
               THE EXTRA - PROFESSIONAL ROLE OF THE LAWYER
                 (UNITED STATES).=
               THE AMERICAN JOURNAL OF SOCIOLOGY, 61, (JANUARY 1956),       56
                 PP. 304-307.
               ELEL, ELNOEL, ELPRNOR
WARNWL-55-BBL  WARNER, WL          ABEGGLEN, JC
               BIG BUSINESS LEADERS IN AMERICA.=
               NEW YORK, HARPER AND ROW, 1955.                              55
               COMEL, ELEL, ELPRNOR, METEL
WARNWL-63-AFE  WARNER, WL          ET AL
               THE AMERICAN FEDERAL EXECUTIVE -- A STUDY OF SOCIAL AND
                 PERSONAL CHARACTERISTICS OF THE CIVILIAN AND MILITARY
                 LEADERS OF THE UNITED STATES FEDERAL GOVERNMENT.=
               NEW HAVEN, YALE UNIVERSITY PRESS, 1963.                      63
               COMEL, ELEL, ELPRNOR
WARRJH-51-PSL  WARREN, JH
               THE PARTY SYSTEM IN LOCAL GOVERNMENT(GREAT BRITAIN).=
               PARLIAMENTARY AFFAIRS, 5, (WINTER 1951), PP. 179-194.        51
               ELEL, ELNOEL
WARRRL-55-SYC  WARREN, RL
               STUDYING YOUR COMMUNITY (UNITED STATES).=
               NEW YORK, RUSSELL SAGE FOUNDATION, 1955.                     55
               DEFEL, METEL
WARRRL-63-CA   WARREN, RL
               THE COMMUNITY IN AMERICA.=
               CHICAGO, RAND MCNALLY AND COMPANY, 1963.                     63
               DEFEL, ELEL
WASHSW-59-SPL  WASHINGTON, SW
               STUDENT POLITICS IN LATIN AMERICA --
                 THE VENEZUELAN EXAMPLE.=
               FOREIGN AFFAIRS, 37, (APRIL 1959), PP. 463-473.              59
               COMEL, ELNOEL
WATEJ -67-MPE  WATERBURY, J
               MARGINAL POLITICS AND ELITE MANIPULATION IN MOROCCO.=
               EUROPEAN JOURNAL OF SOCIOLOGY, 8, (1967), PP. 94-111.        67
               COMEL, ELEL, ELNOEL, ELPRNOR
WATSJB-54-SLB  WATSON, JB          SANORA, J
               SUBORDINATE LEADERSHIP IN A BICULTURAL COMMUNITY --
                 AN ANALYSIS (UNITED STATES).=

                      AMERICAN SOCIOLOGICAL REVIEW, 19, (AUGUST 1954),            54
                         PP. 413-421.
                      ELNOEL
WATSRA-67-BPJ    WATSON, RA          DOWNING, RG          SPEIGEL, FC
                 BAR OF POLITICS, JUDICIAL SELECTION AND THE REPRESENTATION
                    OF SOCIAL INTERESTS (UNITED STATES).=
                 THE AMERICAN POLITICAL SCIENCE REVIEW, 61, (MARCH 1967),   67
                    PP. 54-71.
                 COMEL, ELEL, ELPRNOR
WATTDC-55-GDN    WATT, DC
                 THE GERMAN DIPLOMATS AND THE NAZI LEADERSHIP, 1933-1939.=
                 JOURNAL OF CENTRAL EUROPEAN AFFAIRS, 15, (JULY 1955),      55
                    PP. 148-160.
                 COMEL, ELNOEL, ELPRNOR
WATTDC-63-ABF    WATT, DC
                 AMERICA AND THE BRITISH FOREIGN POLICY-MAKING ELITE,
                    FROM JOSEPH CHAMBERLAIN TO ANTHONY EDEN, 1895-1956.=
                 THE REVIEW OF POLITICS, 25, (JANUARY 1963), PP. 3-33.      63
                 DEFEL, COMEL, ELPRNOR
WATTDC-65-PPS    WATT, DC
                 PERSONALITIES AND POLICIES -- STUDIES IN THE FORMULATION
                    OF BRITISH FOREIGN POLICY IN THE TWENTIETH CENTURY.=
                 LONDON, LONGMANS, GREEN AND CO., 1965.                     65
                 COMEL, ELEL, ELPRNOR
WAUGEW-56-SCV    WAUGH, EW
                 SECOND CONSUL -- THE VICE PRESIDENCY -- OUR GREATEST
                    POLITICAL PROBLEM (UNITED-STATES).=
                 INDIANAPOLIS, BOBBS-MERRILL, 1956.                         56
                 ELEL, ELNOEL
WEBBL -53-LLP    WEBB, L
                 LEADERSHIP IN THE LABOUR PARTY (NEW ZEALAND).=
                 POLITICAL SCIENCE, 5, (SEPTEMBER 1953), PP. 45-49.         53
                 FLEL
WEBBS -61-FLG    WEBB, S
                 THE FIRST LABOUR GOVERNMENT (GREAT BRITAIN).=
                 THE POLITICAL QUARTERLY, 32, (JANUARY 1961), PP. 6-44.     61
                 COMEL, ELEL, ELNOEL
WEBEE -58-LFD    WEBER, E
                 LA FIEVRE DE LA RAISON -- NATIONALISM AND THE FRENCH
                    RIGHT.=
                 WORLD POLITICS, 10, (JULY 1958), PP. 560-578.              58
                 ELPRNOR
WEEMB -48-BKE    WEEMS, B
                 BEHIND THE KOREAN ELECTION.=
                 FAR EASTERN SURVEY, 17, (JUNE 23, 1948), PP. 142-147.      48
                 COMEL
WEERID-60-CGE    WEERAWARDANA, IDS
                 CEYLON GENERAL ELECTIONS, 1956.=
                 COLOMBO, MC GUNASENA AND COMPANY, 1960.                    60
                 COMEL, ELEL, ELNOEL
WEIKWF-62-AFP    WEIKER, WF
                 ACADEMIC FREEDOM AND PROBLEMS OF HIGHER EDUCATION
                    IN TURKEY.=
                 THE MIDDLE EAST JOURNAL ,16, (SUMMER 1962), PP. 279-294.   62
                 ELEL, ELPRNOR
WEIKWF-63-ACT    WEIKER, WF
                 THE AYDEMIR CASE AND TURKEY'S POLITICAL DILEMMA.=
                 MIDDLE EASTERN AFFAIRS, 14, (NOVEMBER 1963), PP. 258-271. 63
                 ELEL, ELPRNOR
WEILHN-64-EPN    WEILER, HN (ED)
                 EDUCATION AND POLITICS IN NIGERIA.=
                 FREIBURG IM BREISGAU, VERLAG ROMBACH, 1964.                64
                 COMEL, ELEL, ELNOEL, ELPRNOR
WEINM -57-PPI    WEINER, M
                 PARTY POLITICS IN INDIA -- THE DEVELOPMENT OF A
                    MULTIPARTY SYSTEM.=
                 PRINCETON, NEW JERSEY, PRINCETON UNIVERSITY PRESS, 1957.   57
                 COMEL, ELEL
WEINM -59-CPP    WEINER, M
                 CHANGING PATTERNS OF POLITICAL LEADERSHIP IN WEST
                    BENGAL (INDIA).=
                 PACIFIC AFFAIRS, 32, (SEPTEMBER 1959), PP. 277-287.        59
                 ELEL, ELNOEL
WEINM -59-HPM    WEINER, M
                 SOME HYPOTHESES ON THE POLITICS OF MODERNIZATION IN
                    INDIA.=
                 RL PARK, I TINKER (EDS), LEADERSHIP AND POLITICAL          59
                    INSTITUTIONS IN INDIA, PRINCETON, PRINCETON UNIVERSITY
                    PRESS, 1959, PP. 18-38.
                 ELEL, ELNOEL, ELPRNOR
WEINM -60-PSA    WEINER, M
                 THE POLITICS OF SOUTH ASIA.=
                 GA ALMOND AND JS COLEMAN (EDS), THE POLITICS OF THE        60
                    DEVELOPING AREAS, PRINCETON, PRINCETON UNIVERSITY PRESS ,

```
                         1960, PP. 153-246.
                         COMEL, ELEL, ELNOEL, ELPRNOR
WEINM -62-PSP    WEINER, M
                 THE POLITICS OF SCARCITY -- PUBLIC PRESSURE AND POLITICAL
                    RESPONSE IN INDIA.=
                 CHICAGO, UNIVERSITY OF CHICAGO PRESS, 1962.                   62
                 ELEL, ELNOEL, ELPRNOR
WEINM -64-TRP    WEINER, M
                 TRADITIONAL ROLE PERFORMANCE AND THE DEVELOPMENT OF MODERN
                    POLITICAL PARTIES -- THE INDIAN CASE.=
                 THE JOURNAL OF POLITICS, 26, (NOVEMBER 1964),                 64
                    PP. 830-849.
                 COMEL, ELEL, ELNOEL
WEINM -67-CPE    WEINER, M
                 CONGRESS PARTY ELITES (INDIA).=
                 BLOOMINGTON, THE CARNEGIE SEMINAR ON POLITICAL AND            67
                    ADMINISTRATIVE DEVELOPMENT, DEPARTMENT OF GOVERNMENT,
                    INDIANA UNIVERSITY, 1967.
                 COMEL, ELEL, ELPRNOR
WELCCE-66-SAW    WELCH, CE
                 SHIFTING AUTHORITY IN WEST AFRICA.=
                 CURRENT HISTORY, N.S., 50, (MARCH 1966), PP. 153-159.         66
                 ELEL, ELNOEL
WELLH -55-ILP    WELLS, H
                 IDEOLOGY AND LEADERSHIP IN PUERTO RICAN POLITICS.=
                 THE AMERICAN POLITICAL SCIENCE REVIEW, 49, (MARCH 1955),      55
                    PP. 22-39.
                 ELEL, ELPRNOR
WEN-M -63-IF     WEN-LI, M
                 THE INTELLECTUALS ON FORMOSA.=
                 THE CHINA QUARTERLY, 15, (1963), PP. 65-74.                   63
                 COMEL, ELEL
WERBRP-67-FAR    WERBNER, RP
                 FEDERAL ADMINISTRATION, RANK, AND CIVIL STRIFE AMONG
                    BEMBA ROYALS AND NOBLES (ZAMBIA).=
                 AFRICA, 37, (JANUARY U9LM), PP. 22-49.                        67
                 ELEL, ELNOEL, ELPRNOR
WERNEE-  -WCU    WERNER, EE
                 WOMEN IN CONGRESS, 1917-1964 (UNITED STATES).=
                 THE WESTERN POLITICAL QUARTERLY, 19, (MARCH 1966),
                    PP. 16-30.
                 COMEL
WERTWF-55-CIS    WERTHEIM, WF
                 CHANGES IN INDONESIA'S SOCIAL STRATIFICATION.=
                 PACIFIC AFFAIRS, 28, (MARCH 1955), PP. 42-52.                 55
                 ELEL, ELNOEL, ELPRNOR
WERTWF-59-IST    WERTHEIM, WF
                 INDONESIAN SOCIETY IN TRANSITION -- A STUDY OF
                    SOCIAL CHANGE.=
                 THE HAGUE, W VAN HOEVE, LTD., 1959.                           59
                 ELEL, ELNOEL ELPRNOR
WERTWF-62-NLA    WERTHEIM, WF
                 NATIONALISM AND LEADERSHIP IN ASIA.=
                 SCIENCE AND SOCIETY, 26, (WINTER 1962), PP. 1-14.             62
                 COMEL, ELEL, ELNOEL, ELPRNOR
WERTWF-62-SCJ    WERTHEIM, WF            GIAP, TS
                 SOCIAL CHANGE IN JAVA, 1900-1930.=
                 PACIFIC AFFAIRS, 35, (FALL 1962), PP. 223-247.                62
                 ELEL, ELNOEL, ELPRNOR
WERTWF-64-PPP    WERTHEIM, WF
                 PEASANTS, PEDDLERS AND PRINCES IN INDONESIA --
                    A REVIEW ARTICLE.=
                 PACIFIC AFFAIRS, 37, (1964), PP. 307-311.                     64
                 DEFEL
WESOW -65-RCP    WESOLOWSKI, W
                 RULING CLASS AND POWER ELITE.=
                 THE POLISH SOCIOLOGICAL BULLETIN, 11, (1965), PP. 22-37.      65
                 GNELTH, DEFEL
WESTAF-61-EPI    WESTWOOD, AF
                 ELECTIONS AND POLITICS IN IRAN.=
                 THE MIDDLE EAST JOURNAL 15, (SPRING 1961), PP. 153-164.       61
                 COMEL, ELEL, ELNOEL, ELPRNOR
WESTAF-62-UPC    WESTIN, AF
                 THE USES OF POWER -- 7 CASES IN AMERICAN POLITICS.=
                 NEW YORK, HARCOURT, BRACE, AND WORLD, 1962.                   62
                 ELEL, ELNOEL, ELPRNOR
WESTAF-65-PDI    WESTWOOD, AF
                 POLITICS OF DISTRUST IN IRAN.=
                 THE ANNALS OF THE AMERICAN ACADEMY OF POLITICAL AND SOCIAL65
                    SCIENCE, 358, (MARCH 1965), PP. 123-135.
                 ELEL, ELNOEL, ELPRNOR
WESTFJ-61-PAS    WEST, FJ
                 POLITICAL ADVANCEMENT IN THE SOUTH PACIFIC -- A
                    COMPARATIVE STUDY OF COLONIAL PRACTICE IN FIJI, TAHITI,
```

```
                   AND AMERICAN SAMOA.=
                   NEW YORK, OXFORD UNIVERSITY PRESS, 1961.                    61
                   ELEL, ELNOEL
WESTHB-55-FPP      WESTERFIELD, HB
                   FOREIGN POLICY AND PARTY POLITICS -- PEARL HARBOR TO
                      KOREA (UNITED STATES).=
                   NEW HAVEN, YALE UNIVERSITY PRESS, 1955.                     55
                   ELEL, ELNOEL
WESTJ -45-PU       WEST, J
                   PLAINVILLE, USA.=
                   NEW YORK, COLUMBIA UNIVERSITY PRESS, 1945.                  45
                   COMEL, FLNOEL, ELPRNOR
WEYLN -66-CEA      WEYL, N
                   THE CREATIVE ELITE IN AMERICA.=
                   WASHINGTON, PUBLIC AFFAIRS PRESS, 1966.                     66
                   ELEL, ELNOEL, ELPRNOR
WEYRWO-64-PLC      WEYRAUCH, WO
                   THE PERSONALITY OF LAWYERS -- A COMPARATIVE STUDY OF
                      SUBJECTIVE FACTORS IN LAW, BASED ON INTERVIEWS WITH
                      GERMAN LAWYERS.=
                   NEW HAVEN, YALE UNIVERSITY PRESS, 1964.                     64
                   COMEL, ELEL, ELPRNOR, METEL
WHEAWL-64-IUL      WHEATON, WLC
                   INTEGRATION AT THE URBAN LEVEL -- POLITICAL INFLUENCE
                      AND THE DECISION PROCESS.=
                   PHILADELPHIA, JB LIPPINCOTT, 1964, PP. 120-142.            64
                   DEFEL, METEL
WHEEJW-54-NPG      WHEELER-BENNETT, JW
                   THE NEMESIS OF POWER -- THE GERMAN ARMY IN POLITICS
                      1918-1945.=
                   NEW YORK, ST MARTIN'S PRESS, 1954.                          54
                   ELEL, ELNOEL, ELPRNOR
WHITAH-64-TCL      WHITEFORD, AH
                   TWO CITIES OF LATIN AMERICA -- A COMPARATIVE DESCRIPTION
                      OF SOCIAL CLASSES.=
                   GARDEN CITY, NEW YORK, DOUBLEDAY, 1964.                     64
                   COMEL, ELEL, ELNOEL
WHITAP-56-AUP      WHITAKER, AP
                   ARGENTINE UPHEAVAL -- PERON'S FALL AND THE NEW REGIME.=
                   NEW YORK, FREDERICK A PRAEGER,1956.                         56
                   COMEL, ELEL, ELNOEL
WHITAP-63-LRE      WHITAKER, AP
                   LEFT AND RIGHT EXTREMISM IN ARGENTINA.=
                   CURRENT HISTORY, N.S., 44, (FEBRUARY 1963), PP. 84-88.      63
                   COMEL, ELEL, ELNOEL
WHITCM-57-CCS      WHITE, CMN
                   CLAN, CHIEFTAINSHIP, AND SLAVERY IN LUVALE POLITICAL
                      ORGANIZATION (NORTH RHODESIA).=
                   AFRICA, 27, (JANUARY 1957), PP. 59-74.                      57
                   COMEL
WHITCS-65-TPH      WHITAKER, CS
                   THREE PERSPECTIVES ON HIERARCHY -- POLITICAL THOUGHT AND
                      LEADERSHIP IN NORTHERN NIGERIA.=
                   JOURNAL OF COMMONWEALTH POLITICAL STUDIES, 3, (1965),       65
                      PP. 1-19.
                   COMEL, ELEL, ELNOEL, ELPRNOR
WHITJE-50-TMR      WHITE, JE
                   THEORY AND METHOD FOR RESEARCH IN COMMUNITY LEADERSHIP.=
                   AMERICAN SOCIOLOGICAL REVIEW, 15, (FEBRUARY 1950),          50
                      PP. 50-60.
                   DEFEL, METEL
WHITNE-65-PSS      WHITTEN-JR, NE
                   POWER STRUCTURE AND SOCIOCULTURAL CHANGE IN LATIN AMERICAN
                      COMMUNITIES.=
                   SOCIAL FORCES, 43, (MARCH 1965), PP. 320-329.               65
                   COMEL, ELEL, ELNOEL
WHITRK-65-ICI      WHITE, RK
                   IMAGES IN THE CONTEXT OF INTERNATIONAL CONFLICT --
                      SOVIET PERCEPTIONS OF THE U.S. AND THE U.S.S.R.=
                   HC KELMAN (ED), INTERNATIONAL BEHAVIOR--A SOCIAL            65
                      PSYCHOLOGICAL ANALYSIS, NEW YORK, HOLT RINEHART AND
                      WINSTON, 1965, PP. 238-276.
                   ELPRNOR
WHITTN-44-LFS      WHITEHEAD, TN
                   LEADERSHIP IN A FREE SOCIETY.=
                   CAMBRIDGE, HARVARD UNIVERSITY PRESS, 1944.                  44
                   DEFEL, ELEL, ELNOEL
WHYTWF-61-MW       WHYTE, WF
                   MEN AT WORK.=
                   HOMEWOOD, ILLINOIS, DORSEY PRESS, INC, 1961.                61
                   GNELTH, DEFEL, ELEL, ELNOEL, ELPRNOR
WIARHJ-65-PCM      WIARDA, HJ
                   THE POLITICS OF CIVIL - MILITARY RELATIONS IN THE
                      DOMINICAN REPUBLIC.=
```

                        JOURNAL OF INTER-AMERICAN STUDIES, 7, (OCTOBER 1965),     65
                           PP. 465-484.
                        COMEL, ELEL, ELNOEL, ELPRNOR
WIARHJ-66-DLM   WIARDA, HJ
                        THE DEVELOPMENT OF THE LABOR MOVEMENT IN THE
                           DOMINICAN REPUBLIC.=
                        INTER-AMERICAN ECONOMIC AFFAIRS, 20, (SUMMER 1966),      66
                           PP. 41-63.
                        ELEL, ELNOEL
WIATJJ-66-PSC   WIATR, JJ
                        POLITICS AND SOCIAL CHANGE -- POLAND.=
                        INTERNATIONAL JOURNAL OF COMPARATIVE SOCIOLOGY, 7,       66
                           (MARCH 1966), PP. 237-246.
                        ELEL, ELNOEL, ELPRNOR
WIEDEW-62-WRU   WIEDNER, EW
                        THE WORLD ROLE OF UNIVERSITIES.=
                        NEW YORK, MCGRAW-HILL BOOK COMPANY, 1962.                62
                        COMEL
WIGGCW-67-PPI   WIGGENS, CW
                        PARTY POLITICS IN THE IOWA LEGISLATURE (UNITED STATES).=
                        MIDWEST JOURNAL OF POLITICAL SCIENCE, 11, (FEBRUARY 1967),67
                           PP. 86-97.
                        ELEL, ELPRNOR
WIGHE -59-BUG   WIGHAM, E
                        BRITISH UNIONS AND THE GOVERNMENT.=
                        CURRENT HISTORY, N.S., 37, (AUGUST 1959), PP. 68-73.     59
                        ELEL
WILCRW-63-PPB   WILCOX, RWJ
                        PROBABLES AND POSSIBLES (BRITISH CANDIDATES).=
                        THE POLITICAL QUARTERLY, 34, (JULY 1963), PP. 300-305.   63
                        COMEL
WILDA -61-PDU   WILDAVSKY, A
                        PARTY DISCIPLINE UNDER FEDERALISM -- IMPLICATIONS OF
                           AUSTRALIAN EXPERIENCE.=
                        SOCIAL RESEARCH, 28, (WINTER 1961), PP. 437-458.         61
                        ELEL, ELNOEL
WILDA -64-LST   WILDAVSKY, A
                        LEADERSHIP IN A SMALL TOWN (UNITED STATES).=
                        TOTOWA, NEW JERSEY, BEDMINSTER PRESS, 1964.              64
                        COMEL, ELEL, ELNOEL, ELPRNOR
WILDA -64-PBP   WILDAVSKY, A
                        THE POLITICS OF THE BUDGETARY PROCESS (UNITED STATES).=
                        BOSTON, LITTLE, BROWN AND COMPANY, 1964.                 64
                        ELEL, ELPRNOR
WILDAB-59-MCD   WILDAVSKY, AB
                        A METHODOLOGICAL CRITIQUE OF DUVERGER'S
                           POLITICAL PARTIES.=
                        THE JOURNAL OF POLITICS, 21, (MAY 1959), PP. 303-318.    59
                        DEFEL, METEL
WILDAB-62-SNC   WILDAVSKY, AB
                        ON THE SUPERIORITY OF NATIONAL CONVENTIONS.=
                        THE REVIEW OF POLITICS, 24, (JULY 1962), PP. 307-319.    62
                        COMEL
WILDE -65-SEE   WILDER, E
                        SOCIOLOGY IN EASTERN EUROPE -- POLAND.=
                        PROBLEMS OF COMMUNISM, 14, (JANUARY-FEBRUARY 1965),      65
                           PP. 58-62.
                        ELEL, ELPRNOR
WILEHL-56-ILU   WILENSKY, HL
                        INTELLECTUALS IN LABOR UNIONS (UNITED STATES).=
                        GLENCOE, THE FREE PRESS, 1956.                           56
                        ELEL, ELPRNOR
WILEHL-64-PE    WILENSKY, HL
                        THE PROFESSIONALIZATION OF EVERYONE.=
                        THE AMERICAN JOURNAL OF SOCIOLOGY, 70, (SEPTEMBER 1964), 64
                           PP. 137-158.
                        DEFEL, ELEL
WILKI -66-ABA   WILKS, I
                        ASPECTS OF BUREAUCRATIZATION IN ASHANTI IN THE
                           NINETEENTH CENTURY (AFRICA).=
                        THE JOURNAL OF AFRICAN HISTORY, 7, (1966), PP. 215-232.  66
                        COMEL, ELEL, ELPRNOR
WILKR -62-PLL   WILKINSON, R
                        POLITICAL LEADERSHIP AND THE LATE VICTORIAN
                           PUBLIC SCHOOL.=
                        THE BRITISH JOURNAL OF SOCIOLOGY, 13, (1962), PP. 320-330.62
                        COMEL
WILKR -64-GPB   WILKINSON, R
                        GENTLEMANLY POWER -- BRITISH LEADERSHIP AND THE PUBLIC
                           SCHOOL TRADITION -- A COMPARATIVE STUDY IN THE
                           MAKING OF RULERS.=
                        NEW YORK, OXFORD UNIVERSITY PRESS, 1964.                 64
                        COMEL, ELEL, ELNOEL, ELPRNOR
WILLAR-65-RRC   WILLNER, AR              WILLNER, D

```
                  THE RISE AND ROLE OF CHARISMATIC LEADERS.=
                  THE ANNALS OF THE AMERICAN ACADEMY OF POLITICAL AND          65
                      SOCIAL SCIENCE, 358, (MARCH 1965), PP. 77-88.
                  GNELTH, DEFEL
WILLF -56-OPR     WILLIAMS, F
                  THE OFFICE OF PUBLIC RELATIONS ADVISOR TO THE
                      PRIME MINISTER (GREAT BRITAIN).=
                  PARLIAMENTARY AFFAIRS, 9, (SUMMER 1956), PP. 260-267.          56
                  ELEL
WILLFM-59-REN     WILLSON, FMG
                  THE ROUTES OF ENTRY OF NEW MEMBERS OF THE
                      BRITISH CABINET, 1868-1958.=
                  POLITICAL STUDIES, 7, (OCTOBER 1959), PP. 222=232.            59
                  COMEL, ELEL, ELPRNOR
WILLIG-56-RVP     WILLIAMS, IG
                  THE RISE OF THE VICE PRESIDENCY (UNITED STATES).=
                  WASHINGTON, PUBLIC AFFAIRS PRESS, 1956.                       56
                  COMEL, ELEL, ELNOEL
WILLJH-49-BCP     WILLIAMS, JH
                  THE BRITISH CRISIS -- A PROBLEM IN ECONOMIC
                      STATESMANSHIP.=
                  FOREIGN AFFAIRS, 28, (OCTOBER 1949), PP. 1-17.                49
                  ELEL
WILLJR-52-BGE     WILLIAMS, JR
                  THE BRITISH GENERAL ELECTION OF 1951 -- CANDIDATES AND
                      PARTIES.=
                  PARLIAMENTARY AFFAIRS, 5, (AUTUMN 1952), PP. 480-494.         52
                  COMEL, ELEL
WILLJR-52-RHC     WILLIAMS, JR
                  REPRESENTATION IN THE HOUSE OF COMMONS OF THE
                      TWENTY-FIRST PARLIAMENT -- PARTY AND PROVINCE (CANADA).=
                  CANADIAN JOURNAL OF ECONOMICS AND POLITICAL SCIENCE,          52
                      18, (FEBRUARY 1952), PP. 77-87.
                  COMEL
WILLOP-63-FCS     WILLIAMS, OP         ADRIAN, CR
                  FOUR CITIES -- A STUDY IN COMPARATIVE POLICY-MAKING
                      (UNITED STATES).=
                  PHILADELPHIA, UNIVERSITY OF PENNSYLVANIA PRESS, 1963.         63
                  ELEL, ELNOEL
WILLP -53-CSH     WILLEN, P
                  CAN STALIN HAVE A SUCCESSOR (SOVIET UNION).=
                  COMMENTARY, 16, (JULY 1953), PP. 36-44.                       53
                  COMEL, ELNOEL, ELPRNOR
WILLP -57-CEB     WILLEN, P
                  COMMUNIST EXPERIMENTS WITH BALLOT (POLAND, YUGOSLAVIA).=
                  PROBLEMS OF COMMUNISM, 6, (MARCH-APRIL 1957), PP. 33-37.      57
                  ELNOEL
WILLP -63-ECG     WILLMOTT, P
                  THE EVOLUTION OF A COMMUNITY (GREAT BRITAIN).=
                  LONDON, ROUTLEDGE AND KEGAN PAUL, 1963.                       63
                  ELEL, ELNOEL, ELPRNOR
WILLPM-64-CCP     WILLIAMS, PM
                  CRISIS AND COMPROMISE -- POLITICS IN THE FOURTH REPUBLIC.=
                  3RD EDITION, LONDON, LONGMANS, 1964.                          64
                  ELEL, ELNOEL, ELPRNOR
WILLRC-62-VML     WILLIAMSON, RC
                  SOME VARIABLES OF MIDDLE AND LOWER CLASS IN TWO CENTRAL
                      AMERICAN CITIES.=
                  SOCIAL FORCES, 41, (DECEMBER 1962), PP. 195-207.              62
                  COMEL, ELPRNOR
WILLRC-64-USW     WILLIAMSON, RC
                  UNIVERSITY STUDENTS IN A WORLD OF CHANGE
                      -- A COLUMBIAN SAMPLE.=
                  SOCIOLOGY AND SOCIAL SCIENCE RESEARCH, 48,                    64
                      (JULY 1964), PP. 397-413.
                  COMEL, METEL
WILLRW-55-TUA     WILLIAMS, RW
                  TRADE UNIONS IN AFRICA.=
                  AFRICAN AFFAIRS, 54, (1955), PP. 267-279.                     55
                  COMEL, ELEL, ELNOEL
WILLSM-66-ESS     WILLHELM, SM
                  ELITES, SCHOLARS, AND SOCIOLOGISTS.=
                  CATALYST, (SUMMER 1966), PP. 1-10.                            66
                  ELEL, METEL
WILLV -65-LTR     WILLIAMS, V
                  LEADERSHIP TYPES, ROLE DIFFERENTIATION, AND
                      SYSTEM PROBLEMS.=
                  SOCIAL FORCES, 43, (MARCH 1965), PP. 380-384.                 65
                  DEFEL
WILLWM-56-SEV     WILLIAMS, WM
                  THE SOCIOLOGY OF AN ENGLISH VILLAGE.=
                  LONDON, ROUTLEDGE AND KEGAN PAUL, 1956.                       56
                  COMEL, ELEL, ELNOEL, ELPRNOR
WILML -53-VPU     WILMERDING-JR, L
```

                        THE VICE PRESIDENCY (UNITED STATES).=
                        POLITICAL SCIENCE QUARTERLY, 68, (MARCH 1953), PP. 17-41. 53
                        ELEL
WILSAJ-66-TFP   WILSON, AJ
                        THE TAMIL FEDERAL PARTY IN CEYLON POLITICS.=
                        JOURNAL OF COMMONWEALTH POLITICAL STUDIES, 4,            66
                           (JULY 1966),PP. 117-135.
                        ELEL, ELNOEL, ELPRNOR
WILSCS-59-SBC   WILSON, CS              LUPTON, T
                        THE SOCIAL BACKGROUND AND CONNECTIONS OF TOP
                           DECISION-MAKERS (GREAT BRITAIN).=
                        THE MANCHESTER SCHOOL, 27, (1959).                      59
                        CONEL, ELEL
WILSDA-62-MTP   WILSON, DA
                        THE MILITARY IN THAI POLITICS.=
                        JJ JOHNSON (ED), THE ROLE OF THE MILITARY IN            62
                           UNDERDEVELOPED COUNTRIES, PRINCETON, PRINCETON
                        COMEL, ELEL, ELNOEL, ELPRNOR
WILSFG-62-TPO   WILSON, FG
                        A THEORY OF PUBLIC OPINION.=
                        CHICAGO, H REGNERY, 1962.                               62
                        ELEL, ELNOEL
WILSG -45-ASC   WILSON, G               WILSON, M
                        THE ANALYSIS OF SOCIAL CHANGE -- BASED ON OBSERVATIONS
                           IN CENTRAL AFRICA.=
                        CAMBRIDGE, CAMBRIDGE UNIVERSITY PRESS, 1945.            45
                        DEFEL, ELEL, ELNOEL, COMEL
WILSJQ-60-NPS   WILSON, JQ
                        NEGRO POLITICS -- THE SEARCH FOR LEADERSHIP.=
                        GLENCOE, ILLINOIS, THE FREE PRESS, 1960.                60
                        COMEL, ELEL, ELNOEL, ELPRNOR
WILSJQ-60-TNP   WILSON, JQ
                        TWO NEGRO POLITICIANS -- AN INTERPRETATION
                           (UNITED-STATES).=
                        MIDWEST JOURNAL OF POLITICAL SCIENCE, 4,                60
                           (NOVEMBER 1963), PP. 346-369.
                        COMEL, ELNOEL, ELPRNOR
WILSJQ-62-ADC   WILSON, JQ
                        THE AMATEUR DEMOCRAT -- CLUB POLITICS IN THREE CITIES
                           (UNITED STATES).=
                        CHICAGO, UNIVERSITY OF CHICAGO PRESS, 1962.             62
                        COMEL, ELEL, ELNOEL, ELPRNOR
WINDRB-62-SDC   WINDER, RB
                        SYRIAN DEPUTIES AND CABINET MINISTERS, 1919-1959
                           -- PART 1 -- PART 2.=
                        THE MIDDLE EAST JOURNAL, 16,17, (AUTUMN 1962,           62
                           WINTER-SPRING 1963), PP. 407-429, PP. 35-54.
                        COMEL
WINGR -65-CSC   WINGFIELD, R            PARENTON, VJ
                        CLASS STRUCTURE AND CLASS CONFLICT IN HAITIAN SOCIETY.=
                        SOCIAL FORCES, 43, (MARCH 1965), PP. 338-347.           65
                        COMEL, ELEL, ELNOEL
WINSEM-48-PIS   WINSLOW, EM
                        THE PATTERN OF IMPERIALISM -- A STUDY IN THE THEORIES
                           OF POWER.=
                        NEW YORK, COLUMBIA UNIVERSITY PRESS, 1948.              48
                        DEFEL, ELEL
WIRTJD-64-TBR   WIRTH, JD
                        TERENTISMO IN THE BRAZILIAN REVOLUTION OF 1930.=
                        THE HISPANIC AMERICAN HISTORICAL REVIEW, 44,            64
                           (MAY 1964), PP. 161-179.
                        ELEL, ELNOEL, ELPRNOR
WIRTL -48-CMC   WIRTH, L
                        CONSENSUS AND MASS COMMUNICATION.=
                        AMERICAN SOCIOLOGICAL REVIEW, 13, (FEBRUARY 1948),      48
                           PP. 1-15.
                        ELNOEL
WISEHV-57-GCG   WISEMAN, HV
                        THE GOLD COAST (GHANA) -- MINISTERS AND OFFICIALS -- 3.=
                        PARLIAMENTARY AFFAIRS, 10, (SUMMER 1957), PP. 333-343.  57
                        COMEL, ELEL, ELPRNOR
WISHRL-61-CPM   WISHLADE, RL
                        CHIEFSHIP AND POLITICS IN THE MLANJE DISTRICT OF
                           SOUTHERN NYASALAND.=
                        AFRICA, 31, (JANUARY 1961), PP. 36-45.                  61
                        COMEL
WISHRL-65-SSN   WISHLADE, RL
                        SECTARIANISM IN SOUTHERN NYASALAND.=
                        LONDON, OXFORD UNIVERSITY PRESS, 1965.                  65
                        COMEL, ELEL, ELNOEL, ELPRNOR
WITTK -57-ODC   WITTFOGEL, K
                        ORIENTAL DESPOTISM -- A COMPARATIVE STUDY OF TOTAL POWER.=
                        NEW HAVEN, YALE UNIVERSITY PRESS, 1957.                 57
                        GNELTH, DEFEL, COMEL, ELEL

WITTKA-53-RBO    WITTFOGEL, KA
                 THE RULING BUREAUCRACY OF ORIENTAL DESPOTISM -- A
                   PHENOMENON THAT PARALYZED MARX.=
                 THE REVIEW OF POLITICS, 15, (JULY 1953), PP. 350-359.        53
                 DEFEL
WM      -52-CCB  WM
                 THE CHINESE COMMUNISTS AND THE 'BOURGEOISIE'.=
                 PROBLEMS OF COMMUNISM, 1, (NUMBER 1, 1952), PP. 1-4.          52
                 ELEL
WOHLJ -56-BUS    WOHL, J            SILVERSTEIN, J
                 THE BURMESE UNIVERSITY STUDENT -- AN APPROACH TO
                   PERSONALITY AND SUBCULTURE.=
                 THE PUBLIC OPINION QUARTERLY, 30, (SUMMER 1966),             66
                   PP. 237-248.
                 ELPRNOR
WOHLR -54-FEG    WOHL, R
                 THE FORMATION OF ENTREPRENEURIAN GROUPS IN
                   UNDER-DEVELOPED COUNTRIES.=
                 RL ARONSON AND JP WINDMUELLER (EDS), LABOR                   54
                   MANAGEMENT AND ECONOMIC GROWTH, ITHACA, INSTITUTE OF
                   INTERNATIONAL INDUSTRIAL AND LABOR RELATIONS, CORNELL
                   UNIVERSITY, 1954.
                 ELEL, ELPRNOR
WOLFBD-53-SSS    WOLFE, BD
                 THE STRUGGLE FOR THE SOVIET SUCCESSION.=
                 FOREIGN AFFAIRS, 31, (JULY 1953), PP. 548-565.               53
                 COMEL, ELEL
WOLFBD-55-PCS    WOLFE, BD
                 PROFESSOR CARR'S 'WAVE OF THE FUTURE'.=
                 COMMENTARY, 19, (MARCH 1955), PP. 284-290.                   55
                 ELEL, ELNOEL, ELPRNOR
WOLFBD-56-SVS    WOLFE, BD
                 STALINISM VERSUS STALIN (SOVIET UNION).=
                 COMMENTARY, 21, (JUNE 1956), PP. 522-531.                    56
                 ELEL, ELNOEL, ELPRNOR
WOLFBD-61-CTK    WOLFE, BD
                 COMMUNIST TOTALITARIANISM -- KEYS TO THE SOVIET SYSTEM.=
                 REVISED EDITION, BOSTON, BEACON PRESS, 1961.                 61
                 DEFEL, ELEL, ELNOEL, ELPRNOR
WOLFC -55-CBU    WOLFE, C
                 COLLECTIVE BARGAINING IN THE USSR.=
                 BULLETIN OF THE INSTITUTE FOR THE STUDY OF THE HISTORY       55
                   AND CULTURE OF THE USSR, 2, (JUNE 1955), PP. 16-22.
                 ELEL
WOLFC -65-PEM    WOLF, C
                 THE POLITICAL EFFECTS OF MILITARY PROGRAMS -- SOME
                   INDICATIONS FROM LATIN AMERICA.=
                 ORBIS, 8, (WINTER 1965), PP. 871-893.                        65
                 ELEL
WOLFER-65-AGR    WOLF, ER
                 ASPECTS OF GROUP RELATIONS IN A COMPLEX SOCIETY --
                   MEXICO.=
                 AMERICAN ANTHROPOLOGIST, 58, (DECEMBER 1956),                65
                   PP. 1065-1078.
                 COMEL, ELEL, ELNOEL
WOLFEV-67-PAC    WOLFENSTEIN, EV
                 SOME PSYCHOLOGICAL ASPECTS OF CRISIS LEADERSHIP.=
                 LJ EDINGER (ED), POLITICAL LEADERSHIP IN INDUSTRIALIZED      67
                   SOCIETIES, NEW YORK, JOHN WILEY AND SONS, 1967,
                   PP. 155-181.
                 DEFEL, COMEL, ELPRNOR
WOLFRE-60-RRS    WOLFINGER, RE
                 REPUTATION AND REALITY IN THE STUDY OF 'COMMUNITY POWER'
                   (UNITED STATES).=
                 AMERICAN SOCIOLOGICAL REVIEW, 25, (OCTOBER 1960),            60
                   PP. 636-644.
                 DEFEL, ELEL, ELNOEL, METEL
WOLFRE-63-IPW    WOLFINGER, RE
                 THE INFLUENCE OF PRECINCT WORK ON VOTING BEHAVIOR
                   (UNITED STATES).=
                 THE PUBLIC OPINION QUARTERLY, 27, (FALL 1963),               63
                   PP. 387-398.
                 ELNOEL
WOLFRE-64-ASR    WOLFINGER, RE        WOLFINGER, BK        PREWITT, K
                 AMERICA'S RADICAL RIGHT -- POLITICS AND IDEOLOGY.=
                 DE APTER (ED), IDEOLOGY AND DISCONTENT, LONDON, THE FREE     64
                   PRESS, 1964, PP. 262-293.
                 COMEL, ELPRNOR
WOLFRE-65-SSS    WOLFINGER, RE        HEIFETZ, J
                 SAFE SEATS, SENIORITY, AND POWER IN CONGRESS
                   (UNITED STATES).=
                 THE AMERICAN POLITICAL SCIENCE REVIEW, 59, (JUNE 1965),      65
                   PP. 337-349.
                 COMEL, ELEL, ELNOEL

WOLFTW-64-PPV    WOLFE, TW
                 POLITICAL PRIMACY VS PROFESSIONAL ELAN (SOVIET UNION).=
                 PROBLEMS OF COMMUNISM, 13, (MAY-JUNE 1964), PP. 44-52.        64
                 ELEL, ELPRNOR
WOLIS -57-SSP    WOLIN, S            SLUSSER, RM (EDS)
                 THE SOVIET SECRET POLICE.=
                 LONDON, METHUEN, 1957.                                        57
                 COMEL, ELEL
WOLLP -63-AB     WOLL, P
                 AMERICAN BUREAUCRACY.=
                 NEW YORK, NORTON AND COMPANY, 1963.                           63
                 ELEL, ELNOEL
WOLPJF-65-TSA    WOLPERT, JF
                 TOWARD A SOCIOLOGY OF AUTHORITY.=
                 AW GOULDNER (ED), STUDIES IN LEADERSHIP, NEW YORK             65
                   RUSSELL AND RUSSELL, 1965, PP. 679-701.
                 GNELTH
WOODD -65-PLG    WOOD, D
                 THE PARLIAMENTARY LOBBY (GREAT BRITAIN).=
                 THE POLITICAL QUARTERLY, 36, (JULY-OCTOBER 1965),             65
                   PP. 309-322.
                 ELEL
WOODDM-64-IDM    WOOD, DM
                 ISSUE DIMENSIONS IN A MULTI - PARTY SYSTEM --
                   THE FRENCH NATIONAL ASSEMBLY AND EUROPEAN UNIFICATION.=
                 MIDWEST JOURNAL OF POLITICAL SCIENCE, 8, (AUGUST 1964),       64
                   PP. 255-276.
                 ELPRNOR
WOODN -59-CBI    WOOD, N
                 COMMUNISM AND BRITISH INTELLECTUALS.=
                 NEW YORK, COLUMBIA UNIVERSITY PRESS, 1959.                    59
                 ELEL, ELNOEL, ELPRNOR
WOODP -54-MWR    WOODRUFF, P
                 THE MEN WHO RULED INDIA -- THE GUARDIANS.=
                 NEW YORK, SAINT MARTIN'S PRESS, 1954.                         54
                 COMEL, ELEL, ELNOEL, ELPRNOR
WOODTJ-64-DCU    WOOD, TJ
                 DADE COUNTY -- UNBOSSED, ERRATICALLY LED (UNITED STATES).=
                 THE ANNALS OF THE AMERICAN ACADEMY OF POLITICAL AND           64
                   SOCIAL SCIENCE, 353, (MAY 1964), PP. 64-71.
                 COMEL, ELEL, ELNOEL
WOOTG -58-ESP    WOOTON, G
                 EX - SERVICEMEN IN POLITICS (GREAT BRITAIN).=
                 THE POLITICAL QUARTERLY, 29, (1958), PP. 28-39.               58
                 COMEL, ELEL, ELNOEL
WRAIRE-54-SCQ    WRAITH, RE
                 THE 'SECOND CHAMBER' QUESTION IN THE GOLD COAST (GHANA).=
                 PARLIAMENTARY AFFAIRS, 7, (AUTUMN 1954), PP. 393-400.         54
                 ELEL, ELPRNOR
WRIGAF-55-CMP    WRIGHT, AF
                 THE CHINESE MONOLITH -- PAST AND PRESENT.=
                 PROBLEMS OF COMMUNISM, 4, (JULY-AUGUST 1955), PP. 1-8.        55
                 ELNOEL
WRIGCC-59-CRB    WRIGLEY, CC
                 THE CHRISTIAN REVOLUTION IN BUGANDA.=
                 COMPARATIVE STUDIES IN SOCIETY AND HISTORY, 2,                59
                   (OCTOBER 1959), PP. 33-48.
                 ELEL, ELNOEL, ELPRNOR
WRIGDS-67-ELS    WRIGHT, DS
                 EXECUTIVE LEADERSHIP IN STATE ADMINISTRATION
                   (UNITED STATES).=
                 MIDWEST JOURNAL OF POLITICAL SCIENCE, 11, (FEBRUARY 1967),67
                   PP. 1-26.
                 ELEL, ELPRNOR
WRIGG -58-UAF    WRIGHT, G
                 SOME UNEXPLORED AVENUES IN FRENCH POLITICAL BEHAVIOR.=
                 PROD (THE AMERICAN BEHAVIORAL SCIENTIST), 1,                  58
                   (MAY 1958), PP. 12-14.
                 METEL
WRIGJR-64-MLI    WRIGHT, JR, TP
                 MUSLIM LEGISLATORS IN INDIA -- PROFILE OF A MINORITY
                   ELITE.=
                 THE JOURNAL OF ASIAN STUDIES, 23, (FEBRUARY 1964),            64
                   PP. 253-267.
                 COMEL, ELEL, ELNOEL
WRIGMC-51-CPC    WRIGHT, MC
                 THE CHINESE PEASANT AND COMMUNISM.=
                 PACIFIC AFFAIRS, 24, (SEPTEMBER 1951), PP. 256-265.           51
                 ELNOEL
WRIGMC-55-RRT    WRIGHT, MC
                 FROM REVOLUTION TO RESTORATION -- THE TRANSFORMATION OF
                   KUOMINGTANG IDEOLOGY (CHINA).=
                 FAR EASTERN QUARTERLY, 14, (AUGUST 1955), PP. 515-532.        55
                 ELPRNOR

WRIGMC-59-MCT    WRIGHT, MC
                 MODERN CHINA IN TRANSITION.=
                 THE ANNALS OF THE AMERICAN ACADEMY OF POLITICAL AND          59
                    SOCIAL SCIENCE, 321, (JANUARY 1959), PP. 1-8.
                 ELEL, ELNOEL
WRIGTP-66-MLS    WRIGHT-JR, TP
                 THE MUSLIM LEAGUE IN SOUTH INDIA SINCE INDEPENDENCE -- A
                    STUDY IN MINORITY GROUP POLITICAL STRATEGIES.=
                 THE AMERICAN POLITICAL SCIENCE REVIEW, 60, (SEPTEMBER        66
                    1966), PP. 579-599.
                 ELEL, ELPRNOR
WRIGWE-67-IPO    WRIGHT, WE
                 IDEOLOGICAL - PRAGMATIC ORIENTATIONS OF WEST BERLIN
                    LOCAL PARTY OFFICIALS (WEST GERMANY).=
                 MIDWEST JOURNAL OF POLITICAL SCIENCE, 11, (AUGUST 1967),     67
                    PP. 381-402.
                 COMEL, ELNOEL, ELPRNOR, METEL
WRISHM-54-YMF    WRISTON, HM
                 YOUNG MEN AND THE FOREIGN SERVICE (UNITED STATES).=
                 FOREIGN AFFAIRS, 33, (OCTOBER 1954), PP. 28-42.              54
                 COMEL, ELEL
WRONDH-54-TMS    WRONG, DH
                 THEORIES OF MCCARTHYISM -- A SURVEY (UNITED STATES).=
                 DISSENT, 1, (AUTUMN 1954), PP. 385-398.                      54
                 ELNOEL, ELPRNOR
WU, T -52-ICE    WU, T
                 AN INTERPRETATION OF CHINESE ECONOMIC HISTORY.=
                 PAST AND PRESENT, 1, (FEBRUARY 1952), PP. 1-12.              52
                 COMEL
WURFD -67-SPE    WURFEL, D
                 THE SAIGON POLITICAL ELITE -- FOCUS ON FOUR CABINETS
                    (SOUTH VIETNAM).=
                 ASIAN SURVEY, 7, (AUGUST 1967), PP. 527-539.                 67
                 COMEL, ELEL
WYCKT -60-RML    WYCKOFF, T
                 THE ROLE OF THE MILITARY IN LATIN AMERICAN POLITICS.=
                 THE WESTERN POLITICAL QUARTERLY, 13, (SEPTEMBER 1960),       60
                    PP. 745-763.
                 DEFEL, COMEL, ELEL, ELNOEL, ELPRNOR
WZL    -57-SMA   WZL
                 SYRIA ON THE MOVE -- ASCENDANCY OF THE LEFT WING.=
                 THE WORLD TODAY, 13, (JANUARY 1957), PP. 17-26.              57
                 ELEL, ELNOEL, ELPRNOR
YABELY-63-TIT    YABES, LY
                 TWO INTELLECTUAL TRADITIONS.=
                 ASIAN STUDIES, 1, (1963), PP. 34-104.                        63
                 COMEL, ELEL, ELNOEL
YAGEJW-63-WRO    YAGER, JW
                 WHO RUNS OUR TOWN (UNITED STATES).=
                 NATIONAL CIVIC REVIEW, 50, (MAY 1963), PP. 255-259.          63
                 COMEL
YALLI -67-RED    YALLIER, I
                 RELIGIOUS ELITES -- DIFFERENTIATIONS AND DEVELOPMENTS IN
                    ROMAN CATHOLICISM (LATIN AMERICA).=
                 SM LIPSET AND A SOLARI (EDS), ELITES IN LATIN AMERICA,       67
                    NEW YORK, OXFORD UNIVERSITY PRESS, 1967, PP. 190-232.
                 ELEL, ELNOEL, ELPRNOR
YALMA -47-SMP    YALMAN, A
                 THE STRUGGLE FOR A MULTI - PARTY GOVERNMENT IN TURKEY.=
                 THE MIDDLE EAST JOURNAL, 1, (JANUARY 1947), PP. 46-58.       47
                 ELEL, ELNOEL, ELPRNOR
YANAC -56-JPP    YANAGA, C
                 JAPANESE PEOPLE AND POLITICS.=
                 NEW YORK, JOHN WILEY AND SONS, 1956.                         56
                 ELEL, ELNOEL, ELPRNOR
YANAC -57-JPP    YANAGA, C
                 JAPANESE POLITICAL PARTIES.=
                 PARLIAMENTARY AFFAIRS, 10, (SUMMER 1957), PP. 265-276.       57
                 ELEL
YARRLJ-58-LIC    YARROW, LJ           YARROW, MR
                 LEADERSHIP AND INTERPERSONAL CHANGE (UNITED STATES).=
                 JOURNAL OF SOCIAL ISSUES, 14, (1958), PP. 47-59.             58
                 METEL
YATEWR-58-PPD    YATES, WR
                 POWER, PRINCIPLE, AND THE DOCTRINE OF THE MOUVEMENT
                    REPUBLICAIN POPULAIRE (FRANCE).=
                 THE AMERICAN POLITICAL SCIENCE REVIEW, 52, (JUNE 1958),      58
                    PP. 419-436.
                 ELEL, ELNOEL, ELPRNOR
YEE,R -63-FPP    YEE, R
                 FACULTY PARTICIPATION IN THE 1960 PRESIDENTIAL
                    ELECTION (UNITED STATES).=
                 THE WESTERN POLITICAL QUARTERLY, 16, (MARCH 1963),           63
                    PP. 213-220.

```
                    ELEL
YOUNEP-63-SGP       YOUNG, EP
                    A STUDY OF GROUPS AND PERSONALITIES IN JAPAN INFLUENCING
                        THE EVENTS LEADING TO THE SINO-JAPANESE WAR.=
                    HARVARD UNIVERSITY, EAST ASIAN RESEARCH CENTER, PAPERS       63
                        ON JAPAN 2, 1963, PP. 229-275.
                    COMEL, ELEL, ELPRNOR
YOUNK -55-POF       YOUNGER, K
                    PUBLIC OPINION AND FOREIGN POLICY (GREAT BRITAIN).=
                    THE BRITISH JOURNAL OF SOCIOLOGY, 6, (JUNE 1955),            55
                        PP. 169-175.
                    ELNOEL
YOUNK -60-PSN       YOUNGER, K
                    THE PUBLIC SERVICE IN THE NEW STATES -- AFRICA.=
                    LONDON, OXFORD UNIVERSITY PRESS, 1960.                       60
                    COMEL, ELEL, ELNOEL
YOUNM -53-LRF       YOUNG, M
                    THE LEADERSHIP, THE RANK AND FILE, AND MR. BEVAN
                        (GREAT BRITAIN).=
                    THE POLITICAL QUARTERLY, 24, (JANUARY 1953), PP. 99-107.     53
                    ELEL, ELNOEL, ELPRNOR
YOUNM -58-RMG       YOUNG, M
                    THE RISE OF MERITOCRACY, 1870-2033 (GREAT BRITAIN).=
                    HARMONDSWORTH, MIDDLESEX, PENGUIN BOOK LTD, 1958.            58
                    COMEL, ELEL, ELNOEL, ELPRNOR
YOUNMW-66-DKJ       YOUNG, MW
                    THE DIVINE KINGDOM OF THE JUKUN -- A RE-EVALUATION
                        OF SOME THEORIES (EAST AFRICAN).=
                    AFRICA, 36, (APRIL 1966), PP. 135-151.                       66
                    COMEL
YOUNTC-53-SSC       YOUNG, TC
                    THE SOCIAL SUPPORT OF CURRENT IRANIAN POLICY.=
                    THE MIDDLE EAST JOURNAL, 6, (JANUARY 1953), PP. 125-143.     53
                    ELNOEL
YOUNTC-62-ICC       YOUNG, TC
                    IRAN IN CONTINUING CRISIS.=
                    FOREIGN AFFAIRS, 40, (JANUARY 1962), PP. 275-292.            62
                    ELEL, ELNOEL
YOUNWH-52-GMC       YOUNG, WH
                    GOVERNORS, MAYORS, AND COMMUNITY ETHICS (UNITED STATES).=
                    THE ANNALS OF THE AMERICAN ACADEMY OF POLITICAL AND          52
                        SOCIAL SCIENCE, 280, (MARCH 1952), PP. 46-50.
                    ELPRNOR
ZABIS -65-CI        ZABIH, S
                    COMMUNISM IN IRAN.=
                    PROBLEMS OF COMMUNISM, 14, (SEPTEMBER-OCTOBER 1965),         65
                        PP. 46-55.
                    COMEL, ELEL, ELPRNOR
ZAGODS-58-SRS       ZAGORIA, DS
                    THE SPECTRE OF REVISIONISM (SOVIET UNION, EAST EUROPE).=
                    PROBLEMS OF COMMUNISM, 7, (JULY-AUGUST 1958), PP. 15-21.     58
                    ELEL, ELPRNOR
ZALDMN-65-WSR       ZALD, MN
                    WHO SHALL RULE -- A POLITICAL ANALYSIS OF SUCCESSION
                        IN A LARGE WELFARE ORGANIZATION (UNITED STATES).=
                    PACIFIC SOCIOLOGICAL REVIEW, 8, (SPRING 1965), PP. 52-60. 65
                    COMEL, ELEL
ZAREZ -52-STP       ZAREMBA, Z
                    SOCIAL TRANSFORMATIONS IN POLAND -- THE NEW RULING CLASS.=
                    JOURNAL OF CENTRAL EUROPEAN AFFAIRS, 12, (OCTOBER 1952),     52
                        PP. 226-289.
                    COMEL, ELEL, ELNOEL
ZARIR -60-PFC       ZARISKI, R
                    PARTY FACTIONS AND COMPARATIVE POLITICS -- SOME
                        PRELIMINARY OBSERVATIONS.=
                    MIDWEST JOURNAL OF POLITICAL SCIENCE, 4,                     60
                        (FEBRUARY 1960), PP. 27-51.
                    ELEL, ELNOEL, ELPRNOR, METEL
ZARIR -62-ISP       ZARISKI, R
                    THE ITALIAN SOCIALIST PARTY.=
                    AMERICAN POLITICAL SCIENCE REVIEW, 56, (JUNE 1962),          62
                        PP. 372-390.
                    ELEL, ELNOEL
ZARIR -65-IPC       ZARISKI, R
                    INTRA - PARTY CONFLICT IN A DOMINANT PARTY --
                        THE EXPERIENCE OF ITALIAN CHRISTIAN DEMOCRACY.=
                    THE JOURNAL OF POLITICS, 27, (FEBRUARY 1965), PP. 3-34.      65
                    COMEL, ELEL, ELPRNOR
ZARTIW-64-MPN       ZARTMAN, IW
                    MOROCCO -- PROBLEMS OF NEW POWER.=
                    NEW YORK, ATHERTON PRESS, 1964.                              64
                    ELEL, ELNOEL
ZASLJJ-62-RRS       ZASLOFF, JJ
                    RURAL RESETTLEMENT IN SOUTH VIET NAM -- THE AGROVILLE
```

```
                    PROGRAM.=
                    PACIFIC AFFAIRS, 35, (WINTER 1962), PP. 327-340.                    62
                    ELEL, ELNOEL
ZAWOJK-57-NTW    ZAWODNY, JK
                    A NEW TYPE OF WHO'S WHO FOR A NEW ELITE.=
                    PROD (AMERICAN BEHAVIORAL SCIENTIST), 1,                           57
                       (NOVEMBER 1957), PP. 21-22.
                    METEL
ZEITM -60-MWS    ZEITLIN, M
                    MAX WEBER ON THE SOCIOLOGY OF THE FEUDAL ORDER.=
                    SOCIOLOGICAL REVIEW (NEW SERIES), 8, (DECEMBER 1960),             60
                       PP. 203-208.
                    DEFEL, ELPRNOR
ZEITM -66-ARC    ZEITLIN, M
                    ALIENATION AND REVOLUTION (CUBA).=
                    SOCIAL FORCES, 45, (DECEMBER 1966), PP. 224-236.                  66
                    DEFEL, ELNOEL
ZEITM -66-PGC    ZEITLIN, M
                    POLITICAL GENERATIONS IN THE CUBAN WORKING CLASS.=
                    THE AMERICAN JOURNAL OF SOCIOLOGY, 71, (MARCH 1966),              66
                       PP. 493-508.
                    ELPRNOR
ZELELD-49-SL     ZELENY, LD
                    SOCIAL LEADERSHIP.=
                    SOCIOLOGY AND SOCIAL RESEARCH, 33, (JULY-AUGUST 1949),            49
                       PP. 431-436.
                    DEFEL
ZIEGH -64-IGA    ZIEGLER, H
                    INTEREST GROUPS IN AMERICAN SOCIETY.=
                    ENGLEWOOD CLIFFS, NEW JERSEY, PRENTICE-HALL, 1964.                64
                    ELEL, ELNOEL
ZIEGH -65-IGS    ZIEGLER, H
                    INTEREST GROUPS IN THE STATES (UNITED STATES).=
                    H JACOB AND KN VINES (EDS), POLITICS IN THE AMERICAN              65
                       STATES--A COMPARATIVE ANALYSIS, BOSTON, LITTLE, BROWN
                       AND COMPANY, 1965, PP. 101-147.
                    ELEL, ELNOEL
ZIMMCC-62-RIS    ZIMMERMAN, CC
                    THE RISE OF THE INTELLIGENTSIA -- A STUDY OF THE NEW
                       SOCIAL LEADERSHIP.=
                    POLITICO, 27, (MARCH 1962), PP. 35-49.                            62
                    DEFEL, ELEL, ELNOEL
ZINKH -30-CBU    ZINK, H
                    CITY BOSSES IN THE UNITED STATES.=
                    DURHAM, DUKE UNIVERSITY PRESS, 1930.                              30
                    COMEL, ELEL, ELNOEL, ELPRNOR
ZINKT -55-NIS    ZINKIN, T
                    NEHRUISM -- INDIA-S REVOLUTION WITHOUT FEAR.=
                    PACIFIC AFFAIRS, 28, (SEPTEMBER 1955), PP. 221-234.               55
                    ELEL, ELNOEL, ELPRNOR
ZINKT -59-IMD    ZINKIN, T
                    INDIA AND MILITARY DICTATORSHIP.=
                    PACIFIC AFFAIRS, 32, (MARCH 1959), PP. 89-91.                     59
                    ELNOEL, ELPRNOR
ZINKT -62-CTI    ZINKIN, T
                    CASTE TODAY (INDIA).=
                    NEW YORK, OXFORD UNIVERSITY PRESS, 1962.                          62
                    COMEL, ELNOEL, ELPRNOR
ZINNPE-52-IBS    ZINNER, PE
                    THE IDEOLOGICAL BASES OF SOVIET FOREIGN POLICY.=
                    WORLD POLITICS, 4, (APRIL 1952), PP. 488-511.                     52
                    ELPRNOR
ZISKBH-65-CCG    ZISK, BH           EULAU, H              PREWITT, K
                    CITY COUNCILMEN AND THE GROUP STRUGGLE -- A TYPOLOGY
                       OF ROLE ORIENTATIONS (UNITED STATES).=
                    THE JOURNAL OF POLITICS, 27, (AUGUST 1965), PP. 618-646.   65
                    DEFEL, ELEL, ELNOEL, ELPRNOR
ZNANF -48-WIT    ZNANIECKI, F
                    WILLIAM I THOMAS AS A COLLABORATOR.=
                    SOCIOLOGY AND SOCIAL RESEARCH, 32, (MARCH-APRIL 1948),            48
                       PP. 765-767.
                    COMEL
ZNZ   -51-YPN    ZNZ
                    YOUTH AND POLITICS IN THE NEAR EAST.=
                    THE WORLD TODAY, 7, (MARCH 1951), PP. 102-109.                    51
                    ELEL
ZOLBAR-63-MPN    ZOLBERG, AR
                    MASS PARTIES AND NATIONAL INTEGRATION -- THE CASE
                       OF THE IVORY COAST.=
                    THE JOURNAL OF POLITICS, 25, (FEBRUARY 1963), PP. 36-48.   63
                    COMEL, ELEL, ELNOEL
ZOLBAR-64-OPG    ZOLBERG, AR
                    ONE - PARTY GOVERNMENT IN THE IVORY COAST.=
                    PRINCETON, PRINCETON UNIVERSITY PRESS, 1964.                      64
```

```
                        COMEL, ELEL, ELNOEL
ZOLBAR-66-CPO  ZOLBERG, AR
               CREATING POLITICAL ORDER -- THE PARTY - STATES OF
                  WEST AFRICA (MALI, GHANA, SENEGAL, GUINEA,
                  IVORY COAST).=
               CHICAGO, RAND MCNALLY AND CO., 1966.                    66
               DEFEL, COMEL, ELEL, ELNOEL, ELPRNOR
ZUCKEM-66-SSH  ZUCKERT, EM
               THE SERVICE SECRETARY -- HAS HE A USEFUL ROLE.=
               FOREIGN AFFAIRS, 44, (APRIL 1966), PP. 458-479.          66
               ELEL
ZWEIF -58-TSC  ZWEIG, F
               THE THEORY OF SOCIAL CLASSES.=
               KYKLOS, 11, (1958), PP. 390-404.                        58
               GNELTH, ELNOEL
```

# LIST OF AUTHORS

A HONG KONG CORRES
    A HOHO-52-COC
AARONOVITCH, S AAROS -61-RCS
ABBOTT, RS ABBORS-51-RCP
ABEGGLEN, J ABEGJ -60-LMJ
ABEGGLEN, JC WARNWL-55-BBL
ABELSON, HI ABELHI-58-SDI
ABRAHAM, HJ ABRAHJ-62-JPI
ABRAHAM, PLR ABRAPL-49-GGS
ABRAMS, M ABRAM -61-CPG
    ABRAM -61-SCB
ABRAMS, P ABRAP -65-YAB
ABRAMSON, E ABRAE -58-SPC
ABU-LABAN, B ABU-B -65-RAS
    BARTEA-59-PSN
ABU-LUGHOD, I ABU-I -64-IFA
ABUEVA, JV ABUEJV-59-FPB
    ABUEJV-61-IBL
ACHMINOV, H ACHMH -56-SCT
    ACHMH -58-PPA
    ACHMH -58-SIP
    ACHMH -59-PPR
    ACHMH -59-PPS
    ACHMH -65-ROM
    ACHMH -65-OYW
ACHMINOW, H ACHMH -54-PLC
    ACHMH -63-SCP
    ACHMH -65-CPS
ACZEL, T ACZET -60-RMC
ADAMS, AE ADAMAE-58-BAU
ADAMS, R CLEGHA-61-TUO
ADAMS, RN ADAMRN-  -SCL
ADAMS, S ADAMS -57-OAO
ADAMS, W ADAMW -58-CIF
ADIE, WAC ADIEWA-62-PAN
ADLER, KP ADLEKP-56-IIF
ADLER, MK ADLEMK-53-ICA

ADLOFF, R THOMV -49-SAF
    THOMV -50-LWS
ADORNO, TW ADORTW-65-DLM
ADRIAN, CR ADRICR-59-ILP
    BOOTDA-61-SDE
    BOOTDA-62-PSC
    WILLOP-63-FCS
ADU, A ADU,A -65-CSN
AGGER, R AGGER -64-RRU
AGGER, RE AGGERE-56-LPU
    AGGERE-56-PAL
    AGGERE-58-CPS
    AGGERE-56-PSS
    AGGERE-62-PAL
AGPALO, RE AGPARE-62-PPP
AGULLA, JC CHAME -66-CPP
AHH AHH   -51-PIS
AHMAD, M AHMAM -59-GPP
    AHMAM -60-CPI
AHMED, JM AHMEJM-60-IOE
AITON, EW KREIBW-60-LAR
AKE, C AKE,C -66-CLP
    AKE,C -67-PIP
AKHMINOV, H AKHMH -61-PPN
    AKHMH -63-CSS
    AKHMH -64-RIS
    AKHMH -67-EPD
    AKHMH -61-OKS
    AKHMH -66-ASL
AKISADA, T AKIST -59-WSD
AKZIN, B AKZIB -60-EAU
    AKZIB -61-KI
AL-HABIB, MM AL-HMM-56-LMI
ALAN, R ALANR -58-IAC
    ALANR -59-CDC
    ALANR -62-FSS
    ALANR -60-UBD

BAILER, S          BAILS -65-ULS
BAILEY, FG         BAILFG-60-TCN
                   BAILFG-60-TSR
                   BAILFG-63-PSC
BAILEY, NA         BAILNA-65-CBH
BAILEY, SD         BAILSD-62-SUN
BAILEY, SD (ED)
                   BAILSD-52-PPP
BAILEY, SK         BAILSK-52-CWU
                   BAILSK-66-NCU
BAKER, F           GOLDLC-65-LCU
BAKER, JC          BAKEJC-45-DTF
BALARAMAN, K       BALAK -56-IPF
BALDWIN, DA        BALDDA-66-CIF
BALDWIN, G         BALDG -63-FEI
BALDWIN, HW        BALDHW-55-SN
BALES, RF          BORGEF-54-FRG
BALL, WM           BALLWM-56-DMP
BALLIS, WB         BALLWB-61-PIR
BALMER, DG         BALMDG-62-RPL
BALTZELL, ED       BALTED-65-PEA
                   BALTED-58-PGM
BANFIELD, EC       BANFEC-58-MBB
                   BANFEC-61-PIU
                   BANFEC-63-CPU
                   MEYEM -55-PPP
BANKS, MA          BANKMA-  -PCC
BANTON, M (ED)     BANTM -65-PSD
BARATZ, MS         BACHP -62-TFP
                   BARAMS-56-CGP
BARBER, B          BARBB -61-FSL
                   BARBB -55-SAA
BARBER, JD         BARBJD-65-LRA
                   BARBJD-66-LSL
                   BARBJD-66-PCE
BARBER, JD (ED)
                   BARBJD-64-PLA
BARBU, Z           BARBZ -56-DDT
BARGHOORN, FC      BARGFC-66-CRN
                   BARGFC-66-SRO
BARITZ, JJ         BARIJJ-57-OAS
                   BARIJJ-63-SAF
BARKLEY, R         BARKR -55-TEM
BARNARD, CI        BARNCI-48-OM
                   BARNCI-46-FPS
                   BARNCI-38-FE
BARNES, JA         BARNJA-60-IPC
                   GLUCM -49-VHB
BARNES, SH         BARNSH-59-PFC
                   BARNSH-67-LSP
BARNETT, AD        BARNAD-57-PPC
                   BARNAD-51-MPO
                   BARNAD-62-CCP
                   BARNAD-66-SCC
                   BARNAD-66-MPC
                   BARNAD-67-CBP
                   BARNAD-66-SSA
BARRON, R          BARRR -59-PPM
BARTH, EAT         BARTEA-59-CPT
                   BARTEA-59-PSN
                   BARTEA-61-CIS
BARTH, F           BARTF -59-PLA
BARTHOLOMEW, DJ
                   FINESE-61-BOH
BARZINI, L         BARZL -56-IIA
BASHEER, TM        BASHTM-58-UAF
BASS, BM           BASSBM-60-LPO
BASS, BM (EDS)     PETRL -61-LIB
BASS, R            BASSR -66-EEC
BATES, FL          BATEFL-56-PRS
BATTISTINI, LH     BATTLH-56-PSS
BAUER, ML          EHRLHJ-65-NCR
BAUER, PT          BAUEPT-47-NPM
BAUER, R           BAUER -55-TSA
                   BAUER -63-ABP
                   BAUER -56-HSS
BAUER, RA          BAUERA-53-PCL
                   BAUERA-56-PSM
                   BAUERA-53-ISC
                   BAUERA-58-IES
                   INKEA -59-SCD
                   MARCAS-64-YTA
BAUM, RD           BAUMRD-67-AOC
BAUMAN, Z          BAUMZ -64-EGS

BAUMGARTEL, H      BAUMH -56-LMA
                   BAUMH -57-LSV
BAYHS, TA          BAYHTA-66-NES
BAZELON, DT        BAZEDT-63-NRA
BEAGLEHOLE, E      BEAGE -48-SPC
                   BEAGE -57-SCS
BEALES, HL         BEALHL-53-LPI
BEALL, CP          BEALCP-58-SCC
BEALS, RL          BEALRL-53-SSL
                   BEALRL-54-MSV
BEATTIE, JHM       BEATJH-64-BAF
BEATTY, DW         BEATDW-62-ICG
BECK, C            BECKC -63-BPD
                   BECKC -67-MRB
                   BECKC -61-PCB
                   BECKC -66-PEM
BECKER, H          BECKH -50-CSS
BECKER, RW         BECKRW-62-CLV
BECKER, TL         BECKTL-64-PBM
                   BECKTL-66-SJO
BECKETT, P         BECKP -57-WSS
BEER, SH           BEERSH-52-CPG
                   BEERSH-56-PGP
                   BEERSH-57-RIB
                   BEERSH-57-TCG
                   BEERSH-58-GRB
                   BEERSH-65-BPC
BEHR, E            BEHRE -59-FAP
BELING, WA         BELIWA-64-INC
BELKNAP, GM        BELKGM-58-MAL
                   BELKGM-56-PPR
                   BELKGM-58-SLB
                   SMUCRH-56-LPU
BELL, D            BELLD -58-PER
                   BELLD -48-SLD
                   BELLD -62-EIE
                   BELLD -55-BMH
                   BELLD -56-TMS
                   BELLD -65-NAD
BELL, D (ED)       BELLD -55-NAR
BELL, W            BELLW -60-IUS
                   BELLW -60-AJE
                   BELLW -61-PLU
                   BELLW -62-EAE
                   BELLW -64-JLP
                   BELLW -65-SCE
BELOFF, M          BELOM -53-PPU
                   BELOM -54-ICR
BEN-DAVID, J       EISESN-56-IGT
BENDA, HJ          BENDHJ-49-LCN
                   BENDHJ-58-CRS
                   BENDHJ-60-NWI
                   BENDHJ-65-PMC
                   BENDHJ-64-PEC
                   BENDHJ-61-IPW
BENDIX, R          BENDR -45-BPP
                   BENDR -53-CSP
                   BENDR -47-BPI
                   BENDR -49-HCS
                   BENDR -57-PS
                   BENDR -52-SSP
                   BENDR -57-SMA
                   BENDR -65-WAG
                   BENDR -60-SSP
                   BENDR -67-RCL
                   LIPSSM-51-SSS
BENEDICT, B        BENEB -2 -SPS
BENEDICT, R        BENER -46-CSP
BENNETT, G         BENNG -57-DPO
BENNIGSEN, A       BENNA -59-MIU
BENNIS, WG         BENNWG-60-LTA
                   BENNWG-58-APA
                   BENNWG-61-RTL
                   COHEAM-61-CLC
BENNO, P           BENNP -61-PCL
BENNY, M           BENNM -50-SCP
BENSMAN, G         BENSG -63-MCB
BENSMAN, J         BENSJ -62-PCB
                   VIDIAJ-58-STM
BENSON, M          BENSM -64-APL
BENSON, O          BENSO -59-CPP
BERDAHL, RO        BERDRO-59-BUS
BEREDAY, GZF       BEREGZ-60-PSE
BERELSON, BR       BEREBR-54-VSO

```
CHOUDHURY, GW   CHOUGW-59-FPD                        COLEJS-65-UEC
                CHOUGW-60-RDP                        COLEJS-60-PSS
CHRISTIANSEN, B                    COLEMAN, JS (ED)
                CHRIB  -59-ATF                       COLEJS-65-EPD
CHRISTIE, J     CHRIR  -54-SSM     COLLINET, M      COLLM  -59-FCC
CHRISTIE, M (EDS)                  COLOMBE, M       COLOM  -54-EFK
                CHRIR  -54-SSM     COLSON, E        COLSE  -58-RBN
CHRISTIE, R     CHRIR  -54-SSM     COLTART, J       COLTJ  -63-INT
CHRISTOFF, B    CHRIB  -62-BVS     COLTON, HK       COLTHK-55-WJD
CHRISTOPH, JB   CHRIJB-65-CCB      COLTON, KE       COLTKE-55-CLJ
                CHRIJB-62-CPB      COMFORT, GO      COMFGO-58-PPS
CHRYPINSKI, VC  CHRYVC-66-LCP      COMHAIRE-SYLVAIN,
CHU-WANG, Y     CHU-Y -58-ICC                        COMHJL-55-HCD
CHU, D          CHU,D -57-LCC                        COMHS -59-USH
CHUAN, TSENG-YU                    CONQUEST, R      CONQR -60-SGS
                CHUATS-63-MLS                        CONQR -63-AKC
CHUBB, B        CHUBB -57-IMI                        CONQR -66-IDS
                CHUBB -54-VRI                        CONQR -65-AFL
                CHUBB -63-GAP                        CONQR -61-PPU
CHUNG-LI, C     CHUNC -55-CGS      CONTAS, H        CONTH -62-USS
CHUNG, K        CHUNK -63-NKP      CONVERSE, PE     CONVPE-64-NBS
CHURCHWARD, LG  RIGBTH-62-PMU                        CONVPE-65-EMR
CICOUREL, AV    CICOAV-58-FBO      COOK, SD         COOKSD-57-HSL
CLAGUE, C       GILBCE-62-ECE      COOKE, EF        COOKEF-61-RIP
CLAPP, CL       CLAPCL-63-CHW      COONS, AE        STOGRM-57-LBI
CLAPP, GR       CLAPGR-55-AIG      COPPER, BK       CAMEID-54-WAC
CLARK, KB       CLARKB-65-DGD      COQUIA, JR       COQUJR-55-PPE
CLARK, SD       CLARSD-63-GIC      CORLEY, FJ       CORLFJ-61-PCR
CLARKE, EL      CLAREL-36-RNS      CORMACK, ML      CORMML-61-SWR
CLARKE, P       CARTRE-62-PAO      CORNELL, R       CORNR -65-YCH
CLARKE, RA      CLARRA-67-CUS      CORNWELL-JR, EE
CLAUSEN, AR     CONVPE-65-EMR                        CORNEE-65-PLP
CLEARY, JW      CLEAJW-64-PPS                        CORNEE-57-CPL
CLEGG, E        CLEGE -60-RPP                        CORNEE-64-BME
CLEGG, HA       CLEGHA-61-TUO      CORPUZ, OD       CORPOD-57-BP
CLELLAND, DA    CLELDA-64-EDC      CORRADINI, A     MCCAJL-54-PSD
CLEMENTIN, JR   CLEMJR-50-NDV      CORSON, JJ       CORSJJ-66-MNT
CLEMENTS, RV    CLEMRV-65-CGB      CORWIN, ES       CORWES-56-PTU
CLIFFORD-VAUGHAN,                  COSER, LA        COSELA-65-MIS
                CLIFM -60-FCE      COSIO-VILLEGAS, D
CLIGNET, RP     CLIGRP-64-PEG                        COSID -61-CLA
CLINE, CA       CLINCA-63-RLB      COSMAN, B        COSMB -62-PRS
CLINE, H        CLINH -52-MCS      COSTANTINI, E    COSTE -63-IAC
CLINE, WB       CLINWB-47-NM       COSWELL, R       COSWR -65-RYF
CNUDDE, CF      CNUDCF-66-LBC      COTTAM, R        COTTR -64-NI
COATES, CH      PELLRJ-56-AOC      COTTER, CP       COTTCP-64-PWP
COBBAN, A       COBBA -48-SCF                        SMITJM-57-ARC
COCHRAN, TC     COCHTC-59-PRB      COTTER, CP (EDS)
                COCHTC-62-EAC                        SMITJM-60-PPD
                COCHTC-64-EEC      COUON, AS        BORGEF-54-FRG
COCHRANE, JD    COCHJD-67-MSN      COVERLEY, HM     COVEHM-50-DRG
COCKROFT, JD    ANDEB -66-CCM      COWAN, LG        COWALG-65-ENB
COCKS, PM       COCKPM-63-PMZ                        COWALG-49-TCP
CODDING, GA     CODDGA-60-FSP      COWAN, M         COWAM -62-EGR
COFFIN, TE      COFFTE-44-TCT      COX, EF          COX,EF-62-CDP
COHEN, A        COHEA -66-TEA      COX, OC          COX,OC-50-MWS
COHEN, AA       COHEAA-63-DWR                        COX,OC-62-CAL
COHEN, AM       COHEAM-61-CLC                        COX,OC-65-LAN
COHEN, BC       COHEBC-56-PCJ      CRAIG, GA        CRAIGA-53-D
                COHEBC-57-PPF                        CRAIGA-55-PPA
                COHEBC-63-PFP      CRAIG, JM        CRAIJM-53-ES
                COHEBC-66-MPP      CRAMER, FH       CRAMFH-51-DPM
                COHEBC-55-PFP      CRAMER, MR       CRAMMR-63-SDN
                COHEBC-59-ING      CRANE W          RUECGL-62-CDG
COHEN, EE       COHEEE-49-IJC      CRANE-JR, W      CRANW -60-CRC
COHEN, SP       COHESP-63-SCB                        CRANW -62-ERF
                COHESP-64-RPS      CRANE-JR, WW     CRANWW-60-DRR
                COHESP-64-APP      CRANE, RI        CRANRI-59-LCP
COHN, TS (EDS)  BROWCG-8 -SL       CRANE, WW        CRANWW-64-IPE
COLBERT, ES     COLBES-52-LWJ      CRECELIUS, D     CRECD -66-AAR
COLE, AB        COLEAB-56-JSP      CREEL, HG        CREEHG-64-BBC
                COLEAB-56-SSM      CRICK, B         CRICB -65-RPG
COLE, GDH       COLEGD-50-CMC      CRIDER, JH       CRIDJH-44-BUS
                COLEGD-55-SCS      CROAN, M         CROAM -60-IUU
                COLEGD-50-LSP      CROSLAND, CAR    CROSCA-62-ICC
COLE, T         COLET -49-CBS                        CROSCA-64-FLG
                COLET -55-NWG                        CROSCA-60-LAG
COLEMAN, CP     COLECP-55-CSL      CROSSMAN, R      CROSR -64-SWG
COLEMAN, J      LIPSSM-56-UDI      CROUCH, WW       CROUWW-56-CSI
COLEMAN, JS     ALMOGA-60-PDA      CROW, RE         CROWRE-62-RSL
                COLEJS-57-CCU      CROWLEY, JB      CROWJB-62-JAF
                COLEJS-58-NBN      CROZIER, B       CROZB -60-RSP
                COLEJS-64-PPN                        CROZB -62-DAR
                COLEJS-60-PSD      CROZIER, M       CROZM -64-BPE
```

DOIG, JW            STAN  -67-MWG
DOMENACH, JM        DOMEJM-61-FAP
DONNELLY, TC        DONNTC-50-NEP
DONNISON, DV        DONNDV-54-FLL
DONOVAN, JC         DONOJC-51-CIR
DOOB, LW            DOOBLW-65-PVP
DOOLIN, D           DOOLD - -RFC
DOOLIN, DJ          DOOLDJ-64-CCP
DORE, RP            DORERP-52-ENJ
                    DORERP-64-SMA
DORRILL, WF         DORRWF-65-LSC
DORSEY, JT          DORSJT-63-BPD
                    LAPAJ -57-IFB
DOUGHTY, PL         DOUGPL-65-IPR
DOUGLAS, WA         DOUGWA-64-SKS
DOWNING, RG         WATSRA-67-BPJ
DOWNS, A            DOWNA -62-PII
                    DOWNA -57-ETD
DOWSE, R            DOWSR -63-PDH
DOWSE, RE           DOWSRE-61-LWO
                    DOWSRE-63-MPH
                    DOWSRE-60-PLP
DOWVONA, M          DOWVM -62-WAI
DRAPER, T           DRAPT -65-CTP
                    DRAPT -62-CSR
DRESSLER, A         DRESA -59-PWS
DUBE, SC            DUBESC-58-ISC
                    DUBESC-64-BNB
DUBIN, R            DUBIR -63-PFO
                    TAUSC -65-CAM
DUBIN, WB           DUBIWB-50-PEP
DUBOIS, CA          DUBOCA-59-SFS
DUCHACEK, I         DUCHI -62-CPR
DUEVEL, C           DUEVC -66-DPS
DUNCAN, G           DUNCG -63-ND
DUNHAM, VS          DUNHVS-64-SVS
DUNN, E             DUNNSP-64-RIC
DUNN, SP            DUNNSP-64-RIC
DUPRE, JS           DUPRJS-62-SNP
DURANT, H           DURAH -55-POF
DURHAM, GH          DURHGH-48-VPU
DWH                 DWH   -50-SPE
DYACHKOV, Y         DYACY -61-CCP
DYE, TR             DYE,TR-62-PID
                    DYE,TR-65-SLP
DZIEWANOWSKI, MK
                    DZIEMK-59-CPP
                    DZIEMK-52-FCP
EAGLETON-JR, W      EAGLW -65-IRM
EARLE, EM (ED)      EARLEM-51-MF
EASTON, D           EASTD -59-PA
                    EASTD -65-SAP
                    HESSRD-60-CSC
EATON, JW           EATOJW-47-ETL
EBERHARD, W         EBERW -52-CRS
EBW                 EBW   -54-CYG
ECKHARDT, W         ECKHW -65-WPW
ECKSTEIN, HH        ECKSHH-55-PBM
                    ECKSHH-62-BPS
                    ECKSHH-60-PGP
EDELMAN, M          EDELM -64-SUP
EDELMANN, AT        EDELAT-65-LAG
EDELSTEIN, AS       EDELAS-63-WNS
EDELSTEIN, JD       EDELJD-67-OTU
EDEN, G             EDENG -48-LCG
EDINGER, LJ         DEUTKW-59-GRP
                    DEUTKW-67-FGW
                    EDINLJ-56-GEP
                    EDINLJ-60-PTL
                    EDINLJ-61-CCB
                    EDINLJ-63-MLF
                    EDINLJ-64-PSP
                    EDINLJ-67-ESI
                    EDINLJ-65-KSS
                    EDINLJ-67-PLI
EDINGER, LU         EDINLU-67-SBE
EDWARDS, FG         EDWAFG-59-NPC
EDWARDS, HT         EDWAHT-67-PSI
EFIMENCO, NM        EFIMNM-55-ECD
                    EFIMNM-54-AIU
EGGAN, F (EDS)      GLUCM -65-PSD
EGGER, R            EGGER -49-USB
EH                  EH    -55-TSB
EHLE, EL            EHLEEL-49-TSL

EHRLICH, HJ         EHRLHJ-65-NCR
                    EHRLHJ-61-RAS
EHRLICH, HJ (EDS)
                    D'ANWV-61-PDA
EHRMANN, HW         EHRMHW-54-FTA
                    EHRMHW-48-PFP
                    EHRMHW-61-FBO
                    EHRMHW-63-DDF
                    EHRMHW-57-OBF
EHRMANN, HW (ED)
                    EHRMHW-58-IGF
EISENSTADT, EN      EISEEN-51-YCS
EISENSTADT, SN      EISESN-56-GGA
                    EISESN-56-IGT
                    EISESN-51-PEP
                    EISESN-56-PLS
                    EISESN-58-BB
                    EISESN-56-PSA
                    EISESN-63-PSE
                    EISESN-58-I
                    EISESN-58-ICB
                    EISESN-59-PPS
                    EISESN-58-SOD
                    EISESN-60-BBD
                    EISESN-62-IIP
                    EISESN-62-ROP
                    EISESN-66-DSP
                    EISESN-63-BPD
EKMAN, P            EKMAP -66-CCD
ELDEN, RE           ELDERE-57-PSD
ELDER, N            ELDEN -53-PFP
                    ELDEN -57-SR
                    ELDEN -60-PGS
ELDER, NCM          ELDENC-57-SEO
ELDER, RE           ELDERE-60-PMD
ELDERSVELD, SJ      ELDESJ-58-AIG
                    ELDESJ-64-PPB
                    KATZD -61-ILP
                    MARVD -61-NCL
ELIAS, N            ELIAN -65-EOG
ELKIN, B            ELKIB -60-RIE
ELLING, RH          BLANLV-62-OSC
ELLINGSWORTH, H
                    DEUTPJ-61-MMU
ELLIOTT, O          ELLIO -59-MTU
ELLISON, FP         ELLIFP- -WLA
ELSBREE, WH         ELSBWH-53-JSR
                    ELSBWH-65-PPE
ELWELL-SUTTON, LP
                    ELWELP-49-PPI
EMBER, M            EMBEM -62-PAS
EMERSON, R          EMERR -53-PRG
                    EMERR -60-ENR
                    EMERR -60-NPD
EMERSON, RM         EMERRM-62-PDR
ENCARNACION-JR, V
                    ENCAV -57-TAB
                    ENCAV -62-DAS
ENCEL, S            ENCES -61-PEA
                    ENCES -62-CGA
ENGELMANN, FC       ENGEFC-56-MPP
ENGHOLM, GF         ENGHGF-57-KSF
ENGLEMANN, FC       ENGLFC-67-PPC
EPSTEIN, AL         EPSTAL-58-PUA
EPSTEIN, L          EPSTL -63-BMP
EPSTEIN, LD         EPSTLD-56-BMP
                    EPSTLD-58-PWU
                    EPSTLD-59-CSB
                    EPSTLD-62-BCC
                    EPSTLD-56-CBP
                    EPSTLD-62-NMP
                    EPSTLD-62-WMP
                    EPSTLD-64-BPS
                    EPSTLD-64-CSC
EPSTEIN, TS         EPSTTS-62-EDS
ERASMUS, CJ         ERASCJ-52-LVT
ERDMAN, HL          ERDMHL-64-ISS
                    ERDMHL-66-FPV
EREM, S             PRESRV-58-SAC
ERICKSON, EC        D'ANWV-62-RTM
ERICKSON, J         ERICJ -62-SHC
ERIKSON, EH         ERIKEH-58-YML
ERLICH, V           ERLIV -64-PST
ESMAN, MJ           ESMAMJ-47-JAC

| | | | | |
|---|---|---|---|---|
| ET AL | ABRAE -58-SPC | | FATHALLA EL KHATIB | |
| | ADAMRN- -SCL | | | HIRAGK-58-CPA |
| | ALMOGA-54-AC | | FAWSI, SED | FAWSSE-57-LMS |
| | BECKRW-62-CLV | | FAYERWEATHER, J | |
| | CAMPA -60-AV | | | FAYEJ -59-EOA |
| | CAMPG -52-PSG | | FEDENKO, P | FEDEP -64-RFK |
| | DALLA -64-SUD | | FEI-HSIAO-TUNG FEI- -53-CSG | |
| | DAVISR-54-APP | | FEITH, H | FEITH -54-TEI |
| | DEUTKW-67-FGW | | | FEITH -58-WCT |
| | EKMAP -66-CCD | | | FEITH -62-DCD |
| | EULAH -61-CPA | | | FEITH -63-EIR |
| | FREELC-60-LCL | | | FEITH -63-ISP |
| | FREELC-63-LLL | | FEJTO, F | FEJTF -60-HI |
| | HAIRM -63-CPR | | FELD, MD | FELDMD-64-MSI |
| | HOFFS -63-SF | | | FELDMD-58-PPP |
| | KATZE -57-LSS | | FELD, W | FELDW -66-NEI |
| | KERRC -64-IIM | | FELDMAN, AS | TUMIM -61-SCS |
| | MARTRC-61-DSU | | FELDMESSER, RA FELDRA-53-PSA | |
| | MICACA-64-TPM | | FELSER, JW | FELSJW-62-FFA |
| | MULDM -66-IPP | | FENNO-JR, RF | FENNRF-58-PCR |
| | POOLID-52-SD | | | FENNRF-59-PSC |
| | WARNWL-63-AFE | | | FENNRF-65-IDI |
| | WAHLJC-62-LSE | | | FENNRF-62-ACP |
| ET AL (EDS) | BERGM -54-FCM | | | FENNRF-66-PPA |
| | MERTVK-52-RB | | FERGUSON, LC | EULAH -59-PSA |
| | VIDIAJ-64-RCS | | FEUER, LS | FEUELS-63-SIU |
| ET. AL. | EULAH -59-OTE | | | FEUELS-64-MPS |
| | SNYDRC-64-FPD | | | FEUELS-65-LDC |
| ETZIONI, A | ETZIA -59-FDE | | FF | FF -55-DSW |
| | ETZIA -65-DLC | | FIEDLER, FE | FIEDFE-57-NLT |
| | ETZIA -65-PUC | | FIELD, GL | FIELGL-51-HTP |
| | ETZIA -57-AIS | | FIELDHOUSE, DK FIELDK-62-AEE | |
| | ETZIA -59-ASO | | FIELLIN, A | FIELA -62-FIG |
| | ETZIA -61-CAC | | FILLEY, WO | FILLWO-56-SSC |
| EULAU, H | EULAH -59-PSA | | FILLOL, TR | FILLTR-61-SFE |
| | EULAH -59-OTE | | FINER, H | FINEH -60-PCR |
| | EULAH -56-ICP | | FINER, SE | BERRHB-61-BHC |
| | EULAH -61-CPA | | | FINESE-61-BOH |
| | EULAH -62-BAL | | | FINESE-58-AEG |
| | EULAH -62-CPE | | | FINESE-65-ATB |
| | EULAH -62-OMP | | | FINESE-62-MHR |
| | EULAH -64-LPS | | | FINESE-65-AEL |
| | EULAH -64-LWP | | FINER, SE (ED) FINESE-66-VPS | |
| | PREWK -67-PSP | | FINKELSTEIN, L BRYSL -47-CPM | |
| | WAHLJC-59-LBR | | FINKELSTEIN, LS | |
| | WAHLJC-60-ASL | | | FINKLS-51-IFP |
| | ZISKBH-65-CCG | | FISCHER, G | FISCG -52-SOS |
| EVAN, WM | EVANWM-61-LEB | | | FISCG -58-RLG |
| EVANS-PRITCHARD, E | | | FISCHER, J | FISCJ -61-SPS |
| | EVANEE-40-APS | | | FISCJ -63-UPP |
| | EVANEE-60-EOZ | | FISHER, FM | FISHFM-58-MAS |
| EWING, CAM | EWINCA-48-SGU | | FISHER, SN | FISHSN-62-CPS |
| EYRE, JD | EYREJD-55-CRF | | FISHER, SN (ED) | |
| EZERA, K | EZERK -64-CDN | | | FISHSN-55-SFM |
| FAINSOD, M | FAINM -54-SUS | | | FISHSN-63-MME |
| | FAINM -58-PPS | | FISHER, SN (EDS) | |
| | FAINM -61-KRS | | | TEPAJJ-64-EFL |
| | FAINM -49-PRC | | FITCH, RE | FITCRE-53-IIU |
| | FAINM -65-HRI | | | FITCRE-54-FIU |
| | FAINM -58-SUS | | FITZGERALD, CP FITZCP-63-FLC | |
| | FAINM -56-CPS | | FITZGIBBON, R | FITZR -54-UPD |
| | FAINM -59-WHC | | | FITZR -57-PPL |
| | FAINM -67-RFS | | FITZGIBBON, RH FITZRH-59-SBC | |
| FAIR, DR | FAIRDR-64-PSP | | | FITZRH-60-DDL |
| FAIRBANK, JK | TENGS -54-CSR | | FLEMING, WG | FLEMWG-66-AER |
| FAIRBANK, JK (ED) | | | FLICK, JJ | JACOPE-62-FVP |
| | FAIRJK-57-CTI | | FLINN, TA | FLINTA-64-PRS |
| FAIRLIE, H | FAIRH -65-JIU | | | FLINTA-65-LPL |
| FALK, SL | FALKSL-64-NSC | | FLORO, GK | FLORGK-55-CCM |
| | FALKSL-61-OMP | | | FLORGK-54-TCM |
| FALL, BB | FALLBB-60-NVN | | FLUHARTY, VL | FLUHVL-57-DMM |
| | FALLBB-62-PPG | | FOOT, M | FOOTM -60-FLG |
| | FALLBB-63-TV | | FORCE, RW | FORCRW-60-LCC |
| | FALLBB-55-PRS | | FORDE, D | FORDD -61-GRA |
| | FALLBB-54-LAU | | FORM, WH | CLELDA-64-EDC |
| FALLERS, L | FALLL -55-PMA | | | D'ANWV-65-ITB |
| FALLERS, LA | FALLLA-55-BBS | | | FORMWH-65-IRS |
| FALLERS, LA (ED) | | | | FORMWH-60-ILC |
| | FALLLA-64-KSM | | | FORMWH-60-OLS |
| FALLUS, LA | FALLLA-59-DSC | | | FORMWH-61-CIM |
| FANELLI, AA | FANEAA-56-TCL | | | FORMWH-63-CLI |
| FARIS, REL | FARIRE-60-MCS | | | FORMWH-59-ICA |
| FARNSWORTH, LW FARNLW-66-CFJ | | | FORRESTER, DB | FORRDB-66-CPP |
| FARRIS, CD | FARRCD-58-SAI | | FORSTER, R | FORSR -65-FNO |

| | | | |
|---|---|---|---|
| FORTHAL, S | FORTS -48-PWU | GANTT-JR, F | GANTF -64-CET |
| FOSTER, P | CLIGRP-64-PEG | GARCEAU, O | GARCO -54-PGP |
| FOX, GH | FOX,GH-64-PVP | GARFINKEL, H | GARFH -59-SSE |
| FOX, PW | FOX,PW-59-PPC | GARIGUE, P | GARIP -54-CPL |
| FOX, WTR | FOX,WT-55-CSA | | GARIP -53-WAS |
| | FOX,WT-61-RED | GARTHOFF, RL | GARTRL-57-RMR |
| FRANCIS, WL | FRANWL-65-RCL | | LEITN -51-PIS |
| | FRANWL-62-IIS | GARVEY, G | GARVG -66-TPE |
| FRANCISCO-JR, GA | | GASS, O | GASSO -63-RKA |
| | FRANGA-60-CDF | GASTIL, RD | GASTRD-58-MCI |
| | FRANGA-57-RSP | GAWTHROP, LC | GAWTLC-66-CMP |
| FRANCK, FM | FRANFM-60-RNS | GEERTZ, C | GEERC -63-PPS |
| FRANCK, PG | FRANPG-55-EPM | | GEERC -60-JKC |
| FRANDA, MF | FRANMF-62-ODI | | GEERC -63-OSN |
| FRANK, E | FRANE -66-RBT | GEHLEN, MP | GEHLMP-66-EBC |
| FRANK, VS | FRANVS-NCS | GEIGER, K | INKEA -53-CLE |
| FRANKEL, C | FRANC -64-BDN | GEIGER, T | GEIGT -50-HSO |
| FRANKEL, J | FRANJ -55-CNQ | GEISS, P | BENNM -50-SCP |
| FRANKENBERG, R | FRANR -66-BCS | GELLERMANN, JE | GELLJE-59-GSF |
| | FRANR -66-BC | GELMAN, H | GELMH -66-MPP |
| FREE, L | FREEL -61-IIP | GERMANI, G | GERMG -62-PSS |
| FREE, LA | FREELA-59-SAN | GERMINO, DL | GERMDL-59-IFP |
| | FREELA-58-OPI | GERSCHENKRON, A | |
| FREEDMAN, M | FREEM -60-GPS | | GERSA -62-CDS |
| FREEMAN, D | FREED -64-OKP | GERTH, H | GERTH -60-NPI |
| FREEMAN, FD | FREEFD-48-ASS | | GERTH -54-SL |
| FREEMAN, JL | FREEJL-58-BPP | GERTZEL, C | GERTC -66-PAK |
| | FREEJL-65-PPE | GHAI, D | GHAID -65-AEA |
| | FREEJL-58-LPS | GHAI, DP (ED) | GHAIDP-65-PMA |
| FREEMAN, LC | FREELC-60-LCL | GHAI, Y | GHAID -65-AEA |
| | FREELC-63-LLL | GIAP, TS | WERTWF-62-SCJ |
| FRENCH, JRP | FRENJR-59-BSP | GIBB, CA | GIBBCA-54-L |
| FREUND, PA | FREUPA-49-USC | GIBSON, C | GIBSC -60-AAC |
| FREY, F | HYMAH -58-VTC | GIL, F | GIL,F -62-GMP |
| FREY, FW | FREYFW-63-PDP | GIL, FG | GIL,FG-66-PSC |
| | FREYFW-65-TPE | GIL, G | GIL,G -53-RPL |
| FREYRE, G | FREYG -46-MSS | GILBERT, CE | GILBCE-64-NPA |
| FRIED, MH | FRIEMH-51-MSC | | GILBCE-59-FAR |
| FRIED, RC | FRIERC-63-IPS | | GILBCE-62-ECE |
| FRIEDLAND, WH | FRIEWH-64-SCC | GILBERT, F (EDS) | |
| FRIEDMAN, HJ | FRIEHJ-60-PSE | | CRAIGA-53-D |
| | FRIEHJ-63-AGR | GILBERT, GM | GILBGM-50-PDB |
| FRIEDMAN, J | FRIEJ -60-IDS | GILEAD, B | GILEB -58-PPT |
| FRIEDMAN, RS | FRIERS-65-RCM | GILISON, JM | GILIJM-67-NFS |
| FRIEDRICH, CJ | FRIECJ-63-RR | GILLESPIE, J | GILLJ -61-ARR |
| | FRIECJ-63-PEB | GILPIN, R | GILPR -64-SNP |
| | FRIECJ-56-TDA | GILPIN, RG | GILPRG-62-ASN |
| | FRIECJ-61-PLP | GINSBURGH, VN | GINSVN-64-CMP |
| | FRIECJ-63-PL | GINSBURGS, G | GINSG -64-KRH |
| FRIEDRICH, CJ (ED) | | | GINSG -59-SPF |
| | FRIECJ-58-A | | GINSG -63-LGA |
| FROMAN-JR, LA | FROMLA-63-IPC | | GINSG -59-TAT |
| | FROMLA-65-CPL | GITLOW, AL | GITLAL-52-MPA |
| | FROMLA-63-IIV | GITTELL, M | GITTM -66-TPM |
| FROMAN, LA | FROMLA-61-PPS | GITTINGS, J | GITTJ -67-RCA |
| | FROMLA- -CTC | | GITTJ -67-CAS |
| FROST, RT | FROSRT-61-SCL | | GITTJ -63-PCC |
| FRYE, CE | FRYECE-65-PPG | GLADDEN, EN | GLADEN-53-ACG |
| FRYKENBERG, RE | FRYKRE-65-EGS | | GLADEN-57-PCS |
| FURBER, H | FURBH -51-UI | GLASER, WA | GLASWA-60-DPU |
| FURNISS-JR, EJ | FURNEJ-64-DGF | GLASER, WA (EDS) | |
| GABIS, ST | GABIST-64-LLM | | MCPHWN-62-POC |
| GABLE, RW | GABLRW-58-IGP | GLASS, DV | GLASDV-54-SSS |
| | GABLRW-61-PAI | GLAZER, N | GLAZN -54-NLA |
| GADGIL, DR | GADGDR-51-RTP | | GLAZN -51-APP |
| | GADGDR-59-OMI | GLEITMAN, H | GLEIH -60-HSP |
| GADOUREK, I | GADOI -53-PCC | GLICK, HR | GLICHR-66-PRS |
| GAINSON, WA | GAINWA-66-RRC | GLICKMAN, M | GLICM -54-RRS |
| GALAY, N | GALAN -65-NGS | GLOCK, WP | GLOCWP-63-PEM |
| | GALAN -64-SRS | GLUBB, J | GLUBJ -65-RAT |
| | GALAN -56-MRH | GLUCKMAN, M | GLUCM -65-PLR |
| | GALAN -57-RSA | | GLUCM -49-VHB |
| | GALAN -58-MRS | | GLUCM -65-PSD |
| GALENSON, W (ED) | | GOCHENOUR, TS | GOCHTS-65-NTA |
| | GALEW -59-LED | GODFREY, D | GODFD -55-FFN |
| | GALEW -62-LDE | GOERLITZ, W | GOERW -53-HGG |
| GALESKI, B | GALEB -57-SSR | GOLD, D | GOLDD -61-LPE |
| GALLI, G | GALLG -59-ICC | | SCHMJ -58-SSC |
| | GALLG -66-WRB | GOLDBERG, LC | GOLDLC-65-LCU |
| GALLO, PS | RAVEBH-64-ENC | GOLDENBERG, B | GOLDB -65-CRL |
| GALLOWAY, GB | GALLGB-59-LHR | GOLDHAMER, H | GOLDH -39-TPS |
| GALVAN, ET | GALVET-66-SOS | | GOLDH -50-POP |
| GAMARNIKOW, M | GAMAM -67-PPP | GOLDMAN, EF | GOLDEF-52-PML |
| GAMSON, WA | GAMSWA-66-RRC | GOLDMAN, I | GOLDI -55-SRC |

GOLDMAN, M           GOLDM -64-WCP
                     GOLDM -67-LDC
GOLDMAN, R           GOLDR -62-RCP
GOLDMAN, RM (EDS)
                     DAVIPT-54-PNP
GOLDMAN, S           GOLDS -66-VBU
GOLDRICH, D          AGGER -64-RRU
                     AGGERE-66-CPS
                     GOLDD -61-DPO
                     GOLDD -66-SEE
                     GOLDD -64-ROR
                     GOLDD -62-RNP
GOLDTHORPE, JE       GOLDJE-55-AES
                     GOLDJE-61-EAC
GOLDTHRORPE, JH
                     GOLDJH-63-ABC
GOLDWERT, M          GOLDM -66-DMA
GOLEMBIEWSKI, RT
                     GOLERT-58-TAS
GOMEZ, RA            GOMERA-61-LAE
                     GOMERA-60-GPL
GOODALL, MR          GOODMR-66-ACN
GOODE, CE            GOODCE-51-SRL
GOODLAND, TM         GOODTM-57-MPI
GOODMAN, JS          GOODJS-67-NLR
GOODMAN, P           GOODP -62-IIP
                     GOODP -62-CSU
GOODNOW, HF          GOODHF-64-CSP
GOODSELL, CT         GOODCT-64-ARP
GOODWIN-JR, G        GOODG -62-SML
                     GOODG -59-SSC
GOODY, J             GOODJ -63-FA
GORDEN, M            GORDM -65-SEA
GORDON, BK           GORDBK-61-MBC
GORDON, MM           GORDMM-58-SCA
GORE, WJ             GOREWJ-56-DMF
                     GOREWJ-59-BED
GOSNELL, HF          GOSNHF-50-DCM
                     GOSNHF-48-DTF
GOTTFRIED, A         GOTTA -61-PPU
GOUGH, EK            GOUGEK-52-CKU
GOULDNER, AW         GOULAW-65-BA
                     GOULAW-58-CLT
                     GOULAW-65-I
                     GOULAW-65-LAS
                     GOULAW-65-PSB
GOULDNER, AW (ED)
                     GOULAW-65-SL
GOURLAY, WE          GOURWE-52-CCC
GOUVEIA, AJ          GOUVAJ-67-EDO
GOYAL, OP            GOYAOP-64-CPC
GP                   GP    -65-CSA
GRAEBNER, NA         GRAENA-61-UTA
GRAHAM, GA           GRAHGA-50-PEO
GRAHAM, S            GRAHS -56-CCA
GRAINGER, GW         GRAIGW-58-OBC
                     GRAIGW-57-CBC
GRANICK, D           GRAND -62-EEB
                     GRAND -60-RES
GRANT, JAC           GRANJA-50-JCL
GRAPER, ED           GRAPED-48-HPA
GRASSMUCK, G         GRASG -64-PBI
GRASSMUCK, GL        GRASGL-51-SBC
GRAYSON, GW          GRAYGW-65-CDC
GRAYSON, H           GRAYH -55-CMC
GREEN, P             GREEP -64-SSN
GREENBAUM, JJ        GLEIH -60-HSP
GREENE, LS           GREELS-64-CBP
GREENSLADE, RV       GREERV-63-KES
GREENSTEIN, FI       GREEFI-65-PPS
GREER, S             GREES -53-SPF
                     GREES -62-MSP
                     GREES -62-SSP
                     GREES -63-RMS
                     GREES -63-MSP
GREGG, RW            GREGRW-63-ESC
GREY, DL             GREYDL-67-ICU
GRIFFITH, WE         GRIFWE-62-DFR
GRIFFITHS, R         GRIFR -53-RBC
GRIGG, C             KILLL -64-RCA
GRINDROD, M          GRINM -56-ULC
                     GRINM -55-SMB
GRODZIUS, M          GRODM -60-APP
GROSS, BM            GROSBM-53-LSS

GROSS, F             GROSF -58-SPP
GROSSER, A           GROSA -64-EEP
GROSSMAN, G          GROSG -55-LPP
GROSSMAN, JB         GROSJB-64-FJS
                     GROSJB-65-LJA
                     LADIJ -66-OCP
GROVE, JW            MACKWJ-59-CAB
GROW, SL             GROWSL-63-DPP
GROZDANIC, S         GROZS -66-AMP
GRULIOW, L           GRULL -56-HSN
                     GRULL -63-RPS
GRUMM, JG            GRUMJG-63-FAL
GRUNDSTEIN, NO       GRUNND-62-WIM
GRUNDY, KW           GRUNKW-64-CSA
GRUSKY, O            GRUSO -65-CMM
                     GRUSO -64-ESC
GRZYBOWSKI, K        GRZYK -57-PWS
                     GRZYK -58-RGP
GUBIN, K             GUBIK -61-SSU
GUETZKOW, H          GUETH -53-ACD
                     SAWYJ -65-BNI
GUETZKOW, H (ED)
                     GUETH -51-GLM
GUILLAIN, R          GUILR -52-RME
GUIREY, C            GUIRC -53-SPS
GULICK, CA           GULICA-58-ALS
                     GULICA-58-ASS
GULICK, L            GULIL -63-PAL
GULLAHORN, JT        GULLJT-56-MUO
GULLIVER, PH         GULLPH-63-SCA
GUNLICK, JM          GUNLJM-58-IPS
GUPTA, SK            GUPTSK-57-IPS
                     GUPTSK-62-MIP
GURADZE, H           GURAH -50-LLG
GUSFIELD, JR         GUSFJR-58-EBR
                     GUSFJR-62-MSE
                     GUSFJR-65-PCG
GUSFIELD, MR         GUSFMR-57-PGO
GUTMANN, EE          GUTMEE-61-OPP
GUTTERIDGE, WF       BROWN -64-AMB
                     GUTTWF-59-IRR
                     GUTTWF-57-DCA
                     GUTTWF-63-AFN
                     GUTTWF-65-EML
                     GUTTWF-65-MIP
                     GUTTWF-67-PRA
GUTTSMAN, WL         GUTTWL-54-AMC
                     GUTTWL-60-SSP
                     GUTTWL-61-CBL
                     GUTTWL-63-BPE
                     GUTTWL-51-CSB
GUYOT, JF            GUYOJF-66-BTB
GYR, J               GUETH -53-ACD
HACKER, A            HACKA -60-RYS
                     HACKA -61-EAT
                     HACKA -64-PDW
                     HACKA -57-LDS
                     HACKA -65-DDP
HADDEN, GM           HADDGM-65-RMR
HADLEY, G            HADLG -56-PPW
HADMEN, JG           HADMJG-61-HUN
HAER, JL             HAERJL-56-SSR
HAGEN, EE            HAGEEE-62-TSC
HAGGEN, EE           HAGGEE-62-FAE
HAHN-BEEN, L         HAHNL -65-DTL
HAHN, H              HAHNH -67-TIS
HAHN, L              HAHNL -62-TPP
                     HAHNL -64-NAN
HAHN, WF             HAHNWF-55-SPA
HAIMAN, FS           HAIMFS-51-GLD
HAIMSON, LH          HAIMLH-58-TGS
                     HAIMLH-59-TGS
HAIRE, M             HAIRM -63-CPR
HALAS, F             HALAF -52-NWS
HALL, DGE            HALLDG-54-TCQ
HALL, JW             HALLJW-66-GLP
HALL, R              BLONJ -67-CDM
HALL, RH             HALLRH-63-BSO
HALLGARTEN, GWF
                     HALLGW-54-WDC
HALPERIN, E          HALPE -65-NCC
                     HALPE -59-MNC
HALPERN, B           HALPB -62-RMI
HALPERN, JM          HALPJM-64-GPS

645

| | | | | |
|---|---|---|---|---|
| HOSELITZ, BF | HOSEBF-63-ETE | | JAN, GP | JAN,GP-62-MPC |
| HOTTINGER, A | HOTTA -61-ZAP | | JANDA, KF | JANDKF-60-TEC |
| HOUGH, J | HOUGJ -67-SEG | | JANICKE, M | JANIM -63-EGT |
| HOUGH, JF | HOUGJF-65-SCR | | JANIS, IL | JANIIL-59-DCT |
| | HOUGJF-65-HSR | | JANOSIK, GE | JANOGE-63-BSN |
| | HOUGJF-59-TEV | | JANOWITZ, M | JANOM -55-CPD |
| HOUN, FW | HOUNFW-57-ECC | | | JANOM -56-SSC |
| HOWARD, M | HOWAM -60-CMR | | | JANOM -57-MES |
| HOWARD, M (ED) | HOWAM -59-SGN | | | JANOM -54-SAP |
| HOWE, I | HOWEI -46-LYI | | | JANOM -58-BPS |
| HOWE, JM | HOWEJM-48-GCI | | | JANOM -58-PAP |
| HOWMAN, R | HOWMR -56-ALT | | | JANOM -58-SSM |
| | HOWMR -66-CA | | | JANOM -60-PSS |
| HOWTON, FW | BENDR -57-SMA | | | JANOM -59-CPD |
| HOYLE, E | HOYLE -64-ECK | | | JANOM -65-AFW |
| HSIAO, GT | HSIAGT-67-BDP | | | JANOM -62-CPS |
| HSUEH, C | HSUEC -67-CRL | | | JANOM -65-SME |
| HSUEH, C-T | HSUEC--61-HHC | | JANOWITZ, M (ED) | |
| HSUEH, SS | HSUESS-66-TCD | | | JANOM -61-CPS |
| HUBERMAN, LPM | HUBELP-61-CAR | | | JANOM -64-MPD |
| HUCKER, CO | HUCKCO-51-TCC | | | JANOM -64-NMC |
| HUDSON, MC | HUDSMC-66-EPP | | JANSEN, MB | JANSMB-57-EVP |
| HUELIN, D | HUELD -62-CFA | | JAYNES, W | STOGRM-56-LRE |
| HUGHES, C | HUGHC -56-EPS | | JCC | JCC -51-SWP |
| HUGHES, CA | HUGHCA-59-LCP | | JELAVICH, B (EDS) | |
| | HUGHCA-60-CRF | | | JELAC -63-BTE |
| HUGHES, HS | HUGHHS-56-IIO | | JELAVICH, C | JELAC -63-BTE |
| | HUGHHS-58-DGP | | JELENSKI, KA | JELEJA-59-GPI |
| | HUGHHS-64-NII | | JELENSKI, KA | JELEKA-58-RPG |
| | HUGHHS-59-CS | | JENNINGS, EE | JENNEE-60-ALP |
| HUITT, RK | HUITRK-61-OSA | | | JENNEE-62-EAB |
| | HUITRK-65-IDI | | JENNINGS, MK | JENNMK-64-PAC |
| | HUITRK-54-CCC | | | JENNMK-64-CIE |
| | HUITRK-57-MCA | | | JENNMK-66-TLP |
| | HUITRK-61-DPL | | JENNINGS, WI | JENNWI-57-PGB |
| HULICKA, K | HULIK -62-KSU | | | JENNWI-59-CGG |
| HUNT, RNC | HUNTRN-58-IDS | | | JENNWI-54-PCS |
| HUNT, WH | CRANWW-64-IPE | | JESSIE, B | JESSB -55-DAS |
| HUNTER, F | HUNTF -59-TLU | | JESSUP, PC | JESSPC-55-ICS |
| | HUNTF -53-CPS | | JEWELL, ME | JEWEME-64-SLS |
| HUNTER, G | HUNTG -63-NST | | | JEWEME-62-SPF |
| HUNTINGTON, P | BRZEZ -64-PPU | | | JEWEME-59-EDS |
| HUNTINGTON, SP | BRZEZ -63-CA | | | JEWEME-59-SRP |
| | HUNTSP-56-CCC | | | JEWEME-55-PVA |
| | HUNTSP-57-SST | | JEWELL, ME (ED) | |
| | HUNTSP-61-ICP | | | JEWEME-62-PR |
| | HUNTSP-62-PVW | | JIANG, JPL | JIANJP-62-PCP |
| | HUNTSP-65-CRT | | JOESTEN, J | JOESJ -60-NRP |
| | HUNTSP-66-PMT | | JOFFE, E | JOFFE -65-PAP |
| | HUNTSP-63-PEM | | | JOFFE -64-CBO |
| HUNTINGTON, SP (ED | | | JOHNSON, C | JOHNC -66-RC |
| | HUNTSP-62-CPM | | JOHNSON, CA | JOHNCA-62-PNC |
| HUSSEY, ERJ | HUSSER-46-EPP | | JOHNSON, JJ | JOHNJJ-58-PCL |
| HYMAN, H | HYMAH -58-VTC | | | JOHNJJ-62-LAM |
| HYNEMAN, CS | HYNECS-50-BDU | | | JOHNJJ-61-WLA |
| IGNOTUS, P | IGNOP -59-HIU | | | JOHNJJ-51-FFD |
| | IGNOP -62-LBA | | | JOHNJJ-64-MSL |
| IKE, N | IKE,N -49-DCJ | | | JOHNJJ-65-LAN |
| IKELLE-MATIBA, J | | | | JOHNJJ-64-CCL |
| | IKELJ -64-PYE | | JOHNSON, KF | JOHNKF-65-ICR |
| INAYATULLAH, (ED) | | | JOHNSON, LL | JOHNLL-65-USB |
| | INAY(E-63-BDP | | JOHNSON, P | JOHNP -63-RIW |
| INKELES, A | BAUER -56-HSS | | JOHNSON, SD | BARTEA-59-CPT |
| | INKEA -59-SCD | | JOHNSTON, SD | JOHNSD-62-EPS |
| | INKEA -53-CLE | | JOINER, CA | FOX,GH-64-PVP |
| | INKEA -50-POS | | JOLL, J | JOLLJ -54-IGP |
| | INKEA -50-SSM | | JONES, CO | JONECO-64-PPM |
| INNES, FM | INNEFM-53-POP | | | JONECO-61-RCC |
| IONESCU, G | IONEG -67-PEC | | | JONECO-65-RPA |
| IRISH, MD | IRISMD-58-OMP | | | JONECO-63-IPC |
| | IRISMD-60-POA | | JONES, MWH | JONEMW-63-PGG |
| ISAACS, HR | ISAAHR-51-TCR | | JONES, V | KAUFH -54-MP |
| ISSAWI, C | ISSAC -55-ECM | | JORAVSKY, D | JORAD -60-SSG |
| ITALIAANDER, R | ITALR -61-NLA | | JOSEPH, E | JOSEE -52-ILF |
| IVELLA, V | IVELV -49-PRD | | JOSEY, A | JOSEA -58-PSB |
| JACKSON, C | JACKC -49-YGT | | JULIVER, PH | JULIPH-61-ICS |
| JACOB, CE | JACOCE-63-LPL | | JUMPER, R | JUMPR -57-MBP |
| JACOB, H | BROWRP-64-PMP | | | JUMPR -57-PPA |
| | JACOH -63-GAS | | | JUMPR -57-RPF |
| | JACOH -62-IRE | | | JUMPR -59-SCS |
| JACOB, PE | JACOPE-62-FVP | | JURCZENKO, A | JURCA -60-ARB |
| JACOBINI, HB | JACOHB-59-OPV | | KABYSH, S | KABYS -63-RPL |
| JAHODA, G | JAHOG -54-SBW | | KAHIN, GM | KAHIGM-49-IRE |
| JAMES, RC | JAMERC-58-TUD | | KAMALIZA, M | KAMAM -64-TSV |

| | | | |
|---|---|---|---|
| KAMMERER, GM | KAMMGM-48-EWP | KERR, W | KERRW -48-FLD |
| | KAMMGM-54-GCA | KERSTEN, H | KERSH -58-UIE |
| | KAMMGM-53-ACL | KERSTIENS, T | KERST -66-NEA |
| | KAMMGM-64-ULD | KESSEL, JH | KESSJH-64-WCD |
| KAMPELMAN, MM | KAMPMM-54-LBI | KESSELMAN, K | KESSK -61-PLU |
| KANTOR, H | KANTH -52-ASP | KESSELMAN, M | KESSM -65-PLC |
| | KANTH -59-DAD | KEY-JR, VO | KEY-VO-64-PPP |
| | KANTH -53-IPP | | KEY-VO-61-POD |
| | KANTH -54-APS | | KEY-VO-61-POA |
| KAPLAN, H | KAPLH -63-URP | | KEY-VO-66-RER |
| KAPLINSKY, Z | KAPLZ -54-MBE | KHADDURI, M | KHADM -52-CCC |
| KARAVAEV, A | KARAA -61-SDS | | KHADM -53-RMM |
| KARPAT, KH | KARPKH-62-RPD | KHAMA, T | KHAMT -51-PAT |
| | KARPKH-59-TSP | KHERA, SS | KHERSS-64-DAI |
| | KARPKH-64-SEP | KHERA, SSS | KHERSS-60-AI |
| | KARPKH-67-SLP | KILLIAN, L | KILLL -64-RCA |
| KASHIN, A | KASHA -61-TCA | KILLIAN, LM | KILLLM-60-NPL |
| | KASHA -64-DPS | KILLICK, AJ | CLEGHA-61-TUO |
| | KASHA -64-ISS | KILMUIR, V | KILMV -56-OLC |
| KASSOF, A | KASSA -57-YVR | KILNER, P | KILNP -62-MGS |
| | KASSA -58-AYL | KILPATRICK, FP | JENNMK-66-TLP |
| | KASSA -64-AST | | KILPFP-64-IFS |
| KATRAK, S | KATRS -61-ISC | KILSON, M | KILSM -66-PCW |
| KATTIN, GM | KATTGM-52-NRI | | KILSM -63-APC |
| KATZ, D | KATZD -61-ILP | KILSON, ML | KILSML-63-ASP |
| | KATZD -59-CRP | | KILSML-58-NSC |
| | VALEH -65-PPN | KIM, YC | KIM,YC-66-ACE |
| KATZ, E | KATZE -57-LSS | | KIM,YC-64-CPC |
| KATZ, Z | KATZZ -56-PPE | KIMBROUGH, RB | KIMBRB-64-PPE |
| KATZENBACH-JR, EL | | KIMCHE, J | KIMCJ -64-SLI |
| | KATZEL-50-PPF | KINCAID, HB | KINCHB-57-IBE |
| KAUFMAN, A | KAUFA -54-WAR | KING, A | KINGA -66-GBS |
| KAUFMAN, H | KAUFH -54-MP | KING, A (ED) | KINGA -66-BPP |
| | SAYRWS-60-GNY | KING, JB | KINGJB-60-MCF |
| KAUFMAN, HK | KAUFHK-60-BCS | KING, JK | KINGJK-54-TSB |
| KAUL, JM | KAULJM-64-SCC | KINGDON, JW | KINGJW-67-PBA |
| KAUTSKY, JH | KAUTJH-55-ICP | KINGSLEY, JD | KINGJD-44-RBI |
| | KAUTJH-62-PCU | KINOSHITA, H | KINOH -53-EMJ |
| | KAUTJH-56-MCP | | KINOH -63-URW |
| KAVANAGH, D | KAVAD -67-OCL | KIRCHHEIMER, O | KIRCO -57-WOP |
| KAWAI, K | KAWAK -50-JVN | | KIRCO -58-FFF |
| KAZAMIAS, AM | KAZAAM-67-PET | | KIRCO -59-MMW |
| | KAZAAM-66-PET | | KIRCO -50-CGB |
| KEARNEY, RN | HARRRL-64-CAA | KIRK-GREENE, AHM | |
| | KEARRN-64-BEC | | KIRKAH-65-BCT |
| | KEARRN-64-SNS | KITCHEN, H (ED) | |
| | KEARRN-66-CCB | | KITCH -62-EA |
| | KEARRN-66-MPS | KITCHEN, JD | KITCJD-60-NPA |
| KECSKEMETI, P | KECSP -57-IUB | KITTRELL, ER | KITTER-55-IEE |
| | KECSP -61-URS | KITZINGER, UW | KITZUW-60-SED |
| | KECSP -52-HTG | | KITZUW- -AES |
| KEEFE, WJ | KEEFWJ-54-PPP | KIYOSHI, E | KIYOE -58-JCP |
| | KEEFWJ-56-CSR | KLAPP, OE | KLAPOE-60-PSD |
| | KEEFWJ-64-ALP | | KLAPOE-64-SLP |
| KEEP, JLH | KEEPJL-58-SIT | KLEIN, DW | KLEIDW-60-PSE |
| KEESING, FM | KEESFM-56-ECS | | KLEIDW-60-PSL |
| KEESING, MM | KEESFM-56-ECS | | KLEIDW-64-SEP |
| KEISER, NF | KEISNF-58-PRF | | KLEIDW-62-NGC |
| KELLER, J | KELLJ -60-CGS | KLEIN, LB | DODDSC-62-CIS |
| KELLER, S | KELLS -63-BRC | KLING, M | KLINM -56-TTP |
| KELLEY-JR, S | KELLS -56-PPR | | KLINM -61-MIG |
| KELLY, D | KELLD -52-RF | KLUCKHOHN, C | BAUER -56-HSS |
| KELLY, GA | KELLGA-61-FAR | KNAPP-JR, FA | KNAPFA-64-MML |
| | KELLGA-65-LSF | KNICKERBOCKER, I | |
| | KELLGA-65-FCS | | KNICI -48-LCI |
| KELLY, J | KELLJ -64-SEB | KNIGHT, ME | KNIGME-52-GE |
| KELMAN, HC (ED) | | KNOWLTON, CS | KNOWCS-62-PPP |
| | KELMHC-65-IBS | KOENIG, LW | CORWES-56-PTU |
| KELSALL, RK | KELSRK-54-SBH | | KOENLW-60-IPU |
| | KELSRK-55-HCS | KOFF, D | EULAH -62-OMP |
| KELSON, RN | KELSRN-64-PMP | KOFMEHL, K | KOFMK -62-PSC |
| | KELSRN-54-NZN | KOGAN, N | KOGAN -66-ICW |
| KEMP, T | KEMPT -62-IMC | | KOGAN -53-IAP |
| | KEMPT -64-LCI | KOLARZ, W | KOLAW -61-WAS |
| KENDALL, PL | KENDPL-56-ACN | KOLEGAR, F | KOLEF -67-ERC |
| KENDALL, W | KENDW -60-TMU | KOLKO, G | KOLKG -62-WPA |
| | RANNA -56-DAP | KOLKOWICZ, R | KOLKR -67-SMC |
| KENKEL, WF | CUBEJF-54-SSU | KOLODZIEJ, EJ | KOLOEJ-65-SPA |
| KENNEDY, JJ | KENNJJ-58-CND | KONSTANTINOV, D | |
| KENNEY, CD | KENNCD-56-TCC | | KONSD -63-TPM |
| KENZO, T | KENZT -62-NES | KOOL, F | KOOLF -60-CHS |
| KERANEY, RN | HARRRL-63-BCP | KORAB, A | KORAA -57-PPC |
| KERN, E | KERNE -59-EEC | | KORAA -56-PSI |
| KERR, C | KERRC -64-IIM | KORBEL, J | KORBJ -59-CSC |

| | |
|---|---|
| KORCHIN, SJ | BRUNJS-46-BVC |
| KORMENDI, F | KORMF -56-HSR |
| KORNAI, J | KORNJ -59-OEA |
| KORNBERG, A | KORNA -65-PSN |
| | KORNA -66-CCC |
| | KORNA -65-SBL |
| | KORNA -66-RDP |
| KORNHAUSER, W | KORNW -59-PMS |
| KORT, F | KORTF -57-PSC |
| | KORTF -58-RFS |
| | KORTF -66-MAF |
| KORTON, DC | KORTDC-62-SDL |
| KOSLIN, B | MOOSM -51-PLR |
| KOTHARI, R | KOTHR -66-CSI |
| | KOTHR -67-ICS |
| KRACKE, EA | KRACEA-58-CRC |
| KRAMER, MN | LERND -3 -FEP |
| KREITLOW, BW | KREIBW-60-LAR |
| KRIESBERG, L | KRIEL -63-ELA |
| KRISHNA, G | KRISG -66-DIN |
| KRISLOV, S | KRISS -59-CVC |
| KRISTOL, I | KRISI -67-AIF |
| KROLL, M | KROLM -61-PBS |
| KRUZHIN, P | KRUZP -65-YYC |
| | KRUZP -66-PPG |
| | KRUZP -64-TPR |
| KRYLOV, KA | KRYLKA-66-PPP |
| KUBAT, D | KUBAD -61-STC |
| | KUBAD -61-PLC |
| | KUBAD -65-TYM |
| | KUBAD -61-CUC |
| KUEBLER, J | KUEBJ -63-AP |
| KULSKI, W | KULSW -53-CSS |
| KULSKI, WW | KULSWW-55-CCS |
| KUMALO, C | KUMAC -66-AEI |
| KUNZ, FA | KUNZFA-65-MSC |
| KUO-CHUN, C | KUO-C -59-LCC |
| KUPER, H | KUPEH -47-AAR |
| KUPER, L | KUPEL -50-DAW |
| | KUPEL -65-ABR |
| KURIHARA, KK | KURIKK-46-JSN |
| KURODA, Y | KUROY -65-SPI |
| KUTNER, B | KUTNB -65-EPD |
| KUWAHAMI, T | TOTTGO-65-FFJ |
| KYDIS, S | KYDIS -65-PWP |
| L | L -57-SI |
| LABEDZ, L | LABEL -57-ITP |
| | LABEL -60-SSI |
| | LABEL -59-NSI |
| | LABEL -63-RPS |
| | LABEL -56-RAK |
| LABEDZ, L (ED.) | |
| | LABEL -62-REH |
| LADD-JR, EC | LADDEC-66-NPL |
| LADINSKY, J | LADIJ -66-OCP |
| | LADIJ -63-CLL |
| LAIDLER, HW | LAIDHW-59-LSR |
| LAING, LH | LAINLH-46-NCS |
| LAIRD, RD | LAIRRD-64-PSA |
| | LAIRRD-66-CSL |
| LAKOFF, SA | DUPRJS-62-SNP |
| LAMB, HB | LAMBHB-55-IBC |
| | LAMBHB-59-BOL |
| LAMB, RK | LAMBRK-52-PEP |
| LAMBERT, RD | LAMBRD-59-HCG |
| LANDAU, R | LANDR -53-MPN |
| | LANDR -61-MIU |
| LANDE, CH | LANDCH-59-PAB |
| | LANDCH-65-LFP |
| LANDSBERGER, HA | |
| | LANDHA-67-LEI |
| LANDY, P | LANDP -58-HSD |
| | LANDP -58-RRE |
| | LANDP -62-HPA |
| LANDYNSKI, JW | LANDJW-64-MCL |
| LANE, RE | LANERE-58-ECG |
| | LANERE-49-NTL |
| | LANERE-53-BBU |
| LANG, K | LANGK -64-TCM |
| LANGBAUM, R | LANGR -55-TDM |
| LANGDON, FC | LANGFC-61-BBL |
| | LANGFC-56-CAC |
| | LANGFC-61-OIJ |
| LANGER, PF | LANGPF-63-IOS |

| | |
|---|---|
| LANPERT, E | LANPE -57-SR |
| LAPALOMBARA, J | LAPAJ -54-LWT |
| | LAPAJ -57-IFB |
| | LAPAJ -58-PPS |
| | LAPAJ -57-ILM |
| | LAPAJ -60-ULI |
| | LAPAJ -63-OBP |
| | LAPAJ -64-IFI |
| | LAPAJ -64-IGI |
| LAPALOMBARA, J (ED | |
| | LAPAJ -63-BPD |
| LAPALOMBARA, JG | |
| | LAPAJG-65-PPP |
| LAPIERE, RT | LAPIRT-65-SC |
| LAPONCE, JD | LAPOJD-58-RBC |
| LAPP, RE | LAPPRE-65-NPS |
| LAQUER, WZ | LAQUWZ-57-CNM |
| LAQUEUR, WZ | LAQUWZ-59-NIC |
| | LAQUWZ-59-IGC |
| LAQUIAN, AA | LAQUAA-63-UPP |
| LASCH, C | LASCC -62-ALR |
| LASKER, B | LASKB -50-NFA |
| LASKI, HJ | LASKHJ-48-ADC |
| LASSWELL, H | LASSH -52-CSE |
| LASSWELL, HD | LASSHD-0 -NSI |
| | LASSHD-30-PP |
| | LASSHD-48-APB |
| | LASSHD-36-PWG |
| | LASSHD-48-PP |
| | LASSHD-51-WRO |
| | LASSHD-52-CSS |
| | LASSHD-52-CSE |
| | LASSHD-50-PSF |
| | LASSHD-56-DPS |
| | LASSHD-61-ASP |
| | LASSHD-62-GSH |
| | LASSHD-65-CIA |
| | LASSHD-66-CLP |
| | LASSHD-54-EPP |
| | LASSHD-66-WRE |
| | LASSHD-67-PSS |
| | LASSHD-67-RSC |
| | ROGOAA-63-PCR |
| LASWELL, HD | LASWHD-59-PCC |
| LATHAM, E | LATHE -54-SCS |
| | LATHE -52-GBP |
| LATIF, SA | LATISA-53-ISC |
| LAULICHT, J | PAULJ -63-YOL |
| LAUNDY, P | LAUNP -61-SHC |
| LAUTERBACH, A | LAUTA -65-GDM |
| | LAUTA -66-ELA |
| LAVINE, H | LAVIH -59-SRC |
| LAZARSFELD, PF | BEREBR-54-VSO |
| | LAZAPF-58-AMS |
| LC | LC -62-SMA |
| LEACH, ER | LEACER-54-PSH |
| LEACH, RH | LEACRH-65-LCU |
| LEBED, A | LEBEA -65-SAE |
| | LEBEA -63-EPR |
| LEE, AM | LEE,AM-65-PS |
| LEE, EC | LEE,EC-52-POR |
| LEE, RA | BRANRL-64-LBJ |
| LEE, SC | LEE,SC-47-IC |
| LEEDS, A | LEEDA -64-BCS |
| LEFCOWITZ, MJ | TURKH -62-TTR |
| LEGUM, C | LEGUC -65-BAD |
| | LEGUC -65-SPD |
| LEIDEN, C | LEIDC -65-PIS |
| LEIGHTON, AH | LEIGAH-65-LSS |
| LEISERSON, A | LEISA -58-PPU |
| | LEISA -57-PPS |
| | LEISA -65-SPP |
| LEITES, N | LEITN -51-OCP |
| | LEITN -51-PIS |
| | LEITN -52-PTW |
| | LEITN -59-GPF |
| | LEITN -53-SBS |
| LEITH-ROSS, S | LEITS -56-RNE |
| LEMARCHAND, R | LEMAR -64-PAB |
| | LEMAR -66-SPC |
| LENCZOWSKI, G | LENCG -47-CMI |
| LENSKI, GE | LENSGE-52-ASC |
| LEONHARD, W | LEONW -66-WRN |
| | LEONW -58-TSS |

| Author | Code |
|---|---|
| MEISSNER, B | MEISB -66-TRS |
| | MEISB -65-PGR |
| MELADY, TP | MELATP-61-PAL |
| MELLER, N | MELLN -58-MHS |
| | MELLN -67-RRT |
| MENDEL, DH | MENDDH-59-BJE |
| | MENDDH-61-JPF |
| MENDELSON, EM | MENDEM-60-RAM |
| MENDELSON, W | MENDW -64-UWJ |
| MENG, SM | MENGSM-59-TYI |
| MENZEL, JM | MENZJM-63-CCS |
| MERAY, T | ACZET -60-RMC |
| | MERAT -62-GTH |
| MERCER, P | MERCP -56-ESE |
| MERKL, PH | MERKPH-62-ESI |
| | MERKPH-64-EAP |
| MERRIAM, CE | MERRCE-49-PLU |
| MERRY, HJ | MERRHJ-55-ECS |
| MERTON, VK | MERTVK-52-RB |
| MERTSALOV, VS | MERTVS-56-MSS |
| MESZAROS, J | MESZJ -58-ERH |
| METRAUX, R | METRR -52-AHS |
| MEYER, AG | MEYEAG-65-SPS |
| | MEYEAG-61-UIS |
| | MEYEAG-67-ACP |
| MEYER, AJ | MEYEAJ-58-EED |
| MEYER, P | MEYEP -57-AOC |
| MEYEROWITZ, LR | MEYELR-60-DKG |
| MEYERSON, M | MEYEM -55-PPP |
| MEYNAUD, J | MEYNJ -61-IGS |
| | MEYNJ -58-EMS |
| MICAUD, CA | MICACA-54-FIC |
| | MICACA-57-NLF |
| | MICACA-63-CFL |
| | MICACA-52-OLF |
| | MICACA-64-TPM |
| MICHAEL, F | MICHF -63-KSD |
| | MICHF -67-SPC |
| MICHAEL, FH | MICHFH-46-CMT |
| MICHELS, R | MICHR -27-RSC |
| | MICHR -49-E |
| | MICHR -62-PPS |
| MIDDLETON, J | MIDDJ -56-RCH |
| MIDDLETON, J (EDS) | |
| | TAITD -58-TWR |
| MIKULAK, MW | MIKUMW-64-PSS |
| MILBRATH, LW | MILBLW-60-LCP |
| | MILBLW-63-WLU |
| | MILBLW-58-PPA |
| MILBURN, JF | MILBJF-58-FSB |
| | MILBJF-66-TUP |
| MILLEN, BH | MILLBH-63-PRL |
| MILLER, DC | FORMWH-60-ILC |
| | MILLDC-57-PIO |
| | MILLDC-58-DMC |
| | MILLDC-63-TGP |
| MILLER, J | MILLJ -65-TSI |
| MILLER, N | MILLN -65-JLL |
| MILLER, W | MILLW -50-RAB |
| MILLER, WB | MILLWB-55-TCA |
| MILLER, WE | MILLWE-63-CIC |
| | STOKDE-62-PGS |
| MILLER,WE | CONVPE-65-EMR |
| MILLET, JH | MILLJH-56-RIG |
| MILLETT, JH | MILLJH-59-NFR |
| MILLS, CW | GERTH -54-SL |
| | MILLCW-54-ABE |
| | MILLCW-48-NMP |
| | MILLCW-57-PEC |
| | MILLCW-56-PEU |
| | MILLCW-58-SPA |
| | MILLCW-59-PEM |
| | MILLCW-63-PPP |
| | MILLCW-58-CWW |
| MILNE, RS | MILNRS-55-ACE |
| | MILNRS-58-BNZ |
| | MILNRS-61-COC |
| | MILNRS-61-RGC |
| | MILNRS-62-AET |
| MILNER, J | MILNJ -47-HCC |
| MILOSZ, C | MILOC -52-IPS |
| | MILOC -56-PVD |
| | MILOC -55-SPG |
| | MILOC -57-ASP |
| MINAR, DW | MINADW-66-CBC |
| | MINADW-61-IPB |
| MINDLIN, M | MINDM -58-ISI |
| MINYAILO, V | MINYV -60-JCC |
| MISES, LV | MISELV-44-BAG |
| | MISELV-44-OSR |
| MISRA, BB | MISRBB-61-IMC |
| MITCHELL, C | MITCC -67-RTL |
| MITCHELL, JC | GLUCM -49-VHB |
| | MITCJC-56-YVS |
| MITCHELL, WC | MITCWC-59-ASS |
| | MITCWC-62-APS |
| | MITCWC-58-ORS |
| | MITCWC-58-PPS |
| | MITCWC-59-RTL |
| MITSCHERLICH, A | |
| | MITSA -67-CPP |
| MOISLEY, HA | CAIRJB-61-LCC |
| MONAHAN, EH | MONATP-56-CAN |
| MONAHAN, TP | MONATP-56-CAN |
| MONSEN-JR, RJ | MONSRJ-65-MPP |
| MONTAGUE-JR, GB | |
| | MONTGB-51-ACS |
| MONTGOMERY, JD (ED | |
| | MONTJD-59-CVA |
| MOODIE, GC | MOODGC-57-MSP |
| MOORE-JR, B | MOORB -50-SPD |
| | MOORB -54-TPU |
| | MOORB -58-PPS |
| | MOORB -55-STC |
| | MOORB -66-SOD |
| MOORE, BM | MOORJW-58-RSE |
| MOORE, CH | MOORCH-62-NDP |
| | MOORCH-65-OPM |
| | MOORCH-65-TSI |
| MOORE, JW | MOORJW-58-RSE |
| MOORE, SF | MOORSF-58-PPI |
| MOOS, M | DAVIPT-54-PNP |
| | MOOSM -51-PLR |
| MORA, JF | MORAJF-59-ICS |
| MORGAN, GG | MORGGG-62-SAL |
| MORGENTHAU, RS | MORGRS-64-PPF |
| MORRIS-JONES, WH | |
| | MORRWH-57-PI |
| | MORRWH-59-RPD |
| | MORRWH-64-GPI |
| | MORRWH-66-DDT |
| MORRIS, I (ED). | |
| | MORRI -63-MFJ |
| MORRIS, I (EDS) | |
| | MARHM -63-TBM |
| MORRIS, II | MORRII-60-NRW |
| MORRIS, RT | MORRRT-50-PLI |
| MORSTEIN-MARX, F | |
| | MORSF -57-ASF |
| | MORSF -58-HCS |
| MORTON, L | MORTL -57-DUA |
| MOSCA, G | MOSCG -39-RC |
| MOSKOS-JR, CC | MOSKCC-65-MCS |
| MOSSMAN, J | MOSSJ -61-RPI |
| MP | MP -52-SPS |
| MU-FU-SHENG | MU-F -62-WHF |
| MUELLER-DEHAM, A | |
| | MUELA -57-HRP |
| MUELLER, G | MUELG -65-HCN |
| MUHLEN, N | MUHLN -57-NAN |
| MULDER, M | MULDM -66-IPP |
| MUNEY, LW | MUNELW-47-JPA |
| MUNGER, FJ | MARTRC-61-DSU |
| MURPHY, WF | MURPWF-64-EJS |
| | MURPWF-62-CJT |
| | MURPWF-61-CJP |
| | MURPWF-62-CCC |
| MURRAY, E | MURRE -60-HEC |
| MUS, P | MUS,P -49-RVV |
| MUSGROVE, F | MUSGF -61-EGB |
| MYRDAL, G | MYRDG -44-ADN |
| MYSBERGH, JH | MYSBJH-57-IE |
| MZ | MZ -50-IRR |
| NADEL, SF | NADESF-57-TSS |
| | NADESF-56-CSE |
| NAGEL, SS | NAGESS-62-EAJ |
| | NAGESS-61-PPA |
| | NAGESS-62-TRB |

REY, L                REY,L -57-ILR
REYMAN, K             REYMK -62-OSE
RF                    RF    -52-NTU
RHYNE, EH             RHYNEH-58-PPD
RIBEIRO, D            RIBED -67-USD
RICHARDS, AI (ED)
                      RICHAI-59-EAC
RICHARDS, PG          RICHPG-56-SPA
                      RICHPG-59-HMS
                      RICHPG-63-PBG
RICHARDSON, RJ        RICHRJ-67-RDA
RIENCOURT, A          RIENA -57-CC
RIESMAN, D            RIESD -56-OTI
                      RIESD -59-PPP
RIEZLER, K            RIEZK -54-PDM
RIGBY, TH             RIGBTH-62-HSI
                      RIGBTH-53-CCS
                      RIGBTH-62-PMU
                      RIGBTH-63-ELA
                      RIGBTH-64-TMO
                      RIGBTH-56-SOR
RIGGS, FW             RIGGFW-62-SME
                      RIGGFW-63-BPD
                      RIGGFW-61-PSF
                      RIGGFW-66-TMB
                      RIGGFW-64-ADC
RIKER, WH             RIKEWH-59-MDS
                      RIKEWH-59-TAP
                      RIKEWH-58-VMI
                      RIKEWH-62-SCR
                      RIKEWH-62-TPC
RINGER, BB            RINGBB-52-PEI
RINTALA, M            RINTM -62-TGE
                      RINTM -58-PGF
                      RINTM -62-IEP
RIPLEY, RB            FROMLA-65-CPL
                      RIPLRB-64-PWO
RIPPY, JF             RIPPJF-65-LAS
RITTER, G             RITTG -57-MPG
RITVO, H              RITVH -61-TFP
                      RITVH -63-DDS
                      RITVH -63-PCR
                      RITVH -60-TWC
RIVLIN, B             RIVLB -52-TNM
ROBERT, D             ROBED -64-MSU
ROBERTS, A            ROBEA -66-BWV
                      ROBEA -65-BPS
ROBERTS, BC           ROBEBC-56-TUG
ROBINSON, JA          DAWSRE-63-IPC
                      ROBIJA-59-DMH
                      ROBIJA-62-CFP
                      ROBIJA-60-SIA
                      ROBIJA-61-PSP
                      ROBIJA-59-RRC
                      ROBIJA-63-HRC
                      ROBIJA-65-DMI
                      STANWH-58-IPC
ROBINSON, K           ROBIK -58-CRF
ROBINSON, R           LERND -60-SPT
ROBSON, WA            ROBSWA-48-MGG
                      ROBSWA-46-LDG
                      ROBSWA-50-GBP
                      ROBSWA-53-LLG
                      ROBSWA-64-GG
ROBSON, WA (ED)
                      ROBSWA-56-CSB
ROCHE, JP             ROCHJP-58-PSS
                      ROCHJP-55-BEE
RODNICK, D            RODND -50-NCP
RODNICK, E            RODND -50-NCP
ROFF, WR              ROFFWR-67-OMN
ROGERS, H             ROGEH -65-ERH
ROGERS, L             ROGEL -49-PPO
ROGOW, AA             LUCERD-56-GTA
                      ROGOAA-55-LGB
                      ROGOAA-63-PCR
ROMANO, OI            ROMAOI-60-DMA
ROMNALDI, S           ROMNS -47-LDL
ROSBERG, C            COLEJS-64-PPN
ROSE, AM              ROSEAM-62-APC
                      ROSEAM-66-PSP
ROSE, LE              ROSELE-63-NSE
ROSE, R               ROSER -62-PIE
                      ROSER -61-BGS

ROSER -64-PFT
ROSER -63-CPL
ROSER -66-ETM
ROSE, R (ED)          ROSER -66-SBP
ROSE, S               ROSES -56-PDO
ROSENAU, JN           ROSEJN-62-CBA
                      ROSEJN-61-POF
                      ROSEJN-63-NLF
                      ROSEJN-60-OMO
ROSENBERG, B          BENSG -63-MCB
ROSENBURG, H          ROSEH -66-BAA
ROSENTHAL, CS         ROSECS-55-FPT
ROSENTHAL, DB         ROSEDB-66-FAI
                      ROSEDB-66-DFP
ROSENZWEIG, RM        ROSERM-58-PCU
                      ROSERM-57-PCP
ROSHWALD, M           ROSHM -56-PPS
ROSI, EJ              ROSIEJ-65-MAO
ROSS, RG              ROSSRG-52-EMP
ROSSI, PH             CUTRP -58-POP
                      CUTRP -58-GRP
                      ROSSPH-57-CDM
                      ROSSPH-58-CDM
                      ROSSPH-60-PCS
ROSSITER, C           ROSSC -50-WDP
ROSSITER, CL          ROSSCL-49-CDA
                      ROSSCL-56-AP
ROSSOW, R             ROSSR -62-PND
ROTBERG, R            TUMIMM-57-LLL
ROTBERG, RI           ROTBRI-63-OND
ROTH, G               ROTHG -63-SDI
ROTHCHILD, D          MAZRAA-7 -SSE
ROTHELL, EC           LASSH -52-CSE
ROTHSCHILD, J         ROTHJ -59-CPB
ROURKE, FE            ROURFE-60-ASC
                      ROURFE-65-UNP
ROWAT, DC             ROWADC-59-JPS
ROWE, ET              ROWEET-64-EAC
ROWSE, AL             ROWSAL-45-BLP
ROXAS, GM             ROXAGM-63-PBS
ROY, NC               ROY,NC-58-CSI
ROY, R                ROY,R -61-IPC
ROZMARYN, S           ROZMS -59-PCA
RPH                   RPH   -55-YLC
RS                    RS    -53-WGP
RUBENSTEIN, AH        GOLDLC-65-LCU
RUCHELMAN, LI         RUCHLI-66-LNY
RUDOLPH, LI           RUDOLI-64-GPI
RUDOLPH, SH           RANDLI-60-PRI
                      RUDOLI-64-GPI
RUECKER, GL           RUECGL-62-CDG
RUGG, WD              ABELHI-58-SDI
RUNCIMAN, WG          RUNCWG-63-EO
                      RUNCWG-63-CLO
RUPEN, RA             RUPERA-67-MPS
RUSCH, TA             RUSCTA-59-DSL
RUSH, GB              RUSHGB-63-TDE
RUSH, M               RUSHM -58-RKS
                      RUSHM -59-ECS
                      RUSHM -62-KSP
                      RUSHM -65-PSU
RUSSETT, BM           ALKEHR-65-WPG
                      RUSSBM-62-ICL
RUSTOW, A             RUSTA -65-TMT
RUSTOW, D             RUSTD -63-TSS
RUSTOW, DA            RUSTDA-67-WNP
                      RUSTDA-59-AFT
                      RUSTDA-60-PNE
                      RUSTDA-64-STC
                      RUSTDA-66-SEW
RUSTOW, DA (EDS)
                      WARDRE-64-PMJ
RUTHERFORD, BM        RUTHBM-66-PDM
RYAN, B               RYANB -61-SAE
RYLE, M               RYLEM -65-CHC
RYWKIN, M             RYWKM -64-LAS
RYWKIN, MS            RYWKMS-58-ECL
SACKS, IM             SACKIM-67-RGS
SAFRAN, N             SAFRN -61-ESP
SAHLIN, MD            SAHLMD-58-SSP
SAHLINS, MD           SAHLMD-63-PMR
SAKAI, RK             SAKARK-57-FSM
SALEM, E              SALEE -62-EGA
SALISBURY, R          SALIR -65-UPO

SALISBURY, RH   SALIRH-64-UPN
                SALIRH-60-SLP
SALITAN, E      SALIE -58-ATU
SALTER, JT (ED)
                SALTJT-46-PMO
SAMONTE, AG     SAMOAG-60-EDP
SAMPSON, A      SAMPA -65-ABT
SAMUEL, HD      BAILSK-52-CWU
SANDERS, IT     SANDIT-61-SSP
                SANDIT-56-CDE
SANDERS, R      SANDR -65-MSC
SANDOMIRSKY, V  SANDV -54-SNS
SANGER, C       SANGC -64-KGE
SANORA, J       WATSJB-54-SLB
SANTHANAM, K    SANTK -64-TIO
SAPIN, BM       SAPIBM-4 -RMA
SAPOSS, DJ      SAPODJ-54-SBA
SAQUEUR, W      SAQUW -64-NN
SARTORI, G      SARTG -62-DLE
                SARTG -61-PI
SAUER, WL       FORMWH-63-CLI
                FORMWH-61-CIM
                FORMWH-60-OLS
SAUNDERS, JT (EDS)
                DOWVM -62-WAI
SAWYER-JR, RL   SAWYRL-60-DSC
SAWYER, J       SAWYJ -65-BNI
SAX, JW         SAX,JW-54-ICR
SAYEED, KB      SAYEKB-58-PRP
                SAYEKB-64-PSC
SAYIGH, YA      SAYIYA-62-ELR
SAYRE, WS       SAYRWS-60-GNY
                SAYRWS-54-RTB
SC              SC    -46-PFY
SCALAPINO, RA   SCALRA-53-DPM
                SCALRA-52-JDT
                SCALRA-62-LWJ
                SCALRA-62-PPC
                SCALRA-53-CRA
SCANLON, DG (EDS)
                COWALG-65-ENB
SCARRITT, JR    SCARJR-66-APS
SCARRITT, JR    SCARJR-65-PCT
SCARROW, HA     SCARHA-57-HPS
SCHACHTER, R    SCHAR -61-SPS
SCHACTMAN, M    SCHAM -62-BRR
SCHAPIRO, L     SCHAL -60-PRI
SCHAPIRO, LB    SCHALB-65-GPS
                SCHALB-60-CPS
                SCHALB-55-OCA
SCHAPIRO, M     SCHAM -64-LPS
SCHATTSCHNEIDER, E
                SCHAEE-60-SSP
SCHELLENGER-JR, HK
                SCHEHK-66-GSD
SCHEMEN, LR     SCHELR-63-BLS
SCHER, S        SCHES -60-CCM
                SCHES -61-RAC
                SCHES -63-CLC
SCHERMERHORN, RA
                SCHERA-61-SP
SCHERZ-GARCIA, L
                SCHEL -67-RBP
SCHILLING, WR   SCHIWR-62-SFP
SCHIRRMACHER, H
                SCHIH -59-SLP
SCHLESINGER-JR, A
                SCHLA -60-HL
SCHLESINGER, JA
                SCHLJA-57-HTB
                SCHLJA-57-LAP
                SCHLJA-58-FRS
                SCHLJA-65-PEU
                SCHLJA-60-SCO
                SCHLJA-67-PCP
                SCHLJA-65-PPO
                SCHLJA-66-APP
SCHMIDHAUSER, J
                SCHMJ -62-SDD
                SCHMJ -58-SSC
SCHMIDHAUSER, JR
                SCHMJR-58-SCF
                SCHMJR-59-JSC
                SCHMJR-60-SCI

SCHMIDT, F      SCHMF -62-CNB
SCHNEIDER, RM   SCHNRM-58-CG
SCHOENFELD-JR, BN
                SCHOBN-48-PCL
SCHOENFELD, BN  SCHOBN-63-ERI
SCHOPFLIN, GA   SCHOGA-66-CSP
SCHOR, EL       SCHOEL-61-TB
SCHREIBER, T    SCHRT -62-CLH
SCHUBERT-JR, GA
                SCHUGA-58-TPI
SCHUBERT, G     SCHUG -61-PMS
                SCHUG -62-SIF
                SCHUG -62-TSC
                SCHUG -63-JDM
                SCHUG -67-IAA
                SCHUG -67-JPL
SCHUBERT, GA    SCHUGA-59-QAJ
                SCHUGA-58-SJD
                SCHUGA-57-PIA
                SCHUGA-65-JMA
SCHUCKMAN, HL   JACOPE-62-FVP
SCHUELLER, GK   SCHUGK-51-PSU
SCHULZ, CE      SCHUCE-64-BPO
SCHULZ, JB      EDELAS-63-WNS
SCHULZE, RO     BLUMLA-57-DLP
                SCHURO-57-DLP
                SCHURO-58-RED
SCHUMPETER, JA  SCHUJA-62-CSD
SCHUMPTER, J    SCHUJ -55-ISC
SCHURMANN, HF   SCHUHF-61-PSR
                SCHUHF-59-ORC
                SCHUHF-65-IOC
SCHWARTZ, BI    SCHWBI-60-ICC
                SCHWBI-51-CCR
SCHWARTZ, HG    SCHWHG-66-GPR
SCHWARTZ, MA    ENGLFC-67-PPC
SCHWARZ, SM     SCHWSM-53-NLC
                SCHWSM-59-TUS
                SCHWSM-53-CPS
SCIGLIANO, RC   SCIGRC-60-PPS
SCOBLE, HM      SCOBHM-63-PMS
SCOTSON, JL     ELIAN -65-EOG
SCOTT, DJR      SCOTDJ-54-PRY
SCOTT, EL       STOGRM-56-LRE
SCOTT, EW       GOLDD -60-DPO
SCOTT, RE       SCOTRE-59-MGT
                SCOTRE-67-PEP
                SCOTRE-66-MER
SCRIVEN, T      SCRIT -58-LOS
SEABURY, P      SEABP -54-WSG
SEALE, P        SEALP -65-SSS
SEARING, DD     EDINLU-67-SBE
SEEMAN, M       MORRRT-50-PLI
                SEEMM -53-RCA
SELIGMAN, LG    SELILG-59-PSL
                SELILG-58-RPU
                SELILG-55-DPC
                SELILG-50-SPL
                SELILG-56-PLI
                SELILG-61-PRP
                SELILG-64-ERP
                SELILG-64-LNN
                SELILG-67-PPR
                SELILG-64-PCL
SELVIN, HC      SELVHC-60-ELU
SELZNICK, P     SELZP -49-TGR
                SELZP -51-IVM
                SELZP -43-ATB
                SELZP -52-OWS
                SELZP -57-LAS
                SELZP -65-DLD
SENIOR, DA      SENIDA-64-OSR
SERENO, R       SERER -62-R
SETH, SC        SETHSC-65-CFE
SETON-WATSON, H
                SETOH -51-TCR
                SETOH -54-EES
                SETOH -56-SRC
                SETOH -59-IRH
                SETOH -62-RIS
                SETOH -61-FYA
SHAH, DJ        SHAHDJ-66-CPP
SHANNON, JB     SHANJB-49-SPL
SHAPIRO, I      SHAPI -61-SBP

656